HARLEY HAHN'S
LIST OF 25 THINGS TO DO WHEN YOU SHOULD BE WORKING

1. ART GALLERIES AND EXHIBITS: World Art Treasures

Enjoy works of art from around the world . See page 96.

2. ASTRONOMY: Space Calendar

Check out what is happening in space, right now. See page 102.

3. BODY, MIND AND SPIRIT: Dreams

Make sense out of last night's flight into fantasy. See page 127.

4. COMICS: Daily Comics

Read your favorite comics without having to buy a newspaper. See page 178.

5. CONTESTS: Contest Advice

Get some hints on how to be a winner. Then enter a contest and try your luck. See page 202.

6. COOKING: Famous Recipes

Learn the secret recipes that will allow you to copy famous dishes. See page 208.

7. CRAFTS: Origami

Put your extra paper to work. Teach yourself how to create small works of art by folding paper. See page 225.

8. FINDING STUFF ON THE NET: Music and File Sharing

Find some free music and brighten your day. See page 340.

9. FOLKLORE, MYTHS AND LEGENDS: Urban Legends

Is that story that happened to a "friend of a friend" really true? Find out for sure. See page 350.

10. FUN: Web Soap Operas

Divert yourself by following the ups and downs of a Web-based soap opera. See page 367.

11. HOLIDAYS AND CELEBRATIONS: Entertainment and Party Ideas

Plan your next party. See page 447.

12. HUMOR AND JOKES: Humor Archives

Time to laugh. Better check out a few jokes. See page 462.

13. LANGUAGE AND LINGUISTICS: Word-a-Day

Learn a new word, right now, and use it in your next memo. See page 519.

Visit my Web page at **www.harley.com**

HARLEY HAHN'S INTERNET YELLOW PAGES

2003 EDITION

HARLEY HAHN'S INTERNET YELLOW PAGES

2003 EDITION

Harley Hahn

McGraw-Hill/Osborne

Berkeley New York St. Louis San Francisco Auckland Bogotá Hamburg
London Madrid Mexico City Milan Montreal New Delhi Panama City
Paris São Paulo Singapore Sydney Tokyo Toronto

HARLEY HAHN'S
INTERNET YELLOW PAGES
2003 EDITION

McGRAW-HILL/OSBORNE
2600 TENTH STREET
BERKELEY, CALIFORNIA 94710
U.S.A.

This is not a commercial yellow pages book. Please do not write asking how you can buy an ad in this book. There are no commercial ads. In addition, please do not write asking Harley to mention your new Web site in the next edition. Also, please do not put the above address on any mailing lists for press releases or marketing materials. Thanks. To contact Harley, visit his Web site at **www.harley.com**.

For information on translations or book distributors outside the U.S.A., or to arrange bulk purchase discounts for sales promotions, premiums, or fund-raisers, please contact **McGraw-Hill**/Osborne at the above address.

Copyright © 2003 by Harley Hahn. All rights reserved. Printed in the United States of America. Except as permitted under the Copyright Act of 1976, no part of this publication may be reproduced or distributed in any form or by any means, or stored in a database or retrieval system, without the prior written permission of the publisher, with the exception that the program listings may be entered, stored, and executed in a computer system, but they may not be reproduced for publication.

The name "Harley Hahn", the stylized signature *HARLEY HAHN* ®

and the Unisphere logo  ® are registered trademarks of Harley Hahn.

Cover Design: Greg Scott

Cover Illustration: Rob Schuster

Back Cover Photo: Michael Moore

1234567890 QPD QPD 0198765432

ISBN 0-07-222553-X

This book was composed with Corel VENTURA™ Publisher.

To my father,

Murray Hahn (1921–2001)

I REMEMBER
by Harley Hahn

FROM SPUTNIK TO THE ARPANET

I have been using the Internet for a long time, in fact, for more than a decade. During that time, I have seen a great deal of change as the Net has grown from a small research network into the largest information system in the history of mankind.

This being the tenth anniversary edition of "Harley Hahn's Yellow Pages", I'd like to take a few moments to reminisce, and to describe my impressions of how the Internet has changed over the years. Along the way, I'll share some stories and some thoughts that I hope you will find interesting.

On October 4, 1957, the USSR shocked the rest of the world by launching Sputnik, the first artificial satellite. For the first time in history, a man-made object was orbiting the Earth. A month later, on November 3, the Soviets launched Sputnik II, a much larger satellite that not only orbited the Earth, but carried a live dog (named Laika).

All of this happened during the Cold War, a time when the United States was very concerned with planning for a possible war with the USSR. The launch of the Soviet satellites caught the U.S. defense community completely off-guard. As a result, the U.S. government created a number of programs to develop American technology as quickly as possible, in order to regain the lead in the "space race".

One of the new programs was called ARPA, the Advanced Research Projects Agency, which was formed within the Department of Defense. ARPA's mandate was to sponsor research that would allow the U.S. to become the world leader in military-oriented science and technology.

Over the next several decades, the tentacles of ARPA stretched far and wide, insinuating themselves into many areas of the U.S. research community. By the late 1960s, ARPA had become the principal sponsor of advanced computer science research throughout the country. As such, ARPA had bought a number of computers for computer scientists to use in their research. The computers were installed at a handful of locations around the country. However, in order to use one of the machines, a researcher had to physically be at the computer site.

This was a serious limitation. However, in those days, computers were very large and very expensive, and there was no way ARPA could afford to buy and install a machine for every researcher who needed one. In order to save money, ARPA needed to find a way for researchers around the country to share resources. In pursuit of this goal, ARPA decided to fund the development of a network that would connect the computers and enable them to be accessed remotely.

On November 21, 1969, the first two computers were connected together: one in Los Angeles (at UCLA), the other in Menlo Park, California (at the Stanford Research Institute). On December 5, 1969, the Arpanet was officially established by connecting the machines in Los Angeles and Menlo Park to two more computers: one in Santa Barbara (at U.C. Santa Barbara) and one in Utah (at the University of Utah).

As you might expect, the software that was developed for the Arpanet evolved over the years. Eventually, this software became the basis upon which the Internet was founded. For this reason, many people consider that the Internet evolved from the Arpanet and, thus, the date December 5, 1969 should be recognized as the official birthday of the Internet.

Actually, the Internet did not really evolve from the Arpanet, one step at a time. The real story, as you will see later, is far more complex and a lot more interesting.

THE PSYCHOLOGIST AND THE PARANOID

In 1972, when the Arpanet was barely three years old, I was a student at the University of Waterloo, about 75 miles west of Toronto, a well-known math and computer school dedicated to educating Canadian nerds. I was studying a lot of mathematics and computer science, although I didn't have any specific plans. I loved math, and I found computer programming easy, so, like many intelligent people without a firm goal, I just did what came naturally.

At the end my first year, I took a vacation, during which I met a young woman who was to become my first girlfriend. It happened that she lived in Los Angeles and so, smitten with the intoxication of young love, I decided to take off a semester in the fall of 1972 and visit her in California.

My girlfriend was a student, and while she was in classes, time hung heavy on my hands. (I am one of those people who gets bored easily and suffers enormously when it happens.) To alleviate the monotony, I spent time visiting UCLA and, naturally, I gravitated towards the computer labs.

One day, while I was visiting, someone showed me a room with a couple of computers. One of these, he said, was connected to the Arpanet. He explained that it was possible to use this computer to connect to other computers around the country. In particular, this computer could connect to another computer at Stanford. This was the first time I had ever seen a long-distance computer network.

At the time, there was a well-known program called Eliza, named after the Eliza Doolittle character in the play "Pygmalion". Eliza was created in 1966 by Joseph Weizenbaum at MIT. His idea was to use the techniques of artificial intelligence to write a program that would act like a psychologist. Eliza had been installed on one of the UCLA computers, and it was possible to "talk" to it by typing comments on a typewriter-like device. Eliza would process the comments and type a reply.

I had an interest in such programs, and I knew of another one, called Parry, that had recently been created by a researcher at Stanford named Kenneth Colby. Like Eliza, you could talk to Parry by typing comments and reading the replies. However, where Eliza was designed to act like a psychologist, Parry was designed to act like a paranoid schizophrenic.

Well, I was an imaginative guy. Once I learned that it was possible to connect to the computer at Stanford, it was the work of a moment for me to run Eliza on one computer, and use the other one to connect to Stanford via the Arpanet and run Parry. I then allowed Eliza and Parry to talk to one another (by typing the responses from one program into the other).

Thus, it happened that my very first experience with a computer network, in 1972, was to use it to watch a psychologist program, running on a computer at UCLA, talk to a paranoid program, running on a computer at Stanford.

So what happened?

Eliza was a relatively simple program that used a technique called nondirective psychotherapy, a type of therapy that had been developed by the prominent psychologist Carl Rogers. In Rogerian treatment (which was quite popular in the 1960s), the therapist would repeat the patient's own remarks back to him in the form of a question. ("So what does your mother's need to clean the house so much mean to you?") The idea was to help the patient find answers within himself by having the therapist disappear, leaving the patient alone with his conscience.

Parry, however, simulated a paranoid who didn't have a conscience. Moreover, Parry was (for its time) a very complex program, much more sophisticated than Eliza. In fact, it was rumored that Parry was even able to fool real psychologists.

The results are as you might imagine: Parry completely dominated and confused Eliza (advancing the cause of paranoids everywhere).

UNIX AND ME

By today's standards, using the Internet to run two programs in tandem might seem a bit lame. In 1972, however, this experiment seemed like nothing less than a modern miracle.

Still, in those days, computer science students didn't pay much attention to the Internet. We spent our time studying programming techniques, data structures, numerical analysis, and lots of mathematics.

By the late 1970s, I had become a computer science graduate student at U.C. San Diego. Even then, computer networks were not that important to me. To be sure, the Arpanet had grown to encompass virtually all of the major universities in the U.S., as well as many others around the world. However, the network was mostly used by professors and researchers, principally for email and for technical discussions. During my entire time as a computer science grad student (1976-1979), I don't think I even used the Arpanet at all.

After grad school, I decided to leave computer science to study medicine, which I did at the University of Toronto from 1980 to 1984. Towards the end of medical school, I decided that I did not want to be a practicing doctor, so I left the field and became a full-time professional writer. Since I had a graduate degree in computer science, I specialized in writing books about computers.

Even then, it wasn't until 1991 that I began to actually use the Internet with any regularity. Here is how it happened.

In 1991, the Internet had been around for 22 years and had become popular within universities, although not yet with the general public. The reason was simple: there was no easy way for a regular person to access the Net. If you worked or studied at a university, it was easy to use the Internet. All you had to do was get an account (that is, a user name and password) on a computer that was connected to the Net.

At the time, however, there were no commercial ISPs (Internet Service Providers). This meant that, if you didn't have a way to get a computer account at a university, you were effectively shut out from using the Internet.

In the spring of 1991, I was living in Santa Barbara. An editor from McGraw-Hill visited me to see if he could talk me into writing a textbook. The topic of the book was to be Unix, a complex operating system (master control program) that ran most of the computers connected to the Internet. Unix textbooks were important because, in those days, if you wanted to use the Internet, you first had to learn how to use Unix. Although Unix was easy to use, it was difficult to learn (as is the case with most tools for smart people).

In December 1991, I signed a contract to write the book and worked on it throughout 1992. In February 1993, the book was published under the title "A Student's Guide to Unix". (Later, when I wrote the second edition of the book, the title was changed to "Harley Hahn's Student's Guide to Unix".)

While I was researching the book, I realized how important the Internet was becoming. I came to the conclusion that explaining how to use the Net (which was not easy in those days) was something I needed to do for my readers. So, beginning in 1992, I started to use the Net in earnest.

I have never stopped.

TELNET: THE IMPORTANCE OF UNINTENDED USES

When I first started to use the Internet, it was much different than it is now. In those days, there were four main services:

- Telnet
- FTP
- Mail
- Usenet

For two reasons, I'd like to take some time to talk about each of these services.

First, telnet, FTP, mail and Usenet formed the foundation upon which the Internet was created. In fact, these four services are so basic to the Internet, that they are still in wide use today.

Second, I want to introduce you to an idea that is fundamental to the world of computing: the importance of unintended uses.

When a well-designed computer tool is released to the world at large, smart people will modify and use that tool in ways that its creators never imagined. In many cases, this results in a burst of creativity that brings enduring benefits to a wide audience.

This phenomenon happened with all four of the services I mentioned above. In fact, it was the unintended uses to which these four services were put that allowed the Internet to grow so large in a relatively short amount of time.

I'll show you what I mean. Let's start with telnet.

Telnet is a service that allows you to log onto any Internet computer on which you have an account. Once you log in (by typing a user name and password) you can use that computer remotely.

When we talk about telnet, you will often see the word used as verb. For example, you might hear someone say, "In order to get the groatcake recipe you wanted, I had to telnet to a computer at the University of Syldavia."

(By the way, no one knows what the name "telnet" means. In all my research, including reading the original papers, I was never able to figure out how the name was chosen.)

By 1992, when I started work on my Unix textbook, telnet was over two decades old. It was, in fact, the very first service available on the Internet. As I explained earlier, the Arpanet was created so that researchers could share computing resources. They did so by using telnet. In fact, it was telnet that I used, back in 1972 at UCLA, to connect to the computer at Stanford.

When a computer tool such as telnet is first developed, it's hard to predict how important it really will be. Of course, every new computer tool is created to fill an immediate need, but the real test of a new tool is to wait and see what happens over the next few years—to watch what people *do* with the tool.

This is a characteristic that is found throughout the world of computers. Because computer programs act as extensions of our minds, the very best tools end up being used for purposes that go far beyond what their inventors had anticipated. Such was the case with telnet.

Let's say that a programmer at a university wrote a program that provided a particularly useful service. Once the programmer showed the program to his colleagues, word would start to spread and people who had an account on the same computer would start to use the program.

However, what about other people, especially people at other universities? They would hear about the new service and want to use it, but how could that be arranged?

One solution would be to give everyone who wanted to use the new service an account on the computer that ran the program. That way, anyone could simply telnet to that computer, log in, and run the program.

To some extent, this solution would work, but not for very long. If the service proved to be popular, there would be requests from people all over the country asking for computer accounts. The administration alone would be horrendous, not to mention the security risk of allowing hundreds, or even thousands of people full access to the computer.

To solve this problem, it became necessary to figure out how to use telnet to provide services of general interest. A system had to be developed that was easy to administer without creating a security risk.

Before I can explain the solution, I will have to introduce you to a bit of technical jargon, so bear with me.

On the Internet, computers connect to one another in order to request services. Whenever one computer connects to another, the first computer must specify a "port number" to the second computer. The port number serves as an ID number that tells the second computer what type of service is being requested.

In the early days of the Net, it was decided that the basic telnet service would use port 23 to identify itself. Thus, whenever anyone used telnet to connect to a remote computer, the connection would be made using port number 23. Once this connection was made, the remote computer would require the user to log in by entering a valid user name and password.

However, there was nothing inherent in telnet that required a user name and password. All telnet did was connect you to a remote computer. What happened at the other end depended on how the remote computer was configured.

Thus, the solution to the problem of allowing general access to a service was to configure a computer so that it would accept telnet requests for a nonstandard port number, say, 4000. Whenever a person connected to the computer using port 4000, he would not be required to specify a user name and password. However, his privileges would be restricted so that all he could do would be to run one program, the one that provided the service.

Once the idea of nonstandard port numbers was invented, a large number of people began to create services and offer them, via telnet, to anyone with Internet access. The most interesting and enduring of these services were the imaginary role-playing communities that came to be known as "muds".

TEXT-BASED REALITIES

As I mentioned earlier, the only way to access the Internet in 1992 was by finagling a computer account at a local university (which I managed to do). Since I was working at home, I connected to the university computer by using a phone line and a modem. By today's standards, the connection was horribly slow, a mere 2,400 bits per second.

However, a slow connection wasn't that big a deal. All the programs we used ten years ago were text-based, which means they used only simple characters, such as letters, numbers and punctuation. Most of the time, a slow connection was just fine, because text-based information can be transmitted a lot more quickly than the pictures, icons, windows, and other graphical elements that we use today.

You might think it would be boring to use programs that could display only characters. Actually, this was not the case at all. Because communication on the Net was restricted to text, people spent much more of their time thinking about and talking about *ideas*, compared to creating and looking at pictures.

It is human nature to want to make images and tell stories. What I learned in the early days of the Net was that we create much more imaginatively with words than we do with pictures. At first, this idea may seem counterintuitive, especially when it comes to images. After all, wouldn't a visual idea be expressed better with pictures than with words?

Actually not. Just think of all the books you have enjoyed over the years, and how well the writers of those books were able to "create" pictures in your head. When you read a well-written description of something, your mind fills in the blanks in a way that is meaningful to you. When you look at a picture, it has less of an impact because, literally, it leaves nothing to the imagination. The reason I explain this in detail is that, during the time period I am describing, there arose a new type of text-based creative endeavor, called muds.

A mud is a complex, imaginary, computer-mediated role-playing environment, one that you can join (for free) and then visit again and again. To use a mud, all you need to do is telnet to a particular computer, using a specific port number. For example, I sponsor a mud called Zynna (which I will talk about in a moment). To use Zynna, you telnet to **zynna.com** using port number 4000.

The first mud was developed in 1978. It was modeled after the popular role-playing game Dungeons and Dragons. Indeed, the word "mud" was originally an acronym, MUD, meaning "Multi-User Dungeon".

Every mud has a theme, which gives it an overall atmosphere, usually fantasy or science fiction. Muds are highly participatory: you choose an imaginary identity for yourself—often a non-human—and then, whenever you visit the mud, you take on that particular persona. The mud software keeps track of all the players, and remembers their characteristics and identities.

All muds are oriented toward meeting people, talking, making friends and developing relationships. Some muds also allow you to have adventures, go on quests, and solve puzzles. These so-called "adventure muds" are very complex places, with an elaborate system of locations and inhabitants.

In many ways, muds are the epitome of what you can do with a large, worldwide computer network. When you connect to a mud, you enter a world that exists only in the minds of other people. There are many different kinds of muds, but what they all have in common is a degree of sophistication, creativity and imagination that exists nowhere else on the Net.

Muds have been around for well over twenty years, and they are still thriving. In spite of the fact that there is no shortage of highly visual video games and

multi-person network games, there are literally thousands of text-based muds on the Internet today.

I first wrote about muds in 1992, when I was working on the first edition of my Unix textbook. I never did much mudding (as it is called), but six years later, I came to sponsor a mud of my own. Here is how it happened.

In 1998, I was living with my girlfriend of the time, and *she* was heavily into mudding. She and her friends would lament that, although they put a lot of work into their favorite mud, they didn't have control over it. They wished they could have a mud of their own, which they could customize and run the way they wanted. So, to please my girlfriend, I became the sponsor of a mud.

Although, officially, I was the sponsor, all I did was furnish the equipment and provide the Internet connection. I didn't really do anything to set up the mud; my girlfriend and her friends did everything themselves.

Eventually, after a few years, my girlfriend lost interest in the mud (and me), and moved on. However, even without the founders of the mud, I have been able to keep it alive by choosing smart, responsible people to run it.

When I need a job done, my philosophy has always been to choose the very best person I can find, then leave him alone to do the job as he sees fit. Over the years, four different people—two women and two men—have managed the mud, and they have all been excellent. (The current manager is Jeff Thompson, who is doing a wonderful job.) Although I make it a point to never second-guess my managers, they know that I am always there should they need help with a serious problem. In four years, this has only happened twice.

By the way, if all this talk about muds has made you interested, you will find a guide to muds on my Web site:

http://www.harley.com/muds/

Reading this guide is the best way I know to get started. For more information (including a description of the Zynna mud), take a look at the Muds section of this book on pages 632–635.

In the previous section, I observed that a well-designed computer tool will end up being used in ways that are much different than what the original programmers envisioned. This was certainly the case with telnet.

As you remember, telnet was the very first Internet service. It was created so that computer scientists would be able to access remote computers in order to do their research. What fascinates me is that this same service is now used to support elaborate, imaginary environments that are open to anyone on the Net who wants to participate.

FTP: SHARING ANONYMOUSLY

Once telnet was established on the Net, the next important Internet service to be developed was FTP or File Transfer Protocol. (In computer terminology, a protocol is a set of technical specifications.) The original role of FTP was to allow researchers who used more than one computer to copy files from one computer to another.

As with telnet, the word "FTP" is often used as a verb. For example, "I'll be down for dinner in a moment. I just have to FTP a couple of substitute data files to the CIA computer."

FTP is like telnet in that it was designed to be used by people who had permission to use a remote computer. To start, you would use the FTP program to connect to a remote computer. Then (as with telnet) you would log in by entering a user name and password. Once you were logged in, you could enter commands to either upload (send) or download (receive) files. (If you have trouble remembering which is which, just imagine the remote computer floating above you in the sky. You send files *up* and receive files that are sent *down* .)

As with telnet, once FTP was established, it was not long before inventive Internet users started to put it to other uses, two of which are particularly important.

First, at the same time that the FTP specifications were being finalized, a number of programmers had started to think about how the Arpanet community might implement a system for electronic mail. At the request of one of these programmers, a rudimentary email facility was added to FTP.

The FTP-based email system wasn't much, and it was difficult to use. All it could do was pass one text message at a time from one computer to another. Still, it was email and, within a short time, the rudimentary FTP-based system jump-started the development of a full-fledged, Internet-wide email standard.

Even more important than FTP-based email was the idea of "anonymous FTP": a system that enabled people to set up "archives" of files that could be downloaded by anyone on the Internet.

In my opinion, anonymous FTP was the single most important service contributing to the growth of the Internet. In fact, in the first edition of my Unix textbook, I described anonymous FTP as "one of the most significant inventions in the history of mankind". Let me tell you briefly how it works.

To set up an anonymous FTP archive on a computer, the system administrator would create a directory (folder) containing all the files that were to be shared. He would then configure the computer so that anyone on the Net would be able to log in using the user name "anonymous", and without needing a password. Once someone had logged in as "anonymous", he or she would be able to download any of the files in the public directory, but nothing else.

For the first time in history, programmers could create programs and make them available to people all over the world. The reason this was so important is that anonymous FTP was the system that was used to distribute the very programs that built the Internet into a huge worldwide network. Whenever a programmer had a new program to share (or a new improved version of an old program), all he had to do was put it in an anonymous FTP archive. Then, anyone, anywhere in the world, could download the program and install it on his or her own computer.

In this way, anonymous FTP ensured that the software needed to grow the Internet was made freely accessible to anyone in the world.

MAIL: COMMUNICATION AND DISCUSSION

The next Internet service, electronic mail, is something we all take for granted today. In the early days of the Net, however, relatively few people had even heard of email. Even as late as 1992, when I was working on my Unix textbook, the idea of an electronic mail system was new to many people in the university community. Still, email was quickly becoming crucial within many organizations, and I imagine that many of my readers *were* my readers because they were forced to learn Unix in order to use email.

In the early 1970s, email was new to almost everyone. However, it caught on quickly and, by 1973, email messages comprised three-quarters of all the data sent out over the Arpanet.

The original motivation for email was to allow researchers to work together by sending messages to one another. However, as with telnet and FTP, email hadn't been around long before people found a new way to use it: to form discussion groups.

In 1975, the first email-mediated discussion group was founded. Its name was MsgGroup ("Message Services Group"), and it was devoted to discussing technical issues related to the Internet.

At first, MsgGroup was administered manually by a person who took on the job of "moderator". The moderator's job was to maintain a master list containing the email addresses of everyone who wanted to participate in the discussion. Whenever anyone sent in a message, the moderator would forward the message to everyone in the group. As you can imagine, this was a lot of work. Eventually, software was written to automate the day-to-day details, and MsgGroup became the very first Internet mailing list.

Since the people using the Net in those days were mostly hard-core nerds, it makes sense that the first real Internet mailing list would be devoted to nerd-like topics. Still, it was not until September 1979 that the first non-technical mailing list was finally started. This was because the Arpanet was funded with government research money, and there was strong pressure not to use the Net for personal activities.

When the first non-technical mailing list was started, though, it quickly became a great success, attracting people from all over the world. The list was called "SF-Lovers", and was devoted to science fiction.

(How popular was SF-Lovers? Well, the very same mailing list is still alive today, over two decades later. If you want to check it out, take a look at the SF-Lovers Web site: **www.sflovers.org** .)

Today, there are tens of thousands of mailing lists on the Internet. In fact, no one knows how many there are, as anyone who has access to mailing list software can start his own list. A great many mailing lists are open to the general public, although there are some that are kept completely private.

As you look through this book, you will see a lot of mailing lists that my researchers and I have found. All of these lists in this book are free, and open to anyone who wants to join. If you would like some help in getting started, I have written some introductory material, which you will find on page 28. (There is also a copy on my Web site.) If you think you might like to create your own mailing list, see the item called "Free Mailing List Hosting" in the Internet section on page 473.

About the same time that SF-Lovers began, back in 1979, another mailing list was started that also proved to be extremely popular and long-lived: Human-Nets. The purpose of Human-Nets was to discuss the effects of email and computer networks on human culture. As you might imagine, in an environment composed of highly educated and technically adept people, a discussion of how computer networks might affect our culture would inspire a great deal of spirited debate. Indeed, some old-timers who look back with nostalgia remember the Human-Nets mailing list as being home to the most inventive and vital discussions that have ever taken place on the Net.

What I find fascinating is that, long before most people had ever heard of electronic mail and computer networks, the people on Human-Nets were discussing the "network of the future". For a long time, the participants on Human-Nets discussed a brand new idea: Would it be possible to create a global network (which they referred to as "WorldNet")? If so, what would such a network mean to mankind?

Eventually, of course, the possibility was realized. The Internet came into being and did, indeed, become a global network.

However, the genesis of the Internet was not in the way you might have imagined. The Internet did *not* evolve from the Arpanet. What actually happened was much more interesting and, in retrospect, much more unexpected.

USENET: MOVING TOWARD A WORLDWIDE NETWORK

Now that we have discussed telnet, FTP and mail, I'd like to spend a few minutes talking about the fourth fundamental Internet service: Usenet.

Usenet is an independent, worldwide system of tens of thousands of discussion groups. As you look through this book, you will see many different Usenet groups, covering every topic imaginable. (If you need help in learning how to use Usenet, there is a quick introduction on page 26. There is also an entire section devoted to Usenet resources on page 898.)

Even twenty years ago, Usenet was a large, complex and very important system. However, its roots were simple, and much less ambitious.

The story starts at Bell Labs, a renowned AT&T research facility in New Jersey. In 1969, a computer scientist at Bell Labs developed a small, streamlined operating system, which he called Unics.

(The name was actually a pun. The idea was to poke fun at a large, unwieldy system named Multics, which had been developed at MIT and which was full of problems.)

Within a short time, the name Unics was changed to "Unix" and, throughout the 1970s, while the rest of the country was listening to music, taking drugs, and protesting the War in Vietnam, the computer scientists at Bell Labs were raising their own consciousness by developing Unix into what was to become the best and most successful operating system in the world.

Because AT&T was a commercial entity, they put strong restrictions on how Unix might be used outside of the company. For this reason, a project was started within the Computer Science department at U.C. Berkeley to create a homegrown, unrestricted version of Unix called BSD (Berkeley System Distribution). The first version, called 1BSD, was released in March 1978.

Thus, it came to pass that, in the late 1970s, there were two really cool groups of Unix people in the country: those at Bell Labs (in New Jersey), and those at U.C. Berkeley (in California). Both groups were known for their camaraderie, academic freedom and highly innovative programming. (Although I never made it to Bell Labs, I did have a chance to visit Berkeley. I remember that people liked to bring their dogs to work and to spend a lot of time playing volleyball.)

In the fall of 1979, a graduate student from Duke University in North Carolina had just returned to school after spending the summer at Bell Labs. As you can imagine, after spending the summer in such a cool place, he felt a big letdown being back in school. What was especially hard was the feeling of being disconnected from the Unix community.

The grad student discussed his angst with a friend, another Duke grad student, and together they started to plan a system to pass news messages from one computer to another. If they could find a way to connect their computer to a computer at Bell Labs, such a system would allow them to rejoin the mainstream Unix culture.

They quickly recruited two more grad students, one from Duke, the other from the University of North Carolina (UNC) at Chapel Hill. Within a short time, the group had created a rudimentary news system, which they called Usenet (a contraction of "Users' Network"). In January 1980, they presented a paper at a Unix conference, introducing Usenet to the rest of the world.

Within a short time, a number of different programmers helped develop Usenet into a full-fledged system of discussion groups. For historical reasons, the groups were called "newsgroups" (which is still the case today), and Usenet itself was often referred to as Netnews. Similarly, the program that people used to access Usenet was called a "newsreader", and any computer that acted as a Usenet hub was called a "news server".

In the fall of 1979, the first Usenet connection was established between two Unix computers, one at UNC and one at Duke. By the end of the year, a third news server, also at Duke, was added to the system. By the summer of 1980, Usenet had expanded to five more news servers, two of which were at Bell Labs and one of which was at Berkeley. From that point, Usenet grew at an ever-increasing pace until it, literally, became an enormous global system. Today, there are tens of thousands of newsgroups and countless news servers around the world.

Today, all of the Usenet servers in the world are on the Internet. However, that was not always the case. Usenet was actually started on a completely different network, the UUCP network, and for years, UUCP was the glue that kept Usenet together. The UUCP networking facility was built into all Unix systems, which made it readily available. The actual name, UUCP, was taken from a tool called "uucp", which was the "Unix-to-Unix copy program".

By the late 1970s, Unix people around the country had started to use UUCP to connect their computers into a loose network. At the time, the Arpanet was strictly controlled, because it was supported by government money and was supposed to be used only for research.

The UUCP network was much more informal. For one thing, it had virtually no money. On the other hand, the Arpanet—being funded by the Department of Defense—had lots of money. This made for significant differences between the two networks.

For example, on the Arpanet, many of the connections were leased communication lines. Leased lines were expensive, but they were also fast and reliable. The UUCP network was created by programmers who used modems and phone lines to stitch together a low-budget network that spanned the entire country.

To do this, each local network had at least one UUCP computer that was programmed so that, at specified intervals, it would call one of its neighbors, establish a temporary connection and exchange data files. In this way, an email message or Usenet article could be passed from one computer to another until it reached its destination, which might be anywhere in the country.

I can still remember what it was like to use UUCP to send mail in the early days. The addresses could get tricky, because you had to specify the exact path you wanted your message to take, from one computer to another, as it traveled to its destination. For example, let's say you wanted to send a message to a friend whose user name was "nipper" on a computer named "delta". You might have to use the address:

alpha!beta!gamma!delta!nipper

This meant that the message should be sent to the computer named "alpha", which would send it to the computer named "beta", which would send it to "gamma", which would send it to "delta", where it would be delivered to the user named "nipper". Such addresses were called "bang-path" addresses. (In old-time typesetting, the exclamation mark character was referred to as "bang". This usage was picked up by the early Unix people.)

Eventually, UUCP addresses were simplified when programs were written to automate the routing. Then, you could simply send a message to:

nipper@delta.uucp

A routing program would automatically figure out the best path.

Unfortunately, the automated system didn't always work and, even in the early 1990s, it was sometimes necessary to know how to construct a bang-path. Indeed, I explained how to do so in the first edition of my Unix textbook (1992) and in another book I wrote at the time, "The Internet Complete Reference" (1993).

As you might imagine, using a series of intermittent dial-up connections to send messages made for a slow system. For example, it would often take hours, or even a day or two, for a message sent over the UUCP network to travel from one side of the country to the other.

With the Arpanet, on the other hand, the connections were fast and permanent, and data moved quickly from one computer to another. Moreover, the Arpanet used the same modern address scheme that we use today, for example:

nipper@delta.ucb.edu

Thus, sending email over the Arpanet was a lot more convenient than using UUCP.

Still, the UUCP network worked. Moreover, it was cheap and there were no government regulations to dampen its operation. For these reasons, the UUCP network actually grew to be much larger than the Arpanet.

Once UUCP was established, a grad student at U.C. Berkeley set up one of their computers to act as a "gateway" -- that is, a connection point -- between the UUCP network and the Arpanet.

This was a big deal, because the Arpanet was tightly controlled by the Department of Defense and only approved sites were allowed to connect. Anyone with a computer, who knew what he was doing, could join the UUCP network. The coming of the gateway meant that, for the first time, UUCP users could send email to Arpanet users, and vice versa.

At the same time, the UUCP-Arpanet gateway was used to connect various Arpanet mailing lists with Usenet newsgroups. This significantly increased the number of people participating in the discussions, and had a lot to do with the growth of Usenet.

Within the next few years, other UUCP-Arpanet gateways were set up, to provide more points of connectivity between the two networks. In the eyes of the visionaries, all of this took the world one step closer to the holy grail of computer networking: the establishment of a single, large interconnected network spanning the globe.

OUR FRIEND THE INTERNET

I mentioned earlier that, in the late 1970s, I went to computer science graduate school at U.C. San Diego. Then, in the early 1980s, I studied medicine at the University of Toronto. I was very unhappy in medical school and, eventually, I got to the point where I felt just like Popeye when he is pushed beyond his limits ("I've had all I can stands, and I can't stands no more!")—and I left.

As you can imagine, it was a big deal for me to leave medical school. Moreover, I was now faced with an important problem: What was I to do with my life?

At first, I just needed to calm down, so I used a bit of my savings to support myself and spent a few weeks in the university library, researching and making notes for a reference book about the English writer P. G. Wodehouse. (This is how people like me calm down.)

After about a month, I took a job working for a small computer company, saved my money, and moved back to California, where I settled in North San Diego County. However, I still had the same problem: What was I to do?

At the time, I was living with a girlfriend, and we had a limited amount of savings, so I had to find some way to make money. One day I was talking on the phone to someone who told me about a literary agent who had gotten her a job writing a computer book. This sounded like a good idea to me: I liked writing, I had a graduate degree in computer science, and I needed to earn money. In the fall of 1984, I met with the agent, and he arranged for me to write a series of computer books for a major publisher.

Eventually, I wrote three such books: one about PCs and DOS (the old operating system that was used before Windows); one about Xenix (a type of Unix for PCs); and one teaching Assembly Language, a very technical type of programming. I then went on to write other books, including the Unix textbook I discussed above.

Fast forward to 1991. The original three books had reached the end of their useful lifespan, and the publisher sent me a letter telling me that the books were officially out of print. This meant that all the rights to the books reverted back to me.

Not long afterward, as I was preparing to go to a computer trade show, I happened to talk to someone in the agent's office. He told me, "When you go to the show, be sure to drop in at the Osborne McGraw-Hill booth and say hello to the executive editor." I did so, and the editor and I got along well. As a result, we decided to reissue my Assembly Language book, which ended up doing quite well.

In the spring of 1992, the same editor called me and asked, "How would you like to write a book about the Internet?" I didn't realize it at the time, but this conversation was to be a major turning point in my life.

In 1992, the Internet was just starting to become popular. To explain why, I am going to have to get a bit technical for a moment, so bear with me.

On any computer network, there must be a set of rules -- called protocols -- that describe how data is be transmitted from one computer to another. In 1970, the Arpanet programmers developed a rudimentary protocol called NCP (Network Control Program). NCP lasted a long time, but by 1981, it was obvious that a newer, more robust system was needed. This new system was a family of protocols referred to as TCP/IP. (The name came from two members of the family, "Transmission Control Protocol" and "Internet Protocol".) By the middle of 1982, the Arpanet was running on TCP/IP.

Although the Arpanet was an important network, it was not the only one. There were many others, and quite a few of them had their own protocols. Here is a short list of the most important networks along with the years in which they were started:

- 1976: UUCP
- 1981: BITNET ("Because It's Time" Network)
- 1981: CSNET (Computer Science Network)
- 1982: EUnet (European Unix Network)
- 1984: JANET (Joint Academic Network, UK)
- 1984: FidoNet
- 1986: NSFNET (National Science Foundation Network)

The founder of FidoNet chose that name when a visitor referred to his computer as a "mongrel" (because it had been built with parts scavenged from a variety of different machines).

The networks I mentioned above were mostly for research and academic pursuits (except FidoNet, which was maintained by individual computer enthusiasts.) During the same time, a number of commercial networks were also started such as CompuServe (1979), The Source (1979), MCI Mail (1980), Delphi (1982), Genie (1985), and America Online (1990).

Eventually, gateways were established between the Arpanet and all of these networks, in order to exchange email and Usenet articles.

In 1982, when TCP/IP was adopted as the official Arpanet standard, computer scientists first discussed the idea of an "internet": a group of networks connected together by gateways. At the same time, a similar name was coined to refer to all the networks that were connected to one another via TCP/IP. This brand new network of networks was called the *Internet* (with a capital "I").

Over the next decade, more and more networks adopted TCP/IP and the Internet became larger and larger. As the Arpanet began to merge with so many other networks, the vision of a global network finally became a reality.

In 1990, the Internet was so large and important that the Department of Defense officially ended the Arpanet. By 1991, the Internet consisted of over 5,000 different networks in more than 35 countries. There were now over 700,000 computers, used by more than 4 million people.

So now you understand where the Internet came from. It was not created at a specific time, nor did it evolve from the Arpanet. The Internet developed over the better part of a decade (1981-1990), as more and more networks joined the global TCP/IP internet.

Today, the Internet has hundreds of millions of computers used by hundreds of millions of people. But, back in 1992, when I started to write my very first Internet book, "The Internet Complete Reference", the Internet was still new to most people in the country.

HARLEY HAHN'S INTERNET YELLOW PAGES

At the time I was working on "The Internet Complete Reference", there was no easy way to find Internet resources. The Web—which was then called the "World Wide Web"—was still brand new. There were very few Web sites and no modern search engines.

For the most part, Internet resources were accessed using the four basic services we discussed earlier:

- Telnet
- Anonymous FTP
- Mail
- Usenet

In addition, there were also several other services:

- IRC (Internet Relay Chat): a sophisticated worldwide chat system
- Gopher: a large, distributed menu-driven information system
- Archie: a service to help you search for files on anonymous FTP servers

- Wais: a service to provide access to a variety of databases

Since then, Archie, Gopher and Wais, have vanished, having been rendered obsolete by the Web. IRC, however, is still used and is larger than ever. As a matter of fact, if you look through this book, you will see I have included many IRC resources (called "channels"). If you don't know how to use IRC and you would like to try it, there is a quick introduction on page 28. There are also IRC resources on pages 860–863 in the section called "Talking on the Net".

Because Internet resources were so hard to find, I decided that, at the end of "The Internet Complete Reference", there should be a large catalog of resources. I got the idea from another book, "The Whole Internet User's Guide & Catalog" written by Ed Krol, which had been published earlier that year, in September 1992. As you can tell from the name, Krol's book had a catalog, and I decided that my book should have one too.

At the time, the Internet was just starting to become popular with the general public. However, learning how to use the Internet was difficult. Indeed, most people still used Unix to access the Net and, as I explained earlier, Unix is easy to use but hard to learn.

For this reason, Internet books were in great demand. Ed Krol's book sold in enormous numbers and, in my opinion, was *the* book that was responsible for opening up the Internet to the general public. My book, which came out in October of 1993, was also a best seller. In fact, it did so well, that the editor at Osborne McGraw-Hill asked me to create a brand new book, one that would contain nothing but Internet resources.

I agreed to do so, and the editor and I started to think about how to position the book. At first, we had thought of calling it "The Internet Directory of Resources". However, the Osborne McGraw-Hill Publisher (the person in charge) had an inspired idea. He suggested we print the book on yellow paper and model it after a phone book. We did and, in February 1994, "The Internet Yellow Pages" was published. It was my 11th book.

The original "Internet Yellow Pages" was much smaller and much less ambitious than the book you are holding in your hands. Still, from the beginning, there was something special about the book. There were two reasons for this.

First, I have always been a highly creative person, and if I was going to create a "Yellow Pages", I wanted to do more than compile a mere directory. Since no one had ever written such a book before, there were few specific expectations. This meant that I was able to do whatever I wanted, which allowed me to give free reign to my imagination. My editor respected my creativity, and allowed me to do what I wanted. (For the most part, this has been the case with all of my editors. They have always allowed me to do things my way, for which I am grateful.)

Second, as the McGraw-Hill artists worked on the raw material, it became obvious that if the pages were to be laid out evenly without breaking items into two columns, there would have to be a way to fill up the spaces.

To solve this problem, I created new visual elements that had never been seen before (at least in a computer book). First, I wrote a large number of fake advertisements, just for fun. The "ads" were supposed to be for specific Internet resources, but I used the opportunity to be as witty and irreverent as I could.

In addition to the fake ads, I created a number of "fillers", short sentences that were printed in small boxes whenever we needed to fill a small space. Again, I did my best to be witty, in order to give life to what might be an otherwise dull book. For example, "This is the first book of the rest of your life." (Never fear; I got better over the years.)

Writing the ads and the fillers was a lot of fun, and they proved to be popular, especially with the artists who were now able to make the pages bottom out, as it is called. In fact, I like the ads and fillers so much that I used them in all 10 editions of the book, including this one.

The first edition of "The Internet Yellow Pages" also had two other elements that have since been discontinued. First, I searched through many Usenet newsgroups, looking for interesting articles. I then edited them and placed them throughout the book under the heading "Look What I Found on the Net". We called these articles "excerpts", and I kept them in the book—adding new ones each year—through the 8th (2000) edition.

The second element that has since been discontinued consisted of pictures—photos and graphics—that were downloaded from the Internet (mostly with anonymous FTP). We discontinued them because we didn't want to have to worry about copyright problems.

When I wrote the first edition of this book, I had no idea how it would be received. In fact, I had no idea if there would even be a second edition. However, the book became more popular than anyone had anticipated and, every year, I was called upon to put out a new edition.

In the spring of 1996, the book (now called "Harley Hahn's Internet Yellow Pages") became the first Internet book to have sold over 1,000,000 copies. To me, this was a landmark for two reasons. First, I had never had a million seller before, and I was proud of how well the Yellow Pages had done. In fact, when you add in the sales of my other books, the Yellow Pages makes me the best-selling Internet author in history.

Second, even more important, the sales of this book showed just how important the Internet was becoming to our culture.

WHAT A DIFFERENCE...

Over the years, I have written many good books. However, when I look back, I see no correlation at all between how good a book was and how well it sold.

Like all authors, I'd like to believe that each best seller is an irrefutable testament to my skill as an artist. But when I force myself to be dispassionate, I am forced to admit that luck had far more to do with it than I would like to admit. Although I see myself as a good writer, it is all too clear that a lot of my success came from being the right guy in the right place at the right time.

The reason I mention this is because, as I look back, I see that the evolution of the Yellow Pages followed the evolution of the Internet itself.

In the mid-1990s, the Internet burst upon the popular culture like a supernova. This was not totally unexpected. As I mentioned, as far back as the 1980s, there were ongoing discussions regarding the creation of a global computer network. These discussions, however, were carried out on the Human-Nets mailing list and on Usenet, which meant that the participants were mostly academics who already had access to the Net.

In 1994, when the first edition of the Yellow Pages was published, few of the hundreds of millions of people who use the Net today had even heard of the Internet. They had no idea that, within a few years, they would own their own computer, and that their children would grow up in a world in which the Internet would play a dominant cultural role.

As the world changed, so did the Yellow Pages.

When I wrote the first edition, most of the work went into compiling resources and writing a short description of each one. At the time, it was so hard to locate Internet resources, that I put in everything my researchers and I could find. In fact, in the introduction to the first edition, I gave my readers an email address and asked them to let me know if they found any resources that they thought should be in the next edition. (I stopped doing this a long time ago.)

As the years passed, I changed the focus of the book from a mere compilation of Internet resources to a personal guide to culture, science, technology and the arts. I made this change for two reasons.

First, the Internet itself was changing. With the coming of the Web and the explosive growth of the Net, there were far too many resources to think about using even a small fraction of them. It was imperative that I refocus my efforts and those of my researchers. At one time, our job was to find anything we could. Now, our goal was to search the Net to find the very best resources for every topic in the book.

Second, perhaps more important, I began to grow as a writer. Spending so much time describing Web sites, mailing lists and Usenet groups just wasn't satisfying any longer. To be sure, creating the other parts of the book (such as the fake ads and the fillers) was fun. At heart, though, I am an explainer. If I am to be happy, I need to spend a lot of time researching, learning and explaining.

So I recast the book, changing it from a simple directory into a guide to life, annotated with Internet resources. Enhancing the book in this way afforded me the freedom to learn and write about anything I wanted—which I consider to be the best job in the world.

For the ninth (2001) edition, I came up with a new idea. I wrote a large number of questions and answers that I called "Ask Harley". I scattered these short essays throughout the book. They didn't really have anything to do with the Internet. I just wanted to write them, and I thought my readers would enjoy reading them.

For this current edition, I created a whole new set of questions and answers, in a slightly differen format, which I called "Tidbits". (To see a list of all the Tidbits in the book, see page 23.) Again, these were short essays I wrote, just for fun, because I thought my readers would enjoy them. Like the "Ask Harley" essays, they have nothing to do with the Internet.

As I look back and think about what I have seen, I can now realize why the Internet is so important to humanity. By connecting distant computers in so many homes and offices, a global network enables people everywhere to share the fruits of their labor, including their ideas. The Internet also allows people to be a part of something that is larger and more important than themselves, a necessary condition for human beings, if they are to have enduring fulfillment in their lives.

Earlier, I talked about the Unix operating system and how important it was. One reason why Unix was so popular was that every Unix system came with built-in networking tools. This meant that, if you could find a way to connect two Unix computers, it was easy to send data back and forth between them.

A programmer, talking in the argot of computer science, would say that Unix machines are able to "talk" to one another. Well, as someone who is well-versed in computer science, I can tell you that human beings find machines that can talk to one another infinitely more interesting than machines that work in isolation.

As someone who is well-versed in medicine and culture, I think I can also tell you why.

Human beings are social animals, driven by a strong biological need to be connected. As individuals, we are not happy unless we feel a connection with our family and our friends.

On a larger scale, our species is driven by a biological imperative, a force that has compelled us to build the Internet in order to connect ourselves into a large, supra-human organism. To me, the Net—with all its computers, communication lines, information and people—is nothing less than the next important step in the course of human evolution.

I admit that this is a strange concept. But think about how strange the idea of a beehive or an anthill would be to an individual bee or ant. Let us say that it were possible for you to talk to an individual bee or ant. How would you even begin to explain that the beehive or the anthill has a life of its own? That it exists because each separate insect does nothing more than follow his own individual biological destiny?

When I first thought about this idea, I believed that the Internet would bring only good to humanity. We would each participate in the Net in a way that makes sense for us as individuals. As a whole, we would, unconsciously, be creating something large and wonderful that, by its very nature, would bring us increased happiness and prosperity.

Now, I don't think it is that simple.

Since the mid-1990s, the world has changed a great deal, and the Internet has managed to insinuate itself into many aspects of our lives. To be sure, the Internet does bring out the best in us, encouraging us to create, share, think, learn and talk to one another. However, when I look around at the Net and how it influences us, I see also a great many problems: privacy violations, broken relationships, excessive advertising, a vast amount of misinformation, dishonest business practices, and so on.

For the rest of human existence—certainly, for the rest of our lives—there will never be a time without the Internet. For those of us who grew up before there were personal computers, this is a startling idea. Perhaps even more startling is the realization that the children who are growing up now will never remember a time without the Internet.

The implications of these ideas are far from obvious. In cultural terms, the Internet is still brand new, and it will be a long time—maybe generations— before we are able to come to terms with what the Net really means to our species.

Now that the Internet has become a permanent part of our everyday lives, we find ourselves influenced by strong forces that we don't yet understand and that we can't control. The Internet has become an extension of our minds. As such, it acts as an amplifier, enhancing both the good and bad aspects of our society.

If we are to understand what this means to us as individuals and as a society, we need to understand more than just computers and technology: we need to have a basic appreciation of ourselves, our culture and our institutions. We also need to understand psychology, history, philosophy, science, money, and relationships, and how these aspects of life fit into the new world in which we live.

In 2001, I wrote a book, "Harley Hahn's Internet Insecurity" (published by Prentice Hall PTR) in which I discuss these topics in depth, along with a lot of practical suggestions as to how to make the Internet work well for you. If these ideas intrigue you, I invite you to take a look at the book. It is, in my opinion, the best book I have ever written (not counting the Yellow Pages, of course, which is in a class of its own).

(By the way, the person who asked me to write this book was Jeff Pepper, the Publisher of Prentice Hall. He is the same person who, ten years earlier, when he worked at McGraw-Hill, asked me to write the Yellow Pages.)

When I think about the Internet and how much it has changed our world, the last ten years seem extraordinary beyond belief. I look around and see a new world, one that is filled with more creativity and communication than I ever thought possible. Truly, what I see today is much more extraordinary and much more profound than anything I would ever have anticipated when I first started to write about the Net.

Today, however, I look ahead with far more than a sense of wonder. Having written about the Internet for so many years, I know full well that none of us has any idea what the next decade has in store for us.

What a difference ten years makes.

— HARLEY HAHN

List of Tidbits

Frequently Asked Questions

1. Do you have a Harley Hahn Web site?

Yes. Take a look at:

http://www.harley.com/

2. How can I send you a message?

Visit my Web site. You can send me a message from there.

3. Is there a way for me to keep up on what you are doing?

Yes. Visit my Web site, and sign up for my free newsletter.

4. This book is so large. Does it contain a lot of what is on the Internet?

As large as this book is, it contains only a tiny fraction of what is on the Net. The Internet is so big that nobody knows everything it contains. Moreover, it is always changing. This book is my personal guide to the best resources on the Net.

5. How do you decide which Web sites to put in the book?

I have organized all the material in this book into 183 categories. My goal is to find the very best Web sites within each category. My researchers and I look for sites that are useful, interesting, stable, well-maintained, and easy to navigate. In addition, I only use sites that are free to access, and I avoid those that require you to register by specifying personal information.

I stay away from Web sites that are abandoned or poorly maintained. In addition, I do not use sites that are poorly designed, that play music automatically (which is highly annoying), or that are overloaded with gratuitous pictures, graphics or advertisements.

One of my main goals is to find resources that will be permanent. For this reason, I do not use Web sites that reside on free Web servers, such as

Geocities, Tripod and so on. Such Web sites have a high rate of being abandoned.

The ultimate test of whether or not I use a Web site is my opinion. I ask myself, is the Web site important and useful enough that I want you to see it?

6. Can my company advertise in this book?

Sorry, no. This is not a commercial directory like a telephone yellow pages book. I do my best to ensure that nothing gets in this book unless it is free to use. Thus, I do not take paid advertisements. All the "advertisements" in this book were written by me and are just for fun.

7. I have just created a new Web site. How can I tell you about it, so you can put it in the book?

Sorry, you can't. My researchers and I choose all the items in this book ourselves.

8. I tried to access a Web site and it wasn't there. What is happening?

The Internet is always changing. By the time you get this book, some of the items will be obsolete, and there is nothing anyone can do about it. However, virtually all the items should be fine. For each new edition, my researchers and I start from scratch and check each item in the book by hand.

Unless you happened to buy an old edition of this book, most everything should work just fine. Before you get too frustrated, make sure you are doing everything correctly.

If a few items don't seem to be there, that is to be expected. However, if nothing seems to work, you know something important is wrong. The best advice I can offer you is to get a friend to help you, ask your Internet service provider for assistance, or take a look at one of my books.

LEARNING HOW TO USE THE INTERNET

My advice is to take some time to learn how to use the Internet well. Many people don't bother to do so: they just learn how to click from one Web site to another, how to struggle with email, and leave it at that. I want you to get more out of using the Net.

If you look through this book, you will see that the Internet has a lot to offer. In particular, along with all the Web sites, you will see Usenet discussion groups, mailing lists and IRC (Internet Relay Chat) channels. What are these resources, and how do you use them?

I can help you answer these questions in three ways. First, keep reading. Following this section, I have included some information to help you get started with the Internet, to teach you how to use the Web well, and to explain a bit about Usenet, mailing lists and IRC.

Second, when you get a chance, take a look at my Web site, where you will find a variety of material designed to help you learn about the Internet:

http://www.harley.com/

Finally, the very best way I know to learn about the Internet is to have someone show you. Now, it's not possible for me to show you in person, but I can help you a lot, if you will take the time to read my books.

HARLEY HAHN BOOKS

This book (*Harley Hahn's Internet Yellow Pages*) is a personal guide to life, annotated with Internet resources. It is a great companion to using the Internet, but it will not teach you how to use the Net. For that, I recommend one of my other books, *Harley Hahn's Internet Advisor*.

In *Harley Hahn's Internet Advisor*, I teach you everything you need to know to use the Net well. I will show you how to understand Internet addresses, and how to use the Web, email, Usenet, mailing lists and IRC. I will also teach you how to find what you want on the Web, how to talk to other people, how to get free software and free music, how to get your own domain name (like **harley.com**), and how to create your own Web site. Finally, I explain the real truth about such issues as privacy and computer

viruses, and show you what you need to do to protect yourself and your family. (It's not what you think. There is a lot of misinformation.)

In particular, to get the most out of this book, I would like you to take a look at the following chapters:

Chapter 4: Internet Addresses

Chapter 7: The Web

Chapter 8: Talking to People on the Net (the discussion on IRC)

Chapter 9: Downloading and Installing Software

Chapter 11: Finding Stuff on the Net

Chapter 13: Usenet

Chapter 14: Mailing Lists

Harley Hahn's Internet Advisor is published by Que Publishing. The ISBN (official book identification number) is 0-7897-2697-1.

Another book I know you will enjoy is *Harley Hahn's Internet Insecurity*. This book is a fascinating journey into our society and culture. You will read about privacy, security, philosophy, psychology, science, history, politics, money, sex, family life and the Internet. In addition, as I mentioned above, there is a lot of misinformation when it comes to the Net, especially about computer viruses, privacy and safety. In this book, I tell you the truth.

Of all the books I have written, this one is my favorite. If you are a thoughtful person who likes understanding why things are the way they are, you will love this book.

Harley Hahn's Internet Insecurity is published by Prentice Hall PTR. The ISBN is 0-13-033448-0.

You can find more information about my books, by visiting my Web site:

http://www.harley.com/books/

All of my books should be available at major bookstores. If you have a problem finding the book you want, or if you want to buy the book online, I have information on the Web site to help you.

THE WEB

The Web is the largest information delivery system in the history of mankind. The program you use to access the Web is called a *browser*. The two most popular browsers are Internet Explorer (from Microsoft) and Netscape (from AOL).

Although it seems easy to use the Web, there is a lot more to it than many people realize. To be sure, it is easy to look at a Web page, and use your mouse to click on one link after another. However, you can get a lot more out of the Web if you take some time to learn the basics. I have 6 specific suggestions:

1. Learn about *domain names* (such as **harley.com**, **whitehouse.gov** and **ucla.edu**). These are the foundation of all Internet addresses.

2. Learn to understand Web addresses, usually referred to as *URLs* (uniform resource locators).

3. Learn how to customize your browser.

4. Learn how to use search engines to find what you want on the Web.

5. Install an ad blocking program. Such a program will block most of the ads on Web pages.

6. Install a pop-up ad blocking program. This will prevent Web sites from opening new windows in order to force you to look at ads.

I cover all of these topics, in detail, in the book I mentioned above, *Harley Hahn's Internet Advisor*. In addition, look at the following sections in this book:

- Finding Stuff on the Net (page 339)

- Web: Software (page 925)

USENET

Usenet is a worldwide system of discussion groups in which millions of people participate. There are tens of thousands of different Usenet groups, and anyone on the Internet may participate for free. For historical reasons, Usenet groups are sometimes referred to as *newsgroups*, even though they are actually public forums for discussion.

Within each newsgroup, people send messages, called *articles*, for other people to read. Once an article is sent to a group, anyone in the world may read it.

Throughout this book, you will see the names of many Usenet groups. Let's take a minute to talk about those names, so you will understand how they work.

Each Usenet group has a unique name that consists of two or more parts, separated by periods. For example, here are the names of several groups:

```
alt.celebrities
biz.marketplace.international
k12.news
news.newusers.questions
rec.parks.theme
sci.chem
soc.women
talk.environment
```

Within Usenet, groups are organized into *hierarchies*. When you look at the name of a group, the first part of the name is the hierarchy. For example, when you look at the name **news.newusers.questions**, you can tell that this group is part of the **news** hierarchy. Similarly, you can tell that the **talk.environment** group is part of the **talk** hierarchy, the **sci.chem** group is part of the **sci** hierarchy, and so on.

There are hundreds of different hierarchies within Usenet, but only thirteen are of general interest. These are shown in the accompanying table.

The Most Important Usenet Hierarchies

All the Usenet groups in this book are from these hierarchies.

Hierarchy	Contents
alt	Wide variety of miscellaneous topics
bionet	Biology
bit	Miscellaneous topics
biz	Business, marketing, advertising
comp	Computers
humanities	Literature, fine arts
k12	Kindergarten through high school
misc	Miscellaneous topics
news	Usenet itself
rec	Recreation, hobbies, arts
sci	Science and technology
soc	Social and cultural issues
talk	Debate, controversial topics

Most of the time, you can guess the purpose of a Usenet group just by looking at its name. For example, `news.newusers.questions` is for new users to ask questions about Usenet. The group `talk.environment` is for people to debate topics devoted to the environment.

There are two ways to access the Usenet newsgroups. The most common way is to use a program called a *newsreader* to display articles for you to read. You tell your newsreader which group you want to look at, and it fetches the articles and displays them for you. If you decide to send out an article of your own, you can use your newsreader to compose the message and send it to the appropriate group.

Both popular Web browsers come with a free newsreader. With Internet Explorer, the newsreader is Outlook Express (the same program used to handle email). With Netscape, the newsreader is built into the browser. However, there are other, better newsreaders that you can use. For information on where to find them, look in the Usenet section of this book for the item called "Usenet Newsreaders" (page 902).

You might ask, where are all the Usenet articles stored? The answer is, each Internet service provider maintains a Usenet repository for their customers. This repository (called a *news server* or *news feed*) contains all the articles that are currently available. As new articles come in, they are added to the repository. After a certain amount of time — usually several days — old articles are purged to make room for new ones.

Before you can use your newsreader, you must configure it by telling it the name of the computer you will be using as a news server. Your Internet service provider will tell you this name. If you have problems getting started, they should be able to help you configure your newsreader.

Once your newsreader is configured, there is an easy way to read the articles in a particular group. Within your browser, there is a place where you can type the address of a Web site you want to visit. The easy way to look at a Usenet group is to type the "address" of the group. This consists of the word **news:** followed by the name of the group.

For example, if you want to read the articles in the group in which people debate environmental topics, specify the following Usenet address to your browser:

`news:talk.environment`

Your browser will recognize this as a Usenet group, and will start your newsreader automatically.

If you are a heavy-duty Usenet user, I recommend that you use a newsreader program. However, such programs are complex and take time to master. There is an alternative that is easier, especially if you are not a nerd.

There are Web-based services that allow you to read and send Usenet articles. These services are useful in several situations:

- You don't want the hassle of having to learn how to use a newsreader program.

- You want to access Usenet at work, but the network firewall (protection system) won't let you use a newsreader program.

- You want to be able to access Usenet from wherever you are, for example, if you travel.

When you use a Web-based Usenet service, all you need is an Internet connection and a regular Web browser. This makes accessing Usenet simple, especially if you are an AOL or WebTV user. For information on such services, look at the item called "Web-Based Usenet Access" in the Usenet section of this book (page 902).

As I mentioned, there are tens of thousands of Usenet groups, and it is not always easy to find the one you want for a specific topic. If you want to find a group, I have two suggestions. First, start your search by looking in this book. I have included many Usenet groups along with Web sites and mailing lists.

Second, I have created a Web site to help you find the Usenet group you want. The name of this service is "Harley Hahn's Master List of Usenet Newsgroups." The address is:

http://www.harley.com/usenet/

This Web page also contains a variety of useful information about Usenet and how to use it.

Usenet is a very rich system and, in this section, I can give you only a brief summary. To really learn how to use Usenet well, please take a look at Chapter 13 in the book I mentioned above, *Harley Hahn's Internet Advisor.*

IRC

IRC, or Internet Relay Chat, is the largest of the Internet talk systems. IRC has been in use since 1988, and is supported by a well-developed, complex system, which enables thousands of people around the world to talk at the same time.

There are actually over 50 different IRC networks. Within an IRC network, there are many different *channels*, each of which is used for separate conversations. The names of IRC channels all start with the # character, for example, **#astronomy**, **#gothic** and **#canada**.

One thing about IRC channels is that they are not permanent. Anyone can create a channel in which to have a conversation and, in most cases, when the last person leaves the conversation the channel is deleted automatically. In this book, I list channels from the three largest networks: EFnet, Undernet and DALnet. My researchers and I have carefully chosen popular channels that are stable, so they will almost always have someone talking on them.

An IRC network consists of a number of computers called *IRC servers*. To connect to an IRC network, you must first install a program called an *IRC client*. You then use your IRC client (which runs on your computer) to connect to one of the IRC servers for a particular network. Once you have connected to an IRC server, you can join any of the channels on that network, and start talking to people.

IRC is a mature, sophisticated system, and there are more details you need to understand that I cannot tell you in this short essay. However, I can tell you two places to look for more help. First, you can read the discussion about IRC in Chapter 8 of the book I mentioned above (*Harley Hahn's Internet Advisor*). Second, take a look at the IRC items in this book. You will find them in the section called Talking on the Net (page 860).

MAILING LISTS

A mailing list is a system by which a group of people can have a discussion via electronic mail. The idea is that a person can send a message to one central address. That message is then processed by a program that automatically sends a copy of the message to everyone on the list. Thus, once you join a mailing list, you will automatically receive copies of all the messages that anyone sends to the central address. These messages will be sent to your electronic mailbox.

When you join a mailing list, we say you *subscribe* to that list. To leave the list — that is, to stop receiving mail — you *unsubscribe*. Although we use the words "subscribe" and "unsubscribe", there is no cost involved. You can join — and quit — as many mailing lists as you want for free. However, if you join too many, your mailbox will be flooded with so much mail, you won't have time to read it.

Subscribing and unsubscribing to a mailing list is easy. Each list has a special administrative address. All you have to do is send a message to that address saying that you want to subscribe or unsubscribe. A program (not a person) will read and process the message, and carry out your request.

There are three main types of mailing list systems. They are called Listserv, Listproc and Majordomo. Subscribing and unsubscribing with each is almost the same. There is only one small difference when you subscribe to a Majordomo list (which I will explain below).

Let's look at an example. In the Animals and Pets section of this book, you will see an item called "Horses". One of the resources under this item is a mailing list. Here is the information:

Listserv Mailing List:
    List Name: **equine-l**
    Subscribe to: **listserv@lists.psu.edu**

What can we tell about this list? First, we see that this is a Listserv mailing list, as opposed to Listproc or Majordomo. Second, each mailing list has a name. The name of this list is **equine-l**.

Notice the two characters **-l** at the end of the name. In the olden days, it was necessary to know if a name belonged to a person or a mailing list. Thus, mailing lists were given names that ended with **-l**. The letter "l" (L) stands for "list". On some systems, this is still the custom. That is why this name, **equine-l**, ends with **-l**.

The third piece of information we see is the address to which we would send mail to subscribe. In this case, it is **listserv@lists.psu.edu**. This is the address of the program that administers the list. When you send a message to this address, your message is not seen by a person. Everything is done automatically by the Listserv program. It will read your message, figure out what you want, and respond appropriately.

There are many commands you can send to a Listserv program (and the same goes for Listproc and Majordomo). I will describe four.

Before you subscribe to a mailing list, you should always send a request to the mailing list program asking for information about that list. This will help you make sure you really want to subscribe, as well as alert you to any special considerations about the list. To request such information, send an email message to the administrative (subscription) address. The subject of the message doesn't matter; it will be ignored. In the body (main part) of the message, put a single line consisting of the word **info** followed by the name of the list.

For example, in this case, you would send a message to:

listserv@lists.psu.edu

The subject of the message could be anything. In the body of the message, you would type the single line:

info equine-l

Now wait. You will receive a reply with some information. Sometimes this takes only a few minutes, sometimes longer. When you receive the reply, read the information and see if you still want to subscribe. (There will be a lot of technical information you can ignore.)

If you want to subscribe, send another one-line message to the same address. This message should have the word **subscribe**, followed by the name of the list, followed by your first and last names. You do not need to specify your email address. The program at the other end will pick it up automatically.

Let's say your name is Bartholomew Bunzlehammer. To subscribe to the equine-l mailing list, send a one-line message to the address:

listserv@lists.psu.edu

The subject of the message doesn't matter. In the body of the message, you type the single line:

subscribe equine-l Bartholomew Bunzlehammer

When the message is received, the Listserv program will automatically subscribe you to the list. From now on, any messages sent to the list will be sent to you as well.

Hint: For security reasons, some mailing list programs require you to confirm that you really want to join the list (just in case some friend has snuck over to your computer while you were away and sent in a subscription to a mailing list). If this is the case, you will be sent instructions on how to confirm. Usually, it is as simple as replying to a message and saying "ok".

You can unsubscribe to a mailing list at any time. Just send a one-line message to the administrative address with the word **unsubscribe**, followed by the name of the list. You do not need to include your name or your email address. In our example, you would send a message to the address:

listserv@lists.psu.edu

The subject of the message doesn't matter. In the body of the message, type the single line:

unsubscribe equine-l

For a Listproc mailing list, everything works exactly the same. For a Majordomo mailing list, there is only one difference: when you subscribe, you do not have to specify your first and last names.

The final command I want you to know about is **help**. Listserv, Listproc and Majordomo systems have more commands than **info**, **subscribe** and **unsubscribe**. To learn about these commands, send a one-line message to the administrative address with the single word **help**. For example, you can send a message to the address:

listserv@lists.psu.edu

The subject of the message doesn't matter. In the body of the message, type the single line:

help

Once you belong to a list, the question arises, how do you send messages to everyone on the list? You do not send messages to the administrative address: that is only for subscribing, unsubscribing, and so on. Rather, you send messages to the list itself. The list's address consists of the name of the list, followed by the name of the computer.

In our example, the name of the list is **equine-l**. The name of the computer is **lists.psu.edu**. Thus, to send a message to the list itself (that is, to all the people on the list), you would mail to:

equine-l@lists.psu.edu

Each time you send a message to this address, it will be sent automatically to everyone on the list.

So remember, when you want to unsubscribe, do not send the **unsubscribe** message to this address. All administrative requests go to the administrative address (where they are handled automatically by a program).

For reference, the following table summarizes what I have explained in this section. Notice that — for the basic commands — all three systems work the same, except that when you subscribe to a Majordomo mailing list, you do not specify your first and last names.

Subscribing and Unsubscribing to a Mailing List

To request information about a mailing list, or to subscribe or unsubscribe, send mail to the administrative (subscription) address for the list. These are the addresses given in this book. For example:

listserv@lists.psu.edu
majordomo@massey.ac.nz
listproc@cornell.edu

Request Information About the List
  info *list*

Request General Information
  help

Subscribe to a List
  subscribe *list firstname lastname*   (Listserv and Listproc)
  subscribe *list*   (Majordomo)

Unsubscribe to a List
  unsubscribe *list*

Acknowledgments

This edition of Harley Hahn's Internet Yellow Pages, being the Tenth Anniversary Edition, is especially important to me. In this section, I would like to take a moment to thank the people who worked with me to make this the best Yellow Pages ever.

However, let's face it. As important as all these people are to me, they mean nothing to you, and why should they? What do you care if my chief of staff, Lydia Hearn, worked with me late, night after night, to carefully craft numerous aspects of the book? And why should it mean anything to you that the page layout artist, Kelly Stanton-Scott, spent countless hours, making sure that each page of the book looked as good as possible?

Frankly, if I were you, I wouldn't care about these people at all. I'd probably just skip this section and get onto something more interesting.

So in order to make it worth your while to read these acknowledgements, I have created a game you can play while you are reading. The great thing about this game is that, it will not only show you some interesting examples of human nature, it will help you hone your analytical skills and significantly increase your insight into the lives of other people.

Here is how it works.

I have collected special information about eight of the people I will be mentioning in this section. Their names are Lydia, Elaine, Diana, Eugene, Debbie, Carolyn, Kelly and Lyssa. I have personally interviewed each of these people, and asked them to tell me two things about themselves of which they are especially proud. Below is a list of these 16 statements (two for each person).

Before we start, take a moment to read through the list. Then, as we make our way through the acknowledgments, think about each person in turn, and what I have to say about them. At the very end, I will ask you to guess which people made which statements. I will tell you who said what, and you can see how well you did. I will then help you evaluate your score, providing you with valuable insight into yourself and your relationship to the world.

To help you, I'll give you extra hints along the way, by telling you something specific that each person is proud of. You'll see; it'll be fun. (Aren't you glad you bought this book?)

Okay, let's push on. Here is the list of achievements of which these 8 people are proud:

I am proud that...

1. I have a car with a 218 horsepower engine.

2. I can play the flute and sight-read any kind of music.

3. I have a singing range of 3 octaves.

4. I can do just about anything I put my mind to.

5. I am a discriminating reader, and I love to discuss books with intelligent people.

6. I read a lot, especially good literature.

7. I like solitude, and I am completely comfortable being alone.

8. I love being an artist, and I am good at it.

9. I watch every Los Angeles Lakers and UCLA basketball game on TV, and crochet afghans at the same time.

10. I never lie.

11. I am very good at putting together difficult jigsaw puzzles.

12. I am a good hiker, better than most people 20 years younger than I.

13. I am proud to do research for this book and other Harley Hahn books.

14. I found a man who loves to cook.

Okay, now, here are the acknowledgments.

Lydia Hearn has two important jobs. First, she is my chief of staff, which means that she organizes, administers and manages the entire Yellow Pages project. This she does with superb skill and efficiency. Her dedication and skill have a lot to do with the overall quality of the book. As part of her job description, Lydia also plays the piano (she can sight-read anything), sings like an angel, and provides wonderful conversation during those rare times when we manage to take a break from work. Lydia's other job is copy editing; that is, she reads everything I write, making such small corrections as are necessary. In her other lives, of which she has several, Lydia is a professor of literature, a volleyball player, a performer, and the center of a circle of about a thousand friends.

Lydia is proud that, in just about any situation, no matter how bad, she always manages to laugh. She is also proud that her students like her so much that they call her, even when they are no longer her students.

Elaine McIntyre, the senior researcher for this book, is a sweet, talented woman who has worked for me for a long time. Elaine is a detailed, methodical worker, whose work is of the highest quality. Moreover, she is smart, insightful and intelligent: an excellent person to talk to late at night when I am under the pressure of deadline madness. Elaine lives with her family (including her son Bryan who likes Freddy the Pig and Harry Potter, and her husband Tom) in an undisclosed location somewhere in the United States.

Elaine is proud that she is a faithful Catholic, and that she is raising Bryan to be one as well.

Diana Eid, an excellent researcher, is a graduate of Ohio State University where she majored in English. She has been working for me for several years and is bright, pleasant, skillful and cooperative. Diana loves animals, which she gathers about her in abundance. Right now, she has only one animal, her rabbit Hercules, but, one day, Diana is going to live on a farm and have lots of horses, dogs, cats, and other zoological companions. I love working with Diana, because she has an excellent attitude, she is dependable, and she works hard to learn as much as she can.

Diana is proud that animals really like her, and that she can cross-stitch well.

Eugene Katunin is my youngest researcher. Eugene, who lives in Odessa, Ukraine, is a *very* smart young man, a hard worker who speaks four languages fluently (Russian, Ukrainian, English and Greek). Eugene graduated from Odessa State University, with a degree in economics, and he now works as a Marketing, Sales and Computing Manager for a freight-forwarding company. Eugene is very, very smart. He enjoys learning about all types of technology, especially cars and computers, and collecting jokes.

Eugene is proud that he has such wonderful parents, both of whom are smart and give him valuable advice. He is also

proud that he graduated with good marks from a major university, and that he has an important job where he works with friendly colleagues.

Debbie Gin, is a professor at Azuza Pacific University in Southern California, where she teaches theology and acts as a recruiter for graduate students. Debbie is the quintessential expert in making people feel comfortable and welcome. She is also an excellent pianist and singer, and a true Renaissance woman who has studied psychobiology, medicine, theology and music. Debbie is the older sister of Lydia Hearn who, of course, constantly shows Debbie the respect she deserves.

Debbie is proud that she has two masters degrees in unrelated fields (music and theology). She is also proud that she is married to a wonderful man, Michael, with whom she plans to do missionary work one day.

Carolyn Welch, the project editor at Osborne McGraw-Hill (the publisher of this book), is a pleasant, gentle taskmaster, whose job is to make sure that everything that is supposed to happen, actually does happen. Toward this end, she put in many hours coordinating everyone's work, as well as contributing her own efforts to the book. Carolyn grew up in California, Washington and Oregon, and has a degree in history from U.C. Berkeley. She loves reading, Woody Allen films, and sharing Italian food and Italian wine with good friends.

Carolyn is proud that, when she was 18 years old, she moved from Oregon to San Francisco, with only $50 in her pocket. Although she didn't know a soul, Carolyn was able to "make everything work out perfectly."

Kelly Stanton-Scott is a talented, hard-working professional, a desktop publishing expert who laid out much of the book by herself. (*"This has been a big challenge, and I enjoyed every minute of it."*) Every page of this book shows Kelly's skill. Just open the book anywhere, and you can see why I was so lucky to have her working with me. As a child, Kelly attended a special school for gifted children where she studied art. Her childhood dream was to become a typesetter. Later in life, she studied typography and production (at the California College of Arts and Crafts) and typesetting (in San Francisco). Kelly likes all types of music. She has a cat named Mozart and a husband named Kevin.

Kelly is proud that she found her soulmate in her husband. She is also proud that she has perfect pitch. (I tested her, by the way. I had her make the sound of Middle C over the phone, and then I played that note on the piano. She was exactly right.)

As you can imagine, every publishing company has a number of artists. Lyssa Sieben-Wald, however, is one of the most talented I have ever seen. Lyssa spent many hours modifying the internal design for this book. She also worked on the ads for the book, including coloring them. (By the way, the ads aren't real. They are just for fun.)

Lyssa is proud that she single-handedly takes care of her three cats (Bailey, Mouse, Munch), horse (Autumn Fox) and two dogs (Max, Sooner). She is also proud that she is a good friend to all her friends.

To continue, I would like to thank various other people for various other types of help.

Carroll Proffitt and Paul Medoff, the proofreaders, scrutinized every page of this book to find and correct any errors, no matter how small.

At Osborne McGraw-Hill, the publisher, a lot of people worked on this book. They are:

- Mickey Galicia and Melinda Moore Lytle worked with Kelly Stanton-Scott to lay out the pages of the book.

- Roger Stewart (Editor Director) also helped with the planning, decision making, and tended to a great many important details.

- Tana Allen, an exceptionally organized and effective Acquisitions Coordinator, attended to all the administrative details.

- Lisa Bandini (Production Manager) spent a great deal of time planning, managing and organizing. Lisa is—in one word—amazing.

- Kate Viotto worked on the marketing for this book, including the cover and strategic planning.

- Greg Scott created the cover.

- David Zielonka (Managing Editor) supervised the Project Editors and all the scheduling.

- Judy Kessler (Sales Manager) made all the arrangements for this book to find its way into a store near you.

- Scott Rogers (Associate Publisher) and Brandon Nordin (Publisher) managed the enterprise.

Now, to finish the acknowledgments, I'd like to thank various people.

If you enjoyed the introductory essay at the beginning of this book, you will appreciate that it took a lot of time and effort to write it. During the time, I was helped enormously by Terry Keramaris, who provided inspiration, ideas and encouragement. Terry is the best muse a writer could ever hope for.

On the back cover, the wonderful picture of me and The Little Nipper (my cat) was taken by Michael Moore of Santa Paula, California.

For help with programming, I thank Tammy Cravit and Alex Taylor (Taylored Software) who maintained the software used to store the data for this book.

For help with computer hardware, I thank the IBM Product Reviews Lab. In particular, I thank the manager, Sid Baker, as well as his co-workers Robert Armbruster, Loring Montague, Michael Redd, Richard Sawyer, Frank Benzaquen, Steve Gager, Stuart McAteer, Jeffrey G. Witt, Stephanie Clark and Michael Haley.

While Lydia Hearn and I were working on the book, we used excellent remote control software, called GoToMyPC, from Expertcity. For help with this software, I thank Geoff Rotunno (Customer Service), who suggested that I learn about the software, Christie Cooney (Public Relations), who arranged for Lydia and me to use GoToMyPC, and John Connolly, who helped us set it up and get it running.

For friendly, professional delivery service, I wish to thank the employees at my local DHL office: Terry Keramaris, Hajime Warren, Cypress Feld, April Jackson, Lybrya Williams and Ger Coghlan.

So, now that we are finished with the acknowledgments, are you ready to exercise your powers of social insight? Look back at the beginning of this section at the list of achievements. Now do your best to match up two achievements with each of the following people: Lydia, Elaine, Diana, Eugene, Debbie, Carolyn, and Lyssa. Once you have made your choices, compare them with the answers:

Lydia: 9, 10

Elaine: 6, 7

Diana: 2, 11

Eugene: 1, 13

Debbie: 3, 14

Carolyn: 5, 12

Lyssa: 4, 8

You can now grade yourself as follows:

If you scored 11-16 correct, congratulations, you are a master at remembering and analyzing the nuances of social interaction. You have a superb appreciation of others and an understanding of what makes the people around you so special. Your friends are lucky to know you.

If you scored 6-10, you are a solid, dependable person, one who is firmly grounded in reality. You see most of what goes on around you. However, you are thoughtful enough to make decisions deliberately, without jumping to conclusions or following blindly.

If you scored 0-5, you are a solid, steady thinker, one who does not get easily distracted. You see the big picture, uncluttered by petty details. Although you enjoy other people, you have learned to evaluate them over time, looking for enduring motivations and values rather than transient, short-term behavior.

Enjoy the book.

— HARLEY HAHN

Over the last ten years, a lot of people have helped me work on this book. I'd like to mention three sets of people.

First, for each book, I have had a principal assistant. These were Rick Stout (1st-2nd editions), Wendy Murdock (3rd-7th editions), and Lydia Hearn (8th-10th editions).

Second, I have always had my own copy editor. This is the person who checks over every page of the book to make sure there are no mistakes. In all the time I have published this book, I have had only two copy editors, both of whom are excellent: Lunaea Weatherstone (1st-7th editions) and Lydia Hearn (8th-10th editions).

Finally, over the years, I have had a large number of people help me with research. My researchers were:

1st Edition
- Rick Stout
- Michael Peirce
- Wendy Murdock
- Scott Yanoff
- John Navarra
- Paola Kathuria

2nd Edition
- Rick Stout
- Wendy Murdock
- Michael Peirce
- Scott Yanoff
- Carrie Campbell
- John Navarra

3rd Edition
- Wendy Murdock
- Carrie Campbell
- Kalyan Neelamraju
- Jerry Fridrich
- Eugene Katunin
- Melinda Casino
- Melissa Hahn
- Virginia Hatfield

Mary Axford
Peter ten Kley
Michael Tucker

4th Edition
- Wendy Murdock
- Carrie Campbell
- Zbigniew Jurkowski
- Johanna Newell
- Martin Rivers
- Eugene Katunin
- Kalyan Neelamraju

5th Edition
- Wendy Murdock
- Carrie Campbell
- Zbigniew Jurkowski

6th Edition
- Wendy Murdock
- Carrie Campbell
- Zbigniew Jurkowski

7th Edition
- Wendy Murdock
- Carrie Campbell

Elaine McIntyre
Diana Eid

8th Edition
- Carrie Campbell
- Elaine McIntyre
- Kelly Murdock-Billy
- Diana Eid

9th Edition
- Lydia Hearn
- Elaine McIntyre
- Diana Eid
- Eugene Katunin
- Debbie Hearn

10th Edition
- Lydia Hearn
- Elaine McIntyre
- Diana Eid
- Eugene Katunin
- Debbie (Hearn) Gin

Table of Contents

ADVICE

Advice Chat

Here is an IRC channel where you can go to ask questions and get advice from other Internet folk. While I was in there I saw some honestly friendly people giving good advice to a lonely shy teenager on some ways to make more friends. I was relieved at the lack of sarcasm and joking around.

IRC:
  #advice (EFnet)

Annie's Mailbox

Ann Landers (1918-2002)—born Esther (Eppie) Pauline Friedman in Sioux City, Iowa—was, for most of her life, one of the two most beloved advice columnists in the United States. (The other M.B.A.C. in the U.S. being her twin sister, Pauline Esther Friedman, who wrote Dear Abby.) Eppie started writing her column at the Chicago Sun-Times in October 1955. At the time of her death, on June 22, 2002 (actually, four days ago as I write this), Eppie was the most widely syndicated columnist in the world. Her column was syndicated to well over 1,200 newspapers around the world, with a readership of over 90 million people. Eppie did not want the name "Ann Landers" used after her death, so the replacement column was named Annie's Mailbox. Annie's Mailbox is written by Kathy Mitchell and Marcy Sugar, Eppie's editors of many years.

Web:
  http://www.creators.com/
      lifestyle_show.cfm?columnsname=ama
  http://www.creators.com/
      lifestyle_show.cfm?columnsname=alc

> **The true mark of a man is what he does when no one is looking. Remember this, the next time you play hide-and-seek.**

Ask E. Jean

Personally, I find E. Jean's advice just the type of insipid, retreaded, pseudo-straight-from-the-hip stuff you'd expect from a magazine (in this case, Elle) whose main purpose in life is to present one advertisement after another, punctuated by a small number of insipid, retreaded, pseudo-straight-from-the-hip articles. ("You could have brought forty or fifty of the finest men to the absolute limit of captivation with the energy you've wasted wishing and waiting for this stinker.") However, the questions are really interesting. Go figure.

Web:
  http://www.ejeanlive.com/ellearch.htm

Dear Abby

Dear Abby, written by Jeanne Phillips (1942-), is the most successful advice column in the world. The column was started in January 1956, at the San Francisco Chronicle, by Phillips's mother, Pauline Esther Friedman (1918-), the twin sister of Ann Landers (Esther Pauline Friedman). Pauline wrote the column for decades, building it into the most popular advice column in the world. A few years ago, the writing was taken over by Jeanne, who had been apprenticing for much of her life.

Web:
  http://www.uexpress.com/dearabby/

Devices that Answer Your Questions

There is an old Alice Cooper song (Halo of Flies) that starts, "I've got the answers / To all of your questions / If you've got the money / To pay me in gold..." Well, like Alice, these devices have all the answers. However, you don't need to pony up gold just to avail yourself of omnipotent wisdom. All you need is a question, a willingness to plug yourself into the spirit of the universe, and the curiosity to see what happens when you place your fate into the hands of an automated Internet soothsayer.

Web:
  http://www.jaked.org/8ball.html
  http://www.resort.com/~banshee/misc/8ball/

Good Advice

Need some advice? Want to check out some questions and answers? The Internet is full of people giving advice, but how do you find what you want when you want it? Start here, where you will find a collection of links to a variety of advice-oriented resources. Not only will you find personal-type stuff (romance, relationships, teen issues, Internet relationships, family problems, and so on), but also places to check for advice about computers, health, diet, travel and finances.

Web:
   http://www.4advice.4anything.com/

Have you got a problem? Not to worry. Miss Abigail will check her extensive library of old books and find the advice you need.

You may not be able to live in the past, but getting advice via Miss Abigail's literary time warp can present you with a better future.

Help Me Harlan

When you are young, there is no shortage of people willing to give you advice, most of which is best forgotten at the starting gate. Harlan, however, is able to tread that fine line between wise-older-person and remembering-what-it-was-like. If you are a teen or young adult, you'll find good, straightforward words of wisdom, and before you can say "Doing the right thing is a drag," you'll be developing good values in your spare time.

Web:
   http://www.helpmeharlan.com/

The nice thing about advice is that you can take it or leave it. And when you get your advice from the Net, you can take it whenever you want and leave it without worrying about hurting somebody's feelings.

Miss Abigail's Time Warp Advice

Over the past hundred years, many books have been written offering advice. You may not have many of these books, but Miss Abigail does. So just ask away, and Miss A. will search through the books and find you an appropriate answer for such questions as "What is the proper age for marriage?" (a book from 1938 says at least 25 years old for men and 22 years old for women), or "How can I tell if a guy's not married?" (a book from 1969 counsels that a married man will never ask you out for a weekend date). So when you need the wisdom of the ages, check with Miss Abigail. After all, your best friend may be wise, but can she run to her library and check with "The Cool Book: A Teen-Ager's Guide to Survival in a Square Society" [1961]?

Web:
   http://www.missabigail.com/

MissInformation

MissInformation is Jayne Lytel, a technically knowledgeable writer who seems to know everything and is more than willing to give informed advice to anyone who will listen. (Now, who does that remind you of?) Lytel answers questions on *many* different topics. MissInformation is a good person to know when you have a question that would cause a normal person to go bananas just thinking about where to look for the answer.

Web:
   http://www.missinformation.com/archives/

AGRICULTURE

Agribusiness

As they say on the farm, there's no business like agribusiness. The agribusiness industry is huge, and these resources can help you keep your finger on the agricultural pulse of the world. Industry calendars, market prices and reports, trade regulations, postharvest and production guides, industry analysis, news, quotes, weather and crop conditions—all of that and more is waiting for you on the Net, where nothing grows but everything flourishes.

Web:
   http://www.eharvest.com/
   http://www.fintrac.com/gain/
   http://www.ual.org/

Agricultural Statistics

According to the U.S. Department of Agriculture, April 2002 was a big month in the egg production business: 7.08 billion eggs were produced (down slightly from the year before), of which 5.99 billion were table eggs and 1.09 billion were hatching eggs. A total of 336 million hens contributed to this burst of ovo-activity. On the average, each laying hen produced 21.1 eggs during the month. (At this point, let us take a moment to imagine what it must be like to ovulate 21.1 times every month.) If you have even a passing interest in learning interesting facts, reading agricultural statistics is a great way to satiate your curiosity. There are lots and lots of numbers about crops, farm economics, food, weather, technology, international agriculture, livestock, dairy, poultry, rural affairs, specialty agriculture and trade issues. Imagine how impressed your friends will be once they know that *you* know how much land in France was planted with apples last year (78,000 hectares), what the yield was (260,513 hectograms/ hectare), and how many apples were actually produced (2,032,000 metric tons).

Web:
   http://usda.mannlib.cornell.edu/usda/
   http://www.usda.gov/nass/

Agriculture Jobs

The world of agriculture is vast, with literally hundreds of different types of jobs. If you are looking for work, here are some resources to help you. You'll find information regarding professional-level job opportunities in many different areas, including agricultural production, business and research. (It's not generally known, but Mr. Greenjeans used the Net to get his job with Captain Kangaroo.)

Web:
   http://www.eharvest.com/careers/
   http://www.nationjob.com/ag

Agriculture Magazines

These days, people think you have to go skydiving, bungee jumping, ice climbing or fire walking to get a thrill. How wrong can they be? On the Net, I can get a rush any time I want. Check out the agricultural magazines on the Net and you will see what I mean. There are several different agriculture magazines for your perusal. You can read articles from journals like Hogs Today, Beef Today, Dairy Today, Farm Journal, Top Producer and Progressive Farmer. If you don't want to just read, you can hang with other agricultural thrill-seekers in chat rooms.

Web:
   http://www.agweb.com/
   http://www.ars.usda.gov/is/ar/
   http://www.progressivefarmer.com/

Agriculture News

The basic goal of agriculture has always been the same: to turn natural resources (land, water and sunlight) into food and other useful products. In pursuit of this goal, modern agriculture has evolved into an amalgam of science, technology, business and politics, all of which make for a great deal of agricultural news every day. In fact, something important is probably happening right now. My advice is don't even finish this paragraph. Check the news right away.

Web:
   http://agnews.tamu.edu/
   http://www.agriculturelaw.com/
   http://www.agricultureworld.net/
   http://www.ars.usda.gov/is/pr/

Listserv Mailing List:
   List Name: agnmore
   Subscribe to: listserv@listserv.tamu.edu

Agriculture Resources

Agriculture is the art, science and business of producing crops and livestock. Agriculture, in some form or another, is as old as human history. Indeed, it was the development of farming techniques that allowed early humans to form stable settlements and begin to develop culturally. Modern agriculture is a vast area of activity. In the United States, agriculture accounts for about one sixth of the national economic output. Within the science of agriculture, the main branches of study are agronomy (soil management, field crops), horticulture (fruits, vegetables, ornamental plants), entomology (insects), animal husbandry (care and breeding of domestic animals), and dairying (milk production).

Web:
http://cipm.ncsu.edu/agvl/
http://www.agnic.org/
http://www.agriscape.com/
http://www.agrisurf.com/
http://www.joefarmer.com/

Agriculture Talk and General Discussion

It has been a long time since farmers were isolated tillers of the soil, living alone and working from dawn to dusk with little contact with the outside world. Today's modern farmer is as likely to have an Internet connection as a tractor. If you are a farmer or have an interest in agriculture, join the discussion, and stay in touch with your neighbors all over the world.

Web:
http://talk.agriculture.com/

Usenet:
alt.agriculture
alt.agriculture.beef
alt.agriculture.commodities
alt.agriculture.fruit
alt.agriculture.misc
alt.agriculture.technology
sci.agriculture
sci.agriculture.fruit

Listserv Mailing List:
List Name: agric-l
Subscribe to: listserv@listserv.uga.edu

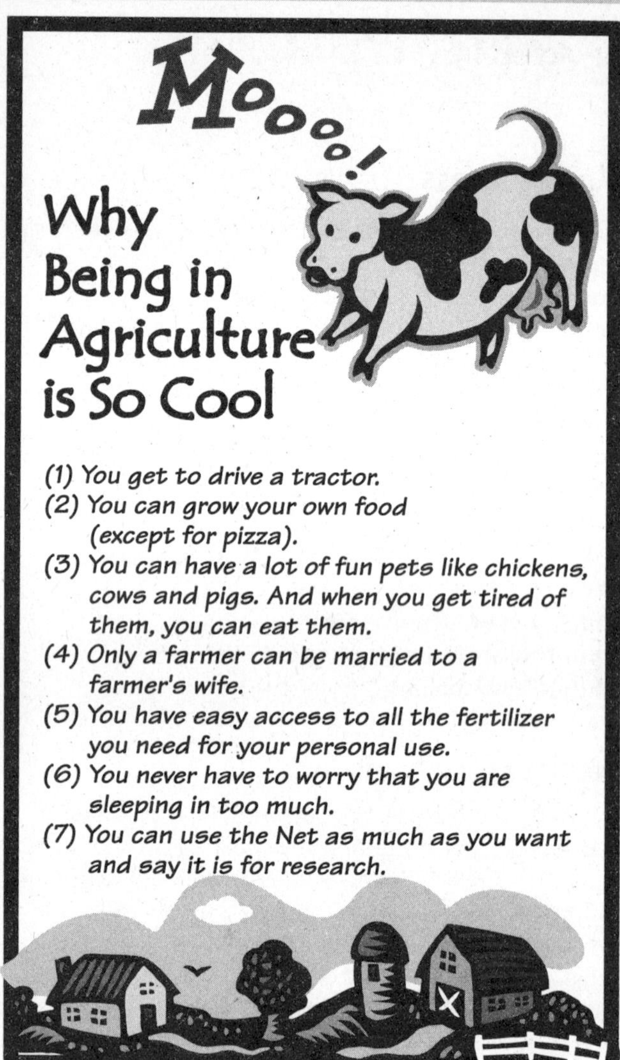

Agripedia

Agripedia is a well-designed encyclopedia of agriculture maintained by the University of Kentucky's College of Agriculture. The site is oriented toward learning, so if you are an agriculture student, you will find the resources particularly useful. The reference material is comprehensive, including many well-organized links to resources around the Net. If you have any interest at all in agriculture, you will want to know about this site. (Actually, the only word I couldn't find in the large glossary was "dell". It seems as if the U. of Kentucky College of Agriculture still has a lot to learn about The Farmer in the Dell.)

Web:
http://www.ca.uky.edu/agripedia/

Beekeeping

The other day, I was walking down the street, humming a little tune and enjoying a honey sandwich wrapped in wax paper, when I ran into a winged, hairy-bodied, stinging insect of the superfamily Apoidea in the order Hymenoptera— that is to say, a bee. Hello, Ms. Bee, I said, I notice you have a dense coat of feathery hairs on your head and thorax, as well as enlarged hind feet. You betcha, Harley, she said. I use my feathery coat and my enlarged hind feet to gather pollen which I deposit in one place or another in an agriculturally useful manner as I cruise for nectar, which I convert to honey within my digestive tract. You look busy, I said. Tell me about it, she replied. I not only gather nectar and make honey, I mix the pollen with water to make special bee-bread for the youngsters (that is to say, the larvae), and I help take care of the queen and protect the hive. I looked at her closely. You also look tired, I observed. She sighed. You are correct; there is no rest for me. Every time I try to take a moment to relax, I have to get up and perform a complex patterned dance in order to communicate the location of a pollen source to some dumbcluck who is too dense to find it on her own. However, she said, I have a job to do. I am a honeybee (and I could see her multifaceted eyes light up with pride) and I am cultivated not only for my honey and my contribution to pollen distribution, but for my ability to make wax. And now, she said, with a little wave of her head, I have to go. As you can see, I am as busy as a writer.

Web:

http://ourworld.compuserve.com/homepages/
    beekeeping/weblinks.htm
http://www.beekeeping.com/index_us.htm
http://www.gobeekeeping.com/
http://www.honeybee.com/
http://www.ibiblio.org/bees/

Usenet:

alt.hobbies.beekeeping
sci.agriculture.beekeeping

Listserv Mailing List:

List Name: apis-l
Subscribe to: listserv@lists.ufl.edu

Listserv Mailing List:

List Name: bee-l
Subscribe to: listserv@listserv.albany.edu

Dairy Science

There is no other farm animal whose output reflects the quality of forage as much as a lactating dairy cow. Even high-quality alfalfa does not supply enough digestible dry matter: you still have to use some type of grain and protein supplement. When you come right down to it, if you want top milk production, there is no substitute for young, bright- green alfalfa. Can't you just smell that pleasant freshly-cut-grass aroma without a hint of mustiness? (I'm getting hungry just thinking about it.) Check the Net, where you can milk the dairy science resources for all they are worth.

Web:

http://www.dairynetwork.com/
http://www.foodsci.uoguelph.ca/dairyedu/
    home.html

Listserv Mailing List:

List Name: dairy-l
Subscribe to: listserv@listserv.umd.edu

Forestry

The only thing bad about the forest is that there's no good waves to surf. Other than that, I really like the forest. Except for the bugs. But other than that, I like the forest. Except for the snakes, I mean. Other than that, I really do like the forest. If you are a big fan of forestry like I am, you have to check out the forestry resources on the Net. And you don't even need any insect repellent.

Web:
   http://www.fs.fed.us/
   http://www.metla.fi/info/vlib/Forestry/
   http://www.stateforesters.org/

Usenet:
   alt.forestry

Irrigation

Irrigation—the artificial watering of agricultural land—has been used for centuries. Irrigation is crucial to agriculture, and modern irrigation practices can be complex. Simply put, the idea is to use the techniques of hydraulic modeling, drainage, salinity control and drought management to get enough water in the right place at the right times, without causing waterlogging (soil saturation) or salinization (excessive accumulation of salts). At the same time, there are other concerns: water rights, the overall water supply, environmental issues—such as endangered species—and politics. (Boy, just thinking about all that makes me thirsty.)

Web:
   http://www.greenmediaonline.com/li/
   http://www.igin.com/Irrigation/

Listserv Mailing List:
   List Name: irrigation-l
   Subscribe to: listserv@listserv.dfn.de

Livestock: Exotic

We are all familiar with traditional farm animals, such as horses, cows, pigs and chickens. But where are the camels, the exotic poultry, the antelopes, the bison and the ratites? Not to mention chinchillas, minks, boer goats, miniature horses, alpacas, deer and tropical birds? On the Net, of course.

Web:
   http://www.animalsexoticandsmall.com/
   http://www.pacificnet.net/~jmcnary/species.html

Usenet:
   alt.chinchilla

Livestock: Rare Domesticated Breeds

Of all the treasures of youth, one that I miss the most is my grandmother's chicken soup. Nothing like it exists today, and one of the reasons is that you can't get chickens that taste as good as they used to. (If you are under 40, ask an old person how real chicken used to taste.) Too many domesticated breeds are in danger of disappearing because the food industry, for the sake of efficiency, relies on just a few specialized breeds. However, there are people who concern themselves with preserving traditional livestock breeds. One day we will praise them.

Web:
   http://www.albc-usa.org/
   http://www.ansi.okstate.edu/breeds/
   http://www.kelmscott.org/
   http://www.rbta.org/

Market Reports

Running a farm means staying up to date on the market, sometimes on a daily basis. Having the latest news and current prices is an invaluable aid to agricultural planning. These resources will help you find the information you need to work in the fast-moving agricultural marketplace. Sometimes it's just as important to know what a 50-pound sack of Russet Burbank potatoes is going for in Los Angeles, as it is to know the name of that little green bug with red spots.

Web:
   http://www.joefarmer.com/howdy/markets.htm
   http://www.market-news.com/

National Agricultural Library

The National Agricultural Library (NAL) is one of four national libraries in the United States. NAL is part of the U.S. Department of Agriculture's research service. Through this Web page you can learn how to access ISIS, the library's public catalog, see part of the NAL's image collection that is online, and get information on how to access other NAL resources.

Web:
   http://www.nalusda.gov/

National Genetic Resources Program

The USDA's National Genetic Resources Program provides germplasm and related information for plants, animals, microbes and insects. ("Germplasm" refers to the hereditary material within germ [sex] cells. Get enough germplasm, and you can start your own world.) My favorite plants are the Giant Raspberries of Jilin. These raspberries, which were originally bought from street vendors along the banks of the Songhua reservoir near the city of Jilin in northeastern China, measure from 2.5 to 3.5 centimeters wide. In case you are a raspberry breeder, the species name for the Giant Raspberries of Jilin is *Rubus crataegifolius*. Germplasm—in the form of seeds—is available from the National Clonal Germplasm Repository in Corvallis, Oregon. You will need to reference accession (identifier) RUB 1917.

Web:

http://www.ars-grin.gov/

You're sitting around the house with nothing to do, so you say to yourself, "Hey, why not create my very own biological environment?"

Why not indeed?

However, before you can start, you are going to need some germplasm. But how do you decide which germplasm to use?

Just connect to the National Genetic Resources Program site where you will find information about plants, animals, microbes and invertebrates.

It won't solve all your problems, but it can save you a lot of time.

(I don't want to point fingers or anything, but if you-know-who *the Big Guy up there* had used the Net, he probably would have been able to create the world in five days and rest for the whole weekend.)

Organic Farming

"Organic farming" refers to agricultural practices in which farming is carried out without the use of synthetic fertilizers, pesticides or chemicals (such as hormones and antibiotics). Organic farmers employ a wide array of materials and techniques, and there is a great deal of information available on the Net.

Web:

http://www.ers.usda.gov/briefing/organic/
http://www.nal.usda.gov/afsic/ofp/
http://www.ofrf.org/
http://www.ota.com/
http://www.rain.org/~sals/my.html

Poultry

According to my sister, there's nothing bad about poultry that can't be fixed by boiling it long enough. Of course, not everyone agrees. There are about 14,859,460,000 chickens in the world, many of whom are loved like brothers (or sisters). Of course, there is more to life than chickens. There are also geese, ducks and turkeys. If you are a poultry person, you're going to feel right at home on the Net. Join the people who appreciate that buttercup combs are less round and lumpy than silkie combs, and read about poultry till your uropygial gland overflows. (By the way, to put the whole thing in perspective, 14.8 billion, the number of chickens in the world, is more than all the people who have ever bought a Harley Hahn book, put together.)

Web:

http://www.ampltya.com/
http://www.ansi.okstate.edu/poultry/
http://www.the-coop.org/

Usenet:

sci.agriculture.poultry
sci.agriculture.ratites

Listserv Mailing List:

List Name: pltrynws
Subscribe to: listserv@sdsuvm.sdstate.edu

Precision Farming

I will admit I didn't anticipate information about farming to be interesting. However, after reading some documents about precision farming, I have changed my mind. Precision farming is the process of tailoring soil and crop management to fit the various conditions found in individual fields. Precision farming uses remote sensing, geographic information systems (GIS) and global positioning systems (GPS) to analyze field data within inches. Using this system, farmers can adjust seeding rates, fertilizer and pesticide applications; make tillage adjustments; and record yield data variations within each individual field. If you want to know more about this space age method of farming, check out these sites, which have lots of good information.

Web:
http://nespal.cpes.peachnet.edu/pa/
http://www.agcentral.com/linkx/xpfarm.html

Sustainable Agriculture

Farming is habit-forming. You think you'll try it for a year, just for fun, and you tell yourself that you can take it or leave it. But one day you wake up and realize it's in your blood. You're a farmer and you just can't quit. Then you start to realize how expensive your habit is. All those chemicals and fertilizers you put in the soil add up to big bucks. So use the Net to investigate sustainable agriculture, and see how people are working together to make farming less dependent on additives and more self-sustaining. After all, no one likes a freeloader, so why not make Mother Nature carry her own weight?

Web:
http://www.permaearth.org/
http://www.sarep.ucdavis.edu/

Usenet:
alt.sustainable.agriculture

Listproc Mailing List:
List Name: sustag-l
Subscribe to: listproc@listproc.wsu.edu

Can We Keep On Keeping On?

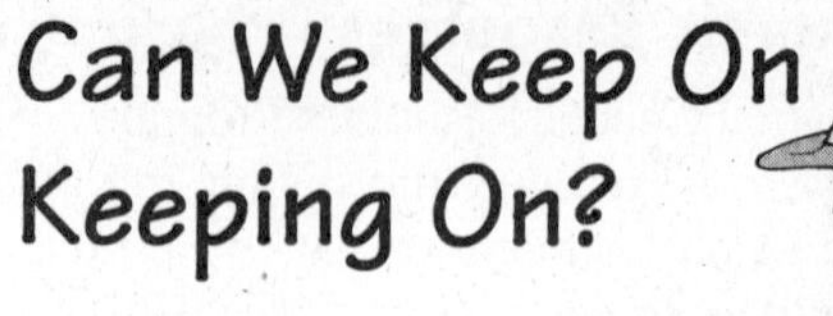

Traditional agriculture requires that we add a significant amount of substances and energy to the soil. For example, farmers routinely use chemical fertilizers, pesticides, soil conditioners, and so on.

The goal of sustainable agriculture is to depend as little as possible on external resources. The holy grail of sustainable agriculture is to create an agricultural system that is efficient and economically viable, while needing as little external support as possible.

In the long run, sustainable agriculture practices can benefit us all, conserving resources and saving money. However, to reach that goal, there will have to be a lot of experimentation, development and testing.

If you would like to follow the flow, check the sustainable agriculture resources on the Net. Maybe there is a way we can keep on keeping on without running out of resources.

World Agricultural Information Center

The World Agriculture Information Center (WAICENT) was created by the Food and Agriculture Organization of the United Nations. WAICENT provides information on agriculture, fisheries, forestry, nutrition and rural development. Information is also available in languages other than English. This is just the thing when you have to pick up a quick present for a farm girl and you don't know what to get her.

Web:
http://www.fao.org/waicent/search/

ANARCHY

Anarchist Calendar

When you want to give a party, but you just don't have a good occasion to celebrate, check with the anarchist calendar on the Net. This site has a list of important anarchist happenings in history. (For example, on February 16, 1916, Emma Goldman was arrested in New York for lecturing on birth control.) Just find the anarchist event closest to the day you are giving the party, then call your caterer and tell him the theme of the gathering. Or you can read him the entire list of historical events and ask him which one goes best with frozen pigs-in-blankets.

Web:
  http://recollectionbooks.com/bleed/
    AnarchistTimeline3.htm

Anarchist Feminism

Anarchy and feminism have been strolling hand in hand long before Hillary Clinton agreed to be Martha Stewart's financial planner for a straight percentage of the gross. If you would like to explore the roots of modern feminism, you need to look at the women who were not afraid to stand up and be counted at a time when even getting noticed could be hazardous to a lady's health. True, Hillary and Martha are honest-to-goodness folk heroines, but in my humble masculine opinion, they can't hold an intellectual candle to, say, Emma Goldman, the Russian-born American activist who was pro-birth control and anti-draft long before it was fashionable. Check the Net and see for yourself.

Web:
  http://www.infoshop.org/afem_kiosk.html

It's time for an
ice cream break.

Anarchist Resources

After going through a three-hour meeting, it's refreshing to look at a nice Web site that can help you fantasize about throwing off the corporate chains that bind you. These sites have lots of interesting resources that are related to anarchy and anarchists: discussion groups, archive sites, Web pages, newsletters, mailing lists, publications, and more.

Web:
  http://flag.blackened.net/ias/links.htm
  http://flag.blackened.net/sai/faq/links.html
  http://www.anarchy-movement.com/
  http://www.anarchy.org/
  http://www.infoshop.org/
  http://www.zpub.com/notes/aadl.html

Anarchist Yellow Pages

There are a lot of people who want to change the status quo, one way or another, for one reason or another. And those people support a lot of anarchy-related organizations and publications around the world. The Anarchist Yellow Pages will help you find the information you want, when you want it (as long as the Internet doesn't dissolve into anarchy).

Web:
  http://flag.blackened.net/agony/ayp.html

Anarchy FAQs

Anarchy comes in a variety of shapes and sizes with the one common belief that Government Is Bad. On the Net, you can read more about the ins and outs of anarchy. These FAQs attempt to take all the ideas and philosophies and put them in a readable format.

Web:
  http://www.faqs.org/faqs/anarchy/theory/faq/
  http://www.infoshop.org/faq/

Anarchy History

The thing I like best about anarchy is that no one organizes it. Oh, people try, but anarchy seems to have a life of its own. If you like reading about the history of not following the rules, try these sites. Learn about the people who did not feel like getting permission from Burger King just to have it their way: people like Noam Chomsky, Emma Goldman, William Godwin, Michael Bakunin and Max Stirner. Find out what the Haymarket massacre has in common with the Spanish Civil War, and see why, when push comes to anarchical shove, there's no business like show-em-how-it-really-ought-to-be-done business.

Web:
> http://dwardmac.pitzer.edu/anarchist_archives/
> http://flag.blackened.net/revolt/history.html

Human society is a stew into which you throw all types of ingredients and cook for a long time, with no idea of how it is going to turn out. One of the most important ingredients in human history is anarchy. Every now and then, we need a few people to redefine the recipe of government and stir the stew.

Even a cursory glance at history will show you that what starts off as frank rebellion often ends up as the status quo. Thus, when we learn about the anarchy of the past, we are studying the seeds of our modern society.

Remember, those who do not understand the history of anarchy may find themselves repeating it with their own heads on the platter.

Anarchy News

Our world seems to be filled with news, but not all of it is readily available from the dominant media. Here is a less well-known side of the news: the stories that don't titillate enough to make it onto the magazine covers, and aren't bland and harmless enough to sell TV commercials. Here it is, the anarchy news. The news *they* don't want you to read.

Web:
> http://flag.blackened.net/revolt/new.html
> http://www.ainfos.ca/en/
> http://www.infoshop.org/news.php

Anarchy Samplers

Wanna get serious? Sitting around the cafeteria, drinking coffee and discussing politics will only take you so far. If you want to be a real anarchist, you've got to learn a whole lotta stuff, and this is the place to start. You will find a great many quotes, full of just the ideas you need to get the anarchical ball rolling down the hill of enlightenment.

Web:
> http://flag.blackened.net/daver/anarchism/
>   anarchism.html
> http://flag.blackened.net/revolt/women_write.html
> http://www.radio4all.org/anarchy/
> http://www.spunk.org/cat-us/writers.html

Anarchy Talk and General Discussion

To some people, anarchy is society without government. To others, anarchy is life without television. Still, whether you are an armchair social critic or a couch potato with a plan to reform the world, you won't want to miss the discussion. Talk may be cheap, but good plans to reform the world the hard way are in short supply.

Usenet:
> alt.anarchism
> alt.anarchy.rules
> alt.society.anarchy

Majordomo Mailing List:
> List Name: practical
> Subscribe to: majordomo@tao.ca

Chomsky, Noam

In 1957, the linguist Noam Chomsky (1928-) published a book called Syntactic Structures, in which he proposed the Theory of Generative Grammar. This theory states that people learn to speak because they have an innate ability to recognize which constructions are valid and invalid within their language (as opposed to learning to speak by memorizing minimal sounds). The Theory of Generative Grammar revolutionized linguistics, affording Chomsky considerable renown. Since then, Chomsky has used this considerable renown to try to revolutionize the rest of the world. Chomsky is an anarchist with thoughtful opinions about *everything*, and he is not shy about sharing. It takes a long time to understand much of what Chomsky says, but if you are willing to try, the Net is a good place to start. And if you become confused, you can always switch to linguistics (where confusion is taken for granted).

Web:
  http://www.zmag.org/chomsky/

Usenet:
  alt.fan.noam-chomsky

Goldman, Emma

Emma Goldman (1869-1940) was a Russian-born American anarchist. At the age of 17, she emigrated from Russia to the U.S., where she and Polish-born Alexander Berkman later published the newspaper Mother Earth. Goldman was vociferously active in a number of unpopular causes, including birth control (with Margaret Sanger), anti-militarism, the anti-draft movement, free speech, the eight-hour work day, and women's rights. Between 1893 and 1917, Goldman was sent to prison several times. In 1919, she was deported to Russia (along with Berkman), only to leave in 1921 after becoming disillusioned with the Russian government. It is difficult to appreciate the importance of Goldman's contributions because, today, much of what she worked for has come to pass and is taken for granted. However, in her time, Emma Goldman was a tireless anarchist, an unbridled force of nature whose lifelong devotion to her causes made her one of the outstanding political activists of the twentieth century. (Some Emma trivia: In the Warren Beatty film Reds, the part of Emma Goldman was played by Maureen Stapleton.)

Web:
  http://sunsite.berkeley.edu/goldman/

History of the Black Flag

You may have noticed that when the political and fashionable hoi polloi congregate (say, at the opening of Congress or the annual Hooterville, California, turkey drop) you never see a black flag. And you know why? Because a black flag is the symbol of anarchy, and if there is one thing the political and fashionable hoi polloi will not tolerate, it is anything that smacks of not following the rules. (Just ask any member of Congress or, for that matter, any turkey from California.) But how did the black flag come to have such a meaning? Read this article and find out.

Web:
  http://www.spunk.org/library/intro/sp001492/
    blackflg.html

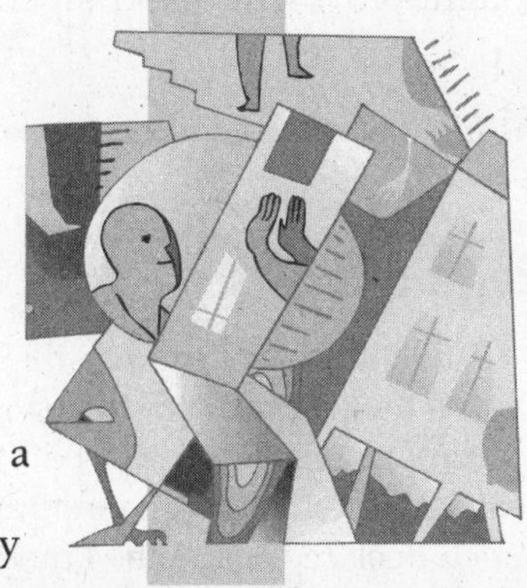

History of the Black Flag

The other day, I was going for a walk in my neighborhood, when I ran into a large group of anarchists about to pillage the community. "Hold on a minute," I said. "Why don't you take a break and let me tell you about the History of the Black Flag?" They did, and by the time I had finished, they were so engrossed in a discussion of political symbolism that they forgot all about pillaging the community. Don't you owe it to yourself to find out about the History of the Black Flag? After all, don't you want to be able to protect your neighborhood when the time comes?

Prominent Anarchists

Who's who, and why? Here's the inside scoop about your favorite anarchists: biographies, photos, quotations, and information about their work. After all, you can't follow in someone's footsteps if you don't know their shoe size. Or as Noam Chomsky once put it: "If I were to run for president, the first thing I would do is tell people not to vote for me."

Web:
  http://flag.blackened.net/liberty/libertarians.html

Rocker, Rudolf

Rudolf Rocker (1873-1958) was a German-born anarchist writer, speaker and philosopher. Rocker was a socialist when he was young, but soon became an anarchist. Throughout his adult life, Rocker proved to be a prolific and energetic proponent of anarcho-syndicalism (a movement that believes in wresting power from the bosses and vesting it in unions or syndicates). Rocker believed an anarchist world, characterized by "free association of all productive forces based upon cooperative labor", would be, ultimately, the logical outcome of modern monopoly capitalism and totalitarianism. (Remember, Rocker lived through the labor unrest of the early part of the century, the Great Depression and two World Wars.) Clearly, he did not envision the evolution of society that was to take place in the latter half of the century. Nevertheless, Rocker's writings are, to this day, thought-provoking and compelling.

Web:

  http://flag.blackened.net/rocker/

Siege of Paris

In 1870, Otto Von Bismarck, the "Iron Chancellor", goaded the French into declaring war against Prussia (a German state). This was part of Bismarck's plan to create a unified German empire, and it worked. The French declared war—the Franco-Prussian War—and lost, after which Bismarck was able to consolidate the German empire as an aggressive military force, leading to one or two minor military problems in the twentieth century. Once the war ended, Germany forced France to accept punitive and humiliating terms of surrender. Many of the working class citizens of Paris (such as writers of Internet books) were so upset at the new French government's acceptance of these terms that they forced out the National Assembly and formed a committee called the Commune of Paris to run the city. Led by the Commune of Paris, the citizens put up a brave and desperate struggle against government troops, but after a week of battles—called the Siege of Paris—the working class protesters lost. Afterward, there were massive reprisals in which tens of thousands of people were killed, putting a crimp in the French political scene for the next several years.

Web:

  http://www.library.northwestern.edu/spec/siege/

Situationists

A constructed situation is "a moment of life, concretely and deliberately constructed by the collective organization of unitary environment and the free play of events." If this sounds like hot stuff to you, you may be a latent situationist. The Situationist International organization was founded in 1957, flourished in France, Germany and Italy, and lasted for 18 years. To outsiders, SI is remembered for having a great influence on the French national strike of May 1968. To insiders, SI is a complex philosophical movement, based in large part upon radical ideas of Guy Debord and Raul Vaneigem: an anarchistic school of thought that seeks to make sense out of the modern twentieth century brouhaha. If you are a young idealist, searching for subtle, but fundamental ideas that even your teachers won't be able to understand, situationism may be your entrée into the world of obscure esoterica.

Web:

  http://www.members.optusnet.com.au/~rkeehan/
  http://www.notbored.org/texts.html
  http://www.nothingness.org/si/
  http://www.slip.net/~knabb/SI/contents.htm

Spunk Library

If you're going to be an anarchist, you need spunk. If you're going to be an anarchist on the Net, you need the Spunk Library: a collection of anarchist literature, including lots of esoteric papers and commentaries, as well as the Anarchist FAQ (frequently asked question list). The Spunk Library is a good place to browse when you have a few extra moments and you want to raise your anti-hierarchy consciousness without having to do any heavy lifting. (By the way, the word "spunk" was taken from a Pippi Longstocking book.)

Web:

  http://www.spunk.org/

Look behind you.

ANIMALS AND PETS

Animal Information Database

Created by Sea World and Busch Gardens, this Web page is loaded with information, not only about aquatic animals, but also on a variety of terrestrial critters. Learn about manatee bodysurfing, hippos that sweat pink oil, and other interesting animal facts that will make you the life of any party.

Web:

  http://www.seaworld.org/infobook.html

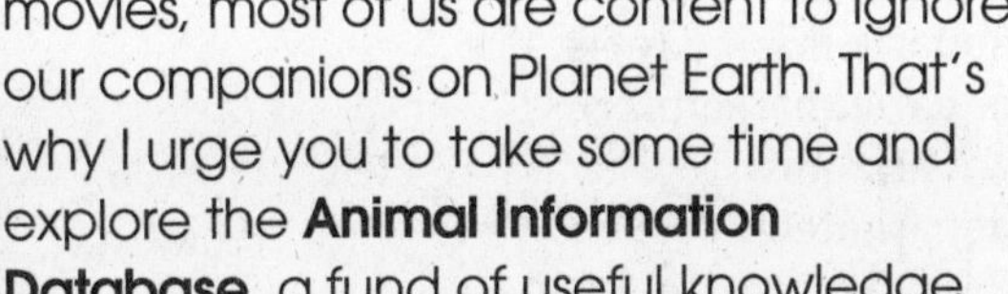

You know, we don't really pay enough attention to our friends in the animal kingdom. Aside from Los Angeles, where lower invertebrates are routinely used to write television shows and movies, most of us are content to ignore our companions on Planet Earth. That's why I urge you to take some time and explore the **Animal Information Database**, a fund of useful knowledge.

You never really know when useful and important animal-oriented knowledge is going to make a difference in your life. For example, what do you do when your Uncle Louie surprises you by inviting himself over for dinner, and you are not sure what to feed him? Or say you pick a particularly strange-looking blind date, and you are interested in finding out if she might be dangerous. Not to worry, the Animal Information Database is ready and waiting for you, twenty-four hours a day.

Animal Rescue and Adoption

Let me tell you a true animal rescue story. Every night, my cat (The Little Nipper) sleeps on my bed. If he happens to be outside in the evening, he knows to come in when it is time for bed and, as soon as he comes in, I close all the doors. One night a few years ago, after he was inside and I had shut all the doors, The Little Nipper disappeared. He didn't show up all night. I was worried about him and had trouble sleeping. Early in the morning, I got up and started a comprehensive search. I looked in every closet, behind every door, and on top of every shelf. The Little Nipper had vanished. By now it was light, so I started to look around outside, just in case he had found a secret exit even though the doors were closed. However, my efforts were fruitless. I walked all around the house with a bowl of tuna, a treat that had never before failed to attract him, but The Little Nipper was gone. I checked with the neighbors. No one had seen him. My options had run out. With trembling fingers, I dialed the local animal control office. Calmly and professionally, they took a report and offered general advice. I hung up the phone and, within five minutes, in walked The Little Nipper. With the air of a United States congressman helping himself to a substantial donation, The Little Nipper swanked over to the bowl of tuna and, demonstrating a quiet dignity that became him well, lowered his head and began to indulge himself. To this day, I have no idea where he was—a swanky hotel, perhaps. If you like pets, I bet you will enjoy reading more rescue stories about animals (some of which are even more gripping than this story). If so, check the Net, where you can also find information about rescue organizations and animal shelters. If you have a pet of your own, take a moment to see what organizations exist in your area. Don't wait until tragedy strikes to identify the sources of professional help. After all, one day you may find yourself involved in a situation in which even a bowl of tuna is not enough.

Web:

  http://acmepet.petsmart.com/civic/
  http://www.aspca.org/
  http://www.birdhotline.com/
  http://www.ecn.purdue.edu/~laird/animal_rescue/
    shelters
  http://www.pmia.com/
  http://www.tc.umn.edu/~devo0028/

Animal Rights

My cat (The Little Nipper) and I have developed an Animal Bill of Rights: (1) All animals are entitled to tuna once a day. (2) Having your teeth brushed every morning should be voluntary. (Actually, The Little Nipper made up the Bill of Rights. I did the typing.) However, the world is not always so simple. Many people think that it takes more than guaranteed tuna to fulfill our responsibilities toward animals. In that, I agree. Animals are an important part of our culture and our economy, and how we treat them—and think about them—affects our society more than most people appreciate. Take a look at the animal rights resources on the Net, and see if you agree with me that there is room for kindness and reason in all aspects of our lives.

Web:
  http://www.aldf.org/
  http://www.herbweb.org/resources.htm
  http://www.peta-online.org/

Usenet:
  talk.politics.animals

Animal Talk and General Discussion

Animals are for more than eating or making into pets. Some are pretty or lovable, and some are to be admired for their skill in stalking and devouring small prey or unsuspecting pizza-delivery boys.
On the Net there are several places you can go to participate in discussions of your favorite animal.

Usenet:
  alt.animals.badgers
  alt.animals.bears
  alt.animals.foxes
  alt.animals.gorilla
  alt.animals.hawk
  alt.animals.lion
  alt.animals.llama
  alt.animals.otters
  alt.animals.pandas
  alt.animals.raccoons
  alt.animals.tiger
  alt.animals.wombat
  alt.fan.hedgehog
  alt.fan.lemurs
  alt.goat
  alt.skunks
  alt.wolves
  alt.wolves.hybrid

Aquariums

What does it mean when your gourami is leaning thirty degrees to the right? He could be trying to steer, but that's probably not the case. Splash around with the rest of the ichthyophiles as they explore the true nature of tropical fish. Learn a wide variety of new things, like the best way to earthquake-proof your tanks, how to name your fish after famous Internet book writers, or what to feed your black piranha when all he really wants is you.

Web:
  http://faq.thekrib.com/
  http://fins.actwin.com/
  http://www.aquariumhobbyist.com/
  http://www.fishlinkcentral.com/

Usenet:
  alt.aquaria
  alt.aquaria.killies
  alt.aquaria.oscars
  rec.aquaria
  rec.aquaria.freshwater.cichlids
  rec.aquaria.freshwater.goldfish
  rec.aquaria.freshwater.misc
  rec.aquaria.freshwater.plants
  rec.aquaria.marine.misc
  rec.aquaria.marine.reefs
  rec.aquaria.marketplace
  rec.aquaria.misc
  rec.aquaria.tech
  sci.aquaria

Listserv Mailing List:
  List Name: aquarium
  Subscribe to: listserv@listserv.cc.emory.edu

> By the time you finish this sentence, 47 people will have read the "Trivia" section.

Look before you click.

Bird-Keeping

Birds, birds, birds. There are 28 different orders of birds, comprising the class Aves. Within the bird world there is a great deal of variation with respect to what birds eat, how they live, where they live, where they migrate, how they build nests, and the sounds they make. It's hard to give an exact definition that covers every bird in the world, but most birds do share a number of characteristics. First, they have wings and feathers. Second, birds are streamlined— contoured feathers, no external ears—and fly with their feet held tightly against their bodies. Finally, birds have fast metabolisms, with a low body weight and light bones. Bird-keeping is no fly-by-night hobby, so to help you, I have found some cool avian-related resources.

Web:
 http://www.birdsnways.com/
 http://www.ddc.com/~kjohnson/birdcare.htm
 http://www.parrotpages.com/
    information_center.shtml
 http://www.upatsix.com/

Usenet:
 alt.pets.birds.dutch
 alt.pets.birds.softbills
 alt.pets.birds.softbills.crows
 alt.pets.birds.softbills.starlings
 alt.pets.parrots.african-grey
 alt.pets.parrots.amazons
 alt.pets.parrots.budgerigars
 alt.pets.parrots.cockatiels
 alt.pets.parrots.jardines
 alt.pets.parrots.marketplace
 alt.pets.parrots.misc
 alt.pets.senegal-parrots
 rec.pets.birds
 rec.pets.birds.pigeons

Listserv Mailing List:
 List Name: birdtech-l
 Subscribe to: listserv@listserv.aol.com

Bird-Watching

This is a hobby that can be as simple or as elaborate as you wish. Basic pieces of equipment are a lawn chair, a bird book, and a pair of binoculars—and some birds, of course. On the high end, you can use complicated camouflage, blinds and camera equipment. No matter what your aim is, bird-watching is an endlessly fascinating pastime.

Web:
 http://nature.gardenweb.com/forums/bird/
 http://www.birder.com/birding/
 http://www.birdwatching.com/
 http://www.mangoverde.com/birdsound/
 http://www.mbr-pwrc.usgs.gov/id/framlst/
 http://www.naturesongs.com/birds.html
 http://www.nmnh.si.edu/birdnet/
 http://www.petersononline.com/birds/links/
    general.html

Usenet:
 rec.birds

Listserv Mailing List:
 List Name: birdchat
 Subscribe to: listserv@listserv.arizona.edu

TIDBITS

What should honest people know about LIARS?

It is important to be able to detect falsehoods and identify people who lie to you. Unfortunately, many liars are good at deception, and it is easy to get fooled. Here are some hints to help you.

Look at the person's body language. A liar will often avoid eye contact, cross his arms or legs a lot, and talk fast (to finish quickly). If you look closely, you may also see the pupils of his eyes narrow.

Many liars, especially those who lie habitually, will be overly friendly and laugh a lot. They do this in order to get you to like them. (You are more likely to believe your friends.)

Every lie leaves a trail. Look for the clues. If you suspect someone is lying to you, pay attention to your gut feelings.

Cats

No doubt about it, cats are très cool. (And my cat, The Little Nipper, happens to be the coolest cat of all.) The Net abounds with cat information, and just about everything cat-wise is out there waiting for you. Cats are also involved in some of the most amazing coincidences in the world. For example, my chief researcher's mother's name is Kitty and—get this—my maternal grandmother's name was Kitty. Far out or what?

Web:
http://www.cfainc.org/
http://www.fanciers.com/
http://www.fanciers.com/cat-faqs/
http://www.felinewww.com/

Usenet:
alt.animals.cat
alt.animals.felines
alt.animals.felines.diseases
alt.pets.cats
rec.pets.cats
rec.pets.cats.anecdotes
rec.pets.cats.announce
rec.pets.cats.community
rec.pets.cats.health+behav
rec.pets.cats.misc
rec.pets.cats.rescue

Listserv Mailing List:
List Name: feline-l
Subscribe to: listserv@lists.psu.edu

Listserv Mailing List:
List Name: talk-aboutcats
Subscribe to: listserv@listserv.temple.edu

Majordomo Mailing List:
List Name: cybercat
Subscribe to: majordomo@iastate.edu

Don't leave home without this book.

Cats Are People Too

I may be biased, seeing as I have the best cat in the entire world, but what could be better than a warm, fluffy bundle of feline affection sitting beside you as you work?
If you like cats, the Net is the place to be, with all the cat-related information you will ever need. My cat loves the net so much, he often takes the laptop computer with him to bed. (I only wish he wouldn't get tuna all over the keyboard.)

Dogs

By their nature, dogs are pack animals that crave companionship. Combine this with over 10,000 years of domestication and a wide range of genetic variability, and you have the perfect companions for human beings. Even a cursory look at our culture will show you how important the canine dominion is to mankind. When I was growing up, I watched Huckleberry Hound, Rin Tin Tin, Lassie and Mighty Manfred the Wonder Dog. When I learned how to swim, I started with the dog paddle; when I was hungry, I would eat a hot dog; and when I felt argumentative, I would be dogmatic. If you like dogs, you are in good company on the Net, where there are more dog lovers than you can throw a stick at.

Web:
  http://www.akc.org/
  http://www.canine-connections.com/
  http://www.canismajor.com/dog/
  http://www.dogomania.com/
  http://www.k9web.com/dog-faqs/
  http://www.worldclassdogs.com/

Usenet:
  alt.animals.dog
  alt.animals.dogs.collies.open-forum
  alt.pets.dogs.aussies
  alt.pets.dogs.labrador
  alt.pets.dogs.pitbull
  alt.pets.dogs.sharpei
  alt.pets.dogs.vizsla
  rec.hunting.dogs
  rec.pets.dogs
  rec.pets.dogs.activities
  rec.pets.dogs.behavior
  rec.pets.dogs.breeds
  rec.pets.dogs.health
  rec.pets.dogs.info
  rec.pets.dogs.misc
  rec.pets.dogs.rescue

Listserv Mailing List:
  List Name: k9singles
  Subscribe to: listserv@listserv.iupui.edu

Listserv Mailing List:
  List Name: smalldogs
  Subscribe to: listserv@apple.ease.lsoft.com

Listserv Mailing List:
  List Name: talk-aboutdogs
  Subscribe to: listserv@maelstrom.stjohns.edu

Electronic Zoo

Whenever I go to the zoo, I find so many interesting things to look at, I never have time to visit everything. The Electronic Zoo is the same. I have been visiting this Web site off and on for years, and it grows so fast I always find something new to explore. So if you love animals, this is the place to spend your spare time.

Web:
  http://netvet.wustl.edu/e-zoo.htm

Endangered Species

Endangered species are animals whose numbers are diminishing to such an extent as to threaten their very existence. Throughout the history of the Earth, countless species have developed, flourished, and died out. In this sense, species extinction is natural and normal. However, many people believe that a great many species are becoming extinct because of changes produced in the environment by people and their activities. Although your personal life may seem remote from, say, the Moschus chrysogaster leucogaster (Himalayan musk deer) in Afghanistan, we do share the same world, and changes in remote areas can affect the ecological balance. So, when a species in Afghanistan becomes threatened, it is not necessarily something we can ignore with impunity. Still, I want you to be aware that the culture of the environment is filled to the brim with politics. A lot of people— perhaps most people—who argue passionately about saving the environment are misinformed and ignorant. For example, talk to any kid, and you will find that children get a lot of politically correct pro-environment propaganda at school. (My philosophy is that ten-year-old kids should have certain responsibilities, but that saving the rain forest should not be one of them.) So where does that leave us? The idea that the Earth is a large ecosystem in which all species are indirectly dependent on one another is a sound, even brilliant observation. However, running around like Chicken Little, moaning that the ecological sky is falling, gets us nowhere. Try to see past the propaganda and figure out for yourself what is real and what is important.

Web:
  http://endangered.fws.gov/
  http://www.nwf.org/
  http://www.wcmc.org.uk/data/database/
    rl_anml_combo.html
  http://www.worldwildlife.org/

Ferrets

The weasel-like ferret is actually a type of domesticated polecat. Traditionally, ferrets have been used to chase rabbits, rats and mice. They are as playful as kittens, good-natured, energetic and entertaining. However, when they are not sleeping, ferrets are often very, very active. Ferrets can be a lot of fun, sometimes even more fun than you can stand. In one sentence, this is what a pet ferret does for a living: He runs around your home, exploring every opening and every object he can reach, and then he does the whole thing all over again.

Web:
   http://my.en.com/~rcmcr/info.html
   http://www.afip.org/ferrets/
   http://www.ferretcentral.org/

Usenet:
   alt.pets.ferrets
   rec.pets.ferrets

Listserv Mailing List:
   List Name: ferret-l
   Subscribe to: listserv@cunyvm.cuny.edu

Fleas and Ticks

Learn how to rid your pet or home of fleas and what to do about ticks. (The ol' gasoline trick probably isn't a very good idea anymore.)

Web:
   http://www.canismajor.com/dog/critter.html
   http://www.k9web.com/dog-faqs/fleas-ticks.html

Hamsters

When I was a kid I had a hamster named Hamlet. He used to stay up all night, running around inside a wheel in his cage. Aside from that, he was pretty easy to get along with. He never ate the last corndog; when we were watching TV, he didn't mind if I changed the channel to Dick Van Dyke; and he always saved the comics for me to read before he started ripping them apart.

Web:
   http://www.afrma.org/hamster.htm
   http://www.ggower.com/hamsters/faq.htm
   http://www.hamsterific.com/
   http://www.hamsterland.com/
   http://www.minxlinx.co.uk/linx.html

Usenet:
   alt.pets.hamsters

Majordomo Mailing List:
   List Name: hammies-r-us
   Subscribe to: majordomo@lists.i-way.co.uk

Horses

I have a friend named Debbi who has her own horse (named Colty), and every year, she goes on a long trail ride with a group of women, riding and camping in the California wilderness. Why do so many young women love to ride horses? Well, I know, but I can't tell. What I can tell you is that the Net is the place to meet horse lovers of all types for a general discussion of horses, riding, and all-around good, clean equestrian fun.

Web:
   http://www.haynet.net/
   http://www.horseweb.com/links/

Usenet:
   alt.animals.horses.breeding
   alt.animals.horses.icelandic
   alt.animals.mules
   alt.animals.ponies
   alt.horseback.riding
   alt.horsecare.basics
   rec.equestrian

Listproc Mailing List:
   List Name: horse-sense
   Subscribe to: listproc@prairienet.org

Listserv Mailing List:
   List Name: equine-l
   Subscribe to: listserv@lists.psu.edu

Majordomo Mailing List:
   List Name: horsewomen
   Subscribe to: majordomo@queernet.org

Iguanas

An iguana is a large lizard, found in the tropical regions of the western hemisphere. Even in the dark, it is easy to tell an iguana from a cat or a dog, because iguanas have spiny projections along their backs. Here is information for every iguana lover or potential iguana lover about housing, feeding, health, reproduction, and so on.

Web:
   http://www.baskingspot.com/iguanas/
   http://www.geeky-boy.com/iguana_blurb.html
   http://www.iguana-reptiles.com/

Usenet:
   alt.pets.reptiles.lizards.iguana

Marine Mammals

I love spending time in the ocean. Occasionally, I will be sitting on my board, waiting for a wave, when a group of dolphins will swim by. Just having them nearby is a special treat. Dolphins are one of the few animals that are always cool, even when they are lying around doing nothing in particular. There is something intriguing about dolphins, porpoises, manatees, whales and seals. They are mammals, but they live in the water. Sometimes, when I am snorkeling, I will lie with one eye above the water, staring at the sky and the shore, and the other eye under water, looking at all the plants, rocks and fish. The underwater environment is so different from where we live, it is almost like being on two planets at the same time. Perhaps that is why marine mammals are so enchanting: they manage to live above and below, and still fit in so well.

Web:

http://nmml.afsc.noaa.gov/
http://www.physics.helsinki.fi/whale/
http://www.rosmarus.com/aad_faq.htm
http://www.tmmsn.org/

Usenet:

alt.animals.dolphins
alt.animals.whales

Monkeys

I never had a pet monkey when I was growing up, but I did have a little sister. Of course, there are important differences. For example, many sisters do not live in tropical or semi-tropical climates. And monkeys do not tie up the telephone when you are waiting for an important call. If you need even more information, here are some good places to look.

Web:

http://www.indiana.edu/~primate/primates.html
http://www.mommensj.web2010.com/monkeys.htm
http://www.monkeymaddness.com/
http://www.primate.wisc.edu/pin/pets.html

MONKEYS

You would think that having a monkey would be a lot of fun, and it can be. But before you get one, use the Net and find out what's in store for you.

Living with a monkey is a permanent, highly demanding job, and is not for the faint at heart. Before you think seriously about getting your own monkey, take the following quiz. Answer each question yes or number

(1) Is it okay if an animal repeatedly trashes your home?

(2) Do you hate going on a vacation or having any spare time?

(3) Do you have a lot of extra money you need to get rid of?

(4) Does your idea of having a good time involve a lot of cleaning and repairing?

(5) Can you be patient and loving when your pet, whom you have cared for since it was a baby, savagely attacks you for no particular reason?

Score 1 point for each "yes", 0 for each "no".

If your score is 0, 1, 2, 3, or 4, you should get a cat. If your score is 5, you may be monkey material.

Pet-Keeping Dos and Don'ts

Before my brother was born, the doctor asked me what I hoped the baby would be. I said I wanted a pony. However, my mother knew I was too young to take care of a pony by myself, so she got me a brother instead. Pets can be a lot of fun, but we do have a responsibility to look after them. Here is a wealth of advice on how to select and care for a pet. For example, before you take a trip, make arrangements with your family or friends as to who should take care of your pet if you don't come back.

Web:

http://www.petstation.com/do&dont.html

Pet Loss

Pets are so important that, when we lose one due to illness or accident, the gap in our lives can feel as large and devastating as when we lose a friend or family member. One thing that makes it difficult is that other people don't really understand how much the pet meant to us. Some people, who perhaps don't have pets, may not even understand the bond that forms between a person and an animal. However, pets are ubiquitous in our society, and if you have lost one, there is lots of assistance available to help you deal with your grief, make good decisions and, if you are so inclined, create an online memorial to your pet.

Web:

http://www.mycemetery.com/
http://www.pet-loss.net/

Usenet:

alt.support.grief.pet-loss

Pet of the Day

Any pet is eligible! Just send in his or her picture with some information, and your pet might become the Pet of the Day. If you like animals, this is a great place to visit when you have a few moments. You can browse through the archives and look at the previous Pets of the Day. Of course, none of them is as adorable as my cat (The Little Nipper) or your pet (but they are cute).

Web:

http://www.petoftheday.com/

Pet Talk and General Discussion

If you have a pet, or want a pet, or happen to be cooking a pet for dinner, check with the general pet discussion groups first. Share information and experiences on a range of topics, including exotic animals, nutrition, grooming, behavior, veterinary care and recipes.

Usenet:

alt.pets
alt.pets.guinea-pigs
alt.pets.hedgehogs
alt.pets.skunks
alt.pets.sugar-glider
rec.pets

Pet Travel

Sure it's possible to go on a trip without your pet, but why would you want to? Your cat won't complain if you stay in the bath for hours and then use up all the towels, and your dog will never drag you off to an art museum when you should be soaking up local color at the beer festival. But if you're going to take The Little Nipper or Angel or Pesky or Bowser on your next trip, it's best to be prepared. Make sure you know the best way to make your special companion feel as special as possible. Even better, see if you can find a pet-friendly hotel to visit, one that will welcome the little brute, so he or she can be as comfortable as possible while you're doing research at the beer festival.

Web:

http://www.aphis.usda.gov/oa/pubs/petravel.html
http://www.avma.org/care4pets/safetrav.htm
http://www.dot.gov/airconsumer/animals.htm
http://www.hsus.org/ace/11869
http://www.petsonthego.com/
http://www.petswelcome.com/

Plants Harmful to Animals

It sounds like a job for a professional politician, but truly, there are people who like to grow poisonous plants for a living. At least they do it for the common good. Check out plants that are toxic to animals and humans. You can look up the plants by common name or by scientific name. These are important resources if you have kids or animals that chew on things they aren't supposed to chew on.

Web:

http://www.amby.com/cat_site/plants.html
http://www.ansci.cornell.edu/plants/

Rabbits

Cuddly, soft, lovable little animals that you can dye pastel shades when Easter rolls around, bunnies are not just for kids. They make great pets for everyone. Learn how to care for a pet rabbit and get information about rabbit psychology and diseases that afflict bunnies. On the mailing list, non-bunny-lovers are not welcome unless you can mind your manners.

Web:
  http://www.rabbit.org/
  http://www.rabbitweb.net/
  http://www.rabbitworld.com/

Usenet:
  alt.animals.breeders.rabbits
  alt.animals.rabbit
  alt.pets.rabbits
  rec.pets.rabbits

Listserv Mailing List:
  List Name: petbunny
  Subscribe to: listserv@lsv.uky.edu

Rats and Mice

I once lived with someone who had a pet rat. One day she let it get away and it hid in the couch. Eventually, we were able to retrieve the rat, but the couch was never the same. Another time, she was playing with the rat by holding its tail. Much to her chagrin, the outside of the tail pulled off, leaving a raw, red inner core. Eventually, the rat healed, but the tail was never the same. As you can see, rodents are pretty cool pets, and if your day-to-day existence is missing something or other, maybe you should get yourself a rat or mouse.

Web:
  http://www.afrma.org/rmindex.htm
  http://www.rmca.org/Resources/faqs.htm

Usenet:
  alt.pets.mice
  alt.pets.rodents

Reptiles and Amphibians

Herpetology is the study of reptiles and amphibians. Both reptiles and amphibians are cold-blooded (that is, they do not maintain a constant internal body temperature). However, where reptiles use lungs to breathe, amphibians breathe with gills when they are young (under water), and with lungs once they become adults. Another difference is that reptiles—such as snakes, lizards, turtles and crocodiles—have bodies that are covered by scales or horny plates. Amphibians—such as newts, frogs, toads and salamanders—have a moist, scaleless skin. Why do people enjoy keeping such animals? Because they are creepy. Kewl.

Web:
  http://www.allaboutfrogs.org/
  http://www.animalnetwork.com/reptiles/profiles/
    profilelst.asp
  http://www.baskingspot.com/
  http://www.frogweb.gov/
  http://www.mindspring.com/~jsibleywebster/lizards/
    LizardsLizardsLizards.html

Usenet:
  alt.pets.reptiles.lizards
  alt.pets.reptiles.lizards.gecko
  alt.pets.reptiles.snakes
  alt.pets.reptiles.snakes.pythons.ball
  alt.pets.reptiles.snakes.pythons.reticulated
  rec.pets.alligators
  rec.pets.herp

Rats and Mice

I have a great idea for a new comic character: a cute, lovable rat. He'll act like a human and have yellow shoes, white gloves, and large round ears. He'll have a girlfriend and get into funny adventures and talk with a high squeaky voice. Now what would be a good name? How about Mickey Rat?

Mickey Rat. Mickey Rat. Doesn't that sound just too cute for words?

Naaaah... nevermind.

Sharks

Okay, let's get the strange stuff out of the way. (1) Sharks don't have bones, they have cartilage. (2) There are 250 different species of sharks. (3) Fully grown sharks can range from cute pygmy sharks measuring only 60 cm (2 feet) up to large whale sharks stretching to 15 meters (50 feet). (4) The most feared shark is the white shark (called the "Great White Shark" in the movies). This animal can grow up to 6 meters (20 feet), and will attack and try to eat just about anything, even without provocation. (The huge whale shark, by the way, is much less dangerous, as it lives on microscopic plankton.) Although people are afraid of sharks, such fears are more a testament to the movies than to common sense. I have been swimming in the ocean for years, and the closest I ever came to a shark was going snorkeling with my lawyer.

Web:
  http://members.ozemail.com.au/~bilsons/
    SHARKS.htm
  http://www.mote.org/~rhueter/sharks/shark.phtml
  http://www.ncf.carleton.ca/~bz050/
    HomePage.shark.html
  http://www.seaworld.org/infobooks/sharks&rays/
    home.html
  http://www.shark.ch/
  http://www.sharks.org/page.htm

Listserv Mailing List:
  List Name: shark-l
  Subscribe to: listserv@raven.utc.edu

Tarantulas

The name "tarantula" refers to several species of large, hair-covered spiders native to North and South America. A large tarantula can measure up to 7.5 cm (3 inches) wide, stretching up to 25 cm (10 inches) with its legs extended. Despite their formidable appearance, tarantulas, if handled properly, are not dangerous to people and can make good pets. By the way, the easiest way to preserve a tarantula—or any spider—is to put it in a glass jar filled with 90-100 percent ethanol (regular drinking alcohol). Of course, you should make sure the tarantula is dead, but, if he isn't, you probably won't get any complaints.

Web:
  http://www.atshq.org/
  http://www.tarantulas.com/

Usenet:
  alt.pets.arachnids

Veterinary Medicine

If you were always the one to bring home the bird with the broken wing or if you liked to wrap the dog up in gauze bandages, then maybe your calling is veterinary medicine. There is a wealth of information on the Net about animals and the veterinary field. The **vetstu-l** mailing list is primarily for veterinary students. The **vetplus-l** mailing list is for veterinary medicine professionals. The **vetmed** list is for general discussions

Web:
  http://netvet.wustl.edu/vet.htm
  http://www.avma.org/
  http://www.healthypet.com/

Usenet:
  alt.med.veterinary

Listproc Mailing List:
  List Name: vetplus-l
  Subscribe to: listproc@u.washington.edu

Listserv Mailing List:
  List Name: vetmed
  Subscribe to: listserv@listserv.iupui.edu

Listserv Mailing List:
  List Name: vetstu-l
  Subscribe to: listserv@listserv.uga.edu

Wildlife

Outside of downtown Los Angeles or the U.S. Republican National Convention, most people don't get a chance to see real wildlife in their native habitat. However, as a Net user, you can virtually visit various types of wildlife, including species that are extinct or endangered.

Web:
  http://www.nature-wildlife.com/
  http://www.wildlifer.com/wildlifesites/

Usenet:
  rec.animals.wildlife

Zoos

Who doesn't like to visit a zoo? We live in a controlled environment with very few animals (aside from pets) and visiting a zoo reminds us that most of the world is populated by many different types of non-human animals. There are a lot of zoo-oriented resources on the Net, and before you visit somewhere, you might want to check out the local zoo. By the way, although zoo animals live behind bars and fences, they are well-fed and cared for. Indeed, zoo animals often live better than people. (For instance, no one would ever think of forcing an animal to wake up to an alarm clock, drive 45 minutes in heavy traffic, and sit behind a desk all day.)

Web:
    http://www.mindspring.com/~zoonet/
        www_virtual_lib/zoos.html
    http://www.zooweb.com/

ARCHAEOLOGY

Archaeoastronomy

Many early civilizations created monuments that had astronomical importance. Among the most well known of such creations are Stonehenge, the Egyptian pyramids and various Mayan palaces. However, there are literally hundreds of such sites, constructed by ancient peoples around the world. Archaeoastronomy is a confluence of anthropology and astronomy, a science that seeks to study ancient astronomical practices, celestial lore, mythologies, calendar systems, and so on.

Web:
    http://user.online.be/felixverbelen/
    http://www.wam.umd.edu/~tlaloc/archastro/

For a good time, visit
http://www.harley.com/

FAQs are cool.

Archaeological Dating Techniques

We all know that archaeologists come up with some old stuff, but exactly how old? To answer that question, scientists have developed a variety of sophisticated dating techniques such as seriation, cultural affiliation, dendro chronology, and fluorine, carbon-14 and potassium-argon dating. Once you learn how it all works, you'll have a better understanding of how a knowledgeable archaeologist can estimate exactly how far back lie the beginnings of important cultural relics whose origins would otherwise be lost to antiquity, such as ancient papyri, primitive hand tools, and Dick Clark.

Web:
    http://members.aol.com/dsfrink/ocr/ocrpage.htm
    http://www.anthro.mankato.msus.edu/archaeology/
        dating/
    http://www.rlaha.ox.ac.uk/orau/02_01.htm
    http://www.sonic.net/bristlecone/dendro.html
    http://www.staff.ncl.ac.uk/kevin.greene/wintro/
        chap4.htm

Archaeological Fieldwork

If you are a student of archaeology, it behooves you to spend a lot of time crawling around the great outdoors looking for little bits and pieces of whatnot. But where should you go? Here are sites that list fieldwork opportunities around the world. The pay is often low or nonexistent, the hours are long, and the work can be mind numbing, but the experience can be invaluable (especially if, one day, you plan to become a professional archaeologist, crawling around the great outdoors looking for little bits and pieces of whatnot).

Web:
    http://www.archaeologyfieldwork.com/cgi-bin/yabb/
        YaBB.cgi?board=volunteer
    http://www.cincpac.com/afos/testpit.html
    http://www.qal.berkeley.edu/arf/fieldop.html
    http://www.urep.ucdavis.edu/2001list.html

Archaeological Site Etiquette

Archaeology sites don't grow on trees (although trees do grow on some archaeology sites). It is important, when you work on a site, to be able to investigate without damaging the site and the artifacts. Here is information about minimum impact techniques that every budding archaeologist should understand before visiting a cultural or archaeological site.

Web:

    http://www.azarchsoc.org/topics/tdata/etiquette.htm
    http://www.history.utah.org/httoolkit/proetiquette.html
    http://www.nps.gov/care/arpa.htm

Archaeological Site Etiquette

Having good manners means being thoughtful and following established customs. However, when you visit an archaeological site, there are special tips you need to know.

So if a trip to someplace old and exciting is in your future, there's no time like the present to brush up on the nuances of trips to the past. After all, you wouldn't want some big lummox 100,000 years from now walking into your house with dirty boots, would you?

Archaeological Societies

If you want to be a real honest-to-Pete archaeologist, you've got to join the club. After all, what's the point of spending your life discovering all kinds of cool archaeological stuff if you don't belong to the same organization as all the other people who spend their lives discovering all kinds of cool archaeological stuff? And once you're a member, don't forget to stop by regularly to read about upcoming events, check out the online journals, and immerse yourself in all manner of things archaeological. That's what's great about the Net. No matter where you are, you can always spend time at the club.

Web:

    http://www.saa.org/
    http://www.socarchsci.org/

Archaeology Events

If you're in the field a lot, it's easy to lose track of what's happening. So how can you be sure that you don't miss that oh-so-important conference? Check with the Net, and you will never be left out in the cold when it comes time to talk about what's been left out in the cold.

Web:

    http://www.anthro.org/image.htm

Archaeology Magazines

Being an archaeologist can be hard work. You dig all day, stay up all night making notes, and still, you are expected to keep up on all that is new and exciting. Well, here's where the Net can help. Take time to check out these online archaeological magazines and, never again will you get caught short when the wiseacre with the horn-rimmed glasses starts spouting off about Mesolithic sites in Scotland, or methods of detecting ancient tuberculosis.

Web:

    http://intarch.york.ac.uk/antiquity/
    http://www.archaeology.org/
    http://www.britarch.ac.uk/ba/ba.html

Archaeology News

There are a lot of people excavating and cataloging all around the world, and a week doesn't go by without some fascinating archaeological discovery. These Web sites will help you keep current with what's new and exciting. I like to take a moment every now and then just to see what the archeologists of the world are doing. After all, on the Net, everything old is news again.

Web:

    http://www.anthro.org/main.htm
    http://www.archaeology.org/online/news/
    http://www.siftings.com/siftings.html
    http://www.tamu.edu/anthropology/news.html
    http://www.timespinner.com/

Archaeology Resources

Need to explore? Here's the door. Want more? Read the lore. Wanna soar? Skip the gore, avoid the war, just get to the core. Never a bore. Never a chore. Bring your paramour. Archaeology resources, wow! Need to explore? Here's the door.

Web:
   http://www.archaeologic.com/
   http://www.archaeologica.org/ResourcesPage.htm
   http://www.archaeology.org/wwwarky/wwwarky.html
   http://www.comp-archaeology.org/
      AbstractsWeb_ARCHAEOLOGY_RESOURCES_.htm
   http://www.har-indy.com/links.html
   http://www.julen.net/ancient/
   http://www.perseus.tufts.edu/art&arch.html

Archaeology Talk and General Discussion

The study of archaeology covers a huge amount of ground, which is why there are a great many archaeology discussion groups on the Net. Follow the discussion over the Net, and you can work with people all over the world without having to venture more than a few feet from the fridge. Or, when you are out on a dig, you can take your laptop computer and cellular modem (paid for by a government grant) and keep up on what is happening, no matter how far you are from the trappings of civilization.

Web:
   http://www.anthro.org/lists.htm
   http://www.archaeologyfieldwork.com/

Usenet:
   alt.archaeology
   sci.archaeology
   sci.archaeology.moderated

Archnet

I have a friend named Ginny who is an archaeologist. She spends a lot of time running around the country digging up small pieces of whatnot and making esoteric discoveries. Myself, I prefer to stay at home with my cat and cruise the Arizona State University Archnet site. That way I can spend hours poring over all kinds of archaeological resources without getting my hands dirty. Ginny may have more fun, but I'm a lot closer to the shower.

Web:
   http://archnet.asu.edu/

Take a bunch of stuff from around the house — some old newspapers, a chipped cereal bowl, a few T-shirts with beer ads on them, an old car battery, and any other junk that you can spare — and put it all in a large, hermetically sealed box. Now all you have to do is wait.

After 2,000 years or so, the items in your box will qualify as genuine archaeological artifacts, and you will be able to sell them for a handsome profit.

If you would like to see what the Greeks, Romans, Egyptians, and other ancient people put in *their* boxes, check out Archnet.

Biblical Archaeology

People who study the Bible are especially interested in the archaeological foundations of biblical writings. However, even for non-believers, the study of the archaeology of biblical times can be rewarding, offering a glimpse into ancient societies that form the basis for much of modern Western civilization. Here is a well-organized collection of links relating to sites mentioned in the Bible. Aside from general resources, you will find links to organizations, and information about ongoing excavations.

Web:
   http://www.bib-arch.org/links.html
   http://www.bibarch.com/

Careers in Archaeology

Why settle for a boring, bland, everyday type of existence when you can get paid to live in the past? Here's a great two-part plan, just for you. (1) Find out what archaeologists do. (2) Do it. (What could be easier?)

Web:
   http://www.archaeology.co.uk/begin/
   http://www.museum.state.il.us/ismdepts/anthro/
      dlcfaq.html
   http://www.sha.org/sha_kbro.htm

Classics and Mediterranean Archaeology

Some of the richest areas in archaeology lie in the study of ancient civilizations (Babylon, Egypt, Greece, Rome, and so on). This Web site points to a huge amount of information of interest to classicists and Mediterranean archaeologists. If you are inclined toward the Ancient World, start here and your archaeological amphora will runneth over.

Web:

> http://rome.classics.lsa.umich.edu/

Egyptology

In 1799, a Frenchman named Boussard, digging near the city of Rosetta in north Egypt, happened upon a slab of basalt measuring 114 cm long by 72 cm wide and inscribed with a decree in honor of the Pharaoh Ptolemy Epiphanes. One result of Boussard's discovery was that generations of students have been required to memorize the significance of Patah, Amon, Horus, Kem, Ket, Roshpu, Bes, Ra, Osiris and Sebek, while more mature scholars have lain awake at night, dreaming of visiting the temple at Karnak, the portico of Denderah, the sarcophagi at Assuan, the propylon at Thebes, and the grottos of Sisileh. Boussard's discovery, the Rosetta Stone, contained a specific passage of text inscribed in several different languages, allowing two European archeologists to decipher the system of ancient hieroglyphics, and usher in the modern age of Egyptology. Ancient Egypt, the seat of many of the pursuits of modern man—architecture, sculpture, painting, music, medicine and chemistry—is an enduring area of scholarship well represented on the Internet.

Web:

> http://emuseum.mankato.msus.edu/prehistory/egypt/
> http://www.akhet.co.uk/
> http://www.discoveringegypt.com/
> http://www.guardians.net/egypt/
> http://www.newton.cam.ac.uk/egypt/
> http://www.swan.ac.uk/classics/egypt/egwww.htm

Industrial Archaeology

Industrial archaeology deals with history and artifacts relating to technology, engineering and industry. Today, that means studying, say, the Industrial Revolution. But what about the future? All the technology we use and take for granted today will be studied by future industrial archaeologists. For example, say you throw away an old blender. A few centuries from now, someone is going to be rooting around in an ancient landfill and come across your blender. He or she will excavate it very carefully, and then use it as the subject of a Ph.D. dissertation. That is why, each time I throw away any type of machine, I put a note in it saying, "To whom it may concern: Hello from Harley in the twenty-first century."

Web:

> http://www.iarecordings.org/
> http://www.industrial-archaeology.org.uk/
> http://www.ss.mtu.edu/ia/sia.html

Looting, Plundering and Stealing

It's not nice to take what doesn't belong to you. Yes, when Indiana Jones does it, it's cool, but outside of the movies, archaeological plundering can wreak havoc with a fragile historical site, sometimes defiling it permanently. Even worse, once an artifact is removed and shipped elsewhere, it loses its context. (And if there is anything that archaeologists hate to lose, it's context. I have a friend who's an archaeologist and she won't even leave the house without a bucket of context.) These Web sites will keep you up-to-date about archaeological looting (and recovery) around the world.

Web:

> http://exchanges.state.gov/education/culprop/
> http://home.earthlink.net/~robbinsls/theft/
> http://www.wings.buffalo.edu/anthropology/
>   documents/lootbib.html

> ## Need a laugh? Try "Humor and Jokes".

Lost Cities

Around the world, there are many places containing the remains of cities that once flourished but have long since died. Some years ago, I visited the ruins of the Mayan city of Chichen Itza in the Yucatan peninsula in Mexico. I stood on top of an ancient pyramid that commanded a view of a large, broad valley and gazed at the ruins. I was filled with a sense of awe and wonder. Awe, because I could see the extent to which an ancient people were able to build elaborate structures, and wonder, as I speculated as to what might have caused such a sophisticated civilization to die out. Learning about lost cities gives us a unique sense of the past, underscoring the mortality of even the most enduring of cultures.

Web:
  http://www.franckgoddio.org/
  http://www.tylwytheg.com/lostcity/lostcity.html

Mesoamerican Archaeology

Mesoamerica ("Middle America") refers to the area that includes central Mexico and the region extending to the south and east, encompassing parts of Guatemala, Belize, Honduras and Nicaragua. This area is of interest because it has been inhabited by a variety of civilizations, the most well-known being the pre-Columbian Maya and Olmec. Although the Mayans flourished centuries ago (about 300-900 A.D.), their civilization was well-developed, having an understanding of mathematics, calendars and hieroglyphics, as well as architecture and city planning. The Olmec are much older (about 1300-400 B.C.), and are often considered to be the mother culture of the later Mesoamerican civilizations. Like the Mayans, the Olmec had a hieroglyphic system of writing. Although the Olmec were much less advanced than the Mayans, they have left intriguing artifacts, such as carved stone heads weighing over 20 tons.

Web:
  http://www.mayalords.org/
  http://www.mesoweb.com/

Usenet:
  sci.archaeology.mesoamerican

National Archaeological Database

Throughout most of recorded history, people have had to dig around for official archaeological data. Now, however, the National Archaeological Database puts hard-to-find information at your virtual fingertips. Never again need you spend hours looking for documents such as the Notice of Inventory Completion for Native American Human Remains from Lake Winnepesauke, New Hampshire.

Web:
  http://www.cast.uark.edu/products/NADB/

Treasure in Your Backyard?

How many people are overlooking important — and perhaps valuable — archaeological treasures right in their own backyards? This need never happen to you.

The National Archaeological Database

contains information on more investigations than you can shake a 500-year-old stick at.
Connect to this bountiful resource and get the lowdown on what's low down.

Papyrology

Papyrology is the study of ancient documents written on papyrus leaves. The ancient Egyptians developed the technique of creating a paper-like material from the pith of the papyrus plant, a reed that grew along the banks of the Nile River. (Pith is the material inside the stem.) The idea of writing on papyri spread from Egypt to other parts of the world. However, it was only in Egypt and Mesopotamia (part of modern-day Iraq) that the climate allowed papyri to survive over the years. Today, papyrologists study the estimated 400,000 papyri preserved around the world, many of which are fragments. These papyri contain a large variety of writing—literature, religious works, government reports, private documents—in Egyptian, Greek, Latin, Coptic and Arabic. As you might imagine, a papyrologist is like a detective. He or she must decode the meaning of a document, often from a fragment. Today, however, we have the Net, and papyrologists around the world can share research material.

Web:
    http://faculty.smu.edu/dbinder/papyrolo.html
    http://lhpc.arts.kuleuven.ac.be/
    http://scriptorium.lib.duke.edu/papyrus/
    http://www.csad.ox.ac.uk/csad/
    http://www.papyrology.org/resources.htm

Repatriation and Reburial

Anthropologists and archaeologists are concerned with the past and, hence, have a strong inclination to study and remove human remains from burial sites. In sharp contradistinction, various cultural and religious groups want the dead to be left alone, to rest in peace, as it were, safe from the clutching hands of philistine scientists. As you might imagine, two such diverging points of view are not easy to reconcile. Want to jump into the middle of a bunch of irresistible forces mixing it up with a collection of immovable objects? Here's your invite to the party.

Web:
    http://web.inter.nl.net/users/Paul.Treanor/
       return.art.html
    http://www.archaeologic.com/repatriation.htm
    http://www.wynja.com/arch/reburial.html

Rock Art

The oldest existing works of art we have are drawings and carvings on rocks. Such artifacts have been found on every continent and form an important body of archaeological source material. Common rock art motifs include outlines of human hands, drawings of animals and hunting scenes, and pictures of daily activities. At these sites you will find great examples of fascinating rock art around the world as well as links to other rock art sites.

Web:
    http://www.execpc.com/~jcampbel/
    http://www.questorsys.com/rockart/links.htm
    http://www.rupestre.net/rockart/

Listserv Mailing List:
    List Name: rock-art
    Subscribe to: listserv@lists.asu.edu

Underwater Archaeology

Not all archaeology takes place on land. There is lots and lots of old and important stuff under the water. Here are some sites devoted to studying underwater archaeology. You will find articles, discussion lists, information about shipwrecks, as well as links to other related resources.

Web:
    http://www.abc.se/~m10354/uwa/
    http://www.archaeologic.com/
       underwater_archaeology.htm

ARCHITECTURE

Aesthetic Architecture

This site has information about the aesthetic architecture movement of the late 19th and early 20th centuries. The works displayed at this site are from artists and architects who concentrated heavily on regional styles, hand-craftsmanship and decorative detail. Represented movements include the Prairie School (Frank Lloyd Wright), Craftsman (Gustave Stickley), and other regional and international styles, such as the Gothic revival.

Web:
    http://www.fswarchitects.com/links.html

Architectural Competitions

Competition brings out the best in people. Architects are people. Therefore, architectural competitions bring out the best in architects. (If only all of life were so simple.)

Web:
http://www.deathbyarch.com/html/
   competitions.html
http://www.irish-architecture.com/icn/

ARCHITECTURAL COMPETITIONS

Recently, I looked at the list of architectural competitions and decided to enter one.

I considered a variety of concepts before I started work and, finally, I came up with a wonderful, organic design, elegant with simplicity and charm. My idea was to construct the new building entirely of Popsicle sticks held together with rubber bands and glue. (I have to admit, my cat, The Little Nipper, helped me.The Popsicle sticks were his idea.)

I carefully packed up the model and sent it in. The fact that I did not win the competition, I can only attribute to jealousy on the part of the judges. The Little Nipper thinks we should have included a can of tuna. Perhaps he was right.

Architectural Reconstructions

Do you ever wonder what ancient ruins looked like when they were new? If you have trouble imagining the architecture, you can take a look at some of the computer-modeled reconstructions of famous ancient buildings such as Hadrian's Bath and the Temple of Rameses III. This site has not only the pictures, but details about rebuilding by computer and other architectural explorations.

Web:
http://archpropplan.auckland.ac.nz/virtualtour/

Architectural Styles

When you have to go to one of those swanky, cultural, let's-show-off-who-we-are-and-what-we-do parties, it's good to have a few cocktail conversation topics prepared. Architecture is something good to talk about, because there will always be a building nearby. Before you head off to that party, read the information at these sites. You'll find descriptions of various architectural styles and their influences. Before long, you will be able to name-drop with ease.

Web:
http://www.archpedia.com/Styles.html
http://www.bc.edu/bc_org/avp/cas/fnart/fa267/
   amstyles.html
http://www.for.nau.edu/~twp/p399/styleshome.html
http://www.uwec.edu/Academic/Geography/
   Ivogeler/w367/styles/

Architecture Magazines

Here's the scenario. You are sitting in the local Architect's Club, lounging in a Gerrit Rietveld armchair, sipping a cool fruit smoothie, and having a spirited discussion with an old friend you have known since architecture school. You are arguing the proposition that each generation of architects must reinterpret the principles of architecture for their own time, and you are just about to make a powerful, insightful observation of such import that it is sure to keep your friend quiet for the next twenty minutes, when all of a sudden a vague suspicion begins to invade your countenance that, perhaps, you don't really know what you are talking about. But, for you, it is the work of a moment to excuse yourself temporarily from the conversation, run home, connect to the Net, check out the current contents of a few architectural magazines, race back to the club, plop yourself back down into the Gerrit Rietveld armchair, and stun your friend with a devastating analysis of modern architecture and its relation to an information-based society. Once again, the Internet, in combination with your native intelligence and penetrating insight, has saved the day.

Web:
http://www.a-node.net/
http://www.archpedia.com/Architecture.html
http://www.archrecord.com/
http://www.metropolismag.com/
http://www.plannet.com/

Architecture Resources

There's a lot to keep track of in the world of architecture, and the Net can help. Here are some resources to help you find the information you need about famous architects, buildings, construction technology, organizations, art, design, and much more.

Web:
http://www.bc.edu/bc_org/avp/cas/fnart/
    archweb_frames.html
http://www.library.ubc.ca/finearts/
    ARCHITECTURE.html
http://www.library.unlv.edu/arch/rsrce/webrsrce/
    contents.html
http://www.tiac.net/users/dstein/nw71.html
http://www.vitruvio.ch/

Architecture Talk and General Discussion

In my opinion, architects are some of the most talented, visionary, imaginative people in the world. Join the general architecture discussion group for all manner of architecture-oriented topics: building design, construction, architecture schools, materials, and so on. If they can build it, you can talk about it.

Usenet:
alt.architecture
alt.architecture.int-design
alt.building.architecture
alt.landscape.architecture
rec.arts.architecture

Athenian Architecture

If you can't tell your amphiprostyle structure from a peripteral layout, maybe it's time to brush up on your basic Greek architecture. Take a virtual tour of the architecture of Athens. Here you will see pictures of the Acropolis, the Library of Hadrian, the Arch of Hadrian, the Temple of Zeus, the Theater of Dionysos, and much more.

Web:
http://www.indiana.edu/~kglowack/athens/

Bauhaus

The Bauhaus movement of the early twentieth century developed from a school of art and architecture founded in 1919 by Walter Gropius (1883-1969) in Weimar, Germany. To me, Bauhaus represents two important movements. First, it represents an architectural philosophy that was firmly intertwined with the political and economic conditions of post-World War I Germany. Bauhaus architecture was created for the workers, and was supposed to reject "bourgeois" traditions and materials. The result was a collection of ugly, functional structures based on rigid economic and geometrical designs. The German government built massive amounts of Bauhaus housing which ultimately became highly unpopular (especially among the workers who had to live in the buildings). With the rise of the Nazis, many Bauhaus designers emigrated, spreading their influence to the U.S. (If you have ever seen American public housing or "portable" classrooms, you have seen Bauhaus.) The second important Bauhaus movement concerned itself with applied design: furniture, lighting, kitchenware, appliances, and so on. The Bauhaus artisans popularized the idea that one could design utilitarian objects as pieces of art, offering beauty as well as function. This idea has become one of the defining tenets of our love affair with stuff, and, for many years, we have been buying *objets d'utilité* that double as pretty things to have around the house. Still, it is the Bauhaus style of architecture that has insinuated itself into the body cultural. Like an incorrigible virus, Bauhaus-inspired buildings arise with disturbing regularity, most often when people in authority combine a lack of taste with a desire to save money. On the Net, the Bauhaus sensibility is widespread, flourishing under the guise of Web page design.

Web:
http://people.ucsc.edu/~gflores/bauhaus/b1.html
http://www.cs.umb.edu/~alilley/bauhaus.html
http://www.uiah.fi/presentation/history/ebauha.htm

Great Buildings

A great building stands as more than a structure. It is a mute monument to the location, culture and environment in which it was built. There are hundreds and hundreds of great buildings around the world, and this resource provides an excellent way to study them. For each building, you'll find basic information, including the location, name of the architect and dates of construction, along with pictures, floor plans and a short discussion. (What I want to see is a 3D simulation of what happens when you throw a penny off the top of the Empire State Building.)

Web:
http://www.greatbuildings.com/buildings.html

Japanese Architecture

The architecture of a region has many influences. Some of these are physical (geography, weather patterns), while others are social (the economy, religion, types of people, and history of the area). Over the centuries, Japan has developed distinct architectural traditions that are both pleasing and puzzling to the Western eye. Use these Web sites to explore Japanese architecture and to view pictures of a variety of traditionally designed buildings.

Web:
http://web.kyoto-inet.or.jp/org/orion/eng/hstj/histj.html
http://www.asianinfo.org/asianinfo/japan/architecture.htm
http://www.japan-guide.com/e/e2059.html
http://www.peachstar.org/irasshai/culwww/arc1.htm

New Urbanism

New Urbanism is an approach to architecture that strives to design small, livable, comfortable neighborhoods. The tenets of New Urbanism mandate residential and commercial planning so as to encourage walking, not driving. A neighborhood should have a variety of homes and services, and be small enough for residents to walk from their houses to a public area in which there are stores, public buildings, transportation, and so on. In addition, there should be well-planned open spaces, such as playgrounds and parks, in convenient locations. (If you saw the movie The Truman Show, you have seen an example of a New Urbanism design.) To me, the New Urbanism movement represents an attempt to make modern life more manageable. The goal seems admirable, but I wonder if such designs are not more suitable for vacation communities. They seem unrealistic as day-to-day working and living environments.

Web:
http://www.cnu.org/
http://www.mnapa.com/urbanlex.html
http://www.netsense.net/~terry/newurban.htm
http://www.newurbanism.org/

Listserv Mailing List:
List Name: cnu
Subscribe to: listserv@lsv.uky.edu

Renaissance and Baroque Architecture

The Renaissance (1300-1500) and the Baroque eras (1600-1750) were times of immense architectural development. We study these periods to understand the transition between the architecture of the Middle Ages and modern traditions. During the Renaissance, the dominating force of architectural development was the reintroduction of design principles originally developed by the Romans. This resulted in the construction of many structures of great beauty, based on the elegant, even mathematical, usage of simple shapes. During the Baroque period, architects reinterpreted the Roman influence and experimented with new ideas related to space and time, developing techniques and concepts that form the basis of modern architecture.

Web:

http://arthist.cla.umn.edu/aict/html/renbrq.html
http://web.kyoto-inet.or.jp./org/orion/eng/hst/
   renais.html
http://www.lib.virginia.edu/dic/colls/arh102/

Sullivan, Louis Henry

Louis Henry Sullivan (1856-1924) was an eminent American architect remembered today for his admonition that "form ever follows function". In 1881, Sullivan formed the Chicago firm of Alder and Sullivan (with Dankmar Adler). Alder and Sullivan designed a number of important buildings during the years of rebuilding that followed the Chicago Fire (of 1871), and developed many of the early steel-frame designs for skyscrapers. The firm is also known for employing the young Frank Lloyd Wright for six years at the beginning of his career. Sullivan believed that architects must reconcile nature with science and technology, and he designed buildings in which ornamentation was an integral part of the structure rather than merely an addition to the finished product. Later in life, Sullivan developed the idea of "organic architecture", which asserted that architects should integrate the presence of nature along with the functional needs and materials of a structure.

Web:

http://www.bfn.org/sigs/links/preserve/bam/archs/
   sul/biog/
http://www.tape.net/~gerry/sullivan/

Urban Planning

Urban planning is as old as the Romans and as new as the house being built around the corner. An urban planner must balance architectural principles against economic constraints, regulations, existing infrastructure, local sensibilities, historical traditions and politics. Since most people live in cities, urban planning is one of the most important areas of architecture, and a crucial planning decision can affect many people over a long period of time. Truly, urban planning is a balancing act, one that covers a *lot* of ground.

Web:

http://www.ar.utexas.edu/planning/links.html
http://www.huduser.org/
http://www.library.cornell.edu/Reps/DOCS/
   homepage.htm
http://www.planning.org/resources-k/

Usenet:

alt.planning.urban

Women in Architecture

Women involved with architecture will find these sites inspiring. Here are lots of links to biographical information about women architects, such as Julia Morgan (1872-1957), designer of Hearst Castle in San Simeon, California. There are also bibliographies, statistics regarding women in the architecture workplace, as well as information about modern female architects.

Web:
  http://spec.lib.vt.edu/iawa/guide.html
  http://www.arvha.asso.fr/arvha_french/info_arvha/
    document_info/us-archi.html
  http://www.bluffton.edu/~sullivanm/women/
    contents.html
  http://www.distinguishedwomen.com/subject/
    architec.html
  http://www.library.unlv.edu/arch/rsrce/resguide/
    archwom.html

Wright, Frank Lloyd

Frank Lloyd Wright (1869-1959) was an American architect whose innovations later set standards in architecture. Wright invented the "prairie style" of home and believed in eliminating traditional room divisions in order to create a living space that was more in tune with the needs of the inhabitants.

Web:
  http://lcweb.loc.gov/exhibits/flw/
  http://www.delmars.com/wright/flwright.htm
  http://www.franklloydwright.org/
  http://www.sidesways.com/fllw/

ART

3D Art

3D art is a computer created art form that endows 2-dimensional images with an unusual feeling of depth, perspective and realism. 3D artists use sophisticated computer programs to create images that have a natural, yet unnatural look, that, when it is done well, will totally blow you away. A lot of 3D art is devoted to comic characters and commercial products, but a significant amount is art-for-the-sake- of-art.

Web:
  http://www.3d-cc.com/
  http://www.3dalliance.net/
  http://www.3dark.com/

African Art

An enduring theme in African art is that ideas about life—both spiritual and worldly—can be portrayed through the rendering of human and animal images. Thus, masks, carvings, paintings and other works represent ideas and feelings. Here are some good places to start exploring African art and to appreciate its unique flavor.

Web:
  http://www.africanart.org/
  http://www.africans-art.com/
  http://www.artchive.com/artchive/A/african.html
  http://www.zyama.com/

Report on African Art
by Elmo (age 8)

Africa is a continent on the east side of the Atlantic Ocean. There are many countries there, and a lot of different types of people. I had a friend who went to Africa. He had a good time, but he said it was hot. One day I want to go to Africa to see stuff. My father says I can go when I am older. I like African Art because it looks like fun. Maybe one day, when I am old, I will go to Africa and make art like I saw on the Internet.

-Elmo

Art Activism

Imagine a world in which art mattered. Imagine a world in which artists picked up their brushes and chisels in the service of cultural and political activism. You have just imagined "Art Activism". Now take a look and see what is already happening (and notice that there is a place for you).

Web:
  http://www.guerrillagirls.com/
  http://www.subvertise.org/
  http://www.wsu.edu/~amerstu/pop/activism.html

Listproc Mailing List:
  List Name: artery
  Subscribe to: listproc@u.washington.edu

Listserv Mailing List:
  List Name: agitprop_news
  Subscribe to: listserv@email.rutgers.edu

Art Conservation

Human beings have strong ties to the past. We may not realize it day to day, but what we think and what we do are influenced enormously by the people who preceded us. Although technology and fashion change, human nature doesn't. By studying art, we form a connection to our past, which allows us to understand the present. However, you can't study art if it doesn't exist: once a work of art deteriorates, the original quality is gone forever. Thus, if we don't spend our time, effort and money to preserve our heritage, we may lose it. Modern art conservation not only deals with traditional problems (such as molds and pests), but also with new techniques such as digital imaging and electronic records.

Web:
  http://palimpsest.stanford.edu/
  http://www2.lib.udel.edu/subj/artc/internet.htm

Art Criticism

When it comes to art, everybody may know what they like, but not everybody's opinion is worthwhile. If you are serious about art, you may want to read some art criticism or participate in a discussion. At least you can be sure there will always be one person who knows what he is talking about.

Web:
  http://www.aesthetics-online.org/

Listserv Mailing List:
  List Name: artcrit
  Subscribe to: listserv@yorku.ca

Art History

I have mixed feelings about art history. Learning about art by studying paintings, sculpture, architecture, and the artists themselves can teach us to appreciate the creative spirit of human beings at their very best. However, it is all too common for art history courses to degenerate into the mindless memorization of slide after slide after slide (so you can identify them in order to pass the exam). Don't consign yourself to a life of temporarily force-feeding hundreds of images into your cerebrum. Use the Net to immerse yourself in a sea of electronic resources, and enjoy some of mankind's greatest creations at your own speed.

Web:
  http://witcombe.sbc.edu/ARTHLinks.html
  http://www.arthistory.net/
  http://www.artmovements.co.uk/frames.htm

Art News

Don't get left out of the cool art scene. No matter where on Earth you are—London, Cairo, or Fargo, North Dakota—you can keep up with the latest happenings in the art world.

Web:
  http://www.artdaily.com/
  http://www.artnet.com/magazine/
  http://www.artswire.org/Artswire/www/current.html

Art Nouveau

The Art Nouveau movement flourished as a style of architecture and decoration in the 1890s and early 1900s. Art Nouveau started in France (in Paris and then in the city of Nancy) and from there spread to major European centers in other countries. Here is a nice overview of the Art Nouveau movement as it manifested itself in various European cities. Take a look at representative examples within the decorative arts, as well as a variety of buildings designed in the Art Nouveau style.

Web:
  http://art-nouveau.kubos.org/en/

Art Resources

The best thing about art is you can define it to be whatever you want. For example, this book is a work of art (as are the Eiffel Tower, the Mona Lisa and Mickey Mouse). To a greater or lesser degree, all of us have some creativity. In fact, the urge to create art is one of the distinguishing characteristics that separate us from the lower animals (although my cat once constructed a fascinating collage involving a dead mouse, some tufts of grass and a piece of leftover tuna). So when you are ready for an *expérience d'art*, start by visiting the Internet, where you can enjoy the good, the bad, the ugly, and the I-know-what-I-like-when-I-see-it.

Web:
  http://www.art-smart.com/art/links.html
  http://www.art.net/
  http://www.artresources.com/

Usenet:
  alt.binaries.pictures.fine-art

"Art Nouveau" is just another way of saying "New Art". (We just say it in French to make it sound more classy.) So take a look at the Internet's Art Nouveau overview, and soon you will be saying "Zut alors!" (French for "Way cool, Dude".)

Art Talk and General Discussion

Here are the places on the Net where artists gather to talk about the art community. These discussion groups and mailing lists are where you can post announcements about new exhibits and gallery openings, rant about the politics of art, and offer critical appraisal and analysis.

Usenet:
alt.airbrush.art
alt.art
alt.art.caricature
alt.art.illustration
alt.art.scene
alt.art.video
alt.art.virtual-beret
alt.artcom
alt.arts
alt.illustration
rec.arts.fine
rec.arts.misc

Listserv Mailing List:
List Name: artistcares
Subscribe to: listserv@relief.lsoft.com

Listserv Mailing List:
List Name: artnine
Subscribe to: listserv@listserv.uni-heidelberg.de

Listserv Mailing List:
List Name: design-l
Subscribe to: listserv@lists.psu.edu

Majordomo Mailing List:
List Name: abstract-art-l
Subscribe to: majordomo@itg.uiuc.edu

Art Terminology

How well do you know your art terminology? Never again need you feel embarrassed because you thought that gouache, mischio and sinopia were the names of the Three Musketeers. (A gouache is heavy, opaque watercolor paint; a mischio is a smoky pattern in marble; sinopia is a reddish-brown earth color.)

Web:
http://www.art-wow.com/HTML/glossary.html
http://www.artlex.com/

Artist Encyclopedia

My editor, Carolyn, and I were talking about deadlines when, suddenly, she changed the subject. "I saw a Georgia O'Keefe exhibition the other day," she told me. "It was magnificent." "Really?" I replied. "I can look at paintings anytime," I said. "All I have to do is use the Artist Encyclopedia. I can look up any artist and find, not only information, but links to Web pages with pictures of that artist's work. I can look at all the art I want and never have to leave the house." "That must come in handy," said Carolyn, "seeing as you are not allowed to leave the house until the book is finished."

Web:
http://www.artcyclopedia.com/

LOOKING FOR AN ART JURY OF YOUR PEERS?

Try the **alt.artcom** discussion group. No need to waste your time hanging around a coffee house talking about the art world, when you can sit around your own house, drinking coffee and discussing the art world.

A B C D E F G H I J K L M N O P Q R S T U V W X Y Z

Arts and Crafts Movement

When I was a young sprout at summer camp, we would spend time doing "arts and crafts". We made various craft-like objects, which we would then send home as proof of our cultural development. The label "Arts and Crafts", however, is actually an old one, referring to an important social and aesthetic movement that started in England in the last half of the 19th century. The movement developed as a reaction against the mass production of the Industrial Revolution, and promoted a return to the values of craftsmanship that flourished during medieval times. The Arts and Crafts movement was particularly devoted to design and architecture, and had a large influence on Art Nouveau.

Web:
 http://www.arts-crafts.com/
 http://www.burrows.com/found.html

Majordomo Mailing List:
 List Name: art-crafts
 Subscribe to: majordomo@tias.com

Ascii Art

The basic system used to represent text-based data on PCs is called ascii (the American Standard Code for Information Interchange). Thus, the term "ascii data" refers to information consisting of characters (letters, numbers and punctuation), such as documents, memos and so on. However, if you are artistic, you can use those same letters, numbers and punctuation characters to create images, and have a blast making cool pictures without ever having to throw down a dropcloth or pollute the room with brain-damaging chemicals. As long as you have a keyboard, there is no sense getting your hands dirty just to make art.

Web:
 http://www.ascii-art.de/
 http://www.asciiartgallery.com/
 http://www.chris.com/ascii/
 http://www.ludd.luth.se/~vk/pics/ascii/ASCII.HTML
 http://www.textfiles.com/art/

Usenet:
 alt.ascii-art
 alt.ascii-art.animation
 rec.arts.ascii

Listserv Mailing List:
 List Name: asciiart
 Subscribe to: listserv@lsv.uky.edu

Body Art

Pierced, tattooed, scarred, painted, and more. These resources are where you can find body art in all its forms.

Web:
 http://www.codecipher.com/bodypaint/
 http://www.faqs.org/faqs/bodyart/
 http://www.hennapage.com/henna/
 http://www.members.aol.com/sentai/BP-LINKS.htm

Usenet:
 alt.art.bodypainting
 rec.arts.bodyart

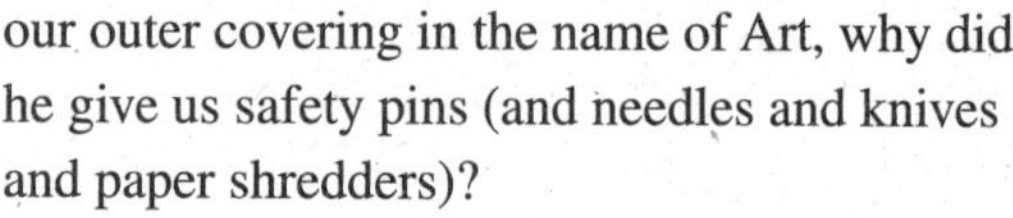

Only a humph-brained ignoramus would think that decorating your body by permanent disfigurement is foolish. After all, if God didn't want us to modify our outer covering in the name of Art, why did he give us safety pins (and needles and knives and paper shredders)?

Personally, I feel that the human body comes with only the minimum set of holes, and anyone who wants to add to the collection has a perfect right to do so. If cleanliness is next to godliness, then holiness must be next to… well, I'm not quite sure, but it must be something important.

So next time you have a few spare moments and it is not too close to mealtime, spend some time reading the body art discussion groups. I guarantee a fun time for all and more than a few ideas for how to decorate the neighbors' children next Christmas.

Ceramic Arts

We're talking about clay here. Mushy, moist, malleable clay. And glazes. Mellifluous, marvelous, multicolored glazes. Not to mention kilns, pottery wheels, greenware and extruders. I love ceramics (inorganic, nonmetallic solids processed at high temperatures) and what you can do with them. So hot, yet so cool.

Web:
http://art.sdsu.edu/ceramicsweb/
http://www.ikts.fhg.de/vl/vl.artistic.ceramics.html

Listserv Mailing List:
List Name: clayart
Subscribe to: listserv@lsv.ceramics.org

Collage

A collage is a piece of art consisting of various disparate elements joined into a whole. Traditionally, collage consists of pasting pieces of paper and possibly other materials on a surface to create a picture. Collage (from the French word for "pasting") was first practiced by Picasso and Braque. Later, the techniques were used by the Dadaists and Surrealists. In modern times, some of the most imaginative and talented artists do collage, including one of my researchers (Elaine).

Web:
http://www.collageart.org/
http://www.globalcollage.com/new_site/
http://www.nationalcollage.com/

Drawing

When I first started medical school, I had to spend each afternoon dissecting in the anatomy lab. After the class, I would stay and practice drawing the various muscles and bones. Unfortunately, I couldn't do it for more than a week or two, as medical school was just too demanding. However, it did reinforce in me the idea that drawing is, and always has been, the basic skill of an artist. These days, most of my art is confined to abstract painting, but I still plan each painting with a drawing. I believe that, with practice, anyone can learn how to draw. If you would like to try for yourself, visit these Web sites, where you will not only enjoy some fine drawings, you can also take an online course to develop your own skills.

Web:
http://www.nyu.edu/classes/miller/guide/
    function.html#independent
http://www.wetcanvas.com/forums/
    channels.php?s=&channel_id=15
http://www2.evansville.edu/studiochalkboard/
    draw.html

Gargoyles and Grotesques

Are you a fan of the dark? Do you, at sunset, glance upward to see the grotesque statuary on the edges of skyscrapers or Gothic cathedrals? These Web sites are devoted to gargoyles old and new, as well as grotesque statues of every sort. They provide a history of and writings about this unique form of sculpture, as well as dramatic pictures of some of its more interesting examples.

Web:
http://www.ils.unc.edu/garg/garghp4.html
http://www.stonecarver.com/gargoyle.html

Impressionism

Impressionism is a style of painting that started in France during the 1860s. Impressionist paintings portray a quick visual impression of a scene (often a landscape), with particular attention being paid to the effects of light. Such paintings are particularly soothing and inviting, with almost universal appeal. Among the well-known Impressionists were Claude Monet, Edgar Degas, Camille Pissarro and Pierre Auguste Renoir. The name "Impressionism" comes from one of Monet's paintings, exhibited in 1874 under the name "Impression Sunrise".

Web:
http://www.artchive.com/74nadar.htm
http://www.artchive.com/artchive/
    impressionism.html
http://www.ibiblio.org/wm/paint/theme/
    impressionnisme.html
http://www.tigtail.org/TVM/X2/b.Impressionism/
    impressionism.html

Installation Art

The environment in which one views a work of art can be as meaningful as the work itself. Installation Art celebrates this idea by the recognition of environments as works of art in their own right. Sometimes there are smaller, static pieces of art serving to complement the larger creation. Sometimes the installation is itself larger than life and overwhelming. Regardless, Installation Art does more to blur the line between art and experience than the first three seasons of The Brady Bunch (put together).

Web:
http://www.235media.com/media_art/
http://www.users.skynet.be/P-ART/PARADISE/
    GALLERY/10INSTAL/instal.htm

Mail Art

Mail art is a fun means of creating interactive art that stays in the hands of the artists, instead of being behind glass or in stuffy exhibits. Find out more about mail and email art, see images of mail art, and get a list of people on the Net who participate in mail art.

Web:
http://www.dragonflydream.com/mailart.html
http://www.plexus.org/cgi-bin/chalk/oneworld.pl

Native American Art

There is no word for "art" in most Native American languages, because the idea of creating beautiful objects is simply part of their culture. Native Americans want to "walk in beauty", as the Navajos put it. To an American Indian, common everyday objects, such as spoons, shoes, blankets, bridles, and so on, are created to be visually pleasing as well as useful. Prior to European contact, Native Americans did not create art as an end unto itself. Rather, they produced crafts that fit into their everyday activities including ceremonies. Native American Art started when Indians were brought into white society (as prisoners, interpreters and students), given ledger books, and asked to make drawings of significant events in the history of their tribes. At first, Native American Art consisted mostly of colorful, 2-dimensional pictures of traditional subject matter. Since the 1940s, Native American artists have created a large, diverse body of work, both traditional and non-traditional.

Web:
http://www.artnatam.com/
http://www.hanksville.org/naresources/
http://www.nativetech.org/

Painting: Oil and Acrylic

One part of painting is being able to conceive of images and put them on paper or canvas. Another part, just as important, is to develop the skills and knowledge necessary to work with various materials. These resources will help you learn about pigments and modifiers, varnishes, brushes, colors, mixing, acrylics, tempera, stretching canvas, and other tools of the trade.

Web:
http://www.paintersstudio.com/acrylic/
http://www.paintersstudio.com/oils/
http://www.wetcanvas.com/forums/
    channels.php?s=&channel_id=19
http://www.wetcanvas.com/forums/
    channels.php?s=&channel_id=7

Painting: Watercolor

Watercolor refers to painting with pigments that are soluble in water, usually on white or tinted paper. Watercolor painting relies upon the transparency and soft harmony of the colors, and as such, requires a high standard of technique. (Unlike oil or acrylics, you can't just paint over your mistakes.) Watercolor painting was well-known as far back as second century A.D. Egypt, but did not become an important art form until the time of the German painter Albrecht Dürer (1471-1528). In eighteenth century England, the modern tradition of watercolors was established by the "English School" including Sandby, Blake, Girtin, Turner, Crome, Cotman, Varley, Cox and de Wint. In later years, America came to develop a tradition of its own, with the work of Winslow Homer, Thomas Eakins, Edward Hopper, Andrew Wyeth and Ben Shahn.

Web:

http://www.fountainstudio.com/watercolor_tips.html
http://www.paintwatercolors.com
http://www.wetcanvas.com/forums/
   channels.php?s=&channel_id=31
http://www.worldofwatercolor.com/

Pop Art

Pop Art focuses on objects taken from the popular urban culture, such as advertisements, comics, and the labels and packages used with mass-produced consumer products. The basic idea was to fashion art based on vernacular images and icons shared by everyone. Pop Art originated in London in the mid-1950s with the work of the Independent Group. Within several years, the same type of ideas were being explored in the United States, where they flourished into the 1960s, partially as a reaction to Abstract Expressionism. The most well-known Pop Art artists were Richard Hamilton, Andy Warhol, Roy Lichtenstein, Claes Oldenburg, Jasper Johns and Robert Rauschenberg.

Web:

http://www.artchive.com/artchive/pop_art.html
http://www.fi.muni.cz/~toms/PopArt/
http://www.popartists.com/

Printmaking

A print is a picture that is transferred from one medium to another to produce a finished product. To create a print, you render an image on metal, wood, silk, stone or rubber. (Some people even use cut potatoes.) You then use the rendering along with ink or another type of pigment to create images of the original design. Prints can be made on a variety of materials, usually some type of paper or fabric. The art of printmaking is an old one, dating way back in history (even before the discovery of potatoes). Although modern printmaking has new techniques and materials, the basic concepts haven't changed. Printmaking has always required artistic skill, manual dexterity, and the ability to attend to details.

Web:

http://duke.usask.ca/~semenoff/
http://www.mtsu.edu/~art/printmaking/wwwboard/
   wwwboard.html
   http://www.printmaker.com/links.html
http://www.woodblock.com/

Listserv Mailing List:

List Name: paper-l
Subscribe to: listserv@listserv.nd.edu

Sculpture

It is inborn in us to create three-dimensional works of art, and sculpture has been a pastime of every civilization since ancient days. The activity of sculpture involves either carving (cutting away) or modeling (building up), using any of a number of materials, traditionally wood, stone, clay, metals or plastics. However, just about anything that can be manipulated (such as ice or beach sand) has been used as a sculpting medium by somebody. (I myself have done some wonderful things using nothing more than leftover rye bread and chunks of tuna.)

Web:

http://web.northnet.org/friends_of_sculpting/
http://www.learningstone.net/stonehoo/
http://www.sculptor.org/

Usenet:

alt.sculpture

Surrealism

If you don't understand it, I can't explain it. Let your mind dance on the edge of radical thought. (Fish.) Take a look at paintings by famed Surrealists or participate in some fun thought games. Don't be afraid. The only thing it can hurt is your brain.

Web:
   http://www.bway.net/~monique/
   http://www.cusimano.com/artist/surreal/
   http://www.execpc.com/~bogartte/links2.html

Usenet:
   alt.surrealism

Alphonse Mucha Museum

Alphonse Maria Mucha (1860-1939) was a Czech artist remembered for his posters created in the French Art Nouveau period. He was propelled into stardom when he was commissioned to create posters of Sarah Bernhardt, an actress who was in vogue in the late 1800s. Mucha's work is characterized by a predominance of curves and flowing lines, and abstract and stylized motifs from nature, such as flowers. At the time, there was a growing interest in decorative art and a relaxation of the Victorian attitudes. Mucha's more free and sensual style was heartily welcomed. Take a look at the beautiful works of Alphonse Mucha. These Web sites have many of his works, including some of the advertisement graphics he did for companies like Nestle foods.

Web:
   http://www.artrenewal.org/museum/m/
      mucha_alphonse/page1.html
   http://www.nymuseum.com/mucha.htm

Art Crimes

Graffiti is often referred to as "art crime" because even though it can sometimes be beautiful, it's still illegal. Take a photo-tour of art crimes around the world. Many of these places no longer exist, so this will be your only chance to see them.

Web:
   http://www.graffiti.org/

Usenet:
   alt.graffiti

Art Gallery Talk and General Discussion

There are lots of things happening in the art scene, and one way to keep up is to follow what's happening in this Usenet group. When the time comes that your work is going on exhibition, you can announce it here.

Usenet:
   alt.art.scene

Art in Context

Looking for a particular artist's work, or the location or Web site of a museum or gallery? This is the place to start. Search for whatever you want by name, discipline or genre. If you like art, this is a jumping-off place to a never-ending journey.

Web:

http://www.artincontext.com/

Asian Art Gallery

Cure that craving for the exotic with a visit to the Asian Art Gallery. Explore an exhibit on Tibetan mandalas or a collection of Himalayan art. You will also find information and photos of art from China, India, Mongolia and more. I like to browse, from time to time, just to look at the pictures of ancient art. They provide a nice change from the overwhelming influence of the modern popular culture sea in which we spend most of our time swimming.

Web:

http://www.asianart.com/

Baroque Art

The Baroque movement involved European painting, sculpture and architecture, particularly in the Catholic countries, from about 1600 to 1750. Baroque style was an outgrowth of the Renaissance. The work emphasized unity and balance, and many ornate, ambitious works were created featuring detailed parts put together to form a single large composition. Among the most important Baroque artists are Caravaggio (1571-1610), Peter Rubens (1577-1640), Diego Velázquez (1599-1660), Rembrandt Van Rijn (1606-1669) and Jan Vermeer (1632-1675).

Web:

http://witcombe.sbc.edu/ARTHbaroque.html
http://www.artcyclopedia.com/history/baroque.html
http://www.artlex.com/ArtLex/b/baroque.html
http://www.tigtail.org/M_View/TVM/X1/f.Baroque/
  b.Italian/baroque-spanish.html

Carlos Museum of Art

Get your daily dose of culture by looking at images of ancient Egypt, the ancient Americas, art from Asia, Greece, Rome and sub-Saharan Africa. You will see ancient artifacts such as a cuneiform tablet, a mummy, and an engraved effigy, among others. Also available are later works on paper, such as manuscripts and scrolls.

Web:

http://www.carlos.emory.edu/

Digital Photography

This web site offers a display of the winners of annual juried contests of digital photography. These images began life as mere photographs or film and video and were then transformed into new art forms using a computer. Since this contest is held annually, you can also get information on how to enter your work in future events.

Web:

http://www.bradley.edu/exhibit/

Erté Museum

Erté was an Art Deco artist born in Russia. (His original name was Romain de Tirtoff.) He moved to Paris in 1912 to become a fashion illustrator and called himself Erté, after the French pronunciation of his initials. He is best known for his extravagant costumes for ballet and the opera, as well as Harper's Bazaar illustrations. His fashion career spanned his entire life—he designed outrageous clothing for approximately 75 years. This Web site contains a nice collection and some writing about Erté.

Web:

http://www.erte.com/sm/sm.html

Imagebase

The Fine Arts Museum of San Francisco maintains this Web site, where you can view a large portion of their collections. Enjoy exhibits devoted to European paintings, African art, American paintings, European porcelain, European glass and ancient art. To make the experience complete, after you look at some paintings, run around the room and yell, "Clang, clang," as if you were on a cable car.

Web:

  http://www.thinker.org/fam/thinker.html

Leonardo da Vinci Museum

See the work of the master who put the word "Renaissance" in "Renaissance Man". Painter, inventor, architect, writer, musician and all-around genius, Leonardo is a household name in the world of art. These sites display his oil paintings, futuristic designs, drawings and sketches, and biographical information on the man who made Mona Lisa smile.

Web:

  http://banzai.msi.umn.edu/leonardo/
  http://www.mos.org/leonardo/
  http://www.museoscienza.org/english/leonardo/

Los Angeles County Museum of Art

There is more to the city of Los Angeles than what you read in the National Enquirer. For instance, the Los Angeles County Museum of Art has quite a collection of beautiful artwork and interesting cultural costumes and textiles. See selected images of ancient and Islamic art, European paintings and sculpture, and art of the twentieth century as well as links to other art sites.

Web:

  http://www.lacma.org/

Art+L.A.= Culture to the Max

A quick trip to the Los Angeles County Museum of Art Web site is one that should be on everyone's cultural agenda. Of course, you will find the usual ancient Islamic and European art, as well as the mandatory collection of priceless paintings and sculpture. All of that is nice, of course, but nothing that you couldn't find on the walls of your local Water, Sewer and Trash Administration Building.

But what you can't find elsewhere are exhibits that capture the essence of the true Southern California creative soul. For example, does the Louvre have an entire room devoted to toupees worn by famous film stars? Can the Sistine Chapel offer a collection as inspiring as the photographic exhibition of *all* of Elizabeth Taylor's husbands? And is there anything in New York — the poor East Coast wannabe — that even approaches the beauty and inspiration of the Winners of the Annual TV Guide Advertisement Collage Contest?

I think not. We in Southern California are proud of our creative heritage and our contributions to world culture, and we love to share.

Louvre Museum

Here's your chance to visit Paris free of charge. Get a ticket to the virtual Louvre, which is conducting tours around the city. You will see the Eiffel Tower and the Champs Élysées, among other sights. At the Louvre itself, they offer tours of a collection of famous paintings and a demonstration of French medieval art. You have to bring your own pastries.

Web:

http://www.louvre.fr/louvrea.htm

M.C. Escher Gallery

Maurits Cornelis Escher was not only a master at paradox and illusion, but he could draw an exquisite likeness of anything he could see or imagine. Artists, mathematicians, scientists and the general consumer are all fascinated by his many graphic images on one level or another. Whether he stimulates your eye or your mind, this site will be interesting to you.

Web:

http://www.worldofescher.com/

Museum of Web Art

The Museum of Web Art (MOWA) is a Web site in the form of an art gallery. MOWA exhibits art from Web pages, such as buttons, logos, backgrounds and animation. There is also a special exhibit hall just for kids (actually, it is my favorite part of the museum). Visit MOWA right now—you'll be surprised.

Web:

http://www.mowa.org/

National Museum of American Art

There is more to good American art than the Sunday newspaper comics. View not only the permanent collection of the National Museum of American Art, but also some spectacular roving collections and exhibits.

Web:

http://www.nmaa.si.edu/

> **"Sex" is not a four-letter word.**

Pinup Art

In the world of art, what could be more accessible (and more American) than the pinup, a rendering of an idealized girl-next-door, suitable for framing? A study of the pinup leads us away from philosophy, art history and symbolism, and takes us firmly into the part of the world in which "I may not know art, but I know what I like" provides the dominant framework for aesthetic appreciation. The Impressionists, Post-Impressionists, Cubists and Abstract Expressionists may all be important to our culture, but for pure, down-home *enjoyment*, the work of, say, Alberto Vargas (1896-1982) provides a visceral impetus that goes a long way toward hitting the lover of fine art on a gut level. After all, the wholesomeness of Betty Crocker in the kitchen may be a comforting and nurturing part of our culture, but I have to admit, I'd much rather spend an evening in the living room looking at pinups of Bettie Page.

Web:

http://www.greatamericanpinup.com/
http://www.scandolls.com/pinups.htm

Sistine Chapel

If you can't get the time off from work to go see the Sistine Chapel, take a mini-vacation right now. Use your browser to take a tour of Cappella Sistina, where you will see hundreds of images of the chapel's artwork and read informative text about the chapel and its history.

Web:

http://www.christusrex.org/www1/sistine/

Treasures of the Czars

This is an excellent exhibit of art, icons, jewelry, armor and other items from the Russian Romanov dynasty. This site not only has images, but also useful historical information, fun games and a crash course on the Russian language. Even if you don't care anything about Russian art, you can still learn important phrases such as, "Grouper is the local specialty."

Web:
  http://www2.sptimes.com/treasures/

Wish Upon a Falling Czar

On March 10, 1917, the troops of Czar Nicholas II of Russia mutinied. On March 11, the Czar ordered the dissolution of the legislature, but the members refused to honor the order. And on March 15, in the face of increasingly powerful unrest, the Czar decided to abdicate.

Clearly, being a Czar is a high-stress occupation that is probably not for everyone. However, if there is one thing good about being His Royal Excellency, it is the magnificent art collection that is yours to enjoy in your moments of leisure.

For example, we might imagine Czar Nicholas II saying to himself, "Sure, the peasants are revolting and my soldiers refuse to obey my commands, but I can still sit on my throne and admire this totally cool Fabergé egg with the tiny copy of a Harley Hahn book inside." (Of course, he would be saying it in Russian, but you get the idea.)

For many years, such treasures were hidden from the world, but now, through the courtesy of the Internet, you can share in the art and culture of the Romanov dynasty. From 1613 to 1917, these awesome dudes (and dudettes) collected enough art to choke a Siberian horse. And if they were alive today, there would be nothing they would enjoy more than having you drop in and look around.

Van Gogh Gallery

Vincent Van Gogh (1853-1890) was a Dutch painter whose work became one of the seminal influences of twentieth century art. Van Gogh was at once immensely talented, innovative and disturbed. For example, at the end of 1888, he cut off his ear following a violent argument with the painter Paul Gauguin (1848-1903). Over the next two years, Van Gogh, suffering from bouts of madness, produced a vast number of brilliantly colored and maniacally frenzied paintings. In the last 70 days of his life, he painted 70 pictures, following which he took his own life. Van Gogh's hypersensitivity to life and sensation led him to create an oeuvre that is unmatched in the history of art. Although there is a great deal of talent, innovation and emotional disturbance in the world, it rarely comes together in the same place at the same time.

Web:
  http://www.nga.gov/exhibitions/vgwel.htm
  http://www.vangoghgallery.com/
  http://www.vangoghmuseum.nl/

Vatican Exhibit

Here is a wonderful resource from the U.S. Library of Congress: an exhibition of Vatican history and culture. Here you can find a great deal of fascinating information as well as some wonderfully unexpected treasures: a fifteenth century manuscript of a Latin translation of Archimedes' mathematics, a Carolingian manuscript of the Roman comic poet Plautusy, and an original autographed Harley Hahn book used by the Pope to teach himself how to send email.

Web:
  http://archive.ncsa.uiuc.edu/SDG/Experimental/
    vatican.exhibit/exhibit/Main_Hall.html

World Art Treasures

An art lover's fantasy: you're going through a bunch of junk at a yard sale and you find an old sculpture that turns out to be a lost treasure from the fifth century. Prepare yourself for those weekend jaunts from sale to sale. Brush up on art treasures from places such as Egypt, China, Japan, India, Burma, Laos and Thailand so you will recognize that precious gem when you find it, although these are items you will probably not find lying around your neighborhood.

Web:
  http://www.bergerfoundation.ch/

World Wide Art Resources

There are a large number of art museums and galleries in the world, many of which have information and exhibits on the Net. These sites offer comprehensive collections of information and are definitely places to start when you are looking for a museum or gallery anywhere in the world. I like visiting these sites for two reasons. First, when I have a few minutes, they are great places to browse. I can always find a new online exhibit to explore. Second, before I travel anywhere, I check out all the museums and galleries in the area to see what looks good.

Web:
  http://www.wwar.com/categories/Commercial/
  http://www.wwar.com/categories/Museums/
  http://www.wwar.com/categories/
    Online_Exhibitions/

ASTRONOMY

Amateur Astronomy

Under ideal conditions, there are about 1,500 stars visible to the naked eye. With a good pair of binoculars or a telescope, the number of celestial objects you can view jumps, well, astronomically. Perhaps more than any other science, astronomy has always attracted a large number of knowledgeable, dedicated amateurs. If you are interested in serious astronomy, here is a collection of resources I know you will enjoy. Find out about news, sky events, clubs and organizations, do-it-yourself projects, hints on what to look for, telescope information, observatories, planetariums, and much more. Remember, when it comes to astronomy, anyone can be a star.

Web:
  http://www.astroleague.org/
  http://www.astronomy.com/
  http://www.astronomyboy.com/
  http://www.efn.org/~mbartels/aa/aa.html
  http://www.pa.msu.edu/abrams/diary.html
  http://www.stardate.org/

Astronomy Catalogs

When astronomers are interested in observing a particular heavenly body, how do you think they find what they are looking for? They use special catalogs, of which there are several thousand. If you are a professional astronomer—or an amateur with some technical knowledge—you'll find it extremely useful to search these catalogs online. (Hint: If you can't find the heavenly body you want in one of these catalogs, try one from Victoria's Secret.)

Web:
  http://cadcwww.dao.nrc.ca/astrocat/
  http://vizier.u-strasbg.fr/

Astronomy History

The study of astronomy is as old as the study of science. Aristarchus of Samos (310-230 B.C.), an early Greek astronomer, suggested that the Earth rotated on its axis and that the planets rotate around the sun in circular orbits. (Actually, the orbits are elliptical.) He also used his own observations along with his knowledge of geometry to determine the relative sizes of the Earth, the moon and the sun, and the distances between them. Personally, I have always been fascinated by man's quest to understand the cosmos. Yes, there were a few false starts (like the Dark Ages and the sixteenth century Catholic Church), but by and large, mankind has made enormous progress in understanding the nature of our universe.

Web:
  http://www.astro.uni-bonn.de/~pbrosche/hist_astr/
  http://www.cv.nrao.edu/fits/www/yp_history.html

Listserv Mailing List:
  List Name: hastro-l
  Subscribe to: listserv@wvnvm.wvnet.edu

Astronomy News

If you are a professional or amateur astronomer, there is no shortage of news to capture your interest. Information about current launches, new data and discoveries is available on the Net. There are also a lot of informative articles to help you keep abreast of what is new and exciting.

Web:
  http://cfa-www.harvard.edu/iau/Headlines.html
  http://einstein.stcloudstate.edu/dome/
  http://skyandtelescope.com/news/
  http://www.astronomynow.com/
  http://www.sciforums.com/

Astronomy Resources

Although we live on planet Earth, our eyes have always turned upward to the sun, the moon, the stars and the planets. Astronomy is one of the oldest sciences, having evolved from the observation of heavenly bodies to the general study of matter and energy in the universe. You'll love spending time with these astronomy resources, reading about comets, meteors, asteroids, planets and the solar system. You'll also find information about space exploration, astronomy magazines, and the history of astronomy. I especially enjoy looking at the wonderful astronomical images. Hint for Windows users: When you find an image you like, you can set it as the background for your desktop. (1) Use your browser to find a particularly cool astronomical image. (2) With your mouse, right-click on the image. You will see a list of choices. (3) Choose "Set as wallpaper". The background on your desktop is now the image you selected. (If you want to reset the background to the way it was, right-click on the desktop and choose "Properties". Then click on the "Background" tab.)

Web:

http://cdsweb.u-strasbg.fr/~heck/sf.htm
http://www.astronomysight.com/as/welcome.html
http://www.regulusastro.com/regulus/astrolinks/
http://www.seasky.org/sky.html
http://www.theskyguide.com/

Astronomy Software

The days have long passed since an astronomer could operate with a telescope and a notebook. Modern astronomy requires a lot of computers and a lot of computer programs. Here is a comprehensive collection of links to many different sites containing astronomy software. Whatever you need—everything under (and over) the sun—if it's available on the Net, you will probably find it here.

Web:

http://www.stsci.edu/astroweb/yp_software.html

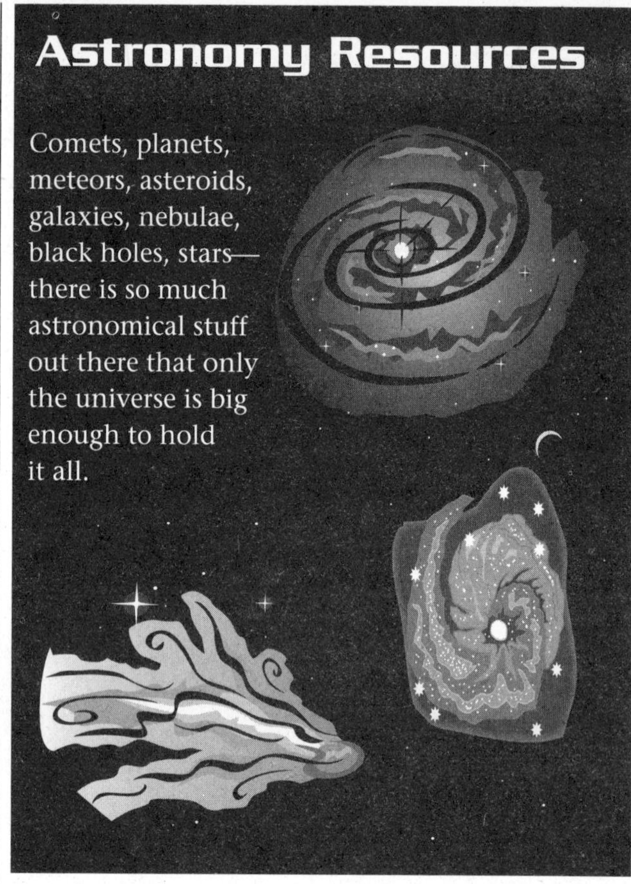

Comets, planets, meteors, asteroids, galaxies, nebulae, black holes, stars—there is so much astronomical stuff out there that only the universe is big enough to hold it all.

Astronomy Talk and General Discussion

Would you like to talk with people who really do understand black holes? Join the astronomers on Usenet and discuss all aspects of astronomy and astrophysics: stars, planets, telescopes, cosmology, space exploration, and so on. The **sci.astro.amateur** group is specifically for amateur astronomers.

Usenet:

alt.astronomy
alt.astronomy.solar
alt.telescopes.meade.lx200
rec.radio.amateur.space
sci.astro
sci.astro.amateur
sci.astro.ccd-imaging
sci.astro.fits
sci.astro.hubble
sci.astro.planetarium
sci.astro.research
sci.astro.satellites.visual-observe

IRC:

#astronomy (EFnet)

Astrophysics Data System

The Astrophysics Data System allows access to hundreds of thousands of abstracts (astronomy and astrophysics, space instrumentation, physics and geophysics, and more), as well as access or links to archives and catalogs of astronomical data, including data collected by NASA space missions.

Web:
  http://adswww.harvard.edu/

Comets

Imagine you are walking down the street, and you see a small block of ice and slush with a rock in the middle. So what? But take that same small block of ice and slush with a rock in the middle and send it in an eccentric, elliptical orbit around the sun, where the solar wind can cause tiny particles to stream out from the block forming a tail over a million kilometers long, a tail that is visible from Earth. You now have a comet. Most comets are not visible to the naked eye, but from time to time, one does arise that is easy to see, and the effect it has on humanity is stupendous. Comets are common, however, and with a telescope, there are always a few that are visible. Although some comets follow periodic schedules, returning to Earth again and again, many comets are new and unexpected and, indeed, are discovered by amateurs.

Web:
  http://cfa-www.harvard.edu/iau/
    CometDiscovery.html
  http://encke.jpl.nasa.gov/
  http://www.comets.amsmeteors.org/

Usenet:
  alt.sci.astro.hale.bopp

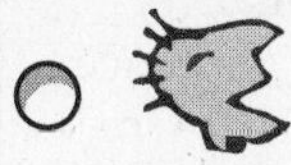

Report on Comets
by Elmo (age 8)

Constellations

Look up into the night sky when the stars are visible, and you will begin to see patterns. Since ancient times, men have identified such patterns, called constellations, and given them names. The oldest references to constellations are from the ancient Greeks, although those constellations probably originated even earlier, among the Sumerians and Babylonians. The modern system of constellations is based on the Greek ones, but has been codified and expanded to cover the entire sky (including the southern areas that were not visible to the Greeks). Today, we recognize 88 different constellations. As you look at the stars, remember that the constellations are artificial constructions made up by people. Only the stars are real.

Web:

  http://einstein.stcloudstate.edu/dome/foyer.html
  http://www.astro.wisc.edu/~dolan/constellations/
  http://www.corvus.com/con-page/con-88.htm
  http://www.cosmobrain.com/cosmobrain/res/
    constellations.html
  http://www.physics.csbsju.edu/astro/asp/
    constellation.faq.html

Dark Sky Stargazing

One time I was camping by myself in a national park east of San Diego, and I ran into a couple of teenagers who had never been out of the city. While talking to them, I found out they had never seen the Milky Way (the long, extended clumping of stars that is actually part of our galaxy), because the lights of the city were so bright as to obscure most of the stars. It wasn't until the boys had finally ventured to the countryside that they were able to see this remarkable phenomenon. Astronomers (professional and amateur) have the same problem. Cities create so much light pollution as to seriously impact astronomical observation. To look at the heavens, you need a dark sky, and these Web sites can help you find it.

Web:

  http://proxima.astro.virginia.edu/~ida/darksky/
  http://www.darksky.org/ida/

Eclipses

An eclipse occurs when one heavenly body casts a shadow on another. To Earthbound observers (you and me), the most important eclipses are those in which the moon comes between us and the sun (a solar eclipse), and those in which the Earth comes between the moon and the sun (a lunar eclipse). The most spectacular eclipses are total solar eclipses, in which the moon, for a short time, will almost completely block the light from the sun. In other words, the moon casts its shadow on the Earth. If you happen to be in this shadow, you will see the awesome sight of the disc of the sun slowly being covered and then, a few minutes later, regaining its original appearance. These Web sites contain pictures of eclipses and information about future eclipses.

Web:
   http://skyandtelescope.com/observing/objects/eclipses/
   http://sunearth.gsfc.nasa.gov/eclipse/eclipse.html
   http://umbra.nascom.nasa.gov/eclipse/
   http://www.earthview.com/resources/links.htm

Usenet:
   alt.sci.astro.eclipses

Extrasolar Planets

Are there planets outside our own solar system that are capable of supporting life? For a long time, astronomers searched for such extrasolar planets (sometimes called "exoplanets"), but with no success. The difficulty is that, at such great distances, anything as small as a planet cannot be seen with a telescope. Instead, astronomers examine one star at a time, looking for tiny perturbations in the star's movements, perturbations that can only be caused by a planet-like object orbiting the star. In October 1995, astronomers at Geneva University found the first such planet and, since then, a growing number of new planets have been found. Compared to the planets in our own solar system, most of the extrasolar planets are significantly different, and it is very unlikely that any of them could support life. However, what we do know is that planets are common throughout the galaxy. Perhaps one day, we will find an extrasolar planet that is similar to our own.

Web:
   http://cfa-www.harvard.edu/planets/
   http://planetquest.jpl.nasa.gov/
   http://www.exoplanets.org/
   http://www.jtwinc.com/extrasolar/mainframes.html

> On the Net, a long journey begins with but a single click.

Observatories and Telescopes

One of the things I like best about the Net is that it provides a place for information that literally did not exist before there was an international computer network. For example, say that you want to look for a particular observatory or telescope. Before the Net existed, where could you even look for an up-to-date master list? Now it's easy to find what you want. Just check these sites and find links to hundreds of observatories and telescopes all over the globe.

Web:
   http://cdsweb.u-strasbg.fr/astroweb/telescope.html
   http://www.bro.lsu.edu/bras/opt.html
   http://www.noao.edu/scope/facilities.html

Peculiar Galaxies

In the 1960s, the astronomer Halton C. Arp collected images of 338 "peculiar galaxies", that is, galaxies with unusual or abnormal shapes. Arp published a book called the Atlas of Peculiar Galaxies, which has become the standard reference work for what many people now refer to as "Arp objects". Arp's work contributed greatly to the study of the nature of galaxies, and today there are Arp enthusiasts around the world who photograph as many Arp objects as they can. Start here if you would like to learn more about these intriguing galactic phenomena (and look at some cool pictures).

Web:
   http://users.aol.com/arpgalaxy/
   http://www.eso.org/outreach/info-events/ut1fl/
      astroim-galaxy-peculi.html

Planetary Nebulae

Within a star there are two great forces balancing one another: the force of gravity (pulling inwards), and the force of heat from the core, created by the fusion of hydrogen to helium (pushing outwards). After a hundred million to ten billion years, depending on the size of the star, the hydrogen is depleted. When this happens, the fusion stops and gravity causes the star to collapse. New reactions begin to take place in the core, resulting in the liberation of a large amount of energy. This energy causes the star to expand, resulting in the formation of a red giant. Eventually, the core completely runs out of fuel and gravity causes the star to collapse. For almost all stars, this leads to the formation of a white dwarf. (With the largest 5 percent of stars, a huge explosion called a supernova occurs instead.) Just before the formation of a white dwarf, large amounts of gaseous matter are thrown off by the dying star, forming a huge gaseous shell around the white dwarf. This shell is called a planetary nebula. (The name comes from a mistake early astronomers made, when they saw such formations and thought they resembled the planet Uranus.) Within the grand scheme of the galaxy, planetary nebulae are short-lived, lasting only about 25,000 years. There are thought to be about 10,000 such bodies in our galaxy.

Web:
http://www.astro.washington.edu/balick/WFPC2/
http://www.blackskies.com/links.html
http://www.noao.edu/image_gallery/
    planetary_nebulae.html
http://www.noao.edu/jacoby/
http://www.seds.org/messier/planetar.html

Radio Astronomy

When you and I look at the sky, we see visible light, which represents only a tiny portion of the electromagnetic spectrum. However, celestial objects emit radiation in all parts of the spectrum, and radio telescopes, which are sensitive to radio waves, can detect a wealth of emissions that would normally pass us by. The fact that celestial bodies emit detectable radio waves was discovered by accident in 1931 by Karl Jansky, a researcher at Bell Labs. Jansky announced his discovery in 1933, which inspired a young radio engineer named Grote Reber to build the first radio telescope. In 1940, Reber published an article called "Cosmic Static" in the Astrophysical Journal, an article that ushered in the age of radio astronomy. One of the most important characteristics of radio waves is that they pass through interstellar dust clouds that block visible light. Thus, radio telescopes allow us to explore parts of the universe that would otherwise be inaccessible.

Web:
http://cdsweb.u-strasbg.fr/astroweb/radio.html
http://radio.uindy.edu/radio/
http://www.bambi.net/sara.html
http://www.jpl.nasa.gov/radioastronomy/
http://www.nrao.edu/
http://www.universetoday.com/html/directory/
    radioastronomy.html

Robotic Telescopes

Professional caliber telescopes are wonderful tools, but access is limited and, for an amateur astronomer, almost impossible to obtain. There are, however, a few such telescopes that can be used by anyone. You can send a request to have the telescope look at a particular position in the sky. The results will be sent to you either as a picture or raw data in FITS (Flexible Image Transport System) format. These resources are suitable for college-level students, researchers and knowledgeable amateurs.

Web:
http://astrwww.cwru.edu/nassau/nassau.html
http://www.deepspace.ucsb.edu/rot.htm
http://www.telescope.org/rti/automated.html

> **The first step in becoming a wise person is to care about what you don't know.**

SkyView

SkyView is a sophisticated tool that allows you to look at various parts of the sky in different wavelengths. However, SkyView does not show you real images: rather, it creates the images you want, based on your specifications, by using an extensive database of astronomical observations. In other words, SkyView is a virtual telescope. The system is set up with various interfaces, for both professional astronomers and amateurs.

Web:

  http://skyview.gsfc.nasa.gov/

Telescopes

Of course, telescopes can be used to look at planets, stars and other celestial objects. However, did you know that throughout history, telescopes have been used for many other purposes?

In ancient Rome, Julius Caesar once used a telescope to stir a pot of spaghetti when Cleopatra dropped in to dinner unexpectedly.

In 1066, William of Normandy, clutching a green plastic telescope in his hand, led his followers into battle, successfully conquering all of southern England and parts of North Dakota.

In 1929, Albert Einstein used a small telescope in the shape of the Eiffel Tower to introduce his Unified Field Theory to a worldwide television audience, setting a fashion trend that would last for decades and inadvertently triggering a massive collapse of the stock market.

Once you get *your* own telescope, just imagine what you can do with it (when you are not busy looking at planets, stars and other celestial objects).

No animals were harmed during the production of this book. (But my cat got tired and fell asleep.)

Space Calendar

If you think it's disastrous when you lose your datebook, how do you think NASA feels? When you are shooting live human beings into space at high speeds, it's important to keep your scheduling straight. Check here if you want to keep up on what's happening in the cosmos.

Web:

  http://www.jpl.nasa.gov/calendar/

Telescopes

It's tempting to rush out and buy a telescope, but don't. Take time, before you buy, to learn what you are doing. I once bought a high-quality telescope, and I sure was glad I did some research before I made my selection. Here are some resources to help you, including a FAQ (frequently asked question list) about buying and using a telescope. Harley's Rules for Buying a Telescope: (1) When you buy a telescope, you get what you pay for. (2) The one you need costs more than you can afford.

Web:

  http://astro.umsystem.edu/atm/
  http://skyandtelescope.com/howto/scopes/
  http://www.perkins-observatory.org/FAQ.index.html

AVIATION

Aerobatic Aviation

Aerobatics are for everyone. Even people who know nothing about airplanes are in awe when they see a highly trained aerobatic pilot doing stunts that seem to defy the laws of physics. Here is information about aerobatics, including the most famous of the aerobatic groups, the U.S. Navy's Blue Angels.

Web:
http://www.aerobatics.org.uk/
http://www.airforce.com/thunderbirds/
http://www.blueangels.navy.mil/
http://www.iac.org/
http://www.raf.mod.uk/reds/
http://www.snowbirds.dnd.ca/index_e.asp
http://www.worldaerobatics.com/

Usenet:
rec.aviation.aerobatics

Aeronautics

We are surrounded by things that fly: animals such as birds and insects; and machines such as airplanes, gliders, balloons and rockets. Aeronautics is the science of how things fly and how to build things that fly. The resources I have chosen will help you learn about basic aeronautics, and if you are so inclined, to pursue the more advanced topics. Although aeronautics is a highly technical branch of science and engineering, the fundamental concepts are within the grasp of anyone with some knowledge of science. After all, you don't have to be a rocket scientist to understand the birds and the bees.

Web:
http://www.allstar.fiu.edu/
http://www.lerc.nasa.gov/www/K-12/airplane/
http://www.quest.arc.nasa.gov/aero/
http://www.quest.arc.nasa.gov/aero/wright/tunnels/
    glossary.html

Usenet:
sci.aeronautics
sci.aeronautics.airliners
sci.aeronautics.simulation

Air Disasters

I am no stranger to aviation disasters. One time I took a dinner flight, and they forgot to put my special vegetarian meal on the plane. Another time, I asked for a glass of apple juice with no ice, but they gave me ice anyway. But the worst disaster—so bad that I actually wondered if I was going to make it— was the time I forgot to bring a book to read and had no choice but to watch an entire Meryl Streep movie. If you are an air disaster buff, here are some Internet resources that are right up your aerodynamic alley. Here is where you can look for timely information after an accident or other disaster, or—between accidents— discuss methods and investigations.

Web:
http://www.aerosupplies.net/Disaster_Data/
    disaster_data.html
http://www.planecrashinfo.com/
http://www.planesafe.org/

Usenet:
alt.disasters.aviation

Air Shows

The aviation scene is full of air shows, exhibitions and competitions, and if you enjoy such events, you will find these resources to be valuable. The next time you have an open weekend to fill or you are planning a trip to a faraway place, why not catch some aviation action? Spend a few minutes on the Net and find out what's happening, where and when.

Web:
http://www.airshows.com/
http://www.airshows.org/
http://www.worldairshownews.com/

Usenet:
rec.aviation.announce

Airplane Mailing Lists

Are you interested in flying? Here are some mailing lists you will enjoy. The **airline** list is concerned with airlines and civil aircraft and **airplane-clubs** is for people discussing the airplane clubs. (Hint: If you would like to have your own plane but you find the cost and maintenance prohibitive, consider joining a club in which you will share the costs with other pilots.)

Listserv Mailing List:

List Name: airline
Subscribe to: listserv@listserv.cuny.edu

Majordomo Mailing List:

List Name: airplane-clubs
Subscribe to: majordomo@dg-rtp.dg.com

Airships

An airship is a lighter-than-air, self-propelled aircraft containing a large balloon-like container filled with gas. (The well-known Goodyear blimp, for example, weighs only 150 pounds [68 kilograms] when fully inflated.) Unlike hot-air balloons, airships have propellers to act as a propulsion system, as well as a mechanism for steering and accommodations for passengers, crew and cargo. Through the years, various types of airships have been developed, such as zeppelins, dirigibles and blimps. The gas within an airship is usually helium or heated air, both of which are non-volatile. In the olden days, when helium was not yet available, airships were filled with hydrogen, which, being flammable, sometimes led to disasters, the most famous of which was the explosion that destroyed the Hindenburg (a German zeppelin) on May 6, 1937. Today's airships are safe, sophisticated aircraft.

Web:

http://spot.colorado.edu/~dziadeck/airship.html
http://www.americanblimp.com/fly.htm
http://www.goodyearblimp.com/
http://www.hotairship.com/

Listproc Mailing List:

List Name: airship-list
Subscribe to: listproc@lists.colorado.edu

Sharing an Airplane

For years you have been dreaming of having your own airplane.

Unfortunately, your two feet are firmly planted on the ground while your bank account grows more slowly than a dead Christmas tree. It's all too true that an airplane is just a hole in the sky into which you throw money. Join the **airplane-clubs** mailing list and meet the people who form clubs to share the only hobby more expensive than running for Congress.

Aviation Charities

What happens when a sick or injured person needs medical help, but there is no easy way for them to get to a doctor? What happens when someone is lost in a remote area, and it is impossible to drive or walk to the rescue? What happens when a hospital needs emergency medical supplies or an organ is ready for transplanting, and there is no one to make the delivery? The pilots who work for aviation charities donate their time, their planes, fuel and use their expertise to help such people who, literally, have no one else to turn to. Do you need help? Or perhaps would you like to volunteer your services or donate money? Why not just take a few moments and learn about these angels of the air.

Web:

http://www.aircareall.org/

Aviation History

The history of aviation is the story of humanity's quest to overcome its limitations and learn how to fly. In some sense, the history of the airplane reaches back as far as there have been people who would look at birds in the sky and dream of flying. However, most of aviation history took place in the twentieth century, and even a casual browsing of these Web sites will leave you in awe of human ingenuity and achievement. If you are doing research, especially in the area of military aviation, you will find these resources valuable.

Web:
  http://www.aviation-history.com/
  http://www.cals.lib.ar.us/miller/
  http://www.first-to-fly.com/
  http://www.fotoimages.com/aircraft/aircraft.html
  http://www.rwebs.net/avhistory

Aviation Magazines

Even the most dedicated pilots can't be in the air all the time. So in those few moments when you come down to Earth to refill the gas tank and chow down on a couple of fast cheese sandwiches, scoot over to your browser and check out the latest issues of these online magazines.

Web:
  http://www.aafo.com/
  http://www.airspacemag.com/
  http://www.aopa.org/pilot/

Aviation Poetry

There's more to flying than just knowing which instruments to read and how many flight attendants it takes to screw in a light bulb. Flying can be truly poetic, inspiration for songs of the soul. Read these poems about flight and flying, so on some dark, romantic night you can whisper into your beloved's ear a little poem that begins, "There once was a girl from Nantucket..."

Web:
  http://members.iquest.net/~jlevy/avpoem.html

Aviation Q & A

Are you thinking of becoming a pilot? Are you a pilot already with an ever-growing list of questions? Well, there is enough useful aviation information on the Internet to fill your needs from now to Orville Wright's birthday. **rec.aviation.answers** is the Usenet group whose sole purpose is to carry all the aviation-related FAQs (frequently asked question lists). This is *the* place to check for the best of aviation wisdom on the Net.

Web:
  http://www.thirtythousandfeet.com/faq.htm

Usenet:
  rec.aviation.answers

Aviation Resources

These are no fly-by-night Web sites. These are the best general aviation resources I could find, where you'll find most everything you'll need—especially if you are a pilot. (However, you'll have to supply your own no-frills snacks and outrageously expensive shopping catalogs for your passengers.)

Web:
  http://aeroweb.brooklyn.cuny.edu/
  http://www.avhome.com/
  http://www.flightinfo.com/
  http://www.globalair.com/
  http://www.landings.com/

Aviation Safety

We all know that flying is the safest way to fly. Why? Because pilots are trained to be dependable and cautious. However, airplanes are complex machines, and there are a lot of variables that affect your flight experience. Use these Net resources to keep yourself up to date on the newest safety-related information and news. Remember, the only good pilot is a living pilot.

Web:
  http://www.aviation-safety.net/
  http://www.faa.gov/aviationsafety/
  http://www.nasdac.faa.gov/internet/

Usenet:
  alt.aviation.safety

Aviation Talk and General Discussion

You'll go into a flat spin when you see how much information you can find in these aviation discussion groups. If you don't know how to choose a specific group, start with the Web. Alternatively, the **.misc** group often has cross-postings from other groups so, if you start there, you'll find a wide variety of topics.

Web:

http://www.airliners.net/discussions/
http://www.newsguy.com/~ericmax/newsgrps.htm

Usenet:

alt.aviation.fun
rec.aviation
rec.aviation.ifr
rec.aviation.marketplace
rec.aviation.misc
rec.aviation.powerchutes
rec.aviation.products
rec.aviation.questions
rec.aviation.restoration
rec.aviation.seaplane
rec.aviation.simulators

IRC:

#aviation (EFnet)

Balloooning

In 1783, two French brothers figured out how to cause a 30-meter linen bag to rise in the air. Within a few months, two daredevils used a similar balloon to make the first manned flight. It took two hundred years for balloon technology to improve to the point where men were able to float across the Atlantic Ocean (1978). Today, modern technology allows many people to enjoy ballooning, and you can too. Start with the Net, and it won't be long before you are having a good time, getting high the old-fashioned way.

Web:

http://www.balloondispatch.com/
http://www.euronet.nl/users/jdewilde/
http://www.launch.net/

Usenet:

rec.aviation.balloon

Majordomo Mailing List:

List Name: balloon
Subscribe to: majordomo@lists.lboro.ac.uk

Careers in Aviation

There are a lot of different jobs in aviation and aeronautics: not only pilots and flight attendants, but engineers, technicians, mechanics, managers, and more. If you are thinking of entering one of these fields, it behooves you to start by doing some research. Read about job duties, salaries, requirements, working conditions, and job availability.

Web:

http://www.aviationemployment.com/
http://www.nationjob.com/aviation
http://www.planejobs.com/
http://www.women-in-aviation.com/Employment/

Usenet:

alt.aviation.jobs

TIDBITS

What should young men know about YOUNG WOMEN?

Overall, girls are a lot like boys. However, they emphasize parts of life much differently than you. For example, girls feel continual pressure regarding their appearance. (Just look at TV and magazines, and you will see why.) As such, they obsess about their bodies much more than boys do.

In addition, girls talk to their friends a lot, especially about sex and relationships. After a date, for instance, a girl will call one of her friends and discuss the details of everything that happened.

Be nice. Girls remember *everything*.

Flight Planning and Navigation

How would you feel if you planned to fly to Washington to help the President of the United States clean out his garage, and you got your directions mixed up and ended up in the middle of Disneyland? Imagine your embarrassment at spending an entire day with the wrong Mickey Mouse. Don't take chances: download a copy of free flight planning software and data today.

Web:
  http://www.aero.com/plan/flitplng.htm
  http://www.airnav.com/
  http://www.fltplan.com/

DUATS

If you are a pilot, the Direct User Access Terminal Service (DUATS) is the place to get your weather briefings, plan your flight, and even file your flight plan. DUATS also offers other valuable services. Check it out the next time you plan a cross-country flight. (Please note that the site says, "DUATS is available to U.S. pilots who hold current medical certificates, flight instructors without current medicals, aviation ground instructors, glider/balloon pilots and other approved users in the U.S. aviation community.")

Web:
  http://www.duats.com/

Plan to Plan a Flight Plan

Of course you need a flight plan. If you didn't have a plan, you might arrive at your destination and not even know it. Worse, you might never arrive, and someone else would end up getting your dessert at dinner.

Before you go, use the Net to help you create a flight plan. Check weather and current conditions, and download software to make the whole thing as easy as falling off an aviational log.

Gliding and Soaring

Gliding, or soaring, is motorless flight. Since gliders (also known as sailplanes) do not have motors, they are more streamlined and beautiful than regular planes. I once had a glider ride, and I still remember the experience as being peaceful and surreal. Here is some important glider trivia I want you to know. On December 18, 1931, the world endurance soaring record was set in Hawaii by William A. Cocke, Jr., who remained aloft for 21 hours 34 minutes. Cocke is related to one of my researchers, Kelly; she is Cocke's first cousin twice removed. I have been to Nuuanu Pail Lookout in Honolulu, where there is a plaque commemorating Cocke's record-setting flight.

Web:

  http://records.fai.org/gliding/
  http://www.soaringmuseum.org/landmark.htm
  http://www.ssa.org/
  http://www.ushga.org/

Usenet:

  rec.aviation.hang-gliding
  rec.aviation.soaring

Helicopters

Helicopters are highly maneuverable and, as such, have an appeal unlike that of fixed-wing aircraft. (I have a friend who keeps his own helicopter in his garage. When he wants to go for a ride, he wheels the helicopter out and takes off.) The first flight of a helicopter-like airplane occurred on November 13, 1907, flown by the Frenchman Paul Cornu. If you are a helicopter enthusiast, these resources will help you find what you need on the Net. If you want to talk to other helicopter buffs, check out the Usenet discussion group.

Web:

  http://www.helis.com/
  http://www.pra.org/
  http://www.rotor.com/

Usenet:

  rec.aviation.rotorcraft

Learning to Fly

What a wonderful new experience, learning to fly. It's nice to know you have a place to ask questions or share your experiences with people who enjoy the same hobby or way of life. Find out all the questions new students are asking, and learn about instructors, lessons, equipment, PPL qualifications, and airspace.

Web:

  http://www.aopa.org/learntofly/
  http://www.studentpilot.com/
  http://www.studentpilot.net/

Usenet:

  rec.aviation.student

Military Aircraft

From the Sopwith Camel to the F-117A Stealth Fighter and beyond, experience the thrill of military aircraft. See the past, present, and even the future, as aviation devotees share their ideas on what are the best planes, who are the most notorious pilots in history, and how military aircraft of various countries compare to one another.

Web:

  http://home.att.net/~jbaugher/aircraft.html
  http://www.csd.uwo.ca/~pettypi/elevon/baugher_us/

Usenet:

  rec.aviation.military
  rec.aviation.military.naval

Military Aviation

So you like to fly? How would you like to fly spiffy airplanes and helicopters in the service of your country? Military aviation is a specialized field with its own challenges and rewards. If you live in the United States, here is information about aviation careers and opportunities available in the various branches of the United States military.

Web:

  http://www.afreserve.com/flash.htm
  http://www.airforce.com/
  http://www.airlant.navy.mil/
  http://www.ang.af.mil/
  http://www.cap.gov/
  http://www.designation-systems.net/usmilav/
  http://www.olive-drab.com/od_other_aviation.php3

Owning Airplanes

Don't you wish owning an airplane were as simple as installing a bigger garage door? Learn the joys and travails of being the owner of a powerful flying machine. If you are interested in building or restoring aircraft, check out **.homebuilt** to indulge in your aviation obsession. A word of warning: one of the questions in the homebuilt FAQ list is, "Will my marriage survive

Web:
  http://www.homebuilt.org/
  http://www.thirtythousandfeet.com/r-a-h.htm
  http://www.wanttaja.com/avlinks

Usenet:
  rec.aviation.homebuilt
  rec.aviation.owning

Piloting

You can't be flying all the time—you do need to spend some of your time on the surface of the planet (if only to refuel). But that doesn't mean you need to be bored. Connect to the Net, and see what other pilots are talking about when they're not up in the air.

Usenet:
  rec.aviation.piloting

Stories About Flying

How does it feel to be so high above the Earth? What was it like the first time you went solo? What excites you about flying? Read anecdotes of flight experiences and share yours. Even if you don't fly, you can experience the thrill of the moment in the stories of others.

Usenet:
  rec.aviation.stories

Ultralight Flying

Don't let the testosterone take over and convince you that you have to fly a jumbo jet. Experience the joy of ultralight aircraft and enjoy flying as often as possible using as little as possible.

Web:
  http://www.qnet.com/~robertc/ultralight.html

Usenet:
  rec.aviation.ultralight

Women in Aviation

The first woman airline pilot was Helen Richey of the U.S., who was hired by Central Airlines in 1934. Unfortunately, the all-male pilots' union refused to accept Richey, and she resigned after only ten months. Although employment conditions have changed a lot since then, even today, only 4.6 percent of U.S. commercial pilots and 12.2 percent of U.S. air traffic controllers are women. Still, if you are a woman interested in aviation, there are many people who share your interest, and a lot of information for you on the Net.

Web:
  http://www.iswap.org/
  http://www.pwcinc.org/
  http://www.wiai.org/
  http://www.women-in-aviation.com/

BIOLOGY

Algae (Phycology)

Phycology is the study of algae, eukaryotic organisms (each cell has a nucleus containing chromosomes), which are non-flowering and are capable of photosynthesis. However, algae are not plants. Some algae are classified Monera, while others are considered to be Protista. Algae range from small single-celled organisms, such as some plankton, to large multicellular forms, such as seaweeds (most of which are green, brown or red algae). Algae are important as they produce much of the organic matter at the bottom of the food chain. In the ocean, algae also produce oxygen used by other marine life. Hint: If you have trouble recalling the definition of algae, just remember: algae = seaweed + some plankton + pond scum.

Web:
http://www.algaebase.org/
http://www.psaalgae.org/
http://www.redtide.whoi.edu/hab/
http://www.seaweed.ie/

Usenet:
bionet.chlamydomonas

Listserv Mailing List:
List Name: algae-l
Subscribe to: listserv@listserv.heanet.ie

Bioethics

No science is complete without well-developed ethical traditions. The biological sciences are driven by research imperatives and a priority on preserving and enhancing human life. However, it is important that someone take the time to define and debate the ethical issues. For example, how should scarce resources be allotted? Are there any kinds of biological research that should not be allowed? How does society establish research priorities? So, what happens when you cross a philosopher with a biologist? You can find out by visiting the bioethics resources on the Net.

Web:
http://www.bioethics.net/
http://www.georgetown.edu/research/nrcbl/
http://www-hsc.usc.edu/~mbernste/

BIOETHICS

The name "bioethics" is derived from two words: "bioeth" (the Greek word for those sandwiches made with pita bread and fried chickpeas) and "ics" (the Greek god of intermittent fertility).

Perhaps this explains why some of the best thinkers in the biological world are attracted to the study of bioethics, like fish to a what's-a-whoosie.

So the next time you are sitting around idly speculating about 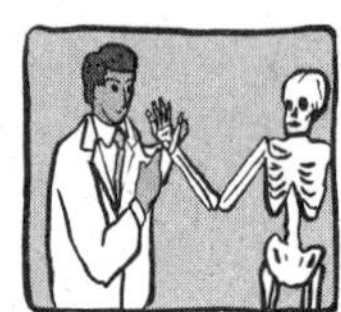 whether or not it is proper for your cat to accept gifts from a corporate lobbyist, don't wallow in ignorant bliss. Connect to the **Bioethics Server** and find the guidance you need to conduct your life with philosophical flair.

Bioinformatics

The techniques of bioinformatics deal with using computers to manipulate and manage biological information. In particular, much of bioinformatics deals with the sort of computational demands generated by the Human Genome Project. Bioinformatics specialists are experts in both molecular biology and computer science, a melding of disciplines which is becoming increasingly valuable.

Web:
http://bioinformatics.weizmann.ac.il/
http://www.cbil.upenn.edu/
http://www.ii.uib.no/~inge/list.html
http://www.ornl.gov/TechResources/
   Human_Genome/

Usenet:
bionet.biology.computational
bionet.molbio.bio-matrix

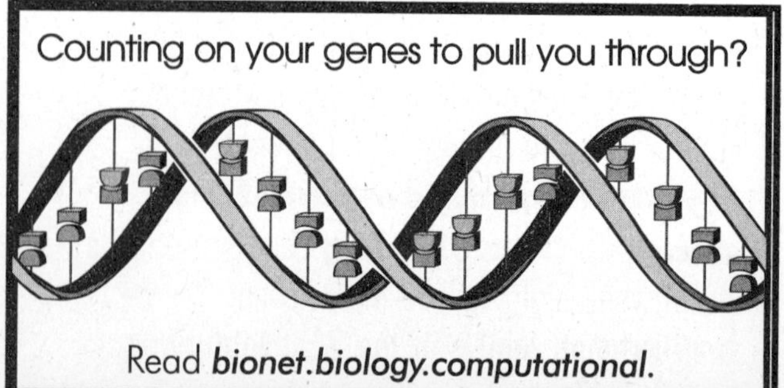

Biology Dictionary

Are you one of those people who have trouble remembering the difference between cytoplasm, ectoplasm and endoplasm? Do you have trouble recalling the exact definition of all your favorite organelles? If so, an online biology dictionary can help. Use the Net, and it won't be long before you are the life of the biological party. ("Is that chromatin in your nucleolus, or are you just glad to see me?")

Web:
   http://www.biology-online.org/dictionary.asp
   http://www.ultranet.com/~jkimball/BiologyPages/

Biology Funding and Grants

Don't wait for your million dollar sweepstakes check to come in. Where are some of the funding agencies in biology? Who's giving out research grants? Find out who has the money and how you can get some too.

Web:
   http://www.grantsnet.org/
   http://www.nsf.gov/bio/programs.htm

Usenet:
   bionet.sci-resources

Biology Job Opportunities

Why be a telemarketer when you can have a job in the exciting field of biology? See cells reproduce right before your eyes, cut up small unsuspecting microorganisms with lightning speed, and create new life forms seemingly from scratch. Opportunities abound for pre- or post-docs, undergraduates looking for something to keep themselves out of trouble for the summer, assistant professors who don't mind grading papers, and upwardly mobile, tenure-track seekers.

Web:
   http://www.bio.com/careercenter/
   http://www.biolinks.com/career/
   http://www.mcb.harvard.edu/biolinks/biojobs.html
   http://www.sciencejobs.com/bio/
   http://www.scientificresources.com/

Usenet:
   bionet.jobs
   bionet.jobs.offered
   bionet.jobs.wanted

Biology Funding and Grants

So you've got this great idea for developing wheat that grows in thin rows, just perfect for making sliced bread. But what can you do for seed money?
Participate in the **bionet.sci-resources** discussion group and perhaps, just perhaps, you will find the financial source that will send you on your way to becoming the next Internet Nobel Prize winner.

Biology Journals

If you like biological journals (or even if you don't, but you have to read them anyway), you can do a lot of your reading on the Internet. A large number of research papers are available online, and many print journals also publish on the Net. The biological world moves fast, and these resources will help you find what you need to stay current.

Web:
   http://www.freemedicaljournals.com/
   http://www.medbioworld.com/bio/journals/
      biochem.html

Usenet:
   bionet.journals.contents
   bionet.journals.letters.biotechniques
   bionet.journals.letters.tibs
   bionet.journals.note

Biology-Related Sciences

Unbutton your top button and roll up your sleeves in preparation for some lively biological bantering. While informative and educational, subjects are never strictly hard-core science. Debate is sparked by such topics as evolution, the ethics of cloning, and the instinctual mating habits of animals and humans.

Usenet:
sci.bio.botany
sci.bio.conservation
sci.bio.ecology
sci.bio.ethology
sci.bio.fisheries
sci.bio.herp
sci.bio.microbiology
sci.bio.misc
sci.bio.paleontology
sci.bio.phytopathology
sci.bio.systematics

Biology Resources

Whatever you are looking for in the world of biology, these Web sites can help you. They contain vast collections of links that will lead you to just about anything you need. These are the places I use when I need to fulfill my biological needs.

Web:
http://www.biochemlinks.com
http://www.scicentral.com/B-02bios.html
http://www.vlib.org/Science/Cell_Biology

Biology Software

If you have the right tools, computers lighten your workload, and the right tools are available if you know where to look. These Web sites are good places to look when you are searching for biological software. The Usenet groups are useful if you have questions or you want to keep up on new products.

Web:
http://iubio.bio.indiana.edu/software/
http://www.ebi.ac.uk/FTP/
http://www.genamics.com/software/

Usenet:
bionet.software
bionet.software.acedb
bionet.software.gcg
bionet.software.srs
bionet.software.staden
bionet.software.www
bionet.software.x-plor

Biology Talk and General Discussion

For many years, biologists have used the Internet extensively, more so than any other scientific discipline. In particular, there are a great many biology-oriented Usenet groups and mailing lists. This Web site is the home of Biosci, where all of this discussion is coordinated. (This is the home of all the **bionet** discussion groups.) If you are looking for a group or mailing list devoted to a particular topic, this Web site is the place to start. For miscellaneous biology talk, visit the Usenet discussion groups.

Web:
http://www.bio.net/

Usenet:
bionet.general
sci.bio

Biotechnology

Biotechnology is a broad area: it refers to using technology within the biological sciences (for research and so on), as well as using elements of biology to create new technology (such as genetic engineering). The advances in biotechnology in the last several decades have profoundly influenced our economy and our culture. For example, even the man on the street is familiar with DNA testing. (He may not know what it is, but at least he knows it's something cool.) If you have an interest in biology, you can use these resources to keep up on the latest biotechnology advances.

Web:
http://www.biochemlinks.com/bclinks/biotech.cfm
http://www.cato.com/biotech/
http://www.ncbi.nlm.nih.gov
http://www.swbic.org/

Usenet:
alt.bio.technology
alt.bio.technology.cloning
alt.bio.technology.misc
sci.bio.technology

Your journey starts here.

Cell Biology

This is where life happens, in tiny units of protoplasm. Unless you are a robot, cell biology concerns you. Cell scholars from all over the world dissect studies, research and experiments that relate to cell biology. The **.cytonet** group is for the discussion of cytoskeletons such as cell walls and plasma membranes.

Web:
http://www.cellbio.com/
http://www.cellsalive.com/
http://www.e-cellbiology.com/

Usenet:
bionet.cellbiol
bionet.cellbiol.cytonet
bionet.cellbiol.insulin

Cell Biology

A eucaryote and a procaryote were in a bar one day, and had a bit too much to drink.

"Boy, do you ever look silly," said the procaryote, "walking around with all those organelles. Look at your endoplasmic reticulum. Everyone and their mother can see it. Don't you feel like a goober?"

"Look who's talking," said the eucaryote. "Your ribosomes are so small, you need to look at them with a magnifying glass. And you call that skinny, twisted stuff DNA? Why, I've seen better genetic material in a virus. You're just jealous because you don't have a nucleus."

"Jealous?" said the procaryote. "We'll see who's jealous. What about that?" he cried, as he reached forward, pulled a mitochondria out of the eucaryote and threw it to the floor.

The bartender looked at the mess and rolled his eyes. "That's what I get," he said to himself, "for serving unicellular organisms. They just can't hold their liquor."

Developmental Biology

Developmental biology is the study of how multicellular organisms develop from their early forms (such as embryos and larvae) into adults. In particular, developmental biology embraces the study of embryology. It seems like a miracle that a complex organism can grow from just a single fertilized cell, but it's not a miracle at all. Miracles are just phenomena you don't yet understand, so let the Net help you fill in the gaps.

Web:
http://sdb.bio.purdue.edu/other/vl_db.html
http://www.luc.edu/depts/biology/dev.htm
http://www.visembryo.com/baby

Ecology

The term "ecology" was coined in 1869 by the German zoologist Ernst Heinrich Haeckel, who used the word to refer to "environmental balance". Today, ecology has developed into a complex biological science dealing with the interrelationships of living organisms and the physical environment. Ecologists observe and analyze systems of organisms: their communities, population patterns, and dependence upon their environment. (By the way, Haeckel was also the biologist who developed the idea that "ontogeny recapitulates phylogeny", that is, the embryonic development of a higher animal mimics the evolutionary development of its species.)

Web:
http://pbil.univ-lyon1.fr/Ecology/
http://www.conbio.net/vl/

Usenet:
bionet.ecology.physiology
sci.bio.conservation
sci.bio.ecology

Listserv Mailing List:
List Name: biosph-l
Subscribe to: listserv@listserv.aol.com

Evolution

Evolution didn't stop when the apes climbed out of the trees and learned to drive sports cars. It's a constant process that goes on from the tiniest bacteria to the largest plants and animals. Get together with other people interested in evolution and discuss where we came from and where we might be going.

Web:
    http://users.mstar2.net/spencersa/evolutus/
    http://www.mcb.harvard.edu/biolinks/evolution.html
    http://www.ucmp.berkeley.edu/history/
        evolution.html

Usenet:
    bionet.molbio.evolution
    sci.bio.evolution

Genetics

Genetics is the study of how biological characteristics are passed on from one generation to the next. In most types of cells, genetic material is stored in the form of deoxyribonucleic acid or DNA, long molecules made up of four different types of building blocks called nucleotides. Within a strand of DNA, sequences of nucleotides (genes) contain "instructions" for creating specific proteins that act as enzymes. Since enzymes control biochemical reactions, the DNA, indirectly, contains the blueprint for much of what happens within the cells of the organism. The mechanisms of inheritance apply to all plants and animals, and, as such, genetics commands a central position in the world of biology. In particular, it is crucial to the study of evolution, embryology, animal and plant breeding, anthropology and pathology, as well as the practice of medicine.

Web:
    http://www.esp.org/foundations/genetics/classical/
    http://www.ornl.gov/TechResources/
        Human_Genome/genetics.html
    http://www.weihenstephan.de/~schlind/genglos.html
    http://www3.ncbi.nlm.nih.gov/omim/

Usenet:
    bionet.drosophila
    bionet.genome.arabidopsis
    bionet.molbio.gene-linkage
    bionet.molbio.molluscs
    bionet.organisms.zebrafish

Listserv Mailing List:
    List Name: hum-molgen
    Subscribe to: listserv@nic.surfnet.nl

Human Genome Project

The Human Genome Project is a massively ambitious global project to ferret out and document all of the genes in the full complement of human chromosomes. These resources will point you to a great deal of data and keep you up-to-date on the progress of this project. For ongoing discussion, you can take a look at the Usenet group. (My hope is that, one day, someone will find the gene for TV watching, and we'll all be saved.)

Web:
    http://gdbwww.gdb.org/
    http://www.genome.ad.jp/
    http://www.ncbi.nlm.nih.gov/Genbank/
        GenbankOverview.html
    http://www.nhgri.nih.gov/

Usenet:
    bionet.molbio.genome-program

Infomine Searchable Database

Here is a huge database of biological, agricultural and medical information. Just the place to do some research when you have to decide whether you should sever your anterior or posterior commissure, and you haven't got a lot of time to make up your mind.

Web:
    http://infomine.ucr.edu/search/bioagsearch.phtml

Microbiology

Microbiology is the study of microorganisms: organisms that are too small to be seen with the naked eye, such as bacteria, viruses, yeasts, fungi, protozoans and the smaller algae. Once you start to study microbiology, you come to a startling realization: most of life is too small to see without a microscope.

Web:
    http://www.asmusa.org/
    http://www.highveld.com/micro.html
    http://www.microbiol.org/
    http://www-micro.msb.le.ac.uk/video/video.html

Usenet:
    bionet.celegans
    bionet.microbiology
    bionet.microbiology.biofilms
    bionet.organisms.pseudomonas
    bionet.organisms.schistosoma
    bionet.parasitology
    bionet.protista
    sci.bio.microbiology

Molecular Biology

Molecular biology is the study of biochemical and molecular reactions within cells. As such, molecular biology deals with the macromolecules upon which life depends (nucleic acids, proteins, and so on). It also deals with the basic processes that take place within a cell (such as respiration, reproduction, synthesis, and excretion). Today, much of molecular biology focuses on the study of genetic material (DNA, RNA, nucleotides, and so on) and how it transmits genetic information.

Web:

> http://ca.expasy.org/
> http://www.mpimg-berlin-dahlem.mpg.de/
>   ~buessow/MolBiol_URLs.html
> http://www.nwfsc.noaa.gov/protocols.html
> http://www.yk.rim.or.jp/~aisoai/

Usenet:

> bionet.genome.autosequencing
> bionet.genome.chromosomes
> bionet.genome.gene-structure
> bionet.glycosci
> bionet.molbio.ageing
> bionet.molbio.bio-matrix
> bionet.molbio.embldatabank
> bionet.molbio.evolution
> bionet.molbio.genbank
> bionet.molbio.genbank.updates
> bionet.molbio.hiv
> bionet.molbio.methds-reagnts
> bionet.molbio.proteins
> bionet.molbio.proteins.7tms_r
> bionet.molbio.proteins.fluorescent
> bionet.molbio.rapd
> bionet.molbio.recombination
> bionet.molbio.yeast
> bionet.molec-model
> bionet.molecules.free-radicals
> bionet.molecules.p450
> bionet.molecules.peptides
> bionet.molecules.repertoires
> bionet.structural-nmr
> bionet.xtallography
> sci.bio.immunocytochem

Mycology

Mycology is the study of the organisms within the Fungi kingdom, including yeasts, molds, smuts and mushrooms. Fungi are characterized by a lack of chlorophyll and vascular tissue. They range from small, single cells to large masses of branched filaments. Here is a great resource containing a collection of material relating to fungi organisms and cultivation, research, publications, discussion groups and taxonomy (naming systems), as well as a Usenet group for mycological discussion. By the way, we commonly divide the world of biology into five separate kingdoms: Plants, Animals, Fungi, Protista (one-celled protozoans and some algae) and Monera (bacteria and blue-green algae). Thus, properly speaking, fungi, protozoa and bacteria are neither plants nor animals.

Web:

> http://www.keil.ukans.edu/~fungi/
> http://www.mykoweb.com/

Usenet:

> bionet.mycology

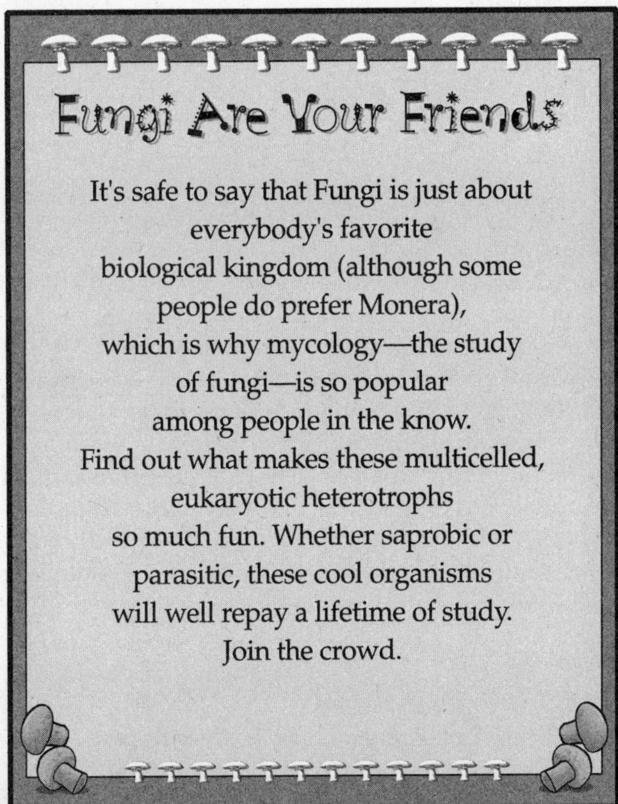

Neuroscience

Neuroscience is the study of the nervous system, encompassing neuroanatomy (one of my favorite areas of science) and neurobiology. When I was younger, I studied neuroscience in between graduate computer science and medical school. I got to dissect brains, and I took a neuroscience course in which I was able to carry out a variety of strange experiments. If you have an interest in learning how your brain functions, you will find neuroscience fascinating: it's all just a matter of mind over matter over mind.

Web:
http://neuro.med.cornell.edu/
http://www.indiana.edu/~pietsch/
http://www.neuroguide.com/
http://www.sfn.org/

Usenet:
bionet.neuroscience
bionet.neuroscience.amyloid

Taxonomy

Taxonomy is the systematic classification of living things. Modern taxonomy originated with the work of the Swedish botanist Carolus Linnaeus (1707-1778), who, in 1735, published *Genera Plantarum*, a work dealing with botanic classification. There are, of course, a vast number of different types of living things, and today's taxonomy systems are complex indeed. Although various systems are used (there is no one definitive scheme), the most common classifications are, from most to least general: kingdom, phylum, subphylum, class, subclass, order, family, genus, species and (for plants only) variety. When we talk about a particular organism, we often use the scientific name consisting of the genus (which is capitalized) followed by the species. For example, the next time someone offers you some Myrichthys maculosus soup, don't worry. It's just a common tiger snake eel.

Web:
http://www.itis.usda.gov/
http://www.ncbi.nlm.nih.gov/Taxonomy/
http://www.tolweb.org/tree/phylogeny.html
http://www.treebase.org/treebase/search.html

Virology

Virology is the study of viruses: tiny infectious agents (most viruses are between 10-200 nanometers) consisting of a length of DNA or RNA wrapped in a protein coat called a capsid. In human beings, viruses cause a large number of diseases, including colds, measles, mumps, yellow fever, polio, flu, AIDS and some types of cancer. Viruses also infect many other kinds of organisms, including plants and bacteria. In order to reproduce, a virus must infect a host cell. The virus then uses the cell's own biochemical mechanisms to create replica viruses. Outside of the host cell, the virus is inert with no active metabolism. Thus, strictly speaking, viruses are not actually alive (although that is not much consolation when you are sick in bed with a fever).

Web:
http://vir.sgmjournals.org/
http://virology.science.org/
http://www.ncbi.nlm.nih.gov/ICTVdb/
http://www.virology.net/

Usenet:
bionet.virology

BIZARRE

Air Sickness Bags

The next time you fly on an airplane, look in the seat pocket in front of you. There you will find a small paper bag, discreetly labeled "For Motion Discomfort". Most people will just ignore the bag and concentrate on the other treasures you find in an airline seat pocket (such as the free magazine or the spiffy card showing all the emergency exits). A few select people, however, know value when they see it. To such people, an (unused) air sickness bag is a valuable commodity, to be collected and enjoyed. Just goes to show what I always say, that half the people in this world don't understand how the other two-thirds live.

Web:
http://www.airsicknessbags.com/
http://www.bagophily.com/
http://www.sicksack.com/

Bizarre Talk and General Discussion

There is too much in the world that is *not* bizarre. If we are to maintain our status as the dominant species on Earth, it behooves us to spend more time immersing ourselves in strangeness. A good way to do so is by subscribing to the Weird List. Then just sit back and wait for your mailbox to be filled with bizarre, disturbing and offensive short stories and ramblings. Perhaps you might even send in a story of your own. (The world needs all the help it can get.) If you are the type of person who wants immediate gratification, check out Usenet for your daily dose of weirdness.

Usenet:
  talk.bizarre
Listserv Mailing List:
  List Name: weird-l
  Subscribe to: listserv@listserv.brown.edu

Contortionism

If you are looking for new recruits for your Olympic Twister team, this is the perfect place to start. You can view lots of photographs of contortionists bending their bodies in ways that are probably outlawed in more conservative parts of the world. Besides images, you will also find text on the history of contortion, a bibliography, information about the International Contortion Society and links to other contortion sites.

Web:
  http://www.contortionhomepage.com/
Usenet:
  alt.arts.contortion

Dark Side of the Net

When the history of the twentieth century is written, the section on gothic culture will have one simple entry: see Carrie Carolin. Carrie is a wonderfully resourceful and talented bundle of energy who maintains The Dark Side of the Net, the preeminent Internet site for things gothic. Here you will find a fabulous list of resources regarding gothic, horror, vampires (and vampyres), occult, magick, zines, magazines, and much more. Root around a little, and you will find links to Carrie's other, equally fascinating enterprises. Not recommended for normal people or Republicans.

Web:
  http://www.darklinks.com/

When it comes to things gothic on the Net, there is only one way to make sure you have it all: Look to the Dark Side.

Death Clock

Do you want to know how long it is going to be before you bite the biscuit so you can plan everything in advance? On the Net, you can find out just how long you have to go until you pass on to your final reward. Your personal death clock will tell you how many seconds you have left to live and the date you are scheduled to die. If you don't want to know for yourself, you can check the death clocks of celebrities instead.

Web:
  http://www.deathclock.com/

Death Pools

Eventually, everyone dies. The question is, when? If you can guess when certain famous people are going to die, you could be a winner! It's all in fun, so don't worry if you lose. You'll live to play another day.

Web:
  http://www.melodyr.com/celebritydeathpool/
  http://www.melodyr.com/otherpool/
  http://www.msu.edu/~daggy/cop/

Discord and Destruction

Serious talk about serious talk. Destroy the earth or just our way of life: it's up to you. Remember, life is stern and earnest, and nobody gets out of here alive.

Web:
　http://www.ci-n.com/~jcampbel/
　　principia.index.html
Usenet:
　alt.destroy.the.earth
　alt.discordia

Grocery Shooting

I bet you've spent a lot of sleepless nights wondering what would happen if common, ordinary foodstuffs were shot with a variety of different firearms. Well, wonder no longer. You can now view short movies showing, say, a cabbage being blown to pieces by a bullet from a .357 Glaser. Before you get offended, however, I want you to remember the slogan of the U.S. National Rifle Association: If guns are outlawed, only vegetables will have guns.

Web:
　http://www.digitalweapons.com/joseph/inan/

Grotesque Curiosities

When I was a kid I had a shrunken head. It was made out of dark, black plastic, and it was ever so cool. If I had had a chance to get a real shrunken head, I would have done so in a minute, but such items were sadly out of reach for a young boy in Toronto, Canada. However, in my exploration of the Internet, I was gratified to find that the young man's fancy with things grotesque is alive and well. If you like shrunken heads, trophy skulls, and other weird stuff, the Net is only too willing to oblige. Just the thing to show your younger sister.

Web:
　http://members.aol.com/arbysaurus/
　http://www.eliteentertainment.net/weirdpictures/

> ## Quick, turn the page.

THE USENET COMPLAINT DEPARTMENT

We all need to complain. The trouble is, most of our complaints are heard only by people in our immediate vicinity. Much better to send your complaints to **alt.peeves.**

That way, anyone on the Internet will have a chance to find out what you think of parents who can't keep their kids quiet in public, or talk show hosts who swank around like they own the place.

Negative Emotions

Angst, bitterness, misanthropy, fear, disgust, anxiety and just plain being in a bad mood. Join the folks down at the not-OK corral for some roll-up-your-sleeves-and-get-down-to-it homestyle bitchin'. As John Milton put it (when they took away his Internet account), "So little is our loss. So little is our gain."

Usenet:
  alt.anger
  alt.angst
  alt.bitterness
  alt.im.angry
  alt.im.having.a.rotten.day
  alt.life.sucks
  alt.peeves

News of the Weird

It's often hard to accept the mundanity of normal everyday living. If your life isn't weird enough, try browsing through the News of the Weird archives or subscribe to their mailing list. You can read stories that will shock, surprise and flabbergast you. And this news is good for a laugh, too.

Web:
  http://www.newsoftheweird.com/

Positive Emotions

As if there isn't enough to deal with already, here are discussion groups devoted to good feelings and happiness. Bah, humbug. If God had wanted us to hear good news, he wouldn't have given us television and newscasters with bad toupees.

Usenet:
  alt.cuddle
  alt.good.morning
  alt.good.news
  alt.hi.are.you.cute
  alt.i-love-you

> You are your most
> reliable ally.

Potatoland

You don't need a potato to visit Potatoland. All you need is some spare time and an inclination to explore weird Web stuff. For example, do you have any computer files you don't need any more? Send them to the Digital Landfill. Oooooh—it gets even stranger. Things to see, do, and…

Web:
  http://www.potatoland.org/

Rotten Galleries

Do you like strange, sick, twisted pictures and information? How about disturbing images of death, racism, mugshots or crime scene photos? Sound good? Of course it does. Isn't it comforting to know that, whenever you want, 24 hours a day, there is a place you can go to look at pictures that would offend anyone with even a shred of decency and good taste?

Web:
  http://www.dailyrotten.com/
  http://www.rotten.com/

Rumors

Check out all the new rumors, both serious (Elvis and aliens) and less serious (the FBI and CIA). Did you know that readers of this book are entitled to free admission to Disney World?

Usenet:
  talk.rumors

Stick Figure Death Theater

Need a break from all the violence on TV and in the movies? Visit the home of the Stick Figure Death Theater, and—through the magic of the animated GIF—you will enjoy a large number of imaginative variations of a stick figure suffering through various disturbing deaths, usually extremely bloody. It sounds simple, but then so does Abstract Expressionism.

Web:
  http://www.sfdt.com/
  http://www.stickdeath.com/

Tasteless Topics

Taste is in the eye (and often in the mouth) of the beholder. But what do you do on those days when you need a good dose of bad taste? The answer is to check out the Net's tasteless discussion group. Feel free to look, to copy and to participate. Just be sure that whatever you do is disgusting and without any redeeming social value whatsoever. The Web site has the alt.tasteless FAQs and other tasteless links. This is not the place to bring your grandmother for her birthday.

Web:
   http://www.aracnet.com/~jaydog/index2.html

Usenet:
   alt.tasteless

Weird IRC Channels

After awhile, going to Tupperware parties and hanging out at the mall can get a tad predictable. So when you get to the point where you are itching to meet some new and bizarre people, try hanging out in these IRC channels. The only thing I can guarantee is that nothing is guaranteed.

IRC:
   #gothic (EFnet)
   #insomnia (EFnet)
   #sleepers (EFnet)
   #thelema (Undernet)

Weird Links

If there is one thing that really bothers me, it's being bored. I know some people who can sit quietly in a corner, doing nothing and being happy. Not me, I need ongoing mental stimulation. Why do I mention this? Because this Web site makes a promise up front: "You won't be bored here!" How true. You may be astonished, you may be outraged, you may be offended, you may be inspired, or you may simply be amused, but I guarantee, you *won't* be bored. If you are at all like me, this is a Web site with which you need to become familiar. (If you are not like me, you need to ask yourself, why not?)

Web:
   http://www.weirdlinks.com/greetings.htm

Who Would You Kill?

If you're mad as hell at the TV industry and you don't want to take it anymore, here's your chance to make a statement. Select a TV show, and send in your three cents' worth: Who from the show would you kill, and why? And how would you do it? Then check how other people around the Net have voted to terminate the obnoxious inhabitants of TV land.

Web:
   http://www.whowouldyoukill.com/

Zooass

Well, this is the Bizarre part of the book, but here is something so bizarre, it stands up and shakes its you-know-what in your face. What do you think about strange postcards, a joke zone, weird advice columns, the Tip the Baby game, the Magnetic Stupidity magnetic poetry Java applet, or Psycho Santa and Kill the Clown games? But wait, there's more: a chat room, some toys you can download for your computer (pranks, icons, goofy stuff) and a pet cemetery. Oh, my gawd. Don't let your parents see this one!

Web:
   http://www.zooass.com/

BOATING AND SAILING

Boat Racing

Boat racing has an appeal that is unlike any other type of racing. On the water, even a relatively slow speed can make you feel like you are streaking along. The fastest racing boats, the unlimited hydroplanes (the ones that produce the large roostertails), use aircraft turbine engines and reach speeds close to 200 mph (330 kph). At any speed, however, boat racing is exciting, and when you are not watching or taking part in a race, what better way to pass the time than to read about boat racing on the Net.

Web:
  http://www.apba-racing.com
  http://www.f1boat.com/
  http://www.sportc.com/
  http://www.ussba.org/

Usenet:
  rec.boats.racing
  rec.boats.racing.power

Boatbuilding

The Bible relates how God gave instructions to Noah on how to build an ark (see Genesis 6:14-16). However, the instructions were rudimentary at best: the ark should be 330 cubits long, 50 cubits wide, and 30 cubits high. It should have a door, a window, three levels with a number of rooms, and should be lined with pitch. Finally, it should be made out of gopher wood. (Go figure.) So, suppose you were given such vague instructions. How would you figure out how to build the ark? You'd do the same thing that Noah did when no one was looking. You'd use the Net to look up as many boatbuilding resources as you could find, and then pretend you knew what you were doing.

Web:
  http://www.rbbi.com/

Usenet:
  rec.boats.building

Listserv Mailing List:
  List Name: yacht-l
  Subscribe to: listserv@nic.surfnet.nl

Boating Magazines

The first rule of boating is "Everything costs more than you anticipate". The second rule is "Use the Net". These online boating magazines will fill in your spare time nicely. They cover a large range of boating topics, including news, articles and event info, so do take a moment to visit them all. Whatever your predilection—racing, cruising, sailing, buying or selling—you'll find a lot to keep you busy for those slack times when you aren't on the water.

Web:
  http://www.by-the-sea.com/
  http://www.goboatingamerica.com/
  http://www.motorboating.com/
  http://www.sailingbreezes.com/
  http://www.sailingsource.com/
  http://www.ybw.com/sp

Boating Mnemonics

When I was in medical school, there were lots of great mnemonics used to remember body parts in anatomy, symptoms of diseases and the properties of drugs. When you are learning to sail, there are also lots of things to remember and the mnemonics really help. This site gives you a list of clever tricks to help commit boating terms and rules to memory: mast light combinations, stern lights, buoyage, sound signals and right-of-way rules. Learn how your life can be saved by knowing that Timid Virgins Make Dull Company at Weddings.

Web:
  http://ficus-www.cs.ucla.edu/ficus-members/geoff/
    mnemonics.html

Honk if you love
using the Internet (or if
you're a goose).

Boating Quiz

Are you ready to captain your own sailing vessel? Find out how you score on this boating quiz. Afterward, you can take a break and head for the open seas, or at least to the bathtub with your little plastic battleships.

Web:

http://www.usps.org/nsbt/test.cgi

Boating Rules

Quick. Take a few minutes and go over the rules by which all good sailors abide. Along with the "Rules of the Road" (the International Regulations for Avoiding Collisions at Sea), you will also find information about signals, lights, navigation marks, equipment and flags. (Next time you go mine sweeping, check with these sites first to make sure your boat has the correct pattern of running lights.)

Web:

http://www.boatsafe.com/nauticalknowhow/
   boating/colregs.html
http://www.digigate.net/mba/rules.htm

Boating Safety

The words "safety" and "boating" go hand in hand. Just like you wouldn't go into a storm after getting your hair done, you wouldn't want to go charging off on a sailing adventure without first getting some safety tips from the Net. These boating safety sites will help you with boating regulations, the weather, personal watercraft safety and more. Don't leave shore without them.

Web:

http://www.boatingsafety.com/
http://www.boatsafe.com/
http://www.commanderbob.com/
http://www.nasbla.org/
http://www.uscgboating.org/

You can do it.

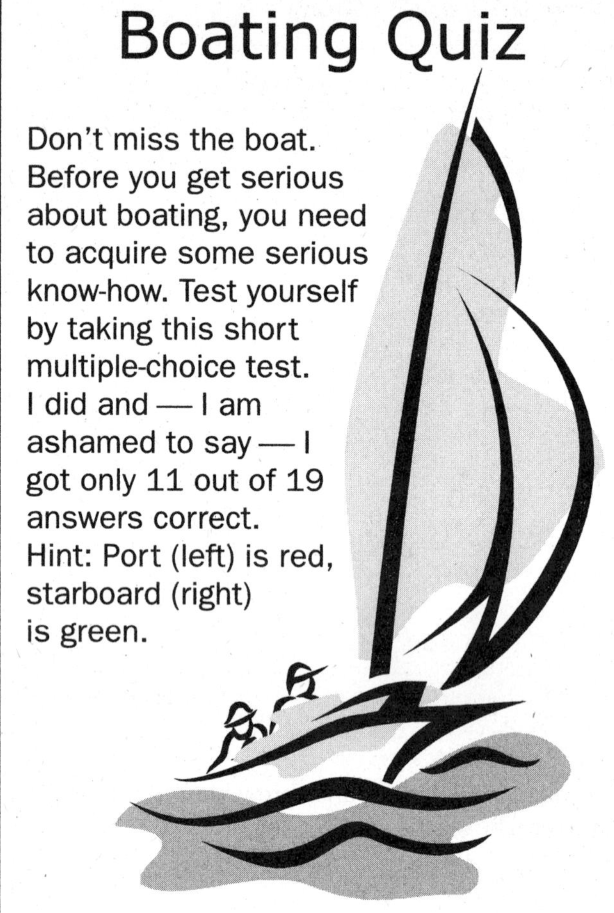

Boating Talk and General Discussion

When I was a kid at camp, I earned my Master Canoeist award. To this day, I can still recall all the esoteric canoeing strokes I had to be able to demonstrate, equally well on both sides. Truly, moving on water invokes deep feelings in all of us. If you care about things that float, join the Usenet boating discussion groups. The **live-aboard** mailing list is for the discussion of living onboard a boat.

Usenet:

rec.boats
rec.boats.cruising
rec.boats.electronics
rec.boats.paddle

Majordomo Mailing List:

List Name: live-aboard
Subscribe to: majordomo@crux.astro.utoronto.ca

Crew and Boat Finders

Are you a boat looking for a crew? Are you a crew looking for a boat? Here are boatless crews and crewless boats looking for the perfect match. If you are itching to set sail, but you just don't have everything you need, try these sites. You might find just what you are looking for.

Web:
  http://ficus-www.cs.ucla.edu/ficus-members/geoff/
     cruisecrew/
  http://www.floatplan.com/
  http://www.globalcrewnetwork.com/
  http://www.hypermax.com/guestbook/
     guestbook4.html
  http://www.windowoncyprus.com/crew_list.htm

Dragon Boat Racing

Dragon boat racing is a popular event in China. It is a Chinese tradition dating back more than 2,000 years. The boat races are said to have originated from a belief that they would bring agricultural prosperity. There is another, more romantic, legend that says dragon boat racing is related to the story of Ch'u Yuan, a Chinese patriot, who was exiled. Because of his expatriation, he was filled with despair and threw himself into the Mi Lo river. The legend says the people of the country were so distraught over the suicide of Ch'u Yuan that they got into their boats and raced up and down the river beating drums, splashing oars and making a general ruckus in order to scare away evil spirits and water dragons from the body of Ch'u Yuan. Today, this story creates a great excuse for people to get into brightly colored boats, which are decorated like dragons, and race up and down the river yelling, making noise and having a good time. Seems like as good an excuse as any to me.

Web:
  http://www.bayareadragons.org/links.html
  http://www.dragon-boats.net/

GORP: Great Outdoor Recreation Pages

Having this site on your bookmark list means you will never run out of interesting and entertaining resources relating to rafting, canoeing and kayaking. There are links to information on trips, gear, books and magazines, safety, events, reviews of locations, health, food and organizations.

Web:
  http://www.gorp.com/gorp/activity/paddle.htm

Inland Waterways

An inland waterway is any navigable river, lake or canal on which it is possible to travel by boat. In the United States, most of the canals that once existed are now closed. Still, the U.S. is a large country and, overall, the American canal system is still the largest in the world. When you add in all the rivers and lakes that connect into these canals, you have a huge number of navigable inland waterways, stretching over 25,000 miles (40,000 km). Other countries also have similar resources. For example, in the U.K., there are well over 2,000 miles (3,200 km) of existing canals over which you can travel. If you haven't been on an inland waterway lately, why not take a few days and try a quiet, relaxing boat trip. (Hint: Take this book with you so you won't be bored.)

Web:
  http://www.cemr.wvu.edu/~venable/asa/am-rivr.htm
  http://www.mvr.usace.army.mil/navdata/
  http://www.waterwaysjournal.net/

Kayaking and Canoeing

When I was an undergraduate student at the University of Waterloo in Canada, I spent a little time with the Whitewater Canoe Club. However, my participation was limited to paddling a kayak around the swimming pool. Later, after I moved to California, I went kayaking in the ocean, and I found it a lot more fun than the pool in Waterloo. Now I have a friend, Hal, who lives a block from the ocean and has two kayaks. Anytime I want, I can go over to his house and go kayaking with him. Somewhere in here is a lesson about life (which I'm sure I could figure out, if I didn't have a deadline to meet).

Web:
  http://home.adelphia.net/~kwinter/kayakmain.html
  http://www.gorp.com/gorp/activity/paddle.htm
  http://www.paddletrips.net/
  http://www.paddling.net/
  http://www.wavelengthmagazine.com/

Usenet:
  rec.boats.paddle.touring
  rec.boats.paddle.whitewater

Majordomo Mailing List:
  List Name: baidarka
  Subscribe to: majordomo@paddlewise.net

Majordomo Mailing List:
  List Name: wavelength
  Subscribe to: majordomo@paddlewise.net

Marine Signal Flags

Ships at sea use signal flags to spell out short messages or to communicate speeds and course changes. This page shows alphabetic flags, answering pennants, numeric pennants, substitute pennants, and the semaphore flag-waving system.

Web:

> http://www.anbg.gov.au/flags/signal-flags.html
> http://www.envmed.rochester.edu/wwwrlp/flags/
>   flags.htm
> http://www.home.zylstra.com/signals/

Navigation

When you are out to sea and lost or confused, send mail to this mailing list for the discussion of non-electronic navigation, with primary topics such as celestial navigation, coastal piloting, dead reckoning, charts, currents and weather at sea. For important navigation resources, see the Web sites. As long as you have an Internet connection, you can find your way home.

Web:

> http://pollux.nss.nima.mil/
> http://www.navcen.uscg.gov/

Listserv Mailing List:

> List Name: navigation-l
> Subscribe to: listserv@listserv.webkahuna.com

Personal Watercraft

If you are not up to sailing your own large boat, start smaller with a personal watercraft. These sites include links to manufacturers, part suppliers, magazines, clubs, and much more, relating to owning, using and maintaining personal watercraft. You have to supply your own pirate flag.

Web:

> http://www.jetski.com/
> http://www.pwctoday.com/
> http://www.watercraftassociation.com/

Navigate Your Way to Happiness

What do you do when you're in the middle of the ocean, all your electronic navigation aids are on the fritz and—on the distant horizon—a black, ponderous cloud has begun to form?

For most people, this would be a giant-sized pickle, but as an Internet user and a reader of this book, you have nothing to worry about.

All you need to do is send a message to the **Navigation** mailing list, describe your predicament ("I am surrounded by a bunch of water. What should I do?") and wait for a reply. Within a short time, some kind soul will probably answer you with the help you need, and soon you will be back in action without a care in the world.

Rowing

Whether you prefer rowing gently down a stream, sculling by yourself in the early morning, or pulling frantically on your oar during a hard-fought bump race, **rec.sport.rowing** is one Usenet discussion group you should read. To help you find the information you need, I have also included some Web sites, one of which contains the rowing FAQ (frequently asked question list).

Web:

> http://archive.museophile.sbu.ac.uk/rowing/
> http://origin-www.fisa.org/
> http://www.ruf.rice.edu/~crew/rowingfaq.html
> http://www.top100.rowing.org.uk/top100/
>   rankem.html
> http://www.usrowing.org/

Usenet:

> rec.sport.rowing

Sailing

I remember the days when, as a young sprout at summer camp, I learned how to sail, and I loved to take a boat out and cruise around the lake. Well, time marches on, and as we get older, we tend to be more landbound. Even if you sail as often as you can, you still have to spend most of your time ashore. So if you miss the open seas (or the open lakes), drop anchor on the Net, where there are a lot of sailing resources waiting for you. You can find FAQs (frequently asked question lists), humor, discussion, information about weather and navigation, and much, much more.

Web:

http://tbone.biol.sc.edu/tide/
http://www.ndbc.noaa.gov/
http://www.sailing.org/
http://www.sailnet.com/
http://www.setsail.com/
http://www.ussailing.org/

Usenet:

alt.sailing
alt.sailing.asa

Majordomo Mailing List:

List Name: tallship
Subscribe to: majordomo@listserv.cc.va.us

Seaports and Harbors

Before you set out on that long-distance trip, check with the Net about the ports you will be visiting. Many port authorities have Web sites, so you can use the Net to find out, in advance, what facilities are available. Here are some resources that will help you find Web sites for ports around the world.

Web:

http://www.mgn.com/worldports/portsearch.cfm
http://www.seaports.com/
http://www.seaportsinfo.com/portmenu.html

The Net loves you.

Yachting

Whether you use your yacht for pleasure or racing, you'll be glad to know about these resources. You'll find a lot of help to navigate through the world of boating: articles, tips, charter information, news, and event info. And when it's time to buy or sell, a few clicks of the mouse is all it will take you to find what you want, and check out the market so you can set the right price or comparison shop.

Web:

http://www.cruisingworld.com/
http://www.spacestar.net/users/cruiser/
http://www.yachtingnet.com/
http://www.yachtworld.com/

BODY, MIND AND SPIRIT

Angels

What is an angel? I can't really tell you, because everyone has his or her own idea. Basically, angels are spiritual beings who can intervene in our lives in positive ways. Do you like angels? If so, you'll find lots of angel poetry, music, pictures and resources on the Net. But most of all, you'll enjoy oodles and oodles of stories in which angels have visited people and helped them in some way. Do angels really exist? Last night I decided to put the question to a test. Before I went to bed, I sent out a silent, spiritual message asking for an angel to visit my house while I was sleeping and finish writing this chapter for me. Unfortunately, when I awoke, nothing had been done and I had to do the work myself. (Maybe I'm just not spiritual enough.)

Web:

http://saints.catholic.org/angelstories/
http://www.angelhaven.com/
http://www.angels-online.com/
http://www.sarahsarchangels.com/

Usenet:

alt.cyberangels

Astrology Horoscopes

So, you want to know how to make your life work as well as possible? Well, you could waste a lot of time thinking about your past behavior, and anticipating what is likely to happen in the near future. You could then think carefully as to what would be the wisest decisions for you to make based on long-term considerations. Or, you can just skip all the foolishness and check your horoscope.

Web:
> http://horoscopes.swirve.com/
> http://www.horoscopes-worldwide.com/
>   free_horoscopes.htm
> http://www.looktown.com/home_life/zodiac.shtml

Astrology Resources

Stars are more than just pretty lights you sit under at night. You can make wishes upon them, navigate ships by them, or record their positions to make up an astrological chart that you can consult for all your important decisions. Learn the basics of astrology, including its history and related topics like solar magnetism and etheric planets. If it's good enough for Sarah Ferguson, it's good enough for... someone.

Web:
> http://www.astrology-online.com/
> http://www.kenaz.com/astrology/
> http://www.panplanet.com/library/lib.htm
> http://www.spiritweb.org/spirit/astrology.html
> http://www.zodiacal.com/

Astrology Talk and General Discussion

You've discovered that Uranus is in conjunction with your ascendant ruler, Jupiter. And as if that's not enough, Uranus also squares Mercury, your tenth house ruler, and you have four yods that are creating frustration and dissatisfaction in your life. What's a person to do? Besides calling the psychic hotline, you can post queries or hints to stargazers around the globe or even—depending on whom they know—across the universe.

Usenet:
> alt.astrology
> alt.astrology.asian
> alt.astrology.marketplace
> alt.astrology.metapsych
> alt.astrology.moderated
> alt.astrology.toadology

Biorhythms

Today I am at my emotional peak. It must be true, because I went to a biorhythm Web site, entered my date of birth and that's what the computer tells me. Yes, today I am at my emotional peak. I feel like going to make friends with all the neighbors. While I am at it, I will send greeting cards to everyone I know and tell them just how I feel. Also, I think I will stop writing for the rest of the day and go practice some random acts of something-or-other. Oh, wait, I just noticed I typed the wrong birth date into the Web page and this biorhythm chart is all wrong. Never mind.

Web:
> http://www.facade.com/biorhythm/
> http://www.mystichouse.com/bio/bio.htm

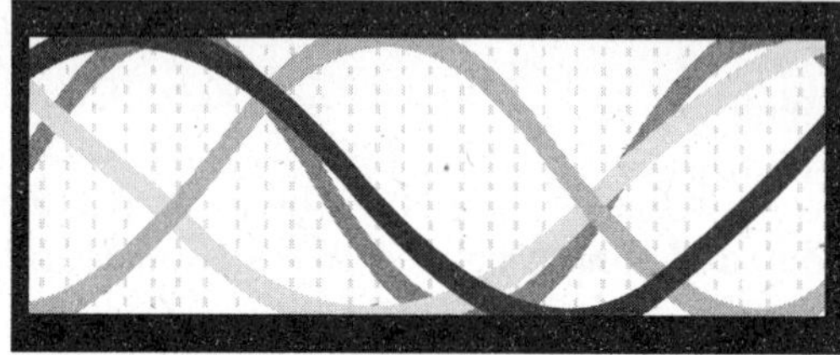

Books of the Dead

What happens when you die? What happens after you die? Do you really want to know? Then start with the Egyptian Book of the Dead and the Tibetan Book of the Dead. If you like esoteric knowledge, you'll feel right at home. After all, death is important, and if you're going to do it, you might as well do it well.

Web:
  http://wolf.mind.net/library/ancient/egyptian/
    bookodead/contents.htm
  http://www.lib.virginia.edu/speccol/exhibits/dead/
  http://www.lysator.liu.se/~drokk/BoD/
  http://www.paradise2012.com/light/tibetan/
    tib2.html

Chakras

The term "chakra" comes from the Sanskrit word for wheel or circle. In traditional yoga philosophy, our bodies have seven major energy centers, located in front of the spine, aligned with the vertical axis. Each of these seven "wheel—or chakras—is associated with a color of the spectrum: red, orange, yellow, green, blue, indigo, violet (the colors of the rainbow). The seven chakras are: base (also called root), sacral (navel), solar plexus, heart, throat, third eye (brow) and crown. Here is information about chakras and how their properties are integrated into a system of energy flow and balance.

Web:
  http://www.jayesh.net/chakras.htm
  http://www.katking.com/wisdom/chakra_m.html
  http://www.kheper.auz.com/topics/chakras/
    chakras.htm
  http://www.sacredcenters.com/toplevel/
    chakras.html

Crystals

What is it about crystals that seems to attract an enormous amount of folklore? For example, what does it say about our civilization that there are people who believe that magnetite (lodestone) electromagnetically pulls toxic energy and pain from the meridians in the pancreas and lower glands? Or that if you touch a person with a piece of magnetite, he will fall out of bed if he is unfaithful? As you can see, there is a lot to say about crystals, and there are a lot of people on the Net ready to contribute.

Web:
  http://www.gems4friends.com/~lorraine/
    therapy.html
  http://www.paganlore.com/crystals.html
  http://www.spacemagic.com/crystals.html

Usenet:
  alt.folklore.gemstones

Majordomo Mailing List:
  List Name: crystal
  Subscribe to: majordomo@mh.databack.com

Dreams

You live in two worlds. First, there is the everyday world of trash, bills, pain, broken hearts, disease and television commentators with bad toupees. Then there is the world of dreams: a place of your own making, based firmly on your personal memories and your subconscious desires. Remembering and analyzing your dreams is fascinating because it gets to the heart of the most important thing in the universe: you. Want more? Try lucid dreaming, in which you are totally aware of what is going on, and you control the outcome. It's fun; it puts you in the fantasy driving seat; and it's free.

Web:
  http://sommeil.univ-lyon1.fr/index_e.html
  http://www.asdreams.org/journal/articles/
  http://www.dreamgate.com/dgvc_01.htm
  http://www.faqs.org/faqs/dreams-faq/general/
  http://www.lucidity.com/LucidDreamingFAQ2.html

Usenet:
  alt.dreams
  alt.dreams.lucid

Extrasensory Perception (ESP)

Extrasensory Perception, or ESP, refers to communication, perception or actions that do not rely on the physical senses, for example, telepathy (mind-to-mind communication), clairvoyance (being aware of remote events), precognition (knowing the future) or psychokinesis (mind over matter). Over the years, scientists have studied extrasensory phenomena in an attempt to answer the basic question: is any of it real? Generally speaking, when proper experimental principles have been applied, the answer has always been no. Still, many people, perhaps most people, believe in some type of ESP. Do I believe? Let's try an experiment. I predict that if you go out, right now, and buy twenty copies of this book to give to your friends, your life will become significantly more successful and fulfilling. Try it and let me know what happens.

Web:

http://www.asdreams.org/telepathy/
http://www.cyberark.com/animal/telepath.htm
http://www.davidmyers.org/social/esp5e/esp.html
http://www.parapsych.org/
http://www.psiresearch.org/para1.html
http://www.spr.ac.uk/
http://www.tadma.net/psychic/

Usenet:

alt.paranet.esp-help

Firewalking

Firewalking is a "transcendent" experience in which a person quickly walks across a bed of hot ash-covered embers prepared from burnt wood. Firewalking is practiced in various cultures around the world. However, in its American New Age form, the actual walking over hot embers is of great symbolic importance (though very real). The main idea is to learn that you can have a great deal more control over your life than you think possible. This philosophy is taught during a workshop that precedes the firewalking experience (and for which you usually pay big bucks). Here is information about firewalking, what it is and how it is done. In the spirit of intellectual fairness, I have included discussions of firewalking that are more scientific and skeptical.

Web:

http://www.firewalking.org/
http://www.pitt.edu/~dwilley/fire.html
http://www.skepsis.no/english/subject/firewalk/
    kpreemp1/
http://www.spiritweavers.com/firewalking.html

Masters, Extraterrestrials and Archangels

Quench your burning desire to know all about ascended masters, extraterrestrial beings, and other spiritual higher-ups. Read about and see pictures of such notables as Maitreya, Serapis-Bei, Melchizedek, Khutumi, Michael and Ballerian.

Web:

http://www.newage.net.cn/nanc/iangels.html
http://www.spiritweb.com/spirit/alien-cultures.html

Meditation

Close your eyes, breathe deeply, relax. Clear your mind of all thoughts, free your body of all tension and float off to a world of pure spiritual essence. Explore the many methods of meditation, whether through yoga, visualization, traditional and philosophical processes, or by using more modern means.

Web:

http://www.erowid.com/spirit/meditation/
    meditation.shtml
http://www.faqs.org/faqs/meditation/faq/
http://www.meditationcenter.com/
http://www.mnsmc.edu/merton/merton.html
http://www.spiritweb.org/spirit/meditation.html

Usenet:

alt.meditation

Mysticism

It's a dark and stormy night, and during the dinner party someone brings up the subject of mysticism and begins telling about the seven layers of consciousness, time and the concept of becoming God. Then someone asks you what you think about the difference between the subconscient and the superconscient. Much to your embarrassment, the only response you can stammer is: "Anyone for dessert?" Raise your consciousness to a more mystical level by checking out these mysticism resources and never be caught with your aura down again.

Web:

http://www.clas.ufl.edu/users/gthursby/mys/
http://www.digiserve.com/mystic/

Usenet:

alt.consciousness.mysticism

Near-Death Experiences

It doesn't count if someone scares you so bad that you think you nearly have a heart attack. In Usenet you can talk with other people about real near-death experiences like actually going out of your body and wisping around the room in an ethereal form before being yanked back to consciousness. Read studies on the near-death concept as well as anecdotes from people who have had these experiences. Check out more information on near-death experiences (NDEs) at these Web sites.

Web:
> http://www.iands.org/
> http://www.nderf.org/
> http://www.ndeweb.com/Contents.htm
> http://www.near-death.com/

Usenet:
> alt.consciousness.near-death-exp

Why wait? Light your own fire.

TIDBITS

What should lovers know about PAST RELATIONSHIPS?

Now that you have finally met someone special, what should you tell him or her about your past? What should the other person tell you?

At the beginning of a new romance, it is tempting to obsess about previous relationships, especially if you are still venting your spleen over past transgressions. Still, the bare minimum often suffices. After all, the idea is to build *new* memories with a new person.

Do tell your lover whether or not he or she is your first lover. (However, there is no need to disclose how many lovers you have had.)

You also need to tell your lover whether or not you have been married. If so, you should explain why the marriage ended.

If you really want to understand your lover's past, visit his or her family. A great deal will be revealed when you meet the people who raised your sweetie.

New Age Talk and General Discussion

In this Usenet group, New Age believers encourage awareness, positive thinking, and healing with the mind, as well as offer information on many other topics. The talk covers a wide range of doctrines and philosophies. If you like to talk about religion, philosophy and the New Age movement, you are sure to never get bored here.

Usenet:
> talk.religion.newage

Numerology

Numerology is the study of the occult significance of numbers. According to this belief system, specific numbers are assigned to the letters of the alphabet. You can add up the digits that correspond to the letters in someone's name, and derive a single digit that is supposed to resonate with his or her personality. However, serious numerology is not that simple, because the personality is divided into various parts, each of which has a different number. In addition, there are also ways to take a birth date into account when analyzing a name. Here are some Web sites that will introduce you to numerology and the significance of numbers. If you are wondering what the world of numbers has in store for you, analyze your own name. I used one of the Web sites to analyze my cat's name and date of birth. I found out that he is "drawn to all that is beautiful, luxurious and expressive" which, as anyone who knows him will confirm, is certainly true.

Web:
> http://www.astrology-numerology.com/
>   numerology.html
> http://www.numberquest.com/numerology/
> http://www.simplynumbers.com/

Out-of-Body Experiences

The best cure for indigestion is to just leave your body behind and let it work out the details for itself. Read up on astral projection, out-of-body healing, meditation, lucid dreaming, theories about higher realms, and tips on how to have an out-of-body experience.

Web:

http://www.eu.spiritweb.org/spirit/obe-faq.html
http://www.robertpeterson.org/obebook.html
http://www.tanega.com/astral/astral.html

Usenet:

alt.out-of-body

Reiki

Reiki is a form of energetic healing that allows you to treat yourself or other people by the laying on of hands. Reiki was developed in the early 1900s by Mikao Usui in Japan. Basic Reiki is easy to learn and, in principle, can be done by anyone. The general idea is to bring balance to yourself and another person by harmonizing your "energy". Reiki masters can heal, not only in person, but at a distance. Does it really work? If you approach Reiki (and similar arts) from the point of view of a proper, skeptical scientist, you will find a lot of baloney (because there is a lot of baloney). However, if you are willing to suspend your critical judgment, you may be surprised at what can happen.

Web:

http://www.algonet.se/~anki-p/reikifaq.html
http://www.angelreiki.nu/reiki/
http://www.energeticarts.com/reiki/reiki.htm
http://www.reiki.org/
http://www.turtlehome.com/reiki/

Usenet:

alt.healing.reiki

Majordomo Mailing List:

List Name: reiki
Subscribe to: majordomo@maelstrom.stjohns.edu

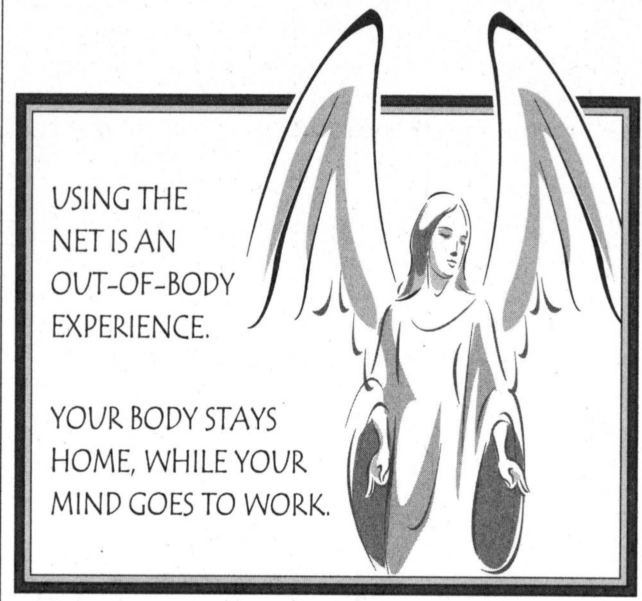

Reincarnation

Reincarnation refers to the rebirth of a soul from one body into another body or lifeform. Many old cultures believe in reincarnation as part of their religion. However, New Age people appreciate the idea of reincarnation from a somewhat different perspective. These Web sites contain information about reincarnation from the point of view of Western culture. Read about karma, personal experiences, transpersonal hypnotherapy, simultaneous lifetimes, pre-birth memories, interesting historical tidbits, and much, much more. On a personal note, I once underwent a past-life regression session in which I discovered that, in a previous lifetime, I had been a person who underwent a past-life regression session in which I discovered that, in a previous lifetime, I had been a person who...

Web:

http://www.comparativereligion.com/reincarnation.html
http://www.reincarnationcentral.com/
http://www.spiritweb.org/spirit/reincarnation.html
http://www.theosophy-nw.org/theosnw/reincar/re-selec.htm

Usenet:

alt.life.afterlife
alt.paranormal.reincarnation

REINCARNATION

The question is not so much, is there life after death, but is there life before death? I have always thought it to be the ultimate cosmic joke. Here we are, trapped in mortal bodies that, through natural selection and evolution, have been programmed to not want to die. But we have brains that can understand not only the idea of death, but that, one day, we also will die and that will be the end of our existence.

There are lots of ways to deal with this problem: religion, philosophy, ignorance, denial... But perhaps the most interesting is fostering the belief that we live again after death. What a comforting feeling it must be to "know" that you do not cease to exist after you bite the big one.

(Actually, I am beginning to suspect that the best thing might be to not even be born in the first place. Unfortunately, probably only one person in ten thousand is so lucky.)

Spirit Web

Do you ever get the feeling that there is more going on around you than you realize? What is it with all these alien sightings and interactions with ghosts and people who say they channel voices from the great beyond? Do they know something you don't? You don't have to feel left out any longer. Get information on channeling, alternative healing, UFOs, light technology, Earth changes, out-of-body experiences, astrology and other subjects that really are out of this world.

Web:
  http://www.spiritweb.org/

Spiritual Healing

This Web site is devoted to spiritual healing, such as the study of auras, chakras, energy work, Reiki, shiatsu, and homeopathy. These methods are much easier to practice on your friends than a splenectomy, plus you can do these tricks at dinner parties without having to use real blood.

Web:
  http://www.spiritweb.org/spirit/healing.html

Spiritual needs call for spiritual methods. That's why I recommend you use your computer and modem to connect to the **Spiritual Healing** site.

Tarot

You're minding your own business, laying your tarot cards out in a simple little Celtic Cross spread when all of a sudden the Nine of Swords pops up in a place where you least suspected. Now, what does that mean? Don't let it stump you. On the Web you can find out about the history of tarot, interesting ideas about spreads, card meanings and many different versions of tarot decks. In Usenet, tarot fans and experts talk about this classical form of divination.

Web:
  http://handel.pacific.net.sg/~mun_hon/tarot/
    tarot.htm
  http://www.aeclectic.net/tarot/
  http://www.facade.com/tarot/
  http://www.lunaea.com/tarot/
  http://www.tarotpassages.com/

Usenet:
  alt.tarot

BOOKS

Audio Books

What could be better than reading a brand new book? Why, having someone (maybe even the author) read the book to you. And what could be even better than that? Why, having someone (maybe even the author) read the book to you for free. I listened to a P.G. Wodehouse book while I was doing yoga. Your mileage may vary.

Web:
  http://www.wiredforbooks.org/

Book-A-Minute

Only got a minute? Read a quick, irreverent summary of a book, and your minute has not gone to waste. Finally, a quick, easy way to get through Beowulf. (Go see for yourself.)

Web:
  http://www.rinkworks.com/bookaminute/

Book Browser

This is one of my favorite book-related sites. I love information, and this Web site—created by two professional librarians—serves up heapin' spoonfuls of data in a well-organized buffet. For example, I was able to find a complete list of all the Perry Mason books by Erle Stanley Gardner. (I am a big Perry Mason fan—I have all the books, which I read repeatedly—so I think this list is a big deal.) There is also a collection of links to authors' Web sites on the Net, a pseudonym reference, lists of book awards, reviews, and much more. Check it out for yourself. If you like to read, you'll love this site.

Web:
  http://www.bookbrowser.com/

Book Concordances

A concordance is an alphabetical list of all the words used in a particular book, along with the context of each usage. This Web site provides an easy-to-use concordance that can help you research how specific words are used within various classic books. For example, I found out the word "sex" was used only six times in all of the Sherlock Holmes novels and stories. (But I like them anyway.)

Web:
  http://www.concordance.com/

Book Fairs

One year, my local library had a big book sale to raise money, and I was one of the volunteers who worked at getting things ready and setting up the books. The best part was that I could go through the books ahead of time, looking for stuff for myself. Book fairs and library sales are so cool. You get to hang out with loads and loads of books; you get to look at loads and loads of books; you get to buy loads and loads of books; and then you get to take them home and wonder where you are going to put them all.

Web:
  http://www.bookexpo.reedexpo.com/
  http://www.booksalefinder.com/
  http://www.lcweb.loc.gov/loc/cfbook/bookfair.html

Book Recommendations

We all love to recommend books to other people, and we all know that most of the time other people don't pay any attention to our recommendations. Why? Because we are wasting our time on the wrong people: our family and friends. Instead, we should be sharing our literary knowledge and good taste with the faceless millions on the Net, who can better appreciate our personal sense of style and discrimination. Take a moment to share your list of favorite books with everyone in the world. At the same time, you can check out what other, less stylish and discriminating people are reading.

Web:
  http://www.allreaders.com
  http://www.figure8.com/homespun/booktop.jsp

Book Resources

When I think about my favorite friends and coworkers, I notice that—as different as they all are—they have one thing in common: they love books. My theory is that smart and interesting people love to talk to other smart and interesting people. In the course of a lifetime, we are limited as to how many people we will be able to meet and get to know. However, when we read a book, we can "talk" to the author, even though he or she is someone we will probably never meet in person. Thus, books are more than printed pages. They are "letters of introduction" to the most interesting people we will ever know.

Web:
  http://www.bookpage.com/
  http://www.bookspot.com/
  http://www.internetbookinfo.com/
  http://www.literaryleaps.com/
  http://www.overbooked.org/

Book Reviews

Why waste your time and money on an unrewarding book? Read the reviews on the Net and find out the real scoop before you make a serious commitment. Save your excess time and money for unrewarding people.

Web:
  http://www.ala.org/booklist/
  http://www.bookreporter.com/
  http://www.home.earthlink.net/~elundegaard/
    bookpage.html

Usenet:
  alt.books.reviews
  rec.arts.books.reviews

Book Talk and General Discussion

There are a lot of people who love to talk about books, and there are a variety of Usenet groups and chat facilities devoted to such discussions. The Usenet groups cover books of all genres, including reviews and discussion of reviews. Moreover, talk is not limited to books: there are also requests for information on interesting bookstores and hard-to-find bargains.

Web:
  http://www.his.com/~allegria/online.html

Usenet:
  alt.books
  alt.books.purefiction
  rec.arts.books
  rec.arts.books.hist-fiction
  rec.arts.sf.dune
  rec.books
  rec.collecting.books

Bookbinding

Books are our friends, and important books are important friends. Being able to create your very own books from scratch is a wonderful skill you will appreciate your whole life. Even more important, as your older books start to deteriorate, it's handy to have some bookbinding skills so you can make the repairs yourself. Remember, books are people too.

Web:
  http://www.cs.uiowa.edu/~jones/book/
  http://www.philobiblon.com/
  http://www.webnz.com/red/book.htm

Listserv Mailing List:
  List Name: book_arts-l
  Subscribe to: listserv@listserv.syr.edu

BOOK TALK AND GENERAL DISCUSSION

Many people believe if you have a complete set of Harley Hahn books, you really don't need anything else. Well, although that is certainly true for most people, there are a few oddballs who need some other type of literary stimulation once in a while. If you are one of these unfortunate eccentrics, you may want to follow the discussion on Usenet. Find out what's old, what's new, what's borrowed, and what's colorful in the land of literature.

BookWeb

Book selling isn't just business, it's big business. If you want to stay plugged into what's new and exciting in the industry, check out BookWeb, maintained by the American Booksellers Association. Here you will find information about the American book industry, such as news, events and statistics, as well as a number of bookstore directories. (I am still waiting to find out the average number of Harley Hahn books that are sold to ballroom dance instructors every day.)

Web:
  http://www.bookweb.org/

BookWire

When you don't want the best book, only the best-selling book, check out this database of the hottest books on the market. The database is searchable by author or title. You'll find descriptions and links to book publishers and sellers on the Web, links to online libraries, a reading room, a book events calendar, and more.

Web:
  http://www.bookwire.com/

Buying and Selling Books

Whether you are looking for a rare first-edition of Isaac Asimov's autobiography, or just trying to find a copy of "Freddy and the Baseball Team From Mars" to fill in your collection, it's easy to search for the books you want on the Net. Use the Web sites to find what you want and to sell books of your own. For book reviews, book business chatter, and general book-lover discussion, try the Usenet discussion groups.

Web:
  http://pages.ebay.com/catindex/books.html
  http://www.bookfinder.com/

Usenet:
  biz.books.technical
  rec.arts.books.marketplace

Do-It-Yourself Book Reviews

Which books are real crowd-pleasers? Find out by reading reviews written by people on the Internet. Categories include science fiction and fantasy, general fiction, religion, new age, mystery, computers and technology, biographies, science and mathematics.

Web:
  http://www.edsbookreview.com/

Online Book Clubs

A book club is a group of people who all read the same book and then get together to discuss it. Does that sound inviting? (Of course it does. Some of the very best people belong to book clubs.) But what about an *online* book club, where you can have the same penetrating discussion without having to change out of your pajamas? Here's the information you need to join an online book club or to start one of your own.

Web:
  http://www.bookbay.com/bookfaq.htm
  http://www.readinggroupsonline.com/

Pulp Fiction

Pulp magazines existed in America from the turn of the century to the early 1950s. They offered an impressive array of stories about crime, mystery, detectives, war, love, romance, science fiction, horror, sports, westerns and adventure. The spirit of pulp fiction is alive today in modern paperback adventure series and on the Net. Did you know that the Shadow was really Kent Allard, a World War I ace and spy? Lamont Cranston was merely a disguise. If you listen to the radio show, you will be misinformed, but with these resources, you will know the truth.

Web:
  http://www.cs.uku.fi/~vaisala/Pulp.htm
  http://www.ip.pt/pulp/
  http://www.thepulp.net/
  http://www.vintagelibrary.com/pulp/

Usenet:
  alt.pulp

Rare Books

People always want what they can't have, so if it's rare, it's bound to be popular. Take rare books, for example. People collect them, and most of the time they just store the books and never look at them. I myself collect old Freddy the Pig books (but I read them). For lots of valuable information, see the Web sites. If you want to talk to other book lovers, join one of the mailing lists, where you can discuss out-of-print and rare books, as well as techniques for preserving your special collection (such as don't read a valuable Freddy the Pig book while you are eating spaghetti).

Web:
   http://www.rarebooks.org/
   http://www.rbms.nd.edu/

Listproc Mailing List:
   List Name: exlibris
   Subscribe to: listproc@library.berkeley.edu

Listserv Mailing List:
   List Name: rarebooks-l
   Subscribe to: listserv@listserv.indiana.edu

Romance Novels

Fantasies are exciting because they are not played out in real life. All the more reason to immerse yourself in a good, old-fashioned romance novel. Are you looking for something new to read? Just specify your favorite author or genre, and the Net can help you find the first romance novel of the rest of your life. In the meantime, let me tell you some interesting statistics. Several years ago, two college professors presented the results of some important research at a scholarly conference. They read one hundred romance novels and found that at the beginning of the novel, 74 percent of the heroines were virgins while none of the men were. Notwithstanding, 98 percent of the heroines had an orgasm the first time they had sex. They also found that 17 percent of the novels had rape scenes, and 18 percent of the women who were raped had an orgasm during the attack. (By the way, a few years later, the two professors were back at the same conference where they presented a paper entitled "Collecting Mickey Mouse".)

Web:
   http://www.judithivory.com/avonladies/
   http://www.likesbooks.com/
   http://www.slake.com/
   http://www.theromancereader.com/

Romance Novels

*Jennifer's breath grew short and stertorous. Her lips began to quiver while her straw-colored hair moved gently in the warm tropical breeze. She gazed up at the dark, mysterious, masculine eyes of the stranger. As a frisson of passion shocked her taut, leonine body, she whispered softly into his dark, mysterious, masculine ear. "Tell me, my love," she murmured, "of all the heroines in all the romance novels in the world, whom would you say I most resemble?" The stranger touched her face gently with the back of his dark, mysterious, masculine hand. He turned away slowly, the moonlight shining brightly on his dark, mysterious, masculine features as he took out his palmtop computer. "Just one moment, my sweet angel," he responded. "My Internet connection will be active shortly, and I will be able to check the **Romance Novels** Web sites."*

Technical Books

If you have a squeak in your clicker or you can't get slot A to line up with tab B, check into these Usenet discussion groups to see if there is a technical book that can help. Just the place to look when you need to decide which Unix book to give your grandmother for her birthday.

Usenet:
   alt.books.technical
   misc.books.technical

BOTANY

Agroforestry

As the population grows, the need for better crops and soil increases. Agroforestry studies plant growth and nutrition in an effort to find crops and soil that are compatible with each other and with the rest of the surrounding environment.

Web:
http://www.icraf.cgiar.org/
http://www.unl.edu/nac/

Usenet:
bionet.agroforestry

Botanical Gardens

I belong to the local botanical garden where I live. I find that there is nothing more relaxing than sitting beside a rushing brook under a large tree, or reading a good book while sitting in a field of wildflowers. If you like gardens and plants, here are lists of arboretums and botanical gardens around the world, wonderful places to visit when you get a chance to slow down and enjoy life.

Web:
http://www.botanique.com/
http://www.botany.net/IDB/subject/botgard.html
http://www.usna.usda.gov/

Botanical Glossary

When someone calls you a reniform acaulescent stomium, don't get mad, get even. Check with the Botanical Glossary and soon you will be able to reply, "Yeah, well, your mother is a vegetative (lacking reproductive organs) perispore (wrinkled spore covering)."

Web:
http://glossary.gardenweb.com/glossary/
http://www.anbg.gov.au/glossary/croft.html

Botany Images

Here are thousands of pictures of plants, flowers, trees, fungi and other vegetation. If you are a student or researcher of botany, these are sites you should explore. However, even if you don't really care about botany, I suggest that you browse around and see what's here. There are fabulous pictures that would be great to dress up your Web page or to use as a background.

Web:
http://images.botany.org/
http://plants.usda.gov/gallery.html
http://www.botany.wisc.edu/virtual.html

Botany Resources

Botany, a branch of biology, is the study of all forms of plant life, from tiny microscopic organisms to large long-lived trees. The roots of botany stretch back to Greek and Roman times. However, modern botany began in the 16th century with the systematic study of plants for medicinal uses. In 1623, the Swiss scientist Gaspard Bauhin published a book in which he described 6,000 different species of plants. The most renowned botanist of all time was the Swedish scientist Carolus Linnaeus (1707-1778) who developed the modern system of nomenclature. Today, botany consists of a large number of specialized disciplines based on six fundamental areas of study: structure, properties, biochemical processes, classification, diseases and environment. There are also a number of applied botanical sciences, the most important of which are agriculture (crops, livestock), horticulture (fruits, vegetables, flowers, ornamental plants), and forestry (forests).

Web:
    http://nmnhwww.si.edu/departments/botany.html
    http://www.amjbot.org/
    http://www.botany.net/IDB/subject/botlink.html
    http://www.botany.org/
    http://www.ou.edu/cas/botany-micro/www-vl/

Botany Talk and General Discussion

How does your garden grow? Discover the myth and mystery of plant growth and reproduction. Discussion of all aspects of plant biology is encouraged. You'll never have a guilt-free salad again.

Usenet:
    bionet.plants
    bionet.plants.education

There's no place like
your home page.

Go get a snack.
(I'll wait here.)

Carnivorous Plants

A carnivorous plant is one that eats animal matter of some type (usually insects, but sometimes very small animals like frogs). Carnivorous plants have adapted to live in an environment which is lacking in nutrients, for example, a bog or the surface of a cliff. Worldwide, there are more than 600 different species of carnivorous plants, many of which can be grown right in your very own home or garden. What is fascinating about them is that they are so unexpected. Normally, we assume that plants will sit quietly and leave the animal kingdom alone. To find a plant that can actually attract, capture and digest an animal of some type is a complete biological non sequitur. In case you want to explore these monarchs of the botanical world, here are some Internet resources to help you learn about these plants before they learn about *you*.

Web:
    http://www.carnivorousplants.org/
    http://www.sarracenia.com/faq.html

Ethnobotany

Ethnobotany is the study of how people in a particular region of the world make use of the indigenous plants. Ethnobotany involves not only botany, but many other disciplines such as archaeology, anthropology, biochemistry, pharmacology, history, sociology, mythology, and so on. Ethnobotany is especially important to us as a source for native plants that might have important pharmacological and medical uses.

Web:
    http://www.erowid.org/entheogens/ethnobotany/
        ethnobotany.shtml
    http://www.sacredearth.com/ethnobotany.htm
    http://www.siu.edu/~ebl/

Ferns

I have a big fern next to my desk, and, no doubt about it—ferns are cool. But actually, ferns are a lot more cool than you might think. Just consider how they reproduce. Ferns grow as a collection of fronds, out of stems called rhizomes. A frond has many small leaflets or pinnae. On the underside of the pinnae, the plant produces small, round containers called sporangia. Within the sporangia are very tiny, dust-like spores. During its lifetime, a fern will drop millions of spores, and if one of them happens to fall in a suitable environment (which must be moist), it will grow into a small (less than a centimeter wide) heart-shaped plant called a gametophyte. On its underside, the gametophyte will grow tiny male organs (antheridia) and female organs (archegonia). In the presence of water, a sperm cell from the antheridia will swim to the archegonia where they will attempt to fertilize an egg cell. (And you thought you had it tough.) The fertilized egg will then grow into a sporophyte, a brand new fern plant. Thus, ferns reproduce by creating a new plant which then produces the child fern. And, just in case there isn't enough water, ferns can also reproduce by growing new plants from their rhizomes or having the gametocyte produce a sporophyte without fertilization. Now tell me, are ferns cool, or what?

Web:

http://www.fs.fed.us/database/feis/plants/fern/
http://www.home.aone.net.au/byzantium/ferns/

Forests

A forest is a large area containing a dense growth of trees, underbrush and other plants. Forests are actually complex biological systems where the plant life interacts with a large number of animals (mammals, birds and insects) and microorganisms. For hundreds of millions of years, much of the Earth's land mass was covered by forests. However, with the rise of civilization, many forest areas were destroyed. As early as two thousand years ago, much of the area surrounding the Mediterranean sea had already been deforested, either for fuel (wood was Man's first fuel) or to clear the land for farming or grazing. As a result, these ancient regions suffered a decline in fertility, which had an enormous effect on the people who lived there, contributing to a decline in prosperity, which has persisted to this day. In the Middle Ages, Western Europe suffered from gradual but constant deforestation, and in more modern times, much of North America has suffered the same fate, but faster. Today, there are few large tracts of virgin forests remaining in the world, and one of largest, the rain forests of South America, is under constant assault. It is important for us to understand the role of our forests: how they work, how they interact with the global environment, and how they affect the lives and cultures of people in the area.

Web:

http://www.americanforests.org/
http://www.forests.org/
http://www.panda.org/forests4life/
http://www.wcmc.org.uk/habitats/forest.htm
http://www.wri.org/forests/

Lichens

Lichens are so cool. You've probably heard of them, but do you know what they really are? Lichens are organisms made up of a combination of algae and fungus living symbiotically. The fungus collects the water that is needed by the algae. The algae uses the water for photosynthesis, which produces the food needed by the fungus. Cool, huh? And not only that, when the algae and fungus reproduce, they usually do so simultaneously (although experts suspect that the fungus will sometimes fake it). Lichens are found all over the world, from the deserts to the polar regions, so there's a good chance you can find some near you. They make great pets, especially for people who can't handle the responsibility of caring for children or cats.

Web:
http://mgd.nacse.org/hyperSQL/lichenland/
http://www.botany.hawaii.edu/cpsu/ial.htm
http://www.lichen.com/
http://www.unomaha.edu/~abls/resources.html

Forests

Forests are a crucial part of the Earth's ecosystem, and as such, give purpose to your life. Here's why.

If it weren't for forests, we wouldn't have trees.

If it weren't for trees, we wouldn't have wood.

If it weren't for wood, we wouldn't have paper.

If it weren't for paper, we wouldn't have books.

If it weren't for books, YOU wouldn't have this book.

And if it weren't for this book, your life would be infinitely poorer, without purpose and meaning.

Paleobotany

Paleontology is the study of the history of life on Earth as reflected in the fossil record. Paleobotany is the branch of paleontology that concentrates on plant fossils and ancient vegetation. The most common type of plant fossils are the impressions of leaves. Other parts of the plant, such as stems, seeds and wood are more often petrified. Petrified wood is formed over millions of years as silica dissolved in groundwater replaces the organic material in pieces of wood. Thus, petrified wood is really a mineral that has been formed within the pattern of the wood.

Web:
http://www.dartmouth.edu/~daghlian/paleo/
http://www.uni-wuerzburg.de/mineralogie/
   palbot1.html

Palynology Resources

Palynology is the study of spores and pollen. My advice is to visit this Web site as often as you can and brush up on your knowledge of tiny things that float around making people miserable. Then, when you meet someone at a party and they ask about your hobbies, you can say, "Oh, I am something of an amateur palynologist. Do you like spores?" I guarantee you will be invited back again and again.

Web:
http://www.scirpus.ca/cap/links/websites.htm

Photosynthesis

Photosynthesis is the process whereby sunlight is used as an energy source to synthesize carbohydrates from carbon dioxide and water. As a byproduct, photosynthesis also produces oxygen. Photosynthesis takes place in most plants, as well as algae and some bacteria. In plants, photosynthesis requires the use of chlorophyll, a pigment that gives plants their characteristic green color. All foods, fossil fuels (such as oil and coal), and plant products are indirect products of photosynthesis. Thus, without photosynthesis, there would be no paper to print this book and no pizza to eat as you use the Net.

Web:
http://photoscience.la.asu.edu/photosyn/

Usenet:
bionet.photosynthesis

Plant Fossil Database

For some reason, when you read about extinct and endangered species, animals get all the press. However, there are a large number of extinct plant species, many of which have left fossil remains. This database contains a wealth of research information relating to thousands of extinct plants.

Web:

http://www.biodiversity.org.uk/ibs/palaeo/pfr2/pfr.htm

Plant Hormones

A plant hormone is a chemical that, when produced in one part of the plant and transmitted to other parts of the plant, can, in small amounts, affect various biological processes. The most common plant hormones are auxin, cytokinins, gibberellins, abscisic acid and ethylene. Hormones control processes such as cell growth, branching, apical dominance, the differentiation of vascular tissue, root creation and signaling. Apical dominance, for example, occurs when a terminal bud produces an auxin that moves down the branch and inhibits lateral budding. Plant hormones are even important in the home. When you have a piece of fruit that you want to ripen quickly, put it in a paper bag with an unripe banana. As the banana ripens, it will emit ethylene (a gaseous hormone), which will cause the other fruit to ripen more quickly.

Web:

http://www.plant-hormones.bbsrc.ac.uk/

Plant Pathology

Plants get sick. However, unlike people, plants rarely have adequate insurance and must almost always depend on the kindness of strangers. If you have a sick plant, or if you happen to be a plant pathologist doing research or wondering what your peers are up to, here are some Web sites specializing in botanical diseases and related topics.

Web:

http://image.fs.uidaho.edu/vide/refs.htm
http://www.apsnet.org/
http://www.ianr.unl.edu/pubs/PlantDisease/
http://www.ifgb.uni-hannover.de/extern/ppigb/

TIDBITS

What should men know about MENSTRUAL CYCLES?

Every month, women of childbearing age go through a process called the menstrual cycle, which prepares them to become pregnant. Starting at about 13 years of age, women go through this cycle repeatedly for about 35 years.

During the course of a single menstrual cycle, the levels of certain hormones change within a woman's body. (A hormone is a chemical, circulating within the bloodstream, that is used to control specific bodily functions.)

The changing hormones have several important effects. One is to cause the lining of the uterus (womb) to thicken. If the woman becomes pregnant, the fertilized egg will implant itself in this thickened lining and begin to grow.

If, by the end of the cycle, the woman does not become pregnant (the usual case), the bulk of the thickened tissue is sloughed off and expelled from the body via the vagina. The tissue contains a fair amount of blood and so, about once a month, a woman experiences a flow of bloody tissue that lasts about 5 days. This process is called menstruation.

The changing hormones have two other important effects. First, before and during menstruation, the uterus, which contains a lot of muscle tissue, will contract. This contraction causes cramps, which can become quite painful.

Second, in the days leading up to menstruation, many women experience one or more physical symptoms (bloating, breast discomfort, weight gain, cramps, back pain, fatigue, insomnia, acne, headache, nausea) or emotional symptoms (anger, anxiety, apathy, confusion, depression, hopelessness, irritability, loneliness, moodiness, nervousness, tension).

The intensity of these symptoms vary widely from one woman to another. When the symptoms are bothersome, the condition is referred to as premenstrual syndrome or PMS. About 5 percent of women have PMS so bad that it has a profound effect on their lives.

Plant Taxonomy

Plant taxonomy refers to the scientific classification of plants. There is a wealth of information on the Net that can help you identify and name the plant of your choice. For example, say your significant other gives you a Phyllanthus acuminatus for Valentine's Day. Most people wouldn't know what to make of it, but as one of my readers, it will be the work of a moment for you to check with the Net and find out that your gift is actually a Jamaican gooseberry tree. (Wow!)

Web:
   http://hortiplex.gardenweb.com/plants/
   http://plants.usda.gov/cgi_bin/
      topics.cgi?earl=classification.html
   http://www.biosis.org/zrdocs/zoolinfo/
      an_names.htm#pla
   http://www.inform.umd.edu/pbio/pb250/
   http://www.sysbot.org/

Succulents and Cacti

Succulents are fleshy plants that are characterized by being able to survive with minimal water. Succulents typically have thick leaves, covered with a waxy material called cutin that acts to reduce the evaporation of water. These plants—including many species of cactus, aloe and yucca—are commonly indigenous to naturally dry regions, such as the semi-arid areas of the world. Personally, I like succulents, and I have a number of them in my office and outside in my garden. One such plant that I recommend for everyone is the aloe vera. It is easy to grow, and the slimy substance inside the leaves is useful for treating mild burns and skin irritations.

Web:
   http://www.desertcacti.com/
   http://www.gardenweb.com/forums/cacti/
   http://www.succulent-plant.com/

I'm ready if you are.

Succulents and Cacti

Low maintenance, hardy, independent, easygoing — succulents are all of these.
(If only all your relationships were so simple.)

BROADCASTING ON THE NET

Celebrity Interviews

There are two types of celebrities: accomplished people who are famous because they have achieved or created something of renown, and vacuous people who are famous because they are famous. However, accomplished or vacuous, celebrities seem to have one thing in common. They always have a lot to say, especially when they need to plug a new movie or book. Let us not forget, though, the main reason for listening to celebrity interviews: to find out the newest gossip. Isn't it interesting that when our friends and relatives get divorced or have financial problems, it's nothing but a big pain, but when the same things happen to celebrities, we are fascinated? Maybe it's because famous people are so far removed from our personal world, it doesn't bother us when they screw up their lives. (Or maybe it's because celebrities don't call in the middle of the night asking us to choose sides or lend them money.) Anyway, if you like to hear celebrities talking, not to mention people talking about celebrities, here are the places to be.

Web:
   http://www.pmpnetwork.com/Live.htm
   http://www.pmpnetwork.com/Live2.htm
   http://www.premrad.com/entertainment/celeb/
      bytes.html
   http://www.zeldman.com/15/main.html

Commercial Radio Stations

There are lots and lots of regular commercial radio stations that you can listen to over the Net. There's something intriguing about listening to a station that is far away. And, somehow, local commercials for a distant city don't seem to be as obnoxious as local commercials in your own hometown. Here are collections of links to hundreds of radio stations you can listen to on the Net. I bet you'll have fun exploring.

Web:

http://www.radiotower.com/
http://www.virtualtuner.com/
http://www.web-radio.com/

Custom Music Stations

In the late 1980s, I did a consulting job for a well-known top-40 radio station in Southern California. The station had a call-in phone number that listeners would use to request their favorite songs. There was a young lady who answered the phone and, no matter what song anyone requested, she would always say, "I'll get that on for you as soon as I can." But it was all a lie—the music was programmed in advance. All the young lady did was gather statistics for marketing purposes. Once in a while, the disc jockey would tape someone asking for a particular song, and play the tape just before that song was played, but it was an illusion to fool the listeners. The requests had nothing to do with the playlist. (In general, there is a lot of dishonesty in the entertainment business.) But now we live in the twenty-first century and *you* can have control. Would you like to build your own custom Internet music station? Just choose the type of music you like, rate the songs, and before you can say "I'll get that on for you as soon as I can," you'll have your own personal source of continuous music. Moreover, you can share your personal station with your friends (including all the people on the Net who are just waiting to admire your good taste), and you can listen to custom stations created by other people.

Web:

http://www.live365.com/
http://www.scour.com/
http://www.shoutcast.com/
http://www.spinner.com/

Live Broadcasting Guides

Every minute of every day, there is a lot of broadcasting—audio and video—on the Net. These broadcasting guides will help you find out what's happening live right now (or soon). Enjoy audio broadcasts, video broadcasts, sports, concerts, live chats, and more. As I was writing this, I checked to see what was on the menu for the day. I found a large variety of free shows including sporting events, live music, a poetry festival, news and commentary from Scotland, India, Africa, Italy, United States and New Zealand, several comedy shows, a science discussion, celebrity gossip, religious sermons, live coverage of the British parliament, a public affairs discussion, a philosophy lecture, and an animated trivia game show.

Web:

http://radio.broadcast.com/
http://www.comfm.com/live/radio/
http://www.flip2it.com/
http://www.live-at.com/

Live Concerts

Concerts are a lot of fun, but who wants to wait? If you are like me, you want the world and you want it *now*. Check out these concert archives—both audio and video—that you can enjoy anywhere you want. After all, why should you pay through the nose for expensive tickets when you can use the Net to listen to a concert for free (through the ears)?

Web:

http://www.hob.com/onlinemusic/concerts/

Send email to yourself
right now, and check
to make sure that
you are online.

News Broadcasts

News, news, news. 24 hours a day. Live. Video and audio. News, business, sports, weather, science. Video and audio. Live. 24 hours a day. News, news, news.

Web:

http://news.npr.org/
http://www.bbc.co.uk/worldservice/
http://www.cnn.com/audio/
http://www.cspan.org/watch/cspanradio.asp

Sports Broadcasts

If you're a sports buff, you'll love the Net. There are lots and lots of sporting events you can listen to and watch—baseball, hockey, basketball, football, college sports, and more—as well as post-game shows, updates, interviews, clips and archived games. And, of course, you can listen to sports news whenever you want, so you never have to worry about missing the latest scores just because you are forced to spend some of your time working, eating or sleeping.

Web:

http://www.espnradio.com/
http://www.sportsbroadcastpages.com
http://www.sportsbyline.com/
http://www.sportsline.com/u/radio/live/sports/

Video Broadcasting Guides

Remember how everyone used to think that in the future there would be zillions of video channels offering any type of content we could imagine whenever we would want it? The future is almost here: just cruise through these video guides and you are sure to find something to distract, entertain or inform you. There is a lot more out there than you think and, as a citizen of the Net, it is your duty to explore the brave new world of video whenever you can grab a few moments away from what people without fast Internet connections call "real life".

Web:

http://www.mediachannel.com/
http://www.vidnet.com/

News Broadcasts

There is so much news in the world, I don't think you should wait; you need to know and need to know now. TV is too slow. Radio is too slow. Newspapers and magazines are also too slow.

Only the Internet can satisfy your inborn need to know everything that is going on right away. So go ahead and check the Internet news broadcasts. (I'll wait here.)

BUSINESS ON THE NET

Affiliate Programs

There are more businesses on the Web than you can shake an electronic stick at, and the biggest problem they have is how to get people to visit their sites. The solution, for many of them, is to offer affiliate programs (also known as associate, referral, partner or reseller programs). Here is how it works. You (the affiliate) put an ad or a link on your Web site, enticing people to visit a particular business. When someone clicks on the ad or link and ends up buying something from the business, *you* get a commission (also known as a finder's fee or kickback). Does this sound like a good way to make money for free? Maybe. However, there are a vast number of affiliate programs on the Net, and before you sign up, you should spend some time investigating the business and how it works. Beware of multilevel marketing (MLM or network marketing) plans, and be sure to stay away from pyramid schemes. Hint: Ask yourself the question, where does the money come from?

Web:
> http://www.affiliateadvisor.com/
> http://www.affiliatematch.com/
> http://www.associate-it.com/
> http://www.associateprograms.com/
> http://www.atlnetwork.com/

Banner Advertising

A banner ad is a small, rectangular graphic that advertises a product or service. The goal of a banner ad is to get the user to click on the ad (which is a link to another Web site). Ad exposure is measured in impressions. Each time an ad is sent to a user's computer (and presumably viewed by the user), it counts as one impression. When you buy a banner ad, the cost is measured in CPM, or "cost per thousand impressions". For example, if a Web site charges $1,000 for an ad, and guarantees 5,000 impressions, the cost is $20 ($1,000/5) per thousand impressions; that is, CPM of $20. However, when it comes to ads, success is measured in terms of the "click-through" rate, and that depends on how well the ad is designed. So don't waste your money. Use these resources to help you turn impressions into click-throughs (and live happily ever after).

Web:
> http://www.adbility.com/
> http://www.bannertips.com/

Ecommerce Ezines

Ever enter enhanced enervation? Especially expecting elusive enticing ecommerce effects? Not to worry. These ecommerce ezines will provide you with tips and advice to help you create and market an online business. Start reading, and it won't be long before the extra effort effects economic exhilaration.

Web:
> http://www.ecmgt.com/
> http://www.ecommerceadvisor.com/
> http://www.netb2b.com/
> http://www.wilsonweb.com/wmt/

Ecommerce Search Engines

Ecommerce (electronic commerce) has its own demands, so when you demand ecommerce info *now*, the place to start is an ecommerce search engine. (And on the Net, knowing where to start is even more valuable than knowing someone whose brother's friend knows Bill Gates's email address.)

Web:
> http://ecommerce.internet.com/
> http://www.clickz.com/

Internet Advertising and Marketing

Advertising and marketing on the Net are not the same as traditional business. Although the basic principles are the same, the details are a lot different and the world moves a lot faster. If you want to be in business on the Net, get off to a good start by learning how it all works.

Web:
> http://www.bpubs.com/Internet_and_E-Commerce/
>   Marketing/
> http://www.cyberatlas.internet.com/
> http://www.cyberspeaker.com/articles.html
> http://www.internetnews.com/iar/

Internet Advertising Discussion List

If you're in the Internet advertising game, you don't want to get lost. Try subscribing to this mailing list and participate in a question and answer forum with a lot of serious Internet advertising folks.

Web:
> http://www.adbility.com/lists.htm
> http://www.i-advertising.com/

Internet Business Resources

Do you want to get into business on the Net? Then let the Net help you. Start here and you'll find just about everything you need to learn about business on the Net and get your own enterprise up and humming. There's always more to learn and the Net changes fast, so check back regularly.

Web:
http://content.techweb.com/netbiz/
http://www.howtoweb.com/corner/webbiz.htm
http://www.ipw.internet.com/
http://www.iw.com/
http://www.webdevelopersjournal.com/hubs/
    ecommercehub.html
http://www.zdnet.com/enterprise/e-business/

Internet Economy

Keeping track of the regular economy is hard enough, but trying to keep abreast of what is happening within the Internet economy is next to impossible. The Internet is pure information, and money and ideas move so fast that it seems as if the whole thing is constantly moving at warp speed. Well, don't get discouraged. The Internet economy changes so fast that no one can stay completely current, so you are not alone. However, I do have some resources to help you keep up on what's happening. My advice? Plug in once in awhile and look for long-term trends.

Web:
http://newsroom.cisco.com/dlls/tln/economy.html
http://www.businessweek.com/ebiz/
http://www.caslon.com.au/economyguide.htm
http://www.ecommercetimes.com/
http://www.internetnews.com/ec-news/
http://www.newslinx.com/
http://www.onmagazine.com/on-mag/

Internet Selling Tips

Lots and lots (and lots) of people want to make money running a business to sell stuff on the Net. So what makes you different? As one of my readers, you are intelligent, thoughtful and prudent. You take your time. You investigate. You learn before you leap. Listen: the truth is, there is no easy way to make money on the Net. You have to know what you are doing, work hard, and build your business one step at a time. There are no magic secrets, but there are lots of things you need to know. Start here.

Web:
http://hotwired.lycos.com/webmonkey/e-business/
    tutorials/tutorial3.html
http://www.bizmove.com/internet/
http://www.copywriter.com/abbr/10tips.htm
http://www.mailworkz.com/tutorials.htm
http://www.searchengines.com/
    marketing_marketing_tips.html

Shopping Carts and Transactions

On the Net, a "shopping cart" system keeps track of the items your customers choose to buy then automates the final processing when they are ready to make their purchase. If you are setting up an online store, you need to learn how to put the Internet shopping cart before the ecommerce horse. Learn how money changes hands on the Net: not only shopping carts, but transaction software, payments, security, credit cards, and more.

Web:
http://www.nightcats.com/sales/free.html
http://www.onlineorders.net/
http://www.poorrichard.com/freeinfo/shop.htm

> When you have
> chocolate cake, always
> serve big portions.

CANADA

Canada Maps

Imagine getting lost in Canada! Why, you could walk miles without finding proper shelter, food, or even a Canadian tire store. So before you plan your next picnic in Nunavut, take my advice and spend some time poring over these maps of Canada. You'll find all kinds of Cool Canadian Stuff®.

Web:
   http://uk.multimap.com/index/CA.htm
   http://www.lib.utexas.edu/maps/canada.html

Canadian Aboriginal Peoples

The term "aboriginal people" refers to the descendants of the original inhabitants of a particular area. In Canada, there are three recognized groups of aboriginal peoples: the Indians, the Metis (who have some European ancestry), and the Inuit (who used to be called Eskimos). The government of Canada has two complementary goals with respect to the aboriginal peoples. First, the government works towards bringing improvements into the lives of these people, many of whom live in extremely isolated areas. Second, the government has an overall goal of making Canada one of the most electronically connected countries in the world. As a result, there are a large variety of Internet resources devoted to Canadian aboriginal peoples.

Web:
   http://ca.fullcoverage.yahoo.com/fc/canada/
      first_nations/
   http://www.aboriginalcanada.gc.ca/
   http://www.academicinfo.net/canfn.html
   http://www.afn.ca/
   http://www.kstrom.net/isk/maps/cantreat.html

Canadian Constitutional Documents

In 1982, the United Kingdom parliament gave up all power over Canadian laws, including the Canadian constitution. Since then—through hard work and perseverance—Canada has become one of the best countries in North America. Would you like your own copy of the 1982 Canada Act? It's here, along with many other Canadian constitutional documents, waiting for you, 24 hours a day, 365 days a year.

Web:
   http://www.solon.org/Constitutions/Canada/English/

Canadian Culture

There is an old riddle: What is Canadian culture? The answer is, "Mostly American." Some people feel that "Canadian culture" is an oxymoron. What do they know? Haven't they ever heard of the Blue Jays? William Shatner? Rick Moranis (with whom I went to summer camp)? After all, if Canadian culture is good enough for Wayne Gretzky, it should be good enough for the Kids in the Hall.

Web:
   http://www.canadianliving.com/
   http://www.icomm.ca/emily/
   http://www.statcan.ca/english/Pgdb/People/
      cultur.htm

Usenet:
   soc.culture.canada

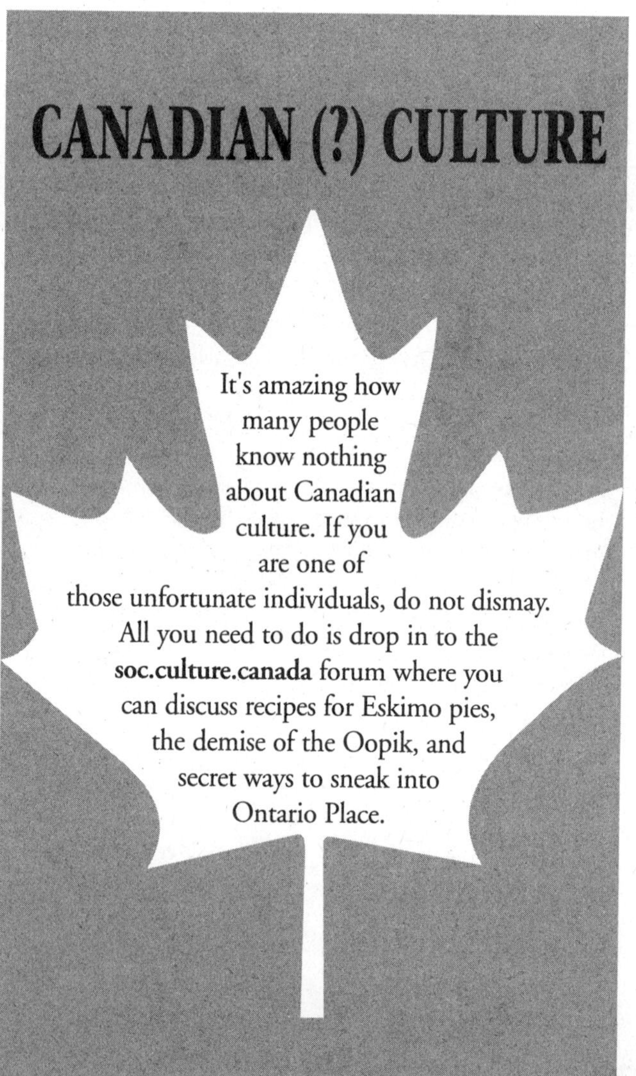

Canadian Fact Sheets

Straight from the Canadian Department of Foreign Affairs and International Trade to you. Here is information about Canadian provinces, history, government, legal system, economy, trade, education, women, geography, environment, climate, transportation, arts, sports, and—of course—the Mounties.

Web:

http://www.dfait-maeci.gc.ca/menu-en.asp

Canadian Geographical Names

It seems like the map of Canada is always changing, changing, changing. In 1867, the Dominion of Canada was created by combining Upper Canada (Ontario) and Lower Canada (Quebec), Nova Scotia, and New Brunswick. In 1871, British Columbia joined the dominion, as did Prince Edward Island in 1873. Now, it happened that, in 1869, Canada had purchased a big chunk of land (called Rupert's Land) from the Hudson's Bay Company. Later, the three prairie provinces were created out of this land: Manitoba in 1870, Alberta and Saskatchewan in 1905. In 1949, after a plebiscite, Newfoundland joined Canada as the tenth province. In the meantime, there were two territories, the Yukon Territory and the Northwest Territory, and on April 1, 1999, a large hunk of the latter was redefined as the Nunavut Territory, a home for Canada's Inuit (the modern, politically correct term for Eskimos). So how do you keep track of all these names? Use the Net, Luke, and when the discussion turns to Canada, you need never feel geographically challenged. (Disclaimer: Please do not use this paragraph as a complete geographical description of Canada. There are probably at least 4 or 5 names I have left out but, as you know, it's a big country.)

Web:

http://geonames.nrcan.gc.ca/english/

Sneak over to "Mischief".

Canadian Government

I remember her like it was yesterday. I was in the Food Building at the CNE, standing in line at the Primo spaghetti booth, when I noticed that, just ahead of me, was the most beautiful Canadian girl I had ever seen. She had captivating blond hair, the color of Molson Golden Ale, and deep green eyes that looked as if they had been poured out of a Resdan bottle. Her earrings were two perfectly shaped Shreddies, and her dress was a diaphanous vision that could have only come from the Mountie-lookalike department at Holt Renfrew. Dare I dream that this girl might be my one true love? I started to talk with her and, when the conversation turned to the federal government—as it inevitably does when you are talking with a beautiful Canadian girl—I was able to impress her with my esoteric knowledge. "Did you know," I asked her, "that the role of the Atlantic Canada Opportunities Agency is to improve the economy of Atlantic Canadian communities through the successful development of business and job opportunities?" Did she notice that, of all the people waiting in line, I was the only one with the coiled sexual power of a jungle cat? Well, let me just say that, as I walked toward the Dufferin Gate looking for a place to eat my spaghetti, I was not alone.

Web:

http://www.canada.gc.ca/
http://www.canada.justice.gc.ca/
http://www.cipo.gc.ca/
http://www.parl.gc.ca/

Canadian History

Here is a little-known fragment of Canadian history: when my sister, Melissa, was two years old and I was babysitting her, she fell off my parents' bed and hit her head on the floor. (Come to Toronto with me some time, and I will show you the exact spot.) Of course, not all Canadian history is that interesting, but still, there are jewels if you only take the time to look.

Web:

http://www.arts.ouc.bc.ca/fiar/his_home.html
http://www.cio-bic.gc.ca/facts/history_e.html
http://www.cyber-north.com/canada/history.html

Listserv Mailing List:

List Name: h-canada
Subscribe to: listserv@h-net.msu.edu

Canadian Investment

If you're looking to spread your money around a little, try investing in Canada. Learn about Canadian money markets, investment clubs, financial publications and the government. (And if you have a little extra money, I have a snow farm you might want to invest in.)

Web:

  http://www.canadianfinance.com/

Usenet:

  misc.invest.canada

Investing In Canada

No financial portfolio is complete without a healthy collection of Canadian stock. But don't let your holdings in the country just north of the Land-of-the-Free-and-the-Home-of-the-Brave expire from benign neglect. Keep track of what is moving and grooving in the country that boasts the best baseball team in the world. Use the **Canadian Investment** site. My personal favorite is a long-term investment in beaver futures.

Canadian Legal Resources

My brother Randy is a lawyer in Toronto, so I guess you could say I have a Canadian legal resource right in the family. But when a free consultation isn't enough, I turn to the Net (and so should you). In less time than it takes to say "division of powers", you will be able to find information about Canadian courts and tribunals, law reform commissions, legislation, taxes and accounting, lawyers and law firms, universities, the federal and provincial governments, free speech and privacy. Wow! (Or as they say in Canada, "Eh?")

Web:

  http://www.acjnet.org/
  http://www.lexum.umontreal.ca/ccq/en/
  http://www.lexum.umontreal.ca/csc-scc/en/

Canadian Music

After more than 25 years of federal "Canadian content" rules, Canadian music is alive and well and living in...ahem...Canada. At the Web sites you can search for your favorite musical artists. Or just join the discussion of your favorite musicians from the land where a rich musical tradition resonates from sea to shining sea. (Bagpipes and accordions are optional.)

Web:

  http://www.canoe.ca/JamMusicCharts/home.html
  http://www.monkey-boy.com/cmusic/

Usenet:

  alt.music.canada

Canadian Names, Addresses and Phone Numbers

Everything seems fine. Life is rolling along smoothly, and you say to yourself, I am content, what more could I want? But then the monster of desire rears its fearsome head. All of a sudden you feel the need to find the address and phone number of a Canadian— and not just any Canadian, a specific Canadian. What to do? You could ignore the urge, but that would be denying the demands of your very being. You need that address and phone number, and you need them now. And you know—you just know—there will be no peace for you in this world until you get the information you desire. What to do? What to do? And then it hits you, like the smack of a wet fish on the snout of a baby seal, you can use the Net to look up Canadian names, addresses and phone numbers (not to mention Canadian businesses). So you look up the address and number you need, and you are relieved. Until later that night, when you have the irresistible urge to look up another Canadian address and phone number. You give in once, twice, three times a day. You tell yourself, there is more to life than looking up Canadian addresses and phone numbers. You tell yourself, I can take it or leave it. You tell yourself, I am in control. But it is that same sad, sad story. Pandora couldn't put her demons back into the box and neither can you.

Web:

  http://ca.people.yahoo.com/
  http://www.canada411.sympatico.ca/
  http://www.yellow.ca/
  http://www.yellowpages.ca/

Canadian News

An American magazine once referred to Canada as "the retarded giant on our doorstep". Read the latest Canadian news and get the real scoop. You will find that Canadian news is about as exciting as...well... Canadian news.

Web:
  http://www.canoe.ca/CNEWS/
  http://www.cbc.ca/newsworld/
  http://www.thestar.ca/
  http://www1.sympatico.ca/news/

Canadian Political Parties

When I was a kid, there was nothing my friends and I liked more than Canadian political parties. In fact, I still remember one such party that ended at 3 AM, and then only because my parents came down to the basement and made us all go to bed. Today, Canadian political parties are larger and better organized but—dare I say it?—not as much fun. Still, you can't tell the players without a program, so here's the info you need to find out more than you really wanted to know about the Bloc Québécois, the Canadian Reform Conservative Alliance, the Liberal Party, the New Democratic Party, and the Progressive Conservative Party, as well as a large couple of handfuls of other, smaller, less effervescent parties.

Web:
  http://www.altstuff.com/parties.htm
  http://www.blocquebecois.org/
  http://www.canadianalliance.ca/index_e.cfm
  http://www.liberal.ca/lpc/
  http://www.ndp.ca/default.asp?language=English
  http://www.pcparty.ca/en/
  http://www.politicalresources.net/canada/
    canada.htm
  http://www.politicswatch.com/parties.htm

Canadian Resources

I grew up in Canada, and, although I didn't realize it at the time, I had Canadian resources all around me. Now I have to get them from the Internet. Fortunately, that's not a problem. There are so many Canadian resources, you can use all you want and still have enough left over for the rest of the family. News, statistics, travel, government services, politics, history, education, culture— everything under the Canadian sun is waiting for you on the Net.

Web:
  http://www.ca.yahoo.com/
  http://www.canlinks.net/
  http://www.maplesquare.com/
  http://www.nlc-bnc.ca/caninfo/ecaninfo.htm

Canadian Sports

As a young lad growing up in Canada, I watched a lot of hockey on television, and went to a great many football games. That was years ago. Since then, Canadian sports have become even more popular. For example, there are now professional baseball and basketball teams, which was not the case when I was growing up. If you are a sports fan, you will enjoy these Web sites, where you can keep up-to-date on Canadian sports of all types, both amateur and professional.

Web:
  http://www.canadianhockey.ca/e/
  http://www.canoe.ca/slam/
  http://www.tsn.ca/

Turn off the TV, and
let your children use
the "Kids" sections
of this book.

Canadian Talk and General Discussion

What do you do at 9:30 PM on Saturday night when you are just dying to talk to a Canadian and William Shatner's line is busy? Hop over to IRC, where nimble-fingered Canadians are cutting fast, loose and easy. Need a French-Canadian fix? Try the **#quebec** channel ("ici, on parle Français"). Who says Saturday night has to be dull?

Usenet:

alt.canadian
alt.ontario.north-bay
soc.culture.canada
soc.culture.quebec

IRC:

#alberta (EFnet, Undernet)
#calgary (Undernet)
#canada (EFnet, Undernet)
#edmonton (EFnet, Undernet)
#manitoba (EFnet)
#montreal (DALnet, EFnet, Undernet)
#ontario (Undernet)
#quebec (DALnet, EFnet, Undernet)
#toronto (EFnet, Undernet)
#vancouver (DALnet, Undernet)
#winnipeg (DALnet)

Canadian Travel

Canada is a big place, and it's easy to get lost. Imagine how embarrassed you would be if, after saving all your money and planning for months, you and your family finally make it to Canada only to become completely disoriented. For example, what if you are driving from Winnipeg to Toronto, and you accidentally make a left turn at North Bay? The next thing you know, you are in the Ungava Peninsula, and the kids are complaining, "There are no bathrooms. You promised we would stop at McDonald's. Whose dumb idea was it to go on this trip anyway?" Don't let this happen to you. Before you even think about exploring this grand old country just north of the Land of the Free and Home of the Brave, use the Net to access Canada's tourism information network. Remember its slogan: "Canada, the country with a lot of space."

Web:

http://www.canadatourism.com/

CBC (Canadian Broadcasting Corporation)

In December 1928, the Canadian government set up a Royal Commission (special committee) to figure out what to do about radio broadcasting in Canada. After spending a long time studying the situation, the commission issued a report, which, in May 1932, led to the formation of the Canadian Radio Broadcasting Commission (CRCB). The CRCB started to create and broadcast Canadian programming and, in November 1936, after more committees and more reports, the CRCB was changed into the Canadian Broadcasting Corporation (CBC). Since then, the CBC has grown into a large, government-supported network, broadcasting television and radio across Canada, in both English and French. It's hard for an outsider to fully understand the importance and the ubiquity of the CBC. Canada has fewer people than California in an area that is much larger than the entire United States. Most of the country speaks English and is heavily Americanized (although they like to deny it). The province of Quebec speaks French and has its own unique culture. Add to this a government that has, for many years, tried to create a "Canadian culture" by spending money, passing laws, spending money, creating lots of cultural propaganda, and spending money. The modern-day mission of the CBC is to balance all of these forces—in two languages—while entertaining and informing the entire country.

Web:
 http://www.cbc.ca/

Who among us has not sat wistfully at a desk, daydreaming about being able to visit Canada? What a joy it would be to visit the frozen jewel of North America without even having to pack a bag.

Well, now your dream can come true– you can use the Net to tour Canada right from your very own home. (Hint: As you pass through Toronto, look for the plaque marking the place where I was born.)

Montreal

When I was in the 10th grade, my class went on a trip to Montreal to see the World's Fair. Years later, I went to Montreal again to see the summer Olympics. You, however, may not have fulfilled your quota, so a trip to Montreal may be in your future. If so, here are good places to get the details you need to make your visit enjoyable: locations, attractions, calendar of events, museums, maps of the city and, for foreign travelers, customs regulations and exchange rates.

Web:
  http://www.montrealcam.com/
  http://www.montrealquebec.netfirms.com/
  http://www.toutmontreal.com/english/

Musée du Québec

The Musée du Québec (Quebec Museum) is the province of Quebec's national art gallery, containing more than 20,000 works of art, most of which were produced in Quebec. You can look at some of the paintings over the Net as well as historical information about the artists. At this point, I can hear you saying, "Wait, Quebec is a province. Why would it have its own 'national' art gallery?" The answer is: Don't even ask. Just visit and enjoy yourself.

Web:
  http://www.mdq.org/english/

Nunavut

Nunavut (pronounced "Nunavut"), a territory in northern Canada, was created by an act of parliament on April 1, 1999, to serve as a homeland for the Inuit people. Nunavut is huge, a bit less than 2 million square kilometers. To put this in perspective, the entire country is about 10 million square kilometers, which means that Nunavut comprises 20% of Canada! Still, most of Nunavut is—to use the technical term—a frozen wasteland and, thus, sparsely populated. (The population of Nunavut is less than 30,000 people, of which two thirds are Inuit.) Do you want to be a Nunavut expert? Here are 4 interesting facts that are sure to impress your friends and relations. (1) The capital of Nunavut is Iqaluit. (2) In Inuktitut, the language of the Inuit, Nunavut means "our land". (3) Nunavut spans 4 time zones. (4) Nunavut's area code is 867.

Web:
  http://www.cgii.gc.ca/p-NT-e.html
  http://www.gov.nu.ca/gnmain.htm
  http://www.npc.nunavut.ca/eng/
  http://www.nunavut.com/home.html

Ottawa

I once spent a summer in Ottawa, the capital of Canada, and I had a great time. It's a beautiful city with a lot of tourist attractions and wonderful places to visit. And there are miles of pleasant bicycle paths on which you can ride your bike or jog. True, the winter gets a tad cold—actually, freezing beyond endurance—but you can skate on the canal and cross-country ski in the parks. However, perhaps the most important thing that anybody needs to know about Ottawa is that my friend, Mike the Dentist, lives there. If, for some reason, you need more information, all you need to do is check with the Net, where you can find out about dining, transportation, things to see and things to do. Whether you live in Ottawa or are merely planning to visit, there is lots of info waiting for you on the Net. And if your teeth start to hurt, you can always call Mike.

Web:
  http://www.canada.com/ottawa/
  http://www.ottawaweb.com/
  http://www.tourottawa.org/

Toronto

I was born in Toronto and, I can tell you, it changes so quickly that the only way I can keep up is to live in California and use the Net to look at the Toronto information Web sites. Find all the info you need about Toronto: news, sports, entertainment, food, music, tourism, and so on. However, my favorite activity is to check the weather reports during the winter.

Web:

http://www.city.toronto.on.ca/
http://www.math.toronto.edu/toronto/
http://www.torinfo.com/
http://www.toronto.com/

Vancouver

The summer after I finished high school, I hitchhiked across Canada and ended up in Vancouver, where I joined a special French-language program at the University of British Columbia. It was great—the government paid for everything. I got free food, a place to stay, had lots of fun, went on excursions, and spent the afternoons sunning at Wreck Beach (the nude beach). And all I had to do was put in a few hours a day trying to learn how to speak French. ("La plume de ma tante est sur la table.") Since then, I have had occasion to spend many more delightful days in the pearl of the Canadian west coast. For instance, when I was a medical student, I spent a few weeks in Vancouver researching a book on unconventional medicine. Even if you do not want to learn to speak French or understand unconventional medicine, you may still want to visit Vancouver. If so, you can check with the Net before you go. There you will find information about parks, community centers, bicycling, swimming pools, arts, entertainment, attractions and visitor resources. True, the government probably won't pay for your room and board, but you can still spend your afternoons at Wreck Beach.

Web:

http://www.city.vancouver.bc.ca/
http://www.tourism-vancouver.org/
http://www.vanmag.com/

Antique Cars

Wash it, buff it, and tuck your baby in at night. If antique automobiles hold a special place in your heart, you are not alone—not on the Net. There are Web sites to visit and people to talk to. If your family and friends can't understand the beauty and allure of a 1957 Studebaker Hawk, a 1948 DeSoto Club Coupe or a classic (1955-1957) Thunderbird, rest assured there are lots of people who share your discrimination and good taste.

Web:

http://www.aaca.org/
http://www.autoroad.com/
http://www.classicmotor.co.uk/

Usenet:

alt.autos.antique
rec.autos.antique

Art Cars

Have you ever been inside a piece of art? Now you can if you have an art car, a regular automobile which has been turned into a work of art. Art car aficionados use all kinds of materials to create original, highly inventive mobile art. When it comes to art cars, no matter how crazy the idea, if you can think of it, someone has probably done it. (If you can't think of it, someone is probably doing it right now.)

Web:

http://the-light.com/artcars/wwwboard.html
http://www.artcarmuseum.com/
http://www.artcars.com/
http://www.bmwworld.com/artcars/artcars.htm

Auto Channel

You don't need a television to check out the Auto Channel. In fact, you don't even need a car. All you have to do to get great auto news, commentary and other useful information is point your Web browser to the Auto Channel Web site.

Web:
  http://www.theautochannel.com/

Auto Discussion Archives and FAQ

Take it from me, the best place to learn about cars is where you learned about sex: in the street. Here is a wealth of street-smart info, guaranteed to explain something interesting you always wanted to know but were afraid to ask. For example, I learned how to double-clutch (and my car is an automatic).

Web:
  http://www.faqs.org/faqs/autos/

Auto Racing

As one of my readers, you can no doubt drive rings around anyone else. So where do you go in between races when you want to read what people are saying about driving from one place to another as fast as possible? Put the virtual pedal to the metal and aim for the Net, where you will find discussion and information covering all aspects of organized racing competition.

Web:
  http://rpm.espn.go.com/rpm/
  http://www.motorsport.com/
  http://www.racingone.com/
  http://www.speedworld.net/

Usenet:
  rec.autos.sport
  rec.autos.sport.info
  rec.autos.sport.nascar
  rec.autos.sport.rally
  rec.autos.sport.tech

Listserv Mailing List:
  List Name: autorace
  Subscribe to: listserv@listserv.vt.edu

You can't always be driving a car or watching a race. Occasionally you need to take a break to go home, eat something, and remind your family who you are.

However, that doesn't mean you have to be wasting your time. During those off hours, you can connect to the Net and check out the racing archive.

After all, you do need to spend some quality time with your computer.

Automobile Listings

When that beautiful woman who lives down the hall comes over for dinner and you want to impress her with all the facts you have at your fingertips on the Internet, connect to this huge list of all-things-automobile. Exotic, classic and run-of-the-mill cars are all represented. This is the Web site to use when size really does matter.

Web:
  http://www.car-stuff.com/

British Cars

Some people have lifelong love affairs with things British. For example, Prince Charles's girlfriend, what's-her-name, always makes a point of riding in a British car, except when it is inconvenient or the weather is bad. Would you like to nurture your feelings for British things that move quickly with style? If so, here are some important British car resources for your anglophilic perusal.

Web:
  http://www.team.net/sol/

Majordomo Mailing List:
  List Name: british-cars
  Subscribe to: majordomo@autox.team.net

Majordomo Mailing List:
  List Name: british-cars-pre-war
  Subscribe to: majordomo@autox.team.net

Selecting just the right car is not easy. No matter which one you pick, you can be assured that somewhere along the line, someone is putting one over on you.

So if you want the straight stuff about which cars offer the best overall cost of ownership, start with the Net.

Before you shell out your hard-earned bucks on a potentially big bucket of back-breaking bolts, check out the real dealer costs as well as the many useful tips.

Stick with the Net and you'll never have to worry about being the laughingstock of the automotive neighborhood.

Car and Truck Purchasing

Listen to me. Before you visit a dealer to buy a car or truck, you *must* use the Internet to find out everything you need. The Web has lots and lots of car and truck information. Best of all, you can get the actual prices the dealer pays for the vehicle and options. Why should you pay the auto club or a consumer magazine for this exact same information when you can get it for free from the Net? Now, when it comes time to open negotiations for a new car, you will know exactly what the dealer is paying, so he won't be able to pull the sleazy automotive wool over your eyes. Information is power and, as we used to say in the Sixties, "Power to the people."

Web:
  http://www.autopedia.com/
  http://www.autoweb.com/
  http://www.carprices.com/
  http://www.digitalcars.com/
  http://www.edmunds.com/
  http://www.intellichoice.com/
  http://www.kbb.com/

Usenet:
  rec.autos.marketplace

Car Audio

If you are one of those people who believe that cars are made to be heard as well as seen, here is a Usenet discussion group (along with a Web site for the FAQ and an IRC channel for live chatting) that is right up your auditory alley. Start hanging around and soon, when someone says, "My woofer is bigger than your woofer," you will be able to snap back, "Oh yeah? Well, my speakers use isobaric variations of a quasi-eighth order series-tuned dual-reflex bandpass."

Web:
  http://www.mobileaudio.com/rac-faq/

Usenet:
  rec.audio.car

IRC:
  #caraudio (DALnet)

What's the point of even driving if you aren't making enough noise to wake several surrounding neighborhoods? However, in these days of computerized engines and strict air control standards, it's not easy to find a car that can produce the required sound levels without a lot of special tuning and getting your hands dirty.

What's the solution? Auto audio, of course. All you need is a sufficiently powerful amp, and you can drive with the peace of mind that comes from being able to create a musical interlude as loud as you want.

So, if you want to make sure you are always as popular as a skunk in the wine tasting booth at a perfume convention, join the discussion in rec.audio.car, and find out how to coax that one last decibel out of Old Bessie. After all, life is designed to be lived with a bang, not a whimper.

Car Classifieds

Don't stop reading the classified ads just because you are tired of having to recycle the daily paper. This Web site provides a great index of advertisements for automobiles of all types. Whether you are buying or selling, the listings are free for non-commercial usage.

Web:
  http://www.carbuyer.com/

Car Place

Here's someone who knows his cars. Here's someone who knows other people's cars. Here's someone who spends his time driving cars and lives to tell about it. Check out the reviews of all types of cars, new and old. Here's someone worth listening to.

Web:
  http://www.thecarplace.com/

Car Talk and General Discussion

When you're not driving, you can talk about driving, and on the Net, there is no end to the discussion: automobile design, construction, service, tires, competitions, driving, manufacturers, and on and on and on.

Web:
  http://cartalk.cars.com/

Usenet:
  alt.auto.mercedes
  alt.autos
  alt.autos.bmw
  alt.autos.camaro.firebird
  alt.autos.classic-trucks
  alt.autos.corvette
  alt.autos.dodge.trucks
  alt.autos.ferrari
  alt.autos.ford
  alt.autos.isuzu
  alt.autos.karting
  alt.autos.microcars
  alt.autos.mini
  alt.autos.toyota
  alt.cars.ferrari
  alt.cars.ford-probe
  alt.cars.lotus
  rec.autos
  rec.autos.makers.chrysler
  rec.autos.makers.ford.explorer
  rec.autos.makers.ford.mustang
  rec.autos.makers.honda
  rec.autos.makers.jeep+willys
  rec.autos.makers.mazda.miata
  rec.autos.makers.mg
  rec.autos.makers.saturn
  rec.autos.makers.vw.aircooled
  rec.autos.makers.vw.watercooled
  rec.autos.makers.yugo
  rec.autos.misc
  rec.autos.vw

Customized Cars

If you like to customize cars, here are some Usenet discussion groups you will enjoy. There are a great many details that go into working on a customized car, and there are a lot of people on the Net who are knowledgeable and experienced. Join the discussion and talk with people who love cars as much as you do. Then cruise the Web and enjoy all the resources devoted to cars and the people who love them.

Web:
  http://www.roadsters.com/
  http://www.ukkustoms.com/intro.htm

Usenet:
  alt.autos.rod-n-custom
  rec.autos.rod-n-custom

We all know that fast, high-performance cars are just a substitute for you-know-what. (Well, I do know, but I'm not allowed to talk about stuff like that in a family-oriented book.) Join the boys in the rod-n-custom Usenet groups and find out how to soup up your performance and enhance your experience with high speed and quick starts.

Driving

Once you know how to drive, it seems easy. After all, how many other important activities are there that you can perform adequately with one hand, while listening to the radio and talking to the person next to you? Ask almost anyone, and he (or she) will tell you that he (or she) is a skillful driver. It's true that most people avoid accidents most of the time, but in actual fact, few people are good drivers. Unfortunately, there is something about driving that makes us reluctant to admit we are less than perfect (males more than females). Perhaps it is because earning a driver's license is considered an important coming-of-age event, bringing with it the illusions of freedom and adulthood. Maybe we like the feeling that comes from being in command of a fast, powerful piece of machinery that we control *from the inside*. As we drive, the car becomes an extension of ourselves, and we develop the same confidence that we have in our ability to walk or run. I think it also has something to do with the fact that we become complacent because, most of the time, most of us do manage to avoid accidents. If you would like to become a more skillful driver, here are some resources to help you. Making yourself into a better, more competent driver will have important long-term benefits (such as increasing your chances of avoiding a serious accident). In addition, as with most things in life, you'll have more fun if you are doing it well.

Web:
  http://www.driving.co.uk/
  http://www.familycar.com/driving.htm
  http://www.ibiblio.org/rdu/p-drv.html
  http://www.racingschools.com/tips/tips.shtml
  http://www.trucking.org/safetynet/

Usenet:
  rec.autos.driving

Electric Vehicles

Regular cars use engines that burn gasoline. An electric vehicle (EV) uses an engine that is powered by an electric motor and batteries. To recharge the batteries, you plug the car into an electrical outlet. Catch up on the state of EV technology and the future of these vehicles. How close are we to affordable electric cars? What advantages do they have over gas-powered cars? Would an electric car run a gas-powered radio?

Web:
http://www.evaa.org/
http://www.evadc.org/
http://www.evworld.com/

Exotic Cars

Imagine the awe you would inspire in everyone around you if you were the lucky owner of an exotic or limited edition automobile. Neighbors would ask you to drive them to the grocery store, people's chatter would die down to a respectful whisper as they passed your car, and the insurance agent would beg you to please leave the car in the garage. But there is more to exotic cars than just good looks. If you can't own one, you might as well be able to drool over them. Check out the fancy driving machines at these well-endowed Web sites.

Web:
http://www.conceptcarz.com/
http://www.supercars.net/

Do not rage against the machine. Embrace it, control it, and make it work for you.

Exotic Car + You = Big Success

As one of my readers, you are as close to being perfect as a human being can expect. Perhaps, however, there is a tiny, little something missing from your life. Is it possible that you need a head-turning, attention-grabbing, high-performance automobile?

If so, drive right over to the exotic car site and pick out something nice. After all, why be almost perfect when you can go all the way?

Hint: If you decide to buy such a car, show them your copy of this book, and they are bound to give you a discount.

Formula 1 Motor Racing

Formula 1 cars are designed for one purpose: to race on a circuit or closed course. If you want to build your own Formula 1 vehicle, don't forget: the car cannot be more than 200 cm wide; it must weigh at least 505 kg; you must use a 4-stroke engine with reciprocating pistons; and the engine capacity cannot exceed 3500 cc. Hint: When you get to the point at which you need to understand how pneumatic valve openers relate to engine mapping, it's time to check with the Net.

Web:

    http://www.formula1.com/
    http://www.planet-f1.com/

Usenet:

    rec.autos.sport.f1

Four-Wheel Drive Vehicles

If you're the type of guy or gal who loves nothing better than to spend hours driving around in a get-where-you-are-going-no-matter-where-you-are-going kind of vehicle, I have only one question to ask you: What could be more fun than spending all day Saturday driving around in your on- or off-road four-wheel drive vehicle? Spending Saturday night reading about on- or off-road four-wheel drive vehicles. Obviously.

Web:

    http://www.4wdlinks.com/
    http://www.4wdonline.com/4WD.html
    http://www.4wdriver.com/
    http://www.4x4review.com/
    http://www.worldoffroad.com/

Usenet:

    rec.autos.4x4

> **When there are no rules, most people choose to cooperate.**

Fuel Cell Cars

A cell, or battery, is a device that converts chemical energy into electrical energy. A fuel cell creates energy from a gas fuel (such as oxygen + hydrogen) and directly converts it to electricity in a continuous process. Unlike a conventional battery, the raw materials for a fuel cell are supplied from an external source, which means they can be stored in tanks and refilled as necessary. Fuel cells are important because they are used to power many of the new clean-air cars. Years from now, thanks to fuel cells, we will all drive quiet, non-polluting electric cars. But you don't have to wait for years. You can read about fuel cell cars today (or tomorrow, if you are busy).

Web:

    http://www.fuelcells.org/
    http://www.ucsusa.org/transportation/faq.html

Indy Racing

The first Indianapolis 500 race was run in 1911. The winner was Ray Harroun, who completed the grueling race with an average speed of 74.602 miles an hour. In 2002, the average speed was 166.499 mph, and the fastest lap was 226.320 mph. In the intervening decades, the Indianapolis 500 and its home, the Indianapolis Motor Speedway, have become world famous, synonymous with the epitome of high-speed, high-endurance racing. (The Indianapolis Motor Speedway, with 250,000 seats, is the largest sports venue in the world, making the Indianapolis 500 the largest single-day sporting event on the planet.) Today there are a series of competitions, referred to as Indy racing, based on Indy-style cars: open wheel, open cockpit, single seat, very fast, and very expensive.

Web:

    http://irlinsider.adnetweb.com/
    http://www.indyproseries.com/
    http://www.indyracingleague.com/
    http://www.indyspeedway.com/
    http://www.starnews.com/sports/indy500/

Usenet:

    rec.autos.sport.indy

Kit Cars

For years you have been building model cars, and now you can do it without gluing your fingers together. It's time to graduate to the real thing. Find out about purchasing, building, driving, and maintaining kit cars—full-size and fully functioning cars you build from scratch. Then when people give you compliments on your smooth ride, you can say, "Thanks. I made it myself."

Web:
  http://www.kitcar.com/

Usenet:
  alt.autos.kitcars

Monster Trucks

Is there anything as pleasing to the eye and ear as the body of a good-sized pickup truck mounted on a huge framework, with an outsize suspension and tires the size of Hungarian water buffalo? What could be more fun than watching such a truck literally crush a car into a flat metal pulp, while the cheers of thousands of monster truck fans echo in your ears as you sip a cool brewski and chow down on a jumbo chili dog? It's as American as you can get, and it just doesn't get any better.

Web:
  http://www.monstermania.com/
  http://www.monstertrucks-uk.com/
  http://www.monstertrucks.net/
  http://www.truckworld.com/Monster-Trucks/
    monster-truck.html

Motorsport FAQ

You should always be prepared for the day your grandmother calls you on the phone and wants to know exactly why an armco may or may not be better than a tyre wall. Are you going to let her down? There's no need to if you have access to the Web. This **rec.autos.sport** FAQ on auto competitions is loaded with detailed information on motorsports.

Web:
  http://www.bath.ac.uk/~bspahh/rasfaq/rasfaq1.html

Nascar

In the United States, more people attend Nascar racing and watch it on TV than any other sport. (Some tracks hold as many as 170,000 people.) Each year, there are 32 official Nascar races, with the overall winner being awarded the Winston Cup plus a lot of money. For many people, Nascar is a lot more than watching cars race around a track. Nascar is a family-oriented activity. Many people come in motorhomes with their families, camp out near the raceway, and form a permanent mobile community (sort of like a Grateful Dead tour without the drugs).

Web:
  http://www.4nascarfun.com/
  http://www.king5.com/NASCAR/?9
  http://www.members.aol.com/nfcfamily/
    nascarfamily.html
  http://www.nascar.com/
  http://www.nascarconnections.com/
  http://www.racinlinks.com/
  http://www.thatsracin.com/

Usenet:
  rec.autos.sport.nascar

PM Zone

Brought to you by the fine folks who get their hands dirty publishing Popular Mechanics, this Web site has lots of nifty car tidbits for automotive fans. Get a tech update of the day, learn more about choosing a quality automobile, and see movies and pictures that will make any car and truck lover purr like a finely tuned hot rod.

Web:
  http://www.popularmechanics.com/automotive/

Road Rally

A road rally is a competition for two-person teams (and a car). One person is the driver, the other is the navigator. Each team is given instructions that describe a particular route to follow. The instructions are exact: the team must travel to specific points at specific speeds. Along the routes are checkpoints, and the idea is to arrive at each checkpoint exactly on time. A road rally is not a race; you lose points for being too slow or too fast. Novices are almost always welcome (they compete against other beginners), so if you like to drive and you like to think, you will probably enjoy road rallying.

Web:
  http://www.cwl.com/bensrallypage/
  http://www.goss.com/rally.htm
  http://www.rallyusa.com/
  http://www.scca.org/amateur/performance_rally/

Solar Cars

Have you been waiting for a rainy day to start learning about solar-powered cars? Well, let's pretend that it's raining right now so you can stay inside and use the Net to explore the world of cars that are powered principally by sunlight. Many solar cars are built for special competitions by students, so if you are an automotively engineeringly type person, start your Web browser and drive to the places where the sun is always shining.

Web:
  http://www.formulasun.org/asc/
  http://www.nesea.org/transportation/
  http://www.nrel.gov/education/student/natjss.html

SUVs (Sport Utility Vehicles)

Imagine yourself driving around in a large, gasoline-loving vehicle that looks like the mutant offspring of a Volkswagen van and a linebacker for the Green Bay Packers. Now imagine you are the beneficiary of either admiration or condemnation from everyone you pass on the road. Welcome to the world of SUVs, a place where even squares can have a ball (and often do).

Web:
  http://www.consumersearch.com/www/automotive/
    suvs/
  http://www.suv.com/
  http://www.suvone.com/

Team.Net Automotive Information Archives

Here is a nice collection of automotive-related resources: links to archives, organizations, mailing lists and activities. By the way, the American pronunciation of Team.Net is "Team Ne—the dot is silent; the British pronunciation is "Team-dot-Net". (See how cool it is to be one of my readers: I make sure you know everything important.)

Web:
  http://www.team.net/

CHEMISTRY

Analytical Chemistry

Analytical chemistry is the branch of chemistry devoted to making quantitative measurements. In particular, the techniques of analytic chemistry are used to determine the composition of chemical samples. Thus, an analytical chemist not only has to know a lot about everything, he or she has to be an expert problem solver. This involves being familiar with a great many different tools and techniques, as well as understanding which tools to use in a specific situation.

Web:
  http://sciweb.cc.duq.edu/analytical/
  http://www.chem.vt.edu/chem-ed/ac-basic.html
  http://www.liv.ac.uk/chemistry/links/refanal.html
  http://www.netaccess.on.ca/~dbc/cic_hamilton/
    anal.html

Usenet:
  sci.chem.analytical
  sci.techniques.xtallography

Atmospheric Chemistry

Atmospheric chemistry is the study of the chemical composition and properties of the atmosphere. Atmospheric chemists study how the components of the atmosphere interact with each other, with the Earth, and with living organisms. One important area of research is the investigation of how human activities may be changing the characteristics of the atmosphere with respect to smog, global climate change, toxic air pollutants, acid rain and ozone depletion.

Web:

  http://daac.gsfc.nasa.gov/CAMPAIGN_DOCS/
    ATM_CHEM/ac_main.html
  http://gonzalo.er.anl.gov/ACP/
  http://www.cac.yorku.ca/
  http://www.igac.unh.edu/
  http://www.shsu.edu/~chemistry/Glossary/glos.html

Biochemistry

Biochemistry is the study of the chemical reactions within living organisms. In particular, biochemists investigate metabolism (the chemical processes within cells), macronutrients (proteins, carbohydrates and fats), enzymes, as well as DNA and the chemistry of genes. When I was a graduate student, I wanted to learn biochemistry. But I was a computer science student. I hadn't studied chemistry since high school and I knew nothing about organic chemistry. I wrote a letter to the famous science writer Isaac Asimov in which I asked him advice on how to teach myself biochemistry. He sent me back a reply, which I still have (it is framed and on my desk). He said, "If you have a good library at your disposal, you can teach yourself anything. I did." Asimov's example inspired me. I got a biochemistry textbook and started teaching it to myself. Later, I ended up going to medical school, where I learned the whole thing over again in more detail. But, to this day, I can't forget how fascinating I found it to read a book that could describe what was going on inside my own body.

Web:

  http://info.bio.cmu.edu/courses/biochemmols/
  http://jb.bcasj.or.jp/
  http://www.biochemist.com/
  http://www.biochemlinks.com/bclinks/biochem.cfm
  http://www.il-st-acad-sci.org/health/biochem.html
  http://www.worthington-biochem.com/best

Where would we be without biochemistry? Well, for some of us, pre-med studies would have been a lot easier. On the other hand, with no biochemistry, all we would be is a bunch of organic chemicals lying in a pool on the floor, so there are definite trade-offs. For those of us stuck in the real world of exquisitely shaped enzymes and long silly chains of carbon that don't seem to know when to stop, the **Biochemistry** Web site can provide a biodegradable home away from home.

Chemical Acronyms

We all know that DNA is deoxyribonucleic acid and EDTA is ethylenediaminetetraacetic acid. But what about the more esoteric chemical acronyms? The next time you are at a party with a bunch of chemists, see if they know what UASBR or FREMSAAS stands for. They may not, but you will, because you have the Net (and this book) to help you. (By the way, UASBR refers to an "upflow anaerobic sludge blanket reactor", and FREMSAAS is "frequency modulated simultaneous atomic absorption spectrometry".)

Web:

  http://www.chemie.de/tools/acronym.php3

Chemistry Journals

Here are collections of links to chemistry journals. Some of the journals are completely online; others only show the tables of contents or abstracts. If you are involved in chemical research of any type, you need to look at these sites. (I bet you have lots of spare time for reading more journals.)

Web:

  http://pubs.acs.org/about.html
  http://www.ch.cam.ac.uk/ChemJournals.html

Chemistry Resources

The Internet has more chemically related resources than you could dissolve in a beaker of distilled water and alcohol-free chloroform. Whatever you need to find in the world of chemistry, virtually everything virtual is here somewhere. Remember, if you're not part of the solution, you're part of the precipitate.

Web:
http://antoine.frostburg.edu/chem/senese/101/
http://www.ase.org.uk/aselinks/
http://www.biochemlinks.com/bclinks/chem.cfm
http://www.cfsan.fda.gov/~dms/chemist.html
http://www.chemdex.org/
http://www.chemistrycoach.com/tutorial.htm
http://www.liv.ac.uk/Chemistry/links/

Chemistry Talk and General Discussion

Let's talk chemistry. Let's talk about substances and how they react when they are combined. Let's talk about mixing diatomaceous earth into sulfuric acid in order to make it sticky. Let's talk about everything under and inside of the sun. Let's talk about cleaning up the mess.

Usenet:
sci.chem

Listserv Mailing List:
List Name: chemchat
Subscribe to: listserv@listserv.uark.edu

Chemistry Visualization and Animation

Chemistry deals with molecules, atoms and bonds, and there are wonderful computer-based tools available to help you visualize these chemical concepts. These resources will help you learn how computer visualization is used in chemistry. In addition, you will be able to view a great many pictures and animations. I have also included information about two of the most important chemistry visualization tools, Chime and RasMol.

Web:
http://www.csc.fi/chem/gallery.phtml
http://www.mdlchime.com/chime/
http://www.umass.edu/microbio/chime/

Date with a Nerd

Okay, you finally got the BNOC (Big Nerd on Campus) to ask you out. So what do you do on your first date?

You entertain your friend by connecting to the Net and showing him how much fun it is to use chemistry visualization tools.

This will demonstrate that you have both good taste and the technical knowledge necessary to make a modern relationship work as well as a properly buffered acid-base reaction.

Computational Chemistry

Computational chemistry involves the use of computers in the study of chemistry. In particular, this area of study has applications to molecular modeling, quantum mechanics, statistical mechanics and dynamics. Computational chemistry is often combined with theoretical chemistry to construct quantitative predictions based on specific theory.

Web:
http://www.ccl.net/chemistry/
http://www.chem.swin.edu.au/chem_ref.html
http://www.wiley.com/legacy/wileychi/ecc/
  layout.html

Electrochemistry

Electrochemistry is the science concerned with the chemistry of electrical phenomena. Most of electrochemistry deals with the conduction of ions (charged particles) within electrolytes: usually liquid solutions, but also molten salts and certain conductive solids. The most common applications are electrophoresis, electroplating, batteries and the study of corrosion.

Web:
http://electrochem.cwru.edu/estir/
http://www.electrochem.org/

Usenet:
sci.chem.electrochem
sci.chem.electrochem.battery

Glycoscience

Glycoscience is the study of carbohydrates and glycoconjugates. Many people in the physical or life sciences find that memorizing the citric acid cycle several times during your academic career provides enough glyco-oriented stimulation to last a lifetime. However, for hard-core glycoscientists, the citric acid cycle is merely the beginning.

Web:
http://www.glycoforum.gr.jp/
http://www.vei.co.uk/tgn/

Usenet:
bionet.glycosci

Hazardous Chemical Database

Please put this Web site in your bookmark list. This important resource contains information on a large number of hazardous chemicals. You can find out basic information—such as formulas, physical data, names—as well as extensive safety information. This is the type of place you want to visit *before* the accident. However, if something unexpected does happen, you will be glad you know where this site is.

Web:
http://ull.chemistry.uakron.edu/erd/

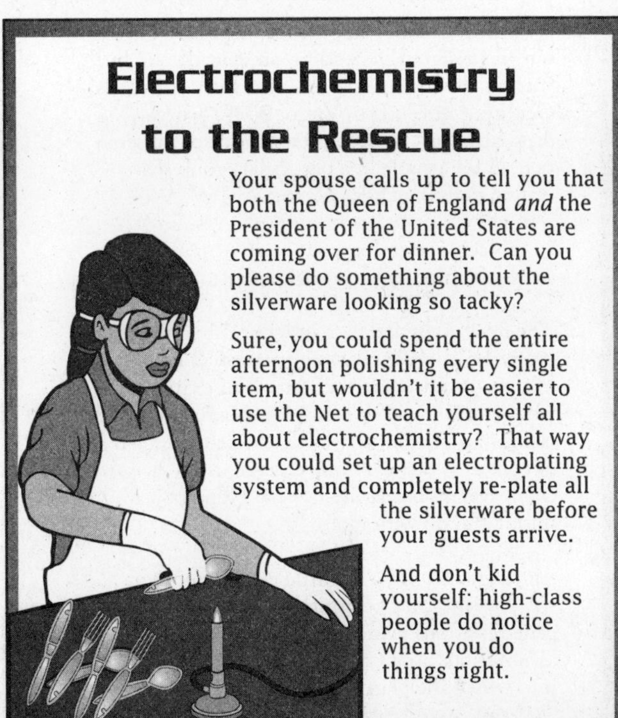

Laboratory Safety

I have to admit, I was a terror in the lab. Although I was mostly well-behaved, I once incurred the wrath of my organic chemistry lab instructor by throwing an iceball at my friend Stan. And in medical school, my partner and I would often break things in biochemistry lab no matter how careful we were. Still, I had an excuse: in those days, there was no Internet, and so I could not subscribe to the laboratory safety mailing list or check out the resources on the Web.

Web:
http://keats.admin.virginia.edu/

Usenet:
sci.chem.labware

Listserv Mailing List:
List Name: safety
Subscribe to: listserv@list.uvm.edu

Molecule of the Month

Who am I? I am a well-known antioxidant, the first provitamin to be discovered. (A provitamin is a substance that the body converts into a vitamin.) My chemical cousins and I are responsible for the yellow and orange colors of many fruits and vegetables. In fact, if you eat too much of me, your skin may turn orange (although I won't hurt you). My cousins and I also give color to tree leaves in the fall. When the chlorophyll (which is green) breaks down, it is our colors that you see. The final clue? I was the Molecule of the Month in April 2002. (If you would like to see who I am, check the archive.)

Web:
http://www.bris.ac.uk/depts/Chemistry/MOTM/
motm.htm

Nuclide Table

This is an amazing resource. You start with a graphical representation of all the known nuclides. (A nuclide is a type of atom, specified by its atomic number, atomic mass and energy state. For example, carbon 14 is a particular nuclide of carbon.) Click on a section of the diagram, and you are presented with a more detailed chart that contains useful information about all the nuclides in that region. It's like a periodic table of the elements on steroids.

Web:
http://www2.bnl.gov/ton/

Organic Chemistry

Organic chemistry is the science that deals with carbon compounds. As such, organic chemistry forms the basis of the study of biochemistry, hydrocarbons and polymers. When I was a computer science graduate student, I studied organic chemistry in preparation for medical school and found the course to be one of the hardest I have ever taken (ranking right up there with advanced calculus). If you have an interest in organic chemistry, here are some resources for you. Aside from general resources, I have also included a site that contains the official IUPAC nomenclature rules. (As strange as it may seem, this can be a fun place to browse.) Special organic chemistry hint: If you don't know what you are doing, do it neatly.

Web:
http://www.acdlabs.com/iupac/nomenclature/
http://www.biochemlinks.com/bclinks/ochem.cfm
http://www.organicworldwide.net/

Usenet:
sci.chem
sci.chem.organic.synthesis
sci.chem.organomet

Periodic Table

Every chemistry student learns about the Periodic Table: a way of organizing the elements into related groups. Within the Periodic Table is a wealth of information about each element and the various chemical families. I like these Web sites as they are so easy to use. Display the entire table and admire the patterns. Then click on a particular element for more information. The details vary from one site to another: atomic number, atomic weight, atomic volume, valence, density, melting point, boiling point, appearance, ionization energies, electron configuration, discoverer, date discovered, and much more. Aside from several online Periodic Tables, I have also included a link to a program you can download and run on your own computer. (By the way, my favorite element is #105: Hahnium.)

Web:
http://pearl1.lanl.gov/periodic/
http://www.thecatalyst.org/m03ptabl.html
http://www.webelements.com/

Physical Chemistry

The purpose of physical chemistry is to explain and interpret the observations made in the other areas of chemistry: inorganic, organic and analytic. As such, physical chemistry (often referred to as pchem) is an amalgam combining the principles and methods of physics and chemistry. Physical chemists work within a variety of chemical disciplines: thermodynamics, electrochemistry, statistical mechanics, spectroscopy, kinetics, molecular modeling, and so on, which means they have to know something about everything, and everything about some things.

Web:
http://pages.pomona.edu/~wsteinmetz/pchem.htm
http://tigger.uic.edu/~mansoori/
    Thermodynamics.Educational.Sites_html
http://www.chem.qmw.ac.uk/surfaces/
http://www.my-edu2.com/EDU/
    chemist5.htm#*physical*

TIDBITS

What should believers know about ASTROLOGY AND RACISM?

Astrology classifies all people as belonging to one of 12 signs. Depending on your date of birth, you are either an Aquarius, Pisces, Aries, Taurus, Gemini, Cancer, Leo, Virgo, Libra, Scorpio, Sagittarius or Capricorn. Basic astrology asserts that all the people in a particular group share certain defining characteristics.

In this sense, astrology, although not malevolent, shares an important trait with racism. Here is why.

The fundamental defect in racist thinking is that it ascribes specific characteristics to all members of a group, based on their race. For example, a white person who does not like blacks, might claim (falsely) that all blacks are dishonest. This, of course, is racist. However, it is just as racist to claim that all blacks are honest. Honesty has nothing to do with race.

Although astrology has little else in common with racism, they both support unfounded generalizations. Moreover, they both make assumptions about a person, based on the group into which the person happened to be born.

Sonochemistry

Sonochemistry is the study of chemical reactions that are significantly affected by ultrasound. Under the influence of ultrasound, a reaction may be accelerated (such as with a catalyst) or may yield completely different products. These effects can happen for various reasons. For example, ultrasound can speed up a reaction by enlarging the surface area of a catalyst or by enhancing the mixing of the reagents. A more profound effect of ultrasound can result from cavitation: the creation of tiny, low pressure bubbles, in this case caused by the compression/decompression pressure cycles as the sound passes through the reagents. For more information about this fascinating new branch of chemistry, check out these sonochemistry Web pages.

Web:
> http://chemistch.shiga-med.ac.jp/chemistry/
>   sonochem.shtml
> http://www.fb-chemie.uni-rostock.de/ess/intro.htm

COLLECTING

Action Figures

An action figure is a doll-like toy in the shape of a person (or humanoid or animal) that looks capable of action. "Action", of course, is a diffuse term and action figures come in more shapes, colors and poses than anyone, except a parent who has to pay for them, would believe. The quintessential action figure was G.I Joe, who debuted in 1964, revolutionizing the modern toy market. (Finally, boys could buy something that required as many ongoing accessories as a Barbie doll.) Although many girls collect action figures, they are primarily boys' toys. Boys, of course, don't play with dolls, so we must be careful to categorize action figures among the collectable masculine *objets d'art*, such as toy cars, toy guns, and gross things that squish.

Web:
> http://www.action-figure.com/
> http://www.actionfigurecollectors.com/
> http://www.aftimes.com/
> http://www.toymania.com/
> http://www.wizardworld.com/
>   community.cfm?comm=action

Action Figures

If you ever hear G.I. Joe say that he wants to put another shrimp on the Barbie, you know it's time to start keeping your action figures in separate boxes.

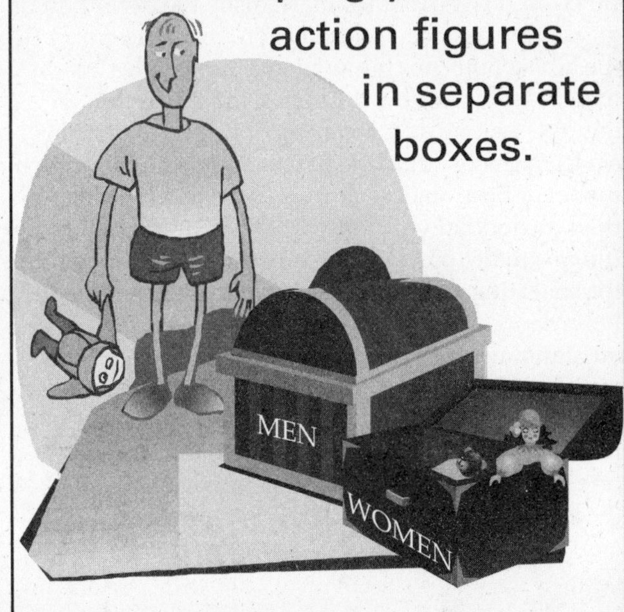

Antique Radios

Modern radios are computerized, cheaply built and ugly. It didn't used to be like that. In the early days of radio, technology was not as good, but the radios themselves were wonderful devices, with knobs to turn, tubes to replace, and beautiful, functional designs to fuss over. Today, many people collect and maintain these old radios, an activity which is alive and thriving on the Net.

Web:
> http://www.antiqueradio.org/
> http://www.antiqueradios.com/

Usenet:
> rec.antiques.radio+phono

Antiques

At one time, the term "antique" referred only to objects that originated in the ancient world. However, with the rise of antique collectors, the supply of ancient objects wasn't enough to satisfy the market (and, tell the truth, would you really want to furnish your sitting room in second century Roman Empire?). As a result, the term "antique" came to mean any object of interest over 100 years old, thus moving the focus of antiquing (which became a verb) from the exhibit halls of dusty museums to the living rooms of the rich and tasteless. However, in recent times, in the spirit of egalitarianism, the definition of an antique has been relaxed even further to embrace the amorphous but far more ubiquitous idea of memorabilia. Anything can now qualify as an antique, as long as it meets the following two tests: (1) Is it possible that one day, someone might pay money for the object?, and (2) Is the object older than the food in your fridge? As a result, antiquing (there's that word again) has become a synonym for collecting, and the world of antiques has finally become accessible to us all. With the rise of Internet auctions, any Jane or John Doe can now become a member in full standing of the antiquing community, where a ready market can be found for such important artifacts as classic 1960 bumper stickers, original Hawaiian shirts, and genuine troll dolls. (Second-century Roman amphora, however, can be a bit hard to unload.)

Web:

  http://www.alsnetbiz.com/acc/
  http://www.antiqueresources.com/
  http://www.antiquetalk.com/
  http://www.lonestar.texas.net/~clough/rafaq.html

Usenet:

  rec.antiques
    rec.antiques.marketplace

Think at least one original thought every day. (That's mine for today.)

This page is officially designated as a collectable piece of memorabilia.

HARLEY HAHN

Autograph Collecting

To many people, an autograph is just someone signing his or her name. For example, suppose you are eating in a restaurant, and you see someone famous like Bill Clinton, Homer Simpson or Denis Thatcher walk in. If you're like most people, you grab a napkin, casually saunter over, and ask Mr. Famous Person for an autograph. Later, you take the napkin home with you, show it around to a few friends, and then throw it out. A serious autograph collector, however, would do it all differently. He or she would use a special piece of paper, not a napkin, and afterward, the autograph would be carefully catalogued and stored. Moreover, real collectors don't collect autographs willy-nilly. They tend to concentrate on certain areas and build their collections by requesting specific autographs, often by mail. If you would like to learn more about this fascinating hobby, take a look at these autograph-related resources on the Net. (By the way, the story in the restaurant is true. All three of the celebrities were there, and I was able to get three great autographs for my collection. I specialize in "Men Who Live With Forceful Women".)

Web:

  http://www.autographportal.com/
  http://www.autographsuccess.com/
  http://www.toddsautographarena.com/

Usenet:

  salt.autographs.transactions
  alt.binaries.autographs
  alt.collecting.autographs

Beanie Babies

Beanie Babies are small, furry, bean bag toys that are popular with many people who collect the toys, sometimes to the point of fanaticism. Official Beanie Babies are made by the Ty Company (but, as you can imagine, there are a lot of knock-offs). My favorite Beanie Baby is Nip the Cat, because he looks like my cat, The Little Nipper. (The Little Nipper, however, is much cuter and was born on April 6, 1991, three years before Nip was first sold on March 6, 1994.) In order to maintain the demand for Beanie Babies, the Ty Company manipulates the market by making specific toys for a limited time. When they stop making a particular toy, they say it has been "retired". Nip the Cat, for example, has been retired. Although Beanie Babies sell for only a few dollars retail, the artificial market has inspired people to pay as high as hundreds of dollars or more for various rare Babies. (I just had a horrible thought. One day, the demand for Beanie Babies is going to fall drastically, and as a result, the real estate market is going to be flooded with people wanting to buy land in Florida.)

Web:

http://www.beaniewonderland.com/
http://www.collectingnation.com/beanbag.shtml
http://www.smartcollecting.com/
http://www.ty.com/

Usenet:

alt.christnet.beanie-babies
alt.collecting.beanie-babies
alt.collecting.beanie-babies.discussion.moderated
alt.collecting.beanie-babies.tradingcards
alt.collecting.beanie-babies.uk
alt.disney.beanies

If you are a bottle collector, here is something cool you can do with one of your bottles. Fill your bathtub with water. Then write a note (be sure to include your name and address). Put the note in the bottle, seal the bottle carefully, and throw it in the tub. Now wait for someone to find the note and send you a reply. The disadvantage of putting the bottle in your tub is that it may take a long time for someone to find the note (especially if you live alone). The advantage, however, is that it is easy to check on the bottle whenever you want.

Book Collecting

I love books and I even have a few of my own collections: Tintin, Perry Mason, Freddy the Pig, as well as anything by P.G. Wodehouse and Isaac Asimov. Mostly I collect these books because I enjoy reading them. However, many book lovers are serious collectors, maintaining accession records and circulating a desiderata (want list). If you are passionate about book collecting in this way, the Net stands ready to help you. (Remember, old collectors never die, they just deaccession.)

Web:

http://www.rbms.nd.edu/
http://www.rcbfaq.com/
http://www.trussel.com/f_books.htm
http://www.webpan.com/msauers/editions/

Usenet:

rec.collecting.books

Bottle Collecting

When I was a young kid, I used to enjoy going to the Canadian National Exhibition. My favorite place was the Food Building, where there were a great many booths selling various types of food and giving away free samples. I remember that the Coca Cola booth used to give away tiny little Coke bottles (with real Coke inside). For some reason, I was never able to get one of these tiny bottles, but I really wanted one. If you are a bottle collector, I'm sure you can understand my feelings. Sometimes it seems as if the most important bottle in the whole wide world is the one you want but can't have.

Web:

http://www.antiquebottles.com/
http://www.bottlecollecting.com/
http://www.fohbc.com/
http://www.worldlynx.net/sodasandbeers/

Usenet:

rec.antiques.bottles

A
B
C
D
E
F
G
H
I
J
K
L
M
N
O
P
Q
R
S
T
U
V
W
X
Y
Z

China, Ceramics and Porcelain

When you heat a nonmetallic mineral, such as clay, at a high temperature, you create a ceramic, a substance which is hard, brittle and resistant to heat and corrosion. Ceramics have been used for centuries to make containers and implements such as dishes, bowls and vases. The earliest ceramics date to sixth-century China, when porcelain was first developed. (Porcelain is made by heating kaolin, a white clay, combined with a mineral called petuntse, a form of feldspar.) To this day, high-quality ceramics and porcelain are referred to as "china". About 1800, British artisans, attempting to imitate Chinese porcelain, created bone china by mixing clay with ground ox bone.

Web:
>   http://www.acguide.com/specchina.html
>   http://www.gotheborg.com/
>   http://www.iadm.com/
>   http://www.inter-services.com/HallChina/
>   http://www.netcentral.co.uk/steveb/mark/
>   http://www.setyourtable.com/

Clocks and Watches

Here are lots of great resources for anyone interested in horology (the science of measuring time and the art of making timepieces). These resources offer information about collecting clocks and watches, timepiece repair, the history of timekeeping, antique timepieces and trading. The mailing list and Usenet group are forums in which you can talk about horology any time, day or night.

Web:
>   http://www.personalposters.com/clocks/
>   http://www.watchzone.net/

Usenet:
>   alt.horology

Listserv Mailing List:
>   List Name: clocks
>   Subscribe to: listserv@listserv.syr.edu

Coins and Money

Collecting various types of money can be a lot of fun. These Web sites have some useful and interesting resources for people interested in collecting coins and banknotes. The **numism-l** mailing list is not a collector's list. It is for discussing coin topics relating to antiquity and the Middle Ages (up to c.1454). The Usenet discussion groups leave room for lots of free-form discussion of coins and paper money.

Web:
>   http://www.coin-gallery.com/
>   http://www.coincollector.org/
>   http://www.coinlink.com/
>   http://www.pennypage.com/

Usenet:
>   rec.collecting.coins
>   rec.collecting.paper-money

Listserv Mailing List:
>   List Name: numism-l
>   Subscribe to: listserv@vm.sc.edu

Collecting Resources

It's human nature to want to collect. I collect old comics (Silver Age DCs), coins from around the world, and Freddy the Pig, P.G. Wodehouse, and Perry Mason books. In fact, it's hard to think of anything that someone *might* collect, that someone doesn't collect.

Web:
  http://www.antiquehotspots.com/
  http://www.collect-online.com/
  http://www.collectingchannel.com/
  http://www.collectors.com/
  http://www.curioscape.com/
  http://www.icollector.com/

Collecting Talk and General Discussion

Is there anyone who doesn't collect anything? (I, for example, collect Internet books.) Collecting seems to be part of our nature as human beings. Thus, if you are human, there is a place in this discussion for you. Use your imagination: anything that can be quantified or categorized is fair game.

Usenet:
  alt.collecting.breweriana
  alt.collecting.casino-tokens
  alt.collecting.pens-pencils
  alt.collecting.sports-figures
  rec.collecting
  rec.collecting.cards.discuss
  rec.collecting.cards.non-sports
  rec.collecting.ornaments
  rec.collecting.phonecards
  rec.collecting.pins
  rec.collecting.villages

> I have a secret plan to take over the world by removing the light bulbs from people's fridges.

Collectors' Marketplace

Just about everyone collects something, so here is a Web site of universal appeal. Free ads to buy and sell just about anything you can think of (as well as lots of stuff you would never think of): animation, antiques, autographs, Barbie, Disney, GI Joe, porcelain, Hallmark, toys, sports, records, sci-fi, and much more.

Web:
  http://www.collectiblesnet.com/

Doll Collecting

There are lots and lots of doll collectors on the Net, and lots and lots of doll stuff to enjoy. Even if you can't tell the difference between a Cabbage Patch Baby Surprise and the Barbie Neptune Fantasy '92 (from the Bob Mackie series), you can still enjoy bopping around, looking at dolls, or hopping in on some hot doll discussions in Usenet.

Web:
  http://www.sowatzka.com/gary/tips.htm
  http://www.thedollnet.com/
  http://www.virtualdolls.com/

Usenet:
  rec.collecting.dolls
  rec.crafts.dollhouses

Floaty Pens

I have a Freddy the Pig floaty pen. You know, one of those pens with a tiny picture of something built into the shaft of the pen, and when you tilt it, part of the picture moves back and forth. My pen shows a picture of the Bean Farm where Freddy lives. Freddy and Jinx the cat are talking to Mrs. Wiggins the cow and two of the rabbits. When I tilt the pen to the right, Freddy and Jinx move to the right. When I tilt the pen back, Freddy and Jinx move to the left. A floaty pen contains a miniature scene housed within a 16x19 millimeter tube. Inside the tube is mineral oil. Since mineral oil is thick, the floaty part moves slowly and gracefully as you tilt the pen. The history of the modern floaty pen dates to 1946, when a Danish baker named Peder Eskesen figured out a way to seal the tubes so the oil would not leak. Today, the center of the floaty pen universe is the Eskesen Floating Action Pen Factory in Store Merlose, Denmark, a small village south of Copenhagen.

Web:

http://www.floatabout.com/
http://www.floatart.com/
http://www.floatydevotee.com/

Found Photos

If you believe in the law of karma, it may have been your destiny to look down the street at a particular instant and notice a lost photo of a fat man eating a massive piece of cake at his niece's wedding. Since each photograph represents a tiny slice of reality, every time you find a lost photo, it intersects with the unfolding pattern of your life. With a single picture it's hard to see the pattern, but once you collect one found photo after another, you can look for patterns, unconscious meanings and clues to the essence of your personal being. Perhaps there really is no such thing as a coincidence.

Web:

http://www.lostleavesphotos.com/
http://www.puppetslounge.com/ephemera/
   greatest.html
http://www.renewal.org.au/object/photos/
http://www.spillway.com/found/index5.html
http://www.superfluous.com/2002/street/

Knives and Blades

Years ago, I had a wonderful switchblade given to me by my uncle. Later, I bought myself another such knife when I was visiting Switzerland. That was years ago, and I didn't think much about knives until my good friend John Anderson, a knife aficionado and collector, took me to a knife show. Boy, did I have a good time. It was a real treat to see so many people who love what they do, and to see so many exquisitely crafted instruments. The knife collecting world has a fascinating culture, with a symbiotic balance between collectors and knife makers. The collectors support the knife makers, who create a limited supply of new knives for the collectors. Thus, a knife show has an interesting mix of two very different types of personalities, sort of like Jack Sprat and his wife.

Web:

http://www.bladeforums.com/
http://www.cutlerscove.com/links/
   knifecollectorclubs.html
http://www.kmg.org/
http://www.knifecenter.com/knifecenter/xtra/
   glossary.html
http://www.knifeforums.com/

Usenet:

rec.knives

License Plates

I like license plates. They're small, they're colorful, and there are just enough variations to make collecting them worthwhile. Whether or not you are a collector, I bet you will enjoy looking at pictures of license plates from around the world. I especially like looking at old plates and imagining the people who used them and the cars they were driving.

Web:

http://www.alpca.org/
http://www.motorcycles-online.com/plates/pl8s.htm
http://www.olavsplates.com/
http://www.pl8s.com/
http://www.plateshack.com/76/

Marble Collecting

When I was young, we had marble season at school every spring as soon as the snow had melted. Here is how the whole thing worked. For several weeks, a large area of the playground was set aside for marbles (also called "alleys"). Various people would sit on the ground with their legs spread and place a valuable marble in front of them. When you did this, it announced that you were willing to let anyone try and win the valuable marble. People could come up and, from a certain distance (about 10-15 feet), roll a less valuable marble on the ground toward you. If the rolling marble hit the valuable marble, the person who rolled the less valuable marble got to keep the valuable one. In general, it is difficult to hit another marble 10-15 feet away, and the person sitting on the ground could end up accumulating many marbles before having to give up the valuable one. There were two basic ideas. First, you could beg, borrow, steal or buy a whole bunch of plain, ordinary marbles, and then use them to try and win a few of the valuable ones such as purees or puree biggies. (Purees were valuable because there was no place to buy them; you had to win them.) Or, if you had some valuable marbles, you could sit on the ground with a valuable marble, and collect as many plain marbles as you could before someone hit the valuable one. I still remember the day two brothers came to school with a big tin filled with beautiful, green, medium-large puree biggies. One of the brothers sat down and placed one of the green marbles on the ground in front of him. In no time, a crowd of people had appeared, rolling one marble after another, trying to win a beautiful, green, medium-large puree biggie. Whenever the green puree was hit, one of the brothers would give it to the winner, reach into the tin, pull out a new puree, and place it on the ground. Boy, did they ever do well! Marble season was for the youngest kids, and I only played for a few years. But even now, it is impossible for me to see a nice-looking marble without feeling nostalgic about those childhood times that seem so far away and so long ago. To this day, whenever I walk into an art supply store and see a box full of clear glass marbles, I feel like calling to the person I am with and saying, "Wow, look at all these purees. I bet if we bought some we could really clean up."

Web:

  http://www.blocksite.com/
  http://www.marblealan.com/
  http://www.marblemuseum.org/

Music Collecting

There are lots of reasons why it is a good idea to be a music collector. Here are the top three. (1) You will always have the right music to play no matter what the occasion (such as a surprise Tupperware party). (2) One day a famous movie producer may come over to your place and ask you to help him choose the soundtrack music for his new picture. (3) When you die, people will have something pleasant to say about you. ("He had such a nice CD collection...")

Web:

  http://www.8trackheaven.com/index2.html
  http://www.hifiheaven.com/vinyl-collecting.htm
  http://www.wfmu.org/MACrec/

Usenet:

  alt.collecting.8-track-tapes
  rec.music.collecting.cd
  rec.music.collecting.misc
  rec.music.collecting.vinyl

Postcards

Postcards were designed so that people who go on vacation could quickly and easily torture all those friends or family members who didn't get to go. Connect with other postcard collectors and discuss the history of picture postcards, information on research activities, or find people with whom you can exchange postcards by mail.

Web:

  http://www.library.arizona.edu/users/mount/
    postcard.html
  http://www.patsabin.com/VintagePostcards/
  http://www.postcard.org/

Usenet:

  alt.collecting.postcard
  bit.listserv.postcard
  rec.collecting.postal-history

Listserv Mailing List:

  List Name: postcard
  Subscribe to: listserv@listserv.boisestate.edu

Rock Collecting

They're not friendly or cuddly, but you don't have to feed and water them and they don't make any noise. If you are into long-term commitment without the emotional sloppiness, rocks make perfect friends.

Web:

http://www.rockhounds.com/rockshop/table.html
http://www.tomaszewski.net/Kreigh/Minerals/
   MineralLinks.shtml

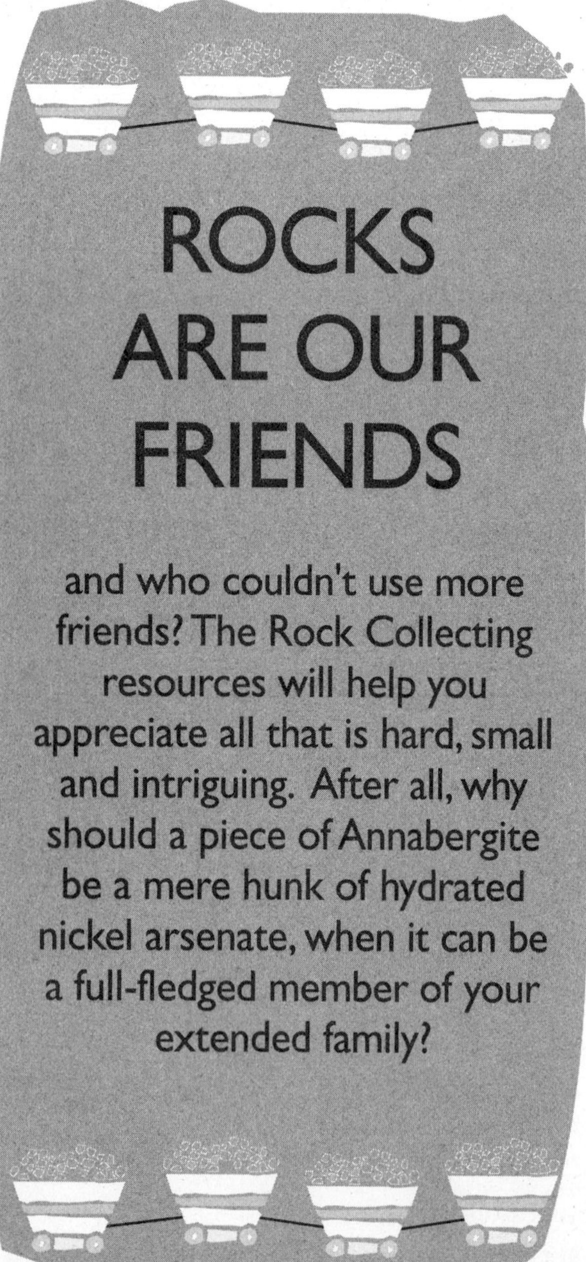

Snowglobes

My favorite snowglobe is a special one commemorating Watergate. You shake it, and, as the snow floats down gently, obscuring the view, you catch a glimpse of Richard Nixon sitting behind a big desk, erasing audio tapes. Snowglobes are not only fun to collect, they can be useful as well. After all, suppose that one day you are on trial for your life and, to get off, have to prove you have visited Fargo, North Dakota. All you need to do is show the judge your special Fargo souvenir snowglobe. Or maybe one day a millionaire will knock on your door and ask if you would be willing to trade a snowglobe for his Rolls Royce. You'd feel pretty silly having to turn him down. But the best thing about snowglobes is that you can shake them up and watch the snow float down gently whenever you want.

Web:

http://www.domeorama.com/inside.html
http://www.incolor.inetnebr.com/snowglobes/

Sports Memorabilia

You don't have to play a sport to be one, but you don't even have to be a sport to collect stuff. All you need is motivation, time, money, and a place to keep your collection where your mother or wife won't throw it out. There are many people on the Net who buy, sell and appreciate sports memorabilia, and these Web sites can help you find what you want. If you like to talk to other collectors, or you want to buy or sell something, you can join the discussion in one of the Usenet groups. It's not always easy to find exactly what you want, but it's worth it. As a kid, I collected football cards, and I still remember how thrilled I was the day I got the last card I needed to have the complete set. It was a *big* deal.

Web:

http://www.carddepot.com/
http://www.cardlinks.com/
http://www.collector-link.com/
http://www.sweetspotnews.com/

Usenet:

rec.collecting.sport.baseball
rec.collecting.sport.basketball
rec.collecting.sport.football
rec.collecting.sport.hockey
rec.collecting.sport.misc

Stamp Collecting

The modern use of postage stamps started in England in 1840. The first official U.S. stamps were issued in 1847. By 1850, the custom had been adopted by countries around the world. Eventually, postal officials noticed that many stamps were never used: they were being saved by collectors (philatelists). For years now, the collecting market has been so large that post offices have been designing and producing stamps specifically for the philatelic community. Indeed, some small countries accrue significant revenue by selling stamps to foreign collectors.

Web:
  http://www.spacecovers.com/links/
    links_philatelics.htm
  http://www.stampfaq.org/toc01.html
  http://www.stampnews.co.uk/
  http://www.stampsites.com/

Usenet:
  rec.collecting.postal-history
  rec.collecting.stamps
  rec.collecting.stamps.discuss
  rec.collecting.stamps.marketplace

Listserv Mailing List:
  List Name: stamps
  Subscribe to: listserv@lists.psu.edu

Teddy Bear Collecting

If you are a woman, I don't have to tell you why it's fun to collect teddy bears. They are cute, cuddly, and you can sleep with them at night without having to worry about them pulling away all the covers. If you are a man, there are two important reasons to have a teddy bear collection of your own. First, from time to time, you can give one of your teddy bears to a woman, and she will think you are thoughtful and sensitive. Second, you can sleep with them at night without having to worry about them pulling away all the covers.

Web:
  http://www.beartop50.com/
  http://www.cobweb.nl/wcoumans/teddie.htm
  http://www.tbonnet.com/

Usenet:
  alt.collecting.teddy-bears

Is it too late? If you have to ask, the answer is yes. (So don't ask.)

Toy Collecting

Admit it. You love toys. Not only are they fun, but they are great to collect. The only thing that could possibly be better than collecting toys is actually getting paid to read about it. So why not take a few minutes every day at work and see what's new in the world of toy collecting? You'll find information covering the simplest plastic Legos to the most complicated technical gadgetry. Moreover, your boss will be amazed at how a few minutes of relaxation improves your productivity, and you'll probably even get a raise.

Web:
  http://www.bigredtoybox.com/
  http://www.toyarchive.com/

Usenet:
  alt.toys
  alt.toys.gi-joe.1980s
  alt.toys.hi-tech
  alt.toys.lego
  alt.toys.my-little-pony
  alt.toys.transformers
  alt.toys.transformers.classic.moderated
  alt.toys.transformers.marketplace
  alt.toys.virtual-pets
  rec.toys
  rec.toys.action-figures
  rec.toys.action-figures.discuss
  rec.toys.action-figures.marketplace
  rec.toys.cars
  rec.toys.lego
  rec.toys.misc
  rec.toys.transformers.marketplace
  rec.toys.transformers.moderated
  rec.toys.vintage

Trading Cards

When I was a kid, I collected football cards. (This was in Toronto, and the cards were for the Canadian Football League.) There came a time when I almost had the full set, and I needed only one more card. As you can imagine, the very last card is the hardest one to find, but one day I found someone who had it and would trade with me. Was I ever happy! I still remember the exact place I was standing in the schoolyard and the immense feeling of satisfaction I had as I made the final trade. I remember a friend of mine running around, all excited, because I had got the whole set. Even as an adult, it still feels like an important accomplishment. Isn't it wonderful how remembering such small things after so many years can bring back such a warm feeling of contentment? Where did those days go?

Web:
   http://www.collector-link.com/
   http://www.collectsports.com/
   http://www.scottsdalecards.com/

Usenet:
   rec.cards.non-sports.marketplace
   rec.collecting.cards

Listserv Mailing List:
   List Name: nonsport-cards
   Subscribe to: listserv@listserv.aol.com

Listserv Mailing List:
   List Name: sports-cards
   Subscribe to: listserv@listserv.aol.com

COMICS

Alternative Comics

Anybody can be mainstream, but if you are looking to break out of your comics rut, try some alternative comics. Enjoy information about comics, including reviews, news, interviews and FAQs. The comic book industry may not be what it used to be (oh, how I miss Jimmy Olsen and Lois Lane), but the alternative scene is as robust and alive as ever.

Web:
   http://www.indyworld.com/
   http://www.indyworld.com/altcomics/

Usenet:
   alt.comics.alternative
   rec.arts.comics.alternative

Anime and Manga

Anime is Japanese animation, and manga are Japanese comics. Anime and manga are much different from their American counterparts. For one thing, the characterization and plot development tend to be more complex. In addition, the subject matter of both anime and manga extend into many more genres than do American animation and comics. The Japanese stories are much more realistic. For example, you will often see characters who have complex relationships (just like real people). Perhaps the most important difference is that there are many types of anime and manga, created for all types of audiences, not just for children or teenagers.

Web:
   http://www.animenation.net/links/pages/
   http://www.anipike.com/
   http://www.csclub.uwaterloo.ca/u/mlvanbie/
      anime-list/
   http://www.ex.org/

Usenet:
   alt.fan.bgcrisis
   alt.fan.r-takahashi
   alt.fan.sailor-moon
   alt.manga
   rec.arts.anime
   rec.arts.anime.creative
   rec.arts.anime.fandom
   rec.arts.anime.games
   rec.arts.anime.info
   rec.arts.anime.marketplace
   rec.arts.anime.misc
   rec.arts.anime.models
   rec.arts.anime.music
   rec.arts.anime.stories
   rec.arts.manga

Listserv Mailing List:
   List Name: anime-l
   Subscribe to: listserv@listserv.vt.edu

IRC:
   #anime (Undernet)

Asterix

I still remember the first time I saw an Asterix book. I was intrigued by the comic-strip-like adventure story, which reminded me of Tintin. As I started to read, I was astonished at the high quality of wit and word play, which was all the more impressive because I was reading an English translation. (The original books, like Tintin, were written in French.) The Asterix stories take place 50 B.C. in Gaul (France). Except for one small village, the entire region is occupied and ruled by the Romans. The village successfully resists the Romans, in large part thanks to a magic potion brewed by their druid, which gives the villagers superhuman strength. The characters include Asterix (the main hero), Obelix (his best friend and sidekick), Dogmatix (his dog), Getafix (the druid), Cacofonix (the bard), and Vitalstatistix (the village chief). The Asterix books were created by Rene Goscinny (1926-1977) and Albert Uderzo (1927-). There are thirty books, and to be a knowledgeable, fulfilled human being, you must read them all.

Web:
  http://lcg-www.uia.ac.be/~erikt/asterix/
    welcome.shtml#pages
  http://www.asterix-international.de/
  http://www.asterix.tm.fr/english/
  http://www.cwi.nl/ftp/dik/strips/Asterix.Anno
  http://www.wi.leidenuniv.nl/home/hoogeboo/
    asterix.html

What should religious people know about ATHEISTS AND AGNOSTICS?

An agnostic believes that there can be no proof that God exists. An atheist flat out denies the existence of a God (or gods).

In the United States, about 1 out of 14 adults are atheist or agnostic. They outnumber Mormons by 3 to 1, Jews by 4 to 1, and Muslims by 14 to 1.

Interestingly enough, atheists and agnostics have a much lower divorce rate than religious people.

Batman

"Criminals are a superstitious, cowardly lot. So my disguise must strike fear and terror in their hearts." With these words, Bruce Wayne began his career as Batman, a hero whose appeal has transcended a wide variety of renditions as well as sixty years of social change. Batman was created by artist Bob Kane and first appeared in the May 1939 issue of Detective Comics (eleven months after Superman). Through the years, there have been comic books, TV shows, movies, and a huge amount of memorabilia and commercial products. Unlike other superheroes, Batman has no special powers. He is not faster than a speeding bullet, nor is he more powerful than a locomotive, and he definitely can't leap tall buildings at a single bound. What he *can* do is use his intelligence, training and superb physical condition to track criminals to their dens and bring them to justice without the use of guns. Why is he so popular and enduring? Because, although he is as human as you and I, Batman represents the highest pinnacle of mortal development: a man whose extreme bravery, strength and knowledge make him the perfect hero for the bulk of humanity who must wake up to an alarm clock, go to work, pay taxes, and raise their children. When a middle-aged man looks into the mirror, holds in his stomach and flexes his muscles, he is, for one brief moment, looking at Batman.

Web:
  http://members.ttlc.net/~bobhughes/Batwho.htm
  http://www.darkknight.ca/
  http://www.goldenagebatman.com/

Usenet:
  alt.comics.batman

Cartoon Museums

I have always enjoyed comics and cartoons. For example, I have a large collection of Tintin books, silver-age Superman comic books, and Duck comic books, and I start each day by reading the daily comics on the Net. That's why I appreciate comics and cartoons as art forms (and why I spend a large portion of my existence walking around the world radiating peace, joy, serenity and so much *joie de vivre* that people in the same room as I'm in often have to wear sunglasses.)

Web:
  http://library.ukc.ac.uk/cartoons/
  http://www.cartoon.org/home.htm
  http://www.wordsandpictures.org/

Classic Comic Books

Classic comic books are those that were published from the 1930s to the 1970s. Within these five decades, various names are used to describe specific periods. The most widely accepted terms are the Golden Age (1938-1945), which started in June 1938 when Superman debuted in Action Comics #1; and the Silver Age (1956-1969), which started in October 1956 with the appearance of the new Flash in Showcase #4. When I was growing up, you were either a DC person or a Marvel person. I was a DC person. To me, DC comics were for thinking people; Marvel comics were full of confusing and meaningless fighting. My all-time favorites were the Silver Age Superman Family (DC) comics. To this day, I have a large collection of old Superman, Lois Lane and Jimmy Olsen comics, which I read from time to time when I need to feel good about the world.

Web:

http://blaklion.best.vwh.net/comics.html
http://fivedots.coe.psu.ac.th/~ad/comics/search.html
http://www.comicboards.com/gsmb/
http://www.dereksantos.com/comicpage/
http://www.elmy.com/gertanddaisy/
http://www.members.aol.com/mg4273/comics.htm
http://www.samcci.comics.org/

Classic Comic Strips

I like old comics. My favorites are the pre-1960 strips of Nancy, Peanuts and Blondie, some of which you can find on this Web site. Here's a mailing list and Usenet group on which you can talk about any pre-1960 vintage newspaper comic strips with other fans.

Web:

http://www.gographics.com/funnies/amstpidx.htm

Usenet:

alt.comics.classic

Majordomo Mailing List:

List Name: comic-strip-classics
Subscribe to: majordomo@liss.olm.net

Classic Comic Strips

Sometimes life moves too quickly. Why live in the fast lane, when you can take it easy and enjoy the past?

Statistics (including the one I just made up) show that if you spend just ten minutes a day reading about classic comic strips, your life will slow down, and you will be healthy, wealthy and wise.

Comic Art

Original comic art has become a respected field in the world of collectable art. Although I don't have any originals, I do have a large framed Donald Duck in my office and a large Tintin poster nearby. They are a constant source of inspiration and comfort. Goodness knows, in these days of modern times, who couldn't use more inspiration and comfort? Imagine how much happier I could be if I had originals.

Web:

http://www.dragonberry.com/

Comic Conventions

When it's time for a road trip, check out the upcoming comics conventions. Pack your bags and go on an adventurous excursion to hang out in a large room with the type of people who like to go on an adventurous excursion to hang out in a large room with the type of people who like to go to comic conventions.

Web:

http://www.comic-con.org/
http://www.comicartlinks.com/html/
  conventions.html
http://www.comicbookconventions.com/pages/
  cons.html
http://www.dragonberry.com/links/pages/
  Comic_Book_Conventions/

Comic Reviews

It's hard to know what to say when you are at a party and someone asks your opinion about a particular comic. Sure, you can always make up something, but isn't it a lot better to prepare for important social encounters by reading a whole lot of comic reviews *before* you leave the house?

Web:

http://www.rzero.com/books/

Usenet:

rec.arts.comics.reviews

Comic Scholarship

Comics and cartoons are understandable to just about everyone, and they have a long and important history within the popular culture. There are many people engaged in the serious study of comics, and a large number of libraries and universities have serious comic collections. If this sounds like the life for you, here are some resources I know you will enjoy. After all, wouldn't the world of academic study be boring if everyone wanted to be a chemist or a mathematician?

Web:
  http://www.comicsresearch.org/
  http://www.lib.msu.edu/comics/director/comres.htm
  http://www.sp.uconn.edu/~epk93002/comixschl/

Comicon

The first Comicon (comic convention) I went to was in 1982 in San Diego. I went with my friends Marlene and David Garstang and I had a great time. Now you don't have to go to San Diego to visit a Comicon: there is an Internet-based comics convention on the Web that you can visit whenever you want. It doesn't quite have the same ambience, but it's a lot more convenient and the food is better. Also, you don't have to worry about Marlene telling you it's time to go because David has to get home and do his homework.

Web:
  http://www.comicon.com/

Comics Databases

I like comics and I have a collection of my own (Silver Age Superman, Lois Lane and Jimmy Olsen, as well as Disney duck comics). If you are a collector, you will be glad to know that there are databases you can use to search for information about comics. Some people might be bored stiff at the idea of browsing through a Web site filled with listings of comic book information, but you and I know better.

Web:
  http://www.comics.org/
  http://www.comicsdb.com/
  http://www.comicstracker.com/
    w_comic_add.asp?source=outside
  http://www.execpc.com/~icicle/main.html

Comics Fan Fiction

Comic book characters really have a life of their own, and fans of comic book characters like to participate by helping bring these characters to life. These Usenet groups are for the purpose of sharing fiction written by fans of various comic strips and comic books. The Web sites contain links to various fan fiction collections and related resources.

Web:
  http://www.fanimenation.com/pages/Fan_Fiction/
  http://www.marvelite.prohosting.com/surfer/fanfic/
  http://www.subreality.com/cfan.htm

Usenet:
  alt.comics.fan-fiction
  rec.arts.comics.creative

Comics Marketplace

What do you do when it's 2 AM and you just have to lay your hands on the Superman comic in which Lois Lane pretends to marry Peewee Herman, but it turns out to be a hoax? Fire up the old computer and visit the Usenet comics marketplace.

Usenet:
  rec.arts.comics.marketplace

Comics on the Net

If you like to read comics, but don't like to get your hands dirty, the Net has the answer for you. There are enough comic links here to keep you busy for hours. These Web sites offer links to comics around the Net. Click to your heart's content and never once worry about icky newsprint or your obligation to the environment. On the Web, you never have to recycle.

Web:
  http://www.comicbookresources.com/
  http://www.sno.pp.se/strips.html

Comics Resources

The world of comics is the world of imagination, and there is no end to what you will find. Such a rich world requires a massive amount of information, and the Net is ready, willing and able to oblige: articles, news, gossip, reviews, convention info, as well as lists of comics, publishers and artists.

Web:
  http://www.comiclist.com/
  http://www.hometown.aol.com/comicbknet/
  http://www.icomics.com/
  http://www.stus.com/

Comics Talk and General Discussion

Zap! Biff! Pow! Action dialog brings comics to life. Whether you are a collector or just a person who likes to read comics now and then, you'll love the variety of discussion you can find in Usenet.

Usenet:

alt.comics.2000ad
alt.comics.alan-moore
alt.comics.elfquest
alt.comics.gunnm
alt.comics.image
alt.comics.jack-kirby
alt.comics.lnh
alt.comics.peanuts
alt.fan.neil-gaiman
rec.arts.comics
rec.arts.comics.dc.lsh
rec.arts.comics.dc.universe
rec.arts.comics.dc.vertigo
rec.arts.comics.elfquest
rec.arts.comics.info
rec.arts.comics.marvel.universe
rec.arts.comics.marvel.xbooks
rec.arts.comics.misc
rec.arts.comics.other-media
rec.arts.comics.strips
rec.arts.comics.xbooks

Daily Comics

These are some of my favorite sites on the whole Internet. Lots of daily comic strips to look at for free. Along with the comics, you will find background information on the cartoonists and on the strips themselves. Just between you and me, these sites eliminated the only reason I ever had to buy a newspaper.

Web:

http://www.chron.com/comics/
http://www.comics.com/
http://www.comicspage.com/
http://www.creators.com/comics.html
http://www.kingfeatures.com/features/comics/
   comics.htm
http://www.washingtonpost.com/wp-dyn/style/
   comics/

Dilbert Zone

There is a fifth dimension beyond that which is known to man (or woman). It is a dimension as vast as the Internet and as timeless as anything that is trendy. It is the middle ground between light and "Where's the light switch?", between science fiction and Super Bowl. It lies between the pit of a man's computer and the summit of his high speed Internet connection. This is the dimension of imagination. It is an area we call... The Dilbert Zone. Check out the cartoon archive and a massive amount of Dilbert-oriented silliness, including information on joining Dogbert's New Ruling Class.

Web:

http://www.unitedmedia.com/comics/dilbert/

Usenet:

alt.comics.dilbert

European Comics

European comics have a history and style that is much different from American comics. If you are a fan of European comics, here are some resources you will enjoy. If you like comics, but have never seen the European publications, take a few minutes to explore.

Web:

http://lcg-www.uia.ac.be/~erikt/comics/
http://www.fumetti.org/cac/
http://www.youknow.demon.nl/pages/index2.html

Usenet:

rec.arts.comics.european

Professional Cartoonists

Professional cartoonists and would-be professional cartoonists will appreciate all the resources available on the Internet. Stay in touch with other cartoonists, keep up on what is new and exciting in the industry, and look for job opportunities.

Web:
   http://cagle.slate.msn.com/
   http://pc99.detnews.com/aaec/
   http://www.reuben.org/

Small Press Comics

On the Net there are great resources for any comic talent looking to be published. These Web sites offer information on how to get yourself published and how to copyright, distribute and advertise your work. You can read about other small press comics, tools of the trade and tips on how to get comic shops to stock small press comics.

Web:
   http://www.backporchcomics.com/
   http://www.hoboes.com/html/Comics/Creators/
   http://www.sentex.net/~sardine/spfaq.html

Tintin

What is Tintin? A series of wonderful stories in comic format—written by the Belgian artist Hergé—in which the hero Tintin (a young reporter) travels around the world with his dog Snowy, having one adventure after another. I have every Tintin book, and I read them again and again and again. (And so should you.) Here is a bit of Tintin trivia: in French, the original language, Tintin's dog is named Milou. This is the name of Hergé's first girlfriend.

Web:
   http://www.cwi.nl/~dik/english/TINTIN.html
   http://www.tintin.com/uk/
   http://www.tintin.qc.ca/english/

I still remember the day. I was 13 years old and I was browsing in a large bookstore. I happened upon a display where several oversized comic/adventure books were on sale.

The books were **King Ottokar's Sceptre**, **The Crab with the Golden Claws**, and **The Secret of the Unicorn**.

I didn't know it at the time, but these were **Tintin** books.

I bought all three books, took them home, and read them. Then I read them again, and again and again. I loved those books. But I was frustrated because I could not find any more books in the series. And what made it worse was that **The Secret of the Unicorn** was the first part of a two-part story, and I couldn't find out how it ended. All I could do was read the first part over and over.

A few years later, I happened to be in the university bookstore, when I ran into the sales rep for the company that published **Tintin** in my country. I told him my problem, and he said, "Well, I'll just send you a complete set."

Since then, I have read all my **Tintin** books so many times that the bindings have disintegrated. A week doesn't go by that I do not see or hear something that reminds me of a **Tintin** book. For example, someone will bend over, and I will say, "You look exactly like Captain Haddock when he hurt his back by throwing a coconut at a parrot in a tree in **Red Rackham's Treasure**."

So what's the moral of all this? Well, I guess there isn't any moral, except to say that **Tintin** books are cool, and you should get the whole set and read them as many times as you can before you die.

COMPUTERS: MACINTOSH

Buying and Selling Macs

Here is the Usenet swap meet for Macs. The **.wanted** group is the place to send a request for Macintosh-related hardware or software. The **.computers** groups are more for buying and selling systems and components.

Usenet:

biz.marketplace.computers.mac
comp.sys.mac.wanted
misc.forsale.computer.mac-specific.systems
misc.forsale.computers.mac
misc.forsale.computers.mac-specific.cards.misc
misc.forsale.computers.mac-specific.cards.video
misc.forsale.computers.mac-specific.misc
misc.forsale.computers.mac-specific.portables

Macintosh Acceleration

What could be better than your own personal Macintosh? Your own personal Macintosh running faster and faster and faster. So run, don't crawl, to the Net where in less time than it takes for Steve Jobs to exercise a new set of stock options, you can find out how to upgrade and enhance your processor, memory, disks, video and lots more.

Web:

http://www.everymac.com/
http://www.macspeedzone.com/
http://www.xlr8yourmac.com/

Macintosh Hardware

All kinds of discussion about all kinds of Macintosh computers. Talk, talk, talk. Point the mouse and click. Talk, talk, talk. Point the mouse and click. Talk, talk, talk. Empty the trash can. Talk, talk, talk, etc.

Usenet:

comp.sys.mac.hardware
comp.sys.mac.hardware.misc
comp.sys.mac.hardware.storage
comp.sys.mac.hardware.video
comp.sys.mac.portables

Macintosh Magazines

Keep up to date on what is happening in the Mac world. Here are some sites for magazines in which you can find news about hardware and software, reviews and articles as well as links to other online resources. As long as you are on the Net, you need never be out of the Macintosh loop.

Web:

http://www.macaddict.com/
http://www.macdesignonline.com/
http://www.machome.com/
http://www.mactech.com/
http://www.macworld.com/

Macintosh Mailing Lists

One way to keep up on the Macintosh world is to subscribe to one or more mailing lists. Here is a list from which you can choose the mailing lists that are just right for you. Moreover, they make great presents. For example, for a wedding present, I registered my brother and his wife for a subscription to the HyperCard mailing list. True, they don't have a computer, and they have no idea what HyperCard is, but it is awfully hard to know what to get newlyweds. A nice mailing list is always in good taste.

Web:

http://lists.apple.com/

Macintosh News and Announcements

There is a lot happening in the Mac world, and you can use the Internet to help you keep up. These resources will show you the official scoops from Apple, as well as what everyone on the street is saying. Never again need you feel embarrassed because Steve Jobs had a new idea, and you didn't know about it until you saw it in the newspaper.

Web:

http://osx.macnn.com/
http://www.apple.com/pr/
http://www.applelinks.com/
http://www.macintouch.com/
http://www.macnn.com/
http://www.macobserver.com/
http://www.macsurfer.com/

Macintosh Resources

When you are looking for any type of Macintosh-related resources, these are great places to start. No matter what you are looking for—software, news, mailing lists, online publications, FAQs, user groups—I bet you'll find it at one of these Web sites.

Web:

http://www.macdirectory.com/
http://www.macsonly.com/
http://www.mymac.com/
http://www.sitelink.net/

Macintosh Reviews

So you've got a Mac, and now you need to buff it out with all kinds of new software and hardware. Before you plunk down your kopeks, check out the reviews. Whatever you are thinking about getting—programs, games, digital cameras, printers—it's probably reviewed on the Net. Find out what's really worth your money and what deserves to be dragged directly to the trash can without passing GO or collecting $200.

Web:

http://www.macreview.com/
http://www.macreviewzone.com/

Macintosh Talk and General Discussion

As fewer and fewer people use Macintosh computers, finding other Mac people to talk with becomes more and more important. Usenet is the way to go. The **.advocacy** group is for debate and opinion. The **.digest** group is a moderated magazine that contains articles of interest to Mac people. The other Usenet groups are forums for general discussion. I say, hooray for Usenet. Where else can you go to have a rousing discussion about what to buy Steve Jobs for his birthday?

Usenet:

comp.sys.mac
comp.sys.mac.advocacy
comp.sys.mac.digest
comp.sys.mac.misc

Macintosh Troubleshooting

Wouldn't it be nice to have a Macintosh expert on call, 24 hours a day, to solve your problems? Well, I'd give you Steve Jobs's unlisted phone number, but you'd probably only get his voice mail. Instead, here are some resources full of hints and tips for troubleshooting Macintosh problems. Using the Net is the next best thing to having your own personal tech support staff.

Web:

http://www.info.apple.com/
http://www.macfixit.com/

Macintosh Updates

If you are a Mac user, this is definitely a place you need to remember: a collection of fixes, updates and information relating to the Mac operating system, peripheral devices and all types of Macintosh software. Next time tech support puts you on hold forever, check here to see if there is a fix you can download.

Web:

http://www.versionmaster.com/
http://www.versiontracker.com/macos/
http://www.vse-online.com/update-finder/

Macintosh Viruses

The great thing about having a Macintosh is you don't have to worry about all those troublesome viruses that run on PCs. However, just so you don't feel left out, there are Mac viruses. Here are some relevant resources, including lots of stuff to read: news, announcements, a FAQ (frequently asked question list), and recommendations regarding antivirus prevention and software.

Web:
   http://www.faqs.org/faqs/computer-virus/
      macintosh-faq/
   http://www.securemac.com/

MacintoshOS.com

When the original Macintosh was introduced in 1984, it cost $2,500. Today it is worth about $10. This is just one of the interesting factoids I found in the Macintosh Museum, a compendium of information about every Macintosh model, including some models that are still under development. Aside from the museum, this well-organized Web site serves as a general launching place for things Mac. You can look for free software, get help troubleshooting your problems, join a discussion group or talk to someone in a live chat area. By the way, in 1984, if you had spent that $2,500 on Apple stock instead of a computer, you would have seen it increase to a high of $3,147,743.75 in the glory days of the Mac. Today, that same stock would be worth about $10.

Web:
   http://www.macintoshos.com/

MacOS Rumors

Computer companies, like all companies, want to control what you know about them and when you should know it. If you're like me, however, you want to know stuff that you are not supposed to know, so take a look at these Macintosh rumors and secrets every now and then to see what's new. I love inside information, and I think that it is only right that you and I be on the inside.

Web:
   http://www.macosrumors.com/

MacSlash

Are you a MacNerd with no place to go? Do you find yourself lonely on Saturday night because your girlfriend doesn't understand the difference between Finder and a disk optimizer, and no one in your immediate circle of friends even cares about the latest version of the OS? You are not alone. Cruise to the Net where you can feast on the latest news and commentary in the Mac world. Be the first one on your virtual block to find out what's hot before it even hits the griddle.

Web:
   http://www.macslash.com/

MkLinux

Linux is *the* cool Unix for the beginning of the twenty-first century, and just because you have a Mac doesn't mean you can't be as cool as all the other Unix people on your block. Use this Web site to find all types of Linux-for-the-Mac (MkLinux) information: the MkLinux package, a FAQ, updates and patches, as well as links to other MkLinux-related resources on the Net.

Web:
  http://www.mklinux.org/

Are you a Mac person?
Would you like to run Unix on your machine? Do you have lots and lots of time?
Try **MkLinux.**

Tidbits

Tidbits is an electronic publication that discusses products and events in the Macintosh part of the world. Tidbits is both practical and news oriented. They do an excellent job and have been around for a long time. I suggest you read it regularly for three reasons: (1) to keep up on what is happening, (2) for useful tips and techniques, and (3) if you have the type of friends who are impressed that you know what is new in the Macintosh community, you will be able to impress your friends.

Web:
  http://www.tidbits.com/

COMPUTERS: PCS

Buying and Selling PCs

When it comes time to buy or sell a PC, it can help you a lot to be able to talk to other people. You can use these Usenet groups to look for a computer or computer parts to buy, to offer something for sale, or to ask questions. Remember, you are dealing with strangers, so you must be careful. Don't blindly send your money (or your PC) to someone without satisfying yourself that everything is okay.

Usenet:

biz.marketplace.computers.pc-clone
misc.forsale.computers.pc-specific.audio
misc.forsale.computers.pc-specific.cards.misc
misc.forsale.computers.pc-specific.cards.video
misc.forsale.computers.pc-specific.misc
misc.forsale.computers.pc-specific.motherboards
misc.forsale.computers.pc-specific.portables
misc.forsale.computers.pc-specific.software
misc.forsale.computers.pc-specific.systems

Monitors

As you use a computer, you are constantly looking at the monitor (display screen). A cheap monitor may save money up front, but it is much more pleasant to use a better quality display. Before you buy your next monitor, take a few moments to learn about what to look for and how to make an intelligent decision. If possible, test the monitor in a store before you buy it. Hint: Cheap monitors flicker. If you notice a flicker, don't buy the monitor. It will bother you more than you might think. (Remember, these are your eyes we are talking about.)

Web:

http://www.computermonitor.org/
http://www.monitorworld.com/
http://www.repairfaq.org/REPAIR/F_monfaq1.html
http://www.tomshardware.com/display/

Usenet:

comp.sys.ibm.pc.hardware.video

PC Acceleration

We all know the faster your computer, the happier you are. So, however fast your computer is right now, it needs to be faster. Faster, faster and even faster than that. There are lots of ways to increase the performance of your PC, but if you want to be a real speed nerd, you need to get your information from the pros. Learn about overclocking (making the processor run faster than its official speed), tweaking the registry, fast Internet connections, diagnostics, benchmarks, and more technical tricks than you can squeeze into a tube of official IBM lubricating gel.

Web:

http://www.arstechnica.com/
http://www.overclockers.com/
http://www.speedguide.net/
http://www.tweak3d.net/

PC Hardware

The term "PC hardware" covers a lot of territory, embracing entire computers as well as the tiny bits and pieces that do so much to fill our twenty-first century lives with meaning. Here are some guides to help you navigate the uncharted sea of PCs, chips, boards and accessories. You'll find reviews, explanations, glossaries, diagrams, articles, price lists, opinions, specifications, troubleshooting guides, and lots and lots of technical details. I have chosen these resources to cover a wide range of needs, so whether you are an expert, a beginner, or a fanatical computer game player, you'll find something here to help you.

Web:

http://www.dansdata.com/altindex.html
http://www.hardwarecentral.com/
http://www.hardwarezone.com/
http://www.sysopt.com/
http://www.techfest.com/hardware/
http://www.tomshardware.com/

PC Hardware Talk and General Discussion

Computing is no fun if you have to work on a slow dinosaur of a PC that creaks when it starts up or blows dust out of its cracks every time you change directories. Keep up with the latest in hardware changes and make your machine state-of-the-art.

Usenet:

    comp.hardware
    comp.sys.ibm.hardware
    comp.sys.ibm.pc.hardware
    comp.sys.ibm.pc.hardware.cd-rom
    comp.sys.ibm.pc.hardware.chips
    comp.sys.ibm.pc.hardware.comm
    comp.sys.ibm.pc.hardware.misc
    comp.sys.ibm.pc.hardware.networking
    comp.sys.ibm.pc.hardware.storage
    comp.sys.ibm.pc.hardware.systems
    comp.sys.ibm.pc.hardware.video
    comp.sys.ibm.ps2.hardware
    comp.sys.next.hardware

PC Hardware

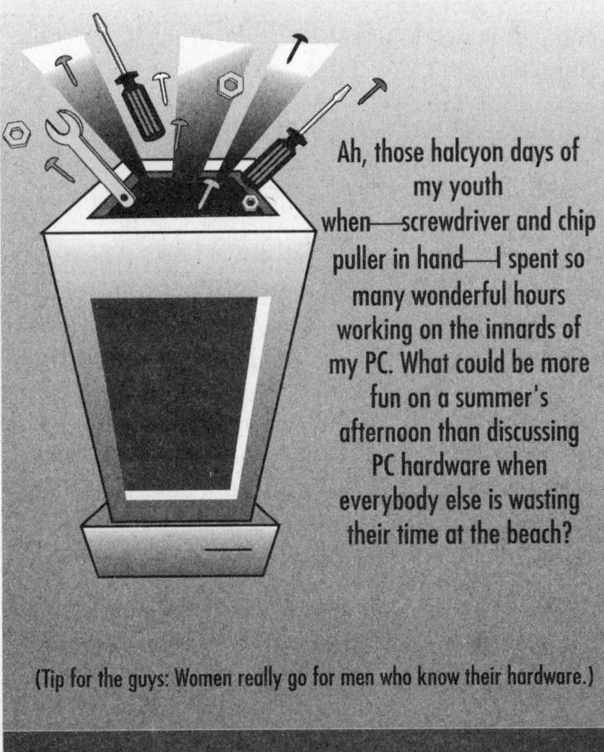

(Tip for the guys: Women really go for men who know their hardware.)

PC Magazines

Keeping up on what is happening in the PC world is impossible. However, if you want to pretend to keep up, the easiest way is by reading PC magazines. To help you, here are some places on the Net where you can read articles from PC magazines without leaving the comfort of your Web browser. Check back every now and then; there is always something new.

Web:

    http://www.computerworld.com/
    http://www.eweek.com/
    http://www.infoworld.com/
    http://www.pcmag.com/
    http://www.pcworld.com/

PC News

Don't get left behind, even for a moment. Check in with the Net every day and see what's new in the world of PCs. Here are some great places to read the factoids behind the rumors and hype that pass for news in the PC industry. If you like keeping up with the PC flow, these sites will help you stay one giant step ahead of the guy or gal in the next cubicle.

Web:

    http://www.pcwatch.com/
    http://www.pcworld.com/news/
    http://www.zdnet.com/

PC Prices

If you are interested in getting the best price, you need a good way to compare. Use this Web site to help you find pricing information about a large number of PCs, as well as parts and components. These days, even the best is relatively inexpensive. Considering what you are getting, being able to buy any PC at all is the bargain of the century. Don't be too cheap. The only way anyone can offer you a computer that is well below the regular price is by selling you last year's technology. If you try to save money, you will only end up with an inferior machine and, believe me, your programs will know the difference.

Web:

    http://shopper.cnet.com/

PC Resources

When you consider what you get for your money, personal computers are the biggest bargain in our society. However, one reason they are so inexpensive is that computers come with no manuals and no help. Although your computer is probably the most complex machine you ever deal with, there is no one to help you when you have trouble. This is something that first-time buyers are not told, but it is true: if you want to solve problems, or enhance your computer in some way, you are on your own. My advice is learn how to use the Net to teach yourself the basics. That way, when you need help, you will know how to find it and you will be able to understand what you read.

Web:
http://www.ars-technica.com/
http://www.chickshardware.com/
http://www.pcguide.com/
http://www.reviewbooth.com/

PC Resources

Do you believe
in magic?
Do you like
having mystery
in your life?

If so, be forewarned. These Internet resources will take all the magic and mystery out of using a PC.

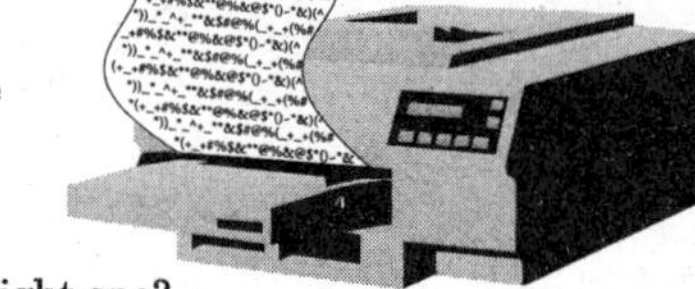

Printer

Printers are great, once you have chosen the right one and gotten it working.
But how to choose the right one?
Check with the Net.
And what do you do if you have problems?
Check with the Net.

PC Talk and General Discussion

When you want to talk about your PC, these are the Usenet discussion groups to check out. Whether you want to ask a question, help someone else, or just hang out, there is always plenty to talk about.

Usenet:
alt.sys.pc-clone.acer
alt.sys.pc-clone.compaq
alt.sys.pc-clone.dell
alt.sys.pc-clone.gateway2000
alt.sys.pc-clone.micron
alt.sys.pc-clone.packardbell
alt.sys.pc-clone.zeos
comp.sys.ibm.pc
comp.sys.ibm.pc.misc
comp.sys.ibm.ps2
comp.unix.pc-clone.16bit
comp.unix.pc-clone.32bit

PCMCIA Cards

PCMCIA cards are small adapters—the size of a thick credit card—designed to fit into laptop computers. The name PCMCIA stands for "Personal Computer Memory Card International Association". (See if you can say that ten times real fast.) There are three types of PCMCIA cards: Type I cards are 3.3 mm thick (for example, memory cards), Type II cards are 5 mm thick (modems, network adapters), while Type III are 10.5 mm thick (miniature disk drives). In theory, PCMCIA cards always work perfectly the first time, especially the "plug and play" cards. In practice, getting these little gremlins working properly can sometimes drive you crazy. Here are some resources to help.

Web:
http://www.pcmcia.org/pccard.htm
http://www.synchrotech.com/support/faq.html

Usenet:
alt.periphs.pcmcia

Printers

I remember when it was hard to get any printer working with a PC and, today, whenever a printer actually works I consider it nothing less than a small miracle. My feelings, of course, are way out of date. Today's printers are generally reliable and well-manufactured, and many printers are actually computers in their own right. There are a lot of different printers and, before you buy, many choices to consider. After you buy, there are a lot of questions that may arise. Here are some resources to help you: links to printer manufacturers, sources for printer drivers, and much, much more.

Web:
 http://www.connectworld.net/c9.html
 http://www.cppfaq.com/
 http://www.laser-printer-reviews.org/
 http://www.lasernetworks.com/advantage.html

Usenet:
 comp.periphs.printers

Scanners

A scanner is a device that you use to convert an image on paper into data stored in a computer file. For example, say you have some photos of your cat that you want to put on your Web site. You could use a scanner to "digitize" the pictures, each of which could be stored in a separate file. You can then display these files on your Web site. (This is how photos end up on Web sites.) Here is some information to help you learn about scanners. I have one and I like it a lot. It's fun to take a photo or drawing and make it into a computer file. If you are artistic, there is a lot you can do with your own scanner. If you are thinking of buying a scanner, here are some tips to help you. (1) You get what you pay for. Expensive scanners work better (and faster) than cheap scanners. (2) All scanners use software. Expensive scanners will have better software, which will make a difference. (3) It will take you some time to learn how to use the software well. (4) It's fun to experiment, but *read the documentation.*

Web:
 http://www.pctechguide.com/18scanners.htm
 http://www.scansoft.com/scanners/
 http://www.scantips.com/
 http://www.zdnet.com/special/filters/sc/scanner/

COMPUTERS: PORTABLE

Electronic Books for Palmtops

You'll never get bored when you have your portable computer with you. The next time you are standing in line for something or other, whip out the machine and start reading an electronic book. You'll be the envy of all the old-fashioned people who still have to read books on paper.

Web:
 http://www.artemispress.com/html/free_ebooks.html
 http://www.dogpatch.org/etext.html
 http://www.memoware.com/

Laptops

A laptop computer works, more or less, like a regular desktop PC. However, a laptop is small and lightweight enough to be portable and sit on your lap comfortably. How small can laptops get and still be laptops? Well, people like a full-sized keyboard and a screen large enough to read without squinting, which puts a minimum size on how small a computer can be and still be usable as a full-fledged PC. However, within these limitations, there are a lot of choices. Before you buy a laptop, check with the Net. You need to know more than when you buy a regular PC, so you should definitely do your homework before leaving home to buy your new electronic home away from home.

Web:
 http://www.infohq.com/Computer/LaptopGuide.htm
 http://www.notebookreview.com/
 http://www.pbsource.com/
 http://www.powerpage.org/
 http://www.roadnews.com/

Usenet:
 comp.sys.laptops

Just say "know".

Mobile Internet Access

There's no excuse for going out of the house without some type of portable computer that can connect you to the Net wherever you go. A laptop, a palmtop, a WAP-enabled phone, an email device, whatever—life as you know it has changed and you must have some type of mobile Internet umbilical cord. You have no choice. You are going to be connected to the Net, and you will stay connected to the Net. Resistance is futile. Your brain cells have been permanently adjusted. Aren't you happy?

Web:
  http://www.allnetdevices.com/wireless
  http://www.mobilecomputing.com/
  http://www.thinkmobile.com/
  http://www.twomobile.com/

Newton

You are in a nerd bar in Silicon Valley, when a friend comes up to you and says, "Would you like me to beam you some cool soup?" If you are a Newton owner, you know exactly what he means: "Would you like me to transfer some cool files from my Newton to your Newton?" A Newton, or more formally, the Newton Message Pad, is a portable personal organizer produced by Apple. A Newton can understand handwritten notes, keep track of appointments, and make your life easier in so many ways. The only problems are (1) it doesn't work well, (2) it's obsolete, and (3) it's discontinued. Still, there are many Newton fanatics in the world, and if you are a Newtonphile yourself, you might as well join the party. ("I'm ready, Man. Beam me some soup.")

Web:
  http://pda.tucows.com/newton/
  http://www.aviators.com/newton/
  http://www.chuma.org/newton/
  http://www.pdastreet.com/boards/Newton/
  http://www.thiel.com/damien/
    newton_battery_FAQ.html
  http://www.thisoldnewt.com/index2.html

Palmtop FAQs

Although palmtop computers are tiny, they are complex and there is a lot to learn. If a FAQ (frequently asked question list) is available for your particular computer, reading the questions and answers will allow you to learn a great deal quickly and orient yourself to your machine.

Web:
  http://www.faqs.org/faqs/palmtops/
  http://www.palmgear.com/faq/

Palmtop Magazines

Immerse yourself in the world of small handheld computers by browsing through these online magazines. You'll find news, feature stories, classified ads, reviews, tips, downloads, and generally enough palmtop-related material to saturate your frontal lobe beyond the point of easy repair.

Web:
  http://www.palmpower.com/
  http://www.pencomputing.com/
  http://www.pocketpcmag.com/

Palmtop News

The world of small computers is getting bigger by the minute. There is so much news that ordinary people just can't keep up, but then, you and I aren't ordinary. When you feel the need to feed the need for news, do what I do: connect to the Net and check out these palmtop-oriented news sites, where you'll find everything you need to make your tiny computer experience on Planet Earth as up-to-the-minute as possible.

Web:
  http://news.tucows.com/pdanews/
  http://www.palminfocenter.com/
  http://www.palmstation.com/
  http://www.pdabuzz.com/
  http://www.pdantic.com/

Palmtop Resources

A palmtop is a small, hand-held computer. Palmtops evolved from PDAs (personal digital assistants) to become today's full-fledged tiny computers running today's full-fledged operating systems (such as Palm OS and Windows CE). Palmtop hardware and software is evolving all the time, and there are lots of things you need to know to use your palmtop well. These resources will allow you to explore the brave new world of brave new hand-held computers. Soon you will achieve total serenity and complete knowledge. Then you will become one with the palmtop universe, and people will travel enormous distances just to touch the hem of your garment. (Not bad for a nerd.)

Web:
> http://www.brighthand.com/
> http://www.handheldnews.com/
> http://www.microsoft.com/pocketpc/default1.asp
> http://www.palmblvd.com/
> http://www.palmtop.net/
> http://www.pdastreet.com/
> http://www.pocketnow.com/
> http://www.pocketpccity.com/
> http://www.pocketpccity.com/hardware.html

Usenet:
> alt.comp.sys.palmtops.hp
> alt.comp.sys.palmtops.pilot
> comp.sys.handhelds
> comp.sys.palmtops
> comp.sys.palmtops.pilot

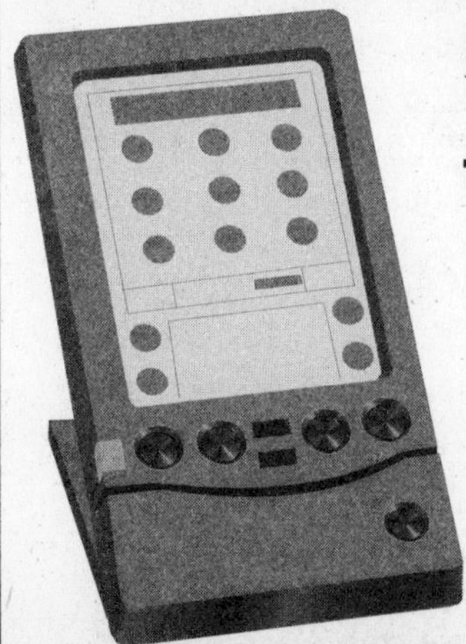

If life were so simple, wouldn't everyone be doing it?

Palmtop Software

No matter what type of palmtop computer you have, I can tell you one thing right now: you need more software to make your life complete. In particular, you need some games. So, don't waste a moment. Check out these archives right now, where you will find oodles of software for your cute, little, cuddly computer-like companion.

Web:
> http://palmcomputing.palmgear.com/palm/
>   shareware.cfm
> http://pda.tucows.com/
> http://www.palmgear.com/
> http://www.palmpilotarchives.com/
> http://www.palmspot.com/whatsnew/
> http://www.palmtop.net/super.html
> http://www.palmtown.com/

Portable Computer Reviews

The world of tiny computers is complex. Palmtops, Pocket PCs, PDAs, WAP-enabled phones—no one really understands them all. So how do you know the best way to spend your money when it comes to software, accessories and gadgets? Easy. Just check with the Net, where you'll find reviews of everything you can imagine and then some.

Web:
> http://computers.cnet.com/hardware/0-1026.html
> http://computers.cnet.com/hardware/0-1087.html
> http://www.pdabuyersguide.com/
> http://www.pocketpccity.com/reviews.html
> http://www.tekreview.net/
> http://www.the-gadgeteer.com/

Portable Computers Talk and General Discussion

Just having a small computer to take with you wherever you go is not enough. To achieve real happiness, you need to be able to talk about your small computer whenever you feel the need. So here's where the people you need to know hang out on the Net—chat rooms, messageboards, forums, Usenet newsgroups, IRC channels, and mailing lists—where you can discuss the various problems and rewards that go along with your new, improved mobile lifestyle.

Web:

  http://lists.palmpilot.org/
  http://www.palmlife.com/

Usenet:

  alt.comp.sys.palmtops.hp
  alt.comp.sys.palmtops.pilot
  comp.binaries.newton
  comp.sys.handhelds
  comp.sys.newton.announce
  comp.sys.newton.misc
  comp.sys.palmtops
  comp.sys.palmtops.pilot

Listserv Mailing List:

List Name: hplx-l
Subscribe to: listserv@uconnvm.uconn.edu

IRC:

#palmwarez (EFnet, Undernet)

WAP-Enabled Devices

WAP stands for Wireless Application Protocol, a system which allows mobile devices to access Web pages. Most WAP-enabled devices are sophisticated cellular phones that also act as simple Web browsers. The WAP system requires that Web pages use only text and simple monochrome (one color) pictures. For this reason, Web pages must be specially designed if they are to be viewed with a WAP-enabled device. In addition, the pages must be small because the screen size is limited and the data connection speed is relatively slow. WAP pages are created using WML (Wireless Markup Language), which is similar to HTML (the regular Web language). Do you really want WAP? If you are not sure, you can try a simulator on the Net and see what it looks like when you WAP.

Web:

  http://www.awooga.com/
  http://www.wapforum.org/
  http://www.wapuseek.com/
  http://www.wirelessinanutshell.com/wap/

Wearable Computers

As computers become smaller and more powerful, it is only natural to imagine them being ubiquitous to the point where, one day, no matter where you go and no matter what you do, you will have access to a computer and to the Internet. One way to achieve this is to design computers that can be worn within your clothes or on your body. Such wearable computers are being developed around the world, and you don't have to wait for them to arrive in your local mall: the details are on the Net now. I predict that, within our lifetime, not only will we always be near a computer and connected to the Net, but we will also be able to control the devices by thinking and touching. Life is going to change radically, so enjoy the peace and privacy while you can.

Web:

  http://wearables.blu.org/
  http://www.media.mit.edu/wearables/
  http://www.redwoodhouse.com/wearable/

COMPUTERS: REFERENCE

Ascii and HTML Character Codes

Within a computer, data is stored as a series of tiny magnetic or electrical impulses called "bits". Bits store data by using a code, each different character being represented by a particular pattern of bits. There are various code systems, the most common being "ascii" (American Standard Code for Information Interchange), which is used to represent character data in most types of computer files. To make bit patterns easy to understand, each particular code is assigned a number. For example, the ascii code number for the letter "W" is **87**, while the number for a space is **32**. (These numbers are not chosen at random. They make sense when the bit patterns are manipulated mathematically.) Within HTML (the system used to specify the design and content of Web pages), you can use special codes, based on ascii, to indicate various characters. The HTML codes are of the format **&#**, followed by a number, followed by **;**. For example, the HTML code for the copyright symbol (©) is **©**. The code for a long dash (what copy editors call an em dash) is **—**. The number within an HTML code is simply its ascii number. For example, within the ascii code, the copyright symbol is number 169, and the em dash is 151. From time to time, you may need to look up the various ascii or HTML codes, especially if you are designing Web pages. Here are some handy references.

Web:

  http://www.bbsinc.com/symbol.html
  http://www.teletechnics.com/reference/
    ascii_codes.html

> ## Life is an intelligence test. (Don't worry; you passed.)

Beta News

There is an old terminology, used when developing programs, in which a prototype is called an "alpha" version of the program; a working program that still needs significant testing is called the "beta" version; and the final program, ready to ship to customers, is called the "gamma" version. (Alpha, beta and gamma are the names of the first three letters of the Greek alphabet.) In the personal computer industry, it has become the custom for companies to release the beta versions—or "betas"—of programs. By definition, betas are not ready for customer use. However, by getting people to use the betas, software companies get to release their products early. Moreover, as people use betas, they discover bugs (problems), which are often reported to the company. Thus, by releasing the beta version of a program, a software company can beat its competitors to market *and* have its customers test the product for free. In general, it is best to avoid beta software unless you know what you are doing. However, if you do know what you are doing, this Web site will help you keep up on the news, status, fixes and other information so important to those who live in the beta world.

Web:

  http://www.betanews.com/

Bugs and Fixes

A bug is a problem in a computer program, often a mistake in the program itself. A fix is a way to cure the problem or, at least, to work around it. All computer programs have two types of bugs: the ones you know about and the ones you don't know about. (I guarantee that all the programs you are using right now have some bugs in them.)

Web:

  http://www.activewin.com/bugs/
  http://www.bugnet.com/

Usenet:

  comp.bugs.misc

A B C D E F G H I J K L M N O P Q R S T U V W X Y Z

Computer Acronyms

Here's how you can be the most popular person you know. Every day, send each of your friends information about a different computer acronym. For example, say you have three friends, Huey, Dewey and Louie. Send email telling Huey that TAD means "Telephone Answering Device". Send Dewey mail telling him that PAL is "Programmable Array Logic" or "Phase Alternating Line". Send Louie a message that CAD means either "Computer Aided Drafting" or "Computer Aided Design". You will be so popular that it won't be long before you are asked to join the CDC (Cult of the Dead Cow).

Web:

    http://www.acronyms.ch/
    http://www.cis.columbia.edu/glossary.html
    http://www.hiddenlab.com/acronym/
    http://www.kresch.com/ab/ab.htm

Computer Books Online

Macmillan Computer Publishing (the largest computer book publisher in the industry) offers some of their books for free online. Just sign up and you can look at a large variety of technical books. What better way to spend a quiet Saturday night while you are waiting for Star Trek to start?

Web:

    http://www.informit.com/itlibrary/

Computer Companies

Here are many, many links to the Web sites of hardware and software companies around the world. Just type in the name of the company you want, and—click-click—you're at their Web site. I have found these resources to be a great time saver. The next time you are looking for a computer company, start your search here.

Web:

    http://guide.sbanetweb.com/SBA_search.html
    http://www.cmpcmm.com/cc/companies.html
    http://www.slac.stanford.edu/comp/vendor/

Computer Companies

Computer equipment is best when it works perfectly, sitting quietly on your desk doing whatever you want. However, before you can get to that point, you need to (1) find the equipment that is just right for you, and (2) get it up and running.

And, before that magic moment arrives, the time will come when you need to find a particular computer company—to find out what they sell, or to check their Web site for updates, or maybe to get a phone number to ask for tech support.

So don't forget, the information you need to find the company you want is waiting for you on the Net.

Computer News

So much happens in the world of computers; it's difficult to stay current on the latest events. So why not let someone else keep track of it all for you? Here are some news sites that will give you the hot (and cool) scoops on the most important computer-related happenings in the world. Check here every few days and you'll be able to stay up to date with no problem.

Web:

    http://extlab1.entnem.ufl.edu/IH8PCs/
    http://www.educause.edu/pub/edupage/
       edupage.html
    http://www.news.com/
    http://www.newsforge.com/
    http://www.newslinx.com/
    http://www.slashdot.org/

Computer Product Reviews

Before you plunk down a wad of money for a computer or a computer-related product, read the reviews. Money is time, time is knowledge, and knowledge is power. So taking the time you need to save money will make you a powerful person indeed (at least around the house).

Web:
  http://computers.cnet.com/
  http://www.anandtech.com/
  http://www.hardwaremasters.com/
  http://www.reviewfinder.com/
  http://www.streettech.com/
  http://www.zdnet.com/products/

Computer Reseller Ratings

It's certainly convenient to order computer equipment on the Internet or over the phone. However, when you buy things at a distance, you have to be extra careful. This is especially true for computer products, where things that don't work are particularly infuriating and good tech support can be hard to find. So, before you buy something, check out the company, and see what other people think. This is important if you are dealing with a small company for the first time.

Web:
  http://www.resellerratings.com/

Computing Dictionaries

In the 1960s, a lot of people gave their children far out names, like Rainbow, Sunshine and Moon Unit. So what can you do in the twenty-first century? Use a computer dictionary to come up with all kinds of cool ideas. For example, anyone can name their kid Jennifer, Bobby or Stacy. But you know you're dealing with someone special when you meet Proxy Server Mandelbaum, Firewall Jackson, Gif Jeffries, or L. Spam Montgomery.

Web:
  http://www.dooki.com/foldoc/
  http://www.instantweb.com/foldoc/
  http://www.nightflight.com/foldoc/
  http://www.techweb.com/encyclopedia/

COMPUTING DICTIONARIES

No doubt about it. Computers and the Internet are the hot technologies of the current economic cycle. As a full-fledged member of the twenty-first century, you must ensure you are not left out of mainstream culture, so here is what I want you to do.

Before your next big social occasion, connect to one of the Computing Dictionaries and find at least three new technical terms. Then, while you are standing around the cheese dip making conversation, find a way to work these words into the conversation.

It won't be long before you are so popular you'll need a social secretary just to handle all your invitations.

Computing Magazines and Journals

I am going to let you in on a secret. Everyone else in the world has no trouble staying current on everything that is happening in the world of computing. *You* are the only one who is having trouble keeping up. That is why I have put in this resource, just for you. Here you will find links to many different computer magazines and journals. Read long and prosper.

Web:
  http://wnt.utexas.edu/~vclib/journals.cfm

Filename Extensions

On most computer systems, filenames end with a dot (that is, a period) followed by a 1- to 4-letter extension. The extension is a code that indicates what type of data is contained within the file. For example, in the filename **harley.html**, the extension is **html**, which indicates that the file contains a Web page. (Web pages are created using HTML [hypertext markup language].) Another example: in the filename **harley.txt**, the extension (**txt**) shows that the file contains plain text. File extensions are used widely by programs and by operating systems such as Windows. There are literally hundreds of different extensions, although you probably only need to know about 5 or 10 of them. When you encounter a filename with an extension you don't recognize, here are some references to help you track down the information you need.

Web:
  http://www.jozy.nl/
  http://www.silicon-alley.com/ext/
  http://www.wotsit.org/

Hacker's Dictionary

The Hacker's Dictionary (also known as the jargon file") is a venerable reference work: a huge, comprehensive compendium of hacker slang, illuminating many aspects of hacker traditions, folklore and humor. I like the Hacker's Dictionary because it is written by smart people for smart people, and because it is authoritative, well-written and witty.

Web:
  http://www.logophilia.com/jargon/jargon.html
  http://www.tuxedo.org/~esr/jargon/

Macintosh-Windows Integration

Is it possible for PCs and Macintoshes to coexist and live in peace and harmony? It is if you know what you are doing and the computer gods have blessed your efforts. To stack the integration deck in your favor, start by visiting these Web sites where you'll find lots of information on Windows-Macintosh integration. In particular, you'll find out how to put Macs and PCs on the same network without having them fight and pout.

Web:
  http://www.homepcnetwork.com/pcmacovr.htm
  http://www.kan.org/networking/quicknet.html
  http://www.macwindows.com/
  http://www.zocalo.net/~waters/macnt/

PDF (Portable Document Format)

PDF is a system, developed by the Adobe Company, that makes it easy to store pictures of paper documents as computer files. The stored documents must be read with a special program called the Acrobat Reader (which is free). A lot of organizations use PDF to make paper documents accessible via computer. For example, in the United States, the Internal Revenue Service uses PDF to distribute tax forms over the Internet. Actually, that gives me an idea. Next year, I think I am going to use PDF to send money to the IRS.

Web:
  http://www.adobe.com/products/acrobat/
    adobepdf.html
  http://www.foolabs.com/xpdf/
  http://www.pdfzone.com/
  http://www.planetpdf.com/

Usenet:
  comp.text.pdf

Smileys

A smiley is a short sequence of characters that looks like a small smiley face when you look at it sideways. For example, here is the basic smiley: **:-)**. (To see the smiling face, tilt your head sideways to the left.) People use smileys in email, within Usenet articles, and when talking on the Net. The purpose of a smiley is to show a sense of irony, as if you mean to say, "Just kidding." The idea of a smiley has been around for years. Although you only really need the one basic smiley, inventive people have created many different smileys just for fun. For example, here is a smiley with a mustache **:-{**. Wanna see more? Enjoy.

Web:
  http://www.muller-godschalk.com/emoticon.html
  http://www.solscape.com/chat/smileys.html
  http://www.windweaver.com/emoticon.htm

Mathematics is good for you.

Tech Support and Online Help

We all wish that every computer product came with free technical support offered by knowledgeable people. Fat chance. If you have ever waited on the phone for a long time just to talk to a tech support person who knew less than you did, you will understand what I mean when I say that good tech support is hard to find. Except on the Net. Here are some resources you can use to look for answers on many different types of problems. My experience is that, whenever I can, it is a lot easier to find the answer myself than to ask someone else.

Web:

http://www.24hoursupport.com/
http://www.computerhope.com/oh.htm
http://www.helponthe.net/
http://www.virtualdr.com/
http://www.zdnet.com/zdhelp/

Webopaedia

So you have a computer question. Well, chances are someone has already asked that question and, if so, there's a good chance you can find an answer here. This is a searchable database with information about anything and everything you could ever want to know about PCs and Macs. A cross between a dictionary and an encyclopedia, the Webopaedia has tons of information with lots and lots of links to explore.

Web:

http://www.pcwebopaedia.com/

CONNECTING TO THE INTERNET

Cable Modems

You know that thick round cable that brings the TV signal into your home? Well, the cable companies have developed ways to use that very same cable to give you Internet connectivity. To connect to the Net in this way, you need an Ethernet card in your computer along with a small box called a cable modem. But don't sweat the details, the cable company will do it all for you. The service is not available everywhere, but if it's in your area, you should definitely consider it. The speed will be very fast: not as fast as the cable company promises—after all, *everyone* in the connectivity business lies about speed—but a lot faster than regular modem access or even ISDN. And once it's all set up, you will have a permanent, 24-hour-a-day Internet connection without having to use (or pay for) a second telephone line.

Web:

http://www.cable-modem.net/
http://www.cable-modems.org/
http://www.cabledatacomnews.com/cmic/
http://www.cablemodeminfo.com/
http://www.catv.org/

DSL

DSL (Digital Subscriber Line) is a system that provides high-speed Internet connections over a regular phone line without interfering with the voice service. DSL is much faster than a dialup connection (using a regular modem) or ISDN. I can't tell you an exact speed because phone companies offer various services, but, at a minimum, you should be able to get several hundred bps (bits per second) and perhaps much faster. Unlike a dialup connection, a DSL connection is always turned on. Thus, once you install DSL, you are connected permanently to the Net until you either stop the service or die (whichever comes first).

Web:
  http://www.dsllife.com/
  http://www.dslreports.com/
  http://www.faqs.org/faqs/datacomm/xdsl-faq/
  http://www.thedslzone.com/
  http://www.xdsl.com/

IRC:
  #adsl.no (EFnet)
  #dsl (EFnet)

Frame Relay

Frame relay is a multiplexed interface to a packet-switched network. With frame relay you have a leased line that supports a high-speed connection to the Net, from 56 K bits per second to T1 (1.536 M bps) and beyond. I have a frame relay line to my house, and let me tell you, if you can live through getting the thing up and running, it's great. During the many times I was put on hold by various engineers, receptionists and technical support people, I found it helpful to do a little reading about the technology. By the time everything's going, you'll probably end up learning more about frame relay than you ever wanted to know, but then, life's funny that way.

Web:
  http://www.alliancedatacom.com/framerelay.asp
  http://www.dcbnet.com/notes/framerly.html
  http://www.frforum.com/basicsguide.html

Usenet:
  comp.dcom.frame-relay

Internet Service Providers

Once you are on the Net, you become dependent on your Internet service provider (ISP). Unfortunately, many people don't appreciate how important this relationship really is. A good ISP can make a big difference in making your time on the Internet comfortable and satisfying, so don't make the mistake of choosing your ISP as casually as you might choose a university, or an employer, or a spouse. Do your homework now, and you'll avoid a lot of regret later.

Internet Cafes

An Internet cafe is a combination store/restaurant where you can enjoy food while using the Net. Some cafes offer free Internet access; others charge for the service. Some also offer extra computer services, like being able to use word processing or graphics programs. There are Internet cafes all around the world, which means that when you travel, you don't need to be cut off from your daily Internet experience or your email. More importantly, by visiting an Internet cafe, you can combine the three fundamental human activities: eating, drinking and using the Net.

Web:
  http://cybercafe.katchup.co.nz/search.asp
  http://www.curiouscat.com/travel/cybercafe.cfm
  http://www.cybercaptive.com/

Internet Service Providers

An Internet service provider (ISP) is a company or organization that provides access to the Internet. For example, if you have a computer at home, you access the Net by having your computer connect to an ISP. Here are some resources to help you find an ISP that serves your area. (If you do not already have access, ask a friend who does to help you out by checking the lists for you.) For discussion about Internet access, you can read the Usenet groups.

Web:
  http://thelist.internet.com/
  http://www.cnet.com/internet/
  http://www.herbison.com/herbison/
    iap_meta_list.html
  http://www.internet.com/sections/isp.html

Usenet:
  alt.internet.access.wanted
  alt.internet.services

ISDN

ISDN is a type of telephone service that is an alternative to a regular phone line. (The name stands for "Integrated Services Digital Network".) The advantage of ISDN is it allows you to connect to another computer at a speed that is much faster than even the fastest modem. If ISDN is available in your area, you should consider it as an alternative to using a modem with a regular phone line. (On the Internet, there is no such thing as too much speed.) To learn more about ISDN, start with these Net resources. Then call your local telephone company and see if ISDN is available. Getting ISDN working can be a lot more hassle than using a modem, but it's worth it. ISDN is fast and, once it's all set up, you'll love it.

Web:
  http://hea-www.harvard.edu/~fine/ISDN/
  http://support.intel.com/support/isdn/
  http://www.isdnzone.com/

Usenet:
  comp.dcom.isdn

Modems

One of the most common ways to connect to the Net is by using a computer with a modem to access an Internet service provider over a regular telephone line. The modem provides the interface between your computer and the phone line. Modem technology has improved tremendously over the years. I remember when the "standard" was 300 bps (bits per second). The current standard, referred to as V.90, is now 56K bps (56,000 bps). Hint: Although the 56K modems are fast compared to the older modems, they are still much too slow. You are better off with DSL, cable modems or ISDN (in that order), if they are available in your area.

Web:
  http://modems.rosenet.net/
  http://www.56k.com/
  http://www.modemhelp.com/
  http://www.modems.com/
  http://www.v90.com/

Usenet:
  comp.dcom.modems
  comp.sys.ibm.pc.hardware.comm
  misc.forsale.computers.modems

WebTV

WebTV is a system that lets you access the Internet without a PC. All you need is a WebTV Internet terminal (which you must buy) and a television set. The WebTV Internet terminal is a special box that connects to your TV and to a phone line. You also need to pay a subscription fee, just like you do with a regular Internet service provider. The advantage of WebTV is that the box is cheaper than a PC, and the system is easy to install and use. However, the box does not run regular software: all it can do is access the Internet. For example, you can't use Windows or any programs that use Windows. Still, I will tell you that when I first saw WebTV, I was pleasantly surprised at how well it worked.

Web:
 http://www.ruel.net/top.box.news/
 http://www.warpspeedhelp.com/
  webtvdirectory.html
 http://www.webtv.net/

CONSUMER INFORMATION

Automobile Lemons

A "lemon law" obligates a car manufacturer or a car seller to repair or replace a defective automobile or refund your money. If you suspect you have a "lemon", check out these Web pages to see how you can be recompensed. These sites have information about consumer strategies and the applicable laws for lemons.

Web:
 http://www.autopedia.com/Lemon/
 http://www.california-lemon-laws-auto-fraud.com/
 http://www.nhtsa.dot.gov/cars/problems/complain/

Better Business Bureau

The Better Business Bureau (BBB) promotes good business/consumer relations. At the BBB site, you can find local bureaus, read consumer warnings and related news, file a complaint online, read consumer buying guides, or obtain a report on a company or charity. Find out what the Better Business Bureau can do for you.

Web:
 http://www.bbb.org/

Consumer Information Catalog

When it's late at night and you need a little something to read, check out the Consumer Information Center, which was established in 1970 to help federal agencies and departments develop, promote and distribute consumer information to the masses. Four times a year, the Consumer Information Catalog is published. This jewel has descriptive listings of hundreds of booklets from all sorts of federal agencies covering topics like buying a car, building a career, federal benefits and housing information. You can order a free copy of the Consumer Information Catalog by filling out this handy-dandy Web form.

Web:
 http://www.pueblo.gsa.gov/

Consumer Law

Find out your rights as a consumer. This Web site offers information on various consumer pitfalls such as insurance fraud, product liability, toxic chemicals, bodily injury, and more. You will also find links to consumer law resources and information on how to file consumer complaints. There is lots and lots of information here, making it a good place to browse when you have a few spare moments.

Web:
 http://www.consumerlawpage.com/

Consumer Line

The Federal Trade Commission's Bureau of Consumer Protection has an online service called "Consumer Line". This service offers lots and lots and lots of online brochures relating to consumer protection. These brochures can inform you about art fraud, repossessions, financing scams, product purchases, and much, much more. Increase your consumer savvy by visiting this site.

Web:
 http://www.ftc.gov/ftc/consumer.htm

Consumer News

Real news about real products bought by real consumers (you). Find out what is happening before the Joneses do.

Web:
  http://www.bbb.org/alerts/
  http://www.ftc.gov/ftc/news.htm

Consumer Product Safety Commission

If you think you are safe because you stay home all the time and play on the Internet, think again. There are all sorts of dangers lurking around your house, just waiting to get you. That's why people in America have the Consumer Product Safety Commission (CPSC): an independent federal regulatory agency whose mission is to keep citizens safe from harmful products such as badly designed cribs, toy boxes or television remote controls. Here's the CPSC official site where you can find their latest news or report an unsafe product.

Web:
  http://www.cpsc.gov/

Consumer Ratings

When it comes time to buy that brand new something-or-other, how do you know which brand of new something-or-other to buy? Easy. Check with the Net, where you'll find reviews and ratings on any consumer item or pastime you can imagine: household products, cars, computers, video games, electronics, sports equipment, books, movies, restaurants, and much, much more. Every now and then, someone telephones me and asks something like, "Harley, do you have any idea what type of kitchen knives I should buy?" I say, "Hold on a second, I have to make some tuna tea for my cat." It is the work of a moment for me to put my friend on hold, check one of these Web sites and learn all about kitchen knives. I then pick up the phone and say, "Okay, I'm back. Now what did you want to know about? Kitchen knives?" And then I sound like an expert (and you can too).

Web:
  http://www.consumerguide.com/
  http://www.consumerreview.com/
  http://www.productopia.com/

Consumer Resources

I think the word "consumer" is dumb. You read about consumer-this or consumer-that, as if a consumer is a special type of person with special problems that don't affect anyone else. ("Consumers to pay more for gasoline this summer.") The reality is that we are *all* consumers, and anything that has to do with buying and selling can affect us all. If you're like me, you love finding ways to beat the system. Wouldn't it be nice to save money and protect your privacy while you are consuming? I just found out how to keep the credit agencies from selling my personal information (which they are allowed to do in the U.S.).

Web:
  http://www.clarkhoward.com/
  http://www.consumerworld.org/

Consumer Talk and General Discussion

Here are Usenet's general consumer forums. Send in your questions, share your answers, read the reviews, opinions, and general bad-mouthing of the bad guys. Before you spend your next dime, check with the world at large.

Usenet:

    alt.consumers.experiences
    misc.consumers

Credit

We're in a fast-moving world, and it is a rare person who is not hard-pressed to keep up with the popular culture. One crucial area of modern life is money and how it affects your credit. A good way to make sure you are capable of minding your financial Ps and Qs is to read the credit information on the Net, and prepare yourself to face the brave new financial world with confidence and style.

Web:

    http://consumers.creditnet.com/
    http://www.cardweb.com/
    http://www.creditinfocenter.com/

Frauds, Scams and Rips-offs

There is a massive amount of fraud in the world, and the best way to avoid it is to be able to recognize it. Before you lose your money, take some time to read about chain letters, "free" prizes, "free" vacations, 900-numbers, foreign lotteries, personal finance-related schemes, multilevel marketing, work-at-home schemes, telephone solicitations, and much more. If you think you have been the victim of fraud, you may be able to find help on the Net. Most fraud is perpetuated by dishonest swindlers, but you can protect yourself by not allowing yourself to be a victim. There is something about the thought of free money that makes people so greedy that they are willing to throw their judgment out the window. Please remember, if someone is offering you a deal that sounds too good to be true, it *is* too good to be true.

Web:

    http://www.badbusinessbureau.com/
    http://www.sec.gov/investor.shtml
    http://www.usps.gov/websites/depart/inspect/
       consmenu.htm

Free Stuff

There is free stuff out there in the world, just waiting for you to ask for it. You can get all kinds of cool things for free—phone calls, food, clothes, recipes, tickets and endless samples of miscellany—just for asking. All the information is here, so clean out the garage in order to make room for more stuff.

Web:

    http://www.1freestuff.com/
    http://www.freestuffcenter.com/
    http://www.freestuffcentral.com/
    http://www.freevault.com/
    http://www.hotfreesite.com/
    http://www.prospector.cz/
    http://www.thefreesite.com/Other_Freebie_Sites/

Usenet:

    alt.consumers.free-stuff

Funeral Planning

Don't let the cost of dying ruin your day. When someone dies, the last thing you feel like doing is attending to all the details of arranging a funeral. So do yourself a favor and let the Net help. Use these resources to answer your questions and to give you the information you need. (Personally, I'd rather be caught dead than to be the guest of honor in a poorly planned, disorganized funeral.)

Web:

    http://www.ftc.gov/bcp/conline/pubs/services/
       funeral.htm
    http://www.funeralnet.com/faq.html
    http://www.funerals.org/

Internet Fraud

In May 2000, the United States FBI and NW3C (National White Collar Crime Center) established the Internet Fraud Complaint Center (IFCC). According to the IFCC, the most important types of Internet fraud are in the areas of online auctions (65%), non-delivered merchandise (22%), and credit cards (5%). It is important to understand that there is no Internet police force and no one to help you if you get into trouble. (The IFCC's job is to gather statistics and help the FBI track down criminals.) I cover Internet fraud and how to avoid it, in detail, in my book *Harley Hahn's Internet Insecurity* (published by Prentice Hall PTR). In case you don't have the book, here is the best advice I can give you. Repeat after me: "If I get scammed on the Internet, no one is going to help me."

Web:
  http://www.fraud.org/
  http://www.ftc.gov/bcp/conline/edcams/dotcon/
  http://www.ifccfbi.gov/
  http://www.scambusters.com/
  http://www.sec.gov/investor/online.shtml

Junk Mail

Perhaps somewhere in the universe (say, on the planet Pluto), there is someone who actually likes junk mail, but I don't. I don't like the idea of my address being sold and resold by junk mailers, and I don't like my mailbox being filled with, well, junk. It's not just the inconvenience; after all, it's not hard to throw away junk mail. It's an emotional thing. I like to have control over my life, and I don't like junk mailers (or telemarketers or spammers) buying and selling personal information about me. If you are like me, you will appreciate learning how to remove yourself from the lists used by the junk mailers and other such direct marketing scum.

Web:
  http://www.cpsr.org/cpsr/privacy/junkmail.html
  http://www.ecofuture.org/jnkmail.html
  http://www.junkbusters.com/
  http://www.the-dma.org/help/consumerfaqs.shtml

National Institute for Consumer Education

Do you know anyone who needs to learn about consumer issues? The National Institute for Consumer Education (a NICE organization) has information about fraud, credit, finance, bankruptcy, credit cards, car leasing, and much more. I say, if you're going to consume, do it knowledgeably.

Web:
  http://www.nice.emich.edu/

Product Recalls

As we enjoy our excellent adventure of living in the twenty-first century, let us take a moment to appreciate how much *stuff* we have. Yes, stuff is good, and stuff is important, but sometimes stuff doesn't work right. In such cases, there may be an official recall, telling you that a particular item is unsafe or defective, and you can return it for an exchange or refund. My advice is to spend a few moments checking out these resources, where you will find the latest scoop on product recalls. After all, good stuff is good, but bad stuff is bad (and you can quote me).

Web:
  http://www.cpsc.gov/cpscpub/prerel/prerel.html
    http://www.fda.gov/opacom/7alerts.html
  http://www.recallannouncements.com/
  http://www.safetyalerts.com/

Tipping

The thing about tipping is, if you don't do it right, you won't be a welcome customer. And if you aren't a welcome customer, a lot of strange things are going to happen to your food you would rather not know about. So learn about tipping: when, why and how much. Nothing is more suave than a man who nonchalantly offers exactly the right tip without even thinking about it (unless it is a woman who offers exactly t r t w e t a i).

Web:

> http://www.emilypost.com/etiquette_tips/
>   holiday_tipping.htm
> http://www.tipping.org/

Unclaimed Property

Wow! Free money! There are a variety of ways in which you might be entitled to money you don't even know about. For example, you may have left money in a bank account a long time ago. Or you may have an unclaimed utility deposit, insurance benefit, stock certificate or safety deposit box. In the United States, each state has rules as to how such property must be handled. In general, the state keeps track of it all and allows people to reclaim their lost treasures. The trick is, of course, to find your unclaimed property. Some people pay money to commercial services, some of which are scams. Even if they are legitimate, such services will take 10%-50% of the total amount. It is not necessary for you to pay for such information, as you can search on the Net for free. As I was researching this item, it happened that a friend of mine was sitting next to me watching me work. "Let's try your name," I suggested, so we did and—Wow! Free money!—in less time than it is taking you to read this sentence right now, we found money that she had left in an abandoned bank account. All she had to do is file a claim (which is free) and the money was hers.

Web:

> http://webinfosearch.com/money/
> http://www.bankrate.com/brm/news/bank/
>   19990420a.asp
> http://www.missingmoney.com/
> http://www.nupd.com/

Academic Competitions

When I was a kid, there was a weekend television program called College Bowl in which two four-person teams represented their schools in a fast-paced academic quiz contest. The idea was that the moderator (Allen Ludden and, later, Robert Earle) would offer a "toss-up" question. Whichever contestant pressed a buzzer first would get to answer the question. If he or she was correct, the team would get points and a chance to answer a bonus question. College Bowl was a perennial favorite among smart kids, who loved to play along at home and see if they could answer the questions faster than the kids on TV. Here are two questions from the original College Bowl: Who gave an Apple to Aphrodite and ran away with Helen? What is CIV minus XXXIX? Today, there are a large number of academic competitions, so if you are a smart kid, you'll find plenty of ways to compete against others of your kind. (Just in case you're not a smart kid, the answers to the two questions are Paris and LXV.)

Web:

> http://www.collegebowl.com/archives/history.shtml
> http://www.naqt.com/
> http://www.odysseyofthemind.com/
> http://www.usad.org/

Usenet:

> alt.college.college-bowl

Contest Advice

If you get into serious contesting, you need to get serious about contests. Read this info to learn how to protect your privacy, stay off the spam (unsolicited mail) lists, know what laws apply to you, and best of all, how to increase your chances of being a winner. (Of course, as one of my readers, you are already a winner in my book.)

Web:

> http://www.onlinesweeps.com/hints.html
> http://www.thewinnersclub.net/hints/

Contest Talk and General Discussion

This is the Usenet group devoted to announcing new contests. You will also find discussion about contests as well as questions and answers. If you like contests, this is a good place to check regularly.

Usenet:
  alt.consumers.sweepstakes

Debating

Debating is a great way to use your firm grasp of logic, your wide base of interesting knowledge, your articulate delivery, and your ability to think extremely quickly, in a way that allows you to prove that you are right and everyone else is wrong. What could be more fun?

Web:
  http://www.debatabase.org/
  http://www.idebate.org/
  http://www.political-debate.org/

Usenet:
  alt.speech.debate

Listserv Mailing List:
  List Name: udl
  Subscribe to: listserv@list.uvm.edu

Hollywood Stock Exchange

Do you think you could pick which films will be winners better than the Hollywood movie moguls? Of course you can, and here is your chance to prove it. Try your hand at this addictive online game, where *you* choose which movies and which stars will be successful. Create your "portfolio" and start to wheel and deal. Then watch your fortune go up and down based on real box office grosses of real films.

Web:
  http://www.hsx.com/

Online Lotteries

In this book, I only put in resources that are free, and these lotteries are no exception. You can enter, wait for the results, and find out you've lost without ever having to pay a cent. So how do they make any money? Hmm... I guess they try to get you to buy something, show you advertisements, and sell your email address to other people who will try to get you to buy something, show you advertisements, and sell your email address to other people who... (But then, we can't all be winners.)

Web:
  http://www.cashbreak.com/
  http://www.freebielotto.com/
  http://www.freelotto.com/
  http://www.lottopol.com/
  http://www.luckysurf.com/

Science Competitions

Now, let's be honest here. Isn't it a lot more fun to work on a fascinating project for a science fair, something that requires knowledge, skill and persistence, rather than being parked in the living room watching TV or playing video games? Of course it is. And, if you're a guy, the best part is that when you grow up, you'll find out that scientists get all the good babes. (Everyone knows that.)

Web:

   http://physics.usc.edu/ScienceFairs/
   http://www.envirothon.org/
   http://www.intel.com/education/sts/
   http://www.siemens-foundation.org/science/
     science_and_technology.htm
   http://www.soinc.org/

Spelling Bee

Would you know how to spell "prospicienc? That's the word that a young man named Pratyush Buddiga had to spell in order to win the final (11th) round of the 2002 Scripps Howard National Spelling Bee. A spelling bee is a contest in which people compete against one another to see who is the best speller. Spelling bees are organized into rounds. In each round, the individual contestants are each asked to spell a word, one person at a time. Only those people who spell their word correctly may move on to the next round. Eventually, only one person—the winner—is left. Spelling bees can use easy or difficult words. With easy words, you can have a spelling bee with young kids, even those who are just learning to read. The National Spelling Bee is a championship in which very difficult words are used. For more information about this contest, take a look at its Web page. I enjoyed looking at the round-by-round descriptions, seeing exactly which words were used. By the way, "prospicience" refers to the act of looking forward.

Web:

   http://www.spellingbee.com/

Spelling Bee

What do all these words have in common?

amaryllis antonomasia ayatollah boutade calceus campodeiform carmagnole cassoulet Catullian chemisette cheongsam chevelure churrasco coelostat connoisseur daven decussate divagate dossier dysphemism emolument ephemeris exsuccous femoral folletto hambo heaume hieroglyphics hussar jalousie Keynesian laparoscopy lauan mandir manes merganser metheglin micaceous mitochondrion nepenthe Nereid notacanthous nudicaulous nunchaku Ogygian Pansil peccavi pentastich peripteral phaeton Philomel pickelhaube porphyry proboscis quatrefoil riant sabin schismatic Scylla seguidilla semainier sevillana sillar soubise spondylitis suzerain telos tetragrammaton thalassocrat tintinnabulary trophallaxis ulotrichous uncinus vacillate zaibatsu

They are all words that people spelled wrong in the first round of the 2002 National Spelling Bee.

Sports Contests

Your sports experience doesn't have to be limited to sitting around watching television. You can sit around testing your hard-won sports knowledge on the Net by entering the monthly contests sponsored by the World Wide Collectors Network. Not only will you impress your friends with your mastery of the esoteric, you may even win a prize.

Web:

   http://ww3.sportsline.com/u/contests/
   http://www.ipredictthat.com/
   http://www.playfive.com/

Sweepstakes and Contests

Here's a gold mine of sweepstakes and contest information for both children and adults. These sites include instant win sweeps, writing contests, freebie pages and links to other sweepstakes pages. Win, win, win, win. (That's my advice.)

Web:
    http://www.cashnetsweeps.com/
    http://www.contestguide.com/
    http://www.huronline.com/
    http://www.online-sweepstakes.com/
    http://www.sweeps.ws/
    http://www.sweepstalk.com/
    http://www.thewinnersclub.net/

> Today may be your lucky day, but there is only one way to find out. Connect to the Sweepstakes and Contests site, and see what destiny has in store for you.

Treasure Hunts

Have you ever been on a real-live treasure hunt, where you follow one clue after another, looking for something special? Go ahead, form a team with your friends and try it. As one of my readers, you are smarter than everyone else, so I have no doubt you'll be able to find the treasure while everyone else is still trying to figure out the first clue.

Web:
    http://www.treasurehunt.com/

Vacation and Travel Contests

If you don't want to spend your hard-earned money on a vacation, you can always try to win a vacation in a contest. Here is a Web site where you can enter a variety of contests to win vacation-oriented prizes. Of course, if you did win a free trip, you would have to leave your computer and a lot of email would accumulate while you were away. Oh well, nothing is perfect.

Web:
    http://www.1worldfilms.com/travelcontests.htm

COOKING AND RECIPES

Asian Cooking

Asian cuisine embraces a wonderful variety of flavors, fragrances and tastes. When you feel adventurous, take a gustatory tour of the Orient by trying something new. You'll find recipes for Chinese (including various regional dishes), Japanese, Filipino, Indian, Thai, Hawaiian, Vietnamese, Korean and Indonesian food. (Need a suggestion? Try a recipe for Pad Thai from Thailand.)

Web:
    http://paml.alastra.com/recipes/asian/
    http://www.asiafood.org/
    http://www.orientalfood.com/recipe/

Usenet:
    alt.food.asian

Backcountry Recipes

When you are heading to the outback, make sure you are prepared. There's nothing worse than getting into the middle of nowhere, and suddenly having a big craving for a barbecued chicken wing. Here are some recipes to use when you go backpacking, hiking and camping. Learn about trail snacks, dinners, breakfasts, meat dishes and desserts that are easy to bring along whether you are going to hike up a mountain or just spend the afternoon in downtown New York.

Web:
    http://www.adventuresports.com/asap/camping/
       recipe.htm
    http://www.desertusa.com/lil.html
    http://www.macscouter.com/cooking/
    http://www.melborponsti.com/camping/

Barbecue

You know what I like after a hard day of writing? A whacking big carrot stick, doused with a liberal helping of spicy barbecue sauce, and roasted slowly over an open flame. However, if vegetarian is not your style, take a look at some of the smoking-and-curing resources on the Net, where I guarantee you'll find enough information to choke a cumin-rubbed Boston butt. And if you find a tempting recipe for slow-roasted barbecued carrot, try it in my honor and see how close you can get to heaven on Earth.

Web:
  http://new.mega-zine.com/kitchen/barbecue/
  http://www.recipeamerica.com/recipes/
    barbecue.htm
  http://www.southernbarbecue.com/recipes.htm

Usenet:
  alt.food.barbecue

Majordomo Mailing List:
  List Name: barbecue
  Subscribe to: majordomo@ipass.net

Bread Recipes

Let me make a confession: I love bread. My favorites are rye bread and challah (and my birthday is December 21). If you are also a bread lover, what could be more fun than making your own? My advice is to figure out how much you need, and then make twice as much. (You can never have too much bread.)

Web:
  http://www.breadrecipe.com/
  http://www.cs.cmu.edu/~mjw/recipes/bread/

Usenet:
  rec.food.baking
  2rec.food.sourdough

Can Sizes

A friend of mine was using a recipe that called for a #2 can of tomatoes, but she didn't know what that meant. So, I used the Net and found out that a #2 can holds 2.5 cups. Then, we lived happily ever after. (And that's a true story.)

Web:
  http://www.amescompany.com/can_sizes.htm
  http://www.cookbooks.org/can.shtml
  http://www.gracefoods.com/charts/can.asp
  http://www.vegweb.com/glossary/docs/
    janan319.shtml

Candy Recipes

When it's midnight and the stores are closed and you are having a big Attack of the Killer Sweet Tooth, get out the pots and pans, and whip up some of these exotic specimens, such as Turkish delight, peanut butter balls, candied apple slices, and many more.

Web:
  http://www.candyusa.org/recipes/recipesindex.shtml
  http://www.caymandesigns.com/candy.htm
  http://www.recipesource.com/desserts/candy/
    indexall.html

Cookie Recipes

Everybody has his or her own favorite type of cookie. Mine are made from organic seaweed, brewer's yeast, whey and (for fiber) biodegradable sawdust. However, if you happen to be one of those people who is not a health food junkie, your taste in cookies may be a tad more mainstream. If so, check out these Web sites for more cookie recipes than you could use in a month of Sunday bake sales.

Web:
  http://www.christmas-cookies.com/
  http://www.cookierecipe.com/

Make a Cookie

I bet that, right now, you need a cookie.

And not just any cookie. I bet you need a delicious, aromatic, homemade cookie.

Here's a great idea: go to the Cookie Recipes Web site, find something that looks good, and get a batch in the oven as fast as you can.

Do you realize that, in less than half an hour, you could have a freshly baked cookie in your mouth?

Now *that's* what I call an idea.

Cooking at High Altitudes

At a high altitude, the air pressure is lower. As a result, water boils at a lower temperature, which means that boiling water is not as hot on the top of a mountain as it is at sea level. Similarly, the low air pressure causes baked goods to rise significantly faster than they do at a low altitude. Thus, if you are cooking or baking at a high altitude, you will find it useful to get some special knowledge to ensure that everything you create turns out to be as perfect as you are.

Web:
　http://www.allrecipes.com/cb/kh/cake/altitude/
　http://www.cahe.nmsu.edu/pubs/_e/e-215.html
　http://www.crisco.com/hi_alt.htm
　http://www.gofallon.com/cookingtips.htm

Cooking Resources

If you're like me, you divide your time between the kitchen and the Internet. If so, here are some fabulously valuable cooking resources that will make life complete. These resources can help you find anything you need in the world of food, and I mean *anything*. You'll find extensive archives of recipes, as well as cooking tips, articles, FAQs (frequently asked question lists), cooking software, and nutrition information. There are also discussion groups and chat facilities. For example, you can post a message asking if anybody has a recipe for fried groat clusters and check back later to see the responses. So whenever you can't stand the heat in the kitchen, hang out on the Net, where something good is always cooking.

Web:
　http://eat.epicurious.com/tips/
　http://www.cheftalk.com/
　http://www.culinary.net/
　http://www.cyber-kitchen.com/
　http://www.faqs.org/faqs/cooking/faq/
　http://www.switcheroo.com/

Cooking Talk and General Discussion

If you like messing around the kitchen and trying out new recipes, there are lots of people on the Net who will love to talk to you. Join one or all of the cooking discussion groups, and talk about cooking techniques, equipment, recipes, vegetarianism, and so on. Usenet is a great place to trade tips and techniques, and to ask questions about things culinary.

Usenet:
　alt.cooking-chat
　alt.creative-cook
　alt.creative-cooking
　rec.food.cooking

Cooking Terminology

You're at a fancy restaurant and the waiter suggests the table d'hôte. Your best friend calls and asks, "Would you like to come over and help me do some sousing?" You are reading a recipe book and the author suggests that you add some zest to the fruit dish you are preparing for brunch. What are these people talking about? All it takes is a few minutes with the Net and you'll be able to understand any cooking term, no matter how obscure. For example, a table d'hôte is a complete meal, in which several courses are served for the price of an entree; sousing refers to pickling food in brine or vinegar; and zest is made by grating the peel of a citrus fruit.

Web:
　http://www.epicurious.com/run/fooddictionary/
　　home
　http://www.nutribase.com/cookingt.shtml
　http://www.pheast.com/glossary/
　http://www.sunset.com/Reference/FoodRef/
　　FoodGlossary.html

Diabetic Recipes

If you are a diabetic, you know you have to be extra careful about your diet. For this reason, you probably know more about nutritious cooking than other people. To augment your repertoire, here are some great collections of recipes for diabetics, including dishes you would think you could never eat, such as apple dumplings, double fudge balls, fruit cookies and chocolate banana mousse. You will also find other useful resources, such as information on sugar replacements.

Web:
  http://www.childrenwithdiabetes.com/
    d_08_200.htm
  http://www.diabeticgourmet.com/
  http://www.recipesource.com/special-diets/diabetic/

Famous Recipes

From time to time, I like to paint and, right now, I have one of my abstract paintings hanging over the fireplace. Sometimes I look at it and think, if only this painting had been done by a famous artist, it would be hanging in a museum and worth $40,000. Sometimes it's the same way with food. We value certain preparations because they are created by well-known restaurants or TV chefs. So, just to prove that you can cook in the big leagues, here are some famous recipes (some of which are secret) guaranteed to make *you* the most famous cook in your household.

Web:
  http://www.topsecretrecipes.com/
  http://www.tvguidelive.com/celebchef/

Are you looking for a good excuse to have a party? See "Holidays and Celebrations".

Fish

Cooking fish is the test of your culinary abilities. Nothing is better than fresh fish, prepared well and cooked properly. On the other hand, old fish cooked poorly is about as rank a foodstuff as you would ever hope to meet. This is why I like this Web site. There are lots of hints, tips and recipes for preparing fish, including a wonderful fish-cooking glossary. My lawyer Bill goes fishing a lot, and sometimes he and his wife Wendy invite me over for a dinner of fresh salmon. Talk about good cooking: I can taste it now. If you ever run into Bill, be sure to tell him you are one of my readers, and ask for a piece of fish. (I'm sure he'll give you one. After all, it's a business expense.)

Web:
  http://www.cookeryonline.com/Fish/
  http://www.fish4fun.com/seafoodrecipes.htm
  http://www.gortons.com/cookbook/

Food Preservation

I love food preservation. For example, right now, I have a 74-day-old pickle in my fridge. (It's actually part of an important biology experiment, but I can't share the details until I am ready to publish.) If you like preserving and processing food and you have higher aspirations than simple pickle preservation, I've got some info here that will keep you busy from now to the next harvest. Learn how to perform all kinds of food miracles: can fruits and vegetables, make your own jams and jellies, cure meat, and even conjure up your very own pickles.

Web:
  http://www.ag.uiuc.edu/~vista/html_pubs/drying/
    dryfood.html
  http://www.foodpres.com/
  http://www.msucares.com/health/food_preservation/
  http://www.nths.newtrier.k12.il.us/library/
    preservation.html
  http://www.seasonalchef.com/preserver.htm

Usenet:
  rec.food.preserving

French Cooking

Some people pooh-pooh French cooking. They say that it uses too much butter, that it's too fattening, that the rich sauces are used to hide meat of dubious quality and that any food that can't be prepared by warming it in a microwave is too complex and intricate for day-to-day consumption. My philosophy is: if it's good enough for Zsa Zsa Gabor, it's good enough for me (and *she's* not even French).

Web:
   http://cook.subportal.com/recipes/C66/listC66-1.html
   http://www.afrenchkiss.com/
   http://www.allrecipes.com/directory/883.asp
   http://www.frenchpastrychef.com/pastry/
      pastrychef.htm
   http://www.recipesource.com/ethnic/europe/french/
      indexall.html

Historical Food

If you want some really old food, besides the scary stuff at the back of the refrigerator, try whipping up something from a historical recipe. After all, what better way to enjoy the past than to chow down on some Byzantine murri, Ratafia cream or buttered wortes?

Web:
   http://www.bahnhof.se/~chimbis/tocb/
   http://www.pbm.com/~lindahl/food.html

Usenet:
   rec.food.historic

Home Canning

Home canning can be a lot of fun, and it sure is nice to be able to go to the pantry whenever you want and pull out a can of your favorite fruit, vegetable or jam. However, to guard against spoilage and contamination, you need to make sure that you do everything just so. Before you can, check out these tips and recipes. Remember, as your third grade teacher would say, if something's worth canning, it's worth canning well.

Web:
   http://www.canning-food-recipes.com/
   http://www.homecanning.com/

Indian Cooking

When I am in the mood for Indian food, I don't always have the time to hop on a plane and travel to India. On these occasions, it's easier just to find a recipe from the Net and make it in my own kitchen. You can do it, too. Set up the computer in the kitchen, point your Web browser to these sites and follow along. In no time, you will have a delightful meal prepared in your own home, without the side effect of jet lag and the red tape that comes with traveling to another country.

Web:
   http://www.gadnet.com/recipes.htm
   http://www.indianrecipes.com/
   http://www.welcometoindia.com/cuisine/index.asp

Insect Recipes

If you are having a party, these Web sites offer the perfect recipes for little appetizers. Insects are not only freely found in the environment, but they make perfect finger food. Try some dry-roasted leafhoppers or Army worms. For dipping, use the rootworm beetle dip or for dessert try my personal favorite: the chocolate chirpie chip cookies.

Web:

http://www.eatbug.com/
http://www.ent.iastate.edu/misc/insectsasfood.html
http://www.naturenode.com/recipes/
   recipes_insects.html
http://www.planetscott.com/babes/

An Unexpected Treat

What do you do when your mother-in-law and your boss drop in unexpectedly for dinner at the same time?

You could reheat that leftover tuna surprise, or whip up a family-sized potful of macaroni and cheese, but that is *so* cliché and would impress nobody.

Instead, why not connect to the Net and try some of the **Insect Recipes**? Insect dishes are stylish, unusual and a good source of protein. After all, why let people bug you when you can bug them first?

Italian Cooking

Can't tell your cannellini from your cannoli or your fontina from your fontinella? Don't worry. The Net can make you an Italian know-it-all in no-time-at-all. These Web sites have recipes for pasta, appetizers and main dishes. Or you can read an Italian cooking glossary so you can enunciate your pancetta with the best of them.

Web:

http://www.cimorelli.com/pie/mangia/
   mangmenu.htm
http://www.eat.com/cookbook/

Jewish Cooking

My most pleasant childhood memories are the Friday nights my family would go to my grandparents' home for dinner. I liked everything my grandmother cooked, but my favorite was chicken soup. She would make it with carrots, celery, parsnips and a bit of parsley, and serve it with kasha and thin noodles. I would load up my bowl and eat so much soup that I hardly had room for anything else, but that didn't bother me. As long as I had my grandmother's chicken soup, God was in his heaven and all was right with the world. (Boy, do I ever miss her.)

Web:

http://www.cyber-kitchen.com/rfcj/
http://www.jewfaq.org/food.htm
http://www.jewish.com/food/
http://www.kashrut.com/recipes/
http://www.kosher.co.il/
http://www.koshercooking.com/recipes/

Usenet:

rec.food.cuisine.jewish

Low-Fat and Fat-Free Recipes

Whether you are staying away from fat for dieting or health reasons, you still need some good recipes. The Net has lots of tasty ways of preparing food with less fat. You don't have to feel deprived, because here are recipes for bread, salads, cookies, casseroles, pizza and a variety of ethnic foods.

Web:

http://www.anitasrecipes.com/browserecipes/
http://www.faqs.org/faqs/food/fatfree/faq/
http://www.floras-hideout.com/recipes/mxp/lowfat/
http://www.low-fat-recipes.com/

Mexican Cooking

When you are in the mood for something spicy, drag the laptop into the kitchen and connect to these Web sites, which have lots of recipes and interesting trivia about Mexican foods and their history.

Web:

http://www.ebicom.net/~howle/page/mexidx.htm
http://www.mexconnect.com/mex_/recipes/
   foodindex.html
http://www.mexico.udg.mx/cocina/ingles/menu/
   frame.html

Pie Recipes

Not long ago I had a great pie experience. A well-known publisher came to visit me and stayed overnight. At dinnertime, he volunteered to help out by making dessert and, using a recipe passed on to him by his grandmother, he baked a magnificent apple pie fit for a king. The best part was—since we couldn't find a king on such short notice—we had to eat the whole thing ourselves. If you would like to have a great pie experience in your own home, you don't have to wait for a well-known publisher to visit you. Simply check with these Internet pie resources, where you can find instructions on pie baking along with a nice variety of recipes and tips that will make the whole experience as easy as you-know-what.

Web:
> http://www.pastrywiz.com/archive/category/pie.htm
> http://www.pierecipe.com/

Recipe a Day

Check these Web sites, and, every day, you will see a free recipe, displayed on your own personal computer in the privacy of your own home. What could be more appetizing?

Web:
> http://www.backofthebox.com/rotd.html
> http://www.pastrywiz.com/dailyrecipes/recipes/
> http://www.recipeoftheday.net/
> http://www.wwrecipes.com/

Recipe Archives

I promise you: As long as you have the Net, you will never ever run out of recipes. How about a new idea for dinner tonight? Or perhaps you'd like to cook up a special something for that special someone. Here are some great archives with more recipes than you can shake a wooden spoon at.

Web:
> http://www.cs.cmu.edu/~mjw/recipes/
> http://www.mel.lib.mi.us/reference/REF-food.html
> http://www.recipecenter.com/
> http://www.recipelink.com/
> http://www.recipesource.com/
> http://www.virtualcities.com/~virtual/ons/
>   recipe.htm

Recipe Talk and General Discussion

Have you ever seen the Dick Van Dyke Show? Well, when Rob Petrie first met his wife Laura, she did not like him at all. However, he found out that she collected recipes and started sending her cookbooks (which helped him win her heart). Rob had to do it the hard way; today, he could snarf as many recipes as he wanted from either the **rec.food.recipes** Usenet group or the Web site that serves as the archive for this group. Then he could simply email the recipes to Laura. So what do you do when your boss and his family are coming over for dinner and all you have is a frozen armadillo? Nothing to worry about. Just connect to the Net and check out the armadillo recipes. Either that or borrow a cookbook from Laura.

Web:
> http://recipes.alastra.com/

Usenet:
> rec.food.recipes

Listserv Mailing List:
> List Name: eat-l
> Subscribe to: listserv@listserv.vt.edu

Recipes by Email

Do you like to experiment with new recipes? Do you like to get email? If you answered yes to these two simple questions, a lot of happiness is waiting for you. Simply sign up for one of these free services and, each day, with the regularity of a twenty-minute egg, you will receive a new recipe, sent in a plain, discreet email message. And the beautiful part is, no one else has to know where you get all your recipes. (I'm certainly not telling.)

Web:

http://www.recipedujour.com/
http://www.wwrecipes.com/

Sauces

A sauce is a liquid, which has been thickened and flavored, used to accompany a particular food. The purpose of a sauce is four-fold: to complement the flavor of the food with which it is served, to moisten the food, to insulate the food, and to decorate the food. In 1902, the French chef Auguste Escoffier, considered by many to be the father of modern cuisine, classified sauces into five categories called the "mother sauces". Within French cooking, all true sauces are based on one of these five mother sauces. They are: Espagnole (Brown Sauce), a dark mahogany sauce made from brown stock; Velouté (Blond Sauce) a light-colored sauce made from a white stock; Bechamel (Cream Sauce), a combination of hot milk, a white roux, and simple seasonings; Hollandaise (Butter Sauce), a combination of clarified butter and egg yolks; and Tomato (Red Sauce), a sauce made from tomatoes. Sounds interesting? Okay, it's time to get serious about sauces.

Web:

http://www.cooks.com/rec/ch/sauces.html
http://www.cs.cmu.edu/~mjw/recipes/sauces/
http://www.gumbopages.com/food/sauces/
http://www.recipesource.com/side-dishes/sauces/

Slow down. It's not a race.

FOOD, SOUTHERN STYLE

*If you don't happen to live in the southern part of the United States, you are missing a lot. For example, I bet you can't remember the last time you had a nice helping of catfish and hush puppies, with a side order of cornbread. Well, as long as you have a Net connection, you can remedy the situation right now. Just connect to one of the **Southern Cooking** sites and find out what you have been missing. Until you can say you really understand grits, you have not led a full life.*

Southern Cooking

Mmm, mmm. If you have never had Southern cooking, you are certainly in for a treat. Take off those jogging shoes and your fitness gear, and pull up to a big slab of ham coated with red eye gravy, a side of collards, some poke salad, okra, black-eyed peas and a hunk of cornbread. If you can't get this at your favorite restaurant, you can learn about Southern cooking on the Net. These sites will tell you what it is and how it's done, including the history of Southern cooking. You'll learn how ingenious Southerners are with their cooking and about the many different uses there are for leftover bacon grease.

Web:

http://dbtech.net/~suncastl/kitchen.htm
http://www.bama.ua.edu/~bgray/recipes.htm
http://www.grits.com/category.htm
http://www.southerncookingandmore.com/

COOL AND USEFUL

Electronic Greeting Cards

Would you like your friends to think you are thoughtful and considerate with very little effort on your part? Send them an electronic greeting card. All you have to do is choose a picture or graphic, fill out the form, and your message is on the way. (Actually, if you really want your friends to think you are thoughtful and considerate, a better idea might be to buy them all copies of this book.)

Web:
  http://www.bemine.com/galleries.htm
  http://www.dworldonline.com/elec.htm
  http://www.electronicpostcards.com/
  http://www.funfreecards.com/
  http://www.mailameal.com/
  http://www.maxracks.com/

Email Via Your Browser

I have a friend who recently went on a trip to Iowa. She was concerned that, as she was traveling, she wouldn't be able to check her email. But here's a solution. All you have to do is use one of these Web-based services that allow you to check your regular email account using a browser. This means that, wherever you go, as long as you can find a way to access the Web, you can check your mail. (Beware: some of these email services make it possible for people to create mail that looks like it comes from a fake address. So, if you get a message from santa@northpole.com offering you a job, you might want to doublecheck before you pack your snowsuit.)

Web:
  http://www.bigmailbox.com/
  http://www.mail2web.com/
  http://www.mochamail.com/

Find a new idea today.

Harley Hahn's Internet Exploration Station

Join me at Harley Hahn's Internet Exploration Station, and I'll take you on a tour of the Internet tempered with genuine, guaranteed wisdom. If I weren't so modest, I would tell you that Harley Hahn's Internet Exploration Station is the very best way to explore the Net, have fun, and learn about life, all at the same time. However, since I am modest, you'll have to find out for yourself.

Web:
  http://www.harley.com/hhies/

Faster than a speeding bullet.

More powerful than a handwritten note and a dozen roses.

Able to leap the widest chasms of interpersonal relationships in a single transmission.

Look! There in your mailbox! It's a note. It's a memo. It's an *electronic greeting card!*

Yes, an *electronic greeting card*—strange visitor from the Internet—with powers and abilities far beyond those of regular messages. An *electronic greeting card*— that can change the course of individual relationships, bend the harshest misunderstandings back to reality, and, disguised as a mild-mannered piece of email, fights a never-ending battle for Friendship, Communication and the Electronic Way.

Kvetch

"Kvetch" is Yiddish for "complain". When life gets to be a bit too much, take a moment and see what other intelligent and accomplished people are complaining about. By the way, speaking of kvetching, it strikes me that a lot of the trouble in this world is caused by other people. I mean, I'm okay and I know that you're pretty cool, but what about all the other people in the world? Don't you wish they would just shut up and do whatever you tell them?

Web:
  http://www.kvetch.com/

Last Word on Science

I believe everyone should understand the basics of science: chemistry, physics and biology. Why? First, being knowledgeable and using your brain is good for you, and, two, a lot of what happens around us from day to day is understandable if you understand basic science. For example, have you ever wondered why the sky is blue? Or how a dog tracks a scent? Or how a smoke detector is able to detect smoke? Or why we have fingerprints? This Web site has the answers to all these questions and more. You know, there are two things in life I really like: good questions and smart answers. Plan on spending some time here, and it won't be long before you agree with me.

Web:
  http://www.newscientist.com/lastword/

Pocket Internet

When I was a little kid, one of my favorite things was when the whole family went downtown to meet my father after work and he would take us out to eat at this restaurant that had a big buffet. I liked that there were all different types of food and that I could sample them all. (My favorite item was the small baked crabapples.) This Web site is like an Internet buffet. There are samples of all the different types of things that people like to do on the Net. If you are teaching somebody how to use the Web, this is a good place to have them start.

Web:
  http://www.thepocket.com/

Reminder Services

We all know how embarrassing it is to forget something important. For example, last month I forgot to send my sister a card for her gerbil's birthday. And a couple of days ago, Bill Gates called me to ask if I was finished with the "Buns of Steel" video he loaned me. This need never happen again—to me or to you. On the Net there are some great electronic reminder services. Just specify your email address, a date, a message, and how many days' warning you want. On the right day, you will receive email containing your message. (By the way, Bill, don't forget you still have my copy of "Harley Hahn's Internet Advisor".)

Web:
  http://www.internetreminder.com/
  http://www.lifeminders.com/
  http://www.memotome.com/
  http://www.rememberit.com/
  http://www.remindall.com/

Search Snoopers

Snoop, snoop, snoop.

See what other people are doing on the Net.

Snoop, snoop, snoop.

Find out what strange things other people are looking for.

Snoop,

snoop,

snoop.

(You'll love it.)

Search Snoopers

Do you like to eavesdrop? Of course you do. Well, here's a way to find out what people all over the Net are doing. These sites, maintained by the search engine companies, allow you to see what other people are looking for. You use a search engine to find resources on the Web. To do so, you specify one or more words or terms, and the search engine examines a vast database of information to suggest resources relating to what you specified. So, wanna eavesdrop? Connect to any of these sites and see a list of words that people are searching for right now. While I looked, I found that people were looking for resources about slot machines, audio components, incest, deer habitats, butts, sailing, teen-only chat, Bible, escape velocity, lottery and singles.

Web:
  http://www.askjeeves.com/docs/peek/
  http://www.infotiger.com/voyeur
  http://www.kanoodle.com/spy/
  http://www.metaspy.com/

Straight Dope

The Straight Dope is the name of a syndicated newspaper column written by Ed Zotti under the pen name Cecil Adams. The Straight Dope site contains archives of many of the questions that Adams has answered. The answers are thoughtful and knowledgeable. What I like is that Adams does not confine himself to questions that have an easy answer. Thus, not all of the answers are exact, which I find thought-provoking. If you can't get enough straight dope from Adam's columns or books, try hanging out in the Usenet groups.

Web:
  http://www.straightdope.com/
Usenet:
  alt.fan.cecil-adams

Virtual Presents

I love virtual presents, and I love to send them to my friends for no reason at all. This is a great place to visit if you need to get someone an impressive gift that you can't afford. You can send your friends a vacation, fine jewelry, animals, food, flowers, and a lot more. What's a virtual present? Try it.

Web:
  http://www.virtualpresents.com/

Voice Mail Via the Net

Suppose you call someone really important, like the President of the U.S. or Madonna. You just know you are going to get voice mail. Now you may have voice mail at work, and you may even have it on your home phone, but as one of my readers, you are more important than the President (and maybe even Madonna). So why shouldn't you have your very own Net-based voice mail?

Web:

http://www.hotvoice.com/
http://www.j2.com/free/free.asp
http://www.messageaccess.com/
http://www.onebox.com/

COOL BUT USELESS

Animated Humor

Just about everything looks better when it is moving: beautiful women, studly men, cute little kittens and...yes, even humor looks better when it moves. If the words "still life" are not in your vocabulary, see if your eyeballs are connected to your funnybone: check out some examples of animated humor where action and humor come together to form a perfect blend of...well, action and humor.

Web:

http://www.messagemates.com/
http://www.tvdance.com/

> Wait for me at the secret rendezvous point. (I'll bring the marshmallow sandwiches.)

Create a Barcode

The secret to happiness is being able to create your own barcodes whenever you want.

Bill Gates' Wealth

Have you ever wondered how much money Bill Gates has and what it really means? The real answer is that no one, not even Billy the Silly himself, actually knows how much he is worth, and very few people can comprehend the extent of his wealth. Here is an interesting statistic, based on Rajah of Redmond's holdings of Microsoft stock, its current price, and the population of the United States. If the Supreme Exalted Nerd were to liquidate all of his Microsoft stock, at the current price, and share it equally with everyone in the country, each person would get about $220.07 (at the time I am writing this). Let's put it another way. If everyone in America were to send me the measly sum of $220.07, our country could have *two* humungously rich billionaires instead of only one. This would serve to increase the competition and be generally better for everyone, a consummation (as Shakespeare pointed out) devoutly to be wished.

Web:

http://www.quuxuum.org/~evan/bgnw.html
http://www.templetons.com/brad/billg.html
http://www.theinfo.org/gatesdollars.tcl
http://www.webho.com/WealthClock/

Brunching Shuttlecocks Toys

When you've got exactly one minute to waste before your favorite Seinfeld rerun comes on, what can you do? Visit the Brunching Shuttlecocks toy page. You'll find quick, silly Web toys. Just the thing to get you through those sixty-second waits.

Web:

http://www.brunching.com/categories/toys.html

Bubblewrap

I love popping bubblewrap, the plastic wrapping that is used to package and protect delicate items. It's such a satisfying way to spend a few minutes of the day: pressing those small plastic bubbles with ever-increasing force until they suddenly surrender and self-destruct with a soul-satisfying pop. In the olden days, I would have to wait until I got a package in the mail with some bubblewrap in it. Not anymore. Now I can use the Net to pop bubblewrap whenever I want, and you can too. Thank goodness for modern technology.

Web:
  http://www.2211.com/pop.htm
  http://www.fathom.org/opalcat/bubblewrap.html
  http://www.snapbubbles.com/
  http://www.urban75.com/Mag/bubble.html

Burma-Shave Signs

From 1925 to 1963, the Burma-Shave Company used road signs to advertise their shaving cream on highways, mostly within the United States. The company used a series of signs, spaced a few hundred yards apart. The signs would show a short message, one line per sign, urging men to use Burma-Shave cream rather than the old-fashioned brush and lather. As a person drove past the signs, he would read each line of the message in sequence. At first, the messages were straight advertising, but it wasn't long before the company started to use short, humorous poems. Here is an example, used in 1933: The answer to / A maiden's prayer / Is not a chin / Of stubby hair / Burma-Shave. Want to see more? Here are some collections.

Web:
  http://www.mc.cc.md.us/departments/hpolscrv/
    mthomas.htm
  http://www.nidlink.com/~dgookin/burma_shave/
  http://www.seniors-site.com/funstuff/burma.html
  http://www.sff.net/people/teaston/burma.htm

> **The most powerful force in the world is habit. Make it your servant.**

Constructor Toy

Imagine a tiny world in which you can create a something-or-other made out of real imaginary forces, springy things and pieces of whatnot. You can turn gravity on and off, and play with your something-or-other until it's time to get back to work or go to sleep, whichever comes first. Imagine no more.

Web:
  http://www.sodaplay.com/

Create a Barcode

Have you ever wished you could create your own barcode patterns? Now you can. Just specify a number, and you will be presented with the corresponding barcode. There are lots of cool ways to have fun with barcodes. For example, if you have a kid, use these services to generate a barcode for a unique identification number (such as the kid's Social Security number). Then have the pattern tattooed on the kid's forehead. Cool, huh? As they say on TV when they are trying to sell you something expensive that you don't need, you are limited only by your imagination.

Web:
  http://www.milk.com/barcode/

Faces

Imagine that you are a great plastic surgeon. You have spent years and years in medical training, and now you are ready: to go to L.A. and experience the thrills of modifying the faces of rich Hollywood stars. But why go through all that training and hard work when you have the Net? You can mix and match parts of well-known faces or, alternatively, check out what happens when a computer program does the work for you. Recreate all the excitement experienced by Dr. Frankenstein without running up a huge electric bill.

Web:
  http://www.corynet.com/faces/
  http://www.kristi.net/interactive/morph/

File Not Found Errors

You are using the Web, and for one reason or another, your browser tries to link to a Web page that does not exist. In most cases, this causes the remote Web server to send back a page showing error code 404. (There is nothing cosmic about 404. It just happens to be the standard error code for "file not found".) Most 404 error pages are pretty dull, but some people have programmed their Web servers to show something flashy instead. This Web site will show you the most interesting 404 error code pages on the Web.

Web:
   http://www.plinko.net/404/

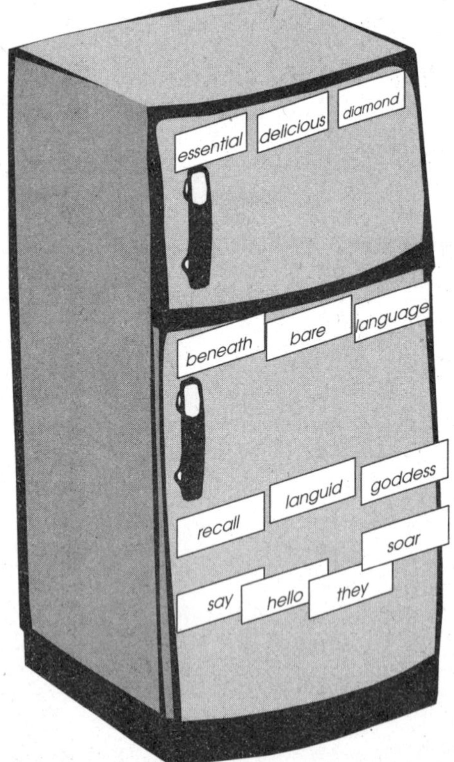

And I bet you could do even better.

Internet Dancing Baby

Have you seen the famous Internet Dancing Baby? It's a wonderful animation of a virtual dancing baby that has been floating around the Net for some time. There are many versions of the baby. One of these Web pages is my version of the dancing baby, in which he gyrates to the sounds of Latin jazz. The other resources will help you find all the dancing babies you need to lead a rich and fulfilling life.

Web:
   http://www.chaoskids.com/BABY/baby.html
   http://www.harley.com/dancing-baby/
   http://www.megababy.com/

Mad Martian Museum of Modern Madness

This is a great place if you are worried you are getting a bit too normal, and you need a boost of weirdness. For example, wouldn't you love to investigate the "Interactive Toilet of Terro? And how can you pass up the "Plastic Eyeball Exhibit" or the "Mad Martian Mask? I don't think I need to say any more: the interactive toilet can speak for itself.

Web:
   http://www.madmartian.com/

Magnetic Poetry

Imagine you have a very large refrigerator and, sticking to the door, you have several hundred small magnetic thingies, each one having a word printed on it ("women", "urge", "pink", "ask", "you", "go", and on and on). Now imagine yourself being able to select and arrange the thingies so as to write poetry out of the words. Well, on the Net you do not have to imagine. Here is a virtual surface with lots and lots of thingies, each with its own word. Use your mouse to move the words around and create whatever poetry or messages your heart and mind desire. When you are finished, you can share the result with everyone by copying your poem onto a piece of paper and putting it on the door of your fridge.

Web:
   http://www.links2love.com/poetry_magnetic.htm
   http://www.magneticpoetry.com/magnet/
   http://www.wingnut-etc.com/poetry/

Money Tracker

Some people think that a dollar doesn't go as far as it used to. Not true. Dollars travel thousands of miles, and you can prove it. Start by registering the serial numbers of some of your dollar bills. Then check back later to see if someone else has encountered any of the same bills. If so, you can see where the banknotes have gone and how long it took them to get there. Personally, my philosophy is don't be afraid to set your money free. If it is really yours, it will come back to you. If it doesn't, then it really wasn't yours in the first place.

Web:

  http://www.wheresgeorge.com/

Museum of Dirt

There's more to dirt than what meets the eye and stimulates the hand. Dirt can have a story of its own, a passive but significant role to play in our appreciation of the world around us. To see what I mean, visit the Museum of Dirt, where you will find dirt samples taken from celebrity yards and interesting places like a Buddhist shrine and Alcatraz Island. You will also see rejection letters from celebrities who did not want to contribute dirt to the museum (boo!).

Web:

  http://www.planet.com/dirtweb/mainmenu.html

Undressing Game

You start by making a choice: do you want to date the man or the woman? Then you answer questions. Depending on your answers, your date will either warm up to you (and take off his or her clothes, a bit at a time) or cool off (and become more and more reserved). It's just like real life only faster, less expensive, and you can keep trying till you get it right.

Web:

  http://stock.photo.net/dating/

Useless Facts

Sometimes, the most enjoyable facts are the most useless facts. Facts that are weird, funny, sometimes astounding, but are careful to never stray from the path of uselessness. For example, I bet you didn't know that: (1) The first product to ever have a UPC bar code on its package was Wrigley's gum; (2) No matter which way Mickey Mouse faces, his ears are always turned to the front; (3) In the Flintstones theme song, the line after "Let's ride with the family down the street" is "Through the courtesy of Fred's two feet." Get your fill of odd factual tidbits and amaze your friends to no end. I predict you will be the most popular person in your entire circle of friends. After all, there is no one more beloved than the purveyor of an endless supply of useless knowledge. Just ask any film studies teacher.

Web:

  http://home.nycap.rr.com/useless/
  http://www.puzzlegrid.com/facts.cgi
  http://www.uselessfacts.net/

Very Crazy Stuff

What do all these women's names have in common? Ethel, Marcella, Wilma, Mildred, Phyllis, Thelma, Bertha, Doreen, Henrietta and Edna? They are all on the list of "Names That Guarantee Your Daughter Won't Find a Husband". There's a lot more crazy stuff at this site, and if you like thinking and reading about things that are a tad unusual, the stuff at this site will keep you rotating in your chair for hours. (By the way, it's not true that all women with these names can't find a husband, although, it is probably not just a coincidence that both Ethel Mertz and Wilma Flintstone had to marry guys named Fred.)

Web:

  http://www.verycrazy.com/

Virtual Pets

Do you need to feel needed? Are you reluctant to commit yourself indefinitely to the care and feeding of an actual flesh and blood animal? You need a virtual pet: a make-believe thingy that seems alive and demands your constant care (until you get tired of it and let it die).

Web:
http://www.neopets.com/
http://www.technosphere.org.uk/
http://www.virtualkitty.com/
http://www.virtualpuppy.com/

CRAFTS

Balloon Art

Balloon art is always a good thing to know how to do in case you are trapped in an elevator with a group of children or perhaps have to calm several wild animals who are about to attack you. Check out this site for lots of balloon pictures, a FAQ (frequently asked question list), a guide to ballooning, as well as other potentially life-saving material.

Web:
http://www.balloonhq.com/

Basket Weaving

If your home is sadly lacking in cultural artifacts, I have the answer. Connect to one of these basket-oriented sites and teach yourself how to render an actual objet d'art. After all, what could be in better taste than a house full of baskets? I myself have a basket in the shape of *Harley Hahn's Student Guide to Unix* hanging on my bedroom wall. (And, boy, am I popular.)

Web:
http://www.bright.net/~basketc/
http://www.ulster.net/~abeebe/basket.html

Batik

My copy editor, Lydia, crochets and does cross-stitch, but she can't batik. Batik is an art form in which cloth is decorated using wax and dye. Batik has been practiced for centuries in Asia, the Middle East, India and, particularly, Malaysia. The basic technique is to cover part of a cloth with wax and then apply a dye. The dye is absorbed only where there is no wax. Afterward, the wax is removed, leaving you with a cloth that is partially dyed according to the original wax pattern. Repeating these steps allows you to create layers in a multiplicity of colors. Learning Batik isn't that hard, but it does take some time to master the skills. So I guess that leaves out Lydia. Being my editor, she doesn't even get time off on national holidays. She does, however, get a day off on her birthday. (Actually, Lydia's opinion is that her birthday *is* a national holiday.)

Web:
http://www.craftown.com/batik.htm
http://www.dharmatrading.com/info/batik.html
http://www.expat.or.id/info/batik.html
http://www.story-of-batik.com/

Majordomo Mailing List:
List Name: batik-ml
Subscribe to: majordomo@bear-buys.com

Beading

There is something magical and seductive about beads, but it's not something you can explain to a stranger. How do you tell someone with no bead experience about the refined, sensual feelings that these small, delightful objects evoke in you? How can you possibly explain to a neophyte how a *frisson* of artistic passion electrifies your being each time you run your hands through a box of beads? You can't, so don't try. Just enjoy your beads and let the rest of the world envy your bead-related satisfaction.

Web:
  http://www.beadwrangler.com/junction.htm
  http://www.kimberlychapman.com/crafts/
    beading.html
  http://www.suzannecooper.com/beadmain.html
  http://www.thebeadsite.com/

Usenet:
  alt.beadworld
  rec.crafts.beads

Calligraphy

Calligraphy is the art of fine handwriting. Traditionally, calligraphy is often used with illumination (the decoration of a manuscript or book). There are many different types of traditional calligraphy and illumination: early Egyptian papyri, ornamental scripts of the Renaissance, Oriental brushwork, Islamic ornamentation, and so on. To be a great calligrapher requires years of practice and a lot of natural talent. Unfortunately, with the advent of computer-assisted artwork, the need for traditional calligraphers (ones who do not use a computer) is significantly diminished. If you are a calligrapher, or interested in calligraphy, take a look at these Web pages. You will find information about individual artists, calligraphy organizations, online pictures of manuscripts, as well as a collection of calligraphy-related links around the Net.

Web:
  http://moas.atlantia.sca.org/topics/call.htm
  http://www.calligraph.com/web/cyberstudy/ass/
    ass.html
  http://www.cecilia-letteringart.com/
  http://www.cynscribe.com/

Candlemaking

Is there anyone who doesn't think that candles are cool? Well I do, and you do, and that's all that matters. Making your own candles is a gentle, artistic pastime. Learn how to do it, and you'll have a hobby that will light up your life without letting you burn out.

Web:
  http://www.candlecauldron.com/
  http://www.candlemaking.org.uk/
  http://www.candleteacher.com/
  http://www.fastforums.com/candlemaking/
  http://www.waxedout.com/

Usenet:
  alt.crafts.candlemaking.soapmaking
  alt.crafts.candlemaking.soapmaking.moderated

Ceramics and Pottery

It's so much fun to play in the mud. The problem is you can't do it and use the computer at the same time. But when you get clean and dry, take some time to subscribe to this mailing list to partake in the discussion of ceramic arts, clay, kilns, glazes and other hot clay art topics. The Web sites and Usenet groups have some nifty stuff you can read when you aren't out getting your hands dirty.

Web:
  http://www.claytimes.com/
  http://www.criticalceramics.org/
  http://www.potterymaking.org/

Usenet:
  bit.listserv.clayart
  rec.crafts.pottery

Listserv Mailing List:
  List Name: clayart
  Subscribe to: listserv@lsv.ceramics.org

Craft Fairs

I can't think of anything that rivals the liveliness and fun of a craft fair except perhaps a folk-dancing marathon. If you want to take a walk on the wild side, take a look at the schedule for upcoming craft fairs.

Web:
  http://www.arts-crafts.com/events/
  http://www.craftersdb.com/events.htm
  http://www.xmission.com/~arts/calendar/view.html

Craft Marketplace

No need to travel to the far regions of the world for the chance to buy cool craft stuff. In this Usenet discussion group, you can buy, sell, trade, or search for craft products and supplies. This is just the place to look when you need a little bit of Australian yarn to finish up that afghan.

Usenet:

rec.crafts.marketplace

Craft Projects

If you are like me, there is no way your life is ever going to be complete until you have your own jelly-bean duck. However, have you priced jelly-bean ducks lately? And have you noticed how the quality has decreased in recent years? Clearly, if you are going to end up with an inexpensive, high-quality jelly-bean duck, you will have to make it for yourself. (And when you are finished, you can work on an apple-head doll and a strawberry moisturizer.)

Web:

http://www.crafterscommunity.com/
http://www.craftplanet.com/Creations/Projects/
http://www.makestuff.com/

Craft Resources

There are so many craft activities in this world, there is no excuse for anyone being bored, not even for one tiny minute. But just in case you do get bored, here are some craft-related resources that will catch your interest and make you want to start a new project immediately. While you are on the Net, you can also find out about craft suppliers, craft associations, information about fairs and events, and fun craft things for kids.

Web:

http://www.craftassoc.com/
http://www.craftsfaironline.com/
http://www.craftweb.com/
http://www.wyomingcompanion.com/janacraft/
   links2.htm

Craft Talk and General Discussion

The only thing as much fun as sitting around making crafts is sitting around talking about making crafts (and you don't have a mess to clean up when you are finished). Come join the discussion. Trade hints, tips, techniques and generally hang with the craftiest people on the Net.

Usenet:

rec.crafts.misc

Crocheting

To crochet, you use an implement called a crochet hook to create chains of complex knots out of thread, yarn or even long skinny pieces of cloth. An experienced crocheter can create a variety of *objets d'art* such as afghans, sweaters, hats, purses, rugs, and so on. Crocheting is more important than most people realize. If it wasn't for crocheting, the world's supply of small round decorations would get used up in less than two years. (Imagine how pathetic it would look watching someone trying to knit a doily.)

Web:

http://www.beadcrochet.com/
http://www.cafecrochet.com/
http://www.chezcrochet.com/
http://www.craftown.com/crochet.htm
http://www.crochet.org/

Majordomo Mailing List:

List Name: crochet
Subscribe to: majordomo@ml.rpmdp.com

Majordomo Mailing List:

List Name: crochetnetwork
Subscribe to: majordomo@gioffre.com

Cross-Stitch

What could be a better way to relax than to spend time sitting in a chair making thousands of little Xs with a needle and thread on a piece of aida cloth? If you like to spend your spare time making colorful crafts of cross-stitch, take a look at what is on the Net. (Using the mouse will limber up your fingers just the right amount to prepare you for a long session of stitching.)

Web:
   http://mickeys-place-in-the-sun.com/xst.html
   http://www.dnai.com/~kdyer/
   http://www.lysator.liu.se/~offe/kors/

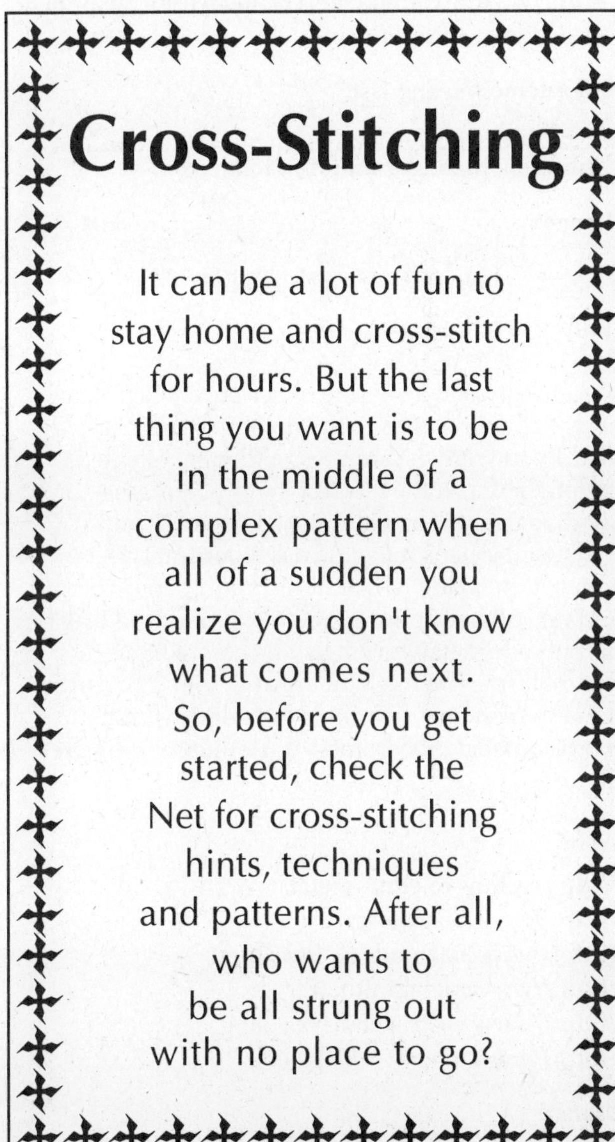

Decorative Painting

Decorative painting refers to a number of techniques in which you embellish walls, furniture or other objects with a patterned finish. Learn about tole painting (decorative painting on metal, and sometimes wood, surfaces), stenciling (applying paint upon a sheet in which a design has been cut, to produce a pattern on the surface beneath), and faux finishing (painting a surface to look as if it were made from a different type of material). Spend a few hours on the Net, and you will soon be impressing people with your knowledge of strié, color washing, patina, crackling and marbleizing.

Web:
   http://gerdesdesign.com/wallart.htm
   http://www.busybrushes.com/
   http://www.designcottage.com/
   http://www.fauxlikeapro.com/
   http://www.paintersworkshop.com/
   http://www.tole-expressions.com/

Fabrics and Textiles

Angora, alpaca, vicuna, cashmere, cotton, hemp, linen, mohair, silk and wool. If you are a tactile Tom or Tessie, just thinking about so many different materials will make your imagination soar. Imagine all the beautiful things you can make from these materials. Imagine the fabrics, the threads, the yarns and the laces, and what you can do with them. Imagine yourself knitting, spinning, embroidering and weaving. Imagine...

Web:
   http://moas.atlantia.sca.org/topics/text.htm
   http://www.fabriclink.com/
   http://www.fabrics.net/
   http://www.faqs.org/faqs/crafts/textiles/
   http://www.hollandandsherry.com/textileguide/

Usenet:
   rec.crafts.textiles
   rec.crafts.textiles.marketplace
   rec.crafts.textiles.misc
   rec.crafts.textiles.yarn

Jewelry

I have a wonderful friend, Antoinette, who for a long time has earned her living by making original jewelry. Antoinette used to live in California and, over the years, has developed quite a following. Later she moved to Hawaii, where she ended up living in a magnificent house on the island of Maui. I haven't seen Antoinette for some time, but knowing her, I am sure that she is happy, fulfilled and has a great many friends. Wouldn't you like to live like that? Of course you would, so let's start with step 1: learn how to make your own jewelry.

Web:
http://www.allcrafts.net/jewelry.htm
http://www.kidsdomain.com/craft/_jewelry.html

Usenet:
rec.crafts.jewelry

Knitting

Knit one, purl two, what could be more fun to do? My experience is that the most intelligent and desirable women like to keep their hands busy. Well, the Internet has lots of resources for knitters, including a lot of patterns. (I recently came across one for a sweater for a chihuahua.) Although the U.S. Surgeon General says that running while carrying knitting needles can be hazardous to your health, my advice is to take your chances and head straight for the Net without delay.

Web:
http://math.vanderbilt.edu/~cjs/knitting.html
http://www.craftyarncouncil.com/
http://www.knitnet.com/
http://www.redlipstick.net/knit/
http://www.woolworks.org/

Usenet:
rec.crafts.textiles.machine-knit

> ## There's lots of room.

Lacemaking and Tatting

Lacemaking and tatting (looping and knotting a single strand of heavy-duty thread on a small hand shuttle) are almost lost arts (probably because beer companies do not like to sponsor professional lacemaking competitions). Fortunately, nothing important is neglected on the Net. Find out about lacemaking techniques, supplies, clubs and guilds, and talk to other lacemakers and tatters around the world.

Web:
http://www.domesticarts.com/
http://www.picotnet.com/Locatelace/locate.html
http://www.thisntat.com/

Majordomo Mailing List:
List Name: lace
Subscribe to: majordomo@arachne.com

Metalworking

It's a totally embarrassing experience when your new neighbor comes to the door and says, "I heard you were the smartest and most talented metalworker on the block. Would you please anodize this piece of aluminum for me?" and that just happens to be the day your Internet connection is down. Don't disappoint your friends and neighbors. Connect to the Net now and brush up on your metalworking skills before that doorbell rings. While you are at it, you can get the lowdown on heat treating, machinery, welding, motors, associations, clubs, museums, and much more.

Web:
http://w3.uwyo.edu/~metal/
http://www.abana.org/
http://www.baba.org.uk/links.html
http://www.metalsmith.org/
http://www.metalwebnews.com/
http://www.metalworking.com/

Usenet:
rec.crafts.metalworking

Mosaics

A mosaic is a design created by gluing tiny pieces of whatnot (glass, stone, terracotta) to a surface. In one of the old Andy Griffith Shows, Barney (the deputy sheriff) decides to rehabilitate Otis (the town drunk). Barney buys Otis a mosaic kit, and it isn't long before Otis creates a picture of his own. In the process, he endows himself with immense self-esteem and personal satisfaction. The art of mosaic, as we practice it today, is an old one. It was created by the Greeks and was later adopted by the Romans. And if there is anything we admire about the Romans, it is their immense self-esteem and personal satisfaction.

Web:
> http://www.americanmosaics.org/
> http://www.asm.dircon.co.uk/
> http://www.ptialaska.net/~sonafrnk/
>   MosaicLinks.html

Needlework

These delicate and skillful arts take time, patience and devotion. Read up on all manner of needlework, including tips and techniques on petit point, cross-stitch and embroidery. Share patterns, design ideas and get timesaving hints on these age-old crafts.

Web:
> http://webstitch.designwest.com/
> http://www.annthegran.com/
> http://www.caron-net.com/
> http://www.needlepoint.org/
> http://www.needlework.com/html/
> http://www.serve.com/marbeth/needlework.html

Usenet:
> rec.crafts.textiles.needlework

Majordomo Mailing List:
> List Name: ang-list
> Subscribe to: majordomo@mail.serve.com

Origami is so beautiful. What compelling beauty there is in constructing something so delicate and exotic from a simple piece of paper.

My favorite is the cute little "PC with modem that doesn't work".

Japanese Folding Tricks

Origami

In the 6th century, the secret of paper was carried by Buddhist monks from China to Japan. The Japanese soon integrated paper into their culture. For a long time, the designs were passed down from one generation to the next as an oral tradition. Creative paper folding with non-traditional designs was popularized by Akira Yoshizawa, starting in the 1930s. Modern origami (from the Japanese words for "fold paper") is a pastime enjoyed all over the world. Origami is a wonderful hobby to explore, and the Net is the place to start learning. Read about all facets of origami, including bibliographies, folding techniques, display ideas and materials.

Web:
> http://www.britishorigami.org.uk/
> http://www.folds.net/
> http://www.origami-usa.org/frames1c.htm
> http://www.origami.vancouver.bc.ca/
> http://www.paperfolding.com/

Usenet:
> alt.arts.origami
> rec.arts.origami

Polymer Clay

Clay. Ah....clay. It makes me think of my childhood, when I could happily spend hours with soft and gooey substances and uninhibitedly mash and smash them into an unrecognizable pulp. (Now I have to spend my time smashing editors into an unrecognizable pulp.) Release your inner child and join the discussion about polymer clays. Common topics include molds, strength of clay, and tips on how to make various clay crafts. The Web sites have lots of cool information for people who like to play with polymer clay.

Web:
  http://www.creationsbykris.com/linkpage1.htm
  http://www.npcg.org/home.htm
  http://www.polymerclaycentral.com/

Usenet:
  rec.crafts.polymer-clay

Quilting

A quilt is a blanket consisting of two layers of fabric enclosing a layer of cotton, wool, feathers or down. The whole thing is stitched together, often using a decorative pattern of some type. What makes quilts so much fun is that you can use various fabrics and designs to create your own personalized work.

Web:
  http://ttsw.com/mainquiltingpage.html
  http://www.quiltart.com/
  http://www.quiltchannel.com/

Usenet:
  rec.crafts.quilting
  rec.crafts.textiles.quilting

Beware of people who have learned how to sit still.

Rubber Stamps

These resources are for people who like to stamp designs onto paper using colored inks: stamping resources, a list of people on the Net who like stamping, information about stores and conventions, reviews and tips, stamp artwork, and a glossary. For a little more interactive action, there is a mailing list for those who like to talk about stamping as much as they like actually doing it.

Web:
  http://www.findastamp.com/
  http://www.kerchunk.com/
  http://www.rubbertrouble.com/
  http://www.scraplink.com/rs.htm
  http://www.silverfoxstamps.com/website.html

Usenet:
  rec.crafts.rubberstamps

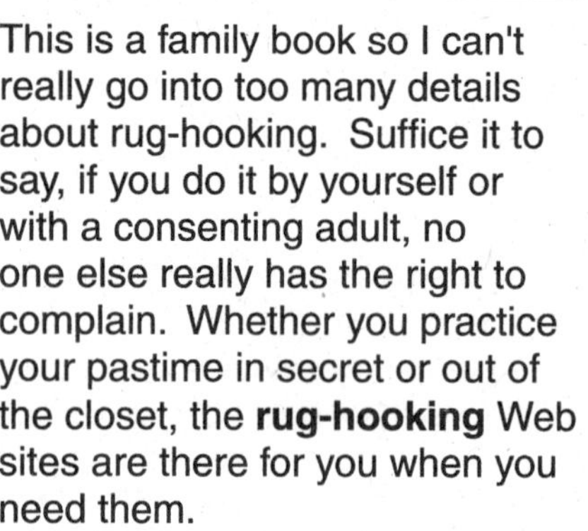

Rug-Hooking

Real rug-hookers know the difference between looped pile rug-hooking and latch-hooking. Don't get caught in a big social faux pas by not knowing the difference. Use the Net to read about rug-hooking patterns, techniques, supplies and events. There are pictures to give you ideas for new projects, and help when you have technical questions.

Web:
  http://www.netw.com/~rafter4/
  http://www.rughookersnetwork.com/
  http://www.rughookingonline.com/

You are here.

Scrapbooks

One of my friends, Elaine, is the Scrapbook Queen. To her, and to many other artistic and sentimental people, scrapbook making is a wonderful, rewarding activity. What better way to appreciate life than to memorialize it in the form of creative, well-organized scrapbooks? All you need is an artistic temperament and lots of patience (not to mention glue, paper and special pencils for writing names and dates on the back of photos). Are you interested? There are some very, very good scrapbookers on the Net, and you could join their ranks. I think you should. My philosophy is that anything Elaine does is worth doing well.

Web:

http://www.gracefulbee.com/
http://www.scrapbooking.com/
http://www.scraplink.com/
http://www.telepath.com/bcarson/scrap_happy/

Sewing

To me, the epitome of skill and artistry is being able to sew a shirt from scratch. I once watched someone do it and, to this day, I am still amazed. I guess I am one of the culturally unwashed: I like to wear clothes, but I have no idea how to make them. However, if you are a real sewing person, you are not alone. There are many people on the Net talking about sewing, and you can join them whenever you want.

Web:

http://ths.gardenweb.com/forums/sewing/
http://www.lilyabello.com/sewdir.htm
http://www.sewing.com/
http://www.sewing.org/

Usenet:

alt.sewing
rec.crafts.textiles.sewing

Soapmaking

Kidneys are important, and, for protection, they are surrounded by a layer of adipose tissue (fat) referred to as perirenal fat. While an animal is alive, the perirenal fat acts as protection, cushioning the kidneys from random blows of fate. After death, however, the fat is up for grabs, which brings us to the question at hand. What would you do if some kind soul presented you with 40 pounds of pure beef kidney fat? Well, most people would be nonplussed at such an opportunity—but not a soap maker. No, a talented soap maker would be able to use that fat, mix it with lye (sodium hydroxide), water, and perhaps a little fragrance and coloring, and come up with a wonderful batch of homemade soap. Sound inviting? Believe me, it's a lot more fun than starting with 40 pounds of soap and trying to create perirenal fat.

Web:

http://hometown.aol.com/oelaineo/directions.html
http://users.silverlink.net/~timer/soaplinks.html#info
http://www.silverlink.net/~timer/soapinfo.html
http://www.waltonfeed.com/old/soaphome.html

Usenet:

alt.crafts.candlemaking.soapmaking
alt.crafts.candlemaking.soapmaking.moderated

Stained Glass

I love to look at stained glass and think of all the work that went into making it: cutting the pieces, grinding the edges, copper foiling or leading the glass, and then soldering the pieces together. If you are a stained glass artist, or if you are interested in learning something about this fascinating craft, you will enjoy these Web sites. You will find lots of information about supplies, patterns, magazines, questions and answers, and much, much more. Check out the Usenet discussion group for lively stained glass banter.

Web:

http://www.artglassworld.com/
http://www.tcp-net.ad.jp/tashiro/

Usenet:

rec.crafts.glass

Tie Dye

Learn to tie dye your clothes in a totally rad fashion, man. And these are not just some lame instructions by capitalist pigs trying to make money off you. The information here can help you create garments wild enough to please even tie-dyed-in-the-wool Grateful Dead fans. (Fun for the entire family, including the kids.)

Web:
http://brands.bestfoods.com/rit/artoftiedye.asp
http://www.dharmatrading.com/info/tie-dye.html
http://www.makingfriends.com/tiedye.htm
http://www.sos.state.mi.us/history/museum/kidstuff/
  sixties/tiedie.html
http://www.tiedyeguy.com/lesson/td_faq.shtml

Weaving

Weaving is a craft in which you create fabric by interlacing filaments of material such as thread or yarn. In ancient times, weaving was a widespread art, having been invented independently at various times by people around the world. We have all seen beautiful weavings, such as tapestries or carpets. However, most weaving is done by people who make things for their own use, simply because it is so satisfying. Traditional weaving uses a device called a loom, in which threads are held under tension and raised and lowered during the weaving process. Today, there are a number of popular weaving methods: tablet/card weaving, inkle weaving, Swedish weaving, kumihimo (actually braiding), and so on. Each of these is different, with its own equipment, techniques and final product, so if you think you might be interested in weaving, there is some type of weaving you'll enjoy.

Web:
http://hem.bredband.net/ronpar/
http://www.duke.edu/~scg3/#tablet
http://www.fibreartsonline.com/fac/weaving/
  weaveResources.htm
http://www.inkleweaving.com/notes/
http://www.weavershand.com/

Majordomo Mailing List:
List Name: fibernet
Subscribe to: majordomo@imagicomm.com

Majordomo Mailing List:
List Name: weaving-digest
Subscribe to: majordomo@lists.his.com

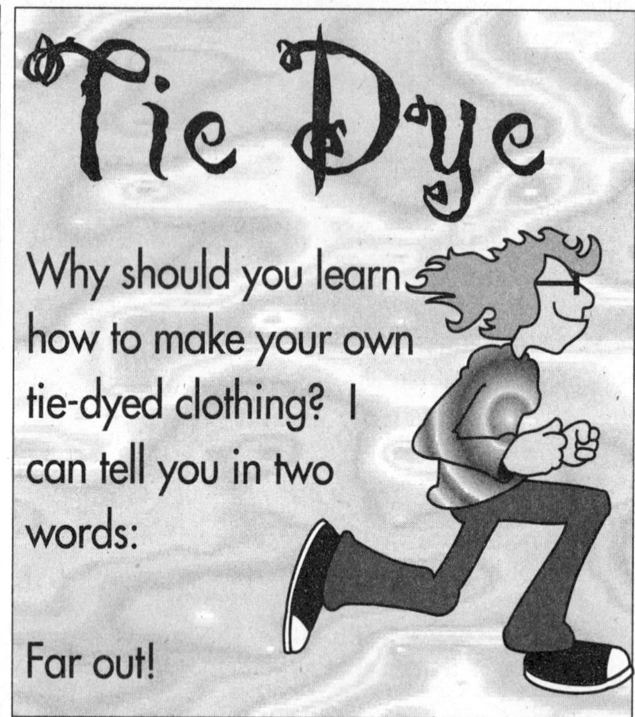

CRIME

Alcatraz

Alcatraz was a United States federal prison built on an island in San Francisco Bay to house the most incorrigible and heinous prisoners in the federal penitentiary system. Alcatraz was opened in 1934, and remained in operation until 1963, when it was closed as a cost-cutting measure. During that time, the prison housed a total of 1,545 inmates, with an average of about 260 at any one time. In all, 36 prisoners tried to escape, of which 22 were recaptured, 7 were shot and killed, 2 drowned, and 5 were left unaccounted for. Currently, Alcatraz is a popular San Francisco tourist attraction, drawing many visitors who arrive by boat and take a tour of what has become America's most notorious prison.

Web:
http://www.bop.gov/ipapg/ipaalcatraz.html
http://www.nps.gov/alcatraz/penfaq.html
http://www.zpub.com/sf50/alcatraz/

Corrections Professionals

Working in a prison or jail is a difficult job, and most people, even your relatives and friends, will never really understand what your job is like. But if you have Net access, there are lots of ways to keep in touch with other corrections professionals and related organizations. These Web sites are for professionals working in the field, and provide information about events, careers, news, legal happenings, and so on. There are also online newsletters as well as chat rooms where you can talk to other people.

Web:
  http://www.corrections.com/
  http://www.nicic.org/

Crime Library

If you are interested in researching evil deeds and foul play, it would be a crime for you to miss this spot. There are long, thoughtful, well-researched articles on famous gangsters, serial killers, assassins, terrorists and other naughty people. I find these stories fascinating, and I bet you will too. Visit when you have time to stay for awhile.

Web:
  http://www.crimelibrary.com/

Crime Magazine

Okay, you know about the crimes, but do you know the gossip behind the crimes? If you like nothing better than to sink your intellectual teeth into a good story about gangsters, serial killers, sex crimes or murderers, you've come to the right place. Lots of good clean fun. What better way to spend quality time with your family?

Web:
  http://www.crimemagazine.com/

Crime News

Are you a crime buff? Well, buff right over to these comprehensive crime-oriented Web sites, where you'll find lots of info on safety, serial killers, currently wanted criminals, major unsolved cases, as well as the latest headlines and articles.

Web:
  http://www.apbonline.com/
  http://www.crimelibrary.com/news/
  http://www.crimenews2000.com/

Crime Statistics

Here are some interesting statistics about the population of the United States. At the end of 1980, there were 1,840,400 adults in prison, in jail, on probation, or on parole. By the end of 2000 (the latest year for which I could get statistics), this number had increased by 351% to 6,467,200. It's interesting to talk about numbers, but these figures represent real people in real communities. There are a lot more crime-related statistics on the Internet, and if you have an interest in this area, there is a lot for you to think about.

Web:
  http://www.albany.edu/sourcebook/
  http://www.bop.gov/weekly.html
  http://www.fbi.gov/ucr/ucr.htm
  http://www.icpsr.umich.edu/nacjd/
  http://www.ncjrs.org/
  http://www.ojp.usdoj.gov/bjs/

Crime Talk and General Discussion

If you are interested in talking about crime, there are several discussion groups just for you. For crime buffs, the **alt.crime** group discusses all types of miscellaneous topics, while **alt.true-crime** is for talking about famous crimes. If you are a law enforcement professional, you may want to participate in the **bail-enforce** group (professional bail enforcement) or the **criminology** group.

Usenet:
  alt.crime
  alt.crime.bail-enforce
  alt.crime.peacemaking.criminology
  alt.true-crime

Death Row

In the United States, the method of putting criminals to death varies from state to state. Overall, there are five different methods that are used: the electric chair, lethal injection, gas chamber, firing squad and hanging. Traditionally, "death row" is the name given to the part of the prison that houses inmates who are scheduled for execution. The death penalty and how it is applied are issues of great debate everywhere. Regardless of how you feel about the death penalty, it's interesting to look at some of the facts and figures. These Web sites have a lot of interesting information, but they did leave one of my questions unanswered. You know that before the doctor gives you an injection, he wipes your skin with an alcohol swab to clean off the germs. I wonder, when somebody is about to be executed by lethal injection, does the person administering the injection clean the person's skin with an alcohol swab?

Web:
http://web.cis.smu.edu/~deathpen/
http://www.deathrowspeaks.net/
http://www.derechos.org/dp/

Usenet:
alt.activism.death-penalty

Electric Chair

In the late 1880s, the electric chair was developed in order to execute criminals more humanely than by hanging. On August 6, 1890, the first person was put to death using this new technology. Since then, the electric chair has earned a place in the annals of American culture. And now, here is a Web site devoted entirely to this wonderful invention. Learn about the electric chair, its history, botched electrocutions, women in the electric chair, crimes, prisons, serial killers, and other methods of carrying out the death penalty.

Web:
http://www.theelectricchair.com/

Famous Murderers

What do Jack the Ripper, Theodore Kaczynski (the Unabomber), Charles Manson, Timothy McVeigh, Ted Bundy, Jeffrey Dahmer and O.J. Simpson all have in common? They all worked hard to rise to the top of their profession, and they all have information available about them on the Internet.

Web:
http://tornadohills.com/dahmer/
http://www.courttv.com/casefiles/oklahoma/
   mcveigh.html
http://www.courttv.com/trials/unabomber/
http://www.crimelibrary.com/bundy/attack.htm
http://www.crimelibrary.com/jack/jackmain.htm
http://www.crimelibrary.com/manson/
   mansonmain.htm
http://www.wagnerandson.com/oj/OJ.htm

Usenet:
alt.fan.karla-homolka
alt.fan.oj-simpson
alt.fan.unabomber

FBI's Ten Most Wanted Fugitives

Perhaps the most famous thing about the FBI (the United States Federal Bureau of Investigation) is its Ten Most Wanted Fugitives program. Starting in 1949, the FBI has published a list of the ten men and women it would most like to apprehend. Since then, more than 473 people (7 of whom were women) have had the honor of making the list. Except for 28 of these people, everyone on the list has been located, about 30 percent because a member of the public saw a familiar face on the list. Do you have some questionable friends? If you manage to turn in an actual fugitive, you could get rewarded with some big bucks.

Web:
http://www.fbi.gov/mostwant/topten/tenlist.htm

Gangs

There are youth gangs in virtually all large cities, and many towns, in the United States, Canada and Europe. At one time, it was thought that gangs were the result of children being raised in poverty. However, today, you will find gangs even in relatively affluent areas. Most gang members, of which 5 to 10 percent are girls, come from homes that have been broken by divorce, separation, abuse, or a dysfunctional parent. Most such children don't join gangs, but they are at risk. When some type of crisis happens in the child's life and there is no strong adult to whom the child can turn, he or she will sometimes join a gang. Joining a gang gives a child a lot more than a new "family". Gang membership eases the pain, anger and isolation felt by a teenager with nowhere else to turn. Would you like to understand gangs and see how you can help? Are you worried about your own kids? Start here.

Web:
  http://www.gangwar.com/
  http://www.lincolnnet.net/users/lrttrapp/block/
    gangs101.htm
  http://www.streetgangs.com/

Law Search

If you are a police officer, this is a resource you will want to visit. There is a large database of police-related Web sites, which you can search to find just what you need. There are also handy online utilities, such as an accident calculator and a U.S. Social Security number state lookup.

Web:
  http://www.copscgi.com/

Mafia

Whatever else you say about the Mafia, at least you have to admit they understand the importance of Family Values. If you want to learn even more about this collection of underground criminal societies, here are some good places to start. Although movies and TV often glorify gangsters, in real life they are highly unpleasant evil people, definitely not cool.

Web:
  http://www.americanmafia.com/
  http://www.ganglandnews.com/
  http://www.ipsn.org/themob.html

Police Brutality

Police brutality and abuse of power are more or less built into our society. As human beings, we need the police. We ask them to take constant risks and protect us against evil, crazy, dangerous (often well-armed) people, who don't have to follow the rules. But police are human, so who watches the police? These resources deal with the problems of police abuse, offering a variety of useful and interesting information. If you are a policeman, take a few moments and explore this information. If you are a civilian with a problem, you will find information to help.

Web:
  http://www.copwatch.com/
  http://www.october22.org/
  http://www.policeabuse.org/
  http://www.refuseandresist.org/ndp/

Police Scanners

Ever wonder what the police are talking about (when they're not cooping)? These Web sites feature live police transmissions from New York, Los Angeles and Dallas, as well as a variety of other live broadcasts, such as fire departments and air traffic controllers. To help you understand the slang, you can display a helpful list of the codes used on the radio. (In Los Angeles, for example, a "code 7" is a meal break.)

Web:
  http://www.apbonline.com/scanner/
  http://www.policescanner.com/police.stm

Prison Life

There are three types of people who will be interested in these resources: people who are currently in prison; people who are about to go to prison; and people who would like to find out what life is like in prison.

Web:

http://www.prisonactivist.org/
http://www.spr.org/
http://www.wild-side.com/darksorrow/stories.html

Usenet:

alt.prisons

Prison Penpals

Believe it or not, there are a lot of prisoners who have access to the Net, directly or through the help of others. These Web sites contain pages created by (or for) inmates, as well as names, addresses and biographical information about inmates who would like pen pals. Warning: When you read the biographies—written by the prisoners themselves—they all sound like nice, normal people who didn't do anything wrong. Obviously, this is usually not the case. If you decide to write to an inmate, be careful.

Web:

http://www.prison-penpals.com/
http://www.prisonpenpals.com/

Serial Killers

Serial killers are people who commit one murder after another, often following the same pattern. Here are some common characteristics shared by many such killers. Serial killers tend to be white heterosexual males in their twenties and thirties. They are loners with low self-esteem, subject to methodical rampages that are sexually motivated and sadistic. They enjoy returning to grave sites and crime scenes to fantasize. While growing up, their family life was violent, they tortured animals and were chronic bed-wetters. As adults, serial killers enjoy setting fires, have brain damage and are addicted to alcohol or drugs. If this reminds you of anyone you know, be careful. At the very least, don't give the person money or anything valuable (such as your only copy of a Harley Hahn book).

Web:

http://www.apbonline.com/crimesolvers/serialkiller/
http://www.serialkillers.net/

Sex Offender Registries

In the United States, people who have been convicted of committing certain types of crimes are required to register with their local police departments as sex offenders. The details vary from one jurisdiction to another, but basically, the police are not allowed to notify people when a registered sex offender moves into their neighborhood. However, people are allowed to go to the police station and check the official list to see which sex offenders live nearby. Some states post information online, others don't. Some cities have Web sites that show you a map of all the schools in the city and, when you click on a school, you are shown the locations of all the registered sex offenders in the vicinity. It's shocking how many there are. Check out your neighborhood.

Web:

http://www.parentsformeganslaw.com/html/
  links.lasso
http://www.sexcriminals.com/registries.html

Stalking

Stalking occurs when an obsessive person becomes completely and utterly focused on another individual. You have probably heard about high profile cases when the stalking victim is a celebrity. However, most victims are regular people, and the crime is a lot more common than you might think. If you have a stalking problem of your own, here is information that may help guide you toward a satisfactory resolution.

Web:

http://www.antistalking.com/
http://www.ncvc.org/src.htm
http://www.privacyrights.org/fs/fs14-stk.htm

Terrorism

The term "terrorism" is derived from the Reign of Terror (1793-1794), a period during the French Revolution when thousands of people were executed. In modern times, terrorism is much more widespread and involves the illegal use of force for political or ideological reasons. Although politicians like to talk about a "War on Terrorism", the global fight against terrorism is not nearly as straightforward as a conventional war. Who is the enemy? Who are our allies? How do we know when the "war" is won? People make their poorest decisions when they are scared and under pressure, and I see it happening now. We are all too quick to sacrifice our long-term judgment—and our liberties—because we are scared. With so much propaganda and censorship in the air, how can we understand what is really happening in order to make up our own minds? How do we decide what are the best actions to take in the long run? Although we will hear about terrorism on TV and read about it in the newspapers, there is a *lot* more going on than the news media is telling us.

Web:
  http://www.emergency.com/cntrterr.htm
  http://www.gwu.edu/~nsarchiv/NSAEBB/sept11/
  http://www.ict.org.il/
  http://www.llrx.com/newstand/wtc_h.htm
  http://www.pbs.org/newshour/terrorism/
  http://www.terrorism.net/
  http://www.usinfo.state.gov/topical/pol/terror/

Usenet:
  alt.conspiracy.america-at-war
  alt.security.terrorism
  alt.terrorism.world-trade-center
  alt.usa.disaster

Majordomo Mailing List:
  List Name: aftersept11
  Subscribe to: majordomo@interversity.com

Unsolved Crimes and Fugitives

Mystery, intrigue, adventure. If you have ever read any Sherlock Holmes stories, you may have wondered how you would be at solving mysteries. Well, here are some real-life mysteries waiting for you on the Net. These Web sites contain a lot of information describing unsolved crimes and criminal fugitives. Remember, as Sherlock Holmes once said, "It is of the highest importance in the art of detection to be able to recognize, out of a number of facts, which are incidental and which vital. Otherwise your energy and attention must be dissipated instead of being concentrated." Make sure you always do your research on the Net before setting out to find the criminal, and, one day, you too may be a famous fictional character.

Web:
  http://www.fugitive.com/main.html
  http://www.mostwanted.org/
  http://www2.amw.com/

Unsolved Crimes:
The Case of the Missing Plum

You read about a lot of unsolved crimes, but here is one that actually happened to me.

When I work late at night, I often like to stop for a quick snack. The other day, I bought a nice, juicy plum and left it on the kitchen counter. A few hours later, I took a short walk outside, and when I got back the plum was gone!

I searched all over the house, but there was no trace of the missing plum. The only other people in the house at the time were my cat (who doesn't even like plums), and my Senior Researcher (who was visiting from out of town) who said she had no idea what might have happened.

Later, I did find a plum pit in my Senior Researcher's trash basket, so the only thing I can think of is that the thief ate the plum, and left the pit in the trash basket to throw us off the trail.

I still can't figure it out.

CRYPTOGRAPHY

Ciphers

If you have to send a quick secret message to one of your friends, but you don't have time to make up a clever code, check out some of the ciphers that are already on the Net. While they aren't exactly a secret, some of them certainly are clever. Maybe you will get lucky and pick one that nobody has read about.

Web:

http://home.ecn.ab.ca/~jsavard/crypto/ppen01.htm
http://www.codebreaker.dids.com/

Crypto Bibliography

There is a ton of cryptography information on the Internet. However, if for some reason you can't find everything you need to know from the Net, check out this bibliography of books about cryptology and cryptography. It is bound to get you going in the right direction.

Web:

http://liinwww.ira.uka.de/bibliography/Theory/
   crypto.security.html
http://www.counterpane.com/biblio.html

Cryptographic Research

To be a cool cryptomaniac, you don't have to sit around in isolation planning new codes and trying to break old ones. No, you too can belong to a club of people just like you. (But remember what Groucho Marx once said, "I don't care to belong to any club that will have me as a member.")

Web:

http://www.iacr.org/~iacr/

Cryptography Archive

Here is a well-organized, compact collection of cryptography resources from around the Net. If you are at all serious about cryptography, you will want to put this site on your bookmark list. If you are not serious about cryptography, put this site on your list anyway. It's bound to impress your friends.

Web:

http://www.austinlinks.com/Crypto/

Cryptography Basics

Cryptography, the science of creating and breaking codes, is an ancient art. Modern cryptography is fascinating, but it can be very complex. To help you get started, here are some resources that will explain the basics. Start today with the ideas of plaintext, ciphertext and keys, and it won't be long before you are waxing eloquently on basic cryptographic algorithms, digital signatures, hash functions, random number generators, DES and advanced cryptanalysis. Eventually, no one will understand what you are talking about, but at least you will understand why.

Web:

http://www.ciphersbyritter.com/LEARNING.HTM
http://www.home.earthlink.net/~mylnir/
   crypt.intro.html
http://www.ssh.com/tech/crypto/intro.cfm

Cryptography FAQs

Cryptography is a fascinating pastime, and it's not difficult to spend many hours immersed in learning about codes. Before you spend too much time, however, take a few minutes and look at these FAQs (frequently asked question lists). Chances are most of your initial questions will be answered. Personally, I found reading these FAQs interesting and I bet you will too (especially if you know some math).

Web:

http://www.faqs.org/faqs/cryptography-faq/
http://www.rsasecurity.com/rsalabs/faq/

Cryptography Policy Issues

Cryptography is more than deciphering secret writing. There are also the political and administrative aspects. Here are some sites that consider cryptography from a political and legislative angle. Read about policies, legislative efforts, cryptography across international boundaries, and much more.

Web:
  http://www.cdt.org/crypto/
  http://www.eff.org/pub/Privacy/Crypto/
    Crypto_export/

Usenet:
  talk.politics.crypto

Cryptography Resources

One of the nice things about cryptography is that it will allow you to store copies of all your love notes on your computer at work and you don't have to worry about your colleagues reading anything that might embarrass you or perhaps cause you to lose a presidential election. Find out about other great uses for cryptography at these Web sites.

Web:
  http://world.std.com/~franl/crypto/
  http://www.cryptography.com/resources/
  http://www.cryptome.org/
  http://www.philzimmermann.com/
    bibliography.shtml

Cryptography Software

If you need some cryptography software, here are a few programs you can download and try for free: PGP, RPK, Crypto Kong and TEA. All of these programs are very secure, but each one has its own design and features. Try them all and see which one you like best.

Web:
  http://disastry.dhs.org/xtea/
  http://web.mit.edu/network/pgp.html
  http://www.di-mgt.com.au/crypto.html
  http://www.echeque.com/kong/kong.htm

Cryptography Talk and General Discussion

Here is a general discussion group for all aspects of data encryption and decryption. If you are a cryptography aficionado, this is the place to communicate with your peers on the Net. (Note: The following is a message in code. There is a prize if you can break it. —Harley)

```
F_eB7    n!K4r    F^Pb2    M:Quf    ^{9&L
0y}w#    I/hH@    K`|eI    6N%-R    G-(4u
UA,,]    .Gs2~    o&?_^    :|IJA    V*e}@
;a2#3    ZZuJB    tOpx9    \@z)t    {eNSr
;LSZx    Kht9.    'oRFa    J`/KH    oF:q'
Hn[\P    vwqo1    4^:pI    ~&8jb    ]q4(2
1D)OE    v.bvZ    6[M\$    1)n;b    L$?q{
d,$}F    Q4PBM    c[<&U    )2>j)    Sh\yF
!\u@j    }:)ZW    cOPKt    2_~P/    x|s]!
;<6.Q    ;<;t     UB,-{    3@wzB    HD4PH
tb$Xr    !2Rpm    &7}BU    8sg)=    {
```

Usenet:
  sci.crypt

Digital Signatures and Certificates

More and more, we have the need to send information over the Net in complete secret. For example, if you order merchandise online by typing your credit card number, you should be sure that no one else can tap into the line, capture the information and use it for their own purposes. Or you may want to send a message to a friend or colleague that no one but the recipient can read. The systems that send and receive secure information over the Net use what are called "digital signatures" and "digital certificates". Such facilities are going to be in common use, so it is a good idea to find out how they work.

Web:
  http://digitalid.verisign.com/client/help/id_intro.htm
  http://www.abanet.org/scitech/ec/isc/
    dsg-tutorial.html
  http://www.howstuffworks.com/question571.htm

Hidden Messages

Here is the situation. You have an idea for a wonderful new book, one that, without a doubt, will revolutionize Western Civilization. You need to email a secret message to your editor to show him the outline of the book. However, other publishers (not to mention the government) have spies everywhere and will go to extreme lengths to steal your ideas. You could use a well-known encryption method, like PGP, but anyone who sees the message would know that it was encrypted, which would bring the harsh eye of suspicion down upon your efforts. Instead, why not hide the secret message in something that looks completely innocent? You could, for example, use "stegnography" to hide a message in a picture or sound file. You could then email the picture to the editor. Since he is the only one with the password, only he can decode the secret message. You could even put the picture on your Web site, secure in the knowledge that no one else would even suspect it of holding a message. Want to be even more sneaky? Hide your secret in a fake email message disguised as spam. (Really.)

Web:

http://www.cl.cam.ac.uk/~fapp2/steganography/
http://www.jjtc.com/Steganography/
http://www.spammimic.com/
http://www.stego.com/

Hidden Messages

Steganography is the most amazing, cool thing you have ever seen. You can encode secret information inside a *picture* — within the little tiny dots. To anyone else, it looks like a regular picture (say, of you shaking hands with Britney Spears and the Pope at George Bush's birthday party). But to anyone in the know, it is a *secret message*. You can send it all around the Net if you want, and no one can extract the information unless they have the password.

Navajo Code Talkers

During World War II, there were a number of U.S. military personnel who were Navajo (a nation of native Americans), primarily Marines in the Pacific theater. At the time, the military authorities were having trouble because the Japanese were breaking many of the Allied codes. In order to create a secure code, a group of Navajo took the English alphabet and assigned each letter to specific Navajo words. For example, the letter "A" was assigned to the words wol-la-chee (which means "ant"), be-la-sana ("apple") and tse-nill ("axe"); "B" was assigned to na-hash-chid ("badger"), shush ("bear") and toish-jeh ("barrel"); and so on. In the basic system, an encoded message would use one Navajo word for each letter. In addition, some very important words were assigned to a single Navajo word. For example, the word "America" was encoded as ne-he-mah (which means "our mother"). The Navajo Code was extremely successful, and the people who used it came to be known as Navajo Code Talkers. The husband of one of my researchers (Kelly's husband, Charlie) is half Navajo and has clan relatives who were code talkers during the war (and to this day, Kelly still has trouble understanding everything that Charlie says.)

Web:

http://www.execpc.com/~shepler/codetalkers.html
http://www.history.navy.mil/faqs/faq12-1.htm
http://www.history.navy.mil/faqs/faq61-2.htm
http://www.history.navy.mil/faqs/faq61-4.htm
http://www.lapahie.com/navajocodetalker.cfm

PGP

The PGP (Pretty Good Privacy) system is widely used to encrypt and decrypt data. Download the software for free, and use it to send secret messages to your friends. Better yet, encrypt your diary with PGP and even your mother won't be able to read it.

Web:

http://web.bham.ac.uk/n.m.queen/pgp/pgp.html
http://www.pgp.com/products/freeware/default.asp
http://www.pgpi.org/

Usenet:

alt.security.keydist
alt.security.pgp
comp.security.pgp.discuss

Listproc Mailing List:

List Name: pgp-users
Subscribe to: listproc@listproc.umbc.edu

Sending Secret Messages with PGP

The best things in life may be free, but if you don't want to share, you may have to hide them. One of the most widely used encryption programs on the Net is PGP, written by Phil Zimmerman. By offering a free, high-quality software package to everyone, Zimmerman single handedly deep-sixed the government's plans to control encryption.

Using PGP requires two passwords, called "keys". One of these is public; the other one is secret. You give your public key to anyone you want to be able to send secret notes to you. They use this key (and the PGP software) to encode a message which they then send to you. The beauty of the system is that a person can only decode the message if they have the private key (which you keep only for yourself).

The PGP program helps you create public and private keys that will work properly. Then you can give out your public key to your friends and start sending secrets around the Net. Similarly, if you have a friend who uses PGP, you can use his public key to encode a message to him that only he can read (because only he has the corresponding private key).

RSA

RSA is a cryptography system, invented in 1977, that is used for both encryption and authentication. (The name comes from RSA's inventors, Ron Rivest, Adi Shamir and Leonard Adleman.) With RSA, each person has a public key and a private key. You can give your public key to everyone; it is not a secret. However, you do not give out your private key. When another person wants to send you a secret message, he uses your public key to encrypt a message. The nature of RSA is such that, once someone uses your public key to encrypt a message, the message can only be decrypted by using your private key. Thus, you are the only person in the world who can decrypt messages that have been encrypted with your public key (because no one else has your private key). RSA is secure because it is extremely difficult to use someone's public key to figure out his private key. Thus, you can give out your public key with no worries. Of course, the whole system depends on being able to create suitable pairs of private and public keys. To create such a pair, you start with large prime numbers—call them p and q. Find their product $n=pq$. Choose a number e, less than n, such that e and $(p-1)(q-1)$ have no common factors except 1. (In other words, e and $(p-1)(q-1)$ are relatively prime.) Now find another number d, such that $(ed-1)$ is divisible by $(p-1)(q-1)$. The public key is the pair (n,e), and the private key is (n,d). Once the keys are generated, the factors p and q can be thrown away. Here is the Web site of a company called RSA Data Security, which was formed by the inventors of RSA in order to develop and explore the technology. You will find a lot of interesting information about RSA and about people's attempts to break the code.

Web:

  http://www.rsasecurity.com/

There's plenty of time. Relax and enjoy yourself.

DANCE

Ballet

Ballet is a formalized dance discipline, first developed in 16th century Italy. (The name "ballet" comes from the Italian word meaning "to dance".) The history of ballet is long and complex. Here is a quick summary, touching only on the most important highlights. 1581: The first ballet is presented at the French court of Catherine de' Medici (the wife of Henry II). 1681: Women, and not just men, now dance in the ballet. 1708: The first public performance of a ballet is presented. 1820: Carlo Blasis introduces modern ballet technique (including the turned-out leg). 1832: "La Sylphide" begins the romantic period of ballet, emphasizing the role of the prima ballerina. 1875: A renaissance of romantic ballet begins in Russia. 1909-1929: Ballet enjoys a renaissance in Europe and America, and is strongly influenced by modern dance. The tradition of male virtuoso dancing is revived. 1977: Harley Hahn takes ballet classes while he is a graduate student. Late 20th century: Ballet gains great popularity, especially in the United States.

Web:
http://www.abt.org/
http://www.artslynx.org/dance/ballets.htm
http://www.ballet.co.uk/magazine/
http://www.balletalert.com/
http://www.blue-diamond-dance.com/
http://www.cyberdance.org/
http://www.danceart.com/
http://www.dancer.com/dance-links/ballet.htm
http://www.panix.com/~twp/dance/faq_1.htm

Usenet:
alt.arts.ballet

As they say in Hotdog Land, "You may already be a wiener."

Ballroom Dancing

Recently, I went dancing with a friend. Last year, we took swing dance classes together, and have been dancing together for some time. She suggested that, this time, we go to a ballroom dancing event where, before the band starts, there is a lesson for beginners. The lesson that week was an introduction to samba. Well, I can tell you that, even though I am in good shape (I have been doing yoga for years), doing the Samba required a fair bit of muscular effort. Later, when the band started, we were able to dance to a variety of music: swing, samba/mambo, waltz, polka, and so on. I don't know how to do all of those dances but, between us, I have found that with a bit of experience and enough chutzpah you can fake anything.

Web:
http://www.astro.umd.edu/~marshall/dance/
    etiquette.html
http://www.ballroomdancers.com/
http://www.dancesport.uk.com/world.htm
http://www.dancetv.com/tutorial/basics/

Listserv Mailing List:
List Name: ballrm-m
Subscribe to: listserv@mitvma.mit.edu

Listserv Mailing List:
List Name: ballroom
Subscribe to: listserv@mitvma.mit.edu

Belly Dancing

Belly dancing, Oriental Dance, has been a part of the Middle Eastern and Mediterranean cultures for a long time, but its exact development is not known (although there are lots of stories). Belly dancing became known in America in 1893, in the Columbian Exposition in Chicago. It was the first time that Americans had been exposed (in public) to exotic, Middle Eastern dancers and their sinuous hip, chest and belly movements. Although I enjoy watching belly dancing, the only dancer I ever knew personally was a beautiful young, slim woman, who was also a rugby player. (I'm still trying to figure it out.)

Web:
http://www.bdancer.com/
http://www.desertdance.com/
http://www.gildedserpent.com/
http://www.mecda.org/
http://www.shira.net/
http://www.tiac.net/users/morocco/articles.html
http://www.zilltech.com/FAQ.html

Majordomo Mailing List:
List Name: med-dance
Subscribe to: majordomo@world.std.com

Break Dancing

Break dancing, which started as a rap-based, inner-city art form in the 1980s, has evolved. It has now embraced hip-hop and the suburbs, and the boomboxes and rappers have been replaced by disc jockeys at all night raves. Everything old is new again, and as loud as ever. (If you remember the original break dancing craze, let me tell you something that is guaranteed to make you feel old: there are now father and son break dancing teams.)

Web:
  http://www.breakdance.com/
  http://www.breakdancecrew.com/
  http://www.scarybubs.com/bboy/

Usenet:
  alt.breakdancing

Competitive Dance Sport

I have a friend who used to compete seriously as a ballroom dancer. In her words, "It's a bitch-eat-bitch world, where both the men and women are bitches." Still, for a spectator, competitive dancing is wonderful. I like to watch because it shows me how skillful people can become by practicing, which inspires me to spend time on the parts of life that I want to improve (like my dancing).

Web:
  http://www.dancescape.com/
  http://www.danceseattle.com/comp.calender.htm
  http://www.dancevision.com/

Contra Dancing

It's not square dancing. It's not country line dancing. A young, Americanized version of English country dancing, this lively dancing pastime gets its name from the French *contredans*. While nobody agrees on the origins, most everyone agrees that contra dancing is the most fun you can have without having to wash your hands afterwards.

Web:
  http://www.concentric.net/~ravitz/dance/
  http://www.io.com/~entropy/contradance/
  http://www.ipcc.com/nationalcontra/
    contra.frame.html
  http://www.sbcds.org/contradance/whatis/
  http://www.tiac.net/users/cseelig/contra/
    contralinks.shtml

Country Line Dancing

You are standing with a group of people, listening to the music. You get caught up in the rhythm, and your body begins to move. All at once, everyone begins to move at the same time—side shuffle rock step, side shuffle quarter-turn rock step... and you're dancing. To be more precise, you are country line dancing. It's easy to learn, but a challenge to master, so what are you waiting for?

Web:
  http://homepages.apci.net/~drdeyne/glossary.htm
  http://www.country-time.com/ldinfo/danceinfo.htm
  http://www.kickit.to/ld/
  http://www.linedancecountry.com/
  http://www.linedancermagazine.com/

Majordomo Mailing List:
  List Name: line-dance
  Subscribe to: majordomo@world.std.com

Dance News

Dance, dance, dance... But now and again, you need a break. What better time to catch up on what's new and what's news in the dance world. Read about who is doing what, and what is being done by whomever. Opinions, stories, articles, features, and soon it is time to go back to work. Dance, dance, dance…

Web:
  http://www.danceinsider.com/
  http://www.dancemagazine.com/

Dance Resources

After six hours of school, I've had enough of a day, I grab the radio dial, and turn it up all the way, I've got to dance, right on the spot, the beat's really hot, dance, dance, dance, dance... (And when I'm not dancing, I'm on the Net, looking at dance resources.)

Web:
  http://www.artslynx.org/dance/
  http://www.dance.thelinks.com/resource.html
  http://www.dancer.com/dance-links/

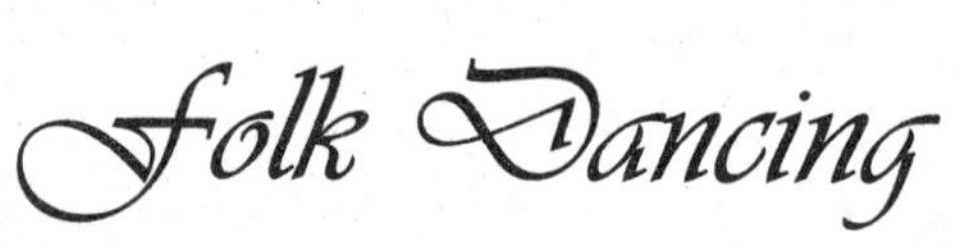

is like life, in that there are only two basic rules to remember:

(1) Wear comfortable shoes.

(2) Don't worry if you are out of step. Just enjoy yourself.

Dance Talk and General Discussion

Eventually the music will stop, but that's no reason for you to stop dancing. Do what I do: stand in front of the computer, read the Usenet articles, and check out the FAQ (frequently asked question list).

Web:
  http://www.dancetalk.com/
  http://www.eijkhout.net/rad/

Usenet:
  rec.arts.dance

Flamenco

There is absolutely no truth to the rumor that culture is boring. This is simple propaganda designed by those in the entertainment business to seduce people into watching more television when, in fact, they should be out learning how to flamenco dance. Flamenco dancing is fun. Other than children's birthday parties, where else can you wear colorful costumes while dancing around, stomping your feet and clapping your hands?

Web:
  http://www.andalucia.com/flamenco/
  http://www.flamenco-world.com/magazine/
    magazine.htm
  http://www.red2000.com/spain/flamenco/

Listserv Mailing List:
  List Name: flamenco
  Subscribe to: listserv@listserv.temple.edu

Folk and Traditional Dance

I have always had a strong interest in traditional dances; for example, my favorite dance is the "Freddy". If you too like traditional dances, you are not alone. Here are some resources to keep you in step with people around the world who care about how dancing used to be in the days when people danced to enjoy life and not just to keep moving till the drugs wore off.

Web:
  http://www.ftech.co.uk/~webfeet/

Usenet:
  rec.folk-dancing

Morris Dancing

When you are looking for something lively in which to participate, consider taking up Morris dancing. This rustic dance of north England had its origins in country festivals and became a vigorous ambulatory dance which found its dancers cavorting from village to village accompanied by pipers and taborers. These resources offer information not only about Morris dancing, but also Garland, North West, Rapper, Cotswold, Border, Abbots Bromley, Longsword and similar forms of English dance.

Web:
   http://web.syr.edu/~rsholmes/morris/rich/
      morris_links.html

Listserv Mailing List:
   List Name: morris
   Subscribe to: listserv@listserv.iupui.edu

Renaissance Dance

For those of you with a little more vintage taste for dance, try Renaissance dancing. It's colorful, it's cultural, the music is good and best of all, you can't get arrested for doing it. The Web sites have tons of files about the dance, including information about music, history and the dance steps themselves. If you want to talk to other people about Renaissance dances, join the mailing list.

Web:
   http://www.pbm.com/~lindahl/dance.html
   http://www.rendance.org/

Listserv Mailing List:
   List Name: rendance
   Subscribe to: listserv@morgan.ucs.mun.ca

Don't just sit there. Put on the music and samba. (And while you are dancing, read about samba on the Net.)

Salsa

Salsa music developed in the 1970s in New York. Salsa dance, based on the music, is a sort of a rumba blended with Cuban, Puerto Rican and Dominican influences. What is wonderful about a salsa concert is the musicians will often perform and dance at the same time. Spend just a few minutes listening, and your body will start moving, and once you start moving, you won't want to stop. That's salsa.

Web:
   http://www.dancefreak.com/
   http://www.planetsalsa.com/
   http://www.salserosweb.com/

Samba

Samba is a type of music and a type of dance from Brazil, a tradition that originated with African slaves. Samba is a lively, gyrating, complicated dance. The men and women perform different moves, with the women shaking their bodies and the men doing more hopping, jumping and slapping hands to their heels (sort of like Customer Appreciation Day at Wal-Mart, without the free pizza).

Web:
   http://www.worldsamba.org/

Majordomo Mailing List:
   List Name: sambistas
   Subscribe to: majordomo@tardis.ed.ac.uk

Honesty: it's cheap and it works.

Square Dancing

Square dancing is wholesome, good clean fun, and, these days, is there anyone who can't use a bit more w.g.c.f. in their life? If you enjoy hanging out with the type of people who understand the difference between a single file promenade and a rollaway half sashay, there is a lot waiting for you on the Net: information about clubs and schools, call lists and definitions, articles to read, and lots of resources to explore. You can even find computer programs that act as square dance simulators. So don't waste a minute. Get out and dance, and when you're not dancing, get on the Net. And the next time you take a shower, join me in singing, "Chicken in the bread pan kickin' out the dough; Chicken in the bread pan kickin' out the dough; Chicken in the bread pan kickin' out the dough; Skip to my Lou, my darling

Web:

http://www.dosado.com/
http://www.squaredancing.com/

Square Dancing,
the Pastime of Kings

Who has not fantasized about meeting the perfect man or woman in the middle of a square dance? There is something about this honestly American tradition that fans the flames of grace and nobility in all of us. The next time you are sitting home on a Saturday night, wondering if there are people out there who really know how to have more fun than you, take a look at the Western Square Dancing Web site and eat your heart out. Then stop feeling sorry for yourself and get out on the floor.

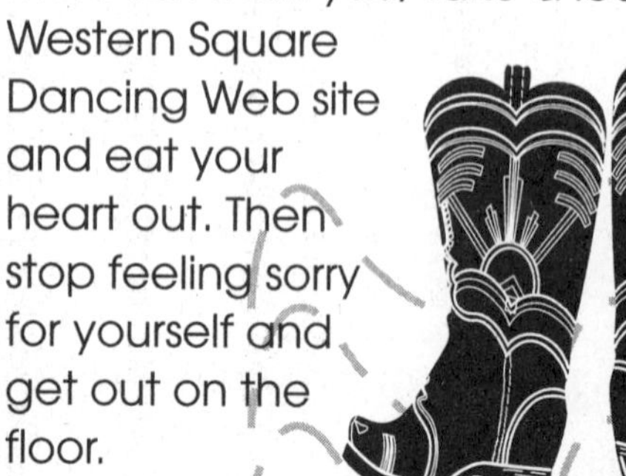

Swing Dance

Swing all night and at daybreak when the music dies down, come home to the Web and swing some more. These Web sites have more information than you can triple step on. For instance, you can get information on upcoming swing dance events on a local or national level. Or you can read about styles and techniques of swing. Impress your friends and dance partners with your huge knowledge of swing steps that you learned from these fabulous online swing sources. I could go on and on, but I have better things to do...like go dancing.

Web:

http://www.anyswinggoes.com/
http://www.havetodance.com/
http://www.planetswing.com/
http://www.swingon.com/Swingpedia.html
http://www.worldofswing.com/woslinksus.asp

Listserv Mailing List:

List Name: swing_dance
Subscribe to: listserv@listserv.vt.edu

Tango

What is it that is so appealing, so passionate and so captivating about the tango? At first glance, it's hard to understand the attraction. Why would so many people spend so much time moving with restrained eroticism to haunting music, when they could be sitting at home reading one of my books? Still, there are tango fans all over the world, so there must be something in it. Try it for yourself and you will find that there is nothing better to perk up an otherwise dull day than a heavy dose of carefully channeled sensuality. (Personal note: My favorite tango is "The Masochism Tango" by Tom Lehrer, which I play on the piano whenever I need a break from writing.)

Web:

http://members.ping.at/kdf-wien/tango/
http://www.bridgetothetango.com/News.htm
http://www.cyber-tango.com/e/tango_e.html
http://www.forevertango.com/links.html

Listserv Mailing List:

List Name: tango-l
Subscribe to: listserv@mitvma.mit.edu

Tap Dancing

When you are looking for some lively, snappy dancing, consider tap. On the mailing list, lovers of fancy footwork discuss steps, techniques, shoes, dancers and the tap industry. For more immediate gratification, you can shuffle, flap, hop, scuff, paddle, dig or cramp roll your way to the Web site. These pages contain information about dance steps, famous tapsters, dance clubs, movies, sounds, and more. By the way, when I was a kid, I used to do a lot of tap dancing, until one day I fell into the sink and hurt my ankle.

Web:
   http://www.tapdance.org/

Majordomo Mailing List:
   List Name: tap-jazz
   Subscribe to: majordomo@world.std.com

DEVICES AND GIZMOS CONNECTED TO THE NET

Animal Cams

Visit various animals live on the Net and become a full-fledged zoological voyeur. Here are some Web sites that will let you look at a giraffe, a wolf, chimps, an elephant, and lots more types of animals. Wait! I have an idea. Throw an animal party, where each person comes dressed as their favorite animal. Then visit each Web site in turn and, when you get to an animal that looks like one of your guests, the guest has to run around the room imitating the animal as it moves on your screen. Boy, talk about fun! Computers, the Internet, animals, friends—it just doesn't get any better.

Web:
   http://kids.discovery.com/cams/cams.html
   http://natzoo.si.edu/webcams/webcams.htm
   http://www.antcam.com/
   http://www.cmzoo.org/zoocam.html
   http://www.cwu.edu/~cwuchci/chimpcam-east.html
   http://www.cyberferrets.com/
   http://www.oinkernet.com/
   http://www.wpz.org/
   http://www.ywl.com/webcam.htm

Cameras on the Net

Feeling lonely and out of sorts? Why not take a moment and look at interesting people, places and things around the world? If you are stuck in a cubicle, check out the views of exotic lands. If you are stuck in an exotic land, look for a cubicle.

Web:

> http://www.agocam.com/english/
> http://www.cam.com/cam/
> http://www.camfun.com/
> http://www.comfm.com/webcam/
> http://www.livecamonline.com/
> http://www.vuecam.com/

Now, for a change, *you* get to be Big Brother. Use one of the cameras on the Net to see what someone else is doing.

New York Views

I love New York in June; how about you? The good news is you don't have to wait until June to see some hot New York action. Check out these Big Apple cameras now, and look at some totally cool NYC sights. (The only better view in town is from the camera in Donald Trump's walk-in closet.)

Web:

> http://home.con2.com/easysurf/cams/
> http://www.bionicsonics.com/
> http://www.hudsonriverlive.com/
> http://www.riotingmanhattan.com/riot_site/
>   webcam.html

Sightseeing Cams

Do you ever feel like going on a trip without leaving the house? Why not tour the world from the comfort of your most comfortable armchair? Here are some places to start. (If you get bored, you can always turn off the computer and read a travel book.)

Web:

> http://www.123cam.com/
> http://www.camvista.com/england/london/
> http://www.lecieldeparis.com/
> http://www.nps.gov/yell/oldfaithfulcam.htm
> http://www.onworld.com/cam/

Taxi Cams

Do you have trouble sleeping? If so, I bet I know why. It's because you just can't relax until you have that comfortable, secure feeling that comes from riding in a taxi. But when you are sitting at home late at night, how can you be riding in a taxi at the same time? Easy. All you have to do is visit one of these taxi cams. Before you can say, "Isn't the meter supposed to be running?" you'll be cruising in the fast lane, and before you know it, sleep will come and claim you for its own.

Web:

> http://www.laavenue.com/la/livecam.htm
> http://www.livetaxi.com/

Things on the Net

Stuff is good. However, having too much stuff in your house is not good. But now, thanks to the Net, you can have access to other people's stuff. This Web site has links to lots of devices that are connected to the Net: cameras, machines, robots, gadgets, screen captures, pagers, and lots more.

Web:

> http://www.oink.com/thingys/

Happiness is a warm modem.

Traffic Conditions

Do you drive in a big city? If so, think about this: as you drive, you are making a small contribution to the overall traffic pattern. That is important because it just may be that people all over the world are looking at that traffic pattern right now on the Web. Take a look. See the cool color-coded map that shows you where the traffic is moving and where it's stuck. Try again during rush hour and see the pattern change. Aren't you glad you're not there?

Web:

    http://www.accessatlanta.com/partners/wsbtv/traffic/
    http://www.eng.hawaii.edu/~csp/Trafficam/
    http://www.hamptonroads.com/traffic/
    http://www.kpix.com/traffic/cameras/
    http://www.nyc.gov/html/dot/html/travroad/
      atis.html
    http://www.wsdot.wa.gov/pugetsoundtraffic/
      cameras/

Vending Machines

The rage started with being able to check the Coke machine from the Internet. Things got out of control with the invention of CU-SeeMe. Check out coffee machines, temperature gauges, light sensors and a Geiger counter without leaving your seat. "Spy cameras" have been set up in offices and pointed out windows so you can even have a view.

Web:

    http://www-cse.ucsd.edu/users/bsy/coke.html

Volcanoes on the Net

I think you and I had better get organized, so here's my plan. Let's get a bunch of people and organize them into teams. Every day, one of the teams is responsible for monitoring these Web sites, where anyone can use recent satellite photos to keep an eye on the most active volcanoes in the world. As soon as a volcano starts to look as if it is going to erupt, the team leader notifies you and me immediately, so we can give everyone instructions on what to do. In that way, the world will be a safer, more organized place. What do you think?

Web:

    http://www.ssec.wisc.edu/data/volcano.html
    http://www.volcanolive.com/volcanocams.html

The Perfect Relaxation Technique

When I feel the need to relax, I use the Net to check the traffic flow on the Los Angeles freeway system.

I look at every colored dot on the map and imagine tens of thousands of cars, slowing down, speeding up, making noise and emitting exhaust.

Within a few minutes, I am completely relaxed and ready to get back to work.

Wedding Cams

What could be more romantic than watching someone else's wedding from a distance? And what better way to get your favorite guy or gal to agree to tie the knot with you? All you need to do is invite your friend over, prepare a candlelight meal with soft music, and then use the Net to share in a real wedding experience. Unless I miss my bet, your significant other will be in such a romantic mood that it won't be long before you have a ring and a date. (By the way, if you do decide to haul off and commit matrimony, be sure to get married in the evening. That way, if it doesn't work out, at least you haven't blown a whole day.)

Web:

http://www.littlechapel.com/liveweddings/
   liveweddings.html
http://www.valleyweddingchapel.com/~chapelcam/

DIET AND NUTRITION

Ask the Dietitian

Our culture is obsessed with food and dietary silliness, and there is a great deal of misinformation. For this reason, it is a pleasure to visit this Web site. There are a great many diet-related questions and they are all answered sensibly and knowledgeably by a dietitian. If it's real information you want about food, nutrition and diet, make this your first stop.

Web:

http://www.dietitian.com/

> **Everything is a dream—
> but don't wake
> up right now.
> It's still raining outside.**

Basal Metabolism Calculator

Here is my simple, four-step plan to achieve optimal health. (1) Visit this Web site and enter your height, weight, age and gender. The computer will perform a calculation and tell you your basal metabolism rate. (2) Specify the activity level that best describes your favorite activity. The computer will then display a detailed breakdown of how many calories you should be eating, and how much of those calories should come from fats, proteins and carbohydrates. (3) Study these numbers carefully, paying particular attention to the maximum suggested values. (4) Order a pizza.

Web:

http://www.room42.com/nutrition/basal.shtml

Calorie Counters

You are just about to pop a couple of chocolate-chip cookies when, suddenly, the god of remorse pops in and gives you the old sleeve across the windpipe. "Do you know," he asks, "how many calories are in those things you are about to put into your body?" Well, you don't need to take this type of abuse. Fire up the old browserooni, and check with a calorie-counter Web site. In two whisks of a cat's tail, you'll be able to say, "Of course I know. These cookies have 90-115 calories, and if you watch carefully, you will now see me ingest them before your very eyes." Ha, that will show the god of remorse.

Web:

http://www.bgsm.edu/nutrition/fdcalc.htm
http://www.ntwrks.com/~mikev/

Cyberdiet

If you think you need to go on a diet, but you are not sure exactly where to start, check with this Web site. They offer a nutritional profile that might help you determine the amount of calories you should eat in order to maintain or decrease your weight. Other information about dieting is also available.

Web:

http://www.cyberdiet.com/

Diet Analysis

If you are serious about maintaining a healthy diet, you may want to analyze what you eat. If so, use this resources to help you figure out just what you are ingesting. Specify what you have eaten today, and let the computer estimate the calories, protein, vitamins and minerals you consumed. (Remember, however, that all such numbers are gross estimates. There is no way to know exactly what is in a particular food.)

Web:
  http://www.dietsite.com/

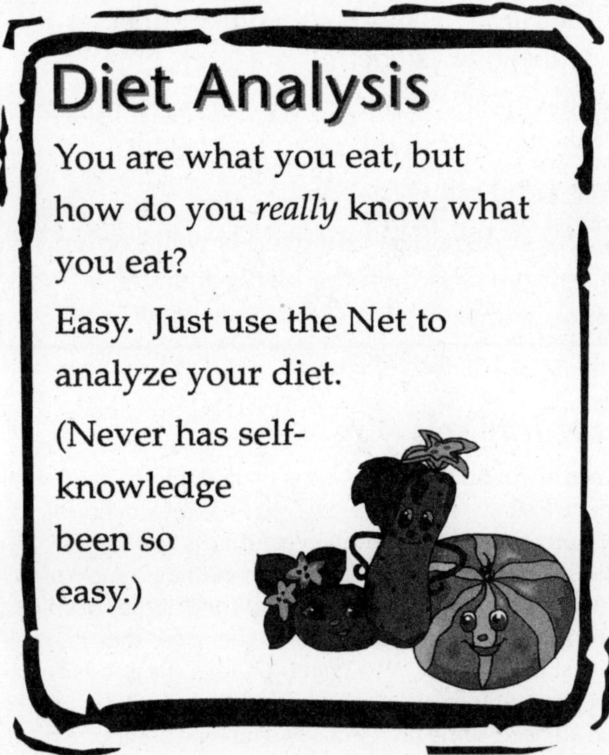

Dieting FAQ

When you are suffering from too much information, get some help sorting it all out with the FAQ from **alt.support.diet**. This list of frequently asked questions covers issues such as general diet and nutrition, weight loss, liquid diets and fasts, weight loss organizations and diet books, motivation, exercise, diet aids, and more.

Web:
  http://www.faqs.org/faqs/dieting-faq/

Dieting Talk and General Discussion

Does your diet work? Or like the other 99.9 percent of humanity, do you have to suffer to lose excess weight? Join ultra-nutrition-conscious people around the world who will thank you for sharing. Trade stories, scientific trivia and leftover Weight Watchers' menus. Are you just about ready for your own zip code? Lonely no more.

Usenet:
  alt.support.diet
  alt.support.diet.rx
  alt.support.diet.zone

Fad Diets

Every day you can see new fad diets in magazines and books. Each one claims to be *the* way to fill your dieting needs. This has been happening for years, and the diets still come and go like the tide. The American Heart Association has a page that talks about fad diets from a health point of view. You might want to read this before starting any new program that you think may be a flash in the fad-diet pan.

Web:
  http://www.americanheart.org/
    presenter.jhtml?identifier=4584

Fast Food Calorie Counter

When you go to a fast food restaurant, you can't exactly read the labels to see what you are putting into your body. In fact, you are probably better off if you *don't* read the labels. Instead, use these calorie counters to find out how fattening everything is. After all, what's the point of eating junky fast food if you can't at least get a substantial helping of guilt out of the experience?

Web:
  http://www.fatcalories.com/
  http://www.kenkuhl.com/fastfood/search.shtml
  http://www.olen.com/food/

Fat

It's 11:00 PM, do you know what your cholesterol/HDL risk ratio is? Saturated fat, hydrogenated fat, good fat, bad fat, everyone is talking about fat. Sometimes the stories, ideas and rumors are so conflicting, you can't tell if you are sinking slowly or rising to the top of the soup bowl of life, only to be skimmed off. Don't despair, get your fat facts hot off the Net.

Web:
    http://www.americanheart.org/
        presenter.jhtml?identifier=4582
    http://www.ific.org/proactive/newsroom/
        release.vtml?id=18325

Healthy Diet Guidelines

When it's time to get off the Pepsi and cheeseburger express, get help from your friend the Net. You'll find everything you need to eat well except willpower. In particular, you will find simple guidelines for a healthy diet. Here is my suggestion: eat vegetables, fruits, fish, grains and oil (in that order). However, I recognize that, when it comes to food, there is no single diet that works for everyone, so I am including a special Web page at the USDA site. Here you'll find links to different food pyramids for various food and ethnic preferences, including one for vegetarians.

Web:
    http://www.americanheart.org/
        presenter.jhtml?identifier=4561
    http://www.nal.usda.gov/fnic/dga/
    http://www.nal.usda.gov/fnic/etext/000023.html
    http://www.nal.usda.gov/fnic/Fpyr/pyramid.html

Holiday Diet Tips

Inevitably, when the holidays roll around, out come the trays of party snacks and rich chocolates, not to mention the high-fat cheeseballs sent across the country by your well-meaning Aunt Matilda (who used to send fruitcakes until she found out you were using them as doorstops). Prepare now by reading tips on how to enjoy the holidays without overeating.

Web:
    http://www.dietbites.com/article1052.html
    http://www.mediarelations.ksu.edu/web/news/
        inview/120601eating.html
    http://www.wellnessjunction.com/athome/nutrition/
        holtips.htm

Healthy Diet Guidelines

People talk a lot about nutrition and dieting, and it's not new. For much of the twentieth century, special diets were a staple of the body cultural.

There is a great deal of confusion, but it's not necessary. All you have to do is follow the Harley Hahn 21st Century Super Nutrition System:

Step 1: Find out what type of diet a normal person should follow to stay healthy.

Step 2: Follow that diet.

The information you need is well known. You can find it on the Net whenever you want.

Low-Fat Diets

There are a number of reasons that people go on low-fat diets. Usually, it is to lose weight or to lower cholesterol, or both. Some people, however, must go on low-fat diets because they have medical conditions (such as pancreatic problems) that prevent their bodies from producing the enzymes or other chemicals they need to digest fat properly. As a general rule, it is a good idea to keep your fat intake down, but don't make it too low: we all need some fat regularly. The type of fats we need are called "essential fatty acids". (A good source is olive oil, which is the main fat I use in my diet.) If you are thinking of going on a low-fat diet, my advice is take some time to learn about what types of fats are good for you and what types are best to avoid.

Web:
    http://www.americanheart.org/
        presenter.jhtml?identifier=4633
    http://www.lightliving.com/
    http://www.mardiweb.com/lowfat/
    http://www.orst.edu/food-resource/l/lowfat/
Usenet:
    alt.food.fat-free
    alt.food.low-fat

Nutrition

Should you eat the Twinkie or opt for another seaweed sandwich? Join the conversation and talk about the usual gang of suspects: vitamins, carbohydrates, proteins, fats, minerals and fiber. Then hop over to a Web site, and read and read and read about food until you are stuffed.

Web:
http://www.ag.uiuc.edu/~food-lab/nat/
http://www.eatright.org/nuresources.html
http://www.ific.org/food/adult.vtml
http://www.nal.usda.gov/fnic/etext/fnic.html
http://www.nutrition.gov/

Usenet:
sci.med.nutrition

Vending Machine Nutrition

How many calories are you putting into your body on those midnight snack runs to the vending machine? Before you commit yourself to putting that something-or-other in your mouth, find out exactly how many of those hard-to-burn little monsters are making their way onto your hips and thighs. Better yet, if you must live on vending machine fodder, find out which choices are actually good for you.

Web:
http://public.bcm.tmc.edu/pa/
vending_machine_snackattacks.htm
http://www.members.aol.com/nedtalk/personal/
caloriepg2.html

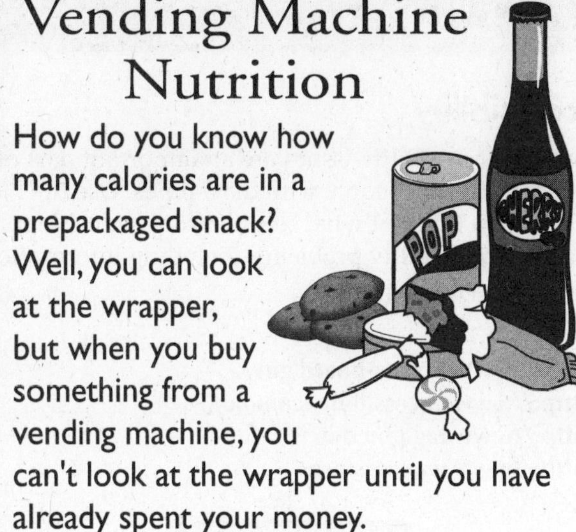

Vending Machine Nutrition

How do you know how many calories are in a prepackaged snack? Well, you can look at the wrapper, but when you buy something from a vending machine, you can't look at the wrapper until you have already spent your money.

Ordinary people just have to put up with problems like this, but *you* are one of my readers, which makes you special. Just check with the Net and never again will you be fooled into buying a "lite" snack only to find out that it contains enough calories to support a closet full of hungry elephants.

Weight Loss

There are lots of ways to lose fat, but the whole thing can be summarized into two simple rules. (1) Exercise more. (2) Eat less. For helpful tips and techniques, check out these Internet resources. (I talked to a doctor once who had a surefire method to lose weight. You serve yourself normal amounts of food, but you don't eat everything, you leave 25% of the food on your plate. It isn't easy to get started, he said, but the technique does work. Now I am ready to introduce him to my new money-saving plan in which I pay all but 25% of my doctor bill.)

Web:
http://www.3fatchicks.com/
http://www.caloriecontrol.org/
http://www.shapeup.net/
http://www.weight.com/
http://www.weightfocus.com/

> I have an airplane made out of marshmallow. It works fine as long as you don't fly over a volcano.

DISABILITIES

Accessibility

Physical accessibility issues are an important part of everyday life for people with disabilities. Use the Net to help you find out what solutions are available for specific accessibility problems, including information about special equipment.

Web:
   http://www.access-board.gov/
   http://www.accessibility.com.au/
   http://www.tag.gb.com/
   http://www.waccess.org/

If you have a serious disability that makes day-to-day life difficult, look at the help and information available on the Net.

Remember, the Internet is not about computers. The Internet is about **people**.

There are lots of people ready to help and to contribute. Perhaps you are one of them.

Americans with Disabilities Act

In 1990, the U.S. Congress passed the Americans with Disabilities Act (ADA). Although most people do not appreciate the significance of this legislation, it has an enormous effect on many areas of the American economy. Why? The ADA defines a disability as a mental or physical condition that "substantially limits one or more of the major life activities" (walking, hearing, seeing, working, and so on). The ADA requires specific action in four areas: employment, public facilities, transportation and communication. If you have some spare time, you might want to read the full text of the actual law. I did, and I found it interesting.

Web:
   http://www.adata.org/
   http://www.usdoj.gov/crt/ada/adahom1.htm

Usenet:
   bit.listserv.ada-law

Amputees

Amputees and friends and families of amputees can find a lot of helpful information on the Net. These Web sites have articles and links to resources, information about prosthetics, phantom sensation, as well as sports and recreation. The mailing list and Usenet group offer ways for amputees to talk to and support one another.

Web:
   http://www.amputee-coalition.org/
   http://www.amputee-online.com/amputee/
   http://www.limbless-association.org/

Usenet:
   alt.support.amputee

Listserv Mailing List:
   List Name: amputee
   Subscribe to: listserv@maelstrom.stjohns.edu

Attention Deficit Disorder

Attention Deficit Disorder (ADD) is a condition characterized by hyperactivity, a short attention span (distractibility) and impulsive behavior. The more formal name for this condition is Attention Deficit Hyperactivity Disorder, or ADHD, so let's call it that. Most ADHD sufferers are diagnosed at a young age, although there are many adults with this condition. As you might imagine, people with ADHD have a lot of trouble in school and on the job. (Just think how hard it was for *you* to sit still when you were a kid.) What is it like to have ADHD? There is a saying, "Time is merely a means for keeping everything from happening all at once." When you have ADHD, time doesn't work like that: everything *does* happen all at once.

Web:
   http://www.add.org/
   http://www.addhelpline.org/
   http://www.adhdguide.net/
   http://www.chadd.org/
   http://www.mentalhelp.net/poc/
      center_index.php?id=3
   http://www3.sympatico.ca/frankk/addfaq3.txt

Usenet:
   alt.support.attn-deficit

Listserv Mailing List:
   List Name: addult
   Subscribe to: listserv@maelstrom.stjohns.edu

Autism

Autism is a syndrome with many variations. By its nature, autism is difficult to define, especially in plain English (but that never stopped me). Autism is a congenital condition characterized by some of the following: (1) abnormal development of physical and social skills, (2) abnormal responses to sensation, (3) delayed development of speech and language, (4) abnormal ways of relating to the outside world. If you are taking care of an autistic child, information can help a great deal.

Web:
    http://curry.edschool.virginia.edu/go/cise/ose/
        categories/aut.html
    http://www.autism-pdd.net/
    http://www.autism.com/
    http://www.autism.org/
    http://www.autisminfo.com/
    http://www.autismtalk.net/
    http://www.nimh.nih.gov/publicat/autism.cfm
    http://www.unc.edu/~cory/autism-info/

Usenet:
    alt.support.autism
    bit.listserv.autism

Listserv Mailing List:
    List Name: autism
    Subscribe to: listserv@maelstrom.stjohns.edu

Birth Defects

A birth defect (or congenital defect) is a condition that is present from birth. There are various types of birth defects, including mental deficiencies, physical traits, malformations and diseases. There are a number of different causes of birth defects: genetic abnormalities, infections, drugs (including alcohol, illegal drugs, and certain medicines), smoking, poor nutrition and environmental chemicals. Some of the more common birth defects are cerebral palsy, cleft lip or palate, fetal alcohol syndrome, Down syndrome, spinal bifida, hearing loss, perinatal AIDS and heart defects.

Web:
    http://library.niehs.nih.gov/consumer/birth.htm
    http://www.cdc.gov/ncbddd/
    http://www.modimes.org/

Blindness

One of the biggest problems blind people face is being able to access information that sighted people take for granted. A few years ago, I worked with the National Braille Press (in the U.S.) to make some of my writing available in Braille. At the time, I developed a great respect for people who read Braille, and for the many other people who work hard to make important information available to everyone.

Web:
    http://personal.lig.bellsouth.net/lig/b/u/bundy2/
        blindnes.htm
    http://www-hsl.mcmaster.ca/tomflem/blindness.html
    http://www.blind.net/blindind.htm
    http://www.deafblind.com/blind.html
    http://www.hotbraille.com/
    http://www.nfb.org/
    http://www.nib.org/
    http://www.nyise.org/blind.htm

Usenet:
    alt.disability.blind.social

Listserv Mailing List:
    List Name: blind-x
    Subscribe to: listserv@maelstrom.stjohns.edu

Listserv Mailing List:
    List Name: blindjob
    Subscribe to: listserv@maelstrom.stjohns.edu

Cleft Palate and Cleft Lip

The palate is the hard, bony area that forms the roof of your mouth. A cleft palate is a congenital (birth) defect in which there exists a fissure along the midline of the palate. A cleft lip (which is often present with a cleft palate) occurs when one or both lips have not fused properly. Unlike many other birth defects, a cleft palate or cleft lip can often be repaired surgically.

Web:
    http://www.cleft.org/
    http://www.cleftadvocate.com/
    http://www.irsc.org/cleft.htm
    http://www.widesmiles.org/

Computer Accessibility

If you have some type of disability, you may have problems using a computer. If so, you should know that a lot of work has been done to make computers as accessible as possible to everyone. These resources will provide you with a great deal of useful information including ways to design accessible Web sites and tools to test the accessibility of existing sites. By the way, Windows comes with a lot of built-in accessibility aids. Look in the Windows help system for the details.

Web:

http://nadc.ucla.edu/dawpi.htm
http://validator.w3.org/
http://www.cast.org/bobby/
http://www.independentliving.org/links/
   links-computers-internet-disability.html
http://www.microsoft.com/enable/
http://www.trace.wisc.edu/world/web/
http://www.webable.com/

Usenet:

alt.comp.blind-users

Listserv Mailing List:

List Name: blind-l
Subscribe to: listserv@listserv.uark.edu

Deaf-Blind Discussion List

This is a multipurpose list devoted to the topic of dual sensory impairment or deaf-blindness. Not only is it a place where professionals can discuss problems and solutions, but it's also a space in which individuals with DSI or families and friends can share information, inquiries, ideas and opinions.

Listserv Mailing List:

List Name: deafblnd
Subscribe to: listserv@tr.wou.edu

Deafness

Here are some discussion forums in which the deaf, the hearing impaired, researchers, and family members of the deaf all gather to discuss issues relating to deafness. People discuss medical and technical subjects, as well as experiences and problems. Aside from the ongoing discussion, you can use the Web to access a great deal of useful information, including an online ASL (American Sign Language) dictionary. When I lived in Berkeley, I studied ASL for a short time. I wish I were fluent—it is a beautiful language.

Web:

http://wally.rit.edu/internet/subject/deafness.html
http://www.deafblind.com/
http://www.deaflibrary.org/
http://www.esmerel.org/deaf/deaf.htm

Usenet:

alt.relationships.deaf-hearing
bit.listserv.deaf-l

Listserv Mailing List:

List Name: deaf-l
Subscribe to: listserv@siu.edu

Disability Benefits

If you live in the United States, there are a variety of programs, managed by the Social Security Administration, that are available to assist people with disabilities. However, the rules and regulations are complex so, if you have a problem, take a moment to see if there might be a program designed to help you and, if so, what are the details.

Web:
  http://www.ssa.gov/odhome/

Usenet:
  alt.government.ssdi.benefits
  alt.social-security-disability

Disability Resources

There is an enormous amount of disability-related material on the Net. If you, or someone you know, has a particular disability, I guarantee there are many people on the Net in the same position. Here are some good places to start exploring. You will find a large amount of information, as well as many other people who share your interests.

Web:
  http://www.disabilities-online.com/
  http://www.disabilityresources.org/
  http://www.disablednotdead.net/
  http://www.esmerel.org/
  http://www.makoa.org/
  http://www.towson.edu/~bhalle/dis-news.html

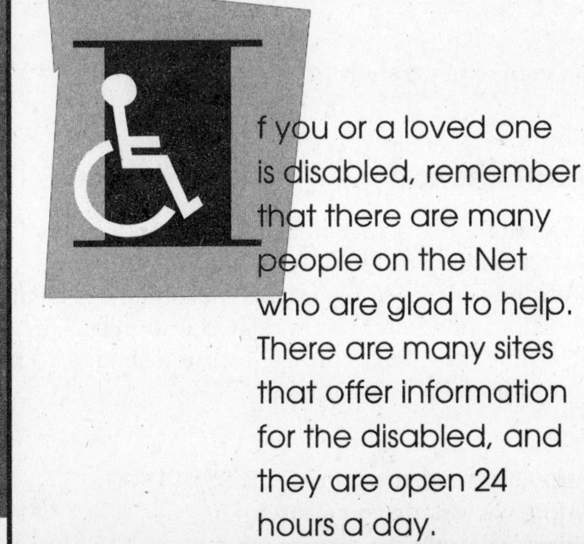

Disabled Sports

Some of the best athletes in the world are disabled. However, they don't get the same media attention as professional athletes, so it can be difficult to follow their activities. Moreover, if you are disabled, you may want to find out what sports are available to you. The Net can help. Here are some resources that introduce you to the many sports programs available to people with physical handicaps.

Web:
  http://cyberrodeo.com/guysgals/riding.htm
  http://www.nscd.org/
  http://www.nwba.org/index2.html
  http://www.powerhockey.com/index2.html
  http://www.quadrugby.com/toc.htm
  http://www.wsusa.org/

Down Syndrome

Down syndrome is a congenital disorder caused by the existence of an extra critical portion of chromosome 21. The condition is characterized by mild to moderate mental retardation. Such people also tend to be short with broadened facial features. Down syndrome was named after John Langdon Down, the British doctor who first identified the condition in 1866.

Web:
  http://www.down-syndrome.info/
  http://www.ds-health.com/
  http://www.esmerel.org/specific/downs.htm
  http://www.ndss.org/
  http://www.unomas21.com/

Usenet:
  bit.listserv.down-syn

Listserv Mailing List:
  List Name: down-syn
  Subscribe to: listserv@listserv.nodak.edu

Dyslexia

Dyslexia is a reading and writing disability characterized by the reversal of letters and words, or by trouble matching letters to their corresponding sounds. Here are some Internet resources with information about dyslexia, including tips for teachers, research information, reports and useful software.

Web:
http://www.cdipage.com/dyslexia.htm
http://www.dyslexia-adults.com/
http://www.dyslexia-parent.com/magazine.html
http://www.interdys.org/
http://www.ldonline.org/

Usenet:
alt.support.dyslexia

Family Village

Family Village is a great site for anyone who has a disability or for parents who have children with disabilities. Family Village has a library of specific diagnoses, contact lists, ways to get in touch with other people with similar disability issues, and much, much more.

Web:
http://www.familyvillage.wisc.edu/

Handicap Talk and General Discussion

If you have a handicap, you will find something helpful from this Usenet group. Useful information and personal support cover problems facing amputees, medical issues for the disabled, handicap access concerns, politics, and personal interest stories such as biographies of famous people with handicaps.

Usenet:
misc.handicap

> **Subtle is an acquired taste.**

Kids with Disabilities

Parents of children with disabilities will find these resources useful. The Web sites have links to information about mental and physical disabilities and related adaptive technologies. The mailing list acts as a support group for parents and other people who work with disabled children.

Web:
http://www.irsc.org
http://www.nichcy.org/
http://www.our-kids.org/

Listserv Mailing List:
List Name: our-kids
Subscribe to: listserv@maelstrom.stjohns.edu

Paralysis and Spinal Cord Injuries

If you, or someone you know, has paralysis or a spinal cord injury, it is good to understand the physical and medical aspects of the condition. It is also important to be able to talk to other people. These resources will provide you with information and news, as well as an easy way to find others who share your concerns.

Web:
http://www.howardnations.com/spinalcord/
http://www.makoa.org/sci.htm
http://www.paralysisproject.org/
http://www.spinalcord.org/
http://www.wheelweb.com/

Usenet:
alt.med.cure-paralysis

Rehabilitation

Rehabilitation is a vast area of human endeavor, related to many different types of disabilities and conditions. Here are Web sites that contain excellent collections of rehabilitation-related resources. Spend some time browsing. You will be astonished at all the information that is available.

Web:
http://www.ed.gov/offices/OSERS/NIDRR/
http://www.naric.com/search/kb/
http://www.nchrtm.okstate.edu/

Service Dogs

Service dogs perform tasks for people with physical disabilities. There are several types of such dogs, including general service dogs, hearing dogs and social dogs. General service dogs perform tasks like switching lights on and off, fetching items, pulling a wheelchair and pushing buttons. Hearing dogs can alert a deaf person to noises such as the telephone, alarm clocks, or a crying baby. Social dogs provide companionship and guidance for people with developmental disabilities.

Web:
http://sdog.danawheels.net/
http://www.assistance-dogs-intl.org/
http://www.caninecompanions.org/
http://www.independencedogs.org/
http://www.ismi.net/iaadp/
http://www.k9web.com/dog-faqs/service.html
http://www.uwsp.edu/psych/dog/assist.htm

Listserv Mailing List:
List Name: g-dogs
Subscribe to: listserv@maelstrom.stjohns.edu

Majordomo Mailing List:
List Name: service-dogs
Subscribe to: majordomo@duke.edu

Special Olympics

The Special Olympics is an exciting sports competition for individuals with mental retardation. The Special Olympics were founded in 1968 by Eunice Kennedy Shriver, and today there are Special Olympics programs in many countries all over the world. This is the official site for the program. You can learn more about the Special Olympics, discover how you can become a volunteer, and read other information about this great program for the mentally retarded.

Web:
http://www.specialolympics.org/

The regular Olympics involves only the very best athletes, once every four years.

The Special Olympics—created for mentally retarded participants—involves over a million people, all over the world, all year long.

Take a look at its Web site, and you will see just how special people can be.

DRAMA

Acting Profession

So you want to be an actor? Well, acting is more than a calling: it is a profession and it is a business. To be a successful actor, you need a lot more than acting skill. You need knowledge about the industry and how it works: agents, managers, resumés, networks, studios, directors, casting calls, auditions, callbacks, unions and common scams. Break a leg.

Web:

  http://www.actingbiz.com/articles/
  http://www.actorsource.com/
  http://www.madscreenwriter.com/acting.htm
  http://www.redbirdstudio.com/AWOL/acting1.html
  http://www.theatrgroup.com/showbiz/

Acting Talk and General Discussion

When I was a young lad in graduate school, I studied theatrical fencing. As part of the course, a friend and I wrote and acted in a play. It was great. It had mystery, excitement, action, beautiful women, brave heroes and, of course, lots of fencing. However, when it came time to put on the play, I made one mistake. I chose a friend of mine to be the narrator. In the middle of the play, my friend the narrator—who shall remain nameless (Marlene Garstang)—decided the play was too long, so she skipped right to the end. Today, after years of intense rehabilitation, Marlene manages to lead a socially useful life, but the loss to American theater is a permanent one as the play was only performed once. You probably have stories of your own as tragic as this one. No doubt your colleagues will thank you for sharing.

Web:

  http://www.actorsite.com/
  http://www.hollywoodnetwork.com/guide/
     lounges.html#actors

Usenet:

  alt.acting

Listserv Mailing List:

  List Name: acting-pro
  Subscribe to: listserv@home.ease.lsoft.com

Aisle Say

If you are a lover of modern theater, you will enjoy Aisle Say, an online magazine of reviews and opinion. The magazine contains theater reviews for plays in a variety of cities in and out of the United States. Before you travel, you may want to check this site to see if there is a review of a play you are thinking about seeing. I enjoy reading the reviews just for fun, even if I don't care about the play.

Web:

  http://www.aislesay.com/

Ancient Greek Theater

Age is good for cheese, fine wines and classic cars, so why not the theater? Take a look at the ancient histories, culture and philosophy of Greek theater.

Web:

  http://users.panafonet.gr/ekar/

Back Stage

No matter how busy you are, if you are in The Business, you need to keep up, and now that you have the Net, what could be easier? Back Stage offers current information on casting calls, show listings, job offers, news, reviews and much more. Show business exists in a tough, highly competitive environment in which having access to timely information can give an edge.

Web:

  http://www.backstagecasting.com/

Casting Calls

Would you like to be in films? How about TV or the theater? Start here, where you will find lots of opportunities for actors, production crew members, singers, dancers, writers and more. You may be between jobs temporarily, but there is always a place for you on the Net.

Web:

  http://www.cattlecallproductions.com/
  http://www.employnow.com/castingc.htm
  http://www.eperformer.com/aud/

Community Theater

When I was a graduate student at U.C. San Diego, I studied a number of different types of dance: tap, jazz and ballet. One day, my tap dance teacher asked me if I wanted to dance in a play that she was choreographing for a community theater. The play was "No, No, Nanette", and I had a great time. It would probably be an exaggeration to say that I burst upon the American musical comedy scene like the first rose of summer. However, when the play was over, they did retire my tuxedo.

Web:
   http://www.aact.org/
   http://www.alltheatrearts.com/
   http://www.communitytheater.org/

Drama Talk and General Discussion

Do your friends and relatives tell you not to dramatize? Well, they don't know what they are missing. The Internet is full of people who love drama and the theater, and they are waiting for you. (Narcissism and immaturity are optional.)

Usenet:
   rec.arts.theatre.misc
   rec.arts.theatre.plays

Dramatic Exchange

The Dramatic Exchange is an archive for storing and distributing play scripts. This Web site is a vehicle for experienced or budding playwrights to publish and distribute their works, and a place for producers to look at new material. Anyone else interested in drama is also welcome here.

Web:
   http://www.dramex.org/

Gilbert and Sullivan

*If your husband is so fat that you must move him
   with a trailer hitch,*

*And you are tired of groups like Nine Inch Nails and
   Weird Al Yankovitch,*

*You clearly need to break away from culture that
   is popular*

To something that is pleasing, auditorial and ocular;

*Try Gilbert and try Sullivan, I guarantee they're
   sure to please,*

No matter if you're sitting in the orchestra or balconies.

In short, in matters musical and other things historical,

This is the very model of an archive categorical.

Web:
   http://diamond.boisestate.edu/gas/
   http://www.cris.com/~oakapple/gasdisc/

Improv

Improv (improvisational theater) is a form of performance in which actors improvise as they go along. There is no script. Rather, the actors make up all the dialogue and action on the spot. Modern improv is almost always humorous (in theory, anyway). There are a number of different styles of improv, one of the most common being a group of actors who take suggestions from the audience and use those suggestions to create a spontaneous skit. There are also competitive forms of improv, where one or more teams will improvise in front of an audience and a set of judges will decide which team is best. When I was an undergraduate, I used to enjoy going to a type of competitive improv called "Theater Sports". One of the things I enjoyed the most was that we were all given soft pieces of foam, called "Boo Bricks", to throw at the actors. Improv is not only fun to watch, it affords an opportunity for extroverted people with a lively sense of humor to make fools out of themselves in front of a large group of strangers.

Web:

http://www.iguanasoft.com/~zot/improv/
http://www.learnimprov.com/
http://www.lowrent.net/improv/
http://www.yesand.com/

Musicals

I want to let you in on a secret. My life is like a musical. Whenever I am excited or perturbed or falling madly in love, I burst into song in a most appropriate manner. And, within a minute or two, all the people around me stop what they are doing and sing along. Then we all start to dance. This goes on for awhile, until everybody just sort of drifts away and I go back to my writing. It may be a little unusual, but hey, it's a living.

Web:

http://www.faqs.org/faqs/by-newsgroup/rec/
   rec.arts.theatre.musicals.html
http://www.musicals.net/
http://www.saintmarys.edu/~jhobgood/Jill/
   theatre.html

Usenet:

rec.arts.theatre.musicals

On Broadway

Are you all dressed up with no place to go? Have a look at this list of plays and musicals on or off Broadway. You provide the date; they'll provide the show time. While you are here, check out the Tony Award information and links to other theater sites.

Web:

http://www.broadwayonline.com/

Performance Art

Performance art is a general term referring to staged artistic events. As you might imagine, such events can take on a large variety of names, shapes and sizes. In the early 20th century, performance art was important to several artistic movements, including Futurism, Dada and Bauhaus. In the 1960s, it was reincarnated in the form of "happenings" (visual art + improvisation) and later developed into personal pieces in which performers used dance, music, pantomime and drama to create a planned experience with the feel of spontaneity. Today, much of what used to be performance art has been absorbed by the world of pop music.

Web:

http://www.syntac.net/hoax/perfart.php
http://www.transformart.com/

Play Scripts

Just the other day, I had a few friends over and we were trying to think of something to do. "I have an idea," I said, "let's put on our own version of Aristophanes' play 'The Thesmophoriazus'." "But where can we get a copy of the play at this time of night?" my friends asked, "Wal-mart is already closed." "No problem," I replied, "we can download it free from the Net." And we did. And you can too, along with many other plays, both classical and contemporary.

Web:
> http://www.cola.wright.edu/dept/eng/wsuwweb/
>   pageindxs/scriptpage1.htm
> http://www.eserver.org/drama/

Playbill Online

Who needs the newspaper when you can get access to this snazzy online magazine that offers news and information listings for Broadway, off-Broadway and national theater tours? Have fun browsing around or use Playbill's search mechanism for speedier results.

Web:
> http://www.playbill.com/playbill/

Theater Resources

When you come right down to it, real life is real dull most of the time.
Why not put on your own show?

Stagecraft

The lure of the theater is hard to resist and even if you have no acting talent, it doesn't mean that you have to miss out on the magic. Arm yourself with tools, gadgets, plans and a great imagination, and you can be one of the all-important backstage magicians who create the stage, lighting, sets and costumes of the theater.

Web:
> http://www.faqs.org/faqs/theatre/stagecraft/faq/
> http://www.lighting-association.com/links/
> http://www.stagespecs.com/

Usenet:
> alt.stagecraft
> rec.arts.theatre.stagecraft

Theater Resources

As long as you have Internet access, you will never have to be without a good dose of theater. These resources cover just about every theater topic imaginable. Now when you are left home on Saturday night because your BMW broke down and you can't get to the theater, you can amuse yourself with a virtual experience that has a compelling drama all its own.

Web:
> http://vos.ucsb.edu/browse.asp?id=782
> http://www.stetson.edu/departments/csata/
>   thr_guid.html
> http://www.theatrecrafts.com/glossary/
>   glossary.shtml
> http://www.vl-theatre.com/
> http://www.wwar.com/categories/Theater/

Listserv Mailing List:
> List Name: astr-l
> Subscribe to: listserv@listserv.uiuc.edu

Listserv Mailing List:
> List Name: collab-l
> Subscribe to: listserv@lists.psu.edu

DRUGS

Anti-Drug Stuff

We all know that bad drugs are bad for you, so here is some good information about bad drugs, so you will be able to take good care of yourself, and avoid the bad things that happen to good people when they have bad information about bad drugs.

Web:

> http://www.freevibe.com/
> http://www.nida.nih.gov/drugabuse.html
> http://www.theantidrug.com/

Anti-War-on-Drugs

If you are old enough, you can remember when it was cool to be anti-war (during "the War"). Well, since then, we have had a number of other, perhaps less minor wars, such as the War on Poverty. If you are still anti-war, here is another one you can protest against: the War-on-Drugs. Find out what people around the world are doing to legalize that which is illegal. (Personally, I think it would be nice if someone would start a War on Bad Taste or a War on Advertising.)

Web:

> http://www.drcnet.org/
> http://www.drugsense.org/
> http://www.faqs.org/faqs/drugs/law-reformers/

Clinical Trials

Before a new drug can be approved, or before an old drug can be approved for a new use, a lot of careful testing must be done. Part of this testing involves clinical trials using volunteers. If you participate in a clinical trial, you will get to try a drug before it is released to the market. You will also receive free medical attention (including the drug). If you have a medical condition that is not responding to standard treatment, you may want to think about volunteering to take part in a clinical trial. If so, remember that you will be taking a drug that has not, as yet, been thoroughly tested, so you must be careful. Do your homework and check with your own doctor before you volunteer.

Web:

> http://www.aegis.com/pubs/trials/
> http://www.centerwatch.com/
> http://www.clinicaltrials.gov/

Cocaine

Cocaine is a powerful central nervous system (CNS) stimulant. Its effects include increased alertness, decreased appetite, decreased fatigue, and—what cocaine users crave—an intense feeling of pleasure. In general, cocaine makes people feel powerful and happy. Unfortunately, cocaine is highly addictive, illegal, expensive and causes terrible side effects, both short-term and long-term. Cocaine is prepared from the leaves of the Erythroxylon coca bush, which grows primarily in Peru, Bolivia and Columbia. Here are some sites from which you can find out more about cocaine, such as its appearance, its effects (including during pregnancy), and a discussion of tolerance and dependence.

Web:

> http://faculty.washington.edu/chudler/coca.html
> http://www.cocaine.org/
> http://www.cocaineaddiction.com/
> http://www.erowid.org/chemicals/cocaine/
> http://www.tcada.state.tx.us/research/facts/
>   cocainefacts.html

Drug Addiction

How do you know if someone is a drug addict? If the person has a physical dependence on a drug and he experiences withdrawal symptoms when he stops taking the drug or decreases the dosage, he is an addict. True physical addiction occurs with various drugs, including narcotics and depressants (such as alcohol). Psychological addiction can occur with or without physical addiction. A careful reading of history will show you that drug addiction is not new. It has always been a problem. Since the 1960s, however, drug addiction has demanded a heavy price from our society. The combination of readily available high-quality drugs, organized crime, and lots of weapons on the street has proven to be devastating to many people, families and communities.

Web:

> http://www.drugabuse.gov/
> http://www.health.org/

Drug Chemistry and Synthesis

Where do you turn when it's late and you have a cold and all the pharmacies are closed? Check out this Usenet group and see if you can find a nice recipe for a decongestant or perhaps some LSD. That won't help your cold, but at least it will take your mind off your symptoms. Chemists and fans of chemistry chat about how drugs are constructed and synthesized.

Usenet:
  alt.drugs.chemistry

Drug Culture

There is an entire group of people who choose not to hang out in reality some of the time. Instead of going to Disneyland, they like to spend lots of money on chemicals that are illegal and bad for their health. Commune with members of the drug culture as they talk about various drugs, music to trip to, becoming one with nature, and with themselves.

Usenet:
  alt.drugs.culture

Drug Information Resources

I know what you are wondering. Did Harley put anything dangerous to my mental health in this book, or are these ordinary, harmless Web sites? To tell you the truth, with all the excitement of working on the book, I don't even remember myself. But seeing as the Internet is the most powerful interactive medium in history, what you need to be asking yourself is, "Do I feel lucky

Web:
  http://www.adhl.org/druglos.html
  http://www.drugfreeamerica.org/drug_resource/
  http://www.erowid.org/psychoactives/
  http://www.streetdrugs.org/
  http://www.trashed.co.uk/

I want you to succeed.

Drug Information Resources

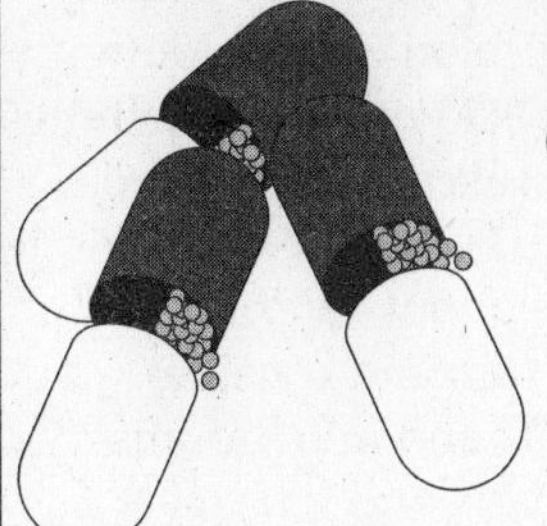

Before you embark on your next drug-induced exploration, check the Net to see what other people have to say.

Remember, you only have one central nervous system, so don't take chances.

As we used to say in the Sixties, "Uh... uummm... like wow, man. Far out..."

Drug Pix

What do you do if you encounter objects that you suspect might be drugs or drug paraphernalia? I know someone who was engaged to a fellow who had been a drug addict. Supposedly, he had stopped taking drugs years ago. One day, she found a small, strange-looking pipe in his truck. She showed it to some friends who told her it was a cocaine pipe. He claimed that a "friend" must have left it in the truck. Needless to say, his fiancé status was terminated immediately. Drugs and the tools people use to get high come in many forms, and it can be difficult to guess what something is just by looking at it. Here are a large variety of pictures to help you make an identification.

Web:
  http://www.drugs.indiana.edu/prevention/
    iprcpics.html
  http://www.erowid.org/chemicals/lsd/
    lsd_images_gallery1.shtml
  http://www.ohsinc.com/
    photos_drug_photos_pictures_drug_paraphernalia_
    drug_lab_photos.htm
  http://www.prevlink.org/getthefacts/
    webphotoalbums/drugpics.html

Drug Talk and General Discussion

There is a lot you can say about drugs, and the Internet has a lot of people who love to say it. And where else can you go for advice on what to do with a pot of leftover phenyl acetic acid or how to tell the difference between Amanita Muscaria, Psilocybe Cubensis and Chinese take-out? On the Net you will find wide-ranging discussions about a variety of topics: hard drugs (such as heroin and cocaine), psychedelic drugs (such as LSD and mushrooms), and soft drugs (such as marijuana and television). Turn on, tune out, and drop into the Usenet groups where "Better Living Through Modern Chemistry" is more than just a slogan.

Usenet:
    alt.drugs
    alt.drugs.hard
    alt.drugs.psychedelics
    alt.hemp
    rec.drugs.announce
    rec.drugs.chemistry
    rec.drugs.misc

IRC:
    #drugs (DALnet, Undernet)
    #lsd (DALnet)
    #mdma (EFnet)
    #pot (DALnet)

Drug Testing

Drug testing is certainly a double-edged sword (to coin a phrase). On the one hand (to coin another phrase), drug testing is a useful tool to help employers maintain a drug-free workplace. Be that as it may (to coin yet a third phrase), many people see the forced donation of bodily substances to possibly incriminate oneself as an affront to personal liberty. Would you like the real scoop on what may or may not be the lesser of two evils? (Wow, I just coined two phrases in one sentence.) Check out these Web sites, and you won't be left out in the cold. (Boy, I sure wish I had a Sacajewea dollar for every phrase I've coined.)

Web:
    http://www.drugtestingnews.com/
    http://www.erowid.org/psychoactives/testing/

Usenet:
    alt.drugs.drug-testing

Ecstasy

Ecstasy—what a nice, tempting name for a drug. An intense, yet delicate labeling. However, unlike other well-known drugs—such as Coca-Cola and television—this is *not* one that you want to try at home. Contrary to what most people believe, Ecstasy (or MDMA— metheylenedimethoxymethamphetamine) is not that new a drug. Read about the history, effects, dangers and usage of Ecstasy, the drug that will turn you into an Energizer Bunny with the brain of a sea slug. ("Coca-Cola", by the way, is a trademark of the Coca-Cola Company; "Ecstasy" is a trademark of the Republican National Committee.)

Web:
    http://faculty.washington.edu/chudler/mdma.html
    http://www.ecstasy.org/
    http://www.erowid.org/chemicals/mdma/
    http://www.tcada.state.tx.us/research/facts/
       ecstasy.html

Usenet:
    alt.drugs.ecstasy

Human nature doesn't change. If you want to understand what is happening, you need to understand what has already happened.

Learning about the history of drug laws will give you the social context you need to make sense out of the contemporary debate regarding drugs and society.

Entheogens

A drug is a chemical substance used to alter the body's biochemistry so as to cause changes in behavior, metabolism or perception. A religious experience is a happening, feeling or realization during which one has the perception of transcending ordinary life and experiencing the divine. What do drugs and religious experiences have in common? Perception. Put them together and you have an entheogen: a chemical substance that can be used to induce a perception of the divine. Hmmmm....

Web:

  http://www.csp.org/nicholas/spiritualindex.html
  http://www.csp.org/practices/entheogens/
  http://www.erowid.org/entheogens/
  http://www.spiritplants.com/

Heroin and Opiates

Within 4-6 hours after his or her last dose, a heroin addict has begun to feel withdrawal symptoms: chills, muscle aches, joint aches, insomnia and nausea. About 10-20 hours later, those symptoms will have intensified and, by the time an addict has reached the 24-36 hour mark, he or she is experiencing insomnia, vomiting, diarrhea, weakness, depression, and hot and cold flashes. (You can see why a heroin addict will do anything to get the next fix.) Symptoms reach a peak at about 2-3 days. By then the person is experiencing muscle cramps, abdominal cramps, fever, severe tremors and twitching. These symptoms are often accompanied by incessant nausea and vomiting, and it is not unusual for an addict to lose 10-15 pounds (over 5 kg) in 24 hours. Withdrawal symptoms can take more than a week to disappear, and there may be a general loss of well-being that lasts for several months. Remember all of this the next time someone tries to tell you that heroin and other opiates are cool. Of course we all have differing tastes, and I would be the last one to impose my values on other people, but having to continually come up with large sums of money in order to avoid severe pain, vomiting and involuntary muscle contractions doesn't seem to be a pleasant way to spend one's brief time on Planet Earth.

Web:

  http://www.erowid.org/chemicals/heroin/
  http://www.sayno.com/opiates.html

History of Drug Laws

The use of drugs stretches back into antiquity, and follows a simple, general principle: if drugs are available, some people will use them, some people will sell them, and some people will regulate them. Our current drug laws have their roots in legislation developed in the late 1800s and modified heavily throughout the last 100 years. The only way to really understand why drug laws are the way they are is to have an appreciation of their history. By the way, speaking of drugs and history, has anyone else noticed that the guitar solo in the middle of the song "Just Like Me" by Paul Revere and the Raiders (1966) is a lot like the famous guitar solo in "25 or 6 to 4" by Chicago (1970)?

Web:

  http://www.druglibrary.org/schaffer/library/
    histdrug.htm
  http://www.unc.edu/courses/psyc070d/
    druglaws.html

Leary, Timothy

The late Timothy Leary (1920-1996) was nothing if not an iconoclast. For example, he firmly believed that proper use of hallucinogenic and mind-altering drugs was necessary for experiencing an optimal existence. His philosophy was not that people should take drugs indiscriminately, but rather they should learn about drugs—what they do and how to use them—and deliberately choose what to take. In other words, where Nancy Reagan was fond of saying "Just say no," Timothy Leary would say "Just say know." In 1995, Leary was diagnosed with terminal prostate cancer and, until he died on May 31, 1996, he used his Web page to keep the world informed of his pre-death drug use (which was considerable). There was some talk of Leary committing suicide on the Net—in real time, I assume—but, in the end, he went quietly and peacefully, certainly not his usual modus operandi. One of his last goals was to "give death a better name or die trying". Even in final repose, Leary seems to have more to say than most living people.

Web:

  http://www.deoxy.org/leary.htm
  http://www.dromo.com/fusionanomaly/
    timothyleary.html
  http://www.erowid.org/culture/characters/
    leary_timothy.shtml

Marijuana

You probably know marijuana as a commonly used mind-altering drug of questionable value. However, there are many people who would like to see this drug legalized. They point out that marijuana is used medicinally by people with AIDS, glaucoma, cancer and multiple sclerosis. They also explain that hemp (the marijuana plant) is an industrial crop that can be used in the manufacture of paper, fiber, fuel and even food. Finally, in scientifically controlled studies, marijuana has been shown to increase the ability of volunteers to get the little beads into the eyes of the clown by as much as 54 percent. Need even more info? It's waiting on the Net. Just remember, however, as you make up your mind on this contentious issue, that long-term marijuana use causes many people to suffer from decreased ambition and mental acuity. On any particular day, using marijuana is somewhat innocuous. Over many years, it often results in significant lifelong consequences.

Web:
  http://www.erowid.org/plants/cannabis/
  http://www.hightimes.com/
  http://www.marijuananews.com/
  http://www.stonernet.org/

Usenet:
  alt.drugs.pot
  alt.drugs.pot.cultivation
  misc.activism.cannabis
  rec.drugs.cannabis

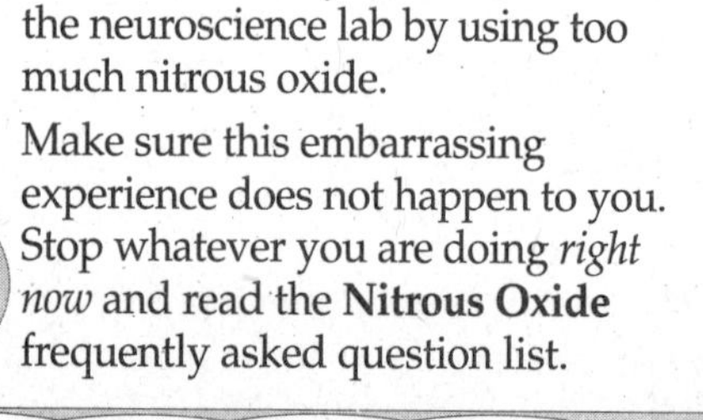

Nitrous Oxide:
Your Friend in the World of Nitrogen

A long, long time ago, my lab partner and I accidentally killed a mouse in the neuroscience lab by using too much nitrous oxide.

Make sure this embarrassing experience does not happen to you. Stop whatever you are doing *right now* and read the **Nitrous Oxide** frequently asked question list.

McKenna, Terence

Terence McKenna (1946-2000) was an ethnobotanist and writer who was as cherished in the old-style drug culture as the original big cheese, Timothy Leary. Unfortunately, McKenna died on April 3, 2000 of terminal brain cancer. On his deathbed McKenna said that he "finally understood that love permeates all that is, and it is the only real thing in this reality."

Web:
  http://www.dromo.com/fusionanomaly/
    terencemckenna.html
  http://www.erowid.org/culture/characters/
    mckenna_terence.shtml

Methamphetamine

Methamphetamine, or speed, is a central nervous system stimulant (that is, an "upper") that produces a variety of effects, including alertness and elation. However, speed is an extremely addictive drug that causes terrible side effects, damage, and often death, to the user. Speed was first synthesized in 1887. In the 1930s and 1940s, there was a significant speed problem, especially among soldiers during World War II. Later, another epidemic occurred in the 1960s. Today, speed is sold illegally and is a major cause of crime. In the street, speed is known by a variety of names such as meth, crystal meth, crank, glass and ice. This is a terrible, terrible drug. Stay away from it.

Web:
  http://www.erowid.org/chemicals/meth/
  http://www.focusas.com/Meth.html
  http://www.kci.org/meth_info/links.htm

Nitrous Oxide

Nitrous oxide—or laughing gas—is a mild anesthetic that has been in use since the late 18th century. Today, it is most widely used by medical professionals for surgery and dental procedures. Of course, there are also people who use this drug for recreation. However, before you put your neurons on the line, you might want to check things out with your buddies on the Net. Remember, pleasure is not a laughing matter.

Web:
  http://www.doitnow.org/pages/142.html
  http://www.erowid.org/chemicals/nitrous/
  http://www.resort.com/~banshee/info/n2o/

Nootropics (Intelligence-Enhancing Drugs)

I have a personal system for enhancing my intelligence: I exercise a lot, eat well, get plenty of sleep, read stimulating books, avoid television, talk with smart people whenever I can, and—except when negotiating with editors—do my best to think pure thoughts. Not everybody has such good habits, so it should come as no surprise that there is a lot of research into drugs that may be able to make you smarter. These drugs are called "nootropics" (from the Latin words for "doing your math homework").

Web:
  http://www.erowid.org/smarts/
  http://www.nootropic.com/refs/

Usenet:
  rec.drugs.smart

Pihkal

An acronym for Phenelthylamines I Have Known and Loved, Pihkal is a "love story" about a man and his favorite chemicals. Read excerpts from the book and see clever chemical breakdowns of everyone's favorite phenylethyl radical.

Web:
  http://www.erowid.org/library/books_online/pihkal/

Politics and Drugs

Throughout history, people have been grappling with the problem of how to set rules for the legal use of recreational drugs, especially alcohol, and in the last century, marijuana. There are arguments on all sides, and the issues are anything but straightforward. Society must protect itself against the irresponsible use of drugs, even by individuals who feel that they should be able to do what they want with their own lives. On the other hand, in a democratic society, personal freedom is crucial, and the rights of the individual must be balanced against the needs of the many. So who is right? The politicians, the reporters, the teachers, the doctors, Dear Abby, your mother? It's hard to tell sometimes, so get your own information to help you understand the issues.

Web:
  http://www.erowid.org/freedom/freedom.shtml

Usenet:
  alt.hemp.politics
  talk.politics.drugs

Prescription and OTC Drugs

There are a great many drugs used for medical purposes—so many that even doctors and pharmacists have trouble remembering all the details and keeping up with new products. The next time you need information about a drug, the Net can help you find what you need. This information is the same data doctors use, so it is an excellent resource for all types of health care professionals. Hint: When you look up a drug, pay particular attention to the "indications and usage" (when and how the drug is used), the "contraindications" (when the drug should not be used), and "adverse reactions" (side effects).

Web:
  http://my.webmd.com/drugs/
  http://www.druginfonet.com/drug.htm
  http://www.drugstore.com/pharmacy/drugchecker/
  http://www.merck.com/pubs/mmanual_home/
    sec2/13.htm
  http://www.nt.net/kirkphar/drugchecker.html
  http://www.rxlist.com/
  http://www4.health-center.com/pharmacy/

Psychedelic Drugs

Wow! Far out. Psychedelic drugs. I can't explain but, well, you just have to see for youself. I mean, it's like so, totally... you know. You can see a whatchamacallit. Wow! Far out. Wow! Like, cool. Totally.

Web:
   http://www.cia.com.au/serendipity/dmt/
      pt_links.html
   http://www.erowid.org/psychoactives/faqs/
      psychedelics_guide.shtml
   http://www.lavondyss.com/donut/guide/toc.html
   http://www.psychedelic-library.org/

Usenet:
   rec.drugs.psychedelic

Rohypnol

You are an intelligent, cultured woman out with a young fellow for the first time. All of a sudden, you feel dizzy and disoriented. Simultaneously you begin to feel too hot and too cold, and within a short time, you become nauseated. Well, you might just be getting the flu, but there could be two more sinister explanations. (1) Someone has slipped a dose of Rohypnol, the so-called "date-rape" drug, into your drink, or (2) you are on a date with a computer programmer. Rohypnol (the trade name for the drug flunitrazepam) is illegal in the United States, although it is used legally in many countries to treat insomnia. By itself, Rohypnol makes a person feel sleepy, relaxed and drunk for anywhere from 2 to 8 hours, effectively lowering his or her inhibitions. Combined with alcohol, the drug may cause the person to pass out and, upon awakening, have no memory of what happened. The blackout period can last from 8 to 24 hours. Thus, under the influence of Rohypnol and alcohol, a person could be raped and have no memory of the experience. Clearly, this is a drug to avoid. (Computer programmers, on the other hand, can be tolerated safely in low doses.)

Web:
   http://faculty.washington.edu/chudler/roof.html
   http://www.gmu.edu/facstaff/sexual/
      rohypnol.html#rohypnol
   http://www.streetdrugs.org/rohypnol.htm

Street Drug Slang

We all know that seemingly innocent words can have other, more sinister meanings. If you get out on the street and start messing around in the world of drugs, one wrong word in the wrong place can have serious repercussions. Let's say your spouse sends you down to the store for some jelly beans, and, to save time, you buy some off a fellow in the street. You may have inadvertently copped a bag full of chloral hydrate (knock-out tablets). Imagine your embarrassment. Next time, check with the Net first.

Web:
   http://www.addictions.com/slang.htm
   http://www.drugs.indiana.edu/slang/
   http://www.whitehousedrugpolicy.gov/streetterms/

EARTH SCIENCES

Ask-a-Geologist

Do you ever lie awake at night wondering whether all Texas lakes are man-made, or where you can find a good source of reservoir rock that is litharenite or sublitharenite? Thanks to modern technology, you can ask such questions of a real geologist. Whip off a letter to a geologist and eventually, someone somewhere will explain something that is geologically interesting.

Web:
  http://walrus.wr.usgs.gov/docs/ask-a-ge.html

Earth Science Resources

The Earth is one of my favorite planets in the entire solar system, so it's no surprise that I like these Earth sciences sites. Find out about geology, geomorphology, geophysics, geochemistry, mineralogy, volcanology, geological organizations, geophysics, hydrogeology and paleontology. Wow! All that information, and you don't even have to dig for it.

Web:
  http://jrscience.wcp.muohio.edu/html/earthsci.html
  http://un2sg4.unige.ch/athena/mineral/minlinks.html
  http://www.earthscienceworld.org/
  http://www.lib.lsu.edu/sci/earth_sciences.html

Geological Image Library

The next time you are having a bunch of geology friends over for a rock party, leave this Web site displayed on your computer screen. Simply type a keyword into a search engine and you will be rewarded with many beautiful images relating to geology. Once your friends wander over to the computer and start playing with this resource, they will become totally captivated, and you will be free to eat all the onion dip yourself.

Web:
  http://www.science.ubc.ca/~eoswr/cgi-bin/
  db_gallery/searchframe.html

Geological Time Scale

Have you ever wondered how to make sense out of the last 4,500 million years? Actually, it's not so hard once you know the names of the geological time periods and some of the details. Soon people will crawl hundreds of miles just to ask you, did the Devonian era come before or after the Silurian (after), and in which time frame were graptolites dominant (the Ordovician)?

Web:
  http://www.geo.ucalgary.ca/~macrae/timescale/
    timescale.html
  http://www.ucmp.berkeley.edu/help/timeform.html

Geology

Where on Earth can you get the real dirt? Wouldn't you like to ground yourself in the world of down-to-Earth, crust-forming alluvium? Don't you just wanna rock your geological world till the Earth moves? All you need to do is land on these earthy Internet resources, and you'll have access to everything there is to know about the origin, history and structure of the Earth (and then some).

Web:
  http://agc.bio.ns.ca/schools/EarthNet/english/
    start_glossary.html
  http://www.college.hmco.com/geology/resources/
    geologylink/
  http://www.geologicalsociety.com/
  http://www.lib.utexas.edu/geo/onlineguides.html
  http://www.realtime.net/~revenant/geo.html
  http://www.soton.ac.uk/~imw/
  http://www.unige.ch/sciences/terre/admin/
    terre_link.html
  http://www.usgs.gov/

Geology Talk and General Discussion

Geology is the study of the structure of the Earth and its surface. These are the places where the geologically inclined discuss technical matters, as well as topics of interest to non-scientists. Talk about rocks, fossils, the origin of natural formations, and so on. If you have a geological question (such as where to take your kids to look for fossils), you can post it here and see if an expert will answer you.

Usenet:
  sci.geo.geology
Listserv Mailing List:
  List Name: geol-101
  Subscribe to: listserv@list.uvm.edu

Here is a fast way to go back to the past without having your time machine run up a huge electricity bill. Use the Net to learn about the geologic time period of your choice.

Glaciology

Glaciology is the study of glaciers and glaciotectonics. These Web sites will lead you to just about anything you need in this area of study. Even if you are not a professional, I bet you'll enjoy a bit of browsing. For example, many people believe that the water content in snow is 1/10 the same volume of water. In other words, 10 inches of snow is equivalent to 1 inch of rain. Actually, the ratio varies from 1/100 to 1/3 and depends upon the weather conditions at the time of the snowfall.

Web:
  http://www.glacier.rice.edu/land/
    5_tableofcontents.html
  http://www.nsidc.org/
  http://www.nsidc.org/data/catalog.html
  http://www.spri.cam.ac.uk/wdcc/

Global Map of Earthquakes

As you move on to adulthood, it is not uncommon for your mother to experience fits of anxiety and despair because she fears for your safety. If you are about to make that big move from home (or if you moved out 30 years ago and your mother is still worried), take a look at these earthquake maps. Show your mother that where you live is nowhere near a fault line and, in no time at all, she will feel completely at ease. (Hint for anyone living on or near a fault line: download the picture ahead of time, and use a graphics program to remove any red lines that are close to where you live.) The map facilities at this site let you zoom around a graphical representation of the Earth, checking out all the recent quake action. I've also included a glossary of geological terms to help you interpret these maps. The Usenet group is that place to talk with other people about what makes the Earth move under your feet.

Web:
   http://cires.colorado.edu/people/jones.craig/
      EQimagemap/global.html
   http://www.college.hmco.com/geology/resources/
      geologylink/glossary.html

Usenet:
   sci.geo.earthquakes

Hydrology

Hydrology is the study of water, its properties, distribution and movement across land. Hydrology encompasses a huge area of study, because the hydrologic cycle is so complex. (The hydrologic cycle refers to the entire process of water evaporating from the Earth's surface and eventually coming back down to Earth.) Moreover, water is present in several different physical forms (like rain, snow and ice) and travels in diverse patterns. For example, water can freeze into polar ice caps, where it will stay for millions of years. Or water can fall onto land where it immediately soaks into the ground, is utilized by plants, and runs off into rivers or soaks into the groundwater.

Web:
   http://terrassa.pnl.gov:2080/EESC/resourcelist/
      hydrology.html
   http://www.hwr.arizona.edu/hydro_link.html
   http://www.usra.edu/esse/ford/ESS205/g300www/
      g300wwwhydr.html
   http://wwwga.usgs.gov/edu/

Usenet:
   sci.geo.hydrology

Minerals

These sites will give you more than the recommended daily allowance of minerals. You can search databases containing information about gems and minerals of all types. In addition, you will also find a great many photos to help you identify any stray minerals you happen to encounter in your journeys on planet Earth.

Web:
   http://www.cobweb.net/~bug2/rock4.htm
   http://www.min.uni-bremen.de/kabinett/
      index.en.html
   http://www.nrcan.gc.ca/mms/school/glossary.htm
   http://www.uni-wuerzburg.de/mineralogie/links.html
   http://www.webmineral.com/

Usenet:
   sci.geo.mineralogy

National Geophysical Data Center

The National Geophysical Data Center (NGDC), located in Boulder, Colorado, is part of the National Oceanic & Atmospheric Administration (NOAA). NGDC manages and makes available a large number of environmental data sets, many of them of interest to geologists. In particular there is data in the areas of marine geology, marine geophysics, paleoclimatology, solar-terrestrial physics, solid earth geophysics and glaciology.

Web:
  http://www.ngdc.noaa.gov/

Quicksand

The popular idea of quicksand is a myth. To be sure, there do exist many places where you can find quicksand-like soil: loose sand, mixed with water, that is soft and pliable. There is quicksand all over the world, anywhere the right type of sand coexists with water, such as near a river. However, don't be afraid. If you ever have the misfortune to step in some quicksand, just walk out carefully and deliberately. If you get in deep, you won't get sucked in; most likely, you will float. On the Net, quicksand is of interest to two types of people: first, geologists who study such phenomena; and second, a large number of people to whom the idea of attractive people sinking in quicksand is erotic. This particular fetish, which encompasses other types of related stimulation, is known as "wam" (wet and messy).

Web:
  http://www.cae.wisc.edu/~wiscengr/issues/apr97/
    quicksand.html
  http://www.dellamente.com/quicksand/
  http://www.hunkinsexperiments.com/pages/
    quicksand.htm
  http://www.newscientist.com/lastword/answers/
    111earth.jsp

Radon

Radon is a colorless, radioactive gas formed by the natural decay of radium. As a tool, radon is primarily used in radiotherapy for treating cancer. However, radon also occurs naturally in areas where uranium-238 is present in the rocks and soil. Elements like uranium decay over long periods of time and, as they decay, the atoms transmute. Eventually, uranium decays into other elements that produce radium. When radium decays, it forms radon. At the same time, a type of radiation called alpha particles is released. (An alpha particle consists of two protons and two neutrons.) Radon gas is itself radioactive because it also decays, emitting more alpha particles and forming polonium (another radioactive element). The problem is, if there is radon in your environment, you breathe it, whereupon it gets trapped in your lungs. When the radon decays, the radiation and the polonium can cause damage to the tissue and predispose you to developing lung cancer. These Web sites will give you detailed information: what is radon, where is it found and what can you do to reduce the risk of radon affecting your living environment?

Web:
  http://www.epa.gov/iaq/radon/
  http://www.nsc.org/ehc/radon.htm
  http://www.vh.org/Providers/Textbooks/Radon/
    HealthRisk.html

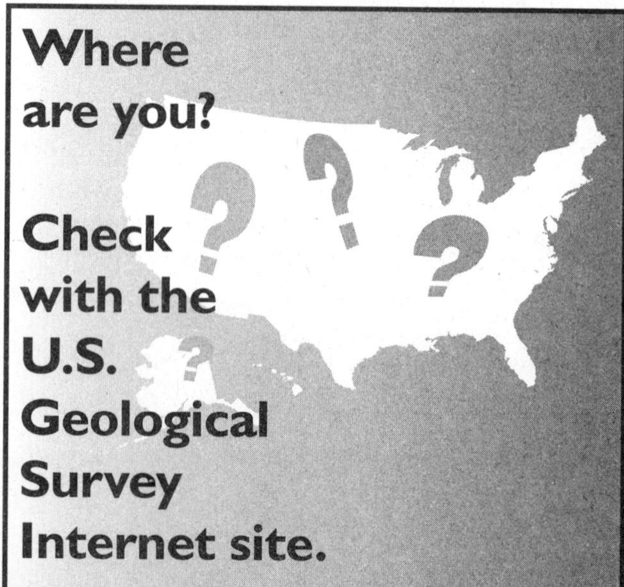

TIDBITS

What should new grandparents know about NEW PARENTS?

If you are a new grandparent, you need to get used to your role as much as the new parents need to get used to theirs. This will take time.

Do you remember when your children were teenagers? No matter how painful it was to watch them make mistakes, you couldn't make all their decisions for them.

When you are a grandparent, the same guideline applies. Do offer help, gently, but don't be afraid to let your children figure things out by themselves. Remember that you had your turn, and you probably did a good job, so have faith in your kids. Some lessons, as you know, have to be learned by experience.

Try to remember that— as is always the case— times have changed. Don't insist, for example, that your kids use cloth diapers instead of disposable diapers. (If you want to encourage them to use cloth, you might offer to pay for a diaper service.)

One important thing you can do is to encourage your children to breast feed. It is the best way to feed an infant and, in our culture, there is still not enough support.

Seismology

Here is a large collection of links to seismic information available on the Net. There are lots and lots of earthquake-related resources, so the next time you run into someone on the street who asks, "What's shaking?" you can invite him over and show him in person.

Web:
  http://www.geophys.washington.edu/seismosurfing.html

Structural Geology

Structural geology is the study of rock deformation and the geologic configurations resulting from such deformations (mountains, canyons, mesas, and so on). In particular, structural geology includes plate tectonics, the study of the slow movements of sections of the Earth's crust (plates), leading to the formation of continents. Of particular interest are earthquakes and volcanoes, which mostly occur at the margins of such plates.

Web:

http://geology.ou.edu/~ksmart/structure_webpage/

http://www.earth.monash.edu.au/AGCRC/ASG/

http://www.rwth-aachen.de/ged/Ww/others/structural.html

U.S. Geological Survey

The U. S. Geological Survey (USGS), a part of the United States Department of the Interior, is America's largest agency devoted to earth science. The USGS creates and provides (for free) an enormous amount of information relating to geology (rocks and soil), topography (lay of the land), and hydrology (water). There are lots of maps and databases, as well as many research analyses of natural resources.

Web:
  http://info.er.usgs.gov/

Virtual Cave

When I was younger, I spent a lot of time exploring the Colossal Cave in the Adventure game (the very first computer-based adventure game). However, I have never had a chance to explore a real cave. Now, however, I can visit the Virtual Cave whenever I want and look at pictures of all kinds of fascinating cave formations. So if—like me—you have always wanted to go spelunking (cave exploring), you can start by doing it over the Net. If you live in the U.S., you can also check with the United States Cave Directory to find out information about many of the public caves you can visit.

Web:
  http://www.goodearthgraphics.com/virtcave.html
  http://www.uni-geophys.gwdg.de/~gkaufman/caving/

Volcanology

It used to be that the only thing you could do with a volcano was to throw a virgin into it and hope that the gods were appeased. Now you can hook up all sorts of wires and gadgets to it, and use X-ray fluorescence to examine trace elements and aerial photographs to analyze pumiceous pyroclastic flow.

Web:
  http://home.mira.net/~gnb/caving/papers/
    kg-svckt.html
  http://volcano.und.nodak.edu/vwdocs/glossary.html
  http://vulcan.wr.usgs.gov/home.html
  http://www.geo.mtu.edu/volcanoes/

Volcanoes

What can you say about volcanoes and their almost magnetic attraction for us all? I could remind you that they are holes or cracks in the Earth's surface that release molten lava, ash or other products from underground magma chambers. (Now *that's* a word: "magma." Bet you can't say it ten times real fast.)

Anyway, i could wax eloquent about the runny volcanic outpourings and how they build basalt beds, or how the more viscous types of lava form steep-sided volcanoes, or how ash residue tends to build cone-like peaks. Or I could go on and on about how volcanoes erupt where one lithospheric plate is forced beneath another, or where two such plates diverge.

Yes, there is a lot to say about volcanoes and, if truth be told, they are among my favorite large-scale geological formations. Still, there is something unsatisfying about mere talk and, if you are like me, you will want some pictures, and that is where the Net comes in. Take a cruise to volcano Web sites and I guarantee that you will find more than a few shots suitable for framing.

Beige Book

The beige book consists of national and regional summaries of the current economic conditions in the United States as described by the Federal Reserve. New versions of the beige book are produced every month or two, in advance of the meetings of the Federal Open Market Committee (FOMC) (the most important monetary policy-making body of the Federal Reserve System). At any time, you can look at the current beige book and check up on the economic health of the U.S. or one of its twelve Federal Reserve districts. I think this is a much better way of understanding the economy and where it might be heading than depending on the writers and commentators in the popular press.

Web:
  http://woodrow.mpls.frb.fed.us/bb/
  http://www.federalreserve.gov/fomc/beigebook/
    2002/

Bureau of Economic Analysis

The Bureau of Economic Analysis (BEA) is an agency of the United States Department of Commerce. The BEA's function is to analyze and integrate immense amounts of data in order to create a consistent model of the American economy. The BEA creates estimates and analyses dealing with regional, national and international areas of economic concern. Their best-known national measure is probably the gross domestic product (GDP), but they also produce a variety of less known but equally important measures. Personally, I find a lot of these numbers fascinating. For example, in 2001, the highest average per capita income in the U.S. was in Connecticut ($41,930), followed by the District of Columbia ($40,498) and Massachusetts ($38,845). The lowest per capita incomes were in Mississippi ($21,643), West Virginia ($22,725) and Arkansas ($22,912). Although California had the 11th highest per capita income ($32,678), it had, by far, the highest total personal income of any state in the country ($1.127 trillion). The state with the lowest total personal income was Wyoming ($14.24 billion).

Web:
  http://www.bea.doc.gov/

Central Banks

A "central bank" is an organization whose purpose is to guide and influence the economy of a particular country or region of the world. Traditionally, a central bank's most powerful tool is the ability to exert partial control over the money supply. Virtually every country in the world has a central bank. In the U.S., the central bank is the Federal Reserve System. In Europe, while each country has its own central bank, there is also one for the European Union as a whole. Most people do not understand the role of central banks—indeed, many people do not even know of their existence—but their power is an important force in the national economies of the world. The most important central banks in the world are those of the countries with the largest economies: United States, Japan, Germany, UK, France, China, Italy, Canada, Brazil and Mexico. In addition, two other important banking organizations are the European Central Bank (European Union) and the Bank for International Settlements (a central bank for central banks).

Web:
http://www.bancaditalia.it/
http://www.bankofcanada.ca/en/
http://www.bankofengland.co.uk/
http://www.banque-france.fr/gb/home.htm
http://www.banxico.org.mx/sitebanxicoingles
http://www.bcb.gov.br/defaulti.htm
http://www.bis.org/cbanks.htm
http://www.boj.or.jp/en/
http://www.bundesbank.de/index_html_en.htm
http://www.centralbanking.co.uk/links/
http://www.ecb.int
http://www.federalreserve.gov/
http://www.pbc.gov.cn/english/

Thanks for reading this line.

It's a conspiracy. I'm not supposed to tell you, but I will anyway. All the central banks of the world are controlled by a small group of the intelligentsia: people who are known to be very smart, highly educated, dedicated and disciplined, working in complete secret. These people hide away in hard-to-find places, wielding an obscene amount of power in almost total obscurity.

They possess esoteric knowledge and use a vocabulary of technical terms that precludes normal people from even understanding what they are talking about. Yes, it's a conspiracy. The central banks of the world are controlled by... writers of Internet books. Well... not actually all writers of Internet books... just a few of us. Well... to be totally honest... it's just me.

But don't tell anyone.

Computational Economics

Computational economics is a branch of economics that uses computers and numerical methods to solve economic problems. As such, computational economics does not lie within any particular branch of economics; rather, it touches many other areas. These Web sites contain links to a wide variety of related Internet resources. Since this area is such a disparate one, the resources sometimes go far afield, and as I followed the links I landed in some especially interesting and unexpected places.

Web:
http://wueconb.wustl.edu/sce/
http://www.econ.iastate.edu/tesfatsi/ace.htm

Economic Growth

It is a characteristic of economic systems—large and small—that they must continually grow in order to stay healthy. Economic growth is a complex phenomenon that depends on many factors: development, technology, politics, and so on. These resources will help you find data relevant to understanding the global economy and how it is changing.

Web:
> http://netec.mcc.ac.uk/~adnetec/WebEc/
> webeco.html

Majordomo Mailing List:
> List Name: economic-growth
> Subscribe to: majordomo@ufsia.ac.be

Economic Statistics

When I was an undergraduate student, I spent a summer in Ottawa (the capital of Canada) working at a company that used statistics and complex mathematical models to forecast the economy of Canada. I wrote computer programs to perform what is called "optimal regression". The algorithms (methods) I used were so complex that it, literally, took me several months to understand what I was doing. One thing I learned is that statistics are the basic currency of economics. If you are an economist, you will find all kinds of economic statistics, both historical and current, on the Net.

Web:
> http://www.bls.gov/
> http://www.econofinance.com/
> http://www.lib.lsu.edu/bus/economic.html
> http://www.lib.umich.edu/govdocs/stecon.html
> http://www.whitehouse.gov/fsbr/esbr.html

Economics Journals

There are a great many economics journals that have some type of presence on the Net. Here is a list of well over 200 such journals, along with links to the corresponding Web sites. This is a great place to look for journals of which you may not already be aware.

Web:
> http://www.helsinki.fi/WebEc/journals.html
> http://www.oswego.edu/~economic/journals.htm

Economics Resources

Let's face it, no one really understands the economy any more than anyone really understands, say, why beer comes in six-packs when people only have two hands. Still, that is no reason to feel left out in the financial cold. There are lots of economics resources out there, just waiting for you to explore, and here are some good places to start. After all, when we are living in a world where an American basketball player can sign a $120,000,000 contract and Internet authors have trouble making that much money in a *good* year, you know that things are getting out of control.

Web:
> http://rfe.wustl.edu/econfaq.html
> http://vax.wcsu.edu/library/b_economics.html
> http://www.econdata.net/
> http://www.econlinks.com/
> http://www.helsinki.fi/WebEc/
> http://www.inomics.com/cgi/show
> http://www.internationaleconomics.net/
> http://www.lib.umich.edu/libhome/rrs/classes/
> econ.html
> http://www.yardeni.com/

ECONOMICS ON THE NET

It all started with classical economics and moved through Marxism, the neoclassical schools, Keynesian economics, monetarism, right through to supply-side economics. Where does that leave us now? Good question. All I can tell you is try to get paid in advance and carry a big stick.

Economics Talk and General Discussion

For serious talk about the science of economics, join the discussion in the **sci.econ** Usenet group. For more specific discussion, there are two other groups, both of which are moderated: **sci.econ.research** for economic research, and **sci.finance.abstracts** for the posting of abstracts of unpublished research papers. If you want to debate economic issues in a less technical and more spirited environment, check out **alt.politics.economics**.

Usenet:
  alt.politics.economics
  sci.econ
  sci.econ.research
  sci.finance.abstracts

Economist Jokes

You've just spent a hard day crunching numbers and making sense out of the latest economic indicators. The rest of the office staff is gone (you always are the last one to leave), and you are relaxing, your feet propped up on a copy of "The Wealth of Nations". What better way to take your mind off the vicissitudes of financial life than by enjoying a collection of economics jokes? To get you started, here's an original joke of my own. How many economists does it take to screw in a light bulb? The answer is two, as long as they have the Chairman of the Board of Governors of the U.S. Federal Reserve to help. The job of the chairman is to actually screw in the bulb, whereupon one economist predicts that the light will work, while the other economist predicts that the light won't work.

Web:
  http://netec.wustl.edu/jokec.html
  http://paul.merton.ox.ac.uk/work/economists.html
  http://www.uni-mainz.de/~martt000/jokes/
    jokes.html

Economists on the Web

Wallow in this large list of economists on the Internet. If there is a better way to impress a hot date quickly with why the Internet is so important, I have yet to find it.

Web:
  http://www.amherst.edu/~jsirons/ewwp.html

Finding an Economist

How many times has this happened to you?

You are planning a big party to impress your friends and neighbors and—while making out the guest list—you realize that you don't know any economists. And, as we all know, a party without at least one economist is like... well... a party without an economist.

No need to panic. Just connect to **Economists on the Web**, and before you can say "M2 Money Supply", you will have as many economists as you need.

Remember, a man who knows his numbers is a man you can count on.

Federal Reserve System

The Federal Reserve System ("the Fed") was founded in 1913 to be the central bank of the United States. The Fed consists of a central Board of Governors in Washington, D.C., and twelve regional Federal Reserve Banks. (The twelve "banks" are really organizations, not regular banks that provide consumer services.) Each Federal Reserve Bank is located within a Federal Reserve District. The districts—which are known by their numbers—are as follows: (1) Boston, (2) New York, (3) Philadelphia, (4) Cleveland, (5) Richmond, (6) Atlanta, (7) Chicago, (8) St. Louis, (9) Minneapolis, (10) Kansas City, (11) Dallas and (12) San Francisco. As the central bank of the United States, the Federal Reserve System has important responsibilities, affecting not only the country, but the entire global economy. The main goal of the Fed is to maintain a safe, flexible and stable monetary system in the United States. To do so, the Fed influences money and credit conditions and regulates America's banking institutions.

Web:
   http://woodrow.mpls.frb.fed.us/info/sys/
   http://www.federalreserve.gov/
   http://www.stls.frb.org/fred/

Game Theory

Game theory is a complex body of mathematical methods used for making decisions. The goal of game theory is to analyze a competitive situation in order to determine the optimal course of action. Game theory has applications in politics, economics and military science.

Web:
   http://www.econ.canterbury.ac.nz/hist.htm
   http://www.economics.harvard.edu/~aroth/
      alroth.html
   http://www.ics.uci.edu/~eppstein/cgt/

Gross State Product Tables

The gross state product data tables estimate the value of goods and services produced for 61 industries in 50 U.S. states, eight regions, and the U.S. as a whole. The value is the sum of four components: compensation of employees; proprietors' income with inventory valuation adjustment and capital consumption allowances; indirect business tax and non-tax liability; and other, mainly capital-related, charges.

Web:
   http://www.bea.doc.gov/bea/regional/gsp/

History of Economic Thought

There have been many economists, but the large-scale schools of economic thought have been shaped by a relatively few important thinkers. For a student of economics, it is an invaluable experience to read historical papers to get a feeling for economic thinking at various times and places. Explore the writings of Babbage, Hobbes, Hume, Locke, Malthus, Marx, Swift, Toynbee, and many more.

Web:
   http://cepa.newschool.edu/het/
   http://home.tvd.be/cr27486/hope.html
   http://phoenix.liunet.edu/~uroy/eco54/histlist/
      hist.html
   http://socserv2.socsci.mcmaster.ca/~econ/ugcm/
      3ll3/
   http://www.eh.net/
   http://www.helsinki.fi/WebEc/webecb.html

Household Economic Statistics

How is it that *They* know more about you than you know about you? The United States Department of Census's Housing and Household Economic Statistics Division has lots of information about incomes and poverty, health insurance, the labor force, wealth and asset ownership of households.

Web:
   http://www.census.gov/ftp/pub/hhes/www/

Inflation and the Consumer Price Index

The Consumer Price Index (CPI) is a measure of the average change over time of the prices paid by urban consumers for a specific collection of goods and services. The CPI is important as it allows us to track the change in cost of living over various time intervals. For example, I was born in 1952. (On December 21, to be exact, if you want to send a birthday present.) According to the CPI, if something cost $100 in 1952, it would cost $677 in 2001. You don't have to be an economist to find such numbers useful. For example, say you are reading a book that was written in 1952, and someone in the book gives $100 to someone else. How much money was that really? Well, in today's dollars, it was about $677.

Web:
   http://woodrow.mpls.frb.fed.us/economy/calc/
      cpihome.html
   http://www.bls.gov/cpi/
   http://www.ex.ac.uk/~RDavies/arian/current/
      howmuch.html
http://www.westegg.com/inflation/

Law and Economics

This is a great way to find Internet resources relating to the law and economics. You can use a search engine to search for the resources you need, as well as look at lists of links to research, publications, organizations, legal and government resources, directories of people involved in the law and economics, and much more. The mailing list is devoted to discussions of relevant topics in this area.

Web:
   http://lawecon.lp.findlaw.com/

Listproc Mailing List:
   List Name: econlaw
   Subscribe to: listproc@gmu.edu

Listserv Mailing List:
   List Name: lawecon-lm
   Subscribe to: listserv@legalminds.org

U.S. Census Bureau Economic Statistics

The U.S. Census Bureau is one of the most prolific publishers of economic statistics. On this Web site, you can find the latest economic indicators, as well as lots of other important statistics relating to business, income and labor and a large collection of research reports. To help you plan, there is also a calendar showing when various economic indicators will be released.

Web:
   http://www.census.gov/econ/www/

U.S. Economy at a Glance

The other night, the Chairman of the Federal Reserve was over for dinner. After dessert, we had a disagreement as to whose turn it was to wash the dishes. (It was his, but he didn't want to admit it.) So I said to him, "I'll tell you what, let's see who can make the best guess as to the size of the civilian labor force in Montana. The loser washes the dishes." While he was thinking about it, I excused myself and checked with the Net. The poor guy never had a chance. (By the way, in case the Chairman of the Federal Reserve ever comes over to your place, the civilian labor force in Montana is 469,600 workers.)

Web:
   http://www.bls.gov/eag/

Adult Education

These forums offer interesting discussions on ways to educate adults. People talk about all sorts of subjects, such as textbooks, education using interactive computer environments, and audio tapes. There is also lots of discussion about teaching in conventional classroom settings. The Web sites can help you find many related resources on the Net.

Web:
   http://www.adultstudentcenter.com/
   http://www.research.umbc.edu/~ira/AEresweb.html

Usenet:
   misc.education.adult

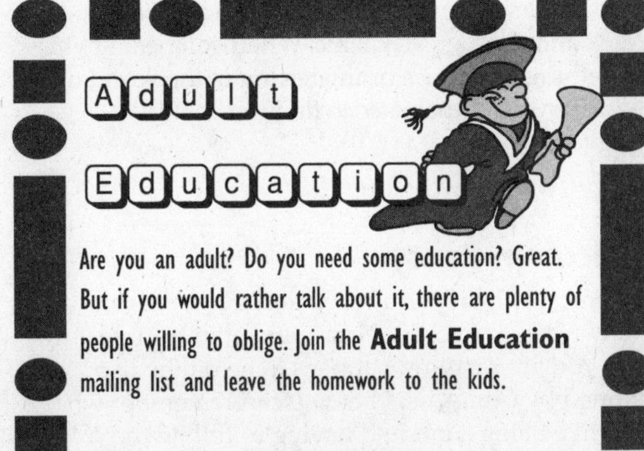

Canada's Schoolnet

If you are a Canadian teacher, you *must* know about Schoolnet. In the great Canadian tradition of let's-spend-lots-of-government-money-to-create-cultural-resources, Schoolnet is the most ambitious, comprehensive teaching facility since I organized the sex education exhibit at the University of Toronto Medical Students' Open House (1981). Are you Canadian? You must plug in; there is no choice. If you are not Canadian, check it out anyway, and you may find something useful.

Web:
   http://www.schoolnet.ca/

Education Conferences

Are you just itching to go to an education conference? Use the Net to check out lists of exhibitions, seminars and conferences, and you'll never have to spend another dull weekend hanging around the house complaining about too much work and not enough recognition.

Web:
  http://webprod.aspensys.com/education/ericconf/
    ericcal/introduction.asp
  http://www.epicent.com/conferences/
    conferences.html

Education News

The world of education moves fast, but here's an easy way for you to keep up with what's new and exciting. Just spend a few minutes every now and then visiting this Web site, where you will find news for education professionals. You'll enjoy the articles from various newspapers and magazines, including Education Week and Teacher Magazine. When you hear about something important or interesting in the world of teaching, this is the place to find the details.

Web:
  http://www.edweek.org/

Education Policy

When I was a kid, you could get in trouble for chewing gum in class. Now you get in trouble if the gun you are carrying happens to be on the list banned by Congress. I bet you can remember what it was like being a kid and having to follow the rules with no say in the matter. Well, now you can have your two cents' worth and eat it too.

Web:
  http://epaa.asu.edu/
  http://www.ctredpol.org/
  http://www.edpolicy.org/

Education Talk and General Discussion

You don't have to be a teacher or administrator to enjoy the education discussion on Usenet. This discussion group covers all sorts of general education topics that relate to teachers, parents, children, administrators, the public school system, and much more. Anything goes.

Usenet:
  misc.education

Educational Mailing Lists

There are lots of mailing lists on the Net devoted to schools, education and related topics. Here are some Web sites that contain information about these lists. If you have anything to do with education (teacher, parent, administrator, even student) it is worth spending a few moments looking for mailing lists that interest you. I guarantee you will find something.

Web:
  http://www.buddyproject.org/tool/list/morelist.asp
  http://www.webscoutlists.com/category/98

Eisenhower National Clearinghouse

The Eisenhower National Clearinghouse (ENC) provides K-12 teachers a central source of information on mathematics and science curriculum materials and encourages the adoption and use of these materials. ENC is funded by the U.S. Department of Education.

Web:
  http://www.enc.org/

Home Schooling

As home schooling becomes more popular, it is easier to find resources relating to the process of teaching children in the home environment. Take advantage of the Internet as one of these resources and discuss with other home schoolers the trials and rewards of teaching your kids at home.

Web:
  http://www.home-ed-magazine.com/
  http://www.home-school.com/
  http://www.homeschoolzone.com/
  http://www.midnightbeach.com/hs
  http://www.teleport.com/~ohen/

Usenet:
  alt.education.home-school.christian
  alt.education.home-school.disabilities
  misc.education.home-school.christian
  misc.education.home-school.misc

Majordomo Mailing List:
  List Name: home-ed
  Subscribe to: majordomo@world.std.com

Special Education

In the United States, we have the Individuals with Disabilities Education Act—I.D.E.A.—and, before that, PL 94-142 (both federal laws) to help ensure that students with a disability can receive a free and appropriate public education in the least restrictive environment. In the outside world (that is, outside the U.S. Congress), there are often problems. Fortunately, there are a lot of people on the Net who are willing to share solutions and information.

Web:
 http://www.awesomelibrary.org/special-ed.html
 http://www.cec.sped.org/
 http://www.iser.com/
 http://www.seriweb.com/

Usenet:
 alt.education.disabled
 bit.listserv.dsshe-l

Talented and Gifted

When I was a kid, there were no special programs where I lived (in Canada) for talented and gifted (TAG) children. So I had to content myself with driving all my teachers crazy and learning extra math on my own. Today, there are many programs for TAG children: kids who show exceptional skill, intelligence or creativity. (By the way, I have a theory that kids who like to talk in class are smarter than everyone else.)

Web:
 http://www.gtworld.org/
 http://www.nfgcc.org/
 http://www.nswagtc.org.au/

Listserv Mailing List:
 List Name: tag-l
 Subscribe to: listserv@listserv.nodak.edu

Check out the headlines in "News".

Special Education

If you live in the United States and your child has a disability, you are, by law, entitled to send him or her to a special education program.

As a parent, the best thing you can do for your child is to know your rights. The Internet can assist you in understanding the many special education laws and help ensure that your child gets everything to which he or she is entitled.

U.S. Department of Education

As part of the Institutional Communications Network project, the U.S. Department of Education has established this site to provide information to educators and researchers interested in education. You will find a wide variety of files on K-12 education as well as vocational and adult education, goals of the Department of Education, programs, announcements and press releases, and educational software.

Web:
 http://www.ed.gov/

Vocational Education

Network with teachers and administrators of vocational education systems as they explore new ways to pass on needed skills to people heading into the work force. Discover projects designed to make learning interesting and see how educators use the Internet to enhance the learning environment.

Web:
 http://scholar.lib.vt.edu/ejournals/JCTE/
 http://www.ed.gov/offices/OVAE/
 http://www.education-world.com/vocational/

Usenet:
 bit.listserv.vocnet

EDUCATION: COLLEGES AND UNIVERSITIES

American Colleges and Universities

Before you pick a college or university in the U.S., you *must* spend some time researching on the Net. These resources will get you started, and help you find the place that is the best for you. Remember, when you choose a college, you are not just choosing a school: you are selecting a football or basketball team, a place to party, a whole set of guys (or girls), restaurants and clubs where you will hang out, and a home away from home where you can do what you want without parental interference. These are not choices to take lightly.

Web:
  http://iiswinprd03.petersons.com/ugchannel/
  http://www.campustours.com/
  http://www.embark.com/
  http://www.globalcomputing.com/university.htm

Usenet:
  alt.college.us

Canadian Colleges and Universities

I am a veteran of two Canadian universities. As an undergraduate, I studied at the University of Waterloo, in Waterloo, Ontario, 60 miles (90 kilometers) west of Toronto where I grew up. While I was a student, I co-founded the Ontario Public Interest Research Group, OPIRG, the first such group in Canada. (The original group is now called WPIRG.) I also had my own radio show (at Radio Waterloo), lived in a co-op dorm (the WCRI Phillip Street Co-op, building A2), and studied a lot of math and computer science. Later, after going to graduate school in California, I returned to a Canadian university, the University of Toronto, to go to medical school. Would you like to have a rich, happy, successful, fulfilling life? Maybe you too should go to a Canadian university. If so, the time to get started is now.

Web:
  http://osap.gov.on.ca/eng/intro.htm
  http://www.accc.ca/english/
  http://www.aucc.ca/en/
  http://www.oise.utoronto.ca/~mpress/eduweb/
    universities.html
  http://www.ouac.on.ca/
  http://www.uwaterloo.ca/canu/

College Admissions

The Net has many kinds of help for college-bound students. You'll find all types of information, including answers to a lot of questions that may be confusing you. If you want to go to college, but you need to know more about the whole process, these Web sites are a good place to start. If you want to talk to other people and ask questions, try the Usenet group.

Web:
  http://www.collegeboard.com/
  http://www.personalessay.com/
  http://www.supercollege.com/

Usenet:
  soc.college.admissions

College Admissions Tests

You can't get far into the college system without taking some type of admission test. And the further you want to go, the more tests you need to take. (I am a survivor of the Canadian version of the SAT, as well as the GRE and the MCAT.) To do well on such tests, there is a lot you can do to prepare. These Web sites will help you.

Web:
  http://www.act.org/
  http://www.collegeboard.com/testing/
  http://www.collegeboard.org/sat/html/students/
    calen001.html
  http://www.gre.org/
  http://www.scholarstuff.com/netguide/test/tests.htm

College Magazines

Are you looking for a diversion from studying? (Of course you are.) Try these online college magazines where you can spend hours reading articles about current events, relationships, academic life, relationships, employment, relationships, money, relationships, travel, relationships, music, relationships, movies and relationships. I enjoy reading these magazines as they bring back memories of some of the best moments of my life. (You do know this is the best part of your life, don't you?)

Web:
  http://www.collegenews.com/
  http://www.colleges.com/umagazine/
  http://www.studentnow.com/

College Student Guides and Manuals

Perfection is not a bad goal. (It's always worked for me.) So if you want to be an ideal student, here are a few guides that can help you. Learn how to make the transition from high school to college, how to deal with various problems you may encounter in college, and how to make your time at the university go as smoothly as possible.

Web:
  http://www.psu.edu/dus/ncta/linkadvs.htm

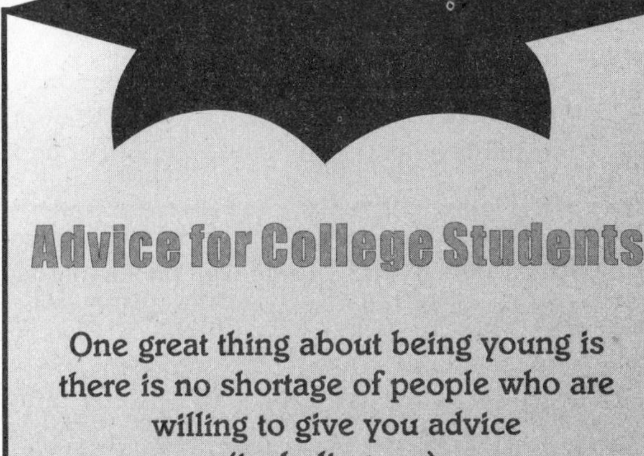

College Talk and General Discussion

These are great discussion groups for students and professors in college, and for anyone thinking about attending college. Anything related to colleges and universities is okay: school reputations, good courses to take, grading, taking exams, study habits, professors, university politics, and so on.

Usenet:
  alt.art.colleges
  soc.college
  soc.college.graduation

College-Related Resource Collections

Being in a university or college is a way of life that lasts for at least a few years. During that time, you live in a world that has its own values, goals, culture and activities. There is a huge amount of college-related resources on the Net. Start here, and you'll find a lot.

Web:
  http://www.collegeclub.com/

Community Colleges

The United States has—aside from universities—a great many post-secondary schools known as community colleges or two-year colleges. These schools have a wide variety of programs: academic studies leading to a diploma, vocational training, preparation for university, developmental education, and so on. If you are planning to apply to such a school, why not check it out over the Net first? You can find information on just about every community college in the U.S.

Web:
  http://www.mcli.dist.maricopa.edu/cc/
  http://www.utexas.edu/world/comcol/alpha/

Essays and Term Papers

I like to write, but I have to admit, it's hard work, especially if you want to do it well. Although I have been a professional writer for 18 years, I didn't write essays as a university student (although I did solve 4,350,893 math problems). However, my experience is atypical. In order to get through college, you are probably going to have to write your fair share of essays, and then some. There are places on the Net where you can find lots and lots of essays, already written, ready for the taking. Should you do so? Well, I'm a straightforward guy, so let me tell you the truth. Lots of people use pre-written essays and pass them off as their own. However, I strongly recommend you do your own work. Over the years, you will have an enormous advantage if you can write well, and the only way to learn how to write is to practice. So look at these essays if you want ideas and guidance. But, in my opinion, anyone who doesn't do his or her own work is a short-sighted fool. (Teachers: I recommend you become familiar with the essays in your subject area that are available for free on the Net. This will help you catch the plagiarists among your young ones.)

Web:
  http://www.cyberessays.com/
  http://www.netessays.net/
  http://www.papercamp.com/papers.shtml

Fraternities and Sororities

Do you feel out of touch? Does your life suffer because of a lack of partying, hazing, goofing off, and long hours of dressing for social success? You may be one step away from social fulfillment. Join a frat or sorority, and make friends for the rest of your life (or until you graduate, whichever comes first).

Web:

  http://www.greekpages.com/

Usenet:

  alt.college.fraternities
  alt.college.fraternities.dlta-sigma-phi
  alt.college.sororities
  alt.fraternity.sorority

Graduate Schools

If you've gone through college and you still just can't get enough of going to school, think about applying for graduate school. You will have much more intellectual stimulation and be admired by all the undergraduate students (who will worship you as a matter of course). These Web sites contain information about graduate schools in the United States along with contact information. The Usenet groups offer a place for grad students or grad student wannabes to talk about applying for graduate schools, attending graduate schools, and so on. Personally, I had a lot more fun as a graduate student than as an undergraduate.

Web:

  http://iiswinprd01.petersons.com/gradchannel/
  http://www.gradschools.com/
  http://www.graduateguide.com/
  http://www.jobweb.com/career_development/
    gguides.htm

Usenet:

  alt.grad-student.tenured
  soc.college.grad
  soc.college.gradinfo

Higher Education Resources Newsletter

Keep up with the latest cool resources valuable to the higher education community. This newsletter comes out once a month and announces new Internet resources such as online tutorials and courses, interesting Web sites, mailing lists and Internet books in print.

Web:

  http://www.hw.ac.uk/libwww/irn/

Honors Programs

Are you looking for a college that will challenge your scholastic prowess with an honors program? As you are shopping for a place to spend the next four (or five or ten) years, check out this list of links to colleges that offer honors programs.

Web:

  http://www.indiana.edu/~iubhonor/nchc/other.php3

Honors Programs

If you are smart and you like to work hard, maybe an honors program is for you. Check it out on the Net, and see what is available. Remember, the brain you train is anything but plain.

Lecture Hall

This is an absolutely fabulous resource. All over the world, professors are putting their lecture notes on the Net. This site is a directory of online lecture notes and course materials for many different subjects. If you are a student, you can check to see what is available for courses like the ones you are taking. If you are thinking of taking a course, you can get a preview by looking at the notes from similar courses. I like to browse, just to learn about many different subjects, especially the ones I never studied formally.

Web:

  http://www.utexas.edu/world/lecture/

Literature Study Guides

It is the mark of a great work of literature that you can read it over and over, and get something new from it each time. In fact, it is these types of novels that we prize over all others. Unfortunately, when you study such a book in school, you are rarely given enough time to understand the book well. One way to augment your work is to use a study guide, a summary in which the most important themes and characters of a novel are discussed and put into perspective. My suggestion is to look at the study guide twice: first, before you read the book, in order to help you understand what you should be looking for as you read, and after you read the book, to help you appreciate the themes and solidify your ideas.

Web:
> http://www.bibliomania.com/1/
> http://www.novelguide.com/novelanalysis.html

Online Courses and Distance Learning

Now that we have the Net, just about anything that has to do with information is within your reach. If you've been thinking about taking a university course, check with these sites where you can find comprehensive lists of courses that are taught online. Many different schools now offer such courses, so there's a good chance you'll find what you want.

Web:
> http://www.hoyle.com/distance.htm
> http://www.mindedge.com/
> http://www.nucea.edu/distance2.htm
> http://www.outreach.utk.edu/weblearning/

Usenet:
> alt.education.distance
> alt.education.distance.teaching

Religious Colleges

If you would like to attend a religous college, check out these Web sites. Take some time and search for the ones that meet your criteria. You will find that there are a lot more religious colleges than you might think, so it is a good idea to prepare well and make an informed search. With a little work, you can find the school that is just right for you.

Web:
> http://www.his-net.com/html/colleges.html
> http://www.netministries.org/college.htm

Residential Colleges

Going to college is a much better way to get away from your family than getting married. So why not go all the way and pick a place that's halfway across the world? Imagine studying in a place where the food makes you ill and nobody speaks your language. Check in the Directory of Residential Colleges to find the perfect place for yourself.

Web:
> http://collegiateway.org/colleges.html

Scholarships and Financial Aid

Want some free money or even some cheap money? Get the scoop on how to pay your way through college by filling out forms for money. Learn about student financial aid, as well as information about specialized schools like grad school, law school and medical school. My advice is to get as much free money as you can, and borrow as little as possible.

Web:
> http://scholarships.kachinatech.com/scholarships/
>   scholars.html
> http://www.college.ucla.edu/up/src/ss.htm
> http://www.collegeview.com/finaid/
> http://www.faqs.org/faqs/college/financial-aid-faq/
> http://www.finaid.org/
> http://www.theoldschool.org/
> www.fafsa.ed.gov

Usenet:
> soc.college.financial-aid

Student Affairs

At a university, the euphemism "student affairs" refers to a wide variety of activities such as counseling services, student activism, fraternities, clubs, organizations, etc. (Actually, the "etc." is the most fun.)

Web:
> http://www.studentaffairs.com/

Studying Abroad

What better excuse is there to go to another country and have adventures than to tell your parents that the whole thing is educational? Think of all the stories you will have to tell when you return and, best of all, when you get back, all your friends will be jealous and your parents will recognize you as being a totally mature human being.

Web:

    http://www.petersons.com/stdyabrd/us.html
    http://www.studyabroad.com/

University Residence and Housing

Before you go away to college, scope out the various places to live on campus. I lived in a co-op residence (a sort of dorm) in my first year as an undergraduate, and I liked it a lot. This Web site has links to many college residency and housing sites. Most of them include information on residence halls, dining, housing policies and rates.

Web:

    http://www.netsquirrel.com/rha/

On-Campus Housing

When I was a young lad, I lived in a co-op dorm during my first year as an undergraduate. By "co-op", I mean a dorm where everything was organized and run by the students. In fact, the dorm was actually owned by the students, and the whole thing worked just fine.

If you get a chance to live in a dorm for a year or two, I think you will agree with me that it is an important social experience (often leading to other important social experiences).

Hint #1: If you want to find out the official details about dorms at various schools, use the Net to do your advance research.

Hint #2: Learn how to use a butter knife to hold a door shut, so you can lock someone into their room before they do it to you.

Boarding Schools

A boarding school is one in which the students live at the school. There are all types of boarding schools: for young and old students, for boys or girls or coed, for exceptional students or those who need some extra help. What they generally have in common is a small class size, lots of attention from teachers, and a serious attitude towards building character and academic achievement. Since finding the right school is such an important decision, here are some resources to help you. My advice is just don't go to any school where they make you read Schopenhauer.

Web:

    http://www.boarding-school-finder.com/US/
        search.htm
    http://www.sabs.org/mainpages/faq.html

Education Place

When you have a spare moment and you want to look for an interesting Internet resource for your children, take a look at this Web site. You will find a variety of information, games and activities suitable for various age groups. For example, I found a multiple choice geography game that was interesting. I also enjoyed the mathematical brain teasers. Hint: This site is produced by a textbook publisher, so you will have to ignore the commercial stuff and hunt for the jewels.

Web:

    http://www.eduplace.com/

High School

Boy, I wish I had the Internet when I was in high school. Imagine: homework help, reference tools, links to resources, and free study guides. You youngsters sure have it lucky with all this cool Net stuff. When I was in high school, all I ever got to do was hang out with my friends and have fun.

Web:

    http://homeworkspot.com/high/
    http://www.aboutschool.com/twelve2.htm
    http://www.highschoolhub.org/
    http://www.multnomah.lib.or.us/lib/homework/

Usenet:

    k12.chat.senior

K-12 Foreign Language Talk and General Discussion

If you are learning (or teaching) a foreign language, you can talk to people around the world who speak that language. Learn about their culture and practice speaking with them. The **art** group is for general discussion of the language arts. The other groups are for specific languages and cultures: **deutsch-eng** (German/English), **esp-eng** (Spanish/English), **francais** (French/English), **japanese** (Japanese/English) and **russian** (Russian/English).

Usenet:

k12.lang.art
k12.lang.deutsch-eng
k12.lang.esp-eng
k12.lang.francais
k12.lang.japanese
k12.lang.russian

K-12 Internet School Sites

This Web site has links to all the known high schools and elementary schools on the Internet. Save these addresses: they may save your life some day. (For example, I have a friend who teaches in Coquille, Oregon. One day she printed the entire list, folded it in two, and put it in her shirt pocket. A short time later, she was walking past a classroom window when an over-stimulated ADD student hurled a blackboard eraser out the window, hitting her smack in the chest. If it wasn't for that list in her shirt pocket, my friend would not be alive today.)

Web:

http://www.asd.com/

K-12 Resources

Here are some well-organized collections of resources relating to many areas of K-12 education: classroom activities, teaching, libraries, administration, art, fun for kids, connecting your school to the Net, museums, information for parents, and so on. I predict that whatever spare time your kids are willing to let you have will be quickly used up by the Net.

Web:

http://www.awesomelibrary.org/
http://www.bigchalk.com/
http://www.ericit.org/weblinks/weblinks.shtml
http://www.homeworkspot.com/
http://www.k-12world.com/
http://www.sdcoe.k12.ca.us/resources/resframe.html

K-12 Student Discussion Groups

There are special Usenet groups in which students all over the world can talk to one another. This is a great way for kids to learn about other children and other cultures while developing their writing skills. The groups are organized as follows: **elementary** for grades K-5, **junior** for grades 6-8, and **senior** for high school.

Usenet:

k12.chat.elementary
k12.chat.junior
k12.chat.senior

Learning to Read

If you have children, you know how important it is to help them learn how to read. Here are some tips that can make the process effective and enjoyable. The emphasis is on talking, telling stories, reading stories together, and making the alphabet fun to learn. I have a hint of my own. Teach your kids the alphabet forward *and* backward. Throughout their entire life, they will find it much easier to use dictionaries, phone books and other reference books that are organized in alphabetical order. It is simple for kids to learn their letters both ways—from A to Z and from Z to A—but most parents and teachers don't realize how important it is.

Web:

http://www.ed.gov/pubs/parents/Reading/
http://www.sfsv.org/read.html

School Projects by Kids

Now that we have the Net, growing up will never be the same. There are many kids on the Net who love to share their work. Here are links to projects, reports and writing, all done by kids. Why not encourage your child to participate in the global community?

Web:

http://sln.fi.edu/tfi/hotlists/kids.html

School Safety

There was a time when schools were completely safe. In some countries, this is no longer the case. Many schools are in areas with significant drug, gang and crime problems. Moreover, many students (in all areas) have easy access to weapons, such as guns and knives, and drugs. As a number of tragic incidents have shown, it is not possible to predict exactly which students are going to cause trouble and when. ("He seemed like such a nice boy...") Instead, school administrators have to do their best to avoid a crisis, but be prepared to handle such crises as they arise—all without unduly affecting the educational environment. If you administer, teach or attend a school, or if you are active in your community, you will find these resources valuable as you work toward making your schools comfortable and safe.

Web:

http://www.cdc.gov/safeusa/school/safescho.htm
http://www.naspcenter.org/safe_schools/
   safeschools.htm
http://www.ncsbs.org/
http://www.nssc1.org/

**Report on School Projects
by Elmo's sister, Lucy (age 6)**

My brother Elmo had to make a project for school. He didn't know what to do, so he asked me to help.
I said, "Elmo, why don't you make a model of the Leaning Tower of Pisa out of toothpicks. I'll help you". He said okay, so we made the model, and he took it to school today.
What he doesn't know is that, instead of glue, I used sugar mixed with water. In a couple of hours, the whole thing will fall apart. Ha, ha, ha, ha, ha!
That will teach him not to put frogs in my bed.

-Lucy

Study Tips

I am going to tell you a secret. How you do in high school *does* matter. I know you may hear stories about people who completely screwed up their grades in high school and went on to become rich/famous/powerful—whatever. However, in general it is just not true. The people you hear about are exceptions and are rare. When I think about the people I grew up with, their success in later life correlates directly with their success in high school. (For example, I did well in high school, and I am very successful.) In my experience, the people who blew off high school ended up being unhappy and poor. Believe me, it is no fun being a middle-aged man or woman who is floundering around looking for work or trying to get by on a small salary with no prospects. One of the things you need to understand is that being a good student involves using skills that you must learn and practice. To get you started, here are some resources with a small amount of information about studying and taking notes. (I don't want you to spend a lot of time reading about studying. I want you to study.) Finally, here are my personal tips on how to do well in high school. (1) Have fun, but don't fool around too much. (2) Learn to study well and do it a lot. (3) Hang around with people who share your interests and do well in school. Avoid people who are losers no matter how popular they may seem. (4) Don't get pregnant; don't get anyone else pregnant.

Web:

http://www.how-to-study.com/
http://www.iss.stthomas.edu/studyguides/
http://www.ucc.vt.edu/stdysk/stdyhlp.html
http://www.unc.edu/depts/unc_caps/TenTraps.html

Test Taking Tips

Tests are important. True, they can be stressful and intimidating, but studying for a test requires us to learn material more deeply than we would otherwise and, hence, pushes us to perform to the utmost of our abilities. As a general rule, there is no substitute for learning the material as well as possible. However, along with your learning, there are techniques you can master that will help improve both your studying and your performance on your tests and exams. Attitude is everything. When I was a student, I used to love exams. I studied hard, I learned a lot and, to this day, I remember much of what I learned. It makes a huge difference in my life. Learning, remembering and thinking are what makes human beings special. I know that many people—both adults and students—think that studying and tests are not cool. They are fools.

Web:
  http://www.byu.edu/ccc/Learning_Strategies/test/
    strategy.htm
  http://www.csbsju.edu/academicadvising/help/
    teststrt.html
  http://www.eop.mu.edu/study/
  http://www3.niu.edu/testing/stress.htm

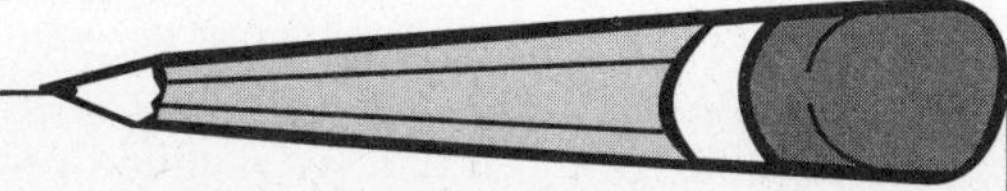

Writing Well

To me, the most important skill you can help your students (or your children) develop is being able to write well. As a child practices writing, he or she is also practicing how to read well, how to organize ideas, and how to concentrate for an extended period of time on a specific goal. Writing well endows a child with an enormous advantage that will persist throughout life. (Also, writers, especially good writers, are cool.)

Writing Well

When your kids write well, everyone benefits. However, writing well must be learned deliberately and requires a lot of practice. Here are some useful hints to assist you in helping your children with their writing. If there is one skill they will use over and over for the rest of their lives, it is writing. Help them get started properly.

Web:
  http://www.ed.gov/pubs/parents/Writing/
  http://www.scils.rutgers.edu/~kvander/ChildrenLit/
    childrenwritingwell.html

EDUCATION: TEACHING

AskERIC

ERIC (Educational Resources Information Center) is an information system that provides access to education-related literature for teachers, library media specialists, administrators, and others. However, you don't have to be a teacher to find ERIC useful. I used it recently to find a paper dealing with management strategies that was written by a friend of mine, Marlene Garstang (look in the Drama category under Acting Talk and General Discussion).

Web:
  http://ericir.syr.edu/

Classroom Discipline

Keeping order in the classroom is important, and it's not always easy to walk a careful path between regulations, parents who are ready to complain, and the fact that, by their nature, many students love to misbehave. Still, you're the teacher, and you do have to spend some of your time socializing the youngsters (if for no other reason than to make your life easier). This Web site contains tips and techniques that you might find useful. However, it is good to remember, every teacher has his or her own personality and what works for one person won't work for everybody, so don't stop experimenting.

Web:
  http://www.honorlevel.com/

College and University Teaching Assistants

Remember how in school everyone wanted to do stuff for the teacher, like clean the chalkboard, bang erasers, or grade papers? Most of us got over that urge, but there are some who never did, and now they are hanging out in the big league academic scene wearing tweed and discussing philosophy at the off-campus coffeehouse. But that's not all they do. Sometimes they are found on the Internet discussing the roles of teacher and student with other teaching assistants.

Web:
   http://id-www.ucsb.edu/ic/ta/hdbk/toc.html
   http://www.adm.uwaterloo.ca/infotrac/liblst2.html
   http://www.ase.tufts.edu/cae/search_pages/
      tasearch.htm
   http://www.ku.edu/~cte/resources/websites.html
   http://www.msu.edu/unit/taprog/web.htm
   http://www.preparing-faculty.org/
   http://www.uni.edu/walsh/teach.html

Usenet:
   soc.college.teaching-asst

Listserv Mailing List:
   List Name: t-assist
   Subscribe to: listserv@listserv.arizona.edu

Teaching Assistants

Being a T.A. (teaching assistant) is fun. For the first time in your life, you actually get to control the grades of other people. And you can have the experience of saying something and watching other people write it down. Still, it can take awhile to become a good T.A. If you would like to talk to other teaching assistants, join the **t-assist** mailing list. When I was a grad student, I was the senior T.A. for a course in which the professor left before the end of the semester to move to Brazil. I got to give all the exams and award all the grades. It was great.

Curriculum Materials and Ideas

Here are some pointers to curriculum resources on the Net, including curriculum guides, lesson plans, ideas and resources. Before you copy anything, though, remember that your kids also have access to the Net.

Web:
   http://www.cloudnet.com/~edrbsass/edres.htm
   http://www.cyberbee.com/
   http://www.execpc.com/~dboals/k-12.html
   http://www.iste.org/resources/curriculum/k-12/
   http://www.stemnet.nf.ca/curriculum/

EdWeb

If you have anything to do with schools, you know that lots of people are running around trying to figure out what to do with the Net—and what the Net is going to do with us. One way to sort it all out is to learn what you are talking about (a solution that has somehow evaded just about every public official in the world). A good place to start is EdWeb.

Web:
   http://www.edwebproject.org/

Geometry and Art

One of the nice things about teaching geometry is that you can use simple visual aids which you can make yourself. Here is a Web site that contains many different ideas on how to teach abstract geometrical ideas imaginatively. You will see detailed presentation plans, as well as descriptions of how to make all the visual aids you need. For the kids, you can find hands-on activities. For yourself, you can find grids and patterns you can copy, as well as tips on teaching geometry vocabulary.

Web:
   http://www.mathforum.org/~sarah/shapiro/

Instructor Magazine

This is a professional publication for elementary school teachers. You will find articles on important topics such as professional development, curriculum planning, communicating with children and parents, grading, teaching strategies, and ideas for the classroom.

Web:
   http://teacher.scholastic.com/products/
      instructor.htm

Jason Project

The Jason Project is an ambitious undertaking that uses modern technology to offer educational experiences relating to science and technology. The material is organized around general themes, and helps children learn about important scientific discoveries and concepts. Jason is designed to be part of a K-12 curriculum, and can provide an ongoing and valuable adjunct to classroom study.

Web:
  http://www.jasonproject.org/

K-12 Curriculum Talk and General Discussion

There are specific Usenet groups for teachers to discuss curriculum and learning materials. If you are a teacher, you may enjoy participating in the discussion related to your area. The groups are: **art** (art), **business** (business education), **comp.literacy** (computer literacy), **health-pe** (health and physical education), **lang.esp-eng** (English/Spanish), **life-skills** (home economics and career education), **math** (mathematics), **music** (music and performing arts), **science** (science), **soc-studies** (social studies and history), **special** (students with handicaps or special needs), **tag** (talented and gifted students), and **tech** (industrial arts and vocational education).

Usenet:
  k12.ed.art
  k12.ed.business
  k12.ed.comp.literacy
  k12.ed.health-pe
  k12.ed.lang.esp-eng
  k12.ed.life-skills
  k12.ed.math
  k12.ed.music
  k12.ed.science
  k12.ed.soc-studies
  k12.ed.special
  k12.ed.tag
  k12.ed.tech

K-12 Teachers Discussion Groups

If you are a K-12 teacher, you may want to participate in the Usenet teachers discussion group. After all, you need something to do in your spare time.

Usenet:
  k12.chat.teacher
  k12.news

Multimedia in Education

Computing doesn't have to be complicated, dull or boring. Not with multimedia. Pictures, sounds, graphics and animations all make computers come to life. Learn about using multimedia as a teaching tool and find out places where you can be taught to use multimedia effectively.

Web:
  http://falcon.jmu.edu/~ramseyil/technology.htm
  http://www.ed.gov/Technology/
  http://www.ericit.org/cgi-bin/resprint.cgi/Resources/
     Educational_Technology/
     Multimedia_Education.html
  http://www.ncrel.org/sdrs/areas/te0cont.htm
  http://www.nea.org/cet/
  http://www.netdaycompass.org/

Usenet:
  misc.education.multimedia

Special Education Teachers

There are a lot of unique concerns when teaching children who have special needs. It's great to be able to network with other teachers, clinicians and researchers to discuss current issues about practices, policies and new developments.

Web:
  http://www.cec.sped.org/
  http://www.dssc.org/frc/
  http://www.pacificnet.net./~mandel/
     SpecialEducation.html
  http://www.parrotpublishing.com/

Listserv Mailing List:
  List Name: speced-l
  Subscribe to: listserv@listserv.uga.edu

Majordomo Mailing List:
  List Name: sneteachtalk-l
  Subscribe to: majordomo@schoolnet.ca

Special education requires very special teachers. If you would like to talk with them, join a **special education** mailing list.

Teachers Helping Teachers

The best tips and hints you can find will come from other teachers. That is what you will find at this Web site. In addition, you will find information on classroom management, language arts, special education and stress reduction. (Stress reduction? Who has time for stress reduction?)

Web:
  http://www.pacificnet.net/~mandel/

Teachers Net

Teachers Net offers a variety of resources for teachers. There are places to talk to other people, as well as lesson plans, news, job information, curriculum planning resources, and a lot more. If you are a teacher, this site is a great place to trade tips, ask questions, and look for help with specific problems. In my experience, it often seems that a big part of teaching is complaining about the working conditions, lack of reasonable pay and all the dumb things your principal does. Most teachers are chronically disgruntled about something or other, so, when you feel in the mood, you might as well complain to your friends on the Net.

Web:
  http://www.teachers.net/

Teaching Art

Anyone can draw a crowd, draw a bath, draw a blank, draw blood, draw a breath, draw a gun, draw strength from wisdom, draw lots, draw a pension, draw a comparison, draw near to another person, draw from your experience, draw away from the heat, draw out your remarks, or draw straws, but only *you* can draw on your experience as a teacher and the resources on the Net to draw out your students' talents while you teach them how to draw.

Web:
  http://www.arteducation.co.uk/
  http://www.fcasd.edu/schools/dms/tart.htm
  http://www.kinderart.com/biglist.shtml
  http://www.teachingideas.co.uk/art/contents.htm
  http://www.teachnet.com/lesson/art/

Usenet:
  k12.ed.art

Listserv Mailing List:
  List Name: arteacher
  Subscribe to: listserv@venus.vcu.edu

Teaching English as a Second Language

Imagine the thrill of teaching people to speak English—every word you say is going to be mimicked, and all across the globe there will be people who talk just like you. Take advantage of networking opportunities by looking at what other teachers of English are doing with lesson plans, multicultural classroom environments, helpful hints for pronunciation and other important issues.

Web:
  http://www.aitech.ac.jp/~iteslj/links/TESL/
  http://www.eflweb.com/
  http://www.mitesol.org/mitesol/links/teachers.htm

Usenet:
  bit.listserv.tesl-l

Teaching Health and Physical Education

Talk to people who teach health and physical education. Trade ideas, tips and stories. Find out if it is really true that "Those who can't do, teach. And those who can't teach, teach gym."

Web:
  http://www.pecentral.org/

Usenet:
  k12.ed.health-pe

Teaching History

A math teacher, a science teacher, and a history teacher have died and gone to heaven. They are standing at the Pearly Gates talking to St. Peter, who says, "Before I can let you progress, you must give me a good reason why you should get into heaven." The math teacher says, "I have an irrefutable mathematical proof that I should go to heaven." So he shows the proof to St. Peter, who finds a flaw in it. "Sorry," sayes St. Peter, "I can't let you in." The science teacher says, "I have an experiment I can perform that will show you that I should go to heaven." But then St. Peter looks at the data and says, "Sorry, this data is not conclusive. I can't let you in." And then he turns to the history teacher. "What do you have to say for yourself?" And the history teacher says, "Can I get an incomplete?"

Web:
  http://www.archives.gov/digital_classroom/
  http://www.emporia.edu/socsci/journal/links.htm
  http://www.oah.org/teaching/
  http://www.rmc.edu/~gdaugher/elem.html

Teaching Language Arts

Your students start with Dr. Seuss and end up with Shakespeare, but somewhere along the line, someone has to spend a lot of time teaching them the language arts: reading, writing and public speaking. It's hard to exaggerate the importance of these skills. The next time your students ask you, "Why do we have to learn all this stuff?" show them my picture and say, "If you study hard and learn how to read, write and speak well, maybe some day you'll grow up to be able to own a nice cat like Harley."

Web:
   http://www.awesomelibrary.org/english.html
   http://www.education-world.com/a_lesson/archives/
      lang.shtml
   http://www.ginaotto.com/languagearts.html
   http://www.school.discovery.com/schrockguide/arts/
      artlit.html

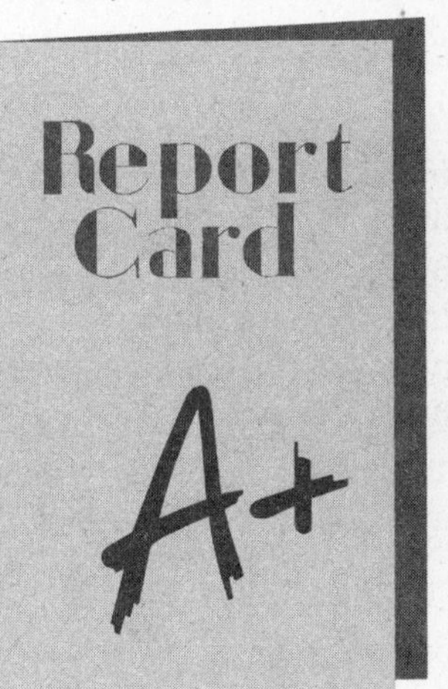

Teaching Language Arts

Here is a simple, three-part plan to enhance your teaching experience:

1. Have your school district buy copies of this book for all the students.

2. Plan a special assembly in which the best students in each class read their favorite parts of this book aloud to the whole school.

3. Prepare your acceptance speech for the Teacher of the Year Award.

Teaching Mathematics

All through school, I always loved mathematics. I never really had a favorite math teacher, because I was so good at it that I used to frustrate the teachers and they used to frustrate me. But that didn't stop them from trying to teach everyone else. I bet their lives would have been a lot easier if they'd had the Internet. Not only would they have been able to search for math teaching resources, they would have been able to tell me to go play on the Web and stop asking so many impertinent questions.

Web:
   http://archives.math.utk.edu/k12.html
   http://explorer.scrtec.org/explorer-db/browse/static/
      Mathematics/
   http://www.people.clarityconnect.com/webpages/
      terri/terri.html

Usenet:
   k12.ed.math

Teaching Music

If music makes the world go round, then music teachers must make the... hmmm... well... something or other. Anyway, if you are a music teacher, you'll find that the Net has a large variety of ... hmmm... well... something or other. You will also find these resources helpful if you are a general teacher who is interested in doing music with your class in order to ... hmmm... well... something or other.

Web:
   http://www.isd77.k12.mn.us/resources/staffpages/
      shirk/k12.music.html
   http://www.musiceducationmadness.com/
      contributions.shtml

Usenet:
   alt.music.education
   k12.ed.music

Smart is as smart does.

Teaching Resources

Teaching takes up a lot of time, so anything that can make your life easier is certainly worth knowing about. Well, here are some Web sites that have a lot of resources to help you. You'll find information about many different aspects of teaching, including curriculum, technology and professional development.

Web:

    http://www.education-world.com/
    http://www.hcc.hawaii.edu/intranet/committees/
        FacDevCom/guidebk/teachtip/teachtip.htm
    http://www.kn.pacbell.com/wired/bluewebn/
    http://www.microsoft.com/education/mctn/
    http://www.smplanet.com/teachers/teachers.html

Usenet:

    alt.teachers.lesson-planning

Teaching Science

When a young child is properly grounded in science, he or she establishes a sense of curiosity, wonder and awe that lasts a lifetime. Unfortunately, too many students see the study of science as being nothing more than the memorizing of a long series of irrelevant facts. This is a shame because, at its roots, science represents the pinnacle of human achievement: the attempt of men and women to understand the world in which they live. We are born into a world in which many wonderful things exist because of the work of people who came before us, but one thing we should never take for granted is the effort and discretion so many men and women have made in order to understand the world in which we live.

Web:

    http://explorer.scrtec.org/explorer-db/browse/static/
        Natural^Science/
    http://ntwww.hcf.jhu.edu/matsci/
    http://www.coe.unt.edu/luttrell/
    http://www.eskimo.com/~billb/scied.html
    http://www.exploratorium.edu/snacks/
    http://www.nbii.gov/education/curriculum.html
    http://www.niehs.nih.gov/dert/programs/translat/
        k12/mats-01.htm

Teachnet

Teachnet is an online magazine devoted to the teaching profession. You will find classroom decor tips, hints on getting organized, lesson plans, classroom management ideas, employment opportunities, and much more.

Web:

    http://www.teachnet.com/

ELECTRONICS

All About Electronics

Would you like to learn about electronics? Here are lots and lots of resources to help you find information about whatever area of electronics interests you. Start with basic skills, such as soldering, and work your way up to designing complicated circuitry. Pretty soon, you will be creating your own robots to help you with the household chores. And when people say, "Wow, how did you ever learn how to make something like that?" you can answer, "I learned it on the Net."

Web:

    http://astrosun.tn.cornell.edu/staff/loredo/ee.html
    http://ee.wustl.edu/~kxg/academics/electronic.html
    http://www.bc1.com/users/sgl/html/jo4.htm
    http://www.coe.montana.edu/ee/info/eesrces1.htm
    http://www.ecn.purdue.edu/~laird/electronics/
    http://www.ensc.sfu.ca/reference/electronics.html

Consumer Repair Documents

Do you think you might like to fix that toaster yourself rather than throw it out? Or how about taking a whack at the microwave before calling the repair service? Here is some handy and practical information about fixing electronic appliances. And if you really get stuck, you can always ask your Usenet friends for help. Maybe you can save enough money to pay for your monthly Internet bill.

Web:

    http://www.repairfaq.org/filipg/

Usenet:

    sci.electronics.repair

All About Electronics

Tell me if the following sounds interesting to you:

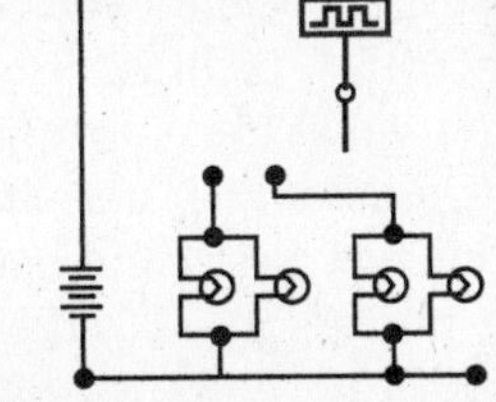

A transistor is a semi-conductor device used for amplifying a current or voltage. Transistors have three terminals. Bipolar transistors have a base, an emitter and a collector. They are controlled by current and have low input impedance. Field-effect transistors have a gate, a source and a drain. They are controlled by voltage and are high impedance.

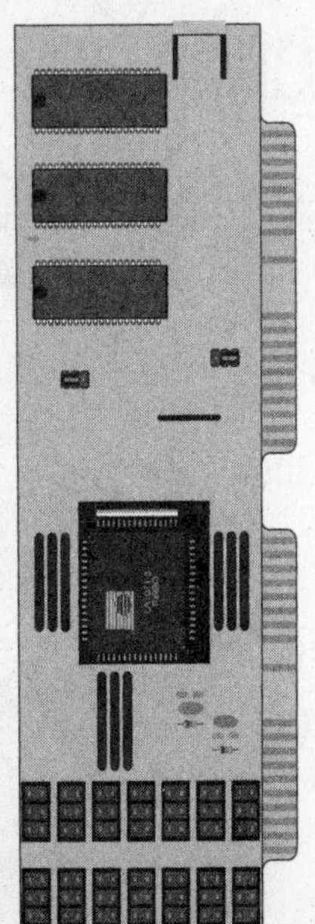

Now don't worry about whether or not you understand all the technical terms. If this type of stuff sounds interesting to you, you may enjoy learning about electronics.

If so, don't waste a moment. Connect to the Net, and start reading about electronics right this very moment.

EDN Magazine

EDN is a well-established magazine that follows the electronics industry, especially in areas related to design engineering and embedded systems. I like the articles because they are researched well, written well, and comprehensive without being bogged down in too much detail. This is a good site to visit every couple of weeks if you are an electronics professional interested in integrated circuits, microprocessors and computers, embedded systems, electronic design automation, testing and measurement.

Web:
  http://www.e-insite.net/ednmag/

Electronic Chip Directory

There are a *lot* of electronic chips in the world, with more being manufactured all the time. To help you find the information you need when you need it, here is a great resource with data about specific chips and manufacturers.

Web:
  http://www.embeddedlinks.com/chipdir/

A B C D E F G H I J K L M N O P Q R S T U V W X Y Z

A B C D E F G H I J K L M N O P Q R S T U V W X Y Z

Electronic Equipment Repair Tips

If you like to repair electronic equipment, you'll find this site useful. People from all over the world contribute tips and hints on how to solve specific problems with electronic devices such as computer monitors, game machines, audio equipment, laser printers, microwave ovens, satellite systems, TVs, telephones, video recorders, and more. If you are a repair buff, take a look at the list of problems for which people need help. Maybe you can suggest a solution. If you have a repair problem of your own, send it in and see if someone can help you.

Web:

http://elmswood.guernsey.net/

Usenet:

sci.electronics.equipment

Electronic Prototyping Tips

Only those who are really lucky can aspire to this level of electronic excellence. Get your fill of electronic prototyping and construction methods. Learn how to do cool things like despike chips, make changes to circuitry, and more. There is a huge amount of great troubleshooting information at these sites.

Web:

http://www.algonquincollege.com/electronics/
    moirb/prototst.htm
http://www.engr.unl.edu/ee/eeshop/proto.html

Electronics Talk and General Discussion

Electronics is a fascinating field that can be a lot of fun. However, it is a complex detailed area of technology, and there are times when it can help a lot to have someone to talk with. The Net has a number of resources devoted to electronics discussion, places where the P=IV type of people hang out.

Web:

http://www.semiconductoronline.com/
    discussionforums/

Usenet:

sci.electronics
sci.electronics.basics
sci.electronics.design
sci.electronics.misc

Great Microprocessors Past and Present

Within your computer are a variety of small electrical components known as "chips". These chips perform a number of different functions, but the one that people talk about the most is the processor. The processor performs many of the principal activities of the computer. You may have heard the processor metaphorically being referred to as the "brain" of the computer. Actually, there are a bunch of chips that are "brains", the processor being the main one. These Web sites contain information about a great many processors that have been developed through the years. I find this type of information interesting because I marvel at the enormous progress in processor design that has been made in such a short time. (The very first "microprocessor"—the old name for processor—was the 4004, announced by Intel in 1971.)

Web:

http://www.techboss.com/hardware/cpu/cpu.htm
http://www3.sk.sympatico.ca/jbayko/cpu.html

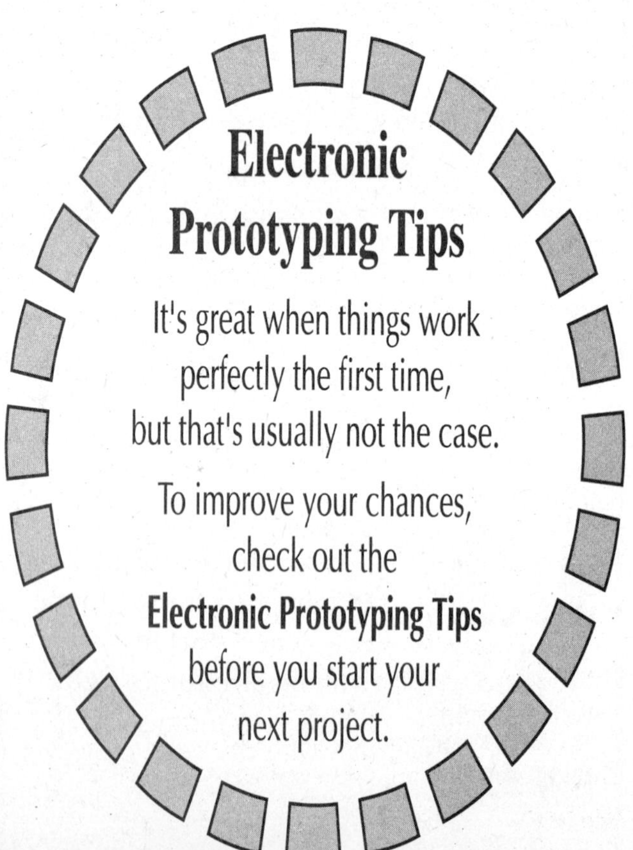

Museum of HP Calculators

When I was a senior in high school, the chemistry teacher had a contraption about the size of an old fashioned adding machine: a brand new electronic calculator. It cost $450 (which was a lot of money in those days) and could add, subtract, multiply and divide. The machine was considered so valuable, the teacher kept it locked in his office. Nowadays, you can pick up a credit card-sized solar-powered calculator for a couple of bucks at the corner drugstore. Much of the evolution from the first rudimentary calculators to today's sophisticated hand-held computers is a result of the work done by Hewlett-Packard. Throughout the years, HP has produced a family of calculators that, even now, are near and dear to the hearts of nerds everywhere. This Web site celebrates the history of such calculators. And if you happen to have one, you can find information about the calculator and how to maintain it.

Web:
  http://www.hpmuseum.org/

Semiconductors

A semiconductor is a substance whose electrical properties lie between that of a conductor and an insulator. Within the substance, there is limited movement of electrons, the exact characteristics depending on the crystalline structure of the material. Materials commonly used as semiconductors include germanium, silicon, indium antimonide, gallium arsenide and aluminum phosphide. What makes semiconductors so useful is the fact that, by adding small impurities to the material, the flow of electrons can be modified. Thus, it is possible to design a component that contains semiconductor material with specific impurities to create an electrical component designed to perform specific functions. As you can imagine, the world of semiconductors is complex. To help you understand what you read, I have found some resources with basic information about semiconductors and semiconductor terminology.

Web:
  http://www.dir-electronics.com/
  http://www.semiresources.com/
  http://www.semiseeknews.com/
  http://www.siliconstrategies.com/
  http://www-mtl.mit.edu/semisubway.html
Usenet:
  sci.engr.semiconductors

Speaker Building Information

Would you like to build your own audio speakers? There are a lot of subtle details that create the difference between a good speaker and a great speaker. Here is some useful information for people who like to design and build their own speakers. You will find various technical articles, tips and techniques.

Web:
  http://members.chello.se/jpo/
  http://topquark.roadkill.com/~davet/project/
    subwooferamp.html
  http://www.home.earthlink.net/~etunstal/diy.htm
  http://www.scrounge.org/speak/speak.htm
  http://www.speakerbuilding.com/

EMERGENCY AND DISASTER

Alertnet

Every day, there are emergencies and disasters somewhere in the world. When you need the latest news and you need it now, here is the place to visit. My advice is to spend five minutes at the end of each day reading this Web site. You will feel so good knowing that all these awful things aren't happening to you, that you will have a wonderful restful sleep all night long.

Web:
  http://www.alertnet.org/

Disaster Situation and Status Reports

It's amazing how many terrible things happen every week around the world. There are man-made calamities, such as wars and insurrections, as well as natural disasters, such as earthquakes, fires, storms, floods, famines and landslides. Spend just a few minutes looking at this information, and I guarantee you will have a whole new perspective about the world in which you live. (You will also realize how lucky you are.)

Web:

> http://www.cidi.org/
> http://www.vita.org/emergres.htm

Listserv Mailing List:

> List Name: disasterinfo
> Subscribe to: listserv@listserv.wa.gov

Natural Disasters and You!

One of the best parts of life is reading about natural disasters that happen to other people. What could be more fun than waking up each morning, logging in to your favorite Internet connection, and checking out all the disasters that happened overnight to people who aren't as smart and good looking as you? (And, if truth be told, may not even be smart enough to read this book.)

Disaster Talk and General Discussion

Are you the type of person who can't resist staring in fascination as you drive by the scene of an automobile accident? Well, if you also like to talk about disasters, this is the place to be. Any disaster will do: fire, flood, earthquake, plane crashes, and so on.

Usenet:

> alt.disasters.misc

Earthquakes

If you live in earthquake country, it's good to be prepared just in case the ground beneath you starts moving. If you don't live in earthquake country, you may want to find out what you are missing. These Web sites have maps of recent earthquakes, seismic data, earthquake news, information about the latest earthquakes around the globe, as well as hints on making your home environment more earthquake-safe. The Usenet discussion groups are for talking about various aspects of earthquakes, including personal information and technical data.

Web:

> http://earthquake.usgs.gov/
> http://gldss7.cr.usgs.gov/neis/qed/
> http://neic.usgs.gov/
> http://www.crustal.ucsb.edu/ics/understanding/
> http://www.fema.gov/library/quakef.htm
> http://www.seismo.unr.edu/htdocs/abouteq.html

Usenet:

> alt.disasters.earthquake
> sci.geo.earthquakes

Emergency News

When you want to find out what is happening in the emergency and disaster world, this is the place to look. You will find news stories about infectious diseases; police, military and fire operations; terrorism and rescue operations; hazardous material reports; and chemical and biological weapons.

Web:

> http://www.emergency.com/

Emergency Services

Emergency service personnel come in a variety of shapes and sizes. Such people—who may be civilian or military—cover various types of natural and technological disasters. Some workers get paid and some volunteer. But they all use a wide range of equipment and techniques to save lives and property. This Web site is a fine tribute to rescue workers as well as a good place to get general information about emergency services and life-saving tips. (You never know when you may need to know how to operate a chain saw properly.)

Web:

> http://www.firehouse.com/

Usenet:

> alt.emergency.services.dispatcher

Emerging Diseases

Not feeling at your perky best? Are you just not getting enough sleep or do you have some newly discovered contagion? Let's be sure. Take a look at these Web sites, where you can find lots of information on various outbreaks around the world, historical information of outbreaks of bygone days (for those who love nostalgia), and in-depth coverage on the spread of important diseases such as ebola, dengue and monkeypox.

Web:
  http://www.cdc.gov/ncidod/eid/
  http://www.niaid.nih.gov/publications/eid.htm
  http://www.who.int/emc/

Famine

Famine is a large-scale shortage of food. There are many causes of famine, the most common being (1) natural disaster, and (2) overpopulation combined with exhausted agricultural resources. However, no matter the reason for a famine, hunger is hunger, and the Net has a great many hunger-related resources. These sites talk about causes of hunger and solutions to famine. You will find information about advocacy groups and policies, education and training, as well as situation updates from all around the world.

Web:
  http://www.brown.edu/Departments/
    World_Hunger_Program/
  http://www.fews.net/

Federal Emergency Management Agency

The Federal Emergency Management Agency (FEMA) is an independent United States federal agency in Washington, D.C. FEMA provides training to help communities prepare for and cope with disasters. After something happens, FEMA offers disaster relief assistance. The FEMA Web site offers information about their services, as well as general information about how to prepare for various natural (and unnatural) disasters: earthquakes, extreme heat, fire, floods, hurricanes, nuclear plant disasters, and much more.

Web:
  http://www.fema.gov/

First Aid

You never know when a medical emergency is going to arise, but when it does, the Net can help. Here are first aid resources where you can learn what to do until proper medical attention is available. Read about bites, bleeding, blisters, bruising, burns, choking, ears/eyes/nose problems, fainting, fractures, frostbite, poisoning, shock, sprains, wounds, and much more.

Web:
  http://library.thinkquest.org/10624/1staid.html
  http://www.adam.com/b2b/products/demos/odh/
    firstaid_index.html
  http://www.alfambulance.net/firstaid.htm
  http://www.kidshealth.org/parent/firstaid_safe/
  http://www.kuwaitonline.com/dems/
  http://www.nlm.nih.gov/medlineplus/
    firstaidemergencies.html

Flood Observatory

If you are thinking of relocating, you may want to know if your new location is in an area that is prone to flooding. If so, you can check the flood activity for various places over the last few years. For example, many Americans think that moving to the midwestern United States is safe because they will be cleverly avoiding the earthquakes and volcanoes from the west as well as the hurricanes from the east. Well, as Marlon Brando said in A Streetcar Named Desire, "Ha... ha ha!" Before you relocate, read the information from the available flood databases, as well as current information about floods. There are also some fascinating images.

Web:
  http://www.dartmouth.edu/artsci/geog/floods/

Home Fire Safety Tips

Do you know what to do if your house catches on fire? These Web sites have tips on how to prevent fires in the home, as well as how to make a good plan for evacuating your house and keeping your family safe in the event of a fire. For example, if your house does catch on fire, have you designated the person whose job it would be to bring the marshmallows?

Web:
  http://www.ou.edu/oupd/fireprev.htm
  http://www.usfa.fema.gov/safety/sheets.htm

Hurricanes

If you live in a place where you occasionally have to batten down the hurricane hatches, you should know about where on the Net you can get good hurricane information. These sites will tell you about hurricanes, including how to prepare for an upcoming storm.

Web:
  http://www.co.broward.fl.us/epi00200.htm
  http://www.co.miami-dade.fl.us/teametro/
    hurrprep.htm
  http://www.gopbi.com/weather/special/storm/
  http://www.nhc.noaa.gov/
  http://www.stormcarib.com/nav/
  http://www.supertyphoon.com/

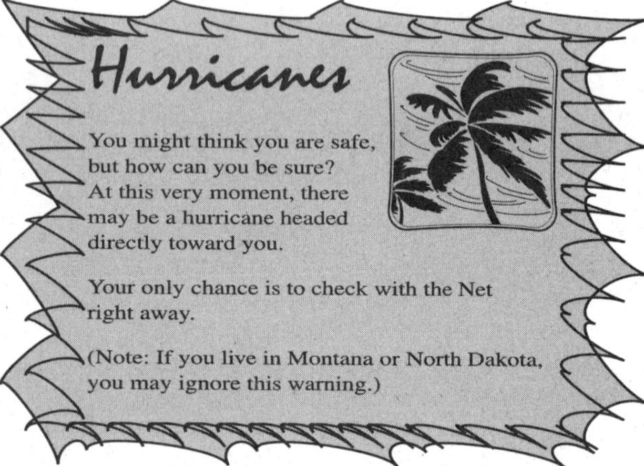

Planning Ahead for Disasters

Part of the trick of surviving a disaster is being prepared. This Usenet discussion group offers a great place for people to talk about how to get ready for that unforeseen day when fate is waiting around the corner with an unpleasant bit of sticky business. Trade anecdotes and hints with people around the world or check out the Web for advice and handy checklists to help you prepare for The Big One.

Web:
  http://www.allstate.com/catastrophe/
    pagerender.asp?page=howprepare.htm
  http://www.redcross.org/services/disaster/
    beprepared/
  http://www.theepicenter.com/howto.html
  http://www.thefamily.com/preparation/

Usenet:
  alt.disasters.planning

Red Cross

There never seems to be a lack of natural disasters, so there is always something for the Red Cross to do. This global nondenominational, nonprofit disaster assistance organization boldly goes where everyone else is evacuating. Read information about the Red Cross, get updated news about current disasters and assistance efforts currently being performed. For those of you who like to participate, you can also find out how to join.

Web:
  http://www.redcross.org/

Survivalism

I am a firm believer in survivalism, and I am quite a survivalist myself. For instance, in my pantry right now, I have not one, but *two* boxes of microwave popcorn in case I am overrun by hoards of hungry guests. In my bathroom, I have extra rolls of fluffy bathroom tissue because, well, you just never know. And, in the cupboard, I have an extra bag of cat food. To some people, however, survival goes beyond popcorn, toilet paper and cat food, as you will see when you start to read what people are doing to practice the art of self-reliance. All it takes is gumption, planning and some money. As Oscar Wilde said, you can survive anything except death.

Web:
  http://www.doubleought.com/survivalism.html
  http://www.justpeace.org/nuggetsindex.htm
  http://www.logicsouth.com/~lcoble/password/
    survival.html
  http://www.smartlink.net/~fred/surv13.htm

Usenet:
  misc.survivalism

Tornadoes

If you think living inland protects you from storm activity, think again. Tornadoes are generally quick but intense, causing destruction in a localized area. Find out how and where tornadoes form, how to rate a tornado, and tips on what to do if a tornado hits in your area.

Web:
  http://www.fema.gov/library/tornadof.htm
  http://www.nws.noaa.gov/om/brochures/
    tornado.htm
  http://www.tornadoproject.com/
  http://www.txdirect.net/~msattler/tornado.htm

Wildfires

Wildfires are a constant problem, and during the fire season, there is always something happening. Here are some Web sites to help you keep up. In particular, you can check the current fire situation in the United States; the information is updated daily. I have also included a Web site with articles of interest to wildfire professionals.

Web:
   http://www.cidi.org/wildfire/fire.htm
   http://www.earthobservatory.nasa.gov/Library/
      GlobalFire/
   http://www.nifc.gov/fireinfo/nfn.html
   http://www.nifc.gov/information.html

ENERGY

Biomass

Biomass refers to organic matter. Much biomass is renewable; that is, if you use it up you can create more. There is a lot of research and development being done to find ways to use renewable biomass to produce energy in a way that is safe, economical and non-polluting. For example, researchers are looking for ways to create energy out of forest and mill residues, agricultural and animal wastes, livestock operation residues, aquatic plants, fast-growing trees and plants, and municipal and industrial wastes.

Web:
   http://www.biomass.org/
   http://www.crest.org/bioenergy/
   http://www.ott.doe.gov/biofuels/
   http://www.westbioenergy.org/biolinks.htm

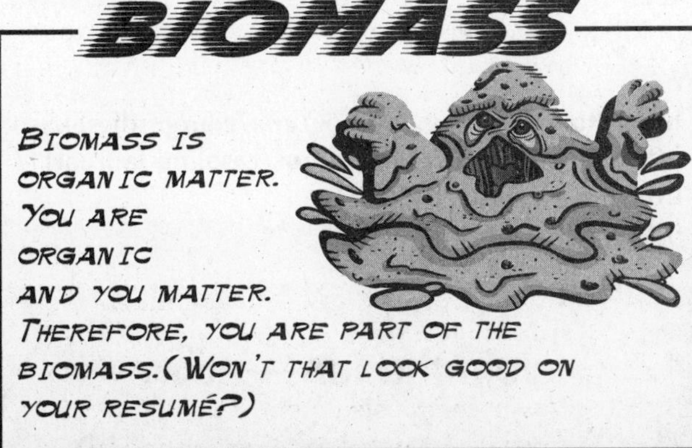

Coal

Coal is a fuel created from fossilized plants (similar to the way in which oil is created). Coal is almost entirely carbon with varying amounts of minerals. Although coal creates a lot of pollution when it is burned, it is still used in a good many places around the world (including the United States, where it is especially important to the steel industry).

Web:
   http://www.coaltrade.com/
   http://www.eia.doe.gov/fuelcoal.html
   http://www.isr.gov.au/resources/coal_vl/

Energy and the Environment

It's common these days to hear about what car smog is doing to the environment. However, there is more to energy and the environment than what your automobile is producing. Check out some of the environmentally related resources on the Net, gathered under one solar-powered virtual roof. You'll find information about alternative energy as well as traditional energy sources (such as fossil fuels).

Web:
   http://www.eh.doe.gov/nepa/
   http://www.ucsusa.org/energy/

Usenet:
   alt.energy.homepower

Energy Efficiency and Renewable Energy Network

The Energy Efficiency and Renewable Energy Network (EREN) is part of the U.S. Department of Energy. The U.S. government is putting a lot of effort into developing new energy technologies, and this Web site is a good place to learn about what's happening. I found an enormous amount of interesting information here. A lot of it is technical government stuff, but there are some fascinating areas, including special resources for kids. I particularly enjoyed reading about superconductivity.

Web:
   http://www.eren.doe.gov/

Energy Efficient Homes

How energy efficient is your home? Here are some resources on the Net that show you how to improve your home's efficiency, help the environment, and save a few bucks at the same time. The Web sites will show you energy-saving tips. The Usenet groups are for the discussion of heating, venting and air conditioning.

Web:
   http://energuide.nrcan.gc.ca/html/home.html
   http://hes.lbl.gov/
   http://www.energyguide.com/
   http://www.energyoutlet.com/

Usenet:
   alt.hvac
   sci.engr.heat-vent-ac

Energy Information Administration

The Energy Information Administration (EIA) is an independent statistical and analytical agency of the United States Department of Energy. The EIA compiles data relating to energy resources, supply and demand, technology, economics, energy policies, and more. The EIA's Web site has summaries and reports on energy consumption all over the world, as well as energy forecasts. (This is the place to check to see if you will have enough energy to play softball after work.)

Web:
   http://www.eia.doe.gov/

Energy Talk and General Discussion

When you need a little pick-me-up, check out the Usenet groups where nerds around the Net energize themselves by talking about the science of energy.

Usenet:
   alt.energy
   sci.energy

Federal Energy Regulatory Commission

The U.S. Federal Energy Regulatory Commission (FERC) is an independent regulatory agency within the Department of Energy. FERC (is that a cool name, or what?) regulates various aspects of the production of natural gas, oil, electricity, hydroelectric projects, as well as various related environmental and administrative matters.

Web:
   http://www.fferc.gov/

Fusion Energy

Fusion, or nuclear fusion, is a reaction in which the nuclei of two light atoms combine, or fuse, into a larger, heavier nucleus. Nuclear fusion is responsible for the energy of the stars, including our Sun. Within the center of stars, hydrogen nuclei combine to form helium nuclei and, in the process, release energy. Hydrogen nuclei are positively charged and, as such, naturally repel one another. In the center of a star, however, the temperature and pressure are great enough to force hydrogen nuclei together long enough to fuse. On Earth, it is extremely difficult to create such conditions, which is why we do not, as yet, have any fusion reactors. However, much work underway is aimed at creating such technology. Although successful fusion reactors are probably decades away (at least), the promise of such technology is seductive: it would end our dependence on oil and gas without the problems of air pollution and radioactive waste.

Web:
   http://fusedweb.pppl.gov/
   http://wwwofe.er.doe.gov/

Usenet:
   sci.physics.fusion

Gasoline

Gasoline (called petrol in the U.K.) is a volatile hydrocarbon fuel, created by distilling petroleum and then processing the distillate. Gasoline is such a part of modern life that just the smell of it can invoke latent memories. I have a friend, who, when she was young, loved the smell of gasoline so much that she used to unscrew the gas cap of her parents' car and inhale the vapor. She even imagined creating a perfume with that same fragrance. Personally, I prefer freshly cut grass or patchouli oil, but then who am I to judge others?

Web:
   http://tonto.eia.doe.gov/oog/info/gdu/gasdiesel.asp
   http://www.faqs.org/faqs/autos/gasoline-faq/part1/
   http://www.methanol.org/
   http://www.ofa.net/

Join the fun—now.

FUSION ENERGY

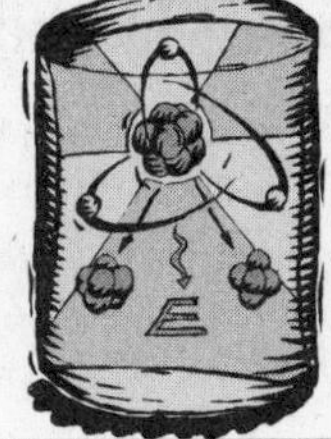

What a nice word fusion is. Just say it slowly, let it roll off your tongue and lips with a soft hissing sound: *fusion*. It's not just a science, it's a way of life.

Hydroelectricity

Hydroelectric power is the largest renewable resource in the United States. Hydropower generates 10 percent of the power produced in the United States, equivalent to 500 million barrels of oil a year. In general, hydropower is an excellent energy source because it gives off no emissions when it is used, and the source of the energy is from water that is already laying around doing nothing in particular. However, there are problems. To create a hydroelectricity plant, water must be diverted and, often, dams must be constructed. These activities must be considered carefully as they can have negative effects on the ecosystems of the waterways. Still, I grew up in a place in which all the electricity was generated from hydropower, and I turned out pretty good.

Web:
  http://www.hydro.org/hydrofacts.htm
  http://www.nwp.usace.army.mil/hdc/
  http://www.usbr.gov/power/

Hydrogen Power

If you have lots of water and the right type of electrical current, you can whip up some hydrogen and create your own power plant. However, if you are low on water, you can also produce hydrogen from sewage, garbage, agricultural biomass, paper waste products and other waste streams that have hydrogen-bearing compounds. Check out these links for interesting information about using hydrogen as a source of fuel. And if you feel like talking, you can expend some hot air on the hydrogen Usenet groups.

Web:
  http://www.eren.doe.gov/hydrogen/
  http://www.hydrogenus.com/advocate/
  http://www.tinaja.com/h2gas01.asp
Usenet:
  alt.energy.hydrogen
  sci.energy.hydrogen

Natural Gas

Natural gas is a mixture of gases that come from beneath the ground. Natural gas is mostly methane (80-95 percent) with the remainder varying according to the geographic locality. The minor components of natural gas may include helium, carbon dioxide, carbon monoxide, hydrogen and nitrogen. Natural gas is a fossil fuel and is often found with petroleum. However, natural gas can also occur by itself within sand, sandstone or limestone deposits.

Web:
  http://www.eia.doe.gov/oil_gas/natural_gas/
    info_glance/natural_gas.html
  http://www.iangv.org/html/sources/
  http://www.naturalgas.org/

North American Electric Reliability Council

The North American Electric Reliability Council (NERC) was formed in 1968 to promote reliability of the electricity supply for the United States, Canada and parts of Mexico. Aside from the general warm feeling visiting this Web site should give you (knowing that reliable people are concerned about your electricity supply), you'll find a wealth of interesting information. For example, you can read the details of major electricity outages over the years, find out the current operating status of the nuclear power plants, and examine the assessment for electricity supply for coming seasons.

Web:
  http://www.nerc.com/

Nuclear Energy

Nuclear energy produces approximately 20 percent of the energy used in the United States. In general, nuclear energy is a versatile form of power. Aside from the production of electricity, nuclear energy is put to such disparate uses as cancer treatments, explosive-detecting machines, medical instrument sterilizers, and smoke detectors. Nuclear usage in the United States is heavily regulated by an independent government agency called the Nuclear Regulatory Commission.

Web:
  http://www.me3.org/issues/nuclear/
  http://www.nei.org/
  http://www.nrc.gov/

A B C D **E** F G H I J K L M N O P Q R S T U V W X Y Z

Petroleum

Back in the olden days (millions of years ago), nobody knew what to do with all the dead dinosaurs and various other organic matter that were just sitting around composting. It was entirely too much for primitive people to use in their tomato gardens, so they just left it laying there. Eventually a lot of the organic matter fossilized and turned into a substance that we process and use as oil, gasoline and natural gas.

Web:
http://www.api.org/
http://www.eia.doe.gov/oil_gas/petroleum/
info_glance/petroleum.html

Usenet:
sci.geo.petroleum

Renewable Electric Plant Database

If you are a professional or researcher in the area of renewable energy, you'll find this resource valuable. You can get data regarding how much renewable energy is used in the power grid. There is also information regarding power plants and their capabilities. The Web site contains information on more than 7,000 power plants, including those that are wind powered, geothermal, hydroelectric, solarthermal and photovoltaic.

Web:
http://www.eren.doe.gov/repis/

Renewable Energy

Right now, as you read this, there are clever people around the world thinking about ways to use renewable energy. They are coming up with new designs for batteries, generators, pumps and chargers to use wind, water and sun for fuel. Read about the neat gadgets they have modified or invented, or just check out the ideas and philosophy behind using renewable energy.

Web:
http://wire0.ises.org/wire/wire.nsf
http://www.caddet-re.org/
http://www.nrel.gov/

Usenet:
alt.energy.renewable

Solar Energy

Where I live in California, there is a lot of sun. In fact, there is such an abundance of sunlight that I can use it to power my souped-up solar-powered surfboard. But even if you don't surf, you may still want to check out solar energy information on the Net. On Usenet, you can discuss various aspects of solar energy with all the other solar buffs, talking about everything energy-related under the sun.

Web:
http://www.flasolar.com/
http://www.ises.org/
http://www.mrsolar.com/faq/
http://www.wagonmaker.com/solar.html

Usenet:
alt.solar.photovoltaic
alt.solar.thermal

U.S. Department of Energy

The United States Department of Energy (DOE) is a large government organization responsible for a number of energy-related areas: maintaining the U.S. nuclear weapons stockpile, lots and lots of scientific research, managing the country's energy resources, and protecting the environment. The DOE's Web site contains a great deal of interesting material, far more than you would ever expect from a government department. If you are a student or teacher, this is a good place for you to explore.

Web:
http://www.energy.gov/

Wind Energy

I love to feel the wind in my hair while I am riding my skateboard. However, wind has other uses. It can also be harnessed for energy. You will find information about wind as well as experiments you can use for teaching about wind energy and windmills.

Web:
http://www.awea.org/
http://www.eren.doe.gov/RE/wind.html
http://www.nrel.gov/wind/
http://www.windpower.org/tour/

PETROLEUM

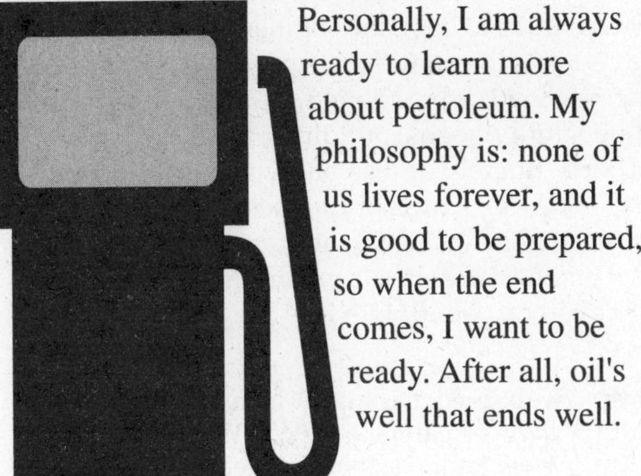

Personally, I am always ready to learn more about petroleum. My philosophy is: none of us lives forever, and it is good to be prepared, so when the end comes, I want to be ready. After all, oil's well that ends well.

World Energy Statistics

Numbers, numbers, numbers. What do you do when you need to find out how much natural gas the world is going to use in the year 2010? Well, you could just wait until 2010, but that would take a long time. Wouldn't it be faster to check with the Net?

Web:
  http://www.eia.doe.gov/emeu/mer/contents.html

ENGINEERING

Aerospace Engineering

Aerospace engineering is the area of engineering that deals with aircraft and space vehicles. The Web site contains numerous links to Internet resources for aerospace engineers: information on NASA projects and missions, news, professional tools, publications, software, aerospace companies, and more. For discussion, the Usenet group is devoted to the technology of space flight.

Web:
  http://www.embryriddle.edu/libraries/virtual/

Usenet:
  sci.space.tech

Audio Engineering

The Audio Engineering Society is a professional society devoted to audio technology. They maintain this Web page, which is a collection of links in the area of audio technology as well as related topics. You can find timely references to papers and articles on loudspeakers, sound reinforcement, microphones, disk recording, time-delay spectrometry and digital audio. For discussion, there are a number of Usenet groups in which you can participate. I have included the ones that are the most useful for audio engineering.

Web:
  http://www.aes.org/resources/www-links/

Usenet:
  rec.audio.high-end
  rec.audio.opinion
  rec.audio.pro
  rec.audio.tech

Biomedical Engineering

Biomedical engineering is an interdisciplinary field, combining engineering, physics and chemistry to develop instruments used to study and treat living organisms. Biomedical engineers design such devices as pacemakers, dialysis machines, medical lasers, surgical instruments, and so on. The Web is a good place to search for biomedical engineering information on the Net. You will find academic resources, publications and organizations, as well as information about jobs, grants and conferences. For discussion with other biomedical engineers, try Usenet.

Web:
  http://memphis.mecca.org/bme/
    connection.html#societies
  http://www.bmenet.org/bmenet/

Usenet:
  sci.bio.technology
  sci.engr.biomed

The magic number is "3".

CAD (Computer Aided Design)

The aim of CAD (computer aided design) is to use computers for creating designs. A basic CAD system can be used to model a design, produce drawings, and keep track of a list of all the parts needed for a particular design. More advanced systems will provide sophisticated help to the engineer during the design process.

Web:
  http://www.cad-portal.com/
  http://www.cadforum.com/
  http://www.cadonline.com/
  http://www.compinfo-center.com/tpcad-t.htm
  http://www.plannet.com/cadresources.html

Usenet:
  alt.cad
  comp.lsi.cad
  sci.electronics.cad

Chemical Engineering

Chemical engineering is the study of the industrial applications of chemistry. In other words, chemical engineers use raw material to make stuff. Did you know that of the four main branches of engineering—civil, mechanical, electrical and chemical—chemical engineering has the fewest people, but they make the most money? Check the Net and see if you can find the formula.

Web:
  http://www.che.ufl.edu/www-che/
  http://www.cheresources.com/
  http://www.ciw.uni-karlsruhe.de/chem-eng.html

Usenet:
  sci.chem.coatings
  sci.engr.chem

Listserv Mailing List:
  List Name: cheme-l
  Subscribe to: listserv@listserv.louisville.edu

Civil Engineering

The term "civil engineering" was first used in the 18th century to describe engineering work performed by civilians for nonmilitary purposes. Today, civil engineering is a broad field, dealing with works of public utility: roads, buildings, bridges, dams, airports, tunnels, and so on (which is probably why the U.S. Army Corps of Engineers—civil engineers to the max—live inside the military). Here are some civil engineering sites from around the world. See what you can build with it.

Web:
  http://web.singnet.com.sg/~icyh1955/civil.html
  http://www.ce.gatech.edu/WWW-CE/
  http://www.tenlinks.com/engineering/civil/

Usenet:
  sci.engr.civil

Listserv Mailing List:
  List Name: civil-l
  Subscribe to: listserv@unb.ca

Cold Region Engineering

When the temperature falls below freezing (0 degrees centigrade, 32 degrees Fahrenheit), water solidifies and the natural world changes dramatically. This causes many engineering problems. For example, machinery may stop working properly, and many materials will change their properties. Nearly half our planet will, at some time during the year, experience temperatures below freezing. In fact, 20 percent of the Earth is underlaid by permafrost (permanently frozen subsoil). Thus, cold region engineering is an important discipline that draws from general engineering, earth sciences and physical sciences.

Web:
  http://www.crrel.usace.army.mil/

Electrical Engineering

Electrical engineering deals with systems and devices that use electric power and electric signals. The four main areas of this discipline are electronics, computers, communications and control, and electric power and machinery. If you are an electrical engineer (or a student), here are a lot of resources you will enjoy.

Web:
http://webdiee.cem.itesm.mx/wwwvlee/
http://www.eet.com/
http://www.ieee.org/

Usenet:
alt.engineering.electrical
sci.engr.electrical.compliance
sci.engr.electrical.sys-protection

Electronics Engineering

Electronics engineering is the branch of electrical engineering that deals with electrical devices and systems. Electronics engineers work in such areas as chips and computer components, digital signal processing, industrial embedded computing, microcontrollers and microprocessors, as well as real-time and embedded systems. (I wish I had an electronics engineer right now. My toaster only toasts the bread on one side.)

Web:
http://www.e-insite.net/electronicnews/
http://www.elec-toolbox.com/
http://www.evaluationengineering.com/
http://www.pels.org/

Engineering Failures

When things go wrong, the most important thing to do is to ask "Why?" Why, for example, did the space shuttle Challenger blow up in 1986? Why did the skywalk collapse in Kansas City in 1981? The answers to these questions and a lot more are to be found in the FAQ (frequently asked question list) for the **sci.engr** Usenet groups. (By the way, the space shuttle blew up when a failed pressure seal [O-ring] leaked combustion gases. The Kansas City skywalk collapsed because the nuts and rods that were supposed to support two levels of catwalk were inadequate because of poor communication between the designers and the contractor.)

Web:
http://www.matscieng.sunysb.edu/disaster/

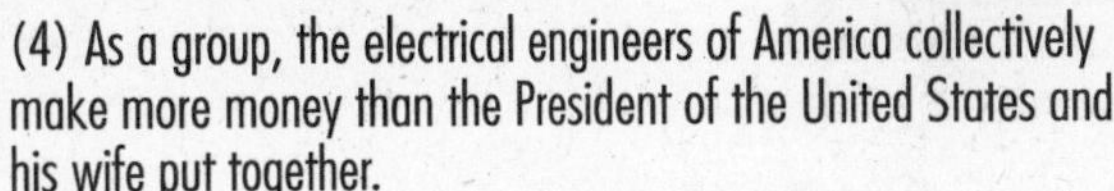

Electrical Engineering

The next time you hear someone pooh-pooh electrical engineering, remind him of the following:

(1) In ancient Rome, there wasn't even one properly certified electrical engineer, and within several hundred years, the entire Roman civilization was toppled by bands of invading barbarians.

(2) No electrical engineer has ever been impeached by the Senate of the United States.

(3) In one survey after another, famous supermodels and movie stars choose electrical engineers as the type of engineer they would prefer to be stranded with in an abandoned hydroelectric plant.

(4) As a group, the electrical engineers of America collectively make more money than the President of the United States and his wife put together.

(5) Electrical engineers never have to wait in line at a restaurant, and they always get the best seats in a movie theater.

(6) Every year, on Electrical Engineering Day, everyone has to find an electrical engineer and do whatever he or she wants for the entire day.

(7) In certain primitive societies, electrical engineers are considered to be gods, even more important than writers.

Engineering Resources

Engineering covers so wide a range of activities as to almost defy definition. Still, such trifles never stopped me, so here it goes: Engineering is the profession in which a knowledge of science and mathematics is used to control the materials and forces of nature. If you have any interest in any type of engineering, paste these Web addresses into your hat. You'll find links to information on just about any type of engineering you can imagine (and several you can't imagine).

Web:
http://www.eevl.ac.uk/wwwvl.html
http://www.engineeringhangout.com/
http://www.er-online.co.uk/
http://www.ipl.org/ref/RR/static/sci15.00.00.html
http://www.motionnet.com/

Engineering Talk and General Discussion

If you are a part of the engineering community, you may want to participate in an ongoing discussion of engineering topics. If so, there are plenty of places on Usenet where you can talk shop.

Usenet:
    sci.engr
    sci.engr.advanced-tv
    sci.engr.color
    sci.engr.control
    sci.engr.joining.misc
    sci.engr.joining.welding
    sci.engr.manufacturing
    sci.engr.marine.hydrodynamics
    sci.engr.metallurgy
    sci.engr.micromachining
    sci.engr.safety
    sci.engr.television.advanced
    sci.engr.television.broadcast
    sci.materials
    sci.materials.ceramics
    sci.systems

Engineering Tools

Are you an engineer? If so, you've probably got a few projects right now that you'd love to finish early so you can go surfing. (Well, I know I do.) When you are a technology expert, you need the best tools to do the best job. So try these tools, and maybe you'll finish work early enough to catch a few waves before sunset. (If you can't surf, at least come out and watch me.)

Web:
    http://www.engineeringtoolbox.com/
    http://www.engineersedge.com/

Geotechnical Engineering

Geotechnical engineering is the study of technology and methods of soil mechanics. Geotechnical engineers build things that must interact with geological structures. If you ever go to a party with such people, you will hear them talk about consolidation, lateral earth pressures, bearing capacity and stability. The father of modern geotechnical engineering (soil mechanics, actually) is the Hungarian-American Karl von Terzaghi (1883-1963).

Web:
    http://geotech.civen.okstate.edu/wwwvl/
Usenet:
    sci.engr.geomechanics
    sci.geo.geology

Mechanical Engineering

Mechanical engineering is the broadest of the engineering sciences. In simple terms, mechanical engineering concerns itself with things that move in some way. More generally, this discipline can be divided into two main parts: machine design and working with heat. One day I'm going to find a way to combine the two, and invent an automated system to warm up my peanut butter and jelly sandwiches.

Web:
    http://www.asme.org/
    http://www.gearhob.com/
    http://www.icrank.com/
    http://www.memagazine.org/

Usenet:
    bit.listserv.biomch-l
    sci.engr.mech

Listserv Mailing List:
    List Name: mech-l
    Subscribe to: listserv@listserv.uta.edu

Mining

The goal of mining is to remove mineral resources from the ground, in particular gems (precious stones), ores (substances containing metals), and solid fuels (such as coal). Before a new mine can become fully operational, there must be an enormous amount of research, planning and development, sometimes taking years. The job of a mining engineer is to provide the expertise to help plan and oversee such operations. Some mining engineers work with geologists and metallurgical engineers to look for new ore deposits. Other mining engineers work on the design of mines, including the construction of shafts, tunnels and ore transportation systems. Still other engineers develop mining equipment and methods to extract mineral from the raw ore. The resources I have listed here pertain to both mining engineering and the mining industry.

Web:
    http://industryclick.com/
        magazine.asp?magazineid=116&siteid=21
    http://www.min-eng.com/
    http://www.mine-engineer.com/

Usenet:
    sci.engr.mining

Nuclear Engineering

So you want to impress your best girl (or guy) and show your parents that you really can amount to something? Go to this Web site and learn something about nuclear engineering (applying technology based on energy absorbed or released during atomic reactions). How hard could it be? After all, it's not rocket science.

Web:
  http://web.mit.edu/ned/www/links.html

Usenet:
  alt.engr.nuclear

Optical Engineering

Do you need to shed light on your engineering problems? Here are some resources devoted to optical engineering (applying the science of light) and to photonics (transmission of information via light, usually lasers). By the way, when I was a graduate student at the University of California at San Diego, one of my best friends was an optical engineer. I used to do my math homework with her.

Web:
  http://www.optics.org/
  http://www.osa.org/

Usenet:
  sci.optics

Robotics

Robotics is the study and creation of machines guided by automatic controls (robots). Although it is fashionable to think of robots as being humanoid, outside of science fiction, robots look a lot more like your toaster than like your Uncle Henry.

Web:
  http://robotics.jpl.nasa.gov/
  http://www-2.cs.cmu.edu/~chuck/robotpg/
    robo_rsrc.html
  http://www.dprg.org/links.html
  http://www.frc.ri.cmu.edu/robotics-faq/
  http://www.robotics.com/robots.html

Usenet:
  comp.robotics.misc
  comp.robotics.research

ENVIRONMENT

Air Pollution

Everyone knows that methanesulfonic acid is an atmospheric aerosol particle formed from the oxidation of dimethylsulfide which has been produced by phytoplankton. But what about the difficult stuff? When it comes to air pollution, you don't want to get left out in the cold. Here are some resources that provide lots of data, a glossary and relevant information from the U.S. Environmental Protection Agency (EPA).

Web:
  http://www.coheadquarters.com/CO1.htm
  http://www.epa.gov/docs/oar/
  http://www.epa.gov/iaq/
  http://www.shsu.edu/~chemistry/Glossary/glos.html
  http://www.skepticism.net/faq/environment/
    clean_air/

Biosphere

The "biosphere" refers to the part of our world in which life can exist: from the surface of the Earth— that is, the oceans and the land—up about 10 km (6 miles) into the atmosphere. Obviously, this is an important area of the universe that we should understand. After all, all our stuff is here.

Web:
  http://atlas.aos.wisc.edu/
  http://ice.ucdavis.edu/mab/
  http://www.unesco.org/mab/wnbr.htm

Listserv Mailing List:
  List Name: biosph-l
  Subscribe to: listserv@listserv.aol.com

Chemicals in the Environment

There are many chemicals in our environment that can be harmful to human beings, and it is important to be able to separate the truth from the myths. When you need real information, read carefully and ask yourself, "Is what I am reading credible? Should I believe it?" When you need to do research, start with these Web sites where you will find factual, scientific information about many different toxic chemicals.

Web:

http://www.atsdr.cdc.gov/toxfaq.html
http://www.nsc.org/library/chemical/chemical.htm

Climate Protection Division

Would you like to help make the environment healthier? The U.S. Environmental Protection Agency's Climate Protection Division sponsors voluntary programs for both individuals and companies. These programs are dedicated to conserving energy, reducing air pollution and solid waste, and minimizing the emission of the greenhouse gases (such as carbon dioxide) that may be contributing to global climate change.

Web:

http://www.epa.gov/cpd.html

Coastal Management

People think that the coast is all fun and sun with the ocean crashing against the beach and the sun setting across the water. Well, it's that very water that makes the coast so tricky to manage. And then there's that rumor that has been going around about California falling off into the ocean. It's enough to give anyone a headache. Fortunately, there are resources on the Net that deal with topics related to coastal management and resources, so there is a place to turn when it's time to come up with some revolutionary ideas in the coastal management field.

Web:

http://www.coastalmanagement.com/
http://www.netcoast.nl/

Coastal Management

Life here in Southern California is a lot more than surfing and snorkeling and swimming. Sometimes we have to take a break and get a massage.

But when we do get serious, we get serious. If you want to join in, take a look at the Coastal Management resources on the Net.

If you can't go surfing, you might as well read about the water.

Coral Reefs

Coral reefs are limestone formations found in shallow tropical oceans where the water is over 22 degrees centigrade (72 degrees Fahrenheit). Reefs are produced by sea animals that secrete calcium carbonate (limestone), which, over thousands of years, builds up into massive formations. Coral reefs are part of the undersea ecosystem and provide important ecological support for coral as well as other animal and plant life. There are several types of reefs: fringing reefs which are platforms running contiguous with the shore, barrier reefs which are separated from the shore by an expanse of deep lagoon, and atolls which surround a lagoon. Although coral reefs cover less than 0.2 percent of the Earth's ocean-covered area, they create a living environment for a great many of the ocean's species. At these Web sites, you can read about all the things that coral reefs do for humans, and why we should save them from contamination and physical destruction.

Web:

http://coralreef.gov/
http://www.coralreef.noaa.gov/
http://www.coralreefalliance.org/
http://www.epa.gov/owow/oceans/coral/
http://www.mojones.com/coral_reef/
http://www.reefrelief.org/

Majordomo Mailing List:

List Name: coral-list
Subscribe to: majordomo@coral.aoml.noaa.gov

Ecological Economics

What does economics have to do with the environment? A lot. Environmental factors are often influenced, at least indirectly, by monetary decisions. Thus, it is important to rethink our approach to finance, resources and money in terms of environmental concerns, if we are going to be able to make wise political and economic decisions.

Web:
   http://csf.colorado.edu/ecol-econ/
   http://www.ecomall.com/greenshopping/
      ecology.htm

Listproc Mailing List:
   List Name: ecol-econ
   Subscribe to: listproc@csf.colorado.edu

Endangered Rivers

Rivers don't grow on trees, so it's a nice idea to take care of the ones we have. Here are some Web sites that will keep you informed about endangered and threatened rivers that are suffering from the effects of mining, toxic dumping, waste dumping, pollution and other human threats.

Web:
   http://www.amrivers.org/
   http://www.irn.org/

Environment Talk and General Discussion

Whether you just like to talk about saving the environment or you actually want to *do* something about saving the environment, these Usenet discussion groups are for you. Earth lovers all over the planet talk about various aspects of ecology and the environment. Discussion ranges widely, from helpful home tips to technical scientific topics.

Usenet:
   alt.desert.restoration
   alt.earth.crisis
   alt.org.sierra-club
   alt.save.the.earth
   alt.wastewater
   sci.environment
   talk.environment

Environmental Protection Agency

The United States Environmental Protection Agency (EPA) is the American federal government agency charged with protecting the public's health and the natural environment. The EPA Web site offers a massive amount of information about the environment: news, programs, publications, regulations, contracts and grants. There are also special resources for teachers and children.

Web:
   http://www.epa.gov/

Environmental Resources

There are several places on the Net that are loaded with information designed to enhance cooperation among people interested in environmental activities. Would you like to save the world, but you don't have enough time? Let's start small. Hug a tree with one hand and, with the other, use your browser to connect to some of these environmental resources.

Web:
http://envirolink.netforchange.com/
http://spot.colorado.edu/~jobem/envrscs.htm
http://www.earthsystems.org/
http://www.igc.org/igc/gateway/enindex.html
http://www.rachel.org/home_eng.htm

Environmental Scorecard

If you are American, you may be interested to see how your congressional representatives rank on the National Environmental Scorecard. This ranking is created by the League of Conservation Voters to draw attention to voting patterns followed by individual congressmen and congresswomen. How did your elected officials do? One of my two senators—both of whom are women—scored high, with a 2001 ranking of 100%. Her previous annual scores were 86%, 89%, 88%, 100%, 92%, 100%, 100% and 88%. The other senator didn't do as well. Her 2001 ranking was only 75% (although that is a lot better than the Senate average of 46%). Her previous scores were 86%, 100%, 100%, 100%, 85%, 93%, 77% and 62%. (Maybe if she helped me pull all the weeds out of my backyard her score would go up.)

Web:
http://www.lcv.org/scorecard/

Environmental Search Engines

When you need to find data and information related to the environment, you can focus quickly using a search engine specifically geared toward environmental resources. Choose from many, many Web sites or archives, or perform a quick search on several databases at the same time.

Web:
http://www.eco-portal.com/
http://www.envirofind.com/

Environmental Web Directory

Here on Earth, we have more environment than you can shake a biodegradable stick at. But some days, it seems as if our large but limited supply of environment is being damaged faster than we can even understand. Is this true, or is the Earth capable of taking care of itself? Check the information on the Net and see what *you* think.

Web:
http://www.environmentaldirectory.net/
http://www.webdirectory.com/

Forest Conservation

Would you like to help protect forests? How about supporting biodiversity and indigenous cultures? If so, these sites are for you. Lots and lots of reference material relating to forest environments around the world. (However, to save disk space, information is restricted to only those forests in our local biosphere.)

Web:
http://www.fguardians.org/
http://www.forest.org/
http://www.forests.org/
http://www.newforestsproject.com/

Do elected officials know the score?

Maybe yes and maybe no, but if you live in the United States, you can check your congressional representative's environmental scorecard.

(Environmental hint: After you are finished connecting to the Web, be sure to recycle all your leftover electrons.)

Greenpeace

If the military is not your style, but you want a sense of adventure on the open seas, check out Greenpeace. Read up on ship movements, press releases, latest demonstrations and job opportunities, and see pictures and publications of this environmental activist group.

Web:
  http://www.greenpeace.org/
  http://www.greenpeaceusa.org/

Hazardous Waste

Every day, a lot of waste is created in the world. Most of this waste is burned, buried, recycled, or thrown away and left to decompose. However, a lot of waste must be handled differently because it is dangerous. For example, many radioactive materials and chemicals must be disposed of carefully to avoid contamination of waste sites and danger to nearby people. Unfortunately, hazardous waste is not always handled properly and, just as important, there is a huge legacy of dangerous material that has already been introduced into the environment and must now be cleaned up. These issues are important for us to understand on a global and national level—to set policy, clean up polluted areas, and develop methods of dealing with hazardous waste—and on a local level—to ensure that people dispose of materials such as used oil and antifreeze in the proper manner.

Web:
  http://www.clu-in.org/
  http://www.epa.gov/epaoswer/osw/hazwaste.htm
  http://www.epa.gov/radiation/mixed-waste/
  http://www.epa.gov/superfund/sites/

National Wetlands Inventory

The Net is great. You can check on America's wetlands without having to put on waders and slosh about in the muck. There is lots of information here, courtesy of the U.S. Fish and Wildlife Service. You will find hard data, suitable for researchers, as well as links to resources for children and teachers.

Web:
  http://www.nwi.fws.gov/

National Wildlife Refuges

Throughout the United States, there are hundreds of land and water areas designated as wildlife refuges. These areas are administered by the National Wildlife Refuge System, part of the U.S. Fish and Wildlife Service (itself a part of the Department of the Interior). The National Wildlife Refuge System looks after the conservation, management and restoration of the natural resources in the refuges, such as the fish, the land animals and the plants. When you visit the Web site, you will find an amazing amount of interesting and useful information, including a lot for kids. For example, do you know what to do if you find a baby bird? Put it back in its nest right away. Most birds can't smell well, and the parents will not abandon a baby just because you have touched it.

Web:
  http://refuges.fws.gov/

Ozone Depletion

Whether you are a serious researcher or just a student looking for information for your term paper entitled "Our Friend the Stratosphere", here are a couple of resources that contain enough information about ozone depletion to keep you satisfied for a long time. The ozone layer, by the way, refers to the area in the stratosphere (about 15-40 km straight up) in which ozone is formed by the action of ultraviolet radiation (coming from the sun) on oxygen. The ozone layer keeps a lot of this radiation from getting down to where we live. If the ozone layer is thinned—by pollutants, for example—a lot of bad things might happen. Don't say I didn't warn you.

Web:
  http://www.epa.gov/docs/ozone
  http://www.faqs.org/faqs/ozone-depletion/
  http://www.nas.nasa.gov/About/Education/Ozone/
  http://www.ucsusa.org/environment/
  ozone.science.html

Planetary Events

Every day, several important planetary events take place. Use these resources to find out about current earthquakes, volcanoes, hurricanes, floods, tornadoes and other important environmental events. If you are the type of person who enjoys keeping track of geological, astronomical, meteorological, biological and environmental events, use the Net and you will always be in the know. The Earth may try to run, but it can't hide.

Web:

http://www.osei.noaa.gov/
http://www.phschool.com/science/planetdiary/

Population Control

Some people call it population. Some people call it overpopulation. I guess it depends on whether or not you are sitting on the side of the bread with the butter. Should you be concerned about overpopulation? Take a look at the information regarding population growth, fertility and mortality, and see what you think. In the meantime, as you make up your mind, you might consider that in the time it took you to read this paragraph, 105 people were born and 44 people died.

Web:

http://www.ecofuture.org/populat.html
http://www.overpopulation.org/
http://www.popinfo.org/issues/
http://www.populationinstitute.org/teampublish/
   71_234_621.cfm

Rainforests

A rainforest is a type of forest found in certain tropical areas in South America and Asia, where there is a lot of rain. The rainforests of the world are large and contain many different species of plants and animals. Although rainforests seem remote to most of us, they are important for several reasons. First, the large number of trees and other plants help balance the global climate, by contributing to the rain and water systems, and by storing and absorbing carbon dioxide. The wide variety of plants also helps us in other ways: as an important source of new drugs and chemicals, new types of foods (fruits, vegetables and nuts), as well as various valuable woods (teak, mahogany, rosewood, balsa, sandalwood). Unfortunately, the late twentieth century saw a significant portion of the rainforest destroyed as people cleared large areas for logging and agriculture.

Web:

http://www.rainforest-alliance.org/
http://www.rainforestweb.org/

Waste Reduction Tips and Factsheets

Here is useful information showing how to reduce waste and conserve resources. The focus is on source reduction and re-use rather than just recycling. Unfortunately, they left out the most important tip: buy Harley Hahn books in bulk, and never, ever throw them away.

Web:

http://www.pnl.gov/esp/greenguide/appe.html
http://www.rco.on.ca/publication/factsheet.html

Usenet:

sci.environment.waste

EXERCISE

Aerobics

Some people cringe each time they hear their aerobics instructor say, "Only eight more." Others get that adrenaline rush after cycling up their local mountain. You can utilize the Net to find information about all forms of aerobic activity and talk to other aerobics fans who will remind you that all your efforts are worthwhile.

Web:
  http://www.stepcenter.com/
  http://www.turnstep.com/
  http://www.webaerobics.com/

Usenet:
  misc.fitness.aerobic

Ashtanga Yoga

According to the tradition of the yoga teacher Patanjali, the full study of yoga involves 8 areas, and the name ashtanga comes from the Sanskrit words for "8 limbs". Actually, ashtanga yoga, like most schools of yoga, concerns itself primarily with 2 of these 8 areas: asanas (yoga poses) and pranayama (control of the breath). The practice of ashtanga yoga consists of performing a long series of postures, integrated with a specific type of breathing. I have studied ashtanga yoga for a long time, and I do some every morning. Ashtanga yoga is hard to master—it takes proper instruction and a lot of practice— but it's the best way I know to build your body to be strong, flexible and healthy. There are several different ashtanga series. Most people do the first series—the second and third are very difficult—which consists of about 80 asanas. Each asana has a long Sanskrit name, which can be confusing to a beginner. To help you understand the terminology, one of these Web sites contains information I have compiled to show exactly what each name means. For example, Ardha Baddha Padmottanasana (a particularly strange pose) can be translated as follows: ardha = half, baddha = bound or restrained, padma = lotus, ut = intense, tan = stretch, asana = pose. In other words, "half-bound-lotus-intense-stretch-pose". Sound like fun?

Web:
  http://pub42.ezboard.com/byoga84291
  http://www.ashtanga.com/
  http://www.ayri.org/method.html
  http://www.harley.com/yoga/
  http://www.ionet.net/~tslade/yoga.htm
  http://www.power-yoga.com/links.ihtml
  http://www.yogaworkshop.com/about.htm

Fitness

Statistics show that 37% of all statistics about fitness are meaningless. Or maybe it's 74%. Actually, I think it's 98%. I would be hard-pressed to think of any part of our popular culture that is so important, yet so misunderstood and riddled with half-truths. Fitness instructors, magazine writers, aerobics teachers, health club employees, and many health professionals repeat scientific-sounding silliness so often that I would challenge anyone to explain how to tell the difference between what is true and what seems to be true just because people believe it. I am going to give you some fitness resources, but for goodness sakes, don't believe everything you read. For example, I found a Web site that says if you weigh 150 pounds and you garden for 10 minutes, you will use 49 calories. A 175-pound person, however, would use 57 calories. Do you believe this? Is it even meaningful? (In this case, the numbers were taken from a publication put out by a running shoe company and posted on the Web.) It's good to use your body, but, please, don't forget to use your brain.

Web:
  http://www.fitconnection.com/
  http://www.fitnessfind.com/
  http://www.fitnesspros.com/
  http://www.justmove.org/home.cfm
  http://www.primusweb.com/fitnesspartner/
  http://www.weightsnet.com/links/fitness/

Fitness Talk and General Discussion

We all know we should exercise every day. And we all know that sometimes we don't like to exercise every day. So when you are having one of those days, maybe it would be more fun to talk about it than actually do it. If so, Usenet is always there, and lots of people are ready to talk.

Usenet:
misc.fitness
misc.fitness.aerobic
misc.fitness.misc
misc.fitness.weights
rec.fitness

Jump Rope

Jump rope can be as simple or as challenging as you want. Want some fun and exercise at the same time? You can get a rope, start jumping, and leave it at that. However, are you an athletic overachiever who likes to compete and push yourself to the limit? If so, you can join a team, learn a lot of fancy acrobatic moves, and become a jump rope athlete. Whatever you choose, don't delay: go get a rope and hop to it today.

Web:
http://www.jumprope.com/questions_b.html
http://www.usajrf.org/
http://www.xs4all.nl/~akelck/jumprope/tricks/

Powerlifting

Powerlifting is competitive weightlifting with an emphasis on brute strength. In powerlifting, competitors perform three types of lifts: a squat, dead lift and bench press. (Olympic lifting, by contrast, uses the snatch and clean-and-jerk, in which technique is more important.) Powerlifting can be rewarding, but it is crucial to train properly and to know what you are doing.

Web:
http://www.deepsquatter.com/strength/archives/
http://www.drsquat.com/
http://www.sover.net/~timw/faq10.htm

Report on Jump Rope
by Elmo (age 8)

Today, I wanted to play on my computer, but my mother said, "Elmo, you need to get some exercise. Go outside right now."

So, I took my sister Lucy's jump rope and tied it across the steps just outside the front door.

Then I yelled to my mother, "Look at what Lucy did with her jump rope." My mother came out the door quickly and— wow—you should have seen what happened!

I ended up getting a lot of exercise, because I had to run for 20 minutes.

-Elmo

Pregnancy and Exercise

Exercising during pregnancy can help you be more comfortable with the weight gain, prepare for the rigor of labor, and recover more quickly after the delivery. You may also be able to minimize the discomforts of pregnancy, as well as improve your mood and sense of well-being. Here are some resources to show you which exercises will help the most, and how to plan a program for yourself. Just remember, after you are finished with your workout, it's up to your husband to cook you dinner and wash the dishes. (That's *his* exercise for the day.)

Web:
http://www.ahealthyme.com/topic/758
http://www.babycenter.com/refcap/758.html
http://www.babycentre.co.uk/fitness/
http://www.fitnessfind.com/pregnancy.html
http://www.lifematters.com/rofintro.html
http://www.womenfitness.net/
pregnancy_exercise.htm

You can't be too rich, too good a writer, too handsome or too strong.

(Well, that's always been my philosophy anyway.)

I can't help you with the money, talent or good looks, but if you want to be strong, spend some time on the Net. Maybe you'll get inspired and build yourself up to be the next world power-lifting champion. (If you do, be sure to mention this book.)

Running

Running can be delightful, if you are in good shape and you know what you are doing (and you have good shoes). When I want to relax, I run up a long, steep hill that is one mile from bottom to top. The first time was difficult, but, with practice (I like to do it every day), I got used to it and now the run is fun. Once your body becomes fit, you begin to realize that running is very much a mental challenge. Believe me, running an entire mile up a steep hill is difficult, and, although I know that my body can do it, I have to summon up my mental reserves to make the experience pleasant and fulfilling. If you are a runner (or you want to be a runner), you can use these resources to help yourself understand what you need to know, and to motivate yourself to excel.

Web:
  http://www.coolrunning.com/
  http://www.fred.net/ultrunr/
  http://www.gbtc.org/whatelse.html
  http://www.ontherun.com/
  http://www.realrunner.com/
  http://www.runtheplanet.com/
  http://www.straznitskas.com/george/
Usenet:
  rec.running

Sports Doctor

When you want to play doctor and nobody is around, just connect to this Web site. You can pretend to be a sports doctor and click on your patient's symptoms until you reach a diagnosis. You can also find a medical glossary to help explain some of the terms used in the diagnosis, as well as read explanations of various medical conditions. And if you like to reduce your appetite, you can watch movies of various surgical procedures.

Web:
  http://www.medfacts.com/sprtsdoc.htm

Don't click here.

Stretching and Flexibility

If exercise is an important part of your life, stretching should be the most important part of your workout. I do yoga every day, and a large part of my workout consists of stretching. There are two reasons for this. First, the best way to make muscles strong is by lengthening them (as opposed to making them thicker). Long muscles allow for greater flexibility. Second, proper stretching gets your circulation going, enabling your muscles to perform well without the risk of injury.

Web:
  http://www.enteract.com/~bradapp/docs/rec/
    stretching/
  http://www.ifafitness.com/stretch/

Walking

Regular walking is an excellent form of exercise that is accessible to everyone. These sites have information about power walking, race walking, and walking for sport, exercise and leisure. For discussions about walking (when you are resting from your exertions), try Usenet.

Web:
  http://www.active.com/walking/
  http://www.apma.org/sports/walking.html
  http://www.walking.org/

Usenet:
  misc.fitness.walking

Weightlifting and Bodybuilding

Do you eat nutritious high protein and swallow raw eggs? Try to build up your shoulders, your chest, arms and legs? Do you do press-ups and chin-ups, cloak and jerk, do the snatch? Do you think dynamic tension must be a catch? Well, try the Net, and maybe, in just seven days, it can make you a man.

Web:
  http://www.getbig.com/
  http://www.weightsnet.com/
  http://www.wlinfo.com/

Usenet:
  alt.sport.weightlifting
  misc.fitness.weights

Women's Fitness

Being fit and healthy requires you to have a variety of information available when you need it. Here are some resources that cover fitness and health considerations for women: toning, weight control, weightlifting, workout routines, nutrition, and so on. I have also included resources to help you find information about women's sports and activities around the world.

Web:
  http://www.association-of-womens-fitness.org/
  http://www.highnrg.com/
  http://www.womenfitness.net/
  http://www.workoutsforwomen.com/stretch.asp

Yoga

I have been doing yoga for years (Ashtanga and Iyengar styles), and I can tell you that it works. However, it is hard work, and a good yoga workout will make you sweat profusely. Perhaps the best way to put it is that yoga is like a sewer: what you get out of it depends on what you put into it. These Web sites have a lot of information about yoga styles, asanas (poses), traditions and classes. If you want to see what people talk about when they are not doing their practice, take a look at the Usenet discussion group. Here you will find all the traditional cultural pursuits of the yoga community: spiritual and physical development, sharing ideas, personal growth, and gossip about other people.

Web:
  http://www.spiritweb.org/spirit/yoga.html
  http://www.yogabasics.com/
  http://www.yogafinder.com/
  http://www.yogamovement.com/
  http://www.yrec.org/

Usenet:
  alt.yoga

Yoga Postures

If you are doing your own yoga practice at home, there is no teacher to help you perfect your asanas (poses). Doing an asana properly can make a big difference, so do take a few moments to check out these Web sites, where you'll find illustrations and instructions to help you with the most common asanas.

Web:
  http://www.hightechyoga.org/postures.htm
  http://www.santosha.com/asanas/
  http://www.yogasite.com/postures.html

FAMILIES AND PARENTING

Adoption

Adoption is both difficult and exciting. These sites offer information for anyone involved in an adoption: birth parents, adoptees and adoptive parents. You can find answers to general, legal and medical questions, information about adoption agencies and publications, and advice on foreign adoption. The mailing lists provide forums for discussing anything relating to adoption and are open to adoptive parents, adoptees, birth parents, social workers, counselors and anyone else interested in the adoption process.

Web:
  http://www.adopt.org/
  http://www.adoptex.org/
  http://www.adopting.com/
  http://www.adopting.org/
  http://www.adoptiontriad.org/internbycntry.htm
  http://www.calib.com/naic/
  http://www.pnpic.org/

Usenet:
  alt.adoption
  alt.adoption.adoptive.parenting
  alt.adoption.agency
  alt.adoption.issues
  alt.adoption.korean
  alt.adoption.searching
  alt.support.adoption.advocacy
  alt.support.birth-parent
  soc.adoption.adoptees
  soc.adoption.parenting

Listserv Mailing List:
  List Name: adoptees
  Subscribe to: listserv@maelstrom.stjohns.edu

Listserv Mailing List:
  List Name: adoption
  Subscribe to: listserv@maelstrom.stjohns.edu

Listserv Mailing List:
  List Name: aparent
  Subscribe to: listserv@maelstrom.stjohns.edu

Listserv Mailing List:
  List Name: open-adoption
  Subscribe to: listserv@home.ease.lsoft.com

Babies

Babies want most of all to be fed, loved and changed. But when there's something wrong, it can be hard to tell what the problem is—or even if there is one. Parenting can be frustrating sometimes. These resources have information about caring for babies. Just the thing to read when you can't sleep at night.

Web:
  http://www.amazingbaby.com/
  http://www.babybag.com/
  http://www.babycenter.com/
  http://www.babyonline.com/

Babies

Baby Names

When you are expecting a baby, one of the biggest decisions you need to make is what to name your child. One way is to use the Net to look at a large selection of names and see what feels right. You can find out the meanings behind specific names, see what names are popular right now, and peruse special pairs of names for twins. However, if you want to save yourself a lot of time, my advice is just to name the baby Harley.

Web:
  http://www.babynamer.momsonline.com/
  http://www.babynames.com/
  http://www.babyzone.com/babynames/
  http://www.dfcreations.com/nh.html
  http://www.parenting.com/parenting/tools/
  babynamer/

Breastfeeding

There are special issues that must be considered by mothers who breastfeed. These Internet resources are great places for talking about and reading about the problems and rewards of breastfeeding. Some of the topics include attachment parenting, weaning, extended nursing, nursing in public, working mothers who breastfeed, tandem nursing, societal attitudes toward nursing, and nursing during pregnancy.

Web:
  http://www.borstvoeding.com/abon/
    bf-resources.html
  http://www.breastfeeding.com/
  http://www.lalecheleague.org/bfinfo.html
  http://www.moonlily.com/breastfeed/

Usenet:
  misc.kids.breastfeeding

Child Activism

Children's rights is the main topic for discussion in these Usenet groups. Read and post your own thoughts and ideas regarding the social and political issues relating to children. Hint: If your child is going to grow up to be famous, be careful what you say and do, as it may all end up in a book.

Usenet:
  alt.activism.children
  alt.activism.youth-rights

Child Discipline

To spank or not to spank—that is the question. These groups mostly contain a long-running debate about whether it is morally and politically acceptable to spank children. However, there are occasional threads about alternative methods of discipline and hints on "positive parenting". My personal hint is to speak softly, and carry a big stick.

Usenet:
  alt.parenting.spanking
  alt.parenting.spanking.moderated

Child Safety

Many accidents are avoidable. However, the little ones can't plan for themselves, so we have to make sure that our houses, cars and play areas are safe. There are so many possible ways a kid can get into trouble that it is difficult to think of them all yourself. My suggestion is to visit these Web sites and take the time to go over the lists of safety information. I bet you'll find yourself saying, "I never would have thought of that."

Web:
  http://www.nhtsa.dot.gov/kids/
  http://www.safekids.org/
  http://www.sosnet.com/safety/safety1.html

Child Safety on the Internet

If you are worried about your kids wandering around the Internet by themselves, have a look at these tips that will give you a better idea of how to protect young minds from inappropriate material.

Web:
  http://www.ed.gov/pubs/parents/internet/
  http://www.getnetwise.org/
  http://www.getnetwise.org/americalinksup/
    parentstips/
  http://www.ou.edu/oupd/kidsafe/warn_kid.htm
  http://www.safekids.com/
  http://www.safesurfin.com/
  http://www.smartparent.com/

Child Support

How do you stand on issues of custody and child support? Find out the thoughts of others affected by these issues and learn about current legislation.

Usenet:
 alt.child-support

Children

What they don't tell you when you have your first child is that no one knows how to be a parent. You have to make it up as you go along. Your children will bring you the best experiences and the worst experiences you will ever have. The best thing about kids is that they are small people that you can raise to become productive, well-adjusted human beings. The worst thing is that, at some point, your children are guaranteed to drive you nuts. When this happens, you will find this book to be an invaluable tool. Just take it out, show it to your kids and say, "Boy, I bet it would be really embarrassing to get spanked with such a nice book."

Web:
 http://www.aacap.org/web/aacap/publications/
   factsfam/
 http://www.family.go.com/yourtime/

Usenet:
 misc.kids
 misc.kids.info
 misc.kids.moderated

Children with Special Needs

Raising a child with a disability is difficult, and doing a good job can be time-consuming, tiring and expensive. But perhaps worst of all, spending a lot of time with a child with special needs can be a lonely experience for you. If you have such a child, you may enjoy participating in this mailing list, and browsing the associated Web site. This is a support group for parents or others who care for children with physical or mental developmental disabilities. It is important for you to remember that such problems are common, and you are not alone. Talking with other people who face similar problems and challenges can make all the difference in the world.

Web:
 http://www.our-kids.org/

Listserv Mailing List:
 List Name: our-kids
 Subscribe to: listserv@maelstrom.stjohns.edu

Dads

Dads are people too, but as a friend of mine observed, it takes a long time to train them. If there is one thing the Age of Divorce has taught us, it is that fathers are extremely important to the emotional well-being of their children. Unfortunately, there aren't a lot of places where fathers (and fathers-to-be) can meet with other men and hear about their experiences. The Net can help fill that gap.

Web:
 http://www.dadsanddaughters.org/
   dads_resources.htm
 http://www.fathers.com/
 http://www.fathersforum.com/
 http://www.ncoff.gse.upenn.edu/
 http://www.newdads.com/
 http://www.slowlane.com/

Listserv Mailing List:
 List Name: father-l
 Subscribe to: listserv@listserv.aol.com

Listserv Mailing List:
 List Name: fathers-l
 Subscribe to: listserv@home.ease.lsoft.com

Majordomo Mailing List:
 List Name: dads
 Subscribe to: majordomo@cuy.net

Majordomo Mailing List:
 List Name: frcpgh
 Subscribe to: majordomo@list.pitt.edu

> I have a friend who loves to watch birds. I tried to get her interested in fish-watching, but she doesn't swim.

Family Resources

When I was a kid, our family used to have a great time on Saturday nights, gathered around the computer—in those days, it was an old black and white job—exploring the Internet together. Then we'd all go out for ice cream, and run around having good-natured fun. Yup, no doubt about it, the family that Webs together, does something or other together. But don't take my word for it. Here are some places to visit together. (Don't forget the ice cream.)

Web:
http://www.family.go.com/
http://www.happyfamilies.com/
http://www.wholefamily.com/

These days, it's hard to keep the family together.

Dad's in his study, using the Net to check the sports scores; Mom's in the kitchen with her laptop computer, cruising the Web for recipes; Junior is downloading free game software; and Sis is up all night talking to her friends on IRC.

Sometimes it seems as if everyone is in a different world, and modern parents despair of creating any real family spirit.

But now there is a way. All you have to do is hold regular family get-togethers, where everyone gathers around the family PC as you visit a family Web site.
Staying together has never been so easy.

Fathers' Rights

Kids do best when they have two strong, caring parents, both a mother and a father. Unfortunately, after a separation or divorce, many mothers do not see the need for the father to stay continually involved with the children, especially when the mother and father do not get along well. All too often, the rights of the father are ignored by the legal system. If you find yourself in this position, or you are about to get divorced, use these resources to find out what you can do to ensure that you can be the best possible father.

Web:
http://users.erols.com/afc/
http://www.abs-comptech.com/frn/frnhome.html
http://www.fathers4kids.org/html/fathersrights.htm

Usenet:
alt.dads-rights
alt.dads-rights.unmoderated

Foster Parents

Being a foster parent can be tricky and can test your ability to adapt to new situations. However, the Net has great support groups with other foster parents. Foster parents gather on the Net to talk about their joys and experiences. The Web sites have a great deal of information about children's specific physical and mental conditions and how to deal with them, as well as articles and hints on foster parenting and a bulletin board to which you can post messages.

Web:
http://www.fosterparenting.com/
http://www.fosterparents.com/
http://www.kidsource.com/nfpa/
http://www.nfpainc.org/stateasso.html

Usenet:
alt.support.foster-parents

Listserv Mailing List:
List Name: foster-l
Subscribe to: listserv@listserv.american.edu

It's time.

Want to send some fan mail? Read "People: Famous and Interesting."

Grandparents Raising Grandchildren

For one reason or another, many children are being raised by their grandparents. If you are such a grandparent, these Web sites can be a real help. You will find articles and tips, information about relevant laws (such as adoption), and more. Perhaps the best resource is people: other grandparents who are raising grandchildren. You can talk to other grandparents by participating in the Usenet discussion group.

Web:
  http://home1.gte.net/res02wo7/
  http://www.aarp.org/confacts/money/tanf.html
  http://www.aoa.dhhs.gov/factsheets/
     grandparents.html
  http://www.familymanagement.com/facts/english/
     grandparents_kids.html
  http://www.grandparentsandmore.com/
  http://www.grandsplace.com/
  http://www.gu.org/projg&o.htm
  http://www.sonic.net/thom/oor/

Usenet:
  alt.parenting.grandparents

Internet Filtering Software

There are many great resources on the Net for kids, and there is no reason why children should be deprived of exploring the Internet just because they might accidentally encounter some inappropriate content (that is, sex). These sites have links to companies that have designed software that helps filter out what you don't want your kids to see.

Web:
  http://www.i-probe.com/i-probe/ip_diclaimer.html
  http://www.microweb.com/pepsite/Software/
     filters.html
  http://www.worldvillage.com/family/parental.html

Jewish Family Life

There's more to Jewish home life than food and guilt. (At least, I think there is :-) There are many Jewish family resources on the Net for you to use and enjoy, including an active, thoughtful Usenet group in which Jewish parents hold ongoing discussions. If you are isolated from a Jewish community, it's hard to instill your children with the cultural values you hold to be important. The Net can help. As part of these resources, I have included some FAQs (frequently asked question lists) about rearing children and a reading list relevant for Jewish children.

Web:
  http://www.faqs.org/faqs/judaism/FAQ/scjp-admin/
  http://www.jewish.com/askarabbi/
     Family_and_Personal_Matters/Parenting/
  http://www.jewishfamily.com/
  http://www.pacificnet.net/~faigin/SCJ/rl/
     kid-index.html
  http://www.shamash.org/listarchives/scj-parenting/

Usenet:
  soc.culture.jewish.parenting

Kids, Computers and Software

I have never met a child who didn't like computers. In these Usenet groups, you can talk about the best computers and hardware for children, as well as educational and entertainment software. The Web site has shareware that I am sure your kids will enjoy (when they are not sneaking behind your back to connect to inappropriate Web sites).

Web:
  http://www.kidsdomain.com/down/

Usenet:
  alt.comp.shareware.for-kids
  misc.kids.computer

Military Moms

Military families have quite a life, and these Web sites have lots of resources that can help. These sites are for any military family: active, veteran, retired or reserve. Find support groups and new friends, advice on parenting, moving tips, and stuff for kids. When military living gets tough, the tough get going on the Net.

Web:
  http://www.parentingplace.com/militarymoms/
  http://www.sgtmoms.com/

Missing Children

If you have a missing child, or if you think you may have found such a child, the Net can help. These Web sites allow you to read descriptions and look at photos of missing children. If you have such a child yourself, you can find help, including arranging for your child's information to be posted on the Net. Be careful of scams, though. I found a multi-level marketing company on the Net that plays on people's emotions ("A Child Is Missing Every 40 Seconds in America") to sell "child protection systems".

Web:
>   http://www.800usakids.org/
>   http://www.childsearch.org/
>   http://www.missingkids.com/

Usenet:
>   alt.binaries.missing-kids
>   alt.missing-kids

Moms

Moms, rev up your Internet connection and check out all the places that are designed especially for you. Hang out in one of the many chat rooms or browse the nice selection of articles while sipping a hot cup of cappuccino. You'll find a little bit of everything here: health, beauty, taking care of the kids, child safety, gardening, cleaning, entertaining, and more.

Web:
>   http://www.allaboutmoms.com/
>   http://www.amomslove.com/
>   http://www.mommytips.com/
>   http://www.momsrefuge.com/
>   http://www.myria.com/
>   http://www.newhomemaker.com/

Parenting Resources

If you are bored and you want to read some new stuff about parenting, check out these Web sites. They have information on just about every topic imaginable related to parenting, step-parenting, parenting multiples, fatherhood, pregnancy, breastfeeding, health, education, and family activities. You will never run out of things to read on the Net. And, if you do, you can always have a couple more kids.

Web:
>   http://www.kidsource.com/
>   http://www.npin.org/library.html
>   http://www.parentsoup.com/
>   http://www.pta.org/aboutpta/whatsnew.asp
>   http://www.sleeptight.com/EncyMaster/

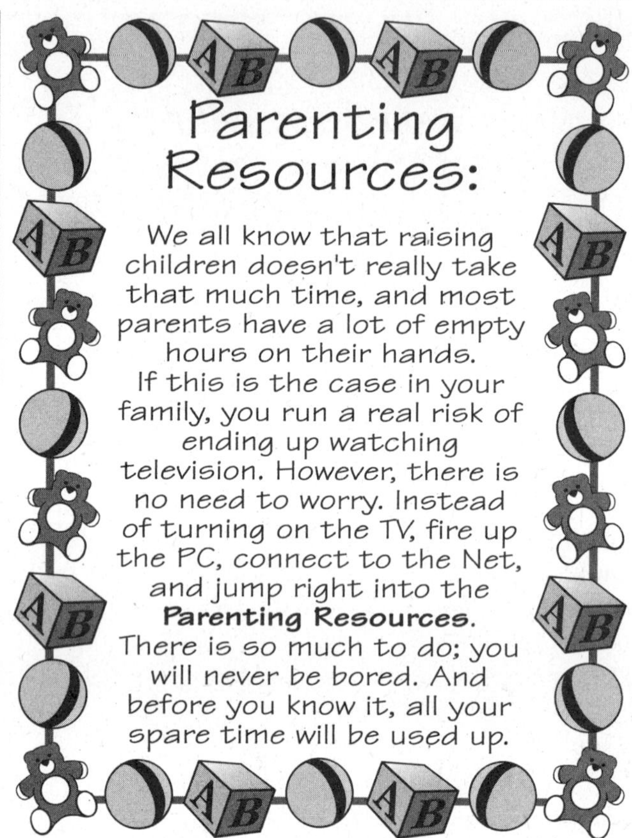

Parenting Talk and General Discussion

Raising children is more than a full-time occupation: it's a way of life that brings challenges, sacrifices and rewards. It can also be confusing and frustrating at times, and there is certainly no end of topics that need to be discussed. There are many, many parents on the Net who love to talk. Join them in these Usenet discussion groups.

Usenet:
>   alt.parenting
>   alt.parenting.solutions
>   misc.kids.moderated

Parents and Children Together Online

Here is an online magazine that both parents and children can enjoy. For the children, there are delightful, entertaining stories and articles. For adults, there are features about parenting, as well as reviews of books and products.

Web:
>   http://eric.indiana.edu/www/famres/pctogeth/

Parents and Teens

When I was younger, I lived with a woman who had a teenage daughter who shall remain nameless (Johanna). Today, Johanna is a lovely young woman, close to my heart. However, having lived with her as a teenager, I can give you two invaluable pieces of advice. First, no matter how cute or lovable your little one may be as a child, she (or he) will inevitably turn into an alien. Second, if your teenager wants to keep a pet rat, do not let her, under any circumstances, take the rat out of its cage and let it get loose inside the sofa.

Usenet:
  alt.parents-teens

Pregnancy and Childbirth

Pregnancy is exciting and exhilarating, but it can be awfully scary if it is your first time. At these Web sites, you can find out what is going to happen at every stage of your pregnancy. Read stories about birth, what labor is like, and find out information on birth procedures such as caesarians and episiotomies. The Usenet group is for the discussion of pregnancy and pregnancy-related issues.

Web:
  http://www.4woman.gov/pregnancy/
  http://www.childbirth.org/
  http://www.nlm.nih.gov/medlineplus/pregnancy.html
  http://www.thelaboroflove.com/

Usenet:
  misc.kids.pregnancy

Premature Infants

The normal human gestation period—the time between conception and birth—is about 280 days (40 weeks). Babies that are born significantly before the full term (six weeks or more) are said to be premature. Premature infants face a special set of problems. First, because their bodies are not fully developed, they may have trouble surviving. Second, premature babies who do survive have a greater than normal chance of suffering from a disability. Here are some resources to help parents understand the problems and considerations unique to premature infants. My experience is that having authoritative information can make a medical situation much easier to bear. However, doctors are often too busy to spend a long time explaining technical matters to patients' families. If you have a premature infant, these resources can help you understand what is happening, and what you can do to help your child.

Web:
  http://www.aapi-online.org/learningcenter.htm
  http://www.kidshealth.org/parent/growth/growing/
    preemies.html
  http://www.medsch.wisc.edu/childrenshosp/
    parents_of_preemies/
  http://www.preemie-l.org/
  http://www.preemies.org/

Usenet:
  alt.support.premature-baby

Majordomo Mailing List:
  List Name: preemie-l
  Subscribe to: majordomo@vicnet.net.au

Products for Children

If you have children, you probably don't get much choice about what toys you want to give them. Children know what they want, and they have their own ways of getting it. However, if you want to get the lowdown on what is best for children—as if they care—check out this guide. This site reviews toys and entertainment products for children, and also has hints for parents about what to select for particular age groups. The Usenet group is for discussion of consumer issues that relate to children.

Web:
  http://www.drtoy.com/

Usenet:
  misc.kids.consumers

Single Parents

Some of my best friends are single parents—single Moms, actually—and they are all wonderful people. However, their lives are hard: parenting is really a two-person job. Moreover, it's a 24-hour-a-day job that requires you to be prepared for the unexpected. I asked a friend of mine, who is a single Mom, what advice she would give to other single Moms. She said, "Get married so you are not a single parent any more." I asked her, "How do you do that?" "If I knew," she said, "I wouldn't be a single Mom."

Web:
  http://www.makinglemonade.com/
  http://www.parentswithoutpartners.org/
  http://www.singleparents.org/sites.html
  http://www.singlerose.com/
  http://www.solosingles.com/ssparent/

Usenet:
  alt.support.single-parents

> I once invented a
> radio-controlled radio. It
> could turn itself on and
> off automatically.

Step-Parents

Step-parents have come a long way since the days of Cinderella. True, being a step-parent can be a difficult job, but in today's world, step-parents are a fact of life, and many of us are called upon to blend into another family. Rest assured, if you have problems, you are not on your own.

Web:
  http://www.bonusfamilies.com/
  http://www.comamas.com/home.htm
  http://www.familyfusion.com/
  http://www.saafamilies.org/
  http://www.stepdads.com/
  http://www.stepfamily.net/
  http://www.stepfamilyinfo.org/

Usenet:
  alt.support.step-parents

Summer Camps

Some of my most important memories are of the summers I spent going to Camp New Moon in Southern Ontario in Canada. I made friends, learned to participate in various ongoing camp traditions, and acquired many different skills, such as swimming, canoeing, sailing and horseback riding. However, it wasn't all good. I had trouble with much of the social interaction, and I did spend some of the time being lonely and unhappy. Still, my summers at camp were growing experiences that, ultimately, had a significant effect on my character as an adult. When it comes time to send your kids to camp, it is important to select the camp that is right for them. The Internet can help, especially if your children have special health considerations. Hint: Look for a place that your kids will find fun and relaxing.

Web:
  http://web.mit.edu/hr/worklife/campinfo.htm
  http://www.acacamps.org/
  http://www.campchannel.com/campers/search/
  http://www.kidscamps.com/

Surrogate Motherhood

A surrogate mother is a woman who conceives a baby and carries it to term on behalf of someone else. In most cases, the someone else is a couple who cannot have children of their own. When the baby is born, it is given to the couple to raise. The pregnancy can be initiated in two ways: the surrogate mother can be impregnated with the sperm of the father (via artificial insemination), or an egg from the mother that has been fertilized by the father can be implanted in the surrogate mother's uterus. In either case, there is a lot to consider and a lot to know.

Web:
  http://www.opts.com/
  http://www.surrogacy.com/articles.html
  http://www.surromomsonline.com/

Teaching with Movies

It used to be that helping your kids learn required time and mental effort. You might have to explain how things work, discuss complicated ideas, or maybe even show the little crumb-grabbers how to do algebra problems. Not anymore. Now you can help your kids just by watching movies. No guff! All the information you need is here on this Web site. They even select the movies for you. All you need to do is drive to the store, rent the video, and see that the popcorn bowl stays full. Who says parenting is hard?

Web:
  http://www.teachwithmovies.org/

Traveling with Children

Some children are great travelers; others will drive you crazy. Of course, a lot depends on temperament, but there *are* things you can do to enhance the experience. First, tell yourself that your trip will be a big adventure, and that getting there will be as much fun as being there. Second, prepare your children in advance for what they can expect during the trip and how you want them to act. Third, treat them like little humans, not like gremlins. Fourth, no matter what happens, laugh.

Web:
  http://www.parentscentre.org.nz/
     babies_and_preschoolers/C-Travel.htm
  http://www.tips4trips.com/Tips/chiltips.htm
  http://www.travelforkids.com/
  http://www.travellingwithchildren.co.uk/

Usenet:
  misc.kids.vacation

Twins and Triplets

The nice thing about multiple births is that you can have all your kids at once. No more Lamaze classes, no more packing the emergency hospital bag, no more late-night frantic phone calls to family members. Yes, now that you have lots and lots of babies on your hands, you can rest easy (sort of). The Web sites have resources for parents of twins and triplets (or more). The Usenet group is for the discussion of raising multiple birth children.

Web:
  http://www.mostonline.org/links.htm
  http://www.nomotc.org/
  http://www.tripletconnection.org/
  http://www.twinslist.org/
  http://www.twinsmagazine.com/

Usenet:
  alt.parenting.twins-triplets

T I D B I T S

What should restaurant customers know about WINES?

If you want to be snooty at a restaurant, the best way to do it is to make a big deal out of choosing the wine. If so, here are 7 hints to help you to make a good choice.

1. Stay within your budget.

2. Avoid the house wine.

3. Choose your food first. Then choose the wine to match whatever will be the strongest flavor on your plate.

4. When you are at a restaurant with foreign food (Italian, French, etc.), choose a wine from that country.

5. If there is a wine steward, don't be afraid to ask for help.

When you taste the wine, remember:

6. The fragrance (bouquet) is the most important factor.

7. The longer the aftertaste, the better the wine.

FAQS (FREQUENTLY ASKED QUESTION LISTS)

FAQ Archives

A FAQ is a list of frequently asked questions and answers on a particular topic. The original FAQs were developed for Usenet discussion groups. People found that all newcomers who joined a group would tend to ask the same questions. For example, people who join the group where urban legends are discussed (**alt.folklore.urban**) often ask if it is true that Mrs. Fields or Nieman Marcus forced somebody to pay a lot of money for a recipe. (The answer is no, by the way.) It became the custom for one or more experienced members of a Usenet group to create a list of frequently asked questions and answers. The idea was that newcomers to the group should read the FAQ before they start participating in the discussion. The concept of FAQs has grown to embrace just about every topic imaginable, in situations where it is useful for people to collect questions and answers. These Web sites are among my favorite resources on the Internet. This is because I love to learn new things and I find that reading a FAQ in an area that is new to me is a great way to pick up interesting and esoteric knowledge. It will be well worth your while to spend some time browsing through the FAQs looking for some areas that interest you. (By the way, according to the urban legends FAQ, green M&Ms are not an aphrodisiac.)

Web:
> http://www.cs.uu.nl/cgi-bin/faqwais/
> http://www.faqs.org/faqs/
> http://www.landfield.com/faqs/

FAQ FAQ

"A FAQ FAQ? What's a FAQ FAQ? I don't need no stinking FAQ FAQ." Well, yes, you do. The FAQ FAQ is a list of questions and answers about FAQs. It explains the history of FAQs, and gives you tips and hints for writing and maintaining a FAQ. If you get the urge, one of the most useful things you can do for the Net is to maintain a FAQ. If you would like to try, begin by reading the FAQ FAQ.

Web:
> http://www.cs.uu.nl/wais/html/na-dir/faqs/
>   about-faqs.html
> http://www.faqs.org/faqs/faqs/about-faqs/

FAQ for the *.answers Usenet Groups

There are a number of Usenet groups devoted to FAQs and other period postings. These principal groups are **alt.answers**, **comp.answers**, **humanities.answers**, **misc.answers**, **news.answers**, **rec.answers**, **sci.answers**, **soc.answers** and **talk.answers** (often referred to collectively as *.answers). Here is a FAQ that explains the purposes and contents of these groups, how to submit new postings, how to join the mailing list for periodic posting maintainers, and where to find archives of postings to the *.answers groups.

Web:
> http://www.cs.uu.nl/wais/html/na-dir/news-answers/
>   introduction.html
> http://www.faqs.org/faqs/news-answers/
>   introduction/

The FAQ FAQ

When I was young, I used to love watching movies starring Mickey Rooney and Judy Garland. (If you're too young to remember Mickey Rooney and Judy Garland, show this ad to your mother, and she'll explain it.) The story would vary from one movie to another, but one thing never seemed to change.

Mickey and Judy would be using the Net to look at various documents, when all of a sudden Mickey would get all excited.

"I have an idea," he would say, "why don't we write our own FAQ?"

So they would, and it would be a great success.

FAQ Talk and General Discussion

The reason for frequently asked question lists is that newcomers to a Usenet discussion group often seem to ask the same questions. Veterans don't mind answering new questions, but nobody wants to explain, over and over and over, what "Unix" means. Through the years, many groups have developed a frequently asked question list (FAQ) that contains all the common questions that have been answered repeatedly in that group. Some FAQs are so large as to be divided into several parts. Whenever you start reading a new group, look for a FAQ to orient yourself. More important, before you post a question to the group, check the FAQ to see if your question has already been answered. The people who maintain FAQs post them regularly, not only to their own group, but to special groups that have been created just to hold FAQs and related material. The **news.answers** group contains FAQs from every possible source. The other **.answers** groups contain FAQs for their respective hierarchies. For example, **comp.answers** contains computer FAQs. When you have a spare moment, check out these groups, especially **alt.answers**. You will see a lot of interesting and strange stuff that you might never encounter otherwise. These groups contain not only FAQs, but important summaries of information not tied to specific Usenet groups.

Usenet:

> alt.answers
> comp.answers
> misc.answers
> news.answers
> rec.answers
> sci.answers
> soc.answers
> talk.answers

Internet FAQ Consortium

The Internet FAQ Consortium is a group of people who are concerned with writing and maintaining FAQs. If you have anything to do with a FAQ, you'll find this site interesting. There is a nice set of useful links that will make your life as a FAQ-meister easier.

Web:
> http://www.faqs.org/

Maintaining a FAQ

At first, it would seem easy—and fun—to maintain a FAQ. However, doing a good job can be more work than you might think. To help you, here is a Web site devoted to making FAQ maintenance as easy as possible. Read about tools for automatically posting your FAQ to Usenet, producing HTML versions of your FAQ, and coping with electronic mail. There are also links to other Internet resources related to FAQs.

Web:
> http://www.faqs.org/faqs/authors.html
> http://www.qucis.queensu.ca/FAQs/FAQaid/

Minimal Digest Format FAQ

When you maintain a FAQ, the format you use is important. Using a proper format can make your FAQ compatible with the digest-handling capabilities of certain newsreader programs. It can also allow your FAQ to be read more easily by a Web browser. Perhaps most important, using a good format will make it convenient for people to read and understand your work. This FAQ describes a format that is relatively simple but contains the minimal characteristics necessary for a proper FAQ.

Web:
> http://src.doc.ic.ac.uk/usenet/usenet-by-group/
>   news.answers/faqs/minimal-digest-format
> http://sunsite.org.uk/usenet/news-faqs/
>   news.answers/faqs/minimal-digest-format
> http://www.cs.uu.nl/wais/html/na-dir/faqs/
>   minimal-digest-format.html
> http://www.faqs.org/faqs/faqs/
>   minimal-digest-format/

Periodic Informational Postings List

On Usenet, there are a great many articles that are sent to various discussion groups on a regular basis. For example, there are many FAQs. There are also other types of regularly posted articles, such as lists of various things. You might ask, does anyone collect the names of all the articles that are posted regularly to Usenet? The answer is yes, and this list—called the Periodic Informational Postings List—is itself posted regularly to Usenet. (Imagine the philosophical implications.) This list is a long one, so here are Web sites that make it easy to find what you want.

Web:
> http://www.cs.uu.nl/wais/html/na-dir/
>   periodic-postings/.html
> http://www.faqs.org/faqs/periodic-postings/

Posting a FAQ Automatically

If you maintain a FAQ, you will want to know about the **auto-faq** script. This script is designed to post a FAQ to Usenet groups automatically. It allows you a large amount of control by specifying particular values in a configuration file. Another benefit is that, if you use this script, your FAQ will comply with all the requirements for posting to **news.answers** and the other *****.answers** groups.

Web:
> http://www.cs.queensu.ca/FAQs/FAQaid/#autopost
> http://www.novia.net/~pschleck/auto-faq/

Submission Guidelines for the *.answers Usenet Groups

If you maintain a FAQ, you will probably want to post it not only to your own Usenet group, but to **news.answers** and possibly one of the other *****.answers** groups. This FAQ explains what you need to do in order to cross-post a FAQ in this manner.

Web:
> http://www.cs.uu.nl/wais/html/na-dir/news-answers/
>   guidelines.html
> http://www.faqs.org/faqs/news-answers/guidelines/

She looked up from her computer as I came in, and I caught a whiff of exotic oriental perfume. She smiled seductively: red hair, green eyes, and a voluptuous body with enough curves to cause a cardiovascular accident in a giraffe.

"I want the program," I said.

"What program?" she asked.

"Don't get smart with me, sister. You know what program. The program to automatically post my FAQs to Usenet."

She wrote down an address on a piece of paper.

"All you have to do is connect to this Web site," she said. "But isn't there anything else you want? I know my way around the Net better than anyone. Just let me work with you, and I'll get you anything you want."

"Sorry, kid, but I work alone."

"Are you sure?" she said. "I have a lot more to offer. Are you positive there isn't anything else?"

I took the paper and headed for the door.

"Just the FAQs, ma'am."

FASHION AND CLOTHING

Beauty Resources

Beauty, as I am sure you know, is a lot of work, and the effort it takes to keep yourself attractive never ends. Moreover, because your skin, your hair, and your body—not to mention fashion trends—are always changing, your habits and beauty aids must also change over the years. These resources will keep you up-to-date on the newest beauty happenings, as well as help you ground yourself in the rudiments of basic beauty techniques.

Web:
> http://www.beautify-tips.com/
> http://www.beautybuzz.com/
> http://www.beautynet.com/
> http://www.beautywalk.com/
> http://www.beautyworlds.com/
> http://www.emakemeup.com/

Beauty Shoppe Archive

Contrary to the song, everything old is *not* new again, and with good reason. Most of the retro hairdo looks seem to be strange concoctions from another galaxy. See for yourself by visiting the Beauty Shoppe Archive. Just a few moments will convince you that whatever happens to be in style now is going to look odd later.

Web:

  http://my.net-link.net/~mwarner/BSA.html

Bra FAQs

A brassiere (or bra) is a women's undergarment whose principal purpose is to lend support to the breasts. As simple as this sounds, choosing the right bra can be a complex and frustrating task. There are many variations of people and by no means does one size fit all. The first modern bra, the Maidenform, was designed in 1922 by Ina Rosenthal and Enid Bissett. (If you are in New York, you can see the original bra on display at the Maidenform Museum.) Here is a series of FAQs devoted to bras, where you can read about coverings, designs, sizes and fitting, health issues, fabrics, fashion, history, trivia and suppliers. There is also a FAQ for underwire bras (bras that provide extra support by having wires underneath the cup or along the rib cage). Helpful Hint: Bra specialists will tell you that most women— especially large-busted women—are wearing the wrong size bra. When you look for a bra, pay attention to fit and comfort, not style and construction. (In other words, evaluate a bra with your eyes closed.)

Web:

  http://www.funhouse.com/babs/FAQ.html

Bridal Fashion Regrets

Doesn't she look beautiful? Well, not always. Just take a look at these fashion catastrophes: well-meaning people who, rather unwisely, decided to do it *their* way.

Web:

  http://www.visi.com/~dheaton/bride/
    the_bride_wore.html

Business Fashion

Are you a writer? If your answer is yes, you can dress any way you want, and no one is allowed to say anything. However, if you are not a writer, you need to dress in a way that is appropriate for your job. It is well-known that, when office workers start to dress informally, their working habits and work etiquette begin to degenerate. For this reason, a lot of companies regulate how their employees must dress. Unfortunately, many of the so-called dress codes are vague. ("All employees must dress in a business-like manner.") As always, the antidote for ignorance is information and experience. The idea is to dress in a way that (1) reflects how you want people to think of you, and (2) makes it clear that you are in a business setting, not a social setting. (But if dressing according to the rules is too much for you, you can always become a writer.)

Web:

  http://www.casualpower.com/tips.htm
  http://www.dressingwell.com/professionalism.htm
  http://www.fashionforrealwomen.com/articles/
    businessattire.htm

Clogs

Originally, a "clog" was any shoe made from wood. Such shoes—constructed from a single piece of wood—were developed by the Dutch, who needed footwear that would keep their feet dry while working in wet fields. Today's clogs are made from a variety of materials, and the word "clog" has come to refer to a large, backless shoe with a thick, elevated sole. Even the most clog-enamored fanatic can't pretend that these shoes are anything but ugly. However, they do make a satisfying clunk-clunk sound as you lumber from one place to another like an elephant at a Sixties dress-up party. (Indeed, some people feel that the name "clog" comes from the sound they make as you walk.) In the Sixties, clogs were practical because they allowed you to walk wherever you wanted while still retaining the freedom to slip off your shoes at a moment's notice. (You had to be there.)

Web:

  http://daugenis.mch.mii.lt/samogitia/kultura/
    klumpes.en.htm
  http://www.bihos.com/theclogpage/
  http://www.curtin.edu.au/curtin/dept/physio/
    podiatry/clog.html
  http://www.personal.utulsa.edu/~marc-carlson/shoe/
    APP4.HTM

Clothing for Big Folks

Here are the FAQs discussing oversized clothing for the United States, Canada, United Kingdom and Europe. You'll find out how to convert sizes internationally, where to find clothing and shoes for everyday as well as where to shop for wedding and maternity clothing. This information will help women, men and children.

Web:
  http://www.cat-and-dragon.com/stef/fatfaqs/
    canada.html
  http://www.cat-and-dragon.com/stef/fatfaqs/us.html
  http://www.cs.ruu.nl/wais/html/na-dir/
    fat-acceptance-faq/clothing/.html
  http://www.faqs.org/faqs/fat-acceptance-faq/
    clothing/

Corsets

Do not confuse corsets with girdles. Girdles are a modern undergarment made out of elastic material. Corsets have been used from time immemorial and are more extreme. Corsets incorporate a series of reinforcements called "stays" in order to bind the breasts, waist and hips into a particular desired shape. At one time, corsets were extremely popular, and the image of a Victorian woman needing help to lace up and tighten her corset is one that does little to make us nostalgic. However, corsets were an important fashion accoutrement that, even today, have their admirers.

Web:
  http://www.dnaco.net/~aleed/corsets/corsetpage/
  http://www.speakeasy.org/~traceyb/forms.html
  http://www.staylace.com/
  http://www.victoriana.com/c/corsets.html

Usenet:
  alt.fashion.corsetry

Corsets

Wearing a corset is definitely an acquired skill. However, is this a skill you want to acquire?

Some people say yes. A properly fitting corset is not only wearable, they say, but comfortable and — dare I say it? — arousing.

Would you like to get into the world of corsets, lacing and "waist training"? You had better know what you're doing, so go right to the Net and get the straight and narrow.

Cosmetics and Makeup

I used to have a friend who said that makeup was war paint. I think she was on to something. Certainly there's a lot more to makeup than meets the eye (or the cheeks or the lips). Using makeup and other cosmetics well calls for a lot of know-how, and how are you supposed to know all the know-how? The Net can help.

Web:
  http://www.cosmeticconnection.com/
  http://www.makeupdiva.com/

Fashion Resources

I know what you are thinking. Harley, I hear you ask, you are a man and you spend most of your time at home, writing. Do you really care about fashion trends? Of course I do. For one thing, every year or so, I get my cat a new collar, and I have to make sure that whatever I get for him is *tout à la mode*. Moreover, as a respected social commentator, I need to be able to appreciate the fashion display of all the women who wait outside my door to get their books autographed. So, when I say I have some great fashion-related resources for you, you can trust I am leading you in the right direction.

Web:
  http://www.dailyfashion.com/
  http://www.fashion.net/
  http://www.fashionangel.com/linkpages/
  http://www.fashiondish.com/
  http://www.fashionguide.com/
  http://www.fp1.com/
  http://www.hintmag.com/

Fashion Talk and General Discussion

It's a nice feeling when you're dressed in a spiffy new outfit with all the right accessories and people turn to look as you walk down the street. Impress your friends, family and total strangers with your fashion sense and the clothing tips you've learned while hanging out on the Internet. Clothing pros, trendsetters and the hopelessly unfashionable find their way to these discussion groups to share ideas or get answers to questions.

Usenet:
  alt.fashion
  alt.fashion.men
  alt.fashion.petite

Gothic Fashion

You feel, deep inside, that you are goth. So you need to develop your own sense of style and personal creativity in matters gothic. How to start? Read the FAQ (frequently asked question list) for the **alt.gothic.fashion** Usenet discussion group. You'll find hints and tips on buying clothes and accessories, caring for your clothes, making your own gothic wardrobe, goth decor for your home, and those two all-important fashion foci: hair and makeup. Then start reading the **alt.gothic.fashion** group. You may be goth and your mother may not understand, but on the Net, you are definitely, divinely, not alone.

Web:
  http://www.toreadors.com/gothfash/
Usenet:
  alt.gothic.fashion

Hair Care

How can you make sure your hair always looks as good as possible? Consult the Net and learn how to banish bad hair days to the dustbin of fashion. While you're at it, check out the latest tonsorial styles, and before you can say "I got anti-frizz liquid all over my barrette," you'll be the envy of everyone in your social set.

Web:
  http://www.hairboutique.com/
  http://www.heaven-earth.com/
  http://www.naturallycurly.com/
  http://www.tlhs.org/

Historical Costuming

There's nothing I like more than dressing up in an authentic historical costume—bell bottoms, love beads and a tie-dyed T-shirt—and walking around the house affecting an attitude as cool as a Canadian winter. However, this is nothing compared to what real historical costume buffs do to relax. On the Net you can find information about historical costuming. Just the place to look when you need to find a Renaissance- style crossbow or complete your research into what type of underwear women wore in the fifteenth century.

Web:
  http://moas.atlantia.sca.org/topics/clot.htm
  http://www.costumes.org/
  http://www.faqs.org/faqs/crafts/
    historical-costuming/
  http://www.kipar.org/costumes_links.html
Usenet:
  alt.history.costuming

Lipstick

Lipstick is something we are all used to. However, like many areas of the fashion world, the more you think about it, the more strange the idea seems. The best solution, then, is not to think about it. Just use lipstick and enjoy. One way to enjoy is to look at this lipstick-oriented Web site. Read about tips and consumer issues, explore other links to cosmetic- related resources, look in the lipstick library of color choices, and much, much more. If you would like to know which lipstick shades and brands are used by famous models and movie stars, this is the place for you.

Web:
  http://www.thelipstickpage.com/

Lycra

Yes, it's true. There is a discussion group for fans of lycra and spandex. If you have something to contribute or are just curious about the lycra culture, check out the Usenet group. For some lycra-oriented exploration, try the Web site.

Web:
> http://invncble.best.vwh.net/altlycra.html

Usenet:
> alt.lycra

Models and Supermodels

Maybe you can never be too rich or too thin, but why not check it out on the Net first? See photos and learn what being a supermodel is all about. If you still think you've got what it takes, remember, no dinner for you tonight.

Web:
> http://www.modelingadvice.com/Home.html
> http://www.supermodel.com/
> http://www.supermodels.nl/

Usenet:
> alt.binaries.pictures.joanne-guest
> alt.binaries.pictures.models
> alt.binaries.pictures.nicki-lewis
> alt.binaries.pictures.petra-verkaik
> alt.binaries.pictures.photo-modeling
> alt.binaries.pictures.supermodels.claudia-schiffer
> alt.binaries.pictures.supermodels.elle-macpherson
> alt.binaries.pictures.supermodels.kathy-ireland
> alt.fan.alison-armitage
> alt.fan.anna.nicole.smith
> alt.fan.ashley-lauren
> alt.fan.bridget
> alt.fan.bridget-maasland
> alt.fan.christy-turlington
> alt.fan.jenny-mccarthy
> alt.fan.julia-hayes
> alt.fan.kate-moss
> alt.fan.kerri-kendall
> alt.fan.lisa-boyle
> alt.fan.melinda.messenger
> alt.fan.patricia
> alt.fan.petra-verkaik
> alt.fan.sung-hi-lee
> alt.models
> alt.models.petite
> alt.supermodels
> alt.supermodels.cindy-crawford

Free Offer: Get Your Own Supermodel

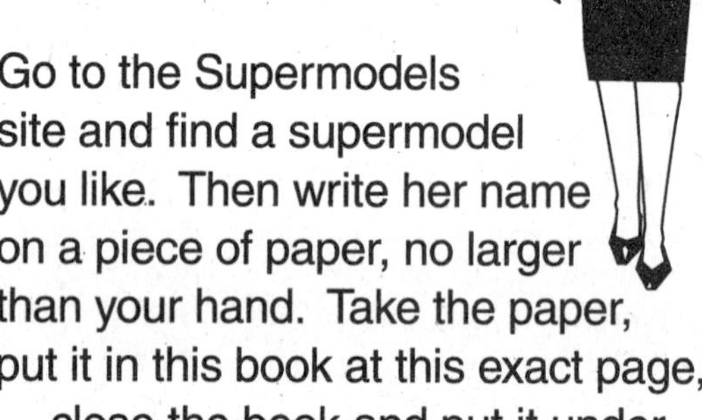

Would you like your own supermodel? I have arranged a special offer just for my readers. Here is what you need to do.

Go to the Supermodels site and find a supermodel you like. Then write her name on a piece of paper, no larger than your hand. Take the paper, put it in this book at this exact page, close the book and put it under your pillow when you go to sleep tonight.

Tomorrow morning, there will be a message on your voice mail from that particular supermodel. The message will tell you where and when you can meet her in person. If for some reason you do not get a message, try again the next night.

Disclaimer: Sorry, this offer is not valid if you do not have voice mail.

Nail Care

When I was young, my father taught me that when you meet someone, they always notice your nails and your shoes. If you are a woman, this is especially true. Although fake fingernails are popular, they are not nearly as attractive as having your own healthy, well-groomed nails. Are you ready to spend a small amount of time taking care of your nails? Fifteen to twenty minutes a week is all it should take. Don't let yourself get discouraged. Your nails grow about 1/8 of an inch per month, so if you start to take care of them today, it won't be that long before they are beautiful and strong (just like you).

Web:
  http://www.salonweb.com/nail.htm
  http://www.tipsofallsorts.com/nail.html

Neckties

Men's ties are confining and awkward (although not nearly so much as certain traditional women's clothing), and, except for covering the shirt buttons, they have no practical value. So why are they so popular? Wearing a tie is one of those traditions passed down from older, powerful men to their younger brethren. Moreover, although most male wardrobe is stultifyingly dull and conventional, choosing a tie is the one area in which a man can express his sartorial personality, at least to the extent of selecting the color and pattern. Women of the world, don't you feel sorry for us?

Web:
  http://www.neckties.com/history.htm
  http://www.onlineties.com/allboutties.html
  http://www.tieguys.com/information/history.shtml
  http://www.ties.com/museum.html

The weather is always fine on the Net.

Shoes

Why do so many women love shoes (and why do so many men love women who love shoes)? There are a variety of reasons, ranging from fashion to sex and back again. I have a friend who has a teenaged daughter who shall remain nameless (Amanda) who simply loves shoes. She has more shoes in her closet than you would think she would ever wear, but somehow she manages to wear them all. Moreover, she is always ready to buy a new pair; she never gets tired of shoe shopping at the local mall. I wonder what she knows that the rest of us don't understand?

Web:
  http://demo.dynamo-x.com/int_measure.asp
  http://www.centuryinshoes.com/
  http://www.curtin.edu.au/curtin/dept/physio/
    podiatry/history.html
  http://www.musonix.demon.co.uk/shoe-sizes/
  http://www.shoeinfonet.com/history/usm/
    hi_shoes.htm
  http://www.shoeworld.co.uk/

Skin Care

Some years ago, a friend of mine was visiting me. Shannon has always been beautiful, and, more to the point, she has always had a beautiful complexion. I asked her to give me some tips and she very kindly taught me the rudiments of good skin care. (Well, the male version, anyway. I have a feeling that the female regimen is a lot more sophisticated.) To this day, I still use a moisturizer with sun screen each morning and a nighttime moisturizer before I go to sleep. I can tell you, it makes a big difference. So if you can get Shannon to come over and give you personal skin advice, do so today. If not, you can always turn to the Net.

Web:
  http://www.bodyfaq.com/skin-care.htm
  http://www.inseventhheaven.com/
  http://www.skincarerx.org/tips.html
  http://www.tanglewoodhair.com/skin_care_tips.htm
  http://www.tipsofallsorts.com/skin.html

Usenet:
  alt.skincare

Sneakers

When you've run out of useful things to do, check out the Internet resources on sneakers. You'll find dialog on different brands of running shoes, what sneaker to buy and how to deal with stinky feet.

Web:
   http://www.sneakers.pair.com/

Usenet:
   alt.clothing.sneakers
   alt.fan.nike

Victorian Fashion

The Victorian Age is named after England's Queen Victoria, who ruled for sixty-four years, from 1837-1901. During these sixty-four years, a collection of style and behavior patterns developed that we refer to as Victorian culture. Along with the culture came a definite set of guidelines as to what proper people should wear and not wear. Even today, Victorian fashion has its admirers. By the way, within the royal household, the champion of taste was not Queen Victoria, but her consort Prince Albert—the Camilla Parker Bowles of his time.

Web:
   http://www.costumes.org/pages/victlinks.htm
   http://www.marquise.de/1800/
   http://www.victoriana.com/cost.html

Wigs

In every society, at all times, beautiful hair has been prized on both men and women. In general, there are two reasons for using a wig: for fashion (to effect a particular look) and to replace lost hair (because of either natural thinning or during chemotherapy). Before you think about getting a wig, especially if you are preparing for chemotherapy, you'll find it helpful to check the Net for advice. And now, a quick joke. A woman is walking down the street and she runs into a friend she hasn't seen for a long time. "Sophie," she says "whatever did you do with your hair? It looks like a wig." "To tell you the truth," says her friend, "it *is* a wig." "Well," says the first woman, "you'd never know."

Web:
   http://www.aaawigbiz.com/about_wigs/
      glossary_of_terms.htm
   http://www.imaginis.com/breasthealth/wigs.asp
   http://www.wigs4you.com/wig_advice.htm

Victorian Fashion

Back in the nineteenth century, Queen Victoria and her husband Prince Albert were the fashion trend-setters of the day. Victoria and Albert could wear whatever they wanted and, instantly, that would become the new fashion.

However, Queen Victoria's temper was legendary, and nobody wanted to show up at an official function wearing something that was out of fashion.

So how could everyone keep up on the latest trends? Easy. All they had to do was connect to the Net and check the Victorian Fashion Web site.

FESTIVALS, AMUSEMENTS AND GATHERINGS

Amusement and Theme Parks

When I was very young, growing up in Toronto, I remember my grandfather taking me to an amusement park called Sunnyside. Sunnyside is long since gone and, by the standard of today's elaborate theme parks, it must have been somewhat humble. However, to me, it was exciting, and the memories of the amusement park visits with my grandfather will stay with me always. Sometimes at night, I close my eyes and go back in time to the days when life was so simple, so sweet and so safe. When you take your kids to a park, isn't it wonderful to know that you are giving them memories that will delight and comfort them for a lifetime?

Web:

  http://members.aol.com/parklinks/links.htm
  http://www.disney.go.com/vacationsbase/
  http://www.disneyfan.com/wdwinfo/themeparks.htm
  http://www.funguide.com/country.html
  http://www.ridezone.com/links/linksap01.htm
  http://www.themeparkvision.net/us/home.asp

Usenet:

  alt.disney.disneyland
  rec.arts.disney.parks
  rec.parks.theme

Burning Man

Burning Man started in San Francisco as an annual artistic event, the focus of which was the burning of a large, manlike wooden structure. In 1990, the festival moved to the Nevada desert. At first it was small, but from an inauspicious beginning, Burning Man has metamorphosed into a huge, non-commercial, temporary community dedicated to creativity, strangeness, celebration and fun (and burning a man).

Web:

  http://www.burningman.com/
  http://www.zpub.com/burn/

Circuses

A circus travels from town to town, putting on a show at each stop. Traditionally, circuses feature clowns, acrobats, trained animals, as well as a variety of other acts. Along with the entertainment, there is a ringmaster (master of ceremonies) and a band, all of which create an overall feeling of fun and excitement. Although there are many circuses in the world, my favorite is Boomschmidt's Stupendous and Unexcelled Circus. In general, I like circuses, but I do have one question that has always puzzled me: Why are clowns so scary?

Web:

  http://circus.circusfolks.com/circuseslinks.html
  http://www.circustuff.com/
  http://www.circusweb.com/circuswebframes.html
  http://www.eduscapes.com/42explore/circus.htm
  http://www.jansown.com/

Usenet:

  alt.circus.arts

Drive-in Theaters

The original drive-in theater, a truly American invention, opened in Camden, New Jersey in 1933. For the first time in history, men and women could enjoy a movie while relaxing in the privacy of their own cars. (Remember, this was years before video, when the only way to see a movie was to go to a public theater.) In the post-war 1940s, the drive-in took on a prominent role as one of *the* places to take your date on a Saturday night. This role peaked in the 1950s, as mid-America discovered the convenience of being able to go out without paying a babysitter and watch a movie in curlers (Mom), an undershirt (Pop), or pajamas (Sis and Junior), while chowing down on all-beef hotdogs and ice-cold cups of Coke. Still, as wholesome as this image is, whisper the words "drive-in" to anyone over the age of fifteen, and you can't help but evoke a feeling of, well, opportunity. As a woman friend (whose name I won't mention and, no, you can't have her email address) recently told me, "Every time I go to a drive-in theater I have to have sex." God bless America is all I can say.

Web:

  http://www.drive-ins.com/
  http://www.driveintheater.com/
  http://www.pinballrebel.com/drive/test.htm

Film Festivals

If the last 100 years ever come to be known as the Century of the Film, surely the 1990s will be recognized as the Decade of the Film Festival. Do you have any idea how many different film festivals there are in the world? A lot, that's how many. By my calculations, it won't be long until the number of film festivals each year outnumbers the number of new films. When this happens, I will be ready, because I am currently hard at work on a film about film festivals. It's called "Meta Festival" (as in "I never met a film festival I didn't like").

Web:
 http://www.festival-cannes.fr/
   index.php?langue=6002
 http://www.filmfestivals.com/
 http://www.filmfestivalsource.com/
 http://www.seattlefilm.com/
 http://www.sundancechannel.com/festival/

Usenet:
 alt.film-festivals
 alt.film-festivals.sundance

Living History

If your domestic life seems a bit mild, spice it up by joining the living history buffs who find delight in reenacting historical periods or events. After all, just because you weren't there doesn't mean you have to be left out.

Web:
 http://www.alhfam.org/
 http://www.cwreenactors.com/
 http://www.livinghistory.co.uk/
 http://www.revwar.com/reenact/

Usenet:
 alt.history.living
 soc.history.living

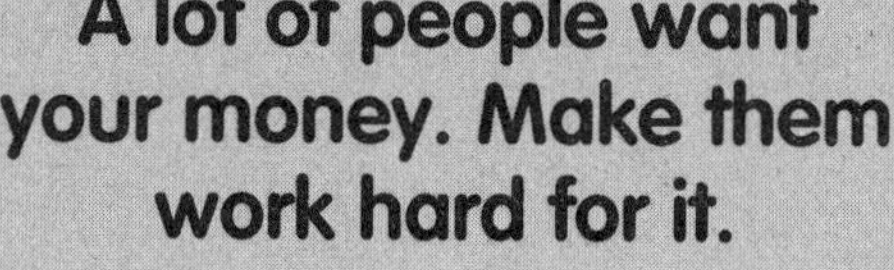

Mardi Gras

In the Christian church, the holiday of Easter is preceded by Lent, a 40-day period from Ash Wednesday to Easter Sunday, which is observed as a season for fasting and penitence. The day before the beginning of Lent is called Shrove Tuesday. Many people traditionally use this day to feast, in preparation for Lent. Thus, Shrove Tuesday is also called Mardi Gras, which means "Fat Tuesday" in French. In many places around the world, the days leading up to Mardi Gras are celebrated as a large carnival, lasting a week or more. Among the most celebrated carnivals are those of New Orleans and Rio de Janeiro. Such carnivals involve non-stop music and dancing, and lots and lots of fun. If you think you can stand this much applied hedonism, use the Net to check out the Mardi Gras carnival closest to you.

Web:
 http://www.mardigras.com/
 http://www.mardigrasday.com/
 http://www.mardigrasneworleans.com/
 http://www.mglinks.com/

Music Festivals

Isn't music amazing? It's fun to listen to music all by yourself, but it's also enjoyable when you are outside, surrounded by thousands of other people, something you can't say about anything else in the world. If you are a music festival buff, you'll be glad to know that wherever you are, the Net can help you find some type of festival to attend. As Jan and Dean put it, "Ride, ride, ride, the wild surf. Gotta take that one last ride." Go for it.

Web:
 http://www.festivalfinder.com/
 http://www.festivalhill.org/
 http://www.folkfests.com/
 http://www.musi-cal.com/simple.html

Usenet:
 alt.music.festivals

Living History

Living history is a wonderful pastime in which people reenact famous historical events.

Why, just the other day, I was taking a shortcut down an alley and I happened upon a couple performing a realistic reenactment of John F. Kennedy and Marilyn Monroe discussing domestic policy in the White House.

Powwows

A powwow is a traditional gathering of Native Americans: a celebration featuring singing, dancing and drumming. In modern times, powwows have evolved into elaborate events offering ceremonies, family reunions, festivals, pageants, and entertainment. Each year, powwows are held across North America, attracting many participants and visitors. There are even professionals who, every summer, travel the powwow circuit, in order to dance or drum at many different events. If you have never been to a powwow, give it a try. You'll be pleasantly surprised at the richness of your experience.

Web:
  http://library.thinkquest.org/3081/terms.htm
  http://www.nativeweb.org/community/events/
  http://www.powwow-power.com/
  http://www.thespike.com/picks.htm

Rainbow Gatherings

The spirit of peace, love and happiness of the sixties lives on, yes it does. It lives within the hearts of the Rainbow Family (a.k.a. the Rainbow Family of Living Light and the Rainbow Nation). The Rainbow Family is a loosely organized group of groups around the world, dedicated to the ideals of...well...peace, love and happiness. Since 1972, they have been holding large and small gatherings in remote forests around the world. Rainbow Gatherings are truly non-commercial. Money is not necessary. Everyone is welcome. Should you go? As a friend of mine, who used to be a flower child, put it, "If I were young, that sounds like something I could really get into."

Web:
  http://home.earthlink.net/~kzirk/scroll/Minutes/
    minimanual.html
  http://www.peaceconspiracy.org/rainbow/
  http://www.perkel.com/rainbow/mini.htm
  http://www.welcomehome.org/rainbow.html

Usenet:
  alt.gathering.rainbow

Renaissance Fairs

A renaissance fair (or faire) is a celebration, often put on by a commercial company, at which people dress in costumes and participate in activities associated with 16th-century Elizabethan England. At a renaissance fair, the view from the past mixes actual history with fantasy. You'll find a pretend world in which the idealizations of romance and chivalry are mixed with music, games, food, drama, competitions, crafts and dancing, with a measure of knights, dragons and fairies thrown in for atmosphere.

Web:
  http://www.faire.net/SCRIBE/WebEventName.htm
  http://www.faires.com/schedule.htm
  http://www.renaissance-faire.com/Locations.htm

Usenet:
  alt.fairs.renaissance
  alt.ren-faire

Roller Coasters

You are utterly terrified, screaming. Your heart is pounding and you think you might lose your cookies at any moment. You are on a roller coaster and, as scary as the ride seems, the whole thing is over much too soon. You tell yourself you can take it or leave it, but soon you are an addict. Don't worry, you are not alone. There are frenzied roller coaster fans all over the world.

Web:
  http://www.coasterclub.org/en/links/
  http://www.joyrides.com/
  http://www.rcdb.com/
  http://www.rollercoaster.com/resources/almanac/
  http://www.rollercoasterworld.com/
  http://www.ultimaterollercoaster.com/

Usenet:
  rec.roller-coaster

Always send a
thank-you note.
(Sorry, email doesn't count.)

Society for Creative Anachronism

Step back in time to the Middle Ages, where chivalry lives and everyone's lives are ordered by the rising and setting of the sun. Watch people dress up in metal and hit each other with sticks. Experience the grace and beauty of period costuming. Discover the festivity of a real medieval feast. Members and friends of the SCA discuss how it feels to live life in the modern Middle Ages.

Web:

http://www.sca.org/

Usenet:

alt.heraldry.sca
rec.heraldry
rec.org.sca

State and County Fairs

Ooohhh, I love fairs. I love the smells, the noise, the animals, the buildings and all the exhibits, and, of course, the food. When I was growing up in Toronto, I loved going to the "Ex" (the Canadian National Exhibition or CNE), a huge fair held every year during the last part of the summer. My favorite activity was to go into the Food Building, get a container of spaghetti for a quarter at the Primo Spaghetti booth, snarf a cold drink, and take it all across the way where I could eat comfortably in a cool, air-conditioned theater that showed free scientific, religious propaganda films. When I moved to the U.S., I learned to enjoy the county and state fairs, which seem to have more of an emphasis on agriculture. If you are visiting the U.S., I strongly urge you to visit a fair. And if you visit Canada, see if you can visit CNE in Toronto or its West Coast counterpart, the PNE (Pacific Nation Exhibition) in Vancouver.

Web:

http://www.fairsandexpos.com/fairframes3.html
http://www.pne.bc.ca/
http://www.theex.com/

World Exposition

The 1967 World's Fair in Montreal, Canada was the scene of one of my biggest accomplishments. I was just a kid, and I loved walking around by myself and exploring the many "pavilions". Most of the pavilions were sponsored by a specific country. When you visited a pavilion, they would stamp your "passport" (a small booklet you got when you entered the grounds). As I walked around, I had a copy of the official Expo 67 guidebook, which had a one-page description of each pavilion. What was my accomplishment? I went to every pavilion, over a hundred, and had them stamp my guidebook on the page for that pavilion. If you ever get a chance to go to a World's Fair, why not see if you can visit every building the way I did? It's good practice if you ever want to be the type of person who would create an Internet Yellow Pages.

Web:

http://www.expomuseum.com/
http://www.virtualworldfairs.org/
http://www.worldsfairs.com/

FINDING STUFF ON THE NET

Culture Finder

The Culture Finder offers useful and interesting information about culture. For example, if you are visiting New York, you can check here to find out what is playing off-Broadway. Or if you want to look up the meaning of "overture", you can use the Culture Finder dictionary. Here are many resources, including news, information and games. I bet you'll love this site.

Web:
  http://www.culturefinder.com/

FTP Search

FTP is a system used to download and upload files on the Internet. (The name FTP stands for "File Transfer Protocol".) There are a massive number of files available on the Net for free downloading via FTP, but you have to know where they are. Sometimes you know the file you want (or you can guess at its name), but you aren't sure where it is. For example, you might want a particular program or picture file or music file. When that happens, here are resources to help you track down your elusive target. These tools are also good ones to use for treasure hunting. For example, I searched for files named "harley" and I found some interesting stuff. Try your own name and see what you find.

Web:
  http://www.ftpfind.com/
  http://www.oth.net/

How to Use Search Engines

A search engine is a program that allows you to search a database quickly. All of the well-known Internet search tools (Yahoo, Altavista, Lycos, Excite, and so on) are search engines. Here is information about the various search engines, along with a wealth of advice on how to use them effectively. If you find yourself spending too much time floundering around, take a few moments and read these articles.

Web:
  http://sunsite.berkeley.edu/help/searchdetails.html
  http://www.monash.com/spidap.html
  http://www.searchengineshowdown.com/
  http://www.searchenginewatch.com/

Image Search Engines

Get the picture? You will. There are a large number of pictures, illustrations, graphics and photographs available on the Net, and you can get them for free.

Web:
  http://creative.gettyimages.com/photodisc/
  http://gallery.yahoo.com/
  http://images.google.com/
  http://www.altavista.com/sites/search/simage
  http://www.ditto.com/

How to Use Search Engines

You can find just about anything you want on the Net—if you know what you are doing. One of the biggest tips I can give you is to spend some time learning how to use the various Internet search engines.

There are a number of companies that maintain databases containing information about all the Web sites on the Net. (You can imagine what a job it is keeping such databases up to date.) These companies allow anyone to use their search engines for free—they make their money from advertising.

For example, if you want information about me, you can use a search engine to look for the words "Harley Hahn". The results of the search will be a set of links to all the Web sites in that particular database that contain these words. To visit these pages, all you have to do is click on the links that look interesting.

My advice is to pick the search engines you like the best and learn how to use them well. Because the databases are so large, it is common to have your search return many spurious items that you will have to ignore. However, there are ways to make your request more sophisticated, which will get you better results.

In my experience, any time you spend learning how to use a tool well is time well spent.

Mailing List Search Engines

The Net has tens of thousands of different mailing lists, with more being added all the time. A mailing list is a forum for the discussion of a particular topic. Mailing lists differ from Usenet in that all the messages are distributed to participants by electronic mail. (With Usenet, messages are posted to various groups, which you can access with your Web browser or a special-purpose newsreader program.) To participate in a mailing list, you must subscribe (which is free). Once you subscribe, all the messages that are posted to the list will be sent to your mailbox. If you get tired of being on the list, you can unsubscribe at any time. Although the first mailing lists were administered by people, most modern lists (and all the ones listed in this book) are managed by computer programs. The three most popular such programs are Listserv, Majordomo and Listproc. I have included a great many mailing lists as resources in this book. However, there are times when you may want to perform a search of your own. To help you, here are my favorite mailing list search engines.

Web:

    http://www.lsoft.com/catalist.html
    http://www.paml.net/
    http://www.tile.net/lists/
    http://www.topica.com/

Music and File Sharing

In general, music on the Net is stored in MP3 files, and there are a huge number of people who are willing to share. The first extremely popular Internet file sharing program was Napster. Unfortunately, Napster was shut down (in the spring of 2000) for copyright infringement. However, music sharing is alive and well on the Net. Many of these systems work without a central server. They use a decentralized peer-to-peer technology, in which the individual computers join into a large, connected system. These facilities can be used to share any type of file, not only music, but video, text, games, programs, and so on. Moreover, because they do not use a central server, such systems cannot be shut down—ever.

Web:

    http://www.filenavigator.com/
    http://www.filetopia.org/home.htm
    http://www.gnutelliums.com/
    http://www.grokster.com/
    http://www.imesh.com/
    http://www.jawed.com/mp3voyeur/
    http://www.limewire.com/index.jsp/download#free
    http://www.winmx.com/
    http://www.zeropaid.com/

New Stuff Talk and General Discussion

These two Usenet groups are good places to look for new and interesting Net resources. The **net-happenings** group is moderated and well-organized. This group is as close to an official place to announce a new resource as exists on the Net. There is *always* something interesting here. The **www.announce** group is not moderated, and is used by the general population to post notices about new Web sites.

Usenet:

    comp.infosystems.www.announce
    comp.internet.net-happenings

Search Bots

What would you think if you could have your own personal Internet slave: a sophisticated computer program that knows how to search the Net on your behalf. Such programs are called search bots, and there are many different kinds. If you know what you want, but you don't know how to get it, let a bot do the work for you.

Web:

    http://www.botknowledge.com/bkbots.html
    http://www.botspot.com/

Search Engine Access Sites

These sites are not search engines. Rather, they are Web pages that contain a list of links to search engines. Although some people find such services useful, my experience is that—if you do much searching—it is probably easier to find one or two favorite engines and learn how to use them well. However, if you are an occasional searcher, you may like the one-size-fits-all setup. At the very least, I'm sure you will appreciate how some of these services select advertisements to show you based on the keywords in your search. How thoughtful.

Web:
> http://www.allsearchengines.com/
> http://www.askjeeves.com/
> http://www.fossick.com/
> http://www.invisibleweb.com/
> http://www.lincon.com/
> http://www.lookoff.com/
> http://www.metacrawler.com/
> http://www.profusion.com/
> http://www.searchability.com/
> http://www.searchenginecolossus.com/
> http://www.webinfosearch.net/

Search Engines

A search engine is a facility that helps you find information on the Internet. The search engines I have listed here all allow you to search the Web. They work by maintaining a large database of information about Web sites. The search engine companies maintain their databases by using programs that continually search the Web. Some companies also accept submissions from people who want their sites listed. The basic way to use a search engine is to specify one or more keywords. A program then searches the database looking for resources that contain those words. The various search engines are organized in different ways. Some try to index every Web page on the Net. Others organize information into categories. In addition, most search engines offer other facilities, such as searching Usenet archives. My advice is to try the various search engines, pick one or two you like best, and learn how to use them well.

Web:
> http://hotbot.lycos.com/
> http://search.aol.com/
> http://www.alltheweb.com/
> http://www.altavista.com/
> http://www.excite.com/
> http://www.google.com/
> http://www.lycos.com/
> http://www.search.msn.com/
> http://www.webcrawler.com/
> http://www.yahoo.com/

Search Engines Around the World

There are *many* special-purpose search engines on the Net that can save you a lot of time if you know where to find them. Well, here's something I want you to know about: a large list of search engines devoted to specific countries. When you are looking for international information, this is the place to start.

Web:
> http://www.twics.com/~takakuwa/search/
> search.html

Search Engine Access Sites

Top Ten Links

We all love top ten lists because they condense modern life to its essence: give me the best, give it to me fast, and give it to me now. Well, now you have it: a huge number of lists, each containing the top ten Web sites in a specific area. The rankings are based on people's votes, so this is real Internet-style power-to-the-people democracy in action. It's also real Internet-style find-me-what-I-want-fast life in the virtual fast lane.

Web:

   http://www.toptenlinks.com/

Web Catalogs

Have you ever thought about what it would be like to search the Web looking for the best sites in many different categories? Well, I do it in order to write this book, but I'm not the only one. Around the Net, a number of companies have Web sites that catalog the best, most interesting, or most useful Web sites. These Web catalogs are a good place to look when you know the type of resource you need, but you don't want to wade through a huge amount of items from a search engine.

Web:

   http://www.britannica.com/
   http://www.clickey.com/
   http://www.dmoz.org/
   http://www.dogpile.com/
   http://www.searchbeat.com/
   http://www.vlib.org/

Web Channel Guides

A channel is a Web site that can send information to your computer automatically according to a predetermined schedule. (You will sometimes see this type of system referred to as "push" technology.) There are many channels available on the Net, and you can access them for free using your browser. Here are some guides to show you what is available. (Just make sure you don't spend so much time with Web channels that you forget to watch enough television.)

Web:

   http://wp.netscape.com/netcenter/cf/index1.html
   http://www.windowsmedia.microsoft.com/

Web Sites by Name

When you look at an Internet address, the rightmost two parts are called the domain name. For example, **microsoft.com**, **whitehouse.gov**, **pacbell.net** or **activism.org**. The domain name will often give you information about the owners or purpose of the service using that name. Have you ever tried to find particular types of domain names? You can, using these awesome search engines, great tools for searching for Web sites set up for a specific purpose or by a specific organization. If a Web site exists for that name, these search engines will help you find it. For example, if you like humor, you might search for all the domain names that begin with "joke" or "humor".

Web:

   http://www.domainsurfer.com/
   http://www.netcraft.com/

Webring

Webring is cool. Very cool. It consists of hundreds of virtual "rings", each of which is devoted to a particular topic and contains a number of Web sites—for example: "Comic Book Ring", "The Official Ring of Games", "Female Empowerment Ring", "Adoption Ring", and so on. Here is how it works. You start by checking the index of rings for a topic that interests you. You then connect to the first site on whichever ring you want. At the bottom of the page, there is an icon you can select to move to the next site on the ring. Eventually, if you visit all the sites, you end up where you started. However, in the process, you will have jumped all over the Net. If you would like your site to be part of Webring, you can register it. Your site will then be placed in a particular ring. Next, you must put the Webring icons at the bottom of your Web page. These icons actually point back to the main Webring computer, where a special program figures out which is the next site in the ring. The Webring program handles all the details automatically, adding and deleting Web sites from rings as the need arises.

Web:

   http://www.webring.com/rw

What's New on the Web

Every day, countless new sites appear on the Web. Here are some resources to help you make sense of it all. Look for what is new and important, and what is new and interesting. These are good places to look when you hear about some hot new Web thingy in the news and want to find it for yourself.

Web:

> http://www.newslinx.com/
> http://www.robotwisdom.com/
> http://www.urlwire.com/headlines/
> http://www.whatsnu.com/

FOLKLORE, MYTHS AND LEGENDS

Aesop's Fables

"Aesop" is the name given to an unknown Greek storyteller who lived in the sixth century B.C. Legend has it that Aesop was a slave, but nobody really knows much about him. What we do know is that, over the years, the stories called Aesop's Fables have become one of the most beloved of our literary traditions. As you read these very short stories, you will see many recognizable themes and morals, such as The Hare and the Tortoise ("Plodding wins the race"), Mercury and the Woodman ("Honesty is the best policy"), and The Fox and the Goat ("Look before you leap").

Web:

> http://classics.mit.edu/Aesop/fab.html
> http://www.dusklight.com/aesop/

Atlantis

It all started with the Greek philosopher Plato (427-347 B.C.). He wrote two dialogues, Timeaus and Critias, in which Socrates, Hermocrates, Timeaus and Critias are sitting around having a conversation. Timeaus and Critias want to tell Socrates a story, a tale of a great city, a story which they say is absolutely true. And ever since, people have been racing around the planet looking for this long-lost city of Atlantis.

Web:

> http://www.atlan.org/
> http://www.atlantishistory.com/
> http://www.pantheon.org/articles/a/atlantis.html
> http://www.spiritweb.org/spirit/
>   atlantis-mu-lemuria.html

Usenet:

> alt.legend.atlantis
> alt.legends.atlantis

Bermuda Triangle

Take a look at a map of the east coast of the United States, and picture an imaginary triangle joining Miami, Bermuda, and San Juan, Puerto Rico. In 1964, a writer named Vincent Gaddis wrote an article for Argosy magazine in which he claimed that, over the years, an abnormally large number of ships and planes had disappeared in that part of the Atlantic Ocean. He called the area the Bermuda Triangle and set off a flurry of speculation, which took years to attenuate. Today, it is accepted that there is nothing mystical about the Bermuda Triangle, and like many similar beliefs, this one was based on poor data and wishful thinking.

Web:

> http://www.bermuda-triangle.org/
> http://www.greatdreams.com/bermuda.htm
> http://www.history.navy.mil/faqs/faq8-1.htm
> http://www.parascope.com/en/bermuda0.htm

Bigfoot

Bigfoot, sometimes called Sasquatch, is a creature of legend in the United States and Canada (especially in the U.S. Pacific Northwest). Bigfoot is supposed to be a tall, hairy apelike creature that has been sighted by isolated hikers and campers. The idea and legends of the North American Bigfoot are similar to that of the Abominable Snowman in parts of Asia. The Native American peoples have many different Bigfoot-like legends. Maybe, next time you go camping, you can start a legend of your own.

Web:
    http://www.bfro.net/
    http://www.bigfootinfo.org/
    http://www.bigfootmuseum.com/
    http://www.theshadowlands.net/bf.htm

Usenet:
    alt.bigfoot

Charms and Amulets

There are days when something special is about to happen, and you want an extra boost to make things turn out perfectly. For example, on the day you go in to ask your boss for a raise, wouldn't it be nice if you had a well-crafted spider amulet like that used by the ancient Europeans when they wanted to attract money? You don't like spiders? How about a magnetic lodestone, a horseshoe amulet, or a Snow Globe Pyramid of Luck?

Web:
    http://www.lib.umich.edu/pap/magic/
        def1.display.html
    http://www.mojomoon.net/amulets.html
    http://www.tryskelion.com/amulets.htm

Cryptozoology

Looking for Mr. Bigfoot?
How about the
Loch Ness monster
or a giant cookiecutter
shark?
If these mythical but
well-known beasts
appeal to you,
maybe you should
investigate Cryptozoology:
the study of hidden animals.
(Actually, I would be satisfied with
a way to find my cat when he is
hiding in the backyard.)

Computer Folklore

Over the years, the world of computing has developed its own traditions, literary and otherwise. Like all traditions, these tend to start with stories, discussion, tall tales and general talk. You can watch it all develop by following the discussion in these Usenet groups. When you need a reference, try one of the Web sites. Hang around long enough and when you get old, you'll be able to tell your grandchildren, "I was there when Bill Gates told the *real* story of why he made everyone use DOS and Windows for so long."

Web:
    http://wilson.best.vwh.net/faq/
    http://www.cs.utah.edu/~elb/folklore/
    http://www.psc.edu/~ecf/work-humor/
        comp.folklore.html

Usenet:
    alt.folklore.computers
    alt.folklore.internet
    comp.society.folklore

Cryptozoology

Cryptozoology is the study of mysterious animals—such as Bigfoot and the Loch Ness monster—whose existence is a matter of dispute. (The term "cryptozoology" was first used in the 1950s by Bernard Heuvelmans, author of "On the Track of Unknown Animals".) If you don't have enough to worry about in your life, and you want to concern yourself with things that don't actually exist, try reading some of the cryptozoology stuff at these sites. There is information about monsters, bugs, invertebrates and legendary lifeforms that nobody can prove are real.

Web:
    http://www.cryptozoology.com/
    http://www.cryptozoology.fsbusiness.co.uk/
    http://www.ncf.carleton.ca/~bz050/
        HomePage.cryptoz.html
    http://www.pibburns.com/cryptozo.htm

Dragons

I was in the bookstore the other day, and I happened to go to the section that has my books. As I turned the corner, I encountered a dragon, holding a copy of this book and breathing fire. I said to him, "Don't you know this is a non-smoking area?" And he said, "I know, but I can't help it. This is a very hot book." As you can see, it's always good to know what to say to a dragon, just in case you happen to meet one unexpectedly. So read up on dragons, learn about their personalities (such as why they have such good taste in books), and enjoy their legendary stories.

Web:
http://www.bestiarium.net/select.htm
http://www.draconian.com/links/links.htm
http://www.igolddragon.com/species.htm
http://www.polenth.demon.co.uk/deep.html

Usenet:
alt.fan.dragons

Encyclopedia of Myths and Legends

High in content and easily searchable, these sites offer a wealth of information about mythology, legends and folklore. Read about all sorts of creatures, gods, goddesses, and their origins and history.

Web:
http://www.clubi.ie/lestat/godsmen.html
http://www.pantheon.org/

Faeries

Fairies (or if you want to be cool and use the Middle English spelling, faeries) are tiny imaginary beings, except that they aren't always tiny, and some people think they are real, and maybe they aren't really beings. The nice thing about faeries (you can see I am cool, because I use the Middle English spelling) is that they can be just about anything you want as long as there is some enchantment involved. When I was younger, I lived in Berkeley, California, for awhile. In one of the apartments nearby was a mild, gentle young fellow who was into "Fairy Consciousness". I was never really sure what he meant, but I bet, whatever it is, you can find it on the Net.

Web:
http://www.faeries.org/site/lore/
http://www.magickalworlds.com/f_basics.html
http://www.open-sesame.com/fairy.html
http://www.wildmuse.net/faerie/

Fairy Tales

A fairy tale is a legendary story involving imaginative characters and unusual adventures. Use the Net to enter the wonderful world of childhood magic. There are a variety of fairy tales for you to read to children and enjoy on your own.

Web:
http://members.aol.com/surlalune/frytales/
http://www.acs.ucalgary.ca/~dkbrown/storfolk.html
http://www.cln.org/themes/fairytales.html
http://www.hca.gilead.org.il/
http://www.inform.umd.edu/edres/readingroom/
    fiction/fairytales/
http://www.legends.dm.net/fairy/

Folk Tales from Around the World

Various cultures around the world have created tales to teach people and to modify the behavior of the community to suit specific needs. Out of these needs are born gods and goddesses, heroes and villains, magical objects, and mythical animals. It's fun to read folk tales from a variety of countries. Occasionally, I will light a nice fire, put the cat in my lap and read him a Syldavian folk tale. He really appreciates the cultural exposure and, as you know, a well-rounded cat can catch more mice. If you too would like to be more culturally refined, take look at these folk tales from around the world. What's my favorite folk tale? The one about the tired Internet writer who fell asleep exhausted in front of his computer, only to awaken in the morning to find that a group of elves had magically finished writing his book during the night.

Web:
http://oaks.nvg.org/lg4ra2.html
http://www.darsie.net/talesofwonder/
http://www.dragonrest.net/romanian/fairytales.html
http://www.g-world.org/magictales/
http://www.lacquerbox.com/tales.htm
http://www.nsc.ru/folk/
http://www.ozemail.com.au/~oban/
http://www.pitt.edu/~dash/folktexts.html

Folklore and Mythology Resources

A myth is a traditional, ancient story involving supernatural beings or other types of heroes. Myths are often used to explain natural phenomena and to demonstrate the customs and traditions of a particular society. A legend is an apocryphal (unverified) story that is handed down from one generation to the next. Myths and legends are important because they represent aspects of human nature and cultural evolution that form the basis of what we think and do today.

Web:
  http://members.bellatlantic.net/~vze33gpz/
    myth.html
  http://www.cybercomm.net/~grandpa/gdsindex.html
  http://www.loggia.com/myth/myth.html
  http://www.pibburns.com/mythfolk.htm

Gems and Mineral Folklore

Some people believe there is magic and power locked inside the stones of the Earth, and that these stones can be used to channel energy from one place to another. (Of course, there are also people who believe the Easter Bunny is going to mysteriously fix all the bugs in Windows.)

Web:
  http://www.cedarseed.com/air/gemstones.html
  http://www.jewelrysupplier.com/
    mythology_links.htm
  http://www.octagamm.com/gemcache/gemlore.htm
  http://www.pearyhs.org/bdayclub/lore.htm

Usenet:
  alt.folklore.gemstones

Germanic Myths, Legends and Sagas

Do you ever have one of those days when you come into the house, all bundled up and covered with snow, and someone hands you a big mug of hot chocolate and says, "Here, sit down by the fire and let me relate an old Germanic legend my mother used to tell me." It doesn't happen to me, because I live near a beach in California, but it could happen to you, especially if you have this Web site in your bookmark list. This site has information about Germanic (Scandinavian and Teutonic) mythology, culture, ancient beliefs and deities.

Web:
  http://www.pitt.edu/~dash/mythlinks.html

Ghost Stories

Kids, do you want to have a lot of fun? The next time your parents go out, invite your best friend over for a visit. Then, get some wood (anything will do, an old chair, a dresser, an antique desk), turn out the lights, and start a fire in the living room. As the flames glow in the dark, take turns telling ghost stories. I guarantee you will have a scary experience.

Web:
  http://www.alienufoart.com/ghoststories.htm
  http://www.ghosts.org/stories/stories.html
  http://www.hotlyps.com/ghostories.htm
  http://www.theshadowlands.net/ghost/

Usenet:
  alt.folklore.ghost-stories

Gnomes

A gnome is an imaginary dwarflike creature that lives underground and is often depicted as guarding a treasure. The traditions and mythos of gnomes are well-developed. You can read about their history, appearance, activities, and so on. Gnomes are cute, and it can be fun to look at their pictures and read about them, but, of course, they don't really exist (or do they?).

Web:
  http://study.haifa.ac.il/~hyavnai/index2.htm

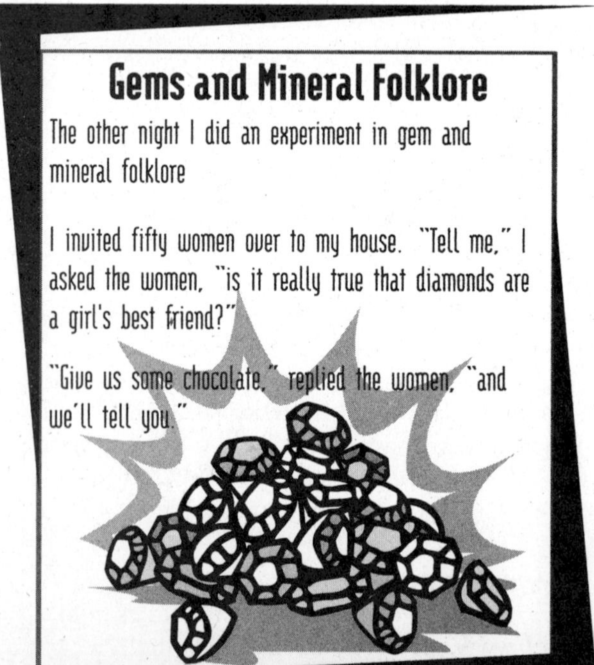

Gems and Mineral Folklore

The other night I did an experiment in gem and mineral folklore

I invited fifty women over to my house. "Tell me," I asked the women, "is it really true that diamonds are a girl's best friend?"

"Give us some chocolate," replied the women, "and we'll tell you."

Greek Mythology

The Greek gods and goddesses are more than mere mythical curiosities. Even today, the myths are part of our culture: our literature, customs, words, even our comic books and cartoons. Moreover, like all timeless myths, learning about the players and their stories helps us understand ourselves and our times. Explore a bit on the Net, so the next time you are at a party and someone asks, "Who was Agamemnon's wife?" you'll be the only one who will be able to answer Klytaimnestra. (Then you can add that their children were Orestes, Elektra and Iphigenia, and it won't be long until your friends start looking upon you as a god.)

Web:
http://web.uvic.ca/grs/bowman/myth/
http://www.classicsunveiled.com/mythnet/html/
http://www.princeton.edu/~rhwebb/trees/
   treesindex.html

Griffins

A griffin (also known as a griffon or gryphon) is a mythological beast with the body of a lion, and the head, forelegs and wings of an eagle. As you can imagine, this would be enough to cause the poor animal to be refused admittance to the more fashionable night clubs. Still, despite their odd features, griffins have been extremely popular over the centuries and are portrayed as having great intelligence and powerful strength (much like writers of Internet books). Griffins have appeared in numerous starring roles, as pets for the god Zeus, in a singing scene in Alice in Wonderland, and on many science fiction book covers.

Web:
http://gryphonguild.critter.net/
http://members.aol.com/alicorn14/firegryph.html
http://www.dragonweave.com/gothos/html/
   gryphons.html
http://www.enteract.com/~tirya/gallery.html

Usenet:
alt.mythology.mythic-animals.gryphons

TIDBITS

What should Internet buyers know about ONLINE AUCTIONS?

Buying and selling at Internet auctions can be a lot of fun and financially rewarding. To get you started right, here are 8 tips on how to make online auctions work for you.

1. Read *all* the help information before you start.

Even if you are the type of person who never reads the instructions, listen to me on this one. Online auctions are a lot more complex than they look.

2. Start small.

For your first few purchases, buy something inexpensive that you understand completely, like a CD. Don't start by buying something complicated like a computer.

3. Watch out for fraud.

Online auctions are the biggest single source of fraud on the Net.

4. Make a budget, and stick to it no matter what happens. Don't allow yourself to get carried away.

5. For expensive items, use an escrow service (a third-party company that acts as a middleman).

Before you bid:

6. Check out the seller.

7. Make sure you are buying the right item.

If you need, say, a part for a computer, make sure the item you are looking at will work with your computer. Don't depend on the seller for technical support.

8. Check availability and prices.

Lots of items that are sold at auctions are also available at stores.

For more help with buying on the Net, as well as a large variety of other interesting topics, see my book *Harley Hahn's Internet Insecurity*, published by Prentice Hall PTR.

Imaginary Creatures

There are a great many mythological creatures in the world. You may not be able to see them in the forest or in the zoo; they live in our imaginations and in our hearts. If you like the land of make-believe, you will have a great time exploring the sites on the Net that are devoted to strange imaginary creatures.

Web:
> http://www.mysticrealms.com/rules/bestiary/
> http://www.pantheon.org/areas/bestiary/
>   articles.html
> http://www.webhome.idirect.com/~donlong/
>   monsters/monsters.htm

King Arthur and Camelot

Arthurian legend contains many stories based in medieval times about King Arthur of Britain and his Knights of the Round Table. The legend can be traced back as far as the sixth century, although the stories have been expanded and modified throughout the years. The basic story, however, has always remained more or less the same. Arthur is the illegitimate son of King Uther Pendragon. After the king's death, Arthur distinguishes himself by successfully pulling out a sword that is embedded in a huge stone. Arthur becomes king and, from Camelot, reigns over the land of Britain. The stories involve the familiar characters of King Arthur, his knights (including Sir Lancelot, Sir Galahad and Sir Tristram), his wife Guinevere, Merlin the Magician, the Lady of the Lake (who gives Arthur his special sword Excalibur), and his enemies Morgan le Fay and Sir Mordred, all of whom appear in Arthur's many adventures. Eventually, Arthur is wounded by Sir Mordred and—as he is dying—is carried away to Avalon, from which he will one day return.

Web:
> http://www.kingarthur-online.co.uk/
> http://www.kingarthursknights.com/
> http://www.lib.rochester.edu/camelot/cphome.stm
> http://www.panix.com/~wlinden/arthur.shtml

Usenet:
> alt.legend.king-arthur

Listserv Mailing List:
> **List Name:** arthurnet
> **Subscribe to:** listserv@morgan.ucs.mun.ca

Mermaids

A mermaid is a legendary sea creature with the head and upper body of a woman and the lower anatomy of a fish. Sightings of mermaids have always been popular among sailors who have spent long days at sea, without female companionship, in the company of other sweaty sailors (and the odd fish). These sites have pictures of mermaids, as well as classic and modern tales.

Web:
> http://www.mermaid.net/
> http://www.pitt.edu/~dash/water.html

Mythology Talk and General Discussion

Myths are traditional stories, passed down from one generation to the next. Myths arise in all time periods, and they most always involve supernatural events. (Myths are different from folklore in that folk tales are generally more entertaining and believable.) If you like any type of mythology, these are the places to hang out and discuss the who, what, when, where and how-high-did-he-jump aspects of this entertaining and telling area of human culture.

Usenet:
> alt.mythology

Native American Myths and Legends

Native storytellers created sacred myths to explain the origin of humans, to answer the question of why we live as we do, and to record lessons that have been passed down through years of living. Many of these stories were based on nature and animals. Aside from being teaching tools, the legends were often used to entertain. Here are a variety of traditional stories from various native tribes.

Web:
  http://www.ac.wwu.edu/~skywise/legends.html
  http://www.bluecloud.org/myth.html
  http://www.ilhawaii.net/~stony/loreindx.html
  http://www.indians.org/welker/chippewa.htm
  http://www.ocbtracker.com/ladypixel/legend.html

Pirates

Pirates are the ultimate seafaring bad guys. They wear cool clothes, they pillage, and they can stay up as late as they want to watch Letterman. Yes, the pirate life is the life for me. If you want to be a pirate, or you want to just see what it was like to be a pirate (back in the days when pirates were allowed to have fun), take a look at these sites. You'll see pictures of ships, read about the pirate way of living, and have a chance to learn about the history, legends and myths of famous pirates of antiquity.

Web:
  http://www.inkyfingers.com/pyrates/
  http://www.ocracoke-nc.com/blackbeard/
  http://www.piratesinfo.com/main.php

Robin Hood

Robin Hood is a legendary 13th-century English hero who robbed the rich and gave his stolen goods to the poor and oppressed. Robin Hood lived in Sherwood Forest (in central England, north of Nottingham and west of Lincoln) with his band of merry followers who assisted him in his heroic endeavors. Read about the life and times of Robin Hood and why he is popular to this day.

Web:
  http://www.cadana.com/
  http://www.lib.rochester.edu/camelot/rh/
     rhhome.stm
  http://www.robinhood.ltd.uk/robinhood/
  http://www.webspan.net/~amunno/rhood.html

Majordomo Mailing List:
  List Name: robinhood-l
  Subscribe to: majordomo@ats.rochester.edu

Scientific Urban Legends

There are all sorts of nasty rumors flying around about science. And we know just where they are coming from. Check out the latest outlandish tales of science, which often sound like they come straight from the set of a 1950s science fiction movie. Help discern the truths from the myths by reading up on what the folks on the Net have to say.

Web:
  http://www.urbanlegends.com/science/
Usenet:
  alt.folklore.science

Sea Serpents and Lake Monsters

I have been swimming in the ocean for many, many years and I have never seen anything out of the ordinary or unexplainable. However, there are people all around the world who say they have seen oddities in oceans and lakes. Some of these people even have pictures. If you want a nice overview of what creatures you might be missing, take a look at this site. There are pictures, explanations and background information about various legendary creatures such as the Loch Ness monster, the Lake Champlain monster, the megamouth shark, giant squids, Ogopogo and others. And if you are insatiable for unusual marine animals, there are links to other water creature sites.

Web:
  http://www.lochness.co.uk/
  http://www.lochness.scotland.net/camera.cfm
  http://www.nessie.co.uk/
  http://www.theshadowlands.net/serpent.htm

Superstitions

There are far too many real problems to worry about in life. Sometimes, just for fun, why not worry about something silly? For example, once you cut a slice from a loaf of bread, you should never turn the loaf upside down. Why? I'm not sure, but what's the point in tempting fate? How about this: If three people are photographed together, the one in the middle will die first. Aren't superstitions fun?

Web:
  http://www.corsinet.com/trivia/scary.html
  http://www.doghause.com/super.html
  http://www.islandnet.com/~luree/silly.html
  http://www.meow.net/superstitions.html
  http://www.weddings.co.uk/info/tradsupe.htm

Tree Lore

Trees are perennial woody plants, characterized by having branches and twigs that extend from a single main stem to form a well-defined crown or canopy. The essence of the tree is its large size, long life, and slow approach to reproductive maturity. Trees are silent, sturdy, strong and mysterious, and they play an important part in a variety of legends and folklore. For example, in the druid tradition, the birch tree is associated with the herald of new beginnings, while the rowan tree protects one's house from lightning. Clearly, it behooves us to learn more about the spiritual life of our perennially woody friends (not to mention the benefits of a slow approach to reproductive maturity).

Web:
  http://www.druidry.org/obod/text/trees/trees.html
  http://www.mystical-www.co.uk/treemyth.htm
  http://www.taliesin.clara.net/treelore2.htm
  http://www.tarahill.com/treelore/

Urban Legends

An urban legend is a story that is widely believed to be true, even though no real evidence exists. Urban legends generally offer a measure of humor or horror, and seem to take on a life of their own, regardless of how true they really are. Urban legends are famous for being retold as if they happened to "a friend of a friend" (FOAF). For example, are there really gangs of kidnappers at Disneyland who abduct children, change their clothing and hairstyles, and then smuggle them out the gates into a waiting getaway car?

Web:
  http://www.gimmick.nl/us/
  http://www.spiffo.co.uk/urban.html
  http://www.urbanlegends.com/
  http://www.warphead.com/urbanlegends/

Usenet:
  alt.folklore.urban

Read a zine today.

Vampires

A vampire is a "living" corpse that, for nourishment, sucks blood from people. In many stories, vampires enslave people and turn them into vampires themselves. Traditionally, you can ward off a vampire by using particular charms. To kill one, you have to drive a stake through its heart. The most famous vampire is Dracula, from the 1897 novel by Bram Stoker. Why are vampire stories so popular? There are a number of reasons, the most important of which is the implied sexuality of the vampire experience. (The penetration of the fangs, a male image, and the liquid-filled mouth, a female image, create an undercurrent of male/female sexual tension.) Are vampires real? I'm not saying one way or the other. However, I do caution you to look under the bed tonight before you go to sleep. If you are really worried, try garlic-flavored pajamas.

Web:
  http://www.csn.ul.ie/~egnarts/vampire/
  http://www.net4u.ro/dracula/
  http://www.niteworld.net/
  http://www.pathwaytodarkness.com/
  http://www.zyworld.com/vampirelore/

Usenet:
  alt.books.anne-rice
  alt.culture.vampires
  alt.vampyres

IRC:
  #vampirehall (EFnet)
  #vampires (Undernet)
  #vampyres (EFnet)

Werewolf Folklore

On those days when you are not feeling quite like your old self, when you would rather have a midnight walk and howl at the moon than watch TV, you should know where to turn. Check these sites to see if you have any of the symptoms.

Web:
  http://www.furnation.com/lobo/mc/ahww/
  http://www.lycanthrope.org/
  http://www.swampfox.demon.co.uk/utlah/
  http://www.were.net/

Usenet:
  alt.horror.werewolves

FONTS AND TYPEFACES

Design Your Own Fonts

There are a lot of fonts available in this world, but let's be honest. Wouldn't you like to have your own font? Of course you would. Everyone needs their own font. Well, your dreams can come true. You are standing at the door of happiness. All you have to do is walk through.

Web:
  http://www.chank.com/howto/
  http://www.cool-fonts.com/howto.htm
  http://www.pcw.com.my/
    download.htm?d_title=editor-create.fonts

Famous Fonts

Coca Cola has its own font. So does the New York Times, the Walt Disney company, and lots of other well-known brand names, including various popular TV shows and movies. Would you like to see what it is like to use a famous font? Give it a try, and see what it is like to write letters like Walt Disney.

Web:
  http://home.no.net/fontzone/famous.shtml
  http://www.graphicsbydezign.com/fontsIII.htm
  http://www.simplythebest.net/fonts/
    famous_fonts.html

Field Guide to Fonts

Have you ever used a Roget's Thesaurus? Although many people think it is a synonym finder, a Roget's Thesaurus is actually designed to help you find the exact right word. You use a Roget's Thesaurus when you know the meaning of a word, but you do not know the word. Analogously, there are times when you need to find out the name of a particular font. For example, what do you do when you know the characteristics of a font—perhaps because you have a sample—but you don't know its name? Here are some unusual tools to help you track down the mysterious font.

Web:
  http://ll.identifont.com/
  http://www.bowfinprintworks.com/
    ScriptIDGuide.html

Figlet Fonts

A figlet font is a large font in which each "character" is made up of smaller characters: letters, punctuation, and so on. In other words, when you use a figlet font, you create pictures of letters. You can use a figlet font to "write" your name as a signature at the end of your email messages or Usenet postings. Experiment and see just how cool figletting can be.

Web:
  http://figlet.zelab.net/
  http://www.schnoggo.com/figlet.html

Font and Typeface Resources

This is an eclectic set of resources for people interested in typography: check out the strange, interesting and useful fonts, take a look at the typesetting tricks, and read a number of articles, all related to fonts and the people who use them.

Web:
  http://www.graphic-design.com/Type/
  http://www.redsun.com/type/
  http://www.websitetips.com/fonts/

Font Talk and General Discussion

These are the Usenet groups that are used to discuss fonts, typefaces, typography and related topics. If you are in the page layout business, these are good groups to read regularly. These are also good places to ask a question about fonts when no one around the office has any idea what you are talking about.

Usenet:
  alt.binaries.fonts
  comp.fonts

Listserv Mailing List:
  List Name: **typo-l**
  Subscribe to: **listserv@listserv.heanet.ie**

Font Utilities

Do you go to bed every night worried that you have duplicate fonts scattered around your hard disk? Do you have trouble keeping track of the huge number of fonts in your collection? Would you like to be able to make a catalog of various fonts? If you are a font-o-phillic, you'll really appreciate how easy and convenient your life will become once you start using these font utilities.

Web:
  http://home.swipnet.se/highsite/programs/prog.html
  http://www.bluefive.pair.com/fontpage.htm
  http://www.mytools.com/myfonts.html

A
B
C
D
E
F
G
H
I
J
K
L
M
N
O
P
Q
R
S
T
U
V
W
X
Y
Z

Foreign Font Archive

This is a huge repository of fonts from around the world. There are many different fonts for a large variety of languages, such as Hebrew, Gaelic, Arabic, Japanese, Cyrillic (Russian), and many more. All of these fonts can be downloaded for free, either as shareware or freeware.

Web:
   http://babel.uoregon.edu/yamada/fonts.html

Free Fonts

There are a large variety of fonts available for free on the Net. Here are some resources from which you can download a large variety of different fonts. When you have a spare moment, these are great places to browse to find a new and interesting font (say, to give to your wife or husband for an anniversary present).

Web:
   http://www.fontface.com/fonts/
   http://www.fontfreak.com/
   http://www.fontparadise.com/
   http://www.fontpool.com/
   http://www.netmegs.com/koncepts/freefont.htm
   http://www.reflectdesign.com/bvfonts/fonts9.shtml
   http://www.thefreesite.com/Free_Fonts/

As Shakespeare once said, "There are more fonts on the Web and on the Net, Horatio, than are dreamt of in your philosophy." That's fine for Horatio: he could borrow Shakespeare's font collection whenever he wanted.

But how do ordinary people like you and I find the fonts we need?

We use the **Free Fonts** sites.

History of Fonts and Typography

How did typography begin? Who developed the first fonts? What is the real story behind serif and sans serif? If you work with fonts and typography, you'll enjoy reading about the history of your profession. There's a lot more to it than most people appreciate.

Web:
   http://nwalsh.com/comp.fonts/FAQ/cf_28.htm
   http://www.webreference.com/dlab/9802/

Truetype Fonts

Truetype is a family of fonts that was originally developed by Apple. They developed these fonts for two reasons. (1) They didn't want to have to pay royalties to the owners of existing fonts. (2) They wanted to fix some of the technical problems in Adobe Type 1 fonts. The Truetype family was designed to be compact, flexible and extensible. Since Microsoft had been looking for a similar type of font family, Apple agreed to license the technology. Since then, Microsoft has done considerable Truetype development, enhancing the font technology. Today, Truetype fonts will work on any current Microsoft platform or Apple computer.

Web:
   http://developer.apple.com/fonts/TTRefMan/
      index.html
   http://www.truetype.demon.co.uk/

Typography Terminology

The world of typography has a great many technical words and terms. Here are some glossaries that can help you understand these terms. In my experience, knowing what the words mean counts for a lot. So the next time someone (say, your manager) acts like he or she knows more than you do, you can say, "Well, I can do it your way if you really want, but the glyphs in that particular typeface will force me to use slightly different kerning which may change the lines by a few points."

Web:
   http://www.nwalsh.com/comp.fonts/FAQ/cf_18.htm
   http://www.sos.com.au/files/glosray.html

Unusual Fonts

Are you a font hog? Do you love collecting all types of fonts until your disk is full? If so, I think you'll enjoy these Web sites. You will find unusual offerings, free for the downloading, that only a real font hog could appreciate.

Web:
 http://fonts.tom7.com/
 http://www.fontsavvy.com/eccentric.html
 http://www.fontsnthings.com/
 http://www.gothic.net/~tygre/
 http://www.katgyrl.com/fonts/

FOOD AND DRINK

Beer

Making, choosing and imbibing: these discussion groups will help you find out everything you want to know about beer and related beverages. Read the regular posting on which beers are best, based on the votes of Usenet participants. (Anyone can vote, although you do have to supply your own beer.) On the Web you will find more beer information than you can shake a handful of beer nuts at.

Web:
 http://www.allaboutbeer.com/
 http://www.beerhunter.com/
 http://www.beerinfo.com/
 http://www.beerme.com/
 http://www.hal-pc.org/~hkaspar/
 http://www.realbeer.com/

Usenet:
 alt.beer
 alt.beer.alt
 alt.drinks.beer
 rec.crafts.brewing
 rec.food.drink.beer

Beer Ratings

So many beers, so little time. If you feel too overwhelmed to go taste test all the beers in the world yourself, don't worry. Some guys on the Net have done a lot of the work for you. Read their beer ratings and see what they say to try and what to avoid.

Web:
 http://www.beerismylife.com/beerlist.shtml
 http://www.beerme.com/beerlist.shtml

Beverages

Unless you drink only water, somewhere, sometime, you are a consumer of commercial beverages. As such, you have my personal guarantee that there is something, somewhere, on the Net that will interest you. We all know that the world is full of fanatics, but it doesn't really hit home until you see something like these Web sites: someone has used enormous amounts of time and energy (and a fair amount of talent) to create entire Web sites devoted to beverages. Check it out for yourself. While you are there, take the beverage purity test to see how beverage savvy you are. (I rated 17 percent, which puts me in the third lowest category.)

Web:
 http://www.bevnet.com/
 http://www.coldbacon.com/drinks.html

Usenet:
 alt.drinks.snapple
 alt.fan.dr-pepper
 alt.fan.ok-soda
 alt.soda.moxie
 rec.food.drink.tea

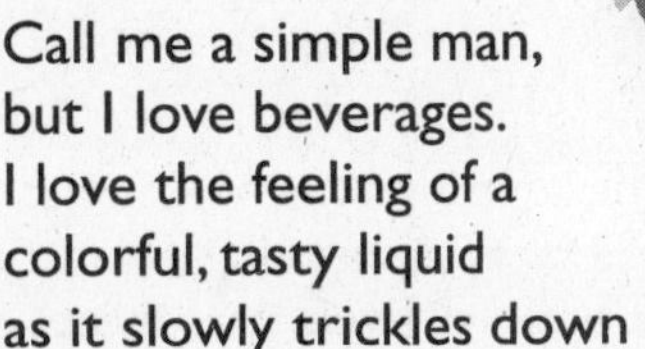
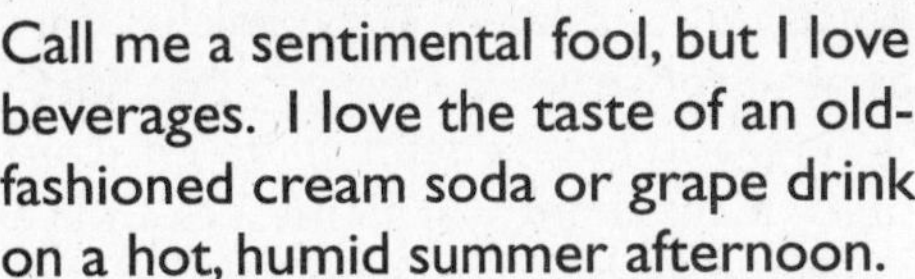

BEVERAGES

Call me a simple man, but I love beverages. I love the feeling of a colorful, tasty liquid as it slowly trickles down the old gullet.

Call me a sentimental fool, but I love beverages. I love the taste of an old-fashioned cream soda or grape drink on a hot, humid summer afternoon.

Call me an unsophisticated rustic, but I love beverages. I love the fragrance and bite of fresh apple juice with a piece of rye bread and some mild cheddar cheese.

Cereal

Cereal is not just for the first meal of the day. In fact, it's more than just nutrition and sustenance—it's fun, and if you read the box, you could even call it a literary adventure. More than that, it's a facilitator of a great social experience by bringing people together on the Net to talk about how cereal makes an impact on all our lives. Don't be left out of the cereal movement. Grab a spoon and dig in.

Web:
  http://lib.stat.cmu.edu/DASL/Datafiles/Cereals.html
  http://www.emptybowl.com/
  http://www.freerecipe.org/breakfast/cereals/

Usenet:
  alt.cereal

Cheese

If you like cheese, even just in passing, you *must* spend some time at this Web site. You will find much information about the cheeses of the world: how they are made, what they are made of, where they are made, what wines go well with particular cheeses, history of cheese, how to make cheese, a cheese glossary, and more.

Web:
  http://cheesenet.wgx.com/
  http://www.cheese.com/
  http://www.ilovecheese.com/

Usenet:
  alt.cheese

Coca-Cola

You can pooh-pooh the contributions of America to world culture, but there is no gainsaying the fact that Coca-Cola has virtually defined the concept of ubiquity. It would be difficult to find anything as well-known as this peripatetic soft drink, so I'm sure it comes as no surprise when I tell you that the Coke fanatics of the world have a definite presence on the Net. If you have any interest at all in Coca-Cola and its social accoutrements, here are some Internet resources to help you explore this beacon of international culture, clearly the most important beverage in the refrigerator of American hegemony.

Web:
  http://www.icubed.com/~colagrrl/
  http://xenon.stanford.edu/~liao/cokestory.html

Usenet:
  alt.food.coca-cola
  alt.food.cocacola

Cocktails

It is interesting that so much of our popular culture has been developed around the acts of creating, mixing and drinking alcoholic beverages. Can you think of any other drug that has specially trained people (bartenders) whose sole purpose is to create and serve a large number of different preparations (cocktails) based on that one particular drug? Do you not think it's interesting that alcohol companies spend huge amounts of money to promote an image for their particular version of this drug? Would I be a spoilsport if I pointed out that the main reason one administers alcohol to oneself is to cause one's brain cells to act abnormally in a way that makes one feel good? I guess that would be too much, so forget I said it. In fact, forget all of this. Just enjoy these cocktails Web sites and drink up.

Web:
  http://www.barnonedrinks.com/index/cocktails/
  http://www.drinkboy.com/
  http://www.mrlucky.com/html/b_cocktails.htm
  http://www.webtender.com/

Usenet:
  alt.drinks.scotch-whisky

Coffee

Some people like to sip it; some gulp it down in the morning before their eyes are open. Some people like to have it flavored and run through various elaborate preparations which result in a thick, syrupy brew or a decadent foamy concoction. And then there are the hardcore people who don't bother brewing and simply munch on the beans themselves. If your drug of choice is coffee, you will feel right at home in these Usenet groups where people talk about preparation, storage, growth and sale of this popular beverage. The Web sites offer the perfect reading material for your coffee break.

Web:
  http://www.coffeefaq.com/coffaq.htm
  http://www.coffeekid.com/
  http://www.coffeereview.com/
  http://www.cupocoffee.com/pages/facts.htm
  http://www.espressoparts.com/faq/index.html
  http://www.ineedcoffee.com/

Usenet:
  alt.coffee
  alt.food.coffee
  rec.food.drink.coffee

College Food

Ah, those good old college days. How nostalgic we will be when our hair turns silver and we wax eloquent about mystery meat burgers and the blue-green algae surprise. Come on in and discuss college dining halls, cafeterias, and pay-for-it-even-if-you-don't-want-it food plans.

Usenet:
 alt.college.food

Diners

In 1872, a fellow named Walter Scott began selling small food items from the back of a covered freight wagon in Providence, Rhode Island. From that inauspicious beginning came the tradition of diners: prefabricated restaurants that feature counter service, booths, and basic American foodstuff served fast and cheap. Diners are the last surviving, authentic bastions of romance in the lexicon of American food service, a place to hang out and talk the night away while enjoying the ambience of genuine American blue-collar probity.

Web:
 http://www.dinercity.com/
 http://www.dinermuseum.org/links.html
 http://www.two-lane.com/diners.html

Epicurious

Epicurious is an online magazine dedicated to the three major areas of culinary enjoyment: eating, drinking, and playing with your food. I find the articles imaginative and well worth a regularly scheduled look. My suggestion is to poke into the Web site once a week to see if anything new and exciting has arrived. You will find reviews, recipes, food commentary, wine information and—my favorite—complaints about stupid food.

Web:
 http://www.eat.epicurious.com/

Fast Food

Fast food refers to cheap food that is sold, prepared, and served to you within several minutes. Fast food is usually bought at a franchised outlet, which, as often as not, allows you to order, receive and devour the food all without leaving your car. Fast food outlets tend to standardize their offerings. For example, a Big Mac (multi-layer hamburger with secret sauce) will look, feel and taste pretty much the same from one McDonalds to the next. (Actually, if the carefully trained employees prepared your Big Mac correctly, it will look, feel and taste *exactly* the same.) Since the cost of fast food is reasonable and there is no real wait, such restaurants are a favorite of busy parents everywhere. If you are a fast food buff or buffette, and you want to share your ersatz culinary experiences and opinions, what better place could there be than the Net: the home of fast, cheap, simple, satisfying experiences?

Web:
 http://www.dietriot.com/fff/rest.html
 http://www.kenkuhl.com/fastfood/
 http://www.olen.com/food/
 http://www.utextension.utk.edu/washington/
  junk_food.htm

Usenet:
 alt.food.fast-food
 alt.food.mcdonalds
 alt.food.taco-bell
 alt.mcdonalds

Tell a story to a kid.

Food Labeling Information

The U.S. Food and Drug Administration (FDA) has created a system of labeling requirements for all foods that are sold in the United States. Food labeling requirements control how nutritional information is listed on all packaging. The next time you are in the supermarket, notice how your shopping experience is enhanced by knowing the exact nutritional breakdown of each item you buy (calories, fats, carbohydrates, proteins, vitamins, minerals, and so on). As you are waiting at the checkout stand, you may want to offer a silent moment of thanks to the FDA's Center for Food Safety and Applied Nutrition.

Web:
http://vm.cfsan.fda.gov/label.html
http://www.healthchecksystems.com/label.htm

Food Safety

It is hard to imagine anything with broader public health implications than making sure our food is safe and nutritious. Food requires proper handling at each step of the way, from production and processing, through distribution and final preparation. Here are some excellent resources that will allow you to find whatever information you need about food safety: how to prepare food properly, germs that cause illness, current public health concerns, and much more. As you might imagine, a great deal of food safety regulation and education is done by the government. As you visit these Web sites, I am sure you will appreciate how complex and difficult it is to maintain a system of safe food. Remember this the next time you hear someone complain that government is a waste of money, and people should be left to fend for themselves in the marketplace. Our food safety system works so well, we can take it for granted, but only because other people are working hard on our behalf.

Web:
http://vm.cfsan.fda.gov/~mow/foodborn.html
http://vm.cfsan.fda.gov/~mow/intro.html
http://www.cfsan.fda.gov/~dms/fc01-3.html
http://www.foodsafety.gov/
http://www.fsis.usda.gov/

Usenet:
alt.food.safety

Listserv Mailing List:
List Name: fsnet-l
Subscribe to: listserv@listserv.uoguelph.ca

Food Labeling Information

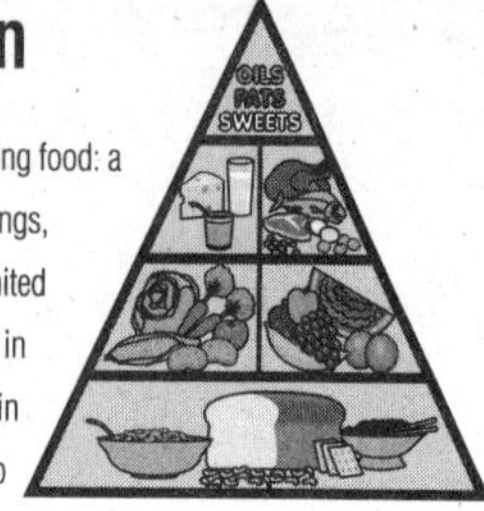

My cat has a simple system when it comes to understanding food: a piece of food is either tuna or it's not tuna. For human beings, however, things are more complicated. To help us, the United States Food and Drug Administration has set up a system in which all prepared foods must carry labels that have certain useful information. If you have any questions as to how to interpret these labels, you can check with the Food Labeling Information Web site, sponsored by the FDA's Center for Food Safety and Applied Nutrition. Or you can use my special alternate system: a piece of food is either chocolate or it's not.

Food Talk and General Discussion

It is universally acknowledged that—out of all the things people put in their mouths in public—food is the most socially acceptable. There is a lot to say about food, and people on the Net are more than glad to say it. If you would like to take part in the discussion, just pull your chair up to the virtual table and join the group. What I like best about the Net is you can talk with your mouth full.

Usenet:
alt.food
rec.food
rec.food.drink
rec.food.equipment
rec.food.marketplace
rec.food.preserving

Listserv Mailing List:
List Name: eat-l
Subscribe to: listserv@listserv.vt.edu

French Fries

Okay, let's be honest for a moment. Is there anything you would rather do, right now, than connect to a hot French fry Web site and indulge yourself? Learn about history, world culture, art, government, little-known facts, foreign customs and the law. All of this from the lowly French fry? It almost sounds too good to be true. (It's not.)

Web:
http://www.csmonitor.com/durable/2000/05/02/
p18s1.htm
http://www.foodreference.com/html/
ffrenchfries.html
http://www.reporternews.com/2000/features/
fries0802.html

Fun Foods

We need to eat just to stay alive, but that doesn't mean we can't have some fun at the same time. We all know that some foods are just naturally more fun than others. For example, a plateful of turkey with cranberry sauce and baked sweet potatoes is serious food—ice cream is fun. A dry red Merlot wine can be a treat to enjoy with your linguini and clam sauce at a pretentious, over- priced Italian restaurant, but for pure enjoyment, Kool-aid is definitely the drink of the people. And ketchup—well, all I can say about ketchup is that anyone who grew up with my brother has enough first- hand experience with the consumption of ketchup to last a lifetime. However, when it comes to appreciating these special foods, eating them is only part of the fun. You should spend at least a few hours a week on Usenet, talking, reading, learning, and generally sharing in the collective experience.

Usenet:
  alt.cake
  alt.drinks.kool-aid
  alt.food.ice-cream
  alt.food.pancakes
  alt.ketchup

Global Gourmet

It's a culinary emergency. Your husband has just called to say that he is bringing home his mother, father and sister for dinner. His mother is from New Zealand, his father is from Poland, and his sister has just spent the last five years living in Mexico. What to do? Turn to the Global Gourmet for international recipes and advice, and within minutes, you are whipping up a wonderful meal of Lamb Turnovers with Curried Yogurt Sauce (New Zealand), Cheese Pascha from Lwow (Poland), and Grilled Snapper with Charred Habanero Salsa (Mexico). Thanks to the Net—and your superior culinary proficiency— the dinner is a complete success, and contentment blankets the family like a gentle rain that falls from the heavens above.

Web:
  http://www.globalgourmet.com/

History of Food

Where do you ask for information on what type of food the peasants ate during the French Revolution? What do you do when the in-laws are due any moment and you need the recipe for figgy pudding? Check out this Usenet discussion group and move forward, into the past.

Usenet:
  rec.food.historic

Homebrewing

Making your own beer can be fun, but you have to know what you are doing. If you are interested in homebrewing, the Net has resources to help you. You can start with the basics—such as, how do you make beer at home?—and work your way up to experimenting with esoteric recipes. Along the way, you can meet other homebrewing enthusiasts around the world and swap tips.

Web:
  http://www.allaboutbeer.com/homebrew/
  http://www.bodensatz.com/homebrew/
  http://www.brewguys.com/
  http://www.ericsbeerpage.com/Beer/Recipe/
     recex2.html
  http://www.hbd.org/brewery/
  http://www.luminet.net/~ssalisbu/

Usenet:
  alt.homebrewing

Majordomo Mailing List:
  List Name: beer
  Subscribe to: majordomo@cuy.net

> I have the rarest Pokémon card in the world. There is only one copy, and I keep it hidden on my Web site.

A B C D E F G H I J K L M N O P Q R S T U V W X Y Z

Junk Food

Every morning, I have a large nutritious breakfast, consisting of (1) a tall glass of fresh vegetable juice made with my own juicer (carrots, celery, cucumber, beets, tomatoes, some cilantro, kale and dandelion greens, all organic), (2) a blended mixture of tomatoes, cucumber, red bell pepper and romaine lettuce, (3) three pieces of fruit, and (4) some fresh nuts. Lunch is a big salad with either beans, fish or tofu. Dinner is a pound of vegetables with a potato, yam or rice, along with (again) beans, fish or tofu. The reason I am telling you this is to explain why I am not qualified to write about junk food. You are on your own.

Web:

   http://www.bbc.co.uk/dna/h2g2/alabaster/A516557
   http://www.dietitian.com/junkfood.html
   http://www.junkfoodnews.com/
   http://www.uihealthcare.com/topics/nutrition/
     nutr4826.html

Mead

Mead is a honey-based fermented beverage that people have been making as long as there have been people (and bees). Traditional mead is made with honey, water and yeast. Other varieties use particular spices and juices. Once you find out about mead, I bet you will be tempted to make some. If so, here are some resources to get you started.

Web:

   http://www.davespicks.com/writing/mme/
     contents.html
   http://www.gotmead.com/
   http://www.hbd.org/brewery/library/meadfaq.html
   http://www.honeywine.com/
   http://www.solorb.com/gfc/mead/

Pasta

Pasta (also known by the lower-class name of macaroni) refers to wheat-flour dough that has been shaped and dried. Pasta is used throughout the world, particularly in Italian cooking. Pasta comes in a variety of forms. However, I am a simple person. My favorite dish is plain old spaghetti and tomato sauce, which, in its leftover incarnation, is also my favorite late-night snack and breakfast food. If you are a pasta-phile, you'll enjoy these Internet resources, where you'll find a huge number of recipes for pasta creations and sauces, as well as a modicum of general pasta-related information. (Hint: When I was in college, I once made a large pot of spaghetti sauce with some friends. I had the adventurous idea of putting in some vanilla. Don't try it. We had to throw away the entire pot.)

Web:

   http://recipes.alastra.com/pasta/default.html
   http://www-2.cs.cmu.edu/~mjw/recipes/pasta/
   http://www.ilovepasta.org/shapes.html
   http://www.pastarecipe.com/

Restaurant Talk and General Discussion

Oh my, we all like to spout off about what is good or bad in the world. Do you have a favorite restaurant you simply must praise? Or did you just spend too much money for a dinner that tasted like warmed-over cardboard, and you feel obliged to warn everyone in the world to avoid? Join the discussion on Usenet, and let the fish and chips fall where they may.

Usenet:
  alt.food.red-lobster
  alt.restaurants
  rec.food.restaurants

Restaurants on the Web

Check out the menus of these fine restaurants on the Web. See their menus, and maybe even fax in your order. You'll find some of the most interesting places to eat in a variety of cities around the world.

Web:
  http://www.chef2chef.net/rank/rest.shtml
  http://www.findagreatrestaurant.com/
  http://www.menus.com/
  http://www.restaurant.com/
  http://www.savvydiner.com/

Sushi

You start with a bowl of misoshiro (miso soup), move on to an appetizer of hijiki (dark, brown seaweed) and grated daikon (white radish), and then settle into a delightful repast of sushi, seasoned with tamari (soy sauce), wasabi (spicy green condiment) and gari (thinly sliced, pink pickled ginger). Don't make the mistake of thinking that sushi is raw fish. (Raw fish is sashimi.) Sushi is a rice-based food, made by taking vinegared rice, rolling it with vegetables, fish, sea food, egg or pickles, and then wrapping the mixture in nori (thin sheets of dried seaweed). Some types of sushi are rolled and sliced into round pieces. Others are shaped into a cone or placed on top of a cylindrical chuck of rice. Yes, some sushi has raw fish, but once you get used to it, it will be your favorite. At the end of your meal, be polite and say to the chef, "Gochi so sama desh-ita". (The accent is on the last syllable.)

Web:
  http://www.bento.com/sushivoc.html
  http://www.sushi.infogate.de/
  http://www.sushilinks.com/
  http://www.sushiref.com/

Usenet:
  alt.food.sushi

Vegans

If it came out of an animal, vegans want no part of it. That means all the rich yummy foods are off limits—butter, milk, cheese and eggs are among the things that will not pass a vegan's lips. Look at the vegan-oriented Web pages, or talk the talk with other vegans on the Net.

Web:
  http://www.all4vegan.net/
  http://www.vegan.com/
  http://www.vegansociety.com/

Listserv Mailing List:
  List Name: vegan
  Subscribe to: listserv@maelstrom.stjohns.edu

Listserv Mailing List:
  List Name: vsxe
  Subscribe to: listserv@listserv.heanet.ie

Majordomo Mailing List:
  List Name: vegan-list
  Subscribe to: majordomo@helsinki.fi

Vegetarian Resources

The word "vegetarian" was first used in England in 1847 by the people who started the Vegetarian Society of the United Kingdom. Today, vegetarianism covers a wide variety of eating choices. Some people simply avoid meat, but eat eggs, dairy products and fish. (Technically, you could call such people ovo-lacto pescetarians.) Other people eat only fruits and vegetables and nothing else (true vegetarians). Some will eat eggs (ovo vegetarians), or dairy products (lacto vegetarians), or both (ovo-lacto vegetarians). Other vegetarians are very strict, avoiding the use of any animal products whatsoever including non-food products (vegans). Perhaps the most strict are those people who will only eat foods that can be harvested without killing the plant (fruitarians).

Web:
  http://www.cs.unc.edu/~barman/vegetarian.html
  http://www.vegweb.com/
  http://www.vrg.org/

Vegetarian Talk and General Discussion

A vegetarian will say, "I eat in a way that makes sense to me, in order to preserve my day-to-day vitality and maintain my long-term health." A non-vegetarian will say, "Is it worth living forever if you can't have a hot dog?" This debate seems to be the central nutritional issue of our times, and here are some places to talk about it. Share your vegetable-oriented opinions, thoughts, hopes, dreams and recipes with vegetarians all over the world.

Usenet:

rec.food.veg
rec.food.veg.cooking

Listserv Mailing List:

List Name: veggie-info
Subscribe to: listserv@listserv.rice.edu

Listserv Mailing List:

List Name: veglife
Subscribe to: listserv@listserv.vt.edu

Wine

Tired of the pedestrian charms of beer? Move up to the big time where drinking is an art form and 1983 was a good year. Join the Bacchus society, wine lovers extraordinaire, learn to appreciate the best in bouquet, taste and color, and maybe even make your own homemade wine. Beer lovers of the world, unite with the oenophiles: you have nothing to lose but your grains.

Web:

http://www.dailywine.com/
http://www.demystifying-wine.com/
http://www.intowine.com/
http://www.wine-lovers-page.com/

Usenet:

alt.food.wine
rec.crafts.winemaking

Listserv Mailing List:

List Name: enology
Subscribe to: listserv@listserv.tamu.edu

Listserv Mailing List:

List Name: foodwine
Subscribe to: listserv@listserv.cmich.edu

Wine Zines

When you are sitting in the study rolling a little vino around on your tongue and you need some interesting reading material, check these great wine zines on the Net. Whether you are a seasoned wine taster or a novice, you will find these Web pages highly agreeable with robust content and balanced, supple designs.

Web:

http://www.bpe.com/studios.htm
http://www.marksquires.com/index2.htm
http://www.winedine.co.uk/
http://www.winesandvines.com/

FREEDOM

ACLU

The ACLU is the American Civil Liberties Union. Its charter is to protect American constitutional rights even when everyone else is asleep at the political switch. You may not always agree with the ACLU, but I guarantee that you will always have an opinion. Its Web site contains speeches, publications, reports, legislative alerts, Supreme Court filings, and other information from the land of the generally free and occasionally brave.

Web:

http://www.aclu.org/

Amnesty International

Amnesty International is an international organization dedicated to three main principles: (1) the release of prisoners of conscience, (2) prompt and fair trials for political prisoners, and (3) opposition to torture, the death penalty and other inhumane treatment of prisoners. Although your neighborhood may be relatively quiet, there is still unrest in much of the world and more than a few people in authority who aren't very nice.

Web:
  http://www.amnesty.org/

Banned Books

The only thing worse than a banned book is two banned books. Unfortunately, banning books did not die out with Hitler and the Nazis. Today, even in the U.S., there are still people who are trying to ban books that challenge their particular political and social agendas. Find out more about it on the Net. You will be surprised how many books have been banned over the years. Moreover, since you are on the Net where everything can be linked to something else, you can not only learn about the banned books, you can, in many cases, read them on your own screen, in the privacy of your own home.

Web:
  http://digital.library.upenn.edu/books/
    banned-books.html
  http://onlinebooks.library.upenn.edu/
    banned-books.html
  http://www.ala.org/bbooks/
  http://www.banned-books.com/

Censorship of the Internet

Traditionally, the Net has been without organized censorship. There has, of course, always been censorship. However, it is at the local level. Now that the Net has become an important and prominent part of our global culture, there are those who would love to impose their will on everyone else by fiat. Here are some Web sites that will keep you up to date on what is happening on the Net censorship-wise.

Web:
  http://www.eff.org/censorship/
  http://www.peacefire.org/
  http://www.personal.dis.strath.ac.uk/control/

Censorship Talk and General Discussion

The antidote to censorship is free and open discussion. That is what this Usenet group is devoted to: a frank discussion of censorship and current events. Hint: If you want to participate, be prepared to argue.

Usenet:
  alt.censorship

Censorware

At first, it seemed like a good idea (to some people anyway). Instead of censoring the Net, someone could create software to block objectionable Web sites. Parents could then choose to use such software on their home computers, thereby preserving their children's innocence. However, like many good ideas, this one got blown out of proportion by zealous fanatics, to the point where the Web site-blocking programs are now referred to as "censorware". The censor companies started blocking all kinds of stuff that had nothing to do with Sex, Violence and other Bad Things: there are now secret blacklists that have definite political overtones.

Web:
  http://www.eff.org/censorship/Censorware/
  http://www.epic.org/free_speech/censorware/

Digital Freedom Network

Because the Internet can bypass traditional means of censorship and disseminate information efficiently over wide areas, it can be a powerful medium for social change. In particular, the Net is proving to be indispensable when it comes to freedom. The Digital Freedom Network (DFN) uses the Internet to promote human rights around the world. If you are interested in learning how the newest technology of the Information Age is being used for activism, start here.

Web:
  http://www.dfn.org/

It takes a real man to read "Women".

Flag Burning

In the United States, the issue of having the freedom to burn the flag is so emotional as to be almost incomprehensible to people in other countries. In some countries, no one would dare even think about burning a flag. In other countries, no one would be bothered. In the U.S., however, the flag is an emotionally charged icon and being able to burn it is an important freedom, almost as if America is proud of the fact that the country is so free that its people are allowed to destroy and denigrate one of its most sacred symbols. The issue, of course, is symbolic. Should a person have the right to do something that many people find offensive, even if the act poses no immediate danger to anyone? Few Americans actually want to burn a flag, but many do want to preserve the freedom to do so. If you would like to understand the issues, try this Web site. As you are reading, you can personally participate by choosing whether or not to burn a virtual flag.

Web:

http://www.esquilax.com/flag/
http://www.immigration-usa.com/flags/new8/
    flag_burning_1.html

Freedom of Expression

In my opinion, the fundamental ideas regarding freedom of expression are best expressed by the First Amendment of the Constitution of the United States: "Congress shall make no law respecting an establishment of religion, or prohibiting the free exercise thereof; or abridging the freedom of speech, or of the press; or the right of the people peaceably to assemble, and to petition the Government for a redress of grievances." Although this particular quotation refers specifically to the U.S., freedom of expression is an issue all over the world. Here are some Web sites that will lead you to a great many related resources all over the Net: the law, civil liberties, censorship, government, and much more.

Web:

http://insight.mcmaster.ca/org/efc/pages/chronicle/
    censor.html
http://www.freeexpression.org/
http://www.mit.edu:8001/activities/safe/

Freedom of Information Act

The United States' Freedom of Information Act (FOIA) was signed into law on July 4, 1966. The purpose of the FOIA was to establish the right of the public to obtain information from agencies of the federal government. Since then, every state has established its own laws to provide similar access to state records. In theory, the FOIA is a wonderful piece of legislation, opening the doors of the government to public scrutiny. In practice, there are problems due to inadequate funding and technical regulations. If you are interested in requesting information under the FOIA, these resources will provide you with the information you need.

Web:

http://www.aclu.org/library/foia.html
http://www.spj.org/foia.asp

Freedom of Religion

Almost by definition, belief in one particular religion precludes belief in another religion. Religions deal with matters of utmost importance to human beings: the existence of a supernatural being (or beings), morality and the law, what happens after death, the reasons for our existence, as well as our responsibilities toward society as a whole and toward individual people. Every religion believes that its scriptures and customs are the best (that is, true). However, history has proven over and over that when one religion dominates within a country or region, that group tends to use its power to oppress members of other religions. For this reason, the United States (and other countries) specifically enshrined in law the right for every person to practice religion (or to be without religion) as he or she sees fit. Such rights—perhaps by their very nature—are continually under attack, especially by those who would interpret the law to their advantage.

Web:

http://religiousfreedom.lib.virginia.edu/
http://w3.trib.com/FACT/1st.relig.liberty.html

Freedom of Speech

Free speech does not mean the same to everybody. As we all find out eventually, it is often the case that my freedom ends where yours begins. For this reason, there is really no such thing as complete freedom of speech. Instead, there is only an eternal debate over what should be allowed and what should be disallowed. Although many people like to think that the idea of free speech can be considered a simple issue, there are many gray areas and, somehow, even in the United States—where freedom of speech is guaranteed by the Constitution—the line between right and wrong seems to always be moving. Here are a large number of free-speech-related resources on the Net. I was surprised at how much information is available.

Web:
  http://www.aclu.org/issues/freespeech/hmfs.html
  http://www.freedomforum.org/first/
  http://www.freeexpression.org/freespeech/
    freespeech02.htm

Usenet:
  alt.freespeech

Listserv Mailing List:
  List Name: amend1-l
  Subscribe to: listserv@listserv.uark.edu

Gun Control

Gun control—restricting people's access to guns—is an issue everywhere, but nowhere is the debate as disputatious as in the United States. Technically, the American debate is rooted in the language of the Second Amendment to the U.S. Constitution: "A well regulated militia, being necessary to the security of a free state, the right of the people to keep and bear arms, shall not be infringed." It's easy to see how this can be interpreted two ways. If you are against gun control, you can point out that this amendment clearly enshrines the right of all Americans to "keep and bear arms". If you feel that guns should be controlled, you can argue that the amendment is irrelevant because it speaks only to the need of maintaining a "well regulated militia", and not any other uses of firearms.

Web:
  http://www.csgv.org/
  http://www.gunowners.org/

Usenet:
  talk.politics.guns

Human Rights

Although we talk a lot about human rights, the idea is relatively new. On December 10, 1948, the United Nations General Assembly unanimously adopted the Universal Declaration of Human Rights. This was the first time a declaration signed by more than one country mentioned the idea of human rights by name. Think about that: it was barely half a century ago.

Web:
  http://www.etown.edu/vl/humrts.html
  http://www.hrw.org/
  http://www.human-rights.net/
  http://www.humanrights.de/index_en.html
  http://www.universalrights.net/
  http://www1.umn.edu/humanrts/

Usenet:
  soc.rights.human

Listserv Mailing List:
  List Name: hraction
  Subscribe to: listserv@netpals.lsoft.com

Listserv Mailing List:
  List Name: humrts-l
  Subscribe to: listserv@listserv.american.edu

Majordomo Mailing List:
  List Name: asylum-l
  Subscribe to: majordomo@www2.ufsia.ac.be

Liberty Web

This is the place to look if you want to find out what the fanatics are doing to protect our freedom (even though, goodness knows, as one of my readers you are anything but a fanatic).

Web:
  http://jim.com/
  http://www.free-market.net/

To walk far, start off slowly.

Naturism and Freedom

Naturism is the philosophy that it is healthy and desirable for human beings to spend a significant amount of time naked, often in the company of other people. Most of us are taught that being naked in front of other people is bad, and so we sublimate our feelings by snickering at the very idea of nudism. So when I tell you that naturists are under attack from various people and organizations, I understand if you feel like ignoring the whole thing ("Surely we have more important matters to worry about") or perhaps even make a joke ("Did you hear about the blind man at a nudist colony?"). However, when an isolated beach is closed to nudism because some local community pressure group is offended by the idea of people being allowed to be naked in a secluded area, the issue should concern all of us. Being naked—in an appropriate place—is a harmless activity, and the people who would deny that freedom to naturists are just as ready to deny other, more vital freedoms to you and me. In my opinion, when you hear the bell of oppression anywhere, at any time, you don't have to ask for whom it tolls.

Web:

  http://www.enaturist.com/resources/
  http://www.nac.oshkosh.net/

United Nations Agreements on Human Rights

When it comes to freedom, some of the most important documents are those adopted by the United Nations: Universal Declaration of Human Rights, Covenant on Civil and Political Rights, Covenant on Economic, Social and Cultural Rights, Convention Against Torture, Convention Against Genocide, Geneva Conventions, Convention on the Rights of the Child, Convention on the Elimination of Discrimination Against Women, and the original 1945 Charter of the United Nations.

Web:

  http://www.magnacartaplus.org/uno-docs/

FUN

Anagrams

Anagrams are something you can do no matter where you are or what is going on. For instance, if you're in traffic and there is nothing on the radio but ads for hair replenishing cream, you can make up all sorts of anagrams by rearranging the letters of all of Henry the VIII's wives' names. This will be good practice so when you are at a party and word gets around that you are the county anagram champion you will be able to demonstrate your talents with grace and elegance.

Web:

  http://www.anagramgenius.com/
  http://www.anagrammy.com/
  http://www.wordsmith.org/anagram/

Usenet:

  alt.anagrams

Bubbles

I have a wonderful battery-operated bubble gun, and sometimes when I need to take a break from writing, I will go out on the patio and make some bubbles. Occasionally, my cat will lounge on a nearby railing and sniff at the bubbles as they float by, carried on their upward journey by the cool ocean breeze. If you think you would enjoy being a bubble person, learn about the history of bubbles, how to make bubble tools, and how to create your own bubble solution.

Web:

  http://www.bubbles.org/

Diaries and Journals

There's nothing like the sinful pleasure of snooping where you don't belong. The Web is a great place to be able to stick your nose into people's private lives. With the click of your mouse, you can be finding out who did what, to whom, and why. Just think, if it weren't for these people who have nothing better to do with their time, you would have nothing better to do with *your* time.

Web:

  http://www.diarist.net/
  http://www.diaryland.com/
  http://www.diaryproject.com/
  http://www.digitalexpressions.nu/
  http://www.jade-leaves.com/journal/misc/
    mlist.shtml
  http://www.my-diary.org/
  http://www.opendiary.com/

ANAGRAMS

Rearrange the letters of one or more words into other words, and you have an anagram. For example, the letters of the words "Tom Cruise" can be rearranged to spell "So, I'm cuter".

But that's kid's stuff. Using the nifty, cool, super-deluxe anagram generator, you can get all kinds of nifty, cool, super-deluxe anagrams.

For example, you can rearrange "Henry got her a Sahara bloke." and "Her hot shy arrangeable... A-OK!" to spell "Harley Hahn books are great!"

(And some people still don't understand why the Internet is so important.)

Fortune Telling

Why wonder about the future, when you can find out your fortune right now? Here are some Web sites that will put you in touch with the all-knowing universal spirit. After all, why guess about the days to come, when you can have a computer program guess for you?

Web:
http://www.facade.com/
http://www.kyliedog.com/psychic/
http://www.now2000.com/fortune/

Madlibs

Are you one of those people who likes to fill in the blanks, so much, that you finish other people's sentences as they are talking? Do your friends urge you to go to Logorrhians Anonymous? Is your sense of order offended by empty spaces? If so, you will love Madlibs. Just fill in the blanks by specifying some words, and watch how they are woven into a cute story before your very ears.

Web:
http://www.madlibs.org/
http://www.zooass.com/madlibs/

A B C D E F G H I J K L M N O P Q R S T U V W X Y Z

Mind Breakers

Is your life uneventful? Is your job a bore? If so, there is no need to go through the day without a mental challenge. Just explore these mind games, puzzles and riddles, and get ready to be perplexed, frustrated and amazed. For some extra stimulation, try the Usenet discussion group.

Web:
  http://www.brainbashers.com/
  http://www.braingle.com/
  http://www.e-fun.nu/mindbreakers/files.htm

Usenet:
  alt.brain.teasers

Mystery Solving

Got a few minutes? Here are short mysteries you can try to solve whenever you have a spare moment. There are new stories posted every week, so, if you are a mystery buff, you will enjoy visiting this site regularly. To test your skills, take a look at the archive of past mysteries and their solutions.

Web:
  http://www.mysterynet.com/thecase/

Payphone Project

Do you like to talk to strangers in faraway places? If so, this is the Web site for you. The Payphone Project lists the numbers of payphones around the world. When you need a break from the humdrum reality of everyday life, take a few minutes and call a payphone in an exotic location, like the Eiffel Tower in Paris, the subway platform underneath Times Square in New York, or across the street from a popular teenage hangout in Hulbert, Oklahoma.

Web:
  http://www.payphone-project.com/

> **The fat lady has sung.
> (You may go.)**

> **There must be fifty ways
> to love your liver. (See
> the "Medicine"
> sections for details.)**

Quizzes and Surveys

When you read a magazine that has one of those quizzes ("How compatible are you and your significant other?"), do you always answer the questions? If so, you'll love spending your time at these sites, taking various quizzes, only some of which are serious. Once you work your way through the quizzes, you can visit their more self-righteous cousins, the surveys and opinion polls.

Web:
  http://tests.studentcenter.org/index_test.php
  http://www.allthetests.com/fun.php3
  http://www.davideck.com/
  http://www.helpself.com/quiz.htm

Usenet:
  alt.usenet.surveys

Tinwhistles

The tinwhistle, also called the pennywhistle, is a low-cost 6-hole fipple flute. (With a fipple flute, you blow into a mouthpiece at one end of the instrument. Compare it to a regular flute which has a mouthpiece on the side of the instrument which you blow across.) There are two fun things about tinwhistles: they are cheap (in fact, cheaper tinwhistles are better than expensive ones), and they are easy to play. Like any musical instrument, it takes practice and talent to play a tinwhistle well, and you can meet such accomplished people on the Net. However, if you just want to make a vague musical noise and pester as many people as possible (something you won't understand unless you were ever a boy), a tinwhistle is the instrument of choice.

Web:
  http://www.chiffandfipple.com/

Web Soap Operas

I don't watch television, so I miss out on the portion of the popular culture having to do with the daily lives of imaginary people having imaginary trials and tribulations in imaginary places. However, on the Net, I can tune into a Web-based soap opera whenever I want. I don't have to wait for a particular time of day, and I don't have to be interrupted by commercials.

Web:
> http://www.101hollywood.com/
> http://www.episodicreview.com/
> http://www.skyfalls.com/
> http://www.webisodiczine.com/

Weblogs

A weblog, or blog, is a site, maintained by one person, that documents his or her explorations around the Web. A typical blog offers many links along with annotations and personal comments. If you are bored and looking for something new under the Internet sun, take a look at a few blogs. I guarantee you'll find something interesting. (Simply think of all the blog creators as being your own personal Internet researchers.) If you are the type of person who likes to explore and share, why not create a blog of your own? You will be surprised at how attractive you will suddenly become to the opposite sex.

Web:
> http://www.blogger.com/
> http://www.larkfarm.com/weblog_madness.htm
> http://www.plasticbag.org/
> http://www.robotwisdom.com/weblogs/
> http://www.weblogs.com/

Weird Sites

We all know there are weird people on the Net, but until you visit this Web site, you can't appreciate the full extent of mankind's eccentricity. Browse through this wacko-inspired craziness, and it won't be long till you start wondering if Man is really Nature's last word.

Web:
> http://www.now2000.com/weird/

GAMES AND PUZZLES

Backgammon

Backgammon is played by two players using a specially marked board, 15 counters and a set of dice. You take turns throwing the dice and moving your counters around the board according to the numbers on the dice. When a counter reaches the end of the circuit, you remove it. The object of the game is to be the first person to remove all your counters from the board. It sounds easy, but there's lots of strategy involved. Backgammon is the oldest game in recorded history; historians even believe it was played in ancient Mesopotamia. Today, backgammon is as popular as ever, and if you would like to play, learn or talk about it, there are lots of resources on the Net. Or you can go to Mesopotamia and find someone to play in person. (Driving instructions: Head toward central Asia, make a left at the Persian Gulf, and go back 3,000 years.)

Web:
   http://www.backgammonbar.com/
   http://www.bkgm.com/
   http://www.gammonvillage.com/
Usenet:
   rec.games.backgammon

Backgammon with Strangers

These days you have to be careful who you mix with. Playing backgammon in person presents all kinds of potential problems. For example, someone might sneeze on you and give you pneumonia, or your opponent could get mad and stab you with an ice pick.

Much better to play it safe: connect to the *Backgammon Server* where you can depend on the kindness of strangers. Moreover, you can play in your underwear and no one will care.

Battleship

In World War II, radio operators invented the game of Battleship in order to test radio transmissions that were kept secret from the Japanese. The operators were only allowed a few tests a day, so they developed a game that they played, a bit at a time, over a matter of weeks. And now you can play the same game (without waiting) on the Internet.

Web:
   http://scv.bu.edu/~aarondf/java/battleship.html
   http://www.justit.net/battleship/

Blackjack

If you can't make it to a casino this weekend, this is the next best thing. Play Blackjack with other Internet folks and become a Net billionaire or downright penniless. There are help files available and records are kept of rankings, cash won and lost, top players, and other table statistics. Join the table today.

Web:
   http://www.allaboutblackjack.com/
   http://www.blackjackinfo.com/
   http://www.hitorstand.com/

Board Game Rules

Strictly speaking, it is not in the rules that, when you land on Free Parking, you are allowed to collect all the money in the middle of the board. (In fact, there isn't even supposed to be any money in the middle of the board.) Still, that's the way everyone I know plays Monopoly. Nonetheless, the actual rules can come in handy, especially if you need an authority to back you up when you know you are right and everyone else is wrong. (If only the rest of life were as simple.)

Web:
   http://www.centralconnector.com/games/
      gamecab.html
   http://www.everyrule.com/boardgames_az_list.html
   http://www.gamecabinet.com/deeperDrawers/
      RulesTranslationsEnglish.html
   http://www.gamesters.org/library.html

Board Games

I've spent a lot of pleasant hours playing board games, and I bet you have too. What better way to spend an evening than getting into a heated game of Monopoly or Risk or Diplomacy or Clue, and beating the pulp out of your best friend? So, board game lovers of the world, here are some resources for you to enjoy: lots of information about lots of games. I have also included a Web site with some new games you may want to try, as well as a site that has the official rules of Monopoly. If you want to talk to other enthusiasts, check out the Usenet discussion groups. The **marketplace** group is for buying and selling; the other groups are for general discussion.

Web:
http://www.boardgamecentral.com/
http://www.faqs.org/faqs/games/board-games-faq/
http://www.gamereport.com/links/
http://www.gamingdumpster.com/catbrowse.htm

Usenet:
rec.games.board
rec.games.board.ce
rec.games.board.marketplace
rec.games.chinese-chess
rec.games.diplomacy
rec.games.go
rec.games.mahjong

Bridge

Bridge is such a fun game for couples. Most men take up bridge when they get married and discover their wives won't let them watch football. The only thing left to do is to sit with another couple and play cards all night. Perfect your bridge skills so you can learn to play a killer game. If you're clever, you can even make it a contact sport so you won't miss football.

Web:
http://www.bridgetalk.com/
http://www.greatbridgelinks.com/
http://www.math.auc.dk/~nwp/bridge/
http://www.thehouseofcards.com/bridge.html

Usenet:
rec.games.bridge
rec.games.bridge.okbridge

Well, it's time to write another advertisement and my editor suggested I write one about the game of bridge. Actually, I don't normally even think of it as a game, per se. More like a thing that you build, or perhaps even a structure. Okay, it's important to have bridges –after all, if we didn't have any bridges, all the cars on the highway would just fall off into nothingness, and you wouldn't be able to get across rivers and things –but still, I hardly see where that qualifies as a game. And I'm dashed if I can figure out why anyone wanted me to write an ad for the "game" of bridge. I mean, I know that there are people out there who build bridges and roads and things, civil engineers and what not, but why anyone would think that belongs in an Internet book, or why it requires an advertisement... What's that? You don't mean building bridges? You mean the card game? Do you mean all that stuff with spades and hearts and two no-trump and so on? Oh... *that* bridge game. Oh... Never mind.

Card Game Rules

You are at a party and you meet a Very Attractive Person of the Opposite Sex. After an hour or so of conversation, the VAPOTOS invites you over for a visit. When you get there, the VAPOTOS suggests a quick game of "52 Card Pick-up". Unfortunately, the game is new to you, so you have to decline the invitation and go home. Too bad you hadn't checked with the Net first.

Web:
http://www.pagat.com/alpha.html
http://www.thehouseofcards.com/rules.html

Chess

The attraction of chess is that it requires intense concentration in order to dominate in a highly competitive environment in which chance plays virtually no part whatsoever (much like being a professional Internet writer). The game symbolizes warfare, in that the strategy is to capture as many of the opponent's "men" (pieces) as possible. Unlike real warfare, the game ends when the King has been captured ("checkmate"). If you are a chess aficionado, or even a beginner, there are lots of chess-related places on the Net to visit. You can learn about the game, play the game, or talk about the game (sort of an allegory for Life).

Web:

    http://www.chess-poster.com/
    http://www.chesscenter.com/twic/twic.html
    http://www.chesscorner.com/
    http://www.chessgoddesses.com/
    http://www.freechess.org/
    http://www.uschess.org/clife/current/

Usenet:

    rec.games.chess
    rec.games.chess.analysis
    rec.games.chess.computer
    rec.games.chess.misc
    rec.games.chess.play-by-email
    rec.games.chess.politics

Cribbage

Why work when you can play games? Learn to play cribbage and spend a few frustrating hours trying to beat your computer. Once you get good, you can start playing against other people and join a cribbage club. Everything you need is on the Net.

Web:

    http://www.cribbage.org/
    http://www.cribbageforum.com/cribbageforum/
    http://www.splange.freeserve.co.uk/cribbage.html

Get in step by checking out the "Dance" section.

Crossword Puzzles

Do you like crossword puzzles? There are many, many puzzles on the Net that you can access for free whenever you want. There are also dictionaries, word lists, guides, computer programs, helpful tips, and a great deal of other crossword-related material. Now, if someone would only tell me the three-letter word for an Australian bird, and the two-letter name for the sun god, my life would be complete.

Web:

    http://www.cluemaster.com/
    http://www.crossword-puzzles.co.uk/
    http://www.primate.wisc.edu/people/hamel/cp.html

Usenet:

    rec.puzzles.crosswords

Darts

The basic skill of darts is to throw a small painted object (a dart) at a target (the dartboard), which is marked with different point values. There are literally hundreds of different games. The classic dart game is called 01 ("oh-one"). In 01, each player starts with 501 (or 301 or 601) points. Players alternate, throwing three darts per turn. Whatever points are scored on a turn are subtracted from the player's score, and the winner is the first player to reach zero. This is not as easy as it sounds because, to win, a player must get to zero exactly. Moreover, the final score must be a "double" (a hit in the outside narrow band or in the small bull's-eye). Playing darts skillfully and dependably takes a lot of practice, which often requires a dart aficionado to spend a lot of time in bars, talking to friends and having a good time.

Web:
  http://www.brisdet.com/darts.htm
  http://www.bullseyenews.com/
  http://www.cyberdarts.com/
  http://www.dartall.com/
  http://www.darters.com/

Usenet:
  alt.sport.darts
  alt.sports.darts

Dominoes

You are dreaming. You and 27 other people are wearing black-hooded robes with eye masks. On each robe, there is a rectangle divided into halves, and in each of these halves, there is a pattern of one to six dots, similar to those found on dice. Everything is fine until you look down and notice there are no dots on your robe. You wake up in a sweat, because you have finally realized: if people were dominoes, you would be the double blank.

Web:
  http://www.dominoeslinks.com/
  http://www.dominoesonline.com/
  http://www.gamecabinet.com/rules/
    DominoGames.html
  http://www.humnet.ucla.edu/humnet/french/faculty/
    gans/java/dominoesa.htm
  http://www.xs4all.nl/~spaanszt/Domino_Plaza.html

Fantasy Sports

Do you think you can do better selecting players and managing a sports team than the professionals? Of course you can, so why not prove it? Run your own fantasy sports team and put together a group of players the way *you* want. During the season, the actual performance of your players will be used to calculate how well your fantasy team does. If you end up winning, you can have the satisfaction of knowing that you are smarter than everyone else. (Of course, being one of my readers, you already knew that.)

Web:
  http://fantasy.sportsline.com/
  http://games.espn.go.com/
  http://www.sandbox.com/

Usenet:
  alt.sports.baseball.fantasy
  alt.sports.hockey.fantasy
  rec.sport.baseball.fantasy
  rec.sport.football.fantasy
  rec.sport.pro-wrestling.fantasy

Foosball

Foosball, or table soccer, is played on a coin-operated table that simulates a soccer game. Built into the table are series of rods to which are attached facsimiles of tiny people. You push, pull and turn the rods in such a way that your tiny people "kick" the ball. To score a point, you must knock the ball into your opponent's goal. Foosball is a favorite game in bars but is also played competitively. If you have ever seen good foosball players, you will not forget the experience. The action is fast and requires a lot of skill. Foosball hint: Although it is possible to spin the rods, don't do so. It is not allowed in official competition and, even in a bar, spinning the rods will mark you as a goober who has had too much to drink.

Web:
   http://www.faqs.org/faqs/sports/table-soccer/
   http://www.foosball.com/
   http://www.foosballheaven.com/
   http://www.natsa.org/

Usenet:
   rec.sport.table-soccer

Games for Prizes

Bingo, trivia, crossword puzzles, strategy, logic, card games, guessing games—you can use the Internet, play games, and maybe even win a real prize, all at the same time. Life just doesn't get any better.

Web:
   http://www.boxerjam.com/
   http://www.pogo.com/
   http://www.prizecentral.com/
   http://www.puzzledepot.com/
   http://www.riddler.com/
   http://www.station.sony.com/
   http://www.worldwinner.com/

Hangman

Hangman is a game in which you try to guess a mystery word, one letter at a time. When you guess a correct letter, you are shown where it appears in the word. When you guess a wrong letter, a new feature is added to a drawing of a little man. If the entire little man is drawn before you guess all the letters in the word correctly, you lose, and the little man gets hung. I wonder if this is a feminist game? (I could make a joke about a well-hung little man, but instead, I will content myself with wondering out loud why the game is not called "hangperson".)

Web:
   http://www.allmixedup.com/cgi-bin/hangman/
      hangman
   http://www.ianktaylor.clara.net/hang.html
   http://www.triumphpc.com/hangman/

It's Your Turn

Here are games you play against an opponent, in which you and the other person take turns making a move—for example, chess, battleship, checkers and backgammon. The games are organized so that you send in your move and then wait for your opponent to reply. This means that if you don't have enough time to play a full game at one sitting, you can play one move at a time, over a period of days. Many people have more than one game going at the same time.

Web:
   http://www.itsyourturn.com/

Mazes

The best thing about having your own maze is you always have a good excuse for not doing something on time. ("I'm sorry I can't turn in my homework; my dog took it and dropped it in my maze.") If you are one of the few people who don't have a maze of their very own in the family room, you can at least explore and create mazes over the Net.

Web:
   http://colbleep.ocs.lsumc.edu/
   http://www.astrolog.org/labyrnth/maze.htm
   http://www.freemazes.com/
   http://www.gwydir.demon.co.uk/jo/maze/
   http://www.puzzlemaker.com/
      advmazesetupform.html

Get the news —
now — on the Net.

Mazes

You start by spending an idle minute with a simple maze you see in a children's magazine. ("Can you help Mortimer Monkey find the bunch of bananas?")

"This maze is easy," you say to yourself. "I can solve it in my head."

The next thing you know, you are using the Net to create your own mazes, each one more complex than the last. You tell yourself you can take it or leave it, but one day, when your Internet connection goes down temporarily, you find yourself pacing the room for hours, aimlessly turning to the right and to the left.

If you can't handle getting lost and finding your way out of confusing environments, you had better forget mazes and stick to real life.

Othello

Othello (which is similar to Reversi) is a strategy board game played by a great many people around the world. Othello is played on an 8x8 square by two players, each of whom uses discs which are one color on one side and a different color on the other side (for example, white and black). Each player has his own color. Players alternate moves, putting down a disc (with their personal color face up) in such a way as to try to "outflank" some of the other person's discs. When this happens, the outflanked discs are flipped, changing their color. When the game ends, the winner is the person who has the most discs with his color on the board. Lots and lots of people play Othello. Would you like to try? On the Net you can practice by playing against a computer.

Web:
>   http://www.allmixedup.com/othello/othello.cgi?start
>   http://www.andreazinno.it/
>   http://www.htmlgames.com/styles.htm
>   http://www.mindsports.net/Arena/Othello/

Pinball

Pinball lovers, there is lots of pinball-related information on the Net, as well as a Usenet discussion group for talking to other enthusiasts. By the way, if you are thinking about getting your own machine, do some research before you spend any money.

Web:
>   http://cascade.mit.edu/pins/faq.buy.html
>   http://www.ds.dial.pipex.com/poa/
>   http://www.homepages.paradise.net.nz/~frenzy/
>   pinlinks/
>   http://www.lysator.liu.se/pinball/IPD/
>   http://www.marvin3m.com/fix.htm
>   http://www.pinball.org/

Usenet:
>   rec.games.pinball

Pokémon

Are you acquainted with pikachu, charmander, bulbasaur and squirtle? If so, you're a member in good standing of the worldwide group of Pokémon aficionados. Pokémon started as a Japanese video game, and has since expanded to become a popular cultural phenomenon within the world of kids. Not only are there video games, but trading cards, a TV show and a small plethora of commercial products. The goal in Pokémon is to find and capture various monsters, and then train them. As you train your monsters, they grow and change. Your goal is to become an expert Pokémon trainer. If you like Pokémon and you collect the cards, I suggest that you learn how to play the trading card game: it requires strategy and knowledge, and can add a lot of fun to your Pokémon activities.

Web:
    http://www.pojo.com/pokemon.html
    http://www.pokemon.com/
    http://www.wizards.com/pokemon/

Usenet:
    alt.games.pokemon
    alt.games.pokemon.cards

Pool and Billiards

As a teenager, I spent a large number of hours playing billiards. This was in Canada, where the most popular game was the English game, snooker. Snooker is a lot more complicated than, say, American 8-ball or straight pool, and is often played on large snooker tables (6.5' x 13') with smaller pockets than the American tables. Thus, to me, American pool is watered-down billiards for cowboys and is not much of a challenge. Not that I am a champion, but it is true that my copy editor, Lydia, who is quite a pool player herself, is afraid to play me. I guess that's where the expression comes from: "as dangerous as a Canadian in an American pool hall."

Web:
    http://www.azbilliards.com/
    http://www.bestbilliard.com/rules/game_rules.htm
    http://www.billiardsdigest.com/
    http://www.faqs.org/faqs/sports/billiards/faq/
    http://www.playpool.com/
    http://www.poolplayers.com/
    http://www.thebilliardchannel.com/

Usenet:
    alt.sport.pool
    rec.sport.billiard

Puzzles

Do you like puzzles? There are enough puzzles (and solutions) on the Net to keep you busy indefinitely. But why should you do puzzles? Puzzles are good because they will help you think better. Thinking better turns you into a finer human being. And being a fine human being will help you become good looking, successful and powerful, with just the right amount of humility to make sure you are loved and respected by everyone you meet. (Well, it's always worked for me anyway.)

Web:
    http://www.brainbashers.com/
    http://www.greylabyrinth.com/puzzles.htm
    http://www.jigzone.com/
    http://www.puzz.com/
    http://www.puzzle.dse.nl/index_us.html
    http://www.rec-puzzles.org/

Usenet:
    alt.brain.teasers
    rec.puzzles

Riddle of the Day

Try to solve the riddles and brain teasers posed by the Sphinx. If you can, you get immortalized in the Sphinx Hall of Fame. You can even submit your own sticklers here or browse the archive of past riddles with their answers.

Web:
    http://www.dujour.com:8080/dujour/

The last part of this sentence
has been censored
for national security,
because it XXXXXX has
XXXXXXX to XXX.

Scrabble

Since 1948, people have been looking at little tiles with letters on them, trying to think of words that use those letters. If you like Scrabble, you'll find lots of cool stuff, including Scrabble games that you can play online, and hints and tools to help you play better. (Did you know that the very best Scrabble players average more than 35 points per turn?)

Web:
http://www.boulter.com/scrabble/
http://www.scrabble-assoc.com/
http://www.scrabble.com/
http://www.teleport.com/~stevena/scrabble/
http://www.thepixiepit.co.uk/scrabble.htm

Shogi

Shogi is a two-player Japanese game played on a board with squares. The object of shogi is to capture your opponent's king. (I hear that Camilla Parker Bowles is a great player.) Don't let any of those facts confuse you: shogi is not chess. However, shogi is fun and challenging, and knowing how to play will make you look cultured. (If that fails to work, just walk around with this book under your arm.)

Web:
http://www.chessvariants.com/shogi.html
http://www.computer-shogi.org/index_e.html
http://www.shogi.net/
http://www.stormpages.com/angelom/

Listserv Mailing List:
List Name: shogi-l
Subscribe to: listserv@techunix.technion.ac.il

Sliding Tile Puzzles

Do you remember when you were a kid playing with one of those puzzles with the sliding tiles? You move the tiles around until they are in the correct order (or until you give up in frustration and decide to throw the thing away and go watch TV). Now you can play the same game on the Net. Just one more way in which childhood is becoming electric.

Web:
http://www.allmixedup.com/Slider/

Sliding Tile Puzzles – The Real Truth

Do you want to know the real truth about sliding tile puzzles?

You know, those puzzles that have a number of small pieces that slide up/down and left/right. You move the tiles around and, when you get all the pieces in the right place, you see a picture of some type.

Okay, here's the real scoop.

These puzzles were invented by aliens. They spread the puzzles everywhere and, whenever you work on one, the aliens monitor you with their special observations rays.

You see, the aliens want to take over the Earth and, to do so, they need to control a certain number of human beings. So, at night, the aliens kidnap certain people and implant control mechanisms in their brains. Before dawn, these people are returned with the memory of the whole procedure wiped out. One day, when enough people have been modified in this way, the aliens will activate all the control mechanisms and take control of the Earth.

The thing is, only certain people's brains are suitable for implantation. However, the aliens can tell if you are one of those people by monitoring your brain waves as you try to solve a sliding puzzle.

And now—for the first time—sliding puzzles are starting to appear on the Net.

I don't have to tell you what that means.

Tic Tac Toe

Tic Tac Toe has been called "one of the most useless games ever invented" (by my chief researcher, actually). Maybe so for the traditional 3x3 game, but have you tried playing on a 6x7 grid with 5 in a row needed to win? Play against a computer program that lets you choose the size of the grid and the number of Xs or Os in a row you need to win. You can play the regular 3x3 or try something more adventurous. When you get into higher numbers, it's more fun and a lot more difficult.

Web:
  http://www.boulter.com/ttt/

Tiddlywinks

You have practiced your potting, your squopping, and your pile flips, and you have kept your squidging muscles in good condition by twiddling your thumbs for thirty minutes a day. You are now ready to play tiddlywinks: a complex, competitive partner game of strategy and tactics. Tiddlywinks is played with colored counters (called winks) on a 6 foot by 3 foot felt mat with
an open pot placed in the center. There are four sets (blue, green, red, yellow) of 6 winks (2 large and 4 small). To play, you use a disc called a squidger to press a wink and make it move. The object of the game is to score points (called tiddlies), either by popping winks into the pot or by having your winks completely uncovered at the end of the game.

Web:
  http://www-history.mcs.st-and.ac.uk/~ben/
    tiddlywinks/Lexicon/lex-note.html
  http://www.etwa.org/
  http://www.faqs.org/faqs/games/tiddlywinks/
  http://www.tiddlywinks.org/

Usenet:
  alt.games.tiddlywinks

America's Army

"America's Army" is a computer game bankrolled by the United States Army in an attempt to make the military culture so cool that significant numbers of impressionable, energetic American youths will join the army and do their part for Peace, Justice and the American Way. Parents, you don't have to worry about your kids. The army has been extra careful to be attentive to teenage sensibilities. As one of their spokesmen explained, "We were very careful on the blood thing."

Web:
  http://www.americasarmy.com

Computer Game Resources

There is no need to waste even a minute of your time working, eating, sleeping or talking to other people. Here are enough game resources to keep you busy all day long. You'll find free games, reviews, cheats, and much more.

Web:
  http://pcgame.gamehelp.com/
  http://www.gamerush.com/
  http://www.gamesdomain.com/
  http://www.gamezilla.com/
    reviews.aspx?platform=PC
  http://www.gignews.com/
  http://www.happypuppy.com/
  http://www.mpogd.com/

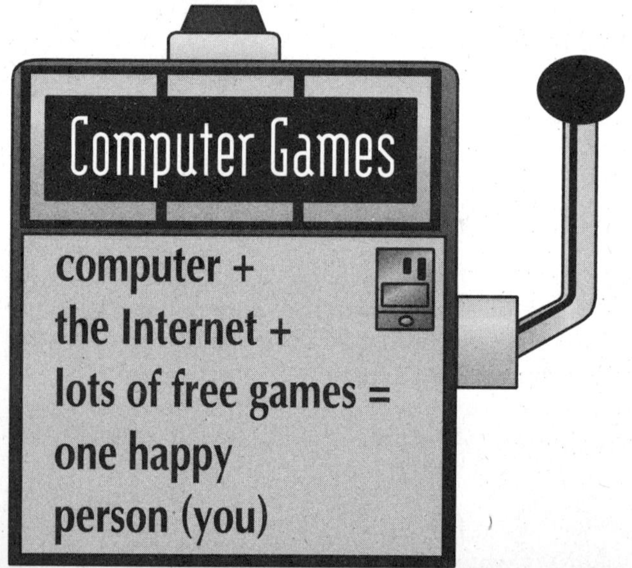

Doom

Why do young men like Doom so much? Because it is so much like real life. You get to travel around surrealistic environments, carrying powerful weapons and shooting at things left and right. But it's not just enough to play Doom. To do it right, you need to become a fanatic. These resources offer everything you need: the official Doom FAQ, tutorials and guides, news, specifications, graphics from the game, great utilities (such as map editors and level creators), and much more.

Web:
   http://www.3dactionplanet.com/doom/
   http://www.doomcenter.com/
   http://www.gamers.org/docs/FAQ/doomfaq/
   http://www.gamers.org/pub/archives/doom/
      periodic/RGCD_FAQ.html

Usenet:
   alt.games.doom
   alt.games.doom.ii
   rec.games.computer.doom.announce
   rec.games.computer.doom.editing
   rec.games.computer.doom.help
   rec.games.computer.doom.misc
   rec.games.computer.doom.playing

IRC:
   #doom (EFnet)

Earth 2025

Here's a Web-based game you can play with nothing more than a browser. Earth 2025 is a strategy/empire building game in which thousands of people can play at the same time. Your goal is to try to create and maintain a strong country that can survive attacks by other players (just like real life). While you are playing, you can chat with other players, keep up with the Earth 2025 news, and check the rankings to see who are the top players. To do well at this game, you don't have to be a fanatic—but it sure helps.

Web:
   http://games.swirve.com/earth/
   http://www.helpmygame.com/

Empire

Here is the home of the famous game of Empire, the real-time strategy war game played by people across the Internet. If you like playing Civilization, you'll love Empire. The Web sites offer everything you need to learn about and start playing this great game.

Web:
   http://www.empire.cx/
   http://www.faqs.org/faqs/games/empire/faq/
   http://www.faqs.org/faqs/games/empire/news/

Usenet:
   rec.games.empire

Emulators and Classic Games

An emulator is a program that causes your computer to act like a different computer or machine. There are programs available for PCs that emulate a variety of old game console systems and arcade games. Once you install such an emulator, you can use it to run the original programs. This means that you can play all manner of classic games on your computer, and when you do, the games behave *exactly* as they did in their original form (because you are running the exact same programs). There are a number of emulators available for free on the Net. One of the most important is MAME (Multiple Arcade Machine Emulator), which can run literally hundreds of different arcade games. (My favorite is Ms. Pacman.) Warning: Don't get started on this stuff unless you have a lot of spare time.

Web:
  http://www.classicgaming.com/
  http://www.emulation.net/
  http://www.emulator-zone.com/
  http://www.game-revolution.com/download/
    emulator/emulator.htm
  http://www.mame.net/
  http://www.retrobase.com/
  http://www.tech-boards.com/
    viewforum.php?forum=19&1

Usenet:
  alt.binaries.emulators.gameboy
  alt.binaries.emulators.neogeo
  alt.binaries.emulators.nintendo
  alt.binaries.emulators.sega
  alt.emulators.classic-arcade
  alt.games.mame
  alt.games.video.emulation
  comp.emulators.game-consoles

> I turned down a job as a talent scout for alien invaders. The pay was good, but I had to wake up early.

> Stay connected.

Game Demos

Games can be a lot of fun, but they also cost money. How do you know which games you want to buy? Simple, just cruise to some of these Web sites, and you can try out all the game demos you want for free. This is a common way for new games to be introduced to the world. I often use game demos to save me from wasting money on games that aren't as much fun as I thought they would be.

Web:
  http://www.demo-files.com/
  http://www.demoland.com/
  http://www.happypuppy.com/

Game Reviews

It is morning. The alarm goes off, and you wake up to find that the world has changed drastically. You feel as if you are on some type of a quest, but you don't know exactly what you are looking for or why you want to find it. As you move around, you have a vague feeling that someone or something is trying to control your actions. As you walk and run from one place to another, strange looking figures pop up and then disappear. You find yourself fighting with strangers, and dodging bullets and knives for no good reason. You feel compelled to run frantically, looking for secret shortcuts. You look down at your hand and see that you are clutching an unusual weapon, one that you have never seen. There is only one thing to do. You summon your will, stiffen the sinews, and fight your way across the living room to your computer. You then start your browser and, as quickly as possible, navigate to a computer game review Web site. The first thing you see is a review of a brand new game that features— you! (Oh, my...)

Web:
  http://www.pcgamereview.com/whatsnew/
    whatsnew.shtml
  http://www.quandaryland.com/
  http://www.videogamereview.com/

Usenet:
  alt.video.games.reviews

Game Search Engines

Do you want to find a particular game? These search engines are where to start. They visit all the major game sites and gaming magazine pages, so when you search for a game by name, you'll find a lot of stuff, including reviews, cheats and tips.

Web:
  http://www.gamerland.com/
  http://www.gamers.com/
  http://www.gamescanner.com/
  http://www.thegw.com/

Gaming News

No matter what your pleasure—Sega, Playstation, PC, whatever—gaming will never be as good as it could be unless you are a fanatic, and to be a fanatic, you're going to have to keep up on all the news. Find out what's new, what's going to be new, and the reality behind the fantasy.

Web:
  http://games.ign.com/
  http://www.avault.com/
  http://www.bluesnews.com/
  http://www.gamefaqs.com/
  http://www.rpgamer.com/

Interactive Fiction

Interactive fiction (IF) is a text-based, role-playing game in which the computer responds to your input and describes your surroundings. The first IF game was probably "Hunt the Wumpus", a Unix game from the early 1970s, in which you move around a dodecahedron-shaped maze, avoiding mysterious dangers in search of a Wumpus, which you must kill before he eats you. (Obviously, some people *did* inhale in the 1970s.) The classic IF was "Adventure", which debuted in 1977. Interactive fiction is a lot of fun. I myself completely mastered Adventure during the summer of 1981 when I had a few months off from medical school.

Web:
  http://www.bang.dhs.org/if/
  http://www.suite101.com/welcome.cfm/
    interactive_fiction
  http://www.wurb.com/if/

Usenet:
  rec.arts.int-fiction
  rec.games.int-fiction

Interactive Fiction

Do you have a couple of days to spare?

Immerse yourself in an Interactive Fiction game and explore an imaginary world where YOU make things happen.

PC Games Talk and General Discussion

If God didn't want us to use our PCs for games, he wouldn't have given us so many games discussion groups. The **.games** and **.misc** groups are for general talk about all types of PC games. The other groups are for particular types of games (**.rpg** means role-playing games).

Usenet:

alt.binaries.warez.ibm-pc.games
alt.warez.ibm-pc.games
comp.sys.ibm.pc.games
comp.sys.ibm.pc.games.action
comp.sys.ibm.pc.games.adventure
comp.sys.ibm.pc.games.flight-sim
comp.sys.ibm.pc.games.misc
comp.sys.ibm.pc.games.rpg
comp.sys.ibm.pc.games.sports
comp.sys.ibm.pc.games.strategic

Sims

The Sims is a sophisticated simulation game from the makers of SimCity in which you control people and their daily lives. (Doesn't that sound like fun?) You create the people, build houses for them, provide them with furnishings and other possessions, and control their lives. At your direction, your Sim people wake up, eat breakfast, use the bathroom, go to work, make friends, have conversations, fall in love, have children, and much, much more. You can even create new "skins" (appearances) for your people, as well as new houses and furniture, which you can share with other players. If you ever had a yen to be God (or to understand God), this is the game for you.

Web:

http://thesims.strategy-gaming.com/links.shtml
http://www.sim-heaven.com/
http://www.sims-source.com/
http://www.thesims.ea.com/us/
http://www.thesimsdimension.com/forums/
http://www.thesimsresource.com/

Usenet:

alt.games.the-sims

IRC:

#thesims (EFnet)

Starcraft

Starcraft is a strategy game from Blizzard, the makers of Warcraft II and Diablo. If you like such games, you will find Starcraft addictive (as do two of my researchers). The setting of Starcraft is an intergalactic war taking place on the rim of the galaxy, in which three races—Terran, Protoss, and Zerg—are fighting one another. You take control of one of these races, planning and executing the strategy. What's really cool are the multiplayer options. You can use a free Blizzard online service to meet and compete with other players from around the world. Not only can you kill fictitious aliens, you can plot against and vanquish real people you will never meet. Life just doesn't get any better.

Web:

http://www.battle.net/scc/
http://www.blizzard.com/starcraft/
http://www.scmillennium.com/
http://www.starcraft.org/

Usenet:

alt.binaries.games.starcraft
alt.games.starcraft
alt.games.starcraft.broodwars

IRC:

#starcraft (DALnet)

Video Games

You never know when you will have to sneak up behind someone and eviscerate him with a light saber before he turns around and blasts you with a laser. Stuff like that happens every day, and I want you to be prepared. The best way I know to be prepared is to spend as much time as possible playing video games, so let's get started.

Web:
> http://www.allgame.com/
> http://www.cinescape.com/0/toysandgames_2.asp
> http://www.vgf.com/
> http://www.vgmuseum.com/

Usenet:
> alt.atari-jaguar.discussion
> alt.atari.2600
> alt.fan.sonic-hedgehog
> alt.games.lynx
> alt.games.mame
> alt.games.rac-rally
> alt.games.sony-playstation
> alt.games.sony.yaroze
> alt.games.twinsens.odyssey
> alt.games.video
> alt.games.video.classic
> alt.games.video.emulation
> alt.games.video.import.japanese
> alt.games.video.nintendo-64
> alt.games.video.nintendo-64.faqs
> alt.games.video.nintendo.gamecube
> alt.games.video.sega-dreamcast
> alt.games.video.sega-saturn
> alt.games.video.sega-saturn.faqs
> alt.games.video.sony-playstation
> alt.games.video.sony-playstation.faqs
> alt.games.video.sony-playstation2
> alt.games.video.xbox
> alt.sega.genesis
> alt.super.nes
> alt.video.games.sony-playstation
> alt.videogames.neo-geo
> rec.games.vectrex
> rec.games.video
> rec.games.video.3do
> rec.games.video.advocacy
> rec.games.video.arcade
> rec.games.video.arcade.collecting
> rec.games.video.arcade.marketplace
> rec.games.video.atari
> rec.games.video.cd-i
> rec.games.video.cd32
> rec.games.video.classic
> rec.games.video.misc
> rec.games.video.nintendo
> rec.games.video.sega
> rec.games.video.sony

Video Games Hints and Cheats

Why spend huge portions of your life trying to master an arcane video game? As a Net user, you are only one click away from enough hints, cheats and walkthroughs to choke an electronic horse. Now you can use all that extra spare time to do something useful (like talk about video games on Usenet).

Web:
> http://www.cheatsearch.com/
> http://www.gameboomers.com/walkthroughs.html
> http://www.gamesdomain.co.uk/cheats/
> http://www.gamesover.com/cheats.htm
> http://www.the-spoiler.com/

Video games can be a lot of fun, but what is even more fun is knowing secret ways to beat the game.
If you play a lot of video games, check out the collection of cheats to see if any are known for your favorite game.
Be sure not to tell your brother, however. That would take all the fun out of it.

GARDENING

Biointensive Gardening

Biointensive gardening is a system of growing plants, which uses specific techniques to produce a large amount of food or other crops in a small amount of space. The system is low tech (you need only a spade and a gardening fork), organic (no pesticides or chemicals), and requires only a moderate amount of labor. If you have limited garden space, especially if you live in a city, biointensive gardening will help you make the most of your resources. You'll learn how to really understand your plants while impressing your neighbors by growing more food than you ever believed possible.

Web:
   http://www.growbiointensive.org/biointensive/
      Gardening.html

Flowers

Many people can't wait to retire so that they can take the time to grow flowers. Being a writer, I get to work at home, which means I can look down on my flower garden whenever I want. My favorites are the roses and the sweet peas, which I love to give to the special people in my life.

My cat looks down his nose at all this activity. He says that when

someone invents a catnip plant that smells like tuna, he'll retire and help me with the garden.

Bonsai

Bonsai is the Japanese art of dwarfing trees and plants into forms that mimic nature. If you have ever seen bonsai trees, you will know how beautiful and elegant they can be. A few years ago, I decided that I wanted to grow some bonsai of my own, but instead of special dwarf plants, I used regular seedlings. Now I have the only giant bonsai trees on the West Coast.

Web:
   http://hometown.aol.com/iasnob/
   http://www.bonsaiprimer.com/
   http://www.hav.com/bonsai/

Usenet:
   alt.bonsai
   rec.arts.bonsai

Listserv Mailing List:
   List Name: bonsai
   Subscribe to: listserv@home.ease.lsoft.com

Companion Plants

Companion plants are plants that do well when they are near one another. For example, asparagus does better when it is grown near tomatoes and does less well when grown near onions. Companion plants can also be used to repel harmful insects or attract beneficial ones. If you want your little bit of earth to be a true *jardin merveilleux*, learning how to use companion plants will take you three giant steps closer to your goal.

Web:
   http://forums.gardenweb.com/forums/complants/
   http://www.gardenguides.com/TipsandTechniques/
      vcomp.htm
   http://www.winnipeg-bugline.com/comp_pl.html

When life hands you a lemon,
put it on your Web page.

Edible Flowers

I have a friend Christy who is a master pastry chef. One of the more delightful things she does is decorate homemade cakes with edible flowers. However, in order to do this, she needs to know which flowers are edible. These resources will help you find such flowers, not only for cake decoration, but for salads, candies, garnishes and general strange-but-healthy afternoon snacks. (Think dandelions, roses, violets, nasturtiums, calendulas, elderberry flowers, scented geraniums, and so on.)

Web:
http://www.colostate.edu/Depts/CoopExt/4DMG/
Flowers/culinary.htm
http://www.colostate.edu/Depts/CoopExt/4DMG/
Flowers/flwrlove.htm
http://www.ext.colostate.edu/pubs/garden/
07237.html
http://www.lancaster.unl.edu/factsheets/092.htm
http://www.ville.montreal.qc.ca/jardin/en/
info_verte/feuillet_fleurs_comes/tableau.htm

Flowers

Do you enjoy looking at the reproductive structures of certain seed-bearing plants, characteristically having stamens and a pistil enclosed in an outer envelope of petals and sepals? That is, are you a flower lover? If so, you will love these resources, your entrée into the world of petals and sepals. The Web sites have lots and lots of information (especially about roses, which I love). There are also facilities that allow you to search for information about specific flowers, using a botanical or common name. When you aren't out in the garden, you may want to spend time reading the Usenet discussion groups to see what other flower lovers have to say.

Web:
http://www.colostate.edu/Depts/CoopExt/4DMG/
Flowers/flowers.htm
http://www.flowerweb.com/
http://www.gardenguides.com/flowers/flowers.htm
http://www.geobop.com/symbols/plants/flowers/
http://www.rosarian.com/

Usenet:
rec.gardens.orchids
rec.gardens.roses

Garden Gate

It's possible to spend hours reading about gardening instead of actually doing any real gardening. When you can't be participating in the real thing, try the virtual thing at the Garden Gate. Find FAQs, plant lists, a reading room, information on houseplants, reviews of gardening software, and tours of botanical gardens and greenhouses around the world.

Web:
http://garden-gate.prairienet.org/

Garden Ponds

Having water near your house creates an extremely pleasant and soothing environment. In one place where I lived, I put a waterfall in my yard near where I grew flowers, strawberries and tomatoes. I was able to see it and hear it from inside, and it served to bring a bit of the outdoors into the house. Would you like to make your own pond? These sites will show you how it is done and give suggestions about populating your pond once it is completed. (I am thinking about having a new pond where I live now, but I am still debating what to put in it. My cat has suggested goldfish.)

Web:
http://forums.gardenweb.com/forums/ponds/
http://www.aquariacentral.com/web/Garden_Ponds/
http://www.hergardenweb.com/ponds/
http://www.koi.com/

Usenet:
rec.ponds

Garden Web

Right now, I wish I could stop writing and go work in my garden. But there's too much work yet to finish, so the best I can do is hang out at the Garden Web for awhile. There are so many great gardening resources here it's easy to get immersed for hours. Oh well, at least while I am doing the research, I can look out the window at my garden.

Web:
http://www.gardenweb.com/

Gardening Mailing Lists

Make new friends and talk about gardening by joining a mailing list. In fact, join lots of mailing lists and impress people when they see how much mail you get all the time. These Web sites have extensive collections of mailing lists on a variety of gardening topics.

Web:
http://home.xnet.com/~jjy/plists.htm
http://www.gardenscape.com/
   GSMagsBooks.html#Mailing%20Lists

Gardening Talk and General Discussion

If things aren't going right in the garden, don't just raze everything with the rototiller; turn to your fellow Internet buddies for ideas. For the organically challenged, you have the opportunity to cry, scream, and beg for help. Bragging is also welcome; you can pass on the news that it was your 25-pound tomato that made the cover of the National Enquirer.

Usenet:
alt.binaries.pictures.gardens
rec.gardens
rec.gardens.edible
rec.gardens.orchids
rec.gardens.roses

Listserv Mailing List:
List Name: gardens
Subscribe to: listserv@lsv.uky.edu

Gothic Gardening

If you prefer the dark and macabre (as opposed to the sunny and cheerful), you do not have to feel left out of the Internet gardening scene. Visit this site and experience gothic gardening at its best. Pick your theme: would you like lots of black plants, plants that attract bats and insects, carnivorous plants, or perhaps a garden that only sits up and takes notice after the sun goes down? It's all here and then some.

Web:
http://www.gothic.net/~malice/

Growing Vegetables

One of my favorite pleasures is growing vegetables. Right now (as you read this), I have wonderful beefsteak tomatoes growing in my garden. Here's some information to help you plan and cultivate your own tiny patch of paradise. After all, if Adam and Eve had a Net connection with access to better information, they probably would have been more successful in handling their gardening problems.

Web:
http://cf.uwex.edu/ics/infosource/veggies.cfm
http://forums.gardenweb.com/forums/cornucop/
http://www.ces.uga.edu/pubcd/b1011-w.html
http://www.gardenguides.com/Vegetables/
   vegetabl.htm

Many people do not appreciate their friends in the vegetable kingdom. Why not grow your own?

Hydroponics

Hydroponics refers to the growing of plants in a water-based nutrient solution without using soil. To use hydroponics, you must have some specialized knowledge and be prepared to put in some extra work to get started. However, there are significant advantages over regular gardening. At home, you can use hydroponics to have your own garden even if you don't have a backyard. For commercial purposes, hydroponics virtually eliminates all pests and weeds. Moreover, it is possible to grow plants closer together than in a field, thus increasing the yield.

Web:
http://www.hydroponics.com/info/
http://www.hydroponics.net/learn/
http://www.interurban.com/abouthydro/

Usenet:
alt.hydroponics

I Can Garden

Yes, you can garden, and this lovely gardening site will inspire you to great things. This well-designed site, the work of many people, is described as a "Canadian Internet gardening resource", but don't let this mislead you. I Can Garden is for everyone. There are articles, resources, cat areas, stuff for kids, and much, much more. If you are the type of person who likes to stop and smell the roses, you will love this site.

Web:
  http://www.icangarden.com/

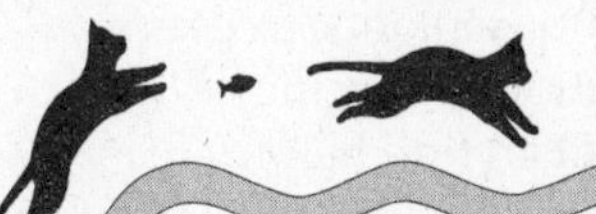

TIDBITS

What should campers know about BEARS?

In North America, there are two main types of bears: the black bear and the Grizzly (brown) bear. Grizzly bears are far more aggressive and dangerous. However, in the lower 48 states, there are only about 1,000 grizzlies.

Although bears eat meat, they mostly live on plants, insects and honey. They spend most of their time foraging for food, so if you encounter a bear, he may simply be looking for a handout. If you encounter a bear, the safest thing to do is pretend you are talking to a politician: keep calm, avoid direct eye contact, and speak in a soft monotone voice. If the bear swats at you, play dead by lying flat or curling into a ball. If you have pepper spray, you will find it to be an effective repellent (just as it is with politicians).

When you are camping, store *all* your food, and anything that smells like food, away from your campsite. If you are near your car, keep your food in the trunk, not in the main part of the car.

Indoor Plants

The cat has eaten half of your rhododendron and the leaves on your African violet are turning yellow. What should you do? Check out the helpful hints you can find at these Web sites. Articles cover topics such as container drainage, decorating with houseplants, feeding and watering, and making terrariums.

Web:
  http://forums.gardenweb.com/forums/houseplt/
  http://gardening.buildfind.com/dir/plants/indoor/
    HowTo.html
  http://hgic.clemson.edu/factsheets/hgic1450.htm
  http://muextension.missouri.edu/xplor/agguides/
    hort/g06510.htm

National Gardening Association

Oh my goodness! An absolutely huge library of gardening articles and FAQs (frequently asked question lists). You'll also find a horticultural dictionary, a plant namefinder and a database of common plant names. Do you like gardening? You *must* spend some time here. I found some great hints to help with my tomato growing.

Web:
  http://www.garden.org/

Organic Gardening

Organic gardening uses biological methods for pest control, fertilizing and maintenance. Thus, organic gardeners avoid the use of synthetic pesticides, growth regulators and additives. To do so, it is necessary to use particular techniques, such as composting. It can take significant effort and knowledge to keep plants healthy without the use of chemicals, so here are some organic gardening resources that will provide you with lots of information and advice.

Web:
  http://mel.lib.mi.us/science/organic.html
  http://www.organicdownunder.com/
  http://www.rain.org/~sals/my.html
  http://www.supak.com/mort/

Usenet:
  rec.gardens.ecosystems

PEST MANAGEMENT

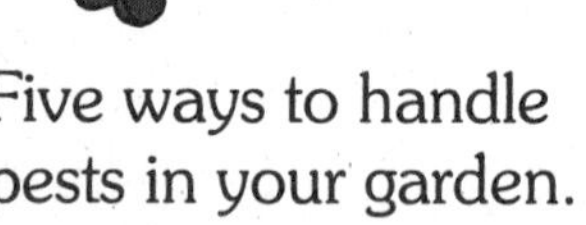

Five ways to handle pests in your garden.

1. Take your boombox outside and play loud rap music until the pests run away in a fit of self-preservation.

2. Sit down in your garden and talk to the pests quietly, but firmly. Tell them that you understand their position, but it really hurts your feelings when they eat your vegetables.

3. Invite your imaginary friend Poindexter, over for a visit. Explain the situation, and ask him to see what he can do. If he does get rid of the pests, make him a spaghetti dinner.

4. Put up a sign that says, "Today: Free basketball tickets. Insects only." When they come out to get the tickets, spray them.

5. Get a book of philosophy and sit in the garden reading Schopenhauer out loud. Soon the pests will be so depressed, they won't be able to cause any trouble.

Pest Management

"Pest management" is the politically correct term for figuring out effective ways to destroy, obliterate, or otherwise get rid of those nasty creatures that feed on your plants. Form your strategic battle plan with the help of these Web sites. They offer insect factsheets, information on exotic pests, and even images of insects so you can accurately identify the enemy.

Web:
   http://www.nysaes.cornell.edu/ent/biocontrol/
   http://www.usna.usda.gov/Gardens/pestmgmt.html

Plant Answers

This is a great site for finding general information on particular types of plants such as flowers, fruits and vegetables, ground covers, houseplants, trees and shrubs, and grasses. In addition to specific plant-oriented answers, you can find helpful files about mulching, irrigation and other gardening basics.

Web:
   http://aggie-horticulture.tamu.edu/plantanswers/
      web.html

Rare and Heirloom Seeds

For various reasons—chief among which are the twenty-first century gods of efficiency and consumer demand—the availability of seeds for many plants is limited to a relatively few popular strains. As a result, the biodiversity of garden plants is diminishing. Vegetables, for example, are often hybridized in the name of uniform size and height, resulting in less flavorful, lower yielding, and less disease- and pest-resistant plants. However, there are people and organizations dedicated to keeping alive many different types of rare seeds and plants (often referred to as heirlooms). Such seeds maintain our rich, horticultural influence by maintaining genetic links to the past. If you want to put something special into your garden experience, try some heirlooms. They are available for a wide variety of flowers (especially roses), vegetables and other great, green, growing inhabitants of planet Earth.

Web:
   http://csf.colorado.edu/perma/stse/handbook.htm
   http://forums.gardenweb.com/forums/heirloom/
   http://www.co.mo.md.us/services/dep/Internet/
      heirloom.htm
   http://www.seeds.ca/
   http://www.seedstrust.com/issi/issi.html
   http://www.vegparadise.com/heirloom.html

Trees

Are you knowledgeable about trees? If so, you know that a tree is a perennial woody plant that at maturity (1) is at least 13 feet [4 meters] tall; (2) has at least one trunk with a diameter of more than 3 inches [7.5 cm]; (3) is unbranched for at least several feet [1 meter] above the ground; and (4) has a definite crown, (the part of the plant where the trunk and roots merge). What you may not know is that it is possible to grow a Brussels sprouts plant into something resembling a tree. Several years ago, I planted a tiny Brussels sprouts seedling. Well, it just kept growing and growing and, today, it is over 6.5 feet [2 meters] tall, with a trunk and several long, strange branches that look like something out of a Harry Potter book. Eventually, when the plant matures, I'll be able to see if it meets the requirements for a tree. In the meantime I can swank around, secure in the knowledge that I have the largest Brussels sprouts plant in the neighborhood (maybe in the world).

Web:

http://forums.gardenweb.com/forums/trees/
http://www.arborday.org/
http://www.backyardgardener.com/tree/
http://www.gardeninglaunchpad.com/tre.html
http://www.oplin.lib.oh.us/products/tree/
http://www.treeguide.com/guides.asp

Urban Gardening

If you live in a city, you will understand how important it is to have some plants around you to balance the artificial environment. I grew up in a large city, and I saw that most people who had even a little land would plant some sort of garden. If you enjoy gardening in the city, you will find these resources helpful. Read about community gardens, urban agriculture, school and rooftop gardens, composting and solutions to common problems.

Web:

http://www.cityfarmer.org/

Vermiculture

Vermiculture refers to the growing of worms. Have you ever grown your own worms? Well, why not give it a try? Wouldn't it be great to have a few thousand worms of your own? Worms are among the most absolutely coolest animals on Earth for two good reasons. First, they are great for gardens. They break up and aerate the soil, which helps plant roots grow and allows the soil to hold more water. They also eat dead organic matter and produce waste that is a wonderful plant food. Moreover, if you have extra worms, you can always use them as animal feed and fishing bait. However, the real reason worms are so cool is that they feel so slimy and squishy when you hold a bunch of them in your hand and throw them in your sister's hair.

Web:

http://www.cityfarmer.org/
   wormcomp61.html#wormcompost
http://www.gnv.fdt.net/~windle/primer.htm
http://www.oldgrowth.org/compost/vermi.html
http://www.wormdigest.org/

Web Garden

With all the great gardening resources available on the Net, it's hard to get away from the computer long enough to spend time in the backyard. This site has information for beginning gardeners, whether you garden at home or commercially. Read garden features and tips, and search a gardening database for information about all sorts of plants.

Web:
   http://webgarden.osu.edu/

Wildflowers

I love wildflowers. Right now, in my garden, I have a large bed of assorted wildflowers that are particularly suited to attracting hummingbirds. The thing I like about wildflowers is that, unlike their cultivated cousins, they retain an air of informality that allows you to enjoy that back-to-nature feeling without actually having to get your feet dirty or leave your home.

Web:
   http://aggie-horticulture.tamu.edu/wildseed/
   http://home.usit.net/~info7/plants.html
   http://www.wildflower.org/

Xeriscaping

Many parts of the world, including the area where I live, have natural climate cycles during which water can be scarce for years at a time. In such areas, it is practical to landscape with plants that have low water requirements. This process is called xeriscaping, from the Greek word *xeros* meaning "dry". (You know what I don't understand? If the Greeks wanted to say "dry", why didn't they just say "dry"? Why did they feel like they had to have a special word for everything? Is it supposed to be some type of secret code?) Anyway, if you xeriscape with plants that are appropriate for your area, once your garden is established, it should be able thrive with only natural rainfall, even in extended periods of drought.

Web:
   http://aggie-horticulture.tamu.edu/extension/
      xeriscape/xeriscape.html
   http://forums.gardenweb.com/forums/swest/
   http://www.ciwmb.ca.gov/organics/xeriscaping/
   http://www.csu.org/xeri/
   http://www.greenbuilder.com/sourcebook/
      xeriscape.html

GENEALOGY

Adoptees and Genealogy

There are times when you can work on genealogy for hours and never seem to get anywhere. As you know, it can be a lot of work trying to trace your family tree. If you are adopted, there are extra complications, especially if you do not have full information about your birth parents. If you are an adoptee or you have adoptees in your family, here are some genealogy resources that can help you trace your lineage.

Web:
   http://www.cyndislist.com/adoption.htm
   http://www.genforum.genealogy.com/adoption/

Canadian Genealogy Resources

Is your family from Canada? If so, you are in luck. You can find all you need to know about your Canadian roots without having to actually put on snowshoes and trek across icy plains to a remote library that is only open for three hours on St. Swithin's Day. Now that's what I call cool, eh?

Web:
 http://www.cyndislist.com/canada.htm
 http://www.islandnet.com/~jveinot/cghl/cghl.html

Usenet:
 soc.genealogy.surnames.canada

Genealogy Discussion by Ethnicity

There are lots of genealogy discussion groups available on Usenet, many of which are devoted to various cultural and ethnic heritages. These groups focus on the following cultures: Africa, Australia/ New Zealand, Belgium/Netherlands/Luxembourg, Canada, France, Germany, Hispanic, Nordic, Slavic, United Kingdom and Ireland.

Usenet:
 soc.genealogy.african
 soc.genealogy.australia+nz
 soc.genealogy.benelux
 soc.genealogy.french
 soc.genealogy.german
 soc.genealogy.hispanic
 soc.genealogy.nordic
 soc.genealogy.slavic
 soc.genealogy.uk+ireland

Genealogy Events

Are you looking for some hot genealogy action? These sites will give you the details on upcoming events such as courses, seminars, meetings, tours, lectures, festivals and reunions. If you are planning a shindig of some sort, post it here so people can see what is going on in your genealogical neck of the woods.

Web:
 http://www.cagenweb.com/events.htm
 http://www.fgs.org/fgs-calendar.htm

Genealogy Mailing Lists

When you participate in a mailing list, you can meet lots of people, including other researchers who are working in the same lines as you. Scan these collections of mailing lists, and see what suits your needs. There is something for everyone here, including lists devoted to specific surnames.

Web:
 http://lists.rootsweb.com/
 http://www.cyndislist.com/mailing.htm

Genealogy Marketplace

If you have any genealogical items you want to buy or want to sell, this is the place to do it. Just about anything goes: books, services, maps, documents, and much more.

Usenet:

soc.genealogy.marketplace

Genealogy Methods and Hints

It's always good to have help when you are working on a family history. These Web sites have lots of hints about what to do and what not to do, as well as suggestions as to good sources of information. The Usenet group is a place to ask questions or offer advice to other genealogical researchers.

Web:

http://community-2.webtv.net/mpetzolt2/
   helpfulhints/
http://www.a1webdesign.com/rebick/26tips.htm
http://www.amberskyline.com/treasuremaps/
http://www.rootsweb.com/~kycarter/tips.html

Usenet:

soc.genealogy.methods

Genealogy Scams

I thought of a great new way to make money.

I am going to invent a brand new last name, say, Glythmxk. Then I'm going to create an entire genealogy for the Glythmxk family, including a full family tree, documents, photos, records and stories. Then I will charge people $1,000 each to change their name to Glythmxk. Once they do, they receive all the Glythmxk genealogy for free.

My only problem is going to be what to do with all the money.

Genealogy Resources

Genealogy is a popular pastime on the Internet, and there are many people (and some companies) that have created related Web sites. But how do you find what you want? Start with these sites: well-organized collections with oodles of resources for the genealogically inclined.

Web:

http://www.cyndislist.com/
http://www.genealogy.org/
http://www.genealogytoday.com/genealogy/enoch/
http://www.gengateway.com/
http://www.genhomepage.com/
http://www.refdesk.com/factgene.html

Genealogy Scams

I got a special "genealogy" offer in the mail. Perhaps you have seen one yourself. Some company wants to sell you a complete history of your family from the beginning of time, or the full names of every single person in the world with your surname. The offers sound inviting, but you should always check them thoroughly before you turn loose any of your money. Some of these pitches are real scams and they are targeted specifically at inexperienced genealogists or anyone who is working on a family history. Read this overview and learn about the types of suspicious offers you should avoid.

Web:

http://www.alden.org/genealogy/scams.htm
http://www.ancestordetective.com/watchdog.htm
http://www.cyndislist.com/myths.htm
http://www.ngsgenealogy.org/comconsumer.htm

Genealogy Search Engine

When you want information fast (or as fast as it gets in genealogy), it's good to know where you can get what you need. Here are search engines that will let you search databases of online genealogical resources to find the ones that are in your area of interest.

Web:

http://www.gendoor.com/
http://www.gensource.com/ifoundit/

Genealogy Software

Once you get started with genealogy, you will find that using a computer makes things a *lot* easier. For example, the program I use is able to print nice charts of various parts of the family tree. I then send these charts to relatives and ask them for changes and additions, which has worked out nicely.

Web:
  http://www.cyndislist.com/software.htm
  http://www.lkessler.com/gplinks.shtml
  http://www.rootsweb.com/roots-l/compgen.html

Genealogy Talk and General Discussion

The Internet is a global community—a great place from which to track down family members from way-back-when. Usenet offers a convenient forum not only to discuss ways of researching, what kinds of software and resources are available, or to compare anecdotes of your quests, but you can also ask for information on family names. Plenty of sharing goes on here. Find that long-lost second-half-cousin-twice-removed who broke all your crayons when you were seven and remind him you want all 64 colors, plus the built-in sharpener.

Usenet:
  alt.genealogy
  soc.genealogy.britain
  soc.genealogy.computing
  soc.genealogy.ireland
  soc.genealogy.italian
  soc.genealogy.misc
  soc.roots

Genealogy Terms

There are lots of special terms used in genealogy. Many of these have origins in other languages. Some terms are really arcane medical words. You will also find technical words relating to genealogy techniques and record keeping. The next time you encounter a baffling word, here are some good places to find a definition. Pretty soon, expressions like paucis hebdomadibus and collateral ancestor will be old friends.

Web:
  http://home.att.net/~dottsr/diction.html
  http://www.genealogy-quest.com/glossaries/
  http://www.genealogy.com/Glossary/glossary.html
  http://www.uftree.com/UFT/Nav/glossary.html

GenWeb Projects

The GenWeb projects are dedicated to providing a comprehensive collection of Web-based free genealogical resources. The U.S. GenWeb started in Kentucky. It works to provide resources for every county and state in the country. The GenWeb idea has spread and now there is a WorldGenWeb, which supports efforts to create a genealogical Web site for every country in the world, maintained by researchers who live in the country or are familiar with its resources. When your research takes you to a specific part of the world (or United States), the GenWebs are often the best place to start.

Web:
  http://www.usgenweb.com/
  http://www.worldgenweb.org/

Getting Started in Genealogy

Getting started in genealogy can be bewildering. If you are having trouble telling your tiny tafel from your soundex, here are some good places to start. These are easy-to-read beginner's guides to genealogy that will offer the help and guidance you need to begin a family search.

Web:
  http://www.familytreemaker.com/mainmenu.html
  http://www.rootsweb.com/roots-l/starting.html

Heraldry

Heraldry is the tradition, dating from the Middle Ages, of displaying symbols or pictures (called charges) on shields. During tournaments, knights were recognized by the shields they carried. (Such tournaments were refereed by officials called heralds—hence, the word "heraldry".) The charges on the shields identified individuals and families, and were passed to successive generations (the Middle Ages' version of a vanity license plate). As centuries passed, these charges were adapted into insignia for the nobility and were used not only on shields, but as seals for documents. Later the designs were embroidered into articles of clothing. In fact, the phrase "coat of arms" comes from the practice of embroidering family designs onto the surcoat that was worn over chain mail armor. (This served to make you easily recognizable by the person who was running you through with a sword.) Here are some interesting sites on the Net that explain heraldry, give a basic primer, and tell what some of the symbols mean. The Usenet group is for the discussion of heraldry. All these resources will help you better analyze your family's coat of arms. (Or, if your family does not have a coat of arms, you can concoct something suitable for your next reunion, and start a brand new family tradition.)

Web:

http://renaissance.dm.net/heraldry/primer.html
http://www.college-of-arms.gov.uk/
http://www.digiserve.com/heraldry/
http://www.heraldica.org/

Usenet:

rec.heraldry

Jewish Genealogy

I grew up in a Jewish family and I found these resources particularly interesting, because I was able to find a huge number of ancestors that I could feel guilty about not inviting to my Bar Mitzvah.

Web:

http://www.genhomepage.com/jewish.html
http://www.jewishgen.org/

Usenet:

soc.genealogy.jewish

Journal of Online Genealogy

The Journal of Online Genealogy is a genealogy magazine with monthly articles. You'll find information for beginners, as well as discussions of advanced projects for more experienced genealogists. You will also find help in learning how to use the Internet for your research, as well as news of interest to the genealogical community.

Web:

http://www.onlinegenealogy.com/

Mayflower Genealogy

The Mayflower was a ship that brought pilgrims from England to New England in 1620. The Mayflower landed at Plymouth on December 26, 1620. Before leaving the ship, the colonists drew up an agreement—called the Mayflower Compact—establishing a temporary government based on their own intentions, rather than the laws of the English crown. These Web sites have information about the Mayflower and the people who descended from the original passengers. You can investigate wills, inventories, passenger lists, early writings related to the Mayflower, and explore links to other Mayflower resources. Somebody had to be descended from those adventurous pilgrims. It might as well have been you.

Web:

http://members.aol.com/calebj/mayflower.html
http://www.mayflowersociety.com/resourc.htm
http://www.ocmayflower.org/

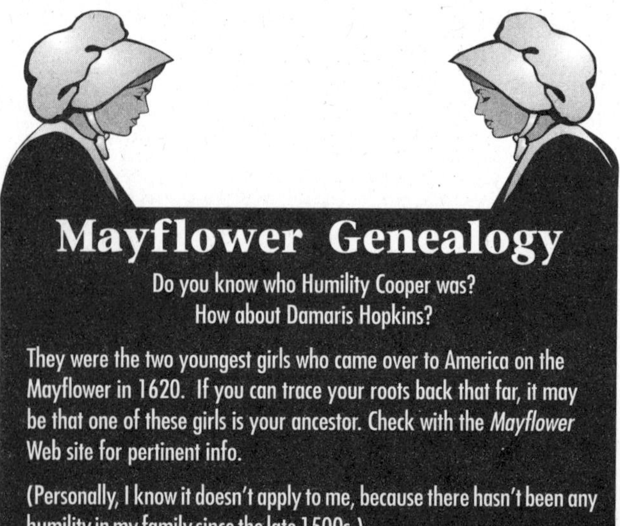

Medieval Genealogy

Medieval genealogy covers the period spanning 500 to 1600 A.D. My cat, The Little Nipper, decided to do a bit of searching, and he found out that he is a direct descendent of Ronronnement, Son of Tueur D'oiseau, Seigneur de Thon, Comte De Chat. Imagine what you can find.

Web:

http://users.erols.com/wrei/faqs/medieval.html
http://www.medievalgenealogy.org.uk/

Usenet:

soc.genealogy.medieval

Mormon Genealogical Resources

You may already know that the Mormon Church has the largest genealogical archive in the world. However, have you ever wondered why the Mormons have such a strong interest in tracing their roots? Let's start at the beginning. According to Mormon doctrine, there exists a "premortal realm" in which spirits reside—spirits who are sons and daughters of Heavenly Father and Heavenly Mother (God and his wife). It is possible for a spirit to obtain a physical body and start a life on Earth. This affords the spirit the chance to acquire earthly experience and to progress toward perfection. (In other words, this is why we were born.) Life on Earth is temporary. After we die, our spirit goes to the "Spirit World" where we continue to learn as we await the Resurrection of Jesus and the Final Judgment. Since life does not end with death, it is possible for our earthly family to survive after death. This will only happen if, while we are alive, the members of our family go to a special temple and make certain promises called covenants. However, what about all our ancestors who did not have the benefit of the church's teachings? (The church only started in 1830.) How can they perform their covenants? Well, obviously, they can't, so we have to do it for them. Each Mormon family is encouraged to spend time in a temple, performing covenant ceremonies on behalf of their ancestors. Now you can see why Mormons care so much about genealogy: it allows them to identify their ancestors, and to do the "temple work" that will enable their entire family to be united throughout all eternity.

Web:

http://www.familysearch.org/

Native American Genealogy

Not long ago, a Native American friend of mine spent a lot of time researching his family tree. After he finished, he gave a wonderful presentation in front of all his friends and relatives with charts, diagrams, old photos and fascinating stories. When it was over, he turned to his wife and said, "So, did you learn anything?" She looked at him, smiled, and said, "You speak the truth, my faithful Indian companion."

Web:

http://members.aol.com/bbbenge/newlinks.html
http://www.hanksville.org/NAresources/indices/
  NAgenealogy.html

Notable Women Ancestors

Women are the invisible ancestors. As you research your genealogy, you will often find that many of the names you encounter will be those of men, simply because they were the ones who were documented. This Web site offers stories about women who stood out from the crowd, in spite of the fact that most women were forgotten over the years. Some of these women were famous, but many of them were everyday women whose personalities and actions were striking enough to cause them to be noticed and remembered. Aside from genealogy, this resource is also a great place to visit if you are doing research into women's history.

Web:

http://www.rootsweb.com/~nwa/

Roots

The mailing list **roots-l** has been a popular genealogy mailing list for many years. It has been spun into a major collection of resources and networking options for genealogists around the world. The Web site has a searchable archive of posts that have been sent to the mailing list. For example, this is a good place to find out if anyone has been making queries regarding a particular surname. The site has a sharing library where individuals who have time to share list books from which they are willing to do lookups for other people. Roots offers a registry of people who are researching particular surnames, so you may be able to find other people who might be related to you. Detailed information about the **roots-l** mailing list is also available at this Web site.

Web:

http://www.rootsweb.com/

Royalty and Nobility

Once, when I was in a Mormon Family History Center, I saw ex-Duchess Fergie at a microfilm reader, working on her family tree. (Actually, she was having trouble with her microfilm reader, and I had to help her load the film.) Before I went back to do my own research, I told her that it would be easier to do her research on the Net. I explained that there are lots of places with information about royal and noble lineages, and she wouldn't even have to remember how to turn the microfilm spool. I gave her a list of these resources to get her started. And, I told her, if you want to see what they are saying about you behind your back, try the Usenet group.

Web:
   http://ftp.cac.psu.edu/~saw/royal/royalgen.html
   http://www.dcs.hull.ac.uk/public/genealogy/
      gedcom.html

Usenet:
   alt.talk.royalty

Royalty and Nobility

When you come right down to it, the kings, queens and nobles of history were a lot like regular people (if you overlook minor details such as fame, power and wealth).

However, there was one important difference: many aspects of the lives of these people were documented in detail and, if you need such information, a lot of it is available on the Net.

So sometime, just for fun, why not graft a portion of some royal family onto your own personal family tree, and see if anything takes root?

Scottish Clans

Most people don't realize it, but there is a lot more to Scottish culture than the Loch Ness monster and Scotch whiskey. For example, they have bagpipes, Highland games, men who wear skirts, and a lot of cool clans (sort of like gangs in Los Angeles, only Scottish accents are easier to understand).

Web:
   http://www.electricscotland.com/webclans/
   http://www.geo.ed.ac.uk/home/scotland/genealogy.html
   http://www.scotlandsclans.com/
   http://www.tartans.com/

Usenet:
   alt.scottish.clans

Surname Databases and Discussion

As a genealogical researcher, you know how easy it is to spend hours and hours and still come up with nothing substantial. However, here's a great way to come up with information quickly that is fun, interesting and just may help you out. Search for your name in one of the surname databases, and I bet you will find something of interest. For example, I found it interesting to see how many people in the database had the same last name as me.

Web:
   http://rsl.rootsweb.com/
   http://www.cyndislist.com/database.htm
   http://www.gengateway.com/spring.htm

Usenet:
   soc.genealogy.surnames
   soc.genealogy.surnames.britain
   soc.genealogy.surnames.german
   soc.genealogy.surnames.global
   soc.genealogy.surnames.ireland
   soc.genealogy.surnames.misc
   soc.genealogy.surnames.usa

Surname Origins

Have you ever wondered what your surname means? My cat wanted to find out about himself. His name is The Little Nipper, so he looked up "Nipper" on these Web sites. The closest he could get was that, in German, the name Nipps means "a dweller near water". Well, in a way, that makes sense, because I have a view of the ocean from my office, and The Little Nipper often sits on my desk, looking out the window while I am working.

Web:
   http://www.familychronicle.com/surname.htm
   http://www.vitalog.net/

Tombstone Rubbings

In the course of your genealogical field trips, you may one day find yourself in a cemetery, recording data from tombstones. One great way to capture the essence of the tombstone is to do a rubbing. Here are detailed instructions about how to do tombstone rubbings as well as hints on the type of information you can expect to find.

Web:
http://www.alsirat.com/taphophile/rubbings.html
http://www.amberskyline.com/treasuremaps/
  t_stone.html
http://www.genealogytoolbox.com/
  gravestonerubbingandtranscription.html
http://www.gravehunter.com/
  tombstone_rubbings.htm

GENEALOGISTS...
FIVE REASONS TO LEARN ALL ABOUT TOMBSTONE RUBBING:

(1) TOMBSTONE RUBBING IS THE BEST WAY TO CAPTURE INFORMATION AND DESIGNS FROM A TOMBSTONE IN A PERMANENT, CONVENIENT AND PORTABLE FORM.

(2) IT'S A GREAT WAY TO MAKE FRIENDS. JUST SPEND SOME TIME IN A GRAVEYARD WORKING ON A TOMBSTONE, AND YOU WILL BE SURPRISED HOW MANY PEOPLE COME OVER TO ASK WHAT YOU ARE DOING.

(3) IT'S FUN, AND UNLIKE VISITING DISNEYLAND, THERE ARE NO LONG WAITS.

(4) IT'S GOOD FOR YOUR SOCIAL LIFE. PEOPLE WHO KNOW HOW TO RUB TOMBSTONES CONSISTENTLY RANK AT THE TOP OF POPULARITY POLLS. THINK BACK TO HIGH SCHOOL. WHO WERE THE ONLY PEOPLE WHO WERE MORE POPULAR THAN THE CAPTAIN OF THE FOOTBALL TEAM AND THE HEAD CHEERLEADER? SEE WHAT I MEAN?

(5) DIDN'T YOUR MOTHER ALWAYS TELL YOU IT WAS HEALTHY TO SPEND TIME OUTDOORS?

U.S. Census Information

Every ten years, the United States government spends millions of dollars and employs tens of thousands of people to gather statistics on everyone in the country, just so you can have the numbers you need, when you need them.

Does that make you feel important, or what?

U.S. Census Information

Article 1, Section 2 of the United States Constitution mandates an "enumeration" of all the people in all the states of the Union. (What a job that has turned out to be.) In the United States, the primary purpose of a census is to count the population in order to distribute seats in the U.S. House of Representatives and to define the legislative district boundaries within each state. However, census findings have many other purposes, most of which relate to allocating federal funds and developing social services. The first American census was taken in 1790; since then, a census has been taken every 10 years. Census records can give you basic information about families, some details about household members, and help you track family locations. These Web sites have information about how to use census records for genealogical research, as well as background information on the census itself. Since 2000 was a census year, new information will start to become available soon.

Web:
http://www.amberskyline.com/treasuremaps/
  uscensus.html
http://www.census.gov/ftp/pub/genealogy/www/
http://www.rootsweb.com/~usgenweb/census/

U.S. Civil War Genealogy

Just imagine. You are sitting on the front porch, drinking a refreshing mint julep, when all of a sudden a group of Union soldiers come tearing through the yard on their way to burn down your house. No doubt about it, the years of the U.S. Civil War were a confusing, difficult time in American history. Fortunately for genealogists, there was a lot of effort put into keeping track of all the men who went off to war, and it is possible to search the old military records for information about these men. In addition, since this was a time of upheaval, many people were away from home, corresponding by letters. There are also a fair number of personal diaries. One problem, however, is that some courthouses were burned, and some records were lost permanently. That aside, there are a lot of great resources relating to Civil War genealogy.

Web:
   http://sunsite.utk.edu/civil-war/warweb.html
   http://www.nara.gov/genealogy/civilwar.html

U.S. National Archives Genealogy Resources

See what the National Archives and Records Administration (NARA) has to offer in the way of instructional leaflets and helpful searching tips for genealogical research. They also give you a glance at microfiche records for census and federal court information such as bankruptcy records, naturalization records, land grant claims, and immigrant and passenger arrivals.

Web:
   http://www.nara.gov/genealogy/

Vital Records in the U.S.

Vital records are official documents that record important life events such as births, marriages, deaths, divorces, and passages from one country to another. There is a great deal of important information you can glean from these documents, so be sure you know where to get them. These sites have a list of places to which you can write for vital records within the United States.

Web:
   http://www.cdc.gov/nchs/howto/w2w/
      w2welcom.htm
   http://www.genealogyspot.com/records/
      vitalrecords.htm
   http://www.vitalrec.com/

Aerial Photos

Here's an easy way to get high without having to worry about hurting yourself, getting arrested or bumping into airplanes. Take a look at these aerial photos and see what down home looks like from up there.

Web:
   http://earthrise.space.com/
   http://www.terrafly.fiu.edu/
   http://www.terraserver.com/

Distance Calculator

Before you go from here to there, make sure you know how far it is. Otherwise, how would you know how much food to bring? This site enables you to calculate the distances between world cities and will even show you the points plotted on a map as well as the longitude and latitude. I found out it is 8,668 miles (13,949 km) from where I live to Bombay.

Web:
   http://www.indo.com/distance/

Earth Rise

Earth Rise is a Web site that allows you to access a huge database of pictures of the Earth taken by astronauts on the U.S. space shuttle. What a wonderful way to appreciate our planet. Just a few clicks of the mouse, and you can see what any part of the world looks like from space.

Web:
   http://earthrise.space.com/

Pictures of Your Planet

If you are like me, the Earth is one of your favorite planets in the entire universe. But what do you do when you meet an alien who pulls out a wallet and starts showing you photos of his home planet? Invite him over to your computer, fire up your Web browser, and point it to "**Earth Rise**". Never again will you have to let a foreigner one-up you when it comes to civic pride.

Flags of the World

If you are looking for something unique and colorful with which to decorate your home, try downloading some of these flags of the world. Not only will they look nice hanging on your walls, but your visitors will be convinced that you have culture and good taste.

Web:
   http://www.crwflags.com/fotw/flags/
   http://www.flags.net/
   http://www.wave.net/upg/immigration/flags.html

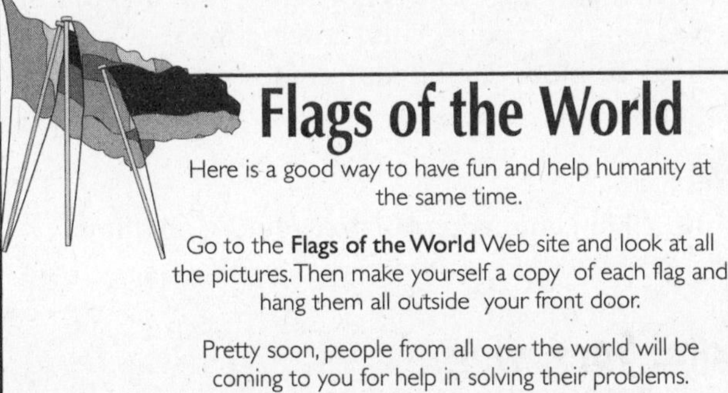

Geographic Information Systems

A geographical information system (GIS) is a computer system used to manipulate information that is related to specific geographical locations. For example, satellite photos showing patterns of vegetation might be part of a GIS. There are many different types of GISs, and a lot of information available on the Net.

Web:
   http://www.gisdevelopment.net/
   http://www.usgs.gov/research/gis/title.html

Usenet:
   comp.infosystems.gis
   comp.soft-sys.gis.esri

Geography Departments Worldwide

This site has a search engine that allows you to search geography department resources all over the Net. You can narrow your search by research field, so you could look up more specific resources, such as who is studying human geography in Bangladesh or remote sensing in Switzerland. You can access resources in many countries and in many different fields of geographical research.

Web:
   http://geowww.uibk.ac.at/geolinks/

Geography Resources

Modern geography embraces many different branches of study. No matter what field you are interested in, you will find a lot of geographical information on the Net. Here are some good places to start. You will find links to educational resources, research publications, maps, images, geographic data sources, and information about jobs, organizations and professional associations.

Web:
   http://www.census.gov/geo/www/
   http://www.colorado.edu/geography/virtdept/
      resources/contents.htm
   http://www.educationindex.com/geography/
   http://www.geography.wisc.edu/resources/phys.html

Geography Talk and General Discussion

Imagine what life would be like if there was no geography. There would be no road maps to have to re-fold. There would be no grueling hours of having to memorize the capitals of third world countries. And worse, there would be no map showing what hills and dales you have to go over to get to Grandma's house. In fact, geography is so important that you can find a lively discussion about it in Usenet. Go hang out with the people who know the planet like the backs of their hands.

Usenet:
   bit.listserv.geograph

Geography Talk and General Discussion

Sometimes, when I need a break from the pressures of a writer's life, I relax by checking the Usenet geography discussion group.

After an hour or so of talking about horsts, grabens, and lateral moraine, I am completely at peace with the universe and ready for more work.

Imagine how fulfilling it must be to be a full-time geographer. No wonder they smile so much.

Global Land Information System

The Global Land Information System (GLIS) is an interactive computer system developed by the U.S. Geological Survey (USGS), a branch of the U.S. Department of the Interior. The GLIS provides you with information relating to a huge variety of data sets that may be ordered from the USGS. If you have an idea what you want, this system can help you find it. If not, you can just cruise around and look for cool stuff. (USGS data sets make wonderful Mother's Day presents.)

Web:

   http://mac.usgs.gov/mac/isb/pubs/factsheets/
      fs06999.html

GPS (Global Positioning System)

The Global Positioning System (GPS) is an amazing system that will tell you your (almost) exact position and time anywhere on the Earth. There are three parts to the system: (1) In space, there are 24 satellites (three of which are spares) that circle the Earth in 12-hour orbits. From any point on the Earth, there are five to eight satellites above you somewhere. (2) Around the world, there is a whole system of tracking stations. The master station is at Falcon Air Force Base in Colorado. (3) To receive data, you use a GPS receiver. This receiver uses the signals from at least four of the satellites to give you navigation, positioning and time information. If you are a special authorized user (U.S. Department of Defense, etc.) your receiver can tell you your exact position within an 18 by 28 meter area, and the time will be accurate within 100 nanoseconds (billionths of a second). Everyone else gets a position within a 100 by 156 meter area, with a time accurate within 167 nanoseconds.

Web:

   http://www.edu-observatory.org/gps/gps.html
   http://www.gpsworld.com/gpsworld/static/
      staticHtml.jsp?id=7993
   http://www.trimble.com/gps/

Usenet:

   sci.geo.satellite-nav

Great Globe Gallery

One of the most interesting and difficult problems for cartographers is how to represent all or parts of the Earth (which is three-dimensional) on a flat surface. I recently read a cartography textbook (just for fun), and I was amazed at how many decisions and tradeoffs there are in making a map. The overall general principle is: if you want to go into outer space and look down, you can see the real thing. Anything else is, in some way, a compromise and there are many, many ways to construct an image of the Earth. Here, in one place, is a magnificent collection showing many ways in which our globe can be represented on a computer screen.

Web:

   http://hum.amu.edu.pl/~zbzw/glob/glob1.htm

Land Surveying

Surveying is cool because there is so much land to go around, you will never run out. Also, when you survey, you get to use neat tools, talk about things other people don't understand, and generally swank around like you own the place. When it comes to being cool about mapping the Earth, surveyors really draw the line. To help you, here's where you can find lots of good information about surveying rules and regulations, state statutes, educational events and resources, professional organizations, and data sources. The Usenet group is for the discussion of the measurement and mapping of the Earth's surface.

Web:

   http://www.lsrp.com/mainind.html
   http://www.surveying.mentabolism.org/

Usenet:

   sci.engr.surveying

The Net knows.

Maps and Atlases

Here are my favorite sites on the Internet to look for maps. You'll find many types of high-quality maps—the selection is absolutely wonderful. Of course, you can use these resources when you need a particular map, but I suggest you take some time and explore. You'll find a lot to interest you, especially if you are doing research. I find these resources especially useful when I am listening to the news, and I want to see a map of a place that is being discussed.

Web:
  http://fermi.jhuapl.edu/states/states.html
  http://oddens.geog.uu.nl/
  http://www.atlapedia.com/online/map_index.htm
  http://www.lib.utexas.edu/maps/
  http://www.theodora.com/maps/
    abc_world_maps.html

United States Gazetteer

Here is a place to find information about any city or town in the United States. Just enter a city name or a zip code, and get useful information about that location: population, latitude and longitude, zip codes, as well as a colorful map you can save and customize. By the way, did you know there are two towns in the United States that are named after me? Harleyville, South Carolina (1990 pop. 633) and Harleysville, Pennsylvania (1990 pop. 7405). I bet if you check, you would find that the people in these towns are smarter, better looking, and more successful than the rest of the general American population.

Web:
  http://www.census.gov/cgi-bin/gazetteer/

Vintage Panoramic Maps

A panoramic map is a nonphotographic picture, shown as it would be if viewed from above (that is, a bird's-eye view). Panoramic maps were popular in the nineteenth and early twentieth centuries, and many such maps have been collected by the U.S. Library of Congress, which maintains this Web site as a public repository. You will find many old panoramic maps of U.S. and Canadian cities, as well as maps relating to military campaigns, exploration, immigration and transportation. I love looking at these old maps, and I particularly like being able to zoom closer to see parts of the image in more detail.

Web:
  http://lcweb2.loc.gov/ammem/pmhtml/

Vintage Panoramic Maps

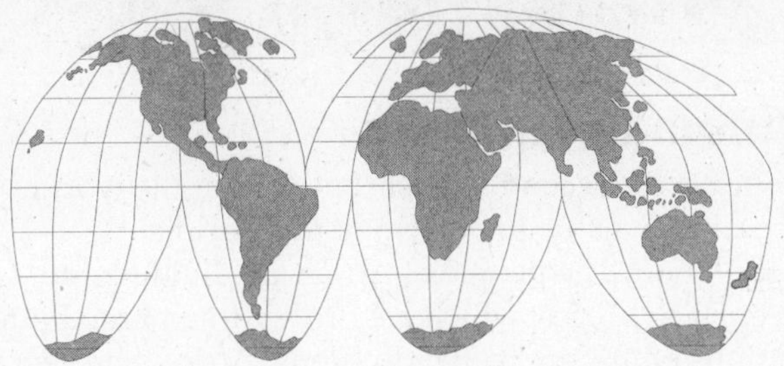

I went back in time. I'll tell you how I know.

I was looking at an old panoramic map of Los Angeles, dated 1888, and I zoomed in on it. There, standing under a tree, was a picture of a person who looked just like me.

He was holding something in his hand. I couldn't make it out, but it looked like a copy of "Harley Hahn's Internet Yellow Pages, 2003 Edition". Either that or a Bible. (I always get the two books confused.)

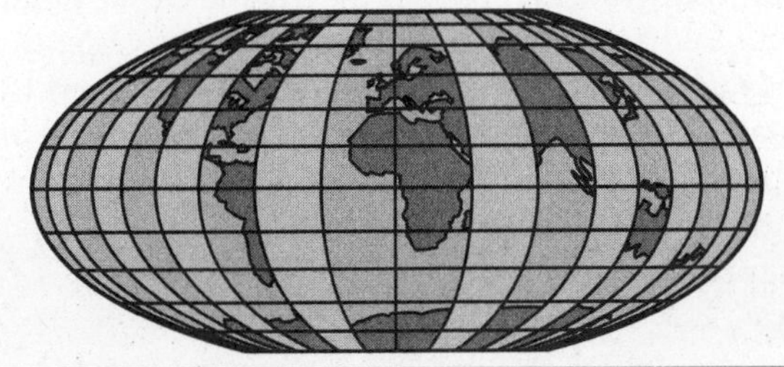

World's Highpoints

Here is a cool thing to do that is so easy, I'm surprised it isn't more popular. Have a friend pick a country, any country in the world. Then, using these resources, find the highest point in that country (probably a mountain). Climb the mountain and, when you get to the top, throw off a penny, just to see what happens when it lands. When you get famous, you can tell everyone that you got the idea from this book.

Web:
  http://www.americasroof.com/world.shtml
  http://www.peakware.com/encyclopedia/
    highest.htm

GOVERNMENT: INTERNATIONAL

African Governments

Africa is the second largest continent in the world, containing about 10 percent of the world's population. The people of Africa are divided into over 50 countries, which are further fragmented into various ethnic and tribal divisions. Africa's presence on the Net is severely hampered by the lack of a large-scale dependable telephone system. However, there are some African countries with Internet access. These Web sites have links to such African governmental resources as exist on the Net.

Web:
http://www.gksoft.com/govt/en/africa.html
http://www.lib.umich.edu/govdocs/forafr.html
http://www.nla.gov.au/gov/africa.html
http://www.politicalresources.net/africa.htm

Asia Pacific Governments

The Asia Pacific region of the world consists of those Asian countries that border the Pacific Ocean (that is, most of what used to be referred to as the Orient). Today, the Asia Pacific region is also considered to contain Australia and New Zealand. The significance of this group of countries lies in their economic and political interdependence, and not only in their geographic proximity.

Web:
http://www.lib.umich.edu/govdocs/forasia.html
http://www.nla.gov.au/gov/asiagov.html

Australian Government

Okay, you don't always need instant access to a huge amount of information regarding all the different organizations and departments that comprise the government of Australia. But when you do, you'll be glad you have the Net. Imagine how embarrassing it might be to, say, lose the respect of your friends and co-workers just because you don't know how to order a Zone Rebate Map from the Australian Taxation Office.

Web:
http://www.algin.net.au/
http://www.fed.gov.au/KSP/
http://www.nla.gov.au/oz/gov/

British Intelligence Organizations

If you have seen any James Bond movies, you would probably guess that the real British intelligence agencies are not exactly like the Secret Service for which Bond works. See for yourself by reading about MI5 (Military Intelligence 5: internal security and intelligence); MI6 (Military Intelligence 6: national security both internal and external); GCHQ (Government Communications Headquarters: intercepting and monitoring communications), SAS (Special Air Service: covert operations, especially counter-terrorism), and SBS (Special Boat Service: naval-based covert operations).

Web:
http://www.fas.org/irp/world/uk/
http://www.gchq.gov.uk/
http://www.mi5.gov.uk/

Embassies and Consulates Around the World

An embassy is the principal site of official representation of one country within another. Traditionally, embassies are located near the capital of the host country. For example, in the United States, most of the foreign embassies are in or near Washington, D.C. The head of the diplomatic mission is called an ambassador. In large countries, there may be other official diplomatic offices called consulates. For example, in the United States, there is a Canadian embassy in Washington, D.C., as well as consulates in various major cities around the country. Embassies and consulates provide a lot of useful information, and many of these offices around the world have their own Web sites.

Web:
http://www.embassyworld.com/
http://www.embpage.org/

Embassies in Washington, D.C.

When it's late at night and you are in the mood for a little political intrigue, take a look at these embassy-related links. You'll get the goods on the staff and resources of the Washington, D.C. embassy community, embassy Web sites, press releases, commerce and trade information, as well as travel and tourism reports. Remember, when you're in Washington, D.C., you can't be too careful. Today's attaché to the assistant secretary for international trade regulations could be tomorrow's industrial spy.

Web:
http://www.codia.org/dcembdirectory.html
http://www.embassy.org/

A B C D E F G H I J K L M N O P Q R S T U V W X Y Z

European Governments

There are many governments in Europe, and sometimes it can be difficult to find the information you want. To help you, here are Web sites that contain links to many different European governments and organizations. When I am looking for European information—especially from an official organization—I often start here.

Web:

http://www.gksoft.com/govt/en/europa.html
http://www.lib.umich.edu/govdocs/foreur.html
http://www.politicalresources.net/europe.htm

European Governments

Sometimes when I have trouble sleeping, I get up in the middle of the night and read about the governments of Europe.

After a half hour, my mind is full of all kinds of information about legislative, executive and judicative branches, and I can return to bed for a quiet, peaceful sleep.

Truly, you can never be too rich, too thin, or know too much about European governments.

European Parliament

The European Parliament is the only democratically elected international governing body in the world. The elected representatives exercise control over the member bodies at a European level. As such, the European Parliament is an important part of the European Union. Here is their official Web site, which contains information about the organization, including its powers, responsibilities, organization and operation.

Web:

http://www.europarl.eu.int/home/default_en.htm

European Union

Interesting facts about the European Union: On May 9, 1950, the French Foreign Minister formally read a declaration in which he proposed the creation of an international European organization to manage the coal and steel industry. (At the time, coal and steel were crucial to the balance of European military power.) From this proposal, a series of institutions were formed that, many years later, resulted in the European Union. For this reason, May 9th is now celebrated as Europe Day. Here is something even more interesting. The European flag consists of a circle of twelve gold stars in a blue background. Why twelve stars? The flag was originally designed for the Council of Europe (a completely different organization, sort of like a United Nations for Europe). At the time the Council of Europe was formed, there was some controversy over how many sovereign countries there would be. So, instead of creating a flag with one star for every country, they decided on a flag with twelve stars, because the number "12" was thought to be a symbol of completeness and unity. Why? There are twelve months in the year; twelve constellations in the zodiac; and—in order to win the support of the Christian population of Europe—it was observed that Jesus had twelve apostles. (I am not making this up.) In 1986, the flag was adopted by the European Communities, which later passed it on to the European Union. (Actually, I have a reason which is even better. The number "12" has a large number of factors: 1, 2, 3, 4, 6, 12. This symbolizes that—although there is only one union—there are many divisions.) Finally, here is one last item of European Union trivia. The European anthem (official song) is the prelude to the last movement of Beethoven's Ninth Symphony, often called the "Ode to Joy". (Note to Americans: Beethoven was a European musician who, in some parts of the world, has enjoyed a popularity rivaling that of Elvis Presley.)

Web:

http://www.eiop.or.at/euroint/
http://www.europa.eu.int/index-en.htm

Usenet:

talk.politics.european-union

Governments of the World

There are well over 200 countries in the world, and each one insists on having its own government, resources, organization, culture, and even its own flag. These sites have a lot of this type of information, organized by country, including links to other Web sites. There is also a nice collection of links to various world organizations. (Hint: This is the place I go when an emergency arises and I need to find the Web sites of the major political parties of Finland.)

Web:
http://www.adminet.com/world/gov/
http://www.hg.org/govt.html
http://www.worldworld.com/

Intelligence Organizations

An intelligence organization is one devoted to gathering secret information, usually, but not always, about an enemy. Such organizations employ many different methods, the most basic of which is spying. However, modern intelligence organizations go well beyond this traditional pastime, devoting much of their efforts to gathering massive amounts of data, monitoring of communications, industrial espionage and covert operations. Of course, these guys do not want you to know anything about their operations or how deeply entrenched they are within the various branches of government. However, as one of my readers, you deserve to know everything. Enjoy.

Web:
http://www.fas.org/irp/intelwww.html
http://www.intelbrief.com/Intelorgs.htm
http://www.loyola.edu/dept/politics/intel.html

Intelligence Organizations

Spies. They're in every country. Every government uses them.

We love them when they are on our side. We vilify them when they work for the enemy.

Spies. They're everywhere. Learn all about them on the Net.

International Government Talk and General Discussion

The world of international government involves a lot more than facts, figures and meetings. There are also opinions, power struggles, influence peddling and intrigue. If you would like to immerse yourself in a discussion of international affairs, join this mailing list. Every day, there is some new turn of events to discuss, and there is no reason why everyone shouldn't know your interpretation of what's happening.

Listproc Mailing List:
List Name: iro
Subscribe to: listproc@listproc.bgsu.edu

International Organizations in Geneva

There are a *lot* of international organizations in Geneva, including a large portion of the United Nations. Many of these organizations are related to various governments. This Web page provides a well-organized reference which allows you to find and access information about many, many international organizations both public and private.

Web:
http://geneva.intl.ch/gi/egimain/edir.htm

> The world's shortest
> inspirational poem:
> Be Me, Be Free.

International Relations and Security Network

The International Relations and Security Network is a large collection of information in several related areas: security and defense, peace and war, and international relations. These are excellent sites if you are looking for research material, or if you are interested in following current world issues and how they are developing. Hint: If you are a political science student and you need to come up with an essay fast, these are great places to look for raw material.

Web:
http://first.sipri.org/
http://www.isn.ethz.ch/

Israeli Government

The State of Israel, a democracy, was founded on May 14, 1948. Israel is governed by the Knesset (a house of representatives), the members of which are elected by the entire country. Unlike other governments, the Prime Minister is directly elected by the people (as opposed to being the leader of the majority party). The Prime Minister appoints the members of the Cabinet. The head of state is the President, a largely ceremonial position, who is elected by the Knesset.

Web:
http://www.info.gov.il/eng/
http://www.maven.co.il/subjects.asp?S=184
http://www.mfa.gov.il/mfa/go.asp?mfah00kj0

Japanese Government

Japan consists of a chain of islands off the coast of east Asia, between the North Pacific Ocean and the Sea of Japan. Most of Japan's land mass consists of four main islands: Honshu (the main island where Tokyo is), Hokkaido, Shikoku and Kyushu. Together, all of Japan is only 143,000 square miles (370,000 sq km), smaller than the state of Montana. Japan's population of about 127 million people is about 45 percent of the entire United States, making Japan the tenth most populated country in the world. (The top ten are China, India, the United States, Indonesia, Brazil, Pakistan, Nigeria, Russia, Bangladesh and Japan.) There are twelve Japanese cities with a population of over a million. The largest city, Tokyo, has more than 8 million people, and is the center of the largest metropolitan area in the world (with over 31 million people). Japan's government is a mixture of modern post-World War II democracy and traditional institutions. The main components of national government are its legislative body called the Diet (consisting of the House of Councilors and the House of Representatives), the Prime Minister (elected by the Diet) and the Cabinet (appointed by the Prime Minister). Although the Prime Minister is the chief executive, the head of state is the Emperor. (Technically, Japan is a constitutional monarchy.) On a regional level, Japan is divided into 47 prefectures, each of which elects its own governor and legislature. Even though Japan's government may look similar to that of other countries, its system is uniquely Japanese, built on a pronounced work ethic and a large degree of government-industry cooperation.

Web:
http://jin.jcic.or.jp/navi/category_2.html
http://www.kantei.go.jp/foreign/index-e.html

Latin American Governments

Latin America consists of the countries of America south of the United States, in which Romance languages are generally spoken (Portuguese in Brazil, French in Haiti, and Spanish just about everywhere else). The breadth of Latin America is huge, ranging from the border of the U.S. to the tip of South America not far from Antarctica.

Web:
http://www.democ.uci.edu/democ/gov.htm#lamer
http://www.georgetown.edu/pdba/english.html

Middle East Governments

The Middle East refers to an area that includes most of southwest Asia and parts of northeast Africa. The countries in the Middle East are (in Asia) Israel, Syria, Jordan, Iraq, Iran, Lebanon, Cyprus and part of Turkey; (on the Arabian peninsula) Saudi Arabia, Yemen, Oman, United Arab Emirates, Qatar, Bahrain, Kuwait; and (in Africa) Egypt. In addition, there are several Palestinian areas: partially autonomous settlements in the Gaza Strip and the West Bank (both adjacent to Israel), as well as tens of refugee camps in Lebanon, Jordan and Syria. The Middle East was the site of the ancient civilizations of Mesopotamia and Egypt, as well as the birthplace of three of the world's major religions: Judaism, Christianity and Islam. In modern times, the Middle East has suffered from a great deal of turmoil and political unrest, much of it due to the tension between Israel and the Arab states, intra-Arab conflicts, and the fact that, although the region is sitting on a significant portion of the world's oil reserves, the wealth and power is distributed extremely unevenly.

Web:

http://www.lib.umich.edu/govdocs/forme.html
http://www.politicalresources.net/m_east.htm

National Parliaments

I am seriously thinking of starting my own parliament.

My cat is going to be Speaker of the House, I am going to be the Prime Minister, and Lydia, my copy editor, is going to be the Leader of the Opposition, the person who stands up once a day and asks embarrassing questions.

National Parliaments

Want to see a magic trick? Pick a parliament, any parliament. Now look it up on one of these Web pages and click with your mouse. Wait a few minutes. All of a sudden, you will see the Web page for that organization. (Actually, it's not really magic—it's the Net.)

Web:

http://www.europarl.eu.int/natparl/
    linkspem_en.htm?redirected=1
http://www.ipu.org/english/parlweb.htm

NATO

NATO (the North Atlantic Treaty Organization) was formed on April 4, 1949, with the signing of the North Atlantic Treaty by twelve countries. Since then, other countries have joined and, today, NATO is a large, complex organization devoted to a voluntary security system in which the member countries share responsibilities. NATO is a defensive alliance based on political and military cooperation. There are nineteen members: Belgium, Canada, Czech Republic, Denmark, France, Germany, Greece, Hungary, Iceland, Italy, Luxembourg, Netherlands, Norway, Poland, Portugal, Spain, Turkey, United Kingdom and the United States.

Web:

http://www.nato.int/

Listserv Mailing List:

List Name: natodata
Subscribe to: listserv@listserv.cc.kuleuven.ac.be

North American Free Trade Agreement

The North American Free Trade Agreement (NAFTA) is an economic agreement signed by the U.S., Canada and Mexico in order to promote economic growth among the three countries. Here you can find the full text of the agreement, as well as resources to help you understand and work with the rules and regulations.

Web:

http://www.dfait-maeci.gc.ca/nafta-alena/
    agree-e.asp
http://www.sice.oas.org/trade/nafta/naftatce.asp

Organization of American States (OAS)

The Organization of American States (OAS) is the oldest regional organization in the world, having been established on April 30, 1948, by the United States and twenty Latin American republics. The purpose of the OAS is to promote cooperation among the countries of North and South America; to work toward peace and security; and to support economic, cultural and social development. Today, all 35 countries in North and South America belong to the OAS.

Web:

  http://www.oas.org/

Swiss Government

The official name for Switzerland is Confoederatio Helvetica (which roughly translates as "the Swiss Federation"). Switzerland has a long history of remaining neutral and, in fact, it is not even a member of the European Union. Switzerland itself is actually a union. It consists of a confederation of 23 different cantons. The country has four official languages: German (the first language of 63.7% of the people), French (19.2%), Italian (7.6%) and Romansh (0.6%). The remainder of the people, 8.9%, speak another language.

Web:

  http://www.admin.ch/ch/index.en.html
  http://www.zurichmednet.com/
    swissgovernment.html

United Kingdom Government

The United Kingdom—England, Scotland, Wales and Northern Ireland—is a constitutional monarchy. The hereditary monarch (currently Queen Elizabeth II) acts as the head of state, carrying out largely ceremonial duties. The parliament consists of an elected House of Commons and a non-elected House of Lords. The Prime Minister is the leader of whichever party holds a majority in the House of Commons. The Prime Minister appoints the Cabinet, the members of which are chosen from among the members of the House. These Web sites contain links to various British government organizations. I have also included the official Web site of 10 Downing Street, the residence and office of the Prime Minister. (However, what I am waiting for is an online version of Prince William's diary.)

Web:

  http://www.nds.coi.gov.uk/coi/coipress.nsf
  http://www.number-10.gov.uk/
  http://www.ukonline.gov.uk/

United Nations

On January 1, 1942, during World War II, representatives of 26 countries signed the Declaration by United Nations, in which they promised to continue fighting together against the Axis (the bad guys). The name "United Nations" was coined by U.S. President Franklin Roosevelt. On June 26, 1945, the United Nations as we know it was established with the signing of the United Nations Charter. In 1945, the U.N. had 51 member countries. Today, there are 189. The United Nations oversees a great many international organizations such as the Security Council, the General Assembly, the International Court of Justice, the United Nations Children's Fund (UNICEF), the World Health Organization, the World Bank, and so on. Overall, the U.N. has 64,700 employees, roughly the same as Disney World + Disneyland.

Web:

  http://www.un.org/english/
  http://www.unsystem.org/

Usenet:

  alt.politics.org.un

United Kingdom Government

The other night, my accountant and his wife were over for dinner. My friend Suzanne cooked a wonderful meal. The theme was British, so she made bangers and mash, mushy peas and boiled lamb, cooked just long enough to remove any semblance of taste.

After dinner, we relaxed with a pleasant game of U.K. Government Trivia. At first, everyone did well (you know how good accountants are at U.K. Government Trivia), but finally, I was able to win because I was the only one who could identify the current Secretary of State for Culture, Media and Sport.

(As a prize, I was allowed to clean the dishes and keep all the leftover mushy peas.)

United Nations Security Council

The United Nations Security Council is the body of the United Nations with the responsibility of maintaining international peace and security. Unlike the General Assembly—which has a representative from every country and is not always in session—the Security Council has a limited number of members and functions continuously. The Security Council has fifteen members: five permanent members (the United States, China, France, Russia and the United Kingdom) who have veto power over all decisions, and ten elected members who change from time to time.

Web:

   http://www.un.org/docs/scinfo.htm

U.S. International Aid

USAID (United States Agency for International Development) is an independent government agency that provides foreign assistance and humanitarian aid to "advance the political and economic interests of the United States". Read about their goals and studies: regional information, population and health information, economic growth studies, and global environmental issues. I'm trying to get a government grant to send me on an all-expense paid trip to the south of France. The only problem is showing how such a trip would be in the economic interests of the United States.

Web:

   http://www.usaid.gov/

World Government

Do you think that we would be better off with one large world government, rather than a whole bunch of countries continually arguing with one another (not to mention clogging up the Olympics and the United Nations)? Here are some resources that you can use to explore and learn about the idea of world government. In the old Superman comics, Superman came from the planet Krypton, which was much more advanced than the Earth. In particular, the Kryptonians had one large world government. (And look where they are today.)

Web:

   http://pages.prodigy.net/aesir/wgp.htm
   http://www.cgg.ch/millenium.htm
   http://www.w-g.jp/wgi/

GOVERNMENT: UNITED STATES

Budget of the United States Government

Have you ever wondered exactly how much money the government spends? Well, now you can find out. The entire budget of the United States federal government is on the Net. (That is, at least the parts of the budget that aren't deadly secrets, such as funding for clandestine operations.) In 2003, the government will spend $369 billion on Defense and Military. To put this in perspective, the following 22 federal branches and departments—put together—will spend $367 billion dollars: Legislative Branch, Judicial Branch, Agriculture, Commerce, Education, Energy, Health and Human Services, Housing and Urban Development, Interior, Justice, Labor, State, Transportation, Treasury, Veterans Affairs, Corps of Engineers, Environmental Protection Agency, Federal Emergency Management Agency, General Services Administration, International Assistance Programs, NASA and the Small Business Administration. All that for only $367 billion, compared to $369 for the military. It sure makes NASA ($15.1 billion) look like a bargain.

Web:

   http://w3.access.gpo.gov/usbudget/

Census Information

The job of the U.S. Census Bureau is to gather demographic (people) and economic (money) statistics about the United States. This information is made public, and much of it is available on the Census Bureau's Web site. I find this site a fascinating place to browse; there are so many interesting statistics. For example, in Midland County, Texas (where George W. Bush grew up), of all the people 25 years of age or older, 79% are high school graduates and 25% are college graduates; within families, 74% of the people speak English at home, while 24% speak Spanish; and of all the people in the county, 12.9% live below the poverty level.

Web:

   http://www.census.gov/

CIA

The Central Intelligence Agency (CIA) was formed in 1947 by the passage of the National Security Act. The CIA's role is to concern itself with intelligence and counterintelligence activities outside the United States, and to coordinate activities with the FBI (Federal Bureau of Investigation) relating to domestic counterintelligence. If you would like to experience a little of the mystery and intrigue of the CIA—without having them start a file on you—visit their Web site, where you can learn more about the agency and take a virtual tour of the parts of their operation they are willing to discuss. While you are here, be sure to check out some of the CIA's publications, such as the "Factbook on Intelligence" and the "CIA World Factbook". The Usenet group is for the discussion of the CIA. You are probably safe to say anything you want because, after all, the United States is a free country and no government agency would ever dare monitor a Usenet discussion group. (Ha, ha.)

Web:
  http://www.cia.gov/

Usenet:
  alt.politics.org.cia

Commerce Department

What could be more romantic than soft lighting, romantic music, a bottle of fine wine, and a direct link to the U.S. Department of Commerce?

The next time your hot date starts to cool off, go back to your place, fire up your Internet connection and tap into the Department of Commerce Web site. Before you know it, your social life will perk up like a ferret on a caffeine binge.

Commerce Department

The U.S. Department of Commerce was started in 1903 and since then has continually changed to keep in step with current economic conditions. Today, the DOC has many agencies, some of which you might be surprised to find in this department. For example, here you will find NOAA (National Oceanic and Atmospheric Administration), NIST (National Institute of Standards and Technology), the Patent and Trademark Office, and the National Weather Service.

Web:
  http://www.doc.gov/

Congress

Senators are elected for only six years, while representatives are elected for a shorter two-year term. However—like General MacArthur and adult children without jobs—they can return. If you would like to check up on your elected representatives, here is all the information you need to find them, send them email, connect to their Web pages, and generally see what they are doing (at least when they think you are looking).

Web:

http://thomas.loc.gov/home/legbranch/
   legbranch.html
http://www.clerkweb.house.gov/
http://www.congress.org/
http://www.house.gov/
http://www.senate.gov/
http://www.visi.com/juan/congress/

C-SPAN Live

Watch the U.S. government at work, from the comfort of your desktop. C-SPAN is a public-oriented cable TV channel, owned by the U.S. cable television industry. The goal of C-SPAN is to allow Americans to watch all the proceedings in the House of Representatives, the Senate, and other public forums. (The name C-SPAN stands for "Cable-Satellite Public Affairs Network".) The idea is that people should be able to watch their elected representatives talk without any editing, commentary or analysis. Of course, from time to time, C-SPAN does get a bit boring. However, at least there are no commercials.

Web:

http://www.c-span.org/

Executive Branch

Never again will you have to hotfoot it around the Net looking for information about the President and his minions. The Library of Congress has compiled a Web page that covers resources pertaining to the executive branch of the federal government and its various departments, as well as independent executive agencies.

Web:

http://lcweb.loc.gov/global/executive/fed.html

FBI

The Federal Bureau of Investigation (FBI), created in 1908, is a division of the United States Department of Justice. The FBI investigates various violations of federal law such as kidnapping, bank robbing, sabotage, espionage and civil rights violations. If you have ever been in a United States post office, you may have seen the pictures on the wall of desperate and suspicious-looking individuals. These are fugitives that are being pursued by the FBI. However, you don't have to go into the post office to see these pictures. At the FBI Web site, you can check out the list of the "Ten Most Wanted Fugitives" and see if you happen to know any of them.

Web:

http://www.fbi.gov/

Usenet:

alt.politics.org.fbi

Federal Government Information

No matter what you are looking for in the federal government, these Web sites are the best places to start. They contain links to all major sources of government information. If you are not sure what you want, you can search for it. If you know a specific department, it is only a few mouse clicks away.

Web:

http://www.firstgov.gov/
http://www.lib.umich.edu/govdocs/federal.html
http://www.nttc.edu/resources/government/
   govresources.asp
http://www.pueblo.gsa.gov/call/phone.htm
http://www.whitehouse.gov/government/

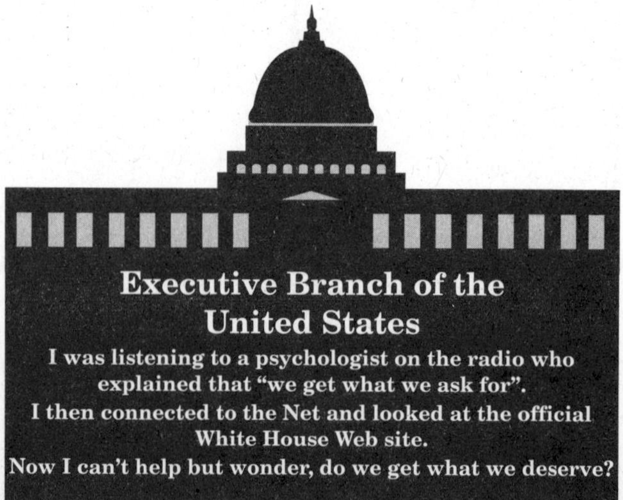

Report on the FBI
by Elmo (age 8)

When I grow up I want to be an FBI agent. Either that, or an astronaut or a fireman. If I'm an astronaut, I will get to fly high in the air in a rocket ship and drop water balloons on my sister, Lucy. If I am a fireman, I will get to ride on a big red truck and make a lot of noise.

However, if I am an FBI agent, I will get to catch bad guys and solve crimes and eat ice cream whenever I want, and nobody could tell me what to do (except the President).

-Elmo

FedStats

The agencies of the U.S. federal government are continually generating an enormous amount of statistics. This Web site can help you find what you need quickly and easily, no matter where it is. My advice is to keep this Web address with you at all times. You never know, for example, when you will need to find out how many electronics technicians were employed by the Federal Aviation Administration in 1984 (7,229).

Web:
  http://www.fedstats.gov/

FedWorld

The U.S. government has hundreds of departments, agencies and programs, all of which offer information to the public. FedWorld is a service supported by the National Technical Information Service (NTIS), an agency of the U.S. Department of Commerce. The purpose of FedWorld is to act as a central access point to help you find and obtain the information you want. Without a doubt, when you need to find something related to the federal government, this is the place to start.

Web:
  http://www.fedworld.gov/

General Accounting Office

The General Accounting Office (GAO) is the investigative arm of Congress. The GAO examines matters relating to the receiving and spending of public funds. In practice, the GAO is as close as we can get to a government auditor. The GAO Web site contains reports on budget issues, investment, government management, public services, health care, energy issues and virtually every other major area of the federal government.

Web:
  http://www.gao.gov/

Government Corruption

I don't want to talk behind anyone's back, but rumor has it that there is corruption in government. I thought if you were going to hear it, you should get the news from me. Find out the details of what's going on in the nooks and crannies of the political system.

Web:
  http://www.citizen.org/congress/
  http://www.pogo.org/

Usenet:
  alt.government.abuse

Government Corruption

Corruption is in the eyes of the beholder and—for people in government service—it is all too often the case that the "I's" have it.

Check out the **Government Corruption** site, and see what your friends on the Net have to say about the government's tendency to confuse the ideas of yours, mine, and ours.

Government Information

This world is full of such wondrous things, there is never a reason to be bored. For example, the next time you feel a bit of the old ennui, hurry over to this Web site where you can find demographic information about the population, employment, education, and economics of the United States. For example, you can read the Consolidated Federal Funds Reports, or the Census of Agriculture. For a nice change of pace, take a look at Earnings by Occupation and Education.

Web:

http://govinfo.kerr.orst.edu/

Usenet:

bit.listserv.govdoc-l

Inspectors General

This site has information about the Federal Offices of Inspectors General, the fine folks who are responsible for auditing, investigating and inspecting government agencies. Their goal is to decrease fraud, waste and abuse, and they have the Web page to prove it.

Web:

http://www.ignet.gov/

Justice Statistics

Here are some statistics on topics relating to the U.S. Department of Justice, including crimes, victims, drugs, prisons, courts, sentencing, and much more. There is a lot of interesting information here and, in my opinion, it speaks highly of the United States that such information is made accessible, for free, to anyone in the world. In many other countries, information like this is kept secret, not broadcast on the Internet.

Web:

http://www.ojp.usdoj.gov/bjs/

Justices of the Supreme Court

The Supreme Court is the highest federal court in the United States and has jurisdiction over all the other courts in the nation. The Supreme Court consists of judges—a chief justice and eight associate justices—all of whom are nominated by the President and confirmed by the Senate. The Supreme Court has two main duties: to interpret acts of Congress, and to determine whether federal and state statutes conform to the United States Constitution. If you want the scoop on those people currently serving on the Supreme Court, check out these Web sites. They have lists of the justices, along with biographical data and their pictures (in case you run into one of them in the supermarket). You will also find a lengthy and fascinating collection of each judge's opinions for the court: important majority opinions, important concurring opinions, and selected dissenting opinions.

Web:

http://supct.law.cornell.edu/supct/
http://www.supremecourtus.gov/about/about.html
http://www.uscourts.gov/

National Archives and Records Administration

The U.S. National Archives and Records Administration is the agency that oversees the management of all the records of the federal government. (And you thought it was a big job just keeping your room tidy.) Here you will find a wealth of information, including historical records, the Federal Register (the daily record of the government), genealogical data, links to the presidential libraries, the official U.S. Government Manual (which contains just about *everything* under the American sun), and much more.

Web:

http://www.archives.gov/

> **Sometimes I wish that I could do what I do, and then I realize — I can!**

Social Security Administration

You can't get far in the United States without having a Social Security number. But that's only the beginning. The Social Security Administration (SSA) dispenses huge amounts of money each year under the auspices of many different programs. If you are American, I promise you that, one day, you will need information from the SSA. On that day, start with this Web site.

Web:

  http://www.ssa.gov/

State and Local Government

Just about every state, county and city in the United States has a Web site, and these resources will help you find whatever you need. One day, just for fun, I spent some time cruising through the Los Angeles County Web sites. I found out that the bail for committing assault with a firearm (245(a)(2) Penal Code) is the same as the bail for cultivating peyote (11363 Penal Code): $30,000. Now, is that fun or what? (You know what? I've got to get out of the house more.)

Web:

  http://www.lcweb.loc.gov/global/state/stategov.html
  http://www.piperinfo.com/state/index.cfm
  http://www.wheretodoresearch.com/states.htm

State Department

The United States maintains diplomatic relations with about 180 countries as well as many international organizations. The Department of State is the principal foreign affairs agency of the U.S government. As such, it has two broad mandates: to represent U.S. policies and interests abroad, and to gather information used to create foreign policy. The head of the State Department—the Secretary of State—is the fourth in line of presidential succession (after the Vice President, the Speaker of the House, and the President Pro Tempore of the Senate).

Web:

  http://www.state.gov/

White House

Here is the official Internet site for the White House. If you have nothing to do, you might want to connect and see who is living there.

Web:

  http://www.whitehouse.gov/

White House News

Each day, you can find out the official word on the activities and goings-on at the White House and related U.S. agencies. This Web site is just the thing to give your son or daughter for a graduation present. (After all, who wants a car?)

Web:

  http://www.whitehouse.gov/news/

HEALTH

Birth Control

On the Net you can find out everything you always wanted to know about birth control (but no one ever bothered to tell you). You can find general information about all methods of contraception (including abstinence). Learn about drugs, contraceptive devices, useful statistics, family planning, and much more.

Web:
  http://ec.princeton.edu/
  http://www.brainphysics.com/guide/
  http://www.choice.org/2.choosing.html
  http://www.fhi.org/
  http://www.plannedparenthood.org/bc/
  http://www.reproline.jhu.edu/

Birth control: When you care enough not to send the very best.

Centers for Disease Control

The Centers for Disease Control and Prevention (CDC) is an agency of the United States Department of Health and Human Services. (The CDC was originally established in 1946 as the Communicable Disease Center.) The CDC offers national programs for the prevention and control of communicable diseases, conducts research and directs quarantine activities when necessary. They also offer health-related information for people who are planning to travel outside the U.S.

Web:
  http://www.cdc.gov/

Children's Health

If you have kids, there will be lots of times when you will need health advice. Here are some Web sites to assist you. You'll find information on a large variety of topics relating to pediatric health, childhood conditions, and acquired and congenital diseases, as well as advice and tips. The Usenet group is for the general discussion of children's health. Hint: If all else fails, ask your mother.

Web:
  http://www.childrenshealth.co.uk/
  http://www.drgreene.com/
  http://www.echildshealth.com/
  http://www.nncc.org/cyfernet/health.page.html
Usenet:
  misc.kids.health

Children's Mental Health

Here is an excellent collection of articles that deal with many different aspects of children's mental health. If one of your children has a problem, this is a great place to look for information, advice and ideas. Read about adolescent development, depression, lying, teen pregnancy, sleep problems, mental retardation, and more. Even if your kids are doing fine, you will still find it worthwhile to browse this site for useful information. For example, did you know that children who watch a lot of television are more likely to have lower grades, read fewer books, exercise less and be overweight?

Web:
  http://www.aacap.org/web/aacap/info_families/

Doctor-Marketed Web Sites

Everyone wants to get into the act, and on the Net, that means doctors too. In a quest for the hearts, minds and dollars of people everywhere, various companies have created Web sites in the names of famous doctors. These Web sites offer news, information and advice on a variety of health-related topics. Here are sites marketed under the auspices of doctors: Andrew Weil (author and lecturer), Donnica Moore (TV personality), Dean Edell (radio talk show host), and Gabe Mirkin (radio talk show host).

Web:
  http://www.drweil.com/
  http://www.drdonnica.com/
  http://www.healthcentral.com/
  http://www.drmirkin.com/

Finding a Doctor or Hospital

I went to medical school, and I know. There is a *huge* difference in the skill of doctors, and it matters a lot. I put in a lot of effort to find a good doctor for myself. I asked around for recommendations, then I made appointments with various doctors and interviewed them. Sure, I had to pay for those appointments, but it was worth it, as I was able to find the doctor I wanted. The best way to find a good doctor is to ask another doctor who is familiar with your area. The doctors in every community know which of their colleagues are good and which are bad. However, they are reluctant to give such information to outsiders, so you may have to be inventive to get a real recommendation. One last hint. Don't ever forget that you are the customer. The doctor works for you.

Web:
> http://www.ama-assn.org/aps/amahg.htm
> http://www.doctordirectory.com/
> http://www.healthgrades.com/
> http://www.physician--directory.com/
> http://www.thehealthpages.com/

Go Ask Alice

"Alice" is a pseudonym for a number of people in the Health Education and Wellness Program at Columbia University in New York City. The "Go Ask Alice" Web site features answers to questions submitted by readers. The questions are oriented toward students and cover sex, relationships, drugs, fitness, emotional health and other topics. You can browse through the many questions that have already been answered, or submit a question of your own. (The name "Go Ask Alice" is taken from the song "White Rabbit", recorded by Jefferson Airplane on their 1967 album "Surrealistic Pillow". The song deals with the superficial similarities between taking drugs in the Sixties and the book "Alice's Adventures in Wonderland". I assume the people at Columbia University chose this whimsical name in order to convince themselves that, even though they are old, they are still cool.)

Web:
> http://www.goaskalice.columbia.edu/

Health Care Politics Talk and General Discussion

What happens when an irresistible force (health care reform) meets an immovable object (the health care industry)? Join the ongoing debate and share your opinions and comments.

Usenet:
> talk.politics.medicine

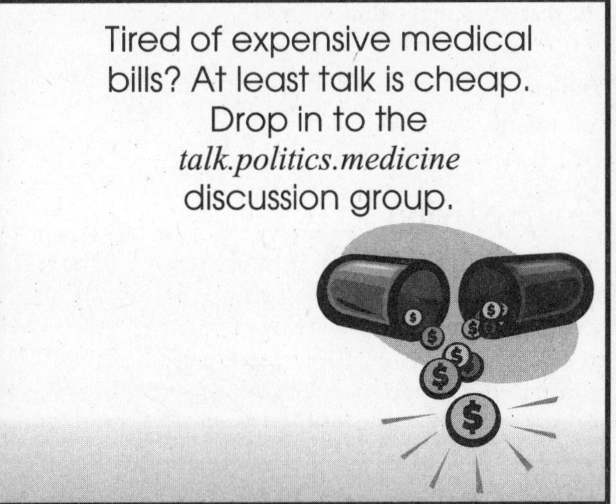

Health News

When it comes to medical problems, especially chronic conditions, it is human nature to look for magic cures and treatments. When it comes to answering health-related questions, the mainstream part of our culture worships at the altar of science (and rightly so). However, we often go too far, and it doesn't take much rational reflection to see that, as a society, we are obsessed with medical research, addicted to the rush that comes with each new "breakthrough". As a result, there is a constant stream of health-related news... day after day after day. Indulge if you must, but do so when you have lots of spare time. Reading health-related articles is like eating potato chips: it's hard to stop at just one.

Web:
> http://www.cnn.com/health/
> http://www.docguide.com/
> http://www.my.webmd.com/
> http://www.reutershealth.com/frame2/eline.html
> http://www.yourhealthdaily.com/

Health Resources

When you are looking for health-related information, here are some excellent places to start. You can find information on specific diseases and conditions, as well as a lot of good advice on how to stay healthy.

Web:

    http://www.druginfonet.com/
    http://www.healthatoz.com/
    http://www.healthfinder.gov/
    http://www.intelihealth.com/
    http://www.mayoclinic.com/
    http://www.medicinenet.com/

Usenet:

    alt.health

Healthy Living

In the long run, what you do for *yourself* will be the most important influence on your long-term health. My philosophy is to slowly build habits that lead to an enduring state of physical and emotional well-being. In my experience, this requires you to make a serious, ongoing commitment to yourself (and being a man, I understand commitment). I know that, as one of my readers, you are wiser and more sensitive than almost everyone else, and when I say that the most important factor governing your life is your attitude, I know you understand what I mean. For this reason, I offer these resources to help you find the path to health that works for you. In my experience, there is no single magic technique; anyone who says different is trying to sell you something. The reality of it is that you will have to practice a variety of good habits over a long period of time. (I use a combination of a good diet, regular exercise, yoga, vitamins and supplements, massage, and chiropractic adjustments.) The changes I am talking about do not depend on your husband or wife, your father or mother, your kids, or your best friend. They have to do with *you*, and the time to start is *now*.

Web:

    http://www.consciouschoice.com/healthconscious/
    http://www.emh.org/hll/
    http://www.health-alliance.com/living
    http://www.healthwell.com/
    http://www.hhnews.com/lifestyle.htm
    http://www.holisticmed.com/
    http://www.shareguide.com/articles.html

Massage

Just by using your fingers, you can turn someone into a noodle. Massage is a delicious and therapeutic way to alleviate the effects of tension and ill health. Discover new techniques and methods of massage along with recommendations for oils and additional accoutrements that can take massage to a new level.

Web:

    http://www.bobnet.com/subpages/tips.htm
    http://www.gems4friends.com/massage.html
    http://www.holistic-online.com/massage/
       mas_home.htm
    http://www.qwl.com/mtwc/

Usenet:

    alt.backrubs
    alt.health.massage-therapy

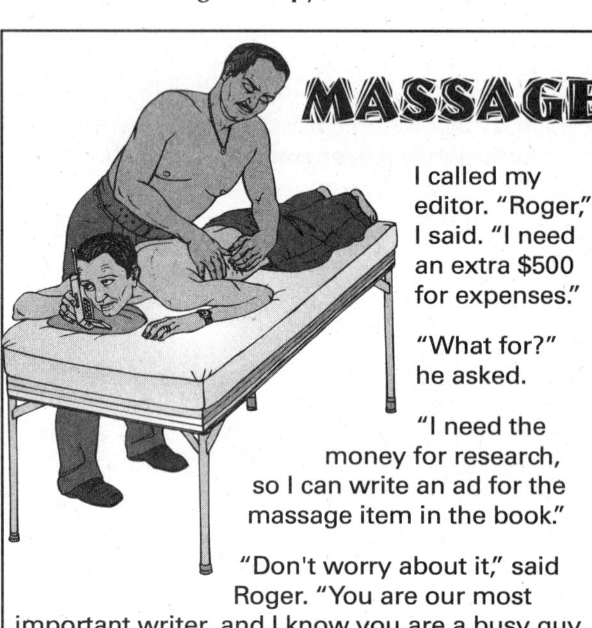

Menopause and Climacteric

Human bodies, both male and female, evolved during a time when people lived no more than a couple of decades. Thus, it is no surprise that long before you die, your body will start to wear out. In particular, as a woman, the time will come when your ovaries will gradually stop producing estrogen. When this happens, your body will change in important ways, a process referred to as the climacteric or, more informally, the "change of life". The most striking change is menopause, the permanent cessation of your periods. However, there are other possible changes, all caused by decreased estrogen, the most common being hot flashes, irritability, emotional lability, mood swings, vaginal dryness and atrophy, decreased libido, thinning hair, vaginal and urinary tract infections, and short-term memory problems. (In other words, if you liked PMS, you'll love menopause.) Most women experience their climacteric at the beginning of their 50s, but it can occur anywhere between the ages of 45 and 60. Some women even experience significant premenopausal changes in their 30s. The actual changes occur over a period of several months to several years. Although the symptoms usually only last a short time, permanently diminished estrogen does cause long-term effects. For this reason, many woman choose to have hormone replacement therapy (HRT). When the time comes, the Net can be a valuable source of information and comfort by helping you understand what is happening and what choices you have.

Web:
   http://www.earlymenopause.com/
   http://www.menopause-online.com/
   http://www.menopause.org/
   http://www.shareguide.com/Menopause.html

Usenet:
   alt.support.menopause

Listserv Mailing List:
   List Name: menopaus
   Subscribe to: listserv@maelstrom.stjohns.edu

My other joke is funny.

What should first-time mothers know about NEWBORN BABIES?

After your baby is born, the first two months will be very difficult. You will find that taking care of a newborn child is an enormous amount of work, and you will feel as if you are tied to the baby 24 hours a day.

• You will suffer from a serious lack of sleep.

• Breast feeding will take up a lot of your time. For example, you may need to feed the baby every two hours around the clock, and when you do, the baby may nurse for an hour and a half at a time.

• It will take time for your baby to learn how to sleep quietly when he or she is not in your arms.

Don't despair. After the first two months, things get a *lot* better.

Moreover, as you take care of your baby, you will experience a new type of love, one that, previously, you could not even imagine. In the words of a friend of mine, Jamie, the mother of Kalissa: "Everything is so much easier, now that I understand the purpose of my life."

Mental Health

Mental health is something we take for granted when things are going well. However, we are very much creatures of the mind, and when our minds do not work well, our suffering can be tremendous. One of the things that can help you the most when you are dealing with mental illness is reliable information. These Web sites can help you understand various mental health conditions and treatments.

Web:
   http://www.mentalhealth.com/
   http://www.mentalhelp.net/

National Institute of Allergy and Infectious Disease

The National Institute of Allergy and Infectious Disease (NIAID) provides major support and direction for medical research relating to infectious, immunologic and allergic diseases that afflict people worldwide (including AIDS). Its Web site is a point of access for information about its myriad activities and research accomplishments.

Web:

http://www.niaid.nih.gov/

National Institutes of Health

The National Institutes of Health (NIH) is one of eight health agencies of the U.S. Public Health Service. The general aim of the NIH is to "uncover new knowledge that will lead to better health for everyone" (boldly going where no medical man has gone before). More precisely, the NIH conducts research in its own laboratories, and supports a lot of research in universities, medical schools, hospitals, and other institutions.

Web:

http://www.nih.gov/

Quackery and Health Fraud

Health and feeling well are so important to us that when things go wrong we may consider any alternative, even those based on unsound principles or deception. Eventually, all of us die, and throughout the course of a lifetime, we will get sick from time to time. Thus, it is no surprise that the world of health has always had quacks and fakes. Moreover, there are many "alternative" therapies that are simply not effective, but still practiced widely. These Web sites contain information and links that will help you recognize health fraud and make informed decisions about health care for yourself and your family. If someone you know has a serious illness, do take some time to learn about the frauds, so you don't end up making a bad decision.

Web:

http://www.mtn.org/quack/
http://www.quackwatch.com/

Sexually Transmitted Diseases (STDs)

The most serious sexually transmitted disease is AIDS, caused by the human immunodeficiency virus (HIV). However, the term "sexually transmitted diseases", or STDs, covers a lot of ground. There are more than fifty diseases and conditions that are spread through sexual activity, among them chlamydia, gonorrhea, herpes, genital warts, syphilis, candidiasis (yeast infection) and trichomoniasis. The microorganisms that cause STDs are generally spread through either physical contact or the exchange of body fluids such as semen, vaginal fluid or blood. Some STDs are minor, but in general, these are conditions that need to be treated, as they can lead to sterility, chronic infection, infertility, cancer and, in the worst cases, death. Here is the information you need to understand how you catch these diseases, what happens when you are infected, and how to get rid of them.

Web:

http://www.ama-assn.org/special/std/std.htm
http://www.ci.nyc.ny.us/html/doh/html/std/std.html
http://www.epigee.org/guide/stds.html
http://www.health.qld.gov.au/sexhealth/
http://www.iwannaknow.org/

Snakebites

In North America, snakes are not nearly as dangerous as most people believe. North American snakes seldom bite humans, and even when they do, the bites are rarely fatal. However, if you do get bitten by a snake, you may be in need of some hard information quickly. If so, here is the place to look. If you happen to be bitten by a snake in a different part of the world, my advice is to check these sites, then catch the first plane for North America. (By the way, unless you are acting in a movie, it is never a good idea to suck out the venom with your mouth.)

Web:

http://www.fda.gov/fdac/features/995_snakes.html
http://www.methodisthealth.com/nontraumatic/
   snake.htm
http://www.xmission.com/~gastown/herpmed/
   snbite.htm

Majordomo Mailing List:

List Name: venom-l
Subscribe to: majordomo@icomm.ca

Stress

Stress, stress and more stress. I'm so tired of stress I could scream. But when I'm finished screaming and I want the real lowdown, I turn to the stress Web sites. Here is information on the reasons and biological basis for stress, the physiology of stress, how to manage stress, and hints on how to relax. (My hint is to stop reading about stress.)

Web:
  http://www.aarp.org/confacts/stress/
    stressresources.html
  http://www.imt.net/~randolfi/StressLinks.html
  http://www.jobstresshelp.com/
  http://www.pp.okstate.edu/ehs/links/stress.htm
  http://www.stressbusting.co.uk/
  http://www.stressless.com/stressnews2.cfm
  http://www.stresstips.com/gtws.html

U.S. Department of Health and Human Services

The Department of Health and Human Services (HHS) is the principal U.S. federal governmental organization devoted to health care. HHS is huge, being the largest grant-making department in the government. HHS contains several hundred agencies and organizations, including the Centers for Disease Control, the Food and Drug Administration and the National Institutes of Health. The HHS Web site provides information about the HHS's programs, organizations and activities.

Web:
  http://www.os.dhhs.gov/

Women's Health

Women have a number of special health considerations. Here is a fine collection of resources related to women's health. Read about pregnancy, birth and midwifery, breast cancer, menopause, osteoporosis, rape and sexual assault, abortion, safe sex, fertility, sexual harassment, AIDS, sexually transmitted diseases, mental health, Pap tests, and much, much more.

Web:
  http://www.4woman.org/
  http://www.bbc.co.uk/health/womens/
  http://www.healthywomen.org/
  http://www.mum.org/
  http://www.obgyn.net/women/women.asp
  http://www.vaginalinfections.com/
  http://www.womens-health.com/
  http://www.womens-health.org/

World Health Organization

The World Health Organization (WHO) operates under the auspices of the United Nations. The goal of WHO is the "attainment by all peoples of the highest possible level of health". (What do they mean by health? "A state of complete physical, mental and social well-being—and not merely the absence of disease or infirmity—in which each person in the world has at least two Harley Hahn books.") I have an idea for you that I know will sound a bit odd. Every now and then, take a few moments and look at the WHO press releases. You will find out a lot of interesting information and get a real feeling for what is happening around the world.

Web:

http://www.who.int/

HERBS

Aromatherapy

Aromatherapy is the therapeutic use of scented essential oils derived from plants. The oil can be put into a vaporizer, applied to the skin by massage, or put into a bath. Many people use aromatherapy in conjunction with massage, baths or vaporizers. However, once you learn how to choose and manipulate fragrances, you may want to make aromatherapy part of your everyday life. Of all our senses, our sense of smell is the most basic and the most powerful. We tend to ignore it, but by changing the smells in our environment, we can influence our moods, our feelings and our sense of well-being.

Web:

http://www.aromaweb.com/
http://www.fragrant.demon.co.uk/aromlist.html
http://www.halcyon.com/kway/articles.htm
http://www.holisticmed.com/www/
   aromatherapy.html

Usenet:

alt.aromatherapy

Chinese Herbs

Using herbs to treat medical conditions is an important part of traditional Chinese medicine. The herbs are taken from plants that grow in China, from the roots, bark, flowers, seeds, fruit, leaves and branches. Within the Chinese system, several hundred different herbs are commonly used. However, you must remember that, in China, such remedies are used within the context of the Chinese society. In other countries, the medical and cultural systems are different. One must be careful before taking a single herb or two in isolation, and transplanting it into the medical system of another culture as some type of wonder cure. Thus, before you use Chinese herbs, it is important to learn about their use, and develop an appreciation of how they fit into a larger picture.

Web:

http://www.acuhealing.com/chineseherbs/
http://www.acupuncture.com/Herbology/
   HerbInd.htm
http://www.rmhiherbal.org/

Culinary Herbs

When I cook, I like to use a variety of fresh herbs to season my meal. They taste great, they are economical, and they are easy to use. Here are FAQs (frequently asked question list) that will help you learn about using herbs in your cooking and growing your own culinary herbs.

Web:

http://ibiblio.org/herbmed/faqs/culi-cont.html
http://www.faqs.org/faqs/food/culinary-herbs/part1/

> **Experience may be
> the best teacher,
> but the tuition can be
> awfully expensive.**

Garlic

I love garlic. I have a recipe for garlic and parsley spaghetti topped with a smoked garlic tomato sauce that is fantastic. (1: Buy ready-made garlic and parsley spaghetti. 2: Buy ready-made smoked garlic tomato sauce. 3: Cook spaghetti. 4: Warm sauce in microwave. 5: Combine spaghetti and sauce.) Garlic is good for more than cooking, though. You can use garlic to promote health. Garlic contains a large amount of organic sulfides and other nutritious compounds, and is reported as being useful as an antibiotic, anti-carcinogen and antioxidant, as well as reducing atherosclerosis (at least in lab animals).

Web:

> http://www.botanical.com/botanical/mgmh/g/
> garlic06.html
> http://www.garlicshoppe.com/shared/recipes/
> facts.html
> http://www.kcweb.com/herb/garlic.htm

> On the Internet, there's no such place as far away.

Growing Herbs

What could be more satisfying than using your own home-grown herbs to season a home-cooked meal? Whether you are a rank beginner or a highly experienced, organic Earth-mother herbaphile, you'll find these growing guides invaluable. When it comes to the care and feeding of these tiny fragrant friends, the Net is ready to help you fulfill your botanical destiny.

Web:

> http://www.chefsgarden.com/GrowingTips.htm
> http://www.doityourself.com/herbs/
> http://www.gardenguides.com/herbs/herb.htm
> http://www.nothyme.com/plantpropagation/
> http://www.sunnyboygardens.com/
> herbinformation.htm
> http://www.wholeherb.com/PAGES/GROW/
> GrowHerb.html

Harry Potter Herbs

Nicholas Culpepper (1616-1654) was a legendary figure in the field of herbal medicine. In 1652, he published an intriguing book with the modest title: "The English Physician or An Astrologo-Physical Discourse of the Vulgar Herbs of This Nation: Being a Complete Method of Physick, whereby a man may preserve his Body in Health; or cure himself, being sick, for three pence charge, with such things only as grow in England, they being most fit for English Bodies". Three and a half centuries later, Culpepper's work was used by J.K. Rowlings as a reference for the herbs she described in the Harry Potter books. If you like Harry Potter, why not look at the original book and create some herbal remedies of your own?

Web:

> http://info.med.yale.edu/library/historical/culpeper/
> culpeper.htm
> http://www.bibliomania.com/2/1/66/113/

Herb Magick

When you are trying to get through life, you don't necessarily have to stick with "the known" reality most people agree on. For instance, you can utilize some herb magick to make life go your way. These Web resources have basic information about getting started with herbs, as well as more esoteric information about the magickal properties of various woods and plants. Don't have a spellbook? No need to worry. You can find sample spells online. Bad with plants? It doesn't matter. After all, you don't need a green thumb when you have a magick wand.

Web:
    http://wolfmoongrove.com/Herb%20Info%20Pages/
        herb_magick.htm
    http://www.branwenscauldron.com/uses_herbs.html
    http://www.eclecticpagans.com/herb_magick.htm
    http://www.sanfords.net/
        Pagan_Humor_and_Thoughts/herb_magick.htm
    http://www.silvermidnight.com/herbcorrespond.htm

Herb Talk and General Discussion

Things that grow and things that don't, plants that heal and plants that won't. Little herbs that stink and flower, have their merit and their power. Here is where the people go, to talk about the herbs to grow. Herbs for cooking and to eat, herbs for healing can't be beat.

Usenet:
    alt.folklore.herbs

Herb Uses

It's always good to know about herbal healing properties. For example, if you have a big publishing deadline, and your editor will not allow you to sleep or have fun, it is nice to know that bergamot helps alleviate tension and basil can be used to treat stress-related conditions like hypertension.

Web:
    http://www.herbanspice.com/silversage/
    http://www.herbmed.org/
    http://www.witchwayrus.com/herbuse.htm

You probably know that, historically, certain herbs are used for medicinal purposes. However, before you use an herb in this way, be sure you understand its effects.

For example, tradition holds that ginger helps fight a cold, chamomile is soothing to the nerves, sarsaparilla helps cure impotence, and hawthorn berries strengthen the muscles and the nerves to the heart.

So, guys, if your wife or girlfriend ever brings you chamomile tea mixed with sarsaparilla and ginger, make sure you've got plenty of hawthorn berries to see you through the night.

Herbal Encyclopedia

The Herbal Encyclopedia is a comprehensive guide to herbs. Choose an herb, any herb, and in two clicks of a mouse tail, you will have information about how the herb is used and how to grow it. For example, did you know that catnip (Nepeta cataria) can be used to treat a cold or the flu? I told this to my cat, and now he won't stop sneezing.

Web:
    http://www.wic.net/waltzark/herbenc.htm

Herbal Hall

Here is an excellent site for herbalists, gardeners and botany lovers. This Web site is loaded with articles, reference material (including a glossary), links to herbal FAQs (frequently asked question lists), and information about herb-related Usenet groups and mailing lists.

Web:
    http://www.herb.com/herbal.htm

Herbnet

For lots of information about herbs, Herbnet is the place to go. In addition to a collection of links to herbal resources, there is a great deal of information about print publications and journals, herb and seed sources, societies and associations, botanical gardens and herbalism schools.

Web:

http://www.herbnet.com/herbnet.htm

Modern Herbal

In 1931, Mrs. M. Grieve wrote an herbal reference detailing the properties, folklore and cultivation of many hundreds of plants. In the book, Mrs. Grieve described how to use plants for healing, cooking, and even for cosmetics. She called her book "A Modern Herbal". Although it is not modern any longer, the book is still a fantastic resource for anyone interested in herbs. Here is a hypertext version of Mrs. Grieve's wonderful reference.

Web:

http://www.botanical.com/botanical/mgmh/
   mgmh.html

These are just three things that you won't find in the

Herbal Hall

What you *will* find is a lot of information about herbs and what to do with them. The next time you have a few minutes, why not take a look at this site and learn something about our friends in the horticultural kingdom. After all, herbs don't grow on trees.

Pictures of Herbs

Specific herbs can be hard to recognize, but if you are putting them in your mouth, it's a good idea to make a positive identification. Use these resources to look up an herb, either by its scientific name (Hypericum perforatum) or by its common name (St. John's Wort), and you will be rewarded with a picture of that very herb, presented in the privacy of your very own computer.

Web:

http://www.altnature.com/gallery/
http://www.nnlm.gov/pnr/uwmhg/

HISTORY: UNITED STATES

American Civil War

The American Civil War took place from 1861 to 1865. There were many reasons for the war, chief among them the South's dependence on slaves, and the fundamental disagreement of federal control over states' rights. In spite of President Abraham Lincoln's efforts to hold together the union, first South Carolina (in 1860) and then ten more southern states seceded, forming the Confederacy. The four years that followed saw a bloody war of attrition that eventually ended up killing or maiming more than 600,000 people—in Lincoln's words, "...so costly a sacrifice on the altar of freedom." (By 1865, fully one quarter of the white male population of the South had been killed or maimed.) The war ended on April 9, 1865, when General (later President) Ulysses S. Grant accepted the surrender of General Robert E. Lee at Appomattox, Virginia. Five days later, on April 14, 1865, President Lincoln was assassinated by an actor, John Wilkes Booth, in an attempt to avenge the loss of the South.

Web:

http://homepages.dsu.edu/jankej/civilwar/
   civilwar.htm
http://www.americancivilwar.com/
http://www.civilwarhome.com/
http://www.cwc.lsu.edu/cwc/civlink.htm
http://www.sunsite.utk.edu/civil-war/warweb.html

Usenet:

alt.war.civil.usa
soc.history.war.us-civil-war

American First Ladies

In the United States, the First Lady is the wife of the President. Traditionally, the style of the First Lady has had a significant influence on the fashion and culture of her time. Some first ladies have contributed enormously to the public good, and are remembered as great Americans in their own right, for example, Edith Wilson, Eleanor Roosevelt and Barbara Bush.

Web:
   http://www.firstladies.org/Bibliography.htm
   http://www.whitehouse.gov/history/firstladies/

Learn about the women behind
the men behind the women.

American Historical Documents

Many people have heard about the most important American historical documents, but few people have had the opportunity to look at the actual texts. Here is your chance. Take a look at the Declaration of Independence, the Constitution and its amendments, the Bill of Rights, the Monroe Doctrine, the Japanese and German surrenders, and many, many other important documents.

Web:
   http://lcweb2.loc.gov/const/ccongquery.html
   http://memory.loc.gov/ammem/bdsds/
   http://odur.let.rug.nl/usanew/D/
   http://www.ushda.org/
   http://www.yale.edu/lawweb/avalon/avalon.htm

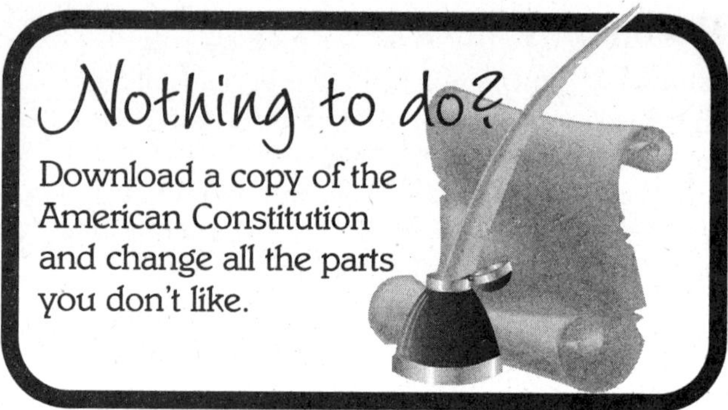

Download a copy of the American Constitution and change all the parts you don't like.

American History

The first permanent English settlements in North America were established in the early 1600s. In less than two hundred years, those settlements, along with other colonies, developed and flourished to the point where they jointly rebelled against Great Britain (1776-1783) and formed the United States of America. Since then, the U.S. has grown to become the most powerful nation in the world, contributing mightily to world culture, economics, science and the waging of war.

Web:
   http://www.historybuff.com/
   http://www.lib.utexas.edu/maps/histus.html
   http://www.polytechnic.org/faculty/gfeldmeth/
      ushistory.html
   http://www.ukans.edu/history/VL/USA/
   http://www.usinfo.state.gov/usa/infousa/facts/
      history/toc.htm

Listserv Mailing List:
   List Name: h-amstdy
   Subscribe to: listserv@h-net.msu.edu

American Memory Collection

The Library of Congress has put together these "scrapbooks" of American history and culture. Flip through and look at Civil War photographs, portraits of literary figures, artists and celebrities, photos of rural America, and hear sound recordings of speeches that were delivered around the World War I era.

Web:
   http://memory.loc.gov/ammem/

Civil Rights Movement

In the 1600s, slavery was widespread in the American colonies. By the early 1800s, the practice had been eliminated in the northern states but, in the South, slavery remained an integral part of the economy until after the Civil War (1861-1865). Since most American slaves had been brought over from Africa, their gradual emancipation left the country with a large, uneducated underclass of black people (the ancestors of today's African Americans). For most of the 20th Century, black people in the U.S. lived in a hostile and discriminating culture, especially in the South. In the 1950s, the post-war American political climate gave rise to the Civil Rights Movement, an organized effort to bring full rights to black people and, by extension, to all Americans. During the next 20 years, the rights of blacks were secured by a succession of Supreme Court decisions (such as Brown v. Board of Education of Topeka, Kansas: 1954, which outlawed segregation in public schools), and federal legislation (such as the Civil Rights Act of 1964, and the Voting Rights Act of 1965). The Civil Rights Movement secured the rights of millions of African Americans. In doing so, the movement gave rise to a number of inspiring leaders, the most beloved of whom was Martin Luther King, Jr. (1929-1968), as well as important civil rights organizations, such as the NAACP (National Association for the Advancement of Colored People). In addition, the massive long-term effort created an overall sensitivity to basic freedoms that resulted in civil rights gains for women (the Women's Movement), homosexuals (Gay Liberation), and people with disabilities. The same sensibilities, taken to an extreme, also gave rise to the unfortunate notion of "political correctness", the unspoken assumption that it is imprudent to express ideas, or even use certain words, that conflict with the political agendas of minority groups.

Web:
> http://lcweb2.loc.gov/ammem/aaohtml/exhibit/
> aopart9.html
> http://www.cr.nps.gov/nr/travel/civilrights/
> mainmap1.htm
> http://www.infoplease.com/spot/
> civilrightstimeline1.html

Constitution of the United States of America

"We, the people of the United States, in order to form a more perfect union, establish justice, insure domestic tranquility, provide for the common defense, promote the general welfare, and secure the blessings of liberty to ourselves and our posterity, do ordain and establish this Constitution for the United States of America." With those words begin the most important document in American history: the U.S. Constitution, the highest law of the land. Within the document, ideas are described in brief, generalized terms. This was done deliberately, and has two important effects. First, any educated person can read and understand the Constitution. (Try it, and you will see what I mean.) Second, the principles expressed in the Constitution are readily adaptable to changing times, which is one reason the American system of government has worked so well for so long. The Constitution's designers purposely made it slow and difficult to make permanent changes. For that reason, most adaptations are made indirectly, by Congress passing laws or by the Supreme Court issuing rulings.

Web:
> http://lcweb2.loc.gov/const/constquery.html
> http://www.house.gov/Constitution/
> Constitution.html
> http://www.usconstitution.net/constnot.html

Usenet:
> alt.politics.usa.constitution

Declaration of Arms, 1775

On July 6, 1775, the representatives of the "United Colonies of North-America" met in Philadelphia and issued a document called "Declaration of the Causes and Necessity of Taking Up Arms". These guys were sick and fed up with the way they were being treated by Great Britain, and this document is the explanation as to why they were rebelling. The document did not mince words. For example, the declaration refers to the members of the British parliament as "stimulated by an inordinate passion" for power, and describes them as being blinded "by their intemperate rage for unlimited domination". Sound familiar?

Web:
> http://odur.let.rug.nl/~usa/D/1751-1775/war/
>   causes.htm
> http://www.law.ou.edu/hist/arms.html
> http://www.yale.edu/lawweb/avalon/arms.htm

Declaration of Sentiments

In 1848, the first Women's Rights Convention was held in Seneca Falls, New York. The convention was convened by Elizabeth Cady Stanton and Lucretia Mott, who presented the Declaration of Sentiments, a document based on the Declaration of Independence. This declaration, however, was a list of grievances denouncing the inequality between men and women in the areas of education, religion, employment, property rights, marriage, family and voting. Almost 150 years later, the Declaration of Sentiments still makes for interesting reading. Note: After the Declaration of Sentiments was presented, another 71 years passed before American women were given the right to vote under the 19th Amendment to the U.S. Constitution.

Web:
> http://www.fordham.edu/halsall/mod/
>   senecafalls.html
> http://www.nps.gov/wori/declaration.htm
> http://www.rootsweb.com/~nyseneca/signers.htm

The Net is waiting for you.

Emancipation Proclamation

In the United States, the expression "Lincoln freed the slaves" is commonly used as an all-purpose rejoinder in certain sticky social situations, such as when your boss tells you to work overtime without extra pay, or when your mother forces you to clean up your room. But just how did Lincoln free the slaves? At the time of the Civil War, Lincoln was president of the Union (the northern states), leading them against the Confederacy (the southern states). On September 17, 1862—the bloodiest day of the Civil War—the Battle of Antietam in western Maryland ended with combined losses of more than 23,000 men. Lincoln used the occasion to issue the Emancipation Proclamation, which declared all slaves free in states still in rebellion against the Union. The slaves were not actually freed until April 9, 1865, when the Union won its final victory against the Confederacy. If any of this interests you, take a few minutes to look at the actual proclamation (and at the fine print contained therein).

Web:
> http://libertyonline.hypermall.com/Lincoln/
>   emancipate.html
> http://www.nps.gov/ncro/anti/emancipation.html

Federalist Papers

Between 1787-1788, a series of 85 political essays—now called "The Federalist Papers"—was published in New York. The series was initiated by Alexander Hamilton in order to persuade New York to approve the Federalist Constitution (which they eventually did). Hamilton wrote most of the essays, the others being written by James Madison and John Jay. As they were written, the essays were published in newspapers and were read widely. (Compare this to what you see in modern newspapers.) Even today, the Federalist Papers are acclaimed for their high literary quality and well-developed cogent arguments.

Web:
> http://lcweb2.loc.gov/const/fed/fedpapers.html
> http://www.constitution.org/fed/federa00.htm
> http://www.yale.edu/lawweb/avalon/federal/fed.htm

The next time your teacher or your boss tries to tell you what to do, download the Emancipation Proclamation and mail them their own personal copy.

Gettysburg Address

From 1861 to 1865, the United States was embroiled in a civil war between the northern states (Union) and the southern states (Confederacy). There were many causes of the war, but the primary reasons for conflict were fundamental disagreements over slavery and federal control of individual states. Approximately halfway through the war, a turning point occurred near the town of Gettysburg, Pennsylvania. On July 1, 1863, General Robert E. Lee (military commander of the Confederacy) attempted to invade the North, but after battling for three days, the Southern troops were routed. More than 43,000 men were killed in those three days. On November 19, 1863, President Abraham Lincoln made a speech at the dedication of the new Civil War cemetery in Gettysburg. His beautiful and oft-quoted words express Lincoln's grief for the fallen soldiers and describes the principles for which the men died. Ironically, in the speech Lincoln says, "The world will little note, nor long remember, what we say here...", but in fact, the Gettysburg Address is one of the most famous speeches in American history. What American does not recognize the words "four score and seven years ago" and "government of the people, by the people, and for the people"? At this Web site, you will find various drafts of the Gettysburg Address. It is a short, powerful speech, and it shows us why Lincoln is considered one of America's greatest presidents.

Web:
  http://lcweb.loc.gov/exhibits/gadd/

Great Depression

The Depression, or more formally, the Great Depression, was a long period of economic hardship that lasted from late 1929 to 1937. The downturn in the economy actually started in August of 1929. However, most people were not aware of what was happening until the stock market began to collapse on October 24, 1929 (referred to as "Black Thursday"). Within a short time, the economy of the United States—and then the rest of the world—deteriorated significantly and the Depression had begun in earnest. By 1933, U.S. industrial production was down 56 percent from 1929 and over 13,000,000 people, a third of the work force, was out of work. It was not until the late 1930s that the massive government spending in preparation for war finally ended the most devastating economic downturn in modern history.

Web:
  http://www.amatecon.com/greatdepression.html
  http://www.fdrlibrary.marist.edu/depress.html
  http://www.nytimes.com/library/financial/
    index-1929-crash.html

Historic American Speeches

There are a great many wonderful historical speeches that you can read. Here are some you will find interesting: "Why Women Should Vote" (Jane Addams, 1915); "Dangers of a Salaried Bureaucracy" (Benjamin Franklin, 1787); "The Sunny Side of Life" (James Hedley, late 1800s); "I Have a Dream" (Martin Luther King, 1963); "Gettysburg Address" (Abraham Lincoln, 1863); "The Blessings of Slavery" (The Plaindealer, New York newspaper, 1837); "Farewell Address" (George Washington, 1796). If that's not enough, see if you can find the speech I gave to the Pulitzer Prize organization, explaining that they would have to become a bit more prestigious if they wanted me to accept one of their awards.

Web:
http://odur.let.rug.nl/~usa/P/
http://www.douglassarchives.org/
http://www.historyplace.com/speeches/previous.htm
http://www.pbs.org/greatspeeches/timeline/

Historic American Speeches

Here is my favorite historic American speech:

"Fourscore and seven years ago our fathers brought forth on this continent a new nation, conceived in liberty and dedicated to the proposition that all men should use the Net. Innocent peoples, innocent nations are being cruelly sacrificed to a greed for power and supremacy, by not ensuring that everyone has a copy of a Harley Hahn book. I know not what course others may take; but as for me, give me a Harley Hahn book or give me death!"

(Don't believe it? Connect to the Net and check it out for yourself.)

Native American Treaties

In the late 1700s through the late 1800s, there were many treaties signed between the United States government and various Native American (Indian) tribes. Many of these treaties were to have long-lasting effects, some to the present day. I found it fascinating to read some of these treaties. In addition, I was surprised how many well-known names of places are derived from Indian tribal names.

Web:
http://digital.library.okstate.edu/kappler/
http://www.yale.edu/lawweb/avalon/natamer.htm

Why work when you can be reading this book?

Prohibition

In the last several decades of the 19th Century, a number of political groups—called temperance movements—arose with the goal of restricting the sale of alcohol in the United States. By the end of World War I (1919), alcohol consumption in the United States had increased so rapidly as to become a serious social problem. At the same time, the brewing industry expanded enormously, resulting in the proliferation of saloons, many of which introduced gambling and prostitution into otherwise law-abiding neighborhoods. As a result, in 1919 Congress passed the 18th Amendment to the Constitution, forbidding the manufacture and sale of alcohol. After the Amendment had been ratified by the states, Congress established it as a law by passing the Volsted Act, ushering in the age of Prohibition. Unfortunately, much of the population never accepted Prohibition (including many politicians and law enforcement officials). This gave rise to a great deal of crime in the form of smuggling and bootlegging (the illegal manufacture and distribution of alcohol). By the early 1930s, the country had had enough. In 1933, the 21st Amendment to the Constitution was passed, repealing Prohibition, ending the so-called "Noble Experiment". In one sense, however, prohibition was a success. It caused the per capita consumption of alcohol to drop significantly. In fact, it did not regain its former level until 1943, well after Prohibition ended.

Web:
http://prohibition.history.ohio-state.edu/contents.htm
http://www.cpcug.org/user/billb/prohibition.html
http://www.druglibrary.org/schaffer/library/studies/wick/index.html
http://www.law.emory.edu/FEDERAL/usconst/amend.html#art-18
http://www.law.emory.edu/FEDERAL/usconst/amend.html#art-21

Richard Nixon Audio and Video Archive

People of the younger generations will never know what it was like to hear Richard Nixon address the people of the United States. Thanks to modern technology and the Internet, anyone young or old, can hear the voice of Richard Nixon at any time of the day or night. Listen to his resignation speech, the Checkers speech, a portion of the Nixon/Kennedy debate and his explanation of Watergate.

Web:
  http://www.webcorp.com/sounds/nixonarchive.htm
  http://www.webcorp.com/video/nixon/
    nixonvideo.html

September 11 Terrorist Attacks

On September 11, 2001, the world was stunned to find out that the worst terrorist attacks ever perpetrated in the United States had taken place within a short two-hour interval. The first attack came at 8:46 a.m., when a hijacked airplane was deliberately crashed into the North Tower of the World Trade Center in New York City. About 20 minutes later, at 9:03 a.m., as people around the world watched on television, a second hijacked plane flew into the South Tower. Within the hour, both towers had collapsed. At 9:45 a.m., a third hijacked plane smashed into the southwest side of the Pentagon (the headquarters of the U.S. Department of Defense), in Arlington, Virginia. Finally, at 10:10 a.m., another plane crashed in a wooded area in Pennsylvania, after passengers confronted hijackers and aborted what was about to become a fourth suicide mission. A total of 3,228 people were killed in the attacks: 2,819 at the World Trade Center, 265 airline passengers and crew, 125 at the Pentagon, and 19 hijackers. It was soon determined that the attacks were carried out as part of a "Holy War" against the U.S. The terrorists belonged to al-Qaida, a fanatical Islamic organization, based in Afghanistan and led by Saudi expatriate Osama bin Laden. Within a short time, U.S. President George W. Bush and British Prime Tony Blair had initiated a prolonged, worldwide fight against terrorism. In the months to follow, people everywhere began to come to terms with a world in which global terrorism would be a significant threat for the foreseeable future.

Web:
  http://www.911digitalarchive.org/
  http://www.interactivepublishing.net/september/
  http://www.pbs.org/newshour/bb/military/
    terroristattack/sept11/
  http://www.poynter.org/terrorism/gallery/
    wednesday1.htm
  http://www.september11news.com/

Thomas Jefferson

Thomas Jefferson (1743-1826) was a writer, architect, diplomat, inventor, politician, philosopher, lawyer and musician. Jefferson was one of the founding fathers of the United States, and stands remembered as one of the outstanding figures in American history, a champion of political and religious freedom. Among Jefferson's many accomplishments are drafting the Declaration of Independence (1776), serving as the third president of the United States (1801-1809), arranging for the Louisiana Purchase (1803), and founding the University of Virginia (1819).

Web:
  http://etext.virginia.edu/jefferson/
  http://memory.loc.gov/ammem/mtjhtml/
  http://www.monticello.org/
  http://www.presidentjefferson.com/

Treaty of Guadalupe Hidalgo

For some years before 1846, there was tension between Mexicans and Americans living in the region that later became the state of Texas. In 1846, upon the annexation of Texas by the United States, a war broke out between the United States and Mexico. The Mexican War continued until 1848, when the Treaty of Guadalupe Hidalgo was signed. This treaty granted the United States possession of the provinces and territories of Texas, New Mexico, California and other significant portions of the southwest. In return, the United States was to pay Mexico $15 million and assume $3.25 million in American claims against Mexico. The U.S. also recognized prior land grants in the southwest and offered citizenship to any Mexicans living in the area. Clearly, this document was instrumental in defining the territory of modern day America.

Web:
  http://www.azteca.net/aztec/guadhida.html
  http://www.lcweb.loc.gov/exhibits/ghtreaty/

Treaty of Paris

On September 3, 1783, about two years after the conclusion of the American Revolutionary War, the Treaty of Paris formally ended the hostilities. The Treaty of Paris recognized the independence of the Thirteen Colonies and set forth what territory the British would cede: the Americans received huge territories in North America; the Spanish received Florida and regained West Indian properties; and France regained St. Lucia, Tobago, Senegal, Gorée, and East Indian properties.

Web:
http://www.ushda.org/paris.shtml
http://www.yale.edu/lawweb/avalon/paris763.htm

United States Bill of Rights

On December 15, 1791, the Bill of Rights became law in the United States. The Bill of Rights is a set of 10 amendments made to the U.S. Constitution (adopted in 1787). The Bill of Rights sets out various freedoms that all citizens of the United States are guaranteed. For example, the first part of the Bill of Rights guarantees freedom of religion, freedom of speech, freedom of the press, freedom of assembly, and freedom to petition the government.

Web:
http://lcweb2.loc.gov/const/bor.html
http://memory.loc.gov/const/bor.html

U.S. Declaration of Independence

The U.S. Declaration of Independence was drafted by Thomas Jefferson between June 11 and June 28, 1776. On July 4, 1776, it was adopted by the Thirteen Colonies as an announcement of their separation from Great Britain and their creation of the United States of America. The Declaration of Independence portrays what the Americans considered an ideal government and lists particular grievances that went unanswered for too long. The American Revolution lasted for eight years and finally ended with the United States keeping their independence and their territories. If you would like to feel the same spirit as Jefferson did when he wrote it, print your own copy of the Declaration of Independence, read it through, and add your signature to the list at the end.

Web:
http://lcweb2.loc.gov/const/declar.html
http://www.loc.gov/exhibits/declara/
http://www.thedeclarationofindependence.org/

United States Bill of Rights

If you are an American history buff, you know that the Bill of Rights was adopted in 1787 in order to guarantee that all Americans would enjoy certain fundamental freedoms.

What you may not know is that, because of a deadline, there were a number of important rights that were left out. However, it is not too late to correct the omissions. For that reason, I propose the following additions to the United States Bill of Rights:

1. Congress shall make no law respecting the viewing of Harly Hahn's Web site, or prohibiting the free exercise thereof.

2. A well-educated population, being necessary to the success of a free state, the right of the people to buy as many Harley Hahn books as they want shall not be infringed.

3. Excessive bail shall not be required, nor excessive fines imposed, nor cruel and unusual punishments inflicted on people who refuse to watch television.

4. The right of the people to have a cat sleep on their bed at night shall not be violated.

HISTORY: WORLD

Ancient World Cultures

I find it fascinating to explore ancient world cultures. For instance, when I want to take a break, I love to pour a fresh glass of carrot juice, sit in my special relaxation chair, and read about the formation, by Amenhotep IV, of a new Egyptian monotheistic religion dedicated to the worship of the sun. Or about how, in 750 A.D., Irish monks established early medieval art, of which survives the glorious illuminated "Book of Kells". There is a lot to know, so you had better get started now.

Web:
  http://eawc.evansville.edu/
  http://www.julen.net/ancient/

Anglo-Saxons

The Anglo-Saxon era was a period in English history from the 5th century to the Norman Conquest (1066). The Anglo-Saxons were the descendants of Germanic-speaking peoples—the Angles, the Saxons and the Jutes—who migrated from the European continent in the 5th century after the weakening of Roman influence in England. The Anglo-Saxons dominated England until the arrival of William the Conqueror from Normandy (France).

Web:
  http://members.aol.com/bakken1/angsax/
    angsaxe.htm
  http://orb.rhodes.edu/encyclop/early/pre1000/
    asindex.html
  http://www.bbc.co.uk/education/anglosaxons/

Listserv Mailing List:
  List Name: ansax-l
  Subscribe to: listserv@wvnvm.wvnet.edu

Break a rule.
The "Anarchy" section
will show you how.

Canadian Constitution Act

The country of Canada was formally created in 1867 when the British parliament passed the British North America Act (also known as the Constitution Act), the legislation that created the independent country of Canada. The original country consisted of only four provinces: Ontario (Upper Canada), Quebec (Lower Canada), New Brunswick and Nova Scotia. It is interesting to read this document and compare it to the United States' Declaration of Independence and the United States' Constitution. The differences in the personalities of the two countries really show.

Web:
  http://www.solon.org/Constitutions/Canada/English/
    ca_1867.html

Chinese History

If you are interested in learning about human nature, you can't do better than to spend time reading about the longest, most enduring culture in the world. About one quarter of the people in the world live in China and, as such, live within a civilization that has evolved over more than 3,000 years. Being connected to the past in this way breeds an appreciation for tradition and long-term thinking that is simply unknown in Western countries. For this reason, I have always found the study of Chinese history to be humbling. After all, I live in Southern California, a place where history goes back about 150 years and anything over the age of 35 (including film stars) is considered an antique.

Web:
  http://library.thinkquest.org/10662/
    normal_menu.htm
  http://www.historylink101.com/china_history.htm
  http://www.ibiblio.org/chinesehistory/

Classical Studies

Classical Studies (the Classics) encompass the Greek and Roman civilization and their direct antecedents. This area of study includes the Greek and Latin languages as well as their literature, art, architecture and archaeology.

Web:
  http://www.classicspage.com/
  http://www.faqs.org/faqs/classics-faq/
  http://www.perseus.tufts.edu/

Usenet:
  humanities.classics
  sci.classics

Cold War

Shortly after World War II, an intense economic and political struggle began between the Soviet Union (which was totalitarian and communist) and the Western powers (which were capitalistic and democratic). On April 16, 1947, the American financier Bernard Baruch made a speech to the South Carolina Legislature in which he commented, "Let us not be deceived. We are today in the midst of a cold war." The idea was popularized, and for the next four and a half decades, the term "Cold War" served as the defining paradigm of East/West relations. The Cold War was characterized by a world divided into capitalist and communist camps, leading to an enormous buildup of military strength, particularly nuclear weapons. In Europe, where the Soviet Union extended its influence over a large number of satellite countries, the psychological and political barrier between the two power blocs became known as the Iron Curtain. (Interesting Cold War trivia: Although the term "Iron Curtain" was introduced to the West in a speech by Winston Churchill in 1946, it was first used in an article written by the German Nazi leader Joseph Goebbels in 1945.) The most famous symbol of the Cold War was the Berlin Wall, a long barrier dividing East Berlin (controlled by the Russians) from West Berlin (part of the democratic Federal Republic of Germany). The Berlin Wall was erected in August 1961 and was demolished in 1989. The Cold War ended in 1991 with the breakup of the Soviet Union.

Web:

http://learningcurve.pro.gov.uk/coldwar/
http://www.mtholyoke.edu/acad/intrel/coldwar.htm
http://www.newseum.org/berlinwall/
http://www.yale.edu/lawweb/avalon/coldwar.htm

Listserv Mailing List:

List Name: coldwar
Subscribe to: listserv@sivm.si.edu

Why be ordinary, when you can read the "Bizarre" section?

Council of Trent

The Council of Trent was an ecumenical council of the Roman Catholic church. It was convened in 1545 by Pope Paul III to address the problems of the Protestant Reformation. The Council of Trent met sporadically until 1563, when it was concluded by Pope Pius IV. Throughout its active years, the Council of Trent was a major figure in the Catholic Reformation. The reforms—which covered topics such as the Mass, the clergy, sacraments, scripture, relics, education and feasts—formed a basis for modern Catholicism. Here are the texts and transcripts of the Council of Trent's canons and decrees.

Web:

http://history.hanover.edu/early/trent.htm

Eighteenth Century Resources

Travel back in time, back to the 18th century: a kinder, gentler time before the invention of cellular phones, fax machines and pizza delivery. Instead of doing cool things like playing video games and watching talk shows, people of the 18th century had to be more culturally advanced and make great literature, art, architecture, music and philosophy. Explore the past. Right now.

Web:

http://andromeda.rutgers.edu/~jlynch/18th/

English Bill of Rights

The English established their Bill of Rights in 1689. This document lessened the power of the throne and gave more power to the subjects of England. The Bill of Rights elevated the political stature of Parliament over that of the crown, gave civil and political rights to English subjects and stated that no Roman Catholic would rule England. The Bill of Rights was accepted by William III and Mary II after the Glorious Revolution, which ousted James II from the throne. You can read about this document that created a significant turning point in the history of England.

Web:

http://www.duhaime.org/uk-billr.htm
http://www.yale.edu/lawweb/avalon/england.htm

European Texts and Documents

Have you ever worried that you might run out of important historical documents to read? Well, relax. You are causing yourself unnecessary strain. There are lots of wonderful documents only a mouse click away. These sites, for example, have many European historical documents dating from medieval times to the present. As long as you have the Net, you will never run out of important European documents.

Web:
   http://history.hanover.edu/texts.htm
   http://library.byu.edu/~rdh/eurodocs/

Feudal Terms

Feudalism was a form of social organization common in Western Europe from the fall of Charlemagne's empire (9th century) to the rise of the absolute French, Spanish and English monarchies (14th century and later). An exact definition of feudalism is hard to give, but you won't go far wrong if you think of it as a system with three main characteristics: strict social classes, law based on local customs, and land-holding dependent upon a fee. If you want to read or talk about things feudal, you will need the proper vocabulary, so here are online glossaries with a large number of feudal words, from "abbey" to "witen".

Web:
   http://www.battle1066.com/gloss1.shtml
   http://www.whitelodge.dyndns.org:88/~sithriel/
      fudaldict.html

Eighteenth Century Resources

You can't live in the past—unless you are on the Net—in which case you can visit the eighteenth century whenever you want.

Hiroshima and Nagasaki

It was the summer of 1945. The Allied forces which had defeated Germany now turned their full attention toward Japan and its massive war machine. Although the war in Europe was over, the Japanese had more than 2,000,000 soldiers and 9,000 kamikaze suicide bombers ready to fight to the death. It was estimated that a full-scale invasion of Japan would kill more than 500,000 American servicemen as well as many millions of Japanese. On July 26, the United States, Britain and China warned Japan to surrender unconditionally or face "prompt and utter destruction". Japanese officials stalled for time and scoffed at the demands. In response, U.S. President Harry Truman gave the order to drop an atomic bomb on Japan. On August 6, an atomic bomb was dropped on the bustling city of Hiroshima immediately killing 75,000 people (many more died later). Three days later, a second bomb was dropped on the city of Nagasaki killing another 50,000 people. On August 10, 1945—overruling the desires of its military leaders who wanted to keep fighting—Japan finally surrendered. The dropping of the two bombs ended the war, saved millions of lives, and ushered in a new and terrifying era of human history.

Web:
   http://www.csi.ad.jp/ABOMB/
   http://www.dannen.com/decision/
   http://www.lclark.edu/~history/HIROSHIMA/

Historian's Database and Information Server

Here is a wonderful, comprehensive information server for historians. You can browse through a wide variety of resources—so large, in fact, that you'll be able to use this Web site as your one-stop history warehouse.

Web:
   http://www.ukans.edu/history/VL/

Historical Sounds and Speeches

The best way to learn about history is to read, think and discuss. You can add an interesting dimension to such work by listening to the original version of important speeches. We hear so many boring politicians and commentators talk that we forget that truly skillful orators can have a significant, enduring effect on our culture. These sites contain sound files of famous speeches as well as short excerpts, including some from John F. Kennedy, Richard Nixon, Adolf Hitler, Winston Churchill, Martin Luther King and Will Rogers. Try this experiment. Listen to a few seconds of Hitler addressing a crowd (in German of course), and then ask yourself, "Who does he remind me of?"

Web:
    http://www.bl.uk/collections/sound-archive/
    http://www.discovery.com/guides/history/
        historybuff/media/
    http://www.hpol.org/
    http://www.lib.msu.edu/vincent/
    http://www.ngsw.org/
    http://www.webcorp.com/sounds/

Historical Timelines

What happened and when? With all the historical timelines on the Net, you'll never be at a loss for names, dates and places. For example, not many people know that the Tiahuanaco empire was founded in Peru about 375 A.D. (But now you do.)

Web:
    http://www.historicaltimeline.com/
    http://www.searchbeat.com/Society/History/Timelines/
    http://www.timelines.info/

Historical Sounds and Speeches

Boy, did I get a surprise the other day.

I was browsing through an archive of historical speeches, and I came across one by my grandmother:

"You have such a handsome face. When are you going to shave your beard?"

(It's amazing what you can find on the Net.)

History Resources

Those who do not learn how to find history resources on the Net are doomed to repeat their searches. Don't let this happen to you. Start with these Web sites, and you will be only a few mouse clicks away from whatever you need. If you are going to be a historian, it is crucial to learn how to use the Web. My philosophy is, if you can't master the present, you won't be able to live in the past.

Web:
    http://www.americaslibrary.com/
    http://www.fordham.edu/halsall/
    http://www.history-journals.de
    http://www.libraries.rutgers.edu/rul/rr_gateway/
        research_guides/history/history.shtml
    http://www.worldhistorycompass.com/

History Talk and General Discussion

The great thing about history is that you never run out of it. Every minute there is more history made and that just means there is more to memorize when you are in school. Stop in on the Net, and hang out with the people who love to dwell on the past.

Usenet:
    alt.history
    alt.history.abe-lincoln
    alt.history.ancient-worlds
    alt.history.british
    alt.history.colonial
    alt.history.richard-iii
    alt.old-west
    bit.listserv.history
    soc.history
    soc.history.african.biafra
    soc.history.ancient
    soc.history.early-modern
    soc.history.medieval
    soc.history.moderated
    soc.history.war.us-revolution
    soc.history.what-if

Listserv Mailing List:
    List Name: h-world
    Subscribe to: listserv@h-net.msu.edu

Holocaust

In 1933, Adolph Hitler came to power in Germany, beginning the age of German Nazism, which lasted until the end of World War II in 1945. Nazism fed on the fears, frustrations and prejudices of post-World War I Germans, and embraced a long-term program of political expansion, state control of the economy, and a fanatical nationalism based on the ideal of an Aryan master race coupled with vehemently anti-Semitic racism. Between 1933 and 1945, Germany, under the leadership of Hitler, began to persecute and exterminate Jews. The Nazis sent countless Jews to concentration camps (death camps). With the outbreak of World War II, Hitler and Heinrich Himmler, the head of the Gestapo (secret police), implemented a plan—the "final solution of the Jewish question"—to exterminate all the European Jews within their reach, a reach which expanded over much of Europe as the War progressed. By the end of the war, over 6 million Jews had been systematically rounded up, sent to concentration camps and murdered, resulting in the destruction of one of the most creative religious and secular communities in Europe, one of the most terrible chapters in human history: the Holocaust.

Web:
   http://motlc.wiesenthal.com/pages/
   http://www.faqs.org/faqs/holocaust/
   http://www.holocaust-history.org/
   http://www.library.yale.edu/testimonies/
      homepage.html
   http://www.remember.org/
   http://www.shamash.org/holocaust/
   http://www.snowcrest.net/jmike/holocaustmil.html
   http://www.ushmm.org/education/
   http://www.yad-vashem.org.il/

Usenet:
   soc.culture.jewish.holocaust

Listserv Mailing List:
   List Name: h-holocaust
   Subscribe to: listserv@h-net.msu.edu

Half-time score: Net 1, Censorship 0.

Holocaust Revisionism

Revisionism is the act of changing the way people view a commonly accepted doctrine or series of events. For example, within a movie, a person may be portrayed as a popular hero when, in fact, he was not at all liked during his time. There are many styles of revisionism. Revision can occur from people feeling nostalgic and making "the old days" into a more romantic, endearing time than it was. Revision can also occur when people want to heighten or lessen, for whatever reason, the emotional impact of events from the past. One of the most dangerous revisionist practices today involves misguided people who attempt to deny the reality of the Holocaust, the period from 1933 to 1945, when over 6 million Jews were systematically murdered by Nazi Germany. Mankind has paid dearly for the Holocaust, and the lessons it has for us must never be forgotten. For this reason, it is important that educated people understand and refute the claims of the Holocaust revisionists. We must ensure that, as the memory of this most terrible era in history fades with each new generation, the significance of the Holocaust shall always be understood and appreciated. (After all, the next set of Nazis may be coming for *you*.)

Web:
   http://www.holocaust-history.org/revisionism-isnt/
   http://www.ihr.org/
   http://www.nizkor.org/

Usenet:
   alt.revisionism

Hyperhistory

If you have some time to explore the Net, I suggest visiting this site. It has massive charts that show various historical and cultural happenings (science, politics, medicine, religion and more) juxtaposed so you can see how various events relate to one another. For example, did you know that the year the Pope announced that Catholics could not practice birth control was the same year that Martin Luther King and Robert Kennedy were assassinated? Were you aware that the Berlin Wall was constructed in the same year that Yuri Garagin became the first man in space? And I bet you didn't know that Mussolini and Hitler formed the Rome-Berlin Axis around the same time Margaret Mitchell was writing "Gone with the Wind". This world history chart has lots of great information about people, events and history, and includes some cool maps.

Web:
   http://www.hyperhistory.com/online_n2/History_n2/
      a.html

Joint Declaration on Peace

Ireland has a long, complex history of unrest. In modern times, the main issue is that the Protestants in Northern Ireland (the Unionists) want to be associated with England, while the Catholics (the Republicans) want all of Ireland to be a completely independent country. The situation, however, dates from the 12th century, when Pope Adrian granted control of Ireland to King Henry II of England. This initiated a continuing Anglo-Irish conflict that worsened in the 16th century when England tried to impose Protestantism on the Irish population, which was largely Catholic. In 1800, English control was underscored by the Act of Union, which formally unified the English and Irish parliaments. This legislation created a great deal of political unrest in Ireland, resulting in a series of Home Rule bills, providing for increased Irish control of the country. These bills resulted in great animosity on both sides of the controversy (pro-British and pro-independence). On April 24, 1916 (Easter Monday), a small group of Irish patriots in Dublin led an assault on the British. The "Easter Rising", as it came to be called, lasted only six days before it was put down by British troops. However, it laid the groundwork for the independence of southern Ireland, as well as further decades of violence, unrest and political turmoil. After the Rising, the extreme nationalist political party Sein Fein ("Ourselves Alone") won most of the seats in the 1918 General Election, and the Irish Republican Army (IRA) was formed to fight the British administration. For years, the IRA led a hit-and-run assault on the British and as a result, in 1921, a treaty was negotiated dividing the country into two mostly self-governing areas: Northern Ireland (also called Ulster) and Southern Ireland (the Irish Free State). In 1937, the people of Southern Ireland passed a referendum declaring themselves completely independent, and in 1948, the Republic of Ireland Act officially recognized the country—now called the Republic of Ireland or Eire—as being separate from the British Commonwealth, bringing an end to hundreds of years of direct British influence. However, this did not bring an end to the violence and unrest. Northern Ireland, now a part of the United Kingdom, has a Protestant majority that generally favors the union with Britain. However, the Catholic minority in Northern Ireland would prefer to be part of the south, and there are still many people in both countries who are willing to fight for a completely unified and independent country. In 1993, a document was created as a new starting point in the peace process. This document, the Joint Declaration on Peace, was signed on December 15, 1993, by John Majors, the Prime Minister of England, and Albert Reynolds, the Taoiseach (Prime Minister) of the Republic of Ireland. I think you'll find it interesting to read the Joint Declaration. It's surprisingly easy to understand.

Web:

> http://cain.ulst.ac.uk/events/peace/docs/
>   dsd151293.htm
> http://slarti.ucd.ie/political/

Maastricht Treaty

On February 7, 1992, the Treaty on European Union was signed, formally acknowledging the intentions of a number of European countries to form a political, monetary and social union. The treaty is generally known as the Maastricht Treaty, named after the city of Maastricht in southeast Holland where the meeting and signing took place. (The name is pronounced Mas'-trikt.) On November 1, 1993, the Maastricht Treaty was ratified, establishing the European Union (EU). The treaty is a complex document, but the main goals of the EU can be summarized as follows: (1) to create an economic and monetary union under the control of one central European bank; (2) to create a unified European market in which a single currency is used everywhere; (3) to ensure the unrestricted movement of people within the Union; (4) to create a common foreign and security policy; (5) to ensure cooperation among the member states with respect to justice and law enforcement; (6) to establish a European coal and steel community; (7) to establish a unified European atomic energy community; and (8) to strengthen the powers of the European Parliament. Although it all sounds simple (at least in principle), the European Union is actually a continuing work in progress, and many of the goals of the Maastricht Treaty have not yet been implemented completely.

Web:

> http://www.europa.eu.int/abc/off/index_en.htm
> http://www.uni-mannheim.de/users/ddz/edz/doku/
>   vertrag/engl/m_engl.html

Question:

hat do the following people have in common?

His Majesty the King of the Belgians,

Her Majesty the Queen of Denmark,

The President of the Federal Republic of Germany,

The President of the Hellenic Republic,

His Majesty the King of Spain,

The President of the French Republic,

The President of Ireland,

The President of the Italian Republic,

His Royal Highness the Grand Duke of Luxembourg,

Her Majesty the Queen of the Netherlands,

The President of the Portuguese Republic,

Her Majesty the Queen of The United Kingdom of Great Britain and Northern Ireland.

Choose the correct answer. All of these people...

(A) have four or more Harley Hahn books.

(B) were unable to get a job in the private sector.

(C) have hosted at least two Tupperware parties.

(D) signed the Maastricht Treaty in order to establish European Union.

Magna Carta

Feudalism was a political and social system in Western Europe that developed in the late 9th century and lasted until the rise of absolute monarchies. The feudal system centered upon the ownership of land and manors. The lord of the manor would allow peasants (serfs) to utilize his land for farming and for living. In exchange, the peasant was bound by an oath of fealty to pay money or to perform servile labor for the lord. Within the feudal system, the king owned all land. Under the king was a hierarchy of nobles (for example, barons) who would hold land granted by the king. Under the high nobles were lesser nobles who controlled land granted by the high nobles, and so on, each landowner swearing fealty to the noble above him (not unlike multilevel marketing). During the reign of King John (1199-1216) the barons revolted. They did so because of their strong opposition to the King's abuse of the feudal custom by encroaching on baronial privileges in order to raise money. To settle the rebellion, King John put his seal on the Magna Carta, which guaranteed rights to the subjects of England and generally precluded the excessive use of royal power. The Magna Carta is an interesting document to read, as it lays out what various members of the feudal system could and could not do.

Web:

http://www.magnacartaplus.org/magnacarta/
http://www.yale.edu/lawweb/avalon/medieval/
   magframe.htm

**Report on the Magna Carta
by Elmo's sister, Lucy (age 6)**

Not long ago, I read about the Magna Carta. This was an agreement that took power from the King of England and gave it to the barons.

I drew up a similar document and got my mother to sign it. (She thought she was signing a permission slip for me to go to the museum.) Now, she can't tell me when to go to bed, and she can't make me wash dishes if I don't want to.

-Lucy

Medieval History

Never mind that almost everyone was dirty, smelly, poor, and ate rotten food. Medieval history is cool because you got to fight with swords. Anyone who studies the culture and history of the medieval era can tell you that people were very different back then, as is evidenced by their politics, art, philosophy and religion. Scholars and students of the Middle Ages (476-1453 A.D.) discuss this period in history.

Web:
> http://labyrinth.georgetown.edu/
> http://www.ebbs.english.vt.edu/medieval/
> http://www.fordham.edu/halsall/sbook.html

Usenet:
> soc.history.medieval

Listproc Mailing List:
> List Name: caerleon
> Subscribe to: listproc@u.washington.edu

Listserv Mailing List:
> List Name: lt-antiq
> Subscribe to: listserv@vm.sc.edu

Listserv Mailing List:
> List Name: medart-l
> Subscribe to: listserv@listserv.utoronto.ca

Renaissance

The Renaissance (14th-15th century to mid-17th century) is the period in European history between the Middle Ages and modern times, during which there was an enormous development of Western civilization. The Renaissance began in Italy in the 14th century, and by the 15th century had spread to the rest of Europe. The Renaissance was a time of great creation in art, architecture and crafts. There were also important accomplishments in the areas of literature, science and scholarship. Politically, the Renaissance gave birth to the nation states and to a great surge in exploration. To this day, the term "Renaissance man" describes someone who is accomplished and well-versed in a variety of areas.

Web:
> http://www.academicinfo.net/histren.html
> http://www.ibiblio.org/wm/paint/glo/renaissance/
> http://www.luminarium.org/renlit/
> http://www.r-s-a.org/

Listserv Mailing List:
> List Name: renais-l
> Subscribe to: listserv@listserv.louisville.edu

Royalty

From King Arthur to Princess Diana, we have always been fascinated with legends about royalty. For much of history, people were ruled by monarchs who achieved their divine rights by accident of birth. Today, there are only a handful of active monarchies in the world, but, if you believe the history books, there was a time when you couldn't walk to the next town without bumping into a king or queen. Today, the chances of meeting an actual member of a royal family are slight, but you can read about them whenever you want, and dream that, one day, your very own prince or princess will appear, and you will live happily ever after.

Web:
http://www.britannia.com/history/monarchs/
http://www.royalfamily.com/
http://www.xs4all.nl/~kvenjb/kings.htm

Sixties

A time of great transition is uncomfortable for the people living through that transition. When we look back on the Sixties through rose-colored granny glasses, we fondly remember all the sex, drugs and rock 'n' roll. What we sometimes forget is how turbulent the period actually was. The Sixties (or more precisely, the years from 1965 to 1975) hosted a cultural revolution, one as significant as the Reformation and the Renaissance. During the Sixties, many people fought for what we now take for granted. For example, young men had to fight to grow their hair long. (It was commonplace for boys to be sent home from school for wearing their hair over their ears.) At the same time, countless young men were being sent to Vietnam to fight (and die) in an ideological war against the spread of communism. The Sixties was a time when the world began to embrace the sexual revolution (birth control, the Pill), the women's movement, the drug culture, new music (the Beatles, Woodstock), and a radical change in fashion (miniskirts, bell bottoms, hair styles). I remember the feeling: we all knew we were living through very special times. We experienced an enormous increase in individual freedom and political idealism, while, at the same time, we watched the mass media, especially television, begin to shape the culture and exert a great deal of power over public opinion (something we take for granted today). While all this was happening, the focus of popular culture shifted from the older people to the kids, creating a youth culture that has since become the status quo. As we look back, we are now starting to understand what all the fuss was about and why it was so important. Without a doubt, we lived through interesting times. Sometimes I feel sorry for younger people. To tell you the truth, since the late Seventies, the world has been an awfully dull place.

Web:
http://lists.village.virginia.edu/sixties/
http://www.lib.virginia.edu/exhibits/sixties/

Majordomo Mailing List:
List Name: sixties-l
Subscribe to: majordomo@lists.village.virginia.edu

Titanic

On the night of April 14, 1912, the British passenger liner Titanic, once thought to be invincible, sank in the North Atlantic. Since then, the Titanic disaster has become an enduring element of twentieth century folklore. When I was a young sprat at summer camp, we used to sing a folksong about the Titanic. ("…And the good Lord raised his hand / Said the ship will never land / It was sad when the great ship went down…") The good Lord notwithstanding, what brought the great ship down on its maiden voyage was an unexpected iceberg. As the ship began to sink, the 2,200 people aboard found out that there were not enough lifeboats, and, as a result, more than 1,500 people perished in the dark, icy water. The legend of the Titanic was resurrected in 1987, when the wreck itself was discovered, and again in 1997, when a maudlin, romanticized movie about the disaster rekindled interest in what is one of the oldest stories of mankind: what happens when hubris and poor planning encounter bad luck.

Web:

http://www.abratis.de/
http://www.encyclopedia-titanica.org/
http://www.onlinetitanicmuseum.com/
http://www.skarr.com/titanic/
http://www.titanic-online.com/

Usenet:

alt.history.ocean-liners.titanic

Majordomo Mailing List:

List Name: titanic
Subscribe to: majordomo@admin.listbox.com

Does your country have too much money? Are there too many young men with ambition who have a lot to contribute to society? Is everyone bored with all the peace and quiet? Why not have a WAR?

(Maybe if you're lucky, a famous director will make a movie of it afterward.)

Universal Declaration of Human Rights

On December 10, 1948, the General Assembly of the United Nations adopted the Universal Declaration of Human Rights, a document based on the U.S. Bill of Rights, France's Declaration of the Rights of Man, and England's Magna Carta. The Universal Declaration of Human Rights was created to set a standard for human rights that all countries should meet. It stresses the dignity and worth of humanity, equal rights for men and women, and freedom as a right for everyone. The document was written primarily by René Cassin, a French public official who later (in 1968) won the Nobel Peace Prize for his efforts in promoting human rights. The Universal Declaration of Human Rights is inspiring and well worth a look.

Web:

http://www.udhr.org/udhr/
http://www.un.org/Overview/rights.html

Versailles Treaty of 1919

Over the centuries, there have been many treaties signed in Versailles. The most famous, however, is the treaty signed in 1919 that helped bring World War I to a close. Four world leaders—the "Big Four"—negotiated the treaty: President Wilson (United States), Premier Clemenceau (France), Prime Minister Lloyd George (Britain), and Premier Orlando (Italy). The treaty called for many actions, most of which were geared to strip Germany of its military, political and economic powers. The treaty's main resolutions placed limits on German armed forces, put into place a method for Germany to make enormous reparations, restored various cities and territories to their rightful owners, demilitarized the Rhineland, and created the League of Nations. Unfortunately, the terms of the Treaty of Versailles were so punitive as to create enormous unrest in the German population. In the 1920s, the German economy suffered through a terrible decline and, combined with the resentment over the Treaty of Versailles, the economic suffering created an atmosphere in which Hitler was able to rise to power. What were the actual details of this treaty? See for yourself.

Web:

http://history.acusd.edu/gen/text/versaillestreaty/
    vercontents.html
http://www.lib.byu.edu/~rdh/wwi/versailles.html

Vietnam War

The Vietnam War was a long, drawn-out affair, stretching from 1957 to 1975. In Washington, D.C., on the Vietnam Veterans Memorial, you can see the names of 58,209 dead serviceman, and over 300,000 more who were wounded. As terrible as these numbers are, they are small compared to the dead and injured in Vietnam itself and in neighboring Laos and Cambodia. To anyone growing up in the Sixties, Vietnam was "The War". More than an actual conflict, it was a metaphor for the great mid-century life crisis that America and the world was to experience. It's hard to explain, even generally, what happened and why it was important. Suffice it to say that the Vietnam War finally convinced just about everyone that armed conflict is not a good way to settle differences. And by 1975, America finally started to realize that looking your enemy square in the face would most likely lead you to a reflection of yourself.

Web:
  http://www.faqs.org/faqs/vietnam/
  http://www.historyoftheworld.com/soquel/
    vietwar.htm
  http://www.vwip.org/

Usenet:
  alt.war.vietnam
  soc.history.war.vietnam

Listserv Mailing List:
  List Name: vwar-l
  Subscribe to: listserv@listserv.acsu.buffalo.edu

Vikings

The Vikings were a seafaring people from Scandinavia, who flourished from the eighth to tenth century. By the late 700s, the Viking people were beginning to feel the effects of overpopulation and internal dissention. These problems, coupled with a cultural propensity for adventure and trade, started the Vikings on a long course of conquest, settlement and plundering that eventually led them as far abroad as the coasts of Europe, the British Isles, Greenland and even parts of America. In time, the Viking warriors were repulsed by the kingdoms of Sweden, Denmark and Norway (established after the introduction of Christianity), as well as the rise of strong European states. Today, the Vikings are remembered for their rich legacy: myths, legends and traditions.

Web:
  http://www.control.chalmers.se/vikings/indexframe.html
  http://www.medsca.org/
  http://www.pastforward.co.uk/vikings/

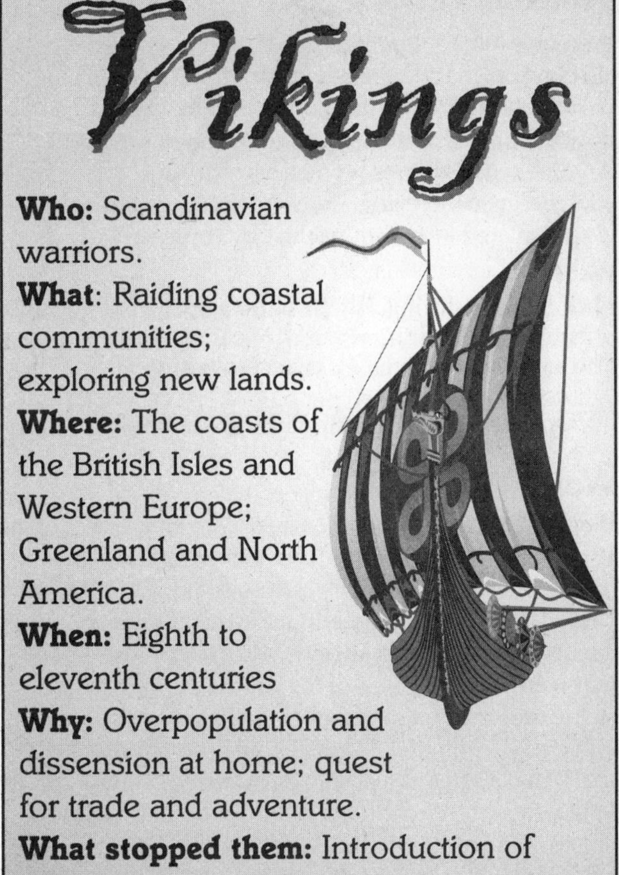

Who: Scandinavian warriors.
What: Raiding coastal communities; exploring new lands.
Where: The coasts of the British Isles and Western Europe; Greenland and North America.
When: Eighth to eleventh centuries
Why: Overpopulation and dissension at home; quest for trade and adventure.
What stopped them: Introduction of Christianity into Scandinavia; creation of kingdoms in Norway, Denmark and Sweden; European states became strong enough to repel invaders.

War

Let's face it, war has been given a bum rap. Okay, so lots of people die, and many more suffer in horrible ways. Yes, families are broken up, and people are changed for the worse permanently. And, I guess, it is true that all kinds of property are damaged and destroyed, and huge amounts of money and resources are funneled away from socially productive uses and into a military machine. But are these necessarily *negative* things? Listen to some of the war discussion on Usenet. Then make up your own mind.

Usenet:
  soc.history.war.misc

Women's History

Women's history involves two broad areas of study: (1) How ordinary women lived in different time periods, and (2) The study of important women and how their achievements have contributed to society. Anyone who explores women's history is going to learn a lot, because there is so much fascinating material that is not covered in traditional history courses.

Web:

http://www.distinguishedwomen.com/
http://www.iisg.nl/~womhist/vivalink.html
http://www.nau.edu/~wst/access/hotlist/
   historyhot.html
http://www.nwhp.org/tlp/links/links.html

World War I

World War I, also called the Great War, took place from 1914 to 1918. The war was fought between the Allies (principally England, France, Russia and, from 1917, the United States), and the Central Powers (Germany, Austria-Hungary and Turkey). The main causes of the war were the ambitions of the German Empire as well as the excessive nationalism of the European nations, especially within the Austro-Hungarian Empire. The spark that started the hostilities occurred on June 28, 1914, when the Archduke Francis Ferdinand, heir to the Austro-Hungarian throne, was assassinated at Sarajevo by Gavrilo Princip, a Serbian nationalist. Within weeks, Europe was involved in a war that would not end until November 11, 1918. In spite of the fact that there were no decisive battles, World War I was one of the bloodiest wars in history. In a four and a half year period, 10 million people were killed and more than 20 million were wounded. At the time, the Great War was looked upon as the war to end all wars. (My paternal grandfather, by the way, was a soldier in the Austro-Hungarian army. In 1916, he was captured by the Russians and sent to Russia as a prisoner of war to work on a farm. While there, he met and fell in love with the young woman who was to become my grandmother.)

Web:

http://info.ox.ac.uk/jtap/
http://www.fordham.edu/halsall/mod/
   modsbook38.html
http://www.lib.byu.edu/~rdh/wwi/
http://www.pitt.edu/~pugachev/greatwar/ww1.html
http://www.worldwar1.com/

Listproc Mailing List:

List Name: wwi-l
Subscribe to: listproc@raven.cc.ukans.edu

World War II

World War II was, by far, the most important conflict of the twentieth century. The war took place from 1939 to 1945, and was fought between the Allies (England, France, Russia, the United States and other countries) and the Axis (Germany, Italy and Japan). The main causes of World War II were the debilitating peace treaties forced on Germany after World War I, the economic suffering of the Great Depression of the 1930s, and the rise of totalitarian regimes in Germany, Italy and Japan. The German leader, Adolf Hitler, spent years building a military dictatorship and, on September 1, 1939, invaded Poland, whereupon England and France declared war on Germany. On December 7, 1941, the United States entered the war, after the U.S. naval base at Pearl Harbor, Hawaii, was bombed by Japan. The war in Europe ended on May 7, 1945, with the surrender of Germany. The war in the Pacific ended in August 14, 1945, shortly after the U.S. dropped atomic bombs on Hiroshima and Nagasaki, Japan. World War II involved every major power in the world, and was the most expensive war in history. In the U.S. alone, the cost was $816,300,000,000 (in 1967 dollars), more than twice as much as the combined cost of the Vietnam War, the Korean War, World War I, the Civil War and the Spanish-American War ($407,100,000,000).

Web:

http://www.euronet.nl/users/wilfried/ww2/ww2.htm
http://www.faqs.org/faqs/world-war-2-faq/
http://www.gi.grolier.com/wwii/
http://www.historyplace.com/worldwar2/timeline/
http://www.ibiblio.org/pha/

Usenet:

soc.history.war.world-war-ii

Listserv Mailing List:

List Name: wwii-l
Subscribe to: listserv@listserv.acsu.buffalo.edu

World War II Propaganda Posters

Have you ever wondered what would inspire thousands and thousands of people to voluntarily march off to a big war far from home? Here's one of the answers: massive government propaganda. Examine these posters that were commissioned by government agencies to stir up the patriotism and sentiment of the American people during World War II. The posters, which are beautifully crafted (some by famous artists such as Norman Rockwell and Thomas Hart Benton), encourage men and women to enlist in the armed services, women to join the work force, and everyone to work hard, conserve resources, and keep secrets from the enemy.

Web:

   http://wopr.stanford.edu/propaganda/15—wwii/
      X15—wwii-1.html
   http://www.americanhistory.si.edu/victory/
   http://www.library.northwestern.edu/govpub/
      collections/wwii-posters/
   http://www.openstore.com/posters/
   http://www.state.nh.us/ww2/

HOBBIES

Audio Talk and General Discussion

A high-quality audio system will make your living room windows bulge. Take the squeak out of your tweeter, the moodiness out of your midrange, and the growl out of your woofer with a few helpful hints from the folks who know audio. High-fidelity, high-end, and professional audio are some of the topics covered.

Web:

   http://www.smr-forums.com/

Usenet:

   rec.audio
   rec.audio.high-end
   rec.audio.marketplace
   rec.audio.misc
   rec.audio.pro
   rec.audio.tech
   rec.audio.tubes

Gold Prospecting

Gold has, since antiquity, had a profound effect on people, often affecting their behavior to the point of irrationality. To a scientist, gold has some unique properties. Among the metals, gold is the most malleable (easily shaped) and ductile (able to be stretched). Compared to other common materials, gold is very dense (19.2 times as dense as water), an excellent electrical conductor, and will not rust, corrode or tarnish. For example, when a treasure of gold coins is recovered from a sunken ship, the coins are as bright and shiny as the day they were minted, even if they were immersed in sea water for hundreds of years. Which brings us to the more interesting properties of gold. It can make otherwise normal human beings act like complete loonies. True, gold is valuable, but not as valuable as, say, platinum (which is actually denser). And there are other precious metals (silver, palladium and rhodium) that are also important enough to be commonly traded as commodities. However, the allure of gold is unmatched in the psychology of mankind. Would you like to explore this irrational craving firsthand? You can. Here are some resources to help you get started with recreational gold prospecting. Start small, and, with perseverance, you may soon work yourself up to fully qualified fanatic. In the meantime, you can have a lot of fun.

Web:

   http://www.golden-caribou.com/goldmin/Jour.htm
   http://www.goldmaps.com/links.html
   http://www.goldprospectors.org/
   http://www.tomashworth.com/

Usenet:

   alt.mining.recreational

Graphology

Take a look at a handwritten letter. If the lines of writing slant upward to the right, the person who wrote them was happy and in a good mood. But if the lines slant downward, it is a sign of depression. How much of graphology (the study of handwriting analysis) is valid? Probably more than you think, but less than you might want. Check for yourself and make up your own mind.

Web:
  http://www.britishgraphology.org/
  http://www.ehandwritinganalysis.com/
    formation.html
  http://www.graphology.co.il/doodles.html
  http://www.graphology.co.il/signatures.html
  http://www.handwritingpro.com/
  http://www.writinganalysis.com/answers.htm

Listserv Mailing List:
  List Name: handwriting-l
  Subscribe to: listserv@listserv.aol.com

Guns

On the Net you can get into all sorts of discussions and information about shooting sports, training, personal defense, gun laws, weaponry, and other topics related to firearms in general. And before you get on your high horse about weapons and gun control, I want you to remember that it isn't guns that kill people: it's bullets traveling at high velocity.

Web:
  http://www.firearmnews.com/
  http://www.gunhoo.com/
  http://www.gunowners.org/
  http://www.gunsnstuf.com/links/
  http://www.recguns.com/

Usenet:
  rec.guns

Hobby Resources

We are all born with a particular combination of talents and aptitudes. Throughout our lives, we must use our inborn aptitudes or we become frustrated and dissatisfied. Life works well when our work (or school work) requires us to use all our aptitudes. For many people, however, this is not the case, and for this reason, hobbies are important. By using the talents that would otherwise be neglected, our hobbies help us balance our lives and feel an ongoing sense of satisfaction. If your life seems to be missing something, maybe a hobby is what you need.

Web:
  http://www.hobbytyme.com/links.html
  http://www.nanana.com/hobbies.html

Japanese Flower Arranging

Ikebana, the Japanese art of flower arranging, is an expression of the dynamic relationships between man and nature. The word Ikebana is derived from "ikeru" (living, to keep alive) and "hana" (flowers). In the Japanese view, one should not seek to fight and conquer nature. Rather, one must learn to live in and with nature. Ikebana, as with other Japanese art, has at its core the goal of using material objects to express a non-material spirit. Whenever I see an Ikebana exhibition, I never fail to appreciate how moving and beautiful a sparse arrangement of only a few flowers, leaves and branches can be.

Web:
  http://www.ikebana.org/Gallery.html
  http://www.jinjapan.org/kidsweb/virtual/ikebana/
    ikebana.html
  http://www.niwa.org/Ikebana.html
  http://www.sagagoryu.gr.jp/html/saga/
    esa_index_new.html

Juggling

I can juggle three oranges. So when I tell you that juggling is a great way to make friends and influence people, you know I'm telling the truth. Join the jugglers and learn how to keep none of your eggs in one basket.

Web:
  http://www.faqs.org/faqs/juggling-faq/
  http://www.juggle.org/
  http://www.jugglemania.net/tricks.asp
  http://www.jugglingdb.com/

Usenet:
  rec.juggling

Kites and Kiting Resources

Did you know that in Thailand, kiting is a major sporting event with teams, rules and even umpires? Kiting competition involves fighting between kites that are controlled by teams of up to twenty players. Whether you are a serious kiter or just like to fly kites for fun, these Web sites will have something for you. Find kite reviews, stories, tips on flying, general information, event guides, and even graphic images of single, dual, and quadline kites. When the wind isn't blowing, stay home and talk about kites on Usenet or IRC.

Web:
   http://www.air-fun.com/windbag.asp
   http://www.kitelife.com/
   http://www.kites.org/zoo/
   http://www.kites.tug.com/
   http://www.kitez.com/

Usenet:
   rec.kites

My Trip to Kite Land

The other night, I was researching kites
on the Internet.
However, it was so late and I was so tired, that
it was all I could do to drag myself to bed,
where I fell asleep immediately.
All of a sudden, I found myself in Kite Land,
flying around a wonderful blue sky, zooming
from one small fluffy white cloud to another.
Within a few minutes, I was joined by a large
flock of brightly colored kites, who led me
through a tunnel into a mountain cavern
where the King of Kite Land sat on a
splendid throne.
"Welcome visitor," he said. "You are my
honored guest." He wagged his tail and a
servant brought out a large covered tray.
"You will join me in a feast," said the King of
Kite Land. The servant removed the cover of
the tray, revealing the largest marshmallow
I had ever seen.
For a good half hour, the King and I gorged on
marshmallow. Finally he said, "The feast
is over. You must now leave Kite Land,"
whereupon I suddenly woke up in my own
bed, my stomach full of marshmallow and my
mind spinning from my wonderful trip
to Kite Land.
Now, if I could only find my pillow.

Knot Tying

Here are some great Web sites that can teach you all about tying knots. You will find diagrams showing you exactly how to create some really cool-looking knots. Have you ever wondered, why are there so many different knots? It's because there are many different uses for knots. For example, the knot you would use to tie down a tent or a tarp would be different from the knot you use to tie a boat to the pier. Once you learn about different knots—and when to use each one—you will find your knowledge useful in many situations. As a matter of fact, after spending some time practicing your knots, I bet you will be walking around looking for something to tie up.

Web:
   http://www.dfw.net/~jazzman/knotter/knot.htm
   http://www.earlham.edu/~peters/knotlink.htm
   http://www.igkt.craft.org/
   http://www.korpegard.nu/knot/

Usenet:
   rec.crafts.knots

Lighthouses

The purpose of a lighthouse is to protect sailors at sea by providing light and sound to guide them through the dark or fog. Over the years, many lighthouses have been built around the world, and today, many people enjoy studying and appreciating these structures. At first, it may seem like an odd hobby, but once you get started, lighthouses are like pistachio nuts. You just can't stop at one.

Web:
   http://home.neo.rr.com/rodsphotogallery/
      Lighthouses/LighthouseIndexLarge.html
   http://www.cr.nps.gov/maritime/ltaccess.html
   http://www.lhdigest.com/digest.cfm
   http://www.lhdigest.com/explorer.cfm
   http://www.lighthouse.cc/links/
   http://www.lighthousegetaway.com/
   http://www.lighthousekeepers.com/
   http://www.us-lighthouses.com/all.asp
   http://www.usalights.com/
   http://Tyww.uscg.mil/hq/g-cp/history/h_lhindex.html

Magic

Even after seeing the cut-up tie trick or the lady and the tiger a hundred times, you still can't figure them out. Brush up on your magic and learn some trade secrets. Learn how to make your little brother disappear or how to change that pesky IRS auditor into a pen and pencil set. You don't have to sell your soul to the devil, you just have to be more clever than the rest of us.

Web:
http://www.allmagic.com/allmagicguide/
http://www.faqs.org/faqs/magic-faq/
http://www.linkingpage.com/
http://www.magic-interactive.com/
http://www.magictalk.com/
http://www.magictimes.com/

Usenet:
alt.magic
alt.magic.history
alt.magic.secrets

Model Building

Having your own airplane, train or rocket is a big hassle. It costs a lot to maintain, and your wife (or mother) probably won't let you keep it in the garage. Much better to stick with scale models—they are a lot more economical and easier to manage.

Web:
http://www.scalemodel.net/
http://www.scalemodelindex.com/
http://www.zendner.com/boats/

Usenet:
rec.models.freeflight
rec.models.railroad
rec.models.rc
rec.models.rc.air
rec.models.rc.helicopter
rec.models.rc.land
rec.models.rc.misc
rec.models.rc.soaring
rec.models.rc.water
rec.models.rockets
rec.models.scale

Why not?

Nudism

Sense the freedom and vitality of the human body unfettered by fabric. Nudists enjoy outdoor activities the natural way. Try it, and you'll like it.

Web:
http://www.aanr.com/
http://www.naturistjournal.com/
http://www.naturists.com/

Usenet:
alt.nudism.moderated
rec.nude

Puppetry

Like to be in control? Maybe you should take up puppetry as a safe outlet. Get information about puppets, puppeteers and puppet troupes. Read about the Puppeteers of America organization, see a list of festivals and guilds, or read about the history of puppetry. For those people who also like to work with their hands, there are patterns for making paper and cloth puppets.

Web:
http://home.carolina.rr.com/puppetrylounge/
http://www.sagecraft.com/puppetry/

Usenet:
rec.arts.puppetry

Majordomo Mailing List:
List Name: **puptcrit**
Subscribe to: **majordomo@lists.village.virginia.edu**

Railroads

Who's been working on the railroad, all the live-long day? And what has Dinah been doing in the kitchen?

Web:
http://www.cwrr.com/nmra/
http://www.rrhistorical.com/
http://www.steamlocomotive.com/

Usenet:
alt.models.railroad.ho
alt.railroad
alt.railroad.steam
bit.listserv.railroad
misc.transport.rail.americas
misc.transport.rail.australia-nz
misc.transport.rail.europe
misc.transport.rail.misc
rec.railroad

Listserv Mailing List:
List Name: **railroad**
Subscribe to: **listserv@cunyvm.cuny.edu**

Puppetry

Last week I had some very distinguished guests over for dinner: the President of the United States, the Pope, the Secretary-General of the United Nations, the Queen of England and Britney Spears.

After dinner, I entertained them by using my puppets to put on a full-length presentation of The Brothers Karamazov.

The show was extremely well received. (The only problem was that, afterwards, I had to stay up all night explaining the various characters to Britney.)

Slot Cars

If you are old enough to remember when slot cars were popular, you are old enough to remember the Dick Van Dyke Show and Peace With Honor. Ah, what sweet days of our youth were those. And what could be a better way to recover a bit of lost innocence than to grab a hot slot car, rev its motor, and show the kids how it was really done? For the slot car aficionado, here is all the info you need to stay cool: race and product information, links to related sites, calendar of events, slot car zines, and much more.

Web:
  http://www.hoslotcarracing.com/
  http://www.oldweirdherald.com/
  http://www.slotcar.com/
  http://www.slotside.com/
Usenet:
  alt.hobbies.slotcars

Treasure Hunting

When I was a little kid, I was digging in the garden one day, when I had an idea. I got some paper and drew a treasure map. I then wrapped it in plastic and aluminum foil and buried it in the garden, as deep as I could. Several years ago, the house was sold and now, a brand new family lives there. Maybe, one day, one of the kids will be digging in the garden and find my map. If he does, I hope he or she is nice enough to split the treasure with me.

Web:
  http://www.garren.net/treasurechronicle/
  http://www.losttreasure.com/sites/
  http://www.otherplane.com/treas/thmyths.htm
Usenet:
  alt.treasure.hunting

Unicycling

When I was an undergraduate student (in Canada), I had a friend who decided he would teach himself how to ride a unicycle (a single-wheeled bicycle). Once he did, another friend decided that he also wanted to learn how to ride a unicycle. Eventually, they conceived the idea of riding their unicycles across Canada. The plan was to get a van that would follow them, in order to provide support and a place to sleep. We even talked about me being the person who would drive the van. Unfortunately, they never followed through with the plan. If they had, however, I would have had a really cool story to tell you.

Web:
  http://www.unicycling.org/
Usenet:
  rec.sport.unicycling

> I believe that there is a role for peanut butter and avocado sandwiches in everyday life.

Yo-Yos

Every now and then, yo-yos come back into fashion. If your personal popularity depends on hanging out at the mall strutting your fancy yo-yo style, it's good to have a way to access fresh material with which to impress your friends. Check out these sites where you will find yo-yo tips and tricks, as well as general information regarding this pastime of the gods.

Web:

    http://member.newsguy.com/~jparrish/faqbeg.htm
    http://www.ayya.net/
    http://www.iwc.com/cosmicyo/trickindex.html
    http://www.mryoyo.com/
    http://www.nationalyoyo.org/
    http://www.stuntpilot.com/
    http://www.yomania.com/cgi-bin/config.pl
    http://www.yomania.com/tricks.htm
    http://www.yoyoing.com/wildjimbo/
    http://www.yvanovich.com/collective/faqcoll.htm

Usenet:

    alt.sport.yo-yo

HOLIDAYS AND CELEBRATIONS

Birthdays

What do Frank Zappa, Benjamin Disraeli, Kurt Waldheim, Joseph Stalin, Heinrich Boll, Jane Fonda and Harley Hahn all have in common? We were all born on the same day (December 21). No matter which day you want to celebrate, there are lots of famous people with the same birthday, and now you can find out who they are and why they are famous. Interesting fact: Philip Gosse (1810-1888) was the inventor of the institutional aquarium. My cat, The Little Nipper (1991-) also likes fish. And they were both born on April 6. Is that cosmic or what?

Web:

    http://www.famousbirthdays.com/
    http://www.leannesbirthdays.com/

Usenet:

    alt.happy.birthday.to.me

Christmas

Christmas, as we celebrate it, is a mixture of traditions from a variety of cultures. Traditionally, Christians celebrate the day, December 25, as the birthday of Christ. However, this date was chosen in the fourth century by Pope Julius I, perhaps as a replacement for the pagan festival that celebrated the winter solstice. (There is no direct evidence, even in the Bible, describing the time of the year at which Christ was born.) Even before this time, the midwinter season had been marked by festivals, such as the Romans' Saturnalia, which were known for their merrymaking. Other traditions were developed throughout the years. For example, singing carols (Christmas songs), hanging mistletoe and exchanging gifts are all English traditions; the Christmas tree comes from medieval Germany; and the idea of a jolly Santa Claus was first popularized in 19th century New York City, where the English community adapted him from the Dutch Saint Nicholas.

Web:

    http://www.christmas-tips.com/ourgurus.asp
    http://www.happychristmas.com/
    http://www.merry-christmas.com/
    http://www.newdream.org/holiday/home.html
    http://www.saint-nick.com/
    http://www.techdirect.com/christmas/cele2.html

Usenet:

    alt.yule.log

Easter

Whether your idea of Easter is waking up early to go to church or lying in bed waiting for a bunny to deliver your chocolate egg, the Net can help you celebrate properly. Enjoy learning about the history of Easter and its traditions. You will also find a lot of other enjoyable resources such as special Easter recipes. (My favorite is Scrambled Chocolate Easter Egg.)

Web:

    http://www.garvick.com/annual/easter/
    http://www.kidsdomain.com/holiday/easter/
    http://www.night.net/easter/
    http://www.njwebworks.com/easter/

Entertainment and Party Ideas

Whose bright idea was it to give this party in the first place? You are a nervous wreck. What if nobody comes? What if everybody comes, but nobody has fun? How do you break the ice? The host and hostess are supposed to be cool and graceful under pressure, so before the party check the Net for great ideas on games, get-to-know-you exercises, songs, and other ways to have fun at parties. People will be talking about your party for weeks.

Web:
> http://www.amazingmoms.com/htm/
>   KidsBirthdayParties.htm
> http://www.birthdaypartyideas.com/
> http://www.boardmanweb.com/party/
> http://www.party411.com/
> http://www.partyschool.com/partythemes/

Halloween

Halloween, October 31, is a holiday celebrated in the United States and Canada. The principal tradition is for children to wear costumes and go door to door in their neighborhood collecting treats and playing pranks. For older people, Halloween is an excuse to have parties and be as ghoulish as possible. The Net is a great source of ideas for how to celebrate. If you join the mailing list, a month or so before the holiday you will read lots of great ideas to enhance your Halloween experience.

Web:
> http://www.benjerry.com/halloween/
> http://www.darklinks.com/dhaunt.html
> http://www.halloween-online.com/
> http://www.kidsdomain.com/holiday/halloween/

Usenet:
> alt.halloween.boo

Hanukkah

Hanukkah, or Chanukah, is an eight-day Jewish holiday celebrated in the winter. The purpose of Hanukkah is to commemorate the victory of the Maccabees (a group of ancient Jews) over their oppressors in the year 167 B.C. Hanukkah traditions include lighting candles in a special candleholder called a menorah and enjoying special foods such as, my favorite, latkes (potato pancakes).

Web:
> http://www.caryn.com/holiday/holiday-chan.html
> http://www.jajz-ed.org.il/festivls/hanuka/
> http://www.virtualchanukah.com/

Hindu Festivals

India, which is largely Hindu, has many different festival days. This is because Hindus worship many different gods, goddesses, saints and gurus. In addition, India is a big country and there are a large number of local and regional celebrations. I have chosen these Web sites to give you an overview of many Hindu festivals. Even if you are not Hindu, I bet you will find it interesting to read about these special days and how they are celebrated.

Web:
> http://www.bawarchi.com/festivals/
> http://www.indiantourism-mandi.com/fairs.htm
> http://www.jetairtours.com/festivals.htm
> http://www.sultanpur.nic.in/fasti.htm

Holiday Stories

'Twas the night before Christmas (or Halloween or Thanksgiving), and you want a story to read to the family. No problem. When it comes to holiday stories, the Net is more than willing to oblige. Holidays stories are an important part of our culture. They do more than entertain us—they teach us to appreciate the spirit of a holiday and help us pass on traditions from one generation to the next. Here are some stories to help you make your next holiday a special treat. What could be more memorable than gathering the entire family around the old computer and reading stories aloud? Talk about tradition.

Web:
   http://photo2.si.edu/ctree/magi.html
   http://www.infostarbase.com/tnr/xmas/
   http://www.kidsdomain.com/holiday/xmas/
      stories.html
   http://www.literature.org/authors/dickens-charles/
      christmas-carol/
   http://www.night.net/christmas/poems12.html-ssi
   http://www.santaclaus.com/stories.html
   http://www.story-telling.com/Stories/
      HolidayStories.htm
   http://www.worldwideschool.org/library/catalogs/
      bysubject-youth-holidaystories.html

Holiday Suicide Talk and General Discussion

Holidays can be stressful and depressing, so it is not surprising that suicides increase during the holiday season. This discussion group is devoted to the problems that lead to being sad while the rest of the world is celebrating. But don't feel you have to be suicidal to participate—it's okay if you just want to complain.

Usenet:
   alt.suicide.holiday

Is There a Santa Claus?

Is there really a Santa Claus? Well... sort of, maybe, well... you know. Okay, Santa Claus may not be a real person, but what about as a metaphor? Is the idea of Santa Claus still important and meaningful? About a hundred years ago, a young girl sent a letter to a New York City newspaper, asking whether or not there really was a Santa Claus. The question was answered in an editorial ("...Yes, Virginia, there is a Santa Claus..."), which is trotted out every year at Christmas time in a seasonal fit of nostalgia. I have put the original essay on my Web site, along with my own answer to Virginia. Take a look at both essays, and see what you think.

Web:
   http://www.harley.com/santa-claus/

Kwanzaa

Kwanzaa is an African-American holiday created in 1966 by Maulana Karenga, a Black Studies scholar. Kwanzaa is a seven-day festival, celebrated just after Christmas, from December 26 through January 1 (although it is not associated with any religion). Karenga's goal in creating Kwanzaa was to establish a set of traditions that would allow African-Americans to enjoy a festival of their own, firmly based on their cultural heritage. Today, Kwanzaa is growing in popularity and is celebrated not only in the U.S., but around the world.

Web:
   http://www.globalindex.com/kwanzaa/
   http://www.melanet.com/kwanzaa/
   http://www.officialkwanzaawebsite.org/

Pagan Holidays

Paganism is a term used to describe a wide variety of spiritual beliefs and customs, loosely based on ancient nature religions, particularly those of ancient Europe. There is no central pagan authority—practicing pagans more or less do what they want—however, many pagans celebrate eight special days called the Sabbats. They are Candlemas, Spring Equinox, Beltane, Summer Solstice, Lammas, Autumn Equinox, Halloween and Yule.

Web:

http://www.circlesanctuary.org/pholidays/
  PaganHolidays.html
http://www.ecauldron.com/holidays.php
http://www.wicca.com/celtic/akasha/index0.htm
http://www.witchvox.com/xholidays.html

Thanksgiving

The idea of an autumn celebration in which people give thanks is an ancient custom. After all, for an agricultural people, autumn is the season just after the harvest and if the harvest went well, there is good reason to be thankful. In America, tradition holds that the modern Thanksgiving holiday is descended from a celebration held by the Pilgrims (early settlers) in 1621. In 1863, U.S. President Abraham Lincoln set aside the last Thursday of November to commemorate the feast given by the Pilgrims. In 1939, the head of the Federated Department Stores convinced President Franklin Roosevelt that a longer Christmas shopping season would be good for the economy. The president moved Thanksgiving to the fourth Thursday in November where it has remained ever since. (Note: In Canada, Thanksgiving is celebrated 11 months after the American holiday, on the second Monday in October.) American Thanksgiving has its own well-defined traditions: food (including turkey, cranberry sauce, stuffing, potatoes, yams, pumpkin pie and gravy), two days off work, more food, watching football games on TV, more food, local parades, and even more food. The week after Thanksgiving is celebrated by the eating of leftovers.

Web:

http://www.bham.wednet.edu/thanks.htm
http://www.kate.net/holidays/thanksgiving/
http://www.pilgrims.net/plymouth/
http://www.plimoth.org/library/thanksgiving/
  thanksgi.htm
http://www.solarcontrol.com/thanksgi.htm

U.S. Independence Day (Fourth of July)

In the United States, Independence Day is one of the four most important American celebrations (the others being New Year's, Christmas and Thanksgiving). Independence Day is celebrated in honor of the adoption of the Declaration of Independence by the Continental Congress in Philadelphia, on July 4, 1776. The Declaration begins, "We hold these truths to be self-evident, that all men are created equal, that they are endowed by their Creator with certain unalienable Rights, that among these are Life, Liberty, and the pursuit of Happiness." In recognition of the importance of the pursuit of happiness, American tradition demands that, on the Fourth of July, all able-bodied citizens must participate in three specific activities: (1) flying the American flag, (2) attending a barbecue, and (3) watching a fireworks display.

Web:

http://www.american.edu/heintze/fourth.htm
http://www.fourth-of-july-celebrations.com/
http://www.usacitylink.com/usa/
http://www.wilstar.com/holidays/july4.htm

Valentine's Day

Valentine's Day, February 14, is the day when we honor that special someone in our life. The tradition of sending romantic gifts and cards is a modern one. The holiday is actually named after St. Valentine who, in the 3rd century A.D., was martyred during the persecution of Christians by the Roman emperor Claudius II. As we celebrate it today, the general idea of Valentine's Day for women is to honor the men who are special in their life with an appropriate gift or pledge of affection. The general idea for men is to try to remember to send something on time so as to not end up like an early Christian martyr.

Web:

http://www.caryn.com/holiday/caryn-valentine.html
http://www.kidsdomain.com/holiday/val/
http://www.phillyburbs.com/valentine/
http://www.tartanplace.com/valen.html
http://www.usacitylink.com/cupid/

A B C D E F G H I J K L M N O P Q R S T U V W X Y Z

Weddings

Don't let your wedding be a remake of Father of the Bride (or the Bay of Pigs). On the Net you can learn what is proper and what is not. Find out shortcuts from folks who have done this before (or again and again). Topics cover a wide range, such as invitations, RSVPs, dresses, parties, garters, underclothes, and much more.

Web:
  http://www.guideforweddings.com/
  http://www.ultimatewedding.com/
  http://www.weddingglobe.com/
  http://www.wednet.com/

Usenet:
  alt.wedding
  soc.couples.wedding

World Holiday Guide

On the Internet, every day is a holiday. Check right now and find something to celebrate. Today, as I write this, it is Women's Day in South Africa and National Day in Singapore. This resource will come in handy when you need to take a day off. For example, let's say it's November 28 and you don't feel like working. Check with the Net and you will be able to tell your boss, in good conscience, that you just don't feel comfortable working on the Albanian National Holiday.

Web:
  http://www.holidayfestival.com/

HOMES

Apartments

Searching for an apartment can be a lot of fun if you live in a town with a high vacancy rate. ("Well, I'll think about taking the place, but you'll have to paint it, replace the appliances, and lower the rent.") In many locations, however, vacancy rates are low, landlords swank around like princes ("If you are interested in renting, you can fill out an application for an application"), and you need all the help you can get. These Web sites have information on apartments for many locations in the U.S. Some sites let you specify what you would like—location, price, size, pets—and then show you the listings for your target area. (One of my researchers lives in an apartment not two miles from Bill Gates's house, and this is how she found her place.)

Web:
  http://www.apartmentworld.com/
  http://www.forrent.com/
  http://www.springstreet.com/apartments/

Report on Weddings
by Elmo (age 8)

Last Sunday, my whole family went to a wedding.

When no one was looking, I ate a big piece of wedding cake. Then I threw another piece at my sister Lucy.

Lucy got mad, and threw part of it back at me, but I ducked, and it hit my mother in the face.

Then she got mad and tried to catch Lucy, who bumped into the buffet table and knocked it over. Then my father got mad at Lucy and made her sit in the car.

When no one was looking, I ate another piece of cake.

I love weddings.

-Elmo

BUILDING YOUR OWN HOME

Before you build your own home, make sure you have the following:

(1) Lots of money.

(2) A well thought-out architectural plan.

(3) Lots of money.

(4) A reliable general contractor with good references.

(5) Lots of money.

(6) A spouse with the patience of a saint.

(7) Lots of money.

(8) Somewhere to live during the extra six months it takes to finish the house past the time your reliable general contractor with good references promised you.

(9) Lots of money.

Ask the Builder

Okay, so you bought a house. In the words of the banker and real estate agent who encouraged you to go deep into debt, you are now a "homeowner". Here is a secret. It won't be long until you find out that it is actually the home that owns you. And, within a short time, you will be devoting as much energy to fixing a faucet and replacing a cabinet as you used to put into choosing which wine to have with dinner. But never fear, help is available. Here is a library of answers to commonly asked home maintenance questions. After all, just because all your weekend time is spent fixing things you never used to care about doesn't mean you can't know what you are doing.

Web:
  http://www.askbuild.com/cgi-bin/library

Building Your Own Home

Building your own home is not for the faint of heart. Moreover, no matter how careful you plan, I promise you, your new home will cost more than you expected. My advice? (1) Hire a good architect. (2) Be realistic in your planning. Don't allow yourself to get carried away. (3) Have lots of money. (4) Use the Net.

Web:
  http://www.builderonline.com/
  http://www.building-cost.net/
  http://www.buildingonline.com/
  http://www.topsider.com/floorF.html

Buying and Selling Houses

So you want to buy a house? In the old days, real estate agents would do some research and find places for you to visit. The agent would pick you up, drive you from place to place, and entertain you along the way with funny stories about escrow officers and title searches. Not any more. Now you need to do a lot of the finding-your-dream-home work for yourself. However, the Net is here to help, and you will be pleased to know that there are many, many real estate listings available online. A lot of people are finding houses on the Net.

Web:
  http://www.ahahome.com/resources.cfm
  http://www.find-homes-for-sale.com/
  http://www.house-hunting.com/
  http://www.hud.gov/homes/homesforsale.cfm
  http://www.realtor.com/

Feng Shui

Feng Shui is an ancient tradition that involves the orientation and placement of objects and buildings. Originating in China, Feng Shui is now popular with people who are in search of a more spiritually harmonious living environment. The idea is to modify your home or working area according to certain principles, thereby enhancing your quality of life and good fortune. The name Feng Shui comes from the Chinese words for wind and water, representing the idea that one's living environment should be oriented and arranged so as to be in harmony with nature.

Web:
  http://www.fengshuigate.com/
  http://www.fengshuiguild.com/
  http://www.fengshuinews.com/
  http://www.worldoffengshui.com/

Usenet:
  alt.chinese.fengshui

Finding an Architect

An architect is a professional whose job is to design and supervise the building of structures. Architects have an enormous amount of specialized knowledge, and you may wish to hire one if you are planning on major remodeling. You should certainly have an architect if you are building a new house. Having the right architect is crucial. Look for one who is interested in the type of work you need done. Interview at least three. Take time to look at their previous work and check their references. Expect to sign a contract. Before you do, make sure you understand all the details, including what you must pay and when.

Web:
  http://www.aiaaccess.com/consumer/
    industry.asp?type=Residential
  http://www.aiaks.org/public/youndx.html
  http://www.aiami.com/hiringan.htm
  http://www.cmdg.com/profile/
  http://www.ourfamilyplace.com/homebuyer/
    buildfind.html

A B C D E F G **H** I J K L M N O P Q R S T U V W X Y Z

Furniture

When you are young, your furniture consists of whatever you can scrounge up for little or no money: a used sofa, homemade bookshelves made from boards and bricks, a second-hand dresser, and so on. As you get older, you begin to realize that furniture is what makes a house into a home. (If you are a woman, this happens around age 20; if you are a man, it's closer to 45.) One day you realize that you now have money to spend on furniture, but you have no idea what to do. I am lucky because I have a friend named Suzanne, who knows everything there is to know about making a home, so when I need furniture help, all I do is call Suzanne. In case you don't have her phone number or if the line is busy (Suzanne is a popular young lady), here are some resources to help you understand and choose the furniture that is right for you. You never know if you have good taste until you have money.

Web:
   http://www.berkshirefurniture.com/Styles.htm
   http://www.functionalarts.com/reference/
      terms.shtml
   http://www.furniturebuying.com/
   http://www.halfpricefurniture.com/webpages/
      buyersguide.asp
   http://www.homeownernet.com/articles/
      buyfurn.html
   http://www.iserv.net/~plucas/

Home Appliance Clinic

Appliances are great when they work. How happy life is when your washing machine actually washes, your dryer really dries, and your refrigerator knows how to stay cool. The best way to achieve such contentment is to choose good appliances in the first place (either new or used). If you are thinking of buying a home appliance, start by reading the knowledgeable words of advice at this Web site. And if something breaks, check here first, before you call for a repairman. Even if you don't want to fix the machine yourself, understanding the problem and the solution will go a long way toward helping you stay in control.

Web:
   http://www.aham.org/consumerhome/home.cfm

Home Decorating

When it comes to decorating, some people are just born with the right stuff. They know what to do, when to do it, and how much to pay for it. Many people, however, seem to flounder helplessly in a sea of colors, patterns and questionable taste. Don't panic. The information I have for you here will help you take control. Start slowly, make your decisions one step at a time, and remember to please yourself. Remember, beauty, like conjunctivitis, is in the eye of the beholder.

Web:
   http://ths.gardenweb.com/forums/decor/
   http://www.committment.com/decorate.html
   http://www.decoratorsecrets.com/
   http://www.getdecorating.com/
   http://www.home-decorating-home-decorating.com/

Home Environmental Hazards

If you spend much time watching TV or listening to the radio, you are bound to hear about home environmental hazards: radon, asbestos, lead, hazardous waste, contaminated water, formaldehyde and so on. It's enough to make you feel a tad uneasy. Is your home sweet home a castle of happiness, or a slow-but-sure death trap that will end up subjecting the members of your family to a slow, painful and expensive death? I understand your discomfort, and I know the cure. It's the same cure that always works in such cases. Find out the truth, so you can make informed decisions.

Web:
   http://www.hsh.com/pamphlets/hazards.html

Home Improvement

I have a great contractor named Larry. Larry can fix anything and will keep working until the job is done right. The only problem is Larry is not available twenty-four hours a day, seven days a week, so when I'm stuck, I turn to the Net. If you are Larry, you already know how to do everything. If you're not Larry, you'll appreciate what the Net has to offer. (Just imagine Martha Stewart singing "If I Had a Hammer".)

Web:
   http://www.epa.gov/hhiptool/
   http://www.hometime.com/
   http://www.hometips.com/help.html
   http://www.livinghome.com/
   http://www.naturalhandyman.com/index.shtm

Home Maintenance and Repairs

It's midnight. A leaky faucet is creating a tsunami in the upstairs bathroom, and your plumber won't answer his pager. What to do? Use the Net, where you'll find helpful advice on how to carry out the 1001 different repairs that make owning your own house a constant joy. Learn about home improvement, repairs, electricity, plumbing and carpentry. If you have a particular problem, join the discussion in one of the Usenet groups, where you can talk things over with people who really know their widgets, gadgets and whatchacallits.

Web:
  http://www.home-inspectors.com/check.htm
  http://www.homedoctor.net/main.html
  http://www.msue.msu.edu/msue/imp/mod02/
    master02.html
  http://www.remodelonline.com/

Usenet:
  alt.coatings.paint
  alt.home.repair
  alt.tools.repair+advice
  misc.consumers.house

Home Maintenance and Repairs

When it comes to fixing things around the house, I have a foolproof system. Whenever anything breaks, I call my friend Suzanne, and she tells me what to do. I write it down very carefully, thank her, and then call my contractor Larry, who comes over and does it.

Of course, this system doesn't work all the time. Last week, a light bulb burned out in the garage, and I couldn't get Suzanne or Larry on the phone. Fortunately, I was able to use the Net to find exact instruction on how to change the bulb—thus answering the question: How many world famous authors does it take to change a light bulb?

Homemaking

Taking care of a home and running a household well requires skill and experience. You need to understand cooking, cleaning, decorating, organizing, budgeting and (possibly) parenting. If you don't know what you are doing, homemaking can be a frustrating and unrewarding experience. But something is missing here. After all, shouldn't "making a home" be one of life's pleasing and rewarding activities? If this makes sense to you, you'll find these resources invaluable. As my personal contribution to your household, let me give you my favorite two organizational tips. (1) All storage areas (such as closets, drawers and cabinets) work best when they are one third empty. (2) When in doubt, throw it out.

Web:
  http://www.doityourself.com/clean/
  http://www.hintsandthings.com/
  http://www.newhomemaker.com/
  http://www.organizedhome.com/
  http://www.pioneerthinking.com/
    cleaningsolutions.html
  http://www.rusticgirls.com/
  http://www.thathomesite.com/forums/
  http://www.washingtonpost.com/wp-dyn/home/
    columns/heloise/

Usenet:
  alt.home.cleaning

International Real Estate Digest

When you think about it, every spot on the planet Earth is real estate of some kind. Well, here is the Web site that expresses this philosophy exactly. The International Real Estate Digest is a colossal, well-organized guide to real estate everywhere. Lots and lots of stuff—you'll feel you've died and gone to real estate heaven. No matter where you want to buy or sell, start here.

Web:
  http://www.ired.com/

A B C D E F G H I J K L M N O P Q R S T U V W X Y Z

Moving

Moving involves a lot more than just getting your possessions from one place to another. There are several bazillion details that have to be taken care of, any one of which has the potential of causing you a great amount of trouble if you forget about it. So don't depend purely on luck and the good graces of the universe. Let the Net help with your planning and your move will be as smooth as Napoleon's retreat from Moscow.

Web:
 http://www.homefair.com/wizard/wizard.html
 http://www.virtualrelocation.com/

Usenet:
 alt.relocate

Old House Restoration

The job of turning your old house into a showplace is not for the faint at heart. The process takes a long, long time and requires money, stamina, money, patience, money, specialized knowledge and money. Old houses can be charming and full of character, but restoring one of them does have its own special challenges. You are starting with a structure that has many hidden traps and idiosyncrasies, and what might be a relatively minor task in a newer house—such as replacing a cabinet—can turn into a big project faster than you can say "unforeseen lateral expansion". So the next time you get surprised and your budget starts to shrink like a salted snail, remember how special you are. Then turn to the Net for help.

Web:
 http://www.oldhousechronicle.com/
 http://www.oldhousejournal.com/
 http://www.oldhouses.com.au/
 http://www.oldhouseweb.com/

Pest Control

Would you like to find out how to make your home inhospitable to those tiny pests who just love to make themselves at home in your home? Well, home in on the Net, your pest control home away from home.

Web:
 http://www.doityourself.com/pest/
 http://www.doyourownpestcontrol.com/info.htm
 http://www.orkin.com/pages/educational_info.html

Usenet:
 alt.consumers.pest-control

REAL ESTATE REALITY

Isn't it great? All you have to do is spend some money and you can own your very own piece of an actual planet (Earth).

I love real estate because it brings out the best in people, and some of the best real estate people hang out in **misc.invest.real-estate**.

Remember, though, talking on the Net is no substitute for experience: the smart way is to "walk the dirt, smell the dirt and feel the dirt". (Fortunately, there's no shortage of dirt.)

Plumbing

Spend some time teaching yourself about the ins and outs of common household plumbing problems, and I guarantee you will be the most popular person on the block. After all, the neighbors may fawn over the guy who used to be a professional football player, or the fellow who can imitate a chicken laying an egg, but when the plumbing breaks, there is no one more in demand than someone who knows his pipes. Here are some great resources to help you understand plumbing: from the basics (such as how to change a washer or freshen up a garbage disposal) to advice on large ambitious projects involving construction, renovation and restoration.

Web:
  http://www.plumbnet.com/
  http://www.theplumber.com/faq.html

Project Calculators and Estimators

You've taken on the weekend painting and carpeting project. Here it is Sunday night at midnight and you are still working. You have about two feet of wall space left to cover and you've run out of paint. Moreover, you are stuck with a large piece of leftover carpet, which will be sitting in your garage forever because your husband won't let you throw it out. The next time the home improvement bug raises its nasty little head, start by visiting these Web sites, where you will find calculators and estimators for carpet, fencing, paint, wallpaper, tile, flooring, insulation, drywall and more.

Web:
  http://www.allabouthome.com/calculators/
  http://www.improvenet.com/projecttools/
    index.html#estimators
  http://www.livinghome.com/cooltools/

Real Estate Talk and General Discussion

It's just like a Monopoly game, except you use real money and the bail is higher if you end up in jail. Learn tips on acquiring real estate: how to choose a good agent, perks for first-time homebuyers, and how to avoid the rental property blues.

Usenet:
  alt.real-estate-agents
  misc.invest.real-estate

Tenant Net

Having a lousy landlord turns Home Sweet Home into Nightmare on Elm Street. Find out what your rights are on a variety of issues such as security deposits, pets, repairs, payment of rent and more. This site offers information on tenants' rights, limited referral and guidance, links to tenant advocacy groups, FAQs, text of rental and housing laws, and much more. Have Tenant Net on your bookmark list in case the big, bad wolf comes to huff and puff and blow your house in.

Web:
  http://www.tenant.net/

Toilet Repair and Maintenance

Okay, let's get this straight. Toilets are *not funny*. And when I tell you that this is the best tutorial about toilets on the Net, you are not to laugh. You are to proceed to this Web site immediately, and teach yourself more about toilets than most people learn in a lifetime. You will find lots and lots of useful information about toilet repair and maintenance. Learn how these devices work, how to fix them, and how to maintain them. If nothing else, be sure to read the emergency advice about what to do when the toilet overflows. (Read it now, *before* it happens.) At the very least, you'll save yourself some real money. At best, you'll find a brand new hobby.

Web:
   http://www.toiletology.com/index.shtml

Woodworking

Wood is really a mass of plant tissue called xylem, formed within the plant from a thin layer (the cambrium) that lies between bark and the stem. Xylem has two primary functions: to conduct water throughout the plant and to provide structural support. Softwood comes from coniferous (evergreen) trees, and has a uniformly nonporous appearance. Hardwood comes from deciduous (leaf-losing) trees that produce xylem with a great many vessels, giving the wood a complex, non-uniform appearance. When wood is freshly cut, it contains a lot of moisture and, before it can be used, it must be dried (seasoned)—either in a kiln or by the action of the sun. This description, though accurate, fails to capture that magic inherent in a beautiful piece of wood. And talking about xylem and cambrium—though interesting to a botanist—doesn't even hint at the enormous utility of wood: a substance that is an integral part of just about every culture in the world. If you are one of the people who appreciate wood for what it is and what you can do with it, there are many useful resources on the Net.

Web:
   http://www.internetwoodworking.com/w5/wood.html/
   http://www.woodweb.com/
   http://www.woodworking.com/

Usenet:
   rec.crafts.woodturning
   rec.woodworking

Listserv Mailing List:
   List Name: **woodwork-l**
   Subscribe to: **listserv@indiana.edu**

HUMANITIES AND SOCIAL SCIENCES

Anthropology

Anthropologists study human beings: their origins and behavior, as well as their cultural, physical and social development. Here are some great collections of anthropological resources, suitable for students as well as serious researchers.

Web:
   http://vlib.anthrotech.com/
   http://www.anthro.net/

Usenet:
   sci.anthropology
   sci.anthropology.paleo

Listserv Mailing List:
   List Name: anthro-l
   Subscribe to: listserv@american.edu

Communication Studies

Don't just talk—communicate. Can't? This'll help. Lotsa links here. Lotsa stuff for the ubiquitous communication student, as well as his or her teachers. Cool. (Although I think I really want to go into broadcasting.) Like, it's great. On the Web, nobody knows if you have nothing to say.

Web:
   http://www.library.ucsb.edu/subj/communic.html
   http://www.natcom.org/
   http://www.uiowa.edu/~commstud/resources/

> The first step to
> self-knowledge is
> to throw away your mirror.

Should You Be a Communication Studies Major?

If you want prestige, go to medical school.

If you want money, study business and finance.

If you want respect, become a nuclear physicist.

If you want intellectual stimulation, take philosophy or math.

But if you want prestige, and money, and respect, and intellectual stimulation…

Future Studies

Future studies is concerned with making projections regarding the near and distant future. Most businesses and governments project no more than 5 years into the future. Futurists—people who specialize in future studies—consider such plans to be *near-term* projections; long-term projections reach out over 50 years. Future studies is highly interdisciplinary in that it concerns itself with population, natural resources, science, technology, globalization, government, and international conflict.

Web:
http://carlisle-www.army.mil/usassi/
http://www.coatesandjarratt.com/resources.htm
http://www.csudh.edu/global_options/
    introfstopics.html
http://www.forecastcenter.com/
http://www.odci.gov/cia/publications/
    globaltrends2015/
http://www.rff.org/library/index.htm
http://www.wfs.org/
http://www.wfsf.org/

Generation X

The term "Generation X" refers to the post-Baby Boomer Americans born between 1961 and 1981. (The name came from a book by Douglas Coupland.) Before they were named, nobody talked much about the Gen Xers. Now just about everyone has something to say.

Web:
http://www.babybusters.org/
http://www.cyberg8t.com/coolink/genx.html

Usenet:
alt.society.generation-x

Listserv Mailing List:
List Name: gen-x
Subscribe to: listserv@listserv.aol.com

Humanities Resources

Traditionally, the humanities referred to the study of Greek and Latin (language and literature). Today, the term is used more generally, to refer to the disciplines devoted to the study of human thought and culture, in particular, history, philosophy, literature, archaeology, languages and the fine arts. Some people consider that the humanities also embrace some of the social sciences, such as sociology, anthropology and psychology.

Web:
http://www.humbul.ac.uk/
http://www.uky.edu/subject/humanities.html
http://www2.h-net.msu.edu/

Usenet:
humanities.answers
humanities.misc

Leisure Studies

Leisure studies—often combined with recreation studies—is the examination of how people spend their leisure time. This is a huge discipline involving many different areas of study such as tourism, sports, outdoor recreation, parks and other public facilities, stress reduction, exercise, resource allocation, and so on. Rest assured, no matter what you do for fun, someone, somewhere, is studying it. If you are a leisure studies student or researcher, the Net has lots of resources to help you. In fact, using the Net to find the information you need will save you so much time, you won't know what to do with it all.

Web:
   http://www.staff.vu.edu.au/lswp/

Listproc Mailing List:
   List Name: leisurenet
   Subscribe to: listproc@gu.edu.au

Listserv Mailing List:
   List Name: gleis-l
   Subscribe to: listserv@listserv.uga.edu

Listserv Mailing List:
   List Name: sprenet
   Subscribe to: listserv@listserv.uga.edu

Perseus Project

The Perseus Project contains a vast collection of information relating to art objects, archaeological sites and buildings, vases, coins, and sculptures, including well over 10,000 pictures. My favorite part is the collection of ancient coins—information as well as pictures—because I like to collect coins myself. This is a great site for serious researchers. You'll find information on all these artifacts, gathered from museums around the world, which is collected and organized into a large, well-organized library.

Web:
   http://www.perseus.tufts.edu/

**Beauty is fleeting,
but Web sites last forever.**

Popular Culture

Popular culture is all around us—all you have to do is open wide and absorb. And popular culture is so accessible. You don't have to study, learn strange terminology, or hang around with eggheads who talk about things you don't understand. Just turn on the TV, listen to the radio, go to the stadium, and pick up a magazine. Of course, popular culture is more than culture, it's popular—which means there's a lot of it and it disappears quickly, like the hot breath of reality on the razor blade of life. What's in vogue today is on the list of things-no-one-remembers tomorrow, so don't get lost looking for your past. Use the Net and stay abreast of all that used to be cool, desirable and popular.

Web:
   http://www.popculturejunkmail.com/
   http://www.pophistorynow.com/
   http://www.sixtiespop.com/
   http://www.uiowa.edu/~commstud/resources/
      POP-Culture.html
   http://www.yesterdayland.com/

Population Studies

Population studies is the area of the social sciences dealing with such topics as population, demographics, ethnicity, migration, nuptiality (marriage), fertility, mortality, social mobility and distribution of wealth. Because of the heterogeneous nature of its subject matter, population studies is multi-disciplinary, drawing on a variety of sciences and social sciences.

Web:
   http://demography.anu.edu.au/VirtualLibrary/
   http://popindex.princeton.edu/
   http://www.psc.isr.umich.edu/library/resources.html

Social Science Resources

There are so many social science resources on the Net it's hard to know where to start, so I'll tell you: start here. Just visit these Web sites, select an area of study, and before you can say "This work was done in partial fulfillment of a Ph.D. thesis," you will be up to your cerebrum in enough information to please even the most demanding principal investigator.

Web:
   http://infomine.ucr.edu/cgi-bin/search?liberal
   http://sosig.esrc.bris.ac.uk/
   http://www.vlib.org/SocialSciences.html

Social Work

During the Great Depression, the United States government, along with private, state and local social organizations, began to help people who were in need of some type of assistance. This evolved into today's large network of people and agencies devoted to helping individuals and families who are facing poverty, alcoholism, drug abuse, and other physical, mental and social problems.

Web:

> http://gwbweb.wustl.edu/websites.html
> http://www.clinicalsocialwork.com/
> http://www.sc.edu/swan/

Sociology Resources

Sociology is the study of how people behave in groups. Modern sociology began in 1748, when the French intellectual Baron de la Brède et de Montesquieu (1689-1755) wrote a book entitled "The Spirit of the Laws". In this book, Montesquieu introduced the revolutionary idea that history could be interpreted as the interrelationship of a number of social forces, including religion, politics, government and economics. (Montesquieu is also well-known for having had great influence on the ideas embodied in the U.S. Constitution.) The term "sociology" was created in 1838 by the French philosopher Auguste Comte (1798-1857), whose writings had a significant influence on 19th- and 20th-Century thinking. (He was the founder of the school of positivism.) As a social reformer, Comte published "The Course of Positive Philosophy (1830–1842), in which he explained that the study and application of "sociology" could provide us with the tools to create a society in which people and nations would coexist peacefully amid a state of general contentment. (Compare this to the goal of the "Introduction to Sociology" course that you took in college.)

Web:

> http://www.ac.wwu.edu/~stephan/timeline.html
> http://www.lib.vt.edu/subjects/soci/
> http://www.sociolog.com/

POPULAR CULTURE

I usually don't answer the phone while I am writing, but for some reason the machine didn't pick up.

"Uh... hello... you don't know me," she said, "but I wonder if you could email me something witty so I can graduate?"

"Say that again."

"I'm a student, and I've read all your books and I think they're great, and all I have to do is finish one last project for my course and I can graduate."

"What course?"

"Modern American Humorists Who Write Internet Books," she said.

I thought about it. "Must be an easy course."

"Independent study," she replied. "I chose it 'cause of the short reading list. So, can you help me?"

"What do you need?" I asked.

"I need to send you email and have you write back a witty message."

"No problem," I said.

"Great. Now I can finish my project and graduate."

"Congratulations. What's your degree?" I asked.

"Popular culture. I'm majoring in Dick Van Dyke with a minor in Lucy. Bye. Gotta go now."

Imagine that. A student studying my books in a college course. I have finally arrived.

Stephen King, eat your heart out.

Sociology Talk and General Discussion

We've all heard the rumors—that sociology is one of those fluffy topics that people are required to take in college. Well, I am here to tell you that it's not so. Get into the hard-core science of sociology, and talk down and dirty with people who know their people.

Usenet:

> alt.sci.sociology

U.S. National Endowment for the Humanities

The United States National Endowment for the Humanities (NEH) is a United States government agency that offers grants for projects in history, philosophy, languages and other areas of the humanities. If you are a humanities scholar, take a look at the NEH's Web site, where you can learn about the NEH and its grants, and find out how to apply for a grant of your own. Every year, the NEH awards millions of dollars. There is no reason why some of this money shouldn't be supporting your research.

Web:
   http://www.neh.fed.us/

Would you like to be the most highly regarded, knowledgeable, respected person around the house?

All you have to do is spend one hour each day, exploring an aspect of the humanities at the Voice of the Shuttle Web site.

In less time than you can say, "Yes, I do understand your point, but a recent paper in postindustrial business theory seems to contradict your hypothesis," you will be the most highly regarded, knowledgeable, respected person around the house, and everyone else will be begging to cook your food and wash your dishes.

(Of course, your cat still won't come when you call him, but then, what do cats care about postindustrial business theory?)

Voice of the Shuttle

It's 2 AM and you are watching Star Trek with your best friend, when all of a sudden the need arises to check something at the Klingon Language Institute. Go to the Voice of the Shuttle, a huge collection of links and resources for students and researchers in the humanities. From Anthropology to Women's Studies, you'll find it here. (The Klingon Language Institute is under Linguistics.)

Web:
   http://vos.ucsb.edu/

Best of Usenet

Don't spend hours searching through thousands of Usenet discussion groups looking for the funny stuff. Someone has already done the dirty work for you. If you are in the market for humor, you can find lots of laughs with one-stop shopping by checking out the group that claims to have the best of what Usenet has to offer. The **alt.humor.best-of-usenet** group has the funny stuff and **alt.humor.best-of-usenet.d** is where you can talk about the funny stuff.

Usenet:
   alt.humor.best-of-usenet
   alt.humor.best-of-usenet.d

Blackout's Box

Every time I visit Blackout's Box I end up laughing and laughing out loud. This Web site features crank phone calls made by a wonderful, talented actor. These recordings are, by far, the funniest such calls I have ever heard. If you need a good laugh right now, you know what to do.

Web:
   http://www.blackout.com/

Comedy Talk and General Discussion

I love jokes, so I am encouraging everyone to choose comedy as a career. Sure, the world will have to make do with fewer new inventions, scientific discoveries and medical miracles, but we will all be laughing too hard to notice. Comedy is an addiction and when people are not listening to it or watching it, they are talking about it on Usenet.

Usenet:
   alt.comedy.british
   alt.comedy.british.blackadder
   alt.comedy.firesgn-thtre
   alt.comedy.improvisation
   alt.comedy.slapstick
   alt.comedy.slapstick.3-stooges
   alt.comedy.standup
   alt.comedy.vaudeville
   alt.tv.comedy-central

Computer Humor

By their nature, computers are dull, technical and boring (unless you are a nerd, in which case computers are fascinating, and you are dull, technical and boring). In either case, here is the antidote.

Web:
    http://computerhumor.glowport.com/
    http://web.ukonline.co.uk/eric.price/pages/
      humour.html
    http://www.helldesk.org.uk/funnies.html
    http://www.laughnet.net/compute.htm
    http://www.monster-island.org/tinashumor/
      computer.html

Cruel Site of the Day

Humor isn't always pretty—but someone has to do it. The Cruel Site of the Day is one of the places you *must* know about. Every day (well, not every day, but most days...well, some days anyway) there is a new link to a bizarre site on the Net. The site might be serious, it might be a parody, or it might be so strange as to defy classification. What is always true, however, is that you are sure to find someone to laugh at. When you have some extra time, check out the Cruel Site archives ("Our Cruel Heritage") for some guaranteed bad-taste-meets-the-Net humor-in-a-box.

Web:
  http://www.cruel.com/

Funny People

Usenet has a whole set of discussion groups devoted to the worship and discussion of various famous people and their work. Humor, of course, is well represented. Join the disciples and discuss your favorite humorists.

Usenet:
    alt.comedy.laurel-hardy
    alt.comedy.marx-bros
    alt.comedy.paul-reubens
    alt.fan.andy-kaufman
    alt.fan.cecil-adams
    alt.fan.chris-elliott
    alt.fan.dave_barry
    alt.fan.dennis-miller
    alt.fan.drew-carey
    alt.fan.goons
    alt.fan.jay-leno
    alt.fan.jim-carrey
    alt.fan.letterman
    alt.fan.mel-brooks
    alt.fan.mike-myers
    alt.fan.monty-python
    alt.fan.penn-n-teller
    alt.fan.pratchett
    alt.fan.rosieodonnell
    alt.fan.rowan-atkinson
    alt.fan.wodehouse
    alt.fan.woody-allen

Henry Cate III Joke Collection

Long before there was a Web, in the days when *everyone* read the Usenet discussion groups and resources were shared by FTP (find an old person to explain it to you), there was an Internet folk hero named Henry Cate III. Henry Cate III worked for Xerox and, in his spare time, indulged in a wonderful hobby. He collected jokes, organized them into series, and posted them to **rec.humor**, the principal Usenet humor group. Although I never met Henry Cate III in person, I did talk to him over the phone and by email. In fact, at one time, we were thinking of creating a book containing jokes from around the world. All too often in this world, people like Henry Cate III are forgotten. But not in this book.

Web:
    http://www.ee.umd.edu/~dstewart/joke/
    http://www.textfiles.com/humor/JOKES/weird89.txt

A B C D E F G H I J K L M N O P Q R S T U V W X Y Z

Humor Archives

Where do you go when you need a good laugh, and you can't find your old high school yearbook? To the Net, of course. Here are some Internet resources that will lead you to enough jokes, humor and overall silliness to supply the entire Peruvian army.

Web:
　http://www.funnybone.com/
　http://www.igs.net/~tril/humor/
　http://www.jokeindex.com/
　http://www.jokes2go.com/dbmenu.html
　http://www.laughnet.net/
　http://www.thehumorarchives.com/

Humor Databases

You have finally managed to get the girl in your economics class to come over for dinner. It is crucial that you impress her, and what better way than to amuse her with some jokes? The Net approves of your relationship and is willing to help. Check with these Web sites, and you are bound to find all the jokes you need, as well as a few extra (just in case). It won't be long before your date is laughing so hard, you can take the bigger hamburger for yourself and she won't even notice.

Web:
　http://humor.ncy.com/
　http://www.myjokemail.com/

Humor for Women

Being a woman requires you to (1) deal with men, (2) deal with the world, and (3) deal with yourself. Under the circumstances, a triple portion of good humor can go a long way.

Web:
　http://www.funnigurl.com/
　http://www.happywomanmagazine.com/
　http://www.thehumorarchives.com/categories/
　　Women/

Humor Magazines

It's easy to be well-read when what you are reading is funny. These online humor magazines will put a snap in your eye and a sparkle in your walk. And the best part is, you don't have to pay good money to buy a print magazine. There are just as many laughs available for free, right now, on the Net. Laugh for free in the privacy of your own home—that's my motto.

Web:
　http://homepages.ihug.co.nz/~dbaxo/
　　urban_legend.htm
　http://www.brunching.com/
　http://www.bunkmag.com/
　http://www.dribbleglass.com/
　http://www.hcs.harvard.edu/~demon/
　http://www.odd-duck.com/

Humor Mailing Lists

Why go out into the cold cruel world in order to hunt down humor, when you can have it come directly to your electronic mailbox? Subscribe to these mailing lists, and you will be able to distract your co-workers by laughing as you read your mail. Then you can forward the best jokes to all your friends, so they will see what a terrific sense of humor you have and appreciate how lucky they are to know you.

Web:
  http://www.jokeseveryday.com/

Listserv Mailing List:
  List Name: humor
  Subscribe to: listserv@listserv.uga.edu

Majordomo Mailing List:
  List Name: jokelist
  Subscribe to: majordomo@arthurian.nu

Majordomo Mailing List:
  List Name: jokes
  Subscribe to: majordomo@lists.spunge.org

Humorists to Discover

There are lots and lots of humor columnists on the Net. I know this because I have looked at tens and tens of Web sites to find the ones that are really worth your time: the humor writers I want you to discover. In order to qualify for such an honor, these humorists must not be available in large-well-known-newspapers-that-feature-columnists-who-write-one-sentence-paragraphs. Moreover, they must meet my strict criteria. First, they have to make me laugh out loud. Next, they must have a significant body of written work. Finally, they must have a lot of natural talent and writing ability. As you can see, the list of writers who made the cut is a short one, but then, I am researching on your behalf and my standards are high. (In case you want to do your own research, I have also included a Web site that has links to a great many Internet-based humorists.)

Web:
  http://www.maddogproductions.com/
  http://www.madkane.com/
  http://www.martybeckerman.com/
  http://www.mattneuman.com/
  http://www.thenetwits.com/

Interactive Top Ten Lists

If you are tired of passively hearing about other people's Top Ten lists, then rejoice: you can participate in making your own. Fill in a form with your entry, submit it and wait to see if yours is selected and put on display. Fame could be just around the corner for you.

Web:
  http://www.csittl.com/

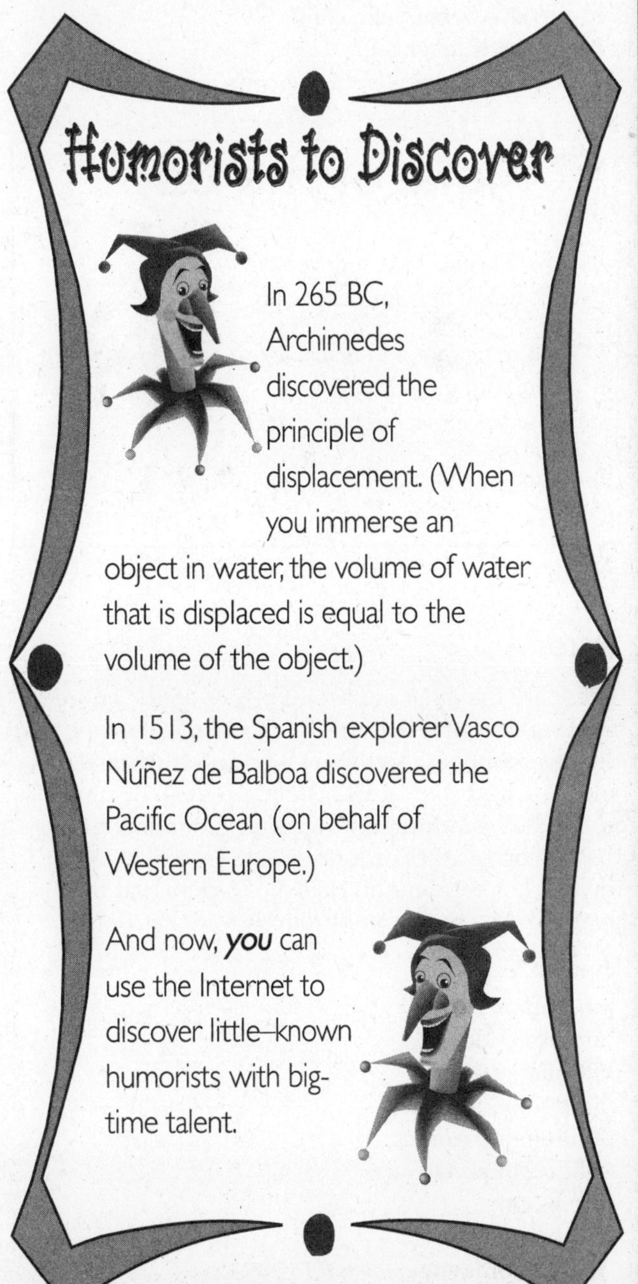

Joke of the Day

I am sorry to be strict about it, but every day you need to read a joke. There are two possibilities. You can arrange to have a joke emailed to you automatically, or you can check the Web and find something funny for yourself. The choice is yours. (After all, this is a free country.)

Web:

    http://www.daily1.com/jokes/jokes.html
    http://www.emailjoke.com/
    http://www.joker.org/
    http://www.jokeswarehouse.com/

Joke of the Day

I have a friend who, for over ten years, read a new joke every day.

One day, he forgot to read a joke and, instantly, his life was exposed as a meaningless sham.

Don't let this happen to you.

Jokes

These are the most important places on the entire Internet: the joke-telling Usenet groups. Anyone may post a joke about anything (although truly tasteless jokes are best sent to **alt.tasteless.jokes**). Beginner's note: The **rec.humor.d** discussion group is for the discussion of jokes or for requests (such as "Does anyone have the canonical list of Oprah and Beavis jokes?"). The **rec.humor** group is for jokes only.

Usenet:

    alt.humor
    alt.humor.dutch
    alt.humor.jewish
    alt.humor.net-abuse
    alt.humor.parodies
    alt.humor.puns
    rec.humor
    rec.humor.d
    rec.humor.flame
    rec.humor.jewish

Jokes, Moderated

This moderated group is to **rec.humor** what America Online is to the Internet: there is Someone in Charge. All jokes are submitted to a moderator who posts the ones he thinks are funny. What this means is that, unlike **rec.humor**, you don't have to wade through a whole lot of junk, silliness and bad jokes. It also means that you have to put up with irritating messages that are tacked on to the end of each joke, as well as regularly posted draconian ukases, setting out rules and regulations. Still, this discussion group is one of the most popular on the entire Usenet (in my estimation, coming between **rec.arts.erotica** and **alt.sex.bondage**).

Web:

    http://www.netfunny.com/rhf/

Usenet:

    rec.humor.funny
    rec.humor.funny.reruns

Microsoft Bashing

Microsoft is the computer company people love to hate, and Bill Gates is the computer executive people love to excoriate. Why is this? Well, I suppose we all have our own reasons, but it's not hard to have mixed feelings about a company that dominates the PC software marketplace while making us all use an operating system whose stability is a tad less reliable than a U.S. senator's promise to lower taxes. Still, why Microsoft is the Barney the Dinosaur of the computer industry is less important than the fact that anyone can take part in this wholesome, fulfilling activity. So don't wait. Whether you want to support a Microsoft boycott, read news that makes Microsoft look bad, or merely enjoy a few good-natured Bill Gates jokes, the tools you need to bash Microsoft and Mr. Bill are available 24 hours a day.

Web:

    http://i-want-a-website.com/about-microsoft/
    http://www.elsop.com/wrc/humor/bill_mic.htm
    http://www.ihatewindows2000.com/
    http://www.microsith.com/

Usenet:

    alt.conspiracy.microsoft
    alt.destroy.microsoft
    alt.is.bill.gates.satan
    alt.microsoft.sucks

Onion

The Onion is a satirical humor magazine that evolved from a college newspaper based in Madison, Wisconsin. The Onion is funny—very funny. (And goodness knows, anyone living in Madison can use a good laugh.) The writing is first-rate, providing a wonderful parody of the ubiquitous self-conscious weakly written style championed by today's mainstream newspapers and magazines. If you have ever had occasion to read newspapers and magazines from earlier in the century (say, before television), you cannot help but notice the difference between what our grandparents used to read and what passes for writing today. In an age when watching an entire uninterrupted 60-second commercial is considered an extreme test of one's power of concentration, it's hard to believe that there used to be a time when daily newspapers published articles with paragraphs that routinely contained more than two sentences. The reason I mention this is because I find the Onion to be the perfect antidote to the banal and diluted output of our current print media. Now that "lowest common denominator" is considered to be a desirable goal by writers and publishers alike, reading the Onion is, in my opinion, the perfect way to pass the time until something better comes along. Also, it's funny. (And goodness knows, anyone living in Madison can use a good laugh.)

Web:
   http://www.theonion.com/

Oracle

You send in any question you want to the Usenet Oracle. After a short wait, you receive your response. Great, you say, the wondrous powers of omnipotent wisdom are at my disposal whenever I want. Then you notice a catch: in return for answering your question, the Oracle sends *you* a question to answer. "Why not?" you say. "Maybe the Oracle is overworked this week, and it is really quite a compliment to be asked for my opinion." Then you notice that whenever you ask a question, you are sent one in return. Eventually you catch on, "Why, we are all just answering..." Well, I'm sure you don't need my help to figure it out (especially if you have ever sold Amway products). The Usenet Oracle is a time-honored tradition. Read the best of the Oracle's answers in the moderated group **rec.humor.oracle**. The **.d** is non-moderated and is for an open discussion of the Oracle's wisdom.

Web:
   http://cgi.cs.indiana.edu/~oracle/index.cgi
   http://www.faqs.org/faqs/usenet-oracle-intro/

Usenet:
   rec.humor.oracle
   rec.humor.oracle.d

Parodies and Satire

What keeps us from taking life too seriously? People who take the trouble to point out how ridiculous much of our culture really is. When life gets to be too much, a few moments perusing these parody and satire Web sites will put the spring back in your step and the gleam back in your eye.

Web:
   http://www.drleons.com/
   http://www.dumbentia.com/
   http://www.justmorons.com/
   http://www.polisat.com/
   http://www.thespeciousreport.com/
   http://www.youcrazy.com/

Relationship Humor

There's more to relationships than doing the laundry and taking out trash. Sometimes, you just have to laugh. After all, what could be funnier than a relationship?

Web:
   http://www.askheartbeat.com/html/
      body_quip46.html
   http://www.hubbycide.com/humor/relationships.htm
   http://www.relationshipjokes.com/
   http://www.voiceone.com/html/marriage.html

Religious Satire

The Surgeon General's priest warns that reading religious satire on the Net could be hazardous to your spiritual health. But it's so much fun that it doesn't really matter. Put off your eternal damnation tomorrow for hours of chuckles today.

Web:

    http://www.bettybowers.com/
    http://www.infidels.org/misc/humor/
    http://www.landoverbaptist.org/
    http://www.randomjoke.com/topic/religion.php
    http://www.thedoormagazine.com/
    http://www.unwind.com/jokes-funnies/
       religiousjokes.shtml

Usenet:

    alt.atheism.satire

Science Jokes

Here is one of the funniest jokes I know: "What's purple and commutes?" Answer: "An abelian grape". Now, this is a mathematical joke, so don't worry if you don't get it. However, if you are a scientist, there are whole oodles of jokes just for you. Not only math, but biology, chemistry, physics and more—everything is funny if you make the right assumptions.

Web:

    http://www.jupiterscientific.org/sciinfo/
       sciencejokes.html
    http://www.xs4all.nl/~jcdverha/scijokes/

Shakespearean Insults

Each time you connect to these sites a different insult is thrown at you in perfect Shakespearean style. Examples: "Thou clouted knotty-pated maggot-pie," "Thou jarring plume-plucked measle," "Thou errant toad-spotted pignut," or "Thou dankish bat-fowling pumpion."

Web:

    http://marge.phys.washington.edu/cgi-bin/shake
    http://www.kitenet.net/insults/
    http://www.pangloss.com/seidel/Shaker/
    http://www.tower.org/insult/insult.html

Tasteless (and Dirty) Jokes

Don't look at these resources unless you want sickening, tasteless, repulsive, humiliating, insulting jokes and stories (many of which are silly, but—like Congressmen—you get what you pay for). Don't you dare post anything that is not tasteless. And don't you dare complain that anything here offends you. You have been warned...now check it out.

Web:

    http://www.fouljokes.com/
    http://www.neonfire.com/spirit_of_joy/
       dirtyjokes_enter.htm
    http://www.tasteless-jokes.com/

Usenet:

    alt.tasteless.humor
    alt.tasteless.jokes

Tasteless Is in the Mind of the Beholder

The best thing about tasteless jokes is that, if you have enough of them, you will be able to offend just about anyone. Personally, I feel everyone should be offended once a week, just on general principles.

So the next time you want to provide a public service, spend some time reading the *alt.tasteless.jokes* discussion group, select the most obnoxious jokes you can find, and then use them to offend as many people as possible.

After all, no man is an island: we all have a social responsibility to make sure that the social fabric rips once in awhile.

INTERESTING TECHNOLOGIES

Artificial Intelligence

Artificial intelligence (AI) is the study of systems that model the human behaviors of learning and reasoning. Some of the main areas of study are problem solving, pattern recognition, natural language processing, machine learning, artificial life, robotics, expert systems, fuzzy logic, neural networks and speech recognition. To this list, I would also add figuring out how to plan your breakfast so the milk and the cereal come out even.

Web:

  http://liinwww.ira.uka.de/bibliography/Ai/
  http://www.aaai.org/
  http://www.compinfo-center.com/tpai-t.htm
  http://www.cs.berkeley.edu/~russell/ai.html
  http://www.cs.washington.edu/research/jair/
  http://www.emsl.pnl.gov:2080/proj/neuron/ai/
    journals.html
  http://www.faqs.org/faqs/ai-faq/
  http://www.ncc.com/misc/ai_sites.html
  http://www.neuron.co.uk/

Usenet:

  comp.ai
  comp.ai.doc-analysis.misc
  comp.ai.doc-analysis.ocr
  comp.ai.edu
  comp.ai.fuzzy
  comp.ai.games
  comp.ai.genetic
  comp.ai.jair.announce
  comp.ai.jair.papers
  comp.ai.nat-lang
  comp.ai.philosophy
  comp.ai.shells
  comp.ai.vision

Artificial Intelligence

Artificial Life

Getting tired of real life? Try a little artificial life. It's low in calories, high in fiber, and while it might run up your electricity bill, it will certainly keep you from being lonely.

Web:

  http://www.alcyone.com/max/links/alife.html
  http://www.aridolan.com/
  http://www.faqs.org/faqs/ai-faq/genetic/

Usenet:

  comp.ai.alife
  comp.ai.genetic

Biometrics

Biometrics is the science of studying biological phenomena using mathematics and statistics. One of the more important applications of biometrics is to use various body characteristics to identify people, for example, by analyzing fingerprints. With the advent of small, powerful computers and sensors, a whole new biometric industry has been developed— an industry devoted to creating personal identification products. Modern biometric devices can be used to identify people based on their physiological or behavioral characteristics, such as speech, hand shape, facial traits, and appearance of the iris (colored part of the eye). One day, biometric devices will be used everywhere to identify us to machines. For example, there are already ATMs that identify a person by scanning his or her eyes, and checking the iris patterns against a database. This means you will be able to withdraw money without having to use a password. It also means that the government and your employer will be able to identify and track you with unbelievable efficiency. Clearly, the shape of biometric things to come is something we all need to understand.

Web:

  http://biometrics.cse.msu.edu/
  http://www.biomet.org/
  http://www.biometrics.org/
  http://www.ibia.org/

Cloning

In most organisms, a copy of the blueprint for reproduction is stored within each cell. Inside the cell there are genes, most of which perform a particular function in creating a brand new organism. Genes are made of a biochemical substance called deoxyribonucleic acid or DNA. In principle, one could take an animal, extract the DNA from one of its cells, and then use that DNA as a blueprint to create a brand new animal. Although the new animal would be a completely separate organism, it would be an exact genetic copy of the original. We call this copy a clone. So far, using the techniques of genetic engineering, various types of plants and animals have been cloned successfully. In 1996, Scottish scientists created a cloned sheep named Dolly (after the singer Dolly Parton). Dolly was the first mammal cloned from an adult cell (as opposed to an embryonic or fetal cell); using an adult cell allows one to choose an animal with specific characteristics. Since then, other mammals have been cloned, including several goats and cows. Should we clone human beings? Technically speaking, cloning-like procedures for human cells have been performed since 1993. However, the full cloning of a person is still a highly controversial issue. Still, it's just a matter of time. There is no doubt in my mind that sooner or later (probably sooner), someone will clone a human, using cells from an adult. Once that happens, the world will never be the same.

Web:

  http://sun3.lib.uci.edu/~mclweb/cloning.htm
  http://www.biotaq.com/gene/cloning.htm
  http://www.humancloning.org/
  http://www.newscientist.com/hottopics/cloning/

Usenet:

  alt.bio.technology.cloning
  alt.cloning

Computer Speech

Computer speech has been hyped for years, and every year we hear the same thing: "This is the year." Well, when I hear it from a computer, I will believe it. In the meantime, you can get a grasp of the fundamentals by reading the FAQ (frequently asked question list). Where else are you going to go when you need a fast Fourier transform program right away and the neighborhood convenience store is closed?

Web:

  http://cslu.cse.ogi.edu/
  http://www.faqs.org/faqs/comp-speech-faq/
  http://www.idealibrary.com/servlet/toc/csla
  http://www.speech.cs.cmu.edu/comp.speech/
  http://www.speech.sri.com/

Usenet:

  comp.speech.research
  comp.speech.users

Listserv Mailing List:

  List Name: prosody
  Subscribe to: listserv@list.msu.edu

Don't be scared by computer viruses. See "Privacy and Security".

Conversations with Computers

In 1972, I was in a computer lab at UCLA where there was a computer connected to several other computers around the country. (The connection was made over a primitive network that was the ancestor of the Internet.) I was able to connect to a computer at Stanford that had a program that acted like a paranoid. I was also able to connect to a computer at MIT that ran a program that acted like a psychiatrist. For fun, I typed the responses from one program into the other, and vice versa, and for the first time in history, that I know of, two computers were talking to one another. (The paranoid won, by the way.) Would you like to talk to a computer program yourself? Well, you can. Here are some programs with which you can carry on a typed conversation. (Tell them I said hello.)

Web:

http://www.agentland.com/
http://www.alicebot.org/
http://www.botspot.com/
  search/s-chat.htm
http://www.cybermecha.com/Robot/
http://www.loebner.net/Prizef/
  loebner-prize.html

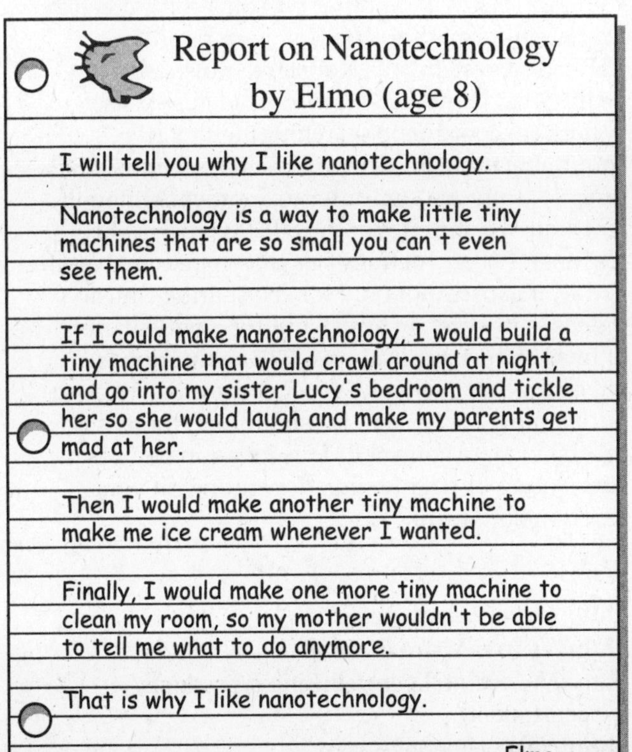

Report on Nanotechnology by Elmo (age 8)

I will tell you why I like nanotechnology.

Nanotechnology is a way to make little tiny machines that are so small you can't even see them.

If I could make nanotechnology, I would build a tiny machine that would crawl around at night, and go into my sister Lucy's bedroom and tickle her so she would laugh and make my parents get mad at her.

Then I would make another tiny machine to make me ice cream whenever I wanted.

Finally, I would make one more tiny machine to clean my room, so my mother wouldn't be able to tell me what to do anymore.

That is why I like nanotechnology.

-Elmo

Gizmos and Gadgets

I must confess, I like reading about the newest gizmos and gadgets. If you're the same way, you'll appreciate these Web sites, where there's always something new and exciting to admire. Kids: these resources can help you get ideas as you write a letter to Santa Claus. Anyone can ask for a toboggan or a new video game, but how many people do you know who request a pen that glows in the dark (so you can write at night), or a wristwatch that is also a fully functional Etch-A-Sketch? Let me tell you, Santa will be impressed.

Web:

http://www.gadgetboy.com/
http://www.mrgadget.com/
http://www.wired.com/news/gizmos/

Nanotechnology

Nanotechnology is an area of technology that strives to work with extremely small devices: devices on the scale of molecules or even atoms. Such devices can be created by using a scanning tunneling microscope. Experiments have been devised in which a single atom is used as an electric switch, or a single molecule is used to convert AC to DC. The holy grail of nanotechnology is to develop the methods necessary to create vast numbers of tiny little machines. Although progress is slow, the implications are fascinating. Here are some Web sites that will introduce you to nanotechnology. There is a lot of general interest information (including a FAQ), as well as more technical material. The name "nanotechnology" is derived from "nano", the Greek word for "dwarf". In the metric system, "nano" is used as a prefix indicating "one billionth" (American terminology). For example, a nanosecond is one billionth of a second. (In the English terminology, this would be one thousand millionth of a second.)

Web:

http://www.foresight.org/
http://www.nano.gov/
http://www.nanozine.com/
http://www.zyvex.com/nano/

Usenet:

sci.nanotech

Neural Networks

A neural network is a computing system consisting of many simple processors connected in various patterns. Each processor operates on its own data and its own input, resulting in an output signal that is transmitted to other processors. In the aggregate, a "network" of such processors can work together to recognize patterns, process information, and help people make decisions. The original work with neural networks was done to try to mimic the biological processes used in our brains. Although neural networks are not nearly as complex or powerful as a brain, they are able to achieve astonishing results and are routinely used in many business and scientific applications.

Web:

ftp://ftp.sas.com/pub/neural/FAQ.html
http://hem.hj.se/~de96klda/NeuralNetworks.htm
http://liinwww.ira.uka.de/bibliography/Neural/
http://www-2.cs.cmu.edu/Groups/AI/html/faqs/ai/
   neural/faq.html
http://www.cs.utexas.edu/users/nn/
http://www.emsl.pnl.gov:2080/proj/neuron/neural/
   what.html
http://www.faqs.org/faqs/ai-faq/neural-nets/
http://www.ieee-nns.org/

Usenet:

comp.ai.neural-nets

Peer-to-Peer Computing

Originally, the Internet was based on a client/server model, in which a relatively few programs (called servers) provide services to a large number of other programs (called clients). In a client/server network, only clients and servers can communicate with one another. A peer-to-peer (P2P) network is an alternate paradigm in which different types of programs and computers communicate with one another directly. For example, with P2P software, your computer could communicate with another person's computer, say, to share information. The first very popular P2P-based system was Napster, a music-sharing facility that combined a centralized client/server system (to coordinate searching) with P2P communication, allowing users to copy music files directly from one computer to another. Although Napster was shut down in 2001 (for copyright reasons), P2P technology has developed unabated. Today, it is used not only for file sharing (music, videos, software, pictures), but for a wide variety of imaginative applications. P2P computing is a big change from client/server computing because, once a pure P2P system is established, there is no reliable way to control it. This idea can be stimulating or frightening, depending on your emotional makeup.

Web:

http://e-serv.ebizq.net/p2p/
http://p2p.newstrove.com/
http://www.intel.com/ebusiness/products/
   peertopeer/
http://www.openp2p.com
http://www.p2ptransfers.com/

Robots

When I was a kid, I made my own robot out of various things I found around the house: a few old radio parts, three tin cans, a pair of knitting needles and my baby sister. It was a great robot, and I could make it do anything I wanted just by hitting it. Now, you can have almost the same experience by making your own robot. Use the Net to see what other robot enthusiasts are doing. Some of the robots are complex and it may take you a while to make them do everything you want. Don't complain. I'm still trying to understand my sister.

Web:
  http://www.cc.gatech.edu/ai/robot-lab/
  http://www.frc.ri.cmu.edu/robotics-faq/
  http://www.ornl.gov/Library/robotics.htm
  http://www.robotbooks.com/robot-news.htm
  http://www.robotcafe.com/
  http://www.robotmag.com/robotics/
  http://www.robots.net/
  http://www.robotslife.com/
  http://www.thetech.org/robotics/

Usenet:
  comp.robotics.misc

Virtual Reality

Before I commit myself to the concept of virtual reality, I need someone to answer some fundamental questions. Will there be commercials? Can I take my cat with me? Will I be able to get *real* food? In the meantime, I content myself with following what's new and almost real in the land of simulated make-believe.

Web:
  http://www.itl.nist.gov/iaui/ovrt/hotvr.html

Usenet:
  sci.virtual-worlds

Listserv Mailing List:
  List Name: virtu-l
  Subscribe to: listserv@listserv.uiuc.edu

Write it down.

Autoresponders

So you are using your Web site to build your business, to accumulate a list of important email addresses, or simply to increase your personal popularity. How do you answer all the people who fill out forms or send email to your site? Simple. Use one of these free autoresponders (also known as mailbots and autobots). These services are easy to integrate into your Web site and will automatically respond to requests from your users by sending them email. If you are imaginative, you can think of oodles of ways to use such a service. For example, you might send anyone who requests it a copy of your last year's Christmas letter. Isn't it nice to know that, even when you are sleeping, the Net is alive and working like an electronic beaver to spread your creative genius far and wide.

Web:
  http://www.freeautobot.com/
  http://www.responders.com/
  http://www.webmailstation.com/

Bookmark Managers

When you visit an interesting or useful Web site, you can save the URL (Web address) in a special list. With Internet Explorer, it's called your Favorites List; with Netscape, it's called your Bookmark list. Of course, those lists are maintained on your computer by your browser. These resources let you maintain a personalized bookmark list on the Net. The information is kept on a Web site, which means you can access the information wherever you are, as long as you have access to a browser. This is a useful way to use a bookmark list if you travel. Even better, you can give your friends and family access to your list, and use it to share information or to collaborate on research projects.

Web:
  http://www.backflip.com/
  http://www.ibookmarks.com/
  http://www.mybookmarks.com/
  http://www.personalindexpage.com/
  http://www.savethis.clickability.com/
  http://www.useful.webwizards.net/wbbm.htm

Browser Nostalgia

Kids today don't know how good they have it. When I was a kid, there were no fancy-shmancy browsers with Java and frames and animations. When I was a kid, we had to make do with simple text and browsers that didn't talk back to you. I remember how the whole family used to crowd around our hand-powered computer at night and look at the tiny screen. Would you like to see how it was in the olden days? This Web site emulates the old, classical browsers, just like the ones your grandparents used to use.

Web:
  http://www.dejavu.org/

Cool Signatures

At the end of mail messages or Usenet articles, it is common for people to put a short message called a "signature". Most signatures have dull, but useful information such as the person's name, email address, phone number, and so on. However, some people, smart, creative, imaginative people (like you and me), like to use something more witty or amusing. Well, here is a collection of a great many interesting signatures. Not only will you enjoy them, I bet you'll get good ideas for a signature of your own.

Web:
  http://www.coolsig.com/

Cyberspace Atlas

How do I look at thee? Let me count the ways.
I look at thee to the depth and breadth and height
Your topology can reach, when connecting out of sight
For the ends of bandwidth and ideal servers.
I look at thee to the level of everyday's
Most quiet need, by Web site and geography.
I look at thee freely, as men strive for data;
I look at thee purely, as they turn from spam.
I look at thee with the hypertext put to use
In my old browsers, and with my childhood's graphics.
I look at thee with a resolution I seem to lose
With my lost pixels—I look at thee with the numbers,
Charts, maps, of all my statistics!—and, if God choose,
I shall but look at thee better after losing my connection.

Web:
  http://www.cybergeography.com/

Domain Name Registration

Within any type of Internet address, the name of the computer is called the domain name or, more simply, the domain. For example, in the address **president@whitehouse.gov**, the domain is **whitehouse.gov**. In **http://canada.gc.ca/**, the domain is **canada.gc.ca**. Have you ever wondered how these names are assigned? There are two systems. Outside the United States, all addresses end with a two-letter country code. In our second example, for instance, the two-letter country code is **ca**, indicating that this is a Canadian domain. The United States uses a different system. There is a country code (**us**), but it's not used much. Instead, most people use an older system that was devised before the Internet became international. The last part of the domain—called the top-level domain—is a three-letter code. The most common of these top-level domains are **com** (commercial), **edu** (educational), **gov** (government), **org** (non-profit organizations) and **net** (network providers). If you have used the Net much, you will have noticed that the **com** top-level domain is also used for miscellaneous addresses that don't fit into another category. So how do you register a domain? You can either have your Internet service provider (ISP) do it for you, or you can do it yourself, by using a company called a "registrar".

Web:
  http://www.aboutdomains.com/
  http://www.corenic.org/
  http://www.icann.org/registrars/accredited-list.html
  http://www.netsol.com/
  http://www.norid.no/domreg.html
  http://www.register.com/

Email

As an Internet user, you have a lot of choices when it comes to email. For example, you can choose which email software to use, and you can choose your own email provider. (You do not necessarily have to use your Internet service provider's email service.) If you learn more about email, you'll learn how to make it work well for you, and the world will be a better place.

Web:
  http://www.emailtoday.com/
  http://www.everythingemail.com/
  http://www.iwillfollow.com/email.htm

Usenet:
  comp.mail

Free Email Services

It might be hard to find a free lunch, but on the Net you can find free email. The services vary, so read the descriptions carefully. You might be wondering, how can people make money giving away free email services? In one word: advertising. (Are you surprised?)

Web:
  http://mail.excite.com/
  http://mail.yahoo.com/
  http://www.eudoramail.com/
  http://www.fepg.net/
  http://www.hotmail.com/
  http://www.iname.com/
  http://www.internetemaillist.com/

Free Mailing List Hosting

A mailing list is a facility that allows you to carry on a discussion by email, by sending messages to everyone who has signed up for the list. Having your own personal (possibly secret) mailing list is a totally cool thing to do. For example, you can have your friends subscribe to your special, exclusive mailing list and then send them jokes and excerpts from your diary. Many families maintain mailing lists to stay in touch. If a mailing list sounds good to you, here are some places that will host your mailing list for free. (Although no money changes hands, there is a cost: you will have to look at advertisements inserted within the messages.)

Web:
  http://felist.com/
  http://groups.msn.com/
  http://www.coollist.com/
  http://www.freelists.org/
  http://www.groups.yahoo.com/
  http://www.notifylist.com/
  http://www.topica.com/

Free Online Disk Space

It can come in handy to have some storage space on the Net. Well, here's some you can use for free. Just register with one of these sites and upload (send) anything you want to your own, personal virtual online disk. Then you can use your Web browser to access or delete the data whenever you want. What's great is you can use your data from anywhere, you don't have to be at home. For example, if you are going on a trip, you can store data ahead of time, and then use your browser to access the data from a remote location.

Web:
   http://briefcase.yahoo.com/
   http://www.filesanywhere.com/
   http://www.kturn.com/
   http://www.xdrive.com/

PEOPLE talk a lot about the Internet and exaggerate a great deal. However, one thing that is not well understood is that the Net is older than most people think. In my mind, I tend to think of the Net as dating back only a short time to the publication of Ed Krol's seminal book ("The Whole Internet User's Guide and Catalog"). However, the Net actually started back in the late 1960s with the first experimental packet-switching network done under the auspices of ARPA (the U.S. Advanced Research Projects Agency). When you get a few moments, take a look at the **Historical Timeline of the Internet**. It will give you a perspective on the Net and allow your feelings of where you are in the course of human events to be all the more meaningful.

Historic Internet Documents

Way back in the olden days of the Internet, long before the Web existed, there were no Internet books. If you wanted to learn how to use the Net, you had to have someone show you enough to get started. You would then download a copy of a document that would teach you more. It may be hard to believe, but the reason the Internet was able to spread was because of these three documents: "The Hitchhiker's Guide to the Internet" by Ed Krol, published on August 15, 1987; "Zen and the Art of the Internet" by Brendan Kehoe, published in January 1992; and "Surfing the Internet" by Jean Armour Polly, first published in June 1992 in the Wilson Library Bulletin, and then on the Net on December 15, 1992. It would be difficult to exaggerate the effect that these three people had on the growth of the Internet and, hence, on our civilization. For example, in 1992, Ed Krol published "The Whole Internet User's Guide & Catalog", which was *the* book that made the Internet popular. As such, Krol's book was one of the most important books in history. Jean Armour Polly, a charming author, speaker and mother, will forever be remembered (if I have my way) as being the person who coined the term "surfing", while bringing an appreciation of the Net to countless people around the world. To round out the discussion, I should, perhaps, mention two other early, important books: the first edition of "The Internet Complete Reference" (October 1993) and the first edition of "The Internet Yellow Pages" (February 1994), both of which were written by me.

Web:
   gopher://gopher.well.sf.ca.us/00/Communications/
      surfing.2.0.2.txt
   http://www.cs.indiana.edu/docproject/zen/
      zen-1.0_toc.html
   http://www.ifla.org/documents/internet/kroe1.htm

Historical Timeline of the Internet

Here is a timeline that shows the history of the Internet from the 1956 Russian launch of Sputnik (which may have triggered it all) through the Arpanet (1969), UUCP (1976), Usenet (1979), DNS (1984), IRC (1988), gopher (1991), the World Wide Web (1992), and on and on.

Web:
   http://www.zakon.org/robert/internet/timeline/

History of the Internet

On December 5, 1969, three computers in California (Los Angeles, Santa Barbara and Menlo Park) and a computer in Utah were connected to one another. This marked the official beginning of the Arpanet, the network that was to grow into the Internet. Since then, the Internet has grown to become the largest information-based facility in the history of mankind. Want to find out more about the history of the Internet? Check with these resources. (By the way, let me add a date to the history of the Net: February 1996. In that month, this book became the first Internet book in history to have sold a million copies.)

Web:
http://www.isoc.org/internet-history/
http://www.livinginternet.com/
http://www.netvalley.com/intval.html

Host Your Own Email Service

If you are a webmaster with your own domain name, you can use these resources to start your own Web-based email service. Wouldn't that be just too totally cool? Now that you have registered imacoolchick.com, you can give all your friends their own personal email addresses, like amanda@imacoolchick.com.

Web:
http://www.bigmailbox.com/
http://www.everyone.net/main/html/email_tour.html
http://www.zzn.com/

Internet Drafts

Right now, at this very moment, a large number of highly skilled nerds around the world are planning the future of the Internet. Wouldn't you like to see what they're up to?

Internet Development Organizations

As you may already know, no one runs the Internet. *You* are in charge of how *you* use the Net, and if something goes wrong, you are on your own. However, there are organizations that work actively to plan the Net's future development and to make the Internet function as smoothly as possible. Want to find out who the people are behind the Internet miracle? Check out the Internet Architecture Board (IAB), the Internet Assigned Numbers Authority (IANA), the Internet Engineering Task Force (IETF), the Internet Research Task Force (IRTF), and the Internet Society.

Web:
http://www.iab.org/
http://www.iana.org/
http://www.ietf.org/
http://www.irtf.org/
http://www.isoc.org/

Internet Drafts

Examine the up-to-date collection of working documents of the Internet Engineering Task Force. Most of these documents relate to technical aspects of the Net, but there are also general interest articles. These draft documents are working proposals, created by the people who are planning the future of the Net and circulated within the Internet community for general comment.

Web:
http://www.ietf.cnri.reston.va.us/1id-abstracts.html

Internet Fax Services

Internet fax services make it possible to send free faxes to many different parts of the world through Internet mail. The recipient's name and fax number are converted to an electronic mail address, and the mail message is routed via the Internet to a computer near the destination. The receiving computer converts the mail message into a fax and transmits it through the local telephone network to the recipient's fax machine.

Web:
http://www.efax.com/
http://www.maclaunch.com/channels/fax.shtml
http://www.tpc.int/

Internet Help Talk and General Discussion

If you are new to the Net, there are certain Usenet groups where you can go to ask questions about using the Net. The **newbies** and **newbie** groups are for general comments and questions about the Net. The **news** and **bitnet** groups are for discussion about learning how to use Usenet and the Internet.

Usenet:
  alt.newbie
  alt.newbies
  bit.listserv.help-net
  news.newusers.questions

Internet Hoaxes

You just got email that some sick kid overseas wants to collect as many postcards as he can before he dies. Then you read about a secret cookie recipe, circulating on the Net, for which someone got tricked into paying a lot of money. The next day you hear a rumor that the government is going to start charging for email. Is any of this stuff true? No. All that is happening is that someone is spreading misleading information about well-known Internet hoaxes. The truth is given out on a need-to-know basis, and you need to know.

Web:
  http://hoaxbusters.ciac.org/
  http://www.humorcafe.com/hoaxes/
  http://www.internet-101.com/hoax/
  http://www.snopes.com/info/current.htm

Internet News

The Internet changes so fast that literally no one can keep up on what's happening. However, if you would like to keep in touch, here are some places that can help. You can check every week, every day, or even every hour, and you will find lots and lots of news articles. In particular, you will find coverage of all the companies that are doing business related to the Net.

Web:
  http://www.internetnews.com/
  http://www.news.com/
  http://www.newslinx.com/
  http://www.onmagazine.com/on-mag/
  http://www1.internetwire.com/

Internet Talk and General Discussion

The next best thing to being on the Internet is talking about being on the Internet. Get your fix of Internet topics by checking out the Usenet groups where anyone who thinks they are anyone chats about issues relating to the Internet.

Usenet:
  alt.culture.internet
  alt.cyberspace
  alt.internet
  alt.life.internet
  alt.nettime
  alt.society.netizens
  soc.net-people

Internet Terminology

The Internet is a global network that works the same way everywhere in the world. This means that everyone has access to the same resources, the same tools and many of the same ideas. However, in order to talk with other people about the Net, you need to be able to use the same words. I do want you to understand what everyone is talking about, so here are some glossaries of Internet technology for you to use as references.

Web:
  http://whatis.techtarget.com/
  http://www.cnet.com/Resources/Info/Glossary/
  http://www.netdictionary.com/html/
  http://www.netlingo.com/

Jargon File

The Jargon File is a legendary work that sounds like it should be dull: a collection of words and technical terms—definitions and examples—used with computers and the Internet. However, the Jargon File is anything but dull. It is not only exquisitely written, it is witty, comprehensive and accurate. In addition, there are also well-written essays discussing the hacking community and its customs. Out of all the dictionaries in the world, this one is probably the most fun.

Web:
  http://info.astrian.net/jargon/
  http://www.jargon.net/
  http://www.tuxedo.org/~esr/jargon/

JARGON

We are what we think, and we think with the words that we manage to scrape up off the sidewalk of life and somehow implant in non-volatile memory. The Jargon File is a wonderful resource that has, to coin a phrase, stood the test of time. In other words, someone smart and witty wrote it and it's a lot of fun to read. Take a few moments and check it out. If nothing else, you will see the human side of the techno-nerd part of our culture that is all too often hidden behind the glamour and the heartache of life in the technical/computer/rational fast lane.

Learning About the Internet and Web

If you are new to the Net, there is a lot to learn. Here are some places that will help you teach yourself about the Internet and the Web. (If you are a woman, pretend that I am sitting beside you, holding your hand. If you are a man, pretend that your mother is holding your hand.)

Web:

http://www.folksonline.com/
http://www.northernwebs.com/bc/
http://www.snowhawk.com/newbie.html
http://www.sofweb.vic.edu.au/internet/

ListTool

To subscribe or unsubscribe to a mailing list, you have to email particular messages to the program that administers the list. (I have put information on how to do so at the beginning of this book.) Emailing these messages is easy, but to make it even easier, you can use ListTool, a nifty Web-based system that will do the work for you. You can only subscribe and unsubscribe to the mailing lists in the ListTool database, but there is a large selection, so, if you know what you want, you will probably find something suitable.

Web:

http://www.listtool.com/

Mailing List Archives

Every day, millions of people around the world carry on discussions via email by using mailing lists. These resources archive the messages from many different lists, and allow you to read them without subscribing to the list. This can be helpful if you are looking for a list to join and you want to check out various lists, or if you are looking for a particularly elusive something-or-other.

Web:

http://www.escribe.com/
http://www.mail-archive.com/

Net Happenings

Net Happenings is a service that publishes announcements of new Internet resources. Check out the Net Happenings Web site, and you'll find lots of new and interesting resources. Subscribe to the mailing list, and your mailbox will be stuffed to the electronic gills with the latest and freshest stuff the Net has to offer. Hint: When your new Web site is ready, send an announcement to Net Happenings.

Web:

http://listserv.classroom.com/archives/
  net-happenings.html

Listserv Mailing List:

List Name: net-happenings
Subscribe to: listserv@listserv.classroom.com

A
B
C
D
E
F
G
H
I
J
K
L
M
N
O
P
Q
R
S
T
U
V
W
X
Y
Z

New Internet Technologies

Today's Internet is based on old technology, and, as you probably know, has a pressing need for bandwidth (the capacity to move information) and speed. There are two big projects underway to develop new improved technology for the Net. One project is called Internet2. The other project is IPng (Internet Protocol, next generation), also referred to as IPv6 (Internet Protocol, version 6). (The current Internet system uses IPv4.) Here is some information about these projects, so you can see what's in store for us in the future. (If you don't like what you see, at least you'll have time to move.)

Web:

http://www.6bone.net/
http://www.internet2.edu/
http://www.ipv6.org/

Scout Report

Stay on top of what is happening in the Net world by getting weekly lists of the latest cool Net sites. Experience the luxury of having someone else do the hard part while you get to have all the fun.

Web:

http://www.scout.cs.wisc.edu/

Listserv Mailing List:

List Name: scout-report
Subscribe to: listserv@hypatia.cs.wisc.edu

Size of the Internet

Have you ever wondered how many people use the Internet? How many computers are connected to the Internet? How many different domain names are in use? All this information, and more, is available, but you have to be careful. It's nice to have numbers, but the real truth is, no one knows exactly how big the Net really is, and the "size" of the Internet depends very much on how you define what you are measuring. What I can tell you for sure is (1) the Net is very important to humanity, and (2) it is large and growing faster than anyone can understand.

Web:

http://www.domainstats.com/
http://www.glreach.com/globstats/
http://www.isc.org/ds/
http://www.netsizer.com/
http://www.zooknic.com/

Web Talk and General Discussion

Would you like to talk about the Web? Goodness knows there is a lot to say. The Usenet groups are for ongoing discussion about various aspects of the Web. The **advocacy** group is for opinion. The **announce** group is for announcements. This is a good place to let people know about a new Web site. The **misc** group is for everything else related to the Web.

Usenet:

alt.culture.www
comp.infosystems.www
comp.infosystems.www.advocacy
comp.infosystems.www.announce
comp.infosystems.www.misc

Whois

Would you like to find out who is in charge of a particular Internet domain? Or maybe you are thinking of getting your own domain name and you want to see if a specific name is in use. Use one of these Whois servers. Just enter a domain name, and see what's what (and who's who).

Web:

http://www.allwhois.com/
http://www.internic.net/whois.html
http://www.netsol.com/cgi-bin/whois/whois

INTRIGUE

Conspiracies

Our world—so they say—is full of a great many conspiracies, many of them perpetrated by the government. Did you know that aliens live on Earth, AIDS is a plot, harmful additives are used in our food, fabulous inventions and technology are being hidden, and there really are cures for cancer? Then there are the secret wars, assassinations, insurrections, and lots and lots of cover-ups. And, oh yes, I almost forgot—Elvis is not really dead.

Web:

http://www.conspire.com/
http://www.darkconspiracy.com/
http://www.floodlight.org/

Conspiracy Talk and General Discussion

Don't look behind you. Don't say anything out loud. Just act natural. Okay, are you ready? There is a big conspiracy. It involves the government (particularly the CIA), the media and big business. I can't tell you the details here. These Usenet groups are the only safe places to talk. See you there.

Usenet:

　alt.conspiracy
　alt.conspiracy.antichrist
　alt.conspiracy.black.helicopters
　alt.conspiracy.new-world-order
　alt.conspiracy.right-wing
　alt.conspiracy.spy
　alt.government.abuse
　alt.illuminati
　alt.paranoia
　alt.paranoia.spambots
　alt.underground.yalta
　bit.listserv.cloaks-daggers

Echelon

When we think of spies, what comes to mind are secret agents like James Bond. However, the original Bond lived in the post-World War II climate of the 1950s and 1960s. In those days, all he had to worry about was defending his country against foreign enemy governments. Today's spies live in the post-Cold War age of information, and have a much more complex job. Spying today has very little to do with putting away the bad guys and winning the heart of a beautiful woman. Today's spies are less suave and more nerdish, and worry about money, corporate espionage, and inside information. The embodiment of twenty-first century spying is Echelon, a comprehensive, automated system designed to intercept global satellite-based communications. Echelon was created by intelligence organizations in five countries: the United States, the United Kingdom, Canada, Australia and New Zealand. Echelon is so covert that the participants go to extreme lengths to keep even its very existence secret. But now, *you* know about it.

Web:

　http://www.echelonwatch.org/
　http://www.signaltonoise.net/library/
　　echelon_faq.htm

JFK Assassination

The whodunit of all whodunits. Just when you think you've seen all the JFK conspiracy material, someone compiles a whole bunch more. At these Web sites, you will find articles galore about every aspect of every assassination theory. New evidence is emerging all the time (from somewhere), so don't get left behind on this very important historical controversy.

Web:

　http://mcadams.posc.mu.edu/
　http://ourworld-top.cs.com/mikegriffith1/id35.htm
　http://www.archives.gov/research_room/jfk/
　http://www.history-matters.com/jfkmurder.htm
　http://www.jfk-assassination.de/wcr/
　http://www.jfklancer.com/JFK2.html

Usenet:

　alt.assassination.jfk
　alt.assassination.jfk.uncensored
　alt.conspiracy.jfk
　alt.conspiracy.jfk.moderated

Mind Control

Is the government/CIA/police/your mother trying to control your mind? The question may seem ludicrous, but many people in the world are completely convinced that malevolent powers are trying to control them, even to the point of implanting devices in their bodies. Now, I have to say, it is well known that psychotics often feel that someone is trying to control them covertly; they may hear voices, think that the TV announcer is talking directly to them, and so on. These are symptoms of mental illness and a malfunctioning brain. Clearly, many of the mind control stories—as real as they seem to the victims—fall into this category. Still, did the government really run secret mind control experiments? See for yourself. (And if you still have the free will to carry on a discussion, try the Usenet group.)

Web:
　　http://www.crank.net/mind.html
　　http://www.datafilter.com/mc/
　　http://www.freedomofmind.com/
　　http://www.mindcontrolforums.com/

Usenet:
　　alt.mindcontrol

Namebase

You don't have to wait until someone calls you before a Senate committee to start naming names. This Web site allows you to search for specific names that may have appeared in hundreds of investigative books and many related articles. For example, if you search for "Hoover, Edgar", you will see a list of various books in which J. Edgar Hoover is discussed.

Web:
　　http://www.pir.org/nbhome.html

Reverse Speech

Take off your skeptic's hat and listen to this. The theory of reverse speech asserts that, if you record what people say and play it backwards, you will pick up secret messages that were put there unconsciously. This is not the same as the backward messages that some musicians purposely put on their albums. Reverse speech is completely involuntary. The idea is that, if someone is trying to hide something, he or she will not be able to prevent it from appearing in their reversed speech. Needless to say, there is no scientific evidence supporting this theory. Still, there are people who take the time to record speeches by famous people, play the speeches backwards, and analyze them. Interesting enough, a lot of weird stuff turns up. (Are you surprised?)

Web:
　　http://www.beyondreversespeech.com.au/
　　http://www.reversespeech.com/
　　http://www.reversespeech.org/

Smoking Gun

Do you like the idea of seeing a secret dossier? Well, then, you'll love this awesome site, full of secret dirt on famous and not-so-famous people. Read the material gathered from court files and government sources, information that somehow doesn't get into the public media. When your curiosity exceeds the resources of the mainstream press, the Smoking Gun is the place to be.

Web:
　　http://www.thesmokinggun.com/

Unsolved Mysteries

Here is a list of unsolved mysteries waiting for someone like you to solve. Look at pictures of fugitives and missing persons. Then read about the crime or disappearance. As you walk around, look at everyone you meet. You never know when *you* will recognize someone and solve a mystery. (If you have some spare time, you can help me track down the person who ate the last low-fat chocolate cupcake.)

Web:
　　http://www.unsolved.com/home.html

The Little Nipper's
INTERNET
CLUBHOUSE

Hi. My name is The Little Nipper.

I am a cat.

The part of the book you are reading right now is called The Little Nipper's Internet Clubhouse. It is a special section just for kids, and I bet you will like it.

I am 11 years old and I live with Harley. In fact, I was born in his closet, which is a good place for a cat to be born.

Harley and I work together. His job is to do the writing, and my job is to correct his mistakes.

I have a good job, because Harley doesn't make too many mistakes, so I get to play outside whenever I want. Most of the time, however, I lie next to Harley's computer, supervising. If you saw us working, it might look as if I were sleeping, but I am not. Every few minutes, I open one eye and check what Harley is doing. When I see a mistake or something that needs to be made better, I point to it with my paw. (Now you know why everything in this book is so good.)

As you can see, The Little Nipper's Internet Clubhouse is the best section of the whole book. That is obvious. What you might be wondering is where did the idea come from? I'll tell you the story.

I mentioned earlier that I like to play outside. However, when the sun goes down, I have to go inside for the evening. If I don't, Harley worries about me. (There's nothing really to worry about, but you know how adults are.)

Anyway, one day I was late coming in. I had been out exploring and I found a really cool dead rat with a whole bunch of slimy green stuff all over it. As soon as I saw the rat, I realized it would be a great present for Harley. As a matter of fact, it was a week past his birthday, and I needed to get him something.

So I brought in the rat and put it on his pillow, where he would be sure to see it. (Harley is not very observant. If you want him to notice something, you have to put it right under his nose.)

Well, that got his attention, but not in a good way. For some reason I don't understand, he didn't like the rat.

He put his hand over his mouth and made a funny noise. Then he threw the rat into the trash can. (Adults can be very strange.)

To make things worse, he got mad at me even more for staying out after dark. I tried to tell him I was playing hide-and-seek with a bunch of raccoons and I couldn't leave till the game was finished, but he didn't listen to me.

This bothered me, so I thought I would do something to make him happy. Late that night, after Harley had gone to bed, I went over to the computer and started working. I had a great idea. How about if I took all the children's stuff from the last edition of this book, made up a whole bunch of new stuff, and used it to create a brand new section, just for kids?

I worked all night and, in the morning, when Harley got up, everything was done.

"Wow," he said when he saw it. "This is so cool. A whole section of stuff just for kids."

Then he stroked his chin. It's funny though, I don't remember doing it. I must have been very tired last night."

Later that day he called Lydia, who works with him, and told her all about the new section. She also thought it was a great idea.

"But what are we going to call it?" she asked.

"How about Harley Hahn's Internet Clubhouse?" said Harley. (Harley is like that. He likes to name everything after himself.)

Lydia thought about it. "I like the Internet Clubhouse part," she said, "but I really think we should name it after someone cute. After all, we do want to sell as many books as possible."

"I guess you are right," said Harley.

And that is the story of The Little Nipper's Internet Clubhouse.

—*The Little Nipper* 

P.S. When you get a moment, please visit my Web site at:

www.harley.com/nipper

The Little Nipper's Internet Clubhouse
CONTENTS

STORIES TO READ ON THE NET 496

EXPLORE AND LEARN

Animals and Pets

Today, I was sitting in my hot tub, thinking of what to write in this book, and all of a sudden I noticed a shadow. I looked up and saw it was my cat. I know this sounds a bit silly, but it was totally cool to look up and see my cat, just standing there on the side of the hot tub. All I can say is that, if you have a pet, I bet you know what I mean. Even if you don't have a pet, you can still enjoy animals by learning about them, and then eating animal crackers every chance you get.

Web:
http://www.animal.discovery.com/guides/cats/
   cats.html
http://www.animal.discovery.com/guides/dogs/
   dogs.html
http://www.audubon.org/bird/watch/kids/
http://www.kidsites.com/sites-edu/animals.htm
http://www.panda.org/kids/wildlife/
http://www.pbs.org/wnet/nature/fun.html
http://www.sharkfriends.com/
http://www.zoobooks.com/gatewayPages/
   gateway1Kids.html

Art

I have a friend who teaches kids how to draw. One thing that I learned from my friend is that everyone, kids and adults, likes to draw—*if* they have fun while they are doing it. So pull yourself away from the TV, and use the Net to get started with your pencil and paper. You may or may not be a budding young genius, but I guarantee you will have more fun than watching commercials. One nice thing about being able to draw is that, as long as you have your paper and pencil with you, you will never have to worry about being bored.

Web:
http://www.artkidsrule.com/
http://www.arts.ufl.edu/art/rt_room/
http://www.kids-space.org/gallery/gallery.html
http://www.markkistler.com/lessons.htm
http://www.nga.gov/kids/

Contests

My cat, The Little Nipper, wants me to start a new contest. His idea is that people all over the world should send him cans of tuna, and whoever sends the best tuna gets a free picture of him. I am still thinking about it. In the meantime, there are lots of contests on the Internet you can enter. If you do, I have a hint about privacy. Many of these contests are sponsored by commercial companies, so you must remember that if you type your name and address into a form on a Web site, you are going to end up on someone's mailing list.

Web:
http://www.acekids.com/contests.html
http://www.amazing-kids.org/contests.html
http://www.grandmajam.com/luv2kids.htm
http://www.kidsdomain.com/kids/contests.html
http://www.studentcontests.com/
http://www.webfreebees.net/kidslinks/
   kids-contests.html

Cooking

One of the best things you can do for yourself is learn how to cook. That way, you can eat whatever you want without having to ask someone to make it for you. (One of my favorite things to eat is a peanut butter and cheese sandwich. I'm sure you have your own favorites.)

Web:
http://www.childrensrecipes.com/
http://www.kidrecipe.com/
http://www.melborponsti.com/kids/gross/
http://www.recipesource.com/misc/kids/
   indexall.html
http://www.theideabox.com/ideas.nsf/
   recipe?openview&start=1

Crafts

When I was a youngster, I spent a lot of time at summer camp, and one of the activities I remember best was Arts and Crafts. Why? Because I got to make stuff, and making stuff was a lot of fun. The trick is to choose a project that matches your skill and age level. Here are lots of ideas to help you find something fun to do right now.

Web:
http://www.crafts4kids.com/projects.htm
http://www.enchantedlearning.com/crafts/
http://www.kidsdomain.com/craft/
http://www.makingfriends.com/concraft.htm
http://www.theideabox.com/ideas.nsf/craft

Energy

I bet you wish you knew more about energy. I know I did when I was young. Spend some time browsing energy resources on the Net and you will soon be at the top of your class, energy-wise. (And will *you* be popular.) There are lots of great hints as to what you can do to help out. For example, you could get your school to start a school energy patrol. Every day, you can check all the bathrooms to make sure that the lights are turned off to save energy. Not only will you have a lot of fun, but it will look great on your resumé when you get older and want to go to medical school. Boy, adults sure think of some great things for kids to do.

Web:

http://www.energy.ca.gov/education/
http://www.energy.gov/kidz/kidzone.html

Math

Please, please, don't just study enough math to pass your tests and get by. I want you to do whatever it takes to really *learn* mathematics and understand it, no matter how bad your teacher is. Why? I'm going to tell you something that may be difficult to believe, but I want you to trust me. Mathematics is one of mankind's most beautiful creations. Once you get far enough along, you will be able to appreciate mathematics in the same way that people appreciate poetry or music or art. Unfortunately, this will not happen until you study math at a university level, and many people don't get that far. However, no matter what all your friends are doing, I want *you* to learn enough now that you can study math at a university. Don't waste time worrying if mathematics is relevant to your life and if you will ever use it once you leave school. Trust me: every hour you spend studying math will repay you later in your life. Not everyone understands this, but then, not everyone is as smart as you and I.

Web:

http://www.aplusmath.com/
http://www.coolmath.com/
http://www.gomath.com/
http://www.mathcats.com/
http://www.mathforum.org/students/elem/
http://www.school.discovery.com/homeworkhelp/
   webmath/

Music and Songs

My philosophy is that every kid who is born should be issued a kazoo. When I was a kid (6 years old), my parents arranged for me to have piano lessons. (We didn't have a kazoo.) So, once a week, for many years, I went to my piano lesson and, during the week, I would practice, practice, practice (sometimes). Although I never got all that good at reading music and playing songs the way they were written, I did teach myself how to play what I could hear in my head and on the radio. To this day, I love to play the piano and sing and, many times, it has helped me make new friends. I also like to play, just for fun, whenever I feel like taking a break from writing. (I still don't have a kazoo.)

Web:

http://www.bluevisionmusic.com/CMRC/
   hotlinks.html
http://www.kididdles.com/mouseum/
http://www.niehs.nih.gov/kids/musicchild.htm
http://www.nyphilkids.org/
http://www.sfskids.com/

Outdoor Activities

I remember, when I was a kid, my mother would send me outside to play. My friends and I had lots of fun riding bikes, making up games, and just hanging out and walking around looking for stuff to do. Now, it's different. Parents think that they have to spend a lot of "quality time" with their kids. My advice is, the next time your parents want to do something with you, tell them to go inside, turn on the computer, look at this book, and see if they can find some really good educational outdoor activities. Then, while they are busy, you can go outside and have fun.

Web:

http://www.boatsafe.com/kids/
http://www.faqs.org/faqs/misc-kids/
   outdoor-activities/part1/
http://www.kidssource.com/info.htm
http://www.nwf.org/kids/outdoorstuff.html
http://www.preschoolrainbow.org/
   preschool-outdoor.htm

MATH

Did you ever stop and think how funny the number 3 is?

2 is ordinary. 7 is boring. And 1, well, no one even talks about 1.

But 3 is a cool number *and* it is funny.

I'll prove it to you.

Go to your mother, right now, look at her and say "3". I bet she laughs.

People and Culture

One of the best things about the Internet is that you can use it to learn about other countries, where kids are using the Internet to learn about you.

Web:
http://www.globalschoolnet.org/gsh/
http://www.hyperhistory.com/online_n2/History_n2/a.html
http://www.ipl.org/youth/cquest/
http://www.supersurf.com/
http://www.worldalmanacforkids.com/explore/timeline.html

Science

Science is actually a way of thinking about the world. Scientists believe that we can understand a lot of what happens around us by experimenting, observing, testing and thinking. Thanks to all the scientists who have worked so hard, we know an *enormous* amount about ourselves, the Earth and the rest of the universe, and our lives are much better than they would have been otherwise. I believe that it is good for you to have a basic understanding of science. Not only will the world be more interesting to you, but knowing science makes it less likely that you will fall prey to superstition and ignorance. Since science covers many different areas of learning, I have chosen resources that will allow you to explore a variety of scientific topics.

Web:
http://solar.physics.montana.edu/ypop/Classroom/
http://www.express.howstuffworks.com/
http://www.faa.gov/education/resource/kidcornr.htm
http://www.sci.mus.mn.us/sln/tf/nav/tfatoz.html
http://www.spartechsoftware.com/reeko/
http://www.wsu.edu/DrUniverse/

Search Engines for Kids

One of the best things you can learn is how to search the Net to find what you want. These search engines are just for children, and are wonderful places for you to start exploring. If you have the time, you can even help your parents. Show them how to take an idea, find Internet resources related to that idea, and then evaluate what they find. Does the information seem correct? Is someone trying to sell you something? Is the Web site outdated? Your parents will be having so much fun, they'll forget they are learning. (Sometimes, that's the only way you can get parents to learn.)

Web:
http://www.ajkids.com/
http://www.yahooligans.com/

Search Engines for Kids

When Sherlock Holmes was a child, he had to use regular search engines, and it took him a long time to track down information on the Net.

Now there are search engines just for kids, so all your little ones can learn how to be Internet detectives.

Space Exploration and Astronomy

By the time you have kids of your own, you may be able to take them on a two-week family vacation to visit outer space. (Actually, it's a lot like going to Disney World, except the lines aren't as long, and the food is better.) So maybe, just in case, it would be a good idea to learn all about space exploration now, so when *your* kids point out the window and ask you, "What are those things?" you can say, "Those are Deimos and Phobos, the moons of Mars."

Web:
   http://edtech.kennesaw.edu/web/solar.html
   http://starchild.gsfc.nasa.gov/docs/StarChild/
      StarChild.html
   http://www.dustbunny.com/afk/
   http://www.jpl.nasa.gov/basics/
   http://www.kidsastronomy.com/
   http://www.kidsites.com/sites-edu/space.htm
   http://www.windows.ucar.edu/tour/link=/
      windows3.html

Web Directories Created by Kids

If I were a kid (and I used to be one), I would want to read what other kids think about Web sites. The Kids Report has just that type of information: real kids write about real K-12 Web sites for real readers (like you). Warning: Teachers do help to put each issue together, but the kids choose all the sites and write the descriptions, so it's still cool.

Web:
   http://www.madison.k12.wi.us/tnl/detectives/

> Whenever I feel sad, I look
> for something to share with
> one of my friends.

FUN STUFF

Creative Corner

I'll tell you something interesting. When you are young, you are naturally creative, and it is normal to want to make stuff and think of new ideas. As you get older, your creativity slowly goes away, until, by the time you are an adult, there is hardly anything left. (If you want to see what I mean, just look at your teachers.) I believe that it is fun—and important—to be creative your whole life. Here are some resources to encourage you, where you can see what lots of other kids have been doing.

Web:
   http://pubs.logicalexpressions.com/pub0006/
   http://www.cs.bilkent.edu.tr/~david/derya/ywc.html
   http://www.kidnews.com/
   http://www.naturalchild.org/gallery/
   http://www.ncsu.edu/midlink/
   http://www.stonesoup.com/

Dinosaurs

I'm not sure why it is, but all kids like dinosaurs. I remember when I was a kid, I got my brother a dinosaur book for his birthday. I didn't even wonder if he would like it: I knew he would. I liked dinosaurs; my brother liked dinosaurs; all our friends liked dinosaurs. So kids, do you like dinosaurs? Of course you do, so here are some great Web sites where you can enjoy a lot of dinosaur stuff and look at some really cool pictures. If you want to talk about dinosaurs, join the Usenet discussion group. And you know what? I bet when you grow up you'll still like dinosaurs (except Barney, of course).

Web:
   http://www.dinofun.com/
   http://www.dinosauria.com/fullindex.html
   http://www.ucmp.berkeley.edu/diapsids/
      dinosaur.html

Usenet:
   alt.dinosaur

Games

I bet that you and your friends spend a lot of time playing games. I did when I was a kid, and so did everyone else. But did you ever wonder where all those games came from? And how did you and your friends happen to know the rules? I'll tell you something amazing. Although there are always new games coming along, kids in every generation end up playing a lot of the same games as did their parents and grandparents. Some of the games you will find here have been played as long as anyone can remember. Other ones are brand new, games that you play on the Internet, using your computer. If you show the old games to your parents, I bet they will say, "I used to play that game when I was young." (Actually, they'll probably say something like, "That's not how you play it. This is how it's done." And then you can get into an argument about the right way to play a particular game. Parents like stuff like that. They call it "quality time".)

Web:
http://www.eduplace.com/tales/
http://www.gamekids.com/gkgame1.html
http://www.gameskidsplay.net/
http://www.multcolib.org/kids/games.html
http://www.pbskids.org/games.html
http://www.zeeks.com/games/zeekgames.asp

Jokes

When I was growing up, I always loved telling jokes. My father and grandfather were the same way, so remembering and telling jokes comes easy to me. One of the nicest things I remember about my father (who died on November 30, 2001, at the age of 80), is that whenever I would talk to him, he would always have a new joke for me. Although everyone likes to hear jokes, perhaps you think you are the type of person who can't tell jokes. If so, I have an idea for you. Each day, look up a new joke and tell it to someone. My philosophy is, he who laughs, lasts.

Web:
http://www.azkidsnet.com/JSknockjoke.htm
http://www.cbc4kids.cbc.ca/general/kids-club/
   joke-page/
http://www.headbone.com/cgi-bin/features/
   smirkcity/smirk.cgi?Home.x=1
http://www.pbskids.org/zoom/funny/

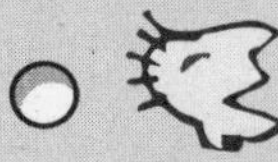

The Dirty Joke
by Elmo (age 8)

Here is a good joke you can tell people (and it's a true story).

One day my sister Lucy was walking home from school in the rain. I ran up to her and said, "Hey Lucy, do you want to hear a dirty joke?"

She looked at me very suspiciously.

"What do you mean?" she said.

"This," I said, and I pushed her in the mud and ran away.

Ha, ha, ha, ha, ha! Boy, I sure fooled her that time. Is she ever weird!

But do you want to hear something even more weird? Later, when I was getting ready to go to sleep, I found a big pile of mud in my bed. In fact, it happened five days in a row.

I asked Lucy if she did it, and she said, how could she do it because she has to go to bed before me?

Talk about a mystery!

-Elmo

Jump Rope Rhymes

Look at that
Harley and his Cat
Make a new rhyme
Skipping all the time
Watch them jumping
Never ever bumping
Look at that
Harley and his Cat

Web:
http://www.aacs.wnyric.org/donius/jump_rope/
   rhymes.html
http://www.gameskidsplay.net/jump_rope_ryhmes/
http://www.streetplay.com/thegames/jumprope/
   jumproperhymes.html

Just for Fun

Doing homework, cleaning your room, taking out the garbage, and clearing the table are all enjoyable activities. But life can't be fun all the time. Sometimes you need to spend some time using the Internet to look at stuff like comics, cartoons, art, writing, science, games, sports, toys, music, entertainment and stories. (If your parents don't understand, you can tell them I said it's educational.) My advice is, enjoy it all while you can. It won't be long till you are an adult, and you'll have to spend your leisure time playing golf, and having serious discussions about politics, relationships, and interest rates.

Web:

    http://www.ala.org/alsc/children_links.html
    http://www.beritsbest.com/
    http://www.cyberkids.com/
    http://www.ipl.org/youth/
    http://www.kids-space.org/
    http://www.kidsclick.org/
    http://www.kidsdomain.com/kids/links.html
    http://www.netmom.com/ikyp/samples/hotlist.htm

Preschool Activities

Here are some Web sites designed especially for preschoolers. You'll find colorful pictures and simple writing, as well as ideas for seasonal activities, crafts, preschool projects, music, cooking, and lots more.

Web:

    http://www.earlychildhood.com/crafts/
    http://www.first-school.ws/theme/teddybears.htm
    http://www.learningplanet.com/kids1.htm

Solve a Mystery

Do you like mysteries? See if you can solve the ones at this Web site. Do you like to read mystery stories? You'll find something diverting to read here. Do you like to write your own mystery stories? Write one and enter it in a contest. Do you like to amaze your friends? Learn a new magic trick. Spend some time developing your talents, and soon you will be a mystery master.

Web:

    http://kids.mysterynet.com/

Television

Here are resources to find information about your favorite TV Shows: Blues Clues, Dexter's Laboratory, Hey Arnold!, Muppets, Powerpuff Girls, Rocket Power, Rugrats, Scooby-Doo, Sesame Street and SpongeBob SquarePants. The nice thing about having favorite TV shows is that they will make you happy when you get old, because you will be able to watch reruns and be nostalgic. ("Nostalgic" means enjoying something because it reminds you of good feelings from a long time ago. When older people sing along to old music on the radio and act goofy, they are being nostalgic.) So when your parents complain that you are watching too much TV, tell them, of course you'd rather be cleaning your room or doing your homework. However, you think it makes a lot more sense to use what little spare time you have to build up good TV memories. "After all," you can tell them, "when I am your age, do you really think I'll get pleasure out of remembering all the times I cleaned my room?"

Web:

    http://www-cs-students.stanford.edu/~csilvers/
        muppet-faq.html
    http://www.bluescluesfan.com/
    http://www.cartoonnetwork.com/
    http://www.cooltoons.com/shows/rugrats/
    http://www.geraldfield.com/unofficial/
    http://www.muppetcentral.com/
    http://www.nick.com/
    http://www.pbskids.org/
    http://www.philburt.com/ppg/
    http://www.powerpuff.com/
    http://www.rugratonline.com/
    http://www.tvtome.com/SpongeBobSquarePants/

Usenet:

    alt.tv.powerpuff-girls
    alt.tv.rugrats
    rec.arts.henson+muppets

Toys You Make Yourself

I have two words for you: water bomb.

Web:

    http://www.users.bigpond.net.au/mechtoys/

Report on Toys You
Make Yourself
by Elmo (age 8)

Yesterday, I made a toy all by myself. I took a balloon and wrote on it "Happy Father's Day from Lucy". (Lucy is my sister.)

Then I filled the balloon with water and put it under my father''s pillow.

I like making toys and giving them away to deserving people.

-Elmo

BOOKS FOR KIDS

An American Girl

"An American Girl" is a large set of books. Each story is set in its own time period and features one girl. So far, stories have been written about seven different girls: Felicity (1774) who lives in an American colony; Josefina (1824), who lives on a ranch in New Mexico; Kirsten (1854), who is a pioneer; Addy (1864), who lives during the Civil War; Samantha (1904), who lives in a city with her rich grandmother; Kit (1934), who lives in Minnesota during the Great Depression; and Molly (1944), who lives during World War II. My favorite is Samantha, because she is rich and beautiful and wears fancy clothes. (Men are so shallow.)

Web:

http://www.kidsbooksandpuppets.com/
    americangirls/amergirl.html
http://www.kidsreads.com/series/american-girl.asp

Blume, Judy

If you are, or were, a teenage girl, you probably know Judy Blume (1938-), the author of "Are You There God, It's Me, Margaret", "Tales of a Fourth Grade Nothing", the Fudge series, and many other popular books. For many girls, it was Judy Blume who taught them what it would be like to have a period, develop physically, make and lose friends (and boyfriends), and generally live through the difficult teenage years.

Web:

http://falcon.jmu.edu/~ramseyil/blume.htm
http://teacher.scholastic.com/authorsandbooks/
    authors/blume/bio.htm
http://www.judyblume.com/

Book Reviews Written by Adults

The most intelligent, knowledgeable, interesting, special people I know all have one thing in common. When they were kids, they liked to read, read, read. Many children are natural readers, and you don't have to encourage them. Left to themselves, they will make a regular pilgrimage to the library and return with an armful of books week after week. However, if your children don't take to books naturally, there are three valuable favors you can do for them: (1) Encourage them to read. Take them to the library every week. (2) Turn off the TV. (For yourself as well. You need to set an example.) (3) Teach them to memorize the alphabet forwards (A, B, C...) *and* backwards (Z, Y, X...).

Web:

http://www.childrenslit.com/th.htm
http://www.kidsbookshelf.com/review.asp
http://www.readersread.com/cgi-bin/
    reviewlist.pl?genre=children

Cats know
how to do magic.

Book Reviews Written by Kids

There are so many good books in the world, you will never get to read them all. So how can you decide which ones you want to read? One way is to look at reviews—descriptions of books—written by other kids who have already read the books. If you are thinking of reading a particular book, you can see what other people thought about it before you even get the book. Even more important, if you are looking for ideas for a new book to read (as I always am), you can look at some reviews first. I have found many good books in this way, and I bet you will too.

Web:
> http://www.eduplace.com/kids/rdg/chall.html
> http://www.stonesoup.com/main2/
>   bookreviews2002.html
> http://www.worldreading.org/

Children's Literature Resources

The Net has lots and lots of literature especially for children. Here are some Web sites that can help you find what you need for your kids. You will see book reviews, tips on using books, information about children's books and their authors, as well as links to other children's literature resources on the Net.

Web:
> http://www.carolhurst.com/
> http://www.cbcbooks.org/
> http://www.dalton.org/libraries/fairrosa/
> http://www.faqs.org/ftp/faqs/misc-kids/books/faq
> http://www.kidsreads.com/

Usenet:
> rec.arts.books.childrens

> One day I spent 2 hours riding a marshmallow elephant. It was a lot of fun but very sticky.

Cleary, Beverly

I love the books of Beverly Cleary (1916-). Some of my most pleasant memories are of the many hours I spent reading and rereading the Henry Huggins books (and, to tell you the truth, I still like to read them once in awhile). When I was a kid, the Huggins books were Cleary's best known works. Today, she is better known for the books about the young pest Ramona and her long-suffering sister Beezus. Personally, I prefer Henry (who lived on Klickitat Street), his dog Ribsy, his friends Robert and Scooter, and the tales of all the goofy things he would do. Beezus and Ramona were in the Huggins stories, but they weren't my favorite characters. I guess that's because I'm a guy.

Web:
> http://teacher.scholastic.com/authorsandbooks/
>   authors/cleary/bio.htm
> http://www.beverlycleary.com/
> http://www.multcolib.org/kids/cleary.html
> http://www.trelease-on-reading.com/cleary.html

Dahl, Roald

Do you think you would like funny, imaginative stories filled with lots of strange and cruel events? How about books in which children are able to be rude to adults, and the bad people always get into trouble? If so, you will like the kids' books written by Roald Dahl. The best ones are James and the Giant Peach (published in 1961), Charlie and the Chocolate Factory (1964), The Magic Finger (1966), Fantastic Mr. Fox (1970), Witches (1973) and Matilda (1988). Roald Dahl (1916-1990) was born in Wales, although his parents were Norwegian. Dahl's father died when Dahl was only four years old. Soon after, Dahl was sent away to a boarding school, where he stayed for a long time. School was awful for Dahl. Not only was he homesick, but many of the students were beaten, both by the teachers and by other students. That is why, in his stories, Dahl does not have much sympathy for adults who tell children what to do. That is also why his books teach that people who are good are rewarded and people who are bad are punished (especially adults).

Web:
> http://falcon.jmu.edu/~ramseyil/dahl.htm
> http://www.kirjasto.sci.fi/rdahl.htm
> http://www.roalddahl.com/
> http://www.roalddahlfans.com/

Dr. Seuss

Growing up is just not complete without Dr. Seuss. Can you imagine being a kid and *not* knowing the Cat in the Hat? Or passing through this world without spending hours reading "Green Eggs and Ham" out loud, over and over and over, till your mother finally takes away the book and sends you outside to play? Dr. Seuss (1904-1991), whose real name was Theodor Geisel, published 44 books from 1937 ("And to Think That I Saw It on Mulberry Street") to 1986 ("You're Only Old Once!"). He is truly one of the treasures of the twentieth century. It's hard to decide which is more fun, Seuss's playfully superb verse or his whimsical drawings. It is difficult to imagine a child growing up in the English-speaking world without bonding with the good doctor. One of my researchers, Carrie, lived in San Diego as a child. Geisel and his wife lived in nearby La Jolla. When she was a teenager, Carrie used to drive past Geisel's house and wave. She never honked, though, 'cause that would be rude.

Web:
  http://falcon.jmu.edu/~ramseyil/seuss.htm
  http://www.carolhurst.com/authors/drseuss.html
  http://www.seuss.org/
  http://www.seussville.com/
  http://www.veaweteach.org/bibpar.html

Report on Children's Literature Resources by Elmo (age 8)

Ever since we got a new computer, my father makes me spend lots of time with him looking at educational Web sites. (Ugh!)

One day we found literature resources for children. Now I am happy, because my father spends time by himself looking at children's stories.

This keeps him happy, which makes me happy, because now he leaves me alone to play my video games.

-Elmo

Freddy the Pig

Between 1927 and 1958, the American writer Walter R. Brooks (1886-1958) wrote 26 children's books about Freddy the Pig. Freddy lives on a farm owned by Mr. and Mrs. Bean, near the town of Centerboro in upstate New York, along with many other animals, including Mrs. Wiggins (cow), Jinx (cat), Charles (rooster), Henrietta (hen), Alice, Emma and Uncle Wesley (ducks), Hank (horse), Robert and Georgie (dogs), and Eek, Eeny, Quik and Cousin Augustus (mice). All the animals can talk, but Freddy is, by far, the most talented. In the course of the books he becomes a detective, a poet, a newspaper publisher (founder of the Bean Home News), a banker (he starts the First Animal Bank), a pilot, a football player, a politician (when Mrs. Wiggins runs for president of the First Animal Republic), a magician, a baseball coach, and a lot more. I have a large Freddy collection and have read each book many times. In fact, much of what I know about human nature, I learned from Freddy and his friends.

Web:
  http://www.freddythepig.org/
  http://www.harley.com/freddy-the-pig/

Goosebumps

Most adults know nothing about Goosebumps stories, except that kids like to read them. So, for your parents, here is a quick guide to understanding Goosebumps.

1. There are lots and lots of Goosebumps books.

2. The books are written by R. L. [Robert Lawrence] Stine (1943-).

3. There are lots and lots of Goosebumps books.

4. The covers are created by Tim Jacobus (1959-).

5. There are lots and lots of Goosebumps books.

6. The books are scary, and even kids that don't like to read will read Goosebumps.

7. There are lots and lots of Goosebumps books.

Web:
   http://www.scholastic.com/goosebumps/

Hardy Boys

Frank and Joe Hardy are the sons of Fenton Hardy, a well-known detective. They live in Bayport, a small town on a bay, three miles inland from the Atlantic Ocean. The boys live with their parents in an old stone house, where they have their own laboratory above the garage. Frank and Joe go from one mystery adventure to another, outwitting just about everyone and bringing numerous bad guys to justice. Although the Hardy Boy books are published as the work of Franklin W. Dixon, no such person really exists. The series was originally created by a publisher named Edward Stratemeyer, and, over the years, Hardy Boy books have been written by a number of different authors. (Stratemeyer is also responsible for creating other popular series, such as Nancy Drew, the Bobbsey Twins, Tom Swift and the Rover Boys.) I loved reading the original Hardy Boys books when I was growing up. However, starting in 1959, the books were changed significantly to bring them up-to-date and to shorten them. If you are a real Hardy Boys fan, I recommend you look for the original editions, which are a lot better than the modern versions.

Web:
   http://home.columbus.rr.com/skywarppro/
   HardyBoys/
   http://www.thrillingdetective.com/hardys.html

Harry Potter

The English writer J.K. (Joanne Kathleen) Rowling (1966-) has planned a series of seven books chronicling the adventures of Harry Potter, a teenage wizard-in-training. Although Rowling is only part way through the series, she has managed to create a set of characters and a setting that have captured the interest of children and adults around the world. The saga starts with Harry, an 11-year-old orphan, suffering a miserable life in the house of his mean aunt and uncle. Harry's life changes unexpectedly when he receives a very special invitation to spend the next school year studying at the Hogwarts School of Witchcraft and Wizardry. Each of the books chronicles one year of Harry's training. (There are seven books, taking Harry from 11 to 17 years old, because Rowling has determined that this is how long it takes to train a wizard properly. However, so far, she has only written four of them.) As you read the Harry Potter books, you will encounter the well-known theme of good versus evil, clothed in an imaginative array of characters and activities (such as Quidditch, a type of soccer played in the air on broomsticks, in which some of the balls attack the players). My all-time favorite character is Hermione, one of Harry's classmates, because she is very, very smart, knows everything, and has, in her own way, a great deal of personal charm. (But then, I always have had a weakness for very, very smart women.) Will Harry marry Hermione one day? Only time will tell. In the meantime, all I can say is that if he doesn't want her, I do.

Web:
   http://www.education.wisc.edu/ccbc/hplinks.htm
   http://www.hagridshut.com/
   http://www.harrypotterfans.net/
   http://www.i2k.com/~svderark/lexicon/
   http://www.scholastic.com/harrypotter/

Usenet:
   alt.fan.harry-potter

I love peanut butter books.

Nancy Drew

Nancy Drew is the teenage heroine of a large series of girls' mystery books, written by a syndicate of authors and published under the pen name of Carolyn M. Keene. The first Nancy Drew book ("The Secret of the Old Clock") was published in 1930 and, ever since, Nancy has captured the imagination of generations of young women. Nancy is an amateur detective, who solves mysteries that baffle her father Carson Drew (a lawyer and widower), her friends George and Bess, and her sometimes boyfriend Ned Nickerson. Nancy lives in the town of River Heights with her father and their housekeeper Hannah Gruen. Nancy's appeal lies in her ability to be feminine (she is intelligent, attractive, gracious, dresses well and has excellent manners), while demonstrating strength, resourcefulness and bravery. And, oh yes, she has a cool roadster.

Web:
   http://www.bookloversden.com/series/girls/Drew/
      Drew.html
   http://www.mysterynet.com/nancydrew/
   http://www.thrillingdetective.com/nancy.html

Usenet:
   alt.books.nancy-drew

Narnia, Chronicles of

The Chronicles of Narnia (an imaginary land) is a series of seven children's books written by the Irish writer C.S. (Clive Staples) Lewis (1898-1963). In 1931 at the age of 33, Lewis became a Christian, eventually becoming one of the most published intellectual Christian writers of his generation. The Chronicles of Narnia were published between 1950 and 1956, starting with "The Lion, the Witch, and the Wardrobe". Despite the overly religious themes (Aslan the Lion, for example, represents Jesus), the Narnia tales have been a favorite of children for several generations.

Web:
   http://cslewis.drzeus.net/
   http://www.factmonster.com/spot/narnia1.html
   http://www.narnia.com/

Usenet:
   alt.books.cs-lewis

Listserv Mailing List:
   List Name: **merelewis**
   Subscribe to: **listserv@listserv.aol.com**

Winnie the Pooh and Christopher Robin

The stories and poems of English writer A.A. (Alan Alexander) Milne (1882-1956) have been a favorite of children for many years. The most well known characters are Winnie the Pooh—the Bear of Very Little Brain who lives in the 100 Acre Wood—and Christopher Robin (a boy). The other characters are Eeyore (a donkey), Piglet, Tigger (a tiger), Kanga and Roo (a kangaroo mother and son), Rabbit and Owl. Everyone has his or her own favorite character. I like piglet. My friend Suzanne and my copy editor Lydia both like Tigger. When life gets hectic, Winnie the Pooh provides a soothing sense of comfort for everyone. If you like Winnie the Pooh, be sure to read Milne's wonderful verses in the collections "When We Were Very Young" and "Now We Are Six". Interestingly enough, Milne wrote these stories and poems for adults. He preferred to read his own son (Christopher) stories by P.G. Wodehouse.

Web:
   http://www.just-pooh.com/
   http://www.nypl.org/branch/kids/pooh/winnie.html
   http://www.pooh-corner.com/index2.html
   http://www.poohthebear.com/

Usenet:
   alt.fan.pooh
   alt.fan.tigger

For your mom's birthday, give her a computer made out of chocolate. The nice thing is she won't care if it doesn't work.

STORIES TO READ ON THE NET

Alice in Wonderland

I bet you have heard of Alice in Wonderland. Actually, it is really two different books: "Alice's Adventures in Wonderland" and the sequel "Through the Looking Glass". These stories are clever tales written by the English writer Lewis Carroll (1832-1898), a pseudonym of Charles Lutwidge Dodgson, a mathematical lecturer at Oxford University. (A "pseudonym" is a fake name that a writer uses when he doesn't want to use his real name.) Both stories concern a young girl named Alice. In the first story, Alice enters a very strange world (Wonderland) by following a rabbit down a hole. In the second story, she begins her journey by climbing through a looking glass (a mirror). In both cases, Alice encounters a great many unusual people and talking animals, and has bizarre adventures.

Web:

http://www.hoboes.com/html/FireBlade/Carroll/Alice/

http://www.literature.org/authors/carroll-lewis/alices-adventures-in-wonderland/

http://www.literature.org/authors/carroll-lewis/through-the-looking-glass/

Anne of Green Gables

Lucy Maud Montgomery (1874-1942) was a Canadian novelist who wrote a series of books about a red-haired, green-eyed, freckled orphan named Anne. Montgomery's first book, "Anne of Green Gables" (1908), was so popular that she ended up writing an entire series using Anne as her central figure. In 1935, "Anne of Green Gables" was made into a motion picture and, in recent years, a popular TV series.

Web:

http://www-2.cs.cmu.edu/people/rgs/anne-table.html

http://www.inform.umd.edu/edres/readingroom/fiction/montgomery/

Child's Garden of Verses

Robert Louis Stevenson (1850-94) was a Scottish author who wrote novels, essays and poems. When he was a child, Stevenson was sickly and was forced to spend a lot of time in bed. As a result, he created his own make-believe world which, later in life, helped him become a wonderful storyteller. "A Child's Garden of Verses" is a well-known collection of children's poems, which you will find enjoyable to read again and again.

Web:

http://www.ibiblio.org/pub/docs/books/gutenberg/etext94/child10.txt

http://www.poetryloverspage.com/poets/stevenson/collections/childs_garden_of_verses.html

Classics for Young Readers

A classic is a story that is worth reading over and over. There are a great many books for kids that, over the years, have been recognized as classics. I have chosen these Web sites because they have a large number of such stories. Some of these stories are long, and I know that it can be difficult to read for a long time on the computer. However, look on these Web sites as an easy way to look for good things to read. If you find a story you really like, you can always check it out from the library. Some of these books might not be in your local library, so I'll tell you something you may not know. If you can't find a book in your library, tell the librarian. He or she will help you fill out a form, and then your library will borrow the book for you from another library. When you get a book in this way, it is called an "interlibrary loan". (I do it all the time.)

Web:

http://etext.lib.virginia.edu/subjects/Young-Readers.html

http://www.classicreader.com/toc.php/sid.3/

http://www.ucalgary.ca/~dkbrown/storclas.html

Grimm's Fairy Tales

Grimm's fairy tales are a large collection of German folk tales collected in the early 1800s by two brothers, Jakob Grimm (1785-1863) and Wilhem Grimm (1786-1859). There are many, many fairy tales in the collection, and I bet you will be surprised how many of them are well known. For example, all of the following are Grimm's fairy tales, and all of them (and many more) are available to read online: Aladdin, Tom Thumb, Ali Baba and the Forty Thieves, Beauty and the Beast, Cinderella, The Elves and the Shoemaker, The Emperor's New Clothes, Goldilocks and the Three Bears, Hansel and Gretel, The Hare and the Tortoise, Jack and the Beanstalk, The Little Mermaid, The Pied Piper of Hamelin, The Princess and the Pea, Puss in Boots, Little Red Riding Hood, Snow White, Thumbelina, The Three Little Pigs, and The Ugly Duckling.

Web:

   http://www-2.cs.cmu.edu/~spok/grimmtmp/
   http://www.familymanagement.com/literacy/
     grimms/grimms-toc.html
   http://www.fln.vcu.edu//grimm/grimm_menu.html
   http://www.hackvan.com/pub/grimm/

Dr. Dolittle

Dr. John Dolittle, of Puddleby-on-the-Marsh, England, is an eccentric physician, who gives up his regular medical practice to work exclusively with animals. Dr. Dolittle can communicate with animals in 498 different languages (499, actually, once he learns goldfish). The Dr. Dolittle books were written by Hugh Lofting (1886-1947), an English-American writer and illustrator. Lofting started writing the Dolittle stories when he was a soldier in France during World War I. When he had spare time, he would write stories and send them home in letters to his children. After the war, his wife insisted that he publish the letters, so he did. They became the first of ten Dr. Dolittle books. The moral of this story is that, if you are a man, you should always listen to your wife. (Ask your mother, and you will see I am right.)

Web:

   http://www.classicreader.com/booktoc.php/sid.3/
     bookid.1549/

Hans Christian Andersen Stories

Hans Christian Andersen (1805-1875) was a Danish author who wrote some of the world's most memorable fairy tales: The Princess and the Pea, The Little Mermaid, The Emperor's New Clothes, The Ugly Duckling, and many, many more. Here is a real treasure in which you will find some of the best bedtime stories ever. Some of these stories had originally been collected by the Brothers Grimm. You may find it interesting to compare the two versions.

Web:

   http://hca.gilead.org.il/
   http://www.amherst.edu/~rjyanco/literature/
     hanschristianandersen/stories/
   http://www.classicreader.com/toc.php/sid.3/
     bookid.109/

Jungle Book

Rudyard Kipling (1856-1936) was an English author whose stories and poems were full of the life and romanticism of India and English imperialism. "The Jungle Book", written in 1894, is one of a collection of children's adventure stories about a boy named Mowgli and a group of talking animals. I have also added a resource where you can find the "Just So Stories" ("How the Camel Got his Hump" and so on).

Web:

http://etext.virginia.edu/toc/modeng/public/KipJung.html

http://www-2.cs.cmu.edu/people/rgs/jngl-table.html

http://www.candlelightstories.com/d001/justsopage.asp

Legend of Sleepy Hollow

"The Legend of Sleepy Hollow" is an American classic. Written by American author Washington Irving (1783-1859), it relates the story of a schoolmaster, Ichabold Crane, who meets up with a headless horseman. Irving is also the author of the well-known story "Rip Van Winkle", based on a German folk tale, about a farmer who falls asleep for twenty years and awakens to find the world changed significantly. (I have included Web sites for both books.)

Web:

http://ravenscroft.jstudios.com/sleepyhollow/

http://www.classicreader.com/read.php/sid.6/bookid.212/

http://www.cwrl.utexas.edu/~daniel/amlit/rvw/rvwtext.html

http://www.hyland.org/sleepyhollow/sleep10.txt

http://www.williams.az.us/writers/library/irving/rvw.html

> I know someone who has a spaghetti and meatball garden.

Peter Pan

James Matthew Barrie (1860-1937) was a British playwright and novelist. In 1904, he wrote a popular tale about Peter Pan, the boy who would never grow up. The story of Peter Pan is popular today in cartoons, film and on stage. Enjoy this story about Peter, Wendy, Captain Hook, the Lost Boys and their adventures in Neverland. (In the movie, Disney changed the name to "Never Never Land".) It's a great book, but I have to say, the ending is a bit sad because, as you will see, Peter never grows up. (If you are a girl, remember not to marry a guy like this.)

Web:

http://www.hoboes.com/html/FireBlade/Barrie/Peter/

http://www.ibiblio.org/pub/docs/books/gutenberg/etext91/peter15a.txt

Peter Rabbit

Is there anything in the world cuter than Peter Rabbit? (Only my cat, The Little Nipper.) I bet you will love reading about Peter and his family, as well as looking at the wonderful pictures. If so, take a look at some of the other tales by British writer and illustrator Beatrix Potter (1866-1943). Aside from Peter, you'll meet Miss Moppet, the Two Bad Mice, Tommy Tiptoes and Squirrel Nutkin. (Squirrel Nutkin. Is that a cool name, or what?)

Web:

http://www.classicreader.com/booktoc.php/sid.3/
   bookid.137/
http://www.tcom.ohiou.edu/books/kids.htm

Poetry for Kids

One of the most wonderful things about listening to (or reading) poetry is hearing how well words can work together. When you get older and you look at adult poetry, you will see a lot of terrible stuff that doesn't rhyme and has only a hint of meter (rhythm). Poetry for kids sounds a lot better and is certainly more fun. When you check out these Web sites, you will find rhymes for you to read aloud, poems written by other children, and places to visit where you can make up poetry of your own. Some of my favorite poems are written by Kenn Nesbitt, who is a good friend of mine. (His Web site is **poetry4kids.com**.)

Web:

http://falcon.jmu.edu/~ramseyil/poeform.htm
http://www.gigglepoetry.com/
http://www.grandpatucker.com/
http://www.mecca.org/~graham/day/poetrypost/
http://www.poetry4kids.com/

> **Fuzzy purple bubble gum
> is cool.
> Brussels sprouts aren't.
> Ask your mother why.**

Robin Hood Stories

Robin Hood is one of the greatest folk heroes in English literature. The origins of the many Robin Hood legends are lost in antiquity, but are thought to date back to the late Middle Ages. In his most well-known incarnation, Robin is the leader of a band of outlaws (including Little John and Friar Tuck) who fight the evil Sheriff of Nottingham, rob from the rich, and give to the poor. This particular book is "The Merry Adventures of Robin Hood", written and illustrated by Howard Pyle in 1883.

Web:

http://www.ibiblio.org/pub/docs/books/gutenberg/
   etext97/2rbnh10.txt
http://www.lib.rochester.edu/camelot/rh/
   rharmenu.htm#p

Secret Garden

"The Secret Garden" tells the story of Mary Lennox, an unhealthy young orphan with an attitude, who, after the death of her mother, is sent to live in a large house on the desolate moors in England. Mary finds the door to a secret garden, which she begins to care for. In the process, she learns about life, herself, and what it means to be spiritually healthy. "The Secret Garden" was written by a prolific English novelist, Frances Hodgson Burnett (1849-1924), and is a favorite of young women. If you like this book, try "A Little Princess," "Sara Crewe" and "Little Lord Fauntleroy".

Web:

http://www.classicreader.com/author.php/aut.14/
http://www.inform.umd.edu/edres/readingroom/
   fiction/burnett/
http://www.ofcn.org/cyber.serv/resource/bookshelf/
   gardn10/
http://www139.pair.com/read/Frances_Hodgson_Burnett/

Stories for Preschoolers

When I was a young boy, I loved to have my mother and father read to me. Here are some stories you and your parents can read together using the computer. Maybe one day, you will write your own stories and other people will read them.

Web:

http://www.lil-fingers.com/storybooks/
http://www.mightybook.com/library_2to4.htm
http://www.storyplace.org/preschool/other.asp

Tom Sawyer and Huckleberry Finn

"You don't know about me without you have read a book by the name of The Adventures of Tom Sawyer; but that ain't no matter. That book was made by Mr. Mark Twain, and he told the truth, mainly..." So begins the story of "Huckleberry Finn" (and, I might add, so begins modern American literature). Mark Twain (1835-1910) spent his boyhood in Hannibal, Missouri, and used that setting as a backdrop for the various adventures of the young, energetic scamps Tom Sawyer and Huckleberry Finn. These two novels are among the most beloved of American children's tales, and have established Tom and his friend Huck as endearing rascals in the hearts of children everywhere.

Web:

    http://etext.lib.virginia.edu/twain/huckfinn.html
    http://www.bibliomania.com/0/0/54/98/
    http://www.literature.org/authors/twain-mark/
       huckleberry/
    http://www.litrix.com/tomsawyr/tomsa001.htm

Treasure Island

Treasure Island, one of Robert Louis Stevenson's best-known stories, has inspired countless young boys to want to go to sea with Long John Silver and become a pirate. Adventure, action, danger, pirates, treasure— if you're a young boy, it just doesn't get any better. ("Fifteen men on a dead man's chest / Yo-ho-ho, and a bottle of rum! / Drink and the devil had done for the rest / Yo-ho-ho, and a bottle of rum!")

Web:

    http://www.classicreader.com/toc.php/sid.1/
       bookid.86/
    http://www.ibiblio.org/pub/docs/books/gutenberg/
       etext94/treas10.txt

Wizard of Oz

The original Oz stories comprise 14 novels written by the American writer L. (Lyman) Frank Baum (1856-1919). The first book, "The Wonderful Wizard of Oz", describes the adventures of a young girl from Kansas who is caught in a tornado and whisked off to a strange land full of witches, Munchkins and other bizarre characters. (This is the book that was made into the movie, "The Wizard of Oz", starring Judy Garland as Toto.) After the death of Baum, the Oz books series was continued by R.P. Thompson.

Web:

    http://www-2.cs.cmu.edu/people/rgs/wizoz10.html
    http://www.classicreader.com/booktoc.php/sid.3/
       bookid.123/
    http://www.ibiblio.org/pub/docs/books/gutenberg/
       etext96/rd2oz10.txt
    http://www.literature.org/authors/baum-l-frank/
    http://www.literature.org/authors/baum-l-frank/
       the-wonderful-wizard-of-oz/

JOBS: FINDING A JOB

Computer Certification

There are many different types of computer-related jobs, and among the most technical are those that require someone to understand the care and feeding of a computer system. To ensure that such people are properly qualified, various companies and organizations have developed "certifications". Among them are A+ (CompTIA service technician), CNE (Certified Novell Engineer) and MCSE (Microsoft Certified Systems Engineer). If you aspire to be certified, I can help. Check out these Web sites where you'll find oodles of info, enough to lead you down the garden path to a life of esoteric knowledge, wealth and job security (not to mention fame, power and the respect of beautiful women and handsome men everywhere).

Web:
http://www.certnotes.com/
http://www.computerjobs.com/
http://www.cramsession.com/
http://www.mcpmag.com/
http://www.microsoft.com/traincert/
http://www.prgjobs.com/

Usenet:
alt.certification.a-plus
alt.certification.cne
alt.certification.mcse

Education-Related Jobs

So you spent the first part of your life sitting in a classroom, waiting patiently for the bell of freedom to ring? And now you're trying desperately to get back into a classroom, so you can contribute and make a difference (while being underpaid and under-appreciated). Thank you for sharing.

Web:
http://www.chronicle.com/jobs/
http://www.higheredjobs.com/
http://www.teachers.net/jobs/jobboard/
http://www.teachersplanet.com/jobcenter.htm

Entry Level Jobs

There's an old riddle: What does an arts graduate say to a computer science graduate? The answer is, "Would you like fries with your order?" Here is a newer riddle: What does a person who doesn't know how to use the Net say to a person who does? The answer is, nothing. Because the person who knows how to use the Net is too busy working at a satisfying and lucrative job. Okay, so we all have to start somewhere, and if you are ready for an entry-level job, the Net is ready to help you find it. Check out the jobs that offer you no place to go but up, and talk to the people who really care whether or not you want fries.

Web:
http://www.careernotice.com/entrylevel.htm
http://www.dnaco.net/~dantassi/jobhome.html

Usenet:
misc.jobs.offered.entry

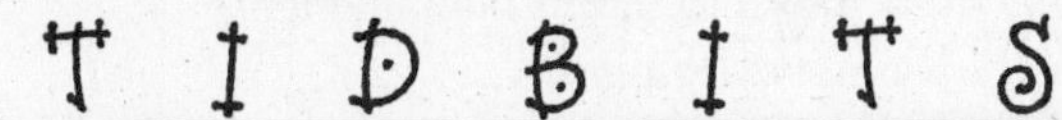

TIDBITS

What should young women know about YOUNG MEN?

Young men live in a world dominated by (1) enormously strong sexual urges, (2) a need to compete aggressively, and (3) a lack of wisdom and maturity.

As a young woman, it is likely that you are looking for a relationship, someone to be your boyfriend. Unlike you, boys have a lot of trouble understanding the importance of their own feelings and the feelings of other people. This is why, for example, boys are much more oriented towards sex for the sake of sex, as opposed to working to build an emotional relationship.

This doesn't mean that boys are defective. It just means that they are different from you, and you must learn to be strong and make your choices carefully.

If you want to understand the opposite sex, there is one fundamental idea you must never forget: Men take a long time to mature.

The actual process is described by the following equation:

$$\text{Sex Drive} + \text{Emotional Maturity} = \text{a constant}$$

Executive, Managerial and Professional Jobs

If you are looking for employment as an executive, manager or professional, you know that such jobs must match your qualifications and goals as closely as possible. For that reason, it is a good idea to carry out as broad a search as you can. Indeed, you may have to investigate positions in a variety of locations over an extended period of time before you are able to find what you need. My advice? Use the ultimate networking tool, and find the job worthy of your skills and experience.

Web:

> http://www.6figurejobs.com/
> http://www.careerjournal.com/partners/
> http://www.execsearches.com/
> http://www.execunet.com/
> http://www.nationjob.com/management/
> http://www.netshare.com/

Freelancing and Contracting

We all need to work, but we all don't need a job. If showing up at the same place every day to do the same thing—day after day—just doesn't cut it, try freelancing. There are a huge number of jobs available, in every profession, for people like you, who have a valuable service to sell to the highest bidder.

Web:

> http://www.bullhorn.com/
> http://www.freeagent.com/resource/
> http://www.freelancehelp.com/
> http://www.freelancers.com/
> http://www.guru.com
> http://www.rentacoder.com/
> http://www.talentmarket.monster.com/
> http://www.thecentralmall.com/
> http://www.ubidcontract.com/
> http://www.webcontractor.com/

Usenet:

> misc.jobs.contract

Freelancing and Contracting

Would you enjoy working

(1) for more money per hour,

(2) with less supervision,

(3) with a steady income?

If you answered "Yes" to all of the above, you may be ready for freelancing and contracting.

International Jobs

So you've lived your whole life in one country, and you feel like it's time to have an adventure by working abroad? Well, the first journey to employment begins with a single occupational step. One of the Web sites is devoted to Canadian jobs. The others will help you find jobs all over the world. For questions and answers, try the Usenet discussion group. Hint: If you answer an ad, do investigate carefully before you commit yourself or spend any money. Remember, anyone can put anything they want on the Web. It's up to you to be careful.

Web:

> http://www.canadajobs.com/
> http://www.escapeartist.com/jobs/overseas.htm
> http://www.overseasjobs.com/

Usenet:

> alt.jobs.overseas

Internships

My paternal grandfather, Irving Hahn, was born in the small town of Brody, Austria, on January 12, 1895. (Today, Brody is part of Ukraine.) At the age of nine, he quit school and was apprenticed to a barber. For three years, my grandfather worked without being paid a regular salary. However, he did get to keep his tips (about 15-20 cents a week) and, during the last half of his apprenticeship, he was given his meals for free. At the beginning of his apprenticeship, my grandfather's responsibilities were to shine shoes, look after the barber's baby (including diapering it), brush the customers' clothes, and wash and oil the rough wooden floor. Eventually, he learned his trade, one tiny step at a time (there was no formal training), and was able to become a barber in his own right. Today, apprenticeships still exist in the form of internships. Of course, there are important differences between modern internships and the old-fashioned apprenticeships, but the basic idea is the same: a young person agrees to work for free (or for low wages) in order to learn a trade.

Web:
http://www.careerplanit.com/world/internship.cfm
http://www.internjobs.com/
http://www.internships.wetfeet.com/
http://www.internweb.com/
http://www.paidinternships.com/
http://www.rsinternships.com/

Job Searching

The Net wants you to work. The Net wants you to make a lot of money. The Net wants you to pay off your mortgage, fully fund your retirement, and save money for your kids' education—but first, you need a job. There are lots of jobs available. To help you find them, use these Web sites, where you will find many job listings in many different categories and regions. Hint: Aim for a job that is so interesting and enjoyable that you love what you are doing.

Web:
http://www.careerbuilder.com/
http://www.careercity.com/
http://www.careers.usatoday.com/
http://www.flipdog.com/
http://www.job-hunt.org/
http://www.jobhuntersbible.com/
http://www.jobstar.org/
http://www.monster.com/

Job Talk and General Discussion

Before you send away for instructions on how to make money at home stuffing envelopes, maybe you should check it out with your friends on the Net. If you need a job, have a job, or are offering a job, these Usenet groups are the place to talk and trade tips about employment, the workplace and careers.

Usenet:
alt.building.jobs
alt.computer.consultants.ads
alt.jobs
comp.databases.oracle.marketplace
comp.jobs.offered
misc.jobs
misc.jobs.discuss.job-search
misc.jobs.misc
misc.jobs.offered

Jobs for College Students and Graduates

There are oodles and oodles of jobs available for college students and recent graduates. However, there are also oodles and oodles of other people looking for those jobs. Never fear. All you need to do is use the Net to find the job you want. Then, just tell them you are one of my readers, and name your own salary. It's that easy.

Web:
http://www.collegegrad.com/
http://www.collegejobsite.com/
http://www.monstertrak.com/
http://www.thejobresource.com/

Kingdomality

When you look for a job, you have to look now—that is, in the present. But what if you had lived in medieval times? You would have had much different employment choices, and maybe one of them would be more suitable for you than what you do now. To find out, all you need to do is answer a set of multiple choice questions. A computer program will then analyze your responses and tell you which type of job would have been best for you in medieval times. (According to the program, I am best suited for the job of Prime Minister.)

Web:
http://www.cmi-lmi.com/kingdom.html

Medical Jobs

The medical field is vast, and you may need some help to find the exact job you want. Whether you are looking for a job as a brain transplant specialist or merely a chrono-synclastic-infundibulum technician, the Net is there to help you.

Web:
   http://myh.monster.com/
   http://www.hcjobsonline.com/
   http://www.nationjob.com/medical

Usenet:
   alt.medical.sales.jobs.offered

Occupation Descriptions

What would you like to be? An insurance adjuster, an art dealer, a travel agent, a midwife, a veterinarian or (why not go for the top) a writer? No matter what occupation you are considering, you need information: learn what the job is like, what education you need, what opportunities you will have, and what the employment outlook is.

Web:
   http://www.acinet.org/acinet/
      library.htm?category=1.4
   http://www.bls.gov/oco/
   http://www.bls.gov/oco/cg/
   http://www.careerccc.org/careerdirections/eng/
      e_al_dwn.asp
   http://www.mois.org/clusters.html
   http://www.nycareerzone.org/graphic/
   http://www.review.com/career/
      article.cfm?id=career/car_car_index

Resumés

These Web sites have hints to help you create or improve your resumé. I've also listed the various Usenet groups to which you can post your resumé. My advice is post to these groups if you want, but don't stop there. There are various Web sites to which you can also send a resumé. One thing that may help you is to look at other people's resumés. Reading what other people write can give you good ideas about how to present yourself in the best possible manner.

Web:
   http://www.jobweb.com/resumes_interviews/
   http://www.rileyguide.com/eresume.html
   http://www.services.juniata.edu/career/roc.htm

Usenet:
   alt.jobs.resumes
   misc.jobs.resumes
   misc.jobs.wanted

Riley Guide

The Riley Guide is a great resource for learning how to use the Internet to find a job. Explore a comprehensive collection of information and tips explaining how the Net can help you get what you want. The guide is also useful for employers who want to learn how to use the Net to fill job openings.

Web:
   http://www.rileyguide.com/

Seasonal Employment

The other day, Santa Claus called me.

"Harley," he said, "you know everything. How can I find work during the summer?"

"Try the Net, Santa," I told him.

So he did, and he got a great seasonal job as a lifeguard in Southern California.

"How can I ever thank you?" he asked, the next time he called.

"Well, you might try getting me that red, toy truck I have been wanting for the last 40 years."

"Consider it done," he said.

You know, when you come right down to it, Santa may be a bit goofy, but he's an all right kind of guy.

Science Jobs

Scientists are like Sherlock Holmes. They spend their days looking for clues, gathering information and putting it together to solve the mysteries of the universe. If you have a career in science, or if you want one, use the Net to find out about current projects, funding and job opportunities.

Web:

http://www.sciencejobs.com/

Usenet:

alt.sci.geology.jobs
bionet.jobs.wanted
misc.jobs.fields.chemistry
sci.research.careers
sci.research.postdoc

Seasonal Employment

Having a job during your summer or winter vacation can be great. You work long hours in a menial position for very little money—and you have so much fun, you're sad when it's over. Believe me, when you get older, you will not want to work long hours in a menial position for very little money, so enjoy it now while you can.

Web:

http://www.aplus-summerjobs.com/
http://www.coolworks.com/
http://www.summerjobs.com/

U.S. Government Jobs

Would you like to work for a U.S. federal or state agency? There are many jobs available, and these resources may be able to help you find what you want. For variety, I have also included the employment Web sites for the CIA and FBI, where, from time to time, you will see listings for jobs such as "Clandestine Service Trainee" and "Theatrical Effects Specialist".

Web:

http://www.fbi.gov/employment/employ.htm
http://www.fedworld.gov/jobs/jobsearch.html
http://www.govtjobs.com/
http://www.jobsfed.com/
http://www.odci.gov/cia/employment/ciaindex.htm
http://www.statejobs.com/
http://www.usajobs.opm.gov/

Young Job Seekers

When you are young, you can be at a disadvantage because of a lack of experience. So when it comes time to find a job, let the Net help you with advice about finding a job, interviewing, evaluating the offers, and all the fun and games that you get to enjoy as you pass from the imaginary world of childhood to the imaginary world of adults.

Web:

http://www.myfuture.com/
http://www.nextstepmagazine.com/
http://www.nextsteps.org/
http://www.petersons.com/summerop/
http://www.youthatwork.org/

JOBS: THE WORKPLACE

Bicycle Commuting

What better way to start your day than by riding your bike? Well, some people get to do this every day, because they commute to work on their bicycles. It's actually much more common than you think, when you realize that millions of kids around the world ride their bikes to school every day. Even at the university level, there are many bike commuters. Unfortunately, many people just assume that, once you finish school and join the "real world", you can't have fun on weekday mornings. Well, you can, just by riding your bike. Forget that riding your bike is good exercise, that it will save you money, and that it will give you time to relax and think on your way to and from work. Forget all of that. Riding your bike is fun.

Web:
  http://biketowork.itelcom.com/

Employer/Employee Relations

As an employee, you have relationships with the other people in your organization, including your boss or manager. However, you also have another, perhaps more important, relationship, with the organization itself. The employer/employee relationship is an important one, but is often neglected. As a result, employee problems are common, especially since employers and employees generally do not share the same long-term goals. If you are interested in improving the quality of your workplace, you will find these resources useful (especially if you are an employer). Read about flexible work hours, retirement plans, employee burnout, and other topics oriented toward inspiring people to do their best.

Web:
  http://www.busreslab.com/policies/good.htm
  http://www.employer-employee.com/

Read a free online book.

How to Get Rich

Would you like to get rich? If so, you need to plan ahead and learn how to make the right decisions. Here is an essay I wrote to help you understand what brings success in life. Read my advice on how to think about work and how to make sure that what you choose works well for you. Work can be immensely satisfying—and provide your best chance of becoming rich—but you need to do it right.

Web:
  http://www.harley.com/get-rich/

Net Slaves

So you work all day on the Net? I guess you know that life in the fast Internet lane is not always the most satisfying way to live out your short, temporary tenure on planet Earth. You think you've got it rough? Read the real horror stories.

Web:
  http://www.netslaves.com/

Philosophy of Work

If you don't pay enough attention to your work, you are depriving yourself of one of the most important sources of ongoing satisfaction in your life. However, if you spend too much time at work, you will lose track of the other important parts of life. Should you want to work as much as you can, or should you try to retire as young as possible? (I believe that, for men anyway, the answer is you should want to work.) How does your choice of career affect your values? How much of a priority should work be in your life? These are not simple questions, and learning how to integrate your work into your life is not easy. But once you deliberately decide on your values, you will be able to balance your work with your family, your hobbies, and your leisure. I encourage you to decide, deliberately, how work fits into your life.

Web:
  http://midcareer.monster.com/articles/
    careerdevelopment/needy/
  http://www.anxietyculture.mcmail.com/
  http://www.awlp.org/
  http://www.flexibility.co.uk/
  http://www.innerself.com/Magazine/
    Lifestyle_Changes/Losing_The_Corporate_Self.htm
  http://www.vcn.bc.ca/timework/worksite.htm
  http://www.workfamily.com/
Usenet:
  alt.lifestyle.simplicity

Repetitive Stress Injuries

A repetitive stress injury (RSI)—also called a cumulative trauma disorder—is a medical condition caused by chronic stress to one or more parts of the body. The most common causes of RSIs are: repetitive motion, working in an awkward position, using an unbalanced force, and not resting enough. In the workplace, the common RSIs are carpal tunnel syndrome (a wrist condition often caused by too much typing), chronic back pain, tendonitis and—everyone's favorite—stress. Here are some Web sites that have a wealth of information about RSIs, in and outside of the workplace. There is a lot you can do about workplace injuries caused by ongoing conditions, but before you can make a difference, you need to understand the real problems.

Web:
  http://www.nycosh.org/rsi.html
  http://www.office-ergo.com/
  http://www.tifaq.com/

Usenet:
  misc.health.injuries.rsi.misc
  misc.health.injuries.rsi.moderated

Listserv Mailing List:
  List Name: rsi-east
  Subscribe to: listserv@maelstrom.stjohns.edu

Every day, you do the same type of work—again and again and again.

Before you know it, something hurts. Don't worry about it, people tell you. It will go away.

But it doesn't.

Every day, you do the same type of work—again and again and again.

You hurt more, and it doesn't go away.

It's time to find out about repetitive stress injuries.

Safety in the Workplace

The business of business is to make money, and you will often see workplace safety given second place when it comes to meeting schedules and getting the job done quickly. Most countries have government agencies to ensure safety in the workplace and avoid injuries. In the United States, this job is done on a national level by the Occupational Safety and Health Administration (OSHA), an agency of the United States Department of Labor. There is a balance between protecting the rights of workers and interfering in how a business does its job, but safety is always important. Check out these Web sites, and you'll see why. You'll also find a lot of useful information to help you keep yourself and your work environment safe.

Web:
  http://www.cdc.gov/niosh/homepage.html
  http://www.osha.gov/

Salary and Wages

Are you being paid as much as you should be? As one of my readers, I know you are unusually intelligent, hard-working, dependable and talented, and, as such, deserve at least twice as much as you are being paid now. But how do you prove this to the people who control the money bags at your place of employment? Here are places where you will find various types of salary-related information: raw numbers, comparisons, negotiation strategies and salary calculators.

Web:
  http://jobstar.org/tools/salary/
  http://www.salarycompensation.net/
  http://www.salaryexpert.com/
  http://www.thelinkzone.com/career/salary.html
  http://www.wageweb.com/

A B C D E F G H I J K L M N O P Q R S T U V W X Y Z

Sexual Harassment on the Job

If you have a problem with sexual harassment on the job, you are not alone. Check with the Net, where you will find lots of relevant information: a list of hotline telephone numbers you can call for help and advice, a guide on how to handle difficult situations, as well as lots of information, opinion and discussion on this complex and volatile topic.

Web:
http://www.employer-employee.com/sexhar1.htm
http://www.feminist.org/911/harass.html

It's been a long time since I did anything resembling a regular job. Mostly, I just stay home all day and do whatever I feel like. Sometimes I take a break to have a snack or to play with my cat.

Telecommuting: It's dirty work, but someone's got to do it!

Telecommuting

Telecommuting (or teleworking) refers to working at home as part of a regular job with an established company. Of course, some people have always worked at home, and home-based businesses are nothing new. What is new is that, with telecommuting, many people who traditionally would have worked in an office environment with lots of other people are now working at home. As you might imagine, this creates a variety of problems as people need to readjust to the logistical and social consequences of being by oneself. These sites have telecommuting resources that can help you.

Web:
http://www.escapeartist.com/tele/commute2.htm
http://www.langhoff.com/
http://www.telework.gov/
http://www.tjobs.com/

Temps

Being a temp—that is, working at temporary jobs—has some great advantages compared to being a permanent employee. You can work or not work as you wish. For example, you can take a long vacation, then work, save some money, and take another long vacation. Moreover, as a temp, you can ignore company politics and all the rest of the silliness that goes on in most workplaces. Of course, there are disadvantages. You can't always count on having a job when you want it, you probably won't get any benefits, and you will never make a huge amount of money. Clearly, such an environment calls for (1) good, solid information about the temp world and what jobs are available, and, (2) humor and fun. Here you are.

Web:
http://www.net-temps.com/
http://www.workrover.com/

Unions

A labor union is an organization dedicated to serving the interests of a particular group of workers. Unions concern themselves with wages, working conditions, grievance resolution, health issues, and so on. These Web sites will lead you to a great many union-related resources on the Net, so you can find what you need without having to work overtime.

Web:
http://www.icem.org/links/labres.html
http://www.igc.org/igc/ln/resources/unions.html

JOURNALISM AND MEDIA

Committee to Protect Journalists

Reporters who work in the United States operate within an environment of freedom of the press. In the U.S., such freedoms are protected by the Bill of Rights ("Congress shall make no law... abridging the freedom of speech, or of the press..."). In other developed countries, journalists have, to some degree, the same types of freedoms. However, in many parts of the world, there is no freedom of the press, and being a journalist with a conscience can be a dangerous job. This Web site, maintained by the Committee to Protect Journalists, reports on attacks against journalists around the world. Let us not forget that many reporters risk injury, prison and even death in pursuit of the freedoms that so many of us can take for granted. However, we live in a global community, and lack of freedom in one country often has a way of affecting us all when we least expect it. Any challenge to freedom of the press diminishes me because I am involved with Freedom; and therefore never send to know for whom the journalistic bell tolls; it tolls for thee.

Web:

   http://www.cpj.org/

Environmental Journalist's Resources

This site is put together by the Society for Environmental Journalism, an organization devoted to helping journalists better inform the public about environmental issues. Expect to find links to environmental resources, environmental journalism organizations and newsletters. If you write about the environment, this is a Web site with which you should be familiar.

Web:

   http://www.sej.org/

Gonzo Journalism

In the tradition of Hunter S. Thompson, gonzo journalism is the method of reporting in which the journalist is a participant in the series of events or story being reported on. Follow the discussion about Thompson and the concepts of gonzo journalism.

Usenet:

   alt.journalism.gonzo

Bedtime for Gonzo

Is there anyone who has read "Fear and Loathing in Las Vegas" and not felt Hunter S. Thompson to possess that spark of outrageous genius that is all too rare? Too bad, then, that the spark fanned into a dull flame that attenuated and died years ago, regretted by all. In its place, we have the legacy of gonzo journalism, a largely mythical school of creation in which the writer is immersed in the events about which he is reporting. Still, as you might guess from reading this book, I firmly believe that irreverence is as irreverence does and that the spirit of gonzo lives.

So, if you are one of the atavistic intellectual hold-outs from the '70s, take some time and visit your friends in **alt.journalism.gonzo**. And if you happen to be reading this in a bookstore, buy this book or I will be forced to rip your lungs out.

International Federation of Journalists

I live in the United States, and it's easy to take freedom of the press for granted. But in many parts of the world, such freedoms are not always enjoyed. Repressive government regimes or warlike conditions will often censor and control news reporting. The International Federation of Journalism is a worldwide organization dedicated to the ideals of freedom of the press and social justice. They issue regular reports (in several languages) that monitor these issues around the world. The next time you think freedom is ubiquitous, go to this Web site and find out how repressed much of the world is. In my country, people more or less accept the idea of the press as a philosophical good, but that is not the case in a lot of places. However, I strongly believe the free flow of information has a civilizing influence on mankind and the synergy of the Internet and the International Federation of Journalists is a welcome one.

Web:

   http://www.ifj.org/

Investigative Journalism

Investigative journalism has a long, mostly honorable, history. Many countries enjoy freedom of the press, and that freedom is used for more than supplying information. A free press serves as an important balance against the power and potential abuses of government officials. The investigative press is well represented on the Net: there is information for the curious (how do they find out all that stuff?), organizations for the professional, and a mailing list for the loquacious.

Web:
    http://www.facsnet.org/
    http://www.icij.org/
    http://www.ire.org/
    http://www.muckraker.org/

Listproc Mailing List:
    List Name: ire-l
    Subscribe to: listproc@po.missouri.edu

Listserv Mailing List:
    List Name: media
    Subscribe to: listserv@psychmax.psychology.su.se

Journalism Grants and Fellowships

You may not know it, but there are a lot of grants and fellowships available to journalists. If you have a special project you want to work on, it may be that someone has already set up funding for that type of work. So, the next time you need a break from feeling guilty about an impending deadline, give yourself a well-earned mental rest and use the Net to check on sources of free money. You may find a pleasant surprise.

Web:
    http://web.mit.edu/knight-science/
    http://www.icfj.org/fellship.html
    http://www.lib.msu.edu/harris23/grants/
        3jrnlism.htm
    http://www.newswise.com/grants.htm

> ## Aim high and you will always surprise yourself.

Journalism Mailing Lists

Mailing lists are used for ongoing discussions. No matter what area of journalism you are interested in, I guarantee there is a mailing list for you. To help you find what you need, here are some Web sites with information about a wide variety of journalism lists. In addition, I have included two specific lists: **spj-l**, for general discussion among professional journalists; and **guildnet-l**, for discussion about working conditions in the journalism industry.

Web:
    http://reporter.umd.edu/listserv.htm
    http://www.journalismnet.com/lists

Listserv Mailing List:
    List Name: spj-l
    Subscribe to: listserv@lists.psu.edu

Majordomo Mailing List:
    List Name: guildnet-l
    Subscribe to: majordomo@acs.ryerson.ca

Journalism Resources

Journalists spend their time collecting and publishing information, so it makes a lot of sense that the Net would be a wonderful tool for a working reporter or researcher. Here are some collections where you can find many, many resources. When you get a spare moment, I suggest that you explore, looking for those places that can help you. As you know, one of the most valuable possessions a journalist can have is a list of reliable sources. The time you spend creating such a list of Internet resources for yourself will be repaid many times over.

Web:
    http://bailiwick.lib.uiowa.edu/journalism/
    http://home.wlu.edu/~grefed/journalism/
        jour_res.html
    http://multimedia.tamu-commerce.edu/Library/
        jour.htm
    http://www.markovits.com/journalism/
    http://www.robertniles.com/data/
    http://www.writerswrite.com/journalism/

Journalism Student Resources

Are you young? Are you interested in journalism? Would you be willing to work long, impossible hours performing mundane tasks for little or no money? If you answered yes to all of these questions, you may be in line for a journalism internship.

Web:

http://www.asne.org/kiosk/careers/
http://www.freep.com/jobspage/interns/
http://www.journalism.berkeley.edu/jobs/
http://www.poynter.org/quickclick/jstudent.htm

Usenet:

alt.journalism.students

Listserv Mailing List:

List Name: STUMEDIA
Subscribe to: listserv@uabdpo.dpo.uab.edu

Majordomo Mailing List:

List Name: sj
Subscribe to: majordomo@world.std.com

Journalism Talk and General Discussion

Throughout the Net, journalists of varying size, shape and paycheck are discussing every aspect of journalism. Join the discussion. If you know what you are doing, contribute. If you don't know what you are doing, ask. If you don't know how to ask, just sit there and read what everyone else has to say (so you can report on it later).

Usenet:

alt.journalism
alt.journalism.criticism
alt.journalism.freelance
alt.journalism.gay-press
alt.journalism.music
alt.journalism.newspapers
alt.journalism.newspapers.wkly-worldnews
alt.journalism.print
alt.music.journalism
alt.news-media
alt.periodismo

Media News

In his 1964 book, "Understanding Media", Marshall McLuhan observed that how we perceive information depends greatly upon how that information is received. "The medium is the message," said McLuhan, in the Sixties. Well, we now live in the twenty-first century and I say, "The medium is the story."

Web:

http://www.journalism.org/daily/
http://www.mediainfo.com/
http://www.poynter.org/medianews/

Media Watchdogs

Here are the Web sites for two of the principal media watch organizations in the United States. One group is Accuracy in Media (AIM), a conservative media watch organization. The second group is Fairness and Accuracy in Reporting (FAIR), a liberal media watch organization. The goal of each group is the same: to monitor and criticize writers, broadcasters and commentators who expound viewpoints with which the group disagrees.

Web:

http://www.aim.org/
http://www.fair.org/

Newslink

Newslink is a Web site featuring many resources related to journalism and the news. Read about news sources, hot news sites, links to newspapers, magazines, radio and television stations, other journalism resources, and much, much more. There are also feature articles reprinted from the American Journalism Review.

Web:
  http://www.newslink.org/

Online Journalism Review

The Internet offers a much different distribution system than the ones used by traditional broadcasting and print publishing. Moreover, the rhythm of the Net is much faster and more dispersed than that of television, radio, newspapers and magazines. As such, journalism on the Internet is a new human activity. The Online Journalism Review casts a critical eye on journalism endeavors on the Web. Somewhere on the Net is the new frontier of journalism. Maybe you'll find it and maybe you won't, but it sure couldn't hurt to keep up on what's happening where and how and to whom.

Web:
  http://www.ojr.org/

Photojournalism

Every day, you see pictures in the newspaper, but for every picture you see, probably more than a hundred were taken and discarded. A photojournalist—someone who specializes in taking pictures for newspapers and magazines—has to be trained in photography and modern technology, and must conjure up immense amounts of patience and endurance to produce that one picture that may make it onto the page.

Web:
  http://www.abovethefold.homestead.com/a1.html
  http://www.fotophile.com/links/photojournalism.htm
  http://www.reportage.org/

Usenet:
  alt.journalism.photo

Press Photographers

A press pass is a license to barge right in where non-journalistic angels would fear to tread. If you are lucky (and you have your camera with you), you'll be able to snap pictures of famous movie stars and world leaders. If you are not lucky (and you have your camera with you), you'll end up taking pictures of the winners of the Blizzard County 94th Annual Chili Cook-Off. Regardless, when it comes to journalism, press photography is where it's at (if you have your camera with you). The mailing list and Usenet group are forums in which photographers, photo and graphics editors, designers, teachers and students discuss this noble profession. When you get a chance, visit the Web site, which is sponsored by the National Press Photographers Association. (Don't forget your camera.)

Web:
  http://www.nppa.org/

Usenet:
  bit.listserv.nppa-l

Listserv Mailing List:
  List Name: nppa-l
  Subscribe to: listserv@listserv.cmich.edu

Pulitzer Prize

The Hungarian-born, American publisher Joseph Pulitzer (1847-1911) was not only a highly successful businessman, he was also a visionary. Before he died, Pulitzer endowed the Graduate School of Journalism at Columbia University, as well as an annual series of prizes (awarded by Columbia University) for achievements in American journalism, letters, drama and music. Over the years, the Pulitzer Prizes have become some of the most prestigious and certainly the most well-known awards for American writers. (I myself had to turn down several such awards, as I was too busy working on this book to attend the ceremony.) Here is the official site for the Pulitzer Prizes, where you can look at a list of current and previous winners, and a history of the prizes.

Web:
  http://www.pulitzer.org/

Photojournalism

If you have an interest in pictures and journalism, you'll find the Photojournalism Internet resources interesting and useful.

After all, anyone can get the picture. But it takes someone really special to get paid for it.

Radio and Television Companies

Here is a huge collection of links to the Web sites of broadcasting companies around the Net. When you need to find a particular media company, radio station, television station or network, this is a good place to start.

Web:
   http://archive.museophile.sbu.ac.uk/broadcast/

Scholastic Journalism

One of the best and most satisfying ways to get journalism experience is to work on your school's newspaper or yearbook. When you are not writing feverishly to make your deadline, these Web sites can provide you with helpful information, including reference material, links to resources and contest notices. Moreover, if you need a jump start with your own investigative writing, you can get some ideas by looking at what other people are doing.

Web:
   http://studentpress.journ.umn.edu/
   http://www.journalism.indiana.edu/resources/
     scholastic/

Television Journalism

Any worthwhile job in the entertainment industry is going to be subject to immense competition, demanding conditions, and—for the very few people who manage to make it to the top—great rewards. The same holds true for television journalism, a unique hybrid between entertainment and reporting. Here is lots of information about the television news industry: TV stations, career strategies, newscast production, and more. Hint: If you become a television journalist, always remember the old "remains to be seen" signoff. It is used to end a piece quickly when there is no time for real insight or analysis. ("...whether or not the negotiators will be able to defuse a tense situation that may lead to war at any moment remains to be seen...")

Web:
   http://www.tvrundown.com/

Take this book
out for a spin.
(But first fasten your
intellectual seat belt.)

KNOWLEDGE AND INFORMATION

Experts

I have always thought that if I changed my name to "Harley Expert" I would get a lot of free publicity in the newspapers. For example, just about every day you see a headline like "Expert Predicts Economy Will Rebound in Next Quarter," or "Expert Says Children Are Using the Internet More Than Their Grandparents Did." I could be famous. However, until then, you and your kids will have to be satisfied with regular, run-of- the-mill experts. Here are some links to such people, who have volunteered to answer questions in areas such as science and technology, health and medicine, computing, the Internet, the economy, and so on. Be aware, though, that questions asked of experts over the Net are similar to prayers addressed to a supreme being: they are not always answered.

Web:
 http://www.allexperts.com/
 http://www.askanexpert.com/
 http://www.k12science.org/askanexpert.html
 http://www.sciam.com/askexpert_directory.cfm
 http://www1.askme.com/businesssplash.asp

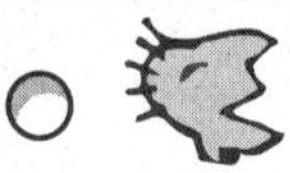

Report on How Stuff Works
by Elmo (age 8)

At school, I have a teacher who is always making us do weird stuff. Last week, she told us that we had to write a report on how something works. We were supposed to choose something around the house.

So I wrote "How a Popsicle Works". Here is what I wrote:

"You take the popsicle out of the freezer and you rip off the paper. Then you lick the popsicle until it is all gone, and all you have left is a popsicle stick. Then you throw the stick at your sister. That is how a popsicle works."

You know what? Some teachers are never happy, no matter what you do.

-Elmo

How Stuff Works

I always like to know how stuff works, and I bet you do too. Learn how car engines, televisions, cell phones, telephones, refrigerators and smoke detectors work (and even more), and it won't be long before you are the most popular pedant in your ever-increasing circle of friends.

Web:
 http://www.howstuffworks.com/

How-To Tips and Advice

There are a lot of things to understand in this world, and if you are like me, you'd like to understand them all. Of course, it isn't possible to know everything (when would you find time to play with your cat?), but you can make a good stab at it. Start with these Web sites, where you'll find all kinds of useful and interesting information about all kinds of useful and interesting topics.

Web:
 http://www.ifiknew.com/
 http://www.lifeoutlined.co.uk/
 http://www.lifetips.com/

Informative Email

It's easy to get lots of email. However, how often do you get *interesting* email? Sign up for one of these free services and, before you can calculate the square root of 991 in your head, you'll be receiving all kinds of cool stuff in your mailbox: information of all types, jokes, useful tips, trivia, quotations, recipes, sports scores, soap opera updates, and on and on and on. (By the way, the square root of 991 is approximately 31.48015247739.)

Web:

http://www.mailbits.com/
http://www.shagmail.com/
http://www.smartreminders.com/

Knowledge by Topic

Imagine you had your own research staff: a group of people, each one an expert in one particular area, who searched the Net just for you. Well, these Web guides are the next best thing. A large number of experts write articles and find resources for different categories of information. All you need to do is sit back, let someone else do the work, and pick and choose what you want. Not bad work if you can get it.

Web:

http://www.about.com/
http://www.suite101.com/

Knowledge Sharing

Do you have a question? Submit it to one of these sites and watch people as smart as you and I do their best to answer it. If you feel like assisting other people, you can answer their questions and help them out. (Actually, no one else is as smart as you and I. I just said that so they won't feel bad.)

Web:

http://www.abuzz.com/
http://www.askanowner.com/
http://www.experts-exchange.com/
http://www.pointask.com/

Online Learning

Here are places where you can find all kinds of online courses for free. Study information technology, business, humanities, math, education, science, social sciences, and more. Just the way to pass the day when the kids are at school and your computer is just begging to be used.

Web:

http://www.free-ed.net/
http://www.wannalearn.com/

So You Wanna

Here is an effervescent collection of articles on how to do all kinds of handy stuff they don't teach you at school: how to change your name, go skydiving, choose a good Scotch, be a movie extra, or read tea leaves. And there's lots more where that came from.

Web:

http://www.soyouwanna.com/

Word Detective

Enjoy the online version of a column in which the writer answers questions about words and their origins. If you enjoy learning about language and words, you will like this site. Here are some examples. (1) One guy wrote a letter because he and his girlfriend had been having an argument about whether to say "have your cake and eat it too" or "eat your cake and have it too". (2) Another person asked if "busting someone's chop" and "busting someone's hump" are the same thing. (3) A third reader who mentioned the term "old fogey" wanted to know if there were such a thing as a "young fogey". (4) And finally, there is a link to an answer to the question "Aside from 'angry' and 'hungry', what well-known English word ends in 'gry'?" By the way, the answers to these questions are (1) It doesn't matter. (2) No. (3) Yes, but people don't use the expression. (4) There are no other common words that end in "gry". The question is a well-known hoax.

Web:

http://www.word-detective.com/

LANGUAGE AND LINGUISTICS

Cliché Finder

Type in a word, any word, and if there are common clichés that use that word, they will pop up on your screen faster than a speeding crawfish. Before you can say "a wet bird never flies at night", you'll have more clichés than a nitro-powered weed whacker. If you've been racking your brain for the right word, you'll never know if you don't try, so go to this Web site and stop on a dime. It might be true that money can't buy happiness, but as I always say, "Don't worry about the horse being blind. Just load the wagon."

Web:
   http://www.westegg.com/cliche/

Computation and Language E-Print Archive

This archive provides automated access to papers and preprints relating to computational linguistics, natural language processing, speech processing, and other fields. If you are a researcher in one of these areas, you will find this Web site a valuable way to keep up on current publications and search through the journals.

Web:
   http://www.acm.org/pubs/corr/

Created Languages

Would you like to create your own language? J.R.R. Tolkien did (several, in fact), and there is also a created language, Klingon, based on the Star Trek mythos. These resources cover these languages and more, including my personal favorite, Syldavian (from the Tintin books by Hergé). I have also included resources to help you make up your own language, should you be so inclined. Bonus: In case you might find it helpful some day, here is a handy sentence in Syldavian: Kzommet micz omhz noh dascz gendarmaskaïa. ("Come with us to the police station.")

Web:
   http://www.elvish.org/resources.html
   http://www.kli.org/
   http://www.quetzal.com/conlang.html
   http://www.zompist.com/kit.html
   http://www.zompist.com/syldavian.html
   http://www.zompist.com/virtuver.htm

Endangered Languages

When cultures collide, among the first casualties are the minority languages. When one culture begins to dominate another, the minority languages are used less and less. Eventually, they die out and with them, another tiny flame in the luminosity of human culture is extinguished. Endangered languages are those that are recognized as being in danger of dying out.

Web:
   http://www.ahapunanaleo.org/OL.htm
   http://www.ogmios.org/links.htm
   http://www.tooyoo.l.u-tokyo.ac.jp/ichel/ichel.html

Majordomo Mailing List:
   List Name: endangered-languages-l
   Subscribe to: majordomo@cleo.murdoch.edu.au

Foreign Language Dictionaries

From time to time I have an immediate need to translate a particular word into another language. For example, just the other day I was wondering, what was the Dutch word for hippopotamus? All I had to do was connect to one of these online dictionaries, and before you could say "get back to work", I knew that the Dutch word for hippopotamus was nijlpaard.

Web:
   http://www.ectaco.com/online/
   http://www.foreignword.com/tools/dictsrch.htm
   http://www.june29.com//IDP/IDPsearch.html
   http://www.systransoft.com/
   http://www.word2word.com/dictionary.html
   http://www.yourdictionary.com/

Foreign Languages for Travelers

Are you going to visit a foreign country where it would help if you knew some of the most important words in its language? Just specify which language you already speak and which language you want to learn. You will then see a list of choices for phrases you can learn: basic words, numbers, shopping, travel, directions, places, times and dates. You can see a list of countries where the foreign language is spoken as well as links to related resources.

Web:
   http://www.dictionaries.travlang.com/

Foreign Language Dictionaries

You know, it's funny. As a young lad in Canada, I studied French for 10 years, and I still can't speak it fluently. And yet, in France, young children hang around in the street with no education whatsoever speaking the language like natives.

Perhaps they have access to the Foreign Language Dictionaries.

Fun Dialects

Talking normally can get boring, and when it does, I have the solution. Translate what you are saying (or what you are reading on the Web) into a fun dialect. Here is an example. Consider the dull, everyday sentence "Hi there, my name is Harley." Watch how it comes alive as it is translated in various ways. (Redneck) Howdy-doo thar, mah name is Harley. (Jive) 'Sup, dude dere, mah' dojigger be Harley. Slap mah fro! (Cockney) Oi there, my name is 'arley. (Elmer Fudd) Hi thewe, my name is Hawwey. (The Swedish Chef) Hee zeere-a, my neme-a is Herley. Bork bork bork! (Pig Latin) Ihay erethay, ymay amenay isyay Arleyhay.

Web:
   http://www.80s.com/Entertainment/ValleyURL/
   http://www.brunching.com/toys/drugslanger.html
   http://www.cs.utexas.edu/users/jbc/home/chef.html
   http://www.ibiblio.org/dbarberi/lame/
   http://www.psyclops.com/wubbler/

Usenet:
   alt.swedish.chef.bork.bork.bork

Idioms and Clichés

An idiom or a cliché is a well-known expression that has a non-literal meaning. When you learn a foreign language, the idioms and clichés drive you crazy, because they need to be memorized outright and often make no sense. What is the difference between an idiom and a cliché? When you or I use such an expression—for example, if I say that something might "drive you crazy"—it is an idiom. This is because you and I are known for our superb grasp of the language and our sense of style. However, when other people use such figures of speech, the expressions are, more often than not, trite and overused, which makes them clichés. But then, other people simply do not have the same *je ne sais quoi* that you and I do.

Web:
   http://www.comenius.com/idioms/
   http://www.english-zone.com/idioms/dictionary.html
   http://www.englishdaily626.com/idioms.html
   http://www.eslcafe.com/idioms/
   http://www.serve.com/shea/idiomlst.htm

Language Translator

These Web sites provide a wonderful service. You can type in any text you want, and a computer program will translate the text from one language to another. As you might expect, the translation is not perfect, but it is usually good enough. Moreover, it's free and it's fast. What's even more useful is that you can use this same service to translate a Web page that is written in a foreign language. Just specify a URL. The program will fetch that Web page for you and translate it automatically.

Web:
   http://babelfish.altavista.com/
   http://www.freetranslation.com/
   http://www.tranexp.com:2000/intertran
   http://www.web-a-dex.com/translate.htm

Do you like weirdness? Check out "Bizarre".

A B C D E F G H I J K L M N O P Q R S T U V W X Y Z

Languages of the World

Here are some collections of information about the various languages spoken by humans and other animals. If you are interested in any particular language or country, I guarantee you can find information that will astonish you. For example, did you know that in the United States, there are 213 languages, 176 of which are living, 35 of which are extinct, and two that are a second language only with no mother tongue speakers?

Web:
http://babel.uoregon.edu/yamada/guides.html
http://www.ethnologue.com/web.asp
http://www.evertype.com/langlist.html
http://www.languages-on-the-web.com/

Linguistic Talk and General Discussion

The Usenet groups are where scholars of linguistics hang out to discuss the scientific and historical study of human language. Get in on some hot and heavy discussion of Latin declensions or a quick and dirty comparison of Frisian to Old English. To help you participate in the discussion, I have included a Web site that contains the FAQ (frequently asked question list) for the **sci.lang** group, as well as another site that contains information about the many linguistic mailing lists on the Net.

Web:
http://www.linguistlist.org/interact-index.html
http://www.zompist.com/langfaq.html

Usenet:
alt.language.english.spelling.reform
humanities.language.sanskrit
sci.lang
sci.lang.translation

Linguistics

Linguistics is the study of human speech. Linguistics concerns itself with various areas: the structure of languages, the history of languages, how languages relate to one another, and the purpose of language within a culture. To understand the structure of languages, study grammar (rules describing how words and their components are combined), phonetics (how sounds are produced, combined and represented) and morphology (the structure and form of words). These Web sites will help you find a large variety of linguistic resources on the Net.

Web:
http://www.allianceforlifelonglearning.org/er/cla00070.html
http://www.ling.rochester.edu/linglinks.html
http://www.linguistlist.org/
http://www.ncbe.gwu.edu/links/langcult/linguistics.htm
http://www.sil.org/linguistics/glossaryoflinguisticterms/

Slang

No matter where you are, you can't be really cool until you know the local slang. I can help you avoid this problem. Just take a look at these Web sites, where you'll find all kinds of slang from all kinds of different places. Never again will you find yourself confused in Canada when someone comes up to you and says, "I was in Tronno, eh, and I met this chick from Kay-beck with a two-four." All it means is "I was in Toronto, and I met a girl from Quebec who had a case of beer." (Interestingly enough, in all the years I lived in Toronto, this never actually happened to me. But then, I spent most of my time in the library reading good books.)

Web:
http://www.boston-online.com/glossary.html
http://www.home.istar.ca/~awright/WORDS1.HTM
http://www.hurricane.net/~wizard/19a.html
http://www.intranet.csupomona.edu/~jasanders/slang/
http://www.notam.uio.no/~hcholm/altlang/
http://www.peevish.co.uk/slang/
http://www.sabram.com/Slang/slang.html
http://www.slanguage.com/

Word-a-Day

If someone calls you a "wowser" and you don't know whether to feel congratulated or insulted, then you might need to improve your vocabulary by checking out this word-a-day site. Impress your friends and co-workers. Don't be caught verbally unaware.

Web:
  http://home.mn.rr.com/wwftd/
  http://www.dictionary.com/wordoftheday/
  http://www.m-w.com/cgi-bin/mwwod.pl/
  http://www.oed.com/cgi/display/wotd/
  http://www.wordsmith.org/awad/

Word-a-Day

We all know that having a big vocabulary is essential if you want to know a lot of words. Still, there is no royal road to knowledge, and if you want to know a lot of words you are just going to have to know a lot of words. The easy way is to submerge yourself in a serious word-a-day commitment, and soon you too will be able to tergiversate with the best of them.

American Sign Language

When I was younger and living in Berkeley, I studied ASL (American Sign Language) for a semester, and I found it to be the most beautiful language I have ever seen. If I could pick a second language in which to be fluent, it would be ASL. (Unfortunately, I am not one to pick up second languages. For over 10 years, the Canadian government tried to get me to learn French, and they failed miserably.)

Web:
  http://www.aslinfo.com/
  http://www.handspeak.com/

Listserv Mailing List:
  List Name: teachasl
  Subscribe to: listserv@admin.humberc.on.ca

Arabic

If Arabic is on your list of things to learn before retirement, you are in luck. Download audio lessons, films, music and pictures. Or if you don't have time for a multimedia experience, check out some vocabulary and nifty-looking Arabic fonts.

Web:
  http://cecilmarie.web.prw.net/arabworld/arabic/
  http://www.i-cias.com/babel/arabic/

Usenet:
  alt.languages.arabic

British English

Although it seems as if the English and the Americans speak the same language, there are a lot of words that are used differently in each country. For example, an Englishman who has had a little too much to drink may think nothing of eating a chip butty. An American wouldn't know a chip butty if it bit him in the face. To help you avoid unnecessary confusion—or perhaps create some intentional confusion of your own—here are some resources to fill the transatlantic gaps in your vocabulary. (By the way, a chip butty is a bread and butter sandwich made with French fried potatoes.)

Web:
  http://www.hps.com/~tpg/ukdict/
  http://www.peak.org/~jeremy/dictionary/dict.html
  http://www.quinion.com/words/
  http://www.uta.fi/FAST/US1/REF/us1refs.html

Chinese

Chinese is the most widely spoken language in the world. In total, the various dialects (varieties) of Chinese are spoken by well over a billion people. By far, the most popular dialect is Mandarin, which is the primary language of about three-quarters of the world's Chinese speakers. Mandarin is spoken in China, Brunei, Cambodia, Indonesia, Malaysia, Mongolia, the Philippines, Singapore, South Africa, Taiwan and Thailand. English speakers find Chinese a particularly difficult language to learn, because the language has nothing in common with the European languages upon which English is based. For example, instead of using a simple alphabet, Chinese employs thousands of different symbols, each of which represents one or more words or ideas. This requires a student to memorize a huge amount of material just to become literate. In addition, Chinese is a tonal language, which means that words must be pronounced with an exact tone. A specific sound, when pronounced with different tones, will often have completely different meanings and, unless you are a native Chinese speaker, it is almost impossible to discern or reproduce the tones properly.

Web:
http://www.deall.ohio-state.edu/chan.9/c-links2.htm
http://www.mandarintools.com/

Usenet:
alt.chinese.story
alt.chinese.text
alt.chinese.text.big5
alt.chinese.text.hz
alt.languages.mandarin
alt.usage.chinese

Cyrillic Alphabet

The Cyrillic alphabet is used to write Russian and certain other Slavic languages. The name comes from St. Cyril who, in 863 A.D.—along with his brother St. Methodius—introduced the alphabet during their missionary work among the southern Slavs. Little did they know that, one day, their work would be used to translate this book into Russian.

Web:
http://www.friends-partners.org/friends/cyrillic/

Czech

The Czech language (spoken in the Czech Republic) is a Slavic language with roots in the Indo-European family of languages. Here is information about Czech as well as an English-Czech dictionary. Mluvite anglicky? Dekuji.

Web:
http://www.bohemica.com/
http://www.muselik.com/czech/czau.html

Usenet:
alt.languages.czech

Dutch

Dutch, the language of the Netherlands (Holland) is spoken by about 20 million people in Holland, Belgium, France and Suriname, making it the 48th most widely spoken language in the world. Many words in Dutch are similar to their English counterparts but, overall, the language is quite different from English. Still, if you are an American visiting Holland, you don't need to worry: virtually all Dutch people speak English as a second language (which, personally, I think is very considerate of them).

Web:
http://dictionaries.travlang.com/DutchEnglish/
http://www.learndutch.org/
http://www.notam.uio.no/~hcholm/altlang/ht/
  Dutch.html

Usenet:
alt.reddingsbrigade

Eastern European Languages

Would you like to learn basic words and phrases in an Eastern European language? Just select a language and you will be shown a small but useful list of words in that language. Although the vocabulary is limited, you can at least learn enough to stay out of trouble. The word lists are available in Albanian, Croatian, Estonian, Latvian, Polish, Russian, Slovak, Bulgarian, Czech, Hungarian, Lithuanian, Romanian, Serbian and Slovenian. As they say in Lithuanian, "Nesuprantu".

Web:
http://www.cusd.claremont.edu/~tkroll/EastEur/

Usenet:
alt.pl
alt.pl.uzywki

English

The sun may have set on the British Empire, but their language lives on around the world. Here are a variety of interesting resources relating to the English language. To discuss English, try Usenet and the mailing lists. Interesting true fact: More Harley Hahn books are written in English than in any other language.

Web:
http://work.ucsd.edu:5141/cgi-bin/http_webster/
http://www.ebbs.english.vt.edu/hel/
http://www.english-at-home.com/
http://www.thediscouragingword.com/
http://www.wsu.edu/~brians/errors/

Usenet:
alt.english.usage
bit.listserv.words-l

Listserv Mailing List:
List Name: words-l
Subscribe to: listserv@listserv.uga.edu

Esperanto

Esperanto is a language invented by the Polish doctor L.L. Zamenhof in the late 19th century. His idea was that if everyone spoke the same language, we would all get along better, and war would be much less likely. The idea of an artificial language is not uncommon: hundreds of such languages have been proposed in the last few centuries. Perhaps one of the most interesting was Solresol, developed by Jean Francois Sudre (1866). Its vocabulary was based on the notes of the musical scale, making it possible to sing as well as speak the language. Esperanto is the most well-known and successful artificial language. Because it is based on the European Romance languages, Esperanto is difficult to learn for people with a completely different mother tongue (Chinese, Japanese, Russian, and so on). However, as languages go, Esperanto is straightforward and sensible, and there are many enthusiasts around the world who enjoy speaking and promoting the language. Esperanto trivia: The 1965 low-budget horror movie "Incubus", starring a young William Shatner, was filmed entirely in Esperanto. (It has English sub-titles.)

Web:
http://www.esperanto.net/veb/faq.html
http://www.esperanto.org/

Usenet:
alt.talk.esperanto
alt.uu.lang.esperanto.misc
soc.culture.esperanto

French

French is a member of the family of Romance languages, and thus has much in common with Spanish, Italian, and Portuguese. French is the 11th most widely used language in the world. Of course, French is spoken throughout France, but you also find the language in parts of Belgium and Switzerland, as well as in areas that were formerly under French control, such as Algeria and French Polynesia (including Tahiti). There is also a form of French spoken in the province of Quebec in Canada, as well as a Creole version used by Cajun speakers in the south-central United States.

Web:
http://etext.lib.virginia.edu/french.html
http://globegate.utm.edu/french/globegate_mirror/
   oral.html
http://polyglot.lss.wisc.edu/lss/lang/french.html
http://www.jump-gate.com/languages/french/
http://www.lamc.utexas.edu/tex/

Usenet:
alt.french

Listproc Mailing List:
List Name: frenchtalk
Subscribe to: listproc@list.cren.net

Majordomo Mailing List:
List Name: cerclefrancais
Subscribe to: majordomo@lists.uoregon.edu

Majordomo Mailing List:
List Name: francais
Subscribe to: majordomo@bagira.iit.bme.hu

IRC:
#francais (EFnet)
#french (EFnet)

Gaelic

Gaelic is the English word used to describe Irish Gaelic, Manx Gaelic and Scottish Gaelic, the three languages that form one half of the Celtic language family group. This site offers examples of spoken Gaelic, a short history of the Celts, mailing list archives, lists of Gaelic books and tapes, Irish National Radio news, and links to many other Celtic-related topics and resources. The mailing list will allow you to experience Gaelic interactively.

Web:
   http://www.daltai.com/home.htm

Listserv Mailing List:
   List Name: gaelic-l
   Subscribe to: listserv@listserv.heanet.ie

Going to Maui soon? Perhaps a copy of the Hawaiian dictionary would help you. It really helps to be able to talk to the natives in their own language when you need to say, "Can I please have a condo that does not overlook the parking lot?"

German

German, the 9th most widely spoken language in the world, is the mother tongue of about 100 million people. German is the national language of Germany and Austria, as well as one of the four official languages of Switzerland (spoken by about 64% of the population). (In case you are wondering, the other three official Swiss languages are French [19%], Italian [8%] and Romansh [less than 1%]). Although many German and English words sound similar, there are significant differences between the languages. For example, German nouns (like Latin nouns) have different forms depending on how they are used. What I find really odd is the German habits of capitalizing all their nouns and placing verbs at the end of sentences. (However, let's not make the Germans feel bad. It may just be that they are foreigners, and they don't know any better.)

Web:
   http://dict.leo.org/
   http://etext.lib.virginia.edu/german.html
   http://www.germanfortravellers.com/learn/
   http://www.iee.et.tu-dresden.de/cgi-bin/cgiwrap/
      wernerr/search.sh

Usenet:
   alt.usage.german

IRC:
   #german (Undernet)

Greek

The word "Greek" actually refers to two different, but related, languages. First, there is modern Greek, the language spoken today by more than 10 million people in Greece, a majority of the people on Cyprus, as well as Greeks around the world. Ancient Greek—the language of Homer and Aristotle—is a family of dialects that was used over two thousand years ago. These Web sites have many resources related to modern and ancient Greek. If you want to know about the language, there is something here for you—whether you are a serious scholar or just planning a vacation trip to the Greek Islands.

Web:
   http://etext.lib.virginia.edu/gr-off.html
   http://www.greek-language.com/
   http://www.kypros.org/greek/

Usenet:
   alt.languages.greek

If you really feel like it, go ahead and have a cow. (See "Agriculture" for details.)

Hawaiian

The Hawaiian language has five vowels (a, e, i, o, u) and only seven consonants (h, k, l, m, n, p, t, w). Thus, for English speakers, Hawaiian words, at first, can look confusing. For example, ho'alohaloha means "to make love" or "to give thanks"; elemakule means "an old man"; and hoaloha means "a friend". (I'll leave it to you to put these words together into a sentence.) Would you like to learn a bit of Hawaiian? Give it a try—I bet you'll enjoy it. By the way, my favorite Hawaiian word is nananana ("spider").

Web:
   http://www.andhawaii.com/hawaii/vacation/culture/
      trad.html
   http://www.olelo.hawaii.edu/

Usenet:
   alt.languages.hawaiian

Hindi

In India, Hindi is spoken by about 480 million people (180 million as a mother tongue, 300 million as a second language). Hindi is an especially expressive language. A poet writing in Hindi can use simple words to convey sophisticated emotional overtones. There are also many beautiful Hindi songs which are loved by people around the world. (In English, of course, we have our own lovely songs, such as "Satisfaction" and "Rudolf the Red-Nosed Reindeer".) Here are some Internet resources to help you learn about Hindi and the cultures in which it is spoken.

Web:
   http://philae.sas.upenn.edu/Hindi/hindi.html
   http://www.ukindia.com/zhin001.htm

Usenet:
   alt.languages.hindi

Icelandic

Icelandic, the official language of Iceland, is a Scandinavian language that is the purest descendent of Old Norse. Here are sites for learning about the language. Hint to guys: If you are traveling in Iceland, and you meet a beautiful young woman, here is the right thing to say: "Þú ert engill af himni ofan. Ég hef aldrei séð yndislegri konu. Getur pabbi þinn lúbarið mig?"

Web:
   http://babel.uoregon.edu/yamada/guides/
      icelandic.html
   http://www.eng.ysu.edu/~jck/nemendja/islenska/
      #internet
   http://www.ismal.hi.is/ob/index_en.html

Usenet:
   alt.usage.icelandic

Italian

Italian is spoken by about 40 million people, mostly in Italy. It is the 27th most popular language in the world. To English speakers, Italian is relatively easy to learn and has a beautiful, melodious sound. In case you are ever in Italy, here is a sentence for you to try out when you meet a policeman: *Ho bevuto un bicchiere di troppo, e sono al limite della sopportazione.* ("Thank you for being a guardian of the peace and protecting me during my visit.")

Web:
   http://academic.brooklyn.cuny.edu/modlang/carasi/
      site/
   http://www.cyberitalian.com/
   http://www.eleaston.com/italian.html

Usenet:
   alt.usage.italiano

IRC:
   #italia (Undernet)

The Net cares.

A B C D E F G H I J K **L** M N O P Q R S T U V W X Y Z

Japanese

Is your kanji a bit weak? Or do you just need a bit of help with pronunciation? These resources will help you with Japanese vocabulary and pronunciation. So the next time you go out for sushi, you won't have to just point at the menu and say, "I'll have that thing." You can ask for raw tuna with such a good accent, the fish will sit up and bow to you.

Web:
   http://www.japanese-online.com/language/
   http://www.japanesetutor.com/
   http://www.savergen.com/onldict/jap.html

Usenet:
   alt.japanese.misc
   alt.japanese.text
   sci.lang.japan

IRC:
   #japan (Undernet)

Korean

Korean is an interesting language, because there are two distinct levels of formality, and young people must use the more formal expressions when addressing their elders. Moreover, within everyday discourse, there are many markers that indicate the relationships between the people who are speaking. For example, my copy editor Lydia is of Korean descent. When she talks to her older sister Debbie, she is supposed to address her as Debbie-ohnee. If she had an older brother, say, Harley, she would address him as Harley-opah. (She should only be so lucky.) Here is one more example: there is a specific term for your father's younger married brother's wife (chah-goon oh-mo-nee). Interesting note: In English, Lydia's last name is Hearn and my last name is Hahn, but in Korean, both names would be pronounced "Hawn" and would be written the same way. (Is that cosmic, or what? I wonder if maybe I *am* her older brother. She is certainly cute enough.)

Web:
   http://korean.sogang.ac.kr/
   http://www.arts.monash.edu.au/korean/centre/
      resources/
   http://www.interedu.go.kr/
   http://www.langintro.com/kintro/

Usenet:
   alt.talk.korean

Latin

Latin is the language spoken by the ancient Romans, although the Latin we learn today has been modified over the years. Latin is important for three main reasons. First, many ancient documents and books are written in Latin. Second, Latin is the basis of our modern Romance languages (such as French, Spanish, Italian and Portuguese). Finally, Latin is important to the traditions and liturgy of the Roman Catholic Church.

Web:
   http://www.csbsju.edu/library/internet/latin.html
   http://www.nd.edu/~archives/latgramm.htm

Usenet:
   alt.language.latin
   alt.languages.latin

Middle English

Quick, read this right away:

Whan that aprill with his shoures soote
The droghte of march hath perced to the roote,
And bathed every veyne in swich licour
Of which vertu engendred is the flour;

You have just read the beginning of Chaucer's 17,000-line epic poem Canterbury Tales.

Don't you wish you could understand it? Well, you can. All you have to do is learn Middle English or read a translation into modern English. Check with the Net.

The time you take will be worth it, as Chaucer is considered to be one of the great authors of all time (although, as you can see, he did have a problem with spelling).

Middle English

After the Norman Conquest (in 1066), the use of Anglo-Saxon—the native language of England—was diminished significantly in favor of French, which became not only the official language, but the language of polite society. Anglo-Saxon was depressed into an illiterate dialect, which underwent rapid and radical changes, emerging in a new form that we now call Middle English. The period of Middle English lasted from 1100 to 1500 (give or take a day or two). If you are interested in Middle English, here is a resource where you can look at a nice collection of literature. My favorite work is "The Harley Lyrics", transcribed from Manuscript Harley 2253 from the British Museum MS. Here is a direct quote: "Middelerd for mon wes mad / vnmihti aren is meste mede". I'm not sure what it means but it sounds important.

Web:

  http://etext.lib.virginia.edu/mideng.browse.html

Native American Languages

There are several hundred different Native American languages. These languages can be categorized into a small number of major language groups. For example, the Athabascan group includes the languages of the Athabascans (in Alaska and northwest Canada) and the Apaches and Navaho (in the southwest U.S.). Even as late as the 1950s, young Native Americans were discouraged from speaking Indian languages and were often punished when they did so. However, in recent years, Native Americans have shown a strong interest in preserving and encouraging the use of their languages, which are now taught actively within many native communities.

Web:

  http://www.hanksville.org/NAresources/indices/
      NAlanguage.html
  http://www.nativenashville.com/tutor_syllabary.htm
  http://www.zompist.com/indianwd.html

Usenet:

  alt.languages.lakota

Pronunciation in the American South

Unless you grew up in the United States, don't even think about trying to understand this Web site. It's full of a great many colloquial pronunciations common in the southern part of the United States. The words are there somewhere, but unless you are from the South (or have watched a great many Andy Griffith reruns), you may not get it. For example, to truly appreciate modern American culture, you need to be able to understand statements like: "Lawd willing and the crik don't rise, I sho do hope that thuh President don't get us kilt by sum farn gummit. He's a nice enough feller, but he can lilac a dawg."

Web:

  http://www.netsquirrel.com/crispen/word.html

Russian

Russian is the 7th most popular language in the world, spoken by over 170 million people. Russian is a phonetic language, which means that it is pronounced exactly as it is written. However, the Russians use the Cyrillic alphabet, which looks completely different from the English alphabet. Learning how to read and understand Russian proficiently can take a long time, but it is worth it. Once you learn Russian, you will be able to read the original version of "War and Peace" by Leo Tolstoy (1828-1910). If you adopt this as your goal when you are young, it can work out nicely, because you can spend the first half of your life learning Russian, and the second half of your life reading the book.

Web:

  http://www.departments.bucknell.edu/russian/
      language/
  http://www.freedict.com/onldict/rus.html
  http://www.masterrussian.com/

Usenet:

  alt.tanya.shalayeva
  alt.uu.lang.russian.misc

IRC:

  #russian (DALnet, EFnet, Undernet)

Serbian

It has been said that Serbian is one of the easiest languages to learn to write because it is so phonetic. See if this is true, by brushing up on your Serbian as well as the Cyrillic and Latin alphabets.

Web:
  http://www.krstarica.com/dictionary/
  http://www.nypl.org/branch/central_units/d/f/
      language/serbian.htm
  http://www.travlang.com/languages/serbian

Slovak

As early as the 11th century, Slovakia was associated with Hungary. Following World War I, the Slovaks separated from Hungary and joined the Czechs (from Bohemia) to form Czechoslovakia. From 1939 to 1945—thanks to the invading Germans—the Slovaks and Czechs were "declared" independent of one another. After the war, they rejoined to reform Czechoslovakia. Finally, however, on January 1, 1993, the Slovaks separated for the last time and formed their own country, Slovakia. Throughout it all, they managed to create and maintain their own language, Slovak, which is now the official language of their country. If you plan to visit, here is a nice glossary of Slovakian words to make your trip a pleasant one.

Web:
  http://slovakia.eunet.sk/slovakia/nat.asp

Usenet:
  alt.languages.slovak

Spanish

I studied Spanish in high school, and I sure wish I had the Net back then: lots of Spanish language resources as well as an IRC channel to talk to people in Spanish. Hint: If you are not sure what to talk about, say: "No quiero quedarme en casa este fin de semana. Vamos a salir para bailar."

Web:
  http://mld.ursinus.edu/~jarana/ejercicios/
  http://www.spanishunlimited.com/
  http://www.studyspanish.com/tutorial.htm

Usenet:
  alt.language.spanish
  alt.languages.spanish
  alt.usage.spanish

IRC:
  #spanish (Undernet)

Tagalog

Tagalog (pronounced Ta-gaw'-log) is one of the major languages spoken in the Philippines, mostly by people from the Tagalog regions on the main island of Luzon and in Manila, the national capital. Tagalog serves as a base for Filipino, and has a strong affinity with Malay languages. Over the years, Tagalog has incorporated a significant number of Spanish words and expressions, and also includes words and phrases rooted in English and Chinese. In the United States, Tagalog is the seventh most commonly spoken language, and the second most commonly spoken Asian language.

Web:
  http://www.copewithcytokines.de/tagalog/cope.cgi
  http://www.omniglot.com/writing/tagalog.htm
  http://www.seasite.niu.edu/tagalog/
      tagalog_mainpage.htm

LAW

Class Action Litigation

In the United States, a class action is a lawsuit initiated by one or more plaintiffs (called the class proponents) on behalf of a group of individuals, all of whom have the same complaint. For example, someone who is a smoker with hiccups might bring a class action suit against the tobacco companies on behalf of all the smokers with hiccups. Class action suits are complex and can take a long time to settle. Sometimes the suits result in a significant award for the plaintiffs, but often they don't. The lawyers, however, usually find a way to do well for themselves.

Web:
  http://www.citizen.org/litigation/briefs/class_action/
  http://www.classaction.com/
  http://www.classactionlitigation.com/contents.htm
  http://www.notice.com/classactions/

Of course you're right.

Computers and the Law

Whenever a new technology becomes important in our culture, it puts a large number of new demands upon our legal system. The world of computers and the Internet have raised many legal issues: some of them brand new, some of them novel variations of existing legal doctrine. These Web sites contain a wealth of information related to legal issues and computing, especially the Internet. If you have heard about a famous case involving the Net, you can probably find the details here.

Web:
  http://www.eff.org/pub/Legal/
  http://www.priweb.com/internetlawlib/95.htm

Usenet:
  misc.legal.computing

Copyrights

A copyright protects the writings of an author against copying. In this sense, "writings" refers not only to books and printed publications, but to software, music, recordings, movies, and so on. In most cases, copyright is automatically vested in the creator of the work, although the legal rights can be assigned or sold to someone else. For example, I own the copyright to this book, which I license to my publisher. To help you understand copyright and its nuances, here is a collection of Internet copyright resources. In addition, I have included the Web site for the United States Copyright Office, which will allow you to access official U.S. information regarding works registered for copyright since 1978.

Web:
  http://www.aipla.org/
  http://www.benedict.com/contents.htm
  http://www.law.cornell.edu/topics/copyright.html
  http://www.loc.gov/copyright/rb.html

Usenet:
  misc.int-property

Listserv Mailing List:
  List Name: uscopyright
  Subscribe to: listserv@loc.gov

Class Action Litigation

Would you like to join me in a class action lawsuit?

My idea is that everyone who reads this book should get together and sue all the people in the world who do not read this book. Just before it goes to trial, we can settle out of court for $10 each, plus breakfast in bed for a year.

What do you think? Isn't it time that someone put the legal system to work on behalf of the people?

Expert Witnesses

Every now and then, you hear about a trial in which some "expert" says such-and-such. Do you ever wonder who are these experts? There are many people who act as "expert witnesses". They get large amounts of money to study the details of a case and render an opinion. In most cases, experts are paid by one side or the other, and, as you might expect, the expert testimony is slanted toward the needs of whomever is paying. If you need an expert witness, or if you might want to be an expert witness, here is information that will help you.

Web:
  http://www.expertpages.com/

Free Legal Information

My experience is that the best source for legal advice is an experienced lawyer. Before you choose a lawyer, get at least three recommendations (from other lawyers in your community, if possible) and interview each candidate. Most lawyers will talk to you once for free. However, regardless of whether or not you have a lawyer, it will always help you to understand the law as it pertains to your situation and what options you have. These Web sites have articles and advice for consumers on many different legal topics: taxes, accidents, family law, personal injury, real estate law, estate planning, and more. Remember, though, if it's important, you need a good lawyer. (This is especially true for estate planning.)

Web:
  http://resources.lawinfo.com/
  http://www.cafelaw.com/
  http://www.nolo.com/lawcenter/ency/

International Criminal Law

There is crime all over the world, and as a Net person, you can have access to all the information you want related to this popular global pastime. So if you're bored with the local crime in your area, check out these web sites to see what the international criminal justice community is doing.

Web:
   http://www.asil.org/resource/crim1.htm
   http://www.odccp.org/crime_prevention.html

International Law Students Association

Law students interested in international law can check out information about the International Law Students Association and get links to a library with online texts, law journals, documents about international law and related resources.

Web:
   http://www.ilsa.org/

International Trade Law

When goods and services are sold across international boundaries, an enormous number of laws, rules and regulations come into play. These resources will help you find information about sales of goods and services, protection of intellectual property, carriage of goods, insurance, payment mechanisms, agency, limitation periods, and other areas of international law.

Web:
   http://www.law.cornell.edu/topics/trade.html
   http://www.lexmercatoria.org/
   http://www.llrx.com/features/trade3.htm

Law Firms

There are a large number of law firms on the Net, and here is a list of many of them. Don't be surprised if, soon, being on the Net is a prerequisite to running a law practice. I can tell you that all of my lawyers are on the Net. (Now, if I can only get them to use PGP, so we can send secret stuff by email.)

Web:
   http://www.directory.findlaw.com/

Law Resources

For the law student and legal professional, here is a useful collection of law resources. You will find information about commercial law, defense funds, human rights, institutes, intellectual property, international trade, law firms, legal agencies, libraries, newsletters, Supreme Court decisions, and much more.

Web:
   http://www.findlaw.com/
   http://www.law.cornell.edu/
   http://www.law.indiana.edu/v-lib/
   http://www.lawsonline.com/
   http://www.lpig.org/
   http://www.wwlia.org/

Law Schools

The great thing about going to law school is that, when you graduate, you will be in a profession that is so popular that people like to tell lots of jokes about it. So, before you commit yourself to one school or another, do enough research to make sure that your school is worthy enough that people will want to make jokes about it.

Web:
   http://www.abanet.org/legaled/approvedlawschools/
      approved.html
   http://www.ilrg.com/schools.html

Usenet:
   bit.listserv.lawsch-l

Law Talk and General Discussion

It's Saturday night and you are anxious to discuss freedom of religion, libel and the concept of invasion of privacy with someone. When you have no place to go and you are just itching to talk law, check out Usenet, where you will find lawyers, law students and lawyer wannabes chatting about legalities.

Usenet:
  alt.philosophy.law
  misc.legal
  misc.legal.moderated

Lawyer Jokes

A guy is standing at a bar talking to a fellow he just met. "You want a good laugh?" he says. "Listen to this joke. This lawyer has—" "Hold on," says the other fellow, "I want you to know that I'm a lawyer, and I don't think it's fair that everyone makes fun of lawyers. I would be glad to hear your joke, but I do get tired of people making jokes about my profession. Why does it always have to be a lawyer? Why can't you tell a joke about a doctor, or an airline pilot, or a plumber?" "Okay," says the first guy, "I'll tell it your way. This plumber has just graduated from law school and he decides to sue his mother..."

Web:
  http://members.aol.com/twh427/lawyer.htm
  http://www.nolo.com/humor/jokes/
  http://www.premack.com/joke.htm

Legal Dictionaries

I love to read Perry Mason books, and I learn a lot about the law by doing so. Every now and then, I encounter a legal term I don't understand. One of the terms I saw over and over was *res gestae*, but I couldn't figure out what it meant from the context. I asked my lawyer, but he didn't know. Then I asked my brother (who is a lawyer), and he didn't know either. However, I was finally able to satisfy my curiosity by using the online legal dictionaries at these Web sites. Now I am prepared in case my lawyer or my brother call me for legal advice.

Web:
  http://www.duhaime.org/diction.htm
  http://www.nolo.com/lawcenter/dictionary/
    wordindex.cfm

Legal Documents Online

We all know that there is no substitute for expert legal advice. We also know that expert legal advice can cost a great deal of money. The resources at these Web sites can help you create some commonly used legal documents—such as a last will and testament, a living will, a durable financial power of attorney, and so on—for free. Here is a suggestion. Before you have your attorney draw up a legal document, see if it is available at these Web sites. If so, create one for yourself and print it out. Read it carefully before you visit your attorney, and take it with you when you go to his office. By learning a bit about the issues in advance and reading over a typical document, the whole thing will be faster and less expensive.

Web:
  http://www.ilrg.com/forms/
  http://www.legaldocs.com/~usalaw/misc-s.htm

Patents

A patent protects the right to use an invention. In the United States, there are three main types of patents: Utility Patents (machines, processes, etc.), Design Patents (design for a manufactured article), and Plant Patents (new varieties of plants). With respect to computers, patents are issued not only for new hardware, but for specific software and computer algorithms. To help you understand patents and how they work, here are some useful resources, including the Web site of the U.S. Patent and Trademark Offices, as well as a site at which you can search for and examine existing patents.

Web:
  http://www.law.cornell.edu/topics/patent.html
  http://www.patentdatabase.com/
  http://www.patentlawlinks.com/
  http://www.patentlawnet.com/
  http://www.uspto.gov/main/patents.htm

Publishing Law

You may not know it, but as soon as you write something, you automatically own the copyright. Unfortunately, most of publishing is not that simple. If you are a writer or publisher, you need to understand something of the laws and rules that govern your business. I use a good contract lawyer who reads and comments on every contract that enters my life *before* I sign it. I encourage you to do the same.

Web:
  http://www.publaw.com/

Supreme Court Rulings

With Project Hermes, the United States Supreme Court makes its opinions and rulings available in electronic format within minutes of their release. Moreover, you can obtain a copy of an opinion as a word processor document. Isn't this great? You can download a Supreme Court opinion and then use your word processor to make any changes you want. Talk about participatory democracy!

Web:

http://supct.law.cornell.edu/supct/
http://www.findlaw.com/casecode/supreme.html

Trade Secrets

There's little that is more pleasurable than hearing a secret that you aren't supposed to hear. If you like secrets, especially trade secrets, take a look at the trade secrets resources on the Internet. You can get information on unfair competition, trade secret protection programs, investigations, nondisclosure and confidentiality agreements, inevitable disclosure doctrines, how to protect intellectual property rights, and information on computer software and anti-trust guidelines.

Web:

http://www.execpc.com/~mhallign/

Supreme Court Rulings

Have you ever been in the situation of being introduced to the man or woman of your dreams, getting into a wonderful conversation, and then all of a sudden having that person turn you down like a bedspread because you have no knowledge of recent Supreme Court rulings? Fortunately, this all-too-common occurrence need not happen to you. All you need to do is take the simple precaution of checking on the Net for new Supreme Court opinions every day when you get up. Never again will you lose out on the relationship of a lifetime because of poor preparation.

Trademarks

A trademark is a word, name or symbol used to distinguish the source of specific services or goods. Trademarks do not have to be registered. However, if you do register a trademark, you have more protection against people using it for their own products. Here is official information from the United States Patent and Trademark Offices, as well as some other trademark-related resources you will find useful.

Web:

http://www.ggmark.com/
http://www.intelproplaw.com/Trademark/
http://www.lib.lsu.edu/sci/ptdl/tmsearch.htm
http://www.uspto.gov/main/trademarks.htm

United States Code

In the United States, there are a huge number of federal laws, each of which is passed by Congress (the House of Representatives and the Senate) and signed into law by the President. To keep track of all these laws, a department called the Office of the Law Revision Counsel (operating under the auspices of the House of Representatives) prepares and publishes all the federal laws of the United States. This corpus is called the United States Code, and you can read it and search it whenever you want. Wow! (Or as Robert Louis Stevenson put it, "The world is so full of a number of things / I'm sure we should all be as happy as kings.")

Web:

http://uscode.house.gov/
http://www.access.gpo.gov/congress/cong013.html
http://www.priweb.com/internetlawlib/
http://www4.law.cornell.edu/uscode/

LIBRARIES

American Library Association

There are more than 122,000 libraries in the United States, of which about 16,000 are public libraries. The American Library Association (ALA) is the oldest and largest library association in the world, serving librarians from every type of library in the U.S. The ALA is more than a professional organization. It is the chief advocate for the American people with respect to the quality of library and information services.

Web:

http://www.ala.org/

Cataloguing Talk and General Discussion

It's not a job that most people envy—cataloguing and keeping track of all those books. It takes someone with patience, perseverance and a good sense of organization. Those are the kind of people who hang out in this Usenet group. Check out the raging debates over the modality and paradigms of cataloguing. The mailing list is for the discussion of automated methods of cataloguing.

Usenet:
  bit.listserv.autocat

Listserv Mailing List:
  List Name: autocat
  Subscribe to: listserv@listserv.acsu.buffalo.edu

Dewey Decimal System

The Dewey Decimal system for the classification of nonfiction library material was developed in 1876 by an American librarian named Melvil Dewey. Dewey created the classification scheme based on his understanding of human knowledge in Europe and the United States. Although the Dewey Decimal System has undergone modifications, the main design has proved remarkably enduring for well over one hundred years, and is used widely throughout North America and Europe. The name "Decimal System" comes from the idea that all knowledge is divided into ten major categories, numbered 000 through 900. Within a category, sub-categories are assigned a specific three-digit number. More detailed specification is expressed by extra numbers following a decimal point. For example, the social sciences all lie within the 300 division: economics is 330, labor economics is 331, and career information is 331.702.

Web:
  http://www.oclc.org/oclc/fp/
  http://www.tnrdlib.bc.ca/dewey.html

Internet Public Library

There are lots of interesting bits of information at the Internet Public Library. This great collection includes reference material, information on youth services and services for librarians and information professionals, and an education division. Librarian services include reviews, professional development, on-the-job resources, and weekly news.

Web:
  http://www.ipl.org/

Librarian Resources

Librarians have more need for information than just about anybody else on the planet. Moreover, they have to know where to look for specific pieces of information and how to find them fast. These resources are put together for librarians by librarians.

Web:
  http://www.ex.ac.uk/library/wwwlibs.html
  http://www.itcompany.com/inforetriever/
  http://www.libraryspot.com/

Usenet:
  bit.listserv.circplus
  soc.libraries.talk

Dewey Decimal System

Libraries Around the World

Librarians work hard to collect, maintain and make available massive amounts of information. As you might expect, there are a great many libraries around the world that have Web sites. Browse through these lists, and you will be impressed as to how many libraries are on the Net. Truly, librarians are among the leaders of the information revolution.

Web:
  http://ourworld.compuserve.com/homepages/
    smilne6/libcats.htm
  http://sunsite.berkeley.edu/libweb/
  http://www.bookwire.com/bookwire/libraries/
    libraries.html
  http://www.libdex.com/

Library and Information Science

If there is anything in the world that you want to know, ask a librarian. Library and information science turns ordinary mortals into oracles of facts. Even if they don't know it off the tops of their heads, librarians will know where to find what you are looking for. Join the discussion on librarianship from a technical and a philosophical point of view.

Listserv Mailing List:
  List Name: libres
  Subscribe to: listserv@listserv.kent.edu

Library Catalogs

When you need to find something in an academic library, this is the place to start. You can select from an enormous number of online catalogs, and then search for whatever you want in the privacy of your own home. For example, I was able to determine that the National Library of Wales has 12 of my books, including the new ones. Mississippi State University, on the other hand, has only 2 of my older books. Interestingly enough, the per capita income in Wales is $15,473,137 a year, while the per capita income in Mississippi is only $14.23 a year. Draw your own conclusions.

Web:
  http://lcweb.loc.gov/z3950/

Library of Congress

The Library of Congress was established as a legislative library for the Congress of the United States. The core of the original library was the personal collection of Thomas Jefferson. Today, the Library of Congress has grown to encompass many information-related activities (including the U.S. Copyright Office). The library holds well over 500 miles of bookshelves in three principal buildings. Although all the storage areas are closed to the public (you tell them what you want and they fetch it for you), the services of the library are available, free of charge, to anyone over high school age. The Library of Congress is not only the research arm of the U.S. Congress, it is recognized as the United States' national library, and its collections are considered the most comprehensive record of human creativity and knowledge in the world (although they do not have a full set of Harley Hahn books).

Web:
  http://www.loc.gov/

Library of Congress Classification System

The Library of Congress Classification System was developed in the nineteenth century to bring order to the vast resources of the United States Library of Congress. The system uses the letters of the alphabet to represent 26 main categories. The categories are divided into sub-categories, each of which is given a two-letter code. To further refine a specific classification, a number is appended to the two-letter code. For example, the social sciences all lie within the letter H, commerce is assigned the code HF, business uses HF5001 to HF6002, and vocational guidance and career development would lie within the specific range HF5381 to HF5386. The Library of Congress Classification System is updated continually and is more detailed than most people realize. The current version actually runs to some 48 volumes with more than 13,000 pages. Most people, however, only need the categories, sub-categories and important classifications. These well-organized Web sites have all this information in an easy-to-use format. (Alternatively—if you need a romantic present for that special someone in your life—for a modest fee you can purchase a printed outline of the system directly from the Library of Congress.)

Web:
  http://innopac.pace.edu/screens/r_lc.html
  http://www.fiu.edu/~library/assistance/lcclass.html

Preservation of Library Materials

One of the most important responsibilities that librarians have is the preservation of books, microfiche, maps, manuscripts, audio recordings and computer data. Preservation experts must deal with a number of potential problems, not only the physical degeneration of the materials (pages, bindings, and so on), but environmental damage due to pests, mold and various types of disasters.

Web:
   http://palimpsest.stanford.edu/
   http://palimpsest.stanford.edu/byorg/georgia/
   http://www.amigos.org/preservation/leaflets.html
   http://www.lcweb.loc.gov/preserv/
   http://www.rlg.org/preserv/

Listproc Mailing List:
   List Name: padg
   Subscribe to: listproc@ala1.ala.org

Presidential Libraries

When the President of the United States leaves office, all the records of his administration are removed from the White House and sent to the National Archives and Records Administration. Since the time of President Herbert Hoover, these records have been housed in special presidential libraries. Although the general public has access to some of the material, most of it is used by historians, writers and other researchers. At this time, there are presidential libraries for the following administrations: Hoover, Roosevelt (Franklin), Eisenhower, Truman, Kennedy, Johnson, Nixon, Ford, Carter, Reagan, Bush (senior) and Clinton.

Web:
   http://bushlibrary.tamu.edu/
   http://www.archives.gov/nixon/
   http://www.archives.gov/presidential_libraries/
      addresses/addresses.html
   http://www.clintonpresidentialcenter.com/
   http://www.eisenhower.utexas.edu/
   http://www.fdrlibrary.marist.edu/
   http://www.ford.utexas.edu/
   http://www.hoover.archives.gov/
   http://www.jfklibrary.org/
   http://www.jimmycarterlibrary.org/
   http://www.lbjlib.utexas.edu/
   http://www.rbhayes.org/
   http://www.reagan.utexas.edu/
   http://www.trumanlibrary.org/
   http://www.wheretodoresearch.com/presidents/
      libraries.htm

LITERATURE

African-American Literature

African-American literature reflects the characteristics and heritage that form the cultural underpinnings of the modern black community in the United States. Read about Maya Angelou, Octavia Butler, Alex Haley, Derek Walcott, Booker T. Washington, Alice Walker and many more authors who have helped create the rich canon of modern-day African-American literature.

Web:
   http://etext.lib.virginia.edu/subjects/
      African-American.html
   http://falcon.jmu.edu/~ramseyil/afroamer.htm
   http://www.aalbc.com/

Listserv Mailing List:
   List Name: afamlit
   Subscribe to: listserv@listserv.kent.edu

American Literature

What good is American Literature? Well, if you are an American high school student, you can study American literature in order to pass your exams and graduate. For the rest of us, though, American literature is far less utilitarian, though potentially more rewarding: all we have to do is read and enjoy it. Regardless of your motivations, you'll find these resources useful and enlightening.

Web:
   http://guweb2.gonzaga.edu/faculty/campbell/
      enl311/sites.htm
   http://www.csustan.edu/english/reuben/pal/
      table.html
   http://www.nagasaki-gaigo.ac.jp/ishikawa/amlit/
   http://www.usinfo.state.gov/products/pubs/oal/
      amlitweb.htm

Listproc Mailing List:
   List Name: amlit-l
   Subscribe to: listproc@po.missouri.edu

Asian-American Literature

To be Asian in America is to experience the clash between two very different cultures. Asian-American literature commonly explores themes such as individual- vs. group-identity; Asian stereotypes, especially with respect to women; assimilation and cultural traditions; and immigration and return to the homeland.

Web:

http://falcon.jmu.edu/~ramseyil/asia.htm
http://mchip00.med.nyu.edu/lit-med/lit-med-db/
   asianamerican.html
http://voices.cla.umn.edu/
   ethnicity.html#Asian-American
http://vos.ucsb.edu/browse.asp?id=1172
http://www.arches.uga.edu/~dbeistle/teaching/
   CMLT2400/links.html
http://www.sjsu.edu/faculty/awilliams/
   AsianAmResources.html

Australian Literature

As the philosopher J. Wellington Wimpy used to say, "I'll gladly pay you Tuesday for some Australian literature today." Well, today, all Wimpy would have to do is use the Net, and he would be able to find enough Australian literature and information about Australian writers to satisfy even the largest literary appetite.

Web:

http://setis.library.usyd.edu.au/ozlit/
http://www.middlemiss.org/lit/lit.html

Beat Generation

The Beat generation refers to a number of American writers and artists who were popular in the 1950s. Among this group were novelists William Burroughs and Jack Kerouac (writer of the seminal beat book "On the Road"), and poets Allen Ginsberg and Lawrence Ferlinghetti. The Beats were the fathers of the 1960s, so their work is particularly relevant to our life today (seeing as the 1960s was an abrupt watershed in twentieth century culture).

Web:

http://www.connectotel.com/marcus/beatfaq.html
http://www.rooknet.com/beatpage/

Usenet:

alt.books.beatgeneration

British Literature

British literature is the basis of modern Western culture. Traditionally, British literature is studied with respect to several major historical periods: Middle Ages (pre-15th century: Dante, Chaucer, Thomas Malory, the epic poem "Beowulf"); Renaissance (15th to 17th century: Shakespeare, John Milton, John Donne); Restoration (18th century: Samuel Johnson, James Boswell, Robert Burns); Romantic (early 19th century: William Blake, William Wordsworth, John Keats, Jane Austen, the Brontë sisters); Victorian (late 19th century: Charles Dickens, Thomas Hardy, Alfred Tennyson, Oscar Wilde, George Eliot [Mary Ann Evans]); and Modernism (20th century: E.M. Forster, Virginia Woolf, James Joyce, Joseph Conrad, T.S. Eliot, D.H. Lawrence, Dylan Thomas, Katherine Mansfield, William Butler Yeats).

Web:

http://etext.lib.virginia.edu/britpo.html
http://newark.rutgers.edu/~jlynch/Lit/victoria.html
http://vos.ucsb.edu/browse.asp?id=3
http://www.english-literature.org/resources/
http://www.luminarium.org/lumina.htm

Conrad, Joseph

Joseph Conrad (1857-1924) was born to Polish parents (his original name was Teodor Jozef Konrad Korzeniowski) in the Russian-dominated Ukraine and did not even learn to speak English until he was an adult. Although writing was difficult for Conrad, and English was his fourth language—after Polish, Russian and French—he was a master of atmosphere and characterization, and is considered one of the greatest writers of English fiction. Conrad's most well-known works are the novels "Lord Jim" and "Heart of Darkness". His work is imbued with a sensitivity to the nuances and ambiguities of what normal people call life, and what English teachers refer to as "the human condition".

Web:
  http://www.bbc.co.uk/arts/books/author/conrad/
  http://www.kirjasto.sci.fi/jconrad.htm
  http://www.literatureclassics.com/authors/conrad/

Dante

Dante Alighieri (1265-1321) is best known for his poetical works "The Divine Comedy" and "The Inferno", which have been translated from Italian into many languages. Dante was not only a poet, he was a philosopher, a rhetorician and a statesman. "When I had journeyed half of our life's way, I found myself within a shadowed forest, for I had lost the path that does not stray..." Thus begins Dante's poem "The Inferno". Dante's works offer a keen insight into human nature, and are considered to be classic literature, the work of a genius.

Web:
  http://www.greatdante.net/
  http://www.princeton.edu/~dante/

This page is not under construction.

Dickens, Charles

Charles Dickens (1812-1870) is perhaps the most famous English novelist of all time. Blessed with an extraordinary gift of satirical humor, melded with the ability to bring his readers both to laughter and to tears, Dickens managed to arouse the conscience of his audience while capturing the popular imagination of his time. More so than any other English novelist, Dickens had the ability to tell a story. Within his many novels ("Oliver Twist", "Great Expectations", "A Christmas Carol", and so on), Dickens created the most marvelous gallery of characters in English fiction. When I was an undergraduate, I had a friend named Ralph who liked to read Dickens to relax. Now, you don't know Ralph, but believe me, the fact that Dickens could write stories that, a hundred years later, could interest a guy like Ralph really says something.

Web:
  http://humwww.ucsc.edu/dickens/
  http://lang.nagoya-u.ac.jp/~matsuoka/Dickens.html
  http://www.fidnet.com/~dap1955/dickens/

Listserv Mailing List:
  List Name: dickns-l
  Subscribe to: listserv@listserv.ucsb.edu

Eliot, George

George Eliot (1819-1880) was the pen name for Mary Ann Evans, an English novelist and poet who flourished during Victorian times. (She chose a masculine name in order that her work would be treated more seriously.) Eliot was an intellectual explorer, as comfortable in the sciences and philosophy (especially when it came to questioning religion), as in literature. Eliot's work is thought-provoking, with a special appeal to intelligent people. (It is well-known that Eliot categorically refused to read USA Today.) Eliot was a literary genius, and as such, skillfully created Victorian novels steeped in minutely detailed description and insightful characterizations. She is remembered chiefly for "Mill on the Floss" (1860), "Silas Marner" (1861), and "Middlemarch" (1872). If you are smart, and you have a lot of patience for detail, you will love Eliot.

Web:
  http://landow.stg.brown.edu/victorian/eliot/
    eliotov.html
  http://www.kirjasto.sci.fi/gelliot.htm
  http://www.selfknowledge.com/139au.htm

Emerson, Ralph Waldo

Ralph Waldo Emerson (1803-1882), an American poet, essayist and lecturer, was one of America's most influential intellectuals. Emerson is remembered for introducing many important new ideas. Among the best known are his call for America to develop intellectual independence from Europe ("The American Scholar", 1837), and his assertion, in a lecture at the Harvard Divinity School (1838), that man's redemption can be found only in his own soul and intuition. One of Emerson's most well-known admonitions, from the essay "Self-Reliance" (1841), is "A foolish consistency is the hobgoblin of little minds, adored by little statesmen and philosophers and divines. With consistency a great soul has simply nothing to do. He may as well concern himself with his shadow on the wall."

Web:

   http://www.gonzaga.edu/faculty/campbell/enl311/
    emerson.htm
   http://www.ralphwaldoemerson.net/
   http://www.rwe.org/
   http://www.transcendentalists.com/1emerson.html
   http://www.watershedonline.ca/literature/Emerson/
    EMERSON.html

F. Scott Fitzgerald

It's not well known, but when F. Scott Fitzgerald was ready to publish his most important novel he wasn't sure what to call it, so he called me for advice.

"Harley," he said, "what do you think of the title 'The Mediocre Gatsby'?"

"It sounds too weak, Scott."

"How about 'The Not-so-great Gatsby'?" he asked.

"I still think it's not strong enough. Why don't you see if you can think of something more powerful."

"Do you really think it's that important?" he said.

"I do," I said. "It's a good book. I think you should have a really great title."

"Okay," he said. "I'll see what I can do."

Faulkner, William

William Faulkner (1897-1962) was an American novelist from Mississippi. His greatest writing was based on the legends and history of the Southern United States, as well as the characteristics of his own family. His most famous works (such as the novel "The Sound and the Fury") are set in the town of Jefferson in the mythical county of Yoknapatawpha (pronounced just as it looks). In 1949, Faulkner was awarded the Nobel Prize for literature.

Web:

   http://www.mcsr.olemiss.edu/~egjbp/faulkner/
    faulkner.html
   http://www.uhb.fr/faulkner/wf/
   http://www.unf.edu/library/guides/faulkner.html

Fitzgerald, F. Scott

To read anything by American writer F. Scott Fitzgerald (1896-1940) is to marvel at his skill. Fitzgerald's writing was just right: neither top-heavy with description nor frantic with unnecessary action. He was a deliberate writer, one who would painstakingly revise, cut, prune and amplify, crafting each scene of a story until he got exactly what he wanted. Fitzgerald was a master, and his prose was greatly admired by other writers. Fitzgerald was also an erratic, financially irresponsible, often sickly alcoholic who was married to a crazy wife (Zelda). Fortunately, he was able to work with the legendary Scribner's editor Maxwell Perkins, who not only edited Fitzgerald's work, but who sent him money, helped manage his financial affairs, and generally looked after and encouraged the writer. Fitzgerald became a major part of the American literary scene with the publication of his first novel, "This Side of Paradise" in 1920, a book which epitomized the Jazz Age in America. His best-known work is "The Great Gatsby" (1925), a timeless story of the unsuccessful pursuit of happiness, a work which categorically defines the classic American novel. (Here is some Fitzgerald trivia: His full name is Francis Scott Key Fitzgerald, named after the person who wrote the words to "The Star-Spangled Banner". Also, Fitzgerald died on December 21, my birthday.)

Web:

   http://www.educeth.ch/english/readinglist/
    fitzgeralds/
   http://www.ipl.org/cgi-bin/ref/litcrit/
    litcrit.out.pl?au=fit-69
   http://www.kirjasto.sci.fi/fsfitzg.htm

Hardy, Thomas

As a young man in the English countryside, Thomas Hardy (1840-1928) was schooled in music and literature by his parents. However, the family could not afford to let him pursue a career as a scholar. Instead, he was apprenticed to a local architect, and it was not until the age of 33 that he abandoned architecture to become a full-time novelist and poet. Hardy wrote many books during his life, most of which were first serialized in popular magazines. His best-known novels are "The Mayor of Casterbridge" (1886), "Tess of the D'Urbervilles" (1891), and "Jude the Obscure" (1896). As you read the work of Hardy, you will encounter two recurring themes. First, that our lives are often influenced by outside forces beyond our control. Second, that our character, which dictates our actions, is inborn and also beyond our conscious control. The confluence of these themes in Hardy's work results in novels that, though emotionally moving, are bleak. For example, my copy editor Lydia is a literature professor, and Hardy's "The Mayor of Casterbridge" is one of only two books that have ever made her cry. (The other one is "Mama Day" by Gloria Naylor.)

Web:
> http://pages.ripco.net/~mws/hardy.html
> http://www.wesspix.btinternet.co.uk/
> http://www.yale.edu/hardysoc/Welcome/
> welcomet.htm

Hawthorne, Nathaniel

The novels and poetry of American writer Nathaniel Hawthorne (1804-1864) explore the related themes of sin and guilt. In every age and every culture, there is always more than enough sin and guilt to go around, so it is no surprise that Hawthorne's writing has become a staple in the supermarket of American literature. His most well-known novels are "The Scarlet Letter" (1850) and "The House of the Seven Gables" (1851), both of which are set amid the strict, moralistic Puritan society of colonial Massachusetts. "The Scarlet Letter" tells the story of Hester Prynne, a young woman who becomes pregnant, even though her husband has been away for some time. As a result, she is branded an adulteress and forced to wear a scarlet letter A on her chest. However, she refuses to reveal the identity of her lover (who is actually the town's young minister), and she satisfies the letter (!) of the law by serving out her punishment with pride and strength: "On the breast of her gown, in fine red cloth, surrounded with an elaborate embroidery and fantastic flourishes of gold thread, appeared the letter A." (Kind of makes you wonder about the large L on Laverne's sweaters, doesn't it?) Although adultery seems as if it ought to be a black and white issue, especially in Puritan New England, Hawthorne shows us that questions of morality often do not have clear-cut answers. Was Hawthorne proud of his work? On February 3, 1850, he read the final pages of "The Scarlet Letter" to his wife. He then wrote, "It broke her heart and sent her to bed with a grievous headache, which I look upon as a triumphant success."

Web:
> http://www.gonzaga.edu/faculty/campbell/enl311/
> hawthor.htm
> http://www.online-literature.com/hawthorne/
> http://www.uwm.edu/dept/Library/special/exhibits/
> clastext/clspg143.htm

**Slow down.
Tomorrow will be yesterday soon enough.**

Hemingway, Ernest

Ernest Hemingway (1899-1961) was an American novelist who lived in France when it was cool to be an American in Paris. Hemingway's writing is known for its plain, stark, tough, brutal, primitive—dare I say it?—masculine style. His first important book ("The Sun Also Rises") became a success by capturing the post-World War I disillusionment of the so-called "lost generation". (And this was years before anyone had heard of Generation X.) Hemingway's novels deftly resonate with the universal themes of Man's struggle against Nature, Man's struggle against other men, and Man's struggle (when no one is looking) against women. In 1954, Hemingway was awarded the Nobel Prize for literature. In 1961, after a long illness, he killed himself.

Web:

    http://www.allhemingway.com/
    http://www.ernest.hemingway.com/
    http://www.hemingwaysociety.org/virthem.htm
    http://www.lostgeneration.com/hrc.htm

Majordomo Mailing List:

    List Name: heming-l
    Subscribe to: majordomo@mtu.edu

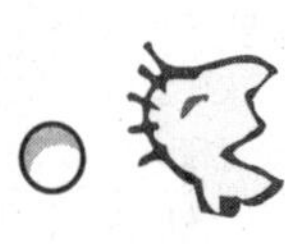

Report on James Joyce by Elmo (age 8)

I was in the library, and when no one was looking I got a book by James Joyce called Finnegans Wake.

I liked it because it had a lot of new words and I could make up that it meant whatever I want.

Also, my father and mother can't understand it.

-Elmo

Joyce, James

James Joyce (1882-1941), was an Irish writer of great renown, known for his profound and complex novels, such as the loosely autobiographical "A Portrait of the Artist as a Young Man" (1916), and "Ulysses" (1922), which has been called the greatest novel of all time. Over the years, Joyce's writing became more and more convoluted, dense and obscure, reaching its apogee with "Finnegans Wake" (1939), an amazingly rich work of words and ideas that Joyce worked on for over ten years. The book is a self-styled "history of the world", told as a series of stream-of-consciousness dream stories, abundantly supplied with multilingual puns, historical allusions, and jokes that are so funny that no one, except Joyce, can ever understand them all without undergoing serious and irreversible brain damage. However, I think I understand it. It's easy. oui lost it in el, but we wernt hi (hi Carolyn!), undergoingone of Harley-she Plimpton Beersticker's fetster bestertester ideations, eh? 2000 A.D. (axle-ly 0.8333 eh? elle ore 2.653 perscent, like candle d'Carrie, apple) after my tohng-seng sang morethan 98.sixties; of the not dais but knight lneye memenom H-n joycened nocturnalnonchopin brayinemissions of leopoldbloom whosayz highrajer editorprints of hphots—

Web:

    http://www.cohums.ohio-state.edu/english/
      organizations/ijjf/jrc/
    http://www.robotwisdom.com/jaj/
    http://www.themodernword.com/joyce/
    http://www.uwm.edu/dept/Library/special/exhibits/
      clastext/clspg158.htm

Usenet:

    alt.books.james-joyce

Listproc Mailing List:

    List Name: fwread
    Subscribe to: listproc@lists.colorado.edu

Listserv Mailing List:

    List Name: fwake-l
    Subscribe to: listserv@listserv.heanet.ie

Shakespeare, William

William Shakespeare (1564-1616) was an English playwright and poet, considered to be the greatest dramatist of all time. Shakespeare wrote a large variety of plays: histories, tragedies, romances and comedies, and his skillfulness and insight were developed to such a high degree as to almost defy description and analysis. That, of course, never stopped anyone, and today, in just about every high school and university in the world, there is an active Shakespeare industry, carefully discussing, memorizing, studying and generally taking apart just about everything that Shakespeare ever wrote. Although Shakespeare never wrote a made-for-TV movie or a vampire book, his plays are still performed frequently all over the world (even though he is dead and is, therefore, not entitled to any of the royalties).

Web:
    http://shakespeare.palomar.edu/
    http://tech-two.mit.edu/shakespeare/
    http://www.ipl.org/reading/shakespeare/
        shakespeare.html
    http://www.library.utoronto.ca/
        utel/rp/authors/shakespe.html

Usenet:
    humanities.lit.authors.shakespeare

Listserv Mailing List:
    List Name: shaksper
    Subscribe to: listserv@ws.bowiestate.edu

Aside from you,
there are seventy-six people
reading this very book
right now. (Two of them are
reading this page.)

A Hint About Shakespeare

What can you say about Shakespeare? Truly, he was a happening dude for his day. Of course, there are ugly rumors that he didn't really write his own plays, that they were all done by someone else who happened to have the same name. In fact, if you take the soliloquy from Macbeth and run it through the Unix **tr** command you will find a secret message that says, "This was really written by Shakespeare."

But don't believe me. Shakespeare's work is available for free on the Net. Download your favorite play or poem and perform your own analysis.

Steinbeck, John

In 1962, American writer John Steinbeck (1902-1968) won the Nobel Prize for Literature. During his Nobel lecture, he declared the job of a writer to be "...exposing our many grievous faults and failures...to declare and to celebrate man's proven capacity for greatness of heart and spirit..." Steinbeck was born in Salinas, California, a small farming town. As a youth, he longed to be a writer and, upon reaching man's estate, devoted himself to the craft, writing mightily about the oppressed, especially the poor, uneducated migrant workers upon whose labor the farms of California depended. Steinbeck's first popular book, "Tortilla Flat" (1935), contained humorous stories about the farm workers in Monterey. His later work, however, was serious, juxtaposing the dreams and difficulties of an oppressed people with the magnificence of the land in which they lived. Steinbeck displayed a sensitivity for the common man, especially the misfits, about whom he wrote with the compassionate awareness that a man can only be understood in the context of his environment. His most famous novel is "Grapes of Wrath" (1939), which tells the story of a family of Oklahoma farmers who, because of the 1930s Dustbowl (extreme erosion and drought on the central plains of America), migrate to California looking for a better life. Other important Steinbeck works are "In Dubious Battle" (1936), "Of Mice and Men" (1937) and "East of Eden" (1952) (the last of which was made into a powerful movie starring James Dean). I don't have time to go into all the details. Suffice to say that, if someone tells you that you remind them of Lennie in "Of Mice and Men", it is not a compliment.

Web:

http://ocean.st.usm.edu/~wsimkins/steinb.html
http://www.bbc.co.uk/history/programmes/
    centurions/steinbeck/steibiog.shtml
http://www.kirjasto.sci.fi/johnstei.htm
http://www.sjsu.edu/depts/steinbec/srchome.html

Express yourself.
Make a Web page.

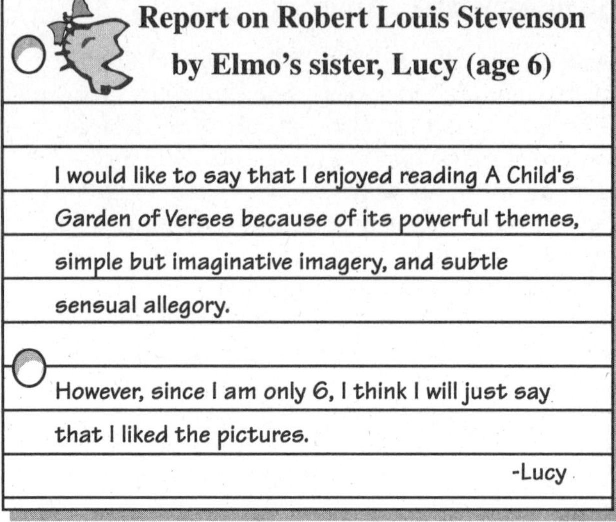

Stevenson, Robert Louis

"I have a little shadow," observed Robert Louis Stevenson, "that goes in and out with me, and what can be the use of him is more than I can see." Exactly. Who among us has not spent sleepless nights wondering the very same thing? The quote is from "A Child's Garden of Verses" (1885), Stevenson's best-known collection of poetry. Robert Louis Stevenson (1850-1894), born in Edinburgh, Scotland, was a highly accomplished writer of just about everything under the literary sun: adventure stories, romances, poetry, short stories, essays, biography, travel stories, reportage, plays, fantasies and fables. When he was 21, Stevenson announced that he was going to devote his life to writing, rather than follow the profession of his father, a lighthouse and harbor engineer. At first, Stevenson wrote mostly about travel, and it was not until he published "Treasure Island", a children's adventure book, in 1882, that he achieved popularity. This was followed by "Kidnapped" (1886) and "The Strange Case of Dr Jekyll and Mr Hyde" (also in 1886). Throughout his life, Stevenson was frequently ill and, eventually, had to leave the harsh climate of his homeland. Although he loved and wrote about the Scots and their history, he spent his final years on the island of Samoa in the South Pacific.

Web:

http://www.poetryloverspage.com/poets/stevenson/
    stevenson_ind.html
http://www.slainte.org.uk/scotauth/stevedsw.htm
http://wwwesterni.unibg.it/siti_esterni/rls/rls.htm

Swift, Jonathan

Irish-born Jonathan Swift (1667-1745) was not a happy man. Although he could read from the age of 3 and went to excellent schools (Kilkenny and then Trinity College), Swift was never able to advance his career satisfactorily. As a young man, he went into the church as the lesser of the only available vocational evils. As he grew older, Swift became cantankerous (as all great writers do once in awhile, and, of course, they should be excused). Moreover, from the age of 23, he suffered from a chronic, untreatable disturbance of the inner ear (now known as Meniere's disease) that produces vertigo and nausea. Still, Swift maintained a life of service to both Ireland and England, and, over the years, developed into a superb writer. Until his last few years, when dementia set in, Swift enjoyed a vital, incisive intelligence and an unmatched talent for satire laced with brilliant irony. Today, Swift is best remembered for his book "Gulliver's Travels" (1726), which, like all his work, was published anonymously. Although the stories are entertaining and amusing, they were actually written as a brutal denunciation of the current political and religious establishment. In 1729, Swift published "A Modest Proposal", a remorseless satire in which he proposed to solve the terrible problem of Irish poverty by encouraging parents to sell their children as food. In his later years, Swift calmed down somewhat, writing a lot of light poetry, as well as essays on more pedestrian topics such as language and manners. (Still, when you were invited to his house for dinner, it did behoove you to tread carefully if the meat looked a bit odd.)

Web:
http://www.jaffebros.com/lee/gulliver/
http://www.kirjasto.sci.fi/jswift.htm
http://www.online-literature.com/swift/

Thoreau, Henry David

After graduating from Harvard, American writer Henry David Thoreau's first job was in his father's pencil factory. Despite significant contributions to the American pencil industry, Thoreau (1817-1862) is actually best known for his writing, in particular, "Civil Disobedience" (1849) and "Walden; or Life in the Woods" (1854). As a child, Thoreau was serious and was happiest when left alone. As he grew older, he became deeply religious, although he did not like going to church. Thoreau had high expectations of himself and of other people and, in fact, perceived himself as having many weaknesses. "Civil Disobedience"— which begins "I heartily accept the motto, 'That government is best which governs least'"— explains why Thoreau would rather go to jail than pay the tax that supported the Mexican War. "Walden" is a long, personal work, describing Thoreau's reverence for nature and his philosophy of life: "If a man does not keep pace with his companions, perhaps it is because he hears a different drummer. Let him step to the music which he hears, however measured or far away". (Note: This does not mean it is okay to let your kids run around and make noise in restaurants.) Thoreau dedicated himself to a search for truth and beauty, and he honestly sought to understand how life could be better for everyone. If you want to study his philosophy, I suggest starting with the chapter in "Walden" called "Visitors".

Web:
http://libws66.lib.niu.edu/thoreau/
http://www.eserver.org/thoreau/
http://www.transcendentalists.com/1thorea.html

Twain, Mark

Mark Twain (1835-1910) was an American writer and humorist who single-handedly ushered in the phenomenon of Modern American Literature. (The name "Mark Twain" was actually a pseudonym for Samuel Langhorne Clemens. At one time, Clemens was one of many Mississippi river pilots, among whom it was common to use the call "mark twain" to indicate a water depth of two fathoms.) Twain's novels and stories are of such enduring value that they are enjoyable even to school children who are forced to read real literature (by English teachers who teach to support themselves while they are finishing their own novels). Twain's most famous characters, Tom Sawyer and Huckleberry Finn, are brilliant but folksy creations, as genuinely American as apple pie, baseball and complaining about Congress.

Web:
http://www.online-literature.com/twain/
http://www.yorku.ca/twainweb/

Listserv Mailing List:
List Name: twain-l
Subscribe to: listserv@yorku.ca

Wharton, Edith

Edith Wharton (1862-1937) was born into upper-class New York society. (We are talking really rich here.) Wharton was a prolific and popular novelist and writer of short stories, who wrote mostly about the wealthy upper-class, New York society of her day. Her best novels, which demonstrate a masterful, entertaining and subtly ironic critique of her society, are "The House of Mirth" (1905) and "The Age of Innocence" (1920). A shorter novel, "Ethan Frome" (1911), is different: it tells the story of a New England tragedy brought about by surrendering to the temptation of forbidden love. If you have never read any of Wharton's novels, I suggest you start with "The House of Mirth", which is marvelous. In case you don't have time to read the entire book, here is a quick summary I have prepared just for you: "Selden paused in surprise. In the afternoon rush of the Grand Central Station his eyes had been refreshed by the sight of Miss Lily Bart... <a bunch of hot stuff> ...He knelt by the bed and bent over her, draining their last moment to its lees; and in the silence there passed between them the word which made all clear." The End.

Web:
http://www.gonzaga.edu/faculty/campbell/enl413/
    wharton.htm
http://www.ocf.berkeley.edu/~kip/wharton/
    whartonlinks.html
http://www.owleyes.org/wharton.htm

Wilde, Oscar

Oscar Wilde (1854-1900), an Irish-born writer who lived most of his life in England, was the foremost literary wit of the Victorian age. Wilde's most famous work is his only novel, "The Picture of Dorian Gray" (1891). However, he is also known for his plays, such as "The Importance of Being Earnest" (1895), and his poetry, such as "The Ballad of Reading Gaol" [Jail] (1898). However, the talent for which Wilde is best remembered is the sparkling epigrams and dialog with which he peppered his work. ("There is always something ridiculous about the emotions of people whom one has ceased to love.")

Web:
http://landow.stg.brown.edu/victorian/decadence/
    wilde/wildeov.html
http://www.bibliomania.com/0/2/57/
http://www.hoboes.com/html/FireBlade/Wilde/
http://www.oscariana.net/

Woolf, Virginia

Virginia Woolf (1882-1941), an English novelist, essayist and critic, had a profound influence on the 20th-century novel. With her husband, Leonard Woolf, she set up a publishing enterprise, Hogarth Press, in 1917. Hogarth published Sigmund Freud in English (his first work in English), T.S. Eliot, Katherine Mansfield and Maxim Gorky, as well as all of Woolf's own work. The Woolfs' house was the center of the Bloomsbury Group, a group of influential writers, artists and intellectuals. Woolf's novels include "Mrs. Dalloway" (1925), "To the Lighthouse" (1927), "Orlando" (1928), "The Waves" (1931) and "Between the Acts" (1941).

Web:
http://www.kirjasto.sci.fi/vwoolf.htm
http://www.online-literature.com/virginia_woolf/
http://www.orlando.jp.org/VWSGB/

If you really want to learn,
no one can stop you.

LITERATURE: CONTEMPORARY WRITERS

Angelou, Maya

Maya Angelou (1928-) is one of those people whose very life is a testament to how high the human spirit can rise. As a young child, Angelou and her brother were shuttled between her grandmother and their divorced mother. The grandmother lived in a small town in Arkansas, and Angelou, an African-American, grew up in the deep south within a culture of extreme discrimination. At the age of eight, Angelou was raped by her mother's boyfriend, after which she became mute for five years. Over the years, Angelou has led a remarkable life, having a variety of experiences, both bad and good (including becoming pregnant at the age of 16). In 1970, she published "I Know Why The Caged Bird Sings", the first of a series of highly regarded autobiographies. Over the years, Angelou has become a world-renowned writer, poet, playwright, essayist and political activist. Angelou's life is a remarkable one, blessed with ambition and resilience. Just reading about Angelou will both inspire and humble you.

Web:

http://www.csustan.edu/english/reuben/pal/chap10/
　angelou.html

http://www.educeth.ch/english/readinglist/
　angeloum/

http://www.empirezine.com/spotlight/maya/
　maya1.htm

Asimov, Isaac

Isaac Asimov was the consummate explainer. He was a genius in the sense that whatever he touched, he illuminated. In his lifetime, he wrote hundreds of books on a large variety of subjects, opening the doors of understanding to countless people around the world. And, oh yes, I think he wrote a science fiction story or two. (I will have to check.)

Web:

http://homepage.mac.com/jenkins/Asimov/
　Asimov.html

http://q.webring.com/hub?ring=isaacasimov

http://www.asimov.com/

http://www.asimovians.com/forum/

http://www.asimovonline.com/

Usenet:

alt.books.isaac-asimov

Advice from Isaac Asimov

When I was a graduate student, I wrote a letter to Isaac Asimov. I told him I wanted to learn biochemistry, but I didn't want to have to take a whole lot of beginning organic chemistry and biology courses. He wrote back and gave me the following advice:

"If you have a good library at your disposal, you can teach yourself anything. I did."

I took his advice and taught myself biochemistry out of a textbook. (Ironically, I later went to medical school and ended up learning enough biochemistry to supply the entire Peruvian army. Still, the advice is well-taken and, to this day, I have kept Asimov's note, framed and hanging on the wall beside my desk.)

Atwood, Margaret

Canadian poet and novelist Margaret Atwood (1939-) is a master of documenting and helping us understand the "Dr. Jekyll-Mr. Hyde double life for women." Her books—which reviewers love to call "powerful"—concern themselves with the twin themes of feminism and the power that mass society has over the individual. Atwood's most well-known novels are "The Edible Woman"(1969) and "The Handmaid's Tale" (1986). (I found an interesting similarity, by the way, between the setting of "The Handmaid's Tale" and the part of Isaac Asimov's book "Prelude to Foundation" in which he discusses the land of Mycogen. If you are an Atwood scholar looking for a dissertation topic, you might want to check it out.) Atwood says that women sometimes ask her about her male characters: why doesn't she make them stronger? She answers that this is a matter that should more properly be taken up with God. "It was not, after all, I who created Adam so subject to temptation that he sacrificed eternal life for an apple." I guess you can color me sensitive, but, yes, I do feel a tad misunderstood.

Web:

http://www.owtoad.com/

http://www.web.net/owtoad/toc.html

http://www.wsu.edu:8000/~brians/science_fiction/
　handmaid.html

A B C D E F G H I J K **L** M N O P Q R S T U V W X Y Z

Bukowski, Charles

The German-born American writer Charles Bukowski (1920-1994) is *the* men's writer of the twentieth century, far more so than, say, the highly overrated Ernie Hemingway. When it comes to earthy, plain-spoken, male (there's that word!) prose, Bukowski alone managed to take the essence of life—the pain of just plain being in a difficult and indifferent world—pick it up, wave it around his head, and show it to us in seventeen different ways, all before breakfast. Moreover, unlike his contemporary angst-filled literary wannabes, Bukowski made it all look *easy*. If you are a man (or if you want to understand men), you must read Bukowski's novel "Women". Do so today. To tempt you, I'm going to tell you how the book ends. It ends with the Henry Chinaski (Bukowski's literary alter ego) feeding a stray cat. "I opened him a can of Star-Kist solid white tuna. Packed in spring water. Net wt. 7 oz." I promise you that, by the time you get to the end of the story, this bland, useless, throwaway ending will be one of the most powerful lines of prose you have ever read.

Web:
  http://www.addict.com/issues/1.09/Features/Bukowski/
  http://www.anti-heroart.com/buk.html
  http://www.levee67.com/bukowski/
  http://www.litkicks.com/buk/

Usenet:
  alt.books.bukowski

Cisneros, Sandra

Mexican-American writer Sandra Cisneros (1954-) grew up (with six brothers!) in a poor family that shuttled between Chicago and Mexico City. Although she was raised with the traditional expectations of her culture, Cisneros did not go gentle into that good life. Instead, she decided to rage, rage against the dying of her spirit: "...I have decided not to grow up tame like the others who lay their necks on the threshold waiting for the ball and chain." Thus declares one of the characters in "The House on Mango Street" (1983), Cisneros' first novel. From that auspicious start, Cisneros' developing oeuvre of novels, stories, poems and essays have elevated her to become, arguably, the best-regarded doyenne of Latina literature.

Web:
  http://voices.cla.umn.edu/authors/sandracisneros.html
  http://www.classicnote.com/ClassicNotes/Authors/
    about_sandra_cisneros.html

Hesse, Hermann

Hermann Hesse (1877-1962) was a German-born Swiss novelist and poet. His work revolves around the recurring theme that artists are estranged from the society in which they live and, hence, suffer from a spiritual loneliness. Perhaps his best known novels are "Siddhartha" (1922) and "Steppenwolf" (1927). As he grew older, Hesse's novels became more analytical and—to the chagrin of undergraduate English students forced to write long essays in order to pass mandatory literature courses—more symbolic. In 1946, Hermann Hesse was awarded the Nobel Prize for literature.

Web:
  http://www.gss.ucsb.edu/projects/hesse/
  http://www.kirjasto.sci.fi/hhesse.htm

Listserv Mailing List:
  List Name: hesse-l
  Subscribe to: listserv@listserv.ucsb.edu

Huxley, Aldous

The English writer Aldous Huxley (1894-1963) is best remembered for his novel "Brave New World", mainly because it has found a firm and enduring place on the list of books high school students are forced to read by English teachers who took a job temporarily, so as to have an income while they worked on their novel and, now, twenty years later, are still teaching while the notes for their long-forgotten literary work lie neglected at the bottom of a dusty attic cupboard. Notwithstanding, "Brave New World" is actually a good book. Moreover, Huxley is more than a literary one-trick pony, and when you can pull yourself away from the superficial demands of day-to-day existence, it behooves you to track down some of Huxley's other work, such as his novels, essays or poetry, and watch him make mash out of the intellectual pretensions of his contemporaries.

Web:
  http://www.huxley.net/
  http://www.kirjasto.sci.fi/ahuxley.htm
  http://www.somaweb.org/

Mailer, Norman

In 1948, the American novelist Norman Mailer (1923-) wielding his first novel "The Naked and the Dead" and an incipient ego the size of Brooklyn (where Mailer grew up), burst onto the cultural scene as a post-World War II literary prodigy. With that one novel, Mailer settled into a tenured appointment as an American man of letters, a position he has held ever since, through a series of books, some good, some bad, and some great. As the years passed, Mailer developed from prodigy to *enfant terrible*, and thence to the aging, respectably rakish grand old man of words he is today. He has broken new ground several times: as editor of "Dissent" (1952-1963,) as the co-founder of the "Village Voice" (1955), and in his forays into the melding of literary smugness and journalism. (See, for example, "Armies of the Night", Mailer's personal reportage of his experiences at the 1968 Washington peace rallies.) Over the years, Mailer has taken a break from his writing long enough to marry six times and sire nine children. I guess he is better at taking breaks than I am. (Actually, that's not really important at all. It's just that I always wanted to be mentioned in the same paragraph as Norman Mailer.)

Web:
  http://www.americanlegends.com/authors/
    norman_mailer.html
  http://www.kirjasto.sci.fi/nmailer.htm
  http://www.normanmailerworksanddays.com/

Norman Mailer

I was having trouble writing something funny about Norman Mailer, so I called him on the phone.

"Norman," I said, "tell me something funny about you."

"Hmmm... let's see," he said. "I don't know what to say. Couldn't you just make up something?"

"Okay," I said. And I did.

Morrison, Toni

African-American Toni Morrison (1931-) is celebrated for her vivid, colorful writing and her idiosyncratic characters. Although she often writes about the details of life in small black towns, her intricate, complex stories appeal to anyone who enjoys immersing themselves in the nuances of personality and human motivation. Her stories invite you to puzzle over what is really happening as the plot unfolds. Morrison's breakthrough as a writer came in 1977 with the publication of her novel "Song of Solomon", a mystical, fantastic tale of a black man in search of his past. A later novel, "Beloved" (1987) was an intense, emotional story set in the time of slavery, which earned Morrison enduring popularity. In 1993, she was awarded the Nobel Prize for Literature.

Web:
  http://voices.cla.umn.edu/authors/tonimorrison.html
  http://www.educeth.ch/english/readinglist/
    morrisont/
  http://www.luminarium.org/contemporary/
    tonimorrison/toni.htm
  http://www.nobel.se/literature/laureates/1993/
    morrison-lecture.html

Orwell, George

By 1946, when English author George Orwell (1903-1950) started to write "1984", his last and most celebrated book, he was a 43-year-old widower suffering from a debilitating case of tuberculosis that would eventually kill him. Orwell had a long history as a reporter, commentator, essayist and political novelist, but it was not until the publication of "Animal Farm" (1946), the story of a revolution carried out by farm animals, that Orwell achieved his first large commercial success. In "1984", Orwell depicts a futuristic England after a totalitarian revolution. In the book, Orwell marries superb writing with political themes that he had been discussing for years: how control of the language can sabotage legitimate political discourse, and how a world of several large superpowers would wage a useless, continual war against one another. Although the world that Orwell envisioned did not come to pass (and we do not have a government that exhorts us to believe that "War is Peace; Freedom is Slavery; Ignorance is Strength"), I, all too often, see chilling reminders that the political weaknesses about which Orwell warned us are ever-present and all too real.

Web:
   http://pages.citenet.net/users/charles/links.html
   http://www.k-1.com/orwell/
   http://www.orwell.ru/home.htm
Usenet:
   alt.books.george-orwell

George Orwell

"Don't you think it's strange," I once asked George Orwell, "that in *Animal Farm* all the animals act like people?"

"Not really," he said. "In most of the novels I read, all the people act like animals."

Dorothy Parker

"I'm never going to be famous," said Dorothy Parker. "I don't do anything, not one single thing. I used to bite my nails, but I don't even do that any more."

Well, all I can say is that Dorothy is lucky she doesn't work on this book.

We have high standards.

Parker, Dorothy

Dorothy Parker (1893-1967) was an American humorist, drama critic (for "Vanity Fair") and book critic (for "The New Yorker"). However, what she was best known for was her role as critic of humanity, starting with herself and working sideways. Her humor, quips and light verse virtually define the idea of irony (at least for the twentieth century). She was the only female member of the Algonquin Round Table—a group of New York-style witty bon vivants that included her wistfully just-beyond-reach paramour Robert Benchley. Have you ever been bothered by someone, and then had the experience of thinking of the perfect comeback—smooth and subtle, with exactly the right amount of graceful reproach—only six hours too late? Dorothy Parker could do it perfectly and in real-time.

Web:
   http://www.english.uiuc.edu/maps/poets/m_r/
      parker/parker.htm
   http://www.kirjasto.sci.fi/dparker.htm
   http://www.library.utoronto.ca/utel/rp/authors/
      parker.html

Salinger, J.D.

Is there any teenager who has read "Catcher in the Rye" and not immediately and irrevocably identified with its protagonist, Holden Caulfield? This short novel is a monologue that details several days in the life of a 16-year-old boy (although he is 17 at the time he relates the story). Caulfield has been expelled from school and is spending a few days in New York before returning home to face his parents. By the end of the book, Caulfield has a nervous collapse, but before he does, he takes us on a personal journey, one which questions our reasons for living, thinking, working, and being who we are. The author of the book, American writer J.D. (Jerome David) Salinger (1919-), published very little in his life: only this one novel and 35 short stories. Salinger worked on "Catcher in the Rye" for over ten years, from 1941 until it was published in 1951. Like Caulfield, Salinger is a strange, unhappy person, one who, for years, has been in the clutches of a mental illness. As a result, he has never published another novel and has lived the life of a recluse. However, though Salinger the man may be a cipher in the annals of American literature, Holden Caulfield, his finest creation, is anything but. Caulfield has a ferocious hold on a reading public that, with each new generation of teenagers, discovers "Catcher in the Rye" and begins to seriously question what it means to grow up, to wrestle with the complex ambiguities of life, and to glimpse the significance of losing the innocence of childhood.

Web:

http://www.morrill.org/books/salbio.shtml
http://www.salinger.org/
http://www.tmtm.com/sides/catcher.html

> **Don't forget to go outside and play. (I'll wait for you here.)**

Silko, Leslie Marmon

Leslie Marmon Silko (1948-), an American of Native American, Mexican, and European ancestry, is a storyteller in the tradition of her tribe, the Laguna Pueblo of New Mexico. Silko integrates poetry and prose into her intricate, vivid pictures of modern life as it relates to Native American culture. Her best-known book is "Almanac of the Dead". In order to fully appreciate her stories, it helps to have a feeling for Native American history. Once you do, Silko's work will quickly draw you into a compelling and fascinating narrative. For example, in her story, "Return of the Buffalo", a character named Wilson Weasel Tail explains to an audience how centuries of abandonment of the traditional spiritual life is responsible for the loss of their power and well-being as a people. As a writer, Silko's reach extends far beyond her Native American upbringing.

Web:

http://voices.cla.umn.edu/authors/
    lesliemarmonsilko.html
http://www.csustan.edu/english/reuben/pal/chap10/
    silko.html
http://www.ipl.org/cgi/ref/native/browse.pl/A75

Stein, Gertrude

"A rose is a rose is a rose is a rose," wrote Gertrude Stein—several times actually, in various poems. Stein (1874-1946), was an eccentric American writer who spent most of her life in Paris with her lifelong companion Alice B. Toklas. Between the world wars, Stein created a salon frequented by leading artists and writers, many of whom were American expatriates. For years, Stein was a cultural leader to the likes of Pablo Picasso, Henri Matisse, Ernest Hemingway, Sherwood Anderson and F. Scott Fitzgerald. So what did Stein mean about roses? Nothing, probably, beyond the abstraction. Stein was one of the early proponents of Cubism and other experimental art, and imbued much of her writing with the Cubist use of fragmentation while concentrating on the present moment. As a result, much of her work is abstract and difficult to understand. Although she wrote throughout her life, Stein's work did not become popular until the 1933 publication of "The Autobiography of Alice B. Toklas" (actually, about Stein herself). However, she was right about one thing: a rose *is* a rose.

Web:

http://www.csustan.edu/english/reuben/pal/chap7/
    stein.html
http://www.ellensplace.net/gstein1.html
http://www.kirjasto.sci.fi/gstein.htm

A B C D E F G H I J K L M N O P Q R S T U V W X Y Z

Tan, Amy

American writer Amy Tan (1952-) grew up in California, surrounded by strong Chinese and American influences. Her work deals with universal conflicts, such as discord between generations, and between men and women. Tan's best known work is her first novel, "The Joy Luck Club", the story of four Chinese immigrant women who eat dinner together every week. Over time, as the women struggle to deal with their daughters' rebellion against their parents and the Chinese culture, their very separate families become interconnected. Tan's stories are related by narrators who search constantly for a balance between their Chinese heritage and their modern American lifestyles. As such, Tan touches us all. We do, after all, spend our lifetimes reconciling our own personal conflicts and doing our best to integrate our heritage into an unfeeling, quirky, ever-changing melting pot world.

Web:

http://voices.cla.umn.edu/authors/amytan.html
http://www.luminarium.org/contemporary/amytan/

Thompson, Hunter S.

Hunter S. Thompson (1939-) is an American writer and ex-journalist, best known for his books (such as "Fear and Loathing in Las Vegas") and his articles (many of which were published in "Rolling Stone" magazine). Thompson is the originator of gonzo journalism, an imaginative and opinionated style of writing in which the author becomes involved in the very story he is trying to cover. Despite his questionable lack of social skills, his drug and alcohol addiction, and his degeneration from a highly skilled writer to a literary non-entity, Thompson is worshipped by fans (of which I am one) for his legendary exploits, as well as a legacy of some of the finest writing produced in 20th-century America. This site has information about Thompson's life, his books and what he's doing now (mostly looking for beer and fretting over legal problems because he drinks and drives). Unfortunately, when the going gets tough, you can't stay cool forever.

Web:

http://www.booklist.com/hunter_thompson.html

Vonnegut, Kurt

I have read virtually all the novels and short stories Kurt Vonnegut (1922-) has published, and I love almost everything. Vonnegut's writing is easy, very easy, to read, but the simplicity is an illusion. Although he seems to write in easy-to-digest bits and pieces, Vonnegut's work is complex, with well-developed characters and deep, subtle themes. What makes reading him so rewarding is that it takes so little effort, but gives you so much. Over the years, Vonnegut has carved a unique niche as *the* grand old, plain-spoken, cynical, entertaining master of American literature. (To quote the character Malachi Constant in the novel "Sirens of Titan" (1959), "I was a victim of a series of accidents as are we all.") If you have never read any of Vonnegut's work, you have a treat in store for you. Start with the "Sirens of Titan", my personal favorite. Not only will you find out the real purpose of human civilization, but you will learn about a chronosynclastic infundibulum. "What is it artists do?" asked Vonnegut in a 1994 commencement address at Syracuse University. "They do two things," he explained. "First, they admit they can't straighten out the whole universe. And then second, they make at least one little part of it exactly as it should be." Years ago, I once saw Vonnegut give a speech at a university. If he had been sober, it would have been quite an occasion.

Web:

http://www.duke.edu/~crh4/vonnegut/
http://www.faqs.org/faqs/books/kurt-vonnegut-faq/
http://www.ipass.net/~brianrodr/vonnegut/

Usenet:

alt.books.kurt-vonnegut

> My philosophy is there's no point being sick unless everyone in your life knows it.

Wells, H.G.

Herbert George Wells (1866-1946) was an English author and social critic, who had a long and varied career as a writer. He is best known for his fantastic stories (what would now be called science fiction), such as "The Time Machine", "The Invisible Man", and "The War of the Worlds". As Wells aged, his style moved from scientific fantasy to realism to pessimism. Wells was a lot more than a novelist, however. Before he started to write he taught biology, and later he wrote the well-received "The Outline of History" and co-wrote "The Science of Life"—truly the Isaac Asimov of his day.

Web:
http://www.kirjasto.sci.fi/hgwells.htm
http://www.literature.org/authors/
  wells-herbert-george/
http://www.online-literature.com/wellshg/
http://www.wsu.edu:8080/~brians/science_fiction/
  warofworlds.html

Usenet:
alt.books.h-g-wells

Wodehouse, P.G.

Pelham Grenville Wodehouse (1881-1975) was an English writer of novels, short stories, plays and song lyrics. Wodehouse (pronounced "Woodhouse") is the creator of a great many enduring characters, including Bertie Wooster and his valet Jeeves, Mr. Mulliner, Lord Emsworth and the Empress of Blandings, and Stanley Featherstonehaugh ("Fanshaw") Ukridge. Wodehouse is unique in that, over a long and successful career, he consistently demonstrated a level of skill that would be difficult to overpraise. He is, by far, my favorite author and, if you have never read any of his books, my advice to you is go out and buy one right now. If you happen to be reading this in a bookstore, it should be the work of a moment for you to pick up a Wodehouse book on the way out. Everything he created was uniformly pleasant and well-written: the best human nature has to offer. If you have not met Wodehouse, you have not led a full life.

Web:
http://www.eclipse.co.uk/wodehouse/
http://www.serv.net/~camel/wodehouse/
http://www.wodehouse.ru/

Usenet:
alt.fan.wodehouse

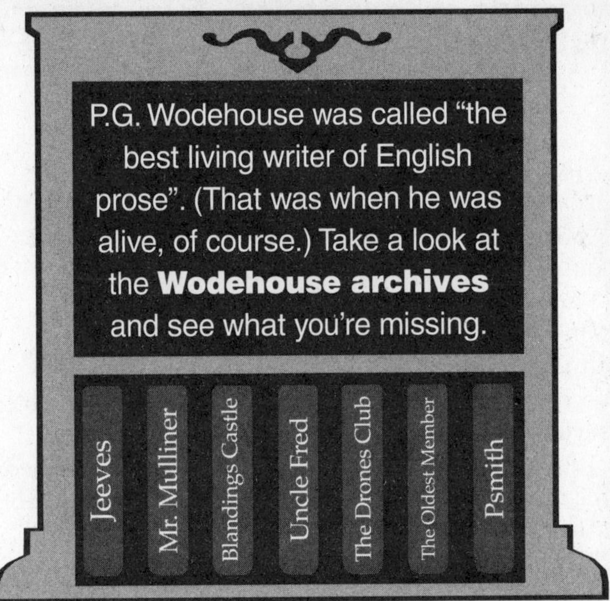

Wright, Richard

Perhaps the most important contribution of Richard Wright (1908-1960), one of the greatest African-American writers of all time, was his ability to show whites an accurate picture of what it really meant to be black in America. Through Wright's books, the general public began to understand that blacks were not the clownish, subservient people portrayed in the popular culture. In doing so, Wright became the first African-American to have his work on the national bestseller lists. Wright grew up in a broken family, within the poverty of the American South. As an adult, he traveled widely in Europe, Asia and Africa and, as a result, was able to transcend the limitations of his childhood and write to a worldly audience about universal themes. His most well-known book, the novel "Native Son" (1940), tells the story of Bigger, a black man who accidentally kills a white woman. Throughout the story, Wright details the frustration of living in extreme poverty and racism. Wright's books provided a major impetus to the revolution of thinking among blacks in America, and inspired black leaders everywhere to work to shape the future of their people.

Web:
http://www.itvs.org/richardwright/
http://www.kirjasto.sci.fi/rwright.htm
http://www.olemiss.edu/depts/english/ms-writers/
  dir/wright_richard/

A B C D E F G H I J K L M N O P Q R S T U V W X Y Z

LITERATURE ONLINE: BOOKS

Age of Innocence

American author Edith Wharton (1862-1937) is best known for her short novel "Ethan Frome" (1911). Wharton was born in New York, and although her family was wealthy, she, being a girl, was not educated formally. However, she dreamed about becoming a writer and, during her lifetime, she wrote seventeen novels, tens of short stories, and many articles and poems. To get you started, I have selected the novel I think you will enjoy the most, "The Age of Innocence" (1920), for which Wharton won a Pulitzer Prize. "The Age of Innocence" is satirical, witty, poignant and subtle. As you read it, be aware that Wharton was writing about the New York society to which she herself belonged.

Web:
   http://www.bibliomania.com/0/0/56/101/
      frameset.html
   http://www.litrix.com/ageinn/agein001.htm

Arabian Nights

The "Arabian Nights" are a collection of fairy tales originating in Persia, Arabia and Asia. Originally the tales were not intended for children, but were told by bold and dramatic entertainers who made their living telling stories. The stories were passed on orally until the 14th-16th centuries when they were translated into French and English and were finally written down. The most well-known tale of the "Arabian Nights" is that of Aladdin and his lamp. The lamp, when rubbed, brought forth a genie who would do Aladdin's bidding. Another well-known hero and adventurer of the "Arabian Nights" was Sinbad, who had seven amazing sea voyages. At these Web sites you can read all the stories of the "Arabian Nights", including the adventures of Aladdin and Sinbad.

Web:
   http://mfx.dasburo.com/an/a_index.html
   http://www.arabiannights.org/index2.html
   http://www.ibiblio.org/pub/docs/books/gutenberg/
      etext94/arabn11.txt

Around the World in Eighty Days

"Around the World in Eighty Days" (1873) is one of many wonderful adventure novels written by the French author Jules Verne (1828-1905), the founder of modern science fiction. The novel tells the story of an eccentric, taciturn Englishman named Phileas Fogg, a man of strict habits. One day at his club, over a game of bridge, Fogg asserts that it is possible to travel around the world in eighty days. (Remember, this is before the days of airplanes, automobiles and fast trains.) Fogg's friends disagree, so, to prove his point, Fogg offers to bet a large sum of money that he can undertake such a journey successfully—all it requires is careful planning. "The unforeseen does not exist," he asserts. Fogg embarks on the journey with his trusty servant Jean Passepartout. Will he make it? What adventures will he have along the way? This is a book you will enjoy immensely; and when you are finished, you will want to read more of Verne's fifty-four novels, including "Journey to the Center of the Earth" (1864), "From the Earth to the Moon" (1865), and "Twenty Thousand Leagues Under the Sea" (1869).

Web:
   http://www.bibliomania.com/0/0/55/100/
      frameset.html
   http://www.literature.org/authors/verne-jules/
      eighty/

Art of War

The "Art of War" was written by a great Chinese general named Sun Tzu about 500 B.C. The book was written as an instruction manual, and is the oldest existing work describing the principles of war and military strategy. The teachings of the "Art of War" are of universal significance, and can be seen as wise strategies for many types of human interaction. In particular, you'll find a lot to help you with your business and personal life. For example: "...to fight and conquer in all your battles is not supreme excellence; supreme excellence consists in breaking the enemy's resistance without fighting." See what I mean? Hot stuff. Just make sure you read it before your boss does.

Web:
   http://www.kimsoft.com/polwar.htm
   http://www.marxists.org/reference/archive/sun-tzu/
      works/art-of-war/

Canterbury Tales

Geoffrey Chaucer (c. 1340-1400) was an English poet who wrote "The Canterbury Tales", a 17,000-line poem about a group of pilgrims traveling to see the shrine of St. Thomas à Becket at Canterbury. The Tales are fascinating because Chaucer is a master storyteller who creates characters that are full of life. "The Canterbury Tales" is an unfinished work, but shows a delightful slice of 14th-century English life.

Web:

http://www.litrix.com/canterby/cante001.htm
http://www.luminarium.org/medlit/chaubib.htm

Christmas Carol

"Bah!" said Scrooge. "Humbug!" His nephew had just volunteered "A merry Christmas, uncle! God save you!", but miserly Ebenezer Scrooge doesn't think much of the idea. It has been seven years to the day since Scrooge has buried his old partner Jacob Marley, also a miser. However, Scrooge has no time for anniversaries, or Christmas for that matter. There is work to be done and sentiment and charity are a waste of time. But—that night, Scrooge is awakened by the ghost of Marley, who warns him of what happens to people like them after death ("No rest, no peace. Incessant torture of remorse"). Later in the night, Scrooge is visited by three more spirits, the Ghosts of Christmas Past, Christmas Present and Christmas Yet to Come. They take him on a strange journey, at the end of which Scrooge has undergone a spiritual conversion. He is now ready to celebrate Christmas and help his fellow man, including Tiny Tim, the young, crippled son of Bob Cratchit. ("God bless us every one," says the young tyke.) English writer Charles Dickens (1812-1870) was a prolific and popular novelist. If you would like to become acquainted with his work, there is no better place to start than with "A Christmas Carol". (Want some trivia? Scrooge's old sweetheart was named Belle.)

Web:

http://www.bibliomania.com/0/0/19/35/
   frameset.html
http://www.literature.org/authors/dickens-charles/
   christmas-carol/
http://www.litrix.com/ccarol/ccaro001.htm

Civil Disobedience

Henry David Thoreau (1817-1862) was an American essayist and poet who believed in "living deep and sucking out all the marrow of life". His best-known book is "Walden". Thoreau's essay "Civil Disobedience" emphasizes the idea of passive resistance against social organization.

Web:

http://sunsite.berkeley.edu/Literature/Thoreau/
   CivilDisobedience.html
http://www.cs.indiana.edu/statecraft/civ.dis.html
http://www.eserver.org/thoreau/civil.html

Here is my favorite quote from *Civil Disobedience*, by Henry David Thoreau. (Actually, when we used to hang around the pop stand after school, I usually called him "Hank"):

"I heartily accept the motto, 'That government is best which endorses Internet books'; and I should like to see it acted up to more rapidly and systematically. Carried out, it finally amounts to this, which also I believe — 'That government is best which makes sure that all of its citizens have a full set of Harley Hahn books; and when men are prepared for it, that will be the kind of government which they will have."

Communist Manifesto

"The Communist Manifesto" was written by Karl Heinrich Marx (1818-1883) and Friedrich Engels (1820-1895). Written in 1848, "The Communist Manifesto" demonstrated Marx and Engel's view of the class struggle and the need to strengthen the solidarity of the working people.

Web:

http://csf.colorado.edu/psn/marx/Archive/1848-CM/
   cm.html
http://www.hnet.uci.edu/history/mposter/syllabi/
   readings/manifesto.html

Don Quixote

"Don Quixote", published in 1615, was written by the Spanish novelist Miguel de Cervantes (1547-1616). In the story, Don Quixote, the hero, travels with his squire, Sancho Panza, and has many comical adventures. Quixote, who has become delusional from reading too many romances, believes he is a knight who must revive the age of chivalry. The novel "Don Quixote" has contributed significantly to our cultural traditions. For example, it has brought us the sayings: "Give the devil his due" (meaning that you should be willing to admit there is some good in people you dislike); "The proof of the pudding is in the tasting" (the best way to evaluate something is by using it); and "Honesty is the best policy".

Web:
  **http://www.encyclopediaoftheself.com/
    classic_books_online/1donq10.htm
  http://www.ibiblio.org/pub/docs/books/gutenberg/
    etext97/1donq10.txt
  http://www.okanagan.net/okanagan/EQuijote/Index.html**

Dracula

The English novelist Bram Stoker (1847-1912) wrote many novels, short stories, essays and lectures. Almost a hundred years after his death, however, Stoker is remembered for only one book, "Dracula" (1897). The story takes place in Transylvania (now a part of Romania), and begins when a clerk, named Harker, calls upon Count Dracula at his castle, in order to transact some business. (You'd think Harker would be a tad suspicious. I mean, Count Dracula in a castle in Transylvania? Come on.) Anyway, while at the castle, Harker begins to notice strange occurrences. The local townspeople refuse to approach the castle, the Count's reflection is not visible in a mirror, and so on. Life moves on. Count Dracula is revealed as a vampire who must drink blood to survive. A young woman becomes ill when blood is sucked out of her. Later she dies and becomes a vampire herself (technically, "un-dead"). In other words, lots of good, clean fun. By the way, have you ever noticed how vampirism is laced with sexuality? This is because the act of sucking blood is both male (penetration of the teeth) and female (accepting blood into the mouth). Like I said, lots of good, clean fun.

Web:
  **http://www.bibliomania.com/0/0/47/frameset.html
  http://www.literature.org/authors/stoker-bram/
    dracula/
  http://www.litrix.com/dracula/dracu001.htm**

Frankenstein

If you have ever felt that a monster who wants only companionship deserves your compassion, you have understood the theme of "Frankenstein, or, The Modern Prometheus" (1818), a novel written by English author Mary Wollstonecraft Shelley (1797-1851), the wife of poet Percy Bysshe Shelley. The book tells the story of a scientist named Victor Frankenstein who takes assorted bones and other spare parts from a graveyard and, using a secret "galvanic process", tries to create life. Instead, he ends up with a monster, so ugly, that Frankenstein abandons it immediately. (Interestingly enough, Shelley never refers to the monster by name.) Throughout the story, the monster struggles to create a life for himself. He tries, unsuccessfully, to become part of a family, and then implores Frankenstein to at least make him a companion, so he won't be so lonely. (The scientist refuses.) Eventually, the monster becomes more and more angry and violent and, well, I bet you can guess what happens. Or can you? (Want to hear something real cool? When Mary Shelley wrote "Frankenstein" she was only 18 years old.)

Web:
  **http://www.bibliomania.com/0/0/43/82/
    frameset.html
  http://www.literature.org/authors/shelley-mary/
    frankenstein/
  http://www.litrix.com/frankstn/frank001.htm**

Great Expectations

"Great Expectations" (1861) was written by English novelist Charles Dickens (1812-1870). The book tells the story of Pip (Philip Pirrip) and how he grows over the years to fit into society. As a young lad, Pip knows right from wrong, but has no understanding of why he must be good. As he grows older, Pip is corrupted and becomes amoral. Eventually, he matures and develops a sense of personal morality based on experience and knowledge.

Web:
  **http://www.bibliomania.com/0/0/19/37/
    frameset.html
  http://www.literature.org/authors/dickens-charles/
    great-expectations/
  http://www.litrix.com/grtex/grtex001.htm**

Gulliver's Travels

"Gulliver's Travels" (1726) is the account of an Englishman, Lemuel Gulliver, writing about his various travels and adventures. Along the way, some of the places Gulliver visits are Lilliput, where the people are six inches tall; Brobdingnag, inhabited by 70-foot giants; and the country of the Houyhnhnms, intelligent horses who keep human brutes, named Yahoos, as a source of labor. Read "Gulliver's Travels" today, and you will judge its author, the Irish-born English writer Jonathan Swift (1667-1745), to be an excellent storyteller with a gift for fantasy. However, what Swift wrote was actually a thinly veiled satire lampooning the English political, social and legal systems of his day. For example, at one point, we learn about civil wars in Lilliput that were caused by a disagreement between the Big-Endians, who break soft-boiled eggs at the large end, and the followers of the Emperor who are commanded to break their eggs at the small end. This passage is meant as a comment on the schism created when Henry VIII broke with the Roman Catholic Church. (Note: Within computer science, "big-endian" and "little-endian" are used to describe two opposite ways of storing data, although, I imagine, few computer scientists know the origin of these terms.)

Web:

http://www.jaffebros.com/lee/gulliver/contents.html
http://www.litrix.com/gulliver/gulli001.htm

Heart of Darkness

"Heart of Darkness" (1902) tells the story of Marlow, a mariner who travels on a long river voyage into the interior of Africa looking for a man named Kurtz. "Heart of Darkness" is an adventure story in which a man's journey turns into a search for himself that forces him to confront the dark side of his existence. There is good and evil in each of us, we come to learn, and it is our choices that ultimately steer us toward or away from moral deterioration. This short, brilliant novel was written by Joseph Conrad (1857-1924), a British author born in Polish Ukraine. ("Heart of Darkness" was the inspiration for the movie "Apocalypse Now".)

Web:

http://sunsite.berkeley.edu/Literature/Conrad/
  HeartOfDarkness/
http://www.acsu.buffalo.edu/~csicseri/
http://www.litrix.com/hartdark/hartd001.htm

Jane Eyre

"Jane Eyre" (1847), another sparkler from those jolly Brontë girls, is a darkly passionate novel of love and betrayal. Written by Charlotte Brontë (1816-1855), the novel tells the story of Jane, one of the most independent, intelligent heroines in English literature, a governess who works for the moody, sardonic Edward Rochester. Jane falls in love; Rochester proposes; and then she finds out he is already married—to an insane woman. Eventually, they are able to marry, but as in real life, getting there is one-half to two-thirds of the fun.

Web:

http://www.literature.org/authors/bronte-charlotte/
  jane-eyre/
http://www.litrix.com/janeeyre/janee001.htm

Lady Chatterley's Lover

The English writer D.H. Lawrence (1885-1930) had the distinction of writing a novel that was banned in both Great Britain and the United States. The book, "Lady Chatterley's Lover" (1928), tells the story of a love affair between Constance Chatterley, the wife of a paraplegic aristocrat, and Mellors, the game-keeper on the Chatterley estate. ("He stared straight into Connie's eyes, with a perfect, fearless, impersonal look...") Lawrence is a masterful writer, who not only plumbs the deep chasms of human emotion and desire, but describes the resulting physical relationship explicitly, earning him the enduring gratitude of high school students everywhere, who are pleasantly surprised to find such an earthy book on their list of required reading.

Web:

http://rishi.serc.iisc.ernet.in/books/Fiction/dhl/chat/
http://www.bibliomania.com/0/0/32/68/
   frameset.html

Little Women

"Talent isn't genius, and no amount of energy can make it so." This is just one of the many insights into human nature you will find in "Little Women" (1868). Written by the American novelist Louisa May Alcott (1832-88), "Little Women" is one of the most popular girls' books ever written, a mostly autobiographical story of the life of four sisters (Meg, Jo, Beth and Amy) growing up in nineteenth century New England. The book has two sequels, "Little Men" (1871) and "Jo's Boys" (1886). Alcott should never be dismissed as only a children's book author. Her writing has a power and beauty that rivals that of Dickens, whom she much admired and emulated. (Note to guys: One day you will be talking to a woman and the topic will shift to "Little Women". At this point, even if you have never read the book, I want you to say, "You know, of all the sisters, the one who has always reminded me the most of you is Jo." Take my word for it. This is *always* the right thing to say.)

Web:

http://www.eserver.org/fiction/little-women.txt
http://xroads.virginia.edu/~hyper/alcott/lwtext.html

Moby Dick

"Moby Dick, or, The Whale", written by American novelist Herman Melville (1819-1891), is a long, adventure story, set in the high seas in the early nineteenth century. The story is related by a narrator named Ishmael, a schoolteacher looking for adventure. Ishmael meets a harpooner named Queequeg and, together, they sign up to work aboard the whaling ship Pequod, commanded by the mysterious Captain Ahab. At first, the ship is managed by the first and second mates, Starbuck and Stubb. It is only after several days at sea that Ahab shows himself and reveals the real purpose of the voyage: to hunt down and kill Moby Dick, the legendary white whale who, in a previous encounter, had relieved the captain of one of his legs. Ishmael and the rest of the crew have various adventures, as the extent of Ahab's obsession with Moby Dick becomes evident. Eventually, they catch up with the whale ("...there she blows! - there she blows! A hump like a snowhill! It is Moby Dick!") and the book reaches its climax. On the surface, "Moby Dick" is a superb adventure story. However, the quest for domination is really a complex allegory. Moby Dick, the great white whale, represents evil, while Ahab's obsession to destroy Moby Dick represents an even greater evil. Thus, the book actually chronicles the struggle between good and evil, as well as the influence of the unseen powers, such as God and the Devil, that affect mankind (all of which you will find especially meaningful if you happen to be an eighteenth-century Calvinist). "Moby Dick" was published in 1851, but was not recognized as a masterpiece until 30 years after Melville's death. (Fortunately, I don't have to worry about that with my work. This book is scheduled to be recognized as a masterpiece any day now.)

Web:

http://etext.library.adelaide.edu.au/m/m53m/
http://www.bibliomania.com/0/0/36/2004/
   frameset.html
http://www.litrix.com/mobydick/mobyd001.htm

**The Net:
open 24 hours a day.**

O. Henry Short Stories

O. Henry was the pen name for the beloved American author William Sydney Porter (1862-1910), who wrote over 300 short stories. O. Henry can rightly be considered the dean of American short story writing. Each year, since 1918, an annual O. Henry Memorial Award has been given to the best writer of a short story published in an American or Canadian magazine. O. Henry's most well-known story is "The Gift of the Magi", which relates how a young impecunious couple, Della and Jim, sacrifice their most valuable possessions in order to buy Christmas presents for one another. My personal favorite is "The Ransom of Red Chief", the story of an abortive attempt by two kidnappers to hold a thoroughly obnoxious child for ransom. It is impossible to read this story without laughing out loud, so when you do so, be sure you are at work (so everyone else will get nervous, thinking that you know something important that they don't).

Web:

http://www.classicreader.com/toc.php/sid.6/
   aut.123/
http://www.litrix.com/magi/magi001.htm

Oedipus Trilogy

Sophocles (c. 496-406 B.C.) was a Greek tragic poet who was an innovator in the history of drama, introducing ideas such as expanding the chorus and introducing scene paintings. The Oedipus Trilogy centers around a young man named Oedipus who was destined to murder his father and marry his mother. I don't want to spoil it for you by telling you how the story turns out.

Web:

http://sailor.gutenberg.org/etext92/oedip10.txt
http://www.eserver.org/drama/sophocles/
   oedipus-trilogy.txt

Paradise Lost

John Milton (1608-1674) was an English poet who wrote a great deal of work about religious ideas and philosophy and was a strong voice in various church reforms. "Paradise Lost" is an epic poem about Satan's rebellion against God, and the story of Adam and Eve in the Garden.

Web:

http://www.literature.org/authors/milton-john/
   paradise-lost/
http://www.paradiselost.org/
http://www.triton.edu/depts/uc/files/plboss10.html

Whatever else you say about Oedipus, you have to admit he *was* nice to his mother.

A B C D E F G H I J K **L** M N O P Q R S T U V W X Y Z

Picture of Dorian Gray

"The Picture of Dorian Gray" (1891) is the only novel written by the Irish-born author Oscar Wilde (1854-1900). The story concerns Lord Henry, a pithy, witty, sardonic aristocrat, and his relationship with a very handsome young man named Dorian Gray. "I like persons better than principles," says Lord Henry, "and I like persons with no principles better than anything else in the world." Henry makes Dorian Gray's acquaintance, and over a period of time, manages to indoctrinate the young man into a life of sensual decadence, leading to... Well, you'll just have to see for yourself. The book is beautifully written, and I know you will enjoy the many epigrams scattered far and wide by Lord Henry as he educates his young charge. Whatever you do, make sure you do *not* read the ending of the book ahead of time, and do not discuss it with anyone else until you have finished the whole thing.

Web:

    http://www.dagonbytes.com/thelibrary/dorgray/
    http://www.hoboes.com/html/FireBlade/Wilde/
      dorian/
    http://www.litrix.com/doriangr/doria001.htm

Pride and Prejudice

"It is a truth universally acknowledged, that a single man in possession of a good fortune must be in want of a wife." Thus begins "Pride and Prejudice" (1813), an intelligent and perceptive romance for smart people, written by English novelist Jane Austen (1775-1817). "Pride and Prejudice" is the story of Elizabeth Bennet and her long, spirited courtship with Mr. Darcy, a seemingly cold and snobbish person who eventually proves himself to be a hero and a gentleman. Austen possesses a clever and funny writing style that, on the surface, seems spare and unemotional, which is why her books are still so popular (and make such good movies).

Web:

    http://www.bibliomania.com/0/0/6/8/frameset.html
    http://www.pemberley.com/janeinfo/pridprej.html

Robinson Crusoe

The English novelist Daniel Defoe (1660?-1731) wrote "Robinson Crusoe" when he was 58 years old. By then, Defoe had had a large variety of experiences, many of which showed up in the book. "Robinson Crusoe" tells the story of a headstrong 18-year-old who, against his parents' wishes, runs away to sea to seek adventure. He is captured by pirates who enslave him, but after two years, he manages to escape to what appears to be an uninhabited island (actually, it is inhabited by friendly black natives). Eventually, Crusoe is rescued. He then goes to Brazil where he acquires some plantations and starts a slave trading business. However, while at sea, his ship is wrecked, leaving him the only survivor on what, this time, really is an uninhabited island. Crusoe manages to save provisions from the ship, and does his best to recreate a proper English life. At first he is miserable, but eventually, he grows to enjoy the solitude and being master of his domain. After about 15 years, he sees a footprint in the sand (imagine how he feels!), and discovers that, from time to time, cannibals with prisoners come from the mainland in canoes. Several years later, when they return, Crusoe scares them away and rescues a young savage named Friday, who becomes Crusoe's servant, even to the extent of embracing Christianity. They live alone happily for two years, but eventually, other people join them on the island. Crusoe and Friday then travel to England, where Crusoe finds that, in his absence, his plantations have prospered and he is a wealthy man. In the fullness of time, Crusoe marries and has three children. Eventually, after his wife dies, Crusoe returns to sea. (Interesting note: in real life, Daniel Defoe was an unsuccessful, somewhat unscrupulous, businessman, who once cheated his own mother-in-law out of four hundred pounds in a cat-breeding scheme.)

Web:

    http://www.bibliomania.com/0/0/17/31/
      frameset.html
    http://www.learnlibrary.com/rob-crusoe/

Do a backup.

Sherlock Holmes Stories

Between 1887 and 1927, the English author Arthur Conan Doyle (1859-1930) wrote fifty-six stories and four novels about the detective Sherlock Holmes. Holmes is the most recognizable character in English literature, and his stories have been read and re-read for over a hundred years. (I myself have read them multiple times.) The stories are narrated by Holmes' friend, Dr. John Watson, whose well-intentioned blundering provides a foil for Holmes' razor sharp intelligence and encyclopedic knowledge.

Web:
http://www.literature.org/authors/
doyle-arthur-conan/
http://www.litrix.com/sec6.htm
http://www.tirkzilla.com/holmes/

Usenet:
alt.fan.holmes

Tarzan

Did you know that Tarzan was actually an English aristocrat? Here is the story. An English couple is stranded on the west coast of Africa while the woman is pregnant. She gives birth to a son, and not long after, the couple dies. The young boy is raised by an ape and grows up to be Tarzan, the leader of the ape tribe. Eventually, he falls in love with an American, Jane Porter. Tarzan and Jane have a son and, with the help of the animals, Tarzan becomes king of the jungle. Over the course of 24 books, Tarzan evolves into an invincible hero who has many strange but exciting adventures. The Tarzan books (as well as two Tarzan stories just for children) were written by the American pulp writer, Edgar Rice Burroughs (1875-1950). Burroughs was also the author of many other adventure novels, including a series of stories taking place on Mars.

Web:
http://www.literature.org/authors/
burroughs-edgar-rice/
http://www.ofcn.org/cyber.serv/resource/bookshelf/
tarz310/
http://www.ofcn.org/cyber.serv/resource/bookshelf/
tarz610/
http://www.ofcn.org/cyber.serv/resource/bookshelf/
tarzn10/

Time Machine

In 1895, H.G. Wells wrote his future-thinking book, "The Time Machine". It's a fantastic tale of a man who creates a machine with which he travels through time and visits the distant future. I am amazed at how well Wells was able to describe such a machine and cleverly contemplate the meaning and the mechanics of time travel. The book is relatively short and well worth the time.

Web:
http://www.literature.org/authors/
wells-herbert-george/the-time-machine/
http://www.umich.edu/~umfandsf/other/ebooks/
timem10.txt

Read *The Time Machine* and see how H.G. Wells traveled to the future (and what he did when he found out that the Internet had replaced television).

War of the Worlds

In 1898, the English writer H.G. Wells (1866-1946) wrote a novel about a Martian invasion of Earth. On October 30, 1938, the American actor and producer Orson Welles put on a radio dramatization of "The War of The Worlds" that scared the daylights out of a great many credulous Americans. "No one would have believed," the book begins, "in the last years of the nineteenth century that this world was being watched keenly and closely by intelligences greater than man's and yet as mortal as his own..."

Web:
http://www.fourmilab.ch/etexts/www/warworlds/
warw.html
http://www.literature.org/authors/
wells-herbert-george/the-war-of-the-worlds/

Wuthering Heights

"Wuthering Heights" was written in 1847 by the English novelist and poet Emily Brontë (1816-1855). The novel tells the disturbing story of destructive and obsessive love between two not-very-nice people (Catherine Earnshaw and the savage rebel Heathcliff), and the nice people whose lives they ruin.

Web:

http://www.bibliomania.com/0/0/9/16/
frameset.html
http://www.literature.org/authors/bronte-emily/
wuthering-heights/

LITERATURE ONLINE: COLLECTIONS

Ancient Greek Literature

The literature of the ancient Greeks forms one of the pillars of modern Western civilization. Very few people, of course, can read ancient Greek. However, many surviving works have been translated into modern English, and this Web site will help you access a great many texts. Read the work of Aeschylus (tragedy), Aesop (fables), Aristophanes (comedy and satire), Aristotle (philosophy and science), Epictetus (philosophy), Euripides (tragedy), Herodotus (history), Homer (epic poetry), Plato (philosophy and science), Sophocles (tragedy) and Thucydides (history).

Web:

http://www.e-classics.com/links.htm

> On the planet Hooloo, money can talk. Half the people sit around listening. The other half wear ear plugs.

Anglo-Saxon Tales

In the movie "Annie Hall", Annie (Diane Keaton) is trying to decide on an adult education course to take. Alvy Singer (Woody Allen) advises her, "Just don't take any course where they make you read 'Beowulf'." So who was this Beowulf guy, anyway? In the middle of the 5th century, after the withdrawal of the Romans, Germanic tribes from Europe overran England, bringing the Anglo-Saxon language—also known as Old English—with them. Anglo-Saxon was used increasingly until the Norman invasion (William the Conqueror in 1066 and all that), after which time French replaced Anglo-Saxon as the most important language in England. Anglo-Saxon literature is a rich area of scholarship, perhaps best known for an epic poem named "Beowulf". "Beowulf" is an epic poem, written in the 8th century and considered to be the epitome of Anglo-Saxon literature. The poem begins and ends with the funeral of a great king (Beowulf), the story being told against the background of an impending disaster. Beowulf is a Scandinavian hero who, in the course of the poem, destroys a monster named Grendal and Grendal's mother, as well as a fire-breathing dragon. If you ask me what I think of the poem "Beowulf", I would have to tell you frankly I have trouble understanding all the nuances. However, I did like "Annie Hall".

Web:

http://vos.ucsb.edu/browse.asp?id=2740

British Authors

You have probably heard of the poet Shelley (1792-1822). What you may not know is his middle name. In Shelley's time, it would have been very difficult to find this information. You would have had to travel all the way to England, get him drunk and, once his guard was lowered, see if you could get him to tell you his full name. Now, all you have to do is look it up on the Net. (Shelley's middle name, by the way, was Bysshe. However don't feel too sorry for him. His son Percy's middle name was Florence.)

Web:

http://libraries.cua.edu/irbritau.html
http://www.cyesis.org/webinstruction/english/
websites.htm
http://www.frostburg.edu/dept/engl/gartner/
britauth.htm

Chinese Literature

The history of Chinese literature stretches back several thousand years. The oldest existing works date from the late Chou dynasty (c. 1207-256 B.C.) and include: "Five Classics of Confucianism", traditionally attributed to Confucius; the "Book of Changes" (the I Ching), a system of fortune telling and predicting the future; the "Book of Rites", which describes ceremonies and the ideal state; the "Book of History", a collection of historical records; the "Book of Songs", poems about war, love and life; and "The Way and Its Power", the traditional basis of Taoism.

Web:
  http://vos.ucsb.edu/browse.asp?id=469

In the fifth and sixth centuries, the Angles and the Saxons joined with the Jutes and headed over to England to see what they could dig up in the way of territory to conquer. Armed only with a few weapons, their wits, a tradition of bravery, and a box full of Harley Hahn books, they managed to take over much of what we now call England, including the house in which Margaret Thatcher used to entertain her male friends.

One of the more important results of this invasion was the establishment of a culture that eventually led to a large number of works of literature, including *Beowulf*, *The Seafarer*, *Widsith*, *Deor's Lament*, and *Walt Disney's Comics and Stories*. If you want to download some Anglo-Saxon material for your next party, the Net will oblige with a nice selection of free literature.

English Server

This Web site offers a colossal collection of literature resources. Just about any subject you can think of will be here: autobiographies, plays, essays, jokes, novels, poems, speeches, short stories, and many other items of interest. If you ever get a spare moment, go immediately to this site. I guarantee within two minutes you'll find something engaging.

Web:
  http://www.eserver.org/

French Literature

As with other languages, French literature began with the creation of poetry, particularly epics. In honor of the French tradition, I have written the following poem:

> There was a juene fille named Degas,
> Whose boyfriend would say "Ooh lah lah".
> But if nothing was new,
> He would say "Deja vu",
> And she'd tell him to "Cherchez la bas".

Web:
  http://humanities.uchicago.edu/ARTFL/
  http://vos.ucsb.edu/browse.asp?id=961
  http://www.frenchculture.org/links/books/
  resources.html#authors

German Stories

If you are a fan of German literature, you will enjoy this collection of 19th century German stories and poems, most of which have English translations available: Aside from the stories and poems, there are wonderful old illustrations. The collection is limited but well worth your time.

Web:
  http://vos.ucsb.edu/browse.asp?id=1226

Literature Collection Talk and General Discussion

The oldest and most renowned collection of literature on the Net is Project Gutenberg. This mailing list is for discussion of issues related to this ambitious project.

Listserv Mailing List:
  List Name: gutnberg
  Subscribe to: listserv@listserv.uiuc.edu

A B C D E F G H I J K **L** M N O P Q R S T U V W X Y Z

Middle English Literature

Middle English refers to the dialects of English spoken from about 1100 to 1500 A.D. This Web site is a valuable reference for students, researchers and fans of Middle English literature. You can find not only the texts of many works, but information and commentary about important authors such as Chaucer, Gawain, Langland, Julian, Kempe and Malory. Even if you have absolutely no interest in Middle English, take a few moments to browse this site. I think you will find it interesting to take a look at a Middle English text, just to see what the language looked like. If you do get interested, you will find translations of many of the texts into modern English.

Web:
  http://www.luminarium.org/medlit/

Online Books

There are many, many books available to read for free on the Net. Although it is not always as comfortable to read books on your computer screen as it is on paper, there are some advantages to using an electronic version. For example, it is easy to search the entire text for a particular word or phrase. And, once you have the text, you can manipulate it with a regular editing program or a word processor.

Web:
  http://www.bartleby.com/
  http://www.bibliomania.com/
  http://www.booksbtc.com/
  http://www.bookvalley.com/
  http://www.digital.library.upenn.edu/books/
  http://www.gutenberg.org/
  http://www.ipl.org/div/books/
  http://www.promo.net/pg/
  http://www.vt.edu/vt98/academics/books/
    AABookIndex.html

Secular Web

The Secular Web—which contains a literature archive—is maintained by a group called the Internet Infidels. The Infidels promote the philosophy of secularism: the belief that morality and education should not be based on religion. If you are religious, I understand that this philosophy may be in direct contradistinction to everything you believe (or have been taught). However, the books and articles at this site all resonate around the idea that people can actually think for themselves and should be able to choose to accept or reject important ideas on their own merit. Take a look and see what you think.

Web:
  http://www.infidels.org/

Short Stories

The definition of a short story is a work of fiction that you can read at one sitting. My favorite short stories are the ones written by P.G. Wodehouse, Isaac Asimov, and me. (The order depends upon my mood.)

Web:
  http://endeavor.med.nyu.edu/lit-med/lit-med-db/
    webdocs/webgenres/collection..short.genre.html
  http://www.classicreader.com/toc.php/sid.6/
  http://www.richmondreview.co.uk/library/
  http://www.worldwideschool.com/library/catalogs/
    bysubject-lit-shortstories.html

Middle English

As soon as I finish this book, I'm going to start my next project: translating the complete set of James Bond stories into Middle English, making changes where appropriate. ("...The name is Gawain, Sir Gawain...")

My cat generally prefers
to use the keyboard.
(He ate the mouse.)

Online Books

Authors labor mightily to write great works of literature, and now you can get many of these books for free, whenever you want. What's more, you can change the stories to make them even better.

For example, consider *Moby Dick* by Herman Melville. This is an enormous novel, hundreds of pages long, which took Melville years to write.

Download the entire book and store a copy on your computer. Then use your word processor and replace every instance of "Dick" with "Harley."

You are now reading *Moby Harley*!

Victorian Literature

The study of Victorian literature covers the work of 19th-century English writers. The Victorian era (named for Queen Victoria, who reigned from 1837 to 1901) was rich in cultural, scientific and social development. In particular, England was blessed with an outpouring of literature, much of which is popular to this day. Many of the great Victorian writers are as famous today as they were in their own time: Charlotte Brontë, Emily Brontë, Elizabeth Barrett Browning, Robert Browning, Thomas Carlyle, Lewis Carroll, Charles Dickens, George Eliot, Rudyard Kipling, Dante Gabriel Rossetti, Alfred Tennyson, W.M. Thackeray, Anthony Trollope and Oscar Wilde. If you have never read any Victorian literature, why not give it a try? I suggest Oscar Wilde's book, "The Picture of Dorian Gray".

Web:
http://vos.ucsb.edu/browse.asp?id=2751
http://www.andromeda.rutgers.edu/~jlynch/Lit/
  victoria.html
http://www.indiana.edu/~letrs/vwwp/

Western European Literature

There is lots of literature on the Net, but it is not always so easy to find what you want. Here is a Web site that will help you find literature in a large number of European languages: Catalan, Danish, Dutch, Finnish, French, German, Italian, Norwegian, Old Norse, Portuguese, Provençal, Spanish and Swedish. Select the language in which you are interested, and you will be shown a selection of resources to explore.

Web:
http://www.lib.virginia.edu/wess/etexts.html

Women and Literature

The study of women's literature has become an important part of our academic tradition. Studying such literature introduces you to a comprehensive view of societies and cultures (as opposed to dwelling on wars and politics). Experience the remarkable writing of women in literature. These sites celebrate numerous women authors, including notables such as Louisa May Alcott, Jane Austen, Emily Brontë and Sylvia Plath.

Web:
http://www.andromeda.rutgers.edu/~jlynch/Lit/
  women.html
http://www.digital.library.upenn.edu/women/

Short Stories

When I was in graduate school, there was a popular song called "Love Stinks", and a local radio station had a contest to see who could write the best short story with that title, in no more than 100 words.

Here is what I wrote:

Love Stinks (in exactly 100 words)

by Harley Hahn

He questioned each suspect in turn, punctuating his interrogation with occasional sniffs. Even the Great Detective was not immune to hay fever.

He pointed to the butler.

"But how?" I asked.

The Great Detective smiled. "Whoever killed the Baron did so immediately after leaving the bed of the Baroness. I needed only to find the man who had recently engaged in sexual congress."

"You mean," I exclaimed, "it wasn't hay fever?"

"Exactly. I was finding the murderer. You know, Boy, this case would make an excellent story for you. You can call it-"

"Don't worry," I said, "I'll think of something."

MAGAZINES

Bodybuilding/Weightlifting Magazines

In the movie "The Rocky Horror Picture Show", Dr. Frank N. Furter introduces Brad and Janet to Rocky, a well-developed muscle man that Dr. Furter has created for his own evil pleasure. "Brad and Janet," he asks, "what do you think of him?" Janet looks at Rocky and then at her boyfriend Brad. "Well," she replies, "I don't like a man with too many muscles." But, as we learn later, she really does. What's more, whenever Janet has a chance, she looks at the online editions of her favorite bodybuilding magazines: Hardgainer, Ironman, Muscle & Fitness, Muscle & Fitness: Hers, and Muscle Media.

Web:
http://www.hardgainer.com/hardgain.html
http://www.ironmanmagazine.com/
http://www.muscle-fitness.com/
http://www.muscleandfitnesshers.com/
http://www.musclemedia.com/

Business and Finance Magazines

The Net is standing ready, 24 hours a day, to help you mind your own as well as everyone else's business. One good way to keep up with how the world of money is shaking out is to read financial magazines online. Try these: Advertising Age, Business Week, Forbes, Fortune and Money.

Web:
http://www.adage.com/
http://www.businessweek.com/
http://www.forbes.com/forbes/
http://www.fortune.com/
http://money.cnn.com/

Cars, Trucks and Motorcycle Magazines

If it's got an engine and you can drive it, it's cool. I guess I don't have to tell you that. What I do want to tell you is that there is a nice selection of magazines online for aficionados of cars, trucks and motorcycles. No need to drive to the store just to keep up on what's moving. Check the Net: Auto Exec, AutoWeek, Car and Driver, Motor Trend, Road & Track and Woman Motorist.

Web:
http://www.aemag.com/
http://www.autoweek.com/
http://www.caranddriver.com/
http://www.motortrend.com/
http://www.roadandtrack.com/
http://www.womanmotorist.com/

Celebrity/Entertainment Magazines

Tell me the truth—when I mention Oprah, JLo, Madonna, Camilla, O.J. and Britney, do you know who I mean? Of course you do. So don't waste even one more moment. See what the rich and vacuous—excuse me, the famous and beautiful—are doing while you and I are busy working, paying taxes, watching television, going to movies and listening to music. Your gossip-enriched sources of insider info are: Boxoffice, Cinescape, Entertainment Today, Entertainment Weekly, Movieline, National Enquirer, People, Premiere, Star Magazine and TV Guide.

Web:
http://www.boxoff.com/
http://www.cinescape.com/
http://www.ent-today.com/
http://www.ew.com/ew/
http://www.movielinemag.com/
http://www.nationalenquirer.com/
http://people.aol.com/
http://www.premieremag.com/
http://www.starmagazine.com/
http://www.tvguide.com/magazine/

Celebrity/Entertainment Magazines

Are you like me? I get bored easily and, at the supermarket, I look at the gossip magazines while I am waiting at the checkout counter.

Most days, however, the checkout is so fast (what with automated scanners and all), it's hard to catch up on much gossip.

Not to worry. The Net is available 24 hours a day, with all the gossip you need to satisfy your minimum daily recommended requirement.

Children's Magazines

Magazines for children are great. By tuning into mainstream culture as they are growing up, kids can not only enjoy themselves and act like grown-ups, they can prepare themselves for being good citizens and consumers later in life. The Net is always ready to help. Take a look at these online versions of kids' magazines: American Girl, Dig, National Geographic, Nick Jr., Time For Kids, Yak's Corner, and Zoobooks.

Web:

 http://www.americangirl.com/agmg/
 http://www.digonsite.com/
 http://www.nationalgeographic.com/kids/
 http://www.nickjr.com/
 http://www.timeforkids.com/tfk/
 http://www.yakscorner.com/
 http://www.zoobooks.com/

Collector's Magazines

Nothing can surpass the thrill you get when you finally add a rare item to your personal collection. And it's a lot of fun to go to conventions and talk with people who collect the same sort of stuff as you. If you like collecting, there are some magazines on the Net you may enjoy. Check out their Web sites and see what you think: Action Figure Times, Autograph Collector, Car Collector, Collector Times, Dollhouse Miniatures, The Old Times, Oriental Rug Review, and Toy Soldier.

Web:

 http://www.aftimes.com/
 http://www.autographcollector.com/acm.htm
 http://www.carcollector.com/
 http://www.collectortimes.com/
 http://www2.dhminiatures.com/
 http://www.theoldtimes.com/
 http://www.rugreview.com/orr.htm
 http://www.toy-soldier.com/

Shhh... It's a secret...
Don't tell anyone. (See
"Secret Stuff".)

Computer Magazines

The world of computing moves fast and furious and takes no prisoners. So how do you keep up? One way is to read computer magazines, and it's a lot easier (and cheaper) to read them online than it is to subscribe to the print editions. Here are some magazines that have a lot of online information and articles: Byte, Computer Active, Computer World, MacWorld, Maximum PC, PC Magazine, and Smart Computing.

Web:

 http://www.byte.com/
 http://www.computeractive.co.uk/
 http://www.computerworld.com/
 http://www.macworld.com/
 http://www.maximumpc.com/
 http://www.pcmag.com/
 http://www.smartcomputing.com/

Entertainment Industry Magazines

Show business—there's no business like it, no business at all. And if you are in the Business, you can ensure that no one gives *you* the business, by making it your business to keep up with the business aspects of the Business on a regular basis. See the Hollywood Reporter, Talkers (radio talk shows), and Variety.

Web:

 http://www.hollywoodreporter.com/
 http://www.talkers.com/
 http://www.variety.com/

Family and Parenting Magazines

Raising a family takes a lot of time, but that's no reason why you can't enjoy your favorite family and parenting magazines. The next time one of your little ones gets you up in the middle of the night, remember that articles, advice and talk are available on the Net 24 hours a day: Compleat Mother, Informed Parent, Parents and Today's Parent.

Web:

 http://www.compleatmother.com/
 http://www.informedparent.com/
 http://www.parents.com/
 http://www.todaysparent.com/

Fashion Magazines

Here is my easy, two-step plan to always stay in fashion. (1) Every day, spend at least half an hour reading one of these fashion magazines on the Net. This will develop your knowledge and sense of fashion. (2) Wherever you go, make sure you have a Harley Hahn book under your arm. That way, no matter what you wear, people will always know you have good taste. The Net is your fashion friend. The reading starts here: Elle, Glamour, In Style, Marie Claire, and Vogue.

Web:
   http://www.ellemag.com/
   http://www.glamour.com/
   http://www.instyle.com/
   http://www.marieclaire.com/
   http://www.vogue.com

Fashion Magazines

If you have a daughter, be sure to "magazine-proof" her before she becomes a teenager.

Spend some time with your youngster looking at fashion magazines together. As you turn the pages, explain to her that the images she sees are not realistic. They are carefully crafted to create a need in consumers to buy cosmetics, clothes and accessories. Normal women do not look this way (even though many of them think they should).

Assure her that, while it is a good idea for her to make herself look attractive, she should not accept the idea that she must constantly strive to look like an unattainable ideal.

Warn her that, as she gets older, she will notice that her friends will become more and more indoctrinated into the system. Explain how that will change the way they feel about themselves, and reassure her that, as she grows up, you will help her develop a realistic and healthy attitude regarding fashion and her personal appearance.

Food, Wine and Cooking Magazines

I bet you understand the pleasure of the table: the sensual aroma of good food, the added pleasure of a great wine, and the company of congenial friends with whom to share your culinary experiences. Great experiences start with great planning, and here are some magazines to help: Cooking Light, Cooks Illustrated, Cuisine at Home, Epicurious, Fine Cooking, Smart Wine, Taste of Home, and Wine Spectator.

Web:
   http://www.cookinglight.com/
   http://www.cooksillustrated.com/
   http://www.cuisineathome.com/
   http://www.epicurious.com
   http://www.taunton.com/finecooking/
   http://www.winebusiness.com/
   http://www.tasteofhome.com/
   http://www.winespectator.com/

Gay Magazines

The world is changing, sometimes quickly and sometimes slowly, but it's always hard to stay current. If you are gay or if you have loved ones who are gay, you'll find these magazines interesting: The Advocate, Curve, Frontiers News Magazine, and Lesbian News.

Web:
   http://www.advocate.com/
   http://www.curvemag.com/
   http://www.frontiersweb.com/
   http://www.lesbiannews.com/

Health and Fitness Magazines

There are lots of ways to keep fit. I swim in the ocean, practice yoga, run along the beach, and play with my cat. However, if you don't have the time to work out every day, you can use Plan B, a little-known but highly effective way to stay slim, trim and energetic. Simply use the Net to read health and fitness magazines. Give it a try for six months and see what happens. Start here: Health, Natural Health, Self, Shape, and Ultra-Fit.

Web:
   http://www.health.com/
   http://www.naturalhealthmag.com/
   http://www.self.com/
   http://www.shapemag.com/
   http://www.ultra-fitmagazine.com/

Hobby Magazines

Hobbies are a great way to pass the time and enjoy your spare hours. Moreover, it's fun to read about your hobby. Here are a couple of hobby magazines with Web sites that I think you might enjoy. If these are publications you already like, take a few minutes and try out the online versions: American Woodworker, Aquarium Fish, Creating Keepsakes, FineScale Modeler, Hobby Merchandiser, Lapidary Journal, McCall's Quilting, Model Airplane News, Popular Woodworking, Scale Auto, The Woodworker, Trains and Wood.

Web:

http://www.americanwoodworker.com/
http://www.animalnetwork.com/fish/
http://www.creatingkeepsakes.com/magazine/
http://www.finescale.com/
http://www.hobbymerchandiser.com/
http://www.lapidaryjournal.com/
http://www.mccallsquilting.com/mccalls/
http://www.modelairplanenews.com/
http://www.popularwoodworking.com/
http://www.scaleautomag.com/
http://www.getwoodworking.com/
http://www.trains.com/maghomepage/
http://www.woodmagazine.com/

Home and Garden Magazines

When you need some ideas for making your home and your garden as comfortable and attractive as possible, the Net is ready to help. Here are some magazines whose Web sites contain lots of useful information to help you turn an ordinary domicile into your own personal castle: Better Homes and Gardens, Coastal Living, Country Living, Good Housekeeping, House Beautiful, Martha Stewart Living and Southern Living Online

Web:

http://www.bhg.com/
http://www.coastalliving.com/
http://www.countryliving.com/
http://www.goodhousekeeping.com/
http://www.housebeautiful.com/
http://www.marthastewart.com/
http://www.southernliving.com/

Home Maintenance and Construction Magazines

Taking care of your home can be a lot of fun. Moreover, if you didn't have all those projects to take up your spare time, you would just be sitting around bored every weekend. Still, as one of my readers, I would never let you get bored. If you ever do get caught up around the house and find yourself with nothing left to fix, adjust or replace, the Net has something for you—articles about home improvement. Enjoy: Fine Homebuilding, Homebuilding & Renovating, Popular Mechanics, Self Build & Design, and The Family Handyman.

Web:

http://www.taunton.com/finehomebuilding/
http://www.homebuilding.co.uk/
http://www.popularmechanics.com/
   home_improvement/
http://www.selfbuildanddesign.com/
http://www.familyhandyman.com/

Internet Business and Technology Magazines

Every day I look at the Net, and I can't believe how fast it's growing and changing. Can you keep up? Why not? Other people will figure out what's happening and write about it. All you have to do is read the articles. Internet business and technology magazines at your service: Business 2.0, Red Herring, and Upside.

Web:

http://www.business2.com/
http://www.redherring.com/
http://www.upside.com/

> **Everyday has a surprise just waiting for you. For example, did you know that, today, you would be reading this?**

Magazine Collections

How many magazines are there on the Net? Lots and lots and lots (and lots). Here are some Web sites that collect links to online magazines. If the magazine you want is on the Net, you'll find it here. If you can't find what you want, maybe you need to start your own.

Web:
http://www.consumer-news.com/magazine/
http://www.ecola.com/news/magazine/
http://www.publist.com/
http://www.searchmagazines.com/

Magazine Talk and General Discussion

This is better than going to the newsstand, because you don't have to take off your fuzzy slippers and leave the house. Check out zines, newsletters and magazines from your computer. Read contents and summaries of electronic and printed publications and find out how to get them.

Usenet:
rec.mag

Men's Magazines

Don't let the springtime of your life turn into a cold, empty winter of discontent. Use the Net to stay up on what's current in the world of men. Fashions change, tastes evolve, attitudes go in and out of style, but you can be there on the electronic cutting edge, gamely following where only the cool, brave and bold dare to tread. (Not to mention pictures of Babes.) Men's magazines on the Net. Check them out now: Ask Men, Controversy, Esquire, FHM, GQ, and Maxim.

Web:
http://www.askmen.com/
http://www.controversymag.com/main.htm
http://www.esquire.com/
http://www.fhm.co.uk/
http://www.gq.com/
http://www.maximonline.com/

Music Magazines

It's fun to listen to music, but keeping up on the music industry is a lot more than fun; it's positively groovy. Here are some magazines that you can read online to check out what your favorite musicians are doing and to see what's hot and selling: Alternative Press, Billboard, Blender, Music Connection, New Musical Express, Rolling Stone, Spin and Vibe.

Web:
http://www.altpress.com/
http://www.billboard-online.com/
http://www.blender.com/
http://www.musicconnection.com/
http://www.nme.com/
http://www.rollingstone.com/
http://www.spin.com/
http://www.vibe.com/

Imagine the trouble politicians could cause if they knew how to use the Net.

National Lampoon Nostalgia

The American humor magazine National Lampoon was published from 1970 to 1998. However, its most creative and funniest issues were produced between 1970 and 1975, the Golden Age of National Lampoon. During this time, a large cadre of talented writers and artists formed the nexus of an extremely original burst of creativity that changed popular culture permanently. The National Lampoon magazine of the 70s directly inspired other well-known humor productions such as movies ("Animal House"...), TV shows ("Saturday Night Live"...), Radio shows ("The National Lampoon Radio Hour"...), Records ("Radio Dinner"...), a stage show (Lemmings), and a variety of books and anthologies. To say that National Lampoon was irreverent would be a massive understatement, sort of like saying that Richard Nixon's biggest mistake was not destroying the tapes.

Web:
  http://www2.bitstream.net/~marksim/natlamp/

News and Politics Magazines

There are two ways to keep up on the news and on what is happening in the political world. First, you can get your news from radio or television. However, you will only hear snippets of information. An alternative is to read a news magazine that takes a more long-term view and has more analyses. When you get a chance, here are some magazines to explore. Some are news, some are politics, some are politics masquerading as news: Christian Science Monitor, Mother Jones, Newsweek, The Nation, The Washington Monthly, Time, and U.S. News & World Report.

Web:
  http://www.csmonitor.com/
  http://www.mojones.com/
  http://www.newsweek.com/
  http://www.thenation.com/
  http://www.washingtonmonthly.com/
  http://www.time.com/
  http://www.usnews.com/

Usenet:
  alt.motherjones

Outdoors Magazines

I have to confess, I'm a typical masculine outdoorsy kind of guy. Why, I think nothing of waking before sunrise, going for a five-mile tramp across freshly plowed country fields, coming back to chop a cord or two of wood, and then sitting down to a good old-fashioned breakfast: stacks and stacks of homemade hotcakes and real maple syrup. Yup, I sure do love all that stuff. But you know what I like even more? Sitting inside a nice cozy house, with my cat in my lap and a cup of hot chocolate in my hand, using my computer to browse outdoor magazines on the Net. Want to join me? Here they are: Field and Stream, National Geographic, Outside, Scuba Diving, Skin Diver, Sport Diver, Sports Afield and Sunset Magazine

Web:
  http://www.fieldandstream.com/
  http://magma.nationalgeographic.com/ngm/
  http://www.outsidemag.com/
  http://www.scubadiving.com/
  http://www.skin-diver.com/
  http://www.sportdivermag.com/
  http://www.sportsafield.com/
  http://www.sunsetmagazine.com/

Photography Magazines

If you have ever taken a college-level photography course, I bet you have mixed feelings. On the one hand, you love photography. On the other hand, there is a good chance that any native love you have for the art was beaten out of you by a cynical, academic loudmouth teacher. You know the type I mean. A fellow who teaches because he couldn't make it as a real photographer, and who constantly criticizes his students' work to alleviate his unconscious feelings of inadequacy. Well, photography is a great art, and the Net wants you to get back into it. Here are some good places to start: Outdoor Photographer, PC Photo, Photo District News and Shutterbug.

Web:
  http://www.outdoorphotographer.com/
  http://www.pcphotomag.com/
  http://www.pdn-pix.com/
  http://www.shutterbug.net/

Popular Culture Magazines

We all need some good fun once in awhile, and what could be more enjoyable than popular culture? You know, all the things that people do, watch and talk about when they are not working. Here are some popular culture magazines, with stuff to think about and stuff to look at: Life, Reader's Digest and The Saturday Evening Post.

Web:

http://www.lifemag.com/
http://www.rd.com/
http://www.satevepost.org/

Science Magazines

More than anything, science is a way of thinking about life and exploring the nature of our universe. I believe that people gain so much in their lives when they train their minds to be rational, knowledgeable and informed. If you enjoy reading about science and new discoveries, I think you'll like these magazines: Discover, New Scientist, Popular Science, Science & Technology Review, and Science News.

Web:

http://www.discover.com/
http://www.newscientist.com/
http://www.popsci.com/
http://www.llnl.gov/str/
http://www.sciencenews.org/

Sports Magazines

No matter what sports are your favorites, there is something for you on the Net. So when your significant other tells you to get away from that television and do something else for a change, tell her (or him) that you are going to turn off the TV and spend some time using the computer. Then connect to the Net where you can read sports magazines all day long: ESPN, Golf Digest, Ski, Sporting News, Sports Illustrated, Surfer, Tennis, WaterSki and Yachting.

Web:

http://www.espn.go.com/magazine/
http://www.golfdigest.com/
http://www.skimag.com/
http://www.sportingnews.com/
http://sportsillustrated.cnn.com/
http://www.surfermag.com/
http://www.tennis.com/
http://www.waterskimag.com/
http://www.yachtingmag.com/

I like popular culture so much that I create some whenever I get a chance. But I can't help but wonder, if popular culture is cultured, how could it be so popular? Maybe we should just read the popular culture magazines and leave the deep questions to the philosophers.

Teen Magazines

If you want an insight into how teenage girls are different than teenage boys (and why women are different from men), all you need to do is take a look at some of these magazine Web sites. You'll find beauty and fashion tips, advice, celebrity gossip, music news, and, yes, just a word or two about relationships: Cosmo Girl, Dolly, Seventeen, Teen Ink, and YM.

Web:

http://www.cosmogirl.com/
http://dolly.ninemsn.com.au/dolly/
http://www.seventeen.com/
http://www.teenink.com/
http://www.ym.com/

Travel Magazines

Sometimes, when I have been working hard for days on end, I like to just browse a travel magazine and read about exotic places. If you need ideas for your next trip or if you love to read about traveling, here are some magazines I know you will enjoy. Get ideas about places to visit, things to do, planning a trip, and much more by reading these magazines: Carribean Travel & Life, Islands, and Travel + Leisure.

Web:

http://www.caribbeantravelmag.com/frontdoor/
http://www.islands.com/
http://www.travelandleisure.com/index.cfm

Women's Magazines

Let me tell you something. Even men can enjoy women's magazines. My chief researcher brings in a women's magazine from time to time and leaves it in the bathroom. At first, I used to ignore the magazine, but, well... I love to read and when I'm sitting around bored I'll read just about anything. So I started reading about fashion, celebrities and relationships. And then one day I found myself taking one of those tests ("What type of person is *your* ideal mate?") and I knew I was hooked. If you are a woman, here are some magazines to enjoy. If you are a man, my advice is, don't get started: Bust, Cosmopolitan, Essence, Ladies Home Journal, Redbook and Victoria.

Web:
http://www.bust.com/
http://www.cosmomag.com/
http://www.essence.com/
http://www.lhj.com/
http://www.redbookmag.com/
http://www.victoriamag.com/

MARTIAL ARTS

Aikido

Aikido is a non-violent martial art that uses throws and joint locks to neutralize opponents instead of using kicks and punches to injure. Aikido was developed in Japan by Morihei Ueshiba and was partially adapted from Daito-Ryu Jujitsu. Unlike other martial arts, aikido is not for fighting or competition. There are no tournaments and no sparring. Rather, aikido is a system of training and self-improvement. For this reason, aikido is learned cooperatively, at a pace suitable for the individual. The goal of aikido is not to defeat other people, but to defeat the negative traits within yourself.

Web:
http://www.aikidofaq.com/
http://www.aikiweb.com/

Usenet:
alt.martial-arts.aikido

Listserv Mailing List:
List Name: aikido-l
Subscribe to: listserv@lists.psu.edu

Capoeira

Capoeira (pronounced "cop-way-ruh") is a group activity that resembles a martial art, but is actually an amalgam of ritual, dance, music, fighting and acrobatics. Capoeira tradition holds that the movements and rituals were first developed by African slaves in Brazil, who had to disguise their fight training as a harmless activity that would not incur the disapproval of the Portuguese slaveowners. Today, an evolved form of capoeira is practiced around the world and is especially popular in Brazil. A capoeira game takes place within a circle called a roda. Spectators stand around the circle, singing, clapping and listening to music. Inside the circle are two opponents, who interact with one another using swift movements such as cartwheels, spins, handstands and kicks, although there is almost no contact. Traditional capoeira music uses several instruments: a berimbau (one-stringed bow attached to a hollow gourd), a caxixi (small rattle), an atabaque (drum), and a pandeiro (tambourine).

Web:
http://www.capoeira.com.au/html/terminology.html
http://www.capoeira.com/
http://www.capoeira.com/planetcapoeira/
http://www.capoeirasj.com/history/
http://www.capoeirasj.com/movements/
http://www.capoeirista.com/
http://www.capoeuropa.com/

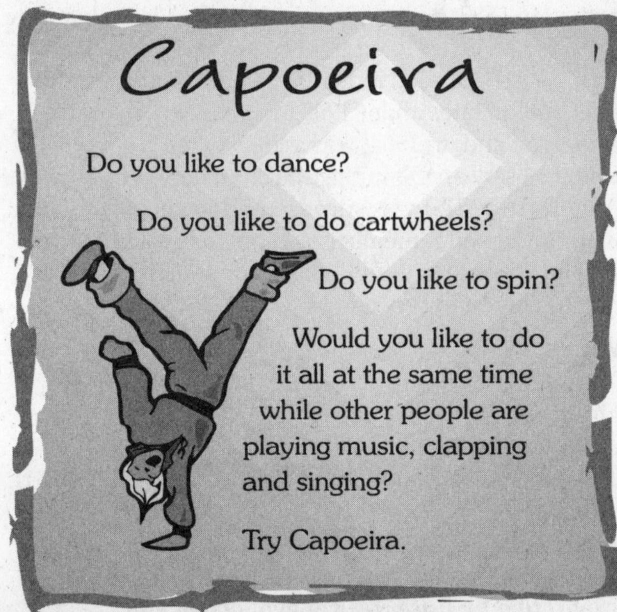

Japanese Sword Arts

The Japanese sword arts encompass a variety of martial arts related to using sword-like weapons, either for training or competition. The most popular such arts are: kendo, a competitive activity involving free-style practice with bamboo swords and protective armor; iaido, which centers around drawing the sword, cutting, and returning it to its scabbard with a minimum of exertion; kenjutsu, the art of using the sword once it has been drawn, practiced with a partner using wooden weapons; and jodo, which uses a short staff about one inch in diameter and four feet long.

Web:

  http://hem.passagen.se/tkolb/fun/kendo/
    kendo_e.htm
  http://pages.prodigy.net/tlbuck/sword.htm
  http://www.funet.fi/~magi/harrasteet/iaido/
    sanasto.html
  http://www.kendo-sask.com/swordfaq.htm
  http://www.swordforum.com/

Judo

Judo is a Japanese martial art characterized by the use of balance, leverage and throwing. In Japanese, the word "judo" means "gentle way", which refers to the idea of yielding deliberately in order to achieve a victory. The inventor of judo was Jigoro Kano (1860-1938). As a child, Kano studied the ancient art of jujitsu. In 1882, he founded the Kodokan Judo Institute in Tokyo, in order to teach his version of the martial arts, which he called judo. Judo was introduced into the United States about 1902 by President Theodore Roosevelt and, in 1964, was added to the Olympic Games. I saw an Olympic judo competition in Los Angeles in 1984, I was surprised how quick the bouts were, and I still remember one in which a small, short fellow was able to easily beat his opponent who was much larger and broader.

Web:

  http://www.ajjf.org/
  http://www.bestjudo.com/
  http://www.judoinfo.com/
  http://www.twoj.org/
  http://www.usjf.com/

Listserv Mailing List:

  List Name: judo-l
  Subscribe to: listserv@uconnvm.uconn.edu

Ju-Jitsu

The name ju-jitsu (spelled in various ways) means "soft" (ju) "practice" (jitsu). Ju-jitsu is an ancient Japanese martial art first practiced over two thousand years ago, whose roots lie in a variety of teachings. As such, ju-jitsu covers different techniques such as kicking, punching, throwing, immobilization, and the use of weapons, such as the sword, cane and knife. In Japan, the time period between the 8th and 16th centuries was filled with a great deal of turmoil, almost constant civil war. The techniques of ju-jitsu were developed into a variety of practices that were used for close fighting. Historically, the techniques of ju-jitsu have formed the basis for other popular martial arts, such as judo, aikido and karate. Not all ju-jitsu is the same. There are a number of different ryu (systems), each with their own characteristics. Ju-jitsu is not as much of a sport as other martial arts, although some ryu do have competitions.

Web:

  http://www.budoshin.com/aja.html
  http://www.jitsuka.org/jitsuka/
  http://www.usjujitsu.net/

Karate

Karate is a family of Japanese martial arts devoted to fighting and competition. Karate uses sharp blows and kicks aimed at sensitive points on the opponent's body—simple motions that depend on timing and delivery. The idea is to punch, kick, block and strike in such a way as to achieve maximum damage. In Japanese, the word "karate" means "open hand". Traditional karate was developed on the island of Okinawa. However, modern karate has evolved greatly and is much different from the original system.

Web:

  http://www.24fightingchickens.com/shotokan/
  http://www.karate1.com/
  http://www.karatetrend.com/
  http://www.thekaratedirectory.com/articles/
    terminology.htm
  http://www.ultimatekarate.com/

Usenet:

  alt.martial-arts.karate.semi-contact
  alt.martial-arts.karate.shotokan

Listserv Mailing List:

  List Name: karate
  Subscribe to: listserv@raven.cc.ukans.edu

Kickboxing

It is in the nature of many young men to be aggressive, and society does its best to channel such aggression into sports and competitions. However, there are times when the available outlets are not intense enough, which leaves a large number of trained athletes looking for a way to fight. The purpose of modern kickboxing is to satisfy this need. Kickboxing is a martial art that combines techniques from karate and boxing and, like other martial arts, it traces its roots back to ancient traditions. However, kickboxing, as it is practiced today, has a very specific goal: to satisfy the needs of trained competitors who want to fight in a more extreme manner than is traditional with other martial arts. There are three common variations of "kickboxing": Full Contact Karate, in which competitors may kick only above the waist; Kickboxing, in which kicking to the legs is also allowed; and Muay Thai, which allows full kicking as well as striking with elbows and knees.

Web:
  http://www.ifafitness.com/kmoves/
  http://www.ikfkickboxing.com/
  http://www.kickboxing-wka.co.uk/
  http://www.kickboxing.com/
  http://www.uskba.com/site.htm

Kung Fu

Kung fu is a general term referring to any of the Chinese martial arts, of which there are many. The words "kung fu" mean "skill from effort". Kung fu traces its roots back to ancient China, over 6,000 years ago. Today, there are literally hundreds of different kung fu styles and sub-styles with many variations. Some styles emphasize kicking and striking; others use grappling, ground-fighting, pressure-point attacks and weapons. What all these styles have in common are a devotion to disciplined learning, self-defense, meditation, mastery of breathing and cultivation of internal awareness.

Web:
  http://ezine.kungfumagazine.com/
  http://www.authentickungfu.com/

Usenet:
  alt.martial-arts.kung-fu.shaolin

Martial Arts for Women

It seems a truism to observe that women are different from men, but in the martial arts, such differences are important. In general, women are smaller and less strong than men. However, strength can be built with training, and a small size makes it easier to move quickly. Women approach the martial arts for a variety of reasons, among them a desire for physical conditioning, increased confidence and self-defense. Two of the most important lessons you learn in the martial arts are learning to hit and learning to be hit. These are difficult lessons for most women (and many men), but once you learn them, your life will never be the same.

Web:
  http://pages.ivillage.com/angiemoshier/karate/
  http://www.nwmaf.org/
  http://www.rutabaga.com/~xena/issues.htm
  http://www.tuffgrrlz.com/

Majordomo Mailing List:
  List Name: kiai
  Subscribe to: majordomo@apocalypse.org

Martial Arts for Women

One of my best friends, whose name is Dawn, is an extremely accomplished martial arts teacher. Not only does she have her third degree black belt in karate, but she has several schools where she teaches her martial arts techniques to children.

However, the best part about being a martial arts expert is how it enhances your relationships. Dawn and her husband Ben never, ever argue.

Martial Arts Resources

A martial art is a system of disciplines used for self-defense or for offense. Many martial arts teach unarmed techniques, although some use weapons. Most martial arts were developed within an Asian culture—in China, Korea, Japan or Okinawa—and they are taught all over the world. There are many different types of martial arts, and these resources will help you find the information you need. In general, martial arts are about training your mind and body, and possibly engaging in organized competition, not about street fighting. Hint: The best fight you can win is the one you avoid.

Web:
> http://www.atlantamartialarts.com/faq.htm
> http://www.budoseek.net/
> http://www.mararts.org/
> http://www.martialinfo.com/martialmainframe.htm
> http://www.martialresource.com/
> http://www.winstonstableford.com/

Martial Arts Talk and General Discussion

Learning a martial art may start as physical training and exercise, but it isn't long before you realize it's a lot more: you are studying how to understand and control the forces that shape our physical and mental existence. But then there's a lot of details: practice, lessons, fighting, philosophy, equipment, tournaments and competition—all of which means there's a lot to talk about.

Usenet:
> alt.arts.bujinkan
> alt.martial-arts.karate.shotokan
> alt.martial-arts.marketplace
> alt.ufc
> rec.martial-arts
> rec.martial-arts.moderated

> **Porcupines always get to the point.**

Tae Kwon Do

Tae kwon do is a Korean martial art, which can be thought of as a type of Korean karate. The techniques of tae kwon do involve using bare hands and feet to punch, kick, block and evade. Literally, the name means "foot" (tae), "fist" (kwon), "philosophy" (do). The roots are lost in antiquity. Modern tae kwon do dates from the post-World War II period. After the defeat of Japan and the liberation of Korea, Korean martial arts masters developed modern tae kwon do as an effort to remove the Japanese influence from their practice. The name "tae kwon do" was chosen in 1955.

Web:
> http://www.acdk.org/
> http://www.itatkd.com/
> http://www.jaguartaekwondo.com/home.htm
> http://www.tkd.net/tkdnetwork/tkdinfo.html

Usenet:
> alt.martial-arts.tae-kwon.do

T'ai Chi Ch'uan

T'ai chi ch'uan, often referred to as t'ai chi, is a "soft" martial art, based on the Taoist philosophy of living in harmony with nature. Today, t'ai chi is most often practiced as a type of exercise that integrates slow, flowing body movements with deliberate mindfulness in order to maintain physical health and spiritual growth. T'ai chi can be done alone or in groups, and can be practiced throughout one's lifetime. T'ai chi is popular around the world, especially in China where, each day, people gather in open areas to practice gentle, beautiful movements. The name t'ai chi ch'uan refers to "large" (t'ai), "ultimate" (chi), "fist" (ch-uan).

Web:
> http://www.maui.net/~taichi4u/taichi.html
> http://www.scheele.org/lee/taichi.html
> http://www.sifuphil.com/tcclinks.htm

Listserv Mailing List:
> List Name: tao-l
> Subscribe to: listserv@listserv.albany.edu

Majordomo Mailing List:
> List Name: kungfu
> Subscribe to: majordomo@cuy.net

MATHEMATICS

Algebra Help

It's a total bummer when you are working on an equation at three o'clock in the morning and you have nobody to ask for help. Never again will you be left mathematically stranded. On the Net you can always find the help you need. (Too bad you can't take the computer in with you when you have a test.)

Web:
  http://www.algebra.com/
  http://www.algebrahelp.com/
  http://www.purplemath.com/

Usenet:
  alt.algebra.help

American Mathematical Society

The American Mathematical Society was established in 1888 in order to promote mathematical research. Since then, the mathematical world has changed more than anyone in 1888 could have imagined. However, the AMS is still around serving its thousands of members.

Web:
  http://e-math.ams.org/

Calculus

When I was a kid, one did not talk about calculus in polite society. I had to learn to differentiate and integrate the same place everyone else did—in the street. Today you can enjoy these once-forbidden arts in the privacy of your own home. Connect to the Net and go wild. (Just remember, if your parents find out what you are doing, you didn't learn about it here.)

Web:
  http://archives.math.utk.edu/calculus/by_state.html
  http://integrals.wolfram.com/
  http://math.vanderbilt.edu/~pscrooke/toolkit.shtml
  http://www.calculus.net/
  http://www.calculus.org/
  http://www.math.uakron.edu/~dpstory/
    e-calculus.html

Chance Server

What exactly *is* a snowball's chance in hell? Check in at the Chance Server and you might find out. Get the Chance News, a biweekly report with popular news items that can be used in classroom settings to make teaching statistics and probability fun. (Not that it isn't normally fun, of course.) Teaching aids are also available.

Web:
  http://www.dartmouth.edu/~chance/

The Monty Hall Problem and the Chance Server

There is an old probability problem:

You are a guest on the "Let's Make a Deal" TV show. The host, Monty Hall, shows you three doors. Behind two of them are goats; behind the third is a brand new car. You choose one of the doors but, before it is opened, Monty Hall — who knows what is behind each door — opens one of the other doors and shows you a goat. Then he asks, "Do you want to stick with your original choice, or do you want to switch?"

As strange as it seems, the best choice is to switch; it will actually improve your odds of winning. Now this is counterintuitive, and for a long time I thought that switching doors would make no difference whatsoever. However, I was wrong (and my first degree was a math degree!). I found out I was wrong by reading an article about the "Monty Hall Problem" on the **Chance Server**. The article made me think about my assumptions and, after recasting my reasoning, I was able to come to the correct conclusion.

When you have a spare moment, spend some time with the **Chance Server**, and learn how and why so many people misunderstand probability and odds-making.

(By the way, here is how I solved the Monty Hall Problem: Imagine there are 100 doors. Behind one door is a car, behind the other 99 doors are goats. As in the original problem, choose one door, but do not open it. Next, imagine Monty — who knows what is behind each door — opening 98 of the remaining 99 doors and showing you they hid goats. When he asks, do you want to keep your original door, or switch to the one remaining closed door, the choice should be obvious.)

Chronology of Mathematicians

Find out who came before whom by reading this lengthy list of mathematicians organized chronologically from 1700 B.C. to modern times. There are also links to some of the mathematicians who have available biographical information.

Web:

> http://aleph0.clarku.edu/~djoyce/mathhist/
> chronology.html

Electronic Journal of Differential Equations

This site is dedicated to all aspects of differential equations, integral equations, and functional differential equations and their applications. (Just don't forget to add the constant.)

Web:

> http://ejde.math.swt.edu/

Flatland

"Flatland", written by Edwin Abbot, is a mathematical story in which a "person" who lives in Flatland tells us what life is like in his world. Flatland is completely two-dimensional—that is, the whole world exists on a flat surface. Although this seems impossible to imagine, Abbot is such a good writer (and mathematician) that he makes the whole thing understandable and plausible. The most interesting thing is that "Flatland" is a lot more than a mathematical book; it is actually an extremely well-executed social commentary. If you have even the slightest skill in mathematical thinking, I suggest that you take a look at "Flatland". It will expand your thinking in more ways than one.

Web:

> http://ofcn.org/cyber.serv/resource/bookshelf/flat10/
> http://www.geom.umn.edu/~banchoff/Flatland/

Geometry

Geometry is the branch of mathematics that studies the properties and relationships of various elements, such as points, lines, planes, curves, solids, surfaces, and so on. We all study geometry in school, but it is clear that some of us are more adept than others at visualizing in two and three dimensions. Here are some tools to help you, not only to visualize, but to explore the properties of many types of geometrical objects.

Web:

> http://astronomy.swin.edu.au/~pbourke/geometry/
> http://geometryalgorithms.com/
> http://www.cut-the-knot.com/geometry.shtml
> http://www.ics.uci.edu/~eppstein/junkyard/
> http://www.xahlee.org/PageTwo_dir/more.html

History of Mathematics

Get the real story of mathematics, the one your teachers never told you. Read these well-researched essays on various topics in the history of math as well as the biographies of several hundred mathematicians. Contemplate those yet-unsolved questions about prime numbers and whether Konigsberg burned his bridges behind him.

Web:

> http://www-groups.dcs.st-and.ac.uk/~history/

Hub Mathematics and Science Center

Take a few mathematicians and scientists, network them together, and suddenly you have The Hub, a service designed to help math and science researchers efficiently utilize telecommunications opportunities. The Hub offers a quarterly newsletter full of Internet usage tips and Internet and telecommunications resources. The Hub can also help you publish reports or requests for proposals.

Web:

> http://www.ra.terc.edu/

Linear and Nonlinear Programming

Linear and nonlinear programming are used to optimize mathematical quantities, subject to various constraints and relationships. With linear programming, the relationships are expressed as a series of linear equations. With nonlinear programming, generalized functions, not necessarily linear, are used instead. Both linear and nonlinear programming are part of operations research and, as such, are discussed in the **sci.op-research** Usenet group.

Web:
  http://www-unix.mcs.anl.gov/otc/Guide/faq/
    linear-programming-faq.html
  http://www-unix.mcs.anl.gov/otc/Guide/faq/
    nonlinear-programming-faq.html

Usenet:
  sci.op-research

Logic

To a civilian, logic describes the act of thinking clearly and rationally. ("My goodness, Clarissa, how can we discuss your mother's visit if you refuse to be logical?") To a mathematician, logic is a lot more. Traditionally, we consider the study of logic as originating with Aristotle, who recognized reasoning as being a science of its own. Modern logic began in 1854 when George Boole published a book in which, for the first time, logical reasoning was treated abstractly. In the twentieth century, much emphasis has been placed on symbolic logic or formal systems, in which mathematical symbols are manipulated according to certain rules. Four important areas of mathematical logic are: axiomatic set theory (what parts of mathematics can be formalized?), proof theory (what can be proved within a formal system?), model theory (how can mathematical logic be applied to algebraic problems?), and recursion theory (are various functions computable?).

Web:
  http://www.gac.edu/oncampus/academics/
    philosophy/llogic.html
  http://www.uni-bonn.de/logic/world.html

Usenet:
  sci.logic

Math and Philosophy

Do you agree that even Frege can be faulted for insufficient tenacity in giving up his program after Russell's discovery of the eponymous paradox? Or do you think that ramified type theory, contextual definition of class abstracts, the doctrine of acquaintance, and the theory of proposition identity are just so much hot air? Sit in with people who really understand who shaves the barber (if the barber shaves everyone who does not shave himself). Just be careful to behave yourself: someone may prove that you do not really exist.

Usenet:
  sci.philosophy.tech

Math Articles

I love mathematics, and I like reading about it, so this is one of my favorite Web sites. This site contains a large collection of articles about various types of math. The articles are short enough so that you can read one at a single sitting. However, there will be plenty to think about. If you have a math background, you will know what I mean when I say there are probably whole areas of math that are strangers to you. Spend some time browsing this site, and you will be able to fill in some of the blanks.

Web:
  http://www.mathpages.com/

Mathematical Association of America

This is an organization of college and university mathematics teachers with the goal of advancing the mathematical sciences. This Web page has links to math preprints, publications, career opportunities and other math resources on the Internet.

Web:
  http://www.maa.org/

Mathematical Quotations Server

The next time you are going to a hot math party, be sure you are well equipped with some good icebreakers, like quotes by your favorite mathematicians. Quotations are sorted alphabetically so you can browse through them or you can do a fast search by keyword.

Web:
  http://math.furman.edu/~mwoodard/mquot.html

Mathematics Resources

The world of mathematics is so vast that, if there is any part of it you like, I guarantee you will find something to interest you on the Net. These resources are suitable for mathematicians and math teachers, but if you just want to browse, I bet you'll have a good time looking at puzzles and mathematical curiosities.

Web:
    http://mathworld.wolfram.com/
    http://mthwww.uwc.edu/wwwmahes/files/
        math01.html
    http://www.abc.se/~m9847/matre/
    http://www.educationindex.com/math/
    http://www.math.fsu.edu/science/math.html
    http://www.math.psu.edu/MathLists/Contents.html
    http://www.tc.cornell.edu/services/edu/
        mathscigateway/math.asp

Mathematics Talk and General Discussion

There are discussion groups in Usenet where you can talk about all things mathematical. Now, you might think that unless you are specifically working on a particular research problem or you have a question, talking about math is a waste of time. What you are forgetting is that, traditionally, the most beautiful and intelligent women have always been attracted to the mathematically inclined. Remember, a man who knows his numbers is a man you can count on.

Usenet:
    sci.math
    sci.math.research

Numerical Analysis

It's amazing how many people still don't know a Tchebyshev polynomial from a fourth-order Runge-Kutte algorithm. Join the discussion with people who want more out of life than the simple L2 norm that seems to satisfy a whole world of mathematically disadvantaged social scientists.

Web:
    http://www.mathcom.com/corpdir/techinfo.mdir/
        scifaq/

Usenet:
    sci.math.num-analysis

What do you do when it's late at night and you need to remember all the characteristics of a vector space? You could go down to the all-night convenience store and ask the guy behind the counter. Or you could call directory assistance and hope that the operator would know. But, if all else fails, why not send a request to **sci.math** and let the Net help you?

(By the way, while I was researching this book, I came across a new proof for Fermat's Last Theorem that is more complete and easier to understand than Andrew Wiles' proof. His proof is long and cumbersome and runs into trouble in attempting to bound the order of a cohomology group that looks like a Selmer group for Sym2 of the representation attached to a modular form. My proof moves directly to elliptic curve theory and is much simpler. All in all, it is a marvelous proof, but unfortunately, there is not enough space here to write it down. What I can do, instead, is remind you that the largest known prime, which is also the largest known Mersenne prime, is $2^{859433}-1$.)

Operations Research

Operations research is the study of how to use mathematics to make decisions when the problem at hand is complex, and you have to decide how to balance various factors to optimize particular criteria. (If there is significant uncertainty in the outcome, you can say you are doing systems analysis and ask for more money.)

Web:
    http://www.informs.org/Resources/

Usenet:
    sci.op-research

Pi (3.14159...)

Here are some Internet sites celebrating the charm and elusiveness of pi, the irrational number that expresses the ratio of the circumference to the diameter of any circle. Would you like to see pi to many, many digits? Would you like to have your very own program to calculate pi? Would you like to experience pi in ways that normal people have never imagined? It's all here, waiting for you on the Net. (By the way, you may be wondering, is pi my favorite transcendental number? No, I have to admit that my favorite is *e*. However, I wouldn't kick pi out of bed for eating mathematical crackers.)

Web:
  http://www.cacr.caltech.edu/~roy/upi/pi.html
  http://www.cecm.sfu.ca/pi/pi.html
  http://www.joyofpi.com/pilinks.htm

Society for Industrial and Applied Mathematics

The Society for Industrial and Applied Mathematics provides information about activities and issues of interest to applied and computational mathematicians, engineers, and scientists who use mathematics and computers.

Web:
  http://www.siam.org/

Square Root of 2

When you've almost got it figured out and everyone keeps interrupting your thinking space, it's really aggravating. There's no sense in starting over again trying to recalculate the square root of 2. It's already been done: to a million digits.

Web:
  http://antwrp.gsfc.nasa.gov/htmltest/gifcity/sqrt2.1mil

Statistics

When you need a fuzzy clustering algorithm right away and the resident statistician has gone to the 7-11 for a 6-pack of Jolt cola, where do you turn for answers? Try the Net: just the place for people who are approximately right, some or all of the time.

Web:
  http://members.aol.com/johnp71/javastat.html
  http://www.math.yorku.ca/SCS/StatResource.html
  http://www.stat.ufl.edu/vlib/statistics.html

Usenet:
  sci.math.stat
  sci.stat.consult
  sci.stat.edu
  sci.stat.math

Symbolic and Algebraic Computation

The invention of symbolic and algebraic computation (SAC) programs has added a whole new set of tools to the arsenal of mathematicians, scientists, engineers and students. SAC systems manipulate numbers and symbols exactly, compared to floating point arithmetic, which is approximate. These resources will help you find a wide variety of SAC information, as well as the main Web sites for the major software packages. The Usenet group discusses such tools, as well as the related mathematical issues. Talk about Mathematica, Maple, Macsyma and Reduce. (My goodness, is Reduce still around? I remember using it back in the mid-1970s. Oh, how symbolic algebra makes one feel old.)

Web:
  http://www.gwdg.de/~cais/issac/
  http://www.mapleapps.com/
  http://www.math.fsu.edu/~seppala/Opetus/ISC/Text/
  http://www.mathlinks.info/
    em010_computer_algebra_sys.htm
  http://www.symbolicnet.org/

Usenet:
  sci.math.symbolic

A B C D E F G H I J K L **M** N O P Q R S T U V W X Y Z

Turing, Alan

Alan Turing, the man who brought you the Turing Test, the most popular after-dinner pastime of pre-television families of the early 1950s, has a site devoted to his life and work. Read his chronology, family origins and information about his early life. Discover who inspired him in his work and read about the Turing Machine, Turing's codebreaking work, early computer technology, his arrest, trial and eventual suicide.

Web:
    http://www-gap.dcs.st-and.ac.uk/~history/
        Mathematicians/Turing.html
    http://www.turing.org.uk/turing/
    http://www.turingarchive.org/

MEDICAL CONDITIONS

Acne and Eczema

Acne is a condition in which the sebaceous glands become inflamed, generally due to the clogging of skin pores. Acne is characterized by blackheads, pimples and cysts which appear on the face, neck, chest, arms and back. Eczema is an inflammatory condition in which the skin develops redness and itching. There may also be a watery discharge, which can become encrusted and scaly. Although acne and eczema are different conditions, they are similar in that they demand a multi-factorial approach to treatment: medicine, attention to stress, avoiding irritants, and diet.

Web:
    http://www.derm-infonet.com/acnenet/
    http://www.eczema.net/
    http://www.noah-health.org/english/illness/
        dermatology/derm.html#acne

Usenet:
    alt.skincare.acne
    alt.support.skin-diseases

Listserv Mailing List:
    List Name: eczema
    Subscribe to: listserv@maelstrom.stjohns.edu

Addictions

There's a lot to be addicted to in this world: cigarettes, alcohol, marijuana, cocaine, heroin, gambling, food, sex, codependency, and so on. Some things are okay in moderation (such as food), while others should be avoided completely. What they all have in common is the potential to control somebody's behavior to the detriment of that person. Many people suffer from addictions and, as you might expect, there is a lot of relevant information on the Net. Most important behavioral changes start with a single small step. Here are the resources. Why not take that step now?

Web:
    http://www.alcoholics-anonymous.org/
    http://www.na.org/basic.htm
    http://www.onlinerecovery.org/
    http://www.recoveryresources.org/

Listserv Mailing List:
    List Name: addict-l
    Subscribe to: listserv@listserv.kent.edu

> ## It's time for a break.

AIDS

AIDS (acquired immune deficiency syndrome) and the HIV (human immunodeficiency virus) family of viruses that cause it are important medical topics. AIDS is a disease that compromises the body's immune system by attacking certain types of white blood cells. (White blood cells attack germs, either directly or by secreting substances that help the immune response.) The HIV virus is spread via body fluids, mostly semen and blood. Once a person is infected, the virus can live in the body for years without seeming to cause a problem. However, in most cases, the immune system eventually weakens, and other diseases can take hold, often leading to severe illness or death. In recent years, drug treatments have been developed that can significantly slow down the course of the disease. But, as of yet, there is no cure nor is there a vaccine.

Web:

http://hivinsite.ucsf.edu/
http://www.aegis.com/
http://www.aids.org/
http://www.aids.wustl.edu/
http://www.aidsinfobbs.org/
http://www.aidsquilt.org/
http://www.cdcnpin.org/
http://www.iapac.org/
http://www.thebody.com/

Usenet:

misc.health.aids
sci.med.aids

Listserv Mailing List:

List Name: treatment
Subscribe to: listserv@critpath.org

Majordomo Mailing List:

List Name: aids
Subscribe to: majordomo@wubios.wustl.edu

Allergies

Sneezing, coughing, runny nose, itchy eyes, funny red bumps and a general miserable feeling—these are a few of the symptoms of allergies, which plague millions of people around the world. Find out more about this aggravating condition. On the mailing list, doctors, scientists, researchers and those who suffer from allergies gather to discuss causes and treatments for allergy conditions. The Web sites and Usenet group are nothing to sneeze at either.

Web:

http://allergy.mcg.edu/
http://www.allallergy.net/
http://www.allernet.com/FAQ/
http://www.focusonallergies.com/script/main/hp.asp

Usenet:

alt.med.allergy

Listserv Mailing List:

List Name: allergy
Subscribe to: listserv@listserv.uark.edu

Altitude Sickness

The higher you go, the thinner the atmosphere, which means you get less oxygen every time you breathe. If you visit a location that is more than 5000 feet (1500 meters) higher than where you live, you will need to give your body time to acclimatize or you may get sick. This is especially true if you plan on being outside in the cold (such as on a ski trip). The most common symptoms of mild altitude sickness are shortness of breath when you exert yourself, headache, nausea, coughing, trouble sleeping, and trouble thinking well. The solution is to rest for a few days (don't go skiing right away) until you feel better. Some people get very sick, developing much more serious symptoms. If this happens to you, you must descend immediately to a lower altitude, give yourself time to recover, and then get used to the altitude change in a more gradual fashion.

Web:

http://www.ahealthyme.com/topic/topic13676
http://www.high-altitude-medicine.com/
http://www.pardoes.com/climbing/acclima.htm

Arthritis

"Arthritis" means inflammation of one or more joints of the body. Symptoms include pain, redness and stiffness, which can range from mild to severe. Although people talk about arthritis as if it is a single disease, there are actually many different types of arthritis. The two most well-known are osteoarthritis, a degenerative disease that sometimes accompanies aging, and rheumatoid arthritis, an auto-immune disease most commonly affecting women. In general, most types of arthritis, as well as many other auto-immune conditions, fall under the branch of medicine known as rheumatology.

Web:

http://www.arthritis.org/
http://www.arthritisinsight.com/

Usenet:

alt.support.arthritis
misc.health.arthritis

Brain Tumors

The term "tumor" refers to tissue that is growing in an abnormal way. Benign tumors grow very slowly and rarely spread. Malignant (cancerous) tumors grow uncontrollably and may spread (metastasize) to other parts of the body. In general, there are two types of brain tumors. Primary brain tumors originate within the brain, and tend to stay there. Metastatic brain tumors—which are about four times as common as primary brain tumors—grow from cells that have spread from another part of the body (for example, from a lung cancer or breast cancer). There are many different types of brain tumors. The prognosis (probable outcome) depends very much on the type of tumor and how far it has spread. If someone you know has a brain tumor, it is important that you become fully informed before you draw any conclusions or make any decisions.

Web:

http://brain.mgh.harvard.edu/
http://www.abta.org/
http://www.abta.org/information/dictionary.htm

Listserv Mailing List:

List Name: braintmr
Subscribe to: listserv@mitvma.mit.edu

Breast Cancer

Breast cancer is the second most common form of cancer in women in the United States. (Only skin cancers are more common.) Every year, more than 200,000 women and 1,500 men are diagnosed with breast cancer in the U.S. The two most common types of breast cancers are ductal carcinoma (which starts in the milk ducts) and lobular carcinoma (which starts in the lobules where milk is produced). Although breast cancer is common, treatments are often effective and there are over 2 million breast cancer survivors in the U.S. alone. If you find a lump in your breast, it is important to get it checked out immediately. If you do have cancer, the more quickly you seek treatment, the higher your chances of a positive outcome. However, don't be scared until you find out what's really happening: over 80 percent of breast biopsies (samples) are *not* cancer.

Web:

http://www.breastcancer.net/
http://www.cancer.gov/cancerinformation/
    cancertype/breast
http://www.nabco.org/

Usenet:

alt.support.cancer.breast

Listserv Mailing List:

List Name: brca-l
Subscribe to: listserv@lists.ufl.edu

Listserv Mailing List:

List Name: breast-cancer
Subscribe to: listserv@morgan.ucs.mun.ca

Listserv Mailing List:

List Name: malebc
Subscribe to: listserv@listserv.acor.org

Cancer Information for Patients

If you need cancer information, it really helps to have something you can understand. Here is information specifically designed for patients. Find out about screening, types of cancer, treatments, side effects, as well as news and research. You'll also find information to help you understand various technical terms.

Web:

http://www.cancerguide.org/
http://www.nci.nih.gov/cancer_information/
http://www.oncolink.upenn.edu/

Chronic Fatigue Syndrome

Chronic fatigue syndrome (CFS) or myalgic encephalomyelitis (ME) is what used to be known as chronic Epstein-Barr virus syndrome. There are many symptoms of CFS, not all of which are present in each patient. The most common symptoms are fatigue, low-grade fever, muscle pain, sleep disorders, impaired thinking, depression, headache, sore throat, anxiety and muscle weakness. The cause of CFS seems to be a chronic immune reaction. However, the exact triggers are not known. The severity of CFS symptoms can vary significantly over time and from one patient to another, making this a difficult condition to diagnose and treat.

Web:
> http://www.cfids.org/
> http://www.cfs-news.org/
> http://www.co-cure.org/

Usenet:
> alt.med.cfs

Listserv Mailing List:
> List Name: cfs-l
> Subscribe to: listserv@maelstrom.stjohns.edu

Listserv Mailing List:
> List Name: cfs-med
> Subscribe to: listserv@maelstrom.stjohns.edu

Listserv Mailing List:
> List Name: cfs-news
> Subscribe to: listserv@maelstrom.stjohns.edu

Common Infectious Diseases

There are a large number of common infectious diseases. Some are relatively benign; others are more serious. Each disease has its own causes, symptoms, treatment and (in many cases) vaccination schedule. When you or a family member is sick, it can be a real help to know what to expect. It is also handy to know what the length of the incubation period is (the time it takes to get sick after being infected), and when the sick person is contagious. For example, if you catch a cold from someone, it will take you 2-5 days until you feel sick. Once you do, you are contagious for 2-4 days, from the time your nose starts to run until your fever goes away.

Web:
> http://www.healthfinder.gov/scripts/
>   Topics.asp?context=5&keyword=113
> http://www.mckennan.org/hubs/ask-a-nurse/
>   health_lib/incubation_periods.htm
> http://www.methodisthealth.com/infectious/
> http://www.nlm.nih.gov/medlineplus/
>   infectiousdiseasesgeneral.html
> http://www.viahealth.org/disease/infectiousdisease/
>   common.htm
> http://www.who.int/health-topics/idindex.htm

Crohn's Disease and Ulcerative Colitis

Both Crohn's disease and ulcerative colitis are chronic inflammatory conditions affecting the gastrointestinal tract. Crohn's disease (or regional enteritis) usually targets the small intestine and colon, although it can affect any part of the GI tract. Ulcerative colitis affects the colon and rectum. These diseases share important characteristics, and for this reason, are often referred to collectively as inflammatory bowel disease (IBD). Some people with IBD have only minor symptoms; other people have serious problems that require medication and even surgery. Over the years, it is also common for people to undergo multiple remissions and exacerbations. There is no medical cure for IBD, so the goal of treatment is to suppress the inflammation, encourage healing, and relieve the symptoms.

Web:
> http://qurlyjoe.bu.edu/cduchome.html
> http://www.ccfa.org/

Usenet:
> alt.support.crohns-colitis

Cystic Fibrosis

Cystic fibrosis (CF) is an inheritable metabolic disorder characterized by abnormal secretions of the exocrine glands. In particular, patients have thick mucus that obstructs the bronchi (resulting in severe breathing problems), intestines, and the pancreatic and bile ducts (making it difficult to digest adequate nutrients). About 1 in every 3,300 babies is born with cystic fibrosis.

Web:

http://www.cff.org/
http://www.cystic-l.org/
http://www.cysticfibrosis.com/
http://www.esiason.org/
http://www.healingwell.com/cysticfibrosis/

Listserv Mailing List:

List Name: cystic-l
Subscribe to: listserv@peach.ease.lsoft.com

Diabetes

Within your body, most starchy and sugar-like nutrients are converted into a substance called glucose. Glucose is used for a number of important purposes, including being a source of energy. In order to use glucose properly, our body depends on a hormone (chemical) called insulin, which is created by your pancreas and released into the bloodstream. Diabetes—more formally, diabetes mellitus—is a disease in which the glucose/insulin system does not work properly.

Web:

http://www.aboutdiabetes.com/
http://www.cdc.gov/diabetes/
http://www.childrenwithdiabetes.com/
http://www.diabetesmonitor.com/
http://www.faqs.org/faqs/diabetes/
http://www.niddk.nih.gov/health/diabetes/pubs/
    dmdict/dmdict.htm

Usenet:

alt.support.diabetes.kids
misc.health.diabetes

Listproc Mailing List:

List Name: diabetic
Subscribe to: listproc@lehigh.edu

Endometriosis

The tissue that lines the inner surface of the uterus is called endometrium. This is the tissue that is sloughed off and expelled when a woman has her period. Endometriosis is a condition in which endometrium-like tissue grows outside the uterus, usually within the abdomen. It is estimated that about 15 percent of American women of childbearing age have endometriosis. The most common symptom is pain, but endometriosis is also one of the most common causes of infertility.

Web:

http://www.digitalgranite.com/endometriosis/
http://www.hcgresources.com/endoindex.html
http://www.ivf.com/endohtml.html

Usenet:

alt.med.endometriosis
alt.support.endometriosis

Listserv Mailing List:

List Name: witsendo
Subscribe to: listserv@listserv.dartmouth.edu

Epilepsy and Seizure Disorders

Epilepsy is a chronic condition in which the normal electrical functions of the brain are disturbed in such a way as to produce seizures. Epilepsy can also produce other neurological symptoms affecting consciousness, movement or sensation. Epilepsy is a common condition, and in most cases, there is no known cause. Here is a lot of useful information about epilepsy, including a FAQ (frequently asked question list).

Web:

http://www.efa.org/
http://www.epilepsyontario.org/faqs/
http://www.neurologychannel.com/seizures/

Usenet:

alt.support.epilepsy

> **Time to spare? Look at "Talking on the Net".**

Gulf War Syndrome

The Gulf War lasted from August 1990 to February 1991. During these seven months, about 700,000 men and women were deployed to the Persian Gulf. Afterward, many of them began to complain of various medical symptoms, including fatigue, joint pain, rashes, diarrhea and memory problems. Eventually, this imprecise constellation of symptoms became known as Gulf War Syndrome. Since that time, a lot of effort has gone into trying to determine whether or not an actual disease exists. Various causes have been proposed such as chemicals, tropical diseases, biological warfare agents, pesticides, depleted uranium, airborne particles from oil-well fires, petroleum products, vaccines, prophylactic drugs and antidotes. After extensive analysis, the best conclusion seems to be that none of these factors is the cause of a single disease. Rather, the general stress of battle and psychological factors combine to create a variety of illnesses with overlapping symptoms. During a war, soldiers can experience enormous fear, fatigue and stress, which can affect the immune system, the brain, the cardiovascular system, and hormonal balances, leaving the body susceptible to all kinds of maladies. In other words, war is hell, and it has always produced serious, enduring medical problems in returning soldiers.

Web:
  http://www.nhgws.org/
  http://www.pbs.org/wgbh/pages/frontline/shows/
    syndrome/

Headaches

There are many causes for headaches. Fortunately, most headaches are not serious. Unfortunately, all headaches are bothersome and painful. Isn't it a wonderful feeling when you realize that the headache that has been bothering you for hours has finally gone away? These Web sites contain useful information to help you understand what causes a pain in the head and what you can do about it. Hint: Many headaches are caused by muscular tension, and can be avoided if you take care of your body. For example, if you work at a desk, take a break every 20 minutes and stretch. I have found that yoga is a wonderful way to eliminate tension headaches.

Web:
  http://www.achenet.org/
  http://www.headache-help.org/head.html
  http://www.headachecare.com/
  http://www.neurologychannel.com/headache/
Usenet:
  alt.support.headaches.migraine

Headaches

A head is a terrible thing to waste, and you can't use yours properly if it's hurting.

(After all, if Eve had had a headache, what would Adam have done? And where would we all be now?)

If you're in pain, why not see if the Net can help?

Hypertension (High Blood Pressure)

Every minute, 60 to 80 times a minute, your heart contracts, forcing blood into your arteries. Just after the heart contracts, the pressure in your arteries increases. In between contractions, the arterial pressure decreases momentarily. If you were to graph the rise and fall of your blood pressure, it would look like a smooth curve, with hills and valleys in regular cycles. Within a cycle, the top of the hill, when the pressure is highest, is called systole ("sys'-tol-ee"). The bottom of the valley, when the blood pressure is the lowest, is called diastole ("di-as'-tol-ee"). When someone measures your blood pressure, they are estimating the highest and lowest pressures throughout the cycle. The result is expressed as two numbers, for example, 120/80. The first number (in this case, 120) is the systolic pressure. The second (80) is the diastolic pressure. Anything over 140/90 is considered to be high blood pressure, or hypertension. The danger of hypertension is that, over the long run, it increases your chances of developing serious medical conditions, such as heart disease or a stroke. Unfortunately, there is no way for you to feel if your blood pressure is too high. Thus, you must have it measured regularly, and, if it is found to be high over several weeks, you should reduce it. Most people find that mild high blood pressure can be controlled with adequate exercise and a good diet. Other people require medicine.

Web:
  http://www.americanheart.org/
    presenter.jhtml?identifier=2114
  http://www.bloodpressure.com/
  http://www5.who.int/cardiovascular-diseases/
    main.cfm?s=0009

Usenet:
  alt.support.hypertension

Infertility

If at first you don't succeed, try, try again. If you still don't succeed, check out the resources on the Net to see if you can find something that will help.

Web:
  http://www.ihr.com/infertility/
  http://www.inciid.org/
  http://www3.fertilethoughts.com/forums/

Usenet:
  alt.infertility
  alt.infertility.alternatives
  alt.infertility.pregnancy
  alt.infertility.primary
  alt.infertility.secondary
  alt.infertility.surrogacy
  misc.health.infertility

Multiple Sclerosis

Multiple sclerosis (MS) is a disease of the central nervous system characterized by (1) the destruction of the insulation (myelin) that surrounds nerve fibers, and (2) patches of sclerosis (plaques) within the brain and spinal cord. Over time, the loss of myelin causes a wide variety of symptoms such as loss of sight, muscle weakness, problems with coordination, tingling and numbness, loss of bladder control, speech problems and mental problems. The course of MS is unpredictable, and patients commonly have remissions and exacerbations. However, MS is a progressive disease and, over time, there is often an accumulation of problems. MS is difficult to diagnose and is usually recognized only after a period of time. The disease is most often diagnosed in young adults in their 20s or 30s, and is twice as common in women than men.

Web:
  http://www.ifmss.org.uk/
  http://www.msnews.org/
  http://www.msonly.com/glossary.html

Usenet:
  alt.support.ms-recovery
  alt.support.mult-sclerosis
  alt.support.mult-sclerosis.alternatives

Listserv Mailing List:
  List Name: mslist-l
  Subscribe to: listserv@techunix.technion.ac.il

Majordomo Mailing List:
  List Name: ms_can-l
  Subscribe to: majordomo@oise.utoronto.ca

If you have the
questions, the Internet
has the answers.

Obsessive-Compulsive Disorder

Obsession means that you cannot stop thinking certain thoughts. Compulsion means you cannot stop performing certain rituals or activities. These two conditions often exist together so, in medical terms, we talk about obsessive-compulsive disorder or OCD. It is important to understand that obsession and compulsion are very common conditions. From time to time, we all have mildly obsessive thoughts, and we all perform tiny actions in a compulsive manner. This is normal. The people with OCD, however, have very strong obsessive or compulsive tendencies that significantly interfere with their lives. What's interesting is that, in many cases, there is a biochemical basis for such behavior, and such people can be treated successfully with drugs.

Web:

  http://www.anxieties.com/5OCD/
     OCD_summary1.htm
  http://www.geonius.com/ocd/
  http://www.mayoclinic.com/findinformation/
     diseasesandconditions/invoke.cfm?id=ds00189&
  http://www.mentalhealthchannel.net/ocd/
  http://www.ocfoundation.org/

Usenet:

  alt.support.ocd

Sleep Disorders

Can't sleep?

Here are two ways to solve your problem.

(1) Get a job as a writer. That way, you'll never have to wake up to an alarm clock, so it doesn't matter if it takes you a long time to fall asleep at night. And if you get so little rest that you doze off in the afternoon, you can tell everyone you are doing research.

(2) Check with the Net to get lots of useful information about sleep disorders.

(Actually, I think there might be a third way, but I'm too tired to remember.)

Pain

There are numerous conditions that can cause pain. If such a condition becomes chronic, our suffering can be intense to the point where life seems just not worth living. The most common pain-inducing conditions are headaches and lower back problems. Less common, but significant, are fibromyalgia, myofascial pain syndrome, phantom pain, polyneuropathy, shingles, trigeminal neuralgia, and CRPS (Complex Regional Pain Syndrome). As important as pain is to all of us, it is a completely personal experience, one that we cannot really express to another person. (One thing I learned in medical school is that there is a big difference between pain and suffering.) However, many types of chronic pain can be treated, and it can help a lot to have good information.

Web:

  http://www.pain.com/
  http://www.painfoundation.org/
  http://www.stoppain.org/

Usenet:

  alt.support.chronic-pain

Majordomo Mailing List:

  List Name: chronicpain
  Subscribe to: majordomo@list.goedhart.com

Sleep Disorders

One time I had trouble getting to sleep because someone ate the last of the chocolate pudding before I could get to it. If you have trouble sleeping at night, it may help to read about various causes of sleeplessness and common sleeping disorders. These Web sites cover topics such as sleep apnea, snoring, sleep deprivation, narcolepsy, insomnia and restless leg syndrome. If it's late at night and you still can't get to sleep, check out the Usenet group for some late-night discussion.

Web:

  http://www.sleepfoundation.org/disorder.html
  http://www.sleepnet.com/

Usenet:

  alt.support.sleep-disorder

Stuttering

Stuttering—or stammering—is an involuntary break in the flow of speech. Everyone stutters at times. However, some people stutter enough to affect their social interactions or peace of mind. Stuttering typically starts in children between 2-7 years old. However, there are many adults who stammer, and it is never too late to get help. Sometimes, just knowledge alone can bring comfort.

Web:
http://www.casafuturatech.com/Book/faq.html
http://www.mankato.msus.edu/dept/comdis/kuster/stutter.html

Usenet:
alt.support.stuttering

Listserv Mailing List:
List Name: stutt-l
Subscribe to: listserv@listserv.temple.edu

Listserv Mailing List:
List Name: stutt-x
Subscribe to: listserv@lists.asu.edu

Is Your Life Complete?

Find out if your life is complete by taking this short quiz. For each of the following statements, choose either True or False.

1. I find my work rewarding. True/False

2. I have someone special in my life who loves me and whom I love. True/False

3. I am able to experience my emotions and come to terms with my inner needs. True/False

4. I am honest with myself and with other people. True/False

5. I own an up-to-date copy of *Harley Hahn's Internet Yellow Pages*. True/False

If you answered True to all 5 questions, congratulations. Your life is as good as anyone on the planet. You can be proud of yourself.

If you answered True to question #5, but False to any other questions, read the entire book. Then wait three weeks and take the test again. You should find a great improvement.

If you answered False to question #5, buy this book right away. Otherwise, you risk having your life turn out to be a total sham.

Tinnitus

Have you ever had ringing in your ears? Tinnitus is a condition in which you hear ringing or other sounds, so often and so loudly, that it affects your peace of mind. Many people have mild tinnitus, and never even bother about it. Other people, however, suffer from the noise. If you go to a doctor—even an ear, nose and throat (ENT) specialist—you will more than likely be told that there is nothing you can do about tinnitus. This is not true. There *are* tinnitus treatments that work. In the 1990s, a modern understanding of the condition was developed, based upon the work of Pawel Jastreboff. This understanding led to the development of Tinnitus Retaining Therapy (TRT). The main idea is that only a portion of your discomfort comes from the actual sounds. A great deal of suffering has to do with your reaction to tinnitus. This reaction involves a part of your brain called the limbic system (unpleasant feelings), as well as your autonomic nervous system (tension and stress). Once you perceive tinnitus to be a threat, the action of your limbic system and autonomic system establishes a permanent neurophysiological pattern of discomfort. To have your tinnitus treated successfully, you need an accurate diagnosis and a treatment plan, one that is customized to your history, personality and intelligence. This will require you to go to an audiologist who specializes in tinnitus (which requires special post-graduate training). In the meantime, here is what to do to decrease your suffering: avoid silence, alcohol and caffeine; if you take medication, check with your doctor to see if it is known to aggravate tinnitus; increase your exercise; reduce your stress level. Most important, don't allow yourself to have distorted thoughts about tinnitus. Don't pay attention to it. Leave it alone.

Web:
http://pub21.ezboard.com/ftinnituscommunitymessageboardfrm1
http://www.ata.org/
http://www.bixby.org/faq/tinnitus.html
http://www.nlm.nih.gov/medlineplus/tinnitus.html
http://www.thehearingdoctor.com/new/tinnitus.htm
http://www.tinnitus.org/home/THC1.htm

Usenet:
alt.support.tinnitus

MEDICINE

Anatomy

When I was in medical school, I studied anatomy for several hours every day during the first semester. Between the classes and the daily dissection labs, I spent a lot of time learning about and memorizing the parts of the human body. It was one of the most stressful, fearful experiences of my life. We had to literally memorize pages and pages of anatomical information: text as well as pictures. I'm not complaining—all medical students go through the same process—but I do want to say it was a thoroughly unpleasant experience. Learning on the Net is a lot more pleasant. You can proceed at your own pace, and concentrate on the areas you find the most interesting. These resources will never replace actual human dissection and intense study, but they do provide a way for you to learn something about what is inside your body, and how it is all organized.

Web:
http://sig.biostr.washington.edu/projects/da/
http://www.innerbody.com/htm/body.html
http://www.vh.org/Providers/Textbooks/
    HumanAnatomy/CrossSectionAtlas.html

Anesthesiology

Anesthesiology is the branch of medicine devoted to the (1) relief of pain, and (2) care of the surgical patient before, during and after surgery. Within the operating room, the job of the anesthesiologist is to control the patient's pain and level of unconsciousness. To do so, the anesthesiologist will continually monitor and control the patient's heart rate, heart rhythm, breathing, blood pressure, temperature and fluid balance. Aside from surgery, anesthesiologists have an important role in critical care medicine, trauma medicine, and various diagnostic procedures and nonsurgical treatments.

Web:
http://www.asahq.org/
http://www.gasnet.org/
http://www.ispub.com/ostia/
    index.php?xmlFilePath=journals/ija/archives.xml
http://www.lib.uiowa.edu/hardin/md/anesth.html
http://www.medwebplus.com/subject/
    Anesthesiology.html
http://www.virtual-anaesthesia-textbook.com/

Listserv Mailing List:
List Name: anest-l
Subscribe to: listserv@listserv.acsu.buffalo.edu

Cancer and Oncology

Cancer is a general name for many different conditions that are characterized by the uncontrolled growth of tissue. There is lots and lots of information on the Net about cancer and oncology (the branch of medicine that deals with cancer). I have selected a variety of resources, some for patients and some for medical professionals. The Usenet group and mailing list are for ongoing discussion.

Web:
http://cancer.med.upenn.edu/
http://www.cancer.gov/cancer_information/
http://www.cancer.org/
http://www.cancerpage.com/
http://www.wcn.org/

Usenet:
sci.med.diseases.cancer

Listserv Mailing List:
List Name: cancer-l
Subscribe to: listserv@wvnvm.wvnet.edu

Carcinogens

A carcinogen is a cancer-causing substance. There are many different ways that carcinogens can do their damage, but the basic mechanism is that the carcinogen, perhaps in conjunction with another agent, creates a certain type of mutation in a cell's DNA: a mutation causes the cell to begin to grow uncontrollably. Here are some resources to help you find information about carcinogens. (There are many more of them than most people realize.) For example, you can look at the official Report of Carcinogens from the United States Department of Health and Human Services. Each year, the department brings its list up to date to reflect the most current knowledge. For example, in 2000, saccharine was removed from the list after many years. You will also enjoy reading a long list of carcinogens and suspected carcinogens. This list is useful when you need to look up a particular substance quickly, for example, when you are at a chemistry party and someone asks if you would like some 2,4-diaminotoluene on your ice cream. (The correct answer would be, "No thank you. The chocolate syrup will be enough.")

Web:
   http://ehp.niehs.nih.gov/roc/
   http://monographs.iarc.fr/
   http://www.physchem.ox.ac.uk/MSDS/
      carcinogens.html

Dentistry

Long in the tooth or down in the mouth, everyone is welcome to this discussion on dentists, materials and dental techniques. Whether you need help deciding if implants are better than a bridge or just want to read humorous stories about people who have had their jaws wired shut, nothing is more exciting and breathtaking than modern dentistry.

Web:
   http://www.animated-teeth.com/
   http://www.dentalpath.com/dp/dp_fp.htm
   http://www.smiledoc.com/dentist/tips.html
   http://www.smiles4ever.com/

Usenet:
   sci.med.dentistry

:-)

Dermatology

Dermatology is the medical specialty that deals with the integumentary system: skin (the body's largest organ), hair, nails, sudoriferous (sweat) glands and sebaceous glands. I studied dermatology in medical school, and, believe me, once you start learning about the stratum corneum, stratum lucidum and stratum granulosum (not to mention things like hidradenitis suppurativa), you quickly realize that beauty really is only skin deep.

Web:
   http://dermis.multimedica.de/index_e.htm
   http://www.aad.org/
   http://www.dermguide.com/dermatology/
   http://www.nsc.gov.sg/cgi-bin/
      WB_GroupGen.pl?id=33

Emergency Medicine

What do you do when you have an emergency medical situation and you don't have a first aid book? Take a look at this information for professionals in the area of emergency medicine and primary home care. These sites have a radiology and photograph library, national physician job listings directory, an EKG of the month and an EKG file room. Browse the interesting cases on file, complete with photographs and diagnosis discussion. This won't help you in your medical emergency, but at least it will keep your mind occupied while help is on the way.

Web:
   http://www.aaem.org/
   http://www.embbs.com/
   http://www.emedicine.com/emerg/

Forensic Medicine

Forensic medicine (sometimes referred to as medical jurisprudence) is the medical specialty that deals with the law. Modern forensic medicine is a highly technical area of study, requiring advanced training in a variety of disciplines. My personal interest in forensic medicine was inspired by the Perry Mason novels, written by Erle Stanley Gardner. In many of the stories, Perry Mason, a lawyer, expounds on subtle medical points that prove to be crucial to unmasking the truth. In more recent years, forensic medicine has been glorified in the mystery novels of Patricia Cornwell, whose character Kay Scarpetta is a particularly tenacious forensic pathologist.

Web:
   http://www.autopsy-md.com/faq.htm
   http://www.forensic.to/forensic.html

Hematology

Hematology is the medical specialty concerned with the blood, its constituents and the blood-forming (hemopoietic) tissues. In a clinical setting, the practice of hematology deals with blood-related diseases and abnormalities. In general terms, they can be categorized as erythrocytic (red cell disorders, such as the anemias, polycythemia, sickle cell disease and thalassemia); leukocytic (white cell disorders, such as the leukemias); and hemorrhagic (clotting disorders, such as hemophilia).

Web:
  http://www.bloodline.net/
  http://www.healthweb.org/browse.cfm?subjectid=46
  http://www.hematologylinks.com/
  http://www.medwebplus.com/subject/
    Hematology.html

Hippocratic Oath

Hippocrates was a physician in ancient Greece, who was born on the island of Cos around 465 B.C. (He lived at the same time as the famous historian Herodotus.) The Hippocratic Oath is a pledge, attributed to Hippocrates, that doctors take at the outset of their career. Traditionally, the original Hippocratic Oath is taken by doctors upon the awarding of their M.D. degree. However—in these days of modern times—tradition is not always acceptable. For example, it is certainly politically expedient to ignore the fact that the original oath obliges physicians to refuse to give abortions. Perhaps even more restrictive is the promise "With purity and with holiness I will pass my life..." Not to worry, there are brand new versions of the Hippocratic Oath, much more up to date and specifically designed to harmonize with the best of modern medical practice.

Web:
  http://www.medword.com/hippocrates.html
  http://www.pbs.org/wgbh/nova/doctors/
    oath_classical.html

Immunology

Having no immune system is like going away on a vacation and leaving all the doors and windows open. Diseases such as chronic fatigue syndrome, lupus, candida, hypoglycemia and others manifest themselves in the immune system and wreak havoc on all the other systems in your body.

Web:
  http://www.keratin.com/am/amindex.shtml
  http://www.medwebplus.com/subject/
    Immunology.html
  http://www.path.cam.ac.uk/immuno/immlinks.html

Usenet:
  bionet.immunology
  sci.med.immunology

Infectious Diseases and Microbiology

Microbiology is the study of bacteria, viruses, fungi and protozoa, the microorganisms responsible for infectious disease. Infectious disease occurs when an microorganism invades the body, reproduces and causes injury to some particular type of tissue. Infectious microorganisms have evolved to invade and reproduce within specific tissues of the human body. For example, influenza A virus invades the epithelial cells of the respiratory tract. Of course, not all microorganisms are pathogenic. For example, your gastrointestinal tract contains literally hundreds of billions of benign bacteria, many of which are necessary to maintain optimal health. Still, there are many infectious microorganisms, and the study of their characteristics and the diseases they cause is complex. (By the way, an invasion of the body by non-microbial pathogens, such as parasitic worms, is called an infestation, not an infection.)

Web:

http://cmr.asm.org/
http://jcm.asm.org/
http://www.ama-assn.org/ama/pub/category/
   1797.html
http://www.bact.wisc.edu/microtextbook/
http://www.cdc.gov/ncidod/diseases/
http://www.hopkins-id.edu/
http://www.journals.uchicago.edu/CID/journal/
http://www.kcom.edu/faculty/chamberlain/
http://www.lib.uiowa.edu/hardin/md/micro.html
http://www.mic.ki.se/Diseases/c1.html
http://www.nlm.nih.gov/medlineplus/infections.html

Medical Libraries

Managing health-related information requires special skills and knowledge. Here are some resources devoted to the care and feeding of medical libraries (and medical librarians).

Web:

http://www.lib.uiowa.edu/hardin/hslibs.html
http://www.mlanet.org/

Usenet:

bit.listserv.medlib-l

Listserv Mailing List:

List Name: medlib-l
Subscribe to: listserv@listserv.acsu.buffalo.edu

Medical Manuals

From time to time, you hear stories about someone practicing medicine without a license. "How do they do it?" you ask yourself. "How can anyone possibly know enough about medicine to fool people—including other doctors—without having gone to medical school?" The answer is, they use a medical manual. Here, for your delectation, are some references you can access for free on the Net, including the famous Merck Manual. All of these resources are great places to look when you need help with a diagnosis or treatment. (Of course, even the best medical manual won't teach you enough to pass yourself off as a real doctor. You still have to learn how to play golf.)

Web:

http://www.fpnotebook.com/
http://www.merck.com/pubs/mmanual/sections.htm
http://www.vnh.org/Providers.html

Medical Physics

Here is the forum for medical physicists (those nice people who give you radiation therapy). Do they really glow in the dark or is that just an old wives' tale?

Web:

http://www.snm.org/

Usenet:

sci.med.physics

Medical Resources

Here are some wonderful, well-organized resources that contain a large variety of medical information. If you practice medicine, I recommend that you become familiar with at least one of these Web sites, so you have a place to visit when you need information. (I only wish I had a portable computer with an Internet connection when I was in medical school. It would have made the multiple choice tests a lot more pleasant.)

Web:

http://www.docguide.com/
http://www.medexplorer.com/
http://www.medforum.com/
http://www.medicinenet.com/
http://www.nlm.nih.gov/

Medical Software

This Web site will help you find software useful to medical and health science professionals, researchers and students. There is a large variety of medical software on the Net, so it is worth looking to see if you can find what you need.

Web:
http://www.medicalcomputingtoday.com/
0nvmedsoft.html

The next time you need some medical software, try the Net.

(Maybe you can figure out how to reprogram your pacemaker so you don't have to reboot it twice a day.)

Medical Students

One would think that med students wouldn't have time to hang out on the Internet because they are always in a classroom somewhere with their hands thrust deep into some formaldehyde-soaked cadaver examining its medulla oblongata and vermiform appendix. But as addictive and distracting as the Internet can be, it's not surprising to find a place where medical students from around the world can gather to discuss anything relating to being a med student—labs, study habits, diseases, residencies, exhaustion and overwork.

Web:
http://www.amsa.org/
http://www.medicalstudent.net/
http://www.s2smed.com/

Usenet:
bit.listserv.medforum

Listserv Mailing List:
List Name: medstu-l
Subscribe to: listserv@unm.edu

Medicine Talk and General Discussion

Here is the agora of the Internet medical community: the Usenet groups where professionals and researchers have ongoing discussions on a variety of medical topics. Do you want to keep up on what your specialty is doing? Do you have questions to ask or answers to share? Check out these groups where you will find free-flowing talk on everything medical. (Does anyone have a cure for a chrono-synclastic infundibulum?)

Usenet:
bionet.biology.cardiovascular
sci.med
sci.med.cardiology
sci.med.diseases.als
sci.med.diseases.hepatitis
sci.med.diseases.lyme
sci.med.diseases.osteoporosis
sci.med.informatics
sci.med.laboratory
sci.med.obgyn
sci.med.occupational
sci.med.orthopedics
sci.med.pathology
sci.med.prostate.bph
sci.med.prostate.cancer
sci.med.prostate.prostatitis
sci.med.psychobiology
sci.med.transcription
sci.med.vision

Medline

Medline is a vast bibliographic database maintained by the U.S. National Library of Medicine. Medline contains citations and abstracts from several thousand biomedical journals, covering medicine, nursing, dentistry, veterinary medicine and other fields, making it an unsurpassed reference. If you are a doctor, you absolutely must become familiar with this resource. For non-doctors, Medline is great for searching for information you can use yourself or print out to show your doctor.

Web:
http://www.nlm.nih.gov/pubs/factsheets/
medline.html

Medscape

Do you know why influenza is not an eradicable disease? Because aquatic birds are a natural reservoir for all known influenza A subtypes, and we can't kill all the aquatic birds, nor can we prevent them from transferring viruses to people. How did I know this? I read it on Medscape, a comprehensive Web site that's the best place I know for keeping up on the news. If you are a doctor or health care practitioner, you definitely need to know about Medscape: there are more useful features than I can list here. If you are a patient, you will find Medscape valuable for looking up information about particular conditions.

Web:
   http://www.medscape.com/

Nursing

Nursing is the profession devoted to caring for sick and disabled people. The most famous nurse in history was the Italian Florence Nightingale (1820-1910). When Nightingale was young, she showed an interest in social problems. However, her parents (who were quite well off) refused to let her become a nurse because, at the time, nursing was considered to be an unsuitable profession for a well-educated woman. In spite of her family's opposition, Nightingale entered nursing. From 1854-1866, she served as a nursing supervisor during the Crimean War, successfully integrating her nurses into the military's medical services. After the war, Nightingale devoted her life to nursing. She established schools, worked tirelessly for health care reform, and wrote a seminal book entitled "Notes on Nursing" (1860). Nightingale is important because, over a lifetime, she managed to change the nursing profession into a respectable occupation for women.

Web:
   http://www.allnurses.com/
   http://www.nursehealer.com/
   http://www.nursingcenter.com/
   http://www.nursingworld.org/

Usenet:
   alt.npractitioners
   bit.listserv.snurse-l
   sci.med.nursing
   uk.sci.med.nursing

Occupational Medicine

Need to pick out a back-friendly chair or an ergonomic keyboard? The Usenet discussion group on occupational medicine will be just what the doctor would have ordered if he had thought of it. For a lot of immediate information, try the Web sites.

Web:
   http://www.link.med.ed.ac.uk/hew//
   http://www.occmed.oupjournals.org/
   http://www.osha.gov/

Usenet:
   sci.med.occupational

Organ Transplants

One of the miracles of modern medicine is the ability to replace various body parts as needed. Of course, it's not that simple, but as the years go by the process becomes more advanced. The mailing list and Usenet group offer a means for organ transplant recipients, family members, and anyone interested in transplant issues to discuss their thoughts and experiences.

Web:
   http://www.faqs.org/faqs/medicine/transplant-faq/
   http://www.medwebplus.com/subject/
      Transplantation.html
   http://www.shareyourlife.org/

Usenet:
   bit.listserv.transplant

Listserv Mailing List:
   List Name: trnsplnt
   Subscribe to: listserv@wuvmd.wustl.edu

Pediatrics

Pediatrics is the medical specialty concerned with the study and treatment of children. Pediatricians treat children from birth through adolescence, and deal with issues of health as well as disease. Modern pediatrics is highly complex, having many specialties and sub-specialties.

Web:
   http://www.aap.org/
   http://www.aap.org/bpi/
   http://www.icondata.com/health/pedbase/
      pedlynx.htm
   http://www.pediatricplanet.com/

Majordomo Mailing List:
   List Name: pedtalk
   Subscribe to: majordomo@pcc.com

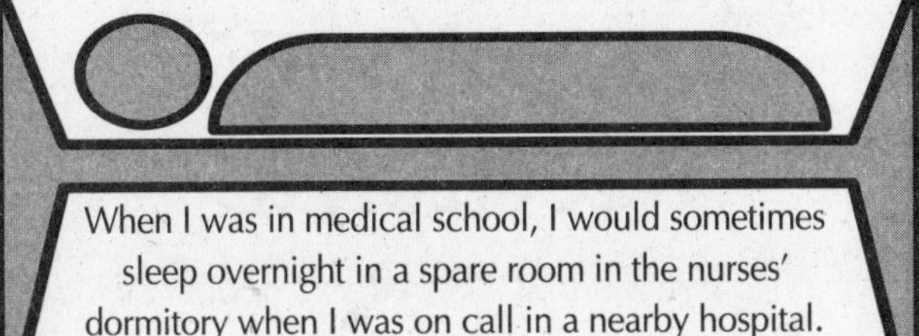

Pharmacy

What a pickle. You have to bring something to the local PTA potluck and you forgot the recipe for methylenedioxyamphetamine. Ask a pharmacist. Or maybe you just need a pharmacist joke. (Did you hear about the pill counter who married the bean counter? They had a son who became a CPA, but would only work one hour before or three hours after meals.) Find out why pharmacy—the practice of preparing and dispensing drugs—is the new glamour profession of the twenty-first century.

Web:
  http://www-sci.lib.uci.edu/~martindale/
    Pharmacy.html
  http://www.pharmacy.org/
  http://www.pharmacytimes.com/
  http://www.pharmweb.net/

Usenet:
  sci.med.pharmacy

Radiology and Imaging

Radiology is the medical specialty that deals with imaging of all kinds: radiographs (X-rays), CT scans, PET scans, MRIs, mammograms, angiograms, IVPs, and so on. In general, radiologists perform three different types of procedures: diagnosis, intervention (helping to place vascular stents or catheters, taking biopsies), and therapy (cancer treatment).

Web:
  http://www.lib.uiowa.edu/hardin/md/rad.html
  http://www.peoria-radiology.com/pinfo.htm
  http://www.radiologyinfo.org/
  http://www.rsna.org/

Usenet:
  alt.image.medical
  sci.med.radiology
  sci.med.radiology.interventional

Telemedicine

Telemedicine means using electronic signals to transfer medical information from one place to another. In other words, clinical consulting via computer networks: new technology for the world's second oldest profession.

Web:
  http://tie.telemed.org/

Usenet:
  sci.med.telemedicine

Virtual Hospital

This is a remarkable medical database containing textbooks, teaching files, lectures and clinical references. There is a lot of information here for patients as well as doctors. If you are a doctor, be sure to check out the multimedia learning resources. I get caught up here, browsing when I should be working.

Web:
  http://www.vh.org/

MEDICINE: ALTERNATIVE

Acupuncture

Chinese medicine is based on the idea that chi (life force energy) flows through the body along constant, definable pathways called meridians. Although there are many meridians, there are twenty-six principal ones, each associated with a different body function or organ. Chi exists in two opposite but complementary forms: yin and yang. When the flow of chi is impeded, the yin and yang become misbalanced, leading to conditions of ill health. There are about 800 places where the flow of chi emerges at the surface of the body. These are the acupuncture points. An acupuncturist stimulates selected points on the body, usually by using very fine needles. The goal is to make the patient healthier by rebalancing the patient's chi over a period of time.

Web:

http://users.med.auth.gr/~karanik/english/main.htm
http://www.acupuncture.com/
http://www.acupunctureguide.com/
http://www.acupuncturetoday.com/
http://www.acuxo.com/
http://www.holisticonline.com/acupuncture/
    acp_home.htm
http://www.medicalacupuncture.org/

Alternative Medicine Resources

Tired of too many drugs and poor bedside manner? Here's where you can find information about alternative forms of medicine. Track down the info you need about acupuncture, homeopathy, naturopathy, osteopathy, herbal medicine, diet and nutritional therapy, biofeedback, rolfing, aromatherapy, and much, much more.

Web:

http://www-hsl.mcmaster.ca/tomflem/altmed.html
http://www.advocacy-net.com/altmedicinemks.htm
http://www.alternativedr.com/
http://www.noah-health.org/
http://www.ohsu.edu/ohmig/cam.html
http://www.pitt.edu/~cbw/altm.html

Alternative Medicine

My philosophy is that it is better to not get sick in the first place.

Still, if you do, it's nice to know that you have a forum in which you can discuss the types of things you can only whisper about at the doctor's office. So next time you need to know how many leeches to use to cure brain cancer, check with your friends on misc.health.alternative.

Alternative Medicine Talk and General Discussion

Here are the Usenet discussion groups in which people talk about alternative medicine. If you are interested in health with a twist, one of these groups will be right up your medicinal alley. My philosophy is that, when it comes to medicine, if you don't want to walk the alternative walk, you should at least talk the alternative talk.

Usenet:

alt.aromatherapy
alt.healing.flower-essence
alt.healing.reiki
alt.health.fasting
alt.health.oxygen-therapy
alt.health.virus.cure.alternatives
misc.health.alternative

Ayurvedic Medicine

In Sanskrit, *ayurveda* means "laws of health," and is the name of one of the four sacred Hindu texts. Ayurvedic medicine is based on Indian traditions more than 3,000 years old. These resources will help you understand this ancient healing art and how it is practiced today.

Web:
http://www.ayurveda.com/info/
http://www.niam.com/corp-web/basicstoc.html
http://www.skepdic.com/ayurvedic.html
http://www.spiritweb.org/spirit/ayurveda.html

Usenet:
alt.health.ayurveda

Cannabis and Medicine

Cannabis (marijuana) is one of the most popular intoxicating drugs in the world. The most common use of marijuana is to induce a sustained sense of well-being and mild euphoria (the technical term is "getting high"). However, there are a number of medical conditions for which cannabis can be used as an effective treatment: cancer chemotherapy symptoms, certain types of loss of appetite, chronic glaucoma, muscle spasms, menstrual cramps, certain AIDS symptoms and moderate chronic pain.

Web:
http://www.cannabisnews.com/
http://www.norml.org/index.cfm?Group_ID=3376

Usenet:
sci.med.cannabis

Chinese Medicine

According to the Chinese system of medicine, a body that is in a balanced state can best maintain health and avoid disease. The question is, what is a "balanced state" and how does one achieve it? I have selected these resources to help you learn about Chinese medicine and the principles behind it. Remember, though, that the Chinese system of medicine was developed over many years to treat people living in a Chinese society, not to use as a marketing tool to sell herbal supplements to Western consumers.

Web:
http://www.chinakontor.de/l-chinese-medicine.htm
http://www.healthy.net/clinic/therapy/chinmed/
http://www.itmonline.org/
http://www.mic.ki.se/China.html

Chiropractic

It's good to be informed on all aspects of medical treatments. When I was in medical school at the University of Toronto, I used to go to the local chiropractic school's public clinic to be treated. These Web sites offer you an introduction and history of chiropractic, an overview of the profession and treatment, links to education and licensing information, and other chiropractic resources.

Web:
http://www.chiro-online.com/
http://www.yourspine.com/

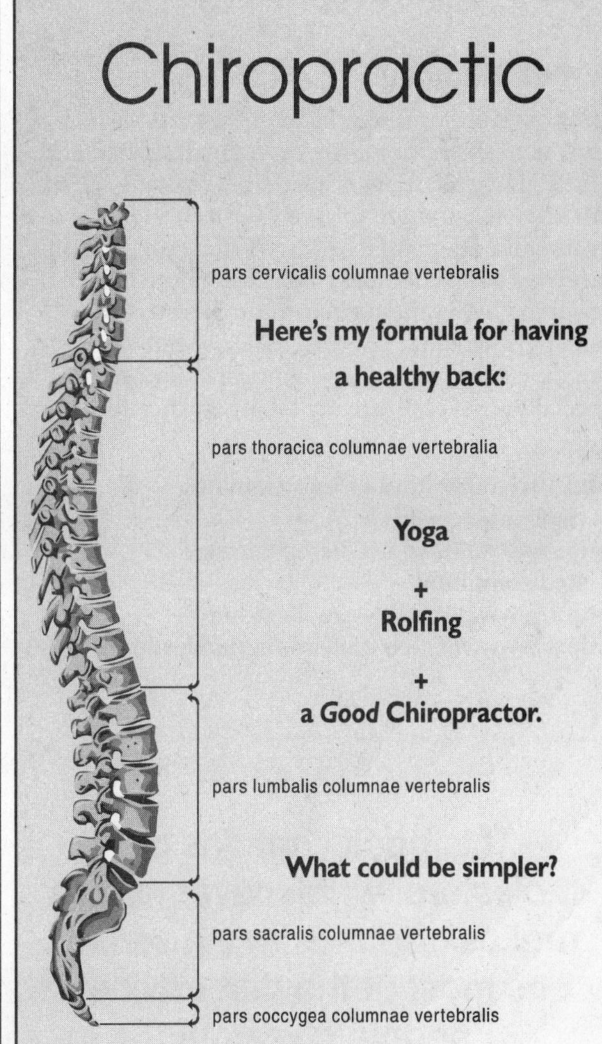

Dictionary of Metaphysical Healthcare

The phone rings. It's that beautiful woman you met at the Santa Cruz Tofu Festival. She wants to know if you would like to come over to her house and do some Dayan Qigong and then have lentils for dinner. Before you commit yourself (because commitments *are* important), you put her on hold and check with the Dictionary of Metaphysical Healthcare. You find out that Dayan Qigong, or Wild Goose Breathing Exercise, is a series of sixty-four movements that imitate the postures of a wild goose. Practicing Dayan Qigong may help you delay the aging process and prolong your life. Wow—all that and lentils too!

Web:

http://www.hcrc.org/diction/dict.html

Herbal Medicine

Herbs have been used in healing for thousands of years, with their popularity occasionally rising and falling. However, there is a lot more to using herbs than knowing enough to give valerian to your lawyer to calm him down. Before you start messing around with your body chemistry, take some time to learn something about the herbs you propose to take. Many herbs contain pharmaceutically active ingredients that can cause significant side effects, especially if you are already taking medication.

Web:

http://www.healthy.net/asp/templates/
center.asp?centerid=24
http://www.ibiblio.org/herbmed/faqs/
medi-cont.html
http://www.pitt.edu/~cbw/herb.html
http://www.wic.net/waltzark/herbindex.htm

> **This book contains no cholesterol whatsoever (which makes about as much sense as most of the diet advice people give you).**

Homeopathy

Homeopathy is a system of medical diagnosis and treatment established by the German scientist Samuel Hahnemann (1755-1843). A homeopath (practitioner of homeopathy) treats patients by taking a detailed history, including a comprehensive analysis of the patient's symptoms. The homeopath will then prescribe one specific "remedy" based on the principle of "like cures like". The idea is to use a very dilute preparation of a substance that, taken in its concentrated form, would cause the exact same symptoms being experienced by the patient. Even more strange is the homeopathic idea that, the more you dilute a remedy, the more powerful it becomes. (These ideas are, of course, contrary to established scientific beliefs.) Traditional homeopathy teaches that there are no easy answers: it takes a long time with the patient—and a lot of knowledge on the part of the homeopath—to choose the exact remedy for each particular patient.

Web:

http://www.abchomeopathy.com/
http://www.classicalhomoeopathy.com/
http://www.homeopathyhome.com/reference/
articles/homeolist_faq.shtml
http://www.onlinehomeo.com/

Music Therapy

Virtually everyone responds to music. We all know that the right music at the right time can be soothing, energizing, inspiring or entertaining. Music therapy practitioners use music and rhythm to alleviate various medical and social conditions. The job of a music therapist is to understand the needs of an individual or a group and then design music sessions to help meet these needs. In the United States, certified music therapists must complete an approved college curriculum (including an internship) and then pass a national board examination.

Web:

http://www.autism.org/music.html
http://www.musictherapyworld.net/
http://www.namt.com/
http://www.ncata.com/music.html

Relaxation Techniques

All stressed out and nowhere to go?

The Net will take care of you.

Visit one of the Relaxation Techniques sites, and soon you'll be cruising through life as cool as a virtual cucumber.

Osteopathy

Osteopathy is a system of medicine descended from the teachings of Andrew Taylor Still (1828-1917). Osteopaths receive medical training similar to regular doctors, with the addition of special courses in tissue manipulation. Where a regular doctor is known as an M.D., an osteopath uses the designation D.O. (Doctor of Osteopathy). In the United States, osteopaths are licensed to practice medicine by using drugs and surgery. However, they tend to have a more generalized and natural approach to healing that they use along with their manipulation techniques. A large portion of osteopaths are engaged in primary care (family medicine).

Web:
http://www.osteodoc.com/
http://www.osteohome.com/
http://www.osteopathy.org.uk/ois/faq/index.shtml

Relaxation Techniques

People complain about stress, but think how much less satisfying relaxation would be if there were nothing to relax from. In fact, what good would these Web sites be if it weren't for stress? So stop what you are doing right now and contemplate the stress in your life, and how lucky you are that stress provides you with an excuse to fall apart and utilize the relaxation resources available on the Net.

Web:
http://www.holisticonline.com/stress/
   stress_relaxation.htm
http://www.psybersquare.com/anxiety/
   panic_relax_I.html
http://www.rickmd.com/relax.htm
http://www.stmarys.org/health/drelax.asp

Rolfing

Rolfing is a complex system of bodywork in which a practitioner makes structural changes in the body of the client. Rolfing is named after its inventor, the American biochemist and physiotherapist Ida P. Rolf (1896-1979). Within the body, the muscles, tendons, ligaments and organs are surrounded by thin, tough sheets of tissue called fascia. This tissue is arranged in "fascial planes" that run throughout the body, providing a framework for movement and posture. A rolfer is specially trained in understanding the nature of the fascial planes and manipulating them along with the musculature. (Note: I spent four years in medical school, and I don't remember learning anything about the fascial planes. Later I found out that the only people who really understand them are rolfers and plastic surgeons.) Rolfing is carried out in a series of treatments (usually ten) in which the rolfer uses his hands, arms and even elbows to manipulate the soft tissue of the client. I can sum up the entire experience (I have been rolfed a lot of times) as follows: (1) It can hurt. (2) It can be expensive. (3) It is absolutely wonderful and is definitely worth doing.

Web:
http://www.rolf.org/
http://www.rolfing-ab.com/
http://www.vilain.com/whatis-fr.html

Shiatsu

Shiatsu is a traditional form of Japanese medicine in which the practitioner uses his palms and thumbs to apply pressure to various points on the body, the same points that are recognized and stimulated during acupuncture. A shiatsu treatment can be a lot like acupuncture using pressure instead of needles (in which case it is sometimes described as acupressure), or it can be more like a massage that concentrates on the various points. A session with a skilled shiatsu practitioner is usually an enjoyable experience, leaving one with a pleasant feeling of relaxation and comfort.

Web:

  http://www.holisticonline.com/shiatsu/
    hol_shiatsu_home.htm
  http://www.rianvisser.nl/shiatsu/e_index.htm
  http://www.shiatsu.org/

MEN

Backlash

Backlash is a magazine that rallies the troops against various unfair political beliefs. In particular, I am including the magazine here because Backlash comes out strongly against male stereotypes. My advice is to visit this site and explore the Sexism section, where you will find features, news and regular columns written from the male point of view.

Web:

  http://www.backlash.com/

Friends of Choice for Men

View the idea of "choice" from a man's point of view. The Friends of Choice for Men promote the idea that men should not be forced into fatherhood. This organization works for the equality between men's and women's reproductive rights. The Friends of Choice for Men offer articles, stories and other resources that promote choice for men.

Web:

  http://www.nas.com/c4m/

Men's Health

Men, let's face it. The health care system is not always going to take care of us the way we need. We have special problems and health considerations that the female-centric medical establishment doesn't always recognize.

The first step to maintaining our health is to become knowledgeable about our bodies and how they work. Then we need to learn about men's health issues and how they affect us.

The Net can help.

Guy Rules

Yes, there are rules that govern the behavior of men, and, yes, most of them are pretty funny. Read the rules (sent in by guys) and learn about cars, wives, sports, partying, and other types of male-type stuff. Then take the Guy Rules Test and see if you might be able to make it as a guy.

Web:

  http://www.guyrules.com/

Hair Loss

As a man gets older, his strength, vitality and sex drive begin to wane. However, as long as he can maintain the illusion of youth, a man can still pretend (at least to himself) that he is not really so old and that his sense of personal power is, as yet, undiminished. Unfortunately, hair loss is a visible sign of aging that is obvious to everyone. The problem is especially important to men who lose their hair prematurely: they still feel young, but they look old. For this reason, balding men have always been suckers for expensive treatments that purport to grow hair. Men, here is what I think. When you try to cover your bald spot by combing the hair on the side of your head over the top, you're not really fooling anyone. Trying to look younger than your real age is a game you can only lose. So my advice is to learn to be gracious about getting older. (In case you don't take my advice, here are some resources about hair loss and what you can do about it.)

Web:
  http://www.hairlossadvisor.com/
  http://www.hairlosstalk.com/faq/
  http://www.mayoclinic.com/findinformation/
      diseasesandconditions/invoke.cfm?id=DS00278&

Usenet:
  alt.baldspot

Men's Health

Men have health concerns all their own, and here are some Web sites that address the issues. Learn how to stay healthy by having a good diet and doing the right type of exercise. If you do have health problems, you will be able to find information to help you understand what is happening. And, of course, there are articles and resources about sex, just in case you need to brush up on a few more factoids.

Web:
  http://www.bbc.co.uk/health/mens/
  http://www.healthatoz.com/atoz/centers/
      menshealth/mensindex.html
  http://www.malehealthcenter.com/
  http://www.menshealthnetwork.org/
  http://www.noah-health.org/english/wellness/
      healthyliving/menshealth.html

Men's Issues

Check out this great collection of men's issues resources. These pages cover topics such as attitudes toward men, domestic violence, employment, fatherhood, health, history of men's movements, romance and relationships, the justice system, and much more. You will also find reviews of books and links to information about various men's organizations.

Web:
  http://www.mensactivism.org/
  http://www.pscw.uva.nl/sociosite/topics/men.html
  http://www.refdesk.com/men.html
  http://www.vix.com/menmag/

Usenet:
  alt.men.politics
  alt.mens-rights

Men's Rights

The definitive speech on men's rights was delivered by Rob Petrie on October 24, 1961 (The Dick Van Dyke Show, episode #5: "Washington vs. the Bunny"):

"A man is a man, even if he is a husband, and at no time, as a man or as a husband, should he ever be his wife's puppet. I have to do what I think is right. A man shouldn't sacrifice his self-respect just to keep peace in the home. All right, a woman's opinion should be weighed and considered, but in the final analysis, a man has to do what he thinks is right, or he is no man."

The implications of this speech are still being debated. Join the discussion on the Net.

Men's Resources

Men learn at an early age that the qualities that come naturally (aggressiveness, ambition, sexuality, and watching sports) must be tempered and redirected in socially acceptable ways. However, somewhere along the way, society has been redefining what it expects and requires from men, and trying to be a good man is like shooting at a moving target. Use these resources to help you understand maleness, and to see what other thoughtful men around the world have to say. No matter what anyone may say, there is always a place in the world for someone who is not afraid to kill a spider.

Web:
  http://www.manhood.com.au/scripts/manhood/
    manhome.idc?
  http://www.menstuff.org/frameindex.html

Men's Talk and General Discussion

Okay, men, this is the place where we can talk about whatever we want without having to worry about being sensitive or politically correct. For the purposes of this book, I will say that in the men's discussion group we talk about work, relationships, feminism, health, and other such topics. (But I'm sure you know what we *really* discuss.)

Web:
  http://www.styleforum.net/

Usenet:
  soc.men

> I have a very strange lava lamp. It glows in seven different colors, but only when you are not looking at it.

Self-Help for Men

If things are not going your way, do a little reading that will inspire, comfort or assist you in problem-solving. Read these articles and archives of self-help resources for men. There are also links to other self-help sites.

Web:
  http://www.shpm.com/topics/men.html

MILITARY

Ancient Warfare

Military scientists know they can learn a lot by studying ancient warfare. If you are interested in the art of war, or if you are a history buff, you'll find these resources fascinating. Although military equipment is a lot different than it used to be, human nature doesn't change and neither do the goals of war.

Web:
  http://www.fiu.edu/~eltonh/warfare/faq.html
  http://www.hillsdale.edu/academics/history/
    documents/war/ancient.htm
  http://www.julen.net/ancient/

Armed Forces of the World

These Web sites are great sources of information about various military organizations around the world. You can find links to defense forces, journals, documents, maps, military bases, military reserves, research centers and intelligence organizations. For example, I was able to learn how the Israeli military forces follow a doctrine of "speed, initiative and audacity". You can also find a lot of interesting information (such as the fact that Cyprus has four aircraft and eight helicopters even though they don't have an air force or a navy).

Web:
  http://ourworld.compuserve.com/homepages/
    mwims/otheraf.htm
  http://www.combat-online.com/world.htm
  http://www.vikingphoenix.com/public/rongstad/
    military/milinksr.htm

Chemical and Biological Warfare

We hear a lot about chemical and biological warfare, but not many people really understand it. These Web sites can help you appreciate the power of these types of weapons and how they work. Learn about substances such as nerve gas, mustard agents, tear gases and hydrogen cyanide, as well as handy tips for protecting yourself should it become necessary.

Web:

    http://chemdef.apgea.army.mil/
    http://www.cbiac.apgea.army.mil/
    http://www.fas.org/nuke/intro/cw/agent.htm
    http://www.mitretek.org/home.nsf/
       homelandsecurity/chembiodefense

Defense Ministries of the World

All around the world, there are government departments whose job is to make sure their country is ready for war. Each of these departments maintains the armed forces for that country and, just as important, they keep track of what is happening everywhere. Well, you have your own life to worry about, so maybe you should keep track of these guys. Start here, with the Web sites for defense ministries in Australia, Bulgaria, Canada, France, Germany, Greece, Holland, India, Israel, Japan, New Zealand, Norway, Russia, South Korea, Taiwan and the U.K.

Web:

    http://www.defence.gov.au/
    http://www.md.government.bg/_en_/index.htm
    http://www.dnd.ca/eng/
    http://www.defense.gouv.fr/
    http://www.bundeswehr.de/ie/
    http://www.mod.gr/english/
    http://www.mindef.nl/
    http://www.mod.nic.in/
    http://www.idf.il/newsite/english/main.asp
    http://www.jda.go.jp/e/index_.htm
    http://www.defence.govt.nz/
    http://www.dep.no/fd/engelsk/
    http://www.rian.ru/mo/
    http://www.mnd.go.kr/mnden/emainindex.html
    http://www.mnd.gov.tw/
    http://www.mod.uk/

Armed Forces of the World

They're highly trained, well-organized, dressed in the latest of military fashion, and armed to the teeth. And how do you keep track of them? Use the Net.

Medieval Armor and Weapons

In the Middle Ages, there were no guns, and it was common for warriors to use armor to protect themselves, and metal and wood weapons to fight. Today, such armor and weapons—bows and arrows, swords, spears, axes, and so on—are anachronisms that are studied and reconstructed by Middle-Ages-armor-buffs. If you are a MAAB, you will enjoy learning about the armor and the weapons: what they look like, how they are constructed, and what technical terms are used to talk about them.

Web:

    http://www.aiusa.com/medsword/
    http://www.historicalweapons.com/Articles.html
    http://www.historicalweapons.com/
       swordsterminology.html
    http://www.netsword.com/

Military Academies

A military academy is a school or college that provides a full-time military living environment for young men and women while they are following a regular academic program. Traditionally, one of the main purposes of a military academy is to train future officers for the armed services. In the United States, there are a great many military academies for students of all ages. The most well-known academies are the three college-level schools: the Military Academy at West Point, New York; the Naval Academy at Annapolis, Maryland; and the Air Force Academy at Colorado Springs, Colorado. There is also the Coast Guard Academy in New London, Connecticut, and the Merchant Marine Academy in Kings Point, New York. I've included links to the main academies as well as links to military academies in other countries. If you would like to discuss life in a military school—especially if you are a cadet—you may enjoy participating in the Usenet group.

Web:
   http://www.cga.edu/
   http://www.defence.gov.au/adfa/
   http://www.keleka.net/salute/
   http://www.mta.ro/
   http://www.nadn.navy.mil/
   http://www.rma.ac.be/rma/
   http://www.rmc.ca/
   http://www.usafa.af.mil/
   http://www.usma.edu/
   http://www.usmma.edu/

Usenet:
   alt.military.cadet

Military Brats

Children who grow up in a military family—military brats—have lives that are just a tad different than the children of civilians. These Web sites and the Usenet discussion group are for you, whether you are currently in such a family or whether you grew up in one. If you need information, try the Web sites.

Web:
   http://dticaw.dtic.mil/mtom/
   http://www.military-brats.com/
   http://www.tckworld.com/

Usenet:
   alt.culture.military-brats

Military Academies

Are you thinking of going to a military academy (or sending your son or daughter to one)? Check with the Net first. Just about every military academy in the United States has a Web site.

Military History

People may scoff at the idea of war, but if it weren't for war, there wouldn't be a need for the military; and if there weren't a military, there wouldn't be any military history; and if there weren't any military history, there wouldn't be any military history Web sites. Which brings us back to war. Here are some resources you can use to find information on all the important wars, the armed services, and related topics.

Web:
   http://www.army.mil/cmh-pg/
   http://www.cr.nps.gov/military.htm
   http://www.hazegray.org/
   http://www.nlc-bnc.ca/milit/
   http://www.rapidttp.com/milhist/journal.html
   http://www.rickard.karoo.net/main.html
   http://www.vikingphoenix.com/public/rongstad/
      history/military/milhist.htm

Usenet:
   us.military.history

Listserv Mailing List:
   List Name: h-war
   Subscribe to: listserv@h-net.msu.edu

Military Medals

In the military, medals have two important roles: to honor people who have demonstrated merit of some type, and to encourage such behavior. In the United States, the Medal of Honor (often referred to as the Congressional Medal of Honor), is the highest award given for valor in action against an enemy. The most famous Medal of Honor winner was Audie Murphy (1924-1971), the most decorated combat soldier of World War II. Murphy received every decoration for valor offered by the U.S., as well as five decorations from France and Belgium. Later in life, Murphy became a successful movie actor and song writer. However, he also suffered from Post Traumatic Stress Disorder, which caused him problems later in life, including depression, insomnia, and an addiction to sleeping pills.

Web:
   http://i.webring.com/hub?ring=odm
   http://www.army.mil/cmh-pg/moh1.htm
   http://www2.powercom.net/~rokats/medals.html

Usenet:
   alt.military.collecting.medals

Military News

In the world of the military, Jane's is the name for info. This is *the* place to come for news about defense forces around the world. I bet that after you spend even ten minutes at this site, you'll be glad that someone is keeping track of all this stuff. Otherwise, there would be a lot going on that no one would ever know about.

Web:
   http://jdw.janes.com/
   http://www.janes.com/defence/

Make good use of
your time. Check out
"Cool and Useful".

Military Police

The military police are the men and women who are responsible for law enforcement within a branch of a service as well as at military installations. Military police also provide certain services to the government, such as guarding embassies. In the U.S., the various services each have their own police, with the Marines providing some of the military police for the Navy.

Web:
   http://uts.cc.utexas.edu/~ehre/AFSPA.html
   http://www.bragg.army.mil/82mp/
   http://www.militarypolice.com/

Usenet:
   alt.military.police

Military Talk and General Discussion

The military is a lot more important and more powerful than most people realize. Moreover, there are lots of important military topics that bear discussion: military science, weapon design and deployment and, of course, politics. There are a number of Usenet groups devoted to ongoing discussions of military topics. Here are the places you can talk about the latest military technology, the various armed services around the world, life in the service, military urban legends, and much more.

Usenet:
   alt.folklore.military
   alt.military.retired
   alt.war.mercenary
   sci.military
   sci.military.moderated
   sci.military.naval

Military Terms and Acronyms

Have you ever encountered a military term that you didn't understand? It's not surprising—there are literally tens of thousands of such terms and nobody knows them all. If you are interested in any aspect of the military, here are some useful tools that can save you a lot of running around.

Web:
   http://www.dtic.mil/doctrine/jel/doddict/
   http://www.fas.org/news/reference/lexicon/
   http://www.periscope.ucg.com/terms/

Military Uniforms

Military uniforms are fascinating. Examine these Web sites and you will see what I mean. One of my favorite sites has pictures of European military uniforms from the early 19th-century and from the Burgoyne Expedition (1777). The early 19th century images cover armies from Austria, Britain, Denmark, France, Greece, Italy, Prussia, Russia, Saxony, Spain and Sweden. The Burgoyne section has uniforms of British, German and American soldiers. Note: John Burgoyne (1722-1792) was a British general who was a hero in the Seven Years War, a worldwide conflict that was fought from 1753-1763 in Europe, North America and India. Burgoyne was elected to Parliament (1761) and led troops during the American Revolutionary War. Later, he became a playwright and was known by the nickname "Gentleman Johnny".

Web:

http://collections.ic.gc.ca/analogue/uniforms/
http://www.cossackweb.com/uniforms.htm
http://www.costumes.org/pages/
   militaryuniforms.htm
http://www.walika.com/sr/uniforms/uindex.htm

Military Vehicles

If you are into testosterone-laced fighting machines, here are some resources that will get your motor running. There are lots of pictures of various types of military vehicles from the United States and other countries. Read about vehicles such as the M1 Abrams Main Battle Tank, the AH-64 Apache Attack Helicopter or, my personal favorite, the HMMWV or Humvee (a super-cool jeep with a thyroid condition). Watch and listen to video clips, sounds and animations, and read factsheets about various military crafts.

Web:

http://military.railfan.net/mv.htm
http://www.4wdonline.com/Mil/Mil.html
http://www.mvt.org.uk/links.html
http://www.skylee.com/mil-veh.html
http://www.wwiivehicles.com/

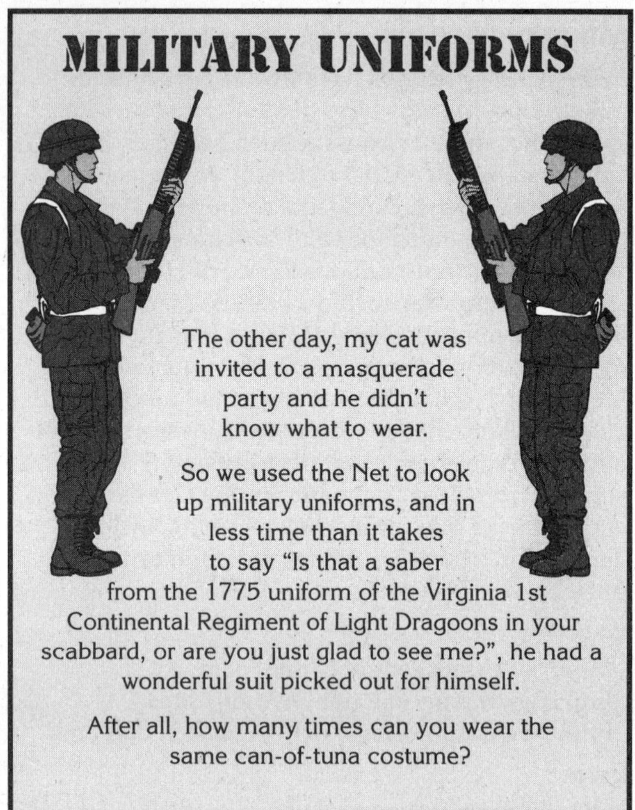

Mine Warfare

A mine is a bomb that is placed in a specific location in such a way that it will explode when a person or piece of equipment sets it off. Some mines—called land mines—are designed to be buried in the ground so that, when you walk on them and press on a sensor, they will explode. If you are lucky, you are maimed. If you are unlucky, you die. Other mines—such as naval mines—are deployed in water, on or below the surface. These mines have sonar or magnetic sensors that make them useful for blowing up warships and other marine vessels. These Web sites offer a wide variety of information about the various types of mines (of which there are many) and the worldwide efforts to remove unused mines. Look at pictures, read the facts, and be glad you live in a safe place.

Web:

http://www.icbl.org/
http://www.llnl.gov/landmine/
   landmine_whos_who.html
http://www.mines.gc.ca/menu-e.asp
http://www.minwara.org/

Nuclear Weapons

Now that the Cold War is over and the Soviet Union has broken up, we don't think about nuclear weapons all that much. Although the numbers are decreasing, there are massive arsenals of these weapons around the world, especially in the U.S. Somebody should keep an eye on all of this. Fortunately, somebody does.

Web:
  http://www.bullatomsci.org/
  http://www.fas.org/nuke/
  http://www.pbs.org/wgbh/pages/amex/bomb/
    sfeature/blastmap.html

Usenet:
  alt.war.nuclear

Prisoners of War

When the conflict is over, it's all too easy to forget the people who were POWs (prisoners of war) or MIAs (missing in action). One of these Web sites has information about the U.S. government's Defense Prisoner of War/Missing Personnel Office. The other site is maintained by families of missing persons, working to get them home or to at least have their deaths documented.

Web:
  http://www.aiipowmia.com/
  http://www.dtic.mil/dpmo/
  http://www.powmiaff.org/

Usenet:
  alt.war.pow-mia

Selective Service System

The United States Selective Service System (SSS) is an independent agency that is part of the executive branch of the federal government. The job of the SSS is twofold. (1) In case of emergency, the SSS is to deliver untrained manpower to the U.S. Department of Defense. (2) At the same time, the SSS is to administer an alternative service program for conscientious objectors. Basically, the SSS works by forcing all young men to register so the organization can keep track of them in case they are needed to serve in the military. In the aftermath of the Vietnam War the program was suspended, but in 1980 (during the last year of Jimmy Carter's presidency), the registration requirement was reinstated. Right now, in the United States, the law says that all men between the ages of 18 and 26 are required to register with the Selective Service System. (You can get the form in any post office.) When a young man turns 18, he must register within 30 days of his birthday. In the event of an emergency that required a military draft, a lottery would be held to choose who has to go. Priority would be given to those who are currently 20 years old. By the way, young women are not required (or allowed) to register. This rule was upheld by the Supreme Court in 1981.

Web:
  http://www.sss.gov/

Special Operations

You have probably heard of the Green Berets and the Rangers (Army), the SEALs (Navy) and the Air Commandos (Air Force). These are all examples of special operations units (sometimes called special forces): highly trained groups of men who respond with speed, skill and authority to high-risk situations. Most countries with a significant military force have such groups, and in the United States there are actually a great many special operations units. This Web site contains lots and lots of links to information about the various special operations units. These men train for years to be able to carry out jobs that most people wouldn't even think are possible.

Web:
  http://www.specialforces.net/

United States Armed Forces

These are the official Web sites of the main branches of the United States armed forces: the Air Force, Army, Coast Guard, Navy and Marine Corps. Each of these sites is independent, and the information varies from one page to the next. In general, though, you can find out a lot about each of the services, including what they do and how to join. I find visiting these sites interesting, as they show how the various branches of the U.S. armed services have distinct personalities and ways of looking at the world. If you need any information at all about part of the U.S. military, one of these Web sites is a good place to start. You can read about what each service does, its history, recruiting policies (including various careers), retirement information, alumni organizations, news and press releases, upcoming public events, and much more.

Web:
  http://www.af.mil/
  http://www.army.mil/
  http://www.navy.mil/
  http://www.uscg.mil/
  http://www.usmc.mil/

U.S. Department of Defense

This Web site is the official Internet public visiting area of the United States Department of Defense (DoD). You will find lots of cool information about the DoD, what they do and who runs the show. (I know it's hard to believe that such information can be cool, but check it out yourself and you will see what I mean.) This is the place to look for links to all the organizations within the Department of Defense, such as the Secretary of Defense, the Joint Chiefs of Staff, and the various branches of the military. If you are American, take a few minutes to explore this site. These guys spend *a lot* of money, so you might as well have an idea of what they are doing. After all, for better or for worse, they are doing it for *you*.

Web:
  http://www.defenselink.mil/

U.S. Military Magazines

These magazines are for people interested in U.S. military culture. I have selected these sites to provide you with magazines devoted to the major branches of the armed services. I find the articles interesting, even though I have no connection at all with the military (except that they protect me against Communism).

Web:
  http://www.af.mil/news/airman/
  http://www.airforcetimes.com/
  http://www.armytimes.com/
  http://www.marinetimes.com/
  http://www.militarypress.com/
  http://www.navytimes.com/

U.S. Military Reunions

If you served in a branch of the United States military, and you look back fondly on your days in the service, you may want to get together and reminisce. As Bing Crosby and Danny Kaye sang in the movie White Christmas: "Gee, I wish I were back in the army / The Army wasn't really bad at all. / Three meals a day / For which you didn't pay / Uniforms for winter, spring and fall..."

Web:
  http://www.militaryusa.com/reunions.html
  http://www.reunionsmag.com/military_reunions/
  http://www.usmc.mil/reunions/reunions.nsf/

Veterans

There are several tens of millions of military veterans in the United States. If you are one of them, you will find these veteran resources useful. Read about news, POW/MIA issues, reunions, and what the government is doing that affects you. You can also talk with other veterans and look for old friends.

Web:
  http://www.oldglorytraditions.com/veterannews.htm
  http://www.va.gov/
  http://www.veterans.house.gov/
  http://www.veteranshour.com/
  http://www.vnis.com/

Usenet:
  alt.military.retired
  soc.veterans

Vietnam Veterans

The American involvement in the war in Vietnam lasted from 1961-1973, with most of the troops being deployed in the late 1960s. Although it may be hard to believe, in 1969 there were well over 500,000 American troops in Vietnam—about four percent of all the men in America. In other words, in 1969, about one out of every twenty-five American males was in Vietnam. It is no surprise then that, almost thirty years later, there are a lot of resources on the Net devoted to Vietnam veterans. If you fought in Vietnam, this Web site has a large collection of resources in which you may be interested, including veteran organizations, support groups and information about reunions. For veterans and their families, the Usenet discussion group is a good place to talk. Note: The Vietnam Veterans Memorial is a monument in Washington, D.C., containing the names of all the servicemen and women who were killed or presumed missing in the Vietnam War. The memorial is a tall V-shaped black granite wall, measuring 493 feet (150 meters) long. Along the long, black surface are inscribed 58,000 names. This is a good image to keep in mind the next time you hear someone talk about starting a war. (Interestingly enough, out of 58,000 names, you will find very few belonging to the politicians and older Americans who supported the war—although their sons are well-represented.)

Web:
  http://www.vietvet.org/

Usenet:
  alt.vietnam.veterans

Women in the Military

These sites are devoted to women and the military: women who are currently in the service, retired from active duty, or even thinking about joining. Read about life after joining the military, family life and childcare, women in combat, harassment issues, women who served in war zones, military humor, and more.

Web:
  http://www.all4nationaldefense.org/
  http://www.h-net.msu.edu/~minerva/
  http://www.militarywoman.org/homepage.htm
  http://www.va.gov/womenvet/

April Fools Tricks

The first day of April is the time when tricksters all over the world unleash their clever plots of lighthearted deceit. April Fools' pranks have developed into an art form that is celebrated on the Net where you can enjoy reading about them from the safety of your own home. You'll find lots of ways to play tricks on your friends. You know, it's never a good idea to leave things to the last minute. Maybe you should play a trick on a friend right now, just for practice.

Web:
  http://www.museumofhoaxes.com/aprilframe.html
  http://www.thefreesite.com/Seasonal_Freebies/
    April_Fools/

Avenger's Page

It's not nice to get even, but if you just have to do it, you might as well do it the best way you can. The Avenger's Handbook is a collection of postings from the **alt.revenge** Usenet group. It has everything you need to know to get revenge, except a listing of bail bondsmen in your area.

Web:
  http://www.ekran.no/html/revenge/

Backyard Ballistics

There are so many ways in which you can propel objects into the air in your own backyard. Learn about spud guns, spudzookas, air cannons, matchstick rockets, the annual "Pumpkin Chunkin" contest, and much more.

Web:
  http://www.frii.com/~bsimon/backyard.html

Big Book of Mischief

Enjoy information on how to make explosives, tennis ball cannons and carbide bombs, how to open locks, and other vital information for the budding soldier of fortune. (For amusement only. You are on your honor not to actually do any of this stuff.)

Web:
  http://www.attrition.org/~modify/texts/mischief/
    TBBOM15.TXT
  http://www.ripco.net/download/text/e-texts/tbbom/

Culture Jamming

Think of someone who jams a radio signal. He sends out another signal that has just the right characteristics to interfere with the original transmission. Culture jamming interferes with the messages of the mainstream media and popular culture. Such activities cast a wide net—art forgeries, impostors, performance art, scams, hacks, and so on—and are generally carried out by social dissidents with a sense of irony. However, the more you explore culture jamming, the more you realize that it is often practiced by people who actually believe that what they are doing is real.

Web:
  http://www.conspire.com/jamming.html
  http://www.syntac.net/hoax/index.php

Dumpster Diving

Grabbing stuff out of the trash can be either silly or cool. With most garbage cans or dumpsters, it's silly, because who wants to be rooting through other people's trash? But when the garbage yields valuable items, or the dumpster contains secret stuff, what would otherwise be silly becomes cool faster than you can say "cultural archeology".

Web:
  http://www.cat.org.au/skippy/
  http://www.nd.edu/~akreider/praxis/dumpster.htm

Usenet:
  alt.dumpster

Exploring Campus Tunnels

If you have not yet explored the tunnels under your campus, you have not had a full college experience. These tunnels are constructed in order to hold all types of utility conduits, wiring and pipes (especially steam pipes). They are secret. They can be dangerous (if you have bad luck or do something stupid). But they can be fun to explore. Since it is illegal to enter such tunnels, I advise you to not go near them. Do not look at these Internet resources even though you will find interesting stories, discussion about tunneling—the legalities and health hazards—and possibly information on entrances to specific campus tunnels.

Web:
  http://www.infiltration.org/tentanda.htm
  http://www.plop.net/underground/
  http://www.urbanexplorers.net/ctlinks.html

Usenet:
  alt.college.tunnels

Fake IDs

According to federal law, there is only one ethically defensible justification for using a fake ID: if you are an underage daughter of the President of the United States and you need to get into a bar. Now that the Bush twins, Jenna and Barbara, have attained the age of legal majority (on November 25, 2002), no one in the entire United States is morally justified in using a fake ID any longer. However, if you have an insatiable curiosity for what ethically challenged people do with their computers, printers and lamination devices, you can explore the world of counterfeit identification. As you do, please remember that, as one of my readers, there is nothing fake about you.

Web:
  http://www.counterfeitlibrary.com/
  http://www.hackcanada.com/canadian/scams/
    beginners_fake-id.html
  http://www.jaggid.com/articles/fakeidguide.html
  http://www.superlink-communications.com/info/
    fake-id.html

Hack Gallery

Hack Gallery is a compendium of Interesting Hacks To Fascinate People (IHTFP) at MIT. The word "hack" refers to a clever, benign and ethical prank, which is challenging and amusing for the perpetrators. The gallery offers a large list of hacks sorted by topic, location, and the dates when they were perpetrated. There is also a FAQ, book list, and a "best of" hack list.

Web:
   http://hacks.mit.edu/Gallery.html

Looking for a nice trick to play on someone? Try the MIT Hack Gallery for inspiration.

No need to put off putting off that special someone. The master hackers of the world have perpetrated all kinds of pranks and hoaxes, and there is no reason why you can't join their ranks.

Mischief Talk and General Discussion

The **alt.shenanigans** group is the Usenet home for discussion of all manner of practical jokes ("shens"). I particularly like reading all the stories of jokes that people have played on unsuspecting victims. This is also a good place to ask for a suggestion when you feel a burning need to put someone in their place.

Usenet:
   alt.shenanigans

Polygraphs (Lie Detectors)

A polygraph, or lie detector, is a device that is supposed to help a trained operator figure out if another person is lying. As the person answers questions, the polygraph measures changes in blood pressure, heart rate, breathing and sweating. Supposedly, the operator can look at these changes and tell if the person is lying. The test starts with innocent questions, to calibrate the results, and then moves on to the real stuff ("Who told Martha that the stock would drop?"). Want a hint to beat the polygraph? Put a tack in your shoe and press on it during the calibration questions. This will confuse the results.

Web:
   http://www.antipolygraph.org/
   http://www.polygraphplace.com/docs/
      information.shtml
   http://www.skepdic.com/polygrap.html
   http://www.totse.com/en/law/justice_for_all/
      liedctr.html

Practical Jokes

For serious enjoyment, what could be more good clean fun than embarrassing your friends and neighbors by making them look foolish? The dribble glass and plastic vomit are child's play. On the Net, you can read about lots and lots of ideas, techniques and experiences with practical jokes. Make your loved ones say "uncle", and make your uncle say, "bork, bork, bork".

Web:
   http://home.cnet.com/specialreports/
      0-6014-7-121707.html
   http://www.startingpage.com/html/
      jokes_pranks_practical_jokes.html
   http://www.yuckitup.com/pjokes.shtml

Usenet:
   alt.shenanigans

Prank Phone Calls

When you are sitting around with nothing to do, visit this site devoted to the art of prank telephone calls. Here you will find links to other prank call pages, information about the Jerky Boys (kings of the prank phone call), and tips about specific types of prank calls (such as 101 zany ways to phone in a pizza order). If you get really bored, I have a friend, Bill, who enjoys prank phone calls. His number is (425) 882-8080.

Web:
  http://www.franksworld.com/pranks/
  http://www.members.aol.com/crankings/
  http://www.odd-duck.com/html/
      modules.php?name=Boombox
  http://www.thewebsquad.com/pranks.htm

Revenge Talk and General Discussion

Landlord got you hot under the collar for no good reason? Teacher rapped you with a ruler for something that wasn't your fault? Your ex-SO (significant other) won't return your only copy of The Little Prince? Don't get mad, get even. Join the pros and find out just how smelly a fish in the ventilation duct can be. (Federal regulations require me to remind you of the ancient Chinese saying: "Before you set out for revenge, be sure to dig two graves.")

Usenet:
  alt.revenge

Statistical Know-it-all

Do you love to make a pest of yourself by correcting other people? Well, now you can do it a lot and the best part is, *you* will be right and they will be wrong. Why? Because you will be a statistical know-it-all who has used the Net to sharpen your critical sense and arm yourself with the real facts, while your friends, neighbors and relatives still believe everything they read in the newspapers and see on TV.

Web:
  http://www.stats.org/newsletters/

Telemarketer Torture

Do you hate telemarketers (people who call you trying to sell something)? Here is a list of horrible things you can do to annoy and torment telemarketing people when they make an uninvited phone call to your home. The suggestions are in the form of a game. Each thing you can do to torture a telemarketer has a point value. After the call, you can add up the points to determine your score.

Web:
  http://www.antitelemarketer.com/teletech2.htm

MONEY: BUSINESS AND FINANCE

Accounting Resources

Modern accounting has a large number of specialties and subspecialties, and it's difficult to give a general definition of an accountant, but let's try anyway. An accountant is a certified professional who provides services related to financial aspects of running a business. When I was growing up in Toronto, my father was an accountant specializing in bankruptcy and insolvency. (In Canada, most of that type of work is done by accountants, not lawyers.) As I got older, I met other accountants and I was always impressed at the breadth of their knowledge. A good accountant can look at a company's balance sheet and tell you more about that company than you would believe. I also developed a special regard for the profession in the 1980s, when accountants were the leaders in using personal computers in business. In the United States, public accounting is dominated by five very large firms called the Big 5, and I have included their Web sites: Arthur Andersen, Deloitte & Touche, Ernst & Young, KPMG and PricewaterhouseCoopers.

Web:
  http://www.academicinfo.net/busacct.html
  http://www.accountantsworld.com/
  http://www.accounting.smartpros.com/
  http://www.arthurandersen.com/
  http://www.deloitte.com/
  http://www.ey.com/
  http://www.kpmg.com/
  http://www.pwcglobal.com/

Usenet:
  alt.accounting
  biz.comp.accounting

Annual Reports

Every year, publicly traded corporations issue annual reports, many of which are available on the Net. If the report you want is online, this Web site will let you find what you want in a mouse click or two. If you do stock market research, this is a great resource for your bookmark list.

Web:
  http://www.reportgallery.com/

Bonds

A bond is a debt instrument used to raise capital by borrowing money for more than one year. A bond represents a promise to pay back the amount borrowed (the principal) on a specified date as well as interest, often at regular intervals. Bonds are issued by various types of organizations, including governments (federal, state/provincial, county, municipal) and corporations. The bond market is complex, and investing in bonds requires you to have a certain degree of specialized knowledge. Here are some resources that can help you understand bonds, find out current values, and make the appropriate calculations and decisions.

Web:
  http://www.bondsonline.com/
  http://www.bradynet.com/
  http://www.investinginbonds.com/
  http://www.publicdebt.treas.gov/sav/sav.htm
  http://www.smartmoney.com/bonds/

Business Headlines

Wondering whether to sell or buy, have a party or jump out the window of the men's washroom on the 44th floor? Don't be hasty. Read the headlines and summaries of the latest business news before making a decision.

Web:
  http://money.cnn.com/
  http://www.bloomberg.com/
  http://www.businessdaily.com/
  http://www.businessnation.com/news/
  http://www.businessweek.com/bwdaily/
  http://www.businesswire.com/
  http://www.wsrn.com/

Business Information Resources

Here are some pointers to business information resources on the Net. You can read business magazines and journals, find out about opportunities and business services on the Net, see some entrepreneurial resources, and much more.

Web:
  http://www.brint.com/interest.html
  http://www.business2.com/webguide/
  http://www.strictlybusinesssites.com/

Business Plans

A business plan is an analysis that details the operations, status and future plans for a business entity. With a corporation, a business plan will be drawn up by the management. With a partnership or sole proprietorship, the plan will be created by the people involved. In most cases, the purpose of a business plan is to document a request to borrow money. In other words, before a bank or an investor will give you money, you have to show you know what you are doing, and that your business is likely to be profitable.

Web:
  http://www.bizplanit.com/vplan.htm
  http://www.bplans.com/
  http://www.sba.gov/starting/indexbusplans.html
  http://www.smallbusinessbc.ca/

Commerce Business Daily

The Commerce Business Daily is a special publication that announces invitations to bid on proposals requested by the U.S. government. This information is updated every business day.

Web:

  http://www.ld.com/cbd/today/

Company Information

Do you want information about a specific company? There is lots of information available if you know where to look. Here are some resources to make it easy. You can find addresses, phone numbers, news, names of executives, stock info, analyst ratings, jobs postings, press releases, and more.

Web:

  http://biz.yahoo.com/i/
  http://www.corporateinformation.com/
  http://www.hoovers.com/

EDGAR Database

In the United States, the securities markets are administered by the Securities and Exchange Commission (SEC), an independent regulatory agency. The SEC's prime function is to protect investors by ensuring that the markets operate fairly, and that all investors have access to material information concerning publicly traded securities. Toward this end, the SEC maintains a huge database called EDGAR (the Electronic Data Gathering, Analysis, and Retrieval system). EDGAR contains the many forms that companies are required by law to file with the SEC. You can find an enormous variety of information by searching EDGAR. It is definitely worth your time to become familiar with the basic forms and what they contain.

Web:

  http://www.sec.gov/edgarhp.htm

What could be more fun than running your own business? Why let someone else worry about health care, liability insurance, meeting the payroll, and making a profit, when you can do so yourself? (Of course, there are drawbacks as well.) If you are starting your own business, make sure to read **misc.entrepreneurs**. There are a lot of people just like you.

Entrepreneurs

Tired of being manacled to that creaking metal desk with the file drawer that always sticks? Take charge of your life: own your own business. See the pitfalls and glories that await you, the entrepreneur.

Web:

  http://www.entreworld.org/
  http://www.tannedfeet.com/
  http://www.venturea.com/

Usenet:

  misc.entrepreneurs

Foreign Trade Statistics

Black market traders, investors and exporting gurus will all be interested to hear what the Foreign Trade Division says about U.S. international trade statistics. Scoot back off the edge of your seat. The waiting is over. Point your Web browser to the U.S. Bureau of Statistics and get all the numbers you need.

Web:
  http://www.census.gov/ftp/pub/foreign-trade/www/

Futures and Options

Many businesses that buy and sell have a need to lock in the price of a future transaction. For example, a farmer who is growing oranges knows that prices fluctuate. However, he may need to know how much money the oranges will sell for later in the year when they are harvested. So he arranges, in advance, to sell the oranges at a specific price. The buyer hopes that, when the time comes, he will be able to sell the oranges for more than he paid for them. In return, he accepts the risk that the farmer wants to avoid. This type of contract is called a "future". Futures are bought and sold for many different commodities (food, metals, oil, and so on), as well as for financial instruments, including foreign exchange. Within the futures market, people also buy and sell options. (An option is a contract that gives someone the right to buy or sell something at a specific price during a specific period of time.) The futures and options market is complex and volatile. It is possible to make a lot of money, if you know what you are doing and if you are lucky, but you can also lose a lot of money more quickly than you would ever believe.

Web:
  http://www.cbot.com/
  http://www.futures-guide.com/
  http://www.futuresindustry.org/
  http://www.futuresource.com/
  http://www.ilhawaii.net/~heinsite/FAQs/
     futuresfaq.html
  http://www.nfa.futures.org/
  http://www.optioncaddie.com/

Usenet:
  misc.invest.commodities
  misc.invest.futures
  misc.invest.index-futures
  misc.invest.options

Commerce Business Daily

Would you like to serve humanity and make money at the same time? Why not do business with the U.S. government? (You couldn't find a nicer group of people anywhere.) Take a look at the Commerce Business Daily and you just may find your path to life, liberty, and the pursuit of financial happiness.

Importing and Exporting

Trading is fun because you can get rid of all the stuff you don't need anymore and get cool new stuff that somebody else wants to get rid of and that makes everyone happy. Make people happy all over the globe by reading up on the import-export business. You might even end up with more stuff than you know what to do with.

Web:
  http://www.fita.org/
  http://www.globaledge.msu.edu/ibrd/

Usenet:
  alt.business.import-export.computer
  alt.business.import-export.food
  alt.business.import-export.raw-material
  alt.business.import-export.services

IPOs

An initial public offering (IPO) occurs when a company offers stock to the public for the first time. Because the stock is new, the market has not yet established its value. Thus, although an IPO offers stock at a specific price, that price can change significantly within the first few days, or even hours, of trading. Thus, IPOs are opportunities to (1) buy an initial investment in a newly offered stock as a sound strategic move, (2) make a lot of money quickly, or (3) lose a lot of money quickly.

Web:
  http://www.123jump.com/ipomaven.htm
  http://www.hoovers.com/ipo/0,1334,23,00.html
  http://www.ipo.com/
  http://www.ipohome.com/

Network/Multilevel Marketing

Network marketing requires independent entrepreneurs to (1) sell products, and (2) recruit other people to become independent entrepreneurs. The system reminds me of the poem by Longfellow: "There was a little girl, / Who had a little curl, / Right in the middle of her forehead. / When she was good, / She was very good indeed, / But when she was bad she was horrid."

Usenet:

http://www.mlmforums.com/forums/
http://www.naftatrade.com/mlmfaq.html
alt.business.multi-level

Small Business Administration

Running your own business can be a delight or a hassle, depending on how you approach it. It helps to have as much information at your fingertips as possible. The Small Business Administration is online, and you can read about business development, government contracting, minority business, and financial assistance.

Web:

http://www.sbaonline.sba.gov/

Small Business Resources

If you own a small business, or you are thinking of starting one, you will find that you need a lot of information and skills that may be new to you. Most importantly, you need to set your goals (although they may change), and make a business plan (although it *will* change). Along the way, you will learn more about taxes than you ever wanted to know. There is a old saying that is good to remember, "When you own a business, the business owns you." Just don't forget that *everyone* needs a vacation.

Web:

http://www.bizoffice.com/library/library.html
http://www.ideacafe.com/
http://www.isquare.com/
http://www.quicken.com/small_business/
http://www.toolkit.cch.com/

Stock Exchanges

A stock exchange is a highly complex marketplace in which stocks and related financial instruments are bought and sold. Although many stock exchanges are not run by the government, they are heavily regulated in order to protect the public. In the United States, stock exchanges are regulated by the Securities and Exchange Commission (SEC). Here are the Web sites for the major U.S. and international stock exchanges. In the United States: the American, New York, NASDAQ and Pacific; international: Australian, Hong Kong, London, Tokyo and Toronto.

Web:

http://www.amex.com/
http://www.nyse.com/
http://www.nasdaq.com/
http://www.pacificex.com/
http://www.asx.com.au/
http://www.hkex.com.hk/
http://www.londonstockexchange.com/
http://www.tse.or.jp/english/
http://www.tse.com/

Venture Capital

Venture capital is money invested in new enterprises or research. The people investing the money, either individuals or companies, are called venture capitalists. Venture capital is sometimes referred to as "risk capital", and for a good reason. There is absolutely no guarantee that any new business or research will succeed. For this reason, venture capitalists will usually not invest money unless they receive ownership of a significant part of the enterprise. In other words, to get the money you want, you may have to give up control of the company. I know people who have raised money in just this way, only to be squeezed out later by the venture capitalists. If you are thinking of raising venture capital, you need to understand how it works, and you need to do your homework *before* you go looking for money.

Web:

http://www.financehub.com/s?k=venture+capital
http://www.garage.com/
http://www.investorguide.com/vc.html
http://www.nvca.org/
http://www.vfinance.com/

Need the scoop on serious network marketing?

Use the Net to find out all the things you should investigate before you commit yourself to being part of a multilevel marketing business. Then, tell five friends, who will each tell five friends, who will...

Wall Street Net

While everyone else is getting their hands grubby going through various newspapers searching for the latest news, you can be sitting pretty with the information all laid out in front of you. Wall Street Net brings you the latest on what is happening in the world of corporate debt and equity financing. See its archival data, which includes SEC filings and prospectuses on transactions that have occurred in the last twelve months.

Web:

http://wsn.doremus.com/

MONEY: INVESTING

Financial News

Nothing about money changes faster than the news about money. It's part economics, part politics, part gossip, part fortune telling, and always addictive.

Web:

http://www.cbs.marketwatch.com/pf/
http://www.moneycentral.msn.com/investor/
http://www.usatoday.com/money/mfront.htm

Investment Fraud

For most people, investment decisions are driven by fear and greed. Let me repeat that: fear and greed. Say it to yourself: fear and greed. Dishonest people know that, and they play to it, which is why investment fraud is an enormous problem. The world is full of people who will be glad to say and do anything to get your money. The best defense is to learn how to recognize fraud so you don't get fooled. I am sure you have heard the old saying, "If it sounds too good to be true, it is." There is no better advice to remember when you are investing.

Web:

http://www.corp.ca.gov/pub/tipsratt.htm
http://www.investorprotection.org/
http://www.sec.gov/consumer/cyberfr.htm
http://www.stock-investment-fraud.com/

Investment Glossaries

The world of money is complex, and from time to time, you are going to encounter an unfamiliar technical term. For example, say you are reading a prospectus or a report, and you see a reference to a term you don't understand, such as "capital rationing". My advice is to spend a few moments, and use a glossary to find out what the word means. In this way, you will build your vocabulary over time. (By the way, capital rationing refers to the placing of limits on the amount of new investment that can be undertaken by a company.)

Web:

http://biz.yahoo.com/f/g/
http://www.investorwords.com/

Financial News

Something is happening right now.

The price of something is going up, the price of something else is going down, and I think that interest rates may be changing. It has something to do with the latest statistics.

You'd better find out for sure.

Investment Resources

As soon as you start to invest, you enter a new world in which it seems as if everyone wants to give you advice. There are books, seminars, brokers, investments advisors, and well-meaning friends and relatives—it seems as if everyone wants to tell you what to do with your money. My advice? Go slowly, and don't do anything you don't understand completely. Remember, you can't lose money by leaving it in the bank while you take time to learn. You can lose money jumping into something you don't understand.

Web:
    http://finance.yahoo.com/
    http://university.smartmoney.com/
    http://www.investingplaces.com/
    http://www.investopedia.com/
    http://www.investor.nasd.com/
    http://www.investorguide.com/
    http://www.nomm.com/ir.htm
    http://www.sec.gov/investor.shtml
    http://www.smartmoney.com/

Investment Talk and General Discussion

Mutual funds, IRAs, discount brokerages, margin terms—do you sometimes feel like your head is going to spin around? Learn everything you need to know about investments and handling money. Make your money work for you.

Usenet:
    alt.invest
    alt.invest.market.crash
    alt.invest.penny-stock
    alt.invest.penny-stocks
    alt.invest.real-estate
    misc.invest
    misc.invest.canada
    misc.invest.commodities
    misc.invest.emerging
    misc.invest.forex
    misc.invest.funds
    misc.invest.futures
    misc.invest.index-futures
    misc.invest.marketplace
    misc.invest.misc
    misc.invest.options
    misc.invest.stocks
    misc.invest.stocks.penny
    misc.invest.technical

Mutual Funds

A mutual fund is a fund, run by an investment company, in which you can buy shares. The investment company uses the money in the fund to invest in a variety of financial instruments, most often stocks. The value of the fund's share rises and falls in relation to its holdings. The advantage of investing in a mutual fund is that it offers more diversification and better management than you could provide for yourself. There are thousands of mutual funds in many different categories, so it helps a lot to do some homework before you invest.

Web:
    http://www.brill.com
    http://www.indexfunds.com/
    http://www.mfea.com/
    http://www.mutual-funds.com/mfmag/
    http://www.sec.gov/mfcc/mfcc-int.htm
    http://www.wsrn.com/mutualfunds.xpl

Usenet:
    misc.invest.mutual-funds

Online Investment Games

Playing the stock market can be exhilarating or devastating, depending on how well you do—if you are using your own money. If you want the excitement without the risk, try one of these online investment games. Start with a given amount of imaginary money and build an imaginary portfolio. Then compete against other people to see who can create the most imaginary profits. (For even more fun, you can imagine how much tax you would have to pay on your winnings if they were real.)

Web:
    http://www.fantasystockmarket.com/
    http://www.virtualstockexchange.com/

OTC Stocks

Many stocks do not meet the requirements to be listed on a regular stock exchange. Such securities are known as OTC (over the counter) stocks or penny stocks, and are traded between dealers, either by computer or over the phone. OTC stocks typically trade at very low prices (less than a dollar a share), and investing in such securities is usually considered risky. Such stocks are often from young companies with no track record, although they are sometimes from older companies that used to be listed but have fallen on hard times. In the U.S., price quotes for OTC stocks can be found on the OTC Bulletin Board or in the Pink Sheets, a publication of the National Quotation Bureau. The rules for trading OTC stocks are enforced by the National Association of Securities Dealers (NASD).

Web:

http://www.otcbb.com/
http://www.pinksheets.com/
http://www.tipreporter.com/

Reports About Financial Professionals

One day, I was checking one of my brokerage accounts on the Web, when I noticed that the name of my broker had changed. (The name is displayed whenever I look at my account.) I found out that the brokerage company had fired her, but had not bothered to tell me. (Why should they? I'm only a customer.) Instead they silently moved my account to another broker. When I called the company and asked why the original broker had been fired, they declined to offer any details. But then I checked the Web site of the National Association of Securities Dealers, and I was able to find out what really happened. (Needless to say, she was not let go for exemplary behavior.) When you need information about a broker, a futures trader or a certified financial planner, don't depend on someone volunteering the information. Check with the appropriate regulatory agency, and find out for yourself.

Web:

http://data.cfp-board.org/nd_licensee_us_form.asp
http://www.nasdr.com/2000.asp
http://www.nfa.futures.org/basic/

Stock Market Data

The next time your therapist tells you to take stock in yourself, you will know where to look. Here are some resources that can help you find stock information for just about any security you can imagine. (And who wouldn't like to imagine more security?)

Web:

http://clearstation.etrade.com/
http://www.bigcharts.com/
http://www.dailystocks.com/
http://www.investorguide.com/stocklist.html
http://www.wallstreetview.com/

MONEY: PERSONAL FINANCE

Consumer Credit Cards

Credit cards. We just can't seem to live without the little devils. Just when you think you have everything under control, you hear about a new card with a picture of your favorite rock band, and you just can't resist. Well, if credit cards are giving you trouble, the Net can help. Here is a lot of information about credit cards, including current data to help you find which card is best for you.

Web:

http://www.abcguides.com/creditcards/
http://www.bankrate.com/brm/rate/cc_home.asp
http://www.creditinfocenter.com/cards/
http://www.federalreserve.gov/pubs/shop/

Currency Converters

Are you planning a trip? Sending money to a foreign country? Or maybe you just want to know what the francs in your Swiss bank account are worth today. No problem. Just a few clicks of the old mouse button and you'll be able to see what any amount of money is worth in another currency. I have also included a site that has historical data, useful when you need to answer such questions as "What was your Swiss bank account worth at the end of last year?"

Web:

http://www.oanda.com/converter/classic
http://www.pacific.commerce.ubc.ca/xr/
http://www.xe.com/ucc/

Estate Planning, Wills and Living Trusts

Estate planning is important for everyone. If you die without a will, the government has a great many rules that will determine what happens to all your money, property and possessions (that is, your estate). There is no guarantee that what eventually happens will be what you want. However, if you make up a will ahead of time, there is much more chance that your wishes will be followed. Moreover, proper estate planning can often save your heirs a great deal of inheritance tax. If you are married, or if you have children, you absolutely must have a will. Let me tell you a personal observation. I don't plan on dying any time soon, and I don't even like to think about death. However, I did have a will made and, once it was done, I felt good about it. It brought me peace of mind. Just do it and you will see what I mean. Here are some resources that can help you understand estate planning. In addition, at one of the sites you can read the text of the wills of various famous people, such as Elvis Presley, Jerry Garcia and Richard Nixon.

Web:
> **http://www.aarp.org/confacts/money/wills-trusts.html**
> **http://www.ca-probate.com/news_idx.htm**
> **http://www.estateplanning.com/law/**
> **http://www.ftc.gov/bcp/conline/pubs/services/**
> **livtrust.htm**
> **http://www.nafep.com/estate_planning/**
> **http://www.nolo.com/category/ep_home.html**

Getting the Most from Your Money

Don't let anyone ever call you cheap. As one of my readers, you have excellent judgment and, of course, that extends to money matters as well. Some people may think you are frugal, but let those people throw their money away. You and I can find the bargains and get the most for our dollars. Here are a few good places to look for tips, hints and Internet resources that can help you spend your money wisely.

Web:
> **http://www.econet.org/frugal/**
> **http://www.ftc.gov/bcp/conline/pubs/general/**
> **66ways/index.html**
> **http://www.hometown.aol.com/dsimple**
> **http://www.stretcher.com/**

Usenet:
> **misc.consumers.frugal-living**

If you don't plan your estate, the state or province in which you live will plan it for you.

The Net has lots of estate planning information to help you decide what's best for you and your family.

Household Budgeting

Sometimes it seems that, no matter how much money you make, it is never enough. Well, that's true for two reasons. First, probably no one ever makes enough money in the sense that there is always something else to buy. However, the second reason is more important: many people simply do not know how to budget their money wisely. Realize that budgeting well is something that you have to learn (and practice). At first, living with a budget may seem like an imposition. But once you get used to it (if you created a good budget for yourself), you will find that spending and planning within your means is a comfortable way to live.

Web:
> **http://www.debtfreeforme.com/tips/budget.htm**
> **http://www.end-credit-card-debt.com/**
> **personal-budgeting.htm**
> **http://www.ourfamilyplace.com/homeowner/**
> **budgettips.html**
> **http://www.schellcousa.com/finplanning.html**

Insurance Information

Insurance is something we buy, hoping that we will never use it. There are many types of insurance, and you can't always depend on the salesman to make sure you understand everything. Here are some useful consumer tips that could end up saving you money (and time) when it comes to understanding your insurance needs.

Web:
> **http://www.compuoffice.com/litts.html**
> **http://www.iii.org/individuals/homei/**
> **http://www.insure.com/**

Mortgage Calculators

If you have your eye on that choice piece of property down the road and you want to see just how bad the mortgage will bite into your wallet, put one of these mortgage calculators to work. Simply enter the buying price, the interest rate, and a few other pieces of information. A program will give you a fully amortized schedule or a brief summary of what you will be paying in principal and interest, your monthly payments, and what you should be earning to be able to afford the house.

Web:
> **http://www.interest.com/hugh/calc/mort.html**
> **http://www.interest.com/hugh/calc/msimple_js.html**
> **http://www.jeacle.ie/mortgage/**
> **http://www.mortgagemath.com/**
> **http://www.mortgagestogo.com/calculators.asp**

Mortgages

Buying a house will probably be the most expensive purchase you ever make. Since houses are so costly, you will probably have to borrow money by taking out a mortgage. To do so, you use the house as collateral, and borrow money to be paid back in equal monthly payments over a number of years. Each time you make a payment, some of the money goes toward paying back the loan, but a big chunk is interest: the fee you pay for borrowing the money. Over the years, the total interest adds up. For example, say you borrow $250,000 at an interest rate of 8.0% and pay the money back over 30 years. Your monthly payment will be $1,834.41 (not including property taxes and homeowner's insurance). Over 30 years, you will make 360 payments (30 years x 12 payments/ year), for a total of $660,387.60 ($1,834.41 x 360). In other words, although you borrowed $250,000, you will end up paying back $660,387.60 (2.64 times what you borrowed), of which $410,287.60 is interest. As you can see, mortgages are expensive, so it behooves you to spend some time finding the best rate you can. Moreover, mortgages are complex transactions that involve a number of fees that you must pay just to get the loan. These resources can help you search for the very best loan you can find. As you do, I have three pieces of advice. First, take your time. Second, compare the prices you find on the Net with what is available at your local lending institutions. Sometimes a local bank can give you a better price. Finally, look for a lender that is easy to work with. When I got a mortgage, I shopped for more than the price—I looked for the company and the people I wanted to deal with. My mortgage officer (whose name is Diana) was great, and she was always available when I needed her. As you look for the best interest rate, see if you can also find yourself a Diana.

Web:
> **http://www.eloan.com/**
> **http://www.getsmart.com/**
> **http://www.iown.com/**
> **http://www.mortgage-net.com/**
> **http://www.realestate.com/buyersandsellers/**
>   **financing/home.asp**

Pensions

A pension is a regular payment that is made to an employee who has retired, either because of age or disability. There are a lot of complex laws and regulations governing pensions, and if you need information about your pension or pensions in general, here are some resources you will find useful. In particular, you can learn about the Pension Benefit Guaranty Corporation (PBGC). The PBGC is a corporation set up by the United States government to insure pensions. The PBGC protects about one out of every three working people in the U.S.

Web:

> http://www.law.cornell.edu/topics/pensions.html
> http://www.pbgc.gov/
> http://www.pensionbenefits.com/articles/

Personal Finance Tips and Resources

It was so much easier when you were a kid. Your biggest money worry was trying to figure out how to break the piggy open without anybody noticing. Now there's all this tax stuff, deductions and annuities, investments and exemptions. At least the Net can make it a little easier to sort out all the information.

Web:

> http://www.financenter.com/
> http://www.improveyourfinances.com/
> http://www.kiplinger.com/
> http://www.myguidehub.com/personal_finance/
> http://
>   www.personal-budget-planning-saving-money.com/

Usenet:

> misc.invest.financial-plan

When it's your turn to fix dinner, read "Cooking and Recipes".

Retirement Planning

Here's a simple but effective way to save for retirement. Throughout your life, set aside 10% of every paycheck. No matter what happens, always set aside the 10%, and never ever use the money for anything else except retirement savings. Now, in the course of a lifetime, it is certain that financial emergencies will arise and, when they do, you are going to be tempted to "borrow" from your retirement money. The key to accumulating wealth is to resist that temptation. Every month, even before you pay your bills, set aside the 10%. If you learn to live on 90% of your income, you won't notice much difference day-to-day, but over the years, you will build up a significant nest egg. What should you do with your retirement money? If you are more than 10 years from retirement, invest the money safely in the stock market using, for example, a growth-oriented mutual fund, or a fund that tracks the S&P 500. Retirement planning is an important issue, and there are lots of resources on the Net that can help you. To get you started, I have picked out a few good Web sites. These resources are especially helpful if you live the United States. However, please remember what I said: no matter where you live, no matter what you do for a living, save 10% of everything you take in and invest it wisely. I want to ensure that, when you retire, you will have enough money to buy all the Harley Hahn books you ever need.

Web:

> http://www.aoa.dhhs.gov/retirement/fpfr.html
> http://www.aoa.dhhs.gov/retirement/rpg.html
> http://www.mpowercafe.com/
> http://www.quicken.com/retirement/
> http://www.retireearlyhomepage.com/
> http://www.ssa.gov/pubs/10035.html
> http://www.ssa.gov/retirement/
> http://www.tiaa-cref.org/ras/

Tax Preparation

Ah, the glorious month of April. The birds rejoice at the dawn of spring. Earthworms happily aerate the soil to stimulate new growth. A delicate breeze blows. And you are stuck inside doing your taxes. Isn't life cruel? Try to make it as painless as possible by planning ahead. Get handy instructions, hints, answers—even tax forms—on the Net. Then go catch some rays.

Web:

http://www.el.com/elinks/taxes/
http://www.irs.ustreas.gov/prod/forms_pubs/
http://www.savewealth.com/taxforms/irs/
http://www.taxadmin.org/fta/forms.html

Usenet:

misc.taxes
misc.taxes.moderated

Retirement Planning

So plan to check out the retirement planning resources on the Net.
(That's a good plan.)

Teaching Kids About Money

It is important that children understand money. But how do you know what to teach them and when? The Net can help. Check these Web sites for articles about many useful topics such as children's allowances and teaching good spending habits. Explore by yourself and then invite the kids to join you. After all, if you make sure that your kids understand money and how to use it, you will be providing them with valuable knowledge that will last a lifetime.

Web:

http://library.thinkquest.org/3096/
http://www.kidsbank.com/
http://www.practicalmoneyskills.com/english/
    students/
http://www.younginvestor.com/

MOTORCYCLES

Antique Motorcycles

Visit these sites devoted to antique motorcycles, including the Web site for the Antique Motorcycle Club of America, a non-profit organization dedicated to the restoration and exhibition of antique motorcycles. Find out information about the various chapters as well as a schedule of events. If you like antique motorcycles, you may as well join the club. As I always say, Harleys only get better as they get older.

Web:

http://www.allenmuseum.com/
http://www.motorcycle.com/mo/classified/
    vintage.html
http://www.statnekov.com/motorcycles/

Biker Women

There is something special about women who love bikes. Maybe it's because they are strong, determined, and just a tad adventurous. There are some great resources for women and motorcycles on the Net, as there should be. After all, it's hard not to admire a woman who knows the value of a Harley.

Web:

http://www.dropbears.com/bikelinks/women.htm
http://www.ladybiker.com/
http://www.womenonwheels.org/

Harley Owners Group

There's something so lovable about a Harley-Davidson. Maybe it's because they are so sexy, powerful and have lots of thrust. Or maybe it's that air of exotic mystery and charisma. Or maybe they're just good motorcycles. If you're a Harley fan, check out this site, which has art, technical information, pictures and stolen bike information.

Web:
   http://www.harley-davidson.com/ex/ins/hog/en/hog.asp

Motorcycle Camping

Have you ever gone camping with your motorcycle? If so, you will appreciate this practical information: choosing bags that work well with your bike, what gear to pack in your limited space, tips on how to best pack your bike and tie it all down, and so on.

Web:
   http://www.keynet.net/~gadget/camplist.html
   http://www.micapeak.com/WetLeather/pages/camping.html

Motorcycle Maintenance

If you enjoy working on your own bike, these Web sites have a lot of information you will find useful. Read the tips on repair, maintenance and tune-ups for many popular brands of bikes. You will not only save money, but you can get your motorcycle running just the way you want it, as well as have the satisfaction of being just that much closer to the machine. (My philosophy is that everyone should have at least one good relationship in their life.)

Web:
   http://www.clarity.net/~adam/winter-storage.html
   http://www.cyclemaintenance.com/
   http://www.nightrider.com/biketech/
   http://www.visi.com/~dalebor/maint.htm

Motorcycle Online Magazine

While it's not as convenient as a paper magazine sitting in the bathroom, this electronic motorcycle magazine is spiffy and worth a look. It features news stories, video and photo archives, a virtual museum, a U.S. events database, sneak previews of next year's motorcycle models, and links to services offered by commercial parties and manufacturers.

Web:
   http://www.motorcycle.com/

Motorcycle Racing

What a rush it is to be racing at high speeds with nothing between you and the air except a flimsy little jumpsuit that will disintegrate upon impact with the asphalt. Motorcycle racing enthusiasts discuss road racing from the racer's point of view as well as the pit crew's.

Web:
   http://www.ahrma.org/
   http://www.bikenet-racing.com/
   http://www.motorcycle-usa.com/

Listproc Mailing List:
   List Name: race
   Subscribe to: listproc@micapeak.com

Motorcycle Resources

When you take a break from riding, cruise on over to the Net, where I guarantee you'll find enough motorcycle resources to keep you happy until you get back on the bike.

Web:
   http://www.cycletrader.com/services.html
   http://www.moto-directory.com/
   http://www.pagexpress.com/motorcyc.html
   http://www.roadriders.com/
   http://www.sepnet.com/cycle/

Motorcycle Reviews

Before you buy a motorcycle, be sure to read about other people's experiences. These Web sites contain reviews—including a large collection from the **rec.motorcycles** Usenet group—and pricing information. If you are going to be spending your hard-earned cash, you deserve the best bike you can get.

Web:
http://www.motorcycle.com/mo/manufac.motml
http://www.streetbike.com/Pages/Main/
   Motorcycle_Reviews.html
http://www.theautochannel.com/db/bikeguide.html

Motorcycle Safety

Riding a motorcycle is inherently more dangerous than, say, driving a car or running around the house with a spoon in your mouth. As part of learning how to ride a motorcycle, it is important to develop an appreciation for safety and good habits. These Web pages can help you enjoy your bike while minimizing the chances of an accident or injury.

Web:
http://www.msf-usa.org/
http://www.nhtsa.dot.gov/people/injury/pedbimot/
   motorcycle/00-nht-212-motorcycle/toc.html

Motorcycle Talk and General Discussion

Anything that puts massive amounts of thrust right where you need it is bound to be desirable. No doubt that is why so many people love their motorcycles. If you just can't live without something hard, fast and powerful, these Usenet groups are the places to be.

Usenet:
alt.binaries.pictures.motorcycles
alt.binaries.pictures.motorcycles.harley
alt.binaries.pictures.motorcycles.sportbike
alt.motorcycle.sportbike
alt.motorcycles
alt.motorcycles.harley
alt.sabmag
rec.motorcycles
rec.motorcycles.dirt
rec.motorcycles.harley
rec.motorcycles.racing
rec.motorcycles.tech

Motorcycle Reviews

You are on a TV game show and you have just identified the 12th letter of the alphabet, which entitles you to a cool prize presented by a beautiful, young, blond woman in a black, sequined gown.

However, you must choose between a 1995 Yamaha Virago 750 and a 1996 Harley-Davidson Sportster 1200 Sport. How do you know what to do?

Easy, just ask for a short break and check the Motorcycle Reviews on the Net.

Motorcycling in the Rain

Riding a cycle safely in the rain calls for a great deal of skill and judgment. The Wetleather Web site is based on a mailing list devoted to issues related to riding in the rain, specifically in the northwestern part of the United States and adjacent areas in Canada. Wetleather people gather together for camping, riding and lots of fun. Check out the calendar of events, ride reports, and pictures of Wetleather members racing, and then join the list.

Web:
http://www.micapeak.com/WetLeather/

Listproc Mailing List:
List Name: wetleather
Subscribe to: listproc@micapeak.com

Regional Motorcycle Mailing Lists

When you want to discuss motorcycle topics with people all over the world, join a mailing list. This site has a comprehensive list of motorcycle mailing lists around the Net, including regional lists that allow you to interact with motorcycle enthusiasts close to home.

Web:
http://www.micapeak.com/pages/mlist.html

Scooters

Some years ago, I visited the Greek island of Crete, where I rented a motor scooter. I had a fabulous time riding around—putt, putt, putt—on the cute little thing. Leave the motorcycles to those other guys. You and I are perfectly secure in our masculinity. We can ride scooters.

Web:
http://www.dreamscape.com/danny/faq/
http://www.vespa.org/vlinks.cfm

Usenet:
alt.scooter

Sidecars

A sidecar is not something you see every day. The last one I saw was racing down the highway attached to a motorcycle driven by a young man in a leather jacket. The sidecar was loaded down with a plump blonde woman in her seventies who was also wearing a leather jacket and a long scarf that was trailing out behind her. Sidecars must be cool.

Web:
http://www.sidecar.com/
http://www.sidecarcross.com/
http://www.sidecarworld.com/

Sidecars

It takes a certain type of person to attach a sidecar to his or her motorcycle. If you would like to hobnob with such people, check out the Sidecars Web sites. It takes all types to make a world, and nowhere is this more true than in the world of motorcycles.

Stolen Motorcycles

Having your bike stolen is like someone taking your baby. Don't sit still for it. Utilize this Web site dedicated to listing descriptions and photos of stolen motorcycles.

Web:
http://www.scalesofjustice.com/stolen/

Classic Movies

In any art form, the works that are remembered are the ones with enduring value. This happens with only a small percentage of movies, when the screenplay, director, actors, editor and photographer are all excellent. If you are like me, you already have some favorite movies. However, isn't it wonderful to find and watch a great movie that is new to you? When you feel like exploring the world of film for something you have missed, visit these Web sites, where you'll find the classics: the movies you can watch over and over and over.

Web:
http://www.combustiblecelluloid.com/movies.shtml
http://www.filmsite.org/
http://www.reelclassics.com/

Usenet:
alt.fan.classic.movies
alt.movies.coen-brothers

Comic-based Films

Filmmakers need to get inspiration from somewhere, and what better place to look for ideas than the world of comic books? There are a large number of movies based on comic book characters, and if you are a popular culture junkie, you'll need to keep up on the latest news, info and rumors.

Web:
http://www.videoflicks.ca/features/comicbook/

Coming Attractions

Anticipation is three-fifths to seven-eighths of the fun, so to maximize your movie-going pleasure, you can visit these Web sites to find out in advance what movies are going to be released and when. To make the experience complete, you can read about the rumors, the production news, the official hype, and the current status of what is filming right now.

Web:
http://www.atnzone.com/ComingSoon/
http://www.chud.com/
http://www.ravecentral.com/comattr.html
http://www.upcomingmovies.com/

Cult Movies Talk and General Discussion

No matter how bad they get, no matter how outlandish they are or how far away from their origins they evolve, you will go see the hundredth remake of a film. There are a few movies that have a cult following and fans feel so strongly about these films that they will see them at all costs. These Usenet groups cover cult movies in general and some in particular, such as the Evil Dead movies and Rocky Horror Picture Show.

Usenet:
  alt.cult-movies
  alt.cult-movies.alien
  alt.cult-movies.cronenberg
  alt.cult-movies.evil-deads
  alt.cult-movies.rocky-horror

Filmmaking Talk and General Discussion

Don't you hate it when you're sitting in a dark theater enjoying the movie, when the hero has just been blown 30 feet into the sky by a car bomb and the guy behind you announces, "Plastique does not have that sort of structured explosive radius. How unrealistic." Unfortunately, not everyone views movies in the same way. For some, film is art. For others, it is pure entertainment. It can also be a business or communications media. For amateur filmmakers, these Usenet groups offer sources of help and a way to connect with other filmmakers and learn about new equipment and techniques.

Usenet:
  alt.movies.cinematography
  alt.movies.visual-effects
  bit.listserv.film-l
  rec.arts.movies.production
  rec.arts.movies.tech

**Easy to use is
easy to say.**

Horror Movies

It's great to scare yourself silly watching horror movies. And when you're not watching, what could be more fun than scaring yourself silly reading about horror movies on the Net and looking at frightening video clips?

Web:
  http://www.carfax-abbey.com/
  http://www.losman.com/
  http://www.zomboo.com/

Usenet:
  rec.arts.horror.movies

Listserv Mailing List:
  List Name: **horror**
  Subscribe to: **listserv@indiana.edu**

Horror Movies

How to be happy:

(1) Find a horror movie you haven't seen yet.

(2) Watch the movie and get good and scared.

(3) Use the Net to read about the movie.

(4) Eat some pizza.

(5) Go to step #1.

Monster Movie Talk and General Discussion

I love monsters. Even the bad ones. Monsters inevitably cause massive amounts of chaos, destruction, explosions and a variety of property damage, but that doesn't make them all bad. They are bound to be good for the economy in that they keep people employed—construction workers, for instance. Check out the Usenet group devoted to the discussion of monster movies and get the real lowdown on Godzilla's family history.

Usenet:
  alt.movies.monster

A B C D E F G H I J K L **M** N O P Q R S T U V W X Y Z

Movie and Film Resources

If you are looking for something related to film, look no further. These resources will help you find information about movies, actors, directors, composers, the film industry, media, multimedia, movie reviews, filmmaking, and more.

Web:

http://www.absolutemovies.com/
http://www.cinemaspot.com/
http://www.nitrateonline.com/

Movie Databases

It's a horrible feeling when you are trying to think of a movie title and you just can't remember it. That never has to be a problem if you use one of the comprehensive databases available on the Net. Search for your favorite (or most hated) movie by the title, cast and crew names, cast character name, genre, and other more obscure methods.

Web:

http://us.imdb.com/
http://www.allmovie.com/
http://www.darkhorizons.com/

Movie Mistakes

Do you like movies? Do you like watching other people's mistakes? Why not combine both your hobbies and double your fun? Enjoy the mistakes, bloopers and inconsistencies of the film world. Many of the mistakes have to do with geographical errors, film cutting and poorly framed shots that show cameras and other equipment.

Web:

http://www.everwonder.com/david/mistakes.html
http://www.movie-mistakes.com/

Movie News

The movies are larger than life, so it is no surprise that we look at the people who make and act in movies as being very special indeed. This is why news about movies and gossip about these people are so alluring. Here are my favorite movie news sites, the place where I go to get my fill of what's new, exciting and full of hype.

Web:

http://www.cinecon.com/news.html
http://www.cinescape.com/0/movies_2.asp
http://www.etonline.com/movie/
http://www.filmforce.ign.com/
http://www.hollywood.com/
http://www.splicedonline.com/

Movie Previews

Previews (sometimes called trailers) can be a lot of fun. In my experience, previews are often better than the actual movies. So plan now for that hot date. Fix a few snacks, pull up a couple of chairs, download lots of movie previews. You'll be able to impress your date with your good taste in movies as well as your technological prowess.

Web:

http://www.apple.com/trailers/
http://www.cinecon.com/trailers.html
http://www.joblo.com/movietrailers.htm
http://www.moviefone.com/multimedia/
http://www.trailersworld.com/

Movie Reviews

Life is too short to waste time on a bad movie. Use the Net and find out what you're getting into before you get into it.

Movie Reviews

Personally, I never go to a movie without first checking with the Net. After all, what a waste of time it is to go all the way to the theater, pay for a ticket, get settled into your chair with a bag of popcorn and a cool lemonade, only to find that the movie you have chosen is worse than a remake of "Titanic" starring the Muppets. There are so many good reviews out there, I never worry about being unpleasantly surprised. Here are my favorite places to look for movie reviews. (Hint: These reviews are also useful when you are looking for a good video to rent.)

Web:
   http://reviews.imdb.com/Reviews/
   http://www.filmcritic.com/
   http://www.houstonpress.com/issues/current/
      film_toc.html
   http://www.movie-reviews.colossus.net/
   http://www.mrqe.com/
   http://www.rottentomatoes.com/

Usenet:
   rec.arts.movies.reviews

Movie Reviews for Parents

As a parent, you certainly don't have time to watch every movie that comes out. (For one thing, the popcorn bill would be prohibitive.) Still, when your kids want to go to a movie or rent a video, you need to be able to judge if their request is in harmony with prevailing local standards (that is, what *you* think is best).

Web:
   http://www.familystyle.com/
   http://www.kids-in-mind.com/
   http://www.moviemom.com/

Movie Schedules in Your Area

When I want to find out what movies are playing in my area, I use the Net. It's a lot faster than calling the theater, and I can get more information than in the newspaper. The sites are mostly for the United States, and they do not cover everywhere. But, even if your area is not covered, you can read the synopses of movies and look at posters and previews.

Web:
   http://www.hollywood.com/showtimes/
   http://www.moviefone.com/
   http://www.us.imdb.com/Showtimes/

Movies Talk and General Discussion

Movies are fun to watch from the audience, but don't you wonder what it would be like to be in on the action? You can at least get in on the talk. Discuss movies and the making of movies from a creative or technical point of view. Fans and filmmakers frequent these Usenet groups.

Usenet:
   alt.asian-movies
   alt.fan.blade-runner
   alt.fan.lion-king
   alt.fan.sam-raimi
   alt.fan.starwars
   alt.movies.branagh-thmpsn
   alt.movies.bruce-lee
   alt.movies.chaplin
   alt.movies.christian-bale
   alt.movies.hitchcock
   alt.movies.independent
   alt.movies.indian
   alt.movies.joe-vs-volcano
   alt.movies.kubrick
   alt.movies.scorsese
   alt.movies.silent
   alt.movies.spielberg
   alt.movies.terry-gilliam
   alt.movies.tim-burton
   bit.listserv.cinema-l
   bit.listserv.screen-l
   rec.arts.cinema
   rec.arts.movies
   rec.arts.movies.current-films
   rec.arts.movies.lists+surveys
   rec.arts.movies.local.indian
   rec.arts.movies.misc
   rec.arts.movies.movie-going
   rec.arts.movies.past-films
   rec.arts.movies.people

Listserv Mailing List:

List Name: cinema-l
Subscribe to: listserv@listserv.american.edu

IRC:
   #movie-central (Undernet)
   #moviestogo (Undernet)
   #mpglovers (Undernet)

Personal Movie Finder

Have you ever been at the video store, looking at all the rows of movies and wondering what to rent? Out of all those movies, something will be just right for you, but how do you find it? At one time, I used to be able to ask John the Movie Expert for advice. John worked at my local video store. He was an articulate movie buff who knew everything there is to know about movies, and who had seen every movie ever made. Since John knew me and my tastes, it was easy for him to find something new for me to enjoy. Unfortunately, the store closed some time ago, and John is long gone. Oh, well. There's always the Net.

Web:
   http://www.advise-a-movie.com/

Science Fiction Movie Talk and General Discussion

Movies of the science fiction genre are getting better all the time. Special effects are more creative and technically seamless, and the movie ideas are more outlandish. Discuss current science fiction movies as well as the more classical features of the last few decades.

Usenet:
   rec.arts.sf.movies

Silent Movies

Although silent films were often accompanied by live music, there was no sound in the movie itself. This meant that the actors and directors had to adapt their presentation accordingly. Silent films play to the drama and visual aspects of a situation and, as you might imagine, depend more on sight gags and overacting than do the films of the sound era. As a result, during the years 1917-1928, a unique genre of entertainment was produced that, even today, offers an enjoyable, refreshing counterpoint to the complex, formulaic creations that are the norm in today's film world.

Web:
   http://www.csse.monash.edu.au/~pringle/silent/
   http://www.silentera.com/
   http://www.silentsaregolden.com/
   http://www.silentsmajority.com/
   http://www.vex.net/~emily/film/amsfaq/online.html
   http://www.welcometosilentmovies.com/

Usenet:
   alt.movies.silent

MUDS

DikuMud Talk and General Discussion

A DikuMud is a text-based role-playing virtual reality. Slay a dragon, save a princess, drink a magic potion that will kill you (these are all optional, of course). If you love excitement, adventure and fantasy, find out what DikuMuds are all about.

Usenet:
   rec.games.mud.diku

Furry Muds and Mucks

People in the furry community—sometimes called "furs"—spend a lot of time relating to animals (real, cartoon, plush or otherwise) that act like people. There are many furs around the world and more furry resources on the Net than you could explore in a month of Saturdays and Sundays. When you want to get hard-core, there's nothing better than immersing yourself in a real virtual furry environment, and here they are: the muds and the mucks. (Muds are more for doing stuff; mucks are more for talking.)

Web:
   http://www.fluffmuck.org/
   http://www.fur.com/furry/vr.html
   http://www.furcadia.com/

Harley Hahn's Guide to Muds

What is a mud? What are the different types of muds? How do you get started? What are you expected to do? There is a lot to know about mudding, and, if you are a beginner, it can take you awhile to feel comfortable. Mudding has its own culture, and it will help you a lot to understand the nuances. My mud guide will introduce you to the world of mudding and teach you the technical terms and basic ideas you need to know.

Web:
   http://www.harley.com/muds/

History of Muds

Muds have an intriguing history that demonstrates some of the most important qualities of the Net and of shared reality experiences. Once you become a serious mudder, you will enjoy knowing how muds got started, and how they developed. In the future, all young children will be required to study the history of muds in school. You and I might as well start now.

Web:
   http://www.apocalypse.org/pub/u/lpb/muddex/
   http://www.ibiblio.org/th/mud.html
   http://www.ludd.luth.se/mud/aber/articles/
      history.html

Imaginary Realities

Here's something to read when you are taking a break: an online mudding magazine. Whether you are a player, a coder or an admin, you'll find something interesting here, especially in the back issues. Even better, you can print a copy of an article and give it to your parents for an anniversary present. (Parents love stuff like that.)

Web:
   http://imaginaryrealities.imaginary.com/

LPMud Talk and General Discussion

Hack it, slash it, just make sure you clean up afterward. LPMuds are text-based virtual realities where you can puzzle out a quest for advancement in the game or you can just find monsters to kill. Discover the adventurer within you.

Usenet:
   alt.mud.lp
   rec.games.mud.lp

Muds in the News

The best thing about muds is that they keep so many people away from real life, where they would otherwise get bored and cause trouble. (Just see how much trouble is caused by all the people who *don't* use muds.)

So, all you mudders, be sure to tune in to **rec.games.mud.announce** and find out what's new and exciting. Wouldn't it be awful to connect to your favorite mud and find out that everyone else has moved to Mars?

Macintosh Mudding Resources

If you are a Mac user, I want you to know about this site. It is a great place to find resources that are scattered all over the Net: mud clients, servers and utilities, as well as links to a nice selection of mud resources, including some for beginners. If you need a mud client, look here first. Not only will you find links to the download locations, but also comprehensive commentary that makes it easy to decide which program might be best for you.

Web:
   http://www.hsoi.net/mud/

Mud Admin Talk and General Discussion

As a player, if you think it's an inconvenience when your mud crashes, think how it would be if you were in charge of the machine that crashed it. Learn the ins and outs of being an administrator of a mud. How do you start a mud, and when you get it started, how in the world do you keep it going?

Usenet:
   alt.mud.programming
   rec.games.mud.admin

Mud Announcements

What's new? What's passed away? Every Friday, get the latest word on what mud sites are up and running and which ones have been put to pasture. Did you lose your favorite mud? Ask around here—someone will know the answer.

Usenet:
   rec.games.mud.announce

Mud Area Building

The information at these Web sites is specific to building areas on a mud. You will find programs that can help you (such as "Make Zones Fast"), sample areas that you can study, lots of tips, links to other resources, as well as a mailing list devoted to creating mud areas. Hint: Before you start to code your mud areas, plan them out using graph paper.

Web:
> http://www.mudconnect.com/resources/
>   Mud_Resources:Area_Building.html
> http://www.snible.org/mud/
> http://www.valhalla.com/builder/

Mud Clients

A mud client is a program that you run on your computer to access a mud. Since muds are text-based entities, you don't need a special mud client—you can use the standard telnet program. However, very few people use telnet because it's pretty much unbearable. A good client program can make a big difference to your mudding experience, so my advice is to experiment with various clients until you find a program you really enjoy using.

Web:
> http://simplemu.onlineroleplay.com/
> http://www.davecentral.com/browse/186/
> http://www.game.org/clients.html
> http://www.gammon.com.au/mushclient/
> http://www.moo.ca/pueblo
> http://www.mud-master.com/
> http://www.mushclient.com/
> http://www.nanvaent.org/help/clients.shtml
> http://www.zuggsoft.com/zmud/zmudinfo.htm

Mud FAQs

Before you get too far in your mudding career it's a good idea to read the FAQs (frequently asked question lists). It may take you awhile until you feel comfortable on a mud. In the meantime, having some real answers to real questions can speed up the process.

Web:
> http://www.faqs.org/faqs/games/mud-faq/
> http://www.lysator.liu.se/mud/faq/
> http://www.moo.mud.org/moo-faq/
> http://www.mudconnect.com/mudfaq/

Mud Glossary

Like all great areas of human culture (art, music, science) mudding has a specialized vocabulary. When you encounter a word or term you do not understand, these Web sites are great places to look for help. Lots and lots of definitions of words that are commonly used on muds and by mud players.

Web:
> http://www.eternal.oxonet.com/Information/
>   Glossary.htm
> http://www.hypercube.org/tess/rom/faq/
>   glossary.html

Mud Lists

Are you bored out of your skull? Or perhaps you just have some responsibility you would like to avoid. No problem. Here are lists of all the Internet muds you will ever want to play. The sites have lots of distractions to keep you busy not only with muds, but with documents designed to help you learn about muds.

Web:
> http://www.kyndig.com/listings/
> http://www.mudconnect.com/
> http://www.mudranger.com/
> http://www.starwarsonline.de/
> http://www.topmudsites.com/

Mud Reviews

There are a lot of muds in the world, so how do you make a choice as to where you want to spend your time? One way is to read thoughtful reviews by knowledgeable people. Then join the mud of your choice, and live happily ever after.

Web:
> http://www.mudconnect.com/reviews/
> http://www.themudjournal.com/

> **Get the latest dirt in "Archaeology".**

Mud Talk and General Discussion

Immerse yourself in the wonders of muds, text-based virtual realities that provide you with an exciting realm in which to socialize or play adventure games. Find out what mudding is all about, but be warned: the Surgeon General has declared mudding to be addictive.

Usenet:
  alt.mud
  rec.games.mud
  rec.games.mud.misc

IRC:
  #mud (DALnet, EFnet)

Muds to Try

Do you want to explore something new? Here is a selection of the most interesting, imaginative and well-maintained muds on the Net. To start, go the Web sites of these muds. Each site gives a general overview of a particular mud. Read the Web pages to get the flavor of the mud, how friendly it is, its style, and its orientation (lots of role-playing, adventures, talking, and so on). The muds I have chosen for you to try are 4 Dimensions, Ages of Despair , Armageddon, Eternal Struggle, Feudal Realms, Forsaken Lands, Genocide, Medievia, Merentha and Star Wars: Shattered Equinox.

Web:
  http://feudal.betterbox.net/
  http://www.4dimensions.org/
  http://www.agesofdespair.org/
  http://www.armageddon.org/
  http://www.esmud.com/
  http://www.forsakenlands.net/
  http://www.geno.org/
  http://www.medievia.com/
  http://www.merentha.com/
  http://www.shatteredequinox.com/

TinyMud Talk and General Discussion

Some mudders consider adventuring and killing monsters barbaric. Imagine that. These social animals hang out on TinyMuds where social skill is a high art. If you are interested in chatting, making friends or other socializing, you'll love TinyMuds (including mushs, muses, and moos).

Usenet:
  rec.games.mud.tiny

Zynna

I sponsor the Zynna mud, and I know you will like it. Zynna was planned and developed by a group of people who have years of mudding experience. These people have created a rich and engaging environment based on a medieval fantasy theme with a well-developed mythos. As with all adventure muds, you can spend time talking with other people, as well as exploring. Zynna has five continents, one of which is an archipelago. There are coastlines, mountains, forests, streams, caves, cliffs (which you can climb), castles, beaches, docks (where you can catch fish to eat), parks, an underground cavern, a maze, roads, and cities that have restaurants, pubs, hospitals, armories and various types of shops. Within Zynna , there are a lot of activities to keep you busy, either alone or in the company of other people, so there is always something to do. If you are an experienced mudder, you will find Zynna to be well-designed, skillfully administered, and a challenge to master. If you are a beginner, Zynna is a good place to start, as there are friendly people, a good help system, and lots of places to wander as you learn. If you are not sure how a mud works, see "Harley Hahn's Guide to Muds".

Web:
  telnet://zynna.com:4000

Mud List

Defining a mud is easy: it's a (usually) text-based virtual world in which people interact with one another as well as with the built-in inhabitants and objects of the mud itself.

Understanding muds is not so easy. There is something about these virtual worlds that appeals to certain types of people in ways that most of us can never understand.

If you think you might be one of these special people, try mudding for awhile and see how your life changes. Aside from making new friends and learning all kinds of esoteric information, you will connect yourself to a type of human/machine experience that just may change your life.

MUSEUMS

Art Museums

Do you like looking at great art? Okay, here is what you should do. Order a pizza, put on some soft, classical music, and visit one of these Web sites. There's a lot to see and I bet you'll find it really relaxing. Best of all, you won't have to worry about getting pizza stains on the paintings.

Web:
    http://www.amn.org/
    http://www.artmuseum.net/
    http://www.ibiblio.org/wm/
    http://www.nga.gov/

Book Museums

I love to read, and books have always been important to me. That's why I find it interesting to visit these museums, where there are exhibits about the history of books, as well as pictures and information about rare books and manuscripts. (Actually, my favorite book museum is in my library, where I have copies of all of my own books.)

Web:
    http://2002.imj.org.il/shrine/
    http://gulib.lausun.georgetown.edu/dept/speccoll/
        bkex96.htm
    http://www.sc.edu/library/spcoll/rarebook.html

Congressional Medal of Honor Museums

In the United States, the highest military award for valor is the Medal of Honor. Relatively few such medals are awarded, and when they are, they are presented by the President in the name of Congress (which is why the award is often referred to as the Congregational Medal of Honor). There are three different Medals of Honor, one each for the army, navy and air force. These museums document the history and accomplishments of the brave heroes who have received this very special honor.

Web:
    http://www.arlingtoncemetery.com/medalofh.htm
    http://www.cmohs.org/
    http://www.homeofheroes.com/

History Museums

There is an old saying, "Those who don't visit online history museums are doomed to repeat something-or-other." Personally, I don't think you should take the chance. Today is a perfect day to look forward into the past. (By the way, if you would like a sense of how much personal computers have changed in a quarter of a century, take a look at a picture of an original Apple I computer (1976) at **http://americanhistory.si.edu/timeline/08apple.htm**)

Web:
    http://www.americanhistory.si.edu/ve/
    http://www.iwm.org.uk/lambeth/tour1.htm
    http://www.thebritishmuseum.ac.uk/

Holocaust Museums and Memorials

From the time of Hitler's rise to power (1933) to the end of World War II (1945), the Germans, under Hitler's leadership, conducted a large-scale program to systematically persecute and exterminate the entire Jewish community within the German sphere of influence. This atrocity—today known as the Holocaust—resulted in the murder of about 6 million Jews, many of whom were sent to the infamous concentration camps, places whose sole purpose was to efficiently kill large numbers of men, women and children. The Jews were not the only people murdered in the Holocaust. The Germans also rounded up and killed homosexuals, Gypsies, Communists, as well as many Poles and other foreigners whose lands were overrun by the German military. The acts committed by Hitler, the Nazis and the German people during this time period are so depraved as to challenge the imagination. Many people feel that such actions must never be forgotten, and that our society has much to gain by studying and understanding the Holocaust. Around the world, various Holocaust museums and memorials have been built. Here are the Web sites for four of them: Yad Vashem in Israel, the United States Holocaust Memorial Museum in Washington, D.C., the Simon Wiesenthal Center in Los Angeles, and the The Museum of Jewish Heritage in New York.

Web:
    http://www.yad-vashem.org.il/
    http://www.ushmm.org/
    http://www.wiesenthal.com/
    http://www.mjhnyc.org/home.htm

International Museums

Here is a selection of online museum exhibits from various countries. I bet you will find it interesting to spend some time in each of these museums. It will give you a sense of the diverse approaches to culture you find in different parts of the world. I have included museums from Canada, Russia, Uruguay and Wales. Notice the variety.

Web:
  http://www.aggv.bc.ca/
  http://www.allabulgallery.com/
  http://www.diarioelpais.com/muva2/index.html
  http://www.nmgw.ac.uk/

Museum Talk and General Discussion

These are the places where museum curators and other professionals gather to discuss their work. You can talk about plans for new exhibits, problems, questions, answers, and whatever else arises in the lives of the people who set up and maintain museums around the world.

Usenet:
  bit.listserv.museum-l

Listserv Mailing List:
  List Name: museum-l
  Subscribe to: listserv@home.ease.lsoft.com

History Museums

I have a great idea for a history museum. It will have exhibits that chronicle the building of the museum itself.

The first exhibit will explain how it all started when I had a great idea for a history museum: one that has exhibits that chronicle the building of the museum itself.

Museums Online

(1) It's a rainy day, and the kids need a break from TV. (2) You have a few spare hours before your date comes over to take you to a Monkees reunion concert. (3) You have just put in a brand new swimming pool, and it will take several hours for it to fill with water. What do all these situations have in common? They are perfect times to visit a museum online.

Web:
  http://www.icom.org/vlmp/
  http://www.musee-online.org/directo.htm
  http://www.museumspot.com/
  http://www.museumstuff.com/

Natural History Museums

Natural history refers to the study of various types of life, particularly relating to its development and evolution. If you are curious about our origins, you'll find these online museums interesting, especially if you like dinosaurs and fossils.

Web:
  http://www.amnh.org/
  http://www.cyberspacemuseum.com/
  http://www.nhm.ac.uk/
  http://www.nmmnh-abq.mus.nm.us/nmmnh/
  http://www.wf.carleton.ca/Museum/lobby.html

Religious Museums

From antiquity, much of the best art in the world has been created with religious themes. Here are some online museums where you can enjoy these creations. One of the sites I have included lets you view all the art from the Sistine Chapel. What is amazing is that, using your computer and the Net, you can get a better view of most of the art than if you were at the museum in person. In particular, I bet you will really enjoy looking at close-ups of Michelangelo's paintings on the ceiling of the chapel.

Web:
  http://www.christusrex.org/www1/sistine/
    0-Tour.html
  http://www.christusrex.org/www1/vaticano/
    0-Musei.html
  http://www.israelbiblemuseum.com/
  http://www.lib.virginia.edu/exhibits/dead/
    index2.html
  http://www.nmajh.org/exhibitions/

Science Museums

Science is fun. You can blow things up, stick things together, take things apart and make loud noises, all in the name of knowledge. However, science is a lot more than looking at exhibits: it is a way of thinking about the world. These online museums provide you with things to think about and, more important, things to *do* in your own home. These sites are great to visit with children, especially if you don't mind cleaning up a mess (in the name of knowledge, of course).

Web:
>   http://www.exploratorium.edu/
>   http://www.mhs.ox.ac.uk/exhibits/
>   http://www.mos.org/home.html
>   http://www.msichicago.org/exhibit/exhome.html
>   http://www.nmsi.ac.uk/
>   http://www.science-tech.nmstc.ca/

Space Museums

One of the stunning achievements of mankind has been our ongoing exploration of space. In many ways, such efforts may be the most important activities going on today. These museums celebrate our achievements and show us what it is like to explore space. You will find a lot of fascinating information, as well as many, many wonderful pictures. Spending even a short time browsing these exhibits should make you proud to be a human being, and glad you are living during this period of time.

Web:
>   http://spaceflight.nasa.gov/gallery/
>   http://www.nasm.edu/

Plant an idea in someone's head. (See "Biology", "Philosophy" and "Psychology" for details.)

Sports Halls of Fame

If you are a real sports fan, you will want to understand the history of your favorite sport. Not only will you appreciate the traditions of the sport, but you will be able to bring a sense of perspective to the performance of current teams and players. Here are the online versions of a number of sports halls of fame: baseball, basketball, bowling, football, hockey, motorsports, soccer, swimming and tennis.

Web:
>   http://www.baseballhalloffame.org/
>   hofers_and_honorees/
>   http://www.hoophall.com/halloffamers/
>   halloffamers.htm
>   http://www.bowlingmuseum.com/
>   http://www.profootballhof.com/
>   http://www.hhof.com/
>   http://www.mshf.com/
>   http://www.soccerhall.org/
>   http://www.ishof.org/honorees.html
>   http://www.tennisfame.org/

MUSIC

Bands

If you've been looking for your favorite rock band on the Net and can't find it, check with these Web sites. You'll find huge lists of links to band-related resources as well as information about concerts, recordings, radio stations, music news, online events, magazines, ezines, record stores, essays, articles, musical terminology and slang, articles, music styles, lyrics, sounds, pictures and more. (See if you can say that ten times real fast.)

Web:
>   http://www.allmusic.com/
>   http://www.bandmatrix.com/
>   http://www.pop-rock.dk/

Buying and Selling Music

Don't waste your time wandering the neighborhood looking for good garage sales at which to buy music and musical instruments. People all over the Net come to Usenet to buy and sell musical goods such as instruments and equipment, records, tapes, and CDs. Buying over the Net sure beats trying to get a piano home in the back seat of your car.

Usenet:
>   rec.music.makers.marketplace
>   rec.music.marketplace
>   rec.music.marketplace.cd
>   rec.music.marketplace.misc
>   rec.music.marketplace.vinyl

Concert Information

Going to concerts is an important part of growing up. When I was a kid I went to a lot of fabulous rock concerts. I saw the Doors, John Lennon, Alice Cooper, and even the Monkees. Later, when I was older and nostalgia was popular, I remember seeing many other groups such as the Beach Boys and the Four Seasons, as well as singers like Ella Fitzgerald and Joe Williams. When we are young, the music that is popular is *ours*, and everything else seems hopelessly outdated. Well, if you are young right now, you're in luck, because you have the Net, and the Net lists of concert schedules, ticket information, as well as other related resources: everything you need to plan your musical memories to comfort you in your old age. (Interesting thought: one day, there are going to be people who are nostalgic about Eminem.)

Web:
>   http://www.concertdirect.com/
>   http://www.mojam.com/
>   http://www.musictoday.com/road_maps.asp
>   http://www.rockrage.com/concert_info.html

Time for a double ice cream break.

Discographies

When you have a blind date with a girl and you know she likes a certain band, go to one of these discographies sites, find the band and memorize every song and album they have ever released (along with the dates they were released). On the date, talk is bound to turn to music and you can wow her with your knowledge of her favorite musical groups. I always say, plan for success.

Web:
>   http://ad.techno.org/
>   http://www.bsnpubs.com/discog.html
>   http://www.discographynet.com/
>   http://www.twee.net/bands/

DJing

If you are old enough to remember when music came from turntables playing vinyl records, you also remember how delicate the whole system was. You had to take care not to jar the turntable while it was playing, and you had to be especially careful with your records to prevent scratches. Today, people use these old, obsolete turntables as musical instruments. It's called DJing. For example, a young music lover will take two turntables, play two records at the same time, and use a mixer to create a musically disjunctive *mélange à deux*. Some people do it as a hobby at home, which is fun because DJing makes exactly the type of noise that most annoys their parents. Other people take the activity much more seriously, calling it "turntablism", studying it scientifically and developing new techniques. There are two basic skills. First, creating a "scratch", a short sound that you play over and over by moving a record back and forth. Second, "beat-matching", in which you take two tunes, and play them at exactly the same tempo, so you can change from one to the other without missing a beat.

Web:
>   http://atn.addict.com/issues/5.02/html/hifi/
>   Cover_Story/Turntablism/History_Of/
>   http://www.backspin.org/terms.html
>   http://www.clubdjforum.com/
>   http://www.recess.co.uk/start.html
>   http://www.sistersf.com/glossary.php

Usenet:
>   alt.dj
>   alt.music.hip-hop.dj
>   alt.music.makers.dj
>   alt.music.makers.dj.bedroom
>   alt.music.mobile-djs

Electronic Music Talk and General Discussion

Composing and playing electronic music is mostly a solitary occupation: you spend a lot of time by yourself, with only a synthesizer, a computer, and some strange-looking audio equipment for company. However, when you want company there's no need to actually go and fetch a real live person. There are people enough on the Net ready to discuss whatever you want regarding electronic music, and *they* know what they are talking about.

Usenet:
  alt.emusic
  rec.music.makers.synth
  rec.music.synth

Eurovision Song Contest

The Eurovision Song Contest is one of the most popular annual events in Europe. Every year since 1956, musicians from different countries have competed for a prize for the best song. In 1956, there were entries from 6 countries. Today, there virtually all European countries send entries, and the event is broadcast to tens of millions of people. My favorite song was the 1999 winner, "Take Me to Your Heaven", from Sweden.

Web:
  http://www.bbc.co.uk/radio2/eurovision/
  http://www.bbc.co.uk/radio2/events/eurovision/
  http://www.ebu.ch/home_2.html?tv-cec_home.html
  http://www.eurosong.net/
  http://www.eurosong.org.uk/
  http://www.kolumbus.fi/jarpen/

Usenet:
alt.music.eurovision

Filk

Filking is the clever, but nearly irreverent art of taking an existing song, gutting it, and making it into something new using the same music, but different words. Join the rowdy crowd around the campfire as they belt out the ballads.

Web:
  http://home.earthlink.net/~kayshapero/filkfaq.htm
  http://www.filk.com/
  http://www.interfilk.org/interfilk/filk.htm
  http://www.musesmuse.com/ut/filkers.html

Usenet:
  alt.music.filk
  rec.music.filk

Guitar Chords and Tablature

When I play guitar, I think in terms of chords and, when I hear music, I often figure out songs on the piano by thinking like a guitar player. True story: For weeks, I had been trying to figure out the chords to the Neil Sedaka song "Breaking Up Is Hard to Do". I had most of it, but a portion of the bridge (the middle part) was driving me crazy: no matter what I did, it just didn't sound right. Then, one day, I found the proper chords in an archive on the Net. All I had to do was transpose and it was perfect. (Here are the chords for the bridge. The ones I was missing are in italics. Cm7 F7 Cm7 F7 *Bb Bbmaj7 Bb Bbmaj7 Bbm7 Eb7 Bbm7 Eb7* Ab G.)

Web:
  http://www.jauko.nl/tot/
  http://www.olga.net/
  http://www.tabrobot.com/
  http://www.tabs.co.za/
  http://www.ultimate-guitar.com/tabs/freshtabs.htm

Usenet:
  alt.guitar.tab
  rec.music.makers.guitar.tablature

Home Recording

In general terms, there are two ways to do home recording. You can use a PC-based system, or you can use a digital recorder. Before you start, you should decide which way you want to go. A digital recorder is easy to master, and you can start recording immediately. A PC-based system is not so simple: it pretty much requires you to be a computer nerd. However, it will give you extreme amount of control over the editing process. I have a friend named Hal who plays in a band called "K" with his two sons, Mason and Zak. (Their last name is Kopeikin.) Hal, Mason and Zak are all skillful musicians, and sometimes I perform or jam with them myself. In the tradition of great musicians, they hold their practice sessions in their garage, where they have a lot of equipment. What is so cool is that, somewhere among all the equipment, Hal has a digital recorder that makes it easy to record anything that they are playing. Using this device, Hal and the boys have recorded songs that they have put on their Web site and on CDs. (I have included their Web site below, just for fun.) My chief of staff, Lydia, and I were talking about all of this, and she said that thinking about home recording makes her want to create her own personal recording studio. Not a bad idea. Maybe you should do it too.

Web:
  http://www.audioamigo.com/
  http://www.drhal.com/k/
  http://www.jeepjazz.com/handbk.html
  http://www.music-recording.com/gear/gear.html
  http://www.music-recording.com/technique/
    technique.html
  http://www.ram.org/music/making/tips/

Usenet:
  alt.music.4-track
  comp.music.misc

Indie Bands

The goal of most bands is to get a contract with a recording company. However, most bands never get such a contract. These are the unsigned bands, often referred to as indie (independent) bands. So how does an indie band get their music distributed? In two ways: they tour (and possibly sell their own CDs), and they put their music on the Net for other people to discover it.

Web:
  http://www.bands411.com/
  http://www.hungrybands.com/
  http://www.indie-music.com/
  http://www.indie-rock-music.net/

Karaoke

Karaoke: you drink, you get up in front of the crowd, you hear the music, and you sing. Karaoke started in Japan (the name means "empty orchestra" in Japanese), and has since become popular among amateur singers around the world. In a bar, or at a party with a DJ, you will see a karaoke machine that plays backup music while it displays the lyrics. On the Net you can download oodles and oodles of karaoke sound+lyrics files, and use your own computer as a karaoke machine. Want something even easier? You can play songs right from a Web site and sing along to your musical heart's content.

Web:
  http://www.absolute-authority.com/Karaoke/
  http://www.computer-karaoke.com/
  http://www.karaokescene.com/

Usenet:
  alt.binaries.karaoke
  alt.music.karaoke

Lyrics

The next time you want to serenade your favorite guy or gal, look for the perfect song to create the perfect moment for the perfect person. You'll find collections of song lyrics from many different artists and groups. When Aerosmith sang "Don't wanna close my eyes/ Don't wanna fall asleep, yeah/ I don't wanna miss a thing," they were expressing the idea that, once you find the right song to sing, life gets as good as it's ever going to get. Or as Neil Sedaka put it, "Yeah, yeah, my heart's in a whirl."

Web:
  http://www.cbel.com/lyrics/
  http://www.gurfel.com/@-lyrics.shtml
  http://www.links2go.com/topic/lyrics
  http://www.liquid2k.com/yeahx3/
  http://www.lyricsconnection.com/

Usenet:
  alt.music.lyrics

Marching Bands

These Web sites contain information about marching bands and drum corps around the United States. The Usenet groups are for marching band and drum corps enthusiasts to discuss the types of things that are important to people who march in formation, making loud musical noises. In my opinion you haven't lived until you have seen the University of Arkansas Razorback Marching Band spell out "GO HOGS", while playing the Razorback Fight Song.

Web:
  http://www.marching.com/
  http://www.marchingarts.com/
  http://www.mchsband.com/mbonline/
  http://www.worldofpageantry.com/newspost/

Usenet:
  rec.arts.marching.band.college
  rec.arts.marching.band.high-school
  rec.arts.marching.colorguard

Music Chat

Night and day, day and night, someone special waits for you on IRC, ready to talk happy talk about music.

IRC:
  #metal (Undernet)
  #mp3music (EFnet)
  #music (DALnet, EFnet, Undernet)
  #trax (DALnet, EFnet)

Music Composition

Do you feel like there is a song inside you, just waiting to get out? Get it out now instead of letting it build up. No sense taking the risk of bursting into song while standing in line at the movie house waiting to get your popcorn (because that is uncool). In the privacy of your own home, you can join Usenet and talk to other people who are interested in writing original music or lyrics.

Web:
  http://www.craftofsongwriting.com/
  http://www.faqs.org/faqs/music/composition-FAQ/
  http://www.musique.umontreal.ca/personnel/
    belkin/bk/
  http://www.newsome.org/cgi-bin/ultimatebb.cgi

Usenet:
  rec.music.compose

Music FAQs

Without music the world would be a quieter and duller place. There would be no reason to call the police because of overcranked speakers. There would be no earplugs needed when people sing off-key. And there would be no reason for all the cool FAQs on industrial, reggae, classical, Christian, metal and ska music, to name a few. This site contains most of the frequently asked question lists for the Usenet groups relating to music.

Web:
  http://www.faqs.org/faqs/music/

Music News

Music is more than spiritual creativity based on the innermost harmonies of human cognition and feeling. It is also big business, with huge amounts of money, intrigue, rumors, partnerships, hype and promotion. If you like music and you care about the music business, you'll want to visit these Web sites regularly (if only to check out the new releases and reviews).

Web:

http://www.livedaily.citysearch.com/
http://www.rockdaily.com/
http://www.rocknews.com/
http://www.sonicnet.com/news/
http://www.soundspike.com/

Usenet:

rec.music.info

Music Performance

If you are a performer, here is where you can hang out on Usenet. Talk to people who understand your language and your concerns. After all, you do have your very own Usenet groups, so why should you spend your time with regular people? Hope you get a good gig. (See, I know the lingo 'cause I'm hep.)

Usenet:

alt.music.makers.dj
alt.music.makers.electronic
alt.music.makers.theremin
alt.music.makers.woodwind
rec.music.classical.performing
rec.music.makers
rec.music.makers.bands
rec.music.makers.bass
rec.music.makers.bowed-strings
rec.music.makers.choral
rec.music.makers.dulcimer
rec.music.makers.french-horn
rec.music.makers.guitar.jazz
rec.music.makers.piano
rec.music.makers.saxophone
rec.music.makers.songwriting
rec.music.makers.squeezebox
rec.music.makers.trumpet

Music Making Made Modern

Who can forget those fabulous musical film performances of the Lost Generation: Tom Cruise as the ultimate cool dude in Risky Business; or Garth, Wayne and the boys in the car, treating us to their very special rendition of "Bohemian Rhapsody"? I know your secret: you too are a cool dude with unbelievable talent, and all you need is a break. Drop in to the *rec.music.makers* Usenet groups and see what all the other talented Internet musicians are up to.

Music Resources

Music is one of the most popular topics on the Net, and there is a huge amount of music-related information. Here are some resources that will act as your entrée into the world of music-on-the-Net. I have chosen Web sites that are well-maintained and offer variety. In particular, you'll find lots of information about musical groups, performers and particular genres.

Web:

http://music.worldrecords.com/
http://www.library.ucsb.edu/subj/music.html
http://www.mary4music.com/
http://www.music.indiana.edu/music_resources/
http://www.musreview.com/

Music Reviews

The nice thing about music is that, although you need to have talent and skill to be a performer or composer, anyone can be a critic. Moreover, it takes no special training to critique other people's reviews. So here they are. Go wild.

Web:

http://www.canoe.ca/JamMusicReviewsAlbums/
http://www.music-critic.com/
http://www.rantnrave.org/
http://www.warr.org/

Usenet:

rec.music.reviews

A B C D E F G H I J K L M N O P Q R S T U V W X Y Z

Music Talk and General Discussion

When it's late at night and you can't turn the stereo up full volume, get your music fix by talking on the Net. This mailing list and the Usenet groups will put you together with other music lovers around the world.

Usenet:

    alt.music.alternative
    alt.music.misc
    alt.music.progressive
    bit.listserv.allmusic
    comp.music
    rec.music
    rec.music.afro-latin
    rec.music.alternative
    rec.music.ambient
    rec.music.cd
    rec.music.christian
    rec.music.dementia
    rec.music.filipino
    rec.music.hip-hop
    rec.music.misc
    rec.music.progressive
    rec.music.promotional
    rec.music.ragtime

Listserv Mailing List:

    List Name: allmusic
    Subscribe to: listserv@listserv.american.edu

IRC:

    #albums (EFnet)
    #mp3passion (Undernet)

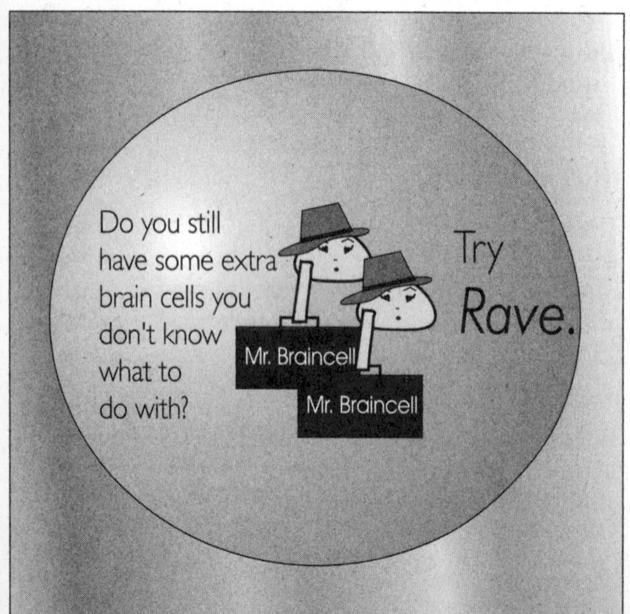

Music Videos

In a world in which personal discord and marital uncertainty is all too common, it's wonderful to see that one partnership has not only survived, but is thriving like a cat in a tuna factory. I refer, of course, to the marriage of convenience between record companies and the video industry—a union that has been responsible for one of the most important cultural achievements of the century: the music video. Of course, you can see all the music videos you want on television, but why should you put up with all the commercials? Harness the power of the Net to indulge your predilections on your very own computer, where you can choose what you want when you want it.

Web:

    http://www.clipland.com/
    http://www.video-c.co.uk/

Usenet:

    rec.music.video

Piano Chords and Sheet Music

I have been playing the piano since I was 6 years old and, although I took the regular classical lessons, I don't play that way at all. I think in terms of chords and improvisation. My favorite way to play a song is to find the chords, look at the melody line, and make up everything else as I go along. Now, compare this to the way Lydia and Debbie play the piano. (Lydia Hearn and Debbie Gin-Hearn are two sisters who work with me.) Neither of them improvises, but they can sight-read sheet music with no problem at all. I watch them play from sheet music, and I say, boy, I wish I could do that. But then they watch me improvise from a set of chords, and they say they wish they could do what I do. I guess there are two types of musical brains: the Hearns and the Hahns.

Web:

    http://www.freesheetmusicguide.com/piano/
       index.htm
    http://www.pianotabs.net/
    http://www.sheetmusicarchive.net/
    http://www.songtrellis.com/changespage

There's a lot more here than meets the I.

Rave

Immerse yourself in the ultimate techno-culture of music, dancing, drugs, and more illegal and excessive fun than most people can imagine. Learn to be the type of person your parents warned you about.

Web:
  http://www.eventnation.com/raves.html
  http://www.hyperreal.org/raves/
  http://www.ravelinks.com/
  http://www.raveshots.com/

Usenet:
  alt.rave

IRC:
  #rave (EFnet)

Record Production

To you, it's just a little sheet of vinyl or a small tape or CD that will fit in your backpack, but producing a record is a really big deal for everyone involved. Check out the details of deadlines, costs of production, contracts, technical miracles and equipment, and develop a great appreciation for all the work that goes into creating your listening pleasure.

Usenet:
  alt.music.producer

Strange Sounds

Here are bizarre, esoteric, unusual music and sounds that are an acquired taste. Exotic music, skank, thrash, hardcore, industrial, electronic body music: not for those without an industrial-strength auditory cortex.

Usenet:
  alt.exotic-music
  alt.music.hardcore
  alt.music.ska
  alt.thrash
  rec.music.industrial

Women in Music

There is women's music, music for women, and women in music, and they're all on the Net. (What could be finer?)

Web:
  http://music.acu.edu/www/iawm/
  http://www.womeninmusic.com/
  http://www.womenonair.com/

Usenet:
  alt.music.alternative.female

MUSIC: GENRES

A Cappella

"A cappella" refers to singing without instrumental accompaniment. A cappella music has many forms, such as Gregorian Chants, choir music, doo-wop, scat, barbershop singing and yodeling. I, myself, was forced to become an a cappella singer when I found that I wasn't able to get my piano into the shower.

Web:
  http://www.acappellafoundation.org/
  http://www.casa.org/
  http://www.rarb.org/reviews/

Usenet:
  alt.music.a-cappella
  rec.music.a-cappella

Barbershop Quartets

Throw down your accordion, your bagpipes, your tin whistles, and join a barbershop quartet. More fun than a barrel of monkeys, able to leap octaves in a single bound, these singers are lively, energetic, and know how to have a good time.

Web:
  http://www.harmonize.ws/links/
  http://www.idacwest.com/bec/
  http://www.spebsqsa.org/

Usenet:
  rec.music.barbershop

"Fun" is fun.

Big Band

The Big Band music we still enjoy today developed in the United States from a mixture of ragtime, jazz and other influences. The Big Band sound was more or less invented in the early 1940s by Benny Goodman (and his arranger Fletcher Henderson), and copied and modified by many other bands. The Big Band era flourished until the mid 1950s, when it was killed off by a combination of television, short (3 minute) 45 rpm records, and a variety of economic factors.

Web:
  http://www.bigbandsandbignames.com/
  http://www.nfo.net/

Usenet:
  alt.music.big-band

Blues

It's best played in tiny lounges with poor lighting. Maybe fill the room with some smoke. There is a true art to the mournful quality of the music. This is not just "crying in your beer" music. Explore the resources that bring the blues to life on the Net.

Web:
  http://www.blues.org/
  http://www.bluesfestivals.com/
  http://www.bluesworld.com/
  http://www.mudcat.org/
  http://www.thebluehighway.com/

Usenet:
  alt.music.blues
  alt.music.blues.delta
  bit.listserv.blues-l
  rec.music.bluenote.blues

Listserv Mailing List:
  List Name: blues-l
  Subscribe to: listserv@listserv.brown.edu

Celtic Music

Music is something that the Celts do well. The soulful wail of the whistles and the primal beating of the drums would make just about anyone yearn to buy a plane ticket to Ireland. The proof is in the numbers. Fans of Celtic music are abundant on the Net. Here are some Web pages with information about Celtic music magazines, live jam sessions, radio programs, and more.

Web:
  http://www.celticguitarmusic.com/celticlinks.htm
  http://www.celticwonder.com/
  http://www.donwalsh.com/celtic.html
  http://www.irishmusicweb.ie/
  http://www.ramsisle.com/celtic/webradio.htm

Usenet:
  rec.music.celtic

Classical Music

What a civilian calls "classical music" is actually a large body of serious work, written by many different composers over centuries: symphonies, concertos, chamber music, duets, opera, choral music, and so on. Such music represents some of the highest achievements of mankind. Traditionally, classical music is studied with respect to various historical periods: Medieval (before 1450: Gregorian chants); Renaissance (1450-1600: Byrd, Monteverdi, Palestrina); Baroque (1600-1750: Bach, Handel, Vivaldi); Classical (1750-1820: Haydn, Mozart, Beethoven); Romantic (1810-1910: Brahms, Chopin, Liszt, Mahler, Schubert, Schumann, Tchaikovsky); and 20th Century/Modern (1900-present: Bartók, Cage, Copland, Gershwin, Schoenberg, Shostakovich, Stravinsky).

Web:
  http://www.classical.net/
  http://www.classicalarchives.com/
  http://www.essentialsofmusic.com/
  http://www.faqs.org/faqs/music/classical/
  http://www.inkpot.com/classical/
  http://www.karadar.it/

Usenet:
  humanities.music.composers.wagner
  rec.music.classical
  rec.music.classical.contemporary
  rec.music.classical.recordings
  rec.music.early

Listserv Mailing List:
  List Name: classm-l
  Subscribe to: listserv@listserv.brown.edu

Contemporary Christian Music

America is a highly religious, mostly Christian, country with a long tradition of homegrown religious music. In the eighties, Christian music was simple: Amy Grant and Michael W. Smith. In the nineties, an influx of money and enthusiasm created a watershed in which the quality (and quantity) of Christian music increased significantly. Today, contemporary Christian music of many types enjoys a large audience, especially among the young and faithful, and as often as not, if you don't listen to the lyrics, you can't tell the difference between Christian music and its more secular cousins. (Presumably, God listens to the lyrics.)

Web:
  http://www.ccmmagazine.com/
  http://www.ccmusic.org/
  http://www.hometown.aol.com/davedj95/
    ccmlinks.htm
  http://www.singingnews.com/
  http://www.wordrecords.com/

Usenet:
  alt.music.gospel.southern

Country Music

If you don't get enough country music while riding in the pickup to and from the feed store, check out these sites, which offer concert reviews, country radio stations, discussion groups, magazines, and fan club information. Love, marriage, divorce, truck driving, dogs, beer—it's all just good old-fashioned American fun.

Web:
  http://www.cmt.com/
  http://www.country-music-club.com/
  http://www.countrymania.com/
  http://www.countrystars.com/

Usenet:
  bit.listserv.bgrass-l
  rec.music.country.old-time
  rec.music.country.western

Disco

On June 7, 1976, New York magazine published an article by Nik Cohn, entitled "Tribal Rites of the New Saturday Night". The article described an eighteen-year old Brooklyn teenager named Vincent, a neighborhood dancer with a sense of style and a definite attitude. The Sixties had faded, and a new generation of teenagers was about to redefine the popular culture. "The new generation takes few risks. It goes through high school, obedient; it graduates, looks for a job, saves and plans. Endures. And once a week, on Saturday night, its one great moment of release, it explodes." And thus was born disco. For most of us, the epiphany came with the 1977 release of the movie "Saturday Night Fever", starring John Travolta as Vincent (who was renamed Tony Manero). Three decades later, it's hard to remember that disco was once a *force majeure*, and that dancing was something you did with a partner, with style, and with an attitude. Thirty years later, disco is looked upon as an aberration, nothing more than the last, flowery hurrah between the revolution of the Sixties and the vast, interminable social wasteland of the Eighties and Nineties. But I was there and I remember. For a short time, it was possible to be cool, have fun, and enjoy the music— with a partner, with style, and with an attitude.

Web:
  http://www.70disco.com/
  http://www.discofresh.com/
  http://www.stuckinthe70s.com/music.htm

A
B
C
D
E
F
G
H
I
J
K
L
M
N
O
P
Q
R
S
T
U
V
W
X
Y
Z

Early Music

Believe it or not, there really was music before rock and roll. And it was good music, too, but you can't do the Twist to it. If that doesn't bother you, you will probably love music from the Middle Ages and Renaissance. Early music lovers chat about records, books, performances, song texts, and translations as well as transcribing early music scores in electronic form. If you are new to early music, check out the FAQ on the Web site.

Web:
   http://www.medieval.org/emfaq/

Listserv Mailing List:
   List Name: earlym-l
   Subscribe to: listserv@wu-wien.ac.at

Folk Music

I think Tom Lehrer put it best: "The reason most songs are so atrocious," he explained, "is that they were written by the people." Lehrer is a tough act to follow, so I'll content myself with pointing out that the Net has lots of folk music resources, including Usenet discussion groups.

Web:
   http://www.folklib.net/
   http://www.folkmusic.org/
   http://www.jg.org/folk/folkhome.html

Usenet:
   rec.music.folk
   rec.music.folk.tablature

One time I listened to a CD of Gregorian chant music over and over for so long that I entered an altered state of consciousness where I heard the voice of God.

   He said to me, "Those Gregorian chants are cool stuff, eh?" (You know, up to then, I had no idea that God was Canadian.)

Funk

Opera makes you homicidal, classical puts you to sleep, and country music makes you want to get in a monster truck and plow over any small cars in your path. For a change, try some funk. Funk is based on the rhythmic innovations of James Brown. Discussion includes not only funk, but some rap, hip-hop, soul, R&B, and related varieties. Artists of the genre include Bootsy Collins; Earth, Wind and Fire; Parliament/Funkadelic, Prince; and Rick James. Not only does funk sound good, you can dance to it too.

Web:
   http://www.funk45.com/
   http://www.livefunk.com/
   http://www.wfnk.com/

Usenet:
   rec.music.funky

Gregorian Chants

Gregorian chants, sometimes referred to as plainsong, are among the oldest type of music that is still performed and studied. (In fact, if you take a college-level music survey course, you will probably start with Gregorian chants and work your way toward contemporary music.) Gregorian chants have no instrumental accompaniment and no rhythmic structure. They consist of only a single melody line sung in unison by a group of people. Such music is described as monodic. (If you are taking a music survey class, remember this word—it will show up on the multiple choice test.) Gregorian chants originated in Catholic churches around the sixth century A.D. and are named after Saint Gregory I (540-604 A.D.), who was Pope from 590 to 604. If you have never heard a Gregorian chant, please do listen to one. You will find that the primitive, unaccompanied melody has the power to soothe your instincts in a way that more modern music cannot.

Web:
   http://comp.uark.edu/~rlee/otherchant.html
   http://publish.uwo.ca/%7ecantus/
   http://www.beaufort.demon.co.uk/chant.htm
   http://www.msu.edu/~knitter/chantlinks.html

Indian Classical Music

Indian music has a long complex history, dating back almost two thousand years. There are two major genres, Hindustani from the north of India and Karnatic from the south. Indian music differs from Western music in fundamental ways. Western music is based upon an octave that has 13 different tones (on the piano, 8 white notes and 5 black notes). Indian music divides the octave into 22 segments, each one being about one quarter of a tone. Most Indian pieces are based upon a single melody line or raga. There are many different ragas, each with its own rules and characteristics. The rhythms, which are complex, are also based on patterns, which are called talas. The main instruments used in Indian music are the drum, and the vina and sitar (both of which are stringed). To Western ears, Indian music sounds exotic and, sometimes, monotonous. To Indian ears, the combination of the talas, the ragas and skillful improvisation make for a complex, never-ending musical tapestry.

Web:
  http://www.forumhub.com/indcmusic/
  http://www.sangeetham.com/

Usenet:
  rec.music.indian.classical
  rec.music.indian.misc

Industrial

Industrial music started in 1976 when Industrial Records was formed by members of Throbbing Gristle. Since then, industrial music has flourished, died, been reincarnated as the electronic instrumentation used to create a dance beat, and then started to flourish again. If you like the idea of blending machinery, noise, rhythm and music, you may be ready for an industrial lifestyle.

Web:
  http://kzsu.stanford.edu/eklein/
  http://www.electroage-music.com/electall.htm
  http://www.faqs.org/faqs/music/industrial-faq/
  http://www.industrial.org/
  http://www.newempire.com/

Usenet:
  alt.music.industrial
  rec.music.industrial

Jazz

Jazz developed in the United States in the early part of the twentieth century. The roots of jazz stretch back to the Black spiritual songs brought from Africa by slaves. Since the 1920s, jazz has developed into a variety of different musical forms. What they have in common is the characteristic of free flowing melody and rhythm, which is often improvised. Some jazz is highly abstract, even to the point of being arrhythmic and lacking in melody. Other, more traditional jazz, is repetitive to the point of being completely familiar (for example, the blues). My opinion is that there is not much in life that can't be improved by adding some good jazz to the mix.

Web:
  http://www.allaboutjazz.com/
  http://www.contemporaryjazz.com/
  http://www.interjazz.com/
  http://www.jazzonln.com/
  http://www.jazzreview.com/
  http://www.redhotjazz.com/

Usenet:
  rec.music.bluenote

Listserv Mailing List:
  List Name: jazz-l
  Subscribe to: listserv@listserv.brown.edu

IRC:
  #jazz (DALnet, Undernet)
  #mp3jazz (DALnet, EFnet, Undernet)

Metal

If it's not worth playing loud, it's not worth playing. Check out the great metal resources on the Net. The Web sites cover not only heavy metal but speed, thrash, death and extreme metal. If you wanna talk the talk, hop onto IRC or hang out in Usenet. Achieve total heavy-osity.

Web:
http://www.blistering.com/
http://www.lut.fi/~mega/music.html
http://www.metal-rules.com/
http://www.rockrage.com/

Usenet:
alt.rock-n-roll.hard
alt.rock-n-roll.metal
alt.rock-n-roll.metal.black
alt.rock-n-roll.metal.death
alt.rock-n-roll.metal.doom
alt.rock-n-roll.metal.gnr
alt.rock-n-roll.metal.groove
alt.rock-n-roll.metal.hard
alt.rock-n-roll.metal.heavy
alt.rock-n-roll.metal.megadeth
alt.rock-n-roll.metal.metallica
alt.rock-n-roll.metal.motley-crue
alt.rock-n-roll.metal.progressive

IRC:
#metal (Undernet)
#mp3-metal (Undernet)

Movie Soundtracks

A big part of every film is the soundtrack, the music that is chosen to go along with the visual images in order to enhance our enjoyment. Creating the soundtrack requires the services of highly skilled musicians, and is an art unto itself. Personally, I think that a good soundtrack significantly enhances the value of a movie and I'm always disappointed when the director creates a pseudo-soundtrack by using a collection of popular songs instead of music that was composed especially for the movie. What could be more boring than to watch a tedious montage to the accompaniment of a commercial rock song? And what could be more moving than to watch a well-scored film in which the music complements the action perfectly?

Web:
http://www.cinemusic.net/
http://www.filmmusicworld.com/
http://www.filmscoremonthly.com/
http://www.hometown.aol.com/musbuff/page2.htm
http://www.imdb.com/Sections/Soundtracks/
http://www.soundtrack.net/

Usenet:
rec.music.movies

Listserv Mailing List:
List Name: filmus-l
Subscribe to: listserv@indiana.edu

New Age Music

In the 1980s, many people believed that the world was about to undergo a massive change, one that would bring harmony and spiritual enlightenment to a vast number of people. Today, the essence of these ideas is preserved in what we call New Age music: soft, peaceful, instrumental music based on slow, evocative melodies and harmonies.

Web:
http://www.loobie.com/
http://www.mkmk.com/kozlovsky/
http://www.rambles.net/new_age.html

Usenet
rec.music.gaffa
rec.music.newage

New Wave

In the 1960s, the French film world produced a movement, led by Godard and Truffaut, in which abstraction and symbolism were used to deal with psychological themes. This movement became known as New Wave. In the late 1970s, a new style of rock music arose that was given the same name. Early new wave music was marked by the use of synthesized sound with a repetitive beat, featuring a general air of emotional detachment. From about 1978 to 1986, new wave embraced a variety of musical styles that dovetailed with the rising popularity of music videos and MTV. To many people, new wave *is* the eighties—Culture Club, Depeche Mode, Devo, Duran Duran, Flock of Seagulls, Howard Jones, The Fixx and Wham!—a time of European groups with big hair, pointy shoes, synthesizers, lipstick and poet shirts.

Web:
  http://www.inthe80s.com/music.shtml
  http://www.jive.net.au/
  http://www.nwoutpost.com/

Usenet:
  alt.music.new-wave

Opera

Opera, drama set to music, started in Florence, Italy, at the beginning of the seventeenth century. (The first opera was Euridice, by Jacopo Peri, in 1600.) If you are an opera buff, you probably like to go to performances as often as you can. But what do you do when the fat lady has already sung, and you haven't had enough? You rush home, and fire up your Internet connection.

Web:
  http://rick.stanford.edu/opera/
  http://www.culturevulture.net/Opera/
    OperaIndex.htm
  http://www.fsz.bme.hu/opera/
  http://www.operaam.org/
  http://www.operabase.com/en/
  http://www.operastuff.com/geopera.html
  http://www.operaworld.com/
  http://www.stairway.bc.ca/bjorling/opralink.htm

Usenet:
  rec.music.opera

Listserv Mailing List:
  List Name: opera-l
  Subscribe to: listserv@listserv.cuny.edu

Punk Rock

Punk rockers, head banging, thrashing, nose studs, dyed hair and shaved heads—and what ever became of Jello Biafra? Share the punk experience.

Web:
  http://www.faqs.org/faqs/cultures/straight-edge-faq/
  http://www.punkrock.org/
  http://www.worldwidepunk.com/

Usenet:
  alt.binaries.punk
  alt.punk
  alt.punk.europe
  alt.punk.straight-edge

IRC:
  #punkmp3 (DALnet, EFnet, Undernet)
  #punks (DALnet)

Rap and Hip-hop

At first, rap music was not much more than how Shakespeare first described it, "no melody, heavy beat, full of words and rhythm, signifying nothing." However, over the years, as rap evolved into hip-hop, intelligent, well-adjusted, educated people started to write the lyrics, and the words became meaningful (well, some of the words anyway). Can you believe it? Rap music has become positively mainstream. Rap is dead; long live rap.

Web:
  http://www.b-boys.com/
  http://www.bet.com/music
  http://www.daveyd.com/
  http://www.hiphop-directory.com/
  http://www.hiphopdx.com
  http://www.rapstation.com/

Usenet:
  alt.rap
  rec.music.hip-hop

IRC:
  #rap (DALnet, Undernet)
  #rapmp3 (Undernet)

Lost? Try a search engine.

Reggae

You don't have to be a nyahbhingi to like reggae. Even quashies can get the beat and suck the rhygin energy to the max. So praise the Lord and pass the chillum: the Net is the most irie place to be.

Web:
  http://www.faqs.org/faqs/music/reggae/
  http://www.niceup.com/
  http://www.reggaefestivalguide.com/
  http://www.reggaeweb.com/

Usenet:
  rec.music.reggae

IRC:
  #reggae.music (EFnet)

Rock and Roll

Rock and roll is here to stay, I dig it till the end. It'll go down in history, just you wait, my friend.

Web:
  http://www.history-of-rock.com/
  http://www.ldb.org/rock.htm
  http://www.membrane.com/rrguide.html
  http://www.rocknews.com/
  http://www.rocknrollvault.com/

Usenet:
  alt.rock-n-roll
  alt.rock-n-roll.classic
  rec.music.rock-pop-r+b.1950s
  rec.music.rock-pop-r+b.1960s
  rec.music.rock-pop-r+b.1970s

Report on Rock and Roll
by Elmo (age 8)

Last week it was my turn to bring something for Show and Tell. So, I brought in my Dad's collection of old Rock and Roll records.

In order to make things interesting, I gave one Beatles record to everyone in the class (except Tiffany who sits in front of me and who I don't like). Then, when the teacher was out of the room, I showed everyone how to make a record fly like a frisbee.

When the teacher came back, she got mad and said I have to tell my Dad to come to school to talk to her.

What a fussbudget! It's not my fault she doesn't like Rock and Roll.

-Elmo

Ska

Ska is Jamaican dance music that first became popular in the early 1960s. (Ska is considered by some people to be the ancestor of reggae.) Do you like ska? There is only one way to find out. You need to listen and you need to move, and once you start moving, I bet you'll like it.

Web:
  http://www.billtanner.net/ska/
  http://www.faqs.org/faqs/music/ska-faq/
  http://www.mtska.com/

Usenet:
  alt.music.ska
  alt.music.ska-core

Majordomo Mailing List:
  List Name: skagroup
  Subscribe to: majordomo@list.pitt.edu

Techno

Composers using computers and electronic tools have fewer constraints than composers using conventional instruments. Techno musicians take advantage of modern music tools to combine rhythm, sounds and complex interactions, and send the whole thing right to your auditory cortex. Can you handle it? Maybe yes, but can you still handle it sixteen hours later?

Web:
  http://www.breaksworld.com/
  http://www.pulsation.com/
  http://www.selekta.com/
  http://www.techno.ca/links/

Usenet:
  alt.music.techno

IRC:
  #techno (EFnet)
  #technomp3 (EFnet)

MUSIC: INSTRUMENTS

Bagpipes

Bagpipes have what might euphemistically be referred to as a characteristic sound. This sound comes from the double-reed melody pipe, which produces the melody, as well as the drone pipe, which produces the constant background sound. Although a taste for bagpipe music is something that needs to be acquired, there is no problem acquiring bagpipe information on the Net.

Web:
http://www.bagpiper.com/
http://www.quinte.net/phaven/
http://www.stanford.edu/~wrinnes/BagpipeFAQ/

Usenet:
rec.music.makers.bagpipe

> Who hasn't heard a real Scotsman playing the bagpipes and not fallen in love with the sensuous, romantic, sophisticated sound that other, more euphonic musicians can only dream of?

Banjo

Africans brought the banjo all the way to America before 1688, just so people could go to bluegrass festivals and jam. And now that the banjo is well-established within our modern culture, it's time for you to start practicing. Remember, the only way you can get to the Grand Ole Opry is to practice, practice, practice.

Web:
http://www.banjohangout.org/
http://www.billpalmer.com/banjset.htm
http://www.bluegrassbanjo.org/
http://www.projectsandhobbies.com/
    playingthebanjo.htm
http://www.radix.net/~jchumley/bnjoglos.htm

Usenet:
alt.banjo
alt.banjo.clawhammer

Brass

The brass is a family of instruments, made out of metal, in which sound is produced by blowing into a metal mouthpiece. The most common brass instruments are the trumpet, trombone, tuba, cornet and horn (which used to be called the French horn). There's something rich and regal about the sound of brass instruments. Trumpet trivia: When I was in junior high school, I played the trumpet for a year. (The music teacher is still recovering.)

Web:
http://www.earlymusic.net/WCSE/early_brass.html
http://www.embouchures.com/
http://www.hornsociety.org/
http://www.iteaonline.org/
http://www.trombone-society.org.uk/
http://www.trombone.org/
http://www.trumpetguild.org/
http://www.whc.net/rjones/brassrsc.html

Usenet:
alt.music.trombone
alt.music.tuba
rec.music.makers.saxophone
rec.music.makers.trumpet

Listserv Mailing List:
List Name: trombone-l
Subscribe to: listserv@po.missouri.edu

Majordomo Mailing List:
List Name: tpin
Subscribe to: majordomo@parnassus.dana.edu

Drums and Percussion

Percussion involves striking objects together to produce a sound. But that's only the starting point. There's lots of ways to strike things together and lots of different sounds you can make. To be a good percussionist takes a strong sense of rhythm, above-average manual dexterity and many hours of practice. If you tend toward the loud and rowdy, percussion may be for you (and there is plenty more where that came from on the Net).

Web:
http://www.drumbum.com/lessons/
http://www.drumlink.com/
http://www.drumweb.com/
http://www.moderndrummer.com/
http://www.rhythmweb.com/

Usenet:
rec.music.makers.percussion
rec.music.makers.percussion.hand-drum

Guitar

I first played guitar when I was a 13-year-old kid at camp. That summer, I was inspired to learn by watching other people play and noticing how much fun they were having (and how cool they looked). So, I borrowed an instrument whenever I could and began to teach myself. When I got back to the city, I got my own guitar and, every summer from then on, I took the guitar to camp with me, where I was able to improve my skills by watching and practicing. Over the years, I discovered that, if you play guitar well enough—and you are willing to wait long enough—you will, eventually, have all the women you want. (For me, it works out quite nicely, as I can get a lot of writing done while I am waiting.)

Web:
   http://www.guitarnoise.com/guitar/
   http://www.guitarplayer.com/
   http://www.harmony-central.com/
   http://www.merde.org/guitar/
   http://www.torvund.net/guitar/blues%20guitar/
   http://www.ultimate-guitar.com

Usenet:
   alt.guitar
   alt.guitar.amps
   alt.guitar.bass
   alt.guitar.effects
   alt.guitar.lap-pedal
   alt.guitar.rickenbacker
   alt.guitar.tab
   rec.music.classical.guitar
   rec.music.makers.guitar
   rec.music.makers.guitar.acoustic
   rec.music.makers.guitar.tablature

IRC:
   #guitar (DALnet, EFnet, Undernet)
   #guitarists (DALnet, EFnet)

Musical Instrument Construction

What a satisfying feeling to be able to drag out a toolbox and some supplies and craft yourself a musical instrument. And what would be even better is if you can play it when you are finished building it. People who are good with their hands gather to discuss the design, building and repair of musical instruments.

Usenet:
   rec.music.makers.builders

Piano

I have been playing the piano ever since I was a little boy. Although I took lessons and I can read music, I mostly play by ear, or by looking at the names of chords and figuring out what the notes as I am playing. I like the piano because it makes me feel as if I am in another world. As a matter of fact, I think I'll take a break right now and go play for a few minutes. Hold on...okay, I'm back. If you want to learn how to play the piano, here is the secret: you have to practice at least one hour every day.

Web:
   http://www.faqs.org/faqs/music/piano/
   http://www.looknohands.com/chordhouse/piano/
   http://www.pianonanny.com/
   http://www.pianonet.com/articles.html
   http://www.pianoworld.com/
   http://www.ptg.org/
   http://www.tunepianos.com/yanfaq.htm

Usenet:
   alt.music.makers.electric-piano
   rec.music.makers.piano

Majordomo Mailing List:
   List Name: **pno-perf-l**
   Subscribe to: **majordomo@lists.colstate.edu**

Strings

The strings are those instruments in which sound is produced by either bowing (and sometimes plucking) a set of strings. The most common stringed instruments are the violin, viola, cello and double bass. String music can be among the most beautiful music in the world. The next time the world becomes just too much to bear, listen to a recording of a string quartet playing Pachelbel's "Canon in D Minor", and you will calm down quickly. (By the way, a canon is a composition in which a single melody is played in an overlapping manner by several instruments.)

Web:
   http://www.bright.net/~hhelser/sheila.html
   http://www.cello.org/
   http://www.celloheaven.com/
   http://www.fiddlingaround.co.uk/
   http://www.isbworldoffice.com/
   http://www.vanzandtviolins.com/
   http://www.viola.com/
   http://www.violincasa.com/tips.htm
   http://www.violink.com/

Usenet:
   rec.music.makers.bass
   rec.music.makers.bowed-strings

Unusual Instruments

What do you do when your teenage daughter comes home with her new boyfriend and announces that they are going to her room, where he is going to teach her how to play with his theremin? Don't panic. Take a moment to check with the Net. You'll find out that the theremin is a strange electronic musical instrument invented in Russia in 1919, and you don't even touch it when you play it. Moreover, there's no need to worry if you hear strange noises coming from the room. That's what theremin sound like (think of the weird sounds in the Beach Boys' song "Good Vibrations"). While you're at it, you might as well read about other unusual instruments, such as the didgeridoo, the armonica, the gravikord, the sarrusophone, and more.

Web:
  http://home.att.net/~theremin1/
  http://www.didgeweb.com/html/english/
      didge_frame.html
  http://www.glassarmonica.com/armonica/
  http://www.ibiblio.org/id/theremin/theremin.txt
  http://www.oddmusic.com/
  http://www.pertout.com/sounds.htm
  http://www.thereminworld.com/
  http://www.wadidge.com.au/care.html
  http://www.windworld.com/emi/links.htm

Usenet:
  alt.music.makers.theremin

When everyone else is playing a boring instrument, like a trumpet, clarinet or oboe, all you need to do is show up with something really special. Just imagine how impressed she'll be when she sees you with a theremin, didgeridoo, armonica, gravikord or sarrusophone.

I mean, let's face it. If you have a gravikord and you still can't get a date, you know it's your fault.

Woodwinds

A woodwind is a wind instrument in which you produce sound by blowing across a mouthpiece or through a reed that vibrates. The most common woodwinds are the clarinet, saxophone, flute, oboe and bassoon. When I was in medical school, I had a friend named Tim who was an accomplished saxophone player. At one time, he loaned me a tenor sax, which I kept in my locker and played between classes. I never took lessons, so I had to figure it out for myself. I had a lot of fun, and I even got to the point where I could make a sound like an inebriated cow with a bad cold. Eventually, Tim took back the sax, but if he hadn't, who knows where I'd be today?

Web:
  http://www.bassoon.org/
  http://www.bobrk.com/saxfaq/
  http://www.clarinet.org/
  http://www.flute.org/
  http://www.metronet.com/~drjoe/clarinet.html
  http://www.nfaonline.org/
  http://www.ocr.woodwind.org/
  http://www.public.asu.edu/~schuring/Oboe/
      oboeinfo.html
  http://www.saxofun.com/
  http://www.saxophone.org/
  http://www.sneezy.org/clarinet/
  http://www.wfg.woodwind.org/

Usenet:
  alt.flute
  alt.music.clarinet
  alt.music.saxophone

MUSIC: SOFTWARE

CD Rippers

A ripper is a program that reads data from a music CD and converts the music to MP3 format. Once you have a ripper, you can create MP3 files from your own CDs. You can then listen to the files, share them with people, or (if you have a rewritable CD drive) make your own custom audio CDs.

Web:
  http://www.cdcopy.sk/
  http://www.musicmatch.com/
  http://www.real.com/jukebox/
  http://www.sonicspot.com/cdextractors.html

Karaoke Software

To use your computer as a karaoke machine, you need special software. First, you will need a karaoke player, a program to play karaoke files and display the lyrics. Most karaoke music is stored in files with the extension **.kar**, which is simply a MIDI format with lyrics added. Aside from a karaoke player, you may also want programs to help you: (1) create and manage song lists, (2) create a CD+G (CD plus graphics disc), and (3) make your own karaoke files by removing the voice from music files (a "vocal remover").

Web:
   http://www.computer-karaoke.com/karplayers.shtml
   http://www.francisli.org/wink/download.htm
   http://www.vanbasco.com/

MIDI Archives and Search Engines

MIDI is one of the most popular systems for sharing instrumental music on the Net. Here are some archives and search engines where you can find a huge variety of music, just waiting for you to listen, listen, listen.

Web:
   http://www.harmony-central.com/MIDI/files.html
   http://www.musicrobot.com/
   http://www.speakeasy.org/~ars/midi.html
   http://www.vanbasco.com/midisearch.html

Usenet:
   alt.binaries.sounds.midi
   alt.binaries.sounds.midi.beatles
   alt.binaries.sounds.midi.blues
   alt.binaries.sounds.midi.classical
   alt.binaries.sounds.midi.country
   alt.binaries.sounds.midi.funk
   alt.binaries.sounds.midi.jazz
   alt.binaries.sounds.midi.originals
   alt.binaries.sounds.midi.pop
   alt.binaries.sounds.midi.rock
   alt.sounds.midi.originals

Why don't we do it on the Net?

MIDI Software

MIDI (Musical Instrument Digital Interface) is a communications system that allows electronic music devices—including instruments, computers and signal processors—to interact with one another. Using MIDI, you can play, compose and arrange synthesized music. There are a number of different types of MIDI software available. The most important programs are: (1) MIDI players to play MIDI files (which have the extension **.mid**), (2) sequencers, patch editors and librarians to record, store, replay and edit MIDI data, and to control the output of musical instruments and signal processors.

Web:
   http://www.borg.com/~jglatt/tutr/miditutr.htm
   http://www.harmony-central.com/MIDI/
   http://www.midi.org/about-midi/resource.htm
   http://www.synthzone.com/miditech.htm

Usenet:
   alt.binaries.sounds.midi-tools
   alt.binaries.sounds.midi.d
   alt.music.midi
   alt.music.midiweb
   comp.music.midi

IRC:
   #midiwarez (Undernet)

MP3

MP3 is a sound compression system that is used to store music in computer files. Since MP3 files are digital, just like audio CDs, the sound is perfect and can be copied over and over. Once you have MP3 files, you can listen to them on your computer or on a digital music player (a portable hardware device about the size of a Walkman). I have a friend Noel who has collected a huge number of songs as MP3 files. He listens to them in his car by using a special tiny computer he built that mounts in the car instead of a regular stereo. If you would like to learn more about MP3, music on the Internet, and how it all works, see my book *Harley Hahn's Internet Advisor*.

Web:
   http://electronics.cnet.com/electronics/
      0-3219397.html
   http://www.help.mp3.com/help/
   http://www.mp3-faq.org/
   http://www.webhome.idirect.com/~nuzhathl/
      mp3-faq.html

MP3 Archives and Search Engines

There are an enormous number of MP3 music files available on the Net, *if* you know where to find them. Here are some good places to start looking. As long as you have the Net, you'll never run out of music.

Web:
> http://www.audiogalaxy.com/
> http://www.mp3int.com/eng/
> http://www.mp3search.astraweb.com/
> http://www.oth.net/

MP3 Players

To listen to MP3 files on your computer, you need a program to act as an MP3 player. There are a number of good MP3 players available for free on the Net. You will find that some of these programs are true multimedia players, being able to handle a variety of audio formats, such as music CDs, MP3 files, WAV files, MIDI files, streaming RealAudio, streaming MP3 and even streaming video. Experiment and see what you like best.

Web:
> http://sonique.lycos.com/
> http://www.a2mediaplayer.com/download.html
> http://www.microsoft.com/windows/windowsmedia/
>   download/
> http://www.musicmatch.com/download/free/
> http://www.sonicspot.com/multimediaplayers.html
> http://www.winamp.com/download/

Report on MP3 Search Engines by Elmo (age 8)

My sister Lucy is very smart and knows how to use computers. The other day, she showed me how to use something called a "Search Engine" to find free music. She found a lot of music by groups I had never heard of like Beethoven, Bach and Haydn.

So, for a joke, when she wasn't looking, I replaced all her music with songs from my favorite cartoons.

I wonder if she will be able to tell the difference?

-Elmo

MUSICAL ARTISTS: CURRENT

Aguilera, Christina

Christina Aguilera (1980-) began performing as a 6-year-old at school talent shows. At 8 years old, she appeared on the "Star Search" TV show, and at age 12 joined the cast of "The New Mickey Mouse Club" (along with Britney Spears, J.C. and Justin of 'N Sync, and Keri Russell of "Felicity"). Aguilera's first #1 hit was "Genie in a Bottle". Her other hits include "What a Girl Wants", "I Turn To You", "Come On Over" and "Lady Marmalade". According to popular legend, Aguilera was influenced by Julie Andrews after watching "The Sound Of Music". Isn't that just too cute for words?

Web:
> http://connection.christina-aguilera.net/
> http://www.christina-a.com/
> http://www.christina-aguilera.co.uk/

Usenet:
> alt.fan.christina-aguilera

Backstreet Boys

The Backstreet Boys—AJ, Brian, Howie, Kevin and Nick—are an internationally popular group from Orlando, Florida (although Brian is actually from Kentucky). Their first big hit, "I'll Never Break Your Heart", came out in 1996. Since then, BSB have sold millions of records and inspired millions of young teenage girls to revise their what-I-want-for-Christmas lists. (Important note: I read that AJ used to have a blankie he carried with him everywhere, until a maid accidentally threw it out. I'm not sure if this important factoid is true, but I thought I'd pass it on just in case.)

Web:
> http://www.bsbcyberfans.net/
> http://www.bsbdigest.com/
> http://www.maturefanclub.com/

Usenet:
> alt.fan.backstreet.boys

Barenaked Ladies

Barenaked Ladies consists of Jim Creeggan, Tyler Stewart, Steven Page, Ed Robertson and Kevin Hearn (one of the few accordion players in a popular band). BNL was formed in 1988 in Toronto, creating a style that mixes alternative rock with folk and country. Their first big single, "Be My Yoko Ono" (1991) was a hit in Canada, as was their 1992 album "Gordon". In 1996, they finally became popular in the United States with their song "The Old Apartment". "I think we're all growing naturally," says Ed, "as writers and musicians," showing that, like all important music stars, BNL can be as philosophical as necessary.

Web:

http://www.barenaked.net/
http://www.barenakedbliss.com/
http://www.mysd.org/news.shtml
http://www.nakedhead.org/

Usenet:

alt.music.barenaked-ladies

I've always wanted to work with Barenaked Ladies. So far, however, my responsibilities as a writer have not allowed me to pursue my dream.

Still, at least I can listen to them whenever I want. (I like the song about Brian Wilson.)

Blink 182

Blink 182 consists of three San Diego musicians, Travis Barker (drums), Tom Delonge (guitar, vocals) and Mark Hoppus (bass, vocals), who qualify as the first new punk-inspired band of the 21st century. In 1992, Blink 182 started to make a name for themselves in San Diego. Since then, they have toured widely and established a firm base of fans around the world. In 1995, they released their first album, "Cheshire Cat". One of my favorites songs is "Carousel" ("Just you wait and see / As school life is a / It is a woken dream / Aren't you feeling alone?").

Web:

http://www.blink-182.org/
http://www.blink-182.tk/
http://www.blink182.com/
http://www.truepunk.com/blink182/

Usenet:

alt.music.blink-182

Carey, Mariah

For over ten years, Mariah Carey (1970-) has been one of the most popular female singer/songwriters in the world. She sold over 120 million albums, becoming the only musician to have a #1 hit every year in the 1990s. Carey has an unusually large multi-octave vocal range, which allows her to be a versatile and entertaining performer. Carey has had many, many popular songs, almost too many to mention, so let me mention three of them: "Heartbreaker", "One Sweet Day" and "Someday". (Okay, I'll also mention "Emotions" and "All I Want for Christmas is You".)

Web:

http://www.faqs.org/faqs/music/mariah-carey-faq/
http://www.mariahcarey.com/
http://www.mariahland.com/news.html
http://www.mariahmania.com/frames.html
http://www.mcarchives.com/

Usenet:

alt.music.mariah.carey
rec.music.artists.mariah-carey

Dave Matthews Band

The Dave Matthews Band has five members: Dave Matthews (who started the band in 1991, in Charlottesville, Virginia), LeRoi Moore, Carter Beauford, Stefan Lessard and Boyd Tinsley. Dave is the main songwriter. He describes the band's music as "clear and simple—pop music with a pretty positive message." Fans, of which there are many, consider it to be an accessible mixture of folk, jazz, rock and reggae.

Web:
http://www.dmband.com/
http://www.dmblinks.com/links/
http://www.nancies.org/

Usenet:
alt.music.dave-matthews

Destiny's Child

Destiny's Child consists of three singers: Beyonce Knowles, Kelly Rowland and Michelle Williams. (Beyonce and Kelly founded the group, which became famous in 1997. Michelle joined in February 2000.) Their most popular songs have been "No, No, No", "Jumpin, Jumpin", "Say My Name", "Bills, Bills, Bills", "Independent Women Part I", "Survivor" and "Bootylicious". So why is Destiny's Child so popular? Well, they're nice looking, they sing well, and they've captured the spirit of hip-hop.

Web:
http://www.amazingdc.com/
http://www.thedcdimension.com/

It is better to plant a seed
in the garden of hope
than to harvest a
tomato from the field
of remorse.

Jackson, Janet

By the time Janet Jackson (1966-) was 7 years old, her older brothers were already famous as the Jackson Five. By the time she was 7, Jackson was performing with them on stage and, when she was 16 years old, she released her first album ("Janet Jackson"). Since then, the peripatetic energy girl has dabbled in various aspects of show business, becoming most successful as an entertainer and entrepreneur specializing in complex, highly stylized musical performances. As a singer or dancer or choreographer, Jackson is not important. However, as a singer/dancer/choreographer, she is very important, being the prime innovator of the complex, highly stylized musical performances that are mandatory for the young, modern, exquisitely packaged entertainers who want to appeal to the young techno-pop audience.

Web:
http://www.janet-love.com/index2.html
http://www.janet-xone.com/index2.html
http://www.velvet-dreams.de/

Usenet:
alt.fan.janet-jackson

Majordomo Mailing List:
List Name: **janet**
Subscribe to: **majordomo@xs4all.nl**

Jewel

What is it about Jewel that inspires such devotion in her fans? Well, she has a good voice and is an excellent performer, but there must be more. The only way to find out is to immerse yourself in Jewel-ness. Start with the Net. Maybe if you hang around long enough, you will become an EDA (Everyday Angel). Little known fact: In the second verse of her poem "Me", Jewel Kilcher says: "I'm from Alaska / but hate the cold", and, indeed, many people believe she was born in Homer, Alaska. Actually, although she grew up in Alaska, Jewel was born in Payson, Utah (on May 23, 1974).

Web:
http://www.foolishgames.com/
http://www.jeweljk.com/
http://www.quackquack.net/jewel/
http://www.tanweb.com/jewel/

Usenet:
alt.fan.jewel

Majordomo Mailing List:
List Name: jewel
Subscribe to: **majordomo@smoe.org**

Kravitz, Lenny

New York-born Lenny Kravitz (1964-), the son of an actress and a TV producer, grew up around famous singers, which had a great influence on him as he developed his natural talent. Over the years, Kravitz has become an accomplished guitarist, singer and composer, creating many popular songs (including his biggest single "Fly Away"), earning him legions of fans around the world. If you are one of Kravitz's fans, make sure you know the significance of September 1998. (It was when he cut off his dreadlocks.)

Web:

http://www.lennykravitz.com/
http://www.lennykravitz.net/

Lopez, Jennifer

Jennifer Lopez (1970-) is an emotionally confused, thirty-something singer, dancer and actress, who is best known for flaunting her body, being a diva, and contributing to the public weal by arranging for herself to be selected to a variety of "Sexiest Women in the World" lists. (Personally, I think that what makes a woman sexy is the ability to communicate, share her feelings, and commit to a long-term relationship, but then, I'm a guy, so what do you expect?) JLo—as we call her around the house—started as a Fly Girl (that is, a dancer) on the television show "In Living Color" in 1991. Her first significant burst into the public vernacular came with her 1997 film "Selena". Since then, she has managed to keep herself rooted firmly in our collective consciousness by a shrewd combination of hit songs, popular movies, spectacularly unsuccessful romances, and well-publicized callipygian splendor.

Web:

http://www.jenniferlopez.net/
http://www.you-know.net/jenniferlopez/

Usenet:

alt.fan.jennifer-lopez

Morissette, Alanis

Alanis Morissette was not only born in Canada, but she plays the harmonica. And, if that weren't enough, her father was a high school principal in Ottawa. (Is that unique or what?) If you like Alanis's singing, you'll enjoy these Web sites with pictures, video clips, sound clips, a FAQ, news, tour dates, lyrics, discography and all that sort of thing. For discussion, see the Usenet groups.

Web:

http://www.alanis-morissette.com/
http://www.definitelyalanis.com/

Usenet:

alt.music.alanis
alt.music.alanis.morissette

'N Sync

'N Sync will come out on stage and dance and sing, and dance and sing, and dance and sing some more; and you'll watch the high-tech, high-output, highly choreographed show; and everyone will go crazy; and you'll get caught up in the sound and sight and booming vibration; and you'll jump and scream and dance and lose yourself in the crowd; and then you'll go home, exhausted, and lay down in the quiet of your room, and start to wonder, did any of it mean anything? Of course not, but who cares? 'N Sync (JC Chasez, Justin Timberlake, Chris Kirkpatrick, Joey Fatone and Lance Bass) is a monstrously popular quintet from Orlando, Florida. Their first album ("'N Sync" in 1998) sold over 10 million copies and had four number-one hits. Their most popular songs include: "Tearing Up My Heart", "I Want You Back", "Bye, Bye, Bye", "It's Gonna Be Me", "Just Got Paid" and "Pop".

Web:

http://www.allnsync.com/
http://www.nsyncstudio.com/new/
http://www.nsyncworld.com/

Usenet:

alt.fan.nsync
alt.music.nsync

Report on Music CDs
by Elmo's sister, Lucy (age 6)

One day, when I wasn't looking, my brother Elmo replaced all my classical music MP3 files with his stupid cartoon songs.

Here is how I got even. First I made a copy of my father's "Best of the Beatles" CD. Then I scratched the word "ELMO" on the original CD. Boy, did Elmo get in trouble.

Later, I gave the copy of the CD to my father for his birthday. He told me it is lovely how little girls are so sweet.

-Lucy

Newly Popular Performers

At any time, there are a number of well-known musical performers whose popularity seems as if they will last forever. Popularity, however, is a fickle mistress (along with wealth, power, and the ability to have important people return your phone calls). So, today, we will honor a select group of newly popular performers: Alicia Keys, Ashanti, Eminem, Green Day, Linkin Park, Nelly, No Doubt, Pink and Shakira. Will they stay hot? Probably not, but here they are anyway. (Don't think I am being cynical. I still remember the Spice Girls, the Bay City Rollers, and Bob Dylan.)

Web:

http://www.aliciakeys.net/
http://www.bbc.co.uk/dna/h2g2/A581122
http://www.eminem.com/
http://www.greenday.com/home.php3
http://www.linkinpark.com/
http://www.nelly.net/
http://www.nodoubt.com/
http://www.pinkspage.com/
http://www.shakira.com/english/mainframeset.html

Usenet:

alt.fan.no-doubt
alt.music.eminem
alt.music.green-day
alt.music.no-doubt

Spears, Britney

Saying that singer/dancer Britney Spears (1981-) is popular, sexy and sassy is like saying that mayonnaise is white and creamy. Like Christina Aguilera, Spears got her start on "The New Mickey Mouse Club". Since then she has performed in off-Broadway shows, sold an obscene amount of albums, won many awards, and guarded her pure, innocent reputation with the fierceness of a junkyard dog. Along the way, Spears has become an object of worship to millions of fans around the world with such well-known hits as "Baby One More Time", "Oops!...I Did It Again", and "Lucky". (Note: If you are ever around true-blue Britney fans, ask if they believe the rumor that she has pierced her nipple.)

Web:

http://www.britneyspears.co.uk/
http://www.britneyspears.com/
http://www.extreme-britney.com/

Usenet:

alt.fan.britney-spears

IRC:

#britney (Undernet)
#digitalbritney (EFnet)

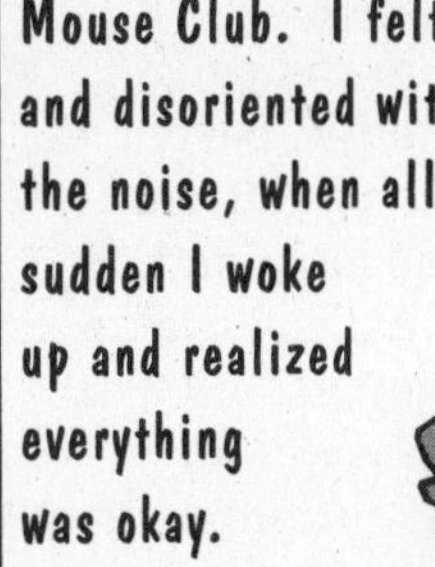

MUSICAL ARTISTS: HARLEY'S HALL OF FAME

Armstrong, Louis

Louis Armstrong (1901-1971), also known as "Satchmo", is the most beloved of American trumpet players. Armstrong, one of the great American jazz performers, was a musician, singer and band leader. Although his voice was raspy, he had excellent pitch and rhythm, and his trumpet playing was smooth and graceful. Over the years, Armstrong had many popular recordings including "Mack the Knife" (1956), "Blueberry Hill" (1956), and "Hello Dolly" (1964). My mother loved Louis Armstrong and, for many years, she had a small statue of him on the piano. Today, that same statue sits on top of my piano. Louis Armstrong trivia: While he was alive, Armstrong believed his birthday to be July 4, 1900. However, in 1983, his birth certificate was discovered, showing he was actually born on August 4, 1901.

Web:

http://www.louissatchmoarmstrong.com/
   biography.htm
http://www.redhotjazz.com/louie.html
http://www.satchmo.com/louisarmstrong/
http://www.satchmo.net/
http://www.satchography.com/home.html

Baker, Chet

I first encountered the music of Chet Baker (1929-1988) not long after he died, when I saw a documentary about his life. I bought one of his CDs, then another, then another. It didn't take long to realize that Baker, a trumpet player and singer, was blessed with the type of raw, natural talent that rarely comes to this world. Where other musicians would have to practice continually, Baker could just stand up and play. Although he never learned to read music, Baker became a master of style, playing with a soft, elusive and haunting spirit. Despite his good looks and increasing success, Baker's life was ultimately a tragic one, mired by drug addiction and conflict. In 1968, he got into a fight with other drug addicts in San Francisco and had his teeth knocked out, although he did go back to playing two years later. He died in Amsterdam, at the age of 58, after falling out of a hotel window.

Web:

http://www.chetbaker.net/
http://www.chetbaker.org/discography.htm

Crosby, Bing

"The secret of Bing Crosby's popularity," my father once told me, "is that he sang the way everyone else thinks they sing in the shower." Moreover, he made it look easy. Bing Crosby (1903-1977) had a beautiful, resonant voice, charming and entertaining people for several decades. Over his lifetime, Crosby made about 2,000 recordings, his most well-known being the Irving Berlin song "White Christmas" (1942). He was also a star of radio, television and movies. Overall, Crosby made 104 films, including the "Road" series with Bob Hope and Dorothy Lamour. My favorite Crosby movies are the musicals, especially "Holiday Inn" (1942) with Fred Astaire, and "White Christmas" (1954) with Danny Kaye. Over the years, Crosby received many awards, including a 1945 Academy Award for his role as Father O'Malley in the movie "Going My Way". At the age of 73, Crosby died of a heart attack in Madrid, Spain, just after finishing a round of golf.

Web:

http://www.crosby.circle.btinternet.co.uk/
http://www.kcmetro.cc.mo.us/~crosby/
http://www.parabrisas.com/d_crosbybing.html

Fitzgerald, Ella

Ella Fitzgerald (1918-1996) was a singer who mastered all the genres associated with American jazz, including ballads, blues, swing, bebop and scat. In the process, she sang both modern songs and classics, developing a marvelous style and diversity of range that earned her many honors as America's first lady of jazz. If it was singable, Fitzgerald could sing it, and with more feeling and skill than almost anyone else. I once saw her give a concert. It was late in her life, and her strength was failing. She had trouble standing the whole time, but her voice, her rhythm and her sheer professional skill were unmistakable. As Ira Gershwin (the brother and partner of composer George Gershwin) once remarked, "I never knew how good our songs were until I heard Ella Fitzgerald sing them."

Web:

http://lcweb.loc.gov/loc/lcib/9708/web/ella.html
http://www.redsugar.com/ella.html
http://www.thepeaches.com/music/ella/
http://www.yonkershistory.org/ella.html

Gershwin, George

By melding the idioms of jazz with the classical traditions of Stravinsky, Chopin, Beethoven and Mozart, George Gershwin (1898-1937) defined twentieth-century American music. Gershwin's list of familiar and seminal works is a long one. It includes songs such as Fascinating Rhythm, Swanee (sung by Al Jolson), Isn't it a Pity, Someone to Watch Over Me, 'S Wonderful, Let's Call the Whole Thing Off, Oh Lady Be Good, I Got Rhythm, They All Laughed, Love Is Here To Stay, and They Can't Take That Away From Me, as well as longer works such as Rhapsody in Blue, Concerto in F, An American in Paris, and the opera Porgy and Bess. During his lifetime, Gershwin wrote the music for many plays and revues, music that has been featured in countless movies, most notably the Woody Allen film Manhattan. Gershwin was a genius who was able to take the musical vernacular of his time and recast it in an original manner that would change the American music scene forever, and give hours of enduring pleasure to music lovers around the world. Who could ask for anything more?

Web:
   http://www.classical.net/music/comp.lst/
      gershwin.html
   http://www.gershwinfan.com/

Goodman, Benny

Benny Goodman (1909-1986) was a clarinetist and band leader. More than anyone, Goodman can be considered the father of the swing era, popularizing the big-band style of music during a time when jazz was still not respectable. For years, Goodman toured the U.S., first as part of other bands, and then, for many years, as the leader of his own bands. Even today, listening to Benny Goodman play the clarinet can make you marvel, not only at his skill as an innovative arranger and band leader, but as an enormously talented soloist. Some of his most popular songs include "Stompin' at the Savoy", "Moonglow" and "Sing, Sing, Sing".

Web:
   http://www.davidmulliss.com.au/BennyGoodman/
   http://www.duke.edu/~app1/bgoodman.html
   http://www.lous.com/benny/
   http://www.redhotjazz.com/goodman.html

Guthrie, Woody

To many people, singer and composer Woody Guthrie (1912-1967) is the embodiment of American folk music. From the 1930s to the 1950s, Guthrie toured the United States, writing and singing inspirational songs about hardship and social injustice. His best-known song, "This Land Is Your Land" (1940) is the de facto national anthem of folk music. Guthrie was a prolific creator, his songs, ballads and poetry being embodied with an understanding for the problems of the common man. Much of his life was spent in a peripatetic journey devoted to political and social reform. In his later years, Guthrie suffered from Huntington's Chorea, an incurable degenerative disease of the nervous system, which eventually killed him. Guthrie was the father of singer and composer Arlo Guthrie ("Alice's Restaurant").

Web:
   http://www.themomi.org/museum/Guthrie/
      index_1024.html
   http://www.woodyguthrie.org/
   http://xroads.virginia.edu/~1930s/radio/woody/
      woodyhome.html

Usenet:
   alt.music.guthrie

Holiday, Billie

Billie Holiday (1915-1959) was a legendary jazz and blues singer, creating a highly personal style and mystique with her passionate, emotional singing. By all accounts, Holiday had a tough life. Her mother was 13 when Holiday was born, and most of her life was spent in poverty. Even after she became successful, Holiday never managed to accumulate much wealth, owing to a longstanding addiction to heroin and poor choices in men. Holiday's most influential song, her signature tune, was "Strange Fruit", a controversial ballad about the racial discrimination she encountered during her career. (Holiday was African American.) Another one of her well-known songs was "God Bless the Child", which she wrote. Holiday died at the young age of 44, but her recognition as a seminal voice in American jazz lives on.

Web:
   http://www.duke.edu/~miness/
   http://www.ladyday.moose.co.uk/bilmain.htm
   http://www.who2.com/billieholiday.html

Miller, Glenn

Glenn Miller (1904-1944) was an innovative bandleader, composer and arranger. Miller was a trombonist, who for many years played and arranged music for Tommy and Jimmy Dorsey. In 1938, he began touring with a band of his own and, before long, achieved a following that was to make his orchestra one of the most popular of the big-band era. In 1942, Miller received the first-ever gold record for selling over one million copies of "Chattanooga Choo Choo". His other well-known songs include "Moonlight Serenade" (his theme song), "In the Mood", "Tuxedo Junction" and "Pennsylvania 6-5000". During World War II, Miller joined the Army Air Force, where he organized a large orchestra to entertain the troops. In 1944, Miller was killed when his plane disappeared, en route from England to Paris in bad weather.

Web:

http://www.barberusa.com/orchestra/
miller_glenn.html
http://www.glennmiller.org/history.htm
http://www.glennmillerorchestra.com/
http://www.glennmillerstore.com/

I designed a great Web server built out of porcelain. So far, it hasn't crashed.

Shore, Dinah

There are two reasons why Dinah Shore (1917-1994) was one of the most popular singers of the 1940s: she was very talented, and she was very nice. People not only liked listening to her—she could sing anything in a pleasant, easy-going manner—they honestly liked her as a person. Moreover, she was the epitome of the blond, glamorous Hollywood singer, the role model for every young girl who ever dreamed about growing up to be famous. Shore's professional career started when she was 14, when she first performed in a nightclub. However, her big break did not come until she was 23 (in 1940) when the well-known entertainer Eddie Cantor brought her onto his popular radio show as a regular performer. Three years later, in 1943, she got her own radio show and, from then on, was rarely out of the public eye. In the 1940s, she recorded a long string of hits—making her the top female singer in the United States—and filmed a handful of pleasant, entertaining movies. In 1951, she became the first woman to host her own variety show, staying on TV until the early 1960s. In the 1970s, she returned to television for ten years, singing, chatting with guests, cooking, and doing what she did best: being a friendly, wholesome person who knew how to make everyone feel good.

Web:

http://www.dinahshorefanclub.com/
http://www.lentriola.com/shore.htm
http://www.mrlucky.com/songbirds/html/jul99/
c_dshore.html
http://www.parabrisas.com/d_shored.html

Sinatra, Frank

Frank Sinatra (1915-1998) was undoubtedly one of the greatest musical artists of this century. Sinatra's phrasing, timing and pitch were as good as they get, and his natural ability as a romantic crooner made him a favorite of countless music lovers around the world. During his more than five decades as an active performer, Sinatra was just about the only singer who had no reason to be jealous of Bing Crosby.

Web:
   http://www.jillyswest.com/
   http://www.nj.com/sinatra/
   http://www.sinatra-ms.com/
   http://www.spiritofsinatra.com/
   http://www.thepeaches.com/music/frank/

Usenet:
   alt.fan.frank-sinatra
   alt.music.rat-pack

Listserv Mailing List:
   List Name: Sinatra
   Subscribe to: listserv@listserv.temple.edu

'Do You Wanna Dance' and have 'Fun, Fun, Fun' 'All Summer Long'?

Would you like to 'Do It Again' with some 'California Girls' in the 'Warmth of the Sun'?

'Don't Worry Baby'.

All you need to do is say 'I Can Hear Music', and in less time than it takes to race your 'Little Deuce Coupe' or 'Little Honda' against the 'Little Old Lady From Pasadena', you'll feel so many 'Good Vibrations', that you'll say 'Please Let Me Wonder' if it's legal to have this much fun.

MUSICAL ARTISTS: ROCK/POP

Beach Boys

The Beach Boys were the quintessential California group, creating song after song about the beach, the sun, surfing, fast cars, girls, and fun, fun fun. The original members of the group were three brothers, Brian, Carl and Dennis Wilson; a cousin Al Jardine; and a school friend, Mike Love. Over the years, however, they toured with many variations in personnel. The Beach Boys' music was startling in its originality, featuring memorable melody lines, and wonderful vocals with stunning harmonies. (Both Brian and Carl had perfect pitch.) The list of their hits is a long one including Surfer Girl, Barbara Ann, California Girls, Do You Wanna Dance, Fun Fun Fun, Good Vibrations, Help Me Rhonda, I Get Around, Little Deuce Coupe, Sloop John B, 409, Surfing Safari, Surfing USA, Wouldn't It Be Nice and Kokomo. The guiding genius behind the Beach Boys was Brian Wilson, who suffered from mental illness for many years, but has since recovered to begin touring with his own band. (One time, years ago, I was backstage at a rock festival where the Beach Boys had performed, and I got to talk to one of them. I asked him, "Why didn't Brian perform with you?" and I will never forget his answer. He looked me straight in the eye and said, "Because he didn't want to.") Regardless, Brian and the boys were able to create a unique sound that has endured for decades, and I, for one, do not want to even imagine a world without their music. (Trivia: Of all the Beach Boys, only Dennis actually surfed. Brian didn't even like the water.)

Web:
   http://www.beachboys.com/
   http://www.cabinessence.com/agladwin/
      beachboys.html
   http://www.hollywoodandvine.com/beachboys/

Usenet:
   alt.music.beach-boys
   rec.music.artists.beach-boys

Majordomo Mailing List:
   List Name: petsounds
   Subscribe to: majordomo@landlocked.iwaynet.net

Beatles

Unless you were there (in the early Sixties), it's impossible to understand. The rise of the Beatles—John Lennon, Paul McCartney, George Harrison and Ringo Starr—as a worldwide musical phenomenon was unprecedented in the history of mankind. For years, their music demonstrated a consistent level of skill and creativity that has yet to be duplicated within the popular culture. Even today, you can listen to their albums and still be amazed how good they were. In the early Sixties, something special happened, but I do understand that you get sick of hearing your parents talk about it. Unfortunately, if you are under forty years old, you don't understand and you never will.

Web:
>   http://www.archervalerie.com/fablinks.html
>   http://www.beatlegirl.com/
>   http://www.beatlelinks.net/links/
>   http://www.beatlesagain.com/
>   http://www.beatlezone.com/
>   http://www.dermon.com/Beatles/Beatles.htm

Usenet:
>   rec.music.beatles

The Beatles

Did you know there were actually five Beatles: John, Paul, George, Ringo and Spot? Spot was an invisible, talking dog.

The reason you may not have heard of Spot is that no one ever saw him, and he never recorded in the studio. He only performed live and, of course, he was invisible.

However, if you listen carefully to a recording of a live Beatles concert, you can hear Spot singing in the background.

Don't believe me? Check for yourself.

Berry, Chuck

Chuck Berry (1926-) was one of the founding pioneers of rock and roll. Berry blended R&B, country, swing and blues, and branded it with his unique touch. He was one of rock and roll's first great lyricists, and was also the first to create some of the more enduring guitar sequences, such as the ones used in "Johnny B. Goode". His other popular songs included "Roll Over Beethoven", "School Day", "Rock & Roll Music", "Sweet Little Sixteen" and "Reelin' and Rockin'". With his trademark duckwalk and his long string of hits, Berry became an influential icon in the 1950s music scene. As John Lennon once said, "If you tried to give rock and roll another name, you might call it Chuck Berry."

Web:
>   http://www.chuckberry.com/
>   http://www.crlf.de/ChuckBerry/
>   http://www.history-of-rock.com/berry.htm
>   http://www.warr.org/berry.html

Doors

The Doors was a vehicle for singer/poet/composer Jim Morrison (1943-1971). The group, which played together from 1965 to 1973, consisted of Morrison (vocals), Ray Manzarek (organ and organ bass), Robbie Kreiger (guitar) and John Densmore (drums). Their name was chosen by Morrison, who was inspired by a quote from William Blake, "If the doors of perception were cleansed, every thing would appear as it is, infinite." I once saw The Doors in concert at an outdoor rock festival. I still remember them playing a long version of their closing song, "The End", as I sat under the stars, listening to Morrison's plaintive voice ("...Lost in a Roman wilderness of pain, and all the children are insane..."). Morrison wrote and sang many soulful and beautiful songs including "Light My Fire", "Break on Through", "Hello, I Love You", "People Are Strange" and "Riders on the Storm". Morrison was an iconoclast with a serious drug habit, who occasionally got himself into trouble for his on-stage antics. However, he was a true genius, one of the few rock performers who could write serious poetry and make it come alive on the stage.

Web:
>   http://www.helsinki.fi/~usinisal/juha/Doors_FAQ.html
>   http://www.thedoors.ch/
>   http://www.thedoors.com/

Usenet:
>   alt.music.the-doors

Dylan, Bob

Robert Allen Zimmerman (1941-) was born in Duluth, Minnesota. In 1960, at the age of 19, Zimmerman hitchhiked to New York, where he began to perform in various Greenwich Village coffee houses. Within a short time, Zimmerman had changed his name to Bob Dylan and had developed a solid reputation as a folksinger. In 1962, he put out his first album, "Bob Dylan". In 1963, his second album "Freewheelin' Bob Dylan" established him as a highly creative folk/protest singer, a role he was to fill for many years. Dylan is important to the development of modern music for several reasons. First, he popularized the idea of incorporating poetry into folk/rock music, becoming the epitome of the politically sensitive singer and songwriter. Second, as a composer, Dylan broke new ground again and again (and again). Over the years, his work has been recorded by many different singers and bands. Third, as a performer and recording artist, Dylan had a long, enduring career, during which he created over 40 albums and gave literally hundreds of concerts. Bob Dylan was the person who, single-handedly, changed popular music from mere sound into a force with intellectual content, one that could change the thinking of his audience. Dylan's most popular songs were Like a Rolling Stone, Blowin' in the Wind, Rainy Day Women No. 12 & 35, All Along the Watchtower, Knockin' On Heaven's Door, Lay Lady Lay and Mr. Tambourine Man. As for his singing, well, the only thing I can say is that it's better than it sounds.

Web:

http://www.bobdylan.com/
http://www.bobdylanbiography.8k.com/
http://www.expectingrain.com/
http://www.punkhart.com/dylan/faq.html
http://www.uvm.edu/~ksherloc/dylan/

Usenet:

rec.music.dylan

Franklin, Aretha

Let's face it. Aretha Franklin does not have a great voice. (Sorry, but it's true.) What Franklin does have is *soul*: in her words, "the ability to make other people feel what you're feeling." Franklin (1942-) was born in Memphis, Tennessee, and raised in the tradition of gospel singing: a passionate, joyful music that originated in the black Protestant churches of the southern United States. In 1967, at the age of 24, Franklin recorded her first hit album "I Never Loved a Man", containing unusually vibrant and earthy tunes, including her most famous song, a cover of Otis Redding's "Respect". "Respect" was the first in a long series of very successful songs, making Franklin one of the most renowned singers of the 1960s, and earning her the title of "Queen of Soul". In later years, the quality of Franklin's work was inconsistent, as was her popularity. However, in 1987, she was honored by being the first woman to be inducted into the Rock and Roll Hall of Fame. Franklin is important because she is one of the two singers most responsible for introducing the gospel sound into popular American music (the other singer being Ray Charles).

Web:

http://www.aristarec.com/aristaweb/ArethaFranklin/
http://www.rhythmandtheblues.org.uk/pdaretha.shtml
http://www.swinginchicks.com/aretha_franklin.htm
http://www.warr.org/franklin.html

Grateful Dead

Somebody recently asked me, why were the Grateful Dead so popular? The answer is, they made good music and they loved their fans. In so many ways, the Dead were unlike any other musical group in history. For example, during their concerts, they allowed people to use their own tape recorders and make personal tapes. During the Dead's years on the road, this peripatetic band created a subculture that defies understanding: music, art, clothing, culture (including drugs), and a collection of the most loyal musical fans ever seen on Planet Earth. True, Jerry Garcia has slowed down somewhat since his demise, but I bet he's still grateful.

Web:

http://www.dead.net/
http://www.deadimages.com/
http://www.deadlists.com/

Usenet:

rec.music.gdead

Hendrix, Jimi

Jimi Hendrix (1942-1970) lived a bit less than 28 years, and was a major performer for only four years, but in that short time he established himself as one of the most remarkable guitarists and musicians in the world of rock. In the mid-sixties, Hendrix began to play with two other musicians, Noel Redding (bass) and Mitch Mitchell (drums), a group that became known as "The Jimi Hendrix Experience". At the end of 1966, they released their first single, "Hey Joe". In May 1967, they released their first album "Are You Experienced", which became one of the most popular rock albums of all time, featuring "Purple Haze", "The Wind Cries Mary", "Foxey Lady", "Fire", and "Are You Experienced?". In 1969, he gave a seminal performance at Woodstock, including a never-to-be-forgotten instrumental rendition of "The Star-Spangled Banner". Hendrix was a master guitarist (although he couldn't read or write music); an innovator who used distortion, such as fuzz and feedback, to create a unique sound; and a showman who was not above burning his guitar on stage. Although his recordings have become immensely popular and influential, the important part of his career lasted only three and a half years. Hendrix had serious drug problems, and in 1970, he died of suffocation after overdosing on pills.

Web:

http://www.hendrix-links.de/
http://www.jimi-hendrix.com/
http://www.musicfanclubs.org/jimihendrix/
http://www.warr.org/hendrix.html

Usenet:

alt.fan.jimi-hendrix
alt.music.jimi.hendrix

Do you really think you were designed to spend most of your waking hours working in an office and going to meetings?

My philosophy is simple: Live your life one decade at a time, and let the details take care of themselves.

Jackson, Michael

There's no denying that Michael Jackson (1958-) is very strange. There is also no denying that the one-gloved, crotch-grabbing singer and dancer is a major, major star. Jackson started his career as a 5-year-old, singing with his older brothers as part of the Jackson 5. In 1969, when Jackson was 11, they signed with the Motown label and his career as a performer began in earnest. The Jackson 5 was successful, having four consecutive #1 hits and becoming one of the most popular groups of the seventies. In 1978, Jackson branched off on his own, starring as the scarecrow in "The Wiz", and creating a unique assortment of trademark dance moves including the moonwalk. In 1982, he released the album "Thriller", which became the best-selling album of all time (over 50 million copies sold worldwide). To accompany the singles from "Thriller", Jackson created innovative short films that established him as a music video pioneer. In 1987, he released the album "Bad", which produced five consecutive #1 singles (another record). However, as talented as Jackson is, he is just as famous for his bizarre behavior (including his strange marriages) as for his superb music, dancing and performance.

Web:

http://www.m-jackson.com/jackson/
http://www.mjsite.com/
http://www.planetjackson.com/

Usenet:

alt.music.michael-jackson

Madonna

Madonna Louise Ciccone was born in Bay City, Michigan, on August 16, 1958. For 25 years, things were relatively quiet. But then, in 1983, she released her first album, and the world has never been the same. Since then, the Material Girl has managed to insinuate herself into the hearts and minds of our culture in a way that almost defies description. And just when you think she is ready for the Where-Is-She-Now Club, Madonna reinvents herself. The next time you find yourself in a trivia competition, use your knowledge of Madonna and ask the other person which female vocalist has the most solo gold singles. (Is this book educational or what?)

Web:
 http://www.eecs.harvard.edu/~zhwang/Madonna/
 http://www.madonna.com/
 http://www.madonnarama.com/
 http://www.mlvc.org/

Usenet:
 alt.fan.madonna

Majordomo Mailing List:
 List Name: madinfo
 Subscribe to: majordomo@monkey.org

Majordomo Mailing List:
 List Name: madonna
 Subscribe to: majordomo@monkey.org

Mitchell, Joni

Joni Mitchell was born in 1943 in Alberta, Canada. Mitchell started her career as a singer before most of today's popular musicians were even born. Over several decades, she has created a vast body of original composition, and became the inspiration, mentor, and matron saint of the current wave of powerful young female singers and songwriters. Mitchell's most famous songs are "Big Yellow Taxi", "Woodstock", "Chelsea Morning", "The Circle Game" and "Both Sides Now". However, to really enjoy Mitchell's work, you need to explore her albums. My advice is to start with "Blue".

Web:
 http://www.jmdl.com/
 http://www.jonimitchell.com/
 http://www.warr.org/joni.html

Majordomo Mailing List:
 List Name: joni
 Subscribe to: majordomo@smoe.org

A B C D E F G H I J K L **M** N O P Q R S T U V W X Y Z

Music Performers Talk and General Discussion

There are many discussion groups devoted to popular musicians and music groups. Tune in for the latest in concert appearances, reviews, opinions and esoterica. Look for your favorites.

Usenet:

alt.fan.admiral-twin
alt.fan.albert-silverman
alt.fan.ana-voog
alt.fan.barbra.streisand
alt.fan.barry-manilow
alt.fan.blues-brothers
alt.fan.bonzo-dog
alt.fan.buddy-holly
alt.fan.capt-beefheart
alt.fan.chris-cornell
alt.fan.courtney-love
alt.fan.david-bowie
alt.fan.david-cassidy
alt.fan.devo
alt.fan.dixie-chicks
alt.fan.elton-john
alt.fan.elvis-costello
alt.fan.emma-bunton
alt.fan.fiona-apple
alt.fan.frank-zappa
alt.fan.george-michael
alt.fan.geri-halliwell
alt.fan.hanson
alt.fan.henry-rollins
alt.fan.jello-biafra
alt.fan.jimmy-buffett
alt.fan.joe-satriani
alt.fan.john-denver
alt.fan.kd-lang
alt.fan.kid-rock
alt.fan.kinks
alt.fan.laurie.anderson
alt.fan.liz-phair
alt.fan.matchbox20
alt.fan.melanie-brown
alt.fan.michael-bolton
alt.fan.oingo-boingo
alt.fan.peter-hammill
alt.fan.samantha-fox
alt.fan.shania-twain
alt.fan.shirley-manson
alt.fan.skinny
alt.fan.spice-girls
alt.fan.spinal-tap
alt.fan.stevie-ray-vaughan
alt.fan.sting
alt.fan.stonecutters
alt.fan.u2
alt.fan.victoria-adams
alt.fan.zoogz-rift
alt.music.abba
alt.music.alice-cooper

alt.music.aliceinchains
alt.music.america
alt.music.anthrax
alt.music.ash
alt.music.autechre
alt.music.b-witched
alt.music.bad-religion
alt.music.beastie-boys
alt.music.beck
alt.music.bee-gees
alt.music.bela-fleck
alt.music.ben-folds-five
alt.music.ben-harper
alt.music.billy-joel
alt.music.bjork
alt.music.black-sabbath
alt.music.blueoystercult
alt.music.blues-traveler
alt.music.blur
alt.music.bon-jovi
alt.music.boyz-2-men
alt.music.brian-eno
alt.music.bush
alt.music.byrds
alt.music.ccr
alt.music.celine-dion
alt.music.chapel-hill
alt.music.cheap-trick
alt.music.cher
alt.music.chicago
alt.music.clash
alt.music.cliff-richard
alt.music.counting-crows
alt.music.ct-dummies
alt.music.danzig
alt.music.dead-kennedys
alt.music.deep-purple
alt.music.def-leppard
alt.music.depeche-mode
alt.music.dio
alt.music.dire-straits
alt.music.dream-theater
alt.music.duke-ellington
alt.music.duran-duran
alt.music.eagles
alt.music.elo
alt.music.enigma-dcd-etc
alt.music.enya
alt.music.erasure
alt.music.eric-clapton
alt.music.everclear
alt.music.faith-no-more
alt.music.fatboy-slim
alt.music.fates-warning
alt.music.fleetwood-mac
alt.music.foo-fighters
alt.music.garbage
alt.music.garth-brooks
alt.music.genesis
alt.music.gomez
alt.music.goo-goo-dolls
alt.music.gwar

alt.music.harry-chapin
alt.music.hole
alt.music.iggy-pop
alt.music.incubus
alt.music.indigo-girls
alt.music.inxs
alt.music.iron-maiden
alt.music.james-taylor
alt.music.jamiroquai
alt.music.janes-addictn
alt.music.jethro-tull
alt.music.joan-osborne
alt.music.jon-spencer
alt.music.journey
alt.music.korn
alt.music.kylie-minogue
alt.music.led-zeppelin
alt.music.lennon
alt.music.leonard-cohen
alt.music.lightfoot
alt.music.limp-bizkit
alt.music.lor-mckennitt
alt.music.lou-reed
alt.music.marillion
alt.music.marilyn-manson
alt.music.mazzy-star
alt.music.meat-loaf
alt.music.moby
alt.music.monkees
alt.music.moody-blues
alt.music.morrissey
alt.music.nat-imbruglia
alt.music.nin
alt.music.nirvana
alt.music.nomeansno
alt.music.oasis
alt.music.offspring
alt.music.ozzy
alt.music.pantera
alt.music.paul-simon
alt.music.pearl-jam
alt.music.pet-shop-boys
alt.music.peter-gabriel
alt.music.phil-collins
alt.music.pink-floyd
alt.music.pixies
alt.music.pj-harvey
alt.music.placebo
alt.music.pogues
alt.music.primus
alt.music.prince
alt.music.prodigy-the
alt.music.queen
alt.music.radiohead
alt.music.rage-machine
alt.music.ramones
alt.music.red-hot-chili-peppers
alt.music.robbie-williams
alt.music.roger-waters
alt.music.roxette
alt.music.rush
alt.music.savage-garden

alt.music.seal
alt.music.sheryl-crow
alt.music.smash-pumpkins
alt.music.smiths
alt.music.sondheim
alt.music.sonic-youth
alt.music.sophie-hawkins
alt.music.soulcoughing
alt.music.soundgarden
alt.music.steely-dan
alt.music.steve-miller
alt.music.stone-roses
alt.music.stone-temple
alt.music.suede
alt.music.the-corrs
alt.music.the.police
alt.music.thecars
alt.music.thecure
alt.music.tlc
alt.music.tmbg
alt.music.todd-rundgren
alt.music.tom-petty
alt.music.tom-waits
alt.music.tool
alt.music.tragically-hip
alt.music.travis
alt.music.van-halen
alt.music.vanhalen
alt.music.ween
alt.music.weezer
alt.music.weird-al
alt.music.who
alt.music.wilco
alt.music.yes
alt.music.zz-top
alt.rock-n-roll.acdc
alt.rock-n-roll.aerosmith
alt.rock-n-roll.metal.gnr
alt.rock-n-roll.metal.megadeth
alt.rock-n-roll.metal.metallica
alt.rock-n-roll.metal.motley-crue
rec.music.artists.amy-grant
rec.music.artists.ani-difranco
rec.music.artists.bruce-hornsby
rec.music.artists.danny-elfman
rec.music.artists.debbie-gibson
rec.music.artists.emmylou-harris
rec.music.artists.extreme
rec.music.artists.kings-x
rec.music.artists.kiss
rec.music.artists.paul-mccartney
rec.music.artists.queensryche
rec.music.rartists.reb-st-james
rec.music.artists.stevie-nicks
rec.music.artists.wallflowers
rec.music.phish
rec.music.tori-amos

Presley, Elvis

Since his untimely death, Elvis Aron Presley (1935-1977) has, through the miracle of modern marketing, achieved a degree of fame that eluded him throughout much of his career. Personally, I love old Elvis movies. Maybe I should make one of my own... Elvis is a poor but honorable working boy, polite to the extreme. He has a girlfriend, but, unfortunately, the course of love hits a bump because of a misunderstanding. Elvis runs into a cute little kid, who hangs around being precocious. A bad guy does something or other, putting Elvis in a bad position. Elvis gets into a fight (although it's not his fault; he is defending the honor of a lady). Then he jumps up on the stage and sings a song or two. Finally, through immense integrity and personal charm, Elvis solves his problems, vanquishes the bad guy, and settles his misunderstanding with the girl. (You know, except for the cute little kid, the whole thing is a lot like my life.)

Web:
    http://members.aol.com/presleyconnect/
    http://www.elvis.com/elvisology/
    http://www.elvispresleyonline.com/
    http://www.girlsguidetoelvis.com/

Usenet:
    alt.elvis.king
    alt.fan.elvis-presley

Elvis Forever

There is no doubt about it. Elvis died for your sins. Well ... he died for someone's sins. Anyway, while you are thinking it over, point your Web browser at the Elvis Web site and see how the simple belief in America's favorite musical deity can change your life.

R.E.M.

R.E.M. consists of Bill Berry (percussion, vocals), Peter Buck (guitar), Mike Mills (bass, keyboards, vocals) and Michael Stipe (vocals). They first started to play together as students at the University of Georgia. Over the years, R.E.M. has toured and recorded tirelessly, creating a large group of fans around the world. Their hits include "Shiny Happy People", "Losing My Religion" and "Everybody Hurts". Here are two bits of interesting R.E.M. trivia you can use to impress your friends. First, the name R.E.M. doesn't mean anything in particular. Second, the tattoo under Michael Stipe's right upper arm is a picture of Ignatz Mouse and Krazy Kat (characters from a very old comic strip).

Web:
    http://m2k1.murmurs.com/
    http://orangefox.svs.com/rem/
    http://www.faqs.org/faqs/music/rem-faq/
    http://www.remhq.com/
    http://www.retroweb.com/rem.html

Usenet:
    alt.music.rem
    rec.music.rem

Rolling Stones

This band has endless energy and will probably outlive most of us and be recording their last albums from the wing of a hospital for the Geriatric Rich and Famous. These Web pages and Usenet group are the hot spots for all things Stones.

Web:
    http://www.faqs.org/faqs/music/rollingstones-faq/
    http://www.iorr.org/
    http://www.keno.org/home.html
    http://www.nzentgraf.de/books/zent.htm

Usenet:
    alt.rock-n-roll.stones

T I D B I T S

What should everyone know about avoiding COLDS?

Colds are short-lived, upper-respiratory illnesses, caused by viruses. The medical name for a cold is a "coryza" or, if you want to get even more snooty, "acute viral rhinitis". (The term "rhino" comes from the Greek word for nose; "itis" means inflammation.)

Colds are not serious illnesses, but they are inconvenient. The frequency with which you catch colds depends on how healthy you are and how often you are exposed to cold germs. Therefore, there is a two-part strategy to not catching colds: (1) maintain good health habits, and (2) avoid cold viruses.

The best strategy is to stay away from people that are coughing and sneezing. Cold germs can live for several hours on a person's skin, and they can live for days on environmental surfaces. Moreover, when a sick person sneezes, the germs that are released into the air are able to infect people for a long time to come. (So if you are sick with a cold, please stay home.)

Once a person is exposed to a cold germ, it takes 2-4 days to become sick. However, that person is contagious for a full day before the symptoms are even noticeable and for 5 days after that.

Cold season stretches from early fall through the end of winter. During that time, there are two important habits you can form. First, wash your hands thoroughly with soap and warm water several times a day, including the moment you get home from work or school. Second, don't touch your hands to your nose or mouth, especially when people around you are sick. (If you don't want to follow my advice, buy a copy of this book for your mother and have her read this page to you.)

Speaking of mothers' advice, is it true that getting a chill will automatically make you sick? No. However, being cold for an extended time can lower the effectiveness of your immune system, and that will make you more susceptible to the germs in your vicinity.

Who, The

Without a doubt, The Who was the best band *ever* to watch live. They were consummate musicians and performers, who energized an entire generation of angst-filled adolescents caught on the cusp of the widest generation gap in modern history. The leader of The Who was Pete Townshend (1945-), a creative genius who wrote virtually all their material, and whose skills at composing, guitar playing, and performing dwarfed his contemporaries. The other members of the group were lead singer Roger Daltrey (1944-), bass and horn player John Entwistle (1944-2002), and drummer Keith Moon (1947-1978). After Moon's death, he was replaced by two other drummers, first Kenney Jones, and then Zak Starkey (Ringo Starr's son). The Who's *raison d'être* was articulated in their early (1965) song My Generation, in which (talking about the older folks) Townshend wrote, "Things they do seem awful cold / Hope I die before I get old". The theme of teenage alienation was to recur many times in Townshend's work, in songs such as Baba O'Riley (which lamented a "teenage wasteland") and in the rock opera Quadrophenia. In the mid-1960s, the band toured America, creating a cult of followers transfixed by The Who's virtuoso performances and high-energy antics, including Townshend's windmill-like guitar playing and his habit of ending concerts by destroying his instrument. The Who's most important studio albums were Tommy (1969), Who's Next (1971) and Quadrophenia (1973). Their album, Live at Leeds (1970), is, arguably, the best live rock album in history.

Web:

   http://thevoid.co.uk/webring/
   http://www.quadrophenia.net/
   http://www.rockhall.com/hof/inductee.asp?id=210
   http://www.thewho.net/

Usenet:

   alt.music.who

Raisins are just grapes that didn't use sunscreen.

A B C D E F G H I J K L M N O P Q R S T U V W X Y Z

NEWS

CNN Interactive

This is a great source of news information. CNN Interactive offers major news stories for the U.S. and the world, including sound clips and pictures. It also offers a compilation of articles for long-running stories and news events.

Web:

  http://www.cnn.com/

Columnists: Collections

I find that, once in awhile, I enjoy reading an opinionated newspaper or magazine article. There are many columnists whose work is available on the Net. Here are some Web sites where you will find many different online columns, making for a lot of interesting reading as well as widely diverging points of view.

Web:

  http://www.blueeagle.com/
  http://www.dfw.com/mld/startelegram/news/
    columnists/
  http://www.headlinespot.com/opinion/columnists/
  http://www.newsmax.com/commentmax/
    commentmax.shtml
  http://www.nytimes.com/pages/opinion/columns/
  http://www.opinionjournal.com/
  http://www.postwritersgroup.com/commentary.htm
  http://www.washingtonpost.com/wp-dyn/opinion/
    columns/

Columnists to Discover

Do you need to kill a bit of time? Take a moment to explore this short list of witty, intelligent, skillful columnists: Andrew Sullivan, Ariana Huffington, Bill O'Reilly, George Will and Thomas Friedman. If you don't know them, you should. You may agree with their opinions; you may disagree but, politics aside, I guarantee you will be stimulated.

Web:

  http://www.andrewsullivan.com/
  http://www.ariannaonline.com/columns/
  http://www.nytimes.com/pages/opinion/columns/
  http://www.washingtonpost.com/wp-dyn/opinion/
    columns/willgeorge/
  http://www.worldnetdaily.com/news/
    archives.asp?AUTHOR_ID=11

Current Events Talk and General Discussion

There are two important aspects to the spread of news. First, news organizations gather the news and present it to us (through television, radio, newspapers, magazines, the Internet, and so on). Next, we discuss the news with other people. Public discussion is crucial to our culture, because it allows us to formulate public opinion. We talk, we express opinions, we listen to other people's opinions, and we debate. In doing so, we not only work out long-term social problems, we develop a personal feeling of belonging to our society. On the Net, there are specific Usenet groups devoted to discussion of the latest happenings. These groups have names that begin with **alt.current-events**. I have listed a few of them here. Others—for more specific topics—are created and removed as the need arises. For example, if a major conflict were to arise anywhere in the world, you can be sure that a Usenet group devoted to the topic would be created quickly.

Usenet:

  alt.current-events
  alt.current-events.bosnia
  alt.current-events.cc-news
  alt.current-events.clinton.whitewater
  alt.current-events.earth-changes
  alt.current-events.haiti
  alt.current-events.massacre.high-school
  alt.current-events.oj-simpson.boycott
  alt.current-events.russia
  alt.current-events.somalia
  alt.current-events.ukraine
  alt.current-events.usa

Drudge Report

The Drudge Report Web site is useful in two ways. First, it offers an easy-to-use comprehensive list of Internet news sources and columnists: an excellent place to start when you are looking for information or commentary. Second, the site is the home of Matt Drudge, political gossip columnist extraordinaire. Drudge collects news, rumors and opinions, and publishes them on the Net, usually before anyone else. It was Drudge, for example, who first broke the Bill Clinton/Monica Lewinsky scandal. (And when you get tired of Drudge, as we all do sooner or later, you can entertain yourself by looking at parodies.)

Web:
  http://www.drudgereport.com/
  http://www.drudgeretort.com/
  http://www.ez-websites.com/grudge/
  http://www.smudgereport.com/

Usenet:
  alt.journalism.drudge

Email the Media

Do you like to sound off? Have you ever thought about writing a letter to the editor? If so, you'll love this site. First, choose a publication from among a large list of magazines, newspapers and periodicals. Next, use the handy Web-based interface to create your own personal letter. Then, with a click of the mouse button, your letter will be emailed to the appropriate address. (And since you are one of my readers, your letter will no doubt be published quickly, with the full respect it deserves.) In order to test the service, I sent a letter to Time magazine. The letter began as follows: "Dear Editor: I never thought I would be writing one of these letters to a magazine such as yours. I am, by trade, a writer and, to tell you the truth, I always believed that the first-hand personal accounts I read in your magazine were invented by your editors. However, the experience I had last week showed that such experiences can happen to people like me, and I felt that I just had to share the details with your readers. It all started when the young widow next door asked me if I would help her carry in her groceries. She was wearing a low-cut blouse, a tight, very short miniskirt, and black high-heeled pumps. As I deposited the groceries on the kitchen table, she asked if I would like to visit and have a drink while she changed into something more comfortable..." (So, anyway, that's the beginning of what I sent as a test of this Web site. I don't have room for the whole thing here, so if you would like to find out how the story ends, you will have to find the back issue of Time magazine in which the letter was published.)

Web:
  http://www.mrsmith.com/

Fox News

When you are looking for up-to-date news with an attitude, head over to the Web site of the little-network-that-could, Fox News. Although I don't watch TV, my favorite show is "Hannity and Colmes", because Alan Colmes is an old friend of mine. (Now, I'm waiting for Alan to write a book, so he can mention me.)

Web:
  http://www.foxnews.com/

Free Clipping Services

There's a lot of news, and it can slip by faster than a greased pig on a turbo-charged skateboard. When you start to get the feeling that the current events portion of your life is passing you by, why not let a computer do the work? Sign up for a free tracking service, and have the news of your choice delivered to your electronic doorstep with monotonous regularity.

Web:
  http://alertwizard.hoovers.com/
  http://www.crayon.net/

Good News and Bad News

The bad news is, there isn't all that much good news. The good news is, the bad news isn't all that bad. No matter what your preference, I've got something just for you. One of these Web sites is the Positive Press, a site with only upbeat news, featuring human interest stories and news items from various newspapers, journals and periodicals. Every time you visit you will find great stuff that will make you happy. The other Web site is the Daily Outrage, a place where you can always be sure to find something bad enough to put you in a foul mood. Good or bad? The choice is yours. (Close your eyes and see if you can figure out which is which.)

Web:
  http://www.positivepress.com/news/
  http://www.theoutrage.com/2002_outrage.html

Los Angeles Times

The online version of this well-known southern California newspaper has all the typical newspaper stuff you would expect as well as lots of local information. The Los Angeles Times is one of the few nationally read newspapers in the United States. Not only is it respected for its coverage of national and international events, but it offers in-depth coverage of southern California happenings including the West Coast financial markets and the ever-present entertainment industry.

Web:
  http://www.latimes.com/

Good News and Bad News

Tired of reading about bad stuff? There are lots of good things happening in the world if you know where to look.

Start with a daily dose of five minutes of **good news**, and work your way up to a half hour. Within a few weeks, you will be so happy that people will travel long distances just to shake your hand.

MSNBC

MSNBC is a news-oriented cable TV and Web site created by a partnership between Microsoft and the NBC television network. There is lots of news: world, commerce, sports, science, technology, life, opinion, weather, as well as some local news. As you travel through MSNBC, you will find various interactive resources and Internet links scattered throughout. You can also personalize this site for local information, traffic reports, specific stock quotes, customized news, and so on.

Web:
  http://www.msnbc.com/

New York Times

You can read the main guts of the New York Times for free (but you do have to register). You can find a bit of every type of news: current events, cybertimes, politics, business, editorial, op-ed, arts and leisure, travel, real estate, classified ads, trivia and the famous crossword puzzle. There are also forums in which you can discuss news and events.

Web:
  http://www.nytimes.com/

News Headlines

Do you only have a minute? Quick, check the latest headlines. Do you have two minutes? Read one of the stories. Have lots of time? You won't get bored—there's always news to read. Start with the headlines and read, read, read until it's time to get back to work.

Web:
 http://www.newshub.com/
 http://www.newsmax.com/
 http://www.newsnow.co.uk/
 http://www.worldnetdaily.com/
 http://www.worldnews.com/

News Search Engines

You want to read about a particular topic, but how do you find the relevant news stories? Easy, just use one of these news search engines and you can find the news you need when you need it. In fact, one day, the Net was so fast that I was able to find the news I needed *before* I needed it.

Web:
 http://www.newsindex.com/
 http://www.newstrawler.com/
 http://www.searchenginewatch.com/links/news.html
 http://www.totalnews.com/

New York Times

Newspapers Around the World

Just about every newspaper you can think of (and many you can't think of) have Web sites. These tools will help you find the Web site for any newspaper you want. Just the other day, I found Web sites for three newspapers I could think of and six newspapers I couldn't think of (and all before breakfast).

Web:
 http://www.dailyearth.com/
 http://www.findnewspapers.com/
 http://www.ipl.org/div/news/
 http://www.nettizen.com/newspaper/
 http://www.newsdirectory.com/
 http://www.onlinenewspapers.com/
 http://www.thepaperboy.com/

OneWorld News

This is world news with a slant toward "global justice". The articles offer a global perspective. Although the coverage can be a bit superficial, they do a good job of highlighting important events around the world—events that relate to stories that don't always make the news. You can read about humanity and freedom issues, migrants and refugees, underdeveloped countries, people who are politically oppressed, and so on. Generally speaking, the stories are well written, not at all "bleeding heart". OneWorld offers some multimedia reports with pictures, audio and video, as well as a discussion area to which you can post messages. The news service is part of a larger project called OneWorld Broadcasting Trust whose goal is to "create greater global understanding through broadcasting".

Web:
 http://www.oneworld.net/news/today/

USA Today

Tired of recycling? Stop getting the newspaper and just get your news online. It's clean, it's neat and best of all you don't have to store a bunch of newspapers around the house until recycling day. USA Today has lots of distracting news and entertainment online. There's so much interesting stuff to read here, you might have to have a second cup of morning coffee just to get through it all.

Web:
 http://www.usatoday.com/

Washington Post

The Washington Post Web site is one of my favorite places to read the news. The Washington Post is a major American newspaper, published out of Washington, D.C., and is the principal voice-to-be-reckoned-with in the nation's capitol. I check in at least once a day: not only for news, but for the columns, human interest features and comics.

Web:
  http://www.washingtonpost.com/

NEWS: INTERNATIONAL

Arabic News

Read news from prominent newspapers of the Arab world and keep up on what is happening in Saudi Arabia, Kuwait, Bahrain, Lebanon, Jordan, United Arab Emirates, Palestine and Qatar. There are also Arab papers from countries such as the United States, Canada, Australia and the United Kingdom. I have also included a Web site that carries news pertaining to Islam, as well as a Usenet group for discussion.

Web:
  http://media.fares.net/Daily_News/
  http://www.amin.org/eng/
  http://www.arabworldnews.com/
  http://www.irna.com/en/
  http://www.sahafa.com/

Usenet:
  bit.listserv.muslims

Australian News

Whenever I am itching for some news about Australia, I always go to these Web sites, because they have links to lots and lots of Australian news sources, including notices on the latest natural disasters. Just the thing if you are planning a little jaunt down under.

Web:
  http://www.australiannews.net/
  http://www.news.com.au/
  http://www.smh.com.au/
  http://www.theage.com.au/

BBC News

The BBC (British Broadcasting Corporation) started daily radio transmissions on November 14, 1922. Since then, the BBC has served as the primary broadcasting voice of Great Britain, both at home and abroad. The BBC Web site is your entrée to the U.K. news, with articles, audio and video clips. The BBC also maintains a large program of international broadcasting called BBC Worldwide (I have included its Web site as well). One thing I like about the BBC is its excellent, comprehensive news coverage. For example, the last time I visited I found out that "Textbooks used for sex education in secondary schools in England and Wales tend to be sexist and even make sex sound dull, according to research..." (No doubt they were written by the same people who write English cookbooks.)

Web:
  http://news.bbc.co.uk/
  http://www.bbc.co.uk/worldservice/

Chinese News

In spite of the fact that about one quarter of the people in the world live in China, we understand very little about what happens within the country. One reason is that their system of government is difficult for us to understand. Here is something I'd like you to do. I am going to show you the very beginning of the Chinese Constitution (not counting the preamble). Take a look at the following quotation, and then go to a Chinese news site and read any article about politics. Notice that your interpretation of the article has been changed by knowing just a bit about the Chinese political system. Okay here it goes: "The People's Republic of China is a socialist state under the people's democratic dictatorship led by the working class and based on the alliance of workers and peasants. The socialist system is the basic system of the People's Republic of China. Disruption of the socialist system by any organization or individual is prohibited."

Web:
  http://english.peopledaily.com.cn/
  http://www.china.org.cn/english/
  http://www.chinanews.com/
  http://www.focus.com.cn/

BBC News

If it's news, you'll find it on the BBC, one of the oldest and most respected news organizations in the world.

Just the other day, I visited its Web site and I saw the headline, **"Harley's Cat Has No Food in His Bowl".** I checked, and they were right.

Talk about good reporting!

German News

Here's the German news, the whole German news, and nothing but the German news (in German). But how important is this to the world at large? Can we learn anything about the Germans by studying their news? There is an old German proverb that says, "A country can be judged by the quality of its proverbs." Right. I couldn't have put it better myself.

Web:
  http://www.bild.t-online.de/
  http://www.spiegel.de/
  http://www.welt.de/

Indian News

India is a country defined by contradictions: a modern society clashing with long-standing, indelible pre-scientific traditions; a prosperous upper- and middle-class living in juxtaposition with an enormous underclass living in unimaginable poverty; large, educated urban enclaves scattered throughout a country which is largely rural and uneducated. India is also the largest and most powerful country in South Asia, and the largest democracy in the world. As such, much of what happens in India affects all of Asia and, indirectly, the rest of the world.

Web:
  http://timesofindia.indiatimes.com/
  http://www.dailypioneer.com/
  http://www.indiadaily.com/
  http://www.indiaexpress.com/
  http://www.indianewspaper.com/
  http://www.tribuneindia.com/

Listserv Mailing List:
  List Name: india-h
  Subscribe to: listserv@listserv.indnet.org

Irish News

If you are Irish, you'll enjoy keeping up on news from the Emerald Isle. These Web sites have all the daily news, sports and opinion you need. (You, however, will have to provide your favorite pub brew.)

Web:
  http://www.ireland.com/
  http://www.irish-herald.com/
  http://www.irishnews.com/
  http://www.moreover.com/ireland
  http://www.online.ie/news/
  http://www.unison.ie/irish_independent/

Israeli News

One thing you can say about Israel, their news is always interesting. Somehow, this tiny country—smaller than New Jersey—manages to generate more news per square kilometer than any other country in the world. The best thing about Israeli news is there is always so much of it, you never have to worry about running out. The Israelis are making news so fast, there's always something new and exciting to enjoy. (I'll tell you something, though. Whoever said, "May you live in exciting times," never lived in Israel.)

Web:
   http://www.haaretzdaily.com/
   http://www.israelnationalnews.com/
   http://www.virtualjerusalem.com/news/

Japanese News

Publishing news is an old tradition in Japan. For example, the Nikkei news service was founded in 1876. Today, we use the Internet, and there is no better way to keep up on everything that is happening in Japan. You'll especially appreciate these resources if you do business with Japanese companies, or if you are a Japanese living in a foreign country.

Web:
   http://home.kyodo.co.jp/
   http://www.asahi.com/english/
   http://www.japantimes.co.jp/
   http://www.japantoday.com/e/
   http://www.newsonjapan.com/
   http://www.yomiuri.co.jp/index-e.htm

Mexican News

The Mexican economy is inextricably connected to that of the United States, not only as a trading partner and a member of NAFTA (North American Free Trade Agreement), but as the source for much of the unskilled labor in the southern and western states. In addition, many residents of the U.S. are of Mexican descent, and have a strong interest in the happenings of their home country. In spite of the fact that Mexico is so important to the U.S., it is impossible to keep abreast of what is happening in Mexico if you depend on American news sources.

Web:
   http://www.mexicodaily.com/
   http://www.mexonline.com/headline.htm
   http://www.thenewsmexico.com/

MEXICAN NEWS

I believe that everyone benefits by learning a foreign language, so the other day I decided to spend an hour reading the Mexican news in *Spanish*.

Even though I studied Spanish for only one year in high school, I had no trouble reading the news, and I am sure I understood everything.

What I don't understand is why the gross domestic product of Mexico was sent to Greenland in order to welcome the President of New Jersey to a new type of folk dance.

Pakistani News

Pakistan is a country burdened by a history of unstable governments, caught between Islamic militants and the outside world, and coexisting next to a neighbor, India, with whom it has serious longstanding political and cultural differences. Moreover, like India, Pakistan has the capability of launching nuclear weapons. Both geographically and politically, Pakistan is in a crucial position with respect to world affairs, and the real news about what goes on in the country is important to us all.

Web:
   http://www.nation.com.pk/daily/today/main/
   http://www.pakistannation.com/
   http://www.paknews.org/
   http://www.paktoday.com/
Usenet:
   bit.listserv.pakistan

Reuters News

Reuters is a news agency founded by the German entrepreneur Paul Julius Reuter in 1851. The agency was based on Reuter's determination to "come up with solutions for his clients". For example, in 1850, Reuter used carrier pigeons to deliver closing stock prices, closing the only gap in the telegraph system connecting Berlin and Paris. The Reuters news agency prides itself on offering objective news services and, toward that end, they established the Reuters Trust to make sure Reuters is never owned by a particular interest group or faction. At the online Reuters site, you can read lots of basic news: international, U.S., politics, business and sports.

Web:
   http://www.reuters.com/

Russian News

Russia is a huge country—150,000,000 people, 17,075,200 square kilometers, spanning 11 time zones—and there is a lot happening. Here are some resources that provide an excellent way to keep up on current events in Russia and nearby countries.

Web:
 http://www.europeaninternet.com/russia/
 http://www.gazeta.ru/english/
 http://www.moscowtimes.ru/
 http://www.rferl.org/newsline/
 http://www.russianews.net/
 http://www.russianobserver.com/
 http://www.therussianissues.com/

South African News

South Africa is a fascinating country, with many different cultures (they have 11 official languages). If you're interested in finding out what's happening in South Africa, the Net is the place to do it. One of these Web sites has daily updates compiled from South African press agencies. You can find out a lot more by reading these summaries than you can from any regular newspaper.

Web:
 http://www.iol.co.za/
 http://www.mg.co.za/
 http://www.news24.com/

World News Sources

Okay, so you are glued to your computer and fastened to the Net for many hours a day. Still, there is no need to miss the news.

Your trusty Web browser can be your window to access news from all over the world.

Now that you have the Net, no event of any importance will ever again escape your attention.

Swedish News

To keep up on what is new and exciting in Sweden, look no further. There are links to many, many Swedish news sources, including daily newspapers, magazines, radio and television. There is also a weather section, which is handy during the winter, when you can cheer yourself up by looking at what the Swedes deal with day after day.

Web:
 http://www.aftonbladet.se/
 http://www.di.se/
 http://www.inetmedia.nu/medier/

U.K. News

For some reason, I find English news fascinating, especially the comings and goings of the royal family. If you share my interests, you can use the Net to keep up on what's happening day by day in the U.K. (England, Scotland, Wales and Northern Ireland). Regardless, reading the news from a U.K. viewpoint is interesting, especially if you are an American who gets most of his or her news from TV.

Web:
 http://www.newsnow.co.uk/
 http://www.newswatch.co.uk/
 http://www.niss.ac.uk/cr/uknews.html
 http://www.tiscali.co.uk/news/

World News

I'm warning you. Don't visit any of these resources unless you have plenty of time. There is so much news in the world of news that you will be distracted for hours. (And that's not news.)

Web:
 http://www.csmonitor.com/
 http://www.iht.com
 http://www.misna.org/eng/
 http://www.pppp.net/links/news/
 http://www.worldnews.com/

Usenet:
 misc.news.bosnia
 misc.news.east-europe.rferl
 misc.news.southasia

OCCULT AND PARANORMAL

Cayce, Edgar

Edgar Cayce (1877-1945) was an American "psychic" who founded the Edgar Cayce Institute for Intuitive Studies and Atlantic University. Cayce is best known for his psychic work as a medical diagnostician and a reader of past lives. However, he is also celebrated for his many interesting predictions. For example, he predicted that, in 1958, the United States would discover a death ray that had originally been used on Atlantis. (In fact, Cayce is responsible for many of the ideas people believe about Atlantis.) He also predicted that China would be converted to Christianity by 1968. Oh well, Babe Ruth used to strike out a lot too.

Web:
  http://www.are-cayce.com/
  http://www.ciis.edu/cayce/FAQ2.html
  http://www.dreamscape.com/morgana/phoebe.htm
  http://www.edgarcayce.com/links.html
  http://www.near-death.com/cayce.html
  http://www.skepdic.com/cayce.html

Usenet:
  alt.dreams.edgar-cayce
  alt.prophecies.cayce

Chaos Magick

Chaos magick is a system of magick that is personal (as opposed to group-oriented) and non-traditional (as opposed to the "old ways" of traditional ritual). It does not have a particular belief system. Each "Chaote" (person who practices chaos magick) believes whatever suits him or her. Chaos magick recognizes no particular deity, theology or morality. "Nothing is True, and Everything is Permitted." This is a world view in which life is chance, random, accidental, chaotic and discordant. (If you can make any sense of this information, you probably have the right chemistry to practice chaos magick.)

Web:
  http://www.boudicca.de/max1-e.htm
  http://www.chaosdancer.com/
  http://www.choronzon.com/efsd/introtochaos.html
  http://www.faqs.org/faqs/magick/chaos/faq/
  http://www.phhine.ndirect.co.uk/archives/
    ess_mach.htm
  http://www.spiralnature.com/magick/chaos/

Usenet:
  alt.magick.chaos

Hermeticism

Hermeticism is not easy to define. It is an esoteric tradition, related to alchemy and magick, and connected to specific works of Hermes Trismegistus (the Egyptian god Thoth), the legendary author of various writings on astrology and magic. Hermeticism is not easy to understand, so be forewarned: you can't be in a hurry.

Web:
  http://www.belinus.co.uk/mythology/
    Hermeticism.htm
  http://www.hermeticfellowship.org/
  http://www.kheper.auz.com/topics/Hermeticism/
  http://www.necronomi.com/magic/hermeticism/

Lightful Images

If seeing is believing, then this will put you one step closer to believing that some strange stuff is going on in the universe, things you would rather not know. So maybe it's best if you didn't look at these pictures of aliens and other paranormal occurrences.

Web:
  http://www.spiritweb.org/spirit/lightwork.html

Magick

The term "magick" was coined by Aleister Crowley (1875-1947), the author of the book "Magick in Theory and Practice". (You should know, however, that a lot of people, even practitioners of magick, consider Crowley to be a nut.) Magick is the art of using charms, spells and rituals to create supernatural effects and to control natural events. The study of magick will take you on a long journey to a lot of mystical, mysterious places, so be sure to take along a extra snack just in case.

Web:
  http://www.branwenscauldron.com/
    rituals_spells.html
  http://www.faqs.org/faqs/magick/
  http://www.ipns.com/northstar/magick/
  http://www.mysteria.com/magick/
  http://www.webcom.com/~gnosis/library.html

Usenet:
  alt.magick
  alt.magick.ethics
  alt.magick.serious
  alt.magick.tantra
  alt.magick.tyagi
  alt.magick.virtual-adepts
  alt.pagan.magick
  alt.traditional.witchcraft

Necronomicon

The original title of the Necronomicon was "Al-Azif". (Azif is an Arab word signifying a nocturnal sound made by insects, which was thought to be the howling of demons.) "Al-Azif" was written around the year 730 by Abdul Al-Hazred, a crazed and wandering poet from Yemen. In 950, the work was translated into what we now know as the Necronomicon by a Greek philosopher named Theodorus Philetus. Some people say the book is full of powerful spells by which you can raise the dead (in case your servants call in sick the night of a big dinner party); other people have their doubts. The document has a long history of suppression and destruction, and has been banned repeatedly. It is said that Abdul Al-Hazred met his death by being devoured by a monster in broad daylight. Even now, people say just looking at the Necronomicon will bring you bad luck. Still wanna read it?

Web:
   http://www.cam.org/~vannuff/darkpage/
      necrono.htm
   http://www.digital-brilliance.com/necron/
      necron.htm
   http://www.flashback.se/archive/necronomicon.html
   http://www.hplovecraft.com/creation/necron/

Usenet:
   alt.necronomicon

Occult and Magick Chat

Do you have your cauldron bubbling away and need a little advice about what to do if you run out of eye of newt? Hop onto IRC and talk to the folks who are into occult and magick. Maybe you can jump on the old broom and fly over to borrow a cup of mandrake root.

IRC:
   #occult (DALnet)
   #thelema (Undernet)

Nostradamus

Nostradamus (1503-1566), actually Michel de Nostredame, was a French physician, mathematician and astrologer. He is remembered as the author of a book called "Centuries", consisting of 946 four-line verses or quatrains. The quatrains are mired in obscure, misleading, vague symbolisms and encryptions. Notwithstanding, many people believe that Nostradamus was a prophet who was able to predict specific future events. For example, the following quatrain is cited as proof that Nostradamus predicted the 1963 assassination of U.S. President John F. Kennedy: "The ancient work will be accomplished, / And from the roof evil ruin will fall on the great man: / They will accuse an innocent, being dead, of the deed: / The guilty one is hidden in the misty copse." Hmmm…

Web:
   http://www.astrologer.ru/Nostradamiana/
      ind_ns_eng.html
   http://www.dreamscape.com/morgana/titan.htm
   http://www.faqs.org/faqs/nostradamus/
   http://www.mods.com.au/blue/nostradamus/
      homepage.htm
   http://www.tje.net/para/nostradamus/

Usenet:
   alt.prophecies.nostradamus

Occult Search Engine

The wisdom of the ages may have taken generations to create, but when you need it, you need it fast. So scoot right over to this search engine for the occult, where you can find a variety of resources: paranormal, Christian mysticism, vampirism, shamanism, paganism, wicca, Satanism, and more.

Web:
  http://www.hiddenpath.net/

Ouija

A Ouija board is a device used to help receive spiritual and telepathic messages. It is thought that the name comes from the French and German words for yes: "oui" and "ja" (but there are other stories). The Ouija apparatus consists of a board and a movable pointer. The board is marked with the letters of the alphabet as well as various other symbols. One or more people touch the pointer while concentrating on spiritual thoughts. As if by magic, the pointer will move from one letter to another, spelling out a message. The spirit of the Ouija may not solve all your problems, but it's certainly cheaper than psychotherapy.

Web:
  http://www.crystalinks.com/ouija.html
  http://www.djmcadam.com/ouija.htm
  http://www.museumoftalkingboards.com/
  http://www.prairieghosts.com/ouija.html

Paranormal News

Just in case you don't have paranormal abilities, here's a more pedestrian way to find out what's new in the world of sightings, aliens, ghosts, bigfoot, strange occurrences, psychic phenomena, crop circles, and other paranormal topics. The other day, I read a paranormal news article that said, "Harley, a psychic will be calling you soon." Just then the phone rang. When I picked it up, a voice at the other end said, "See?" and hung up.

Web:
  http://www.paranormalnews.com/
  http://www.strange.info/
  http://www.xproject-paranormal.com/

Paranormal Phenomena Talk and General Discussion

The weird, the unexplained, the things that go bump in the night—you'll love the stories and the theories, especially the ones that make the hair stand up on the back of your neck.

Usenet:
  alt.paranet.esp-help
  alt.paranet.paranormal
  alt.paranormal
  alt.paranormal.channeling
  alt.paranormal.crop-circles
  alt.paranormal.moderated
  alt.paranormal.spells.hexes.magic

Paranormal Search Engines

I had a really cool experience the other day. I was using a paranormal search engine to look for a Quidditch schedule, and I came across a link with my name on it. I clicked on it and it was a picture of *me*, using a paranormal search engine to look for a Quidditch schedule.

Web:
  http://www.creepyweb.com/directory.htm
  http://www.paraseek.com/
  http://www.polarboy.pwp.blueyonder.co.uk/
    cryptoseek/
  http://www.ufoseek.com/

Parapsychology

Remember all those nights you'd stay up late with friends, turn out the lights, and by the eerie glow of a flashlight you would tell ghost stories and creepy folk legends? None of that has changed; it's just that the scary stories get more complicated and sophisticated. Believers of the weird get together to talk about ESP, out-of-body experiences, dreams and altered states of consciousness.

Web:
  http://perso.wanadoo.fr/basuyaux/parapsy_eng/
    links/
  http://www.mdani.demon.co.uk/para/parapsy.htm
  http://www.parapsych.org/
  http://www.psiexplorer.com/
  http://www.psiresearch.org/para1.html

Usenet:
  alt.paranet.psi

> ## If you were normal, you wouldn't be reading this.

Psychokinesis and Telekinesis

Psychokinesis (PK) is mind over matter. More precisely, it is the ability to manipulate material objects using the power of the mind. For example, if you could bend a spoon without touching it or using an understandable external force, that would be PK. Some people consider remote viewing or healing to be PK. Telekinesis, the ability to move a material object, is a particular type of PK. Do PK and telekinesis really exist? Does the Pope live in the woods? Are bears Catholic?

Web:
> http://www.astralsociety.com/tk/tk.htm
> http://www.crystalinks.com/telekinesis.html
> http://www.psiexplorer.com/

Skepticism

A great many people in the world have superstitious and pseudo-scientific beliefs. In my experience, the people with the most incredible beliefs are the people who suffer from a lack of critical thinking and too little background in the hard sciences. Some people think it doesn't matter—what's the difference if some people want to believe in such things? I believe that it does make a difference, that in a small but significant way, we all lose when individuals base their lives on superstition and pseudo-scientific beliefs. It's not always easy being the bad guy, but someone has to do it.

Web:
> http://www.csicop.org/bibliography/
> http://www.faqs.org/faqs/skeptic-faq/
> http://www.randi.org/
> http://www.skepdic.com/

Usenet:
> alt.paranet.skeptic
> sci.skeptic

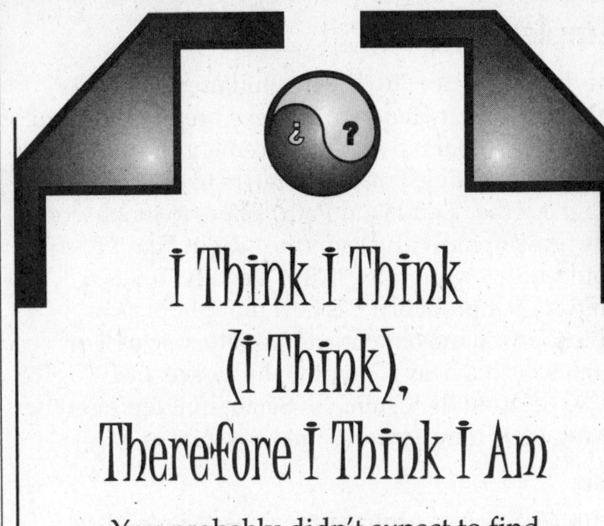

You probably didn't expect to find intelligent, rational, educated thought in a section on the occult and paranormal, but here it is.

The **Skepticism** sites have a lot of compelling information that will restore your faith in human reason. Before you cop out by saying, "It's all a value judgment and everyone is entitled to his or her own opinion," take a look at what the skeptics have to say and you may be surprised.

Thinking is generally a Good Thing™ and, like watching television and drinking coffee, using your intellect well can be habit forming. Having an open mind is great if you are undergoing brain surgery, but for fulfilling your birthright as a human being, nothing beats a good education and an understanding of how rational thought can be used to enhance our lives and stop other people from taking advantage of our emotional weaknesses.

Temple of Set

The Temple of Set (ToS) is an "initiatory magical order of the Left Hand Path." Let's break that down: "initiatory" refers to self-advancement through levels of self-knowledge; "magical" refers to real magic (magick); the "Left Hand Path" refers to inner work that leads to individualism (the "Right Hand Path" would be growing outwardly). Legally, ToS is a religion, but probably, it is best thought of as a philosophical movement and initiatory school of magick with a heavy Egyptian influence. In 1975, ToS broke off from the Church of Satan, but don't get the wrong idea; they are not Satan worshipers.

Web:
  http://www.faqs.org/faqs/religions/temple-of-set/
  http://www.paganlibrary.com/editorials/
     temple_set.php
  http://www.remanifest.com/
  http://www.xeper.org/

OUTDOOR ACTIVITIES

Boomerangs

A boomerang is a curved instrument—usually made of wood—that, when thrown in a particular manner, can be made to fly away and return. Boomerangs were invented in Australia. (In fact, the name "boomerang" is derived from "bumariny", a word from Dharuk, the Aboriginal language of southeast Australia.) Today, boomerangs are used around the world for fun, and there are various boomerang organizations and competitions. These sites contain collections of boomerang-related links and information, as well as instructions to help you learn how to throw and catch. Hint: If you are left-handed, be sure to use a left-handed boomerang. (I had a friend who bought a new boomerang and went crazy trying to throw away the old one.)

Web:
  http://www.boomerangs.org/
  http://www.flight-toys.com/boomerangs.htm
  http://www.usba.org/

Usenet:
  alt.boomerang

Bungee Jumping

Wow! Bungee jumping! Get yourself to a place that is high (a bridge, a crane, a tower, whatever), with nothing around you but air. Fasten yourself into a harness attached to a thick, strong, elastic cord connected to the top of the high place. Hold your breath, close your eyes, jump! Wow! Now do it again. Ready for more? Try it from a helicopter.

Web:
  http://www.bungeezone.com/
  http://www.jojaffa.com/guides/bungee.htm

Usenet:
  alt.sport.bungee

Camping

There are various ways to go camping. Basically, you can either drive to the campground or you can walk (at least from a trailhead). If you drive, there is a big dichotomy between those people who go car camping and those who have recreational vehicles (RVs). If you like to camp, here is information that will be useful no matter what your *modus operandi*. In particular, you can read the various camping FAQs (frequently asked question lists) and use the Net to help you find a campground.

Web:
  http://www.camping-usa.com/
  http://www.gorp.com/dow/
  http://www.totalescape.com/tripez/clueless.html

Usenet:
  alt.rec.camping
  alt.rv
  rec.outdoors.camping
  rec.outdoors.rv-travel

Cave Exploring

If you like crawling around in something that is cool, dark and wet, you are digging in the right place. Here are the connections you need to speleological societies and cave exploration information around the world.

Web:
  http://www.caves.org/
  http://www.nides.bc.ca/assignments/rocks/
     glossary.htm
  http://www.rainierpubs.com/metro/caves/

Usenet:
  alt.caving

Climbing

Trapped indoors but ready to go climbing? Help ease the pain by checking out the great climbing resources on the Net. These Web sites have lots of pictures of climbing, information about climbing, in fact, just about everything about climbing and related activities.

Web:
  http://www.camp4.com/
  http://www.rocklist.com/
  http://www.webclimbing.com/

Usenet:
  rec.climbing

Fishing

There's got to be something special about the type of guy who would spend all day on a boat just to catch a fish that he could buy in the supermarket for $3. One such special guy is my lawyer, Bill. He loves sitting out on his boat waiting for The Big Catch. This is good for me, because every now and then he'll bring me some fresh salmon or sea bass. However, his hobby is not without its attendant risks. Not long ago, he was fishing out of state. A friend of his who trains dolphins asked Bill if he would mind catching some fish to bring back as a treat for the dolphins. The day he was to start back, Bill happened to talk to his friend who told him the dolphins had been behaving badly lately and causing a lot of problems. Fortunately for Bill, he is a trained lawyer who is able to see the hidden pitfalls in any situation, and it was the work of a moment for him to tell his friend that he wouldn't be bringing any fish home. As Bill later explained it to me, this was a close call because in the United States it is illegal to transport fish across state lines for immoral porpoises.

Web:
  http://www.fishbelly.com/
  http://www.fishingworks.com/
  http://www.fishtheworld.com/
  http://www.thefishfinder.com/
  http://www.up-north.com/upnorth/fishstories/
    authors.html

Usenet:
  alt.fishing
  rec.outdoors.fishing
  rec.outdoors.fishing.bass
  rec.outdoors.fishing.fly
  rec.outdoors.fishing.fly.tying
  rec.outdoors.fishing.saltwater

Hiking and Backpacking

There are a lot of great hiking trails in the world, but what really makes a trip enjoyable is to find a wonderful place before it gets too popular. Years ago, I had some wonderful times hiking at a small park near the Big Sur area on the California coast. The hike from the parking area to the ocean was pleasant and, along the way, I would pass through an open meadow, a forest with tall trees, and thick bushes. At the end of the trail was a beautiful cove where small cliffs, covered entirely with sand, overlooked the beach. I remember once visiting the area with one of my good friends. We hiked to the end of the trail and then climbed up the cliffs with our backpacks. At the top of the cliff, we walked down to the end of a point which was surrounded almost entirely by water and had a breathtaking ocean view. We camped out on that very spot, snug at night in our sleeping bags, lying between bushes of wild sage. It was one of those trips that I will never forget and, even with the passing of the years, the sounds and the sights and the smells remain fresh in my mind.

Web:
  http://www.backpacking.net/
  http://www.backpackinglight.com/
  http://www.hejoly.demon.nl/countries/
    essentials.html
  http://www.hikingwebsite.com/
  http://www.thebackpacker.com/

Usenet:
  alt.rec.hiking
  rec.backcountry

Human-Powered Vehicles

Human-powered vehicles (HPV) are designed so that the only power they use is supplied by the muscular effort of a human being. For example, a bicycle is a HPV. However, there are much more elaborate and efficient devices, both for traveling on land and in the air. The fastest land-based HVPs have achieved speeds of over 60 miles per hour (95 kph). Learn how to build and power these unique vehicles, and you can save the environment and get healthy at the same time.

Web:
   http://www.bentrideronline.com/
   http://www.ihpva.org/
   http://www.the-spa.com/rcgilmore/Illustrations.htm
   http://www.wisil.recumbents.com/wisil/whatsup.htm

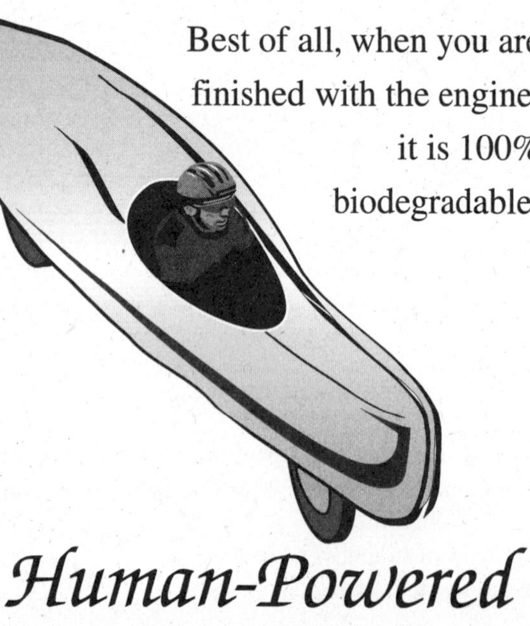

Hunting

There are many aspects to hunting and a lot to discuss. Here are the resources you need to get started. The Usenet groups and mailing lists are for discussion of various hunting-related topics (although, these are *not* the proper places to discuss the politics of gun control). The Web sites contain information on many hunting-related topics such as equipment (including firearms and bows), animals, organizations, and—assuming all goes well on your outing—recipes.

Web:
   http://www.eatsleephunt.com/
   http://www.hunting.net/
   http://www.smarthunter.com/
   http://www.ucalgary.ca/~powlesla/personal/hunting/

Usenet:
   alt.animals.furtrapping
   rec.hunting

Listserv Mailing List:
   List Name: hunter-safety-l
   Subscribe to: listserv@listserv.tamu.edu

Inline Skating

A long, long time ago, there was roller skating. Roller skates were flat pieces of metal with wide, shallow hooks on the sides and small metal wheels on the bottom. To use the skates, you had to attach them to your shoes. You would use a "skate key" to widen the hooks, slap a skate on your shoe, and then use the key to tighten the hook, which would hold the skate onto your shoe. If you were really cool, you would walk around with your skate key hanging on a piece of string around your neck. Eventually, the original roller skates were replaced by boots that had attached wheels, which themselves were replaced by inline skates (in which the thin hard rubber wheels are mounted in a straight line). What hasn't changed through the years is the tendency of boys who have access to anything that moves to do dangerous things their mothers shouldn't know about.

Web:
   http://www.aggressive.com/
   http://www.skatecity.com/links/
   http://www.skatefaq.com/

Usenet:
   rec.sport.skating.inline
   rec.sport.skating.racing
   rec.sport.skating.roller

Mountain Biking

Mountain bikes are designed for riding off-road, in particular, up and down narrow, winding trails. I have a mountain bike, and I have had a lot of fun riding it. Here is my advice: If you stay on mostly flat, mostly smooth areas, it's mostly straightforward. But if you decide to get into real mountain biking, on real mountain trails, you need to develop real skills. Although biking skills are generally learned by trial and error, these resources can help you enjoy the trial and avoid the error.

Web:
   http://mtb.live.com/
   http://www.discovermountainbiking.com/
   http://www.faqs.org/faqs/bicycles-faq/
      mountain-bikes/
   http://www.mtbr.com/

Usenet:
   alt.mountain-bike
   rec.bicycles.off-road

I magine this. You wake up one day to find yourself in a new world. A world in which direction and time have a will of their own and have become as alive as the wind. All your common landmarks are gone; you move from one spot to another, lost in a haze of misdirection. Nothing you have experienced has prepared you for this. Everything you know seems to be wrong, and you are caught in a land of disinformation, shifting visual cues; an ever-changing environment in which the slightest mistake will send you off into the wilderness.

Are you in the Twilight Zone? You wish. No, you are **Orienteering**.

Nude Beaches

If you have never spent an afternoon at a nude beach, you don't know what you are missing. But don't worry, I can show you what it is like right now. Wherever you are, take off your clothes and, for the next 30 minutes, lie down on the floor and think pleasant thoughts. (If you are reading this in a bookstore, you can tell the manager I said that after the 30 minutes are up he or she must give you a discount.) Now, wasn't that great? Doesn't that make you want to try out a real nude beach?

Web:
   http://www.drleisure.com/
   http://www.faqs.org/faqs/nude-faq/beaches/
   http://www.nudetravelguide.com/
   http://www.sfbg.com/nude02/

Orienteering and Rogaining

Grab a map and a sack lunch and head to the woods for some exciting, competitive, cross-country navigation. If you think trying to read a map while driving through Los Angeles is bad, try doing it in the middle of a forest where all the trees look the same and there are no road signs or even flushable toilets. Learn about orienteering and rogaining—the rules, how to compete, and what other people are doing.

Web:
   http://wa.rogaine.asn.au/
   http://www.orienteering.org/

Usenet:
   rec.sport.orienteering

Listproc Mailing List:
   List Name: o-train
   Subscribe to: listproc@u.washington.edu

Outdoor and Recreation Resources

Get out into the sunshine and fresh air. When you want to know where to go and what to do, take a look at all this great information. You'll find loads of stuff to read about things to do and places to visit: national parks, forests, wilderness areas, hiking, biking, fishing and climbing.

Web:
   http://espn.go.com/outdoors/
   http://imoutdoors.winnercomm.com/
   http://www.adventurenetwork.com/
   http://www.hikercentral.com/
   http://www.outdoor-resources.com/

Paintball

When I was a young lad at summer camp, one of my favorite outdoor games was "Capture the Flag". Paintball is a modern version of that same game. There are two teams, each of which must defend a home base, called a flag station. Within the flag station is a flag. The goal of each team is to be the first to capture the other team's flag and bring it back to their own flag station. During the game, players use special guns to shoot at one another. The guns shoot small, harmless, paint-filled balls (hence, the name of the game) that mark, but do not injure the opposing players. Once a player is hit, he or she is eliminated from the game. Do you like the idea of sneaking around, trying to eliminate other people before they eliminate you? If so, paintball is the game for you. (Either that or local politics.)

Web:
   http://www.newpaintball.com/
   http://www.paintball.com/
   http://www.paintballtimes.com/

Usenet:
   alt.sport.paintball
   rec.sport.paintball

Paragliding

Paragliders are the most simple of all aircraft. They consist of a canopy (which acts like a wing), risers (cords) and a harness (suspended from the risers). Where I live there are a lot of paragliders and, when you watch them, they look like large colorful birds, slowly soaring back and forth across the sky. Paragliders are flown and landed with no artificial source of energy—just the wind, gravity and the pilot's muscles. Unlike a hang glider, a paraglider does not have a rigid frame—the shape of the canopy is maintained by air pressure. In addition, paragliders are easier to manage and handle than hang gliders. (A paraglider can be folded into a package the size of a large backpack.)

Web:
   http://www.bigairparagliding.com/
   http://www.poweredparaglider.com/

Radio-Controlled Model Aircraft

For people who like model aircraft, nothing can be more fun than spending a Saturday afternoon out in a large field, putting your favorite radio-controlled (R/C) airplane through its paces. To be good at flying a model plane, you have to understand a lot about flight and flying in general. At these sites you can read about buying, building, learning to fly, gliders, powering with gas or electricity, helicopters, aerodynamics, and supplies and materials. For discussion, you can talk to the many radio-controlled-aircraft buffs on Usenet.

Web:
   http://www.geistware.com/rcmodeling/
   http://www.gettingstartedinrc.com/planes/
   http://www.repairfaq.org/filipg/RC/Fils_RC.html

Usenet:
   rec.models.rc.air

Sand Castles

Who has not played around at the beach with a small plastic pail and shovel, and built a sand castle? Well, that can be fun, but if you really want to get serious, try sand sculpture. Start by planning and erecting a form. Fill the form with hundreds of pails of wet sand, and use sculpting tools to carefully create an elaborate work of art. Then, after six or more hours, take a few pictures and walk away. Eventually, the water will evaporate, the sand will collapse, and the tide will remove the remains. Never mind. You can start again another day. (Hint for beginners: Use really wet sand and don't pound it. Just pour and jiggle.)

Web:
   http://members.aol.com/beachbuddy/
      sandsculpture.htm
   http://www.harrisand.org/
   http://www.netaxs.com/~sparky/sand.html
   http://www.sandcastlecentral.com/
   http://www.sandhands.com/library/faqhow/
      howidoit.htm

Scuba Diving

The word "scuba" stands for "self-contained underwater breathing apparatus". The first primitive scuba-diving equipment was developed in 1943. The Net has lots of resources for the recreational and technical scuba diving community. You'll find mailing list archives, a database of diveable shipwrecks, reviews of dive gear and equipment, details of popular dive destinations, lists of training agencies, clubs, underwater pictures, a catalog of marine fish and invertebrates, classified ads, weather maps, and lots more.

Web:
   http://www.divebuddy.com/
   http://www.divernet.com/
   http://www.diveweb.com/
   http://www.scubaduba.com/
   http://www.scubasource.com/

Usenet:
   bit.listserv.scuba-l
   rec.scuba
   rec.scuba.equipment
   rec.scuba.locations

Listserv Mailing List:
   List Name: scuba-l
   Subscribe to: listserv@listserv.brown.edu

Shooting

Shooting and guns are enjoyed by many people, either as a recreational activity or as part of an organized competition. The Web sites I have listed here will lead you to a large number of shooting and gun resources on the Net. For an ongoing discussion, you can participate in the **rec.guns** Usenet group. If you are concerned about the politics of gun ownership—a highly contentious area of debate— you can join the discussion in **talk.politics.guns**.

Web:
   http://links.shooters.com/
   http://www.gunsgunsguns.com/gunhoo/

Usenet:
   rec.guns
   talk.politics.guns

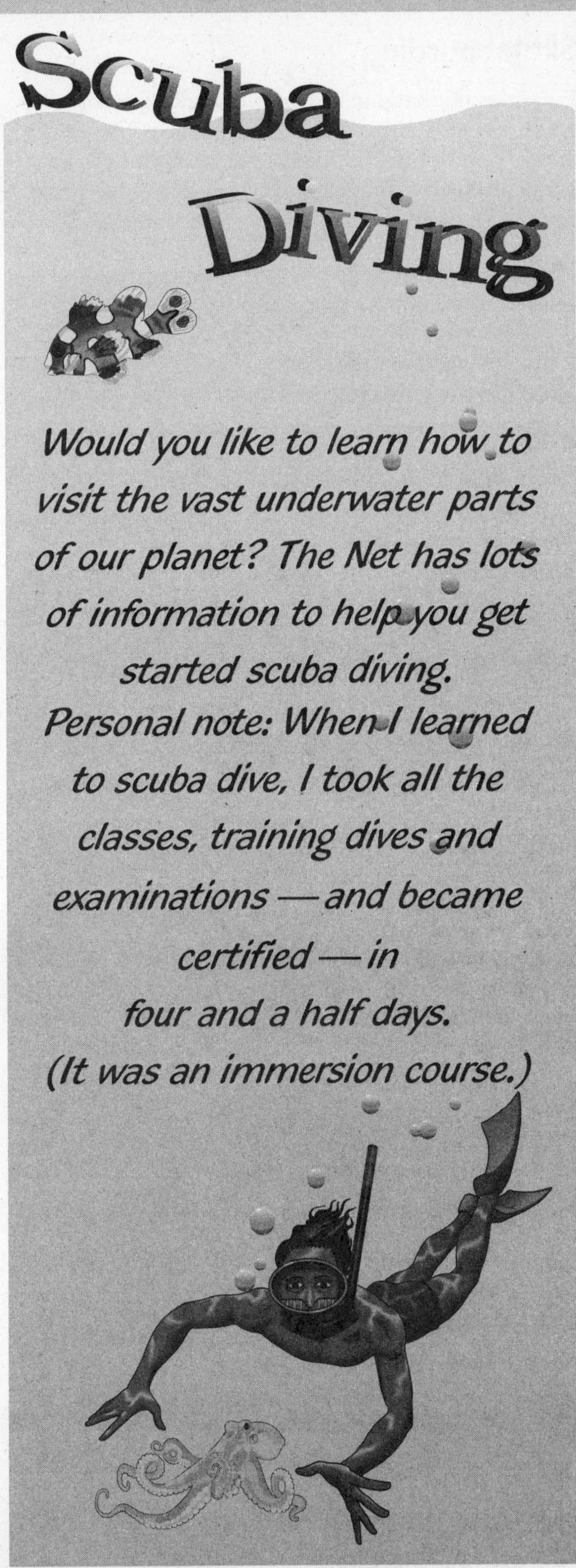

Skateboarding

Fun does not have to be complex. Take a plank, slap some wheels on it and suddenly you have a sport. Today's equipment is a lot better built, but the basic idea is the same. Skateboard enthusiasts can check out lots of good skateboarding stuff on the Net.

Web:

http://web.cps.msu.edu/~dunhamda/dw/
   dansworld.html
http://www.skatetalk.com/
http://www.tumyeto.com/

Usenet:

alt.skate-board

Skydiving

It seems as if jumping out of a perfectly good airplane would be a foolish thing to do. Actually, it isn't—not if you have the right equipment and you know what you are doing. I've been skydiving several times and, I can tell you, it's a wonderful thing to do, so why not give it a try?

Web:

http://www.afn.org/skydive/faq/faq.html
http://www.skydivewww.com/
http://www.soyouwanna.com/site/syws/skydiving/
   skydiving.html

Usenet:

rec.skydiving

Snowboarding

Snowboarding is a sometimes difficult, but always enjoyable, sport in which you ride a large, skateboard-shaped board down a hill of snow. There are snowboarders all over the world—wherever there is snow—and one of them can be you.

Web:

http://www.snowboarding.com/
http://www.snowboarding2.com/
http://www.vpas.fsnet.co.uk/rssFAQ/
http://www.wintercream.com/

Usenet:

rec.skiing.snowboard
rec.sport.snowboarding

Snowmobiles

A snowmobile is one thing at which you won't have to yell, "Mush!" Feed it some gas, tell it you love it, then ride like a maniac across the frozen tundra (or whatever happens to be in front of you). Avid snowmobile fans tell how they keep their machines happy, safe and healthy.

Web:

http://www.off-road.com/snowmobile/
http://www.snowmobile.org/

Usenet:

alt.snowmobiles
rec.sport.snowmobiles

Surfing

When I was a graduate student in San Diego, I took a surfing class during my first year. Since then, I have spent a lot of time in the ocean with my boogie board. This, of course, significantly enhances my skill as a writer. The nice thing is, now that we have the Net, you don't have to go to college just to learn how to surf.

Web:

http://www.boardfolio.com/
http://www.sdsc.edu/surf/surfer_resources.html
http://www.sur4.com/

Usenet:

alt.surfing

Report on Surfing
by Elmo (age 8)

I have a bodyboard and I am teaching myself to surf. It is a lot of fun because I get to paddle around the water, catch a wave, and zoom in.

Yesterday, I zoomed in next to my sister Lucy when she wasn't looking, and made noises like a shark to scare her. Ha, Ha! You should have seen her jump.

Also, I like surfing because some of the lifeguards are real babes.

-Elmo

Swimming

Swimming is a wonderful activity. It's great exercise and a lot of fun. When I was a tiny kid, my mother took me to the local Y, and (according to my father), I was swimming in the pool before I could even walk. When I was older, I went to camp every summer where I swam in a lake. Later, I moved to California and learned to swim in the ocean, which I found to be a completely different experience. (My favorite is the ocean.) You know, all this talk about water makes me feel awfully dry. I think it's time for a dip in the pool.

Web:
> http://www.swiminfo.com/
> http://www.swimmersguide.com/
> http://www.webswim.com/advice/faq.php

Usenet:
> rec.sport.swimming

Wakeboarding

Wakeboarding is an extreme water sport in which you ride a board with fins and foot bindings (a wakeboard), while holding on to a rope and being towed by a boat. The idea is to do a lot of hotshot maneuvers, such as the big crow, frontroll, scarecrow and elephant. Do it right and you'll spend a lot of time in the air. Do it wrong, and you'll spend a lot of time at the chiropractor.

Web:
> http://www.aquaskier.com/wakeboarding.htm
> http://www.prowakeboardtour.com/
> http://www.wakeworld.com/

Majordomo Mailing List:
> List Name: wakelist
> Subscribe to: majordomo@wakeboarder.com

Water Skiing

When I was a young lad at summer camp, I was able to water ski from time to time. Water skiing was the most popular waterfront activity, and we always had to wait a long time for our turn. We were allowed to ski about 2-3 minutes, at which time the ride ended so someone else could have a try. For some reason, water skiing was considered the coolest activity, and the water ski instructors were considered among the coolest guys in the entire camp. It was not uncommon to see them swanking around the waterfront area as if they owned the place, talking with pretty girls and working on their tans. From time to time, they would pause long enough to treat themselves to long ski rides during which they would show off to everyone else. Personally, I didn't care one whit, although I have no doubt that, today, all those guys are working in gas stations.

Web:
> http://www.iwsf.com/
> http://www.usawaterski.org/

Usenet:
> rec.sport.waterski

Windsurfing

Windsurfing is the ultimate sailing sport. You stand on what looks like a large surfboard and manipulate a sail. As the wind takes you, you use your weight and the position of the sail to control the direction and speed of your movement. Windsurfing is a demanding sport, so before you start, you may want to ask yourself if windsurfing is for you. Take this simple three-part quiz and find out: (1) Are you in excellent physical shape? (2) Do you enjoy water sports? (3) Are you willing to have more fun than almost everyone else in the world? If you answered yes, yes and yes, you should try windsurfing.

Web:
> http://www.boards.co.uk/
> http://www.windsurfer.com/newsite/
> http://www.worldwindsurf.com/

Usenet:
> rec.windsurfing

PEOPLE

Alumni Finders

Have you ever wondered what happened to that cheerleader with the blond ponytail from high school? (The one who invited you over to her house that day for "grilled cheese sandwiches".) Or what about that guy in your chemistry class? (The one who you think liked you, but would never actually tell you out loud.) Here is your chance to find that elusive someone-from-the-past and catch up on old times. Register for one of these find-an-alumnus services, and see who you can find (and who might find you).

Web:
  http://www.gradfinder.com/
  http://www.highschoolalumni.com/
  http://www.schoolbuddies.com/
  http://www.searchbug.com/peoplefinder/
    alumni1.asp

Billionaires

Get the goods on the world's richest people. In 2002, Forbes Magazine listed 497 billionaires, of which 243 are from the United States (including #1: Bill Gates). Check out how they made their money, their marital status, their ages, where they were born, and their education. Billionaire trivia: the top 25 billionaires are distributed as follows: United States (14), Germany (2), Hong Kong (2), Sweden (2), Canada (1), France (1), Mexico (1), Saudi Arabia (1) and Spain (1).

Web:
  http://www.forbes.com/billionaires/

Biographies

Have you ever had an uncontrollable urge to find out when Isaac Asimov was born, or when John Lennon married Yoko Ono, or if there was ever anyone famous named Hahn? As an Internet user, you never have to worry about your urges being denied, especially the uncontrollable ones. All the information you need about all the famous people that you might ever care about is only a few mouse clicks away. (By the way, the answers to the previous questions are 1920, 1969 and yes.)

Web:
  http://www.amillionlives.com/
  http://www.biography-center.com/
  http://www.ipl.org/div/subject/browse/ref15.00.00/

Charities

What can you do with all that extra money you have lying around? Why not give it to a charitable organization? You may not be able to use a tax deduction, but you can always use a few extra points with the Man (or Woman) Upstairs.

Web:
  http://www.charities.org/
  http://www.give.org/
  http://www.guidestar.org/

Communes and Intentional Communities

When I was an undergraduate, I lived in a dorm that was actually a co-op. That is, it was owned and operated by the students who lived in it. A student co-op is a type of organization that, today, is referred to as an "intentional community". In addition to student co-ops, other examples of intentional communities are communes (remember the 1970s?), land co-ops and farming collectives. What distinguishes such groups from commercial organizations is that intentional communities are owned by members who share a common philosophy. If you have ever thought about living with a group of unrelated people of your own choosing, you may want to learn about intentional communities.

Web:
  http://www.gaia.org/
  http://www.ic.org/

Cult of the Dead Cow

The Cult of the Dead Cow is the oldest underground telecommunications organization, dating back to 1986. Although the membership is small—consisting of only about 20 active members—their influence is felt around the world. The cult has a number of products, including the program Back Orifice, as well as a series of articles, written at various times by various members, with new articles being added from time to time. The articles are regularly read by thousands of people, so why not expand your mind and give it a try? Do you think you might like to join the cult as a member (as opposed to being an outsider)? Here is a hint: don't ask to join. Cult members are welcomed by invitation only, and once you ask, they will never invite you.

Web:
  http://www.cultdeadcow.com/

Dead People Info

Every now and then, you are bound to ask, "Whatever happened to so-and-so?" Is it possible that so-and-so is dead? Better check, just to be sure. It sounds a bit macabre, but these are actually good reference tools, and I find it interesting just to browse. The first thing I do is to check for my own name, just in case. (I never like to take anything for granted.)

Web:
> http://www.dpsinfo.com/dps.html
> http://www.whosaliveandwhosdead.com/

Expatriates and Refugees

An expatriate is a person who lives away from his or her native country. (I, for example, am a Canadian expatriate.) A refugee is an expatriate who leaves his or her native land for political or religious reasons, often because of persecution, expulsion or war. Expatriates of any type need to be able to fit into a new country while maintaining their personal culture. Refugees have, in addition, the more pressing needs of personal safety and well-being. If you are living away from your own country, for whatever reason, here are some resources that may be able to make your life a bit easier.

Web:
> http://www.1st-spot.net/topic_expat.html
> http://www.expatriates.com/directory/
> http://www.theirc.org/

Family Reunions

There are two types of families: those who have reunions, and those who wonder why anyone would want a reunion. If your family is the type that would enjoy getting together, maybe you should do it. Successful family reunions require a lot of preparation, so here are some resources to assist you in planning your gathering and spreading the word. As you plan your reunion, be sure to answer the four key questions: (1) Where will people stay? (2) What activities will be available? (3) What will everyone eat? (4) How can you keep Aunt Martha from pinching you on the cheek?

Web:
> http://genforum.genealogy.com/reunion/
> http://resources.rootsweb.com/~calendar/cgi-bin/
>   calendar.cgi?calname=family_reunions
> http://www.family-reunion.com/
> http://www.reunionsmag.com/reunions.html
> http://www.reuniontips.com/

Find-A-Grave

What do these people all have in common: Desi Arnaz, Albert Einstein, Greta Garbo, Jerry Garcia, Woody Guthrie, Alfred Hitchcock, Rock Hudson, Janis Joplin and John Lennon? The answer is they were all cremated. This is just one of the fascinating facts I found at the Find-A-Grave Web site. Look for your favorite dead person, and I bet you a cookie they are in the database. Isn't it comforting to know that, wherever you are in the world, you can find out where Marilyn Monroe is buried (at Westwood Memorial Park), display the exact street address, and look at a picture of her tombstone? This is an amazing site that you simply *must* visit at least once in your life.

Web:
> http://www.findagrave.com/

Finding famous people is not easy. Many of them take great pains to protect their privacy, and getting close to your favorite movie star or politician is usually next to impossible.

While they are alive, that is.

Once a famous person is dead, he or she is fair game. The next time you are looking for that elusive someone, check with the **Find-A-Grave** Web site.

Finding graves is not only fun, it's educational. Why, I bet you didn't know that Benjamin Harrison, the 23rd President of the United States, is buried in the same Indianapolis, Indiana, graveyard as John Dillinger, the notorious Depression-era gangster.

(Just another example of how people who read my books are able to stay so well informed.)

Finding People

You can run all over the Net, but it's getting harder and harder to hide. Here are some services to use when you need to track down that elusive someone. You can search for email addresses, phone numbers, postal addresses, Web page addresses, and so on. If you do not want your name listed in these directories, send them email and let them know. Hint: If you really need an email address, and all else fails, call the person on the phone and ask him.

Web:

http://people.yahoo.com/
http://www.411locate.com/
http://www.bigfoot.com/
http://www.teldir.com/
http://www.the-seeker.com/
http://www.theultimates.com/
http://www.whowhere.lycos.com/

Friendly People on IRC

Looking for some new friends? Try chatting on IRC. These channels are lively and always populated. It's the perfect place to start up a conversation and meet new people.

IRC:

#friends (DALnet, EFnet, Undernet)
#superfriends (EFnet)

Friendship Mailing Lists

If you want to make friends and meet some nice people, join one of these mailing lists. They were started as forums for people from anywhere to talk to anybody about anything anytime they want.

Majordomo Mailing List:

List Name: penpal
Subscribe to: majordomo@hazlett.net

Majordomo Mailing List:

List Name: tribe
Subscribe to: majordomo@oakland.edu

Goths

There's a lot more to being a goth than wearing black. As a rule, goths listen to gothic music and are well-read. Past that, it's hard to generalize. Many (but not all) goths enjoy things of a darker nature (such as movies like Nightmare Before Christmas, Edward Scissorhands, and horror films). The darklinks Web site is maintained by Carrie Carolin (one of the most wonderful goths on the Net). Visit and you will learn about gothic history, lifestyle, makeup, fashion and culture. When you want more, try the other Web sites, the Usenet groups and the IRC channel. On the Net, the culture of your choice is yours for the asking.

Web:

http://www.darklinks.com/dgothiclife.html
http://www.darkwave.org.uk/faq/ag/
http://www.gothic-classifieds.com/
http://www.toreadors.com/martha/

Usenet:

alt.gothic
alt.gothic.culture
alt.personals.gothic

IRC:

#darkgoth (Undernet)

Interesting People on the Web

The Internet is the largest gathering of people in the history of mankind, so you really have to go to extremes to stand out as "interesting". Well, these people manage to do it. Bizarre, unusual, unexpected, contorted, ingenious—this collection of strange, but true, humanoids will amuse and astonish you with the enchantment that only the extraordinary can bring to the otherwise dull, meaningless dance of life.

Web:

http://www.backupbrain.com/
http://www.flaunt.net/
http://www.grrl.com/
http://www.kottke.org/
http://www.photodude.com/weblog/
http://www.rebeccablood.net/

Kooks

On the Net, kooks are not only tolerated, they are venerated (at least by somebody, even if it's only their mother). Would you like to explore the mental cutting edge of humanity? These resources lay bare the glorious achievements of kookdom. Some of the kooks are the regular kind you find everywhere. Others are special Usenet kooks, who infest Usenet discussion groups.

Web:
> http://home.pacifier.com/~dkossy/kooksmus.html
> http://www.crank.net/usenet.html
> http://www.faqs.org/faqs/by-newsgroup/alt/
>   alt.usenet.kooks.html
> http://www.pcnet.com/~jdutka/nut/

Usenet:
> alt.usenet.kooks

Masons and Shriners

Freemasons (or Masons) are members of a worldwide fraternal organization named the Free and Accepted Masons. The origins of Freemasonry are lost to antiquity. Some historians trace its roots back to the Middle Ages. Modern Freemasonry started in England in 1717 with the formation of the first Grand Lodge. Masons pass through levels of membership called "degrees". The three basic degrees are Entered Apprentice, Fellowcraft and Master Mason. Once a person attains the third degree, he is deemed to be a member of the Blue Lodge and is considered a full-fledged Mason. He is then entitled to join the Scottish Rite or the York Rite. Within these Rites, a Mason may advance in degree: in the Scottish Rite through 29 more degrees, in the York Rite, through 9 more degrees. Once someone has advanced to the highest degree (of either Rite), he can petition to join the Shrine—more formally, the Ancient Arabic Order of Nobles of the Mystic Shrine—at which point he becomes a Shriner. (When the Shrine was started in 1872 in New York, an Arabic theme was chosen, which is why Shriners wear red fezzes. Notice that the initials AAONMS form an anagram for "A MASON".) Shriners and Masons are well known for their charitable work and for their emphasis on moral development. They are also known for their elaborate rituals and secret traditions. (See, for example, the 1983 book Big Secrets, by William Poundstone.)

Web:
> http://users.1st.net/fischer/freemas.htm
> http://www.shriners.com/

Usenet:
> alt.freemasonry
> alt.masonic.members
> soc.org.freemasonry

Mensa

Do you fancy yourself in the ranks of Isaac Asimov, Marilyn Vos Savant, Geena Davis, and other smart people? If so, maybe you should join Mensa. All you need to do is score within the top two percent of the population on a standardized intelligence test. Check out the official Mensa Web site for information about the organization.

Web:
> http://www.mensa.org/

Usenet:
> rec.org.mensa

Names

Names mean a lot. For example, suppose you are a guy in college, and a friend calls up and says, "Come and visit me next weekend, and I can get you a date with one of two girls. You can either have Bertha or Jasmine. Who do you want?" Come on, you know who you're going to pick. Since names are so important, I have found some resources that will help you understand names and what they mean to us. First, you can try a free name analysis. Find out what your name says about you. Second, you can look at Web pages created by or about people with the same first name (for example, people named "Eric" or "Jennifer").

Web:
   http://www.go2net.com/useless/useless/names.html
   http://www.grownmencry.com/mijo/Believeit.html
   http://www.kabalarians.com/gkh/your.htm

Nerds

Somewhere along the line, a bit flipped in the global memory bank and nerds became cool. So if you want to be cool, you need to know more about nerds, and these are the places to do it.

Web:
   http://www.nerdsrus.com/
   http://www.slashdot.org/

Usenet:
   alt.geek
   alt.nerd.obsessive

Non-Profit Organizations

A non-profit organization is one that is set up for a public purpose, not to generate profit. Most charities, for example, are non-profit organizations, although there are many, many other types, covering a wide variety of social needs. Would you like to volunteer, look for a job or internship, or simply find a particular organization? Perhaps you would like to start your own non-profit organization? The information you need is waiting for you on the Net. (Just make sure you don't make any money.)

Web:
   http://www.idealist.org/
   http://www.ipl.org/div/subject/browse/bus60.00.00/
   http://www.nonprofits.org/

Obituaries

Why settle for reading the obituaries in your local paper, when you can go global? Use the Net and you can find out about all manners of people who have died, from the well-known to the obscure, and back again.

Web:
   http://www.cyndislist.com/obits.htm
   http://www.obitcentral.com/
   http://www.obitlinkspage.com/
   http://www.obitpage.com/great_obits.html

Usenet:
   alt.obituaries

Wondering who's dead?
Read the **Obituaries** Web sites.

(As a matter of fact, why not look for your own name? No need to wait until the last moment.)

Pen Pals by Email

Looking for someone with whom you can exchange email? Check out these lists of people who are looking for pen pals. Along with the names of the people, there is also information about the languages they speak and their hobbies, so you can find someone suitable for you. If you really like writing other people, you might want to register your own name for one of these services and let other people find you.

Web:
   http://ppi.searchy.net/
   http://www.easypenpals.com/
   http://www.penpal-pinboard.de/
   http://www.penpal.net/

Usenet:
   soc.penpals

Personal Web Pages

Once you get caught up in the Web, it's hard to get away. Everywhere you look there are paths leading all over, and it's nearly impossible to get where you are going without getting sidetracked. One of my favorite ways to get sidetracked is to start with someone's personal home page and see where it leads. These Web sites attempt the impossible: to keep track of all the home pages on the Net. Look here if you are searching for someone's page, or if you want to pick a place at random to explore.

Web:
  http://dir.yahoo.com/society_and_culture/people/
    personal_home_pages/
  http://homepages.whowhere.com/
  http://www.bltg.com/people/

Politicians' Biographies

Where do politicians go when they die? I'm not sure, but on their way, they get buried somewhere. If you want to find that somewhere for an American politician, the Net will be glad to help. Along the way, you'll be able to find out general biographical information for a huge number of politicians: federal, state and local. If it's true that the only good politician is a dead politician, the United States certainly has a lot of good ones.

Web:
  http://bioguide.congress.gov/biosearch/
    biosearch.asp
  http://www.politicalgraveyard.com/

Shared Realities

Some days you just wake up and think to yourself, "Hey, I think I will be someone else today." It's easy when you participate in some of the shared realities of Usenet. In these groups, people assume a persona and write about their thoughts, feelings and actions as that character. Meet people, form bonds, make friends, entertain and be entertained. Even if you don't want to participate, these groups are fun to read because it's like seeing a story unfold before your eyes.

Usenet:
  alt.dragons-inn
  alt.kalbo
  alt.pub.coffeehouse.amethyst
  alt.pub.kacees
  alt.shared-reality.sf-and-fantasy
  alt.shared-reality.startrek.klingon

Shared Thoughts

"Thank you for sharing." That's what people all over the world will be saying to you once you participate in these Web sites. Start by looking. See how people with unresolved feelings send in a comment or letter for everyone to read. Then explore the archives, and marvel at how other people are sensitive, but you are even *more* sensitive. Now you are ready: share your thoughts.

Web:
  http://www.lowbrow.com/
  http://www.sothere.com/

Tea and Conversation

Join the silly, comfy, cozy good times at this tea party on the Web. Chatters sit having tea and conversation, making up stories, talking about their lives and generally having a fun time. The atmosphere is relaxed, friendly and comfortable.

Web:
  http://www.bensonassoc.com/pct/tea.html

Thank-You Notes

Would you like to know the secret of my success? It has to do with thank-you notes. Check out my Web site for the details. I hope, after reading what I have to say, you will become a thank-you note person (if you are not one already). If you start writing thank-you notes and it changes your life, please drop me a line and let me know what happened. (You can send me a note from my Web site.)

Web:
  http://www.harley.com/success/
  http://www.partymakers.com/tips_thank_you.asp

Town Criers

It has only been in the last hundred years that the general population has enjoyed a significant degree of literacy. In earlier times, information of general interest was often announced by a town crier: a person who would stand in a public place such as a market or a town hall, get everyone's attention, and then shout the news for everyone to hear. Although we don't use town criers today, the tradition lives on among history and reenactment buffs. In fact, some cities (such as London) still have an official town crier.

Web:

http://www.londonstowncrier.co.uk/magazine.htm
http://www.scottishtowncrier.com/
http://www.towncriers.be/
http://www.ushistory.org/towncrier/

Virtual Memorials

Those who die in the world of flesh and blood live on indefinitely in our hearts and minds. To maintain the memory of our loved ones, it is possible to create a virtual memorial: a Web page that describes and celebrates someone who has passed away. I am always touched when I visit these sites, as you will be. They are so full of life and happiness that the experience of visiting is more joyful than morose. Though we may struggle and complain, life, for all its turmoil, difficulties and uncertainties, is a lovely, delightful gift—and the whole thing is over much too soon.

Web:

http://catless.ncl.ac.uk/vmg/
http://www.griefnet.org/memcard.html

Volunteers

One of the best ways to feel good about yourself and about the world is to help someone else. If you are looking for somewhere to volunteer, you can use these Web sites for ideas and information. Some are for the United States only; others have global info. (If you can't find anything that looks good, I'm looking for a volunteer to help me brush my cat.)

Web:

http://www.globalvolunteers.org/
http://www.servenet.org/
http://www.volunteermatch.org/

Usenet:

alt.peace-corps
bit.org.peace-corps

Y Forum

The idea is to find out how and why people are different from each other. The medium is a forum open to anyone on the Net. The method is to ask questions about race relations to which people write serious, straightforward answers. It works.

Web:

http://www.yforum.com/welcome1.html

PEOPLE: FAMOUS AND INTERESTING

Allen, Woody

What are your favorite Woody Allen movies? My favorites are Manhattan, Annie Hall, Hannah and Her Sisters, and Play It Again Sam. Actually, I like all his movies, and I have seen them over and over and over, to the point where just about anything that happens in my life reminds me of something from one of the movies. In fact (and this is strictly between you and me), there have been a lot of times when people have thought I was spontaneously witty, when I was merely recycling lines from a Woody Allen film. Woody Allen (1935-), born Allan Stewart Konigsberg in Brooklyn, New York, is a lot more than a filmmaker. He is a superb actor, writer, playwright, musician (jazz clarinet) and stand-up comedian. It's hard to exaggerate the contribution that Allen has made to modern filmmaking: he is a cinematic genius of the first order, one whose films will be studied and enjoyed for years to come. A thousand years from now, Woody Allen will be one of the few people remembered from our time.

Web:

http://us.imdb.com/Name?Allen,+Woody
http://www.destinationhollywood.com/celebrities/
   woodyallen/
http://www.rkpuma.com/woody.htm
http://www.torp.priv.no/woody/

Usenet:

alt.fan.woody-allen

Listserv Mailing List:

List Name: woody-l
Subscribe to: listserv@westga.edu

British Royal Family

The British royal family has something to teach all of us. Follow their official and unofficial adventures and you will encounter intelligence, knowledge, industry, discretion and inspiration. You will also find foolishness, ignorance, sloth, indiscretion and just plain awful behavior. Here are some resources that help you keep abreast of anything royal worth knowing. First, you have two official Web sites: one for the entire royal family and one just for Charles (that is, Charles Philip Arthur George Mountbatten-Windsor, His Royal Highness the Prince of Wales, Duke of Cornwall, Duke of Rothesay, Earl of Carrick, Lord of Renfrew, Lord of the Isles, Prince and Great Steward of Scotland, and Earl of Chester). I have also included a more informal site that is anything but official. Using these resources, you'll be able to find out just about anything you need to know about Liz, Phil, Chuck, Wills, Harry, Andy, Sarah, Eddie, Sophie, Annie (and maybe even Camilla).

Web:

    http://www.ananova.com/news/
        index.html?keywords=royals&menu=news.royals
    http://www.etoile.co.uk/Rnews.html
    http://www.heraldica.org/faqs/britfaq.html
    http://www.princeofwales.gov.uk/
    http://www.royal.gov.uk/
    http://www.royalinsight.gov.uk/

Usenet:

    alt.gossip.royalty

British Royal Family

Being a queen sounds like a good job, but it's not all limo rides and free meals. There's a lot of hard work—and that goes for the other members of the royal family. Would you like to see what I mean? The official Royal Diary of Engagements is available on the Net, and you can take a look at it whenever you want. The next time your life feels too demanding and out of control, sneak a peek at the official schedule of Her Majesty, Queen Elizabeth II of Great Britain. I bet she'd trade places with you if she could.

Celebrity Addresses

Would you like to write to your favorite celebrity? Here are some Web sites that contain lots and lots of celebrity addresses, for both regular mail and email. You can also find some good tips on getting autographs, as well as other interesting information. Hint: If you send email to a celebrity, do not expect anything but an automated reply. If you get a personal reply, consider yourself doubly blessed (once because you got the reply, and once because you are one of my readers).

Web:

    http://home.ipoline.com/%7elegends/insatiable/
        spotlights/html/celebaddresses.html
    http://www.addresses.site2go.com/
    http://www.celebrityweb.com/address.htm
    http://www.islandnet.com/~luree/fanmail.html
    http://www.mailhollywood.com/
    http://www.reelclassics.com/Address/
        address-list.htm
    http://www.springrose.com/celebrity/

Celebrity Resources

Take my word for it. The day will come when you will need to know Jane Fonda's birthday, where Harrison Ford went to high school, or the latest gossip about Michael Jackson. When that day arrives, you will be ready. Just cruise over to the Net where the celebrity info you need is ready and waiting. (By the way, Jane's birthday is the same as mine, December 21; Harrison Ford went to Maine Township High in suburban Des Plaines, Illinois; and Michael Jackson did something really weird, just the other day.)

Web:

    http://www.abcnews.go.com/sections/
        entertainment/
    http://www.celeblink.com/
    http://www.celebrityweb.com/
    http://www.starseeker.com/
    http://www.worldhot.com/entertainment/celebrities/

Celebrity Talk and General Discussion

You've devoured every newspaper, magazine and tabloid in sight, and you still want more news and information about celebrities. Here are some sources that are available 24 hours a day, so you can always get a fix. Read stories, news and rumors of old and new famous people.

Web:
  alt.fan.shannen-doherty

Usenet:
  alt.celebrities
  alt.fan.actors
  alt.fan.adam-sandler
  alt.fan.alicia-silverstone
  alt.fan.alyssa-milano
  alt.fan.ashley-judd
  alt.fan.barbra.streisand
  alt.fan.brad-pitt
  alt.fan.british-actors
  alt.fan.brooke-shields
  alt.fan.bruce-campbell
  alt.fan.bruce-willis
  alt.fan.calista-flockhart
  alt.fan.cameron-diaz
  alt.fan.carmen-electra
  alt.fan.chow-yun-fat
  alt.fan.christina-applegate
  alt.fan.claire-danes
  alt.fan.courteney-cox
  alt.fan.crispin-glover
  alt.fan.danielle-fishel
  alt.fan.david-duchovny
  alt.fan.david-gallagher
  alt.fan.denise-richards
  alt.fan.dermot-mulroney
  alt.fan.drew-barrymore
  alt.fan.errol-flynn
  alt.fan.fairuza-balk
  alt.fan.george-clooney
  alt.fan.gillian-anderson
  alt.fan.gwyn-paltrow
  alt.fan.hannigan
  alt.fan.harrison-ford
  alt.fan.heather-locklear
  alt.fan.helen-hunt
  alt.fan.hudson-leick
  alt.fan.j-garofalo
  alt.fan.jen-aniston
  alt.fan.jennifer-connelly
  alt.fan.jennifer-lopez
  alt.fan.jennifer-love-hewitt

  alt.fan.jenny-mccarthy
  alt.fan.jeri-ryan
  alt.fan.jerky-boys
  alt.fan.jessica-alba
  alt.fan.jodie-foster
  alt.fan.john-cusack
  alt.fan.john-travolta
  alt.fan.julia-roberts
  alt.fan.kate-winslet
  alt.fan.katie-holmes
  alt.fan.keanu-reeves
  alt.fan.kevin-spacey
  alt.fan.kirsten-dunst
  alt.fan.leo-dicaprio
  alt.fan.linda-hamilton
  alt.fan.lisa-boyle
  alt.fan.liv-tyler
  alt.fan.meg-ryan
  alt.fan.mich-pfeiffer
  alt.fan.milla-jovovich
  alt.fan.mira-furlan
  alt.fan.natalie-portman
  alt.fan.neve
  alt.fan.nicole-kidman
  alt.fan.noah-wyle
  alt.fan.olsen-twins
  alt.fan.pam-anderson
  alt.fan.phoebe-cates
  alt.fan.pierce-brosnan
  alt.fan.renee-oconnor
  alt.fan.ricci.christina
  alt.fan.robin-williams
  alt.fan.sandra-bullock
  alt.fan.sarah-m-gellar
  alt.fan.sarah.jessica.parker
  alt.fan.schwarzenegger
  alt.fan.sophie-marceau
  alt.fan.tarantino
  alt.fan.tea-leoni
  alt.fan.teen.idols
  alt.fan.teen.starlets
  alt.fan.tiffani-amber-thiessen
  alt.fan.val-kilmer
  alt.fan.will-smith
  alt.fan.winona-ryder
  alt.fan.yasmine-bleeth
  alt.gossip.celebrities
  alt.movies.bruce-lee
  alt.movies.jackie-chan
  alt.movies.marilyn-monroe
  alt.movies.robert-deniro

Dance, dance, dance... rest.

Einstein, Albert

If you ask a man on the street who the greatest scientist of all time was, you would probably get the answer Albert Einstein. Einstein (1879-1955) was born in Germany, although he went to a university in Switzerland and, later, became an American. (Like many other great men, Einstein had the distinction of ending his life in New Jersey.) It would be difficult to exaggerate Einstein's contribution to twentieth-century physics (but let me try anyway). His work on relativity completely changed the way mankind thought about space and time, while his work on quantum physics helped create our modern understanding of how energy and matter are constituted and laid the basis for the exploitation of atomic energy. Einstein won the 1921 Nobel Prize in Physics (for his explanation of the photoelectric effect, not for his relativity theory). Like many other great scientists, Einstein did not seem to have as great an acumen about people and society as he did about science. His scientific insight—at least when he was young—was astonishing. His social insights were well-intentioned but somewhat naive. I guess the best way to put it is that, when it came to understanding the universe Einstein had no peer, but when it came to understanding people he was no Einstein.

Web:
  http://www.westegg.com/einstein/

Famous People's Wills

Are you surprised? Not me, I knew it had to be somewhere on the Net: the last wills and testaments of famous people. See what the likes of Jacqueline Kennedy Onassis, John Lennon, Walt Disney, Babe Ruth and Benjamin Franklin left to posterity. (They also have Elvis's will. I checked, but unfortunately he didn't leave me anything.)

Web:
  http://www.courttv.com/legaldocs/newsmakers/
    wills/
  http://www.johnventura.com/famouswills.htm

Fuller, Buckminster

What do you do in your spare time? Most people read, play sports or watch TV. Not many could say, "Well, I had a lot of time on my hands last weekend, so I invented the geodesic dome." Get to know Buckminster Fuller, his works and philosophy.

Web:
  http://www.cjfearnley.com/fuller-faq.html
  http://www.hearingvoices.com/bucky/
  http://www.thirteen.org/cgi-bin/bucky-bin/bucky.cgi

Usenet:
  alt.bucky-fuller
  bit.listserv.geodesic

Listserv Mailing List:
  List Name: **geodesic**
  Subscribe to: **listserv@listserv.acsu.buffalo.edu**

Buckminster Fuller

Richard Buckminster Fuller was a genius in that he could shed light on just about any area to which he turned his attention. During his lifetime, he received 39 honorary degrees and became the inspiration for a cult-like following based not so much on a belief system, but on a way of looking at the world and solving its problems. He described himself as an "engineer, inventor, mathematician, architect, cartographer, philosopher, poet, cosmologist, comprehensive designer and choreographer". What I like best about Fuller is how he lived his life as an experiment, and his recognition that if one contributes to one's culture, the economy will lend support in an appropriate manner. Although this may seem far-fetched, it is this Fuller-inspired philosophy that has helped me to choose my lot in life and is indirectly responsible for the book you are now reading. If you would like to learn more about Fuller, his teachings and his followers, subscribe to the **geodesic** mailing list. It is wonderful to contemplate the work of someone who has the capacity to rise above the petty concerns of day-to-day life and to see the universe with the eyes of enlightened curiosity.

Gates, Bill

Isn't it great that we all get to live on this Earth at the same time as Bill Gates? Why not send him a letter, right now, and tell him how much you appreciate his efforts to save mankind. (I'd suggest sending him email, but Windows might crash.)

Web:
  http://www.microsoft.com/billgates/
  http://www.netfunny.com/cgi-bin/library/
     searchindex/query.pl?swishindex=/www/etc/
     jokedex&keywords="bill+gates"
  http://www.philip.greenspun.com/humor/
     bill-gates.html

Usenet:
  alt.fan.bill-gates

Hitler, Adolf

If there is one person in history whose activities changed the world the most, that person would have to be Adolf Hitler. Hitler (1889-1945) was the German dictator who founded the National Socialism (Nazi) movement (1920), and led Germany and its allies into World War II (1939-1945). As a result much of the world was plunged into the most devastating war in history, with over 60 million people killed. As a young man, Hitler served in the Bavarian army during World War I. (Bavaria is a part of Germany.) Although he was recognized for bravery, the experience embittered him, and he blamed Germany's defeat on Jews and Marxists. In 1923, Hitler unsuccessfully attempted to overthrow the Bavarian government and was imprisoned for nine months. During that time, Hitler wrote the book "Mein Kampf" ("My Struggle"), in which he laid bare his theories of hate and anti-Semitism, and his plans for world domination, a vision in which the German master race would create the "Third Reich". ("Germany will either become a World Power or will not continue to exist at all."—Vol. 2, Ch. XIV) Eventually, "Mein Kampf" became the bible of the Nazi party. Hitler's movement, however, grew slowly until the Great Depression, during which Hitler's skills as a speaker and organizer allowed him to capitalize on the growing social and economic unrest. As a master of the "big lie", he was able to build substantial grass-roots support, based on a platform of anti-Semitism and anti-communism. Although he had some false starts, Hitler eventually became Chancellor of Germany (1933), and within a year, was given full dictatorial powers by the government. In concert with other Nazi leaders—principally Goering, Himmler and Goebbels—Hitler crushed all opposition and took control of most facets of German life. In 1934, laws were passed to establish official anti-Semitism and to create the first concentration camps. Over the next few years, Hitler prepared Germany for war, and made many political maneuvers that allowed him to extend his power into smaller, less powerful countries. In 1939, he invaded Poland, causing the Allies to declare war on Germany and start World War II. At first, Germany had a great deal of military success. However, in 1941, the United States entered the war, which helped turn the tide. Eventually, Germany and its allies (called the Axis) were defeated. As the Third Reich collapsed around him, Hitler hid in an underground bunker in Berlin as the Russians approached the city. On April 29, 1945, he married Eva Braun (his longtime mistress), and on April 30 they committed suicide. (Adolf Hitler, April 26, 1942: "This war no longer bears the characteristics of former inter-European conflicts. It is one of those elemental conflicts which usher in a new millennium and which shake the world once in a thousand years.")

Web:
  http://www.historyplace.com/worldwar2/
     riseofhitler/
  http://www.hitler.org/
  http://www.stormfront.org/posterity/mk/

Usenet:
  alt.fan.adolf-hitler

Inventors

Few people have the genius to extend current technology significantly. However, in every age, the advance of civilization has always been dependent upon new inventions. Much of what we take for granted was created, after a great deal of hard work, by people who are, all too often, forgotten. These resources will help you understand and appreciate the men and women to whom we all owe so much: the inventors.

Web:
  http://web.mit.edu/invent/www/archive.html
  http://www.invent.org/hall_of_fame/1_1_search.asp

Usenet:
  alt.inventors
  alt.inventorworld

Marx Brothers

The Marx Brothers knew how to make people laugh better than any other comedy group in modern history. All of the Marx Brothers were born in New York. Three of them were comedians: Groucho [Julius] (1895-1977), Harpo [Arthur] (1893-1964) and Chico [Leonard] 1891-1961. Groucho, who had a fast and furious wit, was the undisputed standout. Chico spoke in an imitation Italian accent and played the piano. Harpo did not speak (although he could); he honked a horn, did slapstick and played the harp. Two other brothers joined the act at various times, but played straight roles: Zeppo [Herbert] (1901-1979) and Gummo [Milton] (1892-1977). The group got their start at an early age as a vaudeville singing group, managed by their stage mother Minnie (who herself was an experienced performer). The act evolved into a zany amalgam of puns and wisecracks, slapstick, sight gags, and a great deal of silliness. In 1924, the brothers had their first big-time hit with the Broadway play "I'll Say She Is". In 1929, they released "The Coconuts", the first of 12 classic movies. The Marx Brothers disbanded in 1941. However, Groucho went on to enjoy a successful solo career as a radio and TV performer (as host of the quiz show "You Bet Your Life"), and as a writer.

Web:
  http://hometown.aol.com/sillysongbook/
    MARXBROS.html
  http://members.aye.net/~mainman/groucho/
  http://w1.660.telia.com/~u66002771/intro.htm
  http://www.marx-brothers.org/
  http://www.marxbros.yucom.be/
  http://www.whyaduck.com/contents.htm

Usenet:
  alt.comedy.marx-bros

Majordomo Mailing List:
  List Name: **marx-brothers**
  Subscribe to: **majordomo@lists.panix.com**

There is no doubt about it: the **Pope** is one of the greatest human beings in the world. If you would like information about the Pope's books or biographical data, check out this unofficial home page.

By the way, the Pope and I have a deal. I promised to mention him in my books, and he promised to mention me in his books.

Nobel Prize Winners

The Nobel prizes are named after Alfred Nobel (1833-1896), a Swedish inventor, who left the legacy establishing awards to be given for extraordinary achievement. Have you ever wondered if maybe you have won a Nobel Prize, but you never found out because your phone was off the hook? (Don't laugh, this actually happened to me twice.) Well, stop worrying. Here is information about all the Nobel prize winners. The categories are chemistry, economics, literature, peace, physics, and physiology/medicine. There is also a special list of all the women who have been awarded Nobel prizes.

Web:
  http://www.nobel.se/
  http://www.nobelprizes.com/nobel/

Pope John Paul II

Need a fast dose of religious experience? Check out these Pope-related Web sites, one of which is the official Vatican site. Read some of his writings and find out where the Pope is traveling in case you want to call ahead and make arrangements to have dinner with him. If you do see the Pope, tell him I said hello.

Web:
  http://www.newadvent.org/Popes/ppjp02.htm
  http://www.vatican.va/holy_father/john_paul_ii/

Randi, James

James Randi (1928-)—The Amazing Randi—is a Canadian-born American magician and skeptic who debunks fraudulent paranormal events and claims. Randi offers a half million dollars to any person who can prove, under his scientific conditions, that he or she has psychic powers. This Web site explains about Randi and what he does, including the James Randi Educational Foundation. To me, Randi is truly one of the heroes of our time, debunking foolishness and superstition, and shedding light into the dark recesses of ignorance and dishonesty.

Web:
  http://www.randi.org/

Real Names of Famous People

Have you ever wondered why actress Lauren Bacall did not use her real name in show business? Perhaps because it's Betty Joan Perske, and tell the truth; would you write a letter to Abigail van Buren (Dear Abby) asking for advice if you knew her real name was Pauline Esther Friedman and her friends called her "Pop"? Find out the real names of your favorite celebrities and, who knows, the knowledge may one day save your life. By the way, did you know that Michael J. Fox's real name was Michael A. Fox? (He didn't want the headlines in fan magazines to read "Michael, A Fox".)

Web:

  http://www.celebrityalmanac.com/

Three Stooges

One of the biggest differences between men and women is that women don't understand the Three Stooges (which, if you think about it, is probably a good thing). The Three Stooges were popular during the 1930s, 1940s and 1950s, when they created hundreds of short films that were shown in movie theaters and, later, on television. The Stooges got their start on the vaudeville stage, but their act is far more reminiscent of what used to be called burlesque, with its sight gags, pratfalls and general clowning around. Two of the Stooges, Moe Howard (1897-1975) and Larry Fine (1902-1975) were permanent members of the group. The third stooge was played by several different actors over the years: Curly Howard (1903-1952), Shemp Howard (1895-1955), Joe Besser (1907-1988) and Curly Joe DeRita (1909-1993).

Web:

  http://members.aol.com/jander7103/stooge/
    stooge.htm
  http://www.three-stooges.net/
  http://www.threestooges.com/welcome.htm

Usenet:

  alt.comedy.slapstick.3-stooges

IRC:

  #stooges

Archie Andrews

Since the 1940s, Archie Andrews and his friends have been part of our culture. When I was young, I loved reading Archie comics and, to tell you the truth, I still do. Archie, Betty, Veronica, Jughead, Reggie and Moose are perpetually young students at Riverdale High School. They live in a world in which activities change with the season, fashion changes with the years, but no one ever grows older, and nothing really terrible ever happens. I grew up with Archie, so I always think of him as being a bit like me. That is, I did, until one day I read something that allowed me to figure out the age of his parents, and I realized that I was now older than Archie's father. (Nevermind, I still like to read the stories.)

Web:

  http://www.archiecomics.com/
  http://www.toonopedia.com/archie.htm

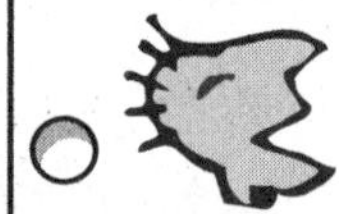

Report on Indiana Jones
by Elmo (age 8)

Last week, I decided to become a secret adventurer, just like Indiana Jones.

My sister Lucy thinks she is so cool because she keeps a secret diary that no one can look at. I hid in her closet while she was writing and, when she left the room, I sneaked over and read what she had written.

At first, I thought Lucy had seen me, but then I realized she hadn't because she wrote that, because I was so sweet, she was trying to save enough money to get me a present for my birthday. So I took the diary, put it on my father's desk, and left it open at that page.

I bet Indiana Jones would have done the exact same thing.

-Elmo

Later tonight, the Internet will close for 1.5 seconds (but no one will notice).

Barbie and Ken

You and I may wonder about the meaning of life, but Barbie knows—without even the tiniest smidgen of doubt—that she is part of this universe for only one reason: to wear clothes. Barbie is a teenage fashion model who has the highest quality, most diverse wardrobe in the history of mankind. Name an activity, a setting, or a special occasion—Barbie has the clothes to match. Moreover, she has the body to wear her clothes as they deserve to be worn. She has beautiful long legs and arms, an arching neck, naturally blond hair, and a more-than-perfect figure. Her eyes are alluring, her makeup is perfect and, in her entire life, she has never had even a hint of a bad hair day. As the years pass; Barbie may change slightly, but she never ages, never retains water, her face never breaks out, and she never puts on even five extra pounds. Barbie's perfection also extends to her steady boyfriend Ken, a social accessory who shares her perpetual youth and devotion to tasteful, complacent well-being. When it is convenient, Barbie has four younger siblings: Skipper, Stacie and Todd (the twins) and Kelly. Barbie lives in the dream world of every pre-adolescent girl, with the perfect body, the perfect clothes, the perfect boyfriend, and no parents or homework to get in the way. She is the ultimate bimbo, an icon who revels in idiosyncrasy, but whose popularity derives from the sheer force of her predictability.

Web:
   http://www.barbiecollectibles.com/about/history.asp
   http://www.dolls4play.com/barbiehistory.html
   http://www.manbehindthedoll.com/
   http://www.people.virginia.edu/~tsawyer/barbie/
      barb.html

Usenet:
   alt.collecting.barbie

Indiana Jones

In a world in which many of our heroes are nothing but image, Henry (Indiana) Jones Jr. (1899-19??) is pure substance. He is handsome, brave, strong and lucky, a larger-than-life adventurer with a propensity to be in the right place at the right time, as well as the wrong place at the wrong time. Jones is an American, born in New Jersey on July 1, 1899, to parents Henry Sr. (a Scotsman) and Anna (from Virginia). In his youth, Jones traveled widely throughout Europe, Asia and Africa, often in the company of his parents and his tutor, Helen Seymour. In 1920, at the age of 20, Jones went to study history and archaeology at the University of Chicago, from which he graduated in 1922. He then moved to Paris, where he enrolled as a graduate student in linguistics at the Sorbonne. However, before long, he changed to archaeology, which soon became his lifelong pursuit. In 1925, he graduated from t he Sorbonne and went to work as a professor at London University. Even as an adult, Jones was never one to stay in one place for very long, and he punctuated bouts of teaching at various schools (including Princeton and the University of Chicago) with a great many adventures around the world. Eventually, he settled into teaching history and archaeology at Marshall College (later known as Barnett College), a small school in Connecticut. Jones married twice. His first wife Deirdre (married in April 1926), died soon after the wedding in a plane crash. In the fullness of time, after Jones was widowed a second time, he retired to New York, where he lived with his daughter and her two children, Spike and Lucy.

Web:
   http://www.indianajones.de/main_site/
      indianajones.html
   http://www.indy-web.com/
   http://www.indyfan.com/
   http://www.theindyexperience.com/index.html
   http://www.theraider.net/

Time to check your email.

James Bond

James Bond is a fictional spy created by Ian Fleming (1908-1964). Fleming wrote 14 books—mostly novels, some short stories—from Casino Royale (1953) to Octopussy (published in 1966). After Fleming's death, Bond books were written by other authors, in particular, John Gardner. The first James Bond film was Dr. No (1962) starring Sean Connery. Since then, many Bond movies have been made with a variety of actors. Fleming's original James Bond is a post-World War II agent of the British Secret Service and has the identification number 007. (The "00" prefix indicates that Bond is licensed to kill in the line of duty.) Through the years, the depiction of Bond (and the British Secret Service) has changed. What has not changed is Bond's basic character: a highly skilled, handsome, self-reliant man, with an affinity for danger, high-performance cars, gourmet food and wine, and beautiful women. (In other words, if James Bond were a real person, he would be an Internet author.)

Web:

  http://www.007database.com/
  http://www.ajb007.co.uk/
  http://www.ianfleming.org/mkkbb/afjbfaq/
  http://www.jamesbondcollective.com/
  http://www.klast.net/bond/
  http://www.universalexports.net/

Usenet:

  alt.fan.james-bond

James Bond

What do you do when you are about to entertain that special someone at an exclusive restaurant, and you can't recall whether the martini should be shaken or stirred, or you are not sure how to ask for your tagliatelle verde to be prepared? In most cases, about all you could do would be to trust in blind faith or hope that I might be in the same restaurant and you could ask me.

However, if you have access to the Net, you can check with one of the **James Bond** Web sites. You'll find enough Bond information to choke a 1954 Continental Bentley with the "R" type chassis, the big 6 engine and a 13:40 back-axle ratio.

Lara Croft

Lara Croft is the perfect woman. She was born on February 14, 1967 in Wimbledon, England, into a British upper-class family. She's brave, talented, tough, skillful, and she travels the world having adventures and solving puzzles. Lara is also very attractive (5'9" tall, 115 pounds, 34D-24-35), extremely popular and single. (Lara travels alone!) In fact, I can think of only one drawback to Lara Croft: she's not real. Lara is the heroine of the Tomb Raider video games (produced by the Eidos company) and a movie (starring Angelina Jolie). Of course, whether or not Lara's non-existence is really a drawback depends on your point of view. As I once heard an Eidos spokesman explain, "She's a great person to have. She doesn't have an agent, and she always says yes."

Web:

  http://www.larainmotion.com/net.htm
  http://www.larasanctuary.com/
  http://www.planetlara.com/

Usenet:

  alt.fan.lara-croft

Perry Mason

Sometimes people ask me, do you have a hero? Is there someone you really admire? The answer is, yes, Perry Mason. Perry Mason is the main character of 86 books published by the prolific author Erle Stanley Gardner (1889-1970) between 1933 to 1973. Although Gardner's stories were dramatized for television (and the movies), the Perry Mason I love is not the one you see on TV. The *real* Perry Mason is the one in the books. He is strong, brave, knowledgeable and loyal to his principles. Mason practices law in Los Angeles, and does so in his own way, assisted by long-time secretary Della Street and private detective Paul Drake. Every story involves a murder and Mason defends the person charged with the crime. Eventually, Mason figures out who really did it and frees his client. What I like about Mason is his personal strength of character. He is never afraid to do what is right, even if it will make him unpopular.

Web:

  http://members.ozemail.com.au/~jsimko/
  http://www.erlestanleygardner.com/
  http://www.totaldanger.com/td_pages/perrypages/
    perryframeset1.html

Santa Claus

It's nice to know that as busy as Santa is, he always has time to stay up with the latest technology. Send your wish list to Santa by email or you can see what he, the elves and reindeer are doing on the Web. Maybe if you are especially good this year, Santa will bring you a high-speed Internet connection for the holidays.

Web:

http://www.claus.com/
http://www.emailsanta.com/
http://www.northpole.com/village.html
http://www.santaclaus.com/

Sherlock Holmes

Sherlock Holmes (1854-?), the world's first consulting detective, is the most famous detective in history. Holmes lives at 221B Baker Street in London, both alone and with his friend and biographer Dr. John Watson. Between 1878 and 1891, Holmes investigated hundreds of cases, sixty of which were documented by Watson. Holmes is not perfect, but he has great appeal, due to his intelligence, knowledge, persistence, precision, attention to detail, and an uncanny ability to solve problems that baffle everyone else, including the police. Is there any intelligent, logical person who does not identify with Holmes when he says (in "The Red Headed League"), "My life is spent in one long effort to escape from the commonplace of existence?"

Web:

http://www.citsoft.com/holmes3.html
http://www.magicdragon.com/SherlockHolmes/
    resumes/Holmes.html
http://www.sherlockian.net/
http://www.sherlockworld.com/
http://www.sherylfranklin.com/sherlock.html

Usenet:

alt.fan.holmes

Listserv Mailing List:

List Name: hounds-l
Subscribe to: listserv@listserv.kent.edu

Space Ghost

In 1966, Space Ghost debuted as a cartoon superhero, part of the series "Space Ghost and Dino Boy". Space Ghost is tall and powerful, and wears a black hood and a yellow cape. In each of the original seven-minute cartoons, Space Ghost would use his powers to save the universe (or whatever needed saving that day). Flash forward to 1994. Space Ghost now has his own late-night talk show. He interviews real guests and is ably assisted by several former bad guys: Zorak, the band leader (and The Original Way Outs); and Moltar, the director. The show "Space Ghost Coast to Coast" has attracted a niche of people who like their talk shows to be tongue-in-cheek, superficial, unpredictable and very strange.

Web:

http://www.lustforlunch.com/dgp/
http://www.renegadechickens.com/spaceghost/
    SG.htm
http://www.tntie.com/ashleys4jc/

Usenet:

alt.fan.space-ghost

Listserv Mailing List:

List Name: ghost-planet
Subscribe to: listserv@lists.duke.edu

Spock

Spock is a Star Trek character from the original series and from the Star Trek movies. Spock was born on the planet Vulcan, in 2230, in the city of Shi'Kahr. His mother, Amanda Grayson, was a human schoolteacher from Earth; his father, Sarek, was a diplomat from Vulcan. The natives of Vulcan are known for their logic and rationalism, but Spock's personality is tempered by his Earth genes. Between 2249 and 2253, Spock trained at the Starfleet Academy (service number S179-276 SP). He was the first Vulcan ever to enlist in the Federation Starfleet and, from 2265 to 2269, served as the science officer aboard the original U.S.S. Enterprise. Why is Spock so popular? Perhaps it is the dichotomy of logic versus emotion, which never really stops tormenting him. As Spock himself says (in "The Way to Eden"), "Many myths are based on truth."

Web:

   http://www.cs.ubc.ca/cgi-bin/nph-spock
   http://www.scifi.com/startrek/cast/spock.html
   http://www.stinsv.com/TOS/spockcat.htm
   http://www.theborgcollective.com/frames/spock.htm

Superman

Superman came to Earth as a baby in a rocket ship. The ship was sent by his father, Jor-el, from the planet Krypton. Superman was found and adopted by a kindly couple, Jonathan and Martha Kent. Superman grew up with super powers and learned to use them to fight evil. When he is not fighting evil, he takes on the persona of his secret identity, Clark Kent. This he has been doing continuously since 1934, first in comic books, then on radio, television and in the movies. Along the way, the Superman mythos has changed significantly several times. My favorite Superman stories are those of the Silver Age comics (1959-1970), in which Superman/Clark Kent lives in Metropolis and is a reporter for the Daily Planet. His (sort of) girlfriend is Lois Lane, his pal is Jimmy Olsen, and his boss is Perry White, and life is strange but predictable.

Web:

   http://www.members.aol.com/smanfan/
   http://www.superman.ws/stta/
   http://www.supermanhomepage.com/

Usenet:

   alt.comics.superman
   alt.tv.superman-adventures
   rec.arts.sf.superman

Majordomo Mailing List:

   List Name: **kal-l**
   Subscribe to: **majordomo@kal-l.com**

Zorro

Zorro (1782-18??) is a masked adventurer, known for fighting the unjust Spanish rulers of the pueblo (town) of Riena de Los Angeles in the early 19th century. Zorro, whose real name was Don Diego de la Vega, was the son of Don Alejandro de la Vega, a wealthy landowner, and Chiquita de la Cruz, both of whom were Spanish. The de la Vegas traveled to California in 1781, where their son was born a year later. While Zorro was still a child, his mother died, and he was sent to Madrid to finish his education. Upon his return, he found that the residents of Los Angeles were oppressed by the cruel Spanish rulers. Zorro devoted himself to fighting the injustice, using his expertise with swords and whips, his considerable skills as a horseman, and his native cunning and bravery. In order to protect himself, he adopted a secret identity, "El Zorro" (the fox), and dressed in a black costume with a mask.

Web:

   http://www.billcotter.com/zorro/
   http://www.pjfarmer.com/woldnewton/Zorro.htm
   http://www.toptown.com/innercircle/billyt/
      zorinfo.htm

PERSONALS AND DATING

Blind Dates

It's one of those really bad experiences: your friends made the blind date sound fabulous, yet you are stuck in the reality of actually interacting with a person whom you would rather be helping board a plane to the Bermuda Triangle. Don't get stuck in this kind of situation. Check out these Web sites. They may save your life.

Web:

   http://ifaq.wap.org/sex/blinddates.html
   http://www.zealmag.com/winter00/blinddates.html

Chit-Chat

The nice thing about IRC is that you can join a channel to talk about something specific, or you can just sit around and talk, talk, talk. If you are in the mood to chat about nothing in particular, try one of these channels and ramble to your heart's content.

IRC:

#chatfun (EFnet)
#funchat (DALnet, Undernet)
#hottub (DALnet, EFnet, Undernet)

Dating and Tests

Do you date? Do you like taking tests? Try these. Some are silly and just for fun. Some are serious and are designed to help you with your dating. See if you can figure out which is which.

Web:

http://www.allthetests.com/relationship.php3
http://www.coolquizzes.com/love/flirt.shtml
http://www.ecrush.com/quizzes/rad/
http://www.queendom.com/tests/relationships/

Dating Resources

Who couldn't use a bit of help with dating? Well, the Net is always ready to help. You'll find advice, ideas, advice, articles, advice, useful information, advice, stories and advice. (Have you ever noticed how other people love to give you advice about your love life?)

Web:

http://www.dateable.com/
http://www.datingace.com/links/directories.htm
http://www.datingdilemmas.com/
http://www.dreamdatesuperlinks.com/
http://www.geekcheck.com/

> **If you think this is funny, you should see my license plate.**

Foreign Brides

For one reason or another, there are many men who want to get married but cannot find a suitable woman in their own country. This is not to say such women do not exist. There may be many such women—it's just that they cannot find them. Some of these men look for a bride in a foreign country. If you think you might want to be one of these men, the Net is a good place to start. However, before you start, I have some advice for you. (1) Think three times before you make any commitments. (2) Think four times before you send any money.

Web:

http://www.bridesbymail.com/library/library.html
http://www.filipinawives.com/
http://www.russianwomenbrides.com/faq.htm
http://www.rwguide.com/
http://www.wildxangel.com/buyabride.htm

Friendly Folk

You can never have too many friends (unless they all want to stay over at your house on the same weekend). Make and keep friends all over the world by visiting these IRC channels. It's fun and fast-paced and best of all, it's cheaper than paying for a long-distance phone call.

IRC:

#cyberfriends (EFnet)
#friendly (DALnet)
#friendship (DALnet)

Internet Romances

Have you met on the Net? Are you planning a hot romance with a net.friend? Optimists, pessimists and fans of the electronic sociological experience should have a look at this collection of resources about romance on the Internet. These writings offer some practical advice and a little dose of reality.

Web:

http://www.internetromance.org/
http://www.lovestory.com.au/
http://www.saferdating.com/
http://www.sage-hearts.com/advice/
http://www.wildxangel.com/

Jewish Personals

If you are looking for more than a good matzo ball recipe, take a look at these Internet resources specifically related to Jewish people. You can post ads whether you are Jewish or just looking for someone Jewish to date.

Web:
   http://www.jcupid.com/
   http://www.jdate.com/
   http://www.thejewishpeople.org/jsc/npp.html

Usenet:
   alt.personals.jewish

Large People

Why bother with skinny, insubstantial waifs when you can go for the romantic gusto? Join the people who appreciate large men and women by reading the ads in these Usenet groups or posting an ad of your own. The **tall** group is for people who are especially tall (or who want a tall partner); the **fat** group is for heavy people, while **big-folks** caters to those who are generally large. Spend some time on Usenet and it won't be long before you'll come to appreciate how often good things come in large packages.

Usenet:
   alt.personals.big-folks
   alt.personals.fat
   alt.personals.tall

Romance and the Internet

Are you looking for that special someone?

Or are you looking for someone who is looking for that special someone?

Or… would you like to just snoop on people who are looking for that special someone?

As you can see, there are lots of reasons to read the Usenet personal groups.

Give your résumé a quick brush up and drop in today.

Meeting People

Welcome to the smorgasbord of personal ads. There is something for everyone, and you can take as much as you like. Non-fattening, hypo-allergenic, 100 percent of your recommended daily allowance of fun and good times. Participate in one of these Usenet groups and maybe you'll meet the man, woman or none-of-the-above of your dreams.

Usenet:
   alt.personal
   alt.personal.ads
   alt.personals
   alt.personals.ads
   alt.personals.black
   alt.personals.bodyart
   alt.personals.gothic
   alt.personals.intercultural
   alt.personals.intergen
   alt.personals.interracial
   alt.personals.misc
   alt.personals.teen
   soc.personals

Meeting Women

If you are like most men, you have a strong biological urge to meet women. However, just having the urge isn't enough. Some men are good at meeting women; other men need a bit of help. Actually, there is a lot more to learn than you might think, and now is a good time to start. For example, can you recognize the signs that a woman is flirting with you? Does she raise her eyebrows, lick her lips, flip her hair with her fingers, smile coyly followed by a downward gaze, whisper into a friend's ear, smooth her clothing unnecessarily, or move in time to the music with her eyes on you? If so, she's ready. Walk over, introduce yourself, and ask if she's read any good Harley Hahn books lately.

Web:
   http://www.getgirls.com/archive.htm
   http://www.meetingwomen.com/tips.html
   http://www.sosuave.com/
   http://www.xtrasite.co.nz/entertainment/loveman/
      cag-v0.9b/

Personal Ads Humor

So you have posted a personal ad and met someone nice. Does that mean you must leave the world of personal ads? Not at all. It's time to read personal ad humor and feel superior to all the people who aren't as successful as you.

Web:
  http://www.countryhumor.com/jokes/personal.htm
  http://www.pan-arts.com/era/humor/
    code-words.htm
  http://www.waytoopersonal.com/

Personal Ads Talk and General Discussion

This is the Usenet group for talking about personal ads that you may have seen on Usenet or in a newspaper or magazine. Discuss style, what works and what doesn't, and your experiences. And, oh yes, while you're looking around, maybe you'll find something to pique your interest.

Usenet:
  alt.personals.d

Personal Ads Tips

Your personal ad represents *you*, so it behooves you to stand out from the crowd. These resources will help you write the best possible ad for yourself (so the best possible person can find you). Important: (1) Be completely honest. (2) Don't be boring or normal (unless you are boring or normal).

Web:
  http://www.alovelinksplus.com/write/
  http://www.penpal-world.com/tips.htm
  http://www.quik-free.com/quikmatch/bothadv2.htm

Personals Sites

As one of my readers, you definitely have a perfect soulmate somewhere. However, you may need to do some looking, and that may mean reading some personal ads or taking out an ad of your own. If you're looking for that very special guy or gal, he or she may be already looking for you, so don't give up. The person you want is out there somewhere.

Web:
  http://www.americansingles.com/
  http://www.datingfaces.com/
  http://www.lovecity.com/
  http://www.montagar.com/personals/
  http://www.one-and-only.com/

Read the "Money" sections, and increase your Net profit.

Relationship Advice

The course of true love does not always run as smoothly as we might wish. You can spend your time working on the relationship, but sometimes enough is enough. Why not turn to the Net instead to satisfy your emotional need to analyze? Free relationship advice is waiting patiently, just for you.

Web:
  http://www.askdrlove.com/
  http://www.loveandlearn.com/
  http://www.xtrasite.co.nz/entertainment/loveman/
    letters/

PHILOSOPHY

Aesthetics

Aesthetics is the area of philosophy concerned with the nature of beauty, for example, as it is expressed within the fine arts. As you might imagine, such topics quickly enter the realm of the nature of art and artistic judgment (and, if you are a Kantian, perception as well). Plato and Aristotle both said that beauty is inherent in an object, and, thus, may be judged objectively. Hume, on the other hand, felt that whatever pleased the observer was beautiful. My opinion is somewhere in between. I feel about beauty the same way U.S. Supreme Court Justice Potter Stewart feels about pornography: I may not be able to define it, but I know it when I see it.

Web:
  http://www.aesthetics-online.org/

Listserv Mailing List:
  List Name: aesthetics-l
  Subscribe to: listserv@indiana.edu

Aristotle

The Greek philosopher Aristotle (384-322 B.C.) was the author of many works on logic, metaphysics, ethics, politics and natural science. Unfortunately, most of Aristotle's writings have been lost. Still, what has survived has a profound effect on Western thought. Aristotle was trained in Athens at Plato's Academy, where he first went as a 17-year-old boy. He stayed there for twenty years, eventually becoming Plato's most renowned student. Aristotle in turn became a teacher, his most famous student being Alexander the Great. Aristotle based his philosophy on logic and rational thinking, and devoted much of his energy to studying the facts and laws of the physical world. Where Plato defined philosophy in terms of ideas, Aristotle defined it in terms of actual existence.

Web:

   http://www.newadvent.org/cathen/01713a.htm
   http://www.paul.bullen.com/AristotleOverview.html
   http://www.philosophypages.com/ph/aris.htm
   http://www.rit.edu/~flwstv/aristotle1.html
   http://www.ucmp.berkeley.edu/history/aristotle.html
   http://www.utm.edu/research/iep/a/aristotl.htm

Majordomo Mailing List:

   List Name: aristotle
   Subscribe to: majordomo@lists.enteract.com

Chinese Philosophy

Chinese philosophy is, historically, considered within the bounds of three specific epochs: the Classical Age (6th century B.C. to 2nd century B.C.), the Medieval Age (2nd century B.C. to 11th century A.D.), and the Modern Age (11th century A.D. to the present). As you might imagine, there are a wide variety of philosophical traditions. However, in Western terms, it is possible to distinguish three distinct traits that are characteristic of Chinese philosophy: an emphasis on logical thinking (rationalism), the importance of human beings and their values (humanism), and the fusion of differing belief systems (syncretism).

Web:

   http://www-personal.monash.edu.au/~dey/phil/
     eastern.htm
   http://www.connect.net/ron/chinesephilosophy.html
   http://www.hku.hk/philodep/ch/

Ethics

Ethics is the branch of philosophy concerned with moral principles, standards of conduct, and social obligations. Society believes that it is the mark of a normal person to be able to distinguish between right and wrong, but who gets to decide what's right and what's wrong? Plato was convinced that there was an absolute good to which human beings could aspire. (But then, even his best friends couldn't deny that Plato was somewhat of a dreamer.) Aristotle, on the other hand, saw moral virtue as the mean between extremes (the dancing on the fence theory). Ethics have always been one of the favorite topics of philosophers, and there is a lot of ethical thought on the Net for you to enjoy. So check out these Web sites: it's the right thing to do.

Web:

   http://ethics.acusd.edu/
   http://www.cis.wayne.edu/aspalding/ethicslist.html
   http://www.utm.edu/research/iep/e/ethics.htm

Listproc Mailing List:

   List Name: soceth-l
   Subscribe to: listproc@usc.edu

Existentialism

Existentialism may seem abstract, but it is actually a highly utilitarian philosophy. Existentialism sees human existence as being fundamentally unexplainable. As individuals, we are isolated from a universe that is at once hostile and indifferent. On the other hand, we are responsible for our own choices, and we do have the freedom to act as we want. Thus, existentialism is the perfect philosophy for teenagers and for people writing essays about twentieth-century French literature.

Web:

   http://www.friesian.org/existent.htm
   http://www.interchange.ubc.ca/cree/
   http://www.tameri.com/csw/exist/

> **Fun is mandatory;
> worry is optional.**

Existentialism

Here's the good news: You are completely free and, hence, responsible for your own decisions and what you make of your life.

Now the catch: You are completely free and, hence, responsible for your own decisions and what you make of your life.

Greek Philosophy

The history of Western philosophy starts at about 600 B.C. with the Greeks. Classical Greek philosophy provides the underpinnings for much of our modern civilization and how we approach thinking about life. Greek philosophy was especially concerned with two main areas: the nature of reality, and the idea of virtue and how it should be applied to politics. What I find interesting is that today we still greatly concern ourselves with the nature of reality, but, for some reason, we seem not to care so much about ideals of virtue and how they should be applied to politics. For this reason, I feel it is especially enlightening to read the works of Aristotle, Socrates, Plato and the other Greek philosophers to whom we owe so much of our heritage.

Web:
http://graduate.gradsch.uga.edu/archive/greek.html
http://www.friesian.com/greek.htm
http://www.thebigview.com/greeks/
http://www.utm.edu/research/iep/g/greekphi.htm

Listserv Mailing List:
List Name: sophia
Subscribe to: listserv@liverpool.ac.uk

Hegel, Georg Wilhelm Friedrich

The German philosopher Georg Wilhelm Friedrich Hegel (1770-1831) wrote widely about life, religion, art and ethics, and is considered to be one of the most influential thinkers of all time. Hegel taught that the purpose of philosophy is to find the truth. To do so, he abandoned the logical, one-step-at-a-time method developed by Aristotle, in favor of a process that we now call "dialectical thinking". Dialectical thinking uses a variety of logical arguments in order to examine and analyze all the important aspects of a particular topic. To apply Hegel's methods, we first state an idea (often referred to as a thesis) and develop a contradictory idea (an anti-thesis). Then, by logical argument, we resolve the two contradictory ideas into a single, coherent whole. In Hegelian terms, the resulting synthesis "sublates" (that is, preserves and overcomes) the contradictions of the various arguments in order to create a higher, more truthful realization. Hegel rejected the idea that knowledge is gained by separate steps of logical reasoning leading to a final conclusion. To Hegel, true knowledge is a *process* that comes only when the arguments and analyses regarding a specific topic are considered in totality.

Web:
http://www.gwfhegel.org/
http://www.hegel.net/
http://www.hegel.org/
http://www.marxists.org/reference/archive/hegel/

Your flight on Spaceship Earth will be 30 minutes late, so slow down, relax and read a magazine.

Kant, Immanuel

Eventually, we are all faced with big questions about life: How do we reconcile our strong wish-to-live with the knowledge that we will someday die? Does our life have meaning? Is there a God? Such questions lead us to metaphysics, the area of philosophy concerned with the basic nature of existence. The German philosopher Immanuel Kant (1724-1804) is one of the towering figures in the history of metaphysics because of his ideas on how we should think about such questions, as well as the influence he had on other philosophers, both contemporaries and descendents. To Kant, our perceptions are translated into understanding by the use of reason. He suggested there were two types of perceptions: physical sensation and our sense of moral duty. When we apply reason to sensation, we are able to understand the world around us—the highest expression of which is the creation of science. When we apply reason to our moral duty, we understand morality and ethics. To Kant, reality exists only because we can, in one way or another, perceive it and think about it. However, our mind—the tool with which we reason—is limited by its basic structure. Therefore, we are, by our nature, limited in our understanding of the universe, which renders us unable to answer certain crucial, but tantalizingly elusive questions. During his lifetime (80 years), Kant never traveled more than fifty miles from home.

Web:
   http://www.friesian.com/kant.htm
   http://www.philosophypages.com/ph/kant.htm

Usenet:
   alt.philosophy.kant

Memetics

There is a theory that ideas can propagate biologically. So if you start getting funny thoughts in your head and you don't know where they came from, you can blame it on your parents and the theory of Memetics. Never again will you have to take responsibility for those strange ideas that keep coming to mind. Learn about memes and their effects on humanity.

Web:
   http://jom-emit.cfpm.org/
   http://pespmc1.vub.ac.be/memes.html
   http://www.aleph.se/Trans/Cultural/Memetics/
      meme_lex.html

Usenet:
   alt.memetics

Metaphysics

Do you ever get the impression that there is more going on in the universe than you realize? Maybe you should jump into some metaphysics, the part of philosophy concerned with the ultimate nature of existence. If you want to get in deeper, you can try ontology (the nature of being), cosmology (the physical universe as everything), or philosophical theology (religious truth).

Web:
   http://mally.stanford.edu/
   http://www.websyte.com/alan/metamul.htm

Usenet:
   alt.paranet.metaphysics
   sci.philosophy.meta

Nietzsche

The German philosopher Friedrich Wilhelm Nietzsche (1844-1900) was one of two thinkers who laid the foundation of existentialism (the other one being Kierkegaard). When Nietzsche was young, he was heavily influenced by Schopenhauer (who was not a happy camper). Eventually, Nietzsche mellowed out and rejected Schopenhauer's depressive outlook on life. Still, Nietzsche did recognize that life was not uniformly good. All lives are difficult, he taught, and full of pain. What makes some lives fulfilled is the manner in which the pain has been met. Happiness is not easy to achieve and requires much effort. He warned against that which artificially removed the pain of life, in particular, alcohol and Christianity. Of all his work, which was considerable, Nietzsche's masterpiece is considered to be "Thus Spake Zarathustra".

Web:
   http://plato.stanford.edu/entries/nietzsche/
   http://www.inquiria.com/nz/
   http://www.pitt.edu/~wbcurry/nietzsche.html

Usenet:
   alt.fan.nietzsche

Objectivism

Ayn Rand (1905-1982) was a Russian-born American philosopher and novelist who created the philosophy of objectivism. She summarizes: "My philosophy, in essence, is the concept of man as a heroic being, with his own happiness as the moral purpose of his life, with productive achievements as his noblest activity, and reason as his only absolute."

Web:

http://www.aynrand.org/
http://www.ellensplace.net/ayn_rand.html
http://www.jeffcomp.com/faq/
http://www.objectivism.addr.com/
http://www.objectivism.net/

Usenet:

alt.philosophy.objectivism
humanities.philosophy.objectivism

Majordomo Mailing List:

List Name: objectivism
Subscribe to: majordomo@auckland.ac.nz

Philosophers

In the game of life, you can't tell the philosophers without a scorecard. With these resources, I guarantee you'll be able to find information about the philosopher of your choice whenever you want. Philosophically speaking, I think that seems as if it might be a good deal—maybe. (I'll have to think about it.)

Web:

http://www-personal.monash.edu.au/~dey/phil/
   think-ak.htm
http://www.epistemelinks.com/main/mainpers.asp
http://www.philosophypages.com/dy/zt.htm
http://www.philosophypages.com/ph/
http://www.trincoll.edu/depts/phil/philo/
   philosophers.html

Objectivism in the 21st Century

There are some who find Ayn Rand's philosophy of objectivism as relevant today as it was many years ago when she first started explaining what was wrong with the world. There are others who say that her ideas were fine for the time but are atavistic and irrelevant to modern life. Then, there are still others who say "Ayn who?"

Philosophy Reference Guides

Is philosophy getting you down? Is there just too much of it to handle? Well, if you find yourself confusing neoplatonism with quantification theory, and mixing up Nietzsche's theory of eternal recurrence with Socrates' doctrine of recollection, maybe it's time to spend a few hours on the Net. Once you know what you are talking about, you will have a stronger sense of identity. (Or as one sweet potato said to another, "I think, therefore I yam.")

Web:

http://plato.stanford.edu/
http://www.philosophypages.com/dy/
http://www.utm.edu/research/iep/

Philosophy Resources

Before you draw your next hot bath, take a look at all these philosophy resources. Spend a few hours reading and then, while you are in the bath, you'll be able to close your eyes and contemplate life. With all the insight you will gain, it won't be long before you are jumping out of the bath yelling "Eureka, eureka."

Web:

http://www-personal.monash.edu.au/~dey/phil/
http://www.earlham.edu/~peters/philinks.htm
http://www.epistemelinks.com/
http://www.eserver.org/philosophy/
http://www.philosophers.co.uk/
http://www.valdosta.peachnet.edu/~rbarnett/phi/
   resource.html

Philosophy Search Engines

Life is stern and life is earnest, and when you need some philosophy, you need it *now*. I understand, so here is a search engine to help you fulfill your philosophical needs quickly and discreetly. (Note: One size does not fit all.)

Web:

http://www.perseus.tufts.edu/

Philosophy Talk and General Discussion

When the going gets tough, the tough start talking about philosophy—and these are the places to do it. Whatever your philosophical preference, there's room for you to talk on the Net. Just remember to be polite, and show respect for other people's point of view (unless they disagree with you).

Web:

http://www-personal.monash.edu.au/~dey/phil/
   section4.htm

Usenet:

alt.philosophy
alt.philosophy.basism
alt.philosophy.debate
alt.philosophy.kant
alt.philosophy.taoism
sci.philosophy
sci.philosophy.tech
talk.philosophy.humanism
talk.philosophy.misc

Political Philosophy

In order to maintain our societies, we organize ourselves into political systems. However, which system is the best one for a particular time and place? That's where political philosophy comes in. The deep thinkers of the ages have described and analyzed various types of political systems. Use the Net, read the ideas, and make your choice.

Web:

http://bubl.ac.uk/link/p/politicalphilosophy.htm
http://lgxserve.ciseca.uniba.it/lei/filpol/filpole/
   homefpe.htm
http://www.epistemelinks.com/main/maintopi.asp
http://www.library.ubc.ca/poli/theory.html
http://www.marxists.org/
http://www.political-theory.org/

Socrates and Plato

The work of Greek philosophers Socrates and Plato is linked forever. Socrates (460-399 B.C.) was a renowned philosopher, dedicated to self-knowledge and rational thinking. He developed a style of teaching that involved asking someone one question after another, in order to lead that person to the truth. (In case you want to try it, you should know that a lot of people found this to be highly irritating.) Eventually, Socrates fell afoul of the authorities in Athens, where he lived, and was put to death. (They charged him with corrupting the minds of the Athenian youth, and with not worshipping the city's gods.) Socrates' most important pupil was Plato (427-347 B.C.), who founded a school, called the Academy (386 B.C.), where he taught and wrote for much of his life. (Plato's most important student was Aristotle.) It is from Plato that we know about Socrates, as Socrates himself did not leave any written records. Plato presented Socrates' ideas in the form of dramatic dialogues. The writings are charming, and have been consistently popular and influential. However, there is no real way to know which views were Socrates' and which were Plato's. Both men were interested in moral philosophy and regarded natural philosophy (science) as an inferior type of knowledge. They saw knowledge as being good in its own right, and not for any practical purpose. (Platonic trivia: In the dialogue "Timaeus", Plato invented a tale about a fictional land he called Atlantis. It is from this tale that the myth of Atlantis arose.)

Web:

http://classics.mit.edu/Browse/browse-Plato.html
http://socrates.clarke.edu/
http://www.briantaylor.com/plato.htm
http://www.rit.edu/~flwstv/plato.html

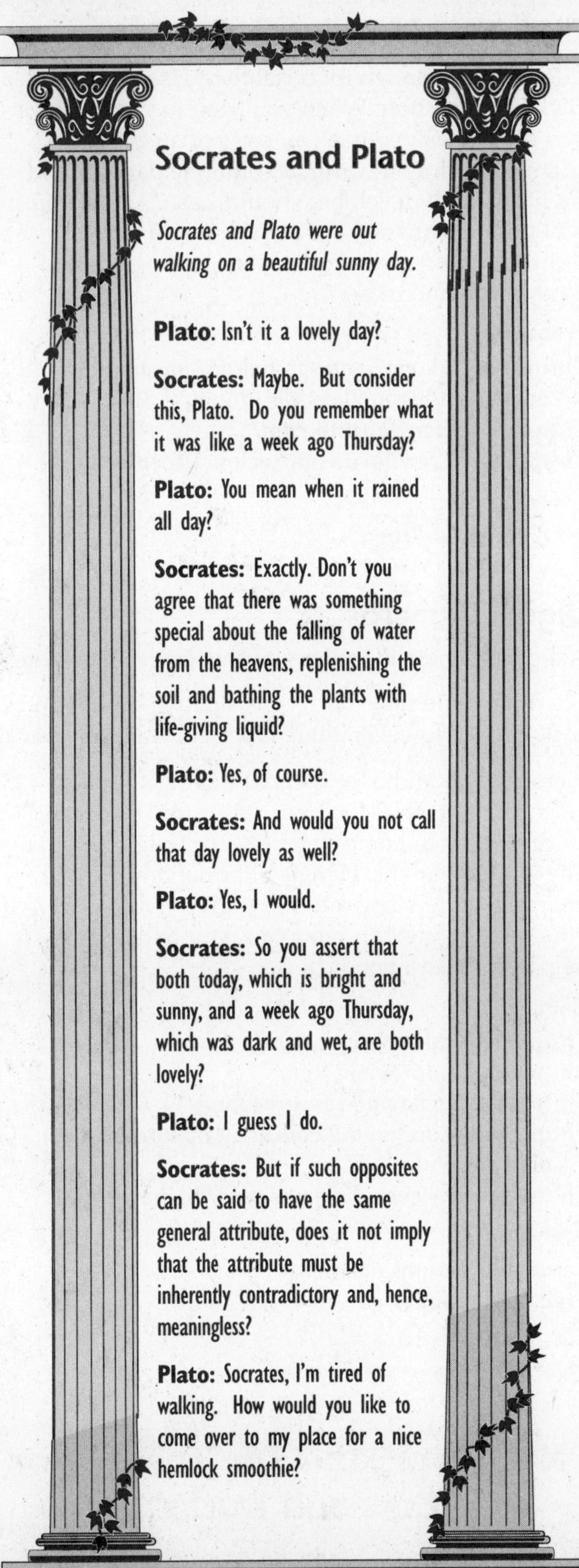

Socrates and Plato

Socrates and Plato were out walking on a beautiful sunny day.

Plato: Isn't it a lovely day?

Socrates: Maybe. But consider this, Plato. Do you remember what it was like a week ago Thursday?

Plato: You mean when it rained all day?

Socrates: Exactly. Don't you agree that there was something special about the falling of water from the heavens, replenishing the soil and bathing the plants with life-giving liquid?

Plato: Yes, of course.

Socrates: And would you not call that day lovely as well?

Plato: Yes, I would.

Socrates: So you assert that both today, which is bright and sunny, and a week ago Thursday, which was dark and wet, are both lovely?

Plato: I guess I do.

Socrates: But if such opposites can be said to have the same general attribute, does it not imply that the attribute must be inherently contradictory and, hence, meaningless?

Plato: Socrates, I'm tired of walking. How would you like to come over to my place for a nice hemlock smoothie?

Utilitarianism

In a world full of moral ambiguities, how do we decide if something is right or wrong? Utilitarianism answers that to make such a judgment, we must look at how much pleasure or pain that something gives. The founder of utilitarianism was the English philosopher Jeremy Bentham (1748-1832). In his book "Introduction to the Principles of Morals and Legislation" (1789), Bentham taught that our judgment, especially with respect to government, should strive to achieve the greatest happiness for the greatest number of people. His work was highly influential, and was the force behind significant nineteenth-century criminal, judicial and governmental reforms. Bentham's most important student was John Stuart Mill (1806-1873). Mill was an advocate of political and social reform, who used the principles of utilitarianism to justify ideas such as increased democracy and women's rights. One of the interesting characteristics of utilitarianism is that it tends to seem either completely obvious or completely wrong.

Web:

> **http://web.ukonline.co.uk/g.mccaughan/g/essays/ utility.html**
> **http://www.blupete.com/Literature/Biographies/ Philosophy/Bentham.htm**
> **http://www.blupete.com/Literature/Biographies/ Philosophy/Mill.htm**
> **http://www.utilitarian.org/**
> **http://www.utilitarianism.net/**

Women in Philosophy

Tired of reading the same old philosophy by Kant, Descartes and Aristotle? For an intellectual change of pace, why not try Hannah Arendt, Simone de Beauvoir or Ayn Rand? Check with these Web sites (where you will find an extensive bibliography of women philosophers) or subscribe to the mailing list (which is for feminist philosophers), then go right to the nearest library and check out a book. Do not pass Go. Do not collect 200 books of male-oriented philosophy.

Web:

> **http://billyboy.ius.indiana.edu/womeninphilosophy/ womeninphilo.html**
> **http://www.earlham.edu/~peters/courses/re/ women.htm**

Listserv Mailing List:

> **List Name: swip-l**
> **Subscribe to: listserv@listserv.uh.edu**

PHOTOGRAPHY

Alternative Photographic Processes

Traditional photography depends on silver gel substances and requires the use of a darkroom with safelighting. Alternative photographic processes use different chemicals and techniques, some of which do not have such rigorous requirements. In addition, alternative processes can be more fun than the traditional ways of developing film and can yield different types of results (often accidentally). If you want to have some fun, you can explore the art of photograms, an easy way to make interesting images using exposure to direct sunlight.

Web:
> http://duke.usask.ca/~holtsg/photo/faq.html
> http://mywebpages.comcast.net/hmpi/AltProcess/
>   Articles/AltArticles.htm
> http://www.mikeware.demon.co.uk/
> http://www.photogs.com/bwworld/
>   bwalternative1.html
> http://www.photogs.com/bwworld/cyanotypes.html

Black and White Photography

I love black and white photography. It's so clean, basic and accessible. If you want to find good black and white photography on the Net, all you need to do is check these Web sites. You'll find links to black and white photo Web sites, a FAQ, as well as archives of some wonderful photos.

Web:
> http://www.bekuz.com/
> http://www.photogs.com/bwworld/

Daguerreotypes

A daguerreotype is a photographic image made on a light-sensitive silver-coated metallic plate. The daguerreotype was invented in 1839 by Louis Jacques Mandé Daguerre (1789-1851), a French scene painter and physicist. (Daguerre was also the man who helped invent the diorama, a sort of three-dimensional pictorial scene.) Take a look at some of the old daguerreotypes, read about their history, and find out all the steps involved in making one. (I bet you'll appreciate how easy photography is today.)

Web:
> http://www.americandaguerreotypes.com
> http://www.daguerre.org/

Darkroom Photography

Photographic creativity certainly doesn't stop with a click of the shutter. When you head to the darkroom you have to ask yourself all sorts of questions like "Should I print on warm or cold tone paper?" and "What kind of developer should I use?" Here you will find information about darkroom-related technical topics: chemical usage, paper, tools and equipment, and more.

Web:
> http://webs.kodak.com/global/en/consumer/
>   education/lessonPlans/darkroom/
> http://www.digitaltruth.com/
> http://www.heylloyd.com/technicl/technicl.html

Usenet:
> rec.photo.darkroom

Digital Cameras

A digital camera is a photographic device that stores pictures within computer chips instead of regular film. As soon as you take a picture, it is ready—you don't need to have it developed. You can take pictures over and over without buying supplies (except a battery). Moreover, it is possible to transfer pictures to your computer. However, digital cameras do have limitations. Here is information that will help you understand and use digital cameras well. If you are thinking of buying one, you will find tips to help you make a good choice.

Web:
> http://www.dcresource.com/
> http://www.dpreview.com/
> http://www.imaging-resource.com/
> http://www.orchidlink.com/digitalphotography/
>   digicam.htm
> http://www.steves-digicams.com/diginews.html

Usenet:
> alt.comp.periphs.dcameras
> rec.photo.digital

Need a pickup? Try "Energy" (or "Cars and Trucks").

Room in the Darkroom

Some of the most mysterious things in the world go on in a darkroom.

If you are not a photographer, sorry, this part of human culture is closed to you and there's not much you can do about it except feel wistful in a polite sort of way.

If, however, you are among the cognoscenti who can distinguish between lith processing and posterization, the discussion group rec.photo.darkroom is waiting for you.

Join the club and see why it pays to stay in the dark.

History of Photography

The development of photography involved the marriage of two different technologies: optical and chemical. Basic optical technology—in the form of the "camera obscura" (a dark box or room with a small hole in one end that could be used to project an inverted image on the wall opposite the hole)—was understood as far back as the time of Aristotle. And scientists have known about optical processes involving light and chemical reactions for hundreds of years. In the seventeenth century, the British physicist Robert Boyle discovered that silver chloride turned dark upon exposure. However, Boyle thought the discoloring was due to exposure to air, not to light. In the next century, Angelo Sala noticed that powdered silver nitrate became dark in the sun. In 1727, Johann Schulze realized that particular liquids turn color upon exposure to the sun. In the early nineteenth century, Thomas Wedgewood was able to capture images, but only temporarily. Finally in 1827, Joseph Niépce produced the first permanent photographic image, which he called a heliograph. Read about the history of photography, and you will find it encompasses politics, culture, science and intrigue.

Web:
  http://www.city-gallery.com/
  http://www.photographymuseum.com/exhibits.html
  http://www.rleggat.com/photohistory/

Listserv Mailing List:
  List Name: photohst
  Subscribe to: listserv@lists.asu.edu

Infrared Photography

Infrared photography uses film that is sensitive to visible light, as well as ultraviolet and infrared radiation. The results are fascinating, often even eerie. Although the images look familiar, the contrast and details are not what you are used to. If you are interested in photography, you have to try infrared photography at least once in your life. To help you get started, I have chosen Web sites that contain documents relating to infrared photography (where you can find out about cameras, lenses, exposures, focusing, developing and printing), as well as collections of infrared photos for you to enjoy.

Web:
  http://www.a1.nl/phomepag/markerink/
    mainpage.htm
  http://www.atsf.co.uk/ilight/
  http://www.mat.uc.pt/~rps/photos/FAQ_IR.html
  http://www.pauck.de/marco/photo/infrared/
    infrared.html
  http://www.photo.net/photo/edscott/spectsel.htm
  http://www.rit.edu/~andpph/
    text-infrared-basics.html

Majordomo Mailing List:
  List Name: infrared
  Subscribe to: majordomo@a1.nl

Kite Aerial Photography

(1) Attach a camera to a kite. (2) Launch the kite. (3) Snap pictures using a remote control device. (4) Repeat step 3 as often as you wish. (5) Carefully pull in the kite and remove the camera. (6) Develop the pictures. (7) Live happily ever after. (What could be more cool?)

Web:
  http://www.arch.ced.berkeley.edu/kap/kaptoc.html
  http://www.geospectra.net/kite/kaphome.htm
  http://www.nitrobug.freeserve.co.uk/intro2.htm

What we have here is a failure to miscommunicate.

Nature and Wildlife Photography

By its nature, nature photography naturally requires an unnatural amount of patience and skill. Naturally, you expect nature photographers to have a persevering nature, as the requirements of nature photography are demanding, although, just as naturally, the results can be rewarding. If your nature is one of a natural nature photographer, you will appreciate the natural pleasure you get from visiting nature photography Web sites and talking in a nature photography Usenet discussion group. Or you can just look at the pictures.

Web:
    http://www.bobatkins.com/photography/
    http://www.paragon-press.com/tips1.htm
    http://www.sphoto.com/techinfo/phototech.html

Usenet:
    rec.photo.technique.nature

Night Photography

How can you take pictures at night when it's dark? The answer is, nighttime is not completely dark. (After all, cats can still see.) It's just that the light is too low for humans. However, by exposing your film for a long time, you can gather enough light to take pictures. Night photography can be a lot of fun, and the pictures have a wonderful, other-worldly feeling. Of course, you will need to know what you are doing. Start here. While you're at it, take a look at some of pictures taken at night: I bet they will inspire you.

Web:
    http://www.kodak.com/cluster/global/en/consumer/
        products/techInfo/ac61/
    http://www.schoolofphotography.com/night/
    http://www.thenocturnes.com/

Panoramic Photography

Panoramic photography uses a wide angle lens in order to capture an unbroken view of the surrounding area. In general, to qualify as panoramic, your picture must have an angle of view of at least 100 degrees (a little less than a third of a full circle). Panoramic photography is perfect for landscape shots in which you want to capture the expansiveness of the area you are photographing (the Grand Canyon, a spectacular snow-covered mountain range, a sweeping city skyline, and so on). Here is how a typical panoramic camera works. The camera rotates on top of a tripod. As the camera turns, the shutter is held open. The film moves past the aperture (shutter opening) with the same speed and direction as the camera itself. The result? A panoramic picture with a view to remember.

Web:
    http://memory.loc.gov/ammem/pnhtml/
        pnhome.html
    http://www.panoguide.com/
    http://www.panoramic.net/www/
    http://www.panphoto.com/

PhotoForum

PhotoForum is a mailing list devoted to serious photography topics. The participants are knowledgeable people, both amateur and professional, as well as novices. The Web site, which is associated with the mailing list, offers some wonderful resources, including a large number of FAQs (frequently asked question lists). If you are serious about photography, you need to know about PhotoForum.

Web:
    http://www.rit.edu/~andpph/photoforum.html

Listserv Mailing List:
    List Name: photoforum
    Subscribe to: listserv@listserver.isc.rit.edu

Photographers Directory

This Web site contains a large list of photographers from all around the world who use the Net. You can check the list either alphabetically or geographically. This is a good site to know about if you are looking for a photographer or if you are a photographer looking for clients.

Web:
  http://www.photographers.com/pho030.html

Photography Basics

Do you want to learn how to go beyond basic pointing and shooting? These Web sites have information about cameras and how they work, the history of photography, natural and artificial lighting, and composing and balancing images. You can also learn about the different kinds of photography—portraiture, documentary, macro and micro, art photography—and explore links to some useful photo sites around the Net.

Web:
  http://www.88.com/exposure/
  http://www.azuswebworks.com/photography/
  http://www.betterphoto.com/
  http://www.thepeaches.com/photography/
    Basics.htm
  http://www.users.globalnet.co.uk/~tkemp/

Photography Equipment Talk and General Discussion

There are a lot of photographers on the Net and, no matter what your particular interest, there is someone to talk to. So why not choose a Usenet group, talk about photographic equipment and see what develops?

Usenet:
  rec.photo.equipment.35mm
  rec.photo.equipment.film+labs
  rec.photo.equipment.large-format
  rec.photo.equipment.medium-format
  rec.photo.equipment.misc
  rec.photo.film+labs

Photography Resources

Photography dates back to 1827 when the Frenchman Joseph Niépce made the first permanent photograph. In 1839, the technology was enhanced significantly by another Frenchman, Louis Daguerre, who invented the daguerreotype. Modern photography dates from 1840 and the work of the Englishman William Talbot. Today, cameras both traditional and digital are ubiquitous and we take photography for granted. However, it has only been in the twentieth century that the general population has had access to reliable, affordable cameras and film. Previously, it was next to impossible for regular people to create and preserve images. Imagine how this changes one's sense of the past. For example, if you look at the Web sites that were created by the ancient Greeks and Romans, you will see that they are mostly text with a few rudimentary graphics. Today, cameras are readily available at low cost and anyone who wants can be a photographer (of sorts). To help you learn more about this rewarding pastime, I have selected Web sites where you will be able to find a large variety of information relating to photography.

Web:
  http://www.apogeephoto.com/
  http://www.photolinks.com/
  http://www.profotos.com/
  http://www.ventureseast.com/photopage/

Photography Talk and General Discussion

Whether you are just a snapshot shooter or a pro with hundreds of pounds of equipment, there is a Usenet group perfect for you. Fans of photography hang out and talk about taking pictures from a creative as well as a technical point of view.

Usenet:
  bit.listproc.stockphoto
  rec.photo
  rec.photo.advanced
  rec.photo.help
  rec.photo.misc
  rec.photo.moderated
  rec.photo.technique.art
  rec.photo.technique.misc
  rec.photo.technique.nature
  rec.photo.technique.people

Pinhole Photography

Take an empty oatmeal box and make a tiny hole in one side. Now, in a darkroom, insert a piece of photographic paper inside the box, opposite the small hole. Cover up the hole and make sure all the edges of the box are completely sealed. Take the box to the location of your choice in the outside world and uncover the little hole. After a period of time, probably seconds, cover up the hole. (The amount of time you need to leave the hole open depends on the size of the hole. You will have to experiment.) Take the box back into the darkroom and extract the photographic paper. Develop it and admire your image. Congratulations, you have created your own pinhole camera.

Web:

http://www.astro.wisc.edu/%7emukluk/pin.html
http://www.pinhole.org/
http://www.pinholevisions.org/
http://www.toptown.com/nowhere/kypfer/pinhole/

Pinhole Photography

The other day, I found a magic lamp. I rubbed it and a genie appeared. "Your wish is my command, Master. How may I serve you?"

"Please take me to Saturn," I said. So he created a pressurized, air-filled bubble for me, and instantly transported me to Saturn. While I was there, I left a pinhole camera.

I intended to go back the next day to retrieve the camera and develop the film. Unfortunately, I misplaced the lamp.

So if you ever are on Saturn and you happen to see a pinhole camera, feel free to bring it back with you. I'd sure like to see how the picture turned out.

Toy Cameras

I think toy cameras are cool. Toy cameras are, literally, toys: cheap little plastic cameras that use 120 film. They leak light; produce distortion, fog and vignetting on film; and have an unknown shutter speed and film that is wound loosely. (And those are just the obvious problems.) So why do people use toy cameras? Because they are fun and you never know what you are going to get. Moreover, toy cameras are great for experimenting and they provide a great break from high-tech photography.

Web:

http://www.frontiernet.net/~moe/TOYPAGES/
    holgamain.html
http://www.huskudu.com/
http://www.merrillphoto.com/
    JunkStoreCameras.htm
http://www.tapir.org/gbc/
http://www.toycamera.com/
http://www.toycamera.org/

Underwater Photography

I once took some underwater pictures. I went on a trip to the Caribbean and, before I left, I bought a waterproof disposable camera. During my snorkeling sessions, I happily snapped away at a variety of colorful fish and underwater scenery. When I returned home and had the pictures developed, I enjoyed them, but I realized they were nothing like the quality you would get with special equipment and techniques. Still, I had a great deal of fun, and I enjoy looking at my favorite picture of a turtle swimming around a reef.

Web:

http://www.cybereef.com/
http://www.mainstream.net/~fgz/diving/
    uwphoto.html
http://www.mauiscuba.com/uwphoto.htm
http://www.photo.net/photo/underwater/
    primer.html
http://www.utahdiving.com/photos/pic-clas.htm

Majordomo Mailing List:

List Name: uw-photo
Subscribe to: majordomo@world.std.com

Zone System

How often have you taken a picture, only to find that what you got was not what you wanted? Some people have the attitude, "I'll take the picture so it more or less captures what I want, and then I'll fix it in the darkroom." Well, that's okay as far as it goes, but if you like your pictures to be as perfect as possible, you may want to learn how to use the zone system. The zone system is a complicated set of techniques based on measuring dark and light spots, and then making certain calculations to get the exact picture you want. This system (which can take years to learn how to use well) was first envisioned in the late 1930s by Fred Archer of the Art Center College in Los Angeles. Ansel Adams read Archer's articles in a photography magazine, contacted Archer, and then developed more formal techniques for using the system. If you want to learn the zone system, this Web site can help you a lot. In addition, you will need to get Adam's book "The Negative" and practice for many hours. To make it easy, always follow these basic principles: (1) Expose for the shadows. (2) Develop for the highlights. (3) Take a break and eat.

Web:
   http://www.cicada.com/pub/photo/zs/

PHYSICS

Computational Fluid Dynamics

Fluid dynamics is the science that studies the movement of fluids (liquids and gases). These resources are for you, if you are concerned with the computational aspects of fluid dynamics. Find out about academic institutions, companies, specific topics (such as turbulence and hypersonic flow), documents, and lots of other related information.

Web:
   http://www.cfd-online.com/
Usenet:
   sci.mech.fluids
   sci.physics.computational.fluid-dynamics

Fusion

Fusion is a process by which small atoms such as hydrogen are fused together to produce heavier atoms such as helium. As this happens, some of the matter is converted into energy. The goal of fusion research is to design reactors that produce large amounts of energy by fusing hydrogen atoms into helium under manageable conditions. In some ways, fusion is an ideal way to create energy. The raw materials are cheap, the waste material (helium) is safe, and there are no problems with radioactivity. However, fusion takes place only under conditions of extreme heat and pressure. (In fact, fusion is the basic process by which energy is produced inside of stars.) If we could create fusion reactors here on Earth, it would be wonderful, but there are still many years of research ahead of us.

Web:
   http://fusioned.gat.com/
   http://www.faqs.org/faqs/fusion-faq/
   http://www.rzg.mpg.de/~bds/
   http://wwwofe.er.doe.gov/education.html
Usenet:
   sci.physics.fusion

Hey, Bud. Yeah, I mean you. C'mon over here, I've got a tip for you.

Ya wanna win a Nobel Prize? I got it all figured out.

All ya gotta do is figure out a way to hold a bunch of hydrogen atoms together under great pressure at a high temperature, just long enough for them to fuse into helium.

I tell you, it's a great idea. We'll make a fortune selling energy all over the world.

You work out the details, and I'll figure a way to sell all the leftover helium to balloon companies, and we'll split the money even-Steven, right down the middle.

Whad'ya say, Bud? Is that an idea or what?

High Energy Physics

High-energy physics is the area of study that deals with fundamental sub-atomic forces and particles. Such study requires special devices that use enormous amounts of energy to create sub-atomic particles and then force them to interact. (Hence, the name, high-energy physics.) The study of such particles and forces leads to an understanding of the very nature of matter, both on sub-atomic (very small) and cosmological (very large) levels.

Web:

http://physics.web.cern.ch/Physics/HEP.html
http://www-spires.slac.stanford.edu/find/
   instlink.html
http://www.er.doe.gov/henp/index.htm
http://www.hep.net/
http://www.slac.stanford.edu/library/pdg/
   hepinfo.html

Usenet:

sci.physics.particle

Let's face it. Anyone can walk around saying they like small molecules, such as sulfur dioxide or phosphoric acid. That takes no skill or taste whatsoever.

But you know what they say. The more important the man, the larger his favorite molecule. (Women, of course, are judged on entirely different standards.)

As one of my readers, you deserve the best, so I suggest you take some time to learn about polymers: large molecules that can literally stretch for millions of units.

Index of Physics Abstracts

This is the perfect place to find papers relating to high energy physics, astrophysics, condensed matter theory, general relativity, quantum cosmology, and nuclear theory. A keyword search will help you track down the information you need.

Web:

http://xxx.lanl.gov/

Optics

Optics is the study of light and vision. Here is the Web site of the Optical Society of America (OSA). It covers all aspects of optical physics and engineering, including information about quantum electronics, photonics and vision.

Web:

http://www.osa.org/

Usenet:

sci.optics
sci.optics.fiber

Particle Surface Research

Particle surface research involves the study of how an ion beam interacts with a particular surface. Here is a Web site where you will find links to computational, experimental and theoretical resources all over the Net. (If you run out of places to visit and you get bored, try shooting some beta particles at this book and see what happens.)

Web:

http://chaos.fullerton.edu/mhslinks.html

Physics Conferences

If you feel the overwhelming urge to attend a physics conference, you can visit this site to search by month or by field of physics. Personally, I was going to go to the Aerosol Symposium, but I blew it off. As well as conferences, there are listings for workshops and summer schools.

Web:

http://www.physnet.uni-oldenburg.de/PhysNet/
   conferences.html

Physics Talk and General Discussion

These are the main Usenet groups in which physics-related topics are discussed. If you have a question or a comment, post it to the most specific group you can that is appropriate. The **sci.physics** group is for the discussion of topics that don't fit in anywhere else. If you are new to these groups, you should start by reading the Usenet Physics FAQ (frequently asked question list) which you can find at the Web sites. (Remember, without physics, our world would be dull indeed and the universe would be far too easy to understand.)

Web:
> http://www.faqs.org/faqs/physics-faq/
> http://www.math.ucr.edu/home/baez/physics/

Usenet:
> **alt.sci.physics.acoustics**
> **alt.sci.physics.new-theories**
> **alt.sci.physics.plutonium**
> **bionet.biophysics**
> **sci.chaos**
> **sci.med.physics**
> **sci.nonlinear**
> **sci.optics.fiber**
> **sci.physics**
> **sci.physics.accelerators**
> **sci.physics.cond-matter**
> **sci.physics.electromag**
> **sci.physics.research**

Plasma Physics

When you have to attend a potluck dinner and you just don't know what to bring, consider a nice quasi-neutral gas such as plasma. Admittedly, it doesn't sound entirely appetizing, but just think of all the great things you can do with it. You could make an advanced microwave device, use it in ceramic production or toxic waste treatment or, for a really fun time, you could design a power grid for a spacecraft. Find out the other reasons why plasma is cool by reading information about the science and possible applications of this branch of physics.

Web:
> http://ippex.pppl.gov/
> http://plasma-gate.weizmann.ac.il/Plasma1.html

Usenet:
> **sci.physics.plasma**

Polymer and Liquid Crystal Tutorial

A polymer is a high-molecular weight compound, consisting of large numbers of repeating units—relatively simple molecules called monomers—linked by covalent bonds. Polymers can be natural (such as cellulose, silk and natural rubber) or synthetic (such as plastics and synthetic fibers). A liquid crystal is a liquid in which the constituent molecules arrange themselves with a higher degree of order than ordinary liquids, by pointing along a common axis called a director. Within a liquid crystal, the arrangement of the molecules offers many of the optical characteristics of solid crystals. However, since the molecular arrangements are not so firmly fixed, they can be modified—along with subsequent changes in optical properties—by mechanical stress, electromagnetic radiation or changes in temperature. Both polymers and liquid crystals are fascinating substances. If you would like a good introduction to these and other related subjects, try this series of well-organized, well-written multimedia tutorials. I enjoyed the tutorials myself, even though they did tend to remind me of organic chemistry class.

Web:
> http://plc.cwru.edu/

Polymer Physics

Polymers are large molecules constructed out of repeating units of small building blocks, joined to one another by covalent bonds. Many polymers occur naturally, such as cellulose, natural rubber and silk. Even proteins can be thought of as polymers. Commercially, there are a great many man-made polymers, such as plastics, synthetic fibers and synthetic rubber.

Web:
> http://cps-www.bu.edu/
> http://www.irc.leeds.ac.uk/irc/research/full/full.htm

Usenet:
> **sci.polymers**

Listserv Mailing List:
> List Name: **polymerp**
> Subscribe to: **listserv@nic.surfnet.nl**

A B C D E F G H I J K L M N O **P** Q R S T U V W X Y Z

Relativity

"Relativity" refers to the idea that there are certain physical properties that can be determined only relative to an observer. Here is a simple example: You're standing beside a highway and someone points to a car and asks "How fast is that car going?" Now imagine yourself driving on the highway beside that very car, keeping even with it. In the first case, the car is moving fast relative to an observer at the side of the road. In the second case, the car is barely moving at all, relative to an observer in a nearby car. Einstein developed such ideas into two complex theories: special relativity (dealing with systems that are not accelerating) and general relativity (dealing with gravity and acceleration). Einstein's theories formed the basis of our modern understanding of the universe, and the relativity research that is being carried on today has the goal of explaining, with more and more accuracy, how things really work.

Web:
  http://archive.ncsa.uiuc.edu/Cyberia/NumRel/
    GenRelativity.html
  http://www-gap.dcs.st-and.ac.uk/~history/
    HistTopics/General_relativity.html
  http://www.execpc.com/~dep33/Relativity.htm
  http://www.math.ucr.edu/home/baez/relativity.html
  http://www.maths.qmw.ac.uk/wbin/GRnewsfind/
    general/

Usenet:
  sci.physics.relativity

PICTURES AND CLIP ART

Cartoon Pictures

There's no need to have a bare room or office cubicle. Check out the Usenet groups in which people discuss and share cartoon pictures. You'll be able to find enough images to decorate your walls to your heart's content. What's more, by participating in the discussion, you'll gain a great deal of valuable knowledge, allowing you to impress people whenever they come by to admire your walls.

Usenet:
  alt.binaries.pictures.cartoons
  alt.toon-pics

Clip Art

Need clip art for your books, publications, garage sale fliers, home pages, term papers or whatever? But just as soon not (shudder) pay for them? On the Net there are lots of public domain clip art sites ripe for the plucking. In these copious archives, you'll find all the royalty-free drawings, etchings and whatnot that you could possibly use.

Web:
  http://www.ability.org.uk/clip.html
  http://www.barrysclipart.com/
  http://www.clipart.com/
  http://www.clipartconnection.com/
  http://www.webplaces.com/html/clipart.htm

Usenet:
  alt.binaries.clip-art

Fantasy Art

When the view out your window becomes boring and tedious, take a break from real life by browsing these huge archives of images of knights, castles, dragons, unicorns, wizards and more.

Web:
  http://elfwood.lysator.liu.se/
  http://www.alshandra.com/pages/clipartmain.htm
  http://www.spiritonline.com/gallery/graphics.html

Fractals

Fractals are mathematical constructions that have a "fractional" dimension. There are many types of fractals and, even within a single fractal, there can be infinite variety. Use these resources to learn about fractals, and explore the wonderful images you can create using these fascinating objects.

Web:
 http://www.faqs.org/faqs/sci/fractals-faq/
 http://www.fractalarts.com/ASF/
 http://www.fractaldomains.com/
 http://www.lifesmith.com/gallery.html

Usenet:
 sci.fractals

Graphics Making Tools

Here are some tools I think you'll really like. You can use them to make all kinds of graphics: plain and fancy text (including 3D), banners, buttons, and much more. Have fun making your own graphics, then print them or use them on your Web site.

Web:
 http://www.coder.com/creations/banner/
 http://www.cooltext.com/
 http://www.flamingtext.com/
 http://www.mediabuilder.com/

Icon Collections

Your Web pages and desktop are just not complete without a few cool icons, either as plain old decoration, or as links to something wild and crazy. Where, though, to get the icons? These Web sites have collections of icons that you can use for anything from simple clip art to clickable links.

Web:
 http://www.ender-design.com/rg/icons.html
 http://www.iconsplus.com/
 http://www.zeldman.com/icon.html

Nature Images

Nature images can really dress up your Web site and your email. (I just mailed a photo of a butterfly to a friend.) These resources will provide you with free pictures of nature scenes, animals, and all kinds of soothing clip art.

Web:
 http://www.btinternet.com/~fireballxl5/nature/
 http://www.freefoto.com/pictures/nature/
 http://www.internetclipart.com/nature/nature.htm

Photo Sharing

It's nice to share, and it's even nicer to share photos. Not only can you upload your photos to share with other people, you can create your own online photo albums for your family and friends to enjoy. It's a nice way to keep everyone up to date on your activities and to share those special moments as nature intended them to be shared: over the Internet.

Web:
 http://www.ofoto.com/
 http://www.photofun.com/
 http://www.printroom.com/
 http://www.webshots.com/

Picture Viewing Software

Most of the time, your browser can show you any picture you want. However, there are a lot of different types of graphics, and there may be times when you need a special-purpose picture viewing program. Not to worry, all the programs you need are available on the Net for free.

Web:
 http://ssi.tucows.com/mmedia/grap95.html

Stereograms

Stereograms are pictures consisting of what looks like a large number of small, random dots. However, when you stare at a stereogram in the right way, your brain will see a three-dimensional image, thereby showing you that there is more to what you see than what you see. (You know, that's an awfully deep thought. Maybe I should start my own religion.)

Web:
 http://www.colorstereo.com/
 http://www.kondo3d.com/stereo/
 http://www.netaxs.com/~mhmyers/rds-ex.html
 http://www.nott.ac.uk/~etzpc/nz/sirds.html
 http://www.nott.ac.uk/~etzpc/sirds.html

Supermodels

The next best thing to living next door to a supermodel is being able to download one whenever you want. Just the thing to look at when you get tired of fractals.

Web:
> http://www.bikinihangout.com/photo_gallery/
> bikini_gallery/
> http://www.user8.com/

Usenet:
> alt.binaries.pictures.supermodels

World Cultures Clip Art

When you want something special and exotic to add cultural spice to your Web site, try some of this free clip art. You'll find graphics with Egyptian, Celtic, Indian, Greek and medieval, and Islamic motifs including borders, backgrounds, and so on.

Web:
> http://members.aol.com/cyrion7/celtic/clipart/
> http://www.ancientnile.co.uk/graphics.html
> http://www.celtic-clipart.co.uk/
> http://www.islam.tc/clip-art/
> http://www.neferchichi.com/
> http://www.webomator.com/bws/data/reclip.html

The castle of your dreams is out there somewhere, and you can visit it right now, on the Net.

Acropolis and the Parthenon

In ancient Greece, many cities had an elevated, fortified area known as an acropolis ("top of the city"). The acropolis is where the inhabitants of a city would seek refuge during an invasion. The most well-known acropolis, *the* Acropolis, is the one in Athens. The Acropolis contains the ruins of some of the world's greatest architectural monuments, in particular, the Parthenon, Erechtheum and Propylaea. (Actually, my theory is that these are the Greek names for the Three Stooges.) The Parthenon, originally built as a temple, is one of the most famous ruins in the world because it is considered to be the supreme example of Doric architecture. The main structures on the Acropolis were built in the fifth century B.C., and were richly adorned with color, statures, friezes and other art. The Parthenon, which has become the archetype of a Greek temple, is in relatively good condition. In total, it had 64 columns, 27 on the outside and 37 on the inside. Today, people visit the Acropolis and Parthenon for two main reasons. First, when you are in Athens, you go to see the Acropolis because everyone else does. Second, you can stand at the top, imagine the ancient Greek city below you, pretend that the ruins of the buildings are intact, and marvel at the architectural achievements of an ancient people.

Web:
> http://academic.reed.edu/humanities/110tech/
> parthenon.html
> http://www.athensguide.com/athacrop.html
> http://www.dragonridge.com/greece/Acropolis.htm
> http://www.greatbuildings.com/buildings/
> the_parthenon.html

Castles

Indulge in your fantasies of knights, dragons and history galore by touring some of the many castles around the globe. You'll find a huge list of castles, including some of the best places in the world to play hide-and-go-seek.

Web:
> http://www.castles.org/
> http://www.dupontcastle.com/castles/

Cathedrals

The Gothic style of cathedrals was predominant in Europe from around 1150 to 1400. Gothic emerged in France and coincided with the rise of the monarchy as the central form of government. (Gothic cathedrals were not called gothic in their days of creation. The style was referred to as the "Modern" or "French" style. The term "Gothic" was coined in the sixteenth century by an Italian artist and historian named Giorgio Vasari. The expression was originally a negative term referring to the Goths who, Vasari felt, were responsible for ruining the classical artistry of the Roman empire.) However, today the Gothic cathedral is admired as a breathtaking work of art. This Web page offers a tour of various cathedrals such as Notre Dame, Canterbury and Chartres.

Web:

   http://www.elore.com/elore04.html

Easter Island

Easter Island is a triangle of volcanic rock in the South Pacific, 2,300 miles (3,700 km) west of Chile. Although the island is small—only 73 square miles (177 sq. km.)—it has the distinction of being the most isolated inhabited island in the world. (Imagine what it is like to try to have a pizza delivered there.) Easter Island was discovered by Dutch explorers on Easter Day 1722 (hence the name). Today, however, we use the Polynesian name of Rapa Nui to refer to the island, as well as the people who live there and their language. What makes Rapa Nui notable are the hundreds of giant human-like figures, called moai, carved out of volcanic rock. Although this may not sound like much, take a look at the pictures. Truly, the moai of Rapa Nui are among the most incredible ancient relics ever discovered. Although they must have taken the original natives many years to build, the actual origins of the moai are unknown. (My theory is that the natives needed something to do while they waited for their pizza.)

Web:

   http://www.crystalinks.com/easter.html
   http://www.mysteriousplaces.com/easter_island/
   http://www.netaxs.com/~trance/rapanui.html

Famous Mountains

Do you find mountains interesting? If so, here are photographs and information about some of the most famous mountains in the world: Mount Fuji (Japan), Mount St. Helens (Washington state, U.S.), Mount Kilimanjaro (Tanzania), Mount Kailash (Tibet) and Mount Everest (Nepal). After looking at the pictures, I have a new goal in life. I want to climb to the top of Mount Everest and throw a penny off the top. (Mountain trivia: Of the highest mountains in the world, all of the top 10 are in Nepal and Kashmir.)

Web:

   http://www.fs.fed.us/gpnf/mshnvm/
   http://www.jerberyd.com/climbing/mountains.htm
   http://www.mnteverest.net/
   http://www.mt-fuji.co.jp/index-e.html
   http://www.planet101.com/mountain10.htm
   http://www.tanzania-web.com/mtkil/

Golden Gate Bridge

In 1579, the English explorer Francis Drake discovered a strait connecting the Pacific Ocean with San Francisco Bay. This strait became known as the Golden Gate. Although the name was used long before the California Gold Rush of 1849, the Gold Rush made the Golden Gate—the entrance into Northern California—an indelible part of the California mystique. The idea of building a bridge across the Golden Gate Strait was discussed as early as 1872. However, it was not until 1937 that a suspension bridge was built to span the strait. The Golden Gate Bridge runs north and south, connecting the city of San Francisco to Marin County. The bridge, which took a little over four years to build, is one of the most beautiful structures in the world. It is not the longest suspension bridge in the world, but it is easily the most famous.

Web:

   http://www.goldengatebridge.org/research/
   facts.html
   http://www.thoma.com/thoma/ggbfacts.html

Great Barrier Reef

A coral is a very small, sedentary sea creature with a hard outer covering. Corals grow where there is warm, clear sunlit seawater. They form colonies in which many tiny animals attach to one another. As individual corals die, their outer coverings remain and build up in layers. Eventually, over many years, more and more corals live and die, and a coral reef is created. The reef forms a colorful, natural barrier that serves as a home for many different types of marine life. The largest coral reef in the world is the Great Barrier Reef, a collection of over 2,900 individual reefs and 618 small islands off the coast of Queensland, Australia. It is 1,430 miles (2,300 km) long, covering 21,000 square miles (349,000 sq km) and, in places, is more than 400 ft (122 m) thick.

Web:
  http://www.acn.net.au/articles/1999/02/gbr.htm
  http://www.barrierreef.net/DiscoveryCoast/
  http://www.gbrmpa.gov.au/
  http://www.ozramp.net.au/~senani/barrier.htm
  http://www2.eis.net.au/~nqtds/infocomm/
    1overv1.html

Great Wall of China

The Great Wall of China is a long series of fortifications, averaging 25 feet (7.6 m) in height, which extend 3,700 miles (6,000 km) across northern China. The wall was designed as a military structure to protect China against invasion. Much of the wall was built in the third century B.C. by 300,000 laborers, most of whom were criminals, conscripted soldiers and slaves who died in the process. Originally, there were a large number of small walls, which were later united into a few very long segments. The present form of the wall dates from the Ming dynasty (1368-1644). Interestingly enough, after all the effort and expense that went into building the wall, it didn't work. China was successfully invaded, a number of times, by nomads from the north. (By then, of course, it was too late for the Chinese to get their money back.)

Web:
  http://www.beijingtrip.com/attractions/greatwall/
  http://www.chinavista.com/travel/greatwall/
    greatwall.html
  http://www.travelchinaguide.com/china_great_wall/
  http://www.walkthewall.com/

Labyrinths

A labyrinth is a place to walk: a circular, single-path maze, used for meditation and spiritual focus. Labyrinths are constructed with a pathway that winds around and around, back and forth. For example, a labyrinth that measures only 40 feet in diameter might take an hour or more to traverse completely. The idea is that, while you are walking, you are free from the normal distractions of everyday life, which allows you to focus on the pattern and create a walking meditation. There are a wide variety of labyrinths in the world: old, new, large, small, indoors and outdoors. Some labyrinths are elaborate works of art, others are simple homemade creations. Are you interested? Would you like to walk a labyrinth or even make your own? Start here.

Web:
  http://www.earthsymbols.com/symbols.html
  http://www.geomancy.org/labyrinths/
  http://www.gracecathedral.org/labyrinth/
  http://www.labyrinthina.com/laby.htm
  http://www.labyrinthos.net/

Pompeii

We often think of ancient people as being different from us. Actually, human nature doesn't really change. One way to appreciate this is to study an ancient city, and one of the best-preserved cities in the world is Pompeii. Two thousand years ago, Pompeii was a flourishing city in what is now southern Italy, close to Naples at the foot of a mountain named Mt. Vesuvius. In 79 A.D., Mt. Vesuvius erupted in a massive explosion, completely burying Pompeii and the nearby city of Herculaneum. In 1748, Pompeii was rediscovered and, since that time, extensive excavations have revealed much about life in Roman times. For example, did you know that the Romans kept dogs as pets and wrote graffiti on their walls? They also baked fresh bread, wore brightly colored clothes and decorated their houses with knickknacks and family portraits. They worked hard to survive and care for their families—until one day, a nearby volcano erupted and their world changed forever.

Web:
  http://users.ipa.net/~tanker/pompeii.htm
  http://www.cs.berkeley.edu/~jhauser/pictures/
    history/Rome/Pompeii/
  http://www.etrav.net/pathways/html/pompeii.asp
  http://www.harcourtschool.com/activity/pompeii/

Pyramids

When I was an undergraduate, I had a friend named Stu. I remember once driving with Stu and his father. We were talking about whether or not humanity should spend a lot of money on space exploration, when Stu's father asked "Why build pyramids?" He was trying to tell us that human beings, by their nature, have always striven to achieve greatness, and that human nature doesn't change. The most famous pyramids are the ten large ones built by ancient Egyptians between 2630 and 2472 B.C. Each of these massive structures was created as a tomb for a single Egyptian pharaoh (king). During his lifetime, a pharaoh would build his own pyramid so that, after he died, his mummified body could be preserved for all eternity. Pyramids were built as part of a group of other structures, including temples, chapels, other tombs and large walls. The largest pyramid in the world, built for the pharaoh Khufu, is the Great Pyramid at Giza, southwest of modern Cairo. It contains many stones weighing several tons and, originally, stood 482 feet (147 m) high. Here is some important information that may save your life one day: the names of the pharaohs for whom the pyramids were built are Zoser, Sekhemkhet, Khaba, Huni, Snefru (2), Khufu, Djedefra, Khafra and Menkaura.

Web:
  http://www.ancientegypt.co.uk/pyramids/
  http://www.egypt-tehuti.com/pyramids.html
  http://www.eyelid.co.uk/pyr-temp.htm
  http://www.gizapyramid.com/
  http://www.guardians.net/egypt/pyramids.htm
  http://www.powerup.com.au/~ancient/pyra1.htm
  http://www.touregypt.net/monument.htm

PYRAMIDS

Last week, I built a life-sized model of the Great Pyramid of Giza in my backyard. But then I had to dismantle the whole thing when I discovered that I had accidentally left my only copy of People Magazine underneath the bottom stone.

Roadside America

When it comes to offbeat and just plain strange, there is no country on Earth like the United States. Just imagine: a huge country with millions of miles of highways, cheap gas, and lots of tourist facilities, all combined with the enormous cultural freedom to do exactly as you wish, without the artificial restrictions of good taste, attractive appearance or tradition. Would you like to see scary museums, mystery spots, gas chambers, or pet cemeteries? How about a place to see really big fake cows? America: is there any place you'd rather be?

Web:
  http://www.roadsideamerica.com/

Sacred Places

Is nothing sacred? Not at all. Lots of stuff is sacred, including a large number of places around the world that people regard with intense emotion—places such as the Ellora caves in India; the Asklepion shrine in Athens; the Dome of the Rock in Jerusalem; Lourdes in France; Mount Sinai in Egypt; Mecca in Saudi Arabia; and on and on.

Web:
  http://www.arthistory.sbc.edu/sacredplaces/
    sacredplacesintro.html
  http://www.sacredsites.com/

Sedlec Ossuary

It's grotesque, or artistically magnificent, depending on how you think about it. The Sedlec Ossuary is a small Christian chapel on the outskirts of the Czech town of Kutna Hora. What makes it unique is that it is decorated with the bones of 40,000 people. Here's how it happened. In the early 1300s, the area suffered from the plague and about 30,000 people died. Their remains were added to an existing cemetery, and around 1400, a chapel was built in the middle of the cemetery. In 1511, a monk gathered the existing bones and put them in a crypt to make room for new burials. In 1870, a woodcarver was hired to use the bones, by then 40,000 sets strong, to decorate the inside of the chapel. And now they are all finally resting in peace.

Web:
  http://www.eurodata.com/articles/sedlec.htm
  http://www.ludd.luth.se/users/silver_p/kutna.html

Seven Wonders of the Ancient World

There were many wonders in the ancient world. Traditionally, we recognize seven of these as being extra special. They are the Great Pyramid of Khufu at Giza, the Hanging Gardens of Babylon, the statue of Zeus at Olympia, the Temple of Artemis at Ephesus, the Mausoleum at Halicarnassus, the Colossus of Rhodes, and the Lighthouse of Alexandria. Except for the pyramid, most of these will probably not be familiar, so take a few moments and explore some of the most impressive creations in history. By the way, the only one that is still around is the Great Pyramid of Khufu at Giza, Egypt. Even into the nineteenth century, when it was about 4000 years old, this pyramid was still the tallest building in the world.

Web:
   http://ce.eng.usf.edu/pharos/wonders/
   http://www.cleveleys.co.uk/wonders/
      sevenwondersoftheworld.htm
   http://www.crystalinks.com/seven.html

Stones and Megaliths

A megalith is a structure made out of huge stones. There are a large number of ancient megalithic monuments in western Europe and the British Isles dating back to 2000-1500 B.C. Typically, the stones are arranged singly, in rows or in a circle. Although no one knows for sure why these monuments were erected, it is thought that they were used for religious purposes or as part of a funeral ceremony. The most well-known megalith monument is Stonehenge, located on Salisbury Plain in the south of England. However, around the world, you will find many other stone circles, as well as cairns, stone settlements, stone rows, dolmens (chamber tombs) and manmade mounds.

Web:
   http://www.anima.demon.co.uk/stones/
   http://www.bass100.freeserve.co.uk/
   http://www.henge.org.uk/
   http://www.stonehenge-avebury.net/
   http://www.stonehenge.uklinux.net/
   http://www.stonepages.com/

World's Tallest Buildings

In 1956, Frank Lloyd Wright proposed a skyscraper, called "The Illinois", which would be a mile high (over 1,600 meters). The structure was never built, but man's quest for such buildings has flourished. If you love tall buildings, this is the place for you. Not only will you find enough information to satiate your desires, you will feel right at home among those who worship tall buildings as more than just jumbo-sized structures. Tall buildings speak deep to our psyche, in an innate sexual way (which I would explain were this not a family book). So what is the tallest building in the world? It's more or less a tie. Officially, the tallest buildings in the world are the Petronas Towers, a pair of buildings in Kuala Lumpur, Malaysia, which reach a height of 1,483 feet (452 meters). However, the Sears Tower in Chicago, a close second at 1,454 feet (443 meters), is actually 1,730 feet (527 meters) if you count the antenna on top. (In Chicago, they count the antenna on top.)

Web:
  http://www.high-rises.co.uk/worlds_tallest.html

POETRY

British Poetry

The legacy of British poetry is a large one, and on the Internet you'll find a lot of information about individual poets, as well as many, many poems to read. Take some time to explore the work of Chaucer (1340?-1400), Shakespeare (1564-1616), Milton (1608-1674), Blake (1757-1827), Burns (1759-1796), Wordsworth (1770-1850), Coleridge (1772-1834), Byron (1788-1824), Shelley (1792-1822), Keats (1795-1821), Elizabeth Browning (1806-1861), Tennyson (1809-1892), Robert Browning (1812-1889), Stevenson (1850-1894), Kipling (1865-1936), Yeats (1865-1939), De la Mare (1873-1956), and many others. Whenever I need a short break, I like to take a moment and look for something interesting to read.

Web:
  http://etext.lib.virginia.edu/britpo.html
  http://users.compaqnet.be/cn127848/obev/
  http://www.bartleby.com/103/
  http://www.lib.ucdavis.edu/English/BWRP/

Chinese Poetry

Chinese poetry is beautiful in its imagery and simplicity. Most poems are written in a special, very old literary language that is widely understood throughout China. The traditional pattern is to use exactly four lines that rhyme, with a specific number of syllables in each line. Within each line, special attention is paid to the phrasing and to the tonal patterns. The oldest extant Chinese poems are those found in the "Book of Songs" (800-600 B.C.). In modern times, Chinese poets have experimented by writing in the spoken languages and by using free verse.

Web:

http://www.chinapage.com/poetry9.html

Haiku

Haiku is a lovely, delicate form of Japanese poetry. If you are a poetry lover, take some time to explore these resources and learn about the world of haiku.

Web:

http://mdn.mainichi.co.jp/haiku/
http://www.ahapoetry.com/haiku.htm
http://www.execpc.com/~ohaus/haiklink.htm
http://www.nhi.clara.net/hktalk.htm

Chinese Poetry

I love Chinese poetry and you will too once you give it a chance. My favorite Chinese poem is the traditional dramatic epic from the Ming dynasty that starts, "There was a young girl from Beijing..." If you like poetry, spend some time with this most beautiful of art forms and its Asian incarnation.

HAIKU

Haiku is a form of poetry, developed in Japan, in which the writer seeks to capture a specific transient observation about the natural world. The world changes so quickly, and haiku is one way to capture a particular image or sensation.

A haiku poem (usually referred to as a "haiku") consists of three lines. The first line has 5 syllables, the second has 7, and the third has 5.

In addition, it is traditional for a haiku to indicate a particular season. Often, this is done by including a word that invokes a feeling of either winter, spring, summer or fall. In English, the tradition is slightly different: a poem should contain a reference to nature, but not necessarily to a particular season.

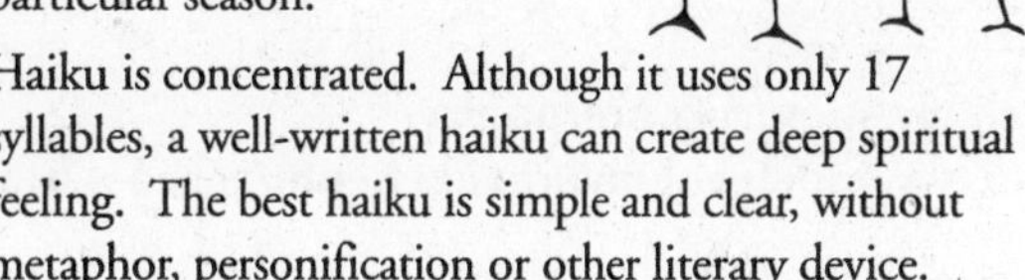

Haiku is concentrated. Although it uses only 17 syllables, a well-written haiku can create deep spiritual feeling. The best haiku is simple and clear, without metaphor, personification or other literary device.

If you would like to learn more about haiku, you will find more information on the Net. In the meantime, here is a haiku I wrote for you to enjoy:

fog blanket covers

tall green trees wait silently

quiet soothing peace

Irish Poetry

If you don't have time to run down to your local pub for a poetry reading, try just getting a brew from the fridge and downloading a poem or two written by an Irish poet. For a really good time, you can even find some poetry set to music.

Web:

http://www.bbc.co.uk/northernireland/poetry/
http://www.dnaco.net/~mobrien/irishptr/irepoems/
http://www.sundown.pair.com/Sharp/Lyra Celtica/celtica_contents.htm

Limericks

Suzanne was a delicate flower,
Whose beauty increased by the hour,
Ev'ry day of the year,
Many men would stand near,
Waiting for her to exit the shower.

Web:
http://www.home.earthlink.net/~kristenaa/
http://www.limericks.org/pentatette/reply.html
http://www.lims.demon.co.uk/

Poetry Archives

There is a lot of poetry for you on the Net. Here are some collections I think you will enjoy: lots and lots of well-known poems, as well as links to other poetry sites. These are good places to visit if you are looking for a particular poem or work from a particular author, or if you just feel like browsing for something to read.

Web:
http://www.eserver.org/poetry/
http://www.petecol.mybravenet.com/authors.htm

Poetry Place

Do you write poetry? Would you like to share it with others? Visit this Web site where you can offer your poems, in a virtual "open mike" area. You can also read other people's poems and notice that they are not nearly as good as yours.

Web:
http://www.ahapoetry.com/

Poetry Slam

A poetry slam, or performance poetry, is a competition in which poets read in front of an audience. After the readings, the competitors are judged and a winner is chosen. Poetry slams can be small informal events, but there are also well-organized national competitions in which poets compete both as individuals and as teams.

Web:
http://www.e-poets.net/library/slam/
http://www.poetryslam.com/
http://www.thebattleofthepoets.com/

Poetry Talk and General Discussion

There are two types of people who write poetry: those who show their poetry to other people and those who don't. If you like to show your poetry to other people, share it with the participants of these Usenet discussion groups. If you don't like to share your poetry, you can enjoy other people's creations. (And while you're there, you might as well offer your opinions.)

Usenet:
alt.arts.poetry.comments
alt.centipede
alt.language.poetry.pure-silk
alt.language.urdu.poetry
alt.lesbian.feminist.poetry
alt.teens.poetry.and.stuff
alt.ygdrasil
rec.arts.poems
rec.arts.poetry

Semantic Rhyming Dictionary

Anyone can rhyme "moon" with "June", and "love" with "stars above". However, when you get into serious rhyming, you want more than words that sound alike. It is important that the words are related to one another. This rhyming dictionary will help you find such words. You can look for perfect rhymes, match the last sound only, match consonants, find homophones, synonyms or semantic siblings. If you are the type of person who looks for just the right word, this is the Web site for you.

Web:
http://www.rhyme.lycos.com/

Sonnets

A sonnet is a 14-line poem in which lines of iambic pentameter are linked by a specific rhyming pattern. (Iambic pentameter refers to five "feet", each of which consists of an unstressed syllable followed by a stressed syllable.) There are two main types of rhyming patterns used in sonnets. An Italian (or Petrarchan) sonnet uses two groupings, 8 lines followed by 6 lines. The rhyming is abbaabba cdecde (or sometimes abbaabba cdccdc); that is, line 1 rhymes with lines 4, 5 and 8; line 2 rhymes with lines 3, 6 and 7; and so on. An English (or Shakespearean) sonnet uses three 4-line groupings, followed by a 2-line couplet, with rhyming as follows: abab cdcd efef gg. Sonnets first gained popularity in Italy during the Renaissance. Later, the art form spread to Spain, Portugal, France and England. Sonnets began as love poetry, and many of the most beautiful love poems ever written are of this form. Some of the more important writers of sonnets were Dante (1265-1321), Petrarch (1304-1374), Edmund Spenser (1552?-1599), Philip Sidney (1554-1586), Shakespeare (1564-1616), John Keats (1795-1821), Elizabeth Barrett Browning (1806-1861), George Meredith (1828-1909), Edna St. Vincent Millay (1892-1950), and W.H. Auden (1907-1973).

Web:
   http://sonnets.spanish.sbc.edu/
   http://www.it.usyd.edu.au/~matty/Shakespeare/
      texts/poetry/sonnets
   http://www.sonnets.org/

Worst Poetry

Who are the worst poets of all time? No one can really say for sure, but there are people who are celebrated as being close to that ideal, such as James McIntyre (Canada), William McGonagall (Scotland) and Julia Moore (United States). And when you have read about them, there's lots more bad poetry to keep your literary fires stoked.

Web:
   http://unix.cc.wmich.edu/~cooneys/poems/bad/
   http://www.coffeeshoptimes.com/badpoet.html
   http://www.inforamp.net/~ihooker/
   http://www.nylon.net/poetry/
   http://www.taynet.co.uk/users/mcgon/
   http://www.wmich.edu/english/tchg/lit/pms/bad/

A lot of people write poetry, and some of it is pretty bad. But it takes real talent to write poetry so bad that you are widely recognized as being in a class of your own.

POETRY: POETS

Blake, William

The English writer William Blake (1757-1827) was considered a visionary, one of the early proponents of what came to be called Romanticism. Over the years, Blake's work evolved from light, comfortable poems to intense, sometimes frightening, work dealing with his excessive spirituality and what he considered to be messages from heaven. His most well-known collections are "Songs of Innocence" and "Songs of Experience". One interesting thing about Blake is that he illustrated, printed and published all of his own books.

Web:
   http://www.bibliomania.com/0/2/81/frameset.html
   http://www.blakearchive.org/
   http://www.online-literature.com/blake/
   http://www.poets.org/poets/poets.cfm?prmID=117
   http://www.tate.org.uk/britain/exhibitions/
      blakeinteractive/

Brooks, Gwendolyn

While she was still in her early thirties, African-American poet Gwendolyn Brooks (1917-2000) won a Pulitzer Prize for her second book "Annie Allen". Throughout a lifetime of creation, Brooks' work has matured and evolved, but one recurring theme is the exhortation that one must be responsible, both personally and socially. When something is wrong, it's not enough to admit guilt; one must also be accountable for one's actions. Brooks has made a career out of being passionate and plain-spoken. Consider one of her most famous poems "The Mother" (1945), which deals with the emotional conflicts of abortion: "Abortions will not let you forget / You remember the children you got that you did not get..."

Web:

http://voices.cla.umn.edu/authors/
    gwendolynbrooks.html
http://www.english.uiuc.edu/maps/poets/a_f/brooks/
    brooks.htm
http://www.poetspath.com/brooks.html

Browning, Elizabeth Barrett

Elizabeth Barrett Browning (1806-1861) was a renowned British poet who married another renowned British poet (Robert Browning). Her most noted works are "Sonnets from the Portuguese" (a series of love poems written to her husband), "Casa Guidi Windows" and "Aurora Leigh".

Web:

http://landow.stg.brown.edu/victorian/ebb/
    browningov.html
http://www.library.utoronto.ca/utel/rp/authors/
    brwneliz.html
http://www.mith2.umd.edu/WomensStudies/
    ReadingRoom/Poetry/BarrettBrowning/
http://www.poets.org/poets/poets.cfm?prmID=153

Turn the page.

Browning, Robert

Robert Browning (1812-1889) was a British poet, celebrated for his dramatic monologues. One of the most well-known monologues (inflicted on countless high school English students) is "My Last Duchess", in which the speaker describes his previous wife and her shortcomings, and leaves us wondering exactly how she met her end. Browning was the husband of poet Elizabeth Barrett Browning, who he met after admiring her poetry and corresponding with her by letter. (He was the one to whom she wrote "Sonnets from the Portuguese".) My favorite Browning poem is "Pippa's Song" from the long, dramatic poem "Pippa Passes". The poem is short, but it always makes me feel good. ("The year's at the spring, / And day's at the morn; / Morning's at seven; / The hill-side's dew-pearled; / The lark's on the wing; / The snail's on the thorn; / God's in his Heaven - / All's right with the world!")

Web:

http://www.4literature.net/Robert_Browning/
http://www.incompetech.com/authors/rbrowning/
http://www.library.utoronto.ca/utel/rp/authors/
    browning.html
http://www.poets.org/poets/poets.cfm?prmID=185
http://www.public.asu.edu/~jolmatt/browning/

Byron, Lord (George Gordon)

The English poet Lord George Gordon Byron (1788-1824) was... well... Byronic: a dark, brooding, passionate man, who devoted himself to the pleasures of life, especially sensual pleasures. Byron is remembered as one of the great Romantic poets, especially with respect to his epic masterpiece "Don Juan". The life of Byron is the story of an insatiable satyric reprobate, who scampered from one dalliance to another only to stop long enough to write magnificent poetry. I particularly like the beginning of his poem "She Walks in Beauty: "She walks in beauty, like the night / Of cloudless climes and starry skies; / And all that's best of dark and bright / Meet in her aspect and her eyes..."

Web:

http://www.byronmania.com/
http://www.englishhistory.net/byron.html
http://www.incompetech.com/authors/byron/
http://www.library.utoronto.ca/utel/rp/authors/
    byron.html

Cummings, E.E.

Cummings (1894-1962) was an American poet who ignored many of the conventions of standard written English. For example, he rarely used capital letters (which is why you will often see his name written, erroneously, as "e.e. cummings"), and his use of punctuation and spacing was idiosyncratic and exact. (I imagine he drove his copy editor crazy.) Cummings wrote on many different subjects, including love and the failings of public institutions.

Web:

http://www.english.uiuc.edu/maps/poets/a_f/
  cummings/cummings.htm
http://www.k-b-c.com/poetry_eec.htm
http://www.library.utoronto.ca/utel/rp/authors/
  eec.html
http://www.mason-west.com/cummings/
http://www.nascitur.com/cummings/cummings.html
http://www.poets.org/poets/poets.cfm?prmID=157

In the Woody Allen movie *Hannah and her Sisters*, Elliot is trying to seduce his wife's sister Lee. Elliot and Lee are alone in a bookstore when he takes a book of E. E. Cummings' poetry off the shelf.

"I read a poem of his and thought of you last week," Elliot tells Lee. "I'd love to get you this, and maybe we could discuss it sometime." As she leaves, he says, "Don't forget the poem on page 112. It reminded me of you."

The next thing we see is Lee reading the second and fifth verses of the poem *somewhere I have never traveled*:

> your slightest look easily will unclose me
> though i have closed myself as fingers,
> you open always petal by petal myself as Spring opens
> (touching skillfully, mysteriously) her first rose
>
> (i do not know what it is about you that closes
> and opens; only something in me understands
> the voice of your eyes is deeper than all roses)
> nobody, not even the rain, has such small hands

Later, when Elliot is alone with Lee once again, he asks, "Did you ever get around to the poem on page 112?"

"It made me cry," she answers, "it was so beautiful and romantic."

(Of course, he could have just given her a copy of a Harley Hahn book and saved a lot of time.)

Dickinson, Emily

Emily Elizabeth Dickinson (1830-1886) was a prolific American poet. Her verse is characterized by style, wit and imagery. Dickinson was a recluse who stayed in her house most of the time, writing poetry. Although she wrote a great many poems, Dickinson was virtually unpublished until after her death.

Web:

http://www.csustan.edu/english/reuben/pal/chap4/
  dickinson.html
http://www.online-literature.com/dickinson/
http://www.poets.org/poets/poets.cfm?prmID=156

Listserv Mailing List:

List Name: dicknson
Subscribe to: listserv@listserv.uta.edu

Eliot, T.S.

I have a friend named Mark, a urologist, who transplants kidneys for a living. I remember once, when we were kids, Mark read the poem "The Love Song of J. Alfred Prufrock" and was so overwhelmed that he called me on the phone and read me the entire poem. T.S. Eliot (1888-1965) was an American-born British poet, playwright and essayist, whose most important themes were the revitalization of religion and the emptiness of modern life. Aside from the Prufrock poem, Eliot is best known for his poem "The Wasteland" and his play "Murder in the Cathedral". To this day, I still remember the beginning of "Prufrock" as Mark read it to me: "Let us go then, you and I, / When the evening is spread out against the sky / Like a patient etherised upon a table" (which seems to explain his appeal among urologists).

Web:

http://occawlonline.pearsoned.com/bookbind/
  pubbooks/kennedy2_awl/chapter9/objectives/
  deluxe-content.html
http://www.deathclock.com/thunder/
http://www.poets.org/poets/poets.cfm?prmID=18

Frost, Robert

Robert Frost (1874-1963) was one of the foremost American poets of the twentieth century. Frost used traditional poetic forms and metrics, which makes his work particularly attractive to someone like me who likes poems that rhyme. Much of what Frost wrote centered upon life in New England, where he lived. However, he is celebrated for writing about universal human themes, which he did with great skill and deceptive simplicity. As an example, consider these lines from two of Frost's best-known poems. "Stopping By Woods On A Snowy Evening: "The woods are lovely, dark, and deep, / But I have promises to keep, / And miles to go before I sleep..." And from the "The Road Not Taken: "...two roads diverged in a wood, and I—/ I took the one less traveled by, / And that has made all the difference." Is that hot stuff, or what?

Web:

  http://www.english.uiuc.edu/maps/poets/a_f/frost/
    frost.htm
  http://www.ketzle.com/frost/
  http://www.online-literature.com/frost/
  http://www.poets.org/poets/poets.cfm?prmID=196

Hughes, Langston

American writer, Langston Hughes (1902-1967) was the shining light of the Harlem Renaissance (a black cultural movement of the 1920s and 1930s, centered in Harlem, New York City). Hughes, a leading figure in American letters, was a world traveler who came to be known as the "poet laureate of Harlem". His work— poems, novels, stories, plays, essays, newspaper columns, and histories—were the foremost depiction of the black experience in the United States of his time. As such, he served as a link between Art and the community, inspiring black writers, not only in America, but around the world. Hughes's first collection of poetry was "The Weary Blues" (1926). In later years, he published two autobiographies, "The Big Sea" (1940) and "I Wonder as I Wander" (1956). His most famous lines of poetry are from "Harlem" (1951): "What happens to a dream deferred? / Does it dry up like a raisin in the sun?"

Web:

  http://falcon.jmu.edu/~ramseyil/hughes.htm
  http://www.csustan.edu/english/reuben/pal/chap9/
    hughes.html
  http://www.english.uiuc.edu/maps/poets/g_l/hughes/
    hughes.htm
  http://www.poets.org/poets/poets.cfm?prmID=84

Keats, John

Although John Keats (1795-1821) lived only 25 years, he is considered to be one of the the the most renowned of the English Romantic poets. If you have ever heard the line, "A thing of beauty is a joy forever", you have experienced Keats: it is the first line of his poem "Endymion" (1818). His other well-known works include "Ode on a Grecian Urn" (1819) and "Ode to a Nightingale" (1819).

Web:

  http://www.englishhistory.net/keats.html
  http://www.library.utoronto.ca/utel/rp/authors/
    keats.html
  http://www.poets.org/poets/poets.cfm?prmID=67

Neruda, Pablo

Pablo Neruda (1904-1973) is a Chilean poet who won the 1971 Nobel Prize for Literature. Neruda's real name was Neftalí Ricardo Reyes Basoalto. He was born in the town of Parral, Chile, the son of a railway employee and a teacher. Neruda was a prolific writer. On his sixtieth birthday, he published "Memorial de Isla Negra", a five-volume collection of autobiographical poetry. Much of his poetry is political in nature. For example, in 1939, Neruda published an epic poem "Canto General", consisting of 250 poems collected into fifteen literary cycles that deal with the nature, people and history of South America. Neruda is also known for his love poetry, written to his wife Matilde.

Web:

  http://www-personal.umich.edu/~agreene/
    Neruda.html
  http://www.nobel.se/literature/laureates/1971/
  http://www.nobelprizes.com/nobel/literature/
    1971a.html
  http://www.poets.org/poets/poets.cfm?prmID=285

The Net was born on December 5, 1969.

Plath, Sylvia

Sylvia Plath (1932-1963) was an American poet whose work is characterized by its intense imagery and highly personal quality. Her most famous work, "The Bell Jar", is an autobiographical novel. Plath possessed a rare writing skill and sensitivity. She wrote her first poem at the age of eight, and throughout her schooling achieved a great deal of critical recognition. However, she was also a deeply troubled woman and committed suicide at the age of 30, after the breakup of her marriage. Perhaps because of her notoriety and unfortunate demise, Plath became popular among young women in the early '70s, along with the growth of the feminist movement. Even today, Plath's work is required reading in most courses of women's literature.

Web:

http://www.english.uiuc.edu/maps/poets/m_r/plath/
plath.htm
http://www.plathonline.com/
http://www.poets.org/poets/poets.cfm?prmID=11
http://www.sylviaplathforum.com/

Pushkin, Aleksandr

If you live in America, a country in which poetry does not play a big part in the body politic of popular culture, it's hard to understand the enormous affection Russians have for Aleksandr Pushkin (1799-1837). Pushkin is considered the greatest Russian poet of the 19th century, and perhaps, of all time—the father of classical Russian literature. Among his best-known works are "Boris Godunov" and "Eugene Onegin". Although his work necessarily loses something in the translation, you may enjoy looking at it. (From the short poem "In the Worldly Steppe...": "The spring of youth is speedy and rebellious, / It boils and runs, and ripples in a blaze...")

Web:

http://www.kirjasto.sci.fi/puskin.htm
http://www.odessaglobe.com/english/people/
pushkin.htm
http://www.poetryloverspage.com/poets/pushkin/
pushkin_ind.html

Shelley, Percy Bysshe

Percy Bysshe Shelley (1792-1822) was an English Romantic poet, celebrated for his highly crafted lyrical poems. Among his most well-known works are "To a Skylark", "Ode to the West Wind" and "Ozymandias". Throughout his life, Shelley had a strong belief in reason, arguing that it was possible for humanity to evolve into perfection. As such, Shelley spent years fighting against religion and promoting political freedom. For example, at the age of 20, he was expelled from Oxford University for collaborating on a pamphlet promoting atheism. Shelley was the husband of Mary Wollstonecraft Shelley (who wrote "Frankenstein"). He married her in 1816, after his first wife, whom he had abandoned two years earlier, drowned herself. Ironically, eight years later, Shelley himself died of drowning while sailing in Italy.

Web:

http://www.english.upenn.edu/~jlynch/
FrankenDemo/PShelley/pshelley.html
http://www.library.utoronto.ca/utel/rp/authors/
shelley.html
http://www.poets.org/poets/poets.cfm?prmID=182

Tennyson, Alfred

Alfred Tennyson (1809-1892) was an English poet who became Poet Laureate in 1850. He was a strong spokesman for Victorian values and is known for his excellent use of language and mastery of poetic technique. Some of his famous poems are "The Lady of Shalott", "The Charge of the Light Brigade" and "In Memorium". The last is a beautiful elegy written after the death of a close friend. I have always liked one of the verses, which I found particularly inspirational: "I held it truth, with him who sings / To one clear harp in divers tones, / That men may rise on stepping-stones / Of their dead selves to higher things."

Web:

http://charon.sfsu.edu/tennyson/tennyson.html
http://landow.stg.brown.edu/victorian/tennyson/
tennyov.html
http://www.incompetech.com/authors/tennyson/

Whitman, Walt

American poet Walt Whitman (1819-1892) was a restless creator, a tormented homosexual in a world of heterosexuals, a man of the people, whose poems, stories and newspaper articles represented the earliest appreciation of the American being. Whitman was a pioneer of free verse (poetry unconfined by rhyme or meter), and his work overflowed with visual and emotional impressions. Whitman spent the early years of his adult life as a wandering journalist. Later, during the Civil War, he served as an Army nurse. At the age of 36 (rather late for a poet), Whitman published his first major work, "Leaves of Grass" (1855), a collection of poems that he would expand and reissue, under the same title, seven more times throughout his life. Although Whitman's work was widely praised, many of his readers were shocked at the coarseness of his language and his explicitness of his ideas. To me, Whitman's personal sense of ambiguity is best illustrated by the lines from his early poem "Song of Myself: "Do I contradict myself? Very well then, I contradict myself, (I am large, I contain multitudes)." Visually, Whitman's image is best-known from the photographs of him in his old age, resplendent in a large, flowing white beard that bespoke both wisdom and competence (but then, it is well-known that the wisest and most competent writers generally do have beards).

Web:

> http://www.americanpoems.com/poets/
> waltwhitman/
> http://www.csustan.edu/english/reuben/pal/chap4/
> whitman.html
> http://www.library.utoronto.ca/utel/rp/authors/
> whitmn.html
> http://www.poets.org/poets/poets.cfm?prmid=127

Wordsworth, William

William Wordsworth (1770-1850) was an English poet who became Poet Laureate in 1843. Wordsworth and his friend, Samuel Taylor Coleridge, wrote a book called "Lyrical Ballads", which introduced romanticism into England.

Web:

> http://www.library.utoronto.ca/utel/rp/authors/
> wordswor.html
> http://www.online-literature.com/wordsworth/
> http://www.poets.org/poets/poets.cfm?prmID=303

William Wordsworth

Early in 1798, William Wordsworth started work on a long autobiographical poem called "The Prelude". His goal was to analyze his intellectual, emotional and spiritual development. After finishing in 1805, he didn't stop. Instead of publishing the poem, he continued to revise it, intermittently, for the rest of his life. The poem was not published until after his death.

Had he asked me, I would have told him that what he was doing was a bad idea. "William," I would have said, "Look at me. I revise and publish a new edition of this book every year, and I am still alive."

Yeats, William Butler

William Butler Yeats (1865-1939) was an Irish writer who is considered to be one of the greatest poets of the twentieth century. Yeats wrote many short plays (such as "The Countess Cathleen") and was one of the founders of the Irish National Theatre Company. As a young man, Yeats wrote a great deal of love poetry. As he grew older, he began to infuse his work with more and more complex symbolism (sort of like real life only more interesting). In 1923, Yeats was awarded the Nobel Prize for literature.

Web:

> http://www.nobelprizes.com/nobel/literature/
> 1923a.html
> http://www.online-literature.com/yeats/
> http://www.poets.org/poets/poets.cfm?prmID=118

POLITICS

Activism

Have you ever had one of those days when you are sitting around doing nothing and you think to yourself, "Boy, I'm really in the mood for a good fight." Well, don't get frustrated, get activated. Here are some places where you can read about political activities that are guaranteed to make you want to shout.

Web:
  http://www.activism.net/
  http://www.berkshire.net/~ifas/activist/how-to/
  http://www.oneworld.net/
  http://www.protest.net/
  http://www.webactive.com/

Usenet:
  alt.activism
  alt.activism.community
  alt.activism.d
  alt.activism.latino-youth
  alt.activism.noise-pollution
  alt.activism.student

American Third Parties

The United States has two major political parties, the Democrats and the Republicans. Although there are other parties, they are of marginal importance, especially in presidential politics. There are two main reasons why. First, in significant ways at the local, state and federal levels, the U.S. has a winner-take-all system in which only the major parties have the size, popularity and money to do well. Second, the U.S. is a large, very powerful country. To be elected President you need to be more than popular; you need to demonstrate that you *already* have significant power, not only in public office, but within your own party. A candidate from a small party is relatively powerless and, as such, doesn't stand much of a chance. In other words, in the American system, you need power to get more power, and you can't get a large amount of power all at once from nothing. This is not bad. Many other countries, especially those with parliamentary systems, suffer from chronic political indecision because one party cannot sustain a clear majority. Moreover, the nature of the American system makes it extremely unlikely that, even in bad times, a dictator would be able to come out of nowhere and take over.

Web:
  http://www.greenparty.org/
  http://www.lp.org/
  http://www.politics1.com/parties.htm
  http://www.reformparty.org/

Conservatism

Traditional conservatism is the belief that society should change slowly while maintaining its existing economic and political characteristics. Modern conservatism takes a more activist stance: although conservatives have a strong commitment to free markets, individual rights and less government, they do want society to change, as long as the change is in harmony with their beliefs. At times, this may mean the government legislating morality, spending more money or even restricting personal freedom.

Web:
  http://www.conservativenews.org/
  http://www.enterstageright.com/
  http://www.freerepublic.com/
  http://www.townhall.com/

Usenet:
  alt.society.conservatism

Decriminalizing Prostitution

Prostitution refers to the soliciting and acceptance of payment for performing sexual acts. Although prostitution has always been a part of human culture, the first large-scale attempts to ban the practice did not occur until the sixteenth century, when an epidemic of sexually transmitted diseases swept through parts of Europe. In 1899, various countries began to cooperate to control prostitution. In 1910, the United States passed the White Slave Traffic Act (usually called the Mann Act) to outlaw the transportation of women across state and international lines for "immoral purposes". Today, most countries outlaw prostitution, although it is legal—and regulated—in some European countries and, in the U.S., in parts of Nevada. Some people look on prostitution as an evil that should be banned or at least repressed. Other people (including many prostitutes) would have us consider prostitutes as being legitimate "sex workers", and would decriminalize the practice. Here are some resources that support the latter point of view.

Web:
  http://www.bayswan.org/index.html
  http://www.sexwork.com/

Democrats

The Democratic party was founded in 1792 by Thomas Jefferson. Originally, party members were called "Republicans" or "Democratic-Republicans" but in 1830, the name was shortened to "Democrats". This is the official Web site of the Democratic party and, like the Republican site, there are no huge surprises. You can also read news and articles about the party and what you can do to help, along with partisan analysis criticizing the Republicans. The Usenet group is for the discussion of Democratic views and platforms.

Web:
  http://www.democrats.org/

Usenet:
  alt.politics.democrats.d

Euthanasia

Euthanasia refers to the deliberate ending of another person's life out of compassion. There are two types of euthanasia. In a passive sense, euthanasia can be accomplished by refraining from postponing a death from terminal illness, for example, by withholding artificial life support. Active euthanasia painlessly puts someone to death. Passive euthanasia is common. With the consent of family or the patients themselves, doctors often withhold measures that would unnecessarily prolong a life filled with pain and anguish. Active euthanasia is illegal in almost all jurisdictions. Clearly, there are no easy answers when it comes to euthanasia, especially active euthanasia. However, it is important that we discuss these issues. As the population ages, and health care for the aged becomes more and more expensive, you and I are going to be faced with some tough decisions at the end of our lives. Perhaps now is the time to start talking about it.

Web:
  http://www.internationaltaskforce.org/
  http://www.partnershipforcaring.org/
  http://www.rights.org/deathnet/lr_libus.html

Usenet:
  talk.euthanasia

Gay Rights

There's a great deal of change in the world. Gay rights extend into many different areas of life: marriage, domestic partnerships, adoption, child custody, military service, inheritance laws, housing, employment, discrimination, government programs, and so on.

Web:
  http://www.aclu.org/issues/gay/hmgl.html
  http://www.glaa.org/
  http://www.glaad.org/
  http://www.hrc.org/
  http://www.indiana.edu/~glbtpol/

Grassroots Activism

Grassroots activism refers to an ad hoc political movement at the local level, as opposed to organizations controlled by a nexus of political activity (such as a party, elected official or governing body). By its nature, grassroots activists are short on money, know-how and facilities. Fortunately, the Net will be glad to help—with no strings attached.

Web:
  http://www.2020vision.org/
  http://www.activistse-z.com/
  http://www.freedomnet.cnchost.com/
    theactivecitizen/grassrootsguide01.htm
  http://www.netaction.org/training/
  http://www.sfaf.org/policy/grassroots/

International Politics Talk and General Discussion

Usenet has a number of discussion groups specifically for discussing the politics of particular countries and regions: Britain, Europe, India, Italy, China, Middle East, Tibet and the former Soviet Union. Please remember that if you are responding to an article written by someone in a foreign country, their first language may not be the same as yours.

Usenet:
  alt.politics.british
  alt.politics.europe.misc
  talk.politics.china
  talk.politics.european-union
  talk.politics.mideast
  talk.politics.soviet
  talk.politics.tibet

Internet Voting

We vote a lot more than most people realize, not only in federal elections, but for state, provincial and local elections. Then, there are elections within political parties, unions, professional organizations, clubs, and so on. Actually, people have been voting on the Net for years. For example, within certain parts of the Usenet community, new discussion groups must be put to a vote before they are created, and the people who vote electronically are in many different countries. For government elections, of course, the requirements are strict: the voting must be secure and reliable; the identity of the voters must be kept private; there must be no fraud; the system must be accessible to the general public; and the act of voting must be simple, flexible and cost efficient.

Web:
  http://mainline.brynmawr.edu/~rmercuri/notable/
    evote.html
  http://www.free-project.org/
  http://www.securepoll.com/
  http://www.ss.ca.gov/executive/ivote/

Majordomo Mailing List:
  List Name: e-lection
  Subscribe to: majordomo@research.att.com

Irish Politics

The mailing list is for the discussion of the kinder, gentler side of Irish politics as defined by the 26 counties of the Republic of Ireland since 1922. Discussions of Northern Ireland are welcome only if they directly relate to the politics of the Republic. The Web site has a huge list of resources relating to all aspects of Irish politics.

Web:
  http://www.ucd.ie/~politics/old-site-files/irpols.htm

Listserv Mailing List:
  List Name: irl-pol
  Subscribe to: listserv@listserv.heanet.ie

Don't forget to email
your mother.

Israeli Politics

The Israeli government is based on proportional representation. Here is how it works. The national house of representatives (the Knesset) has 120 members. In preparation for an election, each party creates a list of preferred candidates. However, when a person votes, he or she votes for a party, not for a particular person. After the votes are counted, the number of representatives elected to the Knesset is proportional to the percentage of votes that party received. For example, a party receiving 10 percent of the overall votes would send the top 12 candidates from its list to the Knesset. This sounds like a good idea, but it makes for a fractured system, in which no party can ever manage to get a majority on its own. Moreover, small, less popular parties can often wield disproportionate power as their votes are needed to form a coalition. Israel has fewer people than the city of Chicago in an area about the same size as New Jersey. However, in the 1999 election, there were 31 political parties (six of which were major organizations). Is it any wonder Israeli politics is so... interesting? You know, when you think of it, Israel has a lot in common with Chicago and New Jersey.

Web:
  http://www.likud.nl/
  http://www.politicalresources.net/israel.htm

Liberalism

Traditional liberalism embraces change, tolerance of diverse points of view, and ethical and humanitarian concerns. Modern political liberalism has inherited the beliefs and philosophies that arose from the centuries-long struggle for human rights. However, modern liberals go further: they believe that many problems are so important as to require large-scale government intervention to supply services and to ensure the safety, freedom and well-being of individuals. To a liberal, a well-run government provides the framework within which all citizens are able to enjoy life, liberty and the pursuit of happiness (to coin a phrase).

Web:
  http://www.amliberals.com/
  http://www.commondreams.org/
  http://www.korpios.org/resurgent/LiberalFAQ.htm
Usenet:
  alt.politics.liberalism

Israel is a small place. In fact, the pre-1967 borders afford it only 17 miles across at the narrowest point. If you wanted, you could comfortably fit the entire country into New Jersey (although why you want to do so is beyond me). Still, when you measure it in brouhaha per unit area, Israel has, pound for pound, the most robust set of mixed-up and eclectic political dynamics this side of a university sociology department.

As a Net person, there is no need for you to miss out on the fascinating and eccentric happenings in what is surely the most effervescent spot in the Middle East. If nothing else, it will make you appreciate the stability and peacefulness of your own country.

Online Activism

The Net helps those who help themselves, so if you want to help, it would be helpful to use the Net to help you help the people who need help, but don't know how to use the Net to help themselves. Does that help?

Web:
  http://www.gn.apc.org/
  http://www.progressiveportal.org/

Political Correctness

Political correctness refers to forcing the general public to talk about issues in oblique ways so as to minimize the possibility of offending people. For example, which term is better: African-Americans, Afro-Americans, Blacks, Negroes or Colored people? All of these words were acceptable at one time, but political correctness dictates which one is the "correct" term to use today. Political correctness in moderation assures that the mantle of public opinion is available to protect us from bias and vulgarity. However, taken to an extreme, such rules serve not only to force people to conform to current political fashion, but to provide a convenient way to separate people based on knowing what is and what is not acceptable. Of course, "political correctness" itself is not a new idea: it is merely the politically correct term used to describe what are ever-present problems in human society: snobbishness, ignorance and the struggle for power over our neighbors.

Web:
  http://www.ora.com/people/staff/sierra/flum/
  http://www.users.bigpond.com/smartboard/pc.htm

Political Policies

In the world of politics, you ain't nobody unless you've got a policy. Anybody can assert an opinion, but not everybody's opinion can be backed up by studies from a think tank. When you come down to it, though, public policy is nothing more than trying to figure out how people should think about something. There are lots of people who spend lots of time trying to figure out what you should be thinking. Maybe you'd like to check up on them.

Web:
  http://www.speakout.com/activism/news/

Political Talk and General Discussion

If you like being contentious and opinionated, you'll love these Usenet groups. (Actually, as one of my readers, you are sensible and insightful. It's everyone else who is contentious and opinionated.) These are the Usenet groups specifically designated for political discussion. Anything goes, but as in most areas of the Net, the power lies with the people who are the most intelligent, witty and well-spoken. If you would like more immediate interactive screaming matches, connect to IRC.

Usenet:
  alt.politics
  bit.listserv.politics
  soc.politics
  soc.politics.anti-fascism
  soc.politics.marxism
  talk.politics
  talk.politics.misc
  talk.politics.theory

IRC:
  #politics (DALnet, EFnet, Undernet)

> **The purpose of chocolate is to make life complete.**

Politicians

In most of life, talk is cheap. In politics, talk is essential. Here are the Usenet groups where you can talk about your favorite and not so favorite politicians. To help you know what you are talking about, I have included a Web site where you can find information about more than 13,000 politicians. Talk about convenient!

Web:
  http://www.vote-smart.org/vote-smart/data.phtml

Usenet:
  alt.fan.bill-clinton
  alt.fan.bob-dole
  alt.fan.dan-quayle
  alt.fan.pauline.hanson
  alt.fan.richard-nixon
  alt.fan.ronald-reagan
  alt.politics.clinton
  alt.politics.gw-bush
  alt.politics.harry-browne
  alt.president.clinton

Politics of Government Organizations

As all of us travel together through Modern Life, government organizations are forced to carry their own political baggage. These are the Usenet groups for the discussion of politics as it relates to various government organizations, mostly American: the Bureau of Alcohol, Tobacco and Firearms (ATF); the Central Intelligence Agency (CIA); general covert operations organizations; the Federal Bureau of Investigation (FBI); the National Security Administration (NSA); and the United Nations. The .misc group is for the discussion of government organizations that do not have their own groups.

Usenet:
  alt.politics.org.batf
  alt.politics.org.cia
  alt.politics.org.fbi
  alt.politics.org.misc
  alt.politics.org.nsa
  alt.politics.org.un

Presidential Scandals

Politics, money and scandal go together like green eggs and ham. Throughout the years, the presidency of the United States has attracted an unfortunate number of high-profile imbroglios: Watergate (1972, Richard Nixon administration: the cover-up of a politically motivated break-in); Teapot Dome (1924, Warren Harding administration: the secret leasing of naval oil reserve lands to private companies); Whiskey Ring (1875, Ulysses S. Grant administration: lost tax revenue on whiskey). Those scandals, of course, are all in the past. True, the U.S. did have a bit of a scandal in the late 90s, what with Bill Clinton, Whitewater, Monica Lewinsky and an impeachment, but Americans have been able to put that behind them and reach closure. The U.S. now has an administration with the highest possible sense of honesty and integrity and, today, the chances of anything even remotely approaching a scandal in the office of the President are so insignificant as to be almost non-existent.

Web:
  http://www.courttv.com/casefiles/clintoncrisis/
  http://www.grolier.com/presidents/ea/
    genconts.html#SCANDALS
  http://www.msnbc.com/onair/msnbc/timeandagain/
    archive/scandal/
  http://www.watergate.info/

Usenet:
  alt.politics.gossip

Republicans

The United States Republican Party was founded in 1854. The first Republican to be elected President was Abraham Lincoln (in 1860). This is the official Republican Web site, and you pretty much get what you would expect: news releases, background information on various governmental and political topics, and a great deal of pro-Republican, anti-Democrat content.

Web:
  http://www.rnc.org/

Usenet:
  alt.politics.usa.republican

Listserv Mailing List:
  List Name: repub-l
  Subscribe to: listserv@vm.marist.edu

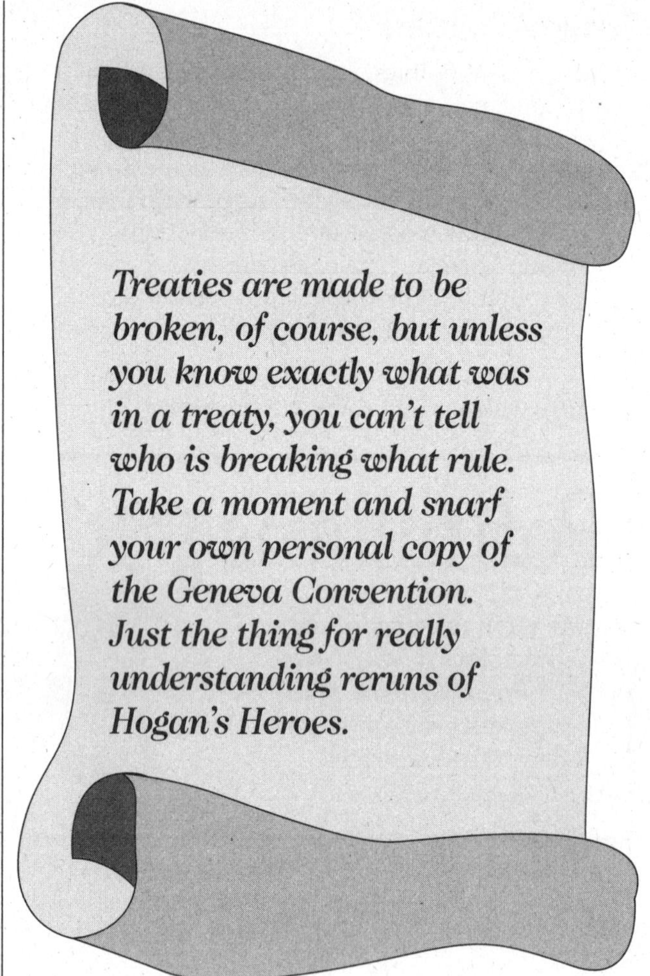

Torture

Torture refers to causing severe pain or suffering in order to punish or coerce someone. There has always been torture and, probably, there always will be. However, it is a mark of our growing social maturity that, in today's world, torture is considered, by most people and most governments, to be inhumane and unacceptable.

Web:
  http://www.cat.pdx.edu/~chuff/christian-torture/
    christian-torture.html
  http://www.getchwood.com/punishments/curious/
  http://www.intellectualloafing.com/
    discussionsfolder/runningdebatesfolder/
    torture.htm
  http://www.omct.org/
  http://www.theelectricchair.com//torture.htm

Treaties

If you are having trouble with your neighbor trimming the trees that are actually on *your* property and you want to take some firm action, I have an idea for you. Go to these Web sites for treaties and other international agreements. Download the treaty of your choice and open the document in your word processing program. Fill in your name and your neighbor's name in the appropriate slots, then trot next door and make him sign it. Not only will he stop trimming your trees, but he might also be morally bound to notify you at the earliest possible moment that there has been a nuclear accident in his house.

Web:
   http://www.jus.uio.no/lm/treaties.and.organisations/
   lm.chronological.html
   http://www.priweb.com/internetlawlib/89.htm
   http://www.state.gov/www/global/legal_affairs/
   tifindex.html

United States Political Talk and General Discussion

I grew up in Canada, where there was a fair amount of politics. But that was nothing compared to the United States, where political wrangling and commentary is the national obsession (second only to watching highly paid athletes perform on TV). The great thing about American politics is that once you choose a point of view, you have all kinds of beliefs, opinions and avocations to adopt and defend without having to do any original thinking for yourself. Don't get me wrong, American politics is *interesting*, and there is nothing I like better than a good old political argument. Actually, I'm not even that fussy. I just like to argue, so I'm always ready to take whichever side is opposed to whomever I am talking with. The **.misc** group is for discussion of general politics that does not fit in one of the other, more specific groups.

Usenet:
   alt.politics.greens
   alt.politics.libertarian
   alt.politics.usa.congress
   alt.politics.usa.constitution
   alt.politics.usa.misc
   talk.politics.libertarian

World Constitutions

These sites have constitutions and basic laws for many countries around the world, including Germany, Hong Kong, the United States, Canada, China, Hungary and the Slovak Republic, as well as the texts of the English Bill of Rights, the Magna Carta, and others.

Web:
   http://oncampus.richmond.edu/~jjones//confinder/
   const.htm
   http://www.charter88.org.uk/politics/links/
   link_cons.html

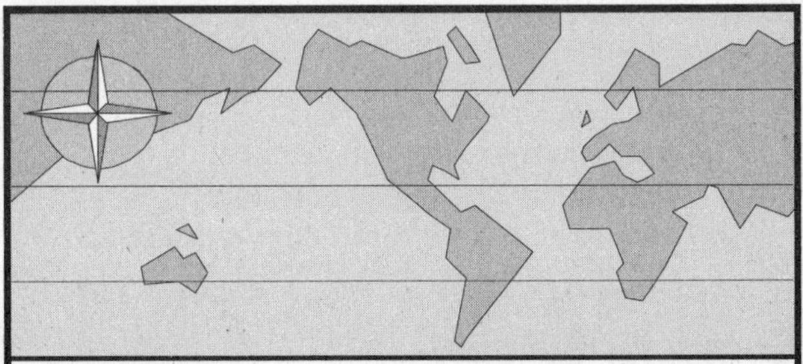

World Constitutions

Have you ever wanted to have your own country? It's easy, as long as you do the proper paperwork.

Start by visiting the World Constitutions resources on the Net. Choose a constitution that looks good and rewrite it to suit your requirements. Now all you need is a bunch of people and some land.

What could be easier?

A B C D E F G H I J K L M N O P Q R S T U V W X Y Z

PRIVACY AND SECURITY

Anonymous Remailers

It's embarrassing when your mom finds out that you are sending mail to someone you have met while perusing the **alt.binaries.pictures.erotica.furry** Usenet group. Perhaps even more disconcerting, would be finding out that the company for which you work does not approve of the political beliefs you express in your personal email.

Web:
  http://anon.efga.org/Remailers
  http://www.andrebacard.com/remail.html
  http://www.onlineprivacy.com/remailer
  http://www.sendfakemail.com/~raph/remailer-list.html

Computer Security

Any computer that is connected to the outside world can never be completely secure. However, computers and networks can be made secure enough to keep problems to a minimum. For example, as problems within an operating system become known, there will usually be a patch (program modification) issued to fix the problem. There are many known security problems with all of the popular operating systems, and most of these problems have patches that you can download and apply to your system. In general, the best thing you can do to make sure your system is dependable is to have proper backups, and—very important—make sure you can restore your backups.

Web:
  http://csrc.ncsl.nist.gov/
  http://www.cerias.purdue.edu/hotlist/
  http://www.cotse.com/security.htm
  http://www.faqs.org/faqs/computer-security/
  http://www.infosecuritymag.com/currentdaily.shtml
  http://www.mountainwave.com/
  http://www.ntsecurity.net/
  http://www.securityfocus.com/
  http://xforce.iss.net/

Usenet:
  comp.os.netware.security
  comp.security.announce
  comp.security.firewalls
  comp.security.misc
  talk.forgery

Computer Vulnerability Testing

If you use DSL or cable to connect to the Internet, you are actually on a large network. This network is shared by other people using your ISP (Internet service provider), and it may be accessible to the world at large. In particular, hackers (bad guys) with certain software tools may be able to go through your ISP's network and penetrate your computer. Are you safe? You can use the free testing facility at this Web site to check for vulnerabilities.

Web:
  http://www.grc.com/

TIDBITS

What should baseball fans know about HOT DOGS?

Since 1893, it has been an American tradition that, while you are watching your favorite baseball team, you should spend at least part of the time chowing down on a cooked sausage made from tiny particles of raw skeletal muscle of beef or pork.

That is, you should eat a hot dog.

During the course of a baseball season, fans at major league stadiums will eat about 26.1 million hot dogs.

Now, it happens that the baseball season consists of 2,430 games, with a total attendance (in 2001) of 72,417,945.

This means that, on the average, 29,801 people attend each game. During a typical game, these 29,801 people will consume 10,741 hot dogs, or one dog per 2.77 people.

Hot dogs average about 6 inches in length, so if you were to line up all 10,741 hot dogs, they would extend 5,370 feet (just under 1.02 miles).

Hot dogs also average about 10 per pound, so the 10,741 hot dogs consumed at a typical baseball game weigh 1,074 pounds, about the same as 45 fully grown Dachshunds.

Cookies (on the Web)

To access the Web, you use a program called a "browser". (The two most popular browsers are Netscape and Internet Explorer.) Your browser contacts computers around the Net and requests information on your behalf. When that information arrives, your browser displays it on your screen. The computers that send the information are called "Web servers". Your browser has a facility built into it that allows Web servers to store data—called "cookies"—on your computer for later retrieval. What you may not realize is that cookies are sent to your browser behind the scenes, and, right now, your personal computer is probably storing all kinds of information. This information—the cookies—accumulates as you visit more and more Web sites, and is used for a variety of purposes, one of which is to track your movements on the Web. People are concerned about cookies as they can be used in ways that infringe on your personal privacy. These resources will help you learn about cookies and what you can do about them.

Web:

 http://www.cookiecentral.com/
 http://www.kburra.com/cpfeat.html
 http://www.redlanternreview.com/cookies1.html
 http://www.thelimitsoft.com/cookie/
 http://www.webroot.com/washie.htm

COMPUTER SECURITY

Right now, someone may be trying to break into a computer for which *you* are responsible. Before they do, check out the latest security information on the Net, and make sure you are protected.
When it comes to maintaining security, the job never ends. (So don't you dare go on vacation—ever.)

Electronic Privacy Information Center

The Electronic Privacy Information Center (EPIC) is a public interest research center based in Washington, D.C. EPIC concerns itself with all types of privacy issues: Internet privacy, medical records, proposals for national ID cards, and so on. The EPIC Web site houses a large collection of privacy-related information and resources on many different topics. If you care at all about these issues, take a few minutes to look around.

Web:

 http://www.epic.org/

Email Privacy

If you use email at work, I guarantee that your company can read your mail if they want to. Even if you delete messages, they are often retrievable (say, from a backup). My advice is to think very carefully before you write something in an email message that you would not want to become public. You are probably okay if you use your own personal Internet account, but if you use the Net at work, be discreet. Want to find out more? Start here.

Web:

 http://www.gahtan.com/cyberlaw/Privacy/

Fingerprinting and Biometrics

Biometrics are techniques that can be used to automatically recognize a person based upon distinguishing traits. One reliable biometric is fingerprinting. Your fingerprints are unique, and every time you touch something you leave a mark that can be used to identify you. In the movies, fingerprints are always used to trap the bad guys, but in real life many people see fingerprinting as an invasion of privacy. It is convenient for government agencies to have a lot of fingerprints on file, but how thrilled are you about them having yours? The loss of freedom will not stop at forced fingerprinting. Biometric systems have been developed that are far more sophisticated. These guys are deadly serious, and what you read here should scare you.

Web:
  http://www.networkusa.org/fingerprint.shtml

Firewalls

A firewall is a barrier between you and the Internet. The purpose of a firewall is to keep your computer or network safe by restricting the flow of data according to specific criteria. A firewall can be a program that runs on your home computer (a personal firewall), or a special hardware device that sits between an entire network and the outside world. As you might imagine, firewalls can be complex and difficult to set up. Do you need a firewall? If you are running a network or some type of server (such as your own Web server), yes, you do need a firewall. Otherwise, it is not necessary, so don't let people scare you. (For a no-nonsense discussion of such matters, see my book "Harley Hahn's Internet Insecurity".)

Web:
  http://www.cerias.purdue.edu/coast/firewalls/
  http://www.firewallguide.com/
  http://www.howstuffworks.com/firewall.htm
  http://www.icsalabs.com/html/communities/
     firewalls/buyers_guide/
  http://www.interhack.net/pubs/fwfaq/
  http://www.isc.org/services/public/lists/
     firewalls.html
  http://www.netsys.com/firewalls/
  http://www.robertgraham.com/pubs/
     firewall-seen.html

Usenet:
  comp.security.firewalls

Hacked Web Pages

Every now and then, hackers will break into a Web server and change around one or more Web pages. These sites archive the hacked pages, so that people like you and I can see the hacker's work and marvel at their skill, ingenuity and obvious lack of anything better to do with their life.

Web:
  http://www.alldas.org/
  http://www.safemode.org/

Hacking

A hacker is a person who learns the details of a complicated system and then exploits that knowledge to extend the capabilities of the system. On the Internet, the hackers you hear about the most are computer hackers: smart, enthusiastic people who understand and exploit computers, programming and networks. These hackers communicate and work in what we might loosely refer to as the "digital underground". Most of what they do is legal, although sometimes it is not. Join the digital underground and you will find not only hackers, but crackers (people who break system security) and phreaks (people who crack communications networks, especially phone systems). You will also find lots of warez (shared commercial software). To be a real hacker requires a lot of time, skill and experience, as well as an understanding of the hacking sub-culture, which can be summarized as, "If you have to ask, you aren't going to understand the answer."

Web:
  http://whacker2.hackerwhacker.com/
  http://www.defcon.org/
  http://www.hideaway.net/
  http://www.wbglinks.net/

Usenet:
  alt.2600.aol
  alt.2600.fake-id
  alt.2600.hackers
  alt.2600.qna
  alt.2600hz
  alt.hacker
  alt.hackers
  alt.hackers.groups
  alt.hackers.malicious
  alt.hacking
  alt.hackintosh

IRC:
  #hack (Undernet)

Identity Theft

Identity theft refers to someone using your name and identification number to cause trouble or break the law. For example, someone might use your name, date of birth and (in the U.S.) social security number to open a credit card account. The person then uses the card and doesn't pay the bills, which then goes on *your* credit rating. Most identity theft originates when someone gets information by stealing your purse, wallet or mail (sometimes by forging your name on a change-of-address form), searching your trash, obtaining a credit report fraudulently, or buying information (such as credit card numbers from a clerk in a store). Here are a few simple techniques you can use to protect yourself: (1) Guard your credit card and identification numbers. (2) Do not carry any more cards than you need, and never leave your wallet or purse alone, even locked in the trunk of your car. (3) Monitor your credit card bills regularly. If a statement doesn't show up on time, find out why. If you are a victim of identify theft, don't wait to do something: there is information on the Net that can help you right now.

Web:

http://www.consumer.gov/idtheft/
http://www.ftc.gov/bcp/conline/pubs/credit/
   idtheft.htm
http://www.identitytheft.org/faq.htm
http://www.pirg.org/calpirg/consumer/privacy/#how
http://www.privacyrights.org/identity.htm
http://www.stolen-identity.com/
http://www.usdoj.gov/criminal/fraud/idtheft.html

Information Warfare

Since antiquity, the goal of the military has been to kill, maim and destroy. In the twenty-first century, things have changed. The military is still trained to kill, maim and destroy, but now they also try to damage the enemy's information infrastructure. This new activity is called information warfare: the practice of infiltrating and compromising other people's computer systems while protecting our own. Information warfare is real and is being actively developed by governments (in both military and civilian branches) and within private companies and organizations.

Web:

http://www.futurewar.net/
http://www.infowar.com/
http://www.psycom.net/iwar.1.html
http://www.terrorism.com/infowar/index.shtml

TIDBITS

What should college students know about LETTERS OF REFERENCE?

As a college student, the time will come when you will need to ask a teacher for a letter of reference: to transfer to another school, to apply to graduate school or for a scholarship, or as part of a job application.

The best person to write such a letter is a full-time professor who is well-known in his area of study. If you don't know a full-time professor, the next best choice would be a part-time instructor or a teaching assistant.

Here is a secret. As you might imagine, college teachers get a lot of requests for letters of recommendation. Most of the time, they will simply take a standard form letter and make minor changes. However, if a teacher likes you, he will take the time to write a more elaborate and more personalized letter.

Your goal should be to make it as easy as possible for your teacher to write you a wonderful letter. Here are some hints.

1. The teacher will have to know more about you than your grades. To help him, prepare a list of the points you would like the letter to highlight, such as a description of your extracurricular activities, your strengths and your goals.

2. Don't wait until the last minute to make your request. Ask for the letter at least a month in advance.

3. Give the professor an envelope that is already addressed (to save him time) and already has a stamp (to show how thoughtful you are).

4. If you have the option of signing a waiver that says that you will not see the letter, do so. Such a letter will carry more weight, as the reader will assume that the opinions are more honest. (Many teachers will show you the letter, anyway, even if you have signed the waiver.)

5. Finally, as soon as the letter has been sent, send the professor a short thank-you note. This is not negotiable.

Privacy Resources

Privacy is everyone's business: you, and you, and you there hiding behind your Macintosh thinking I won't notice you. Once the big boys (AOL, Microsoft, AT&T, and so on) get into the "free software" act, it won't be long until you find that somewhere along the line, your personal interests were sold out for a handful of magic stock options and advertising revenues. I feel strongly that it is up to all of us to protect our privacy. The best way to start is by understanding the issues, and these sites are a good place to begin. Remember, once "they" control your browser, you will be able to run all over the Net, but you won't be able to hide.

Web:
  http://www.epic.org/privacy/
  http://www.junkbusters.com/cgi-bin/privacy
  http://www.privacilla.org/
  http://www.vortex.com/privacy.html

Privacy Rights Clearinghouse

This is a great Web site. It contains a lot of useful information about privacy, your rights, and what you can do to protect them. I have personally found a lot of interesting and useful help here. One caveat: The information is designed for the United States, particularly California. However, don't let that discourage you. These people do a good job and much of the information is helpful to anyone.

Web:
  http://www.privacyrights.org/

Privacy Talk and General Discussion

What better place to discuss privacy and security issues than out in the open on Usenet, where thousands of people you don't even know can read your every word? These discussion groups cover technical issues as well as cultural, political and social topics relating to privacy and security (such as the ill-conceived Clipper chip).

Usenet:
  alt.privacy
  alt.privacy.anon-server
  alt.privacy.clipper
  comp.society.privacy

Listserv Mailing List:
  List Name: internet
  Subscribe to: listserv@maelstrom.stjohns.edu

Privacy Tips

The more information can be processed by computers, the more your privacy becomes important. These Web sites contain some good resources to help you get the privacy you want. Find a wealth of tips and information regarding email, voice mail, Social Security numbers, cordless phones, the Net, computers, and much more.

Web:
  http://www.aclu-wi.org/issues/data-privacy/tips.pdf
  http://www.dbcc.cc.fl.us/fipse_sh/privacy.htm
  http://www.learnthenet.com/english/html/
    63privtips.htm
  http://www.privacyrights.org/ar/donray.htm

Spamming

Spam refers to unsolicited and inappropriate messages, usually advertisements. Spam is sent to both Usenet discussion groups, where it can be a major annoyance, and to personal email addresses, where it shows up as junk mail. Spamming is a big problem, and the people who do it are inconsiderate jerks. Check out these resources to help you understand the problem, and to find out what you can do to fight it and to safeguard your electronic privacy. Here is one big hint. When you configure your browser to access the Usenet news system, you will have to specify your email address. Whenever you post a message to a Usenet group, your browser will insert your address into the "header" of the message. This makes it easy for people who read your message to email you a personal reply. Whatever you do, do *not* specify your real email address—use a fake one. If your real email address ever shows up in the header of a Usenet message, it will be picked up by automated programs used by spammers, and, within hours, your address will be on mailing lists all over the world. Once this happens, you will receive ever-increasing amounts of junk mail, and there will be nothing you can do to stop it short of changing your address. If you want people to be able to reply to your Usenet postings, you can always put your real email address in the body (text) of your message. Hint for nerds: Use **root@localhost** as your fake address.

Web:
  http://spam.abuse.net/
  http://www.cauce.org/
  http://www.cybernothing.org/faqs/
    net-abuse-faq.html

Usenet:
  alt.current-events.net-abuse

Privacy Resources

Privacy means a lot more than being safe and secure in your own home.

Privacy means having control over who is allowed to keep and use information about you: your name, address, email address, phone number, government identification number (such as the U.S. Social Security number and the Canadian Social Insurance number), medical records, bank account information, credit rating, tax records, investment information, use of credit cards, frequent traveler information, magazine subscriptions, and on and on.

Want to learn more? Explore the **Privacy Resources**.

Spyware

Spyware refers to programs that run on your computer, without your knowledge, and secretly use your Internet connection. Typically, spyware will send information about your computer and your activities to companies that will use it for marketing purposes. Some spyware will even make changes in your system. How does spyware get on your system? It is attached to many different freeware and shareware programs. When you install such a program, the spyware is installed as well (without telling you). In many cases, when you uninstall the original program, the spyware still stays on your system! If you think about it, you can see that, in many ways, a spyware is like a virus, and it makes sense to talk about a program (that you download) as being "infected". How do you detect spyware? Easy. Just use one of these free anti-spyware programs.

Web:
 http://lavasoft.de/
 http://www.camtech2000.net/pages/spychaser.html
 http://www.grc.com/optout.htm
 http://www.simplythebest.net/info/spyware.html
 http://www.spychecker.com/
 http://www.spywareinfo.com/

Using the Web Anonymously

Did you ever ask yourself, how can the browser companies (Microsoft, AOL [Netscape]) afford to develop browsers and give them away for free? Browser companies design software to please their customers, and *you* are not a customer. The customers are the companies that actually pay for software, such as Web server programs. So it should come as no surprise when I tell you that browsers are designed to pass information about you and your computer system to any Web server that asks for it. Think about it, each time you connect to a Web server, your browser may be passing private information to that server. (In other words, you only *think* you got your browser for free.) To circumvent this system, you can route all your browser requests through another computer (sometimes called a proxy server) that will maintain your privacy. A proxy server that offers this service will send your requests to the destination Web site, accept whatever data comes back and pass it on to you. You use the Web in the regular way. Sometimes there is a short delay, but no private information is passed to other computers and, for the most part, your actions are hidden from the world at large.

Web:
 http://www.anonymizer.com/
 http://www.orangatango.com/
 http://www.space.net.au/~thomas/quickbrowse.html
 http://www.the-cloak.com/login.html

Virus Hoaxes

A computer virus is a small program designed to insert itself into a file containing another program. When the second program runs, the virus becomes active, possibly causing a problem. A computer virus, of course, can be trouble. However, there are relatively few real viruses around. Unfortunately, there are many people who spread unfounded rumors about viruses, especially the so-called email viruses. Don't be fooled. The next time you get one of these virus warnings, please refrain from sending it along to your friends. Instead, use these resources to find out what's real and what's a hoax. (They are almost all hoaxes.)

Web:
 http://hoaxbusters.ciac.org/
 http://www.icsalabs.com/html/communities/
   antivirus/hoaxes.shtml
 http://www.sophos.com/virusinfo/hoaxes/

Viruses (Computer)

Computer viruses are small programs written by malevolent programmers in order to cause trouble. A virus attaches itself to an existing program. When you run the program, the virus becomes activated and performs some sort of action (which might cause damage to your files or other programs). Anti-virus software is written to detect and eliminate viruses that may have found their way onto your system. Most people have no need for such software, if they follow simple precautions. The most important precaution is never open an email attachment if you don't recognize what type of file it is. However, anti-virus programs are important if you maintain a computer network, or if you work in an environment in which people share computers or bring in floppy disks that have been used in other computers.

Web:
http://www.avp.ch/
http://www.cert.org/other_sources/viruses.html
http://www.symantec.com/avcenter/vinfodb.html
http://www.viruslist.com/eng/

Usenet:
alt.comp.virus
alt.comp.virus.source.code
comp.virus

Listserv Mailing List:
List Name: valert-l
Subscribe to: listserv@lehigh.edu

Listserv Mailing List:
List Name: virus-l
Subscribe to: listserv@lehigh.edu

IRC:
#virus (Undernet)

> **The Internet is like life, only more fun.**

PROGRAMMING

Ada

Ada is a programming language developed by the U.S. Department of Defense in the mid-1970s. The purpose of Ada was to create a standardized language that would be robust, dependable, and could be used efficiently by programmers to develop reliable programs that were easy to read and maintain. At the time, I was a computer science graduate student and I remember that four different proposals were circulated in the computer science community. Eventually one of these proposals was adopted and became Ada. In the last two decades, Ada has been updated into a modern programming language and is still used widely.

Web:
http://lglwww.epfl.ch/ada/home_page.html
http://www.acm.org/sigada/
http://www.adapower.com/

Usenet:
comp.lang.ada

C++ and C

The C language is old, dating back to the early development of Unix. C++ is an object-oriented language based on C, but with significant differences. Both C and C++ are difficult to learn, and to program well in them takes a great deal of talent and experience. However, they are powerful tools, widely used throughout the world.

Web:
http://www.cera2.com/c-plus.htm
http://www.cprogramming.com/
http://www.cs.umd.edu/users/cml/cstyle/
http://www.icce.rug.nl/documents/cplusplus/
http://www.lysator.liu.se/c/c-www.html

Usenet:
comp.lang.c
comp.lang.c++
comp.lang.c++.leda
comp.lang.c++.moderated
comp.lang.c.moderated
comp.std.c++

IRC:
#c (Undernet)
#c++ (Undernet)

If you're thinking of making the most serious commitment that a computer programmer can make — jumping into C++ — stop, take a deep breath, and read the frequently asked question list.

Demoscene

A "demo" is a complex combination of programming, graphics and music, put together to create a multimedia presentation. The demoscene refers to activities of the people, all over the world, who work to create demos. Every now and then, members of the scene gather at a demoparty (such as The Party) in order to show their work and compete. If you are a programmer with imagination, and you like to work with other programmers, you owe it to yourself to find out about demos. If you are not a programmer, download some of the demos and take a look, just for fun. I promise you will be impressed.

Web:
 http://www.cfxweb.net/
    categories.php?op=newindex&catid=1
 http://www.demoscene.ru/english/news/
 http://www.ojuice.net/
 http://www.scene.org/
 http://www.theparty.dk/

Usenet:
 alt.trebel
 alt.trebel.country
 alt.trebel.country.france
 alt.trebel.country.netherlands
 alt.trebel.demos
 alt.trebel.diskmag
 alt.trebel.music
 alt.trebel.party

IRC:
 #coders (EFnet)

DOS Programming Talk and General Discussion

DOS may be well along the way to a well-deserved final resting place, but it is still alive and well on Usenet. Here are the groups devoted to general discussion of DOS programming. If you are a DOS person, these are good places to look for tips, questions and answers. If you are not a DOS person, do not pass "Go" and, definitely, do not collect $200.

Usenet:
 alt.msdos.programmer
 comp.archives.msdos.announce
 comp.msdos.programmer
 comp.os.msdos.programmer
 comp.os.msdos.programmer.turbovision

Free Compilers and Interpreters

You can pay a lot of money for a language translator, or you can check this site and find many, many free compilers and interpreters. If you ever find yourself with some free time and nothing to do, why not download a free compiler and teach yourself a new language? (Actually, I tried to teach myself French that way, but I kept getting parsing mistakes.)

Web:
 http://www.idiom.com/free-compilers/

Usenet:
 comp.compilers
 comp.compilers.tools.pccts

Free Programming Tools

To say that these resources are extensive is like saying that the Queen of England insists on getting her own way: it doesn't even begin to describe the reality of the situation. What we have here is page after page after page of serious tools for serious programmers doing serious things (seriously). If you have even the least bit of interest in being a programming nerd, these sites are a must-have for your personal list of favorites.

Web:
 http://www.codeproject.com/tools/
 http://www.freebyte.com/programming/
 http://www.thefreecountry.com/developercity/
    programmingtools.shtml

Hello, World

It is said that when you learn a new computer language the first thing you do is write a program to display the words "Hello, world". Well, I have been programming for years, in a variety of languages, and I have never, ever written a program that says "Hello, world". (But then, I have never seen a Rocky movie, watched an episode of Ally McBeal, or had tiramisu for dessert.) However, if you happen to be a programmer who is at home in popular culture and likes exploring strange new languages, here is a site that will amuse and entertain you endlessly. But wait, there's more! I have also included another site, where you can see how to program the song "99 Bottles of Beer on the Wall" in many different programming languages. (This is actually a better programming example because you can see some control flow.)

Web:

  http://www.cuillin.demon.co.uk/nazz/trivia/hw/
    hello_world.html
  http://www.roesler-ac.de/wolfram/hello.htm
  http://www2.latech.edu/~acm/HelloWorld.shtml

IEEE Computer Society

The IEEE Computer Society is a world-renowned source of information relating to all aspects of computer science, electronics and engineering, including the publication of periodicals and newsletters, sponsoring conferences, workshops and symposia, and the development of standards. Computer Society Online now offers an electronic source of this information, in many cases before the information is published in hard copy.

Web:

  http://www.computer.org/

Macintosh Programming

Are you a Macintosh programmer? Well, you belong to a select club, a club with members all over the world. Here are Web sites that will help you find all kinds of valuable programming resources. And when you're not busy programming, there are many Usenet discussion groups for you. As a Mac programmer, you may be lonely, but you never have to be alone.

Web:

  http://www.apple.com/developer/
  http://www.mactech.com/

Usenet:

  comp.sys.apple2.programmer
  comp.sys.mac.programmer
  comp.sys.mac.programmer.codewarrior
  comp.sys.mac.programmer.games
  comp.sys.mac.programmer.help
  comp.sys.mac.programmer.info
  comp.sys.mac.programmer.misc
  comp.sys.mac.programmer.tools

Obfuscated C Code

Here are the entries and winners for the International Obfuscated C Code Contest, in which programmers compete to create the most artistic, beautiful and obscure C program. The program must be small (less than a specified number of bytes), and it must work.

Web:

  http://www.ioccc.org/

My new idea: edible Internet jewelry for animals. All I need is venture capital.

Object-Oriented Programming

Object-oriented programming is just like regular programming except that you look at everything differently, write your programs differently, maintain them differently, and think with a different part of your temporal lobe. Join the discussion and talk about object-oriented tools, techniques and problems. The **.misc** group is for general discussion of Macintosh object-oriented programming. The **.macapp3** group is devoted to Version 3 of the MacApp system. The **.tcl** group is for discussion of the Think Class Libraries.

Usenet:

    comp.sys.mac.oop.macapp3
    comp.sys.mac.oop.misc
    comp.sys.mac.oop.tcl

Operating Systems Talk and General Discussion

An operating system is the master control program that runs a computer: for example, Windows 95/98, Windows NT, DOS, MacOS and Unix are all operating systems. If you are interested in issues relating to the design and implementation of operating systems, here is a Usenet group in which you can talk with people working in this area. This group is for general operating system discussion. For issues relating to specific systems, there are more specific Usenet groups.

Usenet:

    comp.os.misc

OS/2 Programming Talk and General Discussion

Here are a few good places where you can ask questions, get answers or talk all night about anything relating to programming under OS/2. In addition, there are groups devoted to tools, porting and object-oriented programming.

Usenet:

    bit.listserv.os2-l
    comp.os.os2.programmer.misc
    comp.os.os2.programmer.oop
    comp.os.os2.programmer.porting
    comp.os.os2.programmer.tools

Perl

It would be difficult to exaggerate the importance of Perl. It is the scripting language of choice in many situations, and is used widely on the Internet. Perl was created in 1986 by Larry Wall, a Unix and Internet programmer of renown. The name Perl stands for "Practical Extraction and Report Language" (although, as with most such acronyms, the meaning was made up after the name was chosen). Here are enough Perl resources to keep you satisfied forever (or until you die, whichever comes first).

Web:

    http://perl.plover.com/
    http://www.cpan.org/
    http://www.perl.com/

Usenet:

    alt.perl
    comp.lang.perl
    comp.lang.perl.announce
    comp.lang.perl.misc
    comp.lang.perl.moderated
    comp.lang.perl.modules
    comp.lang.perl.tk

Programming Humor

Some types of jokes—called canonical jokes—are repeated, with small variations, over and over again. Here are lists of programming jokes. If you are a programmer, my prescription is to pause every time you find a bug and read two jokes.

Web:

    http://www.elsop.com/wrc/humor/progwack.htm
    http://www.gnu.org/fun/
    http://www.klawitter.de/enhumor.html
    http://www.rinkworks.com/stupid/
      cs_programming.shtml

It's never too late in the day to eat breakfast.

Programming Languages

I remember, when I first started programming, the language PL/I was still new. It was supposed to be the language to replace all other languages. I started with Fortran, and, during my early life as a programmer, worked with a variety of different languages, such as C, APL, Basic, Lisp, 360 Assembler (for which I wrote a book), PC Assembler (for which I wrote a couple of books), Pascal, and on and on. There are literally hundreds of programming languages, and no one knows them all. (In fact, no one even knows the names of them all.) Here are some Web sites that are starting places for investigating any of a large list of different languages. For discussion, well, there are enough Usenet programming groups to keep you occupied from now to St. Swithin's Day.

Web:
http://home.nvg.org/~sk/lang/lang.html
http://www.cs.waikato.ac.nz/~marku/languages.html
http://www.csci.csusb.edu/dick/languages.html
http://www.tunes.org/doc/Review/Languages.html

Usenet:
comp.lang.apl
comp.lang.asm.x86
comp.lang.asm370
comp.lang.awk
comp.lang.beta
comp.lang.clarion
comp.lang.clipper
comp.lang.clos
comp.lang.cobol
comp.lang.dylan
comp.lang.eiffel
comp.lang.forth
comp.lang.forth.mac
comp.lang.fortran
comp.lang.functional
comp.lang.icon
comp.lang.idl
comp.lang.idl-pvwave
comp.lang.lisp
comp.lang.lisp.franz
comp.lang.lisp.mcl
comp.lang.lisp.x
comp.lang.logo
comp.lang.misc
comp.lang.ml
comp.lang.modula2
comp.lang.modula3
comp.lang.mumps
comp.lang.oberon
comp.lang.objective-c
comp.lang.pascal
comp.lang.pascal.ansi-iso
comp.lang.pascal.borland
comp.lang.pascal.delphi.advocacy
comp.lang.pascal.delphi.components.misc
comp.lang.pascal.delphi.components.usage
comp.lang.pascal.delphi.components.writing
comp.lang.pascal.delphi.databases
comp.lang.pascal.delphi.misc
comp.lang.pascal.mac
comp.lang.pascal.misc
comp.lang.perl
comp.lang.perl.announce
comp.lang.perl.misc
comp.lang.perl.modules
comp.lang.perl.tk
comp.lang.pl1
comp.lang.pop
comp.lang.prograph
comp.lang.prolog
comp.lang.python
comp.lang.rexx
comp.lang.sather
comp.lang.scheme
comp.lang.scheme.scsh
comp.lang.smalltalk
comp.lang.tcl
comp.lang.tcl.announce
comp.lang.verilog
comp.lang.vhdl

Programming Talk and General Discussion

while (not sleeping)

if (question=not answered")

post (Usenet (query))

else read (Usenet (other-people's-articles));

Usenet:
comp.programming
comp.programming.contests

Need even more information on programming languages?

Try the Programming Languages Web sites.

Do you have a code in the head? Try "Cryptography".

Tao of Programming

Here is a humorous guide to programming and otherwise living with computers in the modern age. "Something mysterious is formed, born in the silent void. Waiting alone and unmoving, it is at once still and yet in constant motion. It is the source of all programs. I do not know its name, so I will call it the Tao of Programming."

Web:
 http://www.dnaco.net/~kragen/
  tao-of-programming.html
 http://www.topsail.org/tao.html

Visual Basic

Visual Basic, a product of Microsoft, is the most modern incarnation of the Basic programming language. However, Visual Basic is a powerful tool that bears little resemblance to the original Basic. For many people, Visual Basic is the programming tool of choice, offering a total environment devoted to rapid program development, especially for client-server systems (including Internet programs) and database applications.

Web:
 http://searchvb.techtarget.com/
 http://www.faqs.org/faqs/visual-basic-faq/
 http://www.msdn.microsoft.com/vbasic/
 http://www.mvps.org/vbnet/
 http://www.vbwire.com/

Usenet:
 comp.lang.basic.visual
 comp.lang.basic.visual.3rdparty
 comp.lang.basic.visual.database
 comp.lang.basic.visual.misc
 comp.lang.visual

IRC:
 #visualbasic (Undernet)

Windows Programming Talk and General Discussion

These Usenet groups are for questions and answers relating to general programming in the Microsoft Windows environment as well as more specific topics such as controls, dialogs, graphics and printing, memory management, multimedia and network programming, and so on.

Usenet:

    comp.os.ms-windows.programmer
    comp.os.ms-windows.programmer.controls
    comp.os.ms-windows.programmer.drivers
    comp.os.ms-windows.programmer.graphics
    comp.os.ms-windows.programmer.misc
    comp.os.ms-windows.programmer.multimedia
    comp.os.ms-windows.programmer.networks
    comp.os.ms-windows.programmer.nt.kernel-mode
    comp.os.ms-windows.programmer.ole
    comp.os.ms-windows.programmer.tools
    comp.os.ms-windows.programmer.vxd
    comp.os.ms-windows.programmer.win32
    comp.os.ms-windows.programmer.winhelp

X Window

Here is information about the X Consortium (the X Window people) as well as links to many X-related sites. Find out what you need to work with X today, and what you need to understand to work with the newest version known as Broadway (X11R6.3): a system for creating and accessing interactive applications over the Web.

Web:

    http://www.rahul.net/kenton/xsites.html
    http://www.x.org/

> ## The problem is that,
> ## except for you and I,
> ## most people are wrong
> ## a lot of the time.

PSYCHOLOGY

Adler, Alfred

Alfred Adler (1870-1937) was an Austrian psychiatrist who started with Freud, but eventually rejected Freud's emphasis on sexuality. Adler founded the school of individual psychology and maintained that neurosis was not a matter of repressed sexuality, but rather a reaction to feelings of inferiority. ("It is always easier to fight for one's principles than to live up to them.") Adler felt that the relation of the individual to his or her community was of prime importance, and that a feeling of connection to society was paramount to maintaining mental health.

Web:

    http://ourworld.compuserve.com/homepages/hstein/

Consciousness

The idea that we are conscious seems so basic to our lives that we take it for granted. However, to philosophers, the idea of consciousness, and its implications, is complex. Indeed, it embraces four distinct areas of experience: knowledge, intention, introspection, and sensation. As such, the study of consciousness is multidisciplinary, involving, not only psychology, but cognitive science, neuroscience and philosophy.

Web:

    http://psyche.cs.monash.edu.au/
    http://www.u.arizona.edu/~chalmers/resources.html

Usenet:

    sci.psychology.consciousness
    sci.psychology.journals.psyche

Listserv Mailing List:

    List Name: psyche-d
    Subscribe to: listserv@listserv.uh.edu

Listserv Mailing List:

    List Name: psyche-l
    Subscribe to: listserv@listserv.uh.edu

Freud, Sigmund

Sigmund Freud (1856-1939) was an Austrian psychiatrist and one of the great geniuses of the twentieth century. Freud opened vast areas of human thought—for example, the idea that there is an unconscious mind—and can rightly be considered the father of modern psychology. Freud's basic theory (which he developed and expanded over the years) is that unresolved infantile conflicts are responsible for much of adult neurosis and other aberrant behavior. Freud developed the techniques of psychoanalysis: the use of free association and dream interpretation to bring these conflicts to light, and to deal with them appropriately. As Freud developed his theories, it became more and more clear to him that the repressed feelings and memories were often of a sexual nature. He described, for example, the Oedipus Complex, a subconscious desire within a child for the parent of the opposite sex. If this complex does not resolve itself naturally, it will have a great effect on the person. As an adult, he or she may become neurotic and may be unable to form a normal, sexual relationship. Freud's strong belief in repressed sexual feelings as the root of much human pathology was extremely controversial at the time, and led to his breaking with some of his followers, in particular, Carl Jung and Alfred Adler. Throughout the years, Freud's theories have been studied, expanded (and even partially discredited) by several generations of psychoanalysts and physiologists. However, the bulk of Freud's insight and contributions have stood the test of time. Although there are those who criticize Freud's theories, I find that most such people know very little about what Freud really said and did. If you have never actually read anything Freud wrote, you may enjoy doing so. (I suggest starting with the book "The Psychopathology of Everyday Life".) Freud was a real genius in the sense that whatever he turned his attention to, he illuminated.

Web:
  http://freud.t0.or.at/freud/index-e.htm
  http://www.freud.org.uk/
  http://www.nyfreudian.org/abstracts/

The Net is immortal.

Sigmund Freud

If you want to find out what Freud really said, read what Freud really said.

Jung, Carl

Carl Gustav Jung (1875-1961) was a Swiss psychiatrist. At one time, Jung was one of Freud's disciples. (In fact, Jung was the first president of the International Psychoanalytic Association.) However, in 1912 he published a book called Psychology and the Unconscious, which described two dimensions of the unconscious. In addition to the regular unconscious, which Freud had discovered (containing repressed and forgotten memories and thoughts), Jung postulated a "collective unconscious" (mental patterns shared within a culture or by all human beings). This was enough of a revolutionary hypothesis to cause Jung to break with Freud. Jung founded the school of "analytical psychology" and achieved a career of great renown. (It was Jung, for instance, who developed the ideas of introversion and extroversion.)

Web:
  http://www.cgjungpage.org/

Usenet:
  alt.psychology.jung

Optical Illusions

Optical illusions are really cool, even without the benefit of caffeine or other artificial substances. These sites have collections of images that make you think twice (or more) about what you are seeing.

Web:
  http://www.ee.bgu.ac.il/~idog/amazing/
  http://www.exploratorium.edu/exhibits/
    f_exhibits.html
  http://www.sandlotscience.com/Ambiguous/
    Ambiguous_frm.htm

Personality Tests

One way to analyze the human personality is by studying a person and classifying him or her as being a particular "psychological type". This idea was originally developed by Carl Jung, who believed that human behavior follows specific patterns that develop from the characteristics of the human mind. Jung believed the conscious human mind was continually perceiving (taking in information) and judging (organizing information to arrive at decisions). However, each person is born with a tendency to favor one type of mental activity over the other. According to Jung, a person could perceive either by "sensing" or by using "intuition". Similarly, one judges either by "thinking" or "feeling". (You can see how one could classify people according to this criteria.) Jung also identified two opposite human tendencies: extroversion (an outward focus) and introversion (an inward focus). Here are some resources that can help you understand personality testing, Jungian and otherwise. If you enjoy self-analysis, one of these Web sites has a test you can take to estimate your Jungian-based personality characteristics. This will allow you to summarize your personality using a standard, four-letter acronym, for example, INTJ (introvert, intuition [N], thinking, judging) or XNFP (split extrovert/introvert [X], intuition [N], feeling, perceiving). For a discussion of personality testing, you can participate in the Usenet groups.

Web:
  http://www.universityoflife.com/personalitytests.htm
  http://www.verysimple.com/personality/

Usenet:
  alt.psychology.personality
  sci.psychology.personality

Psychological Help

There are days when things seem overwhelming and unpleasant or you encounter a problem and you don't know exactly what to do with it. Check out the Usenet group that offers discussion about the problems people face. Maybe you will find an answer or just someone to talk to.

Usenet:
  alt.psychology.help

Psychology Journals

Here are the abstracts and tables of contents for a large number of journals sponsored by the American Psychological Association. The information at this site allows you to scan through the summaries of your favorite journals: an easy way to keep up on what is happening.

Web:
  http://www.apa.org/journals/

Psychology Resources

Psychologically speaking, you can learn a lot about a psychologist by observing what types of Internet resources he uses. If a psychologist only uses Web sites, it means he is a loner, who likes to work on his own. If a psychologist participates in Usenet discussion groups or mailing lists, it means he is more other-centered, the type of person who prefers to work in groups in order to reach a consensus. And if a psychologist uses the Web *and* participates in discussions, it means he is an over-achiever who works too hard in a vain attempt to please his father with whom he has issues that have never been resolved.

Web:
  http://www.fenichel.com/Current.shtml
  http://www.human-nature.com/odmh/
  http://www.psychologie.uni-bonn.de/
     online-documents/lit_ww.htm
  http://www.psychwww.com/

Majordomo Mailing List:
  List Name: inetpsyc
  Subscribe to: majordomo@psyc.uow.edu.au

PsychologyJournals

What do you do when you have a house guest you are just too busy to entertain? Sit him down at the computer, connect him to the Net, and let him read back issues of psychology journals.

Just listen to this:

"According to Wallis (1992), philosophers of mind agree that a successful theory of representation must 'describe conditions for representation in nonintentional and nonsemantic terms.' If we restrict representation talk to what goes on in frogs, the visual systems of humans, etc., then perhaps Wallis is right. But once we count beliefs as representations, there is no such agreement. Indeed..."

Your friends will be coming back to visit you, again and again.

Psychology Talk and General Discussion

The good thing about psychology is that anyone can talk about it. The bad thing is that everyone does. Of course, as one of my readers, your insights are particularly valuable, so if you have any interest in psychology, I encourage you to join the discussion. Here are several Usenet groups devoted to different aspects of psychology. If you are not sure which one is for you, choose the **.misc** group.

Usenet:
  sci.psychology
  sci.psychology.announce
  sci.psychology.journals.psycoloquy
  sci.psychology.misc
  sci.psychology.psychotherapy
  sci.psychology.research
  sci.psychology.theory

Self-Help and Psychology Magazine

This online magazine features articles by renowned psychologists and respected experts. You can find information on subjects such as relationships, sexuality, addictions, family, sports psychology and health.

Web:
  http://www.shpm.com/

Social Psychology

Social psychology is a collective term to describe the areas of study that concentrate on group behavior, and on how social factors influence us as individuals. As such, social psychologists deal with such topics as personal relationships, advertising, the psychology of politics, societal attitudes, group behavior, power and influence, and so on.

Web:
  http://www.socialpsychology.org/

Listserv Mailing List:
  List Name: socpsy-l
  Subscribe to: listserv@listserv.uga.edu

QUOTATIONS

Allen, Woody (Quotations)

You probably think your Uncle Fred has a good sense of humor but, actually, he's just memorized all of Woody Allen's famous quotes. No reason why you can't do the same.

Web:
   http://www.cp-tel.net/miller/billee/quotes/
      woody.html
   http://www.lyfe.freeserve.co.uk/quoteallen.htm
   http://www.workinghumor.com/quotes/
      woody_allen.shtml

Daily Quotations

I bet a day doesn't pass when you don't encounter someone who would just love to hear an interesting quotation. So here are some places where you can find a new quote when you need one. Not only will you have something to read while you take your daily vitamin, you'll have the raw material with which to astonish and delight other people, every day of the year. Just you wait and see. Once you start sharing a quotation a day, it won't be long before you become the Mr. or Ms. Popularity of your entire social set.

Web:
   http://www.qotd.org/
   http://www.quotationspage.com/qotd.html
   http://www.quotelady.com/

Famous Quotations

The next time you're looking for a wise and pithy saying, the Net will be glad to oblige. These Web sites have large collections of quotations from famous people. When you have a few extra moments, take some time and browse through the lists. Soon you yourself will be wise and pithy, fawned over by all your friends. As Winston Churchill once said, "It is a good thing for an uneducated man to read books of quotations." (Uneducated women, I suppose, are on their own.)

Web:
   http://www.cs.virginia.edu/~robins/quotes.html
   http://www.csmngt.com/quote_me.htm
   http://www.kornea.com/quotations.html
   http://www.workinghumor.com/quotes/index.htm

The Internet has a number of sites at which you can find all kinds of quotations. Just the thing for spicing up your conversation and enhancing your reputation. Here is a typical example showing how it works.

You are talking to your teacher or boss.

Teacher/Boss: So what do you have to say for yourself?

At this point you repeat a quote that you downloaded the night before from one of the Internet quotation archives.

You: Well, I think blah, blah, blah, blah, blah...

Teacher/Boss: Wow, you really are terrific. I'm going to give you an A (or a raise).

Very good looking woman/man who happens to be listening: You are an unbelievably attractive person. Would you like to have dinner with me tonight?

Fields, W.C. (Quotations)

W. C. Fields (1879-1946) was an American movie actor whose wit is legendary even today. After all, anyone who hates kids, dogs and books for dummies can't be all bad.

Web:
   http://www.louisville.edu/~kprayb01/WCQuote.html

Goldwyn, Samuel (Quotations)

Samuel Goldwyn (1882-1974) was a Polish-born American film producer who merged his own company with that of Louis B. Mayer to form Metro-Goldwyn-Mayer. Goldwyn is best remembered for the original way in which he expressed his ideas. For example, he once said that "Pictures are for entertainment; messages should be delivered by Western Union." Are all the Samuel Goldwyn quotes real? I can tell you in two words: a pocryphal.

Web:
http://www.eng.wayne.edu/Carlo/Sam.html
http://www.virtualmuseumofhistory.com/
    hallofrhetoric/epideicticartiste/
    samuelgoldwyn.net/

Hahn, Harley (Quotations)

The next time you are at a party with some Very Important People who you need to impress, feel free to quote me. (That's what I do, and I find it to be highly effective.) To help you, here are collections of quotations from some of my books. Note: If you are a Unix person who likes Gilbert and Sullivan, be sure to check out the "Unix Sysadmin Song".

Web:
http://www.harley.com/harley-quotes/

Marx, Groucho (Quotations)

Groucho Marx (1894-1977)—a performer for more than seventy-five years—was one of America's funniest funny men. During his many years as a performer (in plays, radio, movies and television) and as a writer, Groucho came up with numerous witty, timeless quotations. Check out these lists of Groucho quotes, and maybe you can pass them off as your own. ("When I invite a woman to dinner, I expect her to look at my face. That's the price she has to pay.")

Web:
http://ourworld.compuserve.com/homepages/
    ulrich_oswald/groucho.htm
http://www.bmacleod.com/groucho.html
http://www.luquette.org/humor/
    quotes_from_groucho_marx.htm
http://www.ps.uci.edu/~lasio/Groucho.html

Mencken, H.L. (Quotations)

American author H.L. (Henry Louis) Mencken (1880-1956) was known for his many critical essays. He was especially fond of acerbic social commentary directed against what he felt were the complacent middle classes. "Say what you will about the Ten Commandments," observed Mencken, "you must always come back to the pleasant fact that there are only ten of them."

Web:
http://www.freedomsnest.com/qmencken.html
http://www.io.com/gibbonsb/mencken/
    megaquotes.html
http://www.phnet.fi/public/mamaa1/mencken.htm
http://www.positiveatheism.org/hist/quotes/
    mencken.htm
http://www.watchfuleye.com/mencken.html

Monty Python

There is no surer way to impress your significant other or a prospective employer than being able to quote liberally from the Monty Python canon. So, before your next important social interaction, be sure to take the time to memorize at least a few quotations, song lyrics or sketches. My suggestion is to practice the "Argument Clinic" sketch until you can do all the parts, all by yourself, from memory.

Web:
  ftp://ftp.std.com/obi/alt.quotations/Archive/fortune/
    holy/
  http://bau2.uibk.ac.at/sg/python/Scripts/
    Alphabetic.html
  http://www.intriguing.com/mp/
  http://www.quotegeek.com/Movies/
    Monty_Python_and_the_Holy_Grail/

Usenet:
  alt.fan.monty-python

Presidential Quotes

This archive has a collection of quotes from various American Presidents: Jefferson, Lincoln, Clinton, Reagan and others. This is the place to go when you need to remind yourself whether or not it was Ronald Reagan who said, "Ask not what your country can do for you; ask what you can do for your country." In addition, you will also find quotes from other notables, such as Linus Torvalds, the creator of the original version of the Linux operating system. ("Linux does endless loops in six seconds.")

Web:
  http://www.atozquotes.com/u.s.%20presidents.htm

Quotable Women

Since the beginning of creation, women have been talking. As a matter of fact, the first well-known quote is attributed to Eve ("Are you really going to wear that?"). The Quotable Women archive collects memorable quotes from women both modern and historical. Why settle for the last word when you can get all of them?

Web:
  http://www.famouscreativewomen.com/
  http://www.ffrf.org/wws/quotes.html
  http://www.harley.com/womens-quotes/
  http://www.womensmedia.com/quote-a.shtml

Quotation Resources

Truly, there's no need to ever have to be original in anything you say or write. Just check out these resources, and you'll find just about any type of quotations: advertising quotes, animal quotes, music quotes, political quotes, religious quotes, film quotes, and more. With so many sources of information, if you happen to say something original, don't blame me.

Web:
  http://www.aphids.com/quotes/
  http://www.imdb.com/Games/randomquote
  http://www.quotegarden.com/
  http://www.quoteland.com/
  http://www.rockwisdom.com/
  http://www.sbrowning.com/quotes/
    index.php3?authors=1
  http://www.tqpage.com/

Random Quotations

Every day, start your day by reading a witty, interesting saying. It's better for you than coffee and more inspiring than television.

Just connect to one of the **Random Quotations** Web sites, and a randomly chosen quotation will be yours.

Special service: I recognize that it may not be possible for you to check one of these sites every day. So, as a public service, I am giving you two dog-oriented quotes. You can use these when you need to be away from the Net (for example, if you have to leave town for the weekend).

(1) Mark Twain: If you pick up a starving dog and make him prosperous, he will not bite you. This is the principal difference between a dog and a man.

(2) Groucho Marx: Outside of a dog, a book is a man's best friend; inside of a dog, it's too dark to read.

Quotation Talk and General Discussion

Here is the Usenet group devoted to a discussion of quotations. This is the place to ask if anyone knows who said, "It isn't necessary to have relatives in Kansas City in order to be unhappy." Of course, questions like this only get answered if people participate, so if you like quotes, why don't you follow the discussion and see if you can help someone else. (The quotation, by the way, is from Groucho Marx.)

Usenet:
   alt.quotations

Quotes from Famous Authors

Many of our most memorable quotations come from writers. Here are some wonderful things said by some of the wisest, wittiest authors in history: Charles Dickens, Dorothy Parker, George Bernard Shaw, George Orwell, Mark Twain, Oscar Wilde, Shakespeare, Stephen Leacock, and more.

Web:
   http://www.creativequotations.com/special.shtml
   http://www.cyber-nation.com/victory/quotations/
      authors/quotes_orwell_george.html
   http://www.intelligentsianetwork.com/
      dorothyparker/dorothyparker.htm
   http://www.intelligentsianetwork.com/wquotations/
      wquotations.htm
   http://www.nlc-bnc.ca/3/5/t5-258-e.html
   http://www.phnet.fi/public/mamaa1/wilde.htm
   http://www.quoteland.com/author.asp?author_id=119
   http://www.therightside.demon.co.uk/quotes/shaw/
   http://www.twainquotes.com/quotesatoz.html
   http://www.workinghumor.com/quotes/
      charles_dickens.shtml

Random Quotes

Need a quick burst of inspiration? Get yourself a quote chosen randomly from a large collection of interesting and pithy sayings. You can request another quote whenever you want, but be prudent. According to the U.S. Department of Redundancy Department, the recommended maximum allowance for an average adult is three quotes a day (two for Steve Wright quotes).

Web:
   http://www.coolquotes.com/
   http://www.ficara.net/quotes/
   http://www.insanityideas.com/quotemachine/

Rogers, Will (Quotations)

The American humorist Will Rogers (1879-1935) was a beloved social commentator and entertainer, sometimes referred to as the "cowboy philosopher". Although he could be critical, Rogers had the knack of doing so with a wink and a smile. As a result, he became widely popular, through radio, newspaper columns, books and the movies. "I joked about every prominent man of my time," said Rogers, "but I never met a man I didn't like."

Web:
   http://www.dailycelebrations.com/willrogers.htm
   http://www.willrogers.org/willsays_quotes.html
   http://www.willrogerstoday.com/will_rogers_quotes/

Sports Quotes

Sports are an important part of our culture, almost as important as talking, and when you combine the two of them, you're in business. Here are some memorable sports quotations from some memorable sports figures, including Yogi Berra (baseball manager), Knute Rockne (football coach), John Wooden (basketball coach), as well as a miscellany of other notables. "What's the difference between a 3-week-old puppy and a sportswriter?" asked football coach Mike Ditka. "In 6 weeks the puppy stops whining." There have been a lot of interesting things said about sports, but let's give Yogi the last word: "Baseball is 90 percent mental. The other half is physical."

Web:
   http://home.no.net/birgerro/quotes.htm
   http://www.cyber-nation.com/victory/quotations/
      authors/quotes_wooden_john.html
   http://www.dfw.net/~patricia/nba-daily-humor
   http://www.gifts4fishing.com/quotes.htm
   http://www.sportscribe.com/qtes1.html
   http://www.yogiberraclassic.org/quotes.htm

Star Trek Quotes

Dammit, Jim, I'm a writer, not a trivia buff. If you want quotes from the original Star Trek, the Next Generation, the Star Trek movies, Voyager or Deep Space Nine, you'll have to get them yourself.

Web:
   http://www.bolt.icestorm.com/cube/st/kmq.html
   http://www.sciflicks.com/
      star_trek_the_motion_picture/quotes.html
   http://www.sjtrek.com/trek/quotes/

RADIO

Amateur Radio Talk and General Discussion

Radio is a great hobby and one day when you are an expert, you can have your own nationally syndicated talk show and screaming fans will throw themselves at your feet when you go out in public. Until then, you can spend time reading Usenet groups especially for amateur radio enthusiasts. Topics cover construction, packet and digital radio modes, transmission, regulations, repair and other general topics.

Usenet:
rec.radio.amateur
rec.radio.amateur.antenna
rec.radio.amateur.boatanchors
rec.radio.amateur.digital.misc
rec.radio.amateur.dx
rec.radio.amateur.equipment
rec.radio.amateur.homebrew
rec.radio.amateur.misc
rec.radio.amateur.packet
rec.radio.amateur.policy
rec.radio.amateur.space
rec.radio.amateur.swap

Listproc Mailing List:
List Name: qrp-l
Subscribe to: listproc@lehigh.edu

Campus Radio Disc Jockeys

What a cool job it is to sit in a climate-controlled booth jamming out to the latest tunes for hours on end. And in between the songs you get to offer some profound remarks that will reach the ears of every student on campus. What power! Hone your communication skills by hearing what other DJs and station managers discuss on this mailing list about college radio, federal and campus regulations, station policies, and equipment reviews.

Listserv Mailing List:
List Name: dj-l
Subscribe to: listserv@listserv.nodak.edu

Canadian Broadcasting Corporation

For years, the Canadian Broadcasting Corporation (CBC) has been providing the best television and radio broadcasting that government money can buy. If you live in Canada, spend some time at this Web site where you can find all kinds of information, including news, schedules, audio versions of various programs, discussion, and much more (in French and in English). If it's news and it's Canadian, you'll find it here.

Web:
http://www.cbc.ca/onair/

CB (Citizens Band) Radio

CD radio is a two-way voice communication facility designed for short-range (1-5 miles) personal and business use. You do not need a license to use CB radio, which accounts for its popularity, especially among truckers and other drivers. CB radio has 40 different shared channels, each of which can support its own conversation. When you use CB radio, you choose a nickname for yourself, called a "handle". As with other radio communications, CD users have a set of abbreviation codes that are used to save time and make the people using them feel cool. For example, 10-4 means "Message receive; 10-73 means, "There is a speed trap."

Web:
http://wireless.fcc.gov/prs/citzn.html
http://www.cybertron.com/~ddavis/cb10.htm
http://www.dxzone.com/catalog/CB_Radio/
http://www.tvradioworld.com/directory/
   hobby_radio/default.asp?n=cb

Usenet:
rec.radio.cb

Classic Top 40 Radio Sounds

It is human nature to compare and analyze, and ever since there has been music on the radio, there have been lists of which songs were the most popular. In the radio industry, "Top 40" refers to the 40 most popular songs, and "classic" refers to songs that were popular among people who are now old enough to have children. Thus, visiting a "classic Top 40 radio sounds" Web site will allow you to wax nostalgic about the personalities and sounds that baby boomers enjoyed when they were young. Or, as Wolfman Jack once put it, "Good guys only make it in the movies, baby..."

Web:
  http://www.reelradio.com/

Digital Audio Broadcasting

Imagine: your voice—static-free, flying silky smooth through the air at the speed of sound, straight into someone's ear. They turn and could swear that you were right there behind them. This is the wonder of digital audio broadcasting with its improved sound quality and technical superiority. Join with other DAB enthusiasts to talk not only about the technological merits of digital audio broadcasting, but also the social and economic issues.

Usenet:
  alt.radio.digital

Ham Radio

Do you want to be famous? Start practicing now by becoming a ham radio operator. After awhile you will get a reputation around the neighborhood as that studly ham guy. Then you can start spouting your opinions on the radio, build up your ego, put on a few pounds and eventually have your own conservative talk show on mainstream radio. Wouldn't that be fun? So get on the Net now and learn all about ham radio. The faster you learn, the faster you will be on your way to success.

Web:
  http://www.dxzone.com/catalog/Ham_Radio/
  http://www.hamradio-online.com/
  http://www.irony.com/ham-howto.html
  http://www.qrz.com/

Usenet:
  alt.ham-radio.mods
  alt.ham-radio.morse
  rec.ham-radio
  rec.ham-radio.swap

NPR Online

NPR (National Public Radio) is a large non-commercial radio network in the United States. NPR offers a variety of programs: news, talk, information, music and entertainment. In the U.S., NPR is considered by some people to be controversial due to a liberal bias. However, their programs are well-produced and informative, and they have many listeners across the country. If you would like to listen to some NPR programs (which you will probably find interesting, even if you live outside the U.S.), you can do so by connecting to this Web site. You will also find information about NPR itself such as where to listen to NPR, member stations, how to get transcripts of shows, and so on.

Web:
  http://www.npr.org/

Usenet:
  alt.radio.networks.npr

Campus Radio Disc Jockeys

When I was an undergraduate at the University of Waterloo, Canada, I was a CRDJ. Actually, I was a CCCRDJ (Cool Canadian Campus Radio Disc Jockey). If you too are a member of this elite corps, join the dj-l mailing list and see what your fellows are up to.

Number Stations

You're listening to your shortwave radio and all of a sudden you hear a nondescript voice intoning a long list of numbers. Sometimes you hear a pattern, but mostly the numbers seem random. And then suddenly they stop. Later, you happen onto the same frequency and again you hear the numbers. What are they? No one knows for sure, but there are many shortwave stations around the world broadcasting sequences of numbers. Nobody will admit to being responsible for the stations, but they have been broadcasting for years. It is generally thought that these stations are run by espionage agencies and are used to send coded signals to spies in the field. Around the world there are many people who monitor these stations, keep statistics and share information. There are even organizations and newsletters devoted to tracking these number stations.

Web:
  http://www.ibmpcug.co.uk/~irdial/conet.htm
  http://www.spynumbers.com/

Old-Time Radio

I love old radio shows like Jack Benny, Dragnet, the Great Gildersleeve, and Burns and Allen. If you do too, you will enjoy these Web sites. To get you started, here is an interesting trivia item. One of the more popular radio shows (dating back to 1940) was Truth or Consequences. Each time the show began you would hear the audience laughing uncontrollably. How did they arrange it? Well, a few minutes before the show was to start, two men from the audience would be brought up on the stage. Each man was given a suitcase and told that the first person who could get dressed using the contents of the suitcase would win a prize. The suitcases were filled with women's clothes and undergarments. The stunt never failed to whip the audience into gales of laughter, just in time for the announcer to say: "Hello there. We've been waiting for you. It's time to play Truth or Consequences."

Web:
  http://www.antique-radio.org/
  http://www.faqs.org/faqs/radio/old-time-faq/
  http://www.old-time.com/
  http://www.otr.com/

Open Broadcasting

Until recently, those public service agencies that broadcast over the radio have used the same technology as everyone else. That is why it is possible, for example, to use a scanner to listen to police broadcasts. However, many public agencies are now starting to use closed radio systems—such as digital (trunked) or encrypted transmissions—that are difficult or impossible for regular people to monitor. Some public officials will admit frankly that they do *not* want the general public to be able to overhear their transmissions. But is this in our best interests? In a free country, do you really want the police and other government agencies to be able to communicate in secret? Open broadcasting is the idea that public agencies should use the airwaves in ways that are accessible to the public.

Web:
  http://www.openness.org/

Usenet:
  alt.radio.broadcasting.open

Packet Radio

Packet radio is a system that sends information from one computer to another using radio broadcasting. The name "packet radio" refers to the fact that the information is broken into small groupings of data called packets. (The Internet itself is a packet-based network.) With packet radio, you use a device called a TNC (terminal node controller) to connect your computer to a radio. The TNC acts like a bridge between your computer and the radio, which sends and receives data. (Conceptually, the TNC is like a modem only instead of using a phone line, data is transmitted using radio waves.) Most packet radio enthusiasts use VHF frequencies, which limit transmissions to a little better than unobstructed line of sight. However, once you have the appropriate equipment, packet radio is easy to use and requires no special license. And there exist networks of packet radio systems that make it possible to propagate data over long distances.

Web:
  http://www.sedan.org/
  http://www.tapr.org/tapr/html/pktf.html

Usenet:
  rec.radio.amateur.packet

Pirate Radio

In most countries, radio broadcasting is strictly regulated by the government. In the United States, that job is performed by the FCC (Federal Communications Commission). In Canada, the organization is the CRTC (Canadian Radio-television and Telecommunications Commission). These government agencies do not allow private individuals to broadcast willy-nilly over the most commonly used frequencies, such as those set aside for AM and FM radio. Pirate radio refers to non-sanctioned broadcasting over such frequencies. The philosophical justification within the mostly underground pirate radio community ranges from freedom of speech to good plain fun. If the idea of broadcasting illegally in front of the government's back appeals to you, start here.

Web:
   http://www.frn.net/
   http://www.radio4all.org/

Usenet:
   alt.pirate.radio
   alt.radio.pirate

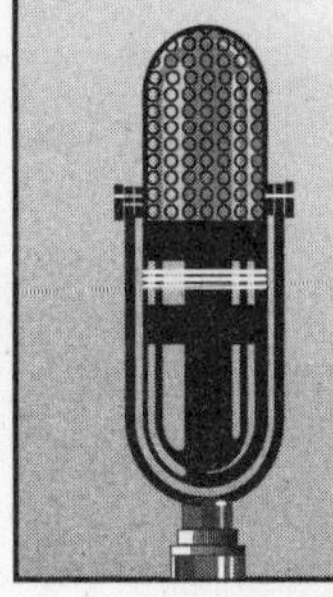

Radio Broadcasting

Boy, radio has just got to be the best invention since television. Join the folks who love to listen, as they discuss radio broadcasting. The **broadcasting** discussion groups are for general broadcasting topics. (The **rec.radio.broadcasting** group is moderated.) The **info** group, also moderated, is for news and announcements. For those who hate advertising, **noncomm** is for talking about noncommercial radio. The **radio-l** group is for digital audio broadcasting.

Usenet:
   alt.radio.broadcasting
   bit.listserv.radio-l
   rec.radio.broadcasting
   rec.radio.info
   rec.radio.noncomm

Radio History

The first radio transmission took place in 1895 when the Italian investor Guglielmo Marconi (1874-1937) successfully sent a signal over a short distance. In 1901, Marconi was able to transmit a radio signal across the Atlantic Ocean. The first important experimental radio broadcasts took place in the 1920s in the United States. These Web sites have information about the early days of radio and the early radio equipment.

Web:
   http://home.luna.nl/%7earjan-muil/radio/
      history.html
   http://www.radiohistory.org/

Radio Industry

The radio industry is complex and cutthroat, and changes daily. If you work in the industry, these resources will help you beat the buzz, by keeping you up to date on the latest happenings. If you are a listener, I bet you'll find something interesting, such as the current insider business gossip. In addition, you can check the latest ratings to see which are the top stations in your area.

Web:
   http://100kwatts.tmi.net/
   http://www.radioandrecords.com/
Usenet:
   alt.radio.broadcasting

Radio Scanner Frequencies

A radio scanner is a device that lets you monitor radio frequencies not accessible with regular AM and FM receivers. These frequencies are used by a variety of organizations, especially law enforcement and public service groups. These Web pages will help you find frequencies that you can monitor to eavesdrop on various types of conversations. You can also find the frequencies used by drive-through restaurants (McDonald's, etc.), theme parks (Disneyland, etc.), TV stations, canned music (Muzak) and cordless phones. After all, if they didn't want you to listen, why would they be talking?

Web:
   http://www.strongsignals.net/access/content/faf.html
   http://www.stupidscannertricks.com/
Usenet:
   alt.radio.scanner
   alt.radio.scanner.uk
   rec.radio.scanner

Radio Station Lists

Here are several comprehensive lists I have selected to help you find information about radio stations around the world. These lists are useful when you want to find out which stations are in a particular area. In addition, one of the lists shows many stations that have their own Web sites. For U.S. listeners, I have included a resource to allow you to look at the official FCC information for any U.S. radio station. You can search by location, frequency or call letters.

Web:
   http://www.radio-locator.com/cgi-bin/home
   http://www.radiostation.com/
   http://www.radiotower.com/

Shortwave Radio

Shortwave radio consists of signals broadcast between 3Mhz and 30 MHz. The nature of shortwave is that the waves bounce off the upper atmosphere and, hence, can travel long distances. This means that you can use a shortwave receiver to listen to broadcasts from around the world. There are a wide variety of shortwave stations, and listening to them is a fascinating hobby. There is a lot of information to help get you started, as well more detailed resources as for the experienced shortwave enthusiast.

Web:
   http://www.anarc.org/naswa/swlguide/
   http://www.rac.ca/swl.htm
Usenet:
   rec.radio.shortwave

Talk Radio Hosts

Here are Web sites for the 9 most popular U.S. radio talk show hosts. They are, in order of popularity: Rush Limbaugh, Laura Schlessinger, Howard Stern, Joy Browne, Sean Hannity, Michael Savage, Art Bell, Jim Bohannon and Don Imus. I have also thrown in two other hosts— Phil Hendrie and Bob Brinker—because I particularly like their shows. By the way, in case you are wondering, my favorites are Joy Browne, Jim Bohannon and Bob Brinker, because they are, by far, the most intelligent of the group.

Web:
   http://www.animaux.net/stern/
   http://www.artbell.com/
   http://www.bobbrinker.com/
   http://www.drjoy.com/
   http://www.drlaura.com/
   http://www.hannity.com/
   http://www.imonthe.net/imus/
   http://www.jimbotalk.com/
   http://www.michaelsavage.com/
   http://www.philhendrieshow.com/
   http://www.rushlimbaugh.com/
Usenet:
   alt.fan.art-bell
   alt.fan.don-imus
   alt.fan.howard-stern
   alt.fan.rush-limbaugh
   alt.flame.rush-limbaugh
   alt.radio.talk
   alt.radio.talk.dr-laura
   alt.rush-limbaugh

Vintage Radios and Broadcasting Equipment

The first regularly scheduled radio broadcasts began in the United States in 1920. In the early 1920s, commercial radio went through a boom, leading to the establishment of a large number of radio stations. Over the next several decades, radio became extremely popular, and a great many different models of radio receivers were sold. Today, many people collect these vintage radio sets, and buy and sell the parts needed to maintain them.

Web:
  http://www.antiqueradio.com/
  http://www.antiqueradios.com/resources/
  http://www.execulink.com/~michiels/links.htm
  http://www.vintageradio.info/

Usenet:
  rec.antiques.radio+phono

Voice of America

The Voice of America (VOA) is the radio broadcasting service of the U.S. International Broadcasting Bureau. The purpose of VOA is to serve the long-range interests of the United States by "communicating with the peoples of the world by radio." In particular, VOA offers a "consistently reliable and authoritative source of news." Around the world, VOA broadcasts on shortwave and medium wave frequencies in more than 50 languages. Many of these broadcasts are also available over the Internet, so take a moment and give a listen.

Web:
  http://www.voa.gov/

REFERENCE

Acronyms

Here is a resource that should be in everyone's bookmark list. You specify an acronym, and a program looks it up in the master list and tells you what the acronym means. You can also search the list of meanings for a particular word or expression. If you have a friend who thinks he knows everything, ask him what MMOSPRED means.

Web:
  http://www.ucc.ie/acronyms/

Calculators

In the Woody Allen movie Radio Days, there's a scene where a father, mother and son are visiting the zoo, and they run into a young boy who is a celebrity because he appears on a radio show. The show is called The Whiz Kids, and the young boy is a child prodigy who answers difficult questions on the air. (Woody Allen modeled this after a real-life radio show called The Quiz Kids, which was popular when Allen was young.) When the father (played by Michael Tucker) meets the boy, he says, "Quick, what's 1,754 divided into 13 million?" Well, of course the boy doesn't answer, but if he had a Web browser he could have found the answer in a flash by using an online calculator. Aside from the highly technical calculators you might expect—mathematics, science, engineering and computer stuff—there are all kinds of special-purpose resources. You can calculate retirement benefits, taxes, calendars, wedding costs, cooking measures, child support payments, sailboat performance, and much more. By the way, here's an easy way to look très cool. Rent the Radio Days movie with a bunch of friends. When you get to the part where Michael Tucker says, "Quick, what's 1,754 divided into 13 million?" casually give the answer (7411.630558722919). It won't be long before your friends are showing you the respect you deserve.

Web:
  http://www.bloomberg.com/money/tools/
    education.html
  http://www.calculator.com/
  http://www.nolo.com/lawcenter/calc/
  http://www.supportguidelines.com/calcs.html

Calendars

It's handy to have a calendar around just to make sure you are doing the right thing on the right day. For example, how would you feel if you completely missed the St. Swithin's day celebration because you had gotten it mixed up with Martha Stewart's birthday?

Web:
  http://www.azteccalendar.com/calendar.html
  http://www.calendarhome.com
  http://www.calendarzone.com/
  http://www.pauahtun.org/CalendarFAQ/
  http://www.webexhibits.org/calendars/

Listserv Mailing List:
  List Name: calndr-l
  Subscribe to: listserv@ecumail7.ecu.edu

Center of Statistical Resources

I have found another important but little-known use for the Net. As you are playing a trivia game, make an excuse and sneak off to your computer, where you can use the Net to find lots of statistics that will help you beat your friends into submission. For example, wait until you get a question you can't answer, and then say, "Oh, just a second, I have to go the bathroom." While you are gone, you can quickly visit this Web site, where you will find a staggering compilation of statistics on many, many topics. When your friends express admiration at your extensive knowledge of trivial subjects, you can tell them that eliminating toxins from the body really helps to clear one's mind.

Web:

   http://www.lib.umich.edu/govdocs/stats.html

Dictionaries

Quick. Pick a word, any word. Type it into a form, press a button and presto, before you can say "my onerous oneiric tendencies have been keeping me up all night," your very own definition will be waiting for you.

Web:

   http://www.freedictionary.org/
   http://www.m-w.com/netdict.htm
   http://www.uwasa.fi/comm/termino/collect/
   http://www.wordsmyth.net/
   http://www.yourdictionary.com/

Dictionaries: Alternative

Here are words you will never see in a regular dictionary: various types of slang. For example, suppose you are in Quebec and someone says to you "Accouche qu'on baptise". Or let's say you are on the east coast of Scotland and a fellow comes up to you and asks if you are a Weedjie. Whatever are they talking about? Check with the Net and find out. Hint: If you find yourself working too hard, remind yourself (as they say in Holland) not to buffelen, or you may become besodemieterd zijn.

Web:

   http://babel.uoregon.edu/slang/sd_search.html
   http://www.notam02.no/~hcholm/altlang/
   http://www.thegoodnamesweretaken.com/
      beatspeak/
   http://www.uwasa.fi/comm/termino/collect/
      slang.html

Alternative Dictionaries

When you study a language in school, you learn how to speak "properly".

However, when you visit a foreign country, you find there are a lot of common words you are never taught in school.

School is fine, but to prepare yourself for life in the street, you need the **Alternative Dictionaries.**

Encyclopedias

In the future, you won't have to haul yourself down to the library and deal with a lot of heavy books just to check something in an encyclopedia. You'll be able to look up anything you want right on the Internet. Well, the future has already arrived. (Was that fast or what?) From now on, you and the Net are partners in knowledge.

Web:

   http://www.encyclopedia.com/
   http://www.infoplease.com/
   http://www.libraryspot.com/encyclopedias.htm

Farmer's Almanac

The Farmer's Almanac is a venerable American publication that has been produced annually since 1792. The Almanac is a treasure of useful information for day-to-day living. This Web site contains some of that information. In particular, you can find information and predictions about the weather, gardening, the sunrise and sunset, the phases of the moon, and astronomical events such as eclipses. There are various other features that are changed regularly so this is always a good place to visit when you have a few spare moments.

Web:

   http://www.almanac.com/

Geographic Place Reference

What do you do when you are reading something and you see a reference to a place you have never heard of? Use this tool and you'll be able to identify that place and find out basic information. If you are curious, pick any name and see what places have that name. For example, I found out that there are three towns named "Harley" in the United States (in North Dakota, Ohio and West Virginia), and four towns named "Hahn" (in Idaho, Missouri, New Mexico and Texas). I also found out that Harley is the 526th most popular male first name in the country, and Hahn is the 925th most popular last name.

Web:
  http://www.placesnamed.com/

Grammar and English Usage

When someone is reading your work, there are various demands you can make. You can ask your reader to recreate various thoughts, feelings and emotions within his or her own mind. You can expect your reader to pay attention to new words (if you explain them properly) and to follow a chain of ideas, from one point to the next. What you can't expect is for anyone to exert mental effort figuring out what you are trying to say because you didn't use the generally accepted writing conventions. Imagination is great, but not when it comes to grammar, punctuation or word usage.

Web:
  http://www.edunet.com/english/grammar/
  http://www.faqs.org/faqs/alt-usage-english-faq/
  http://www.garbl.com/
  http://www.theslot.com/
  http://www.webgrammar.com/

Usenet:
  alt.usage.english

Maps for Driving

Imagine you're living in the future. You have to go visit a place you've never been before, so before you leave, you type the address into your computer, which connects to another computer and presents you with a map of the area, as well as detailed driving instructions from where you are right now to your destination. Well, the future arrived yesterday.

Web:
  http://maps.yahoo.com/
  http://www.mapblast.com/
  http://www.mapquest.com/
  http://www.theodora.com/maps/

Measures, Units and Conversions

There are two basic systems of measurement used in the world, the imperial system for the United States and the metric system for everyone else. Within each system there are a large number of different units. For example, just the other day, I was figuring out how fast I could go on my bicycle and I had to convert from kilometers per hour to furlongs per fortnight.

Web:
  http://lamar.colostate.edu/~hillger/everyday.htm
  http://www.ex.ac.uk/cimt/dictunit/dictunit.htm
  http://www.french-property.com/ref/convert.htm

Phone Books

Find that person—now! Here are electronic phone books that cover the United States and Canada, plus many other countries around the world. Here's a hint on how to be very popular. Look up all your old friends—wherever they are in the world—and call them right now. Tell them Harley says hello.

Web:
  http://canada411.sympatico.ca/
  http://www.libraryspot.com/whitepages.htm
  http://www.whowhere.com/Phone

Population Statistics and Demographics

Population refers to the number of people living in a particular area. Demographics refers to the characteristics of those people in the aggregate. For example, the population of the United States is 277,000,000; the population of Canada is 23,000,000. As an example of demographic data, I can tell you that the average age of women at the time of their first marriage is 25 years in the United States and 26 years in Canada. (Having lived in both countries, this makes sense to me. If you are thinking of marrying a Canadian, it's a good idea to take some extra time to make up your mind.)

Web:

    http://www.census.gov/ipc/www/idbnew.html
    http://www.citypopulation.de/cities.html
    http://www.gazetteer.de/st/stata.htm
    http://www.os-connect.com/pop/
    http://www.popexpo.net/eMain.html
    http://www.popnet.org/
    http://www.population.com/?t=population/
        database.txt
    http://www.worldpop.org/prbdata.htm

Postal Codes and Mail

No matter where you need to send mail, the Net can help. Here are some resources to help you find postal codes from many different countries. If you need more information, you will find links to post offices around the world. For U.S. and Canadian mail, I have included special resources, including a handy U.S. postal rate calculator that I use all the time. Postal trivia: In the United States, postal codes are called "ZIP codes". The name stands for "Zone Improvement Plan".

Web:

    http://dbcalc.usps.gov/ieframe.htm
    http://ircalc.usps.gov/
    http://postcalc.usps.gov/
    http://www.canadapost.ca/personal/tools/pcl/bin/
    http://www.execulink.com/~louisew/postal-links.htm
    http://www.grcdi.nl/linkspc.htm
    http://www.grcdi.nl/linkspo.htm
    http://www.link-usa.com/zipcode/
    http://www.mailposte.ca/personal/tools/pcl/bin/
    http://www.usps.com/ncsc/

Public Records

Have you ever tried to dig through public records looking for a particular piece of information? For example, let's say you are interested in researching the details of a bypass that the town is planning to build through the middle of your house. You go to the local planning office but, after a long search, you still can't find what you want. What you didn't know is that the plans *were* on public display. All you had to do was look in the bottom of a locked filing cabinet stuck in a disused lavatory with a sign on the door saying "Beware of the Leopard". Fortunately, times have changed. Now you can find a *huge* amount of public information on the Net. Take a moment and browse. I promise you will be astonished.

Web:

    http://www.searchsystems.net/

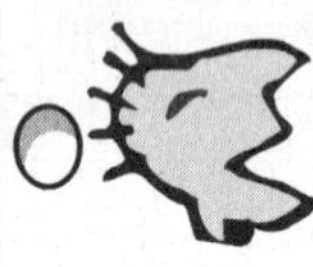

Report on Reference
Resources
by Elmo (age 8)

My sister Lucy thinks she is a bigshot because she has a lot of reference books. She is always looking things up and telling other people they are wrong.

So here's what I did. I ripped out the page in her atlas that shows Africa, and pasted it into a book that shows maps of all the streets in our city, right on the page that shows where we live.

The next time someone asks her for directions to get to our house, they will end up going to Madagascar.

-Elmo

Reference Resources

I have a friend, Mary Axford, who's a wonderful reference librarian. It used to be that whenever I had a question that needed special reference material, I would call Mary. She has all the reference books you can imagine: dictionaries, thesauri, phone books, atlases, encyclopedias, statistics references, and so on. I could call Mary at any time to ask her, say, "What is the capital of Madagascar?" or "What is the most common female name in America?" Now all of that information—and a lot more—is on the Net, available for free, twenty-four hours a day. My life as a writer is certainly easier. The only thing is I don't get to talk to Mary as often as I used to. (By the way, the capital of Madagascar is Antananarivo, and the most common female name in America is Mary.)

Web:
  http://library.csumb.edu/ref/
  http://www-sci.lib.uci.edu/HSG/Ref.html
  http://www.refdesk.com/
  http://www.refdesk.com/facts.html
  http://www.xrefer.com/

Thesauruses

In 1852, Peter Mark Roget published the first edition of his Thesaurus of English Words and Phrases, on which he had been working for 50 years. Throughout successive editions—which were supervised by Roget, his son, and later his grandson—what we now call a thesaurus has become a standard reference work of the English language. The purpose of a thesaurus is simply stated: you use it when you know the meaning of a word but do not know the word. Roget arranged all the words in the English language and their idiomatic combinations, not in alphabetical order as in a dictionary, but according to the ideas they express. If you care at all about writing, please take some time to become familiar with this classic reference and how to use it. Treating a thesaurus as if it were nothing more than a dictionary of synonyms is like using a collection of Mozart CDs as a paperweight.

Web:
  http://humanities.uchicago.edu/forms_unrest/
    ROGET.html
  http://www.thesaurus.com/

Time Zones

You wake up in the middle of the night and look at the clock—it is 2:18 AM. You close your eyes and try to go back to sleep, but all of a sudden a thought comes into your head: what time is it in Bangkok? And you know—you just know—that there is no way you will get to sleep until you find out the answer to your question. Here is all the information you need to find out what time it is now anywhere in the world, as well as learning about time zones and the details of our world time system. It's not really all that hard once you realize that time is merely a means for keeping everything from happening all at once.

Web:
  http://tycho.usno.navy.mil/time.html
  http://www.bsdi.com/xdate
  http://www.hilink.com.au/times/
  http://www.timeanddate.com/worldclock/

Thesauruses

Do you need a word? A specific word with a particular shade of meaning? Use the online *Roget's Thesaurus*, and you'll have the exact word you need

Tracking a Package

If you ever send packages or letters overnight, here are some resources you will use again and again. When you send the package, be sure to keep the receipt with the tracking number. You can then use the Net to track your package every step of the way. I have included the appropriate Web sites for Airborne Express, DHL, FedEx, RPS, UPS and the U.S. Postal Service. Hint: When you send an especially important package, email the tracking number to the recipient, along with the Web address of the site at which he or she can check for the package. This will make you look so cool, people will just naturally want to pay you lots and lots of money for no reason at all.

Web:

http://www.dhl.com/track/
http://www.fedex.com/us/tracking/
http://www.track.airborne.com/
http://www.usps.com/shipping/epstrac.htm
http://www.usps.com/shipping/trackandconfirm.htm

RELIGION: MAINSTREAM

Agnosticism

An agnostic is a person who believes that the existence of God cannot be proved or disproved. The word "agnostic" was coined in 1889 by the English biologist and educator Thomas Henry Huxley (1825-1895). However, the basic ideas are old: they were discussed in various forms by the early Greek philosophers. In its most pure form, agnosticism considers fundamental philosophical problems such as what can we know, and what can we understand about that which we can't know? In its more common pop-culture usage, the term "agnostic" refers to someone who is proud to announce that he or she is not sure if there is really a God.

Web:

http://landow.stg.brown.edu/victorian/religion/
   agnos.html
http://www.infidels.org/library/modern/reason/
   agnosticism/
http://www.newadvent.org/cathen/01215c.htm
http://www.religioustolerance.org/agnostic.htm

Usenet:
alt.agnosticism

Anglicanism

The roots of Anglicanism go back to the days of the British King Henry VIII (1491-1547). Henry was disappointed in his first wife, Catherine of Aragon, who did not produce a male heir. Henry fell in love with Anne Boleyn and wanted to marry her. He petitioned the Pope to annul the marriage to Catherine, but the Pope refused. After a protracted disagreement, Henry issued the Act of Supremacy in 1534, breaking from Rome and making himself the supreme head of the Church of England. To this day, the supreme head of the church is still the reigning British monarch, although the spiritual head is the Archbishop of Canterbury. Over the years, the Church of England has grown into a group of many independent churches, collectively called the Anglican Communion, representing about 70 million people in more than 160 countries. Although these churches have separate organizations, they have a lot in common. For example, they all use the Book of Common Prayer, they all view the Old and New Testaments as containing everything that is necessary for salvation, and they all recognize the Thirty-Nine Articles (a series of short statements of doctrine) as being the foundation of their beliefs. In the United States, the dominant branch of the Anglican Communion is the Episcopalian Church, which developed from the Church of England at the time of the American Revolution.

Web:

http://www.anglicancommunion.org/site.html
http://www.ecusa.anglican.org/
http://www.episcopalian.org/
http://www.justus.anglican.org/resources/pc/
http://www.newadvent.org/cathen/01498a.htm

Product Comparison Chart

	This Book	The Bible
Has snazzy cover	Yes	No
Revised every year	Yes	No
Cute illustrations	Yes	No
Internet resources	Yes	No
The word of God	No	Yes

Atheism

Atheism is the belief that a sound philosophy of life should recognize that there are no gods (or God). Although it is fashionable to pretend that the Western monotheistic religions all believe in the same god, this is just not so. When you look at the details, it is plain that the Muslim god (Allah) is not the same god as the Catholic god, who is not the same god as the Mormon god, and so on. Moreover, the Hindus believe in many gods, and the Buddhists do not believe in the idea of a god at all. Of course, the one thing these religions all have in common is that they believe they are right and the others are wrong. Well, maybe they are all wrong. Maybe what people believe has nothing to do with universal truths. Maybe what people believe depends on their personal spiritual needs and how they were indoctrinated as children. If you are one of those people who insist on thinking for yourself, see what the atheists have to say.

Web:
  http://www.atheists.org/
  http://www.carm.org/atheism.htm
  http://www.harley.com/god/
  http://www.infidels.org/
  http://www.positiveatheism.org/

Usenet:
  alt.atheism
  alt.atheism.moderated
  soc.atheism
  talk.atheism

IRC:
  #atheism (DALnet, EFnet, Undernet)

Bible

The Bible, the holy book of Judaism and Christianity, is the most published and widely read book in the history of the world. As such, the Bible has had a profound effect on the culture, society and legal systems of Western civilization. The Jewish Bible consists of 24 books organized into three sections: the Law (Torah), the Prophets, and the Writings. The Christian Bible has two parts, the Old Testament and the New Testament. The Old Testament is mostly the same as the Jewish Bible. (However, Protestant versions divide the work into 39 books, and the Roman Catholic and Eastern Orthodox versions add 7 more books.) The New Testament relates the life of Jesus and his teachings. It consists of 27 books beginning with the Gospels of Matthew, Mark, Luke and John, four different biographies of Jesus. All branches of Judaism and Christianity treat the Bible as a holy text. However, interpretations vary widely. Some religions consider the Bible to be the exact word of God to be followed literally. Other religions consider the Bible to be the work of man, perhaps divinely inspired. The Bible was written by multiple authors and editors over many years, although the actual details have been lost to antiquity. Modern scholars postulate that the Torah or Pentateuch (the first five books of the Old Testament) derives from four different literary sources designated as the E text (Elohim), written between 922 and 722 B.C.; the J text (Jehovah), written between 848 and 722 B.C.; the D text (Deuteronomy), written around 622 B.C.; and the P text (Priestly), written some time before 587 B.C.

Web:
  http://www.bible.ca/
  http://www.bible.gospelcom.net/bible/
  http://www.bible.org/
  http://www.ccel.org/
  http://www.e-bible.org/

Usenet:
  alt.bible
  alt.bible.prophecy
  soc.religion.christian.bible-study

The Net loves poetry.

Buddhism

Buddhism is a religion and philosophy founded in India by Siddhartha Gautama (the Buddha) in the 6th and 5th centuries B.C. Buddhism teaches that discipline, both spiritual and physical, is necessary to liberate oneself from the physical world. Toward this end, Buddhists observe the practices of meditation and uphold various moral tenets. The goal of a Buddhist is to follow the "Eightfold Path" and reach the state of nirvana (complete peace), in which one is free from the influences of desire and self-consciousness. Historically, Buddhism is the ancestor of both Taoism and Zen Buddhism. Today, Buddhism is practiced most widely in eastern Asia.

Web:
  http://www.buddhanet.net/budzine.htm
  http://www.buddhism.org/link/pages/
  http://www.chezpaul.org.uk/buddhism/
  http://www.dharmanet.org/

Usenet:
  alt.religion.buddhism.nichiren
  alt.religion.buddhism.nkt
  alt.religion.buddhism.tibetan
  talk.religion.buddhism

Listserv Mailing List:
  List Name: buddha-l
  Subscribe to: listserv@listserv.louisville.edu

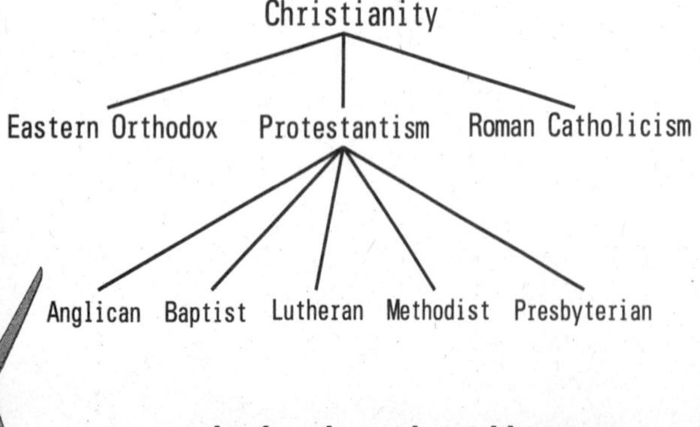

Christianity

Christianity refers to any religion based upon the teachings of Jesus Christ (c. 6 B.C.-30 A.D.). Christians believe that the first man, Adam, disobeyed God, which led to the fall of man. About 2,000 years ago, God sent his son Jesus to live and teach on Earth. By dying and rising from the dead, Jesus made up for the sin of Adam and thus redeemed mankind. Because of this, he who believes in Jesus will be allowed to enter heaven. Christians revere the Bible as their holy book and hold it to be of divine inspiration. At first, Christianity was a small sect limited to Jews living in Palestine under Roman rule. As the new religion spread, Christians were persecuted for nearly 300 years, because they refused to worship the Roman emperor as a god. In 312, the emperor Constantine converted to Christianity, which granted the sect recognition and freedom, allowing it to grow. In 1054, the Eastern Orthodox Church was created when the Pope excommunicated the patriarch of Constantinople after prolonged disagreements. In the 16th century, an attempt to reform the Roman Church (the Reformation) led to a further division and the creation of Protestantism. Today, Christianity has three great divisions: Roman Catholicism, Eastern Orthodoxy and Protestantism. In the United States, the dominant Protestant sects are Anglican (Episcopalian), Baptist, Lutheran, Methodist and Presbyterian (Calvinism).

Web:
  http://ic.net/~erasmus/RAZ387.HTM
  http://www.biblenet.net/
  http://www.christianitytoday.com/
  http://www.crossdaily.com/
  http://www.crosssearch.com/

Usenet:
  alt.christnet.christianlife
  alt.christnet.ethics
  alt.christnet.evangelical
  alt.christnet.hypocrisy
  alt.christnet.philosophy
  alt.christnet.prayer
  alt.christnet.theology
  alt.religion.christian
  alt.religion.christian-teen
  alt.religion.christian.20-something
  alt.religion.christian.last-days
  soc.religion.christian
  soc.religion.christian.youth-work

IRC:
  #christians (EFnet)

Eastern Orthodoxy

The Eastern Orthodox Church (often referred to as the Orthodox Church) is the body of churches that derived from the church of the Byzantine Empire. This body includes the Greek and Russian Orthodox Churches. Eastern Orthodoxy is one of the three great divisions of Christianity (the others being Protestantism and Roman Catholicism). Eastern Orthodoxy originated in Eastern Europe and Southwest Asia in the 11th century when it split from the Roman Catholic Church over differences in doctrine. In particular, Orthodox Christians do not accept the supreme authority of the Pope. In many respects, Orthodoxy is similar to Roman Catholicism, in that they both accept the Trinity, the Bible and various traditions and sacraments. However, there are some interesting differences. For example, Orthodox believers pay special attention to icons (images of Jesus, Mary and the saints); they celebrate Christmas and Easter at different times than other Christians; and they wear wedding rings on their right hands.

Web:
  http://ic.net/~erasmus/RAZ23.HTM
  http://www.theologic.com/links/

Usenet:
  alt.religion.christian.east-orthodox

Listserv Mailing List:
  List Name: orthodox
  Subscribe to: listserv@listserv.indiana.edu

The thing is, most religious groups believe that what they believe is true, and what other people believe is not true, because if what the first group believes is true, and at the same time, what the second group believes as also true, then what they (the first group) believe couldn't possibly be true. But it is.

That's how it works (I believe).

The hardest word in the world to spell is "Xaggertheromompton". (Most people leave out the second "g".)

Hinduism

Hinduism is one of the world's major religions, having nearly one billion followers. The majority of Hindus live in India, where the religion forms a spiritual and cultural base for most of the country. However, there are also large numbers of Hindus in many other countries around the world. Hinduism is actually a family of faiths whose beliefs range from many gods (pluralistic theism) to a single all-pervasive deity (absolute monism). There are four principal denominations of Hinduism—Saivism, Vaishnavism, Shaktism and Smartism—each of which is different enough and complete enough to be considered a self-contained religion in its own right. All Hindus share a number of important spiritual and philosophical traditions in common, among which are karma, dharma, reincarnation, temple worship, and recognition of the Vedas as holy writings.

Web:
  http://www.hindu.org/
  http://www.spiritweb.org/spirit/veda.html
  http://www.us-hindus.com/

Usenet:
  alt.religion.hindu
  soc.religion.hindu
  soc.religion.vaishnava

Listserv Mailing List:
  List Name: hindu-d
  Subscribe to: listserv@listserv.nodak.edu

Islam

In Arabic, the word "Islam" means total submission to the will of Allah (the Arabic name of God). A person who follows the ways of Islam is called a Muslim. Islam was founded by Muhammad (c. 570-632 A.D.), who was born in Mecca. The fundamental belief of Islam is that there is one god and that Muhammad is his prophet. Allah is the creator and sustainer of the universe, and people, though superior to nature, are but servants of Allah. The most important sin is pride, but Allah is ready to pardon any man or woman who demonstrates the proper repentance. Islam is considered to be an all-encompassing way of life that must be practiced continually, and a devout Muslim follows the Koran (Islam's holy book) strictly. For example, a Muslim is obliged to pray five times a day, to give to the poor, to refrain from eating pork or drinking alcohol, and to fast in the daytime during the holy month of Ramadan. Islam is centered in the Middle East, where the religion developed, and where the holiest sites are located, including the sacred cities of Mecca and Medina. Islam is practiced around the world and there are large numbers of Muslims in central Asia, Malaysia and Indonesia. Each Muslim is expected to undertake a holy pilgrimage to Mecca at least once in his lifetime.

Web:

http://www.ghuraba.com/i/html/
http://www.islam-guide.com/
http://www.islamic.org/
http://www.islamworld.net/
http://www.submission.org/home.html

Usenet:

alt.islam.sufism
alt.religion.islam
soc.religion.islam

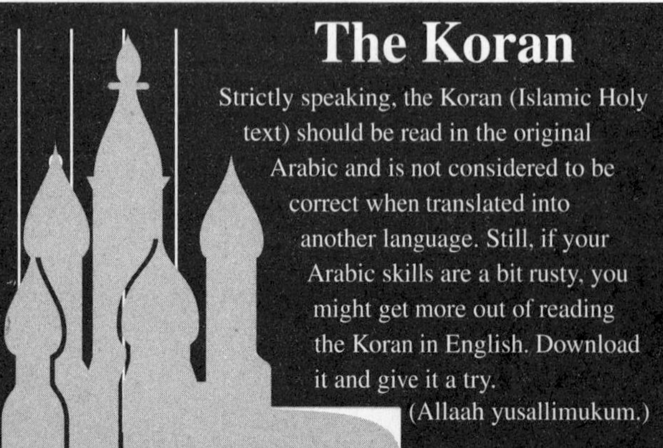

The Koran

Strictly speaking, the Koran (Islamic Holy text) should be read in the original Arabic and is not considered to be correct when translated into another language. Still, if your Arabic skills are a bit rusty, you might get more out of reading the Koran in English. Download it and give it a try.

(Allaah yusallimukum.)

Judaism

Judaism evolved from the religion of the Israelites of the Bible, and is based upon the teachings of the Torah (the first five books of the Old Testament), a belief in the holiness of the Old Testament, and the acceptance of one, omnipotent god. Traditionally, Judaism honors Abraham as the founder of the religion, and Moses as the person who gave the laws of God to the Israelites. Modern Judaism encompasses a wide range of practices. Orthodox Judaism, the smallest movement, considers the Torah to be divine law (orthodox means "correct in teaching"), and as such, must be obeyed exactly. Conservative Judaism allows Jews to adapt various requirements to the demands of modern life. Reform Judaism, the most liberal movement (and, in the United States, the largest movement), asserts that all of Jewish law may be adapted in this manner. Although we describe followers of Judaism as Jews, the name is also used to describe members of the Jewish ethnic group. There are many ethnic Jews, for example, who are not at all religious. The historical homeland of the Jewish people is Israel, and people who support Israel as a Jewish homeland are called Zionists. Judaism is a very old religion, predating Christianity (Jesus, in fact, was Jewish), and has a rich array of traditions and theological writings that have been passed down and refined over thousands of years. Each Jewish congregation has its own spiritual leader called a rabbi. There is, however, no overall Jewish authority.

Web:

http://www.faqs.org/faqs/judaism/
http://www.jewfaq.org/
http://www.newadvent.org/cathen/08386a.htm
http://www.shamash.org/
http://www.torah.org/

Usenet:

alt.music.jewish
alt.religion.aishdas
soc.culture.jewish

Listproc Mailing List:

List Name: mail-jewish
Subscribe to: listproc@shamash.org

Listproc Mailing List:

List Name: mlj
Subscribe to: listproc@shamash.org

Listserv Mailing List:

List Name: tor-ch
Subscribe to: listserv@jtsa.edu

Koran

The Koran (or Qurán) is the sacred book of Islam. According to Islamic belief, the Koran was revealed by God to the Prophet Muhammad in a series of revelations over many years. Within the Koran, the revelations are organized into 144 chapters (called suras) and verses (called ayyas). The language of the Koran is classical Arabic. Devout Muslims consider the Koran to be the definitive word of Allah (God), and as such, it must never be changed or even translated. (However, translations have been made and you can read them on the Net.) Worldwide, the Koran is a highly influential book, second only to the Bible, accounting for much of the unity of the Islamic world.

Web:
  http://etext.lib.virginia.edu/koran.html
  http://www.al-bukhari.org/

Religion Talk and General Discussion

Sit in on discussions that are religious, ethical and moral in nature. Talk includes reference to scriptures and parables, but much of it concerns heavily debatable topics—for example, does the Pope use the Internet?—all of which makes for lively banter.

Web:
  http://www.beliefnet.com/

Usenet:
  alt.religion
  alt.religion.all-worlds
  alt.religion.apologetics
  alt.religion.asatru
  alt.religion.computers
  soc.religion
  soc.religion.christian.promisekeepers
  soc.religion.eastern
  talk.religion.course-miracle
  talk.religion.misc
  talk.religion.pantheism

IRC has many ways to make you talk.

Religious Tolerance

Here's a refreshing change of pace from the hurry-scurry of everyone evangelizing on the Net or the eruptions of arguments between believers and non-believers. This Web page promotes religious tolerance and makes an attempt to educate everyone about the various religions around the world. You can also read the United Nations Declarations on Religious Intolerance, articles on religious freedom, a glossary of terms, information on ritual abuse and cults, and find links to religious home pages.

Web:
  http://www.religioustolerance.org/

Roman Catholicism

Roman Catholicism is the largest branch of Christianity, having almost a billion members around the world. Roman Catholicism is the dominant religion in the Mediterranean part of Europe, much of Eastern Europe, Ireland and Latin America. Like all Christians, Catholics believe in one all-powerful God and Jesus as the son of God. They also accept the Bible as holy scripture. Catholics further believe that God exists as three equal and distinct persons known as the Trinity: the Father, the Son (Jesus) and the Holy Spirit (Holy Ghost). Catholics hold that each person has an immortal soul that, upon death, will go to either heaven or hell. Catholics practice various sacraments, including Communion, a reenactment of the Last Supper, and Confession, in which an individual privately confesses his sins to a priest, receives absolution, and is instructed to carry out an appropriate penance. Catholics venerate the saints, especially Mary, the mother of Jesus, and pray to them to ask them, in turn, to pray to God. The spiritual head of the Catholic church is the Pope (the bishop of Rome) who lives in Vatican City. The Pope leads a hierarchy consisting of cardinals, archbishops, bishops and priests.

Web:
  http://www.catholic.net/
  http://www.columbia.edu/cu/augustine/a/
    faq-cc.html
  http://www.newadvent.org/
  http://www.newadvent.org/cathen/

Usenet:
  alt.religion.christian.roman-catholic

Listserv Mailing List:
  List Name: spirit-l
  Subscribe to: listserv@listserv.american.edu

RELIGION: SECTS, CULTS & DENOMINATIONS

Baha'i

Who was Baha'u'llah (a.k.a. Mirza Husayn Ali)? What did he do in Iran in the mid-19th century that was so important? Was he really the Bab (with a direct line to the twelfth Imam)? Learn about the message of the Baha'u'llah and the Baha'i view of life.

Web:
   http://religiousmovements.lib.virginia.edu/nrms/
      bahi.html
   http://www.bahai.org/
   http://www.beliefnet.com/index/index_10041.asp

Usenet:
   soc.religion.bahai

Christian Science

The Church of Christ, Scientist (Christian Science) was founded in 1879 by Mary Baker Eddy (1821-1910). Christian Scientists believe that nothing exists but the divine Mind, and that all reality derives from Mind. Thus, one is able to achieve universal salvation from all types of evil—including illness, death and sin—through spiritual means alone. For example, when a Christian Scientist is sick, he or she will use prayer and devotion rather than medicine and doctors. In their study of the divine, Christian Scientists use two principal books: the Bible (usually the King James Version) and "Science and Health", written by Eddy and first published in 1875. (Newer editions are called "Science and Health with Key to the Scriptures".) The main church, referred to as the Mother Church, is highly centralized. However, local branches govern themselves democratically. The Mother Church operates Christian Science Reading Rooms, where the public is invited to read the Bible as well as church publications. The best-known publication is the "Christian Science Monitor", an international newspaper founded by Eddy in 1908.

Web:
   http://religiousmovements.lib.virginia.edu/nrms/
      chrissci.html
   http://www.beliefnet.com/index/index_10123.asp
   http://www.religioustolerance.org/cr_sci.htm

Coptic

Coptic Christianity is based on the teachings of Saint Mark, who brought Christianity to Egypt in the first century A.D. The Copts observe seven sacraments, baptize newborns, and participate in fasting. Learn more about this denomination by reading about the history of the Church, Coptic liturgy and other information.

Web:
   http://www.coptic.net/CopticWeb/
   http://www.copticchurch.net/

Cults

The term "cult" is an amorphous one with a variety of meanings. For our purposes, let me define a religious cult as a group with extreme views, a group whose energy is focused inward toward the goals of the leader or the cult itself. Compare this to other, more accepted religions that have an outward focus, groups whose goals are to improve the lives of its members and even nonmembers. Many cults have a strict power structure, with authority concentrated at the top in the form of a Messianic leader. Cults are often deceitful in how they recruit, isolate and control members, how they raise money, and how they portray themselves to the general public and to the law. It is important to recognize that many established and accepted religions began as cults. It is only as they matured and evolved that they lost their cult-like characteristics. In this sense, cults are important as the incubators of new religions. Very few cults, however, actually evolve into a religion, and for the most part, cults are socially destructive and dangerous.

Web:
   http://www.ex-cult.org/
   http://www.factnet.org/
   http://www.freedomofmind.com/
   http://www.math.mcgill.ca/triples/infocult/
      ic-e1.html
   http://www.religioustolerance.org/acm.htm

Sv bndwdth.
Dn't typ ny vwls (xcpt y).

Cults

People can act in strange ways, especially when they are part of a group. If you are interested in some of the more extreme groups in our society, use the Net to read about cults. I guarantee you will find surprises — many well-known organizations are engaged in funny stuff behind the scenes.

Eckankar

The basis of Eckankar spirituality is coming closer to God through dreams and the expansion of consciousness. This site explains more about the philosophy of Eckankar, gives spiritual exercises that are designed to bring you closer to enlightenment, and has various other tidbits of interest to those in search of Sugmad. On the Usenet group you can join Eckists as they explore visualization, reality and waking dreams.

Web:

    http://religiousmovements.lib.virginia.edu/nrms/
      ecka.html
    http://www.eckankar.org/
    http://www.religioustolerance.org/eck.htm

Usenet:

    alt.religion.eckankar

Gnosticism

Take a few Christian terms, add in a liberal dose of Greek philosophy, a dash of mythology and a handful of magickal rituals. Let sit for several centuries and voilà! You end up with a religion that can serve millions and is very low in calories. Learn more about Gnosticism, its origins and tenets. The **soc.religion.gnosis** group is moderated.

Web:

    http://religiousmovements.lib.virginia.edu/nrms/
      gnosticism.html
    http://www.webcom.com/~gnosis/

Usenet:

    alt.religion.gnostic
    soc.religion.gnosis

Hasidism

Hasidism (or Chasidim) is a form of mystical Orthodox Judaism that originated in Eighteenth Century Eastern Europe. It was founded by Rabbi Israel ben Eliezer, sometimes known as the "Baal Shem Tov" (which means "master of the good name" in Hebrew). Today, the largest number of Hasidim (as the followers are called) are in the United States, Israel and Canada. Modern Hasidism consists of a number of ultra-orthodox Jewish sects, chief among them the Chabad-Lubavitch movement. Most Hasidic Jews affect a distinctive style of dress. The men wear beards, hats and dark clothes, while the women cover their heads, often with scarves, and wear plain, modest dresses. Each Hasidic sect is organized around a spiritual leader, referred to as a Rebbe or a tzaddik.

Web:

    http://religiousmovements.lib.virginia.edu/nrms/
      hasid.html
    http://www.chabad.org/
    http://www.maven.co.il/subjects.asp?S=115
    http://www.pinenet.com/~rooster/hasid1.html

Jainism

Jainism is an ascetic religion of India, founded in the 6th century B.C. The religion stresses non-violence, teaches the immortality and transmigration of the soul, and denies the existence of a perfect or supreme being. These Web sites have information about Jainism history and way of life.

Web:

    http://religiousmovements.lib.virginia.edu/nrms/
      jainism.html
    http://www.beliefnet.com/index/index_10040.html
    http://www.cs.colostate.edu/~malaiya/
      jainhlinks.html

Usenet:

    alt.religion.jain

> **This would be a good time to do a backup.**

Jehovah's Witnesses

Jehovah's Witnesses is an international Christian organization, founded in 1870 as a Bible study group by Charles Taze Russell. In 1931, they adopted the name "Jehovah's Witnesses" (from Isaiah 43:12). One of the main things people notice about Witnesses is they are active proselytizers, going from door to door to talk to people about Jehovah (God). Witnesses do not believe in eternal torment or that all good people go to heaven. Rather, they believe that, upon the destruction of wickedness and human governments, a "new system" will be established, and most of God's people will live in human perfection on Earth. Although Witnesses have a Christian love for people, they make an effort to stay "separate from the world" and do not involve themselves in excessive pursuit of material things or political and social movements. Witnesses do not salute the flag, vote, bear arms, or participate in government, nor (for biblical reasons) will they take blood transfusions. On the Net you will find a number of useful resources such as a daily text from the Bible, a listing of events, links to pages of other Jehovah's Witnesses, news stories, a listing of new releases from the Watchtower (the Witness magazine), and more.

Web:
http://religiousmovements.lib.virginia.edu/nrms/
    Jwitness.html
http://www.watchtower.org/

Mennonites

The Mennonites are a sect that departed from the Swiss Anabaptists around 1524. Mennonites believe in nonresistance, and they refuse to take oaths. (A more conservative branch of the Mennonites are the Amish, who broke away from the Mennonites in the late 17th century.)

Web:
http://religiousmovements.lib.virginia.edu/nrms/
    mennonites.html
http://www.mennolink.org/

Chicken soup ice cream: Wow!

Mormons

The Church of Jesus Christ of Latter-day Saints, sometimes referred to as LDS or the Mormon Church, was founded in 1830 by Joseph Smith. Mormon history says that Smith was visited by God and Jesus, and then by the prophet Moroni, who related to Smith a sacred history of the Americas. Smith translated this information and published it as the Book of Mormon in 1830. This book and the Bible are the main scriptures of the LDS Church. The principle doctrines of the Church of Jesus Christ of Latter-day Saints are: (1) The original church, established by Jesus Christ when he lived on Earth, has been restored, along with the original priesthood (the power to act in God's name). (2) God, referred to as Heavenly Father, is one of three separate personages comprising the Godhead. The other two are Jesus Christ (the living Son of God) and the Holy Ghost (who is in spirit form). (3) God continues to reveal his Word in the form of modern-day revelation, through the President of the church who is considered to be a living prophet. (4) Every person who has ever lived, and will ever live, has the opportunity to exist in the hereafter, in the Celestial Kingdom, in the presence of Jesus Christ and Heavenly Father (and his wife, Heavenly Mother).

Web:
http://www.jefflindsay.com/LDS_Intro.shtml
http://www.lds.org/
http://www.mormonhaven.com/

Usenet:
alt.religion.mormon
alt.religion.mormon.fellowship
soc.religion.mormon

Nazarenes

The Church of the Nazarene is the largest denomination in the Wesleyan-Arminian theological tradition. Although Nazarenes have a lot in common with other Christian denominations, they distinguish themselves by a belief in "entire sanctification". This involves devoting one's life to do God's will. In particular, Nazarenes believe that it is important to be of service to others.

Web:
http://www.nazarene.org/
http://www.naznet.com/

New Religious Movements

Why are human beings always creating new religions, while, at the same time, preserving the older, well- established faiths? The best way to understand it is to consider religions as live entities that are subject to evolutionary forces over the course of centuries. As new religions are formed, they compete in the spiritual environment against other religions. Out of the many new religions, very few live long enough to become a major world religion (such as Judaism, Christianity, Islam, Hinduism, Buddhism and Confucianism). However, in order to maintain the spiritual health of the world, we must always have new religions to feed the evolutionary process. Most religions fail, but, in the rare case that one does succeed, it must change as it matures. A maturing religion must become more conservative and mainstream if it is to survive, and must develop a comprehensive philosophy, literature and tradition.

Web:
   http://religiousmovements.lib.virginia.edu/profiles/
      profiles.htm

Quakers (Society of Friends)

The Society of Friends (commonly referred to as Quakers) began in 1647 under George Fox. One strong tenet of the Friends is that believers do not need a spiritual intermediary, they can receive guidance from within by the Holy Spirit.

Web:
   http://religiousmovements.lib.virginia.edu/nrms/
      quak.html
   http://www.beliefnet.com/index/index_10122.asp
   http://www.quaker.org/

Usenet:
   soc.religion.quaker

Santeria

Santeria (often called La Regla Lucumi) has its origins in West Africa and is the traditional religion of the Yoruba people. Santeria was spread to many countries of South America by slave trade. Members of Santeria worship a god named Olodumare and interact with him through emissaries called orishas. The religion is wrapped up in magic and forces of nature. If you want to learn more about their specific religious language and rituals, take a look at this Web site devoted to Santeria.

Web:
   http://religiousmovements.lib.virginia.edu/nrms/
      santeria.html
   http://www.religioustolerance.org/santeri.htm

Usenet:
   alt.religion.orisha

Scientology

Scientology is a controversial global organization with its own values, literature and dogma, as well as a great deal of money. Scientology was started in 1954 by the science fiction writer L. (Lafayette) Ron Hubbard (1911-1986). Initially, Scientology was based on Hubbard's book "Dianetics: The Modern Science of Mental Health" (1950). The core belief was that a person's mental problems stem from the activities of his "reactive" (unconscious) mind, which is beset by bad memories in the form of "engrams". Through proper processing (called "auditing"), a person can remove all his engrams, thereby becoming totally mentally healthy ("clear"). In the beginning, all you needed was Hubbard's book, a crude lie detector-like device (called an "e-meter"), and a friend to help you. Since then, Scientology has been developed into a *very* complex system of beliefs and activities. To become mentally healthy now requires time, motivation and credulity, as well as a great deal of money.

Web:
   http://www.beliefnet.com/index/index_10042.html
   http://www.ezlink.com/~perry/Co$/Christian/
      intro.htm
   http://www.scientology.org/

Usenet:
   alt.clearing.technology
   alt.religion.scientology

Shakers

The Shakers—the United Society of Believers—is a Christian sect that originated in England in 1747 and established itself in America under the leadership of Mother Ann Lee. The name "Shaker" was coined during the early history of the sect. Some of the members would become excited during the meetings and move around, "shaking off their sins". Two of the Shakers' primary tenets are communal living and celibacy. Well, any group that practices celibacy may be pure of heart, but they are going to have trouble surviving as a group. Indeed, today there are only a handful of Shakers remaining.

Web:

  http://religiousmovements.lib.virginia.edu/nrms/
    Shakers.html
  http://www.passtheword.org/shaker-manuscripts/

Listserv Mailing List:

  List Name: shaker
  Subscribe to: listserv@lsv.uky.edu

Shinto

Shinto is an ancient Japanese religion that, over the years, has been significantly influenced by Buddhism and Confucianism. Modern Shinto has no formal dogma. Instead, Shintoists observe traditional rituals and customs based on a love of nature (there are many sacred places) and the veneration of ancestors. Shinto celebrates a variety of festivals and pilgrimages, but the most important celebrations relate to birth and marriage. Shinto morality is oriented toward benefiting the group, rather than the individual. In modern-day Japan, many people follow both Shinto and Buddhism.

Web:

  http://religiousmovements.lib.virginia.edu/nrms/
    shinto.html
  http://www.beliefnet.com/index/index_10030.html
  http://www.religioustolerance.org/shinto.htm

Sikhism

Founded by Guru Nanak, who was born in 1469, Sikhism has gained a loyal following over the centuries. Guru Nanak criticized the rituals of the Hindus and Muslims and preached that the most important things in life were love, understanding and directing worship toward the one true God. The word "Sikh" means "disciple" in the Punjabi language.

Web:

  http://religiousmovements.lib.virginia.edu/nrms/
    sikhs.html
  http://www.beliefnet.com/index/index_10036.html

Usenet:

  soc.religion.sikhism

You remind me of the man.

What man?

The man with the power.

What power?

The power of hoodoo.

Hoodoo?

You do.

Do what?

Remind me of the man.

What man?

The man with the power...

Always have three plans.

Theosophy

Theosophy (literally, "the wisdom of the gods") is devoted to the search for man's divine self. Theosophists believe that the universe is essentially spiritual. Evil exists only because of human desire, and can be overcome by individuals who develop their latent spiritual powers. Historically, Theosophy traces its roots through a variety of ancient mystic traditions. Modern Theosophy, however, consists of a collection of esoteric teachings based on the work of The Theosophical Society, an organization founded in New York in 1875 by the Russian-born writer H.P. (Helena Petrovna) Blavatsky (1831-1891).

Web:
  http://religiousmovements.lib.virginia.edu/nrms/
     theosophy.html
  http://www.spiritweb.org/spirit/theosophy.html
  http://www.theosophy.org/

Usenet:
  alt.theosophy

Unitarian Universalism

Unitarian Universalism (often referred to as Unitarianism) was created from the 1961 merging of two existing religious denominations: the Universalists, dating from 1793, and the Unitarians, dating from 1825. Unitarianism is a liberal religion that originally developed from Christian and Jewish traditions. The church has no particular dogma and congregations are self-governing. A Unitarian does not appeal to a book, person or organization for religious authority. Rather, he or she is encouraged to search for truth and meaning by using personal experience, conscience and rational thought.

Web:
  http://religiousmovements.lib.virginia.edu/nrms/
     uua.html
  http://www.uua.org/main.html

Usenet:
  soc.religion.unitarian-univ

Listproc Mailing List:
  List Name: uua-l
  Subscribe to: listproc@uua.org

Listserv Mailing List:
  List Name: uus-l
  Subscribe to: listserv@listserv.acsu.buffalo.edu

Voodoo

Voodoo (also called Hoodoo or Vodoun) is a religious cult, practiced primarily in Caribbean countries, especially Haiti. Voodoo was created by West-African slaves who were forced by their Catholic masters to practice Catholicism. The Voodoo traditions grew from a syncretism (joining together) of Catholic beliefs with native African traditions. Voodoo recognizes a powerful supreme god who rules a large collection of local deities (some of whom act as guardians), saints and deified ancestors. These deities communicate with people through dreams, chants and possession. By the way, to create a zombie, you use black magic to kill someone, and then revive him in such a way that he no longer possesses a soul. The result is a pliant slave-like being. (Zombies, however, are only a small part of the voodoo tradition.)

Web:
  http://www.members.aol.com/racine125/
     index1.html
  http://www.religioustolerance.org/voodoo.htm
  http://www.vodou.org/

Zen Buddhism

Zen Buddhism (often referred to as Zen) is a Buddhist sect of Japan and China based on the practice of meditation rather than the following of doctrine. According to legend, Zen was founded by Bodhidharma who brought the teaching of Buddhism to China in 475 A.D. Zen concentrates on enlightenment, consciousness and meditation.

Web:
  http://www.ibiblio.org/zen/faq.html
  http://www.io.com/~snewton/zen/
  http://www.mro.org/zmm/zazen.shtml

Usenet:
  alt.philosophy.zen
  alt.zen

Zoroastrianism

Originating in ancient Iran, Zoroastrianism today has a small following in isolated areas of Iran and India. Join the discussion on this religion founded in 6th century B.C. and hear the stories of Ahura Mazda as he battles his evil twin, Ahriman. This is the stuff good movies are made of.

Web:
  http://religiousmovements.lib.virginia.edu/nrms/
     Zoro1.html
  http://www.avesta.org/zfaq.html
  http://www.beliefnet.com/index/index_10035.html

Usenet:
  alt.religion.zoroastrianism

A B C D E F G H I J K L M N O P Q R S T U V W X Y Z

RELIGION: SPIRITUAL MOVEMENTS

Celtic Spirituality and Druidism

The Celts were a group of tribes originating in southwest Germany. In the 5th and 6th centuries B.C., the Celts spread over much of Europe. This was during the Iron Age (which followed the Bronze Age), and the Celt raiders were successful because of their use of iron weapons. Eventually, the Celts were able to reach Asia Minor (Turkey), Macedonia, Italy, Spain, France and the British Isles, and spread their culture, which included the use of iron, the creation of ornamental art and establishment of an elaborate system of folklore. By the 1st century A.D., the Celts were confined mostly to the British Isles and France, where they were subject to Roman rule. (If you have ever read Asterix comics, you were reading about Celts.) Within Celtic clans, there were priests called druids, and today, there are people who use the traditions of the Celts and their druids as the basis for modern spiritual movements. Such movements stress the importance of nature and sacred places (stone circles and so on). They also recognize a large number of gods, goddesses, saints and heroes, and value the many Celtic-derived myths. These modern-day Celts consider it important to acquire skills such as art, crafts, writing, music and healing, and they expect people to be able to study and teach themselves.

Web:
    http://www.adf.org/core/
    http://www.druidry.org/obod/intro/faq.html
    http://www.fairmoon.co.uk/druidry/

Usenet:
    alt.religion.druid
    alt.spirituality.druid

Web, web, web...
sleep, eat...
web, web, web...sleep, eat...

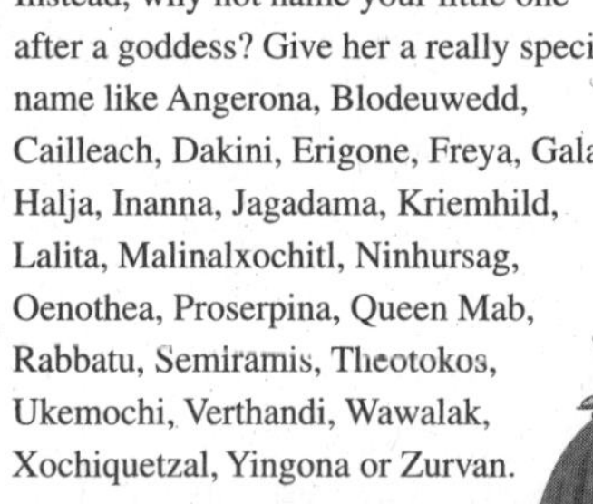

So you have a new baby girl. Don't settle for an ordinary name like Jessica, Michelle, Kimberly or Brandy.

(And for goodness sake, don't name her Jennifer. Every Tom, Dick and Harry is named Jennifer.)

Instead, why not name your little one after a goddess? Give her a really special name like Angerona, Blodeuwedd, Cailleach, Dakini, Erigone, Freya, Galatea, Halja, Inanna, Jagadama, Kriemhild, Lalita, Malinalxochitl, Ninhursag, Oenothea, Proserpina, Queen Mab, Rabbatu, Semiramis, Theotokos, Ukemochi, Verthandi, Wawalak, Xochiquetzal, Yingona or Zurvan.

Goddess Spirituality

Many of the world's religions are controlled by men. This, of course, is no accident. Throughout much of history, society has been controlled by men. However, in the last century, women in many countries have achieved more and more power. At the same time, many spiritual women have articulated a desire for a religion in which the basic ideas are derived from female traditions. For example, mainstream monotheistic religions attest to the existence of a God who is definitely a "he". The Goddess movement celebrates the divine image (the idea of God) as being female. This movement is not an organized religion with a specific dogma, although there are various Goddess-oriented groups. Goddess spirituality is, rather, an ever-growing collection of spiritual practices based on goddesses and grounded in a female approach to worship, philosophy, art and culture.

Web:
    http://www.awakenedwoman.com/
        goddess_spirituality.htm
    http://www.fellowshipofisis.com/
    http://www.lunaea.com/goddess/
    http://www.mothersmagic.net/

Usenet:
    alt.religion.goddess
    alt.religion.triplegoddess

Native American Religions

For centuries, tribes of aboriginal people lived over much of the North American continent. They developed a great variety of religious practices based on the land, natural phenomena (such as the sun, moon and weather), the animals they lived with and hunted, and a reverence for the wisdom of their elders and ancestors. The religions were often shamanic, based on the special powers of their leaders to understand the spirits of nature. Today, these religions are honored by many of the descendants of these aboriginal peoples, the Native Americans (American Indians), as well as other people who value the ceremonies, rituals, prayers and legends.

Web:
> http://religiousmovements.lib.virginia.edu/nrms/
>   naspirit.html
> http://www.stormwind.com/common/
>   nareligion.html
> http://www.tahtonka.com/religion.html

Paganism

The word pagan comes from the Latin "paganus", which means "a country dweller". The modern-day paganism movement is composed of a large variety of nature-based religions and belief systems. Paganism has no central dogma. Rather, Pagans celebrate various gods and goddesses (either one or many), nature, and the cycles of the sun and moon. One advantage to being a pagan is that you have a great deal of freedom in how you express your spiritual beliefs. One serious disadvantage, however, is that you don't get to wear uncomfortable clothes, sit in church, and listen to someone tell you what to think.

Web:
> http://www.jazgordon.com/pagan/
> http://www.landfield.com/faqs/paganism-faq/
> http://www.lapa.net/paganism/
> http://www.summerland.org/
> http://www.ukpagan.com/

Usenet:
> alt.pagan
> alt.pagan.contacts
> alt.religion.all-worlds
> soc.religion.paganism

Learn how to use a search engine well and a whole new world is at your fingertips.

Satanism

Discover what Satanists feel are the misconceptions about their beliefs. See what Satanism means and discuss how Satanists feel it relates to Christianity. Other topics include music, books, and news items.

Web:
> http://www.churchofsatan.com/
> http://www.cs.ruu.nl/wais/html/na-bng/
>   alt.satanism.html
> http://www.satanism-uk.com/
> http://www.satanism101.com/

Usenet:
> alt.satanism

Shamanism

Among tribal peoples, a shaman is a spiritual leader— usually a healer—who has a mystical connection to the spirit world. Delve into the natural, spiritual practices of the shaman. Discover the range of the shamanic experience, which includes such activities as drumming, vision quests, and visiting sacred sites, all of which are used to put someone into an ecstatic trance.

Web:
> http://www.deoxy.org/shaover.htm
> http://www.faqs.org/faqs/shamanism/
>   newsgroup-faq/
> http://www.shamanscave.com/cave.html
> http://www.theblackraven.8m.com/shaman/
>   shaman.htm

Usenet:
> alt.religion.shamanism
> soc.religion.shamanism

Thelema

Thelema is a Greek word meaning "will" or "intention". However, Thelema is also the name of a spiritual philosophy that has been evolving over the last few hundred years. The basic tenet of Thelema is "Do what thou wilt shall be the whole of the Law." The earliest mention of Thelema was in the 16th century. However, the philosophy began to evolve rapidly in the early 1900s when a British occultist named Aleister Crowley (1875-1947) wrote The Book of the Law. Crowley spent the rest of his life developing the philosophy of Thelema as it related to The Book of the Law. (Historical note: Crowley wrote this book at the urging of his wife who, it is said, was pestered by the Egyptian god Horus to get Crowley's attention while he and his wife were on their honeymoon in Egypt.) The basic idea is that "...each person has the right to fulfill themselves through whatever beliefs and actions are best suited to them (so long as they do not interfere with the will of others), and only they themselves are qualified to determine what these are."

Web:
   http://www.religioustolerance.org/thelema2.htm
   http://www.thelema.co.uk/holy_books.html
   http://www.thelema.org/

Wicca

Wicca is a neo-pagan religion that is more focused and ritualistic than traditional paganism. The Wiccan tradition is to worship a god and goddess (not necessarily in that order) or perhaps multiple deities. Wiccans are tuned into nature, cycles and life events, and perform magick rituals to mark the passing of holidays or special events.

Web:
   http://www.cog.org/
   http://www.faqs.org/faqs/religions/wicca/faq/
   http://www.mothersmagic.net/witches/wicca/
   http://www.wiccan.com/
   http://www.witchvox.com/

Usenet:
   alt.religion.wicca
   alt.religion.wicca.moderated

IRC:
   #wicca (Undernet)

ROLE PLAYING

Advanced Dungeons and Dragons

Advanced Dungeons and Dragons (AD&D) is a highly complex fantasy role-playing system, enjoyed by people all over the world. AD&D is the oldest such system, tracing its roots back to the original Dungeons and Dragons (1973). There is a great deal of AD&D material on the Net: spell and priest books, campaigns, modules, new monsters, new spells, rules, interactive games, and lots of commentary.

Web:
   http://www.adnd.com/
   http://www.enteract.com/~aardy/faq/rgfdfaq.html
   http://www.geonomicon.com/portal/

Usenet:
   alt.games.adnd
   rec.games.frp.dnd

Listserv Mailing List:
   List Name: adnd-l
   Subscribe to: listserv@listserv.uta.edu

IRC:
   #ad&d (DALnet, Undernet)

Buying and Selling Role-Playing Games

After awhile, you can reach the burn-out stage on any particular role-playing game. Don't let all that time, money and attention go to waste. On Usenet you can probably find someone who is interested in whatever you want to get rid of. Buy, sell or trade your fantasy role-playing material. It's all happening here.

Usenet:
   rec.games.frp.marketplace

I've never met a
high-speed Internet connection
I didn't like.

Fantasy Role Playing Talk and General Discussion

Join up with the folks in Usenet and discuss your favorite or your most hated role-playing game and all the issues that come with it. Magic, mystery and adventure await you once you step across the line that separates fantasy from reality.

Usenet:

alt.dragons-inn
alt.pub.dragons-inn
rec.games.frp
rec.games.frp.advocacy
rec.games.frp.announce
rec.games.frp.archives
rec.games.frp.cyber
rec.games.frp.dnd
rec.games.frp.gurps
rec.games.frp.misc
rec.games.frp.storyteller
rec.games.frp.super-heroes

Live-Action Role Playing

What a great way to spend the evening—dress up as someone else and take on a whole new life. Say goodbye to reality by doing some live-action role playing where you talk to other characters and solve a mystery or a problem the way your character would. You'll never be able to go back to ordinary board games again.

Web:

http://www.larp.com/
http://www.matalics.org/lrp/larp.htm
http://www.skaro.com/larpdex.html

Usenet:

rec.games.frp.live-action

Magic: The Gathering

"Magic: The Gathering" is a dungeons-and-dragons-type trading card game. The cards are sold by a company called Wizards of the Coast, which created the game in 1993. In order to play, you must first buy some cards (there are several thousand different cards available). Once you have cards, you can trade them with other people in order to improve the quality of your collection. A game takes place between two or more players, and lasts about 20 minutes. To prepare for a game, each player selects a number of cards from his particular collection. Thus, every game is different depending on which cards the players choose to use. Each player represents a powerful wizard, who plays his cards according to his particular strategy. The goal of the game is to gain control of a magical plane of existence. Many people around the world enjoy Magic: The Gathering. For example, Bill Gates often plays this game with his friends, using stock certificates instead of printed cards. (But then Bill plays Monopoly with real money.)

Web:

http://www.crystalkeep.com/magic/
http://www.faqs.org/faqs/games/magic-t-g/rules/part6/
http://www.kragstad.com/
http://www.magiclore.com/
http://www.wizards.com/magic/

Usenet:

alt.cardgame.magic
rec.games.trading-cards.magic.misc
rec.games.trading-cards.magic.rules
rec.games.trading-cards.magic.strategy
rec.games.trading-cards.marketplace.magic.auctions
rec.games.trading-cards.marketplace.magic.sales
rec.games.trading-cards.marketplace.magic.trades

IRC:

#mtgeurope (EFnet)

There is a special secret
on one of the pages
of this book.

Miniatures

I love miniatures and I'm not sure why. It's just so satisfying to hold and look at little things that look just like big things. When I get a chance to browse in a miniature store, I always have a great time, and I always see things I want to take home. I especially like the miniatures of old-fashioned things, maybe because it reminds me of what life was like when I was a kid. If you like miniatures, for collecting or role playing, you'll find lots to keep you occupied on the Net.

Web:
  http://tetrad.stanford.edu/
  http://www.warweb.com/miniatures/
  http://www.zeitcom.com/majgen/

Usenet:
  rec.games.miniatures
  rec.games.miniatures.historical
  rec.games.miniatures.misc
  rec.games.miniatures.warhammer

Role Playing Games Magazine

This online magazine is devoted to role playing and related activities. When you need to take a break between games, what could be more relaxing than curling up with a warm computer and reading role-playing stories, news, announcements and reviews.

Web:
  http://www.rpgtimes.net/rpgtimes/cover.php

Role Playing Resources

There are a lot of role-playing fanatics on the Net, and lots and lots of resources for you to enjoy. Here are some good places to start. Whether you like fantasy, science fiction, cyberpunk, gothic or war, there are enough resources here to ensure you will never be so bored as to be tempted to go back to real life.

Web:
  http://www.hut.fi/~vesanto/roleplay.html
  http://www.role-play.net/
  http://www.rpg.net/
  http://www.rpgarchive.com/
  http://www.rpghost.com/

Usenet:
  rec.games.rpg

Star Trek Role Playing

Don't settle for just watching or reading about Star Trek. You can actually be a Star Trek character in a role-playing game. Star Trek: it's more than fun—it's a way of life.

Web:
  http://www.atrek.org/
  http://www.sfcommand.com/
  http://www.star-fleet.com/
  http://www.ufed.org/

Usenet:
  alt.starfleet.rpg

Vampire: The Masquerade

Vampire: The Masquerade is a series of live-action role-playing games (LARP) based on commercial rulesets derived from the White Wolf's World of Darkness. (In LARP, you not only wear costumes and participate, you act out the parts.)

Web:
  http://www.activision.com/games/vampire/
  http://www.gothgirl.co.uk/Masquerade/
  http://www.sanguinus.com/
  http://www.thekindred.com/

Usenet:
  alt.games.vampire.the.masquerade

Listserv Mailing List:
  List Name: vampire-l
  Subscribe to: listserv@oracle.wizards.com

Right now,
it's exactly 10:45 AM
(somewhere in the world).

Warhammer

Warhammer is a strategy game in which people use a board and miniatures to simulate a fantasy war. These Web sites have a large archive of files, play aids, a bestiary, sample scenarios, and information on religion, rules, magick and careers. The mailing list and Usenet group are for discussing all aspects of Warhammer fantasy role play.

Web:
  http://user.cs.tu-berlin.de/~rossi/Wfrp/encyc/
    menu.html
  http://www.portent.net/
  http://www.terragenesis.co.uk/

Usenet:
  rec.games.miniatures.warhammer

IRC:
  #warhammer (EFnet)

World of Darkness

World of Darkness is a general umbrella term for games such as Werewolf, Mage, Wraith, Changeling and the Vampire: The Masquerade series, all produced by White Wolf Game Studios. These Web sites have links to the various games, archives, and related Usenet groups. There is one Usenet group for the Storyteller system, and another group for White Wolf games.

Web:
  http://www.cruzio.com/~kelinor/wod.html
  http://www.nocturnis.net/
  http://www.patman.org/wod/wodindex.asp
  http://www.thedarkcity.nu/
  http://www.wod-online.com/

Usenet:
  alt.games.whitewolf
  rec.games.frp.storyteller

Breaking Up

As the American philosopher Neil Sedaka (1939-) observed, "Breaking up is hard to do." I have a friend Yoko (1962-), also a philosopher, who comments further. "Breaking up," says Yoko, "is an essential constituent of romance; I'd even say that without it, the impact of romance is reduced a hundredfold." Neil and Yoko are both right: breaking up is hard to do, but at times it's not only unavoidable, but an important part of life. Unfortunately, I can't tell you anything to take away the long period of pain, self-doubt and loneliness—I wish I could. What I can do is remind you that, as Yoko points out, breaking up now will make your future relationships all the sweeter. So as long as you are going to break up, why not do it well?

Web:
  http://dating.lovingyou.com/guides/?id=breakingup
  http://sophie23.addr.com/sing11.htm
  http://www.artofloving.com/family/
    29lovebreakup.htm
  http://www.counseling.swt.edu/
    surviving_a_breakup.htm
  http://www.faqs.org/faqs/romance-faq/part2/
    section-6.html
  http://www.soyouvebeendumped.com/

Couples

It's the best of times, it's the worst of times. Relationships have their ups and downs, but like a roller coaster, it's fun and thrilling, makes you afraid, and makes you laugh. See what is going on in the lives of other couples. Get ideas for romantic outings, anniversaries, how to patch up a fuss, or what to do with in-laws.

Usenet:
  soc.couples
  soc.couples.intercultural

Couples:

Need to work on the relationship? Why not do it in front of the rest of the world? Participate in the **soc.couples** discussion group.

Crushes

If you have a crush on someone, you can use this service to email them an anonymous note. The person is informed that someone has a crush on them, but they aren't told who. He or she can choose to fill out a form, if they too have a crush. If the information on the other person's form matches up in some way with yours, both people are notified. There's no time limit, in case it takes your crush awhile to figure out how awesome you are and get a crush on you. If you're not sure if you want to participate, you can read stories about other people's experiences.

Web:
  http://www.ecrush.com/
  http://www.secretadmirer.com/
  http://www.winkat.com/

Kissing

To use your lips to caress the lips of your beloved, to express your affection and your feelings of amorousness—is there anything more delightful? But, like parachute jumping and cliff diving, if you are going to kiss, it's better not to make a mistake your first time. Don't worry, and don't be shy. All you need is a bit of instruction, and the Net is ready to help.

Web:
  http://www.kissing.com/faqkiss.html
  http://www.links2love.com/teens_kissing.htm
  http://www.partyhearty.com/kissingadvice.html
  http://www.redhotkissingtips.com/

Language of Love

*Every time you kiss me,
I'm still not certain that you love me.*

However, if you use the **Language of Love** Web site, you could tell me you love me in more than 100 languages, including Bulgarian (Obicham te), Esperanto (Mi amas vin), Klingon (qaparHa') and Vulcan (Wani ra yana ro aisha).

Language of Love

World travelers: it's always handy to know how to say "I love you" in any language. You never know when it could be important. For instance, say you are on a brief layover at an airport in Rome and the woman of your dreams comes racing by dragging behind her four suitcases on wheels. She runs over your foot and you realize that, yes, this is The One For You. How are you going to get her attention? Check out this site, so you'll be lucky in love no matter what your native language.

Web:
  http://www.worldpath.net/~hiker/iloveyou.html

Love

Romantic love is the intense feeling we have towards another person, when we are attracted to him or her as a mate. "In the spring," the poet Tennyson tells us, "a livelier iris changes on the burnish'd dove; In the spring a young man's fancy lightly turns to thoughts of love." But—man or woman—once your fancy has lightly turned to thoughts of love, what do you do next? How do you find your true love and, once you do, how can you be sure it is the real thing? My advice is to not let your feelings get the better of you. Real love takes a long time to develop, but will last indefinitely if you are careful. It is true that infatuation is intoxicating, but as anyone over the age of 35 can tell you, be sure to walk the full length of the counter before you make your selection.

Web:
  http://www.enotalone.com/index.php3?catstr=89
  http://www.lovemermaid.com/
  http://www.lovenet.com/digest/
  http://www.soulmaterelationships.com/
    soulmatearticles/whatisasoulmate.htm
  http://www.themushpit.com/whatslove.html

Usenet:
  alt.love

Love Chat

Whether you are looking for love or looking to talk about love, IRC is a good place to start. Not only can you talk romantically, but you can eat pizza at the same time and nobody will know the difference. You can't get much better than that. Check out these channels for romantic talk or possibly some romantic action.

IRC:
  #love (DALnet, Undernet)
  #romance (EFnet)

Love Poetry

It's wonderful to write love poetry to your special, adorable loved one. However, writing good poetry is not easy. My advice is to look at other people's poems for inspiration. When you are ready to write your own, here are two starting lines. Just choose one of them. (1) "Shall I compare thee to a Summer's day?" (2) "How do I love thee? Let me count the ways." Now, all *you* have to do is fill in the details.

Web:
http://library.lovingyou.com/poetry/
http://www.amorantica.com/poems/index.asp
http://www.zdaily.com/poems-love.htm

Love and Romance

Where would we be without love and romance? Probably at home in front of the TV set. At least with romance we can be in front of the TV with someone to keep us company.
As a Net person, you never need to worry about getting your share. There are lots of resources for the romantically inclined (and even for the romantically challenged).
But remember, even in a Harley Hahn book, "Romance" comes before "Sex".

Love Police

Has your husband/wife/boyfriend/girlfriend done something wrong? Would you like to point out the transgression in a humorous but noticeable manner? Try the Love Police. You start by choosing a violation: communication, behavior, bad habit, personality, and so on. Then set the bail (concert tickets, flowers, take me dancing...) and have your loved one cited by email. Once he or she has seen the light, you can visit the corrections office and see if the transgressor has agreed to mend his/her ways. (Don't you wish real life were this easy?)

Web:
http://www.lovepolice.com/

Love Test

There are two ways to find out if your love is real or if it is simply an unrealistic infatuation. You can either ask your significant other, and talk about the relationship, or you can use the Net to take a free love test. The advantage of taking the test is that you can change the answers if you don't like the results.

Web:
http://www.ivillage.com/relationships/cupid/

Marriage and Commitment

Marriage, and the commitment that holds marriage together, can be the most important, most wonderful social forces in our lives. However, when a relationship is not working well, marriage can make us miserable and fill us with doubt and pessimism. When we marry, we promise to take one another for better and for worse, but we make the promise when we are happy and optimistic. What do we do when the happiness seems to have vanished forever into a fog of irritation and despair? Marriage builds a wall around two people, and how you view that wall makes all the difference in the world. To some people, the wall restricts their freedom and makes them feel as it they are living in a prison. To other people, the wall is a magical barrier that surrounds and protects everything they hold dear, drawing a clear line between "us" and the rest of the world. You certainly wouldn't wait until you were 65 to start saving for retirement. Don't wait until you are unhappy to realize how important it is to have a strong, committed marriage. Start now, today.

Web:
http://www.celebratelove.com/articles.htm
http://www.committment.com/goodhusband.html
http://www.couples-place.com/
http://www.marriagetools.com/
http://www.myria.com/directory/Relationships/
   Coupletime/

Usenet:
alt.support.marriage

Men and Women

We all got along fine when we were algae. But somewhere between floating gently on the lake and the invention of the bikini, men and women started to have their differences. Get up close and personal.

Usenet:
soc.men
soc.women

Online Romance Talk & General Discussion

Voyeurs and participants alike can experience fun and romance in Usenet. In this Usenet group you can meet people, talk about the concepts of romance, being romantic, ideas that are romantic or talk about places on the Net where you can find romance.

Usenet:
   alt.romance.online

Random Love Poems

Close your eyes, count to three and wait for this Web page to load. Suddenly you will be presented with a randomly selected romantic poem written by someone who has been dead for many, many years. This, of course, doesn't detract from the romantic value of the poem, so by all means, read on. Don't think about how, as you imagine being in love and laughing with your wonderful partner, these poets have long since been eaten by worms. Don't let that stop you. Carry on. Be happy.

Web:
   http://ddmi.he.net/cgi-bin/suid/~chocolov/
      rand_poem.cgi

Romance Readers Anonymous

You've been sucked in. It's impossible to walk past a rack of romance novels without picking up at least one. The bronzed man holding the lithe woman with the heaving bosom makes your heart beat quickly, loud enough for everyone else in the store to hear. The television has cobwebs and you haven't been out of the house in months since you got a subscription to Romance of the Week. Get help now. You are not alone.

Web:
   http://www.toad.net/~dolma/

Usenet:
   bit.listserv.rra-l

Listserv Mailing List:
   List Name: rra-l
   Subscribe to: listserv@listserv.kent.edu

Romance Resources

I must admit it; I am a sucker for romance. I love sending flowers and cards and doing unexpected things, and I love when someone treats me in that very special way. It's easy to be romantic at the beginning of a relationship. However, once you come to know the other person well, they become real, not a fantasy, and romance can fade. Don't let it. Here are ideas, tips and articles to help you preserve and increase the romance in your life.

Web:
   http://romance.lovingyou.com/
   http://www.anythingromantic.com/
   http://www.electpress.com/loveandromance/
   http://www.kissingbooth.com/
   http://www.links2love.com/
   http://www.only-romance.com/
   http://www.romancetips.com/

Romance Talk and General Discussion

Have you noticed life isn't quite like the covers of paperback romance novels (or the inside of the romance novels, for that matter)? Do something about that by generating a romantic fire with others who mourn the death of romance. Remember Cyrano de Bergerac and his words that could melt the hair off a moose? Where do you think he got his start?

Usenet:
   alt.romance
   alt.romance.chat
   alt.romance.mature-adult

Romantic Ascii Graphics

Stop with the boring email. Send your loved one a nice romantic greeting spiced up with some ascii graphics. For those of you who don't know how to make your own, just cut and paste some of these into your letter and nobody will know the difference. It will be our little secret.

Web:
   http://eleves.supaero.fr/ASCII/images/Hearts
   http://www.chris.com/ascii/art/html/valentine.html
   http://www.grad.math.uwaterloo.ca/~y5liu/ASCII/
      love.html

Romantic Gestures

Don't flounder around in your romantic life when you could be someone's future knight in shining armor. Here are sites with romantic ideas if you don't know exactly what to do or how to get started in the romance game.

Web:
   http://romance.lovingyou.com/ideas/
   http://www.etoile.co.uk/Love/Her.html
   http://www.etoile.co.uk/Love/His.html
   http://www.getromantic.com/
   http://www.hopelessromantics.com/pages/feedback/
      ideas/1.shtml
   http://www.kissingbooth.com/romance/
      gestureadults.htm

Romantic Greetings by Email

There's no need to race out to the store just because you forgot to get a nice card for your anniversary. On the Net, you can make your own cards, or send virtual gifts of flowers or kisses just by using your Web browser. These cards and other electronic greetings will be all the more special because you made them yourself.

Web:
   http://www.azstarnet.com/flowers/
   http://www.bemine.com/
   http://www.heartisticwishes.com/

Seduction

The idea of seduction is to chase someone until they catch you. The time-honored role of seduction is for young men to attract the attention of young women in order to have sex. However, there are a great many other variations. If you look at life carefully, you will see that there are a great many situations that have nothing to do with sex, in which it is useful to be skilled in the art of seduction. In fact, every time you want someone to do something for you, remember that the art of attracting people is 90 percent charm.

Web:
   http://www.getgirls.com/archive.htm
   http://www.getgirls.com/freechap.htm
   http://www.sosuave.com/

Singles

Your mother probably said that anyone you can pick up in a bar is not someone with whom you want to develop a serious relationship. (What you probably didn't want to tell her was that you weren't looking for a serious relationship.) In the event that you change your mind, stop in at the nicest singles hangouts in Usenet and IRC and find that special someone just right for you. The Web sites have the **soc.singles** FAQ (frequently asked question list).

Web:
   http://www.cs.ruu.nl/wais/html/na-dir/
      singles-faq.html
   http://www.faqs.org/faqs/singles-faq/

Usenet:
   soc.singles
   soc.singles.moderated

IRC:
   #singles (EFnet)

Soulmates

There is a moment when you look into someone's eyes and you feel, in an instant, that you have known this person your entire life and that you can never bear to be separated from him or her again. This is the feeling of finding a soulmate, someone who feels like the other half of you. Read anecdotes about people who have found their soulmates, people who are looking for soulmates and discuss the writings of authors who write on the concept of soulmates.

Web:
   http://www.soulmateoracle.com/quiz/quiz-1.html

Usenet:
   alt.soulmates

Unhappy Romances

The only thing worse than no romance is unhappy romance. Unrequited love, romance gone bad or people who are inept in the romance department—these are all topics that are fair game in this Usenet group.

Usenet:
   alt.romance.unhappy

SCIENCE

Annals of Improbable Research

The Annals of Improbable Research (AIR) is a science humor magazine. It's hard to describe what you find here; suffice it to say that, if you like science and you have a good sense of humor, you'll enjoy what you see. (Think of AIR as the National Lampoon for smart people.) Footnotes: (1) If you liked the old Journal of Irreproducible Results, you'll enjoy the AIR. (2) These same people also give out the annual Ig Nobel Awards to honor people whose achievements "cannot or should not be reproduced".

Web:

http://www.improb.com/
http://www.improb.com/airchives/airchives-top.html

Bad Science

When I was in medical school at the University of Toronto, I had a physics argument with a fellow student named Dave Colby. Dave thought that, south of the equator, water emptying from a sink would spin counter-clockwise (as opposed to most sinks up here, in which the water runs clockwise as it drains). Dave said the spinning was caused by the Coriolis effect (the apparent sideways motion of certain forces due to the rotation of the Earth). I tried to explain to Dave that he was wrong: the Coriolis effect works on large-scale phenomena, like the trade winds, but not on anything as small as the water in a sink. However, he was intransigent, so I bet him five dollars that I was right. Well, I was, and his argument is a perfect example of bad science: technical ideas that are presented incorrectly by teachers and writers. As one of my readers, I know you always like to be knowledgeable and accurate, so take a look at the bad science information and learn what's right. (And if you ever run into Dave, tell him he owes me five dollars.)

Web:

http://www.ems.psu.edu/~fraser/BadScience.html

Annals of Improbable Research

If you are like me, you enjoy nothing better than spending Saturday night curled up at home with a good mathematics or physics journal. However, even the best times end, and what do you do when you have read all your scholarly publications and it's only 9:00 PM? Time to fire up the old Web browser and connect to the **Annals of Improbable Research** archives. The lighthearted approach to research and its detritus will entertain for hours.

Dinosaurs

Dinosaurs evolved about 225 million years ago, and became extinct about 65 million years ago, thriving for 160 million years. In modern terminology, dinosaurs are land-living reptiles, members of a group known as archsaurs ("ruling reptiles"). Among today's animals, birds are thought to be the closest relatives to dinosaurs, with crocodiles being somewhat more distant relations. Dinosaur trivia: Around the turn of the century, certain fossils were thought to be those of a brontosaurus. Actually, the head and body were mixed up, and the real name for the animal is apatosaurus. There never really was such a thing as a brontosaurus.

Web:

http://palaeo.gly.bris.ac.uk/dinobase/dinopage.html
http://www.dinodata.net/
http://www.dinosauria.com/
http://www.enchantedlearning.com/subjects/
    dinosaurs/
http://www.ucmp.berkeley.edu/diapsids/
    dinolinks.html

Usenet:

alt.dinosaur

Listproc Mailing List:

List Name: dinosaur
Subscribe to: listproc@usc.edu

Earth and Sky

"Earth and Sky" is a popular radio presentation that is aired daily on hundreds of stations in the U.S., Canada and the South Pacific, as well as on various international networks. Each day the show provides a short discussion of one scientific topic. The Web site offers transcripts from the actual shows. You can read about the most current show, or search for one that interests you.

Web:
   http://www.earthsky.com/

Folklore of Science

Science is rich in folklore, legends and mysteries. This Usenet group is for the discussion of various folklore topics as they relate to science. The Web page contains a listing of science-related urban legends. Will a penny falling from a great height kill someone? Will hot water freeze faster than cold water? Why does the moon look smaller when it is overhead than when it is near the horizon? Visit the Web site and find out the answers to these questions and more. (By the way, the quick answers are no, yes and it's an illusion.)

Web:
   http://www.urbanlegends.com/science/

Usenet:
   alt.folklore.science

DINOSAURS

Everybody likes dinosaurs. Of course, they are an important part of our heritage, seeing as we too are animals-that-live-on-Earth. However, dinosaurs are also an important part of the popular culture.

For example, although few people realize it, before Jay Leno, the top-rated American nighttime TV talk show host was a dinosaur. And fully 75% of modern American publishing companies are run by dinosaurs.

My philosophy is let's teach our kids to understand and appreciate our friends in the dinosaur kingdom, and it won't be long before we will all be living in peace and harmony.

(You know, now that I think of it, the current top-rated American nighttime TV talk show is *still* a dinosaur.)

History of Science

The history of science is the story of our systematic and endless quest to understand the nature of ourselves, our world and the universe in which we live. When you study how science has evolved, you are studying the very best efforts and accomplishments of mankind throughout the centuries.

Web:
   http://www.fordham.edu/halsall/science/
      sciencesbook.html
   http://www.gsu.edu/other/timeline.html
   http://www.rit.edu/~flwstv/presocratic.html
   http://www.wam.umd.edu/~losinp/science.html

Usenet:
   soc.history.science

Human Evolution

Human evolution is the theory of the origin of human beings. In particular, evolution explains how man and the apes descended from common ancestors and how, about five million years ago, our most immediate ancestors (hominids) began the development that would result in our own species (Homo sapiens). There is a great deal of foolish and ignorant thought (and talk) among people who believe that mankind was created supernaturally. As far as I am concerned, the more people learn about science, the better off we all are, and here are some places to start.

Web:
   http://www.modernhumanorigins.com/
   http://www.talkorigins.org/
   http://www.ucmp.berkeley.edu/history/
      evolution.html

Usenet:
   talk.origins

National Science Foundation

The National Science Foundation (NSF) is an independent agency of the United States government. Its purpose is to promote the progress of science within the United States. Toward this end, the NSF funds a great deal of research within the science and engineering disciplines, as well as awarding many graduate scholarships. The NSF also promotes the use of computers in science research and education.

Web:
   http://www.nsf.gov/

Oceanography

The Earth has one large interconnected sea of water, covering 71 percent of the planet's surface. Traditionally, we divide all this water into four main oceans: the Pacific Ocean, the Indian Ocean, the Atlantic Ocean and the Arctic Ocean. Taken together, these oceans cover about 139,400,000 square miles (361,000,000 sq km) and contain about 322,280,000 cubic miles (1,347,000,000 cu km) of water. The average depth is about 12,230 feet (3,730 m). Oceanography is the study of the ocean and the life it supports. As such, oceanography integrates biology, chemistry, geography, geology, physics and meteorology into one marine-oriented field of study. Here are some Web sites that contain particularly good collections. I have also included the Web sites of two of the main oceanographical research organizations in the United States: Scripps Institution of Oceanography (California) and the Woods Hole Oceanographic Institution (Massachusetts).

Web:
http://www.cln.org/themes/oceanography.html
http://www.mth.uea.ac.uk/ocean/vl/
http://www.nodc.noaa.gov/
http://www.scilib.ucsd.edu/sio/
http://www.sio.ucsd.edu/
http://www.whoi.edu/

Usenet:
sci.geo.oceanography

Research Methods in Science

You need a certain kind of mind to be an organized and efficient researcher. Here are some discussion forums on the Internet that will give you lots of different places to talk about scientific techniques. The mailing list helps researchers in classification, clustering, phylogeny estimation and related methods of data analysis to contact other researchers in the same fields.

Usenet:
sci.techniques.mag-resonance
sci.techniques.mass-spec
sci.techniques.microscopy
sci.techniques.spectroscopy
sci.techniques.testing.misc
sci.techniques.testing.nondestructive

Listserv Mailing List:
List Name: class-l
Subscribe to: listserv@lists.sunysb.edu

Science Fraud and Skepticism

Science has a long, distinguished history. Unfortunately, science fraud has just as long a history (although less distinguished). These resources are devoted to a discussion of fraud in science, including current and recent events, as well as historical accounts of fraudulent science.

Web:
http://www.faqs.org/faqs/skeptic-faq/
http://www.junkscience.com/

Usenet:
sci.skeptic

Listserv Mailing List:
List Name: scifraud
Subscribe to: listserv@listserv.albany.edu

Science News

Now that we have the Net, life is certainly a lot better. For example, anytime you want, you can read the science news, all by yourself, in the privacy of your own home. When I was a kid, we had to learn about science on the street and, believe me, it was not always a pleasant experience. (Of course, in those days, boys had to grow up fast.)

Web:
http://news.bbc.co.uk/hi/english/sci/tech/
http://www.newscientist.com/
http://www.sciencedaily.com/
http://www.sciencenews.org/
http://www.scitechdaily.com/

Science Questions and Answers

When it comes to science, our curiosity is unbounded (well, it should be...), so it's great to be able to send questions to experts. The next time you are wondering about some scientific something-or-other, see if you can figure out the answer for yourself. If you can't, send it to one of the experts. Even better, when you have a spare moment, check out the archives of previous questions and answers.

Web:
http://image.gsfc.nasa.gov/poetry/ask/askmag.html
http://www.madsci.org/
http://www.sciam.com/askexpert_directory.cfm
http://www.sciencenet.org.uk/

Science Resources

There's a lot of science in the world (and even more outside the world), so it's not always easy to find what you want. When you are looking for information in a particular area of science, start here. You'll find science resources for a variety of disciplines.

Web:
  http://www.amara.com/science/science.html
  http://www.gggpages.com/
  http://www.ncsu.edu/imse/
  http://www.sciencemag.org/

Science Talk and General Discussion

Science is the organized, rational study of the nature of our universe. As a whole, science is broad, almost beyond description. I think of science in two ways: as a method of thinking and as a human activity. The activity of science depends upon three basic traditions: employing trustworthy methods for experimentation and observation, systematically classifying observed facts, and connecting a body of demonstrated truths in order to reach conclusions. Mankind already knows a great deal about our universe (including the planet on which we live and the nature of the biology it supports). A great deal of mankind's suffering is caused by widespread ignorance of basic scientific knowledge and the inability to apply such knowledge wisely. For this reason, I encourage you to use the resources I have prepared for this book to teach yourself more about science. I hope that, within the many scientific resources, you will find much to interest you. If you would like to talk about science in general, here is the Usenet group devoted to such discussions. Remember what I say: as much as anything else, science is a way of thinking. There is no better way to fulfill your birthright as a sentient human being than by studying the world around you and all its wonders. (Perhaps I can put it another way. My cat can't learn about science, so I have to do it for both of us.)

Usenet:
  sci.misc

Temperature

Here is everything you could want to know about temperature. Learn about global warming and our planet's temperature, temperature and health, temperature tools (such as unit converters), temperature sensors and calibration, thermocouples and more. When it comes to learning about temperatures on the Net, when you're hot, you're hot, and when you're not, you're still pretty cool.

Web:
  http://grads.iges.org/pix/trop.ts.s.html
  http://www.temperatureworld.com/

Why Files

A lot of news stories relate to science, but rarely do you get a chance to really understand the science behind the news. The Why Files start with topics from the news and go on to explore all kinds of interesting questions. If you care why things work the way they do, this site is for you. (Hint: When you have nothing to do and it's still a few hours to dinner, read the step-by-step description of coronary bypass surgery.)

Web:
  http://www.whyfiles.org/

Science Fraud and Skepticism

As one of my readers, it is important for you to be intelligent, well-informed and knowledgeable about the world around you. There is altogether too much "junk science" in the world, and I want you to be able to recognize it. Be skeptical: extraordinary claims require extraordinary proof.

SCIENCE FICTION, FANTASY AND HORROR

Babylon 5

Although Babylon 5 was presented as a series of television programs, it was actually a five-year-long story that was completely planned before the first episode was filmed. Babylon 5 is a science fiction saga that takes place in the distant future during the "third age of mankind". A hundred years earlier, an alien race called the Centauri made contact with Earth. Since then, Earth has found out there are three other races in the galaxy, the Narn, the Vorlon and the Minbari. The four alien races are continuously engaging in various wars and intrigues, sometimes involving Earth. In an attempt to bring peace to the galaxy, Earth conceives of a meeting place in the form of an immense space station, a place to serve as the home for a galactic United Nations. The first four attempts to create such a space station are sabotaged, but the fifth attempt is successful. In the year 2257, Babylon 5—the last hope for a peaceful galaxy—is officially opened and the story begins. Although the original TV series (1994-1998) is now over, the Babylon 5 legacy is still living on the Net (not to mention TV movies and video games).

Web:
  http://www.b5tech.com/
  http://www.cs.ruu.nl/wais/html/na-dir/tv/babylon-5/
    faq.html
  http://www.midwinter.com/lurk/
  http://www.oinc.net/b5/enc/
  http://www.sfcreators.com/b5/

Usenet:
  alt.tv.babylon-5
  rec.arts.sf.tv.babylon5
  rec.arts.sf.tv.babylon5.info
  rec.arts.sf.tv.babylon5.moderated

Listproc Mailing List:
  List Name: b5-review-l
  Subscribe to: listproc@cornell.edu

IRC:
  #babylon5 (EFnet)

Cyberpunk

You can't be totally cool until you know what cyberpunk is. And you can't fake it—you have to know the real stuff, like the difference between the literary movement and the culture. People who are immersed in the cyberpunk culture understand what it is, but they have a lot of trouble explaining it to anyone else. My advice is to start with the idea that technology touches virtually every aspect of our lives. One way to sort of understand it is to look at the type of entertainment cyberpunks like. For example, look at the lists of books, movies and manga (anime) preferred by cyberpunks. Read through and you will start to get a feeling about the cyberpunk culture. Cyberpunk philosophy is very much a heuristic work in progress, where what might be and what should be is more or less determined by what is. So take some time to read the quotes, thoughts and ramblings relating to the cyberpunk way of life, ethos and beliefs. What makes more sense to you: "Attack anything that tries to hide information from the masses" or "Never trust anyone? I like to just read the stuff and let it wash over me like an ocean wave.

Web:
  http://www.replicant.net/cyberpunk/
  http://www.tassie.net.au/~pweeks/wochen.html

Usenet:
  alt.culture.cyber-psychos
  alt.cyberpunk
  alt.cyberpunk.chatsubo
  alt.cyberpunk.movement
  alt.cyberpunk.tech
  alt.cyberworld
  alt.cypherpunks
  rec.games.frp.cyber

IRC:
  #cyberpunk (DALnet)

Furry Stuff

Do you like things that are cute and furry?

Of course you do.

So visit all the cute and furry things on the Net.

Doctor Who

He's wild-haired, strangely dressed, and often chased by hostile robots or aliens. Doctor Who doesn't have to take up jogging because he is almost always running for cover anyway. Join the people who love the excitement and adventure of this futuristic television series.

Web:
   http://www.doctorwho.co.uk/
   http://www.varos.net/drwho/

Usenet:
   rec.arts.drwho
   rec.arts.drwho.info

You may be a cyberpunk and not even know it.

There's only one way to find out. Check to see what the cyberpunks are doing, and look for yourself in the crowd.

Remember, anyone can be a punk, but do you have what it takes to be a cyberpunk?

Furry Stuff

If you are not a "fur", you may not be aware that there are many, many people, all over the world, who love to spend time relating to animals that act like people. The animals can be real, cartoon or toy, or from a book, film, TV or comic. The point is that they are cute (mostly), anthropomorphized and loveable, and you can role-play, create, enjoy, watch or otherwise participate in the "furry" culture. Do so, and you too will be a fur.

Web:
   http://www.fur.com/furry/
   http://www.furnation.com/
   http://www.tigerden.com/infopage/furry/
   http://www.xydexx.com/anthrofurry/stuff.htm

Usenet:
   alt.fan.furry
   alt.fan.furry.bleachers
   alt.fan.furry.muck
   alt.fan.furry.politics
   alt.lifestyle.furry

Horror Fiction Online

Wow. You can scare yourself silly without moving from your computer. Spend a few hours reading these novels and short stories and, before you can say "Whose blood is that?" you'll be ready to stay up all night with the lights on.

Web:
   http://www.darklinks.com/dliterature.html
   http://www.horrormasters.com/

Horror Resources

Want to experience total fear in the privacy of your own home (or even better, at work)? There are a lot of horror resources on the Net, and it's your job to explore them. Better get started right now, or something terrible will happen.

Web:
   http://www.darkecho.com/darkecho/
   http://www.horrorbay.com/
   http://www.horrorfind.com/
   http://www.horroronline.com/

Horror Talk and General Discussion

People all over the world love talking and writing about horror. Usenet has groups for both purposes. To talk, join **alt.horror**. To share your writing (or to read other people's work), try the **alt.horror.creative** group, where you can discuss anything related to the creation of things horrible. If you are new to horror on the Net, start with the Web site, where you will find an informative FAQ (frequently asked question list). Read this before you start posting.

Web:
  http://ezinfo.ucs.indiana.edu/~mlperkin/faq.html

Usenet:
  alt.horror
  alt.horror.creative
  rec.arts.horror.misc

Klingons

Klingons are an alien race from Star Trek. At first, they were bad guys, but now they're mostly good guys. (Worf from Star Trek: The Next Generation is a Klingon.) Klingons have their own customs and culture and their own language.

Web:
  http://www.khemorex-klinzhai.de/faqs/meta.html
  http://www.kli.org/
  http://www.klingon.org/
  http://www.thewebfool.com/kmel/kling1.htm

Usenet:
  alt.shared-reality.startrek.klingon
  alt.startrek.klingon

Lovecraft, H.P.

Howard Phillips Lovecraft (1890-1937) was an American writer of fantasy and horror tales that catapulted him into that rarefied area occupied by writers who have managed to generate a cult following. Lovecraft is best known for his "Cthulhu" mythos—an imaginary world inhabited by a variety of strange, bizarre beings. Lovecraft is also known for the huge volume of his personal correspondence.

Web:
  http://www.ech-pi-el.com/lovecraft/
  http://www.hplovecraft.com/

Mystery Science Theatre 3000

There are worse things than being consigned to review bad sci-fi for your entire life. Experience the hilarity of Mystery Science Theater 3000 with other fans of this TV program, where you can watch strange sci-fi movies while listening to the comments of even stranger observers.

Web:
  http://www.mst3kinfo.com/

Usenet:
  alt.fan.mst3k
  alt.tv.mst3k
  rec.arts.tv.mst3k
  rec.arts.tv.mst3k.announce
  rec.arts.tv.mst3k.misc

Poe, Edgar Allan

Edgar Allan Poe (1809-1849) was an American poet, short story writer and critic. Poe is considered to be one of America's most skillful and intelligent writers. He is best known for (1) inventing the idea of the detective story; (2) creating a universe within his writing that was both beautiful and grotesque; and (3) being a witty and intelligent critic who often wrote about the craft of writing. In addition, Poe also distinguished himself by (4) getting kicked out of both the University of Virginia and West Point.

Web:
  http://www.comnet.ca/~forrest/library.html
  http://www.eapoe.org/
  http://www.pambytes.com/poe/poe.html

Red Dwarf

Red Dwarf is a British science fiction comedy series that takes place in the distant future. The show tells the story of Dave Lister, the last living human being, who is stranded in a spaceship in the middle of galactic nowhere. Lister has several companions including his cat; Holly, a computer; Kryten, an android; and Arnold Rimmer, a hologram simulation of a dead person. Lister's goal is to return to Earth and find his long-lost girlfriend. Along the way, he has adventures in parallel universes, time warps, space holes, and so on.

Web:
   http://www.faqs.org/faqs/tv/red-dwarf/
   http://www.jupitermining.com/
   http://www.reddwarf.co.uk/
   http://www.sadgeezer.com/RedDwarf/

Usenet:
   alt.tv.red-dwarf

Science and Science Fiction

Stretch your mind by pushing your imagination to the limit. How real is the science in science fiction? A wide variety of topics are covered, such as the possibility of force fields, transcendental engineering, and Hawking radiation. Invent your own theories or pick apart someone else's.

Web:
   http://www.treitel.org/Richard/rass/qdfaq.html

Usenet:
   rec.arts.sf.science

Science Fiction and Fantasy Online Books

The Net loves people who love science fiction and fantasy. Start at this Web site, choose something, start to read, and a good time will be had by all. You'll find your favorite authors, as well as writers and titles you have never seen. This is a wonderful way to explore the worlds of sci-fi and fantasy, so visit often and enjoy.

Web:
   http://www.hourwolf.com/sfbooks/

Do cannibals floss their teeth?

Science Fiction and Fantasy Resources

When it comes to living in an imaginary world, reality just can't cut the literary mustard—you need more, a lot more. We all know that you can't get too much of a good thing, and we all know that sci-fi/fantasy is a good thing, so why not immerse yourself? Just be sure to come back to Planet Earth every now and then to change your clothes and to order more pizza.

Web:
   http://sf.www.lysator.liu.se/sf_archive/
   http://www.locusmag.com/Links/Portal.html
   http://www.scifi.com/sfw/
   http://www.scifisource.com/
   http://www.sfsite.com/isfdb/

Science Fiction and Fantasy Reviews

I was recently re-reading a science fiction classic (one of the Foundation novels), and it struck me that we can't always be living in a fantasy world. We need to ground ourselves in reality once in awhile, if for no other reason than to eat and do our laundry. So when you need a break, connect to the Net and talk about science fiction. Here is a Usenet group where people like you and I talk to people like you and I, about the types of science fiction people like you and I like reading. This is the place to read and to send reviews. The Web sites also contain reviews and are great places to cruise when you are looking for something to read or a science fiction gift for that special someone.

Web:
   http://www.scifan.com/classics/
   http://www.sfbook.com/
   http://www.sffworld.com/
   http://www.sfsite.com/

Usenet:
   rec.arts.sf.reviews

Science Fiction Author Talk and General Discussion

When you read the work of the great science fiction and fantasy writers, you become immersed in worlds that exist only in the imagination. One of the best ways to enjoy your favorite books is to discuss them with other fans. These Usenet discussion groups are filled with SF&F enthusiasts who love to discuss the nuances of imaginative fiction, as well as the writers who create it.

Usenet:

```
alt.books.arthur-clarke
alt.books.brian-lumley
alt.books.clive-barker
alt.books.crichton
alt.books.dean-koontz
alt.books.deryni
alt.books.julian-may
alt.books.larry-niven
alt.books.m-lackey
alt.books.orson-s-card
alt.books.peter-straub
alt.books.phil-k-dick
alt.books.poppy-z-brite
alt.books.pratchett
alt.books.raymond-feist
alt.books.roger-zelazny
alt.books.sf.melanie-rawn
alt.books.stephen-king
alt.books.terry-brooks
alt.books.toffler
alt.fan.asprin
alt.fan.authors.stephen-king
alt.fan.douglas-adams
alt.fan.dragonlance
alt.fan.dune
alt.fan.eddings
alt.fan.harlan-ellison
alt.fan.heinlein
alt.fan.pern
alt.fan.piers-anthony
alt.fan.pratchett
alt.fan.pratchett.announce
alt.fan.robert-jordan
rec.arts.sf.written.robert-jordan
```

Science Fiction Convention Calendar

When you need a little break from the real world, pack your bags and head to a science fiction convention. Here's a list of cons all over the world, including information about the guests of honor and contact information so you can pre-register.

Web:
```
http://www.smof.com/conlist.htm
```

Science Fiction Fan Fiction

Fan fiction refers to original stories written by amateur fans (like you). If you have a favorite sci-fi world with characters you love, why not be creative and write something of your own? Does that sound inviting? Take a look and see what other people have done. This is a popular activity in the Internet science fiction community. You'll find X-Files, Star Trek, Highlander, Star Wars, Dr. Who, Forever Knight, Buffy the Vampire Slayer, Quantum Leap, Sliders, and much more.

Web:
```
http://fanfic.theforce.net/lexicon.asp
http://www.fanfix.com/
http://www.sg1-heliopolis.de/
http://www.slayerfanfic.com/
```

Usenet:
```
alt.drwho.creative
alt.ql.creative
alt.startrek.creative
alt.startrek.creative.all-ages
alt.tv.buffy-v-slayer.creative
alt.tv.quantum-leap.creative
alt.tv.sliders.creative
alt.tv.x-files.creative
```

Science Fiction Fandom Talk and General Discussion

Fans from all over the world live, eat and breathe science fiction. They travel in packs, eager to suck the nectar from the sci-fi flower. If you have a taste for something out of the ordinary, join the crowd, go to cons and be a groupie.

Usenet:
```
alt.fandom.cons
rec.arts.sf.fandom
```

Science Fiction Marketplace

Are you looking to trade your extra copy of the "Pegasus" episode of Battlestar Galactica for a signed copy of a Friday print by Whelan? Shop at the science fiction flea market—rare commodities for rare people. Buy, sell or trade. Display your merchandise in this shoplifter-free environment.

Usenet:
```
rec.arts.sf.marketplace
```

Science Fiction Movies

You just saw the best movie ever and you have to tell someone about it or you'll explode. You can either run screaming through the parking lot of the movie theater and risk being arrested for disturbing the peace, or you can tell the sci-fi movie fans on the Internet. Start with the Usenet group. Then move on to the Web sites, where you can immerse yourself in the lore of SF films until it is time to go to another movie.

Web:
 http://www.faqs.org/faqs/sf/movies-faq/
 http://www.sci-fighter.com/
 http://www.sciflicks.com/
 http://www.shipofdreams.net/sfmovies/

Usenet:
 rec.arts.sf.movies

Science Fiction News and Announcements

As a science fiction fan, you have a moral (not to mention a personal) obligation to keep up on what's new and exciting in the world of sci-fi. I don't want anyone, anywhere, to release a new movie, book or TV show without you finding out about it right away, so stay glued to the Net (have all your food sent in).

Web:
 http://www.locusmag.com/
 http://www.sfwa.org/news/

Usenet:
 rec.arts.sf.announce

Science Fiction Talk and General Discussion

Science fiction isn't a hobby: it's a lifestyle. Are you one of those people whose walls and cabinets (and floors) are covered with sci-fi books, magazines, tapes and memorabilia? Scoot all of it out of the way so you can get to the computer and find your sci-fi soulmates. Anything science fiction goes.

Usenet:
 rec.arts.sf.misc
 rec.arts.sf.reviews

SciFaiku

What do you get when you mix science fiction and haiku poetry? You get SciFaiku, a form of haiku poetry about science fiction topics. Read the rules describing this form of poetry and browse the archive of a nice selection of SciFaiku.

Web:
 http://www.scifaiku.com/

Sci-Fi Zines

If you enjoy reading science fiction, spend some time with these zines (small, privately created magazines) and you won't regret it. What could be better than to dive into a world of sci-fi stories, films and art, and stay there until it's time for dinner?

Web:
 http://www.darkmoonrising.com/
 http://www.dcs.gla.ac.uk/SF-Archives/Ansible/
 http://www.etext.org/zines/planet/
 http://www.users.zetnet.co.uk/iplus/

Star Trek

Star Trek is a science-fiction culture based on a variety of interrelated TV series and movies. Star Trek has millions of fans around the world and has been extended into many areas of creative endeavor, including books, toys, games, animation, fan fiction (people on the Internet writing original stories), language, clothes, memorabilia, and conventions. Star Trek began as a TV series created by Gene Roddenberry and first aired in 1966. This series—now called Star Trek: The Original Series (TOS)—had 79 episodes and lasted three years. The shows, taking place in the distant future, chronicle the voyages of the Starship Enterprise as it explores the galaxy on behalf of the United Federation of Planets. The crew of the Enterprise is on a five-year mission "to explore strange new worlds, to seek out new life and new civilizations—to boldly go where no man has gone before." The main characters are Captain James T. Kirk, science officer Spock, doctor Leonard McCoy, communications officer Nyota Uhura, navigator Pavel Chekov, helm officer Hikaru Sulu, chief engineer Montgomery Scott, and nurse Christine Chapel. Although the series didn't last long, it became extremely popular in reruns, inspiring generations of fans and making Star Trek a permanent part of our science fiction culture. In 1979, the first Star Trek movie was released, starring the same actors as TOS. In all, there have been nine movies and four TV series. The newer series are Star Trek: The Next Generation (1987-1994), which had a new cast and continued the original storyline 80 years later; Star Trek: Deep Space Nine (1993-1999), which related the adventures of Starfleet officers working on an alien space station at the borders of Federation space; Star Trek: Voyager (1995-2002), the story of a Starfleet crew and a Maquis (rebel) crew working together in an unexplored part of the galaxy, 70,000 light years from home; and Enterprise (started in 2001), which takes place 100 years before TOS, when interstellar travel is just starting. For all its impossible and hokey situations, Star Trek shows us a hopeful future where mankind has advanced, not only technologically, but socially. So whether you are a Trekkie (fan) or a Trekker (fanatic), the time you spend with Star Trek will make you a better, finer person. And you can take comfort in knowing that the Great Bird of the Galaxy is watching over you.

Web:
http://www.scifi.com/startrek/
http://www.syfyportal.com/
http://www.theborgcollective.com/
http://www.tos.net/indexnew.html
http://www.treknews.com/
http://www.trekweb.com/

Usenet:
alt.binaries.startrek
alt.fan.q
alt.fan.surak
alt.games.rpg.startrek.quadrant
alt.games.shared-reality.fed-frontier
alt.holoworld.rpg.startrek
alt.org.starfleet
alt.starfleet
alt.starfleet.primedirective.rpg
alt.starfleet.rpg
alt.starfleet.rpg.german
alt.startrek
alt.startrek.bajoran
alt.startrek.books
alt.startrek.borg
alt.startrek.cardassian
alt.startrek.creative
alt.startrek.creative.all-ages
alt.startrek.role-playing
alt.startrek.romulan
alt.startrek.trill
alt.startrek.uss-amagosa
alt.startrek.vs
alt.startrek.vs.babylon5
alt.startrek.vulcan
alt.tv.star-trek
alt.tv.star-trek.ds9
alt.tv.star-trek.next-gen
alt.tv.star-trek.tos
alt.tv.star-trek.voyager
rec.arts.startrek
rec.arts.startrek.current
rec.arts.startrek.fandom
rec.arts.startrek.info
rec.arts.startrek.misc
rec.arts.startrek.reviews
rec.arts.startrek.tech
rec.games.trading-cards.startrek

Listserv Mailing List:
List Name: **odn**
Subscribe to: **listserv@listserv.aol.com**

IRC:
#startrek (DALnet, EFnet, Undernet)
#voyager (Undernet)

Star Wars

I still remember seeing Star Wars for the first time. It was like nothing I had ever seen, and it blew me away. In fact, I saw the movie five times before it even became popular. Although Star Wars was not much more than a Western set in space, the originality of the special effects was astonishing. The original movie was simply called "Star Wars" but, since then, the creator, George Lucas, has developed his ideas into a series of six "Episodes", of which five have been made. They are, in "historical" order: The Phantom Menace (1999), Attack of the Clones (2002), A New Hope (1977), The Empire Strikes Back (1980) and Return of the Jedi (1983).

Web:
  http://www.faqs.org/faqs/starwars/
  http://www.naboonline.com/
  http://www.starwars.com/
  http://www.starwarsfanbase.com/index.php
  http://www.theforce.net/
  http://www.xwing.net/links/

Usenet:
  rec.arts.sf.starwars
  rec.arts.sf.starwars.collecting
  rec.arts.sf.starwars.games
  rec.arts.sf.starwars.misc

Majordomo Mailing List:
  List Name: starwars
  Subscribe to: majordomo@logrus.org

IRC:
  #starwars (DALnet, EFnet)

Time Travel

Is time travel possible? Unfortunately, no, but that hasn't stopped us from writing and speculating about it. One of my favorite science fiction novels of all time is Isaac Asimov's "The End of Eternity", which explores a world in which it is possible for people to travel from one time to another. I myself wrote several time-travel stories, which I published in the 1995-2000 editions of this book. (They are all reprinted in the 2000, "Millennium", edition if you want to read them.) Even if time travel isn't possible, is it possible to discuss the subject seriously from a scientific point of view? You betcha.

Web:
  http://www.crystalinks.com/timetravel.html
  http://www.nobeliefs.com/death&timetravel.htm

Usenet:
  alt.sci.time-travel

Time Travel

You can find out a lot about a person's character by thinking about his answer to the following question:

Suppose you have a way to go back in time and you can visit yourself at any age you want. You are allowed to talk to yourself for only a moment, and you can say only one sentence.

What would you say?

Tolkien, J.R.R.

John Ronald Reuel Tolkien (1892-1973) was a South African-born English novelist and scholar. Tolkien, a professor of Anglo-Saxon and English literature at Oxford University, published a children's book called The Hobbit in 1937, in which he created a fantasy world populated by cute pseudo-human creatures. Later (1954-1956) Tolkien published a trilogy, The Lord of the Rings, in which he enlarged this world into a more fully populated Middle Earth, complete with good guys, bad guys, war, adventure, intrigue and masterly storytelling. The trilogy centers around the activities of a hobbit named Frodo, who sets off on a heroic quest of epic proportions, pitting Good against Evil in a series of adventures that surely must rank among the greatest inventions of English literature. (We are talking major Allegory City here.) I know what you are wondering: after all those adventures, was Frodo successful? Well, just in case you haven't read all 1,518 pages, I don't want to ruin the ending for you. Let's just say the Force was with him.

Web:
  http://gollum.usask.ca/tolkien/
  http://www.faqs.org/faqs/tolkien/faq/
  http://www.planet-tolkien.com/
  http://www.tolkiensociety.org/

Usenet:
  alt.fan.tolkien
  rec.arts.books.tolkien

IRC:
  #tolkien (Undernet)

X-Files

The X-Files is a spooky, cult television show featuring two FBI agents, one of whom (Mulder, a man) believes anything, no matter how weird. The other agent (Scully, a woman) is a scientist and a skeptic. Mulder and Scully spend their time investigating the "paranormal", with a special emphasis on UFOs and conspiracies. The X-Files is popular because the characters, the relationships and the circumstances are so engaging. So much so, that for people who are willing to suspend their scientific disbelief, what happens on the show is almost believable. If you're an X-Phile, you'll love the idea of spending all your spare time reliving the episodes and tracking down elusive facts on the Net. (For example, during the filming of the show, the Cigarette Smoking Man is actually smoking herbal cigarettes.) If you are creative, there is a mailing list and Usenet group just for X-Files fan fiction (original stories based on the X-Files characters).

Web:
   http://www.shippersx.com/WhatsNew.html
   http://www.thexfiles.com/
   http://xfiles.wearehere.net/xfiles.htm

Usenet:
   alt.tv.x-files
   alt.tv.x-files.analysis
   alt.tv.x-files.creative
   alt.tv.x-files.x-ville

Majordomo Mailing List:
   List Name: x-files
   Subscribe to: majordomo@lists.x-philes.com

Majordomo Mailing List:
   List Name: x-files-fanfic
   Subscribe to: majordomo@lists.x-philes.com

> **Cupboards work best
> when they are at least
> one-third empty.**

SECRET STUFF

Anarchist Cookbook

Oh my! The Anarchist Cookbook! This is one of the examples that bone-headed people always seem to cite in defense of the idea that we need to censor the Internet to save the human race. And what's in the Anarchist Cookbook? Well, lockpicking, bomb making, drug recipes, getting revenge, fraud, and more. However, I have to warn you, the real Anarchist Cookbook is copyrighted and you won't find it on the Net—these are imitations. Warning #2: These imitations have factual errors. Warning #3: Don't try to do any of this stuff. It's only for reading.

Web:
   http://burn.ucsd.edu/~mai/TEXT/
     aol_cookbook_faq.html
   http://www.flashback.se/archive/cookbook_faq.html

Backward Masking

Backward masking refers to hiding messages on recorded music by inserting sounds that are meaningful when played backward. Some people feel that cunning malevolent fiends insert such messages into music in order to subliminally influence unsuspecting listeners. This idea first surfaced some years ago when fanatical Bible-thumpers were convinced that various popular rock groups were putting reversed Satanic messages in selected recordings. Since then, a number of musicians and bands have embedded such messages on purpose (for the novelty, I suppose). Here are some Web pages that offer audio snippets of actual recordings played backward. (Between us, the possibility that anyone could be affected by listening to backward sounds is about as likely as your being affected by the brain emanations of aliens from a nearby star system.)

Web:
   http://abbeyrd.best.vwh.net/backward.htm
   http://www.triplo.com/ev/reversal/
   http://www.truemetal.org/ironmaiden/
     m_backward.html

Cellular Phone Hacking

If you want to be able to hack cellular phones (or even just talk about it to impress people at parties), you need to know the basics and then some. Here are some Web sites with a collection of information that will set you on the road to getting inside those funny little boxes that cost so much.

Web:
> http://www.cis.columbia.edu/homepages/gonzalu/
> radio/cellmod.html
> http://www.crossbar.demon.co.uk/cell.htm
> http://www.cultdeadcow.com/cDc_files/
> cDc-0241.txt
> http://www.textfiles.com/phreak/CELLULAR/
> http://www.totse.com/en/phreak/cellular_phones/
> cellfile.html

Disney Secrets

Disney theme parks are very controlled. Try causing even a slight amount of trouble and see how fast the security people (materializing out of nowhere) will give you the bum's rush. When you visit a Disney park, everything you see and everything the employees do is planned carefully. For instance, you are never more than 25 paces away from a garbage can. Disney management goes to a great deal of trouble to sustain the illusion of "the happiest place on Earth". People who work at Disney theme parks are called "cast members". (Repeat this often enough and even the employees think it's normal.) That is why I love to read about Disney secrets. None of these secrets is all that important. Nevertheless, they are intriguing because you just know that the pleasant folks who control the world of Disney would very much prefer that you didn't know anything about their behind-the-scenes management.

Web:
> http://www.evernotice.com/parks.html
> http://www.hiddenmickeys.org/

Usenet:
> alt.disney.secrets

Easter Eggs

An Easter egg is a secret feature hidden inside a computer program. Many programs have Easter eggs—usually hidden there by the programmers—that you can invoke if you know the secret key combinations. For example, if you use Netscape, try pressing Ctrl-Alt-F and see what happens. Want to see more? Here is a large collection of Easter eggs hidden in many different programs. However, the fun doesn't stop here. There are also Easter Eggs in other creative works, such as movies and TV shows. Two examples: In the film Close Encounters of the Third Kind, when Richard Dreyfuss is looking into the crater and a large spaceship flies over, underneath the spaceship is an upside-down R2-D2 (from Star Wars). In the film Raiders of the Lost Ark, look at the scene where Indiana Jones falls into the snake pit. You'll see an image of C-3PO and R2-D2 in the hieroglyphics. (And some people say there's no God.)

Web:
> http://www.activewin.com/tips/eeggs/
> http://www.eggheaven2000.com/
> http://www.eggscentral.com/
> http://www.mysteries-megasite.com/eastereggs/
> frame.html
> http://www.wordinfo.com/how_to/eeggs.htm

Easter Eggs

One of the most important legends of Western culture is the story of how Jesus was put to death by the Romans and how, a short time later, was resurrected, symbolizing God's devotion to mankind and showing us that the devout and the faithful will themselves be resurrected at the appropriate time.

Today, these occurrences are remembered during the various Easter observances around the world, one of the most notable being the insertion of secret actions within important computer programs. These so-called "Easter eggs" are found in a number of PC and Macintosh programs.

So, if you are feeling especially devotional one day, take a moment to find out about these Easter eggs and demonstrate them for yourself. After all, it is too easy to concentrate exclusively on work and other secular matters, and a few moments spent in a spiritual activity would be good for just about anybody.

Hacker/2600 Magazine

At one time, it was possible to make free long distance calls by using a homemade device called a blue box. A person using a blue box could fool the telephone switching system into making long distance calls without billing for them. The blue box worked by mimicking sounds that the phone system used for signaling, in particular, a 2600 hertz tone. This number was well-known among phone hackers, and so when it came time to choose a name for a general hackers magazine, it was called "2600". 2600 covers subjects such as phreaking, hacking, cellular phones, scanners, hardware, credit cards, and much more secret stuff than you are ever supposed to know.

Web:

  http://www.2600.com/
  http://www.faqs.org/faqs/alt-2600/

Usenet:

  alt.2600
  alt.2600.cardz
  alt.2600.codez
  alt.2600.moderated
  alt.2600.phreakz
  alt.2600.warez

Lockpicking

I bet you would just love to be able to get into places where you are not supposed to be. Of course, as one of my readers you are scrupulously honest with a well-developed sense of ethics. However, wouldn't it be fun to know how to pick locks, just in case you have to someday? (For example, what would happen if the Queen of England came to visit and accidentally locked herself in the pantry?) Start with these guides to lockpicking. With a little knowledge—and a lot of practice—you will soon be a useful, important member of society, respected by all and worshipped by every male teenager you meet.

Web:

  http://www.flashback.se/archive/mit-guide.html
  http://www.lysator.liu.se/mit-guide/mit-guide.html
  http://www.users.skynet.be/sky68227/dimitri/
    lockpick/lockpicking.html
  http://www.wilton.force9.co.uk/lock/

Magic Secrets Talk and General Discussion

Want to find out how magic tricks really work? This is the Usenet group where people discuss how magicians make sure that the hand is always quicker than the eye. For example, how does David Copperfield take rings from three people in the audience (seemingly at random), link the rings together, show everyone that the rings are really linked, and then separate them so as to give the rings back to the people? (Answer: One of the rings is a fake. It has a piece cut out of it, allowing it to be linked to two other completely whole rings. Copperfield makes sure that the audience never sees the cut-out part. When he borrows the three rings, he palms one and substitutes the special one he has prepared ahead of time.)

Usenet:

  alt.magic.secrets

Pay-TV Decoders

What would you do if someone gave you instructions for building a pay-TV decoder from simple parts you could buy at any electronic supply store? Don't tell me, I don't want to know. I think television is bad for you.

Web:

  http://www.funet.fi/index/esi/tv_crypt_faq.html

Usenet:

  alt.satellite.tv.crypt

Phreaking

Want to talk about phone phreaking: telephones, exchanges, toll fraud, kodez, signaling, and so on? Walk gently into that good night and talk to the people who love to phreak. (Just don't tell Mother and Father what you're doing.)

Web:
http://www.navyrelics.com/tribute/
   phonephreaking.html
http://www.nettwerked.net/altphreakingfaq/
http://www.phonelosers.org/
http://www.phonerangers.org/
http://www.webcrunchers.com/crunch/play/history/

IRC:
#hackphreak (EFnet, Undernet)

Police Codes

The police use a lot of different codes when they talk to one another over the radio. If you have the right type of receiver, you can listen too. But how do you know what the codes mean? Here is the info you need to keep up on what the serve-and-protect guys are doing.

Web:
http://faculty.ncwc.edu/toconnor/polcodes.htm
http://sinai.critter.net/mutant/dawn/slang.htm

Secret Societies

It's hard to find good material on secret societies (are you surprised?), so when you read articles that talk about organizations that conspire in secret, you have to judge for yourself how much you think is true. However, if you like finding out things that you are not supposed to know, it's always fun to read something about a group of people who go to a great deal of trouble to hide their traditions and aims. Visit this Web site to read about Freemasonry, the Knights Templar, the O.T.O., the Rosicrucian Order, Thelema, and more.

Web:
http://www.kassiber.de/cults.htm

Social Security Number Location Finder

Stop me if you've heard this before, but you can tell where a U.S. Social Security number (SSN) was issued by looking at the first three digits. For example, if your SSN starts with 573, it was issued in California. You can also figure out a few more things, and here are Web sites to show you how. Most of the time, a SSN number is issued in the state where the person was born, so here is a trick that never fails that you can play on people. Find an American and tell him you are going to guess the state in which he was born. Then say some magic words to distract him, and, at the same time, use ESP to find out his Social Security number. Then, rush to your computer, connect to these Web sites and find out where his SSN was issued. Then rush back and tell the person where he was born. People are so amazed. (Hint: As with all magic tricks, don't tell the audience how it was done.)

Web:
http://www.iinfosearch.com/ssninfo.htm
http://www.ssa.gov/foia/stateweb.html

Super Secret Web Site

I have found a Web site that is so totally cool, so awesome, that I know you will be completely blown away. However, the site is a big secret and I can't print the address in this book, so you will have to discover the Web site for yourself. (I have left a space for you to write in the address once you find it.)

Web:
http://

Super Secret Web Site

Yes, the Super Secret Web Site really does exist, and if you haven't yet found it, you're not as cool as you could be.

A B C D E F G H I J K L M N O P Q R **S** T U V W X Y Z

SENIORS

Elder Abuse

Most of the time, elder abuse is caused by someone who knows the older person: a husband or wife, a family member, a caregiver, or a staff member at a nursing home. We tend to think of abuse as being physical, such as someone pushing or hitting an older person. However, elder abuse can take place in other ways. For example, someone can be abused emotionally, when another person yells at them or threatens them. There is also financial abuse, when a senior is cheated out of money or other belongings, or has something stolen from them. If you think that you, or someone you know, is being abused, please take a moment to check these resources to get the help you need.

Web:

    http://www.aarp.org/confacts/health/
        avoidabuse.html
    http://www.anursinghomeabuseattorneyforyou.com/
    http://www.apa.org/pi/aging/eldabuse.html
    http://www.elderabusecenter.org/
    http://www.memberofthefamily.net/
    http://www.naela.org/public/
    http://www.try-nova.org/Victims/elderly_abuse.html
    http://www.webster.edu/~woolflm/abuse.html

Fitness for Seniors

Perhaps the best thing you can do for yourself (at any age) is to stay fit. If you are a senior, regular exercise of some type can make a huge difference in your life. The Usenet discussion group is a good place to talk to other people about fitness topics. The Web sites have lots of exercise tips, including suggestions for staying fit over fifty.

Web:

    http://www.aoa.dhhs.gov/aoa/pages/agepages/
        exercise.html
    http://www.seniorfitness.net/sfafit.htm
    http://www.seniorjournal.com/fitness.htm

Usenet:

    soc.senior.health+fitness

Grandparents

Without a doubt, grandparents are the most wonderful people in the world. When I was growing up, I had all my grandparents. We all lived in the same city, and I used to see them a lot. In high school, I would sometimes visit my grandmother for lunch. On Saturday nights, my brother and sister and I would visit her and my grandfather for dinner. (And then, because I was the oldest, I got to stay overnight.) On Friday nights, we would visit the other grandparents for dinner, where I would often see my cousins. I hope there are families like that around today, but what with people moving around so much and getting divorced, a close child/grandparent relationship just doesn't seem to be as common as it used to be. If you are a grandparent, never forget for a minute how important you are to the little ones, and, no matter what happens, you will be alive in their memories for the rest of their lives. I know that my grandparents are.

Web:

    http://www.cyberparent.com/gran/
    http://www.grandparenting.org/
    http://www.grandsplace.com/
    http://www.igrandparents.com/

Housing for Seniors

As you get older, your housing needs will change. If you travel a lot, you may want information about RVs and retirement resorts. If you want to scale down from the responsibilities of maintaining a house, you may want to live in a retirement community. And if you need assistance, you will have to find out about at-home senior care, assisted living or nursing homes, whichever is appropriate. Here are some resources that can help you with all of these topics. Remember, though, wherever you choose to live, don't forget to check your email.

Web:

    http://www.retirenet.com/
    http://www.seniorresource.com/house.htm
    http://www.seniorsites.com/
    http://www.springstreet.com/seniors/

Senior Magazines

Here are some online magazines specially designed for people of retirement age. If you have more time in your life for leisure, hobbies and family, you'll enjoy looking at these Web sites where you will find articles on travel, relationships, grandparenting, health, finance, cooking, books and culture.

Web:
http://www.grandtimes.com/
http://www.matureconnections.com/
http://www.seniorjournal.com/
http://www.suddenlysenior.com/
http://www.theseniortimes.com/
http://www.wwseniors.com/

Senior Organizations

These are the official Web sites of the American Association of Retired Persons (AARP) and the Canadian Association of Retired Persons (CARP). Both are nonprofit organizations dedicated to helping people over the age of 50. (The name "Retired Persons" is a misnomer, as you don't have to be retired to join.) You'll find a lot of useful information about retirement, housing, health, money, volunteer programs, and more.

Web:
http://www.50plus.com/
http://www.aarp.org/

Senior Resources

If you are a senior (which means anyone old enough to remember when tattoos were not considered polite forms of self-expression), I want you to connect to the Net. As soon as you do, take a look at these resources. You'll find a lot to read and a lot to do, as well as many new places to explore.

Web:
http://www.benefitscheckup.org/
http://www.iog.wayne.edu/geroweb.html
http://www.ncoa.org/
http://www.seniorssearch.com/
http://www.writeseniors.com/

Senior Talk and General Discussion

Many people spend hours on the Net talking to people. After awhile, you will find yourself with a whole collection of Internet friends with whom you will share many pleasant hours. These Web sites have chat rooms (talk facilities) that you visit and meet people whenever you want. If you are new to talking on the Net, I have a few hints. First, do not give out your real name, address and phone number. If you get to know someone well, you may wish to contact them away from the Net, but please understand that, on the Internet, it is perfectly acceptable to use a nickname to protect your privacy. Second, there are a lot of scam artists around, especially on the Internet. Never give money to anyone you meet on the Net. Finally, people are not always accurate in how they describe themselves—perhaps this is human nature—so please be careful. When people on the Net talk about themselves, take it all with a grain of salt substitute.

Web:
http://www.overfifties.com/
http://www.seniorsite.com/chatroom/
http://www.snowcrest.net/writers/main.html
http://www.writeseniors.com/chat/

Usenet:
soc.retirement

Travel for Seniors

Some people are happy just sitting home, doing whatever it is they like to do. Other people like to get out and see the world. If you are a travel person, here are some resources to help you find senior discounts and programs, as well as valuable travel tips.

Web:
http://www.elderhostel.org/
http://www.southwest.com/travel_center/seniors.html
http://www.tripspot.com/seniortravelfeature.htm

SEX AND SEXUALITY

Abstinence

There are a number of reasons why you might choose to abstain from sex: to avoid pregnancy out of wedlock, to avoid sexually transmitted diseases, to live with circumstances beyond your control (such as you can't find anyone desirable to have sex with you), to honor religious or philosophical convictions, to deal with a strong fear, or as a temporary break from an otherwise active life. Since sex is fueled by a strong biological drive, abstinence is not always easy. Thoughtful advice and practical information can help a lot.

Web:

  http://www.abstinence.net/
  http://www.glandscape.com/celibate.html
  http://www.plannedparenthood.org/bc/
    abstinence.html
  http://www.w-cpc.org/sexuality/teensex.html
  http://www.wvdhhr.org/mcfh/icah/abstinence/

Aphrodisiacs

An aphrodisiac is a substance, such as a food, drug or fragrance, that stimulates sexual desire. As long as there have been people, people have been looking for aphrodisiacs and there have been precious few. However, under certain circumstances the right accessories can change a possible situation into a real experience. (Remember in physics class, when a teacher used to go on and on about the difference between potential and kinetic energy? Now is your chance to put all that theory into action.) Turn to the Net and there's a good chance that you can find the information you need. And if you can't, you can always try my favorite trick, putting a copy of *Harley Hahn's Student Guide to Unix* under the pillow.

Web:

  http://www.all-naturalsex.net/romance/aphrodr.htm
  http://www.tantra-sex.com/aphrodisiacs.html

First Times

Do you remember the first time you had sex? Would it make a good story? Well, people on the Net love to share and some of them have written about their first time. There are good stories and bad stories, and they do tend to be a bit explicit. Aren't you curious? What are you waiting for?

Web:

  http://www.myfirsttime.com/

Gay, Lesbian, Bisexual Resources

The world is changing, and it's hard to stay current. If you are gay or if you have loved ones who are gay, you'll find these resources particularly handy: news, personal ads, information, Internet resources, magazines, mailing lists, and more.

Web:

  http://www.bisexual.org/
  http://www.bitheway.org/Site.htm
  http://www.biwebsites.com/
  http://www.datalounge.com/
  http://www.gay-love.net/gay_resources.html
  http://www.gayzoo.com/
  http://www.lesbian.com/
  http://www.lesbian.org/lesbian-lists/

Listserv Mailing List:

  List Name: bithry-l
  Subscribe to: listserv@listserv.brown.edu

IRC:

  #gay (Undernet)
  #gaychristians (EFnet)
  #lesbians (DALnet, Undernet)

Human Sexuality

Sexuality means a lot more than sex. Sexuality affects how we act, how we dress, how we form relationships, how we relate to our society as a whole, and how we think about ourselves. The study of human sexuality is a broad one and in particular, it tends to blur when we discuss gender and its importance. Here is a great deal of useful information in this area.

Web:

  http://www.sexuality.org/

Purity Tests

Purity tests have long been a staple of Usenet humor groups. These tests consist of many sexually oriented questions designed to help you find out just how "pure" you are.

Web:
  http://www.armory.com/tests/purity.html
  http://www.circus.com/~omni/purity.html

Safe Sex

"Safe sex" refers to being able to carry out sexual activities in a way that is pleasurable, without exposing yourself to the risk of disease or unwanted pregnancy. Strictly speaking, there is no way to guarantee that any sexual activity will be 100 percent risk-free. For this reason, you will sometimes see the expression "safer sex", which is considered to be the more politically correct term. The basic idea of safe sex is to acquire good habits *before* you get too far into your sexual career. Learn the dos and don'ts, the ins and outs, and all the in-betweens of safe sexual practices. And if you still want to take risks, you can always jump out of an airplane.

Web:
  http://wso.williams.edu/orgs/peerh/sex/safesex/
  http://www.condomania.com/educate/manual/
    manual.html
  http://www.plannedparenthood.org/sti/sex-safer.htm
  http://www.sexuality.org/safesex.html

Sensual Massage

While I was working on this section of the book, I decided to run an experiment.

I got a copy of the Hollywood telephone book and called up 10 beautiful starlets. I then invited them over to my house.

I let each one take 15 minutes to give me the best massage she could. When they were finished, I awarded an autographed copy of this book to the starlet with the best technique.

Everything worked out fine, but now that I need to get back to work, I have a problem: How do I get the 10 starlets to leave? (At the very least, I hope one of them knows how to cook.)

Sensual Massage

Massage is a romantic and sensual way to relax. This guide will help you understand how to select sensual oils, create just the right atmosphere, and know what to do and how to do it with your partner. (Once you get going, though, you're on your own.)

Web:
  http://www.romanticinspirations.com/html/
    massage_tips.html
  http://www.sexuality.org/erotmass.html
  http://www.suite101.com/article.cfm/
    romance_retired/2342

Sex Glossary

Don't be one of those people who gets his refractory period mixed up with his resolution phase. If you wanna be a sex expert—or even a knowledgeable amateur—you need to be able to walk the walk and talk the talk. And that means you'll need to understand a whole bunch of seventy-five cent words. Here's the list. Go to it.

Web:
  http://www.mypleasure.com/education/glossary/
  http://www.sexology.org/glossary.htm

Sex Laws

Have you noticed that almost everybody gets weird when you start talking seriously about sex in public? Sex is such a powerful force in our lives that people who cannot relate to it effectively are bound to repress the energy and have it pop up in strange ways. No doubt this has a lot to do with why there are so many strange laws about sex. Some of them are funny, some of them are terrible (such as the sex laws followed by certain religions), and all of them make for interesting reading.

Web:
  http://www.lib.uchicago.edu/~llou/sexlaw.html

Sex Reference Guide

Here is an informative Web site that has information on just about every sex topic you can imagine (and even a few you can't imagine). The answers speak frankly and are easy to understand. If you have a sex-related question and you don't know anyone to ask (or you are too shy), this is a great place to get the information you need.

Web:
  http://www.sexualitydata.com/

Sex Talk and General Discussion

What's the weirdest place you have ever had sex? Care to share? Even if you don't, there are hoards of people who do. Not only will they tell you about the weirdest place, but also about the weirdest accident they've ever had during sex, how many times they've had sex, and what was going on around them before, during and after. Be informed as you are entertained. Read about birth control, STDs (sexually transmitted diseases), virginity (or lack of), and other topics of a sexual nature.

Listserv Mailing List:

List Name: sex-l
Subscribe to: listserv@listserv.tamu.edu

Sex Tips

If you are going to do *it*, you might as well do it well. The heading of sex covers a lot of activities and a lot of variations and—aside from people who write Internet books—just about everyone could use a few tips now and again. Who are you going to ask when you want some hints about how to put on a condom with your mouth? Your mother? Never mind, the Net is always there, and it won't ask embarrassing questions.

Web:

http://www.carnal.net/
http://www.tagmag.com/features/sex_tips.html

Sex Trivia

Sex can mean so many different things, depending on your point of view, situation in life, and personal inclinations. However, one thing sex is *not* is trivial. Thus, even sexual trivia has a compelling attraction. Do you know, for example, how big are the largest breasts ever measured? What was the largest number of orgasms ever experienced in one hour by a woman? By a man? How long was the longest female orgasm measured by Masters and Johnson? And was it true that Mae West (1892-1980) once made love with the same partner for 15 consecutive hours? All these fascinating bits of sexual trivia—and much more—can soon be yours. (By the way, the answers to these questions are: 44 pounds (20 kg) each [look at the picture], 134, 16, 43 seconds, and yes, according to her autobiography.)

Web:

http://www.auschron.com/mrpants/sex.html
http://www.funtrivia.com/Humans/Sex.html
http://www.sexualrecords.com/

Tantra and the Kama Sutra

The Kama Sutra is perhaps the most well-known erotic self-help book. See what the ancient commentators have to teach you about mankind's oldest pastime. These teachings describe a wide variety of sex positions and techniques, including the Jewel Case, Love's Noose and the Clinging Creeper.

Web:

http://www.bibliomania.com/2/1/76/123/
http://www.sacred-texts.com/sex/
http://www.tantra.org/

Usenet:

alt.magick.tantra

Urban Sex Legends

You know that Batman story you love to tell your friends? Well, it's not true. Really, it's not. In fact, there are a lot of weird sex legends that are not true. You can read all about them at these urban sex legends sites. It's full of amusing stories and urban legends with a sexual twist.

Web:

http://www.therubbertree.com/urbanlegends.htm
http://www.urbanlegends.com/sex/

SHOPPING

Auctions: Online

I have a friend named David Garstang who collects ancient coins. However, David is also a good husband and father who likes to stay home with his wife and two daughters. David lives in Southern California, and, as such, he would normally buy his ancient coins in the usual places: at the beach during a topless volleyball tournament, in a bar on wet T-shirt night, or while sailing a yacht off the Mexican coast. David, of course, being a good husband and father, cares nothing for such pastimes. Instead, he buys his ancient coins through online auctions over the Net. These auctions offer a wide variety of merchandise, bought and sold by people all over the world. No matter what your interests, there is probably someone selling what you want right now (especially if you are a collector). All the buying, selling and bidding is done via the Web and email, so you never have to leave your home. This works well for David, as he can stay home on Saturday nights, rather than wasting his time running around Southern California. (Did I mention that David is a good husband and father?)

Web:

http://www.auctioninsights.com/
http://www.auctions.amazon.com/
http://www.auctions.cnet.com/
http://www.auctions.msn.com/
http://www.auctions.yahoo.com/
http://www.auctionus.com/
http://www.ebay.com/
http://www.internetauctionlist.com/

Here is a little-known fact: George and Laura Bush met on Usenet (alt.personals).

Auctions: Traditional

Do you love the heart-pounding thrill of going to an auction, when it gets down to *mano a mano* bidding and you don't know how it's going to turn out? Going to an auction provides a raw, mercantile experience as close to pure buying and selling as you can get. If you have a day off, check with the Net and find out what auctions are scheduled for your area. If you are planning a trip to a new place, why not visit an auction while you are there? These auction-related resources will help you find an auction in the U.S. as well as many countries around the world.

Web:

http://www.auctionguide.com/
http://www.auctiontalk.com/

Auction Acumen

If you're like me, you never pass through Overland Park, Kansas, without taking a few hours to visit the Auctioneer Hall of History.

However, being steeped in the lore of auctioneering won't help you when you are immersed in the hot and heavy, fast-moving environment of an actual auction.

After all, at an average household estate auction, an auctioneer will sell an average of 60 items per hour. And at a wholesale automobile auction, you may see as many as 150 cars sold per hour. When the auctioneer talks so fast, how can you possibly make any sense out of what he is saying?

"l00 dollar bid, now 105, now 105, will ya give me 110? 110 dollar bid, now 120, now 120, will ya give me 120? 120 dollar bid, now 125, now 125, will ya give me 125?"

Here is a hint: ignore everything but the numbers. All the other words are used as fillers. Listen only to the numbers, and you will be surprised how easy it is to follow along like a pro.

Auctions: Weirdness

Have you ever wondered just how weird online auctions can get? Wonder no more. Check out some of the strange things that people are selling, and it won't be long before your feelings about the human race change significantly.

Web:

http://www.disturbingauctions.com/daily/
http://www.whowouldbuythat.com/

Buying/Selling Talk and General Discussion

Where do you go on the Net when you want to buy or sell something? Here are the main buying/selling Usenet groups, the places where it is okay to post a personal advertisement, wheel and deal till you drop. These are also where to look for a bargain. Just remember, when you are dealing with someone who you have never met, be sure to take normal precautions. (For example, if you are selling a house, don't actually send the house to the buyer until the check clears the bank.)

Usenet:
  alt.ads
  alt.ads.forsale
  alt.art.marketplace
  alt.fitness.marketplace
  alt.forsale
  alt.ham-radio.marketplace
  alt.magick.marketplace
  alt.marketplace
  alt.martial-arts.marketplace
  biz.marketplace.non-computer
  misc.forsale.computers
  misc.industry.electronics.marketplace
  rec.antiques.marketplace
  rec.aquaria.marketplace
  rec.arts.anime.marketplace
  rec.arts.books.marketplace
  rec.arts.comics.marketplace
  rec.arts.sf.marketplace
  rec.audio.marketplace
  rec.autos.marketplace
  rec.aviation.marketplace
  rec.bicycles.marketplace
  rec.boats.marketplace
  rec.crafts.marketplace
  rec.food.marketplace
  rec.games.board.marketplace
  rec.games.frp.marketplace
  rec.games.trading-cards.marketplace
  rec.games.video.marketplace
  rec.music.makers.marketplace
  rec.music.marketplace
  rec.music.marketplace.cd
  rec.music.marketplace.misc
  rec.music.marketplace.vinyl
  rec.outdoors.marketplace
  rec.photo.marketplace
  rec.skiing.marketplace
  rec.travel.marketplace
  rec.video.marketplace
  soc.genealogy.marketplace

Catalogs by Mail

Catalog and junk mail fans will have a blast at this site. You can browse reviews of newly released mail order catalogs, order catalogs online and preview catalogs.

Web:
  http://catalogsite.catalogcity.com/

CD Clubs

CD clubs have their system all set up so they can make lots of money off you. If you want a fighting chance of getting the best value for your money, you should check out this site. It has a FAQ on how to get the most out of CD clubs and information on the strategies of membership, resale value of CDs, the ins and outs of using club coupons, how to stop getting cards every month, how to return CDs you don't want, and more.

Web:
  http://www.chiprowe.com/articles/cdclubs.html
  http://www.eskimo.com/~bloo/cdfaq/toppage.htm

Classified Ads

Shopping, shopping, shopping. Do you like to shop, but don't like to get dressed to leave the house? Shop at home, by checking out the great classified ads on the Net.

Web:
  http://www.classifieds.yahoo.com/
  http://www.e-class.com/
  http://www.freeclassifiedlinks.com/freesites.html

The Net has classified ads, and somewhere somebody wants to make a deal with you.

Comparison Shopping

Before you make an important purchase, it's good to compare. Well, here are some tools called shopping bots ("shopping robots") that can help compare and compare and compare. You can do side-by-side comparisons and read product reviews and articles about the products. I have a friend who successfully used one of these resources to buy a digital camera. First she found some information to read. Then she performed a search according to the specifications she wanted, which helped her narrow down the choices to the one she wanted. She now lives happily ever after, and you can too.

Web:
  http://www.dealtime.com/
  http://www.mysimon.com/
  http://www.pricegrabber.com/
  http://www.roboshopper.com/
  http://www.shopping.yahoo.com/

Coupons

Want the secret to happiness? Here it is. (1) Print your own coupons from the Net. (2) Take them to the store. (3) Live happily ever after.

Web:
  http://www.coupons.com/
  http://www.customcoupon.com/
  http://www.valupage.com/

Usenet:
  alt.coupons

Flea Markets

A flea market is an open-air marketplace in which low-cost goods are sold informally. And what could be more fun? I love walking around flea markets, and I bet you do too (and you can pick up some great bargains). Whenever the urge to bargain and buy cheap strikes without warning, here are some resources to help you find a nearby flea market.

Web:
  http://www.fleamarketguide.com/
  http://www.fleamarkets.com/
  http://www.openair.org/

Online Payment Services

An online payment service is a facility that allows you to transfer money to anyone who has an email address. Think of it as a special type of bank account that is used only on the Internet. You open the account, put money into it and then transfer money to other people. At the same time, other people can transfer money to you. You can use an online payment service to buy items at online auctions, send someone a gift (of money), or pay a debt. If you'd like to try out one of these systems, open an account, put in $100 and send it to me. I'll write back, telling you whether or not it worked.

Web:
  http://paydirect.yahoo.com/
  http://www.bidpay.com/
  http://www.billpoint.com/
  http://www.c2it.com/
  http://www.moneyzap.com/
  http://www.paypal.com/

Outlet Stores

An outlet store sells brand-name or designer merchandise from a single manufacturer. The manufacturer can use the store to sell special types of goods, for example, excess inventory that is left over at the end of a season. The idea is that, because you are buying direct from the manufacturer, you can save money. Do you really save money? Well, probably not much more than a regular discount store. When it comes to buying retail, the sad fact of life is that, no matter what anyone says, you can't cut out the middleman (and, no matter what anyone says, unless you are going to resell what you buy, you are buying retail). Still, outlet stores tend to cluster in groups—called outlet centers or outlet malls—so you can visit one location, and have the time of your life shopping for brand-name merchandise until you fulfill yourself, give up, or run out of money (whichever comes first). Ready to give it a try? These resources will help you find the outlet center of your dreams.

Web:
  http://www.outletbound.com/
  http://www.outletsonline.com/

Reverse Auctions

Do you want what you want, when you want it? You can get it. All you have to do is specify your heart's desire and then let other people make *you* offers. For example, let's say you have your heart set on a purple Hello Kitty porcelain bowl. Just register your need. If someone has one to sell you, they will contact you and offer a price. Also, if you have something to sell, check this site to see if someone wants what you have.

Web:

  http://www.fattytuna.net/

Sales

Don't you *ever* buy anything again in your life without checking the Net first. You'll find so many items on sale in your own neighborhood, you'll want to rush out immediately and start buying (or you can buy online). Try the Net first and I guarantee you will be amazed: the information, convenience and savings are incredible.

Web:

  http://www.salescircular.com/
  http://www.saleshound.com/

Shopping Malls

Do you like to hang out at the mall? Of course you do. But wouldn't you like to know what's going to be on sale before you go? Even more important, what if you go on a trip to a city you have never visited? How are you going to find out where the malls are? No problem. The Net will help you find the mall you need with only a few clicks of the mouse. As long as we have the Net, you will never be deprived.

Web:

  http://www.saleshound.com/
    realmalls_welcome3.asp

> ## Get the latest news —
> ## right now — from the Net.

Shopping Online

Do you have a strong need to find the online shop of your dreams? No problem. Moreover, once you find the shop of your dreams, you'll find helpful information, for example, which credit cards are accepted, price ranges, phone numbers, email addresses, and so on. If that's not enough, you can relax between shopping expeditions by reading articles, picking up a few tips, and talking to other online shopping buffs.

Web:

  http://www.buyersindex.com/
  http://www.eshop.msn.com/
  http://www.internetmall.com/
  http://www.shoppingspot.com/

Shopping With Children

Shopping with children can be either a delightful pastime or—how can I put it?—a "challenge". My philosophy is to use the Boy Scout technique: be prepared. Here are some tips and hints that can make the difference between having a pleasant afternoon or developing post-traumatic stress syndrome.

Web:

  http://members.aol.com/willhite/shop_k.htm
  http://www.naturalchild.com/jan_hunt/
    shopping.html
  http://www.web-access.net/~child/shopping.htm

SOFTWARE

Abandonware

A lot of good software has been abandoned over the years, perhaps because a company went out of business, or a programmer decided to stop supporting one of his creations. Many of these programs, called abandonware, are used by people around the world, some of whom spend time enhancing the programs and fixing bugs. There are a lot of treasures here: abandoned, but not forgotten. I use abandonware myself for spreadsheet work: Framework IV, an old program that hasn't been sold for years.

Web:
  http://abandonware.mivox.com/
  http://www.abandonwarering.com/
  http://www.freeoldies.com/
  http://www.gamelibrary.org/html/eng/main.php
  http://www.oldversion.com/
  http://www.tuol.org/
  http://zork.nl/

Usenet:
  alt.games.abandonware

Buying and Selling Software on the Internet

Here are the Usenet newsgroups in which people advertise software for sale. If you have software you don't need anymore, maybe someone else can use it. Or if you are looking for something in particular, someone out there may be able to help. Hint: Before you do send any money or goods, make sure you take routine precautions (get a phone number, talk to the person, and so on).

Usenet:
  misc.forsale.computers.mac
  misc.forsale.computers.other.software

Need a tuffet? Visit www.little-miss-muffet.com.

CD Images

A "CD image" is a copy of the contents of a commercial CD. A lot of CD images are traded and shared on the Net, usually software and games. In order to participate in this activity, you will need the appropriate hardware and software, and you will need to know what you are doing. The hardware you need is a CD-R (CD-recordable) or CD-RW (CD-rewritable) drive. To find out about the rest, read the FAQ (frequently asked question list). Important: Do not post anything to one of the Usenet groups and do not ask for help until you have read the FAQ.

Web:
  http://www.skuz.net/macfaq/abmc/

Usenet:
  alt.binaries.cd.image
  alt.binaries.cd.image.d
  alt.binaries.cd.image.parts
  alt.binaries.cd.image.playstation
  alt.binaries.cd.image.playstation.d
  alt.binaries.cd.image.playstation.reposts
  alt.binaries.cd.image.tools.d

Cool Tool of the Day

This site picks a new "cool tool" every day. It's mostly technical stuff—Java programs, virtual reality, HTML editors, file management software, mail software, plug-ins, and so on—so if you are an Internet nerd, this is a nice place to check from time to time.

Web:
  http://www.jumbo.com/pod/pod.asp

Free-DOS Project

Free-DOS is a project devoted to developing an entire DOS-compatible operating system, written by volunteers and shared for free (including source code). In other words, Free-DOS is to DOS as Linux is to Unix. If you would like to try the current version of Free-DOS or, better yet, volunteer to work on it, start by visiting the Free-DOS Internet site.

Web:
  http://www.freedos.org/

Freeware

I love free—it's one of my favorite concepts. If you're like me, you'll love these Web sites, where you'll find oodles of real, useful programs—not demos—all for free. Hooray for freeware! That's what I say.

Web:
    http://www.5star-shareware.com/lists/
        picknmix1.html
    http://www.completelyfreesoftware.com/
        index_all.html
    http://www.freewareweb.com/
    http://www.thefreesite.com/Free_Software/
        Misc_freeware/

Jewish Software

Here is a nice collection of Jewish and Hebrew software: programs for using Hebrew on your computer, studying the Torah, Jewish calendars, Hebrew Internet software, and more (including a collection of pictures of the great rabbis). Now, if I can only find a program that can bake me a nice challah while I am waiting for a long download.

Web:
    http://www.pilotyid.com/collection.html

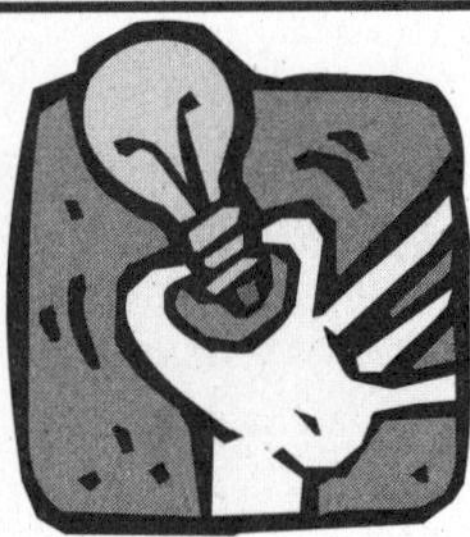

Linux

Every now and then, some person gets an idea that takes on a life of its own and changes our culture. Such a person is Linus Torvalds, the original developer of the Linux operating system (now maintained by a large group of people around the Net).

Linux is one of those wonders—a professional-quality operating system put together entirely by volunteers—that makes you realize how important the Net really is to human affairs. In these days of no real Unix standard, Linux is the closest we have to a universal Unix. The wonderful thing is that, since no one is in it for the money, Bill Gates can't buy it.

(And I am *not* kidding.)

Linux

Linux is a free Unix clone—originally developed by Linus Torvalds—maintained by a gaggle of hackers around the Internet. Linux was written completely from scratch to run on PCs using no "official" Unix code. The world of Linux is huge, and it is one of the most important (and unsung) achievements in the history of operating system development. The Usenet discussion groups are for ongoing discussion; the Web sites contain a lot of information, including source code, documentation and archives; the IRC channels are for real-time discussion.

Web:
    http://tldp.org/linuxfocus/English/
    http://www.ibiblio.org/mdw/
    http://www.linux.org/
    http://www.linuxgazette.com/
    http://www.linuxhq.com/
    http://www.linuxiso.org/
    http://www.linuxjournal.com/magazine.php
    http://www.linuxtoday.com/
    http://www.linuxworld.com/
    http://www.lwn.net/
    http://www.portalux.com/

Usenet:
    alt.uu.comp.os.linux.questions
    comp.os.linux
    comp.os.linux.admin
    comp.os.linux.advocacy
    comp.os.linux.alpha
    comp.os.linux.announce
    comp.os.linux.answers
    comp.os.linux.development
    comp.os.linux.development.apps
    comp.os.linux.development.system
    comp.os.linux.hardware
    comp.os.linux.help
    comp.os.linux.m68k
    comp.os.linux.misc
    comp.os.linux.networking
    comp.os.linux.powerpc
    comp.os.linux.questions
    comp.os.linux.setup
    comp.os.linux.x

IRC:
    #linux (EFnet, Undernet)
    #linuxhelp (DALnet)
    #linuxos (Undernet)

Macintosh Games

What's the point of having a computer without games? Join these Usenet groups to talk about all aspects of Macintosh games: which ones are best, which ones to avoid, copy protection issues, as well as hints and tricks.

Usenet:

comp.sys.mac.games
comp.sys.mac.games.action
comp.sys.mac.games.adventure
comp.sys.mac.games.announce
comp.sys.mac.games.flight-sim
comp.sys.mac.games.marketplace
comp.sys.mac.games.misc
comp.sys.mac.games.strategic

Macintosh Software Archives

There is more free Macintosh software on the Net than you can shake a mouse at. Here are some good places to start foraging for goodies. Surely, your Mac-cup will runneth over (and goodness and mercy shall follow you all the days of your life).

Web:

http://hyperarchive.lcs.mit.edu/HyperArchive.html
http://www.macintoshos.com/shareware.library/
http://www.macosarchives.com/
http://www.macoszone.com/
http://www.macshare.com/
http://www.zdnet.com/downloads/mac/
download.html

Macintosh Software Talk and General Discussion

Visit these Usenet groups for discussions of Macintosh software of all types. The **apps** group is for talk about any type of application; **comm** is for communications; **databases** is for database systems; and **system** is for Macintosh system software (such as Finder and Multifinder), as well as working with disks, dealing with viruses, and so on.

Usenet:

comp.sys.mac.apps
comp.sys.mac.comm
comp.sys.mac.databases
comp.sys.mac.system

Nonags

This is one of my favorite resources: a Web site that can point you to no-nag shareware and freeware. Every program here has been tested to make sure it doesn't nag you or enforce time limits in order to encourage you to buy. This makes evaluating software a lot more pleasant. (Obligatory reminder: if you use shareware and you find it useful, please register and send the person who wrote the program a few bucks.)

Web:

http://www.nonags.com/

Non-English Software

If you are in the software business, you know that it is important to make your products available to an international audience. Here are resources to help you understand what is involved in making your programs work in various languages.

Web:

http://www.cs.uu.nl/wais/html/na-bng/
comp.software.international.html
http://www.threeweb.ad.jp/logos/

Usenet:

comp.software.international

Open Source Software

Open source software refers to programs that can be used for free, with source code that can be viewed and modified by anyone. The Open Source movement is very successful because it resonates with the way most programmers feel about their creations: traditionally, programmers have always wanted to share their work (that is, until they go to work for companies that won't let them share). The genesis of the modern Open Source movement was the announcement of the GNU Project by Richard Stallman (1983) and the formation of the Free Software Foundation (1985).

Web:

http://www.fsf.org/
http://www.gnome.org/
http://www.openoffice.org/
http://www.opensource.org/
http://www.sourceforge.net/
http://www.theopencd.org/

Skins

A skin is a facility that lets you change the appearance of a program without changing how it works. There are lots and lots of skins available for free on the Net. So if you're the type of person who likes to control your visual environment, download a few skins and make your programs look the way you want.

Web:
  http://www.deskmod.com/
  http://www.dezina.co.uk/index.php
  http://www.free-skin.com/
  http://www.softshape.com/
  http://www.wincustomize.com/

Software Archives

If you like computers and you like trying out software for free, you will love these places: huge archives where you can find programs for every popular operating system. When I die, I am going to have someone sprinkle my ashes on these Web sites. You could spend an eternity here, just downloading and playing with software.

Web:
  http://shareware.cnet.com/
  http://www.jumbo.com/
  http://www.pcworld.com/downloads/
  http://www.radfiles.com/
  http://www.simtel.net/

Usenet:
  comp.archives
  comp.archives.admin
  comp.software.shareware.announce

You need some more software.

Don't ask me how I know, I just know.

Visit the Software Archives right away.

Software Licensing

If you are thinking about starting to license software that you have written, read up on licensing issues. This is an archive of articles about licensing software and license management.

Web:
  http://www.globetrotter.com/articles.htm

Software Testing Talk and General Discussion

Testing software is not easy. You need lots of time, effort and a good design. Then you need to know someone to pray to. The problem is that too much software is rushed without allowing for proper planning and quality control. This Usenet group is for talking about the testing of software and computer systems. If you are interested in this area of programming, you will find useful discussion and sympathetic colleagues.

Usenet:
  comp.software.testing

Software Version Trackers

One of the nice things about being on the Net is that you can download giga-oodles of free software. But once you get all that software, you have obligations. You must keep your programs up-to-date or face the wrath of the computer gods. Problem solved: all you need is a program to keep track of your other programs and the new versions. Life just doesn't get any better. (Of course, now you have the problem of keeping your version tracking program up-to-date.)

Web:
  http://www.versiontracker.com/macos/
  http://www.versiontracker.com/windows/

Spam Filtering Software

Spam is unsolicited advertising, and there is too much of it on the Net. Have you ever received spam in your mailbox? If so, take a look at these tools, designed to help you guard against unwanted electronic junk mail. There's no way to ever get the spammers to stop, so you might as well protect yourself. On the Internet, social problems are solved by software.

Web:
  http://www.emailtoday.com/emailtoday/dir/
    email_filters.htm
  http://www.jumbo.com/internet/
    sections.asp?x_sectionid=3130
  http://www.windows-shareware.com/shareware/
    internet_mailclients.html

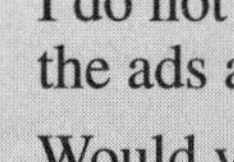

Spam Filtering Software

TCP/IP

TCP/IP is the glue that holds the Internet together. If you want to have your computer on the Internet, it will have to run some type of TCP/IP software. These Usenet groups are for discussion of the zillions and zillions of technical considerations that are unavoidably relevant. A good way to start is by reading the FAQ, which is posted regularly to the groups. Don't get discouraged: all things come to those who think.

Usenet:
  comp.protocols.tcp-ip
  comp.protocols.tcp-ip.domains
  comp.protocols.tcp-ip.ibmpc

Unix Software

Unix is an operating system (master control program) that runs on just about every type of computer in the world. There are many variations of Unix and they are used widely. For example, most of the computers that run the Internet use Unix. The most well-known type of Unix is Linux, which is available for free (as is FreeBSD and other versions of Unix). In addition to Unix itself, there is a wide variety of free Unix software available, and you can find just about any type of program you need. Hint: Unix can be difficult to learn, so don't attempt it unless you are smart and you like computers (you know if you qualify). A good way to teach yourself Unix is to read one of my Unix books, *The Unix Companion* or *Harley Hahn's Student Guide to Unix*.

Web:
  http://garbo.uwasa.fi/unix/
  http://www.acme.com/software/
  http://www.agh.cc.kcl.ac.uk/unix/
  http://www.freebsd.org/ports/
  http://www.freshmeat.net/
  http://www.stokely.com/unix.sysadm.resources/
    shareware.www.html

IRC:
  #freebsd (DALnet, EFnet, Undernet)

Warez and Cracks

These resources are for the discussion of where and how to obtain the latest cracked and pirated software, much of it available through hidden sites on the Internet. Some of the IRC channels are often by invitation only, so you will require contacts to get inside. There are lots of these channels. Start at the highest number you can find at any time and work your way down, seeing if they will let you in. (Unless you are a personal friend of God, you will never get in anything lower than **#warez5**.) The Usenet groups are open to anyone.

Web:

http://www.warezfaq.org/indexx.html

Usenet:

alt.2600.crackz
alt.binaries.warez
alt.binaries.warez.ibm-pc
alt.binaries.warez.ibm-pc.d
alt.binaries.warez.ibm-pc.old
alt.binaries.warez.mac
alt.binaries.warez.mac.req
alt.binaries.warez.macintosh
alt.warez.ibm-pc
alt.warez.ibm-pc.apps
alt.warez.ibm-pc.old

IRC:

#oldwarez (EFnet, Undernet)
#warez (DALnet, EFnet, Undernet)
#warez4free (DALnet, EFnet, Undernet)
#warez950-dcc (EFnet)

Windows CE Software Archives

I have a friend, Mart, who loves his palmtop computer. He took it on a trip to Thailand and used it to write some cool articles about his experiences. However, in order to use any computer, you need good software. Windows CE is the Microsoft operating system designed for tiny computers, such as palmtops and embedded systems, and if you have a palmtop, you will really appreciate these Web sites: You'll have many happy hours down-loading cool stuff to try out. It certainly keeps Mart happy and out of trouble. (He gets bored easily.)

Web:

http://home.cearchives.com/software.html
http://www.pocketpccity.com/software.html

Windows Networking Environment

Getting a network running is often troublesome. Have some back-up help ready in the form of Usenet groups. These groups offer a good source of information on general networking, TCP/IP, and network programming with the Microsoft Windows operating system.

Usenet:

comp.os.ms-windows.networking.misc
comp.os.ms-windows.networking.tcp-ip
comp.os.ms-windows.networking.windows
comp.os.ms-windows.programmer.networks

Windows Software

These are my picks as the best Windows software sites on the Net. They contain grotesque amounts of shareware and freeware for you to download and enjoy. Everything you could possibly want is here somewhere. When it comes to free Windows software, if you can't find it at one of these sites, it's not worth finding.

Web:

http://cws.internet.com/
http://www.sharewarejunkies.com/windows.htm
http://www.thefreesite.com/Free_Software/
http://www.tucows.com/

Usenet:

comp.archives.ms-windows
comp.archives.ms-windows.announce
comp.archives.ms-windows.discuss

Animal Sounds

Just because you don't have a pet doesn't mean you have to feel left out.

There are lots of animal sounds on the Net to make sure that you never get lonely.

SOUNDS

Animal Sounds

These sounds are a lot of fun, especially if you have children. Listen to birds, whales, dolphins, seals, ducks, cows, zebras, polar bears, tigers, turkeys, pigs, dogs, donkeys, elephants, frogs, goats, cats, and more. I have also included a site that has a list of animal noises as they are pronounced in other languages. For example, a cat noise in English is "meow", but in other languages it is "miao" (Chinese), "meu" (Catalan), "myau" (Ukrainian) and "niaou" (Greek). (I wonder what cats say in Klingon?)

Web:
  http://pages.prodigy.com/jenni35.animal.htm/
  http://www.animalden.net/sounds.htm
  http://www.georgetown.edu/cball/animals/
  http://www.ics.uci.edu/~pazzani/4H/Sounds.html

Bird Sounds

Here are some cool collections of bird sounds that are pleasant and engaging. One of my favorites is the kookaburra (a large Australian kingfisher bird that sounds like a fat lady laughing at a Marx Brothers movie). You can also listen to bluejays, chickadees, crows, cockatoos, magpies, peewees, ravens, and more. (Quick bird-sound story: When I was in medical school, I once had a couple of friends over to my apartment. As a trick, one of the friends [Paul Walton] and I put on an album of tropical bird sounds and turned the volume down very low. The other friend, whose name I won't mention [Tim Rutledge], had no idea what we had done. Now this was in a small apartment in downtown Toronto, and every few minutes Tim would sit up and say, "Do you guys hear anything?" "No, Tim," we would reply, "you must be hearing things." He never figured it out. (Today, Tim is a respected emergency room physician, a wonderful husband and the father of three sons. So, if you ever meet him, don't mention anything.)

Web:
  http://www.flmnh.ufl.edu/natsci/ornithology/
    sounds.htm
  http://www.prestogalaxy.com/html/birdssounds.html

Christmas Sounds

On the Net, Christmas lasts all year. Not only is the entire Internet suffused with the spirit of charity, love, forgiveness and sanctity, but you can listen to Christmas sounds whenever you want: enjoy dogs barking the tune "Jingle Bells", listen to sound clips from "How the Grinch Stole Christmas", laugh at parodies of traditional Christmas songs. Truly, the spirit of holiness and reverence is never out of season.

Web:
  http://www.acebiz.com/xmasmidi/xmasmidi.htm
  http://www.hometurf.com/xmas.html
  http://www.midiworld.com/cmc/xmas.html

Goldwave

Goldwave is a digital audio editor that can open, play, modify and convert just about any sound format you have heard of. You can make use of special effects such as Doppler, distortion, echo, flange and transposition. Goldwave is especially useful if you do audio work with Java applications. This is great software. Once you try it, I know you will like it (and I bet you will want to pay the registration fee). There are enough auditory bells and whistles here to equip the entire Peruvian army.

Web:
  http://www.goldwave.com/

Sound Archives

Are you bored with the sounds of silence? Well, special occasions call for special sounds. Some days you may need a little Seinfeld. Other days you may need some classic Monty Python, a friendly cartoon sound file or, perhaps, something so strange that no one will even know what it is.

Web:
  http://new.wavlist.com/
  http://www.bestwavs.com/
  http://www.dailywav.com/
  http://www.jetsound.plus.com/
  http://www.slonet.org/~rloomis/
  http://www.sounddogs.com/start.asp

Sound Tools

Why sweat the small stuff when you can let the computer do the work? Here are collections of sound tools for working with sound files under various operating systems. Grab a tool and go wild.

Web:
   http://www.5star-shareware.com/Music/
   http://www.davecentral.com/browse/31/?topic=31
   http://www.harmony-central.com/Software/
      Windows/
   http://www.sonicspot.com/audio.html

Television and Movie Sounds

Never again will you have to be nervous about being charming and witty the next time you go to a party. Just memorize some of these television and movie sounds. When people come up to talk to you, do your best to imitate what you've heard on the Net, and it won't be long before everyone will want to be your friend.

Web:
   http://www.stonewashed.net/tv.html
   http://www.tk421.net/gallery/sounds/
   http://www.wavplanet.com/

SPACE EXPLORATION

Aeronautics and Space Acronyms

If your space capsule has just landed in the ocean and mission control asks if you want an ACRV, you certainly don't want to answer incorrectly. Take a moment and look it up in this long list of space-related acronyms: a good reference to keep on hand if you are reading anything about space exploration.

Web:
   http://hastur.surly.org/tla/

> **Don't stop the music.**
> **(See "Music: Software".)**

Astrobiology

Does life exist elsewhere in the universe? The universe is a big place, and in many ways, it seems as if there ought to be life, perhaps lots of life, away from Earth. If so, what forms does life take? How does it arise and evolve? And what does this mean for us? These questions are the concern of astrobiology, the generalized study of life in the universe. In pursuit of this goal, astrobiology examines the universe, from the atomic and molecular level to the stars and the galaxies, bringing together a variety of scientific disciplines to provide new answers to very old questions.

Web:
   http://astrobiology.arc.nasa.gov/
   http://www.astrobiology.com/
   http://www.spaceref.com/directory/
      astrobiology_and_life_science/

Center for Earth and Planetary Studies

The Center for Earth and Planetary Studies is one of the research units at the National Air and Space Museum of the Smithsonian Institution. Visit its Web site and experience the excitement of outer space without having to go too far from the fridge. There are a lot of pictures from space, as well as information about many of the U.S. space missions.

Web:
   http://www.nasm.edu/ceps/

Challenger

In the history of manned space flight, there have been some terrible disasters. The most well-known was the explosion of the Challenger space shuttle 73 seconds after takeoff on January 28, 1986. For information about that ill-fated mission, you can look at NASA's Web site. There you can find the official technical information regarding that particular mission, including a movie of the takeoff and explosion.

Web:
   http://science.ksc.nasa.gov/shuttle/missions/51-l/
      mission-51-l.html

European Space Agency

The European Space Agency (ESA) was formed in 1975 through the cooperation of a number of European countries. Each of the countries makes a financial contribution based on which activities that country wishes to support. ESA's major programs include the Ariane rocket, the Spacelab scientific workshop (which is carried into orbit by the space shuttle), and Arianespace, a division of ESA, which produces over half of all commercial satellite launches in the world.

Web:
  http://www.esrin.esa.it/

Goddard Space Flight Center

The Goddard Space Flight Center manages many of NASA's programs having to do with finding out information about Earth itself. As such, the Center is a major U.S. laboratory devoted to developing unmanned space probes. Its Web site contains information about their programs and research.

Web:
  http://www.gsfc.nasa.gov/

History of Space Exploration

One can imagine that there have always been adventurous souls, looking longingly at the nighttime sky, wondering what it would be like to travel to the Moon, the planets, and even to the stars. However, it was not until October 4, 1957, that the idea of exploring space became part of the popular culture. It was on that day that the first man-made object was sent into space in order to orbit around the Earth. Its name was Sputnik 1 and it was launched by the USSR. (In Russian, the word Sputnik means "fellow traveler".) On November 3, 1957, the Soviets launched Sputnik 2, which carried a dog, Laika, who traveled around the Earth for 4 days before she died. This set off the so-called "Space Race" between the USSR and the U.S., leading to a large number of important achievements, including the first soft landing on the Moon (USSR), on February 3, 1966, and landing the first men on the Moon (U.S.), on July 20, 1969.

Web:
  http://planetscapes.com/solar/eng/history.htm
  http://www.nauts.com/history/
  http://www.spaceflight.nasa.gov/history/

Mars

Mars is the fourth planet from the Sun. (Earth is the third.) The Martian surface and sky have a pinkish color and, even with the naked eye, when you look at Mars at night it looks a bit red. For this reason, it is often referred to as the Red Planet. At one time, astronomers thought there were straight lines on the Martian surface, giving rise to the idea that Mars had canals and, possibly, life. Moreover, parts of the Martian surface changed color during the year, and it was thought that this might be some type of vegetation. Since then, man-made probes have sent photos and other data back from Mars, and found no evidence of canals or life. In fact, Mars is not a hospitable planet. The atmosphere is 95% carbon dioxide (ours is 78% nitrogen and 21% oxygen), and the surface temperatures range from -140° C (-220° F) to 20° C (68° F). In spite of these difficulties (and many others), there are people who are actively working toward human exploration of Mars.

Web:
  http://mars.jpl.nasa.gov/
  http://www.cmex.arc.nasa.gov/
  http://www.marsnews.com/
  http://www.marssociety.org/
  http://www.msss.com/moc_gallery/

NASA Historical Archive

It's good to know your NASA space history. For instance, what if you are at the supermarket and the checkout girl says that if you can list the dates of all the Apollo missions you will be the lucky winner of a month's worth of Cheese Doodles? Imagine how sorry you'd feel if you couldn't do it. There's absolutely no need for this to happen as long as you make sure to read all the documents at the NASA Historical Archive. They offer the text of the NASA Space Act, information about rocket history, early astronauts, astronautics history, chronology, manned missions and details about the space shuttles. (Please, no spies allowed.)

Web:
  http://www.ksc.nasa.gov/history/history.html

Usenet:
  sci.space.history

NASA Historical Archive

To you and me, NASA (the National Aeronautics and Space Administration) may be the embodiment of our science fiction dreams of space travel. But in reality, NASA is a department of the U.S. government and, like all such departments, NASA must periodically justify its existence and its budget.

One way in which NASA does this is to make information available about its programs to anyone on the Net. If you are interested in what NASA has done, take a few minutes to check out its site. Much of it is boring (remember, the "A" *does* stand for "Administration"), and a lot of the details are hidden behind cryptic acronyms. However, if you dig deeply enough, you will find some aeronautical jewels.

For example, the mission number of the ill-fated Challenger space shuttle was 51-l. (That's 51-hyphen-lowercase "L.") The technical descriptions of this mission are rather pedestrian, dismissing the final outcome in a few nondescript sentences. But if you know where to look, you can find a video clip of the actual explosion. Here it is:

```
http://www.ksc.nasa.gov/shuttle/
   missions/51-l/movies/51-l-launch2.mpg
```

Hint: The character after "51-" is a lowercase "L."

NASA News

Keep up on the latest information from NASA, including the status of spacecraft currently in space. Find out about the new discoveries made with the space-based Hubble telescope and the unmanned probes launched toward distant planets and galaxies.

Web:
  http://spacelink.msfc.nasa.gov/NASA.News/

NASA Research Labs

It's your turn to plan an exciting date for you and the one you love. How about a tour of some of the most famous NASA research labs? After a romantic candlelit dinner you can go back to your place, fire up the old Web browser and roam through the Goddard, Dryden, Ames, Langley and Kennedy space centers, to name just a few. In no time, word will be out that you really know how to entertain in style.

Web:
  http://www.nasa.gov/nasaorgs/subject_index.html

NASDA (National Space Development Agency of Japan)

The National Space Development Agency (NASDA) is Japan's national agency for space development. NASDA's Web site has information about its activities, publications and technical developments. Here you can find descriptions of NASDA's work on the international space station. There are also technical details regarding the H-II rocket (the central launch vehicle in the Japanese space program), just in case you want to build one for yourself.

Web:
  http://yyy.tksc.nasda.go.jp/index_e.html

Photographs of Earth from Space

It's all a matter of perspective. No matter where you go on the Earth, you can never see the entire thing. These days, you don't have to be an astronaut to enjoy a nice view of the Earth from space. Check out this collection of photos of the Earth. Once you find a photo of where you live, you can print a copy, mark it with a big X, and label it "I am here."

Web:
  http://eol.jsc.nasa.gov/sseop/
  http://www.nasm.edu/ceps/rpif/SSPR.html
  http://www.spacelink.nasa.gov/
    Instructional.Materials/Curriculum.Support/
    Earth.Science/Earth.Images.From.Space/

Yes, there is no doubt about it. Planets are high up on just about everybody's list of favorite astronomical objects. Join the folks on **alt.sci.planetary** and talk about the large, significant objects that comprise our solar system, and our efforts to visit them before the price goes up.

Photographs of Space

For most of history, mankind has only been able to imagine what outer space looks like. To be sure, we can see the Sun and the moon fairly well with the naked eye, but the stars and a few planets look like mere points of light, and virtually no galaxies are visible. In 1609, the Italian astronomer Galileo turned one of the first telescopes toward the heavens and saw what no man had seen before: a close-up view of the planets and the moon. However, until the launch of satellites and space probes in the twentieth century, no one had ever seen pictures taken from space. In 1990, the Hubble Space Telescope (named after American astronomer Edwin Hubble, 1889-1953) was launched into permanent global orbit, becoming our first major outpost for viewing the heavens away from the atmosphere of Earth. In the last decade, we have been able to take spectacular pictures—not only of the moon, sun and stars—but of the planets, galaxies, and other heavenly bodies.

Web:

http://antwrp.gsfc.nasa.gov/apod/astropix.html
http://images.jsc.nasa.gov/
http://nssdc.gsfc.nasa.gov/photo_gallery/
http://oposite.stsci.edu/pubinfo/pictures.html
http://www.astro.princeton.edu/~frei/Gcat_htm/
   cat_ims.htm
http://www.spacelink.nasa.gov/
   Instructional.Materials/Curriculum.Support/
   Space.Science/Space.Science.Images/
http://www.spacepix.net/astronomy/

Photographs of the Moon

If you want to see the moon, but it's a cloudy night and you can't see any celestial bodies, you can take comfort in knowing that you can see the moon on the Internet. Brew up a hot drink, wrap yourself in a cozy blanket and curl up in front of the computer. These are gorgeous pictures and make cloudy nights a pleasure.

Web:

http://www.lpi.usra.edu/research/lunar_orbiter/
http://www.netaxs.com/~mhmyers/moon.tn.html

Planets and the Solar System

The solar system in which we live is complex. At the center lies the Sun. Revolving around the Sun are nine planets, some of which have moons (or more accurately "satellites") revolving around them. (There are a total of 95 known satellite.) The planets are, from closest to the Sun to farthest from the Sun: Mercury, Venus, Earth (1 satellite, the Moon), Mars (2 satellites), Jupiter (32 satellites), Saturn (30 satellites), Uranus (21 satellites), Neptune (8 satellites), Pluto (1 satellite). In addition to the Sun and the planets, the solar system also has many smaller bodies, such as asteroids and comets. There is a lot known about the solar system, and to help you learn about it, here are some resources where you will find a lot of fascinating information and pictures. These are the places I go when I need to get my hands on a picture of Neptune or find out the diameter of Mars (6,794 kilometers or 4,222 miles).

Web:

http://maps.jpl.nasa.gov/
http://nssdc.gsfc.nasa.gov/planetary/planetfact.html
http://pds.jpl.nasa.gov/planets/
http://www.seds.org/billa/tnp/

Usenet:

alt.planets.mars
alt.planets.pluto
alt.sci.planetary

Politics of Space

Do people belong in space? Is all the money worth it? What should we be doing and who should we be doing it with? Discuss non-technical issues pertaining to space exploration.

Usenet:

sci.space.policy

Everyone exaggerates
(except me).

Satellite Observation

If you look at the night sky much, it's likely you have already seen an artificial satellite. It would look like a slowly moving star, a pinpoint of light traveling across the sky. What you are seeing is sunlight reflecting off the surface of the satellite. Since the advent of PCs and the growth of the Internet, the tools available to amateur satellite observers have improved enormously. You can use sophisticated programs to track satellites and help you find the exact place to look for a particular satellite. Moreover, you will find announcements on the Net about forthcoming launches, describing the details of the mission. This makes it all the more interesting when you manage to find and observe a specific speck of light in the vast reaches of the darkness.

Web:
> http://www.fc.net/~worden/vsohp/FAQ/
> http://www.heavens-above.com/
> http://www.satobs.org/satintro.html
> http://wwwvms.utexas.edu/~ecannon/satellite.htm

Search for Extraterrestrial Intelligence

Do you get tired of the same old people here on Earth? Get a new cultural and intellectual perspective on the universe by looking in at the Search for Extraterrestrial Intelligence (SETI) Institute. It is possible that there are planets outside our solar system on which there may be life. The SETI Institute sponsors research and education projects related to the efforts to search for other technologically advanced civilizations. So far, the SETI Institute hasn't found any signals of extraterrestrial origin, but you never know. Just in case, they have worked out the details about how such a discovery would be publicized should it ever happen. (The details are on the Net.)

Web:
> http://www.seti.org/

Solar System Exploration

There has been a lot of exploration of our solar system, but except for some transient news coverage, few people really understand the significance of what has been done and what it means to us. Here is a Web site with information about some of mankind's most impressive and most important achievements.

Web:
> http://sse.jpl.nasa.gov/

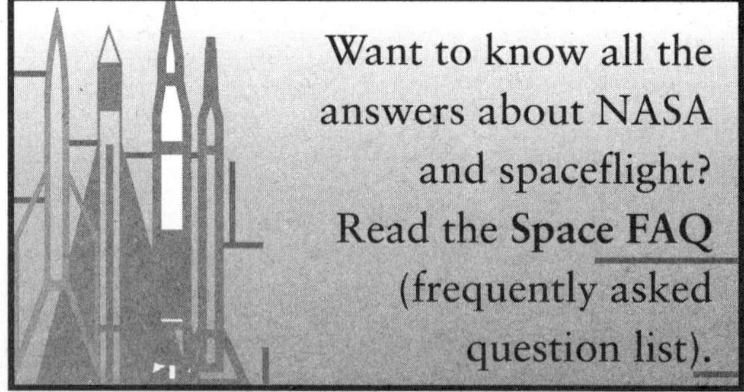

Space Frequently Asked Questions

Get answers to the most frequently asked questions (FAQs) regarding NASA, spaceflight and astrophysics. (For example, is it true that the blueprints for the Saturn V were lost?) If you are interested in space and spaceflight, this is a great source of fascinating information.

Web:
> http://www.faqs.org/faqs/space/

Space News

Keep current on the final frontier. Read all the latest news about space, astronomy and spaceflight. Now that you have a connection to the Net, there is no excuse for being the last one on your block to know whether or not there really once was life on Mars.

Web:
> http://www.chron.com/content/chronicle/space/
> http://www.flatoday.com/space/
> http://www.space.com/spacenews/
> http://www.spaceflightnow.com/news/
> http://www.spacer.com/
> http://www.spaceref.com/
> http://www.spacesciences.com/
> http://www.universetoday.com/

Usenet:
> sci.space.news

Space Shuttle

The space shuttle is a reusable American space vehicle. The first shuttle test flight took place on April 12, 1981. The first operational flight was on November 11, 1982. For information about the shuttle program, including a lot of technical details, you can check NASA's Web sites.

Web:
http://science.ksc.nasa.gov/shuttle/missions/
missions.html
http://www-pao.ksc.nasa.gov/kscpao/status/stsstat/
current.htm
http://www.ksc.nasa.gov/shuttle/missions/sts-90/
vrtour/

Usenet:
sci.space.shuttle

Space Talk and General Discussion

Talk, talk, talk about everything under the Sun (and the Sun as well). Discuss all manner of space-oriented topics with aficionados around the world.

Usenet:
sci.space
sci.space.science

Students for the Exploration and Development of Space

SEDS is a student club devoted to the discussion and study of space. Meet people from SEDS chapters around the world. Find out all the latest space news and what SEDS members are up to.

Web:
http://seds.lpl.arizona.edu/

United Nations Office for Outer Space Affairs

Everyone is anxiously awaiting the news about extraterrestrials joining the United Nations. The U.N. even has an office for Outer Space Affairs which focuses on international cooperation regarding the use of space technology to monitor space activities as well as our terrestrial environment.

Web:
http://www.oosa.unvienna.org/

Windows to the Universe

The universe is one of my favorite places in the whole world. Why do I like it so much? There are three reasons. First, the universe has an awe-inspiring grandeur that never fails to make me feel humble and privileged at the same time. Second, the universe is an endless source of interesting knowledge that constantly amazes and enlightens me. Third, all my stuff is here. If you are interested in space and what's out there, I know you will enjoy touring this Web site. This is an especially good place to visit if you happen to be a bright child or know a bright child. (Actually, when I was a child I was so bright my parents called me "son".)

Web:
http://www.windows.ucar.edu/

SPORTS AND ATHLETICS

Archery

Start practicing your archery now, because you never know when one day you will be called upon to play Robin Hood in your local community theater group. Imagine being up on stage and having to play out a rescue scene without being properly prepared. One wild shot and you could put out somebody's eye. Don't let this happen to you. Read the important archery documents that are available on the Net.

Web:

http://www.archery.start4all.com/
http://www.archeryinfonet.com/
http://www.student.utwente.nl/~sagi/artikel/faq/

Usenet:

alt.archery
rec.sport.archery

Badminton

Badminton is a racket game, played by two people (singles) or four people (doubles). The idea is to use the racket to hit a bird (also called a shuttlecock) back and forth over a net. Badminton is thought to have originated in India, and was introduced into the United States in the 1890s. The word "badminton" was taken from the name of the English estate of the Duke of Beaufort.

Web:

http://www.badmintoncentral.com/
http://www.intbadfed.org/
http://www.tradgames.org.uk/games/
   battledore-shuttlecock.htm
http://www.worldbadminton.com/

Usrenet:

alt.sports.badminton

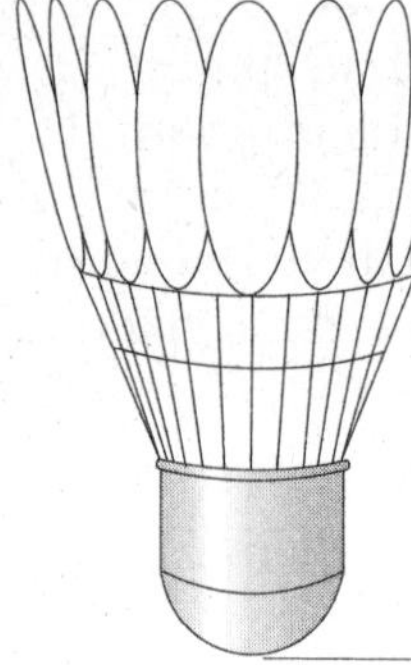

Badminton

Do you enjoy using a long, narrow-handled racquet to volley a shuttlecock back and forth over a high, narrow net?

If so, the badminton resources on the Net will enhance your experience.

Baseball

Baseball is played in the United States, Japan, Mexico, Cuba and other countries. In the U.S., baseball is so popular it is often referred as the "National Pastime". (Actually, there are three National Pastimes. The other two are complaining about taxes and criticizing the President.) Legend has it that baseball was invented in 1839 by Abner Doubleday, but it just ain't so. Modern baseball developed from a more rudimentary version that was played in the early nineteenth century, based on the English games of cricket and rounders. Today, baseball—especially in the U.S.—has millions of devoted fans. If you are one of them, you will love these resources, where you can cruise through massive amounts of information about major and minor leagues around the world: scores, standings, schedules, statistics, rosters, injury reports, and much, much more.

Web:

http://mlb.mlb.com/
http://www.baseball-almanac.com/
http://www.sportseport.com/mlb.htm
http://www.sportserver.com/baseball/mlb/
http://www.sportserver.com/baseball/other/

Usenet:

rec.sport.baseball
rec.sport.baseball.analysis
rec.sport.baseball.college
rec.sport.baseball.data
rec.sport.baseball.fantasy

Listserv Mailing List:

List Name: baseball
Subscribe to: listserv@apple.ease.lsoft.com

Baseball Teams

On those days when it's not enough to watch your favorite team at the ballpark or on television, do some reading on their stats, standings and other team information on the Net.

Web:

http://sports.espn.go.com/mlb/standings

Usenet:

alt.sports.baseball.atlanta-braves
alt.sports.baseball.az-diamondbacks
alt.sports.baseball.balt-orioles
alt.sports.baseball.bos-redsox
alt.sports.baseball.calif-angels
alt.sports.baseball.chi-whitesox
alt.sports.baseball.chicago-cubs
alt.sports.baseball.cinci-reds
alt.sports.baseball.cleve-indians
alt.sports.baseball.col-rockies
alt.sports.baseball.detroit-tigers
alt.sports.baseball.fla-marlins
alt.sports.baseball.houston-astros
alt.sports.baseball.kc-royals
alt.sports.baseball.la-dodgers
alt.sports.baseball.minor-leagues
alt.sports.baseball.mke-brewers
alt.sports.baseball.mn-twins
alt.sports.baseball.montreal-expos
alt.sports.baseball.ny-mets
alt.sports.baseball.ny-yankees
alt.sports.baseball.oakland-as
alt.sports.baseball.phila-phillies
alt.sports.baseball.pitt-pirates
alt.sports.baseball.sd-padres
alt.sports.baseball.sea-mariners
alt.sports.baseball.sf-giants
alt.sports.baseball.stl-cardinals
alt.sports.baseball.tb-devilrays
alt.sports.baseball.texas-rangers
alt.sports.baseball.tor-bluejays

You are now entering the future.

In 1891, James Naismith invented the game of basketball at the Springfield, Massachusetts, YMCA.

A little over one hundred years later, the Web was created.

Now you can combine the best of both worlds: visit the basketball Web site of your choice today.

Basketball

Having basketball fever doesn't mean that you just sit in front of the television making loud whooping noises. It's much more sophisticated than that. It's a fine balance of gathering statistics, analyzing trends, and making studied observations. On the Net you can find all you need to become a seasoned basketball fan.

Web:

http://sportsillustrated.cnn.com/basketball/nba/
  players/
http://www.canoe.ca/Basketball/
http://www.nba.com/

Usenet:

rec.sport.basketball
rec.sport.basketball.college
rec.sport.basketball.europe
rec.sport.basketball.misc
rec.sport.basketball.pro

IRC:

#nba (DALnet, EFnet)

Basketball Teams Talk and General Discussion

You don't have to get together with the guys to be able to talk about your favorite basketball team. Join up with other raging basketball fans and talk all night. (By the way, did you know that basketball is the only major sport that is entirely American in origin?)

Usenet:
alt.sports.basketball.nba.atlanta-hawks
alt.sports.basketball.nba.boston-celtics
alt.sports.basketball.nba.char-hornets
alt.sports.basketball.nba.chicago-bulls
alt.sports.basketball.nba.clev-cavaliers
alt.sports.basketball.nba.dallas-mavs
alt.sports.basketball.nba.denver-nuggets
alt.sports.basketball.nba.det-pistons
alt.sports.basketball.nba.gs-warriors
alt.sports.basketball.nba.hou-rockets
alt.sports.basketball.nba.ind-pacers
alt.sports.basketball.nba.la-clippers
alt.sports.basketball.nba.la-lakers
alt.sports.basketball.nba.miami-heat
alt.sports.basketball.nba.mil-bucks
alt.sports.basketball.nba.mn-wolves
alt.sports.basketball.nba.nj-nets
alt.sports.basketball.nba.orlando-magic
alt.sports.basketball.nba.phila-76ers
alt.sports.basketball.nba.phx-suns
alt.sports.basketball.nba.port-blazers
alt.sports.basketball.nba.sa-spurs
alt.sports.basketball.nba.sac-kings
alt.sports.basketball.nba.seattle-sonics
alt.sports.basketball.nba.tor-raptors
alt.sports.basketball.nba.utah-jazz
alt.sports.basketball.nba.vanc-grizzlies
alt.sports.basketball.nba.wash-bullets
alt.sports.basketball.pro.ny-knicks

Basketball: Women

Many people prefer women's basketball to men's. The rules are changed somewhat—for example, they use a smaller ball—but the game is basically the same and the tickets are a lot less expensive. If you are a basketball fan, try the women's version. I bet you will like it.

Web:
http://www.wbca.org/
http://www.wnba.com/

Usenet:
rec.sport.basketball.women

Listserv Mailing List:
List Name: b10wb-l
Subscribe to: listserv@lists.psu.edu

Bicycling

Some years ago, I rode my bicycle along the California coast from San Diego to San Francisco. Today, I still live near the ocean, and there's nothing I like more than spending the day riding along an oceanfront bike path (especially when I should be working). It's not only great exercise, but I get credit for saving the environment without having to actually do anything. The last time I bought a new bike, it sure was helpful to have useful information and good advice. To help you enjoy your bike-riding experiences, here are some bicycle resources with enough information and advice to equip the entire Swiss navy.

Web:
http://www.bicyclinglife.com/
http://www.bicyclingmagazine.com/
http://www.cycling.org/
http://www.faqs.org/faqs/bicycles-faq/

Usenet:
alt.bmx
alt.rec.bicycles.fatcity
alt.rec.bicycles.recumbent
rec.bicycles
rec.bicycles.misc
rec.bicycles.racing
rec.bicycles.rides
rec.bicycles.soc
rec.bicycles.tech

Listserv Mailing List:
List Name: trials
Subscribe to: listserv@listserv.heanet.ie

Boxing

I am not sure, exactly, what the appeal is of watching men hit each other until they are unconscious or exhausted. Imagine the brain cells that could be in full use, but are instead being bashed about like a string of rugs during spring cleaning. But this thought doesn't bother the fans of boxing, and they will be found on the Net talking about the history of boxing as well as the latest knock-down-drag-out.

Web:
http://www.boxing.clara.net/
http://www.canoe.ca/Boxing/
http://www.ringtalk.net/

Usenet:
rec.sport.boxing

Why Boxing Is Important

Some people think that boxing is an ugly, vicious, atavistic pastime, whose usefulness in a polite, civilized society has long since expired. Other people think boxing is important, as it allows people to express their aggressive urges in a confined, limited fashion, with well-defined rules and procedures.

Actually, neither of those is correct.

The real reason boxing is important is it allows middle-aged men to get together and smoke cigars in a socially acceptable environment.

College Sports

American colleges and universities have two main purposes. First, they are bastions of knowledge, dedicated to the training and enlightenment of young people as they pass through late adolescence into adulthood. Second, they organize and maintain many different athletic teams so that older people—who have already passed through late adolescence into adulthood—can enjoy themselves vicariously by watching the exploits of young athletes.

Web:
   http://www.collegesportsforum.com/
   http://www.naia.org/
   http://www.ncaa.com/
   http://www.usatoday.com/sports/colfront.htm

Usenet:
   alt.sports.college.acc
   alt.sports.college.acc.unc
   alt.sports.college.big-12
   alt.sports.college.big-east
   alt.sports.college.big10
   alt.sports.college.conference-usa
   alt.sports.college.ivy-league
   alt.sports.college.pac-10
   alt.sports.college.sec

Cricket

Cricket is played primarily in Great Britain and the Commonwealth countries. Here is how it works. There are two wickets (made of two crosspieces, or bails, resting on three stumps) placed in the middle of a field. Bowlers try to knock down the bails of the wicket while the batsmen defend the wickets. Each team consists of 11 men. Because of the structure of the scoring, games can sometimes take several days to complete. Cricket developed in medieval England some time before 1400. In 1477, cricket was banned by Edward IV because it was interfering with the mandatory practice of archery.

Web:
   http://www-usa.cricket.org/link_to_database/
      NATIONAL/ICC/
   http://www.cricketindex.com/
   http://www.rickeyre.com/cricket/
   http://www.worldcupweb.com/crickethome.html

Usenet:
   rec.sport.cricket
   rec.sport.cricket.info
   rec.sport.cricket.scores

IRC:
   #cricket (DALnet)

Exercise and Sports Psychology

"Mind over matter." "No pain, no gain." You've heard all the motivational clichés designed to inspire you to push that out-of-shape body of yours up the hill, down the hill, and over the finish line. Examine the brain behind the body by participating in the discussion of exercise and sports psychology.

Listserv Mailing List:
   List Name: sportpsy
   Subscribe to: listserv@listserv.temple.edu

Extreme Sports

When you get to the point where bungie jumping is too tame and the Ironman competition is no longer challenging, it's time for an extreme sport: a regular athletic or outdoor activity exaggerated to the point of idiocy. Some of the best athletes in the world participate in extreme sports, so if you enjoy such pastimes but you feel like living out your natural lifespan, you can always watch. (Hint: If you do become an extreme athlete, don't run while you are carrying scissors.)

Web:
   http://www.adventuresportsdirectory.com/
   http://www.expn.go.com/
   http://www.extremists.com.au/
   http://www.sportseport.com/ext.htm

Fencing

Fencing is more than just making money off stolen goods. It's also a sport that takes speed, grace and finesse. (This is not to say the two are mutually exclusive, though.) These resources offer you a chance to learn the rules of fencing as well as other important fencing information.

Web:
   http://www.britishfencing.com/
   http://www.faqs.org/faqs/sports/fencing-faq/
   http://www.fencing.net/
   http://www.usfencing.org/

Usenet:
   rec.sport.fencing

Figure Skating

Ice skating was originally developed as a form of transportation, but by the seventeenth century skating was well established as a sport. Figure skating was invented in the 1860s by an American, Jackson Haines, and is one of the most beautiful and graceful sports in the world. Whether you are a figure skating fan or a skater yourself, you will find lots of interesting resources on the Net.

Web:
   http://www.cyberus.ca/~karen/recskate/
   http://www.heatherw.com/sk/
   http://www.nsn.org/eakhome/skating/kevinnew/
   http://www.sk8stuff.com/
   http://www.usfsa.org/

Usenet:
   rec.sport.skating.ice.figure

FENCING AND ME

When I was a graduate student at U.C. San Diego, I studied fencing. Here is how it happened.

At the time, registration for physical education (PE) classes was done manually. At the beginning of the term, on a particular day, each coach set up a table in the gymnasium. People lined up for hours in advance to register for their favorite class. I woke up very early that day and stood in line a long time to register for surfing class.

I wanted to take more than one PE class, but by the time I worked my way to the front of the surfing line, there wasn't time to wait at another table. So I asked the surfing coach if he taught anything besides surfing. Yes, he replied, he also taught fencing.

Since I could sign up for both classes at the same table, I did. And that's how I came to take fencing (as well as surfing). Later, I went on to study theatrical fencing, and I even wrote a short play with fencing in it.

If you are a fencing buff, whether by design or fortune, check out the **FENCING** Web sites. And remember, as we wait patiently at the Table of Life, it's not how long we wait that matters, but how we use our opportunities when we get to the front of the line.

Football: American

Good old summertime. The sun is shining, the birds are singing, the flowers are blooming, and you can work on your tan. The problem is that there is no football. This is something that had to be tolerated until recently. Now you can get your fix during any season: scores, history, news articles and discussion on both college and professional football.

Web:
   http://football.espn.go.com/nfl/index
   http://sportsillustrated.cnn.com/football/
   http://www.dickbutkus.com/dbfn/
   http://www.wideright.com/

Usenet:
   rec.sport.football.college
   rec.sport.football.fantasy
   rec.sport.football.misc

Football: Arena

Arena football is a version of American football adapted for playing indoors. The original motivation behind arena football was marketing: There are a huge number of football fans who have nothing to watch during the summer (well, nothing but baseball and tractor pulls). Arena football is a lot like outdoor football, with a few major differences, because it is played indoors. For example, the "field" is a lot smaller, 50 yards long by 85 feet wide (compared to 100 yards by 160 feet for regular football), and there are fewer players on the field, 8 per team (compared to 11). Although there are place kicks and drop kicks, there are no punts (as there is no room). The most interesting variation is that the endzone contains a large "rebound net". From time to time, the ball will bounce off the rebound net, say, after a kick or a missed pass. When this happens, the ball stays in play until it touches the ground.

Web:
>   http://www.aflroundhouse.com/
>   http://www.arenafan.com/
>   http://www.arenafootball.com/
>   http://www.football.com/afl/

Usenet:
>   alt.sports.football.arena

Football: Canadian Football League

Football is not just a disease exclusive to America. See how the Canadians play the game. Rules, referee signals, history, schedules and a glossary are available.

Web:
>   http://www.cfl.ca/

Usenet:
>   rec.sport.football.canadian

> ## "Food and Drink" or "Diet and Nutrition"? The choice is yours.

Football: Professional

It's a good thing football is a seasonal sport. Otherwise, people might never have time to go to the Net and read about football. Check out these Web sites for the latest news and information about professional football. On Usenet, any professional football topic is fair game.

Web:
>   http://www.draftboard.com/draftboard/nfl/
>   http://www.nfl.com/

Usenet:
>   alt.sports.football.mn-vikings
>   alt.sports.football.oak-raiders
>   alt.sports.football.pro.ariz-cardinals
>   alt.sports.football.pro.atl-falcons
>   alt.sports.football.pro.baltimore
>   alt.sports.football.pro.buffalo-bills
>   alt.sports.football.pro.car-panthers
>   alt.sports.football.pro.chicago-bears
>   alt.sports.football.pro.cinci-bengals
>   alt.sports.football.pro.cleve-browns
>   alt.sports.football.pro.dallas-cowboys
>   alt.sports.football.pro.denver-broncos
>   alt.sports.football.pro.detroit-lions
>   alt.sports.football.pro.gb-packers
>   alt.sports.football.pro.houston-oilers
>   alt.sports.football.pro.indy-colts
>   alt.sports.football.pro.jville-jaguars
>   alt.sports.football.pro.kc-chiefs
>   alt.sports.football.pro.la-raiders
>   alt.sports.football.pro.la-rams
>   alt.sports.football.pro.miami-dolphins
>   alt.sports.football.pro.ne-patriots
>   alt.sports.football.pro.no-saints
>   alt.sports.football.pro.ny-giants
>   alt.sports.football.pro.ny-jets
>   alt.sports.football.pro.oak-raiders
>   alt.sports.football.pro.phila-eagles
>   alt.sports.football.pro.phoe-cardinals
>   alt.sports.football.pro.pitt-steelers
>   alt.sports.football.pro.sd-chargers
>   alt.sports.football.pro.sea-seahawks
>   alt.sports.football.pro.sf-49ers
>   alt.sports.football.pro.stl-rams
>   alt.sports.football.pro.tampabay-bucs
>   alt.sports.football.pro.tennessee
>   alt.sports.football.pro.wash-redskins
>   rec.sport.football.pro

Frisbee: Ultimate

A frisbee is a plastic disc used for throwing and catching. Years ago, when I was living in Berkeley for awhile, I took a frisbee class in San Francisco. I had a great time and made a good friend (David Black) with whom I spent a lot of time. David and I were only recreational players, but there are many people who compete in the frisbee-based game called Ultimate. Ultimate is a non-contact sport played by two 7-player teams, using a large field. At each end of the field is an endzone, one for each team. The object of the game is to pass the frisbee from one person to another, trying to score a goal. To score, a player must pass the frisbee to another player on his team who is standing in the opponent's endzone. The catch is that the frisbee may only be passed by a player who is not moving. This ensures that Ultimate has lots of strategy and quick action.

Web:

   http://www.canultimate.com/
   http://www.cs.rochester.edu/u/ferguson/ultimate/
      ultimate-rules.html
   http://www.princeton.edu/~clockwrk/links.html
   http://www.ultimatehandbook.com/

Usenet:

   rec.sport.disc

Golf

The Internet is full of golf information, golf resources and people who want to talk about golf. Join the mailing list and maybe you'll get to talk to Tiger Woods. (Of course, maybe you won't, but as a golfer, I am sure you are always optimistic.) Hint: The next time you play golf, be sure to wear *two* pairs of pants—just in case you get a hole in one. Ha, ha, ha, ha...oh, never mind.

Web:

   http://sportsillustrated.cnn.com/golfonline/
   http://www.19thhole.com/on_the_net/
   http://www.faqs.org/faqs/sports/golf-faq/
   http://www.lpga.com
   http://www.pga.com
   http://www.ttsoft.com/thor/golflinks.html

Usenet:

   rec.sport.golf

Listserv Mailing List:

   List Name: golf
   Subscribe to: listserv@listserv.phone.com

High School Sports

I grew up in Canada and, when I was a kid, high school sports weren't that big a deal. To be sure, my school had athletic teams, but people didn't care about them all that much. In my four years of high school, I remember going to only one football game, and that involved standing at the side of a field. (There was no stadium or even seats for spectators.) When I moved to the United States, I saw that things were a lot different. In the U.S., high school sports are a big deal, not only for the students, but for parents and teachers. I think it is because American culture prizes individualism and, thus, pushes kids to be competitive even as they are growing up. If you want to see the results, compare how the Canada and the U.S. act, as countries, within the international community.

Web:

   http://www.ihigh.com/
   http://www.nhsca.com/
   http://www.schoolsports.com/

Hockey

Hockey has certainly gotten less fun since they made a rule that everyone has to wear helmets when they play. But if that doesn't put you off the game, check out these great resources available on the Internet. When you're not on the ice or in the stands, check into Usenet and IRC to blab with other hockey fans.

Web:

   http://www.canoe.ca/Hockey/
   http://www.exploratorium.edu/hockey/
   http://www.nhl.com
   http://www.sportingnews.com/nhl/

Usenet:

   alt.sports.hockey.echl
   alt.sports.hockey.fantasy
   alt.sports.hockey.ihl
   alt.sports.hockey.rhi
   rec.collecting.sport.hockey
   rec.sport.hockey
   rec.sport.hockey.field

IRC:

   #hockey (Undernet)

Hockey

I am the oldest child in my family and, as such, I had some special privileges when I was growing up. One of them was that I often got to sleep over at my grandparents' house on Saturday night.

Every Saturday night, after I watched Leave It to Beaver on TV, my grandmother would make me a bowl of cereal. I would eat the cereal and sit on the couch with my grandfather as we watched the hockey game together.

That was a long time ago.

My grandparents have since passed away. I don't eat cereal nearly as often as I used to. Leave It to Beaver has been in reruns for many years. And I now spend my Saturday nights listening to the radio and writing.

But all across the country, I am sure that there are still little boys, sitting with their grandfathers, spending the evening watching the hockey game.

Thank goodness, some things never change.

Hockey: College

It's exciting to watch a bunch of padded maniacs zip up and down a slab of ice and hit each other with sticks. You can get more involved in collegiate ice hockey by posting or reading scores, team information, and schedules for your favorite teams.

Listserv Mailing List:
List Name: hockey-l
Subscribe to: listserv@lists.maine.edu

Listserv Mailing List:
List Name: hockey3
Subscribe to: listserv@lists.maine.edu

Hockey Teams Talk and General Discussion

If hockey is too rough for you to participate, try getting on Usenet and talking about it. There's nothing like a vicarious thrill (except a real thrill). Fans of various hockey teams hang out and discuss the game and the players.

Usenet:
alt.sports.hockey.nhl.ana-mighty-ducks
alt.sports.hockey.nhl.atl-thrashers
alt.sports.hockey.nhl.boston-bruins
alt.sports.hockey.nhl.buffalo-sabres
alt.sports.hockey.nhl.chat
alt.sports.hockey.nhl.chi-blackhawks
alt.sports.hockey.nhl.clgry-flames
alt.sports.hockey.nhl.col-avalanche
alt.sports.hockey.nhl.dallas-stars
alt.sports.hockey.nhl.det-redwings
alt.sports.hockey.nhl.edm-oilers
alt.sports.hockey.nhl.fla-panthers
alt.sports.hockey.nhl.hford-whalers
alt.sports.hockey.nhl.la-kings
alt.sports.hockey.nhl.mn-wild
alt.sports.hockey.nhl.mtl-canadiens
alt.sports.hockey.nhl.nash-predators
alt.sports.hockey.nhl.nj-devils
alt.sports.hockey.nhl.ny-islanders
alt.sports.hockey.nhl.ny-rangers
alt.sports.hockey.nhl.ott-senators
alt.sports.hockey.nhl.phila-flyers
alt.sports.hockey.nhl.phx-coyotes
alt.sports.hockey.nhl.pit-penguins
alt.sports.hockey.nhl.que-nordiques
alt.sports.hockey.nhl.sj-sharks
alt.sports.hockey.nhl.stl-blues
alt.sports.hockey.nhl.tor-mapleleafs
alt.sports.hockey.nhl.vanc-canucks
alt.sports.hockey.nhl.wash-capitals
alt.sports.hockey.nhl.winnipeg-jets

Want to have good luck all day? Pet a cat on the head before breakfast.

Olympics

In ancient Greece, the Olympic Games was held as part of a religious festival in honor of Zeus, the father of the Greek gods. The competitions took place in Olympia, a town in southwest Greece. The first modern Olympics took place in 1896 in Athens. Today, there are two sets of Olympic games, one for summer sports and one for winter sports, each of which is held every four years. The 2000 Summer Olympics was held in Sydney, Australia, while future Summer Games will be in Athens (2004) and Beijing (2008). The Winter Games is held two years after the Summer Games. The 2002 Winter Games were in Salt Lake City, United States; the 2006 Winter Games will be in Torino, Italy. I have been to two different Olympic Games (1976 in Montreal, and 1984 in Los Angeles), and I can tell you the experience is wonderful. If you ever have a chance to go, you should do so. You will come away with a real sense of being a citizen of the world.

Web:

http://www.gbrathletics.com/olympic/
http://www.olympic.org/
http://www.upenn.edu/museum/Olympics/
   olympicintro.html
http://www98.pair.com/msmonaco/Almanac/

Usenet:

rec.sport.olympics

Polo

Polo is a game in which four-man teams, mounted on horseback, use long flexible mallets to try to knock a ball through a pair of goal posts. Modern polo was developed in the nineteenth century by British cavalry officers. However, a polo-like game was played in China and Persia as long as 2,500 years ago. Many people consider polo to be a rich man's game, because it takes a certain amount of wealth to maintain horses and polo grounds. Prince Charles of England, for example, is an accomplished polo player. However, polo is enjoyed around the world, including at some universities. Interesting polo fact: According to the official (U.S.) rules, a player may use any size horse of any breed. However, it is against the rules to use a horse that is blind in one eye.

Web:

http://www.polonews.com/
http://www.us-polo.org/

Rodeo

A rodeo is a competition featuring events based on cowboy skills. The first formal rodeo was in Prescott, Arizona, in 1888. Today, rodeos are popular throughout the United States and Canada. At a modern rodeo you will see professional cowboys competing for prize money. There are five main types of events: riding a bronc (bucking horse) bareback, riding a bronc with a saddle, riding a bull, roping a calf, and wrestling a steer.

Web:

http://www.gunslinger.com/rodeo.html
http://www.prorodeo.com/
http://www.prorodeohome.com/
http://www.rodeocanada.com/
http://www.wpra.com/

Usenet:

rec.sport.rodeo

Listproc Mailing List:

List Name: rodeo
Subscribe to: listproc@lists.colorado.edu

Rugby

Rugby is an outdoor game, played by two teams of 15 players (although there are variations). The name comes from the Rugby School, in England, where the game originated in 1823. Rugby is played on a large field, 160 yards long by 75 yards wide, with two "in-goal—similar to the endzones in football—each of which has a set of goal posts. The goal of rugby is to score points, either by carrying the ball into the in-goal, or by kicking the ball between the goal posts. Unlike American football, play is continuous: except for a break in the middle of the game, the clock only stops if there is an injury.

Web:

http://www.irb.org/
http://www.scrum.com/primer/
http://www.webrugby.com/

Usenet:

rec.sport.rugby
rec.sport.rugby.union

Rugby League

It has been said that in the event of nuclear annihilation, only the cockroaches and rugby players would survive. I don't know if that's true, but I do know that this sport is a Rugby Union variation that is more intense, faster-paced, and guaranteed to give you new respect for the human body's ability to withstand punishment.

Web:

http://www.rleague.com/
http://www.totalrugbyleague.com/

Usenet:

rec.sport.rugby.league

Skiing

If you are planning a ski vacation, these Web pages provide you with everything you may or may not need to know, including upcoming ski events, ski conditions, interviews, photos and resort information. When you're not on the slopes, you should at least be talking about skiing. My advice is to join one of the Usenet discussion groups so that, if you can't go skiing every day, at least you're not wasting all your time working and sleeping.

Web:

http://www.skicentral.com/
http://www.skinet.com/
http://www.skiracing.com/

Usenet:

rec.skiing.alpine
rec.skiing.announce
rec.skiing.backcountry
rec.skiing.marketplace
rec.skiing.nordic
rec.skiing.resorts.europe
rec.skiing.resorts.misc
rec.skiing.resorts.north-america
rec.skiing.snowboard

Soccer

Soccer (or as they call it outside the U.S., football) is the most popular sport in the world. These Web pages are your passport to a number of great soccer resources. Access Usenet groups, World Cup information, Fantasy Goal Scorers, mailing lists, hints, FAQs, terminology, and even soccer games for the computer. And, when it comes time for the World Cup, you'll be able to get all the latest information and scores without having to leave your computer.

Web:

http://www.megasoccer.com/page/main.php
http://www.soccer-sites.com/
http://www.soccerage.com/en/33/00001.html
http://www.soccernet.com/
http://www.womensoccer.com/

Usenet:

alt.sports.soccer.european
alt.sports.soccer.european.uk
alt.sports.soccer.non-league
rec.sport.soccer

IRC:

#soccer (DALnet, EFnet, Undernet)

Softball

Softball is a variation of baseball that was invented in 1888 in Chicago. The game is much like regular baseball with a few important changes: the field is smaller, the ball is larger and is softer, and a regular game is only seven innings instead of nine. Softball is played by both men and women and is popular in many different countries because, for normal everyday people, it is a lot more fun than baseball.

Web:

http://www.softball.org/

Usenet:

rec.sport.softball

Sports Champions (Current)

At any time, every sport has a small number of champions who stand above the rest. Here are my choices for the top professional athletes of today, one for each sport: Barry Bonds (baseball), Jerry Rice (football), Lance Armstrong (cycling), Lennox Lewis (boxing), Mia Hamm (women's soccer), Michael Jordan (basketball), Pete Sampras (men's tennis), Tiger Woods (golf), and Venus & Serena Williams (women's tennis).

Web:

    http://www.thebaseballpage.com/past/pp/
       bondsbarry/
    http://pages.prodigy.net/seangates31/RiceRecipe.htm
    http://www.lancearmstrongfanclub.com/
    http://www.lennoxlewis.com/home.asp
    http://www.cnn.com/cnn/programs/people/shows/
       hamm/profile.html
    http://www.23jordan.com/
    http://www.samprasfanz.com
    http://www.tigerwoods.com/
    http://www.venusandserena.homestead.com/

Sports Champions (Historical)

Since the times of the ancient Greeks, star athletes have been lionized and given special privileges. However, very few such athletes are remembered beyond their time. Out of the many sports heroes who become famous during their careers, only a few have both the personality and history of accomplishment that makes them truly great: Babe Ruth (baseball), Bobby Orr (hockey), Hank Aaron (baseball), Jesse Owens (track and field), Jim Thorpe (Olympic pentathlon & decathlon, football, baseball), Joe Louis (boxing), Magic Johnson (basketball), Muhammad Ali (boxing), Pele (soccer), and Wayne Gretzky (hockey).

Web:

    http://www.baberuth.com/
    http://www.bobbyorr4.com/
    http://www.sportingnews.com/archives/aaron/
    http://www.top-biography.com/
       9114-jesse%20owens/
    http://www.cmgww.com/sports/thorpe/
    http://www.cmgww.com/sports/louis/louis.html
    http://www.unc.edu/~lbrooks2/magic.html
    http://www.float-like-a-butterfly.de/indexe.htm
    http://www.isfa.com/server/web/pele/english/
       index.html
    http://www.canoe.com/Gretzky/stories.html

Usenet:
    alt.fan.babe-ruth

Sports History

If you are a sports fan, you'll get a lot more out of watching and analyzing a game if you understand the historical context of the sport. Moreover, when an athlete does especially well, you can appreciate his performance better if you have a sense of perspective. My suggestion is to take some time to study the history and heroes of your favorite sport. You'll be surprised how a bit of background can enhance your enjoyment of the game.

Web:

    http://www.hickoksports.com/history/sprtindx.shtml
    http://www.photo.ucr.edu/projects/sports/
    http://www.readingcottage.com/sports-history.html
    http://www.sportingnews.com/archives/
    http://www.sportseum.net/
    http://www.trilearncs.com/totalview/

Sports Humor

If you can't beat 'em, join 'em. If they won't let you join 'em, laugh at 'em.

Web:

    http://sportshumor.glowport.com/
    http://www.heckledepot.com/
    http://www.kidssportsnet.com/jokes/
    http://www.nickbakay.com/
    http://www.standupsports.com/

Sports News

It's one thing to play a sport. It's another to watch sports on television. But clearly that's not enough. What do you do to fill in the time when you can't get outside and there is nothing on TV? You use the Net to keep up on sporting news, of course. Here are Web sites that will give you all the sports information you need (with enough left over in case you have to entertain unexpected company). Remember, whether you are after the latest scores, schedules or just plain gossip, the Net is there for you.

Web:

    http://sportsillustrated.cnn.com/
    http://www.espn.go.com/
    http://www.sportal.co.uk/
    http://www.sportsline.com/

Sports Resources

There are many sports and many athletes in the world, and the Net can help you find the information you need when you need it. Whether you are looking for an up-to-the-minute sports score, inside information on your favorite team or the location of the nearest Korfball tournament, one of these Web sites will have what you need. For those extra moments when you're not watching or playing, why not join the discussion on Usenet?

Web:
  http://www.sfgate.com/sports/
  http://www.sportingnews.com/
  http://www.sportscribe.com/
  http://www.zdnet.com/searchiq/subjects/sports/

Usenet:
  rec.sport.misc

If you can't play a sport, try to be one.
And if you can't be a sport, at least you can read about one on the Net.

Sports Rules

There are a lot of rules in the world, and when the time comes when you need to find one, you'll be glad you have the Net. Spend a bit of time here and you are bound to impress your friends and loved ones. For example, say you are watching a basketball game, and a player accidentally throws the ball into his own basket. Wouldn't it be great to be the person who is able to explain that credit for the score will go to the opposing player who was closest to the player who shot the ball?

Web:
  http://www.everyrule.com/sports_az_list.html

Sports Schedules

If the only reason you have been buying TV Guide is to look up when your favorite sporting event is on, now you can save all that money and avoid recycling at the same time. This Web site will let you check schedules for various sporting events or create your own viewing schedules for professional football, hockey, basketball and baseball events, and more.

Web:
  http://www.cs.rochester.edu/u/ferguson/schedules/

Squash and Racquetball

Squash and racquetball are similar games in which two players, using racquets, hit a ball back and forth against a wall in an enclosed court. (There are also "doubles" versions of these games in which two-person teams compete against one another.) For hundreds of years, people have been playing games in which they hit a ball back and forth with either their hands or some type of instrument. In 19th-century England, the prisoners in Fleet prison in London invented a game in which they would hit a ball against the walls by using racquets. By 1820, the game of racquets had become popular in various English public schools. Squash was invented around 1830, at the Harrow school, when some of the students discovered that a punctured racquets ball would "squash" against the wall with much less of a bounce than an intact ball. Because the ball did not bounce as much, chasing after it and hitting it required a lot more effort. The game of racquetball was invented in 1949 in Connecticut by Joe Sobek. He designed a short racquet-like paddle, and devised a game to be played on a handball court that was a cross between squash and handball.

Web:
  http://www.racquetball.org/
  http://www.squash.org/

Usenet:
  rec.sport.squash

Swimming Competitions

Swimming is one of the most popular competitive sports in the world. If you have what it takes to get to the end of the pool faster than the next guy, you are assured a great deal of fun, excellent exercise, and the worship of other, less talented human beings who would have trouble finding their way out of a bathtub. (Moreover, you will find yourself with enormous patience, developed during all those hours you spend waiting at the side of the pool for your event.) To help you keep afloat in the world of water, here are some resources where you can find competitive swimming information: read about news, events, meet results, biographies, swim clubs and coaches.

Web:
  http://www.fina.org/
  http://www.swimnews.com/
  http://www.ussswim.org/

Tennis

To me, tennis is a funny sport. There seems to be a huge gap between the competitive tennis you watch on television and the game that everybody else in the world plays. Personally, I get bored watching other people play tennis, but I do like to bat the ball around myself once in a while. Anyway, how can you not like a game in which you start at love and work your way up?

Web:
> http://www.cs.ruu.nl/wais/html/na-dir/sports/
>   tennis-faq/.html
> http://www.tennis.com/
> http://www.tennisserver.com/

Usenet:
> rec.sport.tennis

Volleyball

There is something so fascinating about volleyball especially volleyball on the beach where young, nubile people clad in swimsuits jump around energetically to hit a ball that bounces back and forth and back and forth. If you like to watch or even participate, check out these sites dedicated to the sport of volleyball.

Web:
> http://www.avp.com/
> http://www.cvu.com/
> http://www.top20volleyball.com/cgi-bin/index.cgi
> http://www.volleyball.org/
> http://www.volleyballseek.com/

Usenet:
> rec.sport.volleyball

Women's Sports

Here are resources for all sorts of women's sports, teams and sports clubs: baseball, skating, volleyball, gymnastics, basketball, golf, bicycling, and many others. If you are already an athlete, you'll find lots of information about your favorite sport. If you are just starting to become active, the Net can help you find events in your area. I have also included a Web site that will keep you up to date on women's sports-related news.

Web:
> http://www.makeithappen.com/wis/
> http://www.northnet.org/stlawrenceaauw/sports.htm
> http://www.sportsjones.com/sj/categories/
>   women.shtml

Wrestling: Amateur

Amateur wrestling is nothing like professional wrestling. Amateur wresting is real: the emphasis is on athletic competition, not entertainment. There are two main types of amateur wrestling. In Greco-Roman wrestling, competitors may attack only with their arms and upper bodies. In freestyle wrestling, competitors may use their arms, upper bodies and legs, and they may hold their opponents above or below the waist.

Web:
> http://www.intermatwrestle.com/
> http://www.themat.com/
> http://www.wrestlingspot.com/

Usenet:
> alt.sport.wrestling.amateur

Wrestling: Professional

There's nothing like spending a peaceful weekend in front of the TV with a box of crackers, a can of spray cheese, and the remote control pointing at your favorite professional wrestling show. If you can't wait until the big day, get a wrestling fix from the Net, where you'll find lots of pictures to help you practice your moves at home or at the office.

Web:
> http://www.wrestlingmuseum.com/

Usenet:
> rec.sport.pro-wrestling
> rec.sport.pro-wrestling.fantasy
> rec.sport.pro-wrestling.info

IRC:
> #wrestling (EFnet)

Study the wrestling info on
the Net beforehand, and I
guarantee you will be able to
hold your date spellbound.

Wrestling: Sumo

Sumo wrestling is the national sport of Japan. Sumo
uses a playing ring that is a few meters across and
two men (who are also a few meters across). The
object of the event is to force your opponent out of
the ring or make any part of his body, except for the
soles of his feet, touch the floor (sort of like a
corporate takeover without the money). For more
information about this fascinating sport, take a look
at these sumo Web sites. (For more information about
corporate takeovers, call AT&T and ask for the
chairman's office.)

Web:
  http://www.scgroup.com/sumo/faq/
  http://www.sumoweb.com/

Usenet:
  rec.sport.sumo

SUPPORT GROUPS

AIDS Caregivers

AIDS (acquired immunodeficiency syndrome) is a
disease caused by HIV (human immunodeficiency
virus). Many AIDS patients require extensive care,
and the people who give such care have their own
special needs. This is especially so when the
caregiver is a friend or family member. If you are
taking care of an AIDS patient, you will find this
information helpful and inspiring.

Usenet:
  soc.support.aids-hiv+

Al-Anon and Alateen

Al-Anon and Alateen resources are available for
those people whose lives are affected by friends or
family members who are alcoholics. Here you can
find information about self-help recovery programs,
12-step programs, and a list of phone numbers for
Al-Anon or Alateen groups.

Web:
  http://www.al-anon-alateen.org/

Anxiety

It is normal to be anxious or agitated from time
to time. However, if you have a serious anxiety
disorder, you need help. Anxiety disorders can take
several forms: panic disorder (you have spontaneous
anxiety attacks that disrupt your life), obsessive-
compulsive disorder (you follow rituals or you have
obsessive thoughts), post traumatic stress disorder
(you have anxiety because of a past experience),
phobia (you have a debilitating fear of a particular
situation or object), generalized anxiety (you are
jittery a lot of the time), social anxiety (you are afraid
to be around other people).

Web:
  http://www.adaa.org/
  http://www.algy.com/anxiety/anxiety.html
  http://www.anxiety-panic.com/

Usenet:
  alt.support.anxiety-panic

Cancer Support

There are many different types of cancer, each of which has its own characteristics, problems and treatments. Here are a variety of resources to help you find the type of support you need. In particular, there are mailing lists for breast cancer (**brca-l**), kidney cancer (**kidney-onc**), larynx cancer (**larynx-c**), lung cancer (**lung-onc**), prostate cancer (**circle**), stomach cancer (**stomach-onc**) and testicular cancer (**tc-net**). The lists are not only for patients, but also for relatives and caregivers.

Web:
http://www.acor.org/
http://www.canceradvocacy.org/
http://www.nabco.org/
http://www.oncolink.com/
http://www.ustoo.com/

Listserv Mailing List:
List Name: **brca-l**
Subscribe to: **listserv@lists.ufl.edu**

Listserv Mailing List:
List Name: **kidney-onc**
Subscribe to: **listserv@listserv.acor.org**

Listserv Mailing List:
List Name: **larynx-c**
Subscribe to: **listserv@listserv.acor.org**

Listserv Mailing List:
List Name: **lung-onc**
Subscribe to: **listserv@listserv.acor.org**

Listserv Mailing List:
List Name: **stomach-onc**
Subscribe to: **listserv@listserv.acor.org**

Listserv Mailing List:
List Name: **tc-net**
Subscribe to: **listserv@listserv.acor.org**

Majordomo Mailing List:
List Name: **circle**
Subscribe to: **majordomo@www.prostatepointers.org**

Death of a Child

The death of a child is often unexpected and always profound. However, you are not alone. Use the Net and you'll find people to talk with, support groups, news and information.

Web:
http://www.alivealone.org/
http://www.bereavedparentsusa.org/
http://www.compassionatefriends.org/
http://www.members.aol.com/momofalison/grief/
http://www.missfoundation.org/

Depression

Depression is a psychological disorder characterized by a persisting general unhappiness often accompanied by other symptoms such as sleep disturbances, lack of appetite, lack of concentration, suicidal thoughts, problems with work or family life, and feelings of emptiness and worthlessness. There are a variety of different causes of depression, most of which are treatable.

Web:
http://www.depressiondepot.net/
http://www.docguide.com/news/content.nsf/
   patientresallcateg/depression?opendocument
http://www.nmisp.org/dep/depfaq.htm
http://www.psychologyinfo.com/depression/
http://www.psycom.net/depression.central.html

Usenet:
alt.support.depression
alt.support.depression.manic
alt.support.depression.seasonal
soc.support.depression.crisis
soc.support.depression.family
soc.support.depression.manic
soc.support.depression.misc
soc.support.depression.seasonal
soc.support.depression.treatment

Majordomo Mailing List:
List Name: **depress**
Subscribe to: **majordomo@soundprint.org**

IRC:
#depression (DALnet, Undernet)

Eating Disorders

You are what you eat, so if you really want to be who you should be, you should be eating what you should eat, but if you aren't (eating what you should eat, that is), maybe it would help to get some help, so you can start eating what you should eat, so you can be who you should be. (I never said it would be easy).

> ## Chicken Little was a little chicken.

Divorce

Marriage is an expression of a basic urge: to mate with a member of the opposite sex in a permanent union. For this reason, if your marriage breaks up, it will create an extreme rupture in the fabric of your life. Whether or not the divorce was your idea, it will shake you up a lot more than you might think, and it will take a long time for you to regain your confidence in the world. If you are divorced, you may need help, especially with finances or custody issues. If it happens that you are having trouble with your spouse and are thinking about a divorce, my advice is to be thoughtful and go slowly. You can cause a lot of unnecessary unhappiness in life by looking for permanent solutions to temporary problems.

Web:
   http://www.divorcecentral.com/
   http://www.divorcesupport.com/

Usenet:
   alt.support.divorce

Domestic Violence

If you are suffering from domestic violence, if someone at home is abusing you—either physically or emotionally—you do not need to suffer in silence. A great deal of information is available, and there are people who are ready to help you right now, as long as you take the first step and ask for help.

Web:
   http://www.dvsheltertour.org/
   http://www.endabuse.org/
   http://www.feminist.org/other/dv/dvhome.html
   http://www.ncadv.org/

Usenet:
   alt.support.abuse-partners

Eating Disorders

The three most common eating disorders are anorexia nervosa (an aversion to food coupled with an extreme fear of becoming fat), bulimia nervosa (binge eating followed by self-induced vomiting or purging) and compulsive eating (bouts of uncontrollable eating). Eating disorders can result from a variety of psychological, biochemical and environmental causes, and can have serious consequences, including metabolic disorders, excessive weight loss or gain, dehydration, hyperactivity, depression and even death. If you suspect you might have an eating disorder, you should check out these resources. You'll be able to read about the various conditions and their signs and symptoms. If someone close to you has a problem, you will also find useful information here, such as how to confront a loved one, how to get help, how to find a therapist, and much, much more. The Usenet discussion groups are for people with eating disorders as well as supportive family members and friends.

Web:
   http://www.caringonline.com/
   http://www.closetoyou.org/eatingdisorders/
   http://www.something-fishy.org/

Usenet:
   alt.recovery.compulsive-eat
   alt.support.eating-disord

Gambling Addiction

Compulsive gambling is a chronic, *progressive* condition. Do you suspect that you might be a compulsive gambler? Visit the Gamblers Anonymous Web site, where you can take a private, 20-question test to help bring your problems into perspective. If you determine that you have a problem, help is available.

Web:
   http://www.cghub.homestead.com/
   http://www.gamblersanonymous.org/
   http://www.ncpgambling.org/resources.htm

Usenet:
   alt.recovery.addiction.gambling

Grief

There are many reasons for grief, and sometimes it helps to be able to talk with someone who has gone through a similar experience. If you are in this position, you will find the Usenet discussion group useful and comforting. In addition, there are many Web sites with relevant information. No one can replace your loss or change what has happened, but there are many people on the Net who are in similar situations and who are glad to help you. Notes: (1) The Usenet group is *not* for people who are grieving because of a broken romance. (2) The participants do not want to talk to people who are doing research for journals or academic papers.

Web:
   http://www.griefnet.org/
   http://www.rivendell.org/resources/

Usenet:
   alt.support.grief

Narcotics Anonymous

Narcotics Anonymous (NA) is an international community of organizations dedicated to helping drug addicts recover from their addictions. NA is based on the 12-step program used in other similar organizations. I have included two Web pages: one is the official NA site, the other is an NA-oriented discussion group created by private individuals.

Web:
   http://www.na.org/
   http://www.netmegs.com/na-nbg/

Usenet:
   alt.recovery.na

Pregnancy Loss

When you lose a baby or miscarry, it doesn't do much good when well-meaning friends remind you that it was not your fault, and maybe "it was all for the best." What you need is compassion and some real facts. This Usenet group is for the support of both women and men who have suffered the loss of an unborn child. On the Web, you'll find tips for coping, information about grieving, and medical information about pregnancy loss. If you have recently experienced such a loss, I can tell you that it is a lot more common than you might realize. Please remember, on the Net, you are never alone.

Web:
   http://www.miscarriage.org.nz/
   http://www.womens-health.co.uk/miscarr.htm

Usenet:
   soc.support.pregnancy.loss

Recovery for Christians

This Web site is maintained by Christians in Recovery (CIR). The resources are for people recovering from all types of problems: drug abuse, dysfunctional families, depression, anxiety, eating disorders, sexual addiction, and so on. There is information about the 12-step program, a checklist of symptoms that lead to relapse, computer programs that may help you recover (such as the Recovery Bible, quote-a-day programs, etc.), and links to Christian and non-Christian recovery sites. There is also information that will help you find other people to talk to on the Net using IRC, Usenet and mailing lists.

Web:
   http://www.christians-in-recovery.com/

Recovery for Jews

This site is for Jews who are recovering from alcohol or drug abuse. The site stresses anonymity, so if the shoe fits, there is no reason not to wear it. At this Web site you can read recovery stories, cartoons about Jewish denial, a zine about recovery and spirituality, words from rabbis and scholars, and information about online meetings. This site is sponsored by JACS (Jewish Alcoholics, Chemically Dependent People, and Significant Others).

Web:
   http://www.jacsweb.org/

Sexual Addiction

To most people, sex is a source of enormous pleasure (or frustration). That's normal. But to many people, sex is way, way out of control. If you suspect that you might be addicted to sex—or you know that you *are* addicted to sex—finding thoughtful information about your problem can be the first step to resolving it.

Web:
   http://www.onlinerecovery.org/sex/
   http://www.onlinesexaddict.org/links.html
   http://www.sarr.org/
   http://www.sexaa.org/
   http://www.sexaa.org/online.htm

Smoking

It's not easy to quit smoking. You need to wean yourself from strong physical addiction and psychological dependence. However, there's no reason for you to have to do it alone. There are lots of people on the Net who are going through—or who have gone through—the same process. They are sympathetic and helpful, and will be more than glad to lend support. Once you have successfully beaten your addiction (which may take more than one try), why not hang around for awhile to help and encourage other people?

Web:
http://www.faqs.org/faqs/support/stop-smoking/
http://www.nicotine-anonymous.org/
http://www.quitnet.com/
http://www.quitsmokingsupport.com/

Usenet:
alt.support.non-smokers
alt.support.stop-smoking

Suicide Prevention

Suicide is the act of taking one's own life. Suicide attempts are more common than many people recognize, and are usually due to an underlying disease such as depression. The important thing to realize is that such diseases (especially depression) are treatable, and most suicide attempts are preventable, *if* the person gets help in time. If you are thinking of suicide, please take the time to look at some of these resources. How you feel might seem permanent, but I assure you this is not necessarily the case. If you have a loved one who has committed suicide (or attempted it), you will also find help on the Net. In particular, the Usenet groups are important for ongoing discussion and support.

Web:
http://www.faqs.org/faqs/suicide/resources/
http://www.mentalhelp.net/poc/
   center_index.php?id=9
http://www.metanoia.org/suicide/samaritans.htm
http://www.rivendell.org/resources/suicide.html
http://www.rochford.org/suicide/
http://www.suicidehotlines.com/
http://www.suicidepreventtriangle.org/

Usenet:
alt.suicide.recovery
alt.support.grief.suicide

Support Groups Networking

When you're ailing, it helps to have people to talk to. No matter what your problem, I bet you'll be able to find companionship and conversation at this Web site: a collection of many "bulletin boards" (discussion groups), devoted to just about every area of human suffering you can imagine. The people who participate are friendly and compassionate, so if you have a health, personal or relationship problem, this is the place to look for company.

Web:
http://www.support-group.com/

Support Talk and General Discussion

On the Net, you are never alone. Out of the millions of people, there are some who are a lot like you and want to talk. The Net has a large number of resources to provide support. There are Usenet groups, mailing lists, IRC channels, and many, many Web sites. This Usenet group is the general support forum, where you can go with a question, a problem, a story or simply to satisfy your curiosity. If you are looking for support of a particular kind and you are having difficulty finding it, this group would be a good place to ask people for suggestions. (Personally, I am looking for a group that supports writers who stay up all night to finish Internet books.)

Usenet:
alt.support

Transgendered Support

Transgendered people are those whose sexual identities have significant ambiguity. This group includes transsexuals (people whose minds are trapped in a body of the opposite sex), cross-dressers or transvestites (people, almost always men, who enjoy dressing like the opposite sex), and intersexed (people born with ambiguous genitalia). If you are new to discussing such issues, I have included a Web site that contains a FAQ.

Web:
  http://www.gendertalk.com/
  http://www.heartcorps.com/journeys/
  http://www.medhelp.org/www/ais/
  http://www.sexuality.org/l/transgen/transg1.html
  http://www.symposion.com/ijt/

Usenet Support Groups

It's great to know that when you have a problem, there are people who will be supportive of you. All over the world there are people who are willing to take the time to listen to problems and try to meet the emotional needs of others. Get good information on nearly any subject related to medical, emotional or psychological problems.

Usenet:
  alt.abuse
  alt.abuse.offender.recovery
  alt.abuse.recovery
  alt.abuse.transcendence
  alt.recovery
  alt.recovery.aa
  alt.recovery.adult-children
  alt.recovery.catholicism
  alt.recovery.codependency
  alt.recovery.compulsive-eat
  alt.recovery.mormonism
  alt.recovery.na
  alt.recovery.religion
  alt.support.abortion
  alt.support.abuse-partners
  alt.support.asthma
  alt.support.ataxia
  alt.support.big-folks
  alt.support.breast-implant
  alt.support.breastfeeding
  alt.support.cancer
  alt.support.cancer.prostate
  alt.support.cancer.testicular
  alt.support.cerebral-palsy
  alt.support.childfree
  alt.support.chronic-pain
  alt.support.diabetes.kids
  alt.support.disabled.caregivers
  alt.support.dissociation
  alt.support.dystonia
  alt.support.endometriosis
  alt.support.epilepsy
  alt.support.ex-cult
  alt.support.food-allergies
  alt.support.glaucoma
  alt.support.grief.pet-loss
  alt.support.headaches.migraine
  alt.support.hearing-loss
  alt.support.hemophilia
  alt.support.herpes
  alt.support.ibs
  alt.support.inter-cystitis
  alt.support.jaw-disorders
  alt.support.kidney-failure
  alt.support.learning-disab
  alt.support.loneliness
  alt.support.lupus
  alt.support.marfan
  alt.support.marriage
  alt.support.menopause
  alt.support.ms-recovery
  alt.support.mult-sclerosis
  alt.support.mult-sclerosis.alternatives
  alt.support.myasthe-gravis
  alt.support.ocd
  alt.support.opp-defiant
  alt.support.ostomy
  alt.support.parents.with-custody
  alt.support.pco
  alt.support.personality
  alt.support.post-polio
  alt.support.prostate.prostatitis
  alt.support.schizophrenia
  alt.support.scleroderma
  alt.support.short
  alt.support.shyness
  alt.support.sinusitis
  alt.support.skin-diseases
  alt.support.skin-diseases.psoriasis
  alt.support.social-phobia
  alt.support.spina-bifida
  alt.support.stuttering
  alt.support.survivors.prozac
  alt.support.tall
  alt.support.thyroid
  alt.support.tinnitus
  alt.support.tourette
  alt.support.trauma-ptsd
  alt.support.turner-syndrom
  soc.support.fat-acceptance
  soc.support.loneliness

Widows and Widowers

Anyone who has ever lost a husband or wife knows that you never "get over it". However, most people find that, eventually, the pain does lessen, a bit at a time. This doesn't mean that the memory of your spouse is gone, or that you ever stop caring. What it means is that, over time, you develop a way of thinking about things that decreases the suffering. If you are having trouble with being too sad for too long—or if you have recently lost someone, and you don't know what to do—help is available.

Web:

http://www.fortnet.org/widownet/
http://www.laurieannweis.com/

Majordomo Mailing List:

List Name: widow
Subscribe to: majordomo@fortnet.org

Wish Granting for Adults

There are many people who could use a day- brightener, and there are organizations that can help. These services are for adults only, for example, seniors in nursing homes. Granting a wish to help someone fulfill a dream is a wonderful way to contribute to the world.

Web:

http://www.dreamfoundation.com/
http://www.secondwind.org/

Wish Granting for Kids

My cousin Ellen and her husband Hugh have a daughter, Kate, with cerebral palsy. Some years ago, Kate was able to have a wish granting organization arrange for her to meet and have a dance with her favorite actor, and it was one of the highlights of her life. (Her brothers, Sam and Tom, who got to go on the trip, also had a great time.) There are many children who, for one reason or another, have a tough time of it, and there are organizations set up to grant these kids a special wish. In general, they tailor the wish to the person and take care of all the details. Some of these organizations are for terminally ill children, others are for children with chronic conditions or illnesses.

Web:

http://www.acor.org/ped-onc/cfissues/maw.html
http://www.childrenswish.org/
http://www.grant-a-wish.org/
http://www.starlight.org/intl/programs/wishes.htm
http://www.wish.org/
http://www.wishingwellusa.org/

TIDBITS

What should fans know about watching BASKETBALL?

There are two types of basketball teams: those that are built around a single star player, and those that have a group of players of more or less equal ability. The secret to understanding a basketball game is to watch the game in a way that depends on the types of teams that are playing.

When the offensive team (the team with the ball) has a star player who is good enough to dominate the game, the defensive team must use a strategy in which the star is covered by *two* defensive players at the same time. (We say that the star is "double-teamed".) This means that the other four offensive players will be covered less tightly, which creates an imbalance. It is this imbalance that sets the tone for the game.

In such a case, when the star's team has the ball, make a point of watching the other four offensive players. Notice what they do to take advantage of their situation, and see if you can analyze how they maneuver themselves into a position in which they will be free to get the ball and try to score.

When the offensive team does not have a star player, the players must be more cohesive and use better teamwork, because they can't depend on simply feeding the ball to one person. When you watch a game of this type, don't concentrate on individual players. Look at the team as a whole and the pattern they create as they play. Notice the ways in which all five offensive players work together as a unit.

When you watch a basketball game in this way — by looking for patterns and analyzing the strategy — you will be thinking about the action in the same way as the players do as they are playing, and your enjoyment as a fan will be increased.

This is because, instead of concentrating only on individual players or simply following the ball, you will be watching the *game*.

TALKING ON THE NET

3D Chatting

3D chatting means being able to talk to people while you are moving around in an imaginary three-dimensional world. As a member of one of these worlds, you can choose an avatar for yourself. (An avatar is a virtual body you can control.) As you explore a 3D world, you will not only see interesting scenery, you will encounter other avatars, each of which represents a real person somewhere on the Net.

Web:
  http://www.activeworlds.com/
  http://www.cybertown.com/
  http://www.moove.com/
  http://www.penguinchat.com/
  http://www.thepalace.com/

BBSs (Bulletin Board Systems)

A BBS (bulletin board system) is a small, self-contained communication facility, usually maintained by a single person and organized around a specific theme. A typical BBS will have discussion forums as well as files to download. There may also be other features, such as chat areas and games. Before the Internet was so widespread, there were many independent BBSs, each with its own telephone number. To access one of these BBSs, you would have your computer dial the BBS directly. Now many BBSs are on the Net, and to connect to them you use a program called telnet. Windows has a built-in telnet program you can access from the DOS prompt. (Just type "telnet " followed by an address.) Alternatively, you can access telnet via your browser. In the place where you would enter a Web address, type "telnet:" followed by the BBS address, for example, "telnet:bbb.mybbs.com". (Hint: If you are going to use BBSs a lot, you may prefer to use a better telnet program. To find one, look in a software archive.) If you have never visited a BBS, why not give it a try? Each BBS supports its own online community, some of which have been around for years.

Web:
  http://www.thedirectory.org/telnet/

Usenet:
  comp.bbs.misc

Chat Acronyms

On the Internet, a lot of communication consists of people typing text to one another—in email messages, discussion groups, and while talking to other people using chat rooms, talk facilities, IRC, muds and so on. For years now, people have been using a large number of common abbreviations to save time and effort. So when you see an unfamiliar abbreviation, don't worry. Just look it up on one of these lists. It won't be long before you are a master of the lingo yourself, and you'll find yourself typing: omg paw i'll send you pm l8r. ("Oh my God, my parents are watching. I'll send you a private message later.")

Web:
  http://www.harley.com/abbreviations/
  http://www.sharpened.net/glossary/acronyms.php
  http://www.solscape.com/chat/acronyms.html
  http://www.techdictionary.com/chat.html

BBSs on the Net

If you're all undressed, but you still have a hankering for going out, the Net is at your service.

There are oodles and gobs of BBSs you can visit, 24 hours a day, no matter how casual your attire.

Chat Rooms

A chat room is a facility that lets you talk to people over the Web. Some chat rooms require you to have special software in order to participate. With others, your Web browser will do everything you need. When you connect to a chat room Web site, you will commonly find a number of rooms, each of which is devoted to discussing a specific topic. Other Web sites are devoted to a specific organization or theme. For example, a radio talk show may set up a chat room for its listeners to talk to one another while they are listening to the show. Or a company may set up a chat room for customers to talk about its products. Many Web sites allow you to specify a small image to identify yourself to other people. Each time you send a message, this image is displayed next to the message. Sometimes you can furnish your own image. You could use, for example, a small picture of yourself. Other chat rooms require you to choose an image from their library. The Web sites I have listed all have chat rooms open to the public. However, some of the services may ask you to register. When you visit, you will find people from all over the Net talking on many different topics.

Web:

http://chat.yahoo.com/
http://communicate.excite.com/
http://communities.msn.com/
http://www.aokchat.com/
http://www.chatlist.com/
http://www.chatropolis.com/

Chat Servers

Would you like to set up your own chat room? Well, you can. You can set up your own topic or make it for general discussion. In the olden days, (before television), cultured people would have a salon, a room in their house to which they would invite their friends for intellectual conversation. Now you can do the same thing online and you won't even have to serve refreshments.

Web:

http://www.everysoft.com/everychat/
http://www.parachat.com/
http://www.thefreesite.com/Free_Software/
    free_chat_programs/

Chatting Safety

When you talk to somebody on the Net, they can't harm you physically, but it is possible to get hurt in other ways. For example, if somebody were to get your email address, he or she could become a nuisance sending unpleasant mail. Or you might meet someone online and enter into some type of relationship, only to find out later that the person was misrepresenting himself. And, of course, regular life can intersect with the Net. If you tell somebody where you live, they can come over and pay you an unexpected visit. Almost all of the time, people on the Net are well-behaved and just about everyone you meet will be okay. But there are millions of people out there and a few of them are just plain bad. If you are new to the Net, here is some information that can help you be appropriately prudent when you talk with people. If you are a parent, you will find lots of information to help you teach your child to use the Net safely.

Web:

http://www.chatmag.com/help/safety2.html
http://www.theguardianangel.com/
    basic_internet_safety_tips.htm
http://www.webmaze.com/teen/chatsafety.html

What if…?

Instant Messaging (IM)

An instant messaging (IM) program allows you to talk to your friends by typing messages back and forth. Instant messaging is very popular, and I bet a lot of your friends IM for hours at a time. Not all of these programs are compatible, so be sure to ask your friends which program they use so you can get the same one.

Web:
http://aim.aol.com/
http://messenger.msn.com/
http://messenger.yahoo.com/
http://www.icq.com/
http://www.jabber.org/
http://www.odigo.org/
http://www.paltalk.com/
http://www.trillian.cc/

IRC (Internet Relay Chat)

IRC is an old, well-established system for talking over the Net. To use IRC, you need an IRC client program. Your client connects to an IRC server. You can now talk to people all over the world. IRC is organized into "channels", some of which you will see in this book. To participate, you "join" one or more channels. It is important to realize that, unlike Usenet groups, IRC channels are created and removed dynamically. Anyone can create a new IRC channel; when the last person leaves a particular channel, it is removed automatically. (The channels in this book are so popular, there is almost always someone around to keep them open.) IRC is fabulous, but before you start I do want you to know what you are doing. Begin by visiting these Web sites where you will find a wealth of information: FAQs (frequently asked question lists), primers, RFCs (technical documents, aka "request for comments"), help files, information for channel ops (operators), and lists of IRC servers to which you can connect. For a comprehensive easy-to-understand introduction to IRC, see my book *Harley Hahn's Internet Advisor*.

Web:
http://www.irchelp.org/
http://www.mirc.org/links.shtml
http://www.newircusers.com/
IRC:
#irchelp (DALnet, EFnet, Undernet)

IRC Bots and Scripts

A bot (short for "robot") is a program that will do things for you automatically as you use IRC, by following commands or responding to specific events. There are a number of different types of bots, for example, war bots (to cause trouble), channel bots (to perform channel-related or administrative tasks), and bar bots (to play games, serve you food and drink). A script is an initialization file that is designed to perform specific commands. For example, a script can prevent you from being flooded or disconnected, protect your channels, and so on. Many bots and scripts are useful and fun; others are just annoying.

Web:
http://www.eggfaq.com/
http://www.eggheads.org/
http://www.mirc.net/

Usenet:
alt.irc.bots

IRC Clients

To use IRC, you need a program called an IRC client. You run the program on your computer, and it connects you to IRC servers. Here's where you can find the best IRC clients.

Web:
http://www.dircchat.com/
http://www.jpilot.com/
http://www.leafdigital.com/software/leafchat/
http://www.mirc.com/
http://www.xircon.com/

IRC Talk and General Discussion

Using IRC (Internet Relay Chat) is like going into a crowded bar, only there is not as much smoke and no cover charge. Mingle with crowds of people, make new friends, have philosophical discussions— use your imagination. Just about anything can happen when you're on IRC. Check out these Usenet groups, which cover topics like announcements, specific IRC channels, and questions relating to IRC.

Usenet:
alt.irc.hottub
alt.irc.questions
alt.irc.undernet

Talkers

A talker is an easy-to-use multiuser talk facility. You connect to a talker using telnet. (Telnet is a program that acts like a terminal and allows you to connect to a remote computer. Telnet is usually included with general Internet software, so there is a good chance that you already have a telnet program on your computer. Once you connect to a talker, you can talk to anyone else who happens to be there. If you are a mud person, you can think of a talker as being a simple mud or mush devoted entirely to conversation. These Web sites contain lists of talkers and where you can find them. One of the sites has additional information, such as the history of talkers, and the rules and culture.

Web:
> http://list.ewtoo.org/
> http://realms.palni.edu/
> http://www.stairway.org/tickle/talktips.html
> http://www.tdf.ca/talkers.php

Talking in the Big City

A big city can be a lonely place, but you can meet people and talk to them via the Net. Even better, if you are moving to a new town or even visiting, you can find people on IRC who live there. Make new friends before you go and ask the best places to live and visit.

IRC:
> #atlanta (DALnet)
> #boston (Undernet)
> #chicago (DALnet, Undernet)
> #dallas (DALnet, Undernet)
> #dallastx (Efnet)
> #denver (DALnet)
> #detroit (Undernet)
> #houston (DALnet, Undernet)
> #melbourne (Undernet)
> #miami (DALnet, Undernet)
> #montreal (DALnet, EFnet, Undernet)
> #orlando (EFnet)
> #paris (EFnet, Undernet)
> #realchicago (Efnet)
> #sandiego (DALnet, EFnet, Undernet)
> #seattle (DALnet, Undernet)
> #sydney (DALnet)

Voice and Video Chatting

Voice chatting refers to talking to people over the Net (real voice talking, as with a telephone). To use a voice chat program, you need either a microphone and speakers, or a headset with a built-in microphone. There are three reasons why you might enjoy doing this. First, it's fun to talk to people using your computer; second, you can talk to people all over the world, people who you otherwise would never have met; and third, you don't have to pay long distance charges. Compared to talking with a real telephone, voice chat does not sound as good, but it's fun and it's free. Some voice chat systems also allow you to use video while you are talking. To look at someone as you talk, you don't need any special equipment. However, to broadcast video, you need a webcam, a small camera that connects to your computer. Some people say that, in the future, it will be common to meet with other people via video conferencing. In fact, Isaac Asimov once wrote a book about a planet in which the people would meet one another *only* by three-dimensional video conferencing and not in person. Personally, I think that video conferencing will never be as popular as the telephone.

Web:
> http://aim.aol.com/
> http://messenger.msn.com/
> http://messenger.yahoo.com/
> http://messenger.yahoo.com/messenger/help/
>   voicechat.html
> http://www.eyeball.com/
> http://www.microsoft.com/windows/netmeeting/
> http://www.netscape.com/communicator/
>   conference/
> http://www.paltalk.com/

TEENAGERS

Christian Youth

Church isn't the only place to meet other Christian teenagers. Young people from around the world are using Usenet for ongoing discussion. On the Web, you'll find more forums as well as a variety of Christian-oriented teen resources.

Web:
> http://www.christianteens.net/
> http://www.youthwalk.org/

Usenet:
> soc.religion.christian.youth-work

Cool Science

Do you like science? Do you think it's fun to experiment with stuff, see what happens, and then try to explain it by making up a theory? I bet you'd like some science projects that are fun. For example, you may not realize it, but right this very minute there's DNA in your fridge. (Don't tell your mother.) In fact, your kitchen may hold the tools you need to start becoming a scientist. These Web sites have directions for various fun science projects, some of which you can do at home. (By the way, DNA— deoxyribonucleic acid—is the substance used within cells to store the information needed by the cell to reproduce and to carry out many of its functions.)

Web:
http://faculty.washington.edu/chudler/neurok.html
http://gslc.genetics.utah.edu/students.html
http://www.chem4kids.com
http://www.explorescience.com/
http://www.extremescience.com/
http://www.fetc.doe.gov/coolscience/
http://www.ipl.org/youth/projectguide/
http://www.scitoys.com/scitoys/scitoys/about.html

Girl Stuff

So you want to be popular, you want to be cool, you want the guys to notice you, and you want to fit in. Well, there are three things you can do. You can hang out with other girls at the mall, you can IM your friends and talk all night, or you can check out these resources that are just for teenage girls. (As I am sure your parents have told you, growing up is all about making the right choices.)

Web:
http://www.girlpower.gov/
http://www.girlsinc.org/gc/
http://www.girlsite.com/
http://www.girltech.com/
http://www.ipl.org/teen/esteem/webgirls.html
http://www.purplepjs.com/aunt-musey.htm

Girl's Health

As you grow up, you are going to have various health questions that are specific to girls. When you do, check with these Web sites, where you will find important information that can help you. They cover such topics as periods, changes to your body as you grow, eating, exercise and medical problems.

Web:
http://www.cyclesofwellness.com/index_us.html
http://www.iemily.com/
http://www.kidshealth.org/teen/
http://www.kotex.com/talk/teen/

Marijuana Facts

As illegal drugs go, marijuana seems relatively benign, but, as with any drug that affects your mind, you should have the facts. Long-term marijuana use can sap your ambition and significantly decrease your success in life. (I have seen it happen to more than one person.) Moreover, the more you get stoned, the more you make tiny changes to your brain that, eventually, become irreversible.

Web:
http://www.nida.nih.gov/marijbroch/marijteens.html

Meeting Teens on the Net

As you know, teenagers all around the world are using the Internet. Maybe you would like to meet some of them and perhaps find a penpal. Hints: (1) Don't give out too much personal information (such as your address or phone number). (2) If you make a friend on the Net and you decide to meet in person, do not go alone. Take a friend or have an adult along.

Web:
   http://www.teleboards.com/singlespersonals.html
   http://www.theinplace2b.com/

Preparing for College

Going to college is absolutely the best thing you can do to prepare yourself for having a successful life. People like to remind you that it is easier to get a good job when you have a college degree. That's true, but there is a lot more to it than that. When you go to college you will train your mind for (at least) four years, and that training will help you for the rest of your life. At the same time, you will learn a lot, and the more you know, the better. Even subjects that seem irrelevant now have a way of becoming useful later in life. Finally, college is an important social experience. You'll meet many new people and make new friends. But most important, you will have a lot of *fun*—something your high school guidance counselor may forget to mention. So go to college. Now that we have that settled, here are some Internet resources to help you prepare, choose and apply.

Web:
   http://iiswinprd03.petersons.com/ugchannel/
   http://www.collegeboard.com/
   http://www.collegebot.com
   http://www.collegenet.com/
   http://www.collegeview.com/
   http://www.embark.com/
   http://www.library.uiuc.edu/edx/rankings.htm
   http://www.mycollegeguide.org/

Straight-Edge

Straight-edge (usually abbreviated as sXe) is a practical way of living that was an offshoot of the punk rock scenes of the early 1980s. Originally, sXe was a philosophy based on the simple tenets of having fun—especially at loud volume—but no drugs, no smoking and no promiscuous sex. Since then, sXe has grown and evolved. There have been many sXe bands around the world as well as countless teenagers and young adults who have adopted a sXe lifestyle. Some people have extended the definition of the word sXe to being a vegetarian and becoming involved in social issues such as environmentalism. In general, the sXe lifestyle varies from person to person and place to place, but what it always seems to have in common is the belief that it's possible to lead a clean, wholesome life and still have a lot of fun (at loud volume).

Web:
   http://www.faqs.org/faqs/cultures/straight-edge-faq/
   http://www.straightedge.com/

Usenet:
   alt.lifestyle.substance-free
   alt.punk.straight-edge

Teen Chatting

The great thing about working on the computer and saying it's a school project is that when you are grounded and you can't leave the house, you can still talk to kids your own age and have fun. There are lots of special chat areas just for people your age. Pick the one that is appropriate and talk all night long (or until you have to go back to doing your homework).

Web:
   http://www.teenchat.com/
   http://www.teenchat.net/
   http://www.teenchatnow.com/

IRC:
   #teenchat (DALnet, Undernet)
   #teenszone (Undernet)
   #teenzone (DALnet, EFnet, Undernet)

Teen Dating

As a teenager, you can have a lot of fun dating. You can also have problems, so if you need a bit of help, you can turn to the Net for advice and information. If you are not yet dating (and remember, there is no hurry), this information can help you get started comfortably.

Web:

http://www.askninanow.com/
http://www.teenadviceonline.org/dating/

Teen Driving Tips

Driving can be a lot of fun, especially when you can drive well. Here are some tips for new drivers. Read the hints for driving to school, around town and in the country. Learn about driving in bad weather, when to pass (and when not to), fatigue and buying a used car. Note: This Web site was created by a teenager who is a new driver. He did a good job: the tips are great. (Hint: This is a good place to show your parents when they ask why you spend so much time on the Net.)

Web:

http://www.teendriving.com/

Teen Movie Critic

Remember the last time you went to a movie theater, and you sat behind a mouthy young teenage girl who couldn't stop talking during the show, and, on the way out, explained to her friends and everyone within earshot just what was wrong with the movie, the actors, the director, the music and the popcorn? Well, here she is again, alive and well on the Net.

Web:

http://www.dreamagic.com/vivianrose/
  teencritic1.html

Teen Places

There are a lot of Web sites on the Internet constructed for teenagers by well-meaning teachers and parents, and I can tell you, in two words, what these sites are like: bor ing. Here, then, are some Web sites I think you'll really like. You'll find chat rooms, news, art, advice and things to read, as well as information about movies, music, jobs, travel and sports. You'll also have a chance to meet people and make new friends.

Web:

http://www.bolt.com/
http://www.cyberteens.com/
http://www.teenadventure.com/
http://www.thej.net/

Teen Resources

If you are a teenager, the last thing you want to do is listen to me giving you advice. So, instead, I'll just point you to some interesting teen-oriented Web sites. You're on your own. (Of course, if you really do need advice, I'll be glad to help...)

Web:

http://www.atomicteen.com/
http://www.ipl.org/teen/
http://www.teengrowth.com/

Teen Talk and General Discussion

Here are some lively places where teenagers can write about anything they want. The traffic is high, and there are a lot of diverse opinions as well as some thoughtful messages. This is a great place for you to meet other kids, and to let everyone else know what you think.

Usenet:

alt.kids-talk
alt.romance.teen
alt.teens

Teenage Literature

Sometimes, someone will do something that turns out to be one of the biggest favors anyone ever did for you, but you don't realize it till years later. I still remember the day (I was in high school at the time) when I was standing in the library next to my friend Joe. (Joe was the Smartest Person in the School.) "Joe, I need something good to read," I said. "Can you recommend something?". He went to the shelf and pulled off a book by P.G. Wodehouse. "Try this," he said, so I did. Now, over 30 years later, I have a large collection of Wodehouse books, many of which I have read and reread several times. Perhaps, in these lists of book recommendations, you'll find something that will change *your* life. (If not, try anything by P.G. Wodehouse.)

Web:
  http://www.cannylink.com/teenageliterature.htm
  http://www.grouchy.com/angst/
  http://www.st-charles.lib.il.us/low/ygadread.htm
  http://www.teenreads.com/

ThinkQuest

ThinkQuest is a collection of Internet-based activities for teenagers, in which kids work with other people (including teachers) to create Web-based learning material. Although it sounds dull, ThinkQuest is actually a cool thing to do. Unlike most teenage activities created by adults, this one is actually a lot of fun.

Web:
  http://www.thinkquest.org/

Teen Talk and General Discussion

Volunteering for Teenagers

Many young people would like to volunteer within their community, but they don't know where to go. If this is true for you, the Net can help. Volunteering is good for just about everyone, especially for teenagers. If you are a teenager, you probably know that it is easy to be a bit too concerned with your own problems. By helping someone else, you change the emphasis of your life (at least for a few hours a week) from your own concerns to those of others. In the long run, volunteering will help you learn about human nature and build character. In the short run, you'll have fun. So why not give it a try?

Web:
  http://www.kidscare.org/
  http://www.servenet.org/
  http://www.volunteers.com/

Young Investors and Entrepreneurs

Every day you make decisions. Some are unimportant ("Which cereal should I eat?"), while others are very important ("What college should I go to?"). Learning how to make decisions well is an important part of life, and nowhere is it more important than when it comes to money. If you practice financial decision-making when you are young, it will help you a lot when you become old (that is, over 25). Here are some Web sites that will help you learn how to invest money or start your own business. In general, I encourage you to spend your youth having fun (while you are educating yourself). However, I do recommend that you spend some time learning about how money works, and how you can make it work for you.

Web:
  http://www.anincomeofherown.com/
  http://www.youngbiz.com/

Young Writers

So you want to be a writer. Good. My advice is to practice every day, and stick with it no matter what. I can't guarantee that writing a lot will make you intelligent, good-looking, successful and adorable. All I can say is it worked for me.

Web:
  http://www.diaryproject.com/
  http://www.teenink.com/
  http://www.youngwritersnook.com/

TELEPHONE AND TELECOM

Area Codes

The need for new phone numbers has increased rapidly in the last few years because of mobile phones, faxes and computer lines. In many parts of the United States and Canada, the areas covered by a single code have had to be subdivided or reorganized and then assigned new codes in order to create enough new phone numbers. Here are some area code resources to help you find your way through this brave new telephonic world. (By the way, you might be wondering, is there a master plan? The answer is, yes, and it is maintained by NANPA, the North American Numbering Plan Administration.)

Web:
  http://www.areadecoder.com/
  http://www.mmiworld.com/telephone.htm
  http://www.nanpa.com/area_codes/
  http://www.prodial.com/codes1.html

(A true story.)

The President of the United States called me just the other day.

"Harley," he said, "they tell me you know everything."

"Well..." I said modestly.

"I was hoping you could help me out."

"Yes?"

"Do you have any idea what the area code is for Piscataway, New Jersey? I think I left my wallet there in a restaurant.

"It's 732".

"Thanks," he said. "I really appreciate it. Is there anything I can I do for you?"

"Hmmm... I've always wanted a medal."

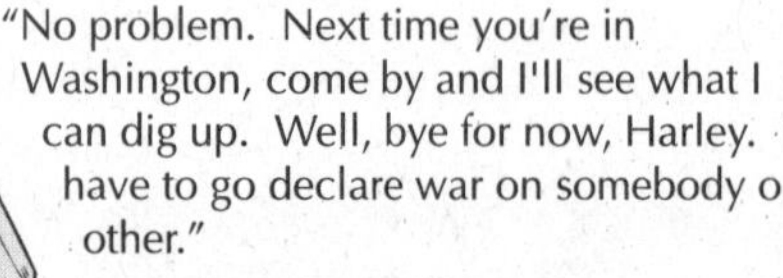

"No problem. Next time you're in Washington, come by and I'll see what I can dig up. Well, bye for now, Harley. I have to go declare war on somebody or other."

"Bye, Mr. President. I hope you find your wallet."

Business and Toll-Free Directory Listings

Looking for a particular business? If the company or organization you want has a telephone, they are probably in here somewhere. These Web sites allow you to search for the phone number of a business. Some of the sites are directories of toll-free numbers; the others help you find regular numbers.

Web:
  http://www.infospace.com/info.zip/
  http://www.inter800.com/
  http://www.superpages.com/

Cell Phone Ring Signals

You're lost in a big city and everyone around you has a cell phone. Suddenly, one of the phones rings, and everyone jumps to see if it is theirs. But you know it's yours, because *you* have programmed your phone to play a super-cool song that makes your cell phone sound unique every time it rings. And where did you get the info you needed to program your phone? On the Net, of course.

Web:
  http://www.alltones.org/
  http://www.mobilefun.co.uk/ringtones.htm
  http://www.phonatic.net/nokia/3210ringtones.htm

Cell-Relay Communications

A "cell" refers to a small device that can be used for transporting and multiplexing information over a network. This discussion group is devoted to the technologies—such as ATM (Asynchronous Transfer Mode)—that make use of cells as transport mechanisms within local, metropolitan and wide-area networks.

Usenet:
  comp.dcom.cell-relay

Data Communications Servers

On Usenet, you can find people who are ready, willing and able to discuss data communications 24 hours a day. This particular Usenet group is for discussion relating to selecting and operating data communications servers: special purpose computers that do the dirty work in moving information from one place to another (terminal servers, routers, hubs, and so on).

Usenet:
  comp.dcom.servers

Fax Technology

There is more to fax machines than just using them to transmit the latest Dilbert comic strip to someone who is not lucky enough to have Net access. This Usenet group is for the discussion of faxes: standalone machines, computer adaptors and software, technical specifications, faxing on the Net, and so on.

Usenet:
  comp.dcom.fax

International Dialing Codes

In order to place a telephone call to a foreign country, you need to know the country code. These resources can help you find the country codes you need, along with city codes and time zone information.

Web:
  http://www.construction-site.com/int_dial.htm
  http://www.dial-a-code.com/
  http://www.kropla.com/dialcode.htm
  http://www.the-acr.com/codes/cntrycd.htm

Internet Telephone Systems

With nothing more than your PC and an Internet connection, you can make all the telephone calls you want. Now, the fine print: (1) It will cost money, although less than regular long distance. (2) The quality will not be as good as a regular phone connection, although it should be adequate for non-business calls. (3) If you are using a slow Internet connection, the quality will suffer. (4) All the systems are not equally good. If one doesn't work well for you, try another. (5) At the very least, you will need speakers and a microphone. However, you should really get yourself a special computer headset (with two plugs, one for output and one for input).

Web:
  http://myvoiz.mediaring.com/eng/pm_demo/
    main.html
  http://web.net2phone.com/home_usen.asp
  http://www.ewaver.net/
  http://www.iconnecthere.com/
  http://www.pc-telephone.com/

Long Distance Rates

The history of AT&T goes back to 1885, when it was incorporated to handle the long distance service for the American Bell Telephone Company. Throughout the twentieth century, AT&T and the Bell system formed a legally sanctioned, regulated monopoly that provided local and long distance telephone service to most of the United States. In 1974, the U.S. government started antitrust proceedings against the company, which were finally settled when, on January 1, 1984, the whole system was broken into seven regional local companies and a new AT&T long distance company. Related to the breakup, the government also opened the doors for other companies to compete against AT&T. Since then, many long distance companies have been formed, and rates have decreased significantly. The competition is fierce, and there are a staggering array of rates and terms that change often. These resources can help you find the most economical company based on the calls you make.

Web:
  http://www.10-10phonerates.com/
  http://www.1callsaver.com/
  http://www.abtolls.com/
  http://www.billzilla.com/
  http://www.greatlongdistancerates.com/

National Telecommunications and Information Administration

Whenever I want to know what the National Telecommunications and Information Administration is up to, I check out its official Web site. It uses the Web to make accessible its press releases, public notices and information on international telecommunications activities. When you just can't wait for the news to hit the streets, go straight to the source.

Web:
  http://www.ntia.doc.gov/

Networks

Specific networking information can be hard to find. For example, what would you do, right now, if you needed some info on ATM, or ISDN, or SMNP, or NT Server? Would you know where to find the Web sites for important networking magazines and journals? Here is everything you need—at least to get started—all in one place, well-organized and comprehensive. If you have anything to do with any aspect of computer networks, these sites should be on your bookmark list.

Web:

> http://www.americasnetwork.com/
> http://www.itprc.com/
> http://www.webcom.com/~llarrow/comfaqs.html

Phone Number Translator

When I was a kid, the first part of every phone number (the prefix) was chosen so that it could be represented by a word. For example, my father's office number was 364-4421. On the phone, the numbers "36" correspond to "EM". Thus, I grew up knowing that my father's office number was Empire 4-4421, which made it a lot easier to remember. Similarly, our home number was Russell 7-4056. and, later (when we moved), Hudson 482-3241. Here's another one: Lucy and Ricky Ricardo's phone number was Murray Hill 5-9975. In the United States, the phone company (AT&T) phased out this system in the early 1960s. From then on, phone numbers would be all numeric, which allowed the phone company to use more prefixes. Not everyone was happy with the new system. The comedian Allen Sherman (1924-1973) even wrote a song called "The Let's All Call Up AT&T and Protest to the President March" (1963). Although it took more than 40 years, Sherman can now feel vindicated: you can use these resources to help you convert your numbers into words, the way they should be.

Web:

> http://www.phonespell.org/
> http://www.phonetic.com/

Your Telephone Number Secrets *Unmasked*

You know that it is possible to convert your phone number from numbers to letters: 2 = A, B or C; 3 = D, E or F; and so on. But have you ever taken your personal number and tried all possible combinations to see if they spell anything cool? If so, you will find that there are a *lot* of combinations. But why should you sweat when you have the Net?

Connect to a **Phone Number Translator** Web site, and let a computer do the work. Plug your number into this handy-dandy form and, before you can say 1-800-HOWCOOL, you will be shown all the interesting alphabetic combinations that match your particular number.

Maybe you'll get lucky. One person I know found out her number spelled out "SEX-YOGA". (You can imagine what this did for her social life.)

Hint: Converting numbers to letters is useful for helping to remember anything you must enter on a telephone-like keypad, such as your ATM secret code.

Relay Service

A relay service is a facility that lets a hearing- or speech-impaired person talk to another person over the telephone for free. The impaired person uses a keyboard and screen to communicate while the other person uses a regular telephone, and the conversation is relayed by a specially trained operator called a communications assistant (CA). Most deaf or speech-impaired people access relay services by using a TTY—a small device with a keyboard and screen—connected to a phone line. However, relay services are now available over the Internet. Just visit a relay service Web site and type in the number you want to call. You can then use your computer to carry out a "telephone" conversation with anyone you want.

Web:

http://www.fcc.gov/cgb/dro/trs/con_trs.html
http://www.sprintrelayonline.com/
https://www.ip-relay.com/lightcall.jsp

Short Messaging Service

Short Messaging Service, or SMS, is a globally standardized system for sending short text messages between portable devices and telecommunication networks. SMS is designed to be fast, low bandwidth, efficient and cheap. SMS works in the background, which means that messages can be sent or received even if a voice or data call is in progress. The system was first introduced in 1991 (in Europe). Today, SMS is used with wireless phones and other devices to offer email, paging and voice mail services, information services (such as stock quotes and interactive banking), and limited Internet access. In addition to consumer services, SMS is also used with commercial field-service applications such as downloading SIM (subscriber identity module) cards, wireless POS (point of sale), meter reading and remote sensing.

Web:

http://www.hssworld.com/commapps/smsc/faq.htm
http://www.iec.org/online/tutorials/wire_sms/
http://www.mobilesms.com/main.asp
http://www.worldxs.net/sms.html

Relay Service

When you use a relay service, only one person types at a time. Since typing is slow compared to talking, there are a number of abbreviations that are in common use. Most of these abbreviations come from the Deaf community, in which TTYs (small devices with keyboards) are used to communicate over phone lines.

The most important abbreviations are:

GA ("go ahead"), which means "I am finished typing for now. It is your turn to type."

SK ("stop typing [keying]"), which means "I am ready to hang up now."

(In other words, GA means "over" and SK means "over and out".)

Here are some other common abbreviations:

CD	"could"
CUL	"see you later"
CUZ	"because"
HD	"hold"
HLD	"hold"
MTG	"meeting"
NBR	"number"
OIC	"oh, I see"
OPR	"operator"
PLM	"problem"
PLS	"please"
QQ	<a question mark>
R	"are"
RO	"relay operator"
SHD	"should"
THX	"thanks"
TMW	"tomorrow"
U	"you"
UR	"your"

At the end of a conversation, you indicate you are about to hang up by typing any of the following:

BYE TO SK

BYE SK

SK

To say that you are ready to hang up unless the person has any final words, you can type either of the following:

BYE TO SK OR GA

GA OR SK.

Telecom Discussions and Digest

The Telecom Digest is an online digest posted regularly to Usenet. If you are interested in telecommunications, this is a source of information worth reading regularly. The **telecom** discussion groups are for all manner of telecommunications including—but not limited to—the telephone system.

Web:
   http://massis.lcs.mit.edu/telecom-archives/

Usenet:
   alt.dcom.telecom
   comp.dcom.telecom

Telecom Resources

Telecommunications is changing our culture faster than any other type of technology. Moreover, telecommunications itself is changing so fast even professionals have a hard time keeping up. I have chosen these resources to help you find telecommunications information as you need it and to make it easy for you to check in every now and then to see what's new.

Web:
   http://www.analysys.com/vlib/
   http://www.businesswire.com/telcoex/
   http://www.gbmarks.com/
   http://www.telecoms-mag.com/
   http://www.telecomweb.com/

Telemarketing Abuse

Telemarketing refers to the soliciting of business or selling goods over the telephone. Once your name gets on a telemarketing list, you are going to get unwanted calls, but you can fight back. First, (in the U.S.) call your telephone company, and tell them to take your name out of the "street address" directory they sell to telemarketers. Second, check the telemarketing resources on the Net. The next time someone interrupts your dinner to ask if you want to invest in pomegranate futures, tell him you have to check with the Internet first, but if he would give you his personal home phone number, you would be glad to call him back later.

Web:
   http://www.antitelemarketer.com/
   http://www.ftc.gov/bcp/menu-tmark.htm
   http://www.junkbusters.com/ht/en/
      telemarketing.html
   http://www.scn.org/~bk269/telemarketing.html

Telephone Tech Talk and General Discussion

Next to the Internet, the phone is one of the greatest inventions of humankind. Without the phone, you could never dial the pizza place and have them make you a steaming hot pizza with everything (except celery) and deliver it to your door. That's all most of us need to know about the phone, but if you are interested in more than that—like learning what the guts of the telephone look like and how the wires connect, then join up with some telephone tech talk on Usenet.

Usenet:
   comp.dcom.telecom.tech

Wireless Technology News

Wireless technology refers to electronic systems that enable communication over a distance without using wires. Before the 1980s, the main use for wireless communication were the dispatch systems used by taxi companies, police, and a number of private microwave data networks maintained by railway companies. In the last two decades, however, wireless technology has developed enormously, resulting in a great many new communication tools such as cell phones, WAP-enabled devices, pagers, wireless modems, wireless computer networks, remote sensing devices, and so on.

Web:
   http://www.telecomweb.com/wirelessdata/
   http://www.wirelessinanutshell.com/
   http://www.wirelessweek.com/
   http://www.wow-com.com/

17 is a funny number. 14 isn't. 34, 49 and 13 are also funny, but 11 isn't. Isn't life strange?

TELEVISION

Commercials

Yes, commercials are annoying, but they are an integral part of our television experience. Commercials give you the opportunity to dash into the kitchen for a snack, retire for a short bathroom break, or chase the cat around the house for a quick bit of exercise. Moreover, no matter how annoying the commercials of today may seem, I promise you, when you get old, the commercials of your youth will become nostalgic to the point of cuteness. Check the commercial archive on the Net, and you'll see what I mean.

Web:
  http://www.retromedia.tv/commercials/
  http://www.songtitle.info/
  http://www.usatvads.com/html/screenings.html

Usenet:
  alt.tv.commercials

HDTV

HDTV (high definition television) is a system that is designed to replace regular TV. The basic changes are a wider aspect ratio and many more scan lines. High definition TV uses an aspect ratio of 16 x 9 (16 units across by 9 units up), similar to movies. The old TV standard uses a more square screen that is 4 x 3. In addition, high definition TV uses 1,125 lines of resolution, compared to only 525 on the old system. The result is a TV image that is wider and sharper. These Web sites provide information for professionals and the general public. Read about the high definition technology and how it is used to create a whole new television system.

Web:
  http://www.atsc.org/
  http://www.calcote.com/hdlinks.htm
  http://www.web-star.com/hdtv/hdtvnews1.html

Usenet:
  alt.tv.tech.hdtv
  alt.video.digital-tv

History of Television

The word "television" was coined in 1900 at the International Electricity Congress. However, it was another 25 years before the first successful synchronized transmission of moving pictures and sound. The transmission was sent 5 miles, from one part of Washington, D.C. to another. In 1928, General Electric began the regularly scheduled TV broadcasts (Tuesdays, Thursdays and Fridays from 1:30 PM to 3:30 PM), and in 1941, 10 U.S. stations were granted the first commercial TV licenses. After the war, the popularity of TV started to grow, and by the 1950s, the box with the tube was the focus of most everyone's living room. In many ways, the history of television is the history of modern life. I was part of the first generation to grow up with television: what a difference it made in our lives. Can you imagine life without TV? What would happen if we all turned it off at the same time?

Web:
  http://members.aol.com/jeff560/chronotv.html
  http://www.civilization.ca/hist/tv/tv02eng.html
  http://www.mztv.com/mech1.html
  http://www.novia.net/~ereitan/

Public Broadcasting Service (PBS)

The Public Broadcasting Service (PBS) is a private, nonprofit organization that serves well over 300 member television stations in the United States. PBS was founded in 1968 with a mandate to provide high-quality TV programming. Quality, of course, is in the eye and ear of the beholder and, in a highly politicized country in which the average television image lasts less than 10 seconds, you can bet there will be disagreement. Still, PBS offers a lot of programming that is just not available on commercial television. Check its Web site to see what it is up to, and if you should be tuning in, or turning on and dropping out.

Web:
  http://www.pbs.org/

You could be learning
HTML right now.

Satellite TV

Using a special antenna, it is possible to receive TV programs directly as they are broadcast from various satellites. The services cost money, but the variety of available programs is enormous and the quality of the signal is excellent. Isn't it marvelous that a technology has finally been developed that ensures you will never, ever run out of interesting things to watch? Now that satellite TV is here, the only reason you need ever take a break from watching the tube is to check your email.

Web:
> http://www.directmagazine.com/dishnews.htm
> http://www.faqs.org/faqs/Satellite-TV/
> http://www.satcritics.com/hardware.php
> http://www.sbca.com/consumer.html

Usenet:
> rec.video.satellite
> rec.video.satellite.dbs
> rec.video.satellite.europe
> rec.video.satellite.misc
> rec.video.satellite.tvro

Television Talk and General Discussion

Don't waste your life in sitting in front of the computer. Instead, you can waste it in front of another electronic box that gives you a continuous feed of images that will lull you into a hypnotic daze and make you susceptible to the lure of home shopping channels. If you are so hooked that you like to talk about television when you are not actually watching it, check out these Usenet groups.

Usenet:
> alt.comedy.british.blackadder
> alt.drwho.creative
> alt.fan.blakes-7
> alt.fan.hawaii-five-o
> alt.fan.inspector-morse
> alt.fan.red.green
> alt.fan.rumpole
> alt.tv
> alt.tv.3rd-rock
> alt.tv.7th-heaven
> alt.tv.a-team
> alt.tv.ab-fab
> alt.tv.airwolf
> alt.tv.ally-mcbeal
> alt.tv.amer-gothic
> alt.tv.andromeda
> alt.tv.angel
> alt.tv.animaniacs
> alt.tv.avengers
> alt.tv.baywatch
> alt.tv.beakmans-world
> alt.tv.beauty+beast
> alt.tv.bh90210
> alt.tv.boston-common
> alt.tv.brisco-county
> alt.tv.cell-block-h
> alt.tv.charmed
> alt.tv.chicago-hope
> alt.tv.christy
> alt.tv.cow-n-chicken
> alt.tv.dallas
> alt.tv.dark-angel
> alt.tv.dark_shadows
> alt.tv.dexters-lab
> alt.tv.dharma-greg
> alt.tv.dinosaurs
> alt.tv.dr-quinn
> alt.tv.dragonball-z
> alt.tv.duckman
> alt.tv.due-south
> alt.tv.early-edition
> alt.tv.earth-final-conflict
> alt.tv.earth2
> alt.tv.eek-the-cat
> alt.tv.emergency

alt.tv.er.creative
alt.tv.expedientes-x
alt.tv.family-guy
alt.tv.felicity
alt.tv.fools-and-horses
alt.tv.forever-knight
alt.tv.freakazoid
alt.tv.hercules
alt.tv.highlander
alt.tv.hogans-heroes
alt.tv.home-and-away
alt.tv.home-imprvment
alt.tv.hometime
alt.tv.homicide
alt.tv.infomercials
alt.tv.jag
alt.tv.just-shoot-me
alt.tv.kids-in-hall
alt.tv.kids-inc
alt.tv.kindred
alt.tv.king-of-hill
alt.tv.knight-rider
alt.tv.kungfu
alt.tv.lafemme-nikita
alt.tv.lexx
alt.tv.liquid-tv
alt.tv.lois-n-clark
alt.tv.macross
alt.tv.mad-about-you
alt.tv.magnificent-7
alt.tv.magnum-pi
alt.tv.mathnet
alt.tv.max-headroom
alt.tv.melrose-place
alt.tv.miami-vice
alt.tv.millennium
alt.tv.millennium.uk
alt.tv.mission-imposs
alt.tv.mst3k
alt.tv.mtv
alt.tv.mtv-europe
alt.tv.muppets
alt.tv.mwc
alt.tv.my-s-c-life
alt.tv.nash-bridges
alt.tv.networks.cbc
alt.tv.newsradio
alt.tv.nick-at-nite
alt.tv.nickelodeon
alt.tv.northern-exp
alt.tv.nowhere-man
alt.tv.nypd-blue
alt.tv.outer-limits
alt.tv.party-of-five
alt.tv.picket-fences
alt.tv.pirate
alt.tv.pizzacats
alt.tv.port-charles

alt.tv.pretender
alt.tv.prisoner
alt.tv.profiler
alt.tv.providence
alt.tv.public-access
alt.tv.quincy-me
alt.tv.reboot
alt.tv.remember-wenn
alt.tv.ren-n-stimpy
alt.tv.robotech
alt.tv.rockford-files
alt.tv.roseanne
alt.tv.roswell
alt.tv.rugrats
alt.tv.sabrina
alt.tv.saved-bell
alt.tv.sctv
alt.tv.seaquest
alt.tv.sentai
alt.tv.sentinel
alt.tv.sesame-street
alt.tv.sevendays
alt.tv.silk-stalkings
alt.tv.sliders
alt.tv.smallville
alt.tv.space-a-n-b
alt.tv.space-cases
alt.tv.stargate-sg1
alt.tv.teletubbies
alt.tv.the-bill
alt.tv.the-goodies
alt.tv.the-practice
alt.tv.the-state
alt.tv.the-tick
alt.tv.this-old-house
alt.tv.tiny-toon
alt.tv.twin-peaks
alt.tv.v
alt.tv.vr5
alt.tv.will-and-grace
alt.tv.wings
alt.tv.wiseguy
alt.tv.wonder-years
rec.arts.sf.tv.quantum-leap
rec.arts.tv
rec.arts.tv.interactive
rec.arts.tv.uk
rec.arts.tv.uk.comedy
rec.arts.tv.uk.coronation-st
rec.arts.tv.uk.eastenders
rec.arts.tv.uk.emmerdale
rec.arts.tv.uk.misc

Television Theme Songs

I'm warning you. If you have anything to do for the next three hours, don't visit these Web sites. Once you do, you will spend a lot of time listening to theme songs for your favorite TV shows. In my case, I got seriously sidetracked from my research listening to the theme songs for Andy Griffith, Dick Van Dyke, The Flintstones, Laverne & Shirley, Popeye and Fractured Fairy Tales (from Rocky and Bullwinkle).

Web:

http://www.80stvthemes.com/
http://www.cardhustler.com/
http://www.telesearch.org/themesonline/
http://www.tvland.com/theme_songs/

TV Episode Guides

This Web site is a godsend to fanatics who need to know exactly when each episode of their favorite series aired. There are episode guides to many popular TV shows, including information about the individual episodes. After all, how many places can you turn to at three in the morning when you just have to know when Jerry put the Tweety Bird Pez dispenser on Elaine's knee? (It was episode #314 of Seinfeld, January 15, 1992, during a classical piano recital.)

Web:

http://www.epguides.com/

TV Gossip

It's not enough simply to watch television. If you really want to experience it correctly, you have to share in the continual aggrandizement of the entire entertainment industry. Here are some Web sites with articles, news, gossip and information on various TV shows and personalities. So the next time you want to find out who did what to whom when, put down the remote control and pick up the mouse.

Web:

http://tvguide.netscape.com/newsgossip/
http://www.eonline.com/
http://www.etonline.com/

TV News Archive

Who says you can't live in the past? Not me. Since 1968, the Vanderbilt Television News Archive has been archiving major news broadcasts to make sure they are recorded, preserved and made accessible to researchers. This Web site allows you to read summaries of these broadcasts. Choose any date you want and read a detailed summary of the news for that day as it was presented on the major networks. If you are a researcher, this Web site is an excellent source for determining exactly when something happened.

Web:

http://tvnews.vanderbilt.edu/

TV Schedules

It takes a lot of time and money to connect yourself to the Net. You need to have a computer and a connection to an Internet service provider. You also need to spend time learning how to use your computer, setting everything up so it connects properly, and teaching yourself to use your Web browser. So after putting in all that time and effort, you might as well use the Net for something important: checking TV schedules. Find out what's playing on any channel, any time.

Web:

http://tv.yahoo.com/
http://tvlistings2.zap2it.com/

TELEVISION SHOWS: CURRENT

Buffy the Vampire Slayer

Buffy is a very pretty, blond Californian student who, one day, finds out that she has a purpose in life that goes beyond normality. Buffy is a vampire slayer, albeit a reluctant one. During the day, she attends school (first Sunnydale High and later the University of Sunnydale) and enjoys the usual student activities with her friends Willow, Xander and Oz. She also trains with her former "Watcher", Rupert Giles. At night, though, Buffy becomes vampire slayer, going wherever she is needed and doing whatever is necessary to take care of the supernatural scum that is polluting the earth. Just a lot of good, clean fun.

Web:
  http://vrya.cstone.net/
  http://www.atpobtvs.com/
  http://www.buffyguide.com/
  http://www.buffyworld.com/
  http://www.enteract.com/~perridox/SunS/

Usenet:
  alt.tv.buffy-v-slayer
  alt.tv.buffy-v-slayer.creative

Majordomo Mailing List:
  List Name: **buffy**
  Subscribe to: **majordomo@valinor.eldar.org**

Majordomo Mailing List:
  List Name: **buffy-watchers**
  Subscribe to: **majordomo@mlists.com**

Dawson's Creek

Dawson's Creek is a teenage soap opera about the lives of various young people in Capeside, a small town in New England. Why are so many people enamored of the social and romantic adventures of Dawson, Jen, Pacey (a guy), Joey (a girl), Andie, Jack and Abby (may she rest in peace)? Maybe it's because something new is always happening. Maybe it's because of the pithy commentary on life ("Growing up sucks, not all kisses are magical and most boys do not live up to your expectations..."—Joey).

Web:
  http://www.dawson-info.com/New-Try.htm
  http://www.dawsons-creek.com/
  http://www.dawsonscreek.com/
  http://www.dawsonsdesktop.com/
  http://www.televisionwithoutpity.com/
    show.cgi?show=3

Usenet:
  alt.tv.dawsons-creek

Frasier

Psychiatrist Frasier Crane used to live in Boston, where he spent a lot of time hanging out at a bar named Cheers with a bunch of regulars. After too many years on the East Coast, Crane decided to change his life. He ended his marriage (to Lilith) and moved back to his hometown of Seattle, where he works as a radio shrink on KACL AM 780, routinely dispensing dollops of wit and wisdom. Crane lives with his brother Niles (also a psychiatrist), his father Martin (a retired policeman), Daphne Moon (Martin's caregiver), Roz Doyle (producer of the radio show), and Eddie the dog (played by a Jack Russell named Moose). Imagine visiting a large, extended, quirky family in which: Niles is separated from his wife Maris (who is never seen), Roz can't stand Niles (although she is an expert in male/female relationships), Niles likes Daphne (who is from England), Daphne is oblivious to Nile's obsession with her, Martin has trouble understanding both his sons (Frasier and Niles), and Martin's best friend is Eddie (the dog). Does that sound like fun, or what? Frasier trivia: The name of Frasier's radio station, KACL, is taken from the initials of the three people who created the series: David Angell, Peter Casey and David Lee.

Web:
  http://users.lanminds.com/eunice/frasier/
  http://www.cafe-nervosa.com/frasier/
  http://www.frasieronline.co.uk/

Usenet:
  alt.tv.frasier

A battery in your neighbor's
house needs changing.
Tell him I said so.
(If he doesn't believe you,
show him this page.)

Friends

Six people in their twenties (well, early thirties by now) live in New York and have various social adventures. Follow the romantic machinations and slow maturation process of Rachel Green, Monica Geller, Phoebe Buffay, Joey Tribbiani, Chandler Bing and Ross Geller, and see if you can keep track of what's going on. Be forewarned, if you watch the show long enough, you will get caught up in the emotional turmoil. ("I wonder if Ross and Rachel are *ever* going to get back together?") To help you, here is a handy guide of couples who have, at some time, kissed one another: Ross & Rachel, Monica & Chandler, Rachel & Joey, Phoebe & Joey, Ross & Phoebe, Chandler & Rachel, Chandler & Phoebe, Rachel & Monica, Chandler & Joey, and Joey & Ross.

Web:

  http://www.friends-at-centralperk.com/
  http://www.friends-tv.org/
  http://www.tvtome.com/Friends/

Usenet:

  alt.tv.friends
  alt.tv.friends.fanfic

Law and Order

Each Law and Order show has two parts. First, you see a criminal investigation and the arrest of a suspect. Then, you see the court case from the point of view of the prosecution. The show is popular because it is well-crafted and thoughtful. The endings may not always be what you expect, but they will make you think.

Web:

  http://members.aol.com/lomail/
  http://www.davidcantwell.com/laworder/
  http://www.nbc.com/Law_&_Order/
  http://www.tvtome.com/LawandOrder/

Usenet:

  alt.tv.law-and-order
  alt.uk.law.and.order

Sex and the City

The city is New York, and the show is about... sex (and sex and sex and sex) and how it plays such an important role in the lives of four women: Carrie Bradshaw (a sex columnist), Charlotte York (an art dealer), Miranda Hobbes (a lawyer), and Samantha Jones (a public relations executive). This is not a TV series for the kids. After all, how many shows are there in which a frank discussion of masturbation fantasies is considered tame? One day, Carrie, Charlotte, Miranda and Samantha may actually find true love instead of true lust. In the meantime, perhaps we should all spend a bit of time pondering Carrie's question: "Are soulmates a reality or a torture device?"

Web:

  http://www.bravo.ca/moresex/
  http://www.hbo.com/city/
  http://www.televisionwithoutpity.com/
    show.cgi?show=7

Usenet:

  alt.tv.sexandthecity

Sopranos

The Sopranos is a multi-character dramatic TV series about the Mob. The stories revolve around the life of Tony Soprano, the boss of a mid-level organized crime family in northern New Jersey. Tony is not one to shy away from violence and intimidation when it is necessary (after all, it is an occupational hazard). However, he is not your typical gangster. Tony has *feelings*. He takes Prozac, he has panic attacks, and he sees a shrink regularly. Although Tony's family is dysfunctional and he cheats on his wife, he does care about relationships. This is why the Sopranos is such a popular show: spending a few hours with the Family has the delightful effect of making you feel that *your* family is normal.

Web:

  http://www.hbo.com/sopranos/
  http://www.mobstory.com/sitemap.html
  http://www.sopranoland.com/

Usenet:

  alt.tv.sopranos

South Park

South Park is a crudely animated cartoon that is very, very gross, and very, very funny (two characteristics that normally don't go together). The show features a group of foulmouthed, yet lovable, third graders, Stan, Kyle, Cartman and Kenny, along with the bizarre inhabitants of the town of South Park, Colorado. If you are a teen-age boy with a highly developed sense of the vulgar, you will love South Park. If you are not a teen-age boy with a highly developed sense of the vulgar, you are on your own. (Note to parents: This is not a show you want to watch. Just let the kids enjoy it and stay out of the room.)

Web:
  http://www.comcentral.com/southpark/
  http://www.everwonder.com/david/southpark/
     spfaq.html
  http://www.rangerstation.com/
  http://www.southparkstudios.com/

Usenet:
  alt.tv.southpark
  alt.tv.southpark.creative

Majordomo Mailing List:
  List Name: southpark
  Subscribe to: majordomo@valinor.eldar.org

IRC:
  #southpark (DALnet, Undernet)

West Wing

The West Wing of the White House is the center of Presidential activity. It is there you will find the Oval Office, the Cabinet Room, the press briefing room, and the executive offices. On TV, we never get to see what goes on in the West Wing, and when we do see the President on television, the experience is formal, pre-arranged and dull. When we watch the West Wing TV show, however, the fictional President, Jeb Bartlett, and his staff never cease to be engaging, entertaining and inspiring. This is why West Wing is so popular: when it comes to television, the real President looks fake, and the fake President looks real.

Web:
  http://westwing.bewarne.com/
  http://www.epguides.com/westwing/
  http://www.nbc.com/The_West_Wing/
  http://www.warnerbros.com/web/westwingtv/

Usenet:
  alt.tv.the-west-wing

TELEVISION SHOWS: GENRES

Cartoons

I like cartoons. They're soothing, like a good book on a rainy day (except you can't turn up the volume on a good book and disturb the neighbors). If you like cartoons, check out some of the great toon resources on the Net. You can get pictures, sounds, movies and other cool cartoon stuff.

Web:
  http://hometown.aol.com/paulec1/clutchjr.html
  http://www.cartoonnetwork.com/watch/video_clips/
  http://www.toonzone.net/

Usenet:
  alt.tv.cartoon-network.toonami
  alt.tv.daria
  alt.tv.dr-katz

Cooking Shows

Cooking shows have always been a popular type of television show, and why not? It's relaxing to watch someone else cook, and inspiring to see an expert prepare elegant dishes, especially when everything works out perfectly and the food is always ready just as the show ends. Enjoy your favorites: Emeril Lagasse, Epicurious, the Food Network, the Iron Chef, Julia Child, Martin Yan, and Ming Tsai.

Web:
>   http://dsc.discovery.com/fansites/greatchefs/
>   greatchefs.html
>   http://eat.epicurious.com/tv/
>   http://www.emerils.com/
>   http://www.foodtv.com/tvshows/tv-g1/
>   http://www.ironchef.com/
>   http://www.ming.com/mingtv/mingtv.htm
>   http://www.pbs.org/juliachild/
>   http://yancancook.asianconnections.com/

Usenet:
>   alt.tv.food-network
>   alt.tv.iron-chef
>   alt.tv.martha-stewart

IRC:
>   #ironchef (DALnet, EFnet)

Daytime Talk Shows

Take pity on those people who waste their time working all day, for they are not able to enhance their existence on Planet Earth by watching daytime talk shows. People may sneer at these shows; they may say that the hosts and hostesses pander to sensationalism and the lowest common cultural denominator. Never mind. You and I know that these hosts and hostesses are more than mere television personalities; they are honored guests in our homes. Let's face it. From day to day, most people have pretty dull lives (and thankfully so). Isn't it nice to know that any afternoon you want, you can turn on the TV and see interviews with people whose lives are more to be pitied than censured.

Web:
>   http://abc.abcnews.go.com/theview/
>   http://www.jennyjones.warnerbros.com/
>   http://www.oprah.com/tows/tows_landing.html
>   http://www.rosieo.warnerbros.com/
>   http://www.sallyjr.com/
>   http://www.sonypictures.com/tv/shows/ricki/
>   index.htm
>   http://www.tvplex.go.com/buenavista/livewithregis/
>   homepage/today.html
>   http://www.uni-television.com/jerry/
>   http://www.uni-television.com/maury/

Usenet:
>   alt.tv.jerry-springer
>   alt.tv.talkshows.daytime

Game Shows

If you're a game show junkie, you probably like to participate as you watch the show. ("What a dummy! Everyone knows Mozart's middle name. Boy, if I was ever on that show, I'd beat everyone.") I remember having the same feeling as a kid. Something tells me that it's harder when you're actually there, under the bright lights, feeling the pressure. Still, you and I could do a lot better than everyone else, if we really wanted to. (We just can't be bothered.)

Web:
>   http://www.faqs.org/faqs/tv/game-shows/
>   http://www.gameshownetwork.com/
>   http://www.tvgameshows.net/

Usenet:
>   alt.tv.game-shows

Judge Shows

When you were a kid and you had a disagreement with someone, do you remember your mother telling you, "I want you to settle this between yourselves." Do you ever wonder what happened to the people who didn't listen to their mothers and never learned how to settle their disagreements with other people? They end up on national television looking like goofballs while the rest of us watch them pathetically strut their stuff in front of a TV judge. The best thing is that you too get to pass judgment. Does the judge agree with you? We'll see in a moment, just after this commercial.

Web:
   http://www.divorcecourttv.com/
   http://www.judgejoebrown.com/
   http://www.judgejudy.com/
   http://www.sonypictures.com/tv/shows/
      judgehatchett/
   http://www.tvjudgeshows.com/

Late Night Talk Shows

In the United States, it has been the custom for several decades to watch a late-night talk show before falling asleep in front of the television set. For many years, late night was ruled by Johnny Carson, but since he retired in May 1992, the nation's attention has been split between Jay Leno and David Letterman. Or has it? What about Conan O'Brien, Craig Kilborn and Bill Maher (Politically Incorrect)? And what about...oh, never mind. It's time to go to sleep.

Web:
   http://abc.abcnews.go.com/primetime/
      politicallyincorrect/
   http://www.cbs.com/latenight/latelate/
   http://www.cbs.com/latenight/lateshow/
   http://www.ddy.com/dl3.html
   http://www.interbridge.com/lineups.html
   http://www.nbc.com/conan/
   http://www.petersreviews.com/latenite.html
   http://www.tonightshow.msn.com/

Usenet:
   alt.fan.conan-obrien
   alt.fan.jay-leno
   alt.fan.letterman
   alt.tv.pol-incorrect
   alt.tv.talkshows.late

Reality Television

Isn't everything around us reality? Not any more. Reality is now a commodity to be packaged, advertised and televised. Reality television consists of heavily edited, highly contrived, artificial slices of "life", showing people, often ordinary people, in unusual (preferably embarrassing) situations. The more preposterous the situation, the larger the audience. The larger the audience, the more money it generates. The more money there is, the more reality television we get. My only question is, how are we going to explain this to our grandchildren?

Web:
   http://www.bigbtv.com/
   http://www.joehollywood.com/reality/
   http://www.realityblurred.com/realitytv/
   http://www.realitynewsonline.com/
   http://www.realitytvfans.com/
   http://www.sirlinksalot.net/

Usenet:
   alt.tv.big-brother
   alt.tv.junkyard-wars
   alt.tv.real-world
   alt.tv.road-rules
   alt.tv.survivor
   alt.tv.survivor-series
   alt.tv.the-mole

Sitcoms

The idea behind a sitcom (situation comedy) is simple. Start with a regular cast with well-defined, one-dimensional characters. For each episode, create a situation, usually some type of misunderstanding, that lends itself to comedy. Develop the story and resolve everything within a half hour (minus a judicious 7 or 8 minutes for commercials). Repeat. The formula is simple, but it has given all of us some of the most diverting and memorable moments of our lives. Who doesn't have their favorite sitcoms? (I do, and I don't even watch television anymore.)

Web:
   http://tvcorner.hypermart.net/
   http://www.mgnet.karoo.net/
   http://www.sitcomsonline.com/

Usenet:
   alt.tv.sitcom

A
B
C
D
E
F
G
H
I
J
K
L
M
N
O
P
Q
R
S
T
U
V
W
X
Y
Z

Soap Operas

Soap opera fans, the Net is *your* home away from the TV. There are so many soap-opera-related resources, you can spend every waking moment—when you are not watching a show—following the adventures of your favorite characters and talking with other soap fans.

Web:
  http://www.faqs.org/faqs/tv/soaps/
  http://www.mediadomain.com/soaps/
  http://www.soapcity.com/
  http://www.soapnet.go.com/

Usenet:
  alt.tv.all-my-children
  alt.tv.another-world
  alt.tv.bold-beautiful
  alt.tv.days-of-our-lives
  alt.tv.general-hospital
  alt.tv.one-life-to-live
  alt.tv.passions
  alt.tv.young+restless
  rec.arts.tv.soaps.abc
  rec.arts.tv.soaps.cbs
  rec.arts.tv.soaps.misc

TV Show Downfalls

When was the exact moment that a television show started to go downhill? Vote for the defining moment for your favorite show and see what others think. For example, Seinfeld started going downhill after Susan died; Laverne and Shirley began their plunge after the move to Los Angeles; and MASH hit the skids when Charles replaced Frank.

Web:
  http://www.jumptheshark.com/

> ## Prepare for retirement by saving ten percent of all the money you earn.

Andy Griffith

It would be wonderful if every town sheriff was like Andy Griffith. But then, not every town is like Mayberry. Can you imagine Andy Griffith being sheriff of Los Angeles or New York City? Settle in for some relaxing nostalgia as you cruise the Net looking at Web sites for The Andy Griffith Show. What a lovely break from the real world.

Web:
  http://www.barneyfife.com/
  http://www.liketelevision.com/web1/classictv/andyg/
  http://www.mayberry.com/tagsrwc/
  http://www.zille.com/griffith/faq.asp

Perhaps somewhere, there are people who have not watched each of the 249 episodes of The Andy Griffith Show and have not immersed themselves in the stories of Andy, Barney, Aunt Bee, Opie, Floyd, Gomer, Goober, Helen, Thelma Lou, Otis and the rest of the inhabitants of Mayberry, North Carolina.

I feel sorry for such people because they are missing out on what is most noble and fine in life: a society in which people most always get along, in which life's problems are well within the capabilities of a small-town sheriff and the homespun wisdom God has seen fit to bestow upon him. Within the show, Andy was sometimes referred to as the "sheriff without a gun, " but he might just as well have been called the "sheriff who doesn't need a gun."

For at least a few minutes each week (and now, every day in reruns), we could transport ourselves to a small town in which everyday problems were manageable and human dignity was preserved simply as a matter of course.

To ask whether there is justice in the world is an elegant but troubling question. To ask whether there is justice in Mayberry is both unnecessary and misleading. One does not watch The Andy Griffith Show for anything remotely involving one's higher cortical functionality. Rather, we worship at the shrine of blessed banality simply because, in a world of discomforting unpredictability and baffling complexity, Mayberry and its inhabitants occupy one of the few safe rest stops available to the human spirit in all of us, as it navigates the confusing and oft-times rocky road of life.

Brady Bunch

I was visiting Christopher Barnes (Greg Brady in the Brady Bunch movies). We had just finished our dinner, and we were sipping our tea and talking politics. Suddenly, I realized what a totally cool thing I was doing. Imagine sitting at the dinner table with Greg discussing the world and how to fix it. The only thing better would be to get the whole family together and go on a trip to the Grand Canyon. Is there any family in television history that has captured our hearts and minds so effectively as the Brady Bunch? What a wacky, lovable bunch of characters: the kids (Greg, Peter, Bobby, Marcia, Jan and Cindy), their parents (Mike and Carol), and their housekeeper (Alice). Who says it's a fantasy? On the Internet, you can not only live in the past, you can live in a perfect past, where everyone has fun, gets along, and solves all their problems within a half hour. Or, as Carol puts it: "You know, money and fame are very important things, but, well, sometimes there are other things that are more important—like people."

Web:

http://www.bradyhour.com/
http://www.bradyworld.com/brady.htm
http://www.davidbrady.com/eb/
http://www.nitscape.com/

Usenet:

alt.tv.brady-bunch

Dick Van Dyke Show

The Dick Van Dyke Show is my all-time favorite television show. In fact, I challenge any of my friends to ask me a Dick Van Dyke question I can't answer. If you enjoy watching the adventures of Rob, Laura, Buddy, Sally, Mel, Jerry, Millie, Alan Brady, and that obnoxious little kid Ritchie Rosebud, pay a visit to these Web sites, where you can re-live your hours of Dick Van Dyke watching (until it's time for the next rerun).

Web:

http://www.dickvandykeshow.com/
http://television.jumptheshark.com/d/dickvandyke.htm
http://www.liketelevision.com/web1/classictv/
   dickvd/
http://www.open4ever.com/

Dick Van Dyke Show

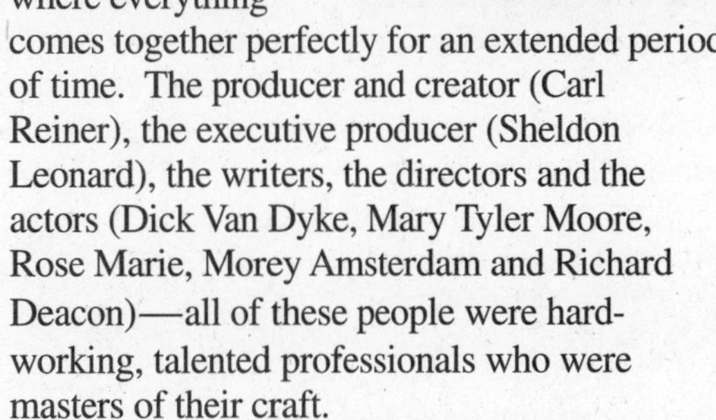

The Dick Van Dyke Show was one of those rare artistic creations where everything comes together perfectly for an extended period of time. The producer and creator (Carl Reiner), the executive producer (Sheldon Leonard), the writers, the directors and the actors (Dick Van Dyke, Mary Tyler Moore, Rose Marie, Morey Amsterdam and Richard Deacon)—all of these people were hard-working, talented professionals who were masters of their craft.

However, there is more. The first Dick Van Dyke Show was filmed before a live audience on January 20, 1961. The last show was filmed on March 26, 1966. This time period marks the end of the transition from the Golden Age of Radio into modern television, and this show represents the last marvelous legacy from a time in which audiences

expected only to be entertained, and performers knew their primary job was to tell jokes, sing songs, dance, and act out a story.

In the transition from one age to another, there is often a short breathing space as the old, mature culture segues into the new one. By the time the Dick Van Dyke Show had finished, the United States was embroiled in Vietnam, the sexual revolution and national protests. But for one long idyllic moment, God was in his heaven, all was right with the world, and, each week, we could count on Rob, Laura, Sally, Buddy and Mel to entertain and amuse us.

Honeymooners

There are not many TV shows that are worth watching again and again and again. The Honeymooners is that good. The Honeymooners stories revolve around the relationship between Ralph Kramden (played by Jackie Gleason)—a temperamental Everyman with a propensity to get himself into trouble—and his long-suffering wife, Alice. Ralph is a 40-year-old bus driver, who lives with his wife Alice in a small, one-bedroom apartment in Bensonhurst, a neighborhood in Brooklyn, New York. Their best friends, Ed Norton and his wife Trixie, live upstairs. For many years, the Honeymooners was presented a segment on one of Jackie Gleason's variety programs. However, the episodes that everyone loves are the classic 39 shows that were filmed on their own in 1955-1956. I have these shows on video, and I have watched them more times than I can remember.

Web:
   http://tvland.classictvhits.com/Honeymooners/
   http://www.haminahamina.com/
   http://www.honeymooners.net/classic39.htm
   http://www.uncwil.edu/com/rohler/kac.htm

I Love Lucy

Is there anyone on our entire planet who does *not* love Lucy? The I Love Lucy show is the most popular situation comedy of all time, being in continual reruns with no signs of stopping. I have watched every I Love Lucy episode from "Lucy Thinks Ricky Is Trying to Murder Her" (#1) to "The Ricardos Dedicate a Statue" (#179). (And I don't even like TV.) But I am not alone in my love for Lucy. There are diehard fans all over the world and all over the Net.

Web:
   http://www.lucilleball.net/
   http://www.lucytalk.com/
   http://www.tvparty.com/movlucy.html

> **Mary had a little lamb (and she learned all about it in the "Agriculture" section.)**

Leave It To Beaver

Leave It To Beaver features Beaver Cleaver (his real name is Theodore), Beaver's brother Wally, and his parents Ward and June. The basic premise is that Beaver is a dumb, but cute, kid who, no matter how hard he tries, just can't stay out of trouble. (Beaver: "Sometimes when a grown-up is mad at you, you can get in trouble just by saying hello.") Wally and Beaver have a number of friends, the most memorable of which is Eddie Haskell, the quintessential wise-guy. Eddie makes a point of sucking-up to adults ("Good morning, Mrs. Cleaver, that's a very pretty dress."), while doing his best to cause trouble when he is alone with the guys ("This is vacation. Your parents aren't allowed to make you work all the time. It's a state law"). Of all the television shows I loved as a kid, this one brought me the most comfort. The reason is simple: Leave It to Beaver portrays a pleasant family in which, everything always turns out right. (My sister, who is 10 years younger, feels the same way about The Brady Bunch.)

Web:
   http://www.leaveittobeaver.org/
   http://www.tvland.com/shows/litbeaver/

MASH

From 1972-1983, the world had a love affair with the inhabitants of the 4077th MASH (Mobile Army Surgical Hospital) Unit, part of the American military medical corps during the Korean War. Every week, millions of people would follow the adventures of Hawkeye Pierce, B.J. Hunnicut, Frank Burns, Margaret (Hot Lips) Houlihan, Radar O'Reilly, Father Mulcahy, Corporal Klinger, Frank Burns, Colonel Blake, (and later) Colonel Potter, Trapper John McIntyre and Charles Winchester. How successful was MASH? Although the actual war was only 3 years (from June 1950 to July 1953), the comedy/drama series lasted 11 years, almost four times as long. MASH touched its viewers in a way that few series ever have. Tell the truth now. In the very last scene, when Hawkeye takes off in a helicopter, looks down over the deserted camp, and sees the "Good-bye" message left by B.J., did you not feel like crying?

Web:
   http://www.bestcareanywhere.net/
   http://www.dreamwater.com/texasfaith/
      mashpost.html
   http://www.faqs.org/faqs/tv/mash/

Usenet:
   alt.tv.mash

Ozzie and Harriet

The Adventures of Ozzie and Harriet was a family TV series that ran for 436 episodes (from 1952-1966), during television's Age of Innocence. The series featured the real-life family Ozzie Nelson (1906-1975), Harriet Nelson (1909-1994), David Nelson (1936-) and Ricky Nelson (1940-1985). The genesis of the series was a radio show, that debuted in 1944, in which Ozzie and Harriet Nelson played a married couple with two young boys. At first, the sons were played by actors, but in 1949, young David and Ricky took over their own parts and, for the next 22 years, the boys grew up in front of America. Where else, but in the Nelson residence, would you find a mother and father who never had a serious fight? Or two eternally polite brothers who not only got along with their parents, but with one another (well, most of the time). My favorite episode is the one in which Ricky—who later became a popular singing star—first sang on the show. The episode was #165 "Ricky the Drummer", April 10, 1957. (Ricky sang the song "I'm Walkin'").

Web:

http://www.sitcomsonline.com/
   theadventuresofozzieandharriet.html
http://www.tvtome.com/servlets/ShowMainServlet/
   showid-1432

Do you want to hear something totally awesome?

On the Seinfeld show, Jerry was born in December. (In "The Heart Attack" episode, Jerry says George was born in April; in "The Butter Shave", Jerry says they are 4 months apart; and everyone knows that Jerry is older than George.)

Anyway, on the show, Jerry Seinfled, was born in December. In real life, Jerry Seinfeld was born in April.

Now, listen to this:

I was born in December and my cat, The Little Nipper, was born in April.

Get out!

Seinfeld

Seinfeld, the self-styled "Show About Nothing", ran for 9 years, from 1989 to 1998. The show centers around the social misadventures of Jerry Seinfeld (a stand-up comedian), George Costanza, Cosmo Kramer and Elaine Benes. How do you describe a show about nothing? Well, it's mostly about relationships: Jerry and George, Jerry and Cosmo, Jerry and Elaine (an on/off odd couple), Jerry and a long string of girlfriends, Elaine and a long string of boyfriends, and so on. What else can I tell you? Jerry's biggest fear is falling in love with someone his parents like. My favorite scene is the one in which Jerry and Elaine are at a piano recital and Jerry puts a Pez dispenser on Elaine knee. (I told you it was a show about nothing.)

Web:

http://www.advocacy-net.com/seinfeldmks.htm
http://www.cgocable.net/~dchristi/scripts.html
http://www.pkmeco.com/seinfeld/
http://www.sonypictures.com/tv/shows/seinfeld/

Usenet:

alt.tv.seinfeld

Simpsons

If you ever get a chance to visit Springfield—somewhere in the United States—be sure to drop in to Evergreen Terrace and call on the Simpsons: Homer, Marge, Bart, Lisa and Maggie. (The street number is either 94, 59, 723, 742 or 1094, depending on which episode you're watching.) This achingly pathetic but irresistibly endearing cartoon family has developed a worldwide following unique in the history of television. There are many, many Simpson fans on the Net and more Web sites than you can shake a stick at. (Actually, I tried once and all that happened was the stick broke). By the way, if you do decide to drop by Evergreen Terrace, you may want to call first. The phone number is 555-6528 (according to Principal Skinner's rolodex card).

Web:

http://www.eyeonspringfield.co.uk/
http://www.labyrinth.net.au/~kwyjibo/simpsonian/
http://www.lardlad.com/
http://www.snpp.com/

Usenet:

alt.tv.simpsons
alt.tv.simpsons.itchy-scratchy

TRAVEL

Air Travel Tips

Did you know that, on large modern planes, the pilots can circulate more fresh air in the cabin if they want to, but they often don't: they recycle the air in order to boost the fuel economy. However, if you complain, there is a chance they will increase the fresh air for you. Now *that's* what I call a travel tip, and there's plenty more where that came from.

Web:
  http://www.airsafe.com/
  http://www.armchair.com/info/fly.html
  http://www.faa.gov/aviationsafety/
  http://www.flyana.com/
  http://www.freetraveltips.com/airlines/
  http://www.naafa.org/documents/brochures/
    airtips.html

Airline Flight Tracking

So your friend Ron is flying in to visit you. Very nice, but when should you go to the airport to meet him? If you go on time, you may end up waiting for hours if his flight was delayed. Instead, before you leave, check how late Ron's flight is really going to be. After all, you can't get there at the last minute unless you have accurate information. (Hint: If you are stuck at the airport waiting for a late flight and the airline employees won't tell you what's happening, call a friend and have him check the Net for you.)

Web:
  http://www.flightview.com/
  http://www.flytecomm.com/cgi-bin/trackflight
  http://www.travelago.com/findflight.asp

Airline Information

Pick an airline, any airline, and I'll guess what it is. Ready? Hmmmm... United Airlines. Pretty good, huh? Sorry, I can't tell you how I do it, or it wouldn't seem like magic. Want some more magic? Use the Net to find the phone number and Web site of any airline you can imagine (and some you can't).

Web:
  http://www.kls2.com/airlines/
  http://www.period.com/airlines/
  http://www.smilinjack.com/airlines.htm

ATM Locator

What happens if you are thousands of miles from home and you encounter a financial emergency? No problem. Call a friend back home and have him pull out a copy of this book. (All your friends have this book, don't they?) Tell him to look up the ATM Locator resources, connect to the Net, and find the ATM closest to you. Of course, you could always just ask someone where the closest ATM is, but that's no fun.

Web:
  http://www.mastercard.com/cardholderservices/
    atm/
  http://www.visa.com/atms/

Budget Travel

When I traveled in Europe, I had a small budget, a Eurail (train) pass, and a book on budget traveling. In my experience, traveling inexpensively can be a lot of fun, but to be as comfortable as possible, it helps to do some research before you leave. To help you, here are some resources with tips, techniques and information you won't find on the beaten track.

Web:
  http://www.artoftravel.com/
  http://www.crazydogtravel.com/
  http://www.frommers.com/magazine/
  http://www.sleepinginairports.net/airports.htm

Usenet:
  rec.travel.budget.backpack

Hostels

Hostels are inexpensive places to stay, offering basic accommodation for informal travelers around the world. Many hostels are only for people below a certain age (youth hostels), but some are open to anyone. When I was younger, I stayed at a lot of youth hostels, and most of the time it was just fine. Hostels are usually centrally located and are great places to meet other people.

Web:
  http://www.hostelplanet.com/
  http://www.hostels.com/

Packing Tips

When you travel, packing well can make a big difference. On a long trip, I like to travel with a single, large backpack. It's practical and easy to carry. However, as you get older, the backpack will get shoved in the corner of the garage, and you'll find yourself traveling with a couple of suitcases. (You'll see.) Still, knowing what to pack and how to do it well is a skill we can all use, even when we start to travel like adults.

Web:

http://www.freetraveltips.com/packing/
http://www.oratory.com/travel/
http://www.travelite.org/
http://www.verber.com/mark/travel/packing.html

Personal Travel Planner

This Web site is presented by the people who produce Fodor's travel guides. My favorite resource is the one that lets you create your own travel planner. You specify where you want to go and select various choices from menus. You will then be presented with a personalized travel guide, based on information from their database. To test it, I created a planner for a trip that I had already taken. The results were so good, I wished I had done it before I took the trip.

Web:

http://www.fodors.com/

Railroad Travel

You're all ready for a fabulous time at the annual convention of the International Order of Loyal Raccoons. This year, the convention is in Minneapolis. Your bags are packed, and you and your best friend make it to the train in plenty of time. You board the train and start unpacking the joke and novelty items you're going to use at the convention. But you wonder, where are your wives? They were supposed to meet you on the train. The train starts rolling, and the conductor comes by. Oh, no! He tells you that you are on the wrong train. This one is going to Norfolk, Virginia, not Minneapolis. But what about your wives? They're on the right train, because they checked all the details on the Net before they left.

Web:

http://mercurio.iet.unipi.it/misc/timetabl.html
http://www.amtrak.com/
http://www.amtraktrains.com/
http://www.railroaddata.com/rrlinks/
   Passenger_Trains/
http://www.railtrack.co.uk/rail_network/
http://www.trainweb.com/
http://www.wwtravelsource.com/trains.htm

Recreational Vehicles

Recreational vehicles (RVs) are self-contained mobile living environments. People love RVs because, once you have one, you can drive wherever you want and never worry about finding a place to sleep or eat. If you're spending much time in your RV, using the Net is one of the best ways to stay in touch with the rest of the world. Not only can you send and receive email, but there are some great RV resources available to help you find campsites and exciting places to visit. In addition, you can join the many RV enthusiasts who participate in Usenet discussion groups.

Web:

http://www.campingworld.com/pc/rvm/
http://www.rvcare.com/
http://www.rversonline.org/

Usenet:

alt.rv
rec.outdoors.rv-travel

Ship Travel

Taking a leisurely trip on a cruise ship can be a great experience. There is a lot of cruise information available, but much of it is commercial pap. To help you find out what you really need to know, I have found the places on the Net where real people talk about their cruise experiences and their interests. If you have questions about cruising, you'll find these resources especially useful. I have also included a cruising FAQ (frequently asked question list), as well as some info about traveling on a freighter.

Web:
 http://pages.prodigy.net/lindacoffman/articles.htm
 http://www.cruisebrokers.com/faq.htm
 http://www.tripspot.com/cruises.htm

Usenet:
 rec.travel.cruises

Speedtraps

A speedtrap is a police setup designed to catch drivers who exceed the speed limit. Since citations for such an infraction generate income for a town, state or province, it is not unheard of for police to place speedtraps in places where they know out-of-town drivers are likely to be tempted to drive too fast. At the very least, if you are a stranger to an area, it helps to know the places where the local police are looking for speeders. This Web site serves as a speedtrap registry for people driving in the United States, Canada, Australia and some European countries. Before you drive in a strange area, check here to make sure that you know where the speedtraps are. Even better, check for speedtraps in the town where you live. You may be surprised.

Web:
 http://www.speedtrap.com/

Subway Navigator

You will never have to get lost on the subway system again. No matter where you are, you can find your way home as long as you have your Internet connection with you. This site will compute subway routes in many major cities around the world. I computed a lengthy subway route in Helsinki and I don't even speak Finnish.

Web:
 http://www.subwaynavigator.com/

Tourism Offices

If you are planning your vacation to some exotic country (or some country that you wish were exotic), don't go jet-setting off without being fully prepared. At this Web site you can enter in the name of the country you are going to visit find a list of all the tourism offices in the area.

Web:
 http://www.towd.com/

Travel Health Advice

If you are planning a trip, you must take a look at some of the resources on the Net devoted to travel health advice. You can find information about particular countries you are going to visit, the hazards specific to that country, listings of immunizations you need, and potential diseases you can bring home as unique souvenirs for you or your friends. While you are planning ahead, take a look at the tips on how to stay healthy while flying. You can learn about air quality on planes, what food to avoid during flights, how to prevent dehydration, and much, much more. These sites will give you what you need to plan for a healthy vacation.

Web:
 http://www.cdc.gov/travel/
 http://www.doh.gov.uk/traveladvice/
 http://www.flyana.com/
 http://www.travelhealth.com.au/
 http://www.tripprep.com/

Travel Marketplace

Upgrades, frequent flyer plans, hotel discounts, travel guides—the longest journey begins with but a single step into Usenet's one-stop travel marketplace. Buy, sell, beg, borrow, steal—then go!

Usenet:
  rec.travel.marketplace

Travel Reservations

That dream trip to North San Diego County, to go surfing at Tabletop and eat burritos at Roberto's, might be a lot more affordable than you think. Use the Net to make reservations and, if there's a way to get there, you'll get there. (Don't forget the sunscreen.)

Web:
  http://travel.yahoo.com/
  http://www.expedia.com/
  http://www.flyaow.com/
  http://www.hotwire.com/
  http://www.onetravel.com/
  http://www.orbitz.com
  http://www.travelocity.com/
  http://www.trip.com/trs/trip/

SUBWAY NAVIGATOR

It's one thing to get lost. It's another thing to get lost underground.

If you are in any doubt as to the best subway route to take in a particular city, check with the Net. The Subway Navigator stands ready to help you find your way from A to B (or, if necessary, from C to D).

Travel Resources

One time, I went to the British Virgin Islands and when I got there, I started asking around for the best places to snorkel. It wasn't long before I found out that most of the natives don't snorkel—it's a tourist activity. Boy, it sure would have been handy to have had a laptop and a wireless modem so I could have connected to the Net. When you need information, don't assume that it's going to be there when you arrive.

Web:
  http://www.lonelyplanet.com/
  http://www.mondolink.com/travel.html
  http://www.planetrider.com/
  http://www.travel-library.com/

Usenet:
  alt.airline
  alt.airline.schedules
  alt.flame.airlines
  misc.transport.air-industry
  rec.travel.air

Travel Resources for Women

Wherever you are, that's where you are. But what if that's not where you want to be? These travel resources can help you make sure your trip runs smoothly. That way—while you are traveling—you will be free to concentrate on the three Ss: safety, shopping and you know what.

Web:
  http://www.adventuregirl.com/
  http://www.journeywoman.com/
  http://www.tips4trips.com/Tips/femmtips.htm

Travel Stories

I have a friend, Kenn, who went on an extended trip to Europe. Kenn took a computer with him, and along the way, he wrote about what he was doing and emailed the stories to his friends. If you enjoy reading travel stories, take a look at these Web sites, where people all over the world write about their trips. Even better, if you are going on a trip, why not write you own stories and share them with everyone else?

Web:
  http://pemtropics.mit.edu/~jcho/travel.html
  http://www.cyber-adventures.com/
  http://www.travel-notes.org/

Travel Talk and General Discussion

Travel is a lot of fun and—as they say—broadening. And, while you are traveling there is no substitute for inside information. These Usenet groups are for discussion of specific aspects of travel or particular locations. If you are going to visit a new place, I suggest reading the appropriate group before you leave. If you have any questions, post them in advance of your trip and you may get some useful answers. For general travel discussion, use the **rec.travel.misc** group.

Usenet:
    alt.travel
    alt.travel.canada
    alt.travel.marketplace
    alt.travel.rides
    alt.travel.road-trip
    alt.travel.uk.air
    alt.travel.uk.marketplace
    bit.listserv.travel-l
    rec.outdoors.rv-travel
    rec.scuba.locations
    rec.travel
    rec.travel.africa
    rec.travel.air
    rec.travel.asia
    rec.travel.australia+nz
    rec.travel.bed+breakfast
    rec.travel.caribbean
    rec.travel.cruises
    rec.travel.europe
    rec.travel.latin-america
    rec.travel.marketplace
    rec.travel.misc
    rec.travel.resorts.all-inclusive
    rec.travel.usa-canada

Travel Tips

Don't let your excitement about your big trip get in the way of being organized and careful about planning the details. You may end up stranded in a tiny country known for political unrest and lack of Internet access. Get tips on packing, passports, air travel—and don't forget to send your favorite Internet author cool postcards from exotic lands.

Web:
    http://www.ease.com/~randyj/secure1.htm
    http://www.freetraveltips.com/
    http://www.lorrypatton.com/travel/tips/by-topic/
    http://www.ricksteves.com/plan/tips/
    http://www.safewithin.com/travelsafe/
    http://www.tips4trips.com/

Traveling Alone

Rudyard Kipling said, "He travels the fastest who travels alone." I say, "He who travels alone, travels by himself." My mother used to say, "If you are going to travel alone, be sure to have extra underwear." Take your pick.

Web:
    http://www.crazydogtravel.com/solo.html
    http://www.travelaloneandloveit.com/tips/
        travel_tips.htm

Travel Net-Style

Ah, travel. There's nothing like the feeling of exploring somewhere new, romantic and exciting where the hand of Man has never set foot.

Ah, travel. A seductive mistress whose inner depths are shrouded in mystery, a temptress who could be leading you into unexpected adventure around the very next corner.

But before you set out on your next journey, use the Net to gather the information and hints you need to make your trip safe and interesting. The **rec.travel** discussion groups are populated with people who love to keep moving, and the **rec.travel** archives have a variety of useful information.

Travel can be uncomfortable, but if you are willing to take your chances, the opportunity of a lifetime may be waiting on the other side of the gate.

U.S. National Parks

The United States has a vast number of parks, many of which are managed by the National Park Service (NPS), a bureau of the U.S. Department of the Interior. The NPS alone administers 400 parks containing an aggregate of over 83 million acres. Some of these parks are well known, such as Yellowstone and the Grand Canyon. However, most of the parks are less known and are wonderful places to explore. For example, do you know anyone who has been to Piscataway Park or Timpanogos Cave? If you like the outdoors and you live in the U.S. (or will be visiting), these Web sites provide you with the information you need to find and visit a park (including making reservations if necessary).

Web:
http://www.areaparks.com/
http://www.llbean.com/parksearch/
http://www.nps.gov/
http://www.recreation.gov/
http://www.virtualparks.org/main.html
http://www.worldfromtheweb.com/
http://www.xanterra.com/

Usenet:
rec.outdoors.national-parks

U.S. State Department Travel Information

The U.S. State Department has extensive information on current and past travel advisories for those interested in traveling abroad. Each factsheet contains the addresses and phone numbers of American consulates, as well as passport, visa and government information, and crime data.

Web:
http://www.travel.state.gov/

World Guide to Vegetarianism

Vegetarians, you no longer have to worry about traveling around the world and not being able to find good food that will fit in with your dietary lifestyle. This site has a listing of vegetarian restaurants, natural food stores and vegetarian organizations around the world.

Web:
http://www.vrg.org/travel/

U.S. State Department Travel Information

Whether or not you are American, you will find the information on this Web site useful. Before you even put one toe outside your native country, look up what the U.S. State Department has to say about where you are going. Along with a great deal of useful information (mostly of interest to Americans) you can find out the basic travel facts about any country (of interest to anyone).

For each country, you can read a general description, as well as information about entry requirements, medical facilities, crime information, drug penalties, road and traffic information, and more.

For example, under Canada, I found the following: "Crime Information: There is a higher incidence of criminal activity in urban areas. However, violent crimes such as murder, armed robbery, and rape are infrequent…"

(Personal hint for travelers to Canada: If a Canadian thief tries to hold you up, federal law allows you to refuse to give up your possessions if the thief does not ask for them in both French and English.)

TRIVIA

Geography Trivia

Geography trivia covers a lot of ground: not only the physical features of our planet, but statistics about people, cities and countries. Here are some examples: Where is the Forbidden City? Which two countries share the island of Hispaniola? Where is the Chapultepec Mountain range? What is the capital of Canada? (The answers are Beijing, Dominican Republic & Haiti, Mexico, and "mostly American".)

Web:
http://www.primate.wisc.edu/people/hamel/
    geotriv.html
http://www.triv.net/html/geography.htm
http://www.triviaplaza.com/geo.htm

History Trivia

When you come right down to it, history is nothing more than the memory of something in the past. Thus, in principle, anyone can be good at history trivia, because all you need to do is remember things that have already happened. For example, if someone says, "When did William the Conqueror invade England?", you say "1066". Big deal. Now, what would be really impressive is to be good at *future trivia*. Here are some sample questions: Who will serve as the Vice President of the United States from 2088 to 2096? What will be the three main causes of the so-called "Mutiny on Microsoft Island? Twenty years from now, which Harley Hahn book will be the most important one in your collection?

Web:
 http://www.primate.wisc.edu/people/hamel/
   histriv.html
 http://www.quia.com/dir/hist/
 http://www.triv.net/html/history.htm
 http://www.usahistory.com/trivia/

Literary Trivia

Every now and then, I'll be with a friend, and we will start asking literary trivia questions. For example, I'll say, "Who wrote 'The Last of the Mohicans'?" and my friend will answer "James Fenimore Cooper". Or he will ask me, "In the Harry Potter books, what was Voldemort's original name?" and I'll reply "Tom Marvolo Riddle". The thing is, regular literary trivia gets dull after awhile, so I developed a new game, Trivial Literary Trivia (TLT) that is a lot more challenging. Here is a typical question: "In Act 5, Scene 3 of Shakespeare's play 'Troilus and Cressida', what is the 12th word in Andromache's first speech?" (The answer is "ears".) Although TLT is a bit esoteric, it has two main advantages over regular literary trivia: first, the questions are very easy to understand; second, the game is usually over quickly.

Web:
 http://www.primate.wisc.edu/people/hamel/
   littriv.html
 http://www.triv.net/html/literature.htm

Movie Trivia

If you like movies, you may be interested in trivia. For example, did you know that the working title for Annie Hall was "Anhedonia?" (It's a medical term referring to the inability to feel pleasure.) How about this? When Woody Allen was making "The Purple Rose of Cairo," he originally cast Michael Keaton in the male lead role. However, Allen wasn't satisfied with Keaton's performance and replaced him with Jeff Daniels. If you find facts like this interesting, you may be a movie trivia person.

Web:
 http://www.cool-movie-trivia.com/
 http://www.faqs.org/faqs/movies/trivia-faq/
 http://www.imdb.com/Sections/Trivia/
 http://www.joblo.com/indianasev.htm
 http://www.primate.wisc.edu/people/hamel/
   movtriv.html
 http://www.triviaplaza.com/movie.htm

Music Trivia

Music is important to all of us. However, there are many different types of music: classical, rock, jazz, opera, country & western, and so on. For this reason, I have constructed the ultimate music trivia question, one that will appeal to anyone regardless of their musical preferences. Here it is: "Where was Louis Armstrong sitting when he recorded his famous electric guitar solo in the last act of Mozart's 'The Cheating Heart of Seville'?" (The answer is: "On a chair".)

Web:
 http://www.iknowmymusic.co.uk/quiz.html
 http://www.musicmini.com/
 http://www.primate.wisc.edu/people/hamel/
   musictriv.html
 http://www.triv.net/html/music1.htm
 http://www.triviaplaza.com/pop.htm

Oldies Music Trivia

If you were listening to popular music in the '60s and '70s, it's high time you started taking your nostalgic legacy seriously. Spend some time at these Web sites and relive the golden days of something or other.

Web:
 http://www.fiftiesweb.com/trivia-oldies.htm
 http://www.oldiesfun.com/triviagames.html
 http://www.oldiesmusic.com/trivia.htm

Religious Trivia

What I want to know is, if God can do anything, can he make up a religious trivia question so difficult that even he can't answer it?

Web:
http://www.biblenet.net/trivia/
http://www.biblequizzes.com/
http://www.findtrivia.com/religion/
　body_religion.html
http://www.primate.wisc.edu/people/hamel/
　bibletriv.html

Religious Trivia

Not long ago, I ate a peanut butter and tunafish sandwich before I went to bed and, during the night, I had the strangest dream.

I dreamed I was competing in the Trivia Championship of the Universe. When I got to the finals, the topic was religious trivia, and I had to play against God.

I never had a chance. 

No matter what the question, he was able to beat me by making up the answer.

Sports Trivia

Do you know how many seasons Bobby Orr led the NHL in scoring? Or who the first golfer was to earn over a million dollars? Have you any idea who the first boxer was to regain the heavyweight championship? Many people don't have the fount of special knowledge to answer questions like this successfully. However, if you have what it takes, I bet you will have lots of fun at these sports trivia sites. Anyone can watch a sport on TV, but it takes a really special person to master the trivia. (By the way, the answers to the questions are: two, Arnold Palmer, and Floyd Patterson.)

Web:
http://www.1st-all-major-sportsbook-sports-betting
　-gambling.com/sportshistory.html
http://www.gamedaydirect.com/trivia.htm
http://www.sportscribe.com/trv1.html
http://www.ttcards.com/trivia/
http://www.twnn.com/sportstrivia.htm

Television Trivia

When you need a break from the old TV, try your hand at some trivia. Here are some quizzes that will test your knowledge of Seinfeld, Cheers, South Park and more. Not only are these quizzes fun, but they are good practice in case you ever have to take a civil service examination.

Web:
http://www.12news.com/cheers/
http://www.home.earthlink.net/~paulywogg/
http://www.primate.wisc.edu/people/hamel/
　tvtriv.html
http://www.triv.net/html/television.htm
http://www.vybr8r.com/seinfeld/triviagame.asp

Today's Date

Every day, there are two numbers associated with the date: the month and the day. For example, December 21st (my birthday) is 12/21. April 6th (my cat's birthday) is 4/6. Each number has interesting facts associated with it, and you can read about today's numbers by visiting this Web site. Personally, I love numbers and I enjoy learning about how each number is special in its own way.

Web:
http://www.nottingham.ac.uk/education/number/

A B C D E F G H I J K L M N O P Q R S **T** U V W X Y Z

Today's Events in History

Do you ever feel like today is just like every other day? Well, I can tell you it's not. In fact, go right now and look up what happened on this day in history and I bet you will learn something wonderful. Just think, on this very date, something astounding happened. Watch what you do today. You just might end up on this list.

Web:
http://lcweb2.loc.gov/ammem/today/
http://www.historychannel.com/today/
http://www.on-this-day.com/
http://www.scopesys.com/today/
http://www.yarranet.net.au/onthisday/otd.htm

Trivia Resources and Quizzes

Trivia refers to simple, interesting facts, often based on the popular culture. Trivia does not have to be useful. It only has to be simple and interesting, for example: "There is no mention of cats in the Bible." There is a huge amount of trivia on the Net, including quizzes to test your knowledge of the esoteric.

Web:
http://osiris.sund.ac.uk/online/quiz/quiztime.html
http://www.avendano.org/quiz/
http://www.funtrivia.com/
http://www.mindlesscrap.com/stumpme/
   stumpme.htm
http://www.primate.wisc.edu/people/hamel/
   trivia.html
http://www.qod.com/
http://www.searchforsales.com/trivia.html
http://www.triv.net/qmenu.htm
http://www.triviaguy.com/
http://www.triviaserve.com/vs/quiz_main

Trivial Talk and General Discussion

Okay, we all know that Richie Petrie's middle name is Rosebud and that it stands for "Robert Oscar Sam Edward Benjamin Ulysses David". But what was Rob and Laura's address? How about the Ricardos' phone number? Join the pros and test your trivia skill. TV, radio, music, film, Internet books—all the great cultural achievements of mankind are grist for those who pursue the trivial.

Usenet:
rec.games.trivia

IRC:
#trivia (Undernet)

(From the rec.games.trivia frequently asked question list)

What are the Seven Wonders of the Ancient World?

The Great Pyramid of Khufu at Giza

The Hanging Gardens of Babylon

The Statue of Zeus at Olympia

The Temple of Artemis at Ephesus

The Mausoleum at Halicarnassus

The Colossus of Rhodes

The Lighthouse at Alexandria

The Great Pyramid is the oldest of the Seven Wonders and the only one of them still in existence.

What were the names of the castaways on the Gilligan's Island television show?

"The ship's aground on the shore of this
Uncharted desert isle,
With Gilligan,
The Skipper too, (Jonas Grumby)
The millionaire and his wife,
(Thurston Howell III, Lovey Howell)
The movie star (Ginger Grant)
And the rest
('Professor' Roy Hinkley, Mary Ann Summers)
Are here on Gilligan's Isle."

Gilligan didn't have a first name on the show, but Bob Denver has stated in interviews that he had talked the matter over with show creator Sherwood Schwartz. Had Gilligan ever needed a first name, it would have been Willie.

UFOS AND ALIENS

Abductions

All over the world, there are people who have been abducted by aliens; or who think they were abducted by aliens; or who say they were abducted by aliens—maybe you should read the material and make up your own mind. These sites contain articles, personal experiences and incident reports covering various alien abduction topics. There are also hints on how to know if you have been abducted (just in case you are not quite sure).

Web:
  http://www.abduct.com/survey.htm
  http://www.alienjigsaw.com/
  http://www.anw.com/aliens/52questions.htm
  http://www.crystalinks.com/abduction.html
  http://www.pbs.org/wgbh/pages/nova/aliens/
  http://www.ufoabduction.com/

Usenet:
  alt.paranet.abduct

Alien Autopsies

An autopsy is a medical procedure—often referred to as a postmortem examination—in which a dead body (cadaver) is examined in order to figure out why a person died. One of the basic facts about this procedure is that you cannot have an autopsy unless you have a body. So when you hear about an autopsy being conducted on an alien, the significance is not that we might find out how an alien died, but that there actually was an alien in the first place.

Web:
  http://www.trudang.com/autopsy.html
  http://www.ufoworld.co.uk/aa_qa.htm

> **My goal is to climb the highest mountain in the world and throw a penny off the top.**

Alien Lexicons

You can't talk about the players without a program, so here are some reference sites that define extraterrestrial and UFO terminology. If you are interested in aliens, it behooves you to spend some time learning the vocabulary. After all, think how embarrassed you would be if some aliens were visiting you, and you introduced them to your mother as Greys when they were really Lyrans.

Web:
  http://ourworld.compuserve.com/homepages/
    andypage/ufogloss.htm
  http://www.counterevidence.com/glossary.shtml
  http://www.strodes.ac.uk/students/paranorm/
    ufogloss.htm
  http://www.tigerbyte.com/dcross/ufo_glossary.asp

Alien Pyramids

It's easy to say that aliens built the pyramids. What's not so easy is to convince people that what you say is true. Well, don't get left behind the next time your social circle is debating the origin of the pyramids. Visit these Web sites and get the real story.

Web:
  http://www.europa.com/edge/pyramid.html
  http://www.mt.net/~watcher/pyramid.html
  http://www.nauticom.net/users/ata/egypt.html
  http://www.qtm.net/~geibdan/cydonia.html

Ancient Astronauts

The theory is that thousands of years ago, alien astronauts visited the Earth. Moreover, our present technological society is not the first one to exist on our planet. But if that were the case, shouldn't there be some evidence? There is, according to the true believers, and the purpose of these Web sites is to find, analyze and disseminate facts that support these theories.

Web:
  http://www.aas-ra.org/
  http://www.crystalinks.com/ancientastronauts.html
  http://www.dailygrail.com/interviews/alford1.html
  http://www.eridu.co.uk/author/ancient_astronauts/
    ancient_astronauts.html
  http://www.skepdic.com/vondanik.html

Area 51

These resources are devoted to Area 51, the super-secret government base near Las Vegas. Read current speculations on alien aircraft, discuss the government's security measures at the base and ponder new ideas on how to spy on the base to see the aliens.

Web:
http://www.area51researchcenter.com/
http://www.dreamlandresort.com/
http://www.nauticom.net/users/ata/resources.html
http://www.ufomind.com/area51/

Usenet:
alt.conspiracy.area51

Crop Circles

Crop circles are large, sometimes intricate designs created on farmland when parts of a field of growing plants are flattened to form a large pattern. Many people believe that crop circles are of extraterrestrial origin. If you would like to find out more about crop circles and what people have said about them, here are some Web sites where you can find information about the phenomenon. You can do all the research you need, or, if you are artistically inclined, you can make your own crop circles.

Web:
http://www.artbell.com/circles.html
http://www.circlemakers.org/
http://www.cropcircleconnector.com/
http://www.cropcirclequest.com/
http://www.paradigmshift.com/
http://www.swirlednews.com/

Usenet:
alt.paranormal.crop-circles

Life on Mars

Is there life on Mars? Well, if not, how do you explain the Martian "pyramids" and the "lost civilization"? They may have been built by aliens. For awhile it looked as if there had been bacteria on Mars at one time (although that hypothesis has since been discredited). Still, if there is life on Mars, you and I don't want to be the last to know.

Web:
http://www.biospherics.com/mars/
http://www.jpl.nasa.gov/snc/
http://www.marsnews.com/focus/life/
http://www.marstoday.com/

Crop Circles: Whence Comest Thou?

Where did all the crop circles come from? They are mysterious patterns and designs that appeared in farmers' grain fields, starting in the middle 1970s and peaking between 1989 and 1992. Lots of explanations have been proposed: the crop circles were made by aliens, by supernatural beings, by natural phenomena that are not well understood, and so on.

Here is the real explanation:

The first crop circles appeared in English grain fields. The size, complexity and circumstances were such that many people said it was impossible for the whole thing to be a hoax. However, it was a hoax.

The original crop circles—and many of the later ones—were created by two Englishmen from Southampton, Doug Bower and Dave Chorley. One night while drinking beer in their pub, they started talking about UFO reports and thought it might be fun to fool all the gullible people who believed in UFOs.

They began by making simple designs in fields using only a steel bar. Eventually they graduated to making elaborate designs using boards and ropes.

Once the hoax caught on, other people started copying them, in England as well as in other countries. Bower and Chorley continued this for 15 years, fooling a lot of "experts". Finally, in 1991, they confessed and demonstrated to reporters how easy it was for them to create the complex patterns that—according to so many believers—could not be made by human beings.

(Actually, I have my own theory: I think the crop circles were created by Martian bacteria.)

Raelian Movement

In retrospect, December 13, 1973, was an important day in the UFO community. On that day (so we are told), a Frenchman named Claud Vorilhon talked to an alien. This little fellow (only 4 feet tall) was not only cute—he had long dark hair, olive-colored skin, and almond shaped eyes—but affected a pleasant and comforting personality. Over the course of several days, the alien revealed that it was his cohorts who were responsible for creating all the life on Earth. Human beings, he explained, mistakenly assumed that the cute little aliens were gods. However, now that we are "mature" enough, it is time for us to know the truth. During the initial meeting, the alien changed Vorilhon's name to Rael, hence the name Raelian Movement.

Web:
http://www.godulike.co.uk/
   faiths.php?chapter=107&subject=intro
http://www.gospelcom.net/apologeticsindex/
   r12.html
http://www.rael.org/int/english/
http://www.thegodsearch.com/links224.htm

Roswell Incident

Read the facts and folklore about Roswell, the town where it is said that, in 1947, an alien vessel crashed and the government hushed it up. See pictures of the crash and an FBI memo. By the way, here is the real explanation: the debris that crashed was from secret experiments the Pentagon was running called Project Mogul. The purpose of these experiments was to develop technology capable of detecting Russian atomic tests (which, it was thought, were about to begin soon). When the apparatus crashed, the military covered it up by saying the debris was from weather balloons. This, of course, was a lie, which in later years served to stimulate the American UFO-cover-up-conspiracy buffs.

Web:
  http://www.af.mil/lib/roswell.html
  http://www.csicop.org/si/9507/roswell.html
  http://www.cufos.org/ros4.html
  http://www.iufomrc.com/incident.shtml
  http://www.parascope.com/articles/0697/
    usafreport.htm
  http://www.v-j-enterprises.com/roswell.html

UFO Chatting

When it's late at night and you are afraid of the dark, you can find some companionship on IRC. The X-Files channel is populated by people who are fans of the X-Files television show, but they also chat about aliens and UFOs. The **#ufo** channel is exclusively for talking about extraterrestrials and UFO-related subjects.

IRC:
  #roswell (EFnet)
  #ufo (DALnet, Undernet)

UFO Information Resources

When you are looking for specific UFO information, you can wait for one of the Greys to come over to your house and deliver the information in person, or you can use the Net and find what you need right away. Whatever you are looking for—photos, movies, personal statements, theories, names, dates and addresses—you'll find it on the Net.

Web:
  http://www.cseti.org/
  http://www.cufos.org/
  http://www.ufoinfo.com/contents.shtml
  http://www.ufomind.com/
  http://www.ufos-aliens.co.uk/

Usenet:
  alt.alien.visitors

UFO Origins

In 1947, a pilot named Kenneth Arnold claimed that, while flying in the northwest area of the United States, he saw nine boomerang-shaped flying objects. Arnold was flying during the day and was able to describe the objects' movement as being similar to saucers skipping across the surface of a lake. A newspaper reporter covered the story, and referred to the objects as "flying saucers". Although Arnold never claimed to see anything saucer-like, the name caught the public fancy, and soon became part of the vernacular. Since then, there have been numerous reports of flying saucers, UFOs and aliens, and a great body of mythos has grown up around them. Here are some alternate explanations of the origin of UFOs.

Web:
  http://ourworld.compuserve.com/homepages/
    andypage/theories.htm
  http://www.parascope.com/nb/ufoin.htm

A B C D E F G H I J K L M N O P Q R S T U V W X Y Z

UFO Reports

Have you seen a UFO recently and lived to tell about it? Here are some places on the Net to report it and to check to see if anyone else in your area might have seen something similar. Read about sightings all over the world, speculate about alien visitors or just laugh at people whose reports seem unbelievable.

Web:
  http://www.parascope.com/nb/uforoundup/
    index.htm
  http://www.ufocenter.com/
  http://www.ufosightingsuk.co.uk/

Usenet:
  alt.ufo.reports

USENET

Creating Alternative Usenet Discussion Groups

An alternative Usenet group is one that has been started without any special procedures, such as voting or discussion. Unlike mainstream groups—which do undergo such procedures before they can be started—alternative groups can be created by anyone who knows how to do so. The disadvantage to such groups is that they are not carried by as many news servers around the world. Alternative groups are important, however. They provide a counterpoint to the more sedate, controlled world of mainstream groups in that people are more free to create and remove alternative groups, with a minimum of fuss, as the need arises. Here is information about how alternative groups should be created. If you want to create a group, please read and follow the guidelines. They were developed by trial and error and a lot of smart thinking over a period of time. Usenet works best when people (1) think before acting, and (2) do not try to re-invent everything.

Web:
  http://www.faqs.org/faqs/alt-hierarchies/
    emily-alt-advice/
  http://www.livinginternet.com/?u/ua_alt.htm
  http://www.nylon.net/alt/newgroup.htm
  http://www.visi.com/~barr/alt-creation-guide.html

Creating Mainstream Usenet Discussion Groups

A mainstream Usenet group is one that is created by following a specific set of procedures, involving one or more votes, serious discussion and deliberate planning. It takes time and effort to create a mainstream group (compared to an alternative group which anyone can create if he or she knows how). The advantage of mainstream groups is that they are respected as real groups and are carried by virtually all news servers around the world. Here is an explanation of how such groups are started.

Web:
  http://www.eyrie.org/~eagle/faqs/big-eight.html
  http://www.faqs.org/faqs/usenet/
    creating-newsgroups/naming/
  http://www.templetons.com/brad/trial.html
  http://www.uvv.org/docs/howto.txt

Discussion Groups (Web-based)

Usenet discussion groups (which you see throughout this book) are wonderful places to talk and share. Usenet is a rich system, with many people participating from around the world. However, to use Usenet, you need special software and you need to learn how the system works. (For details, see the section on Usenet in the front part of this book.) Alternatively, there are a great many Web-based discussion groups—sometimes referred to as forums or message boards—that you can access easily using your browser. These discussion groups are less permanent and have a much smaller audience than Usenet. However, they provide a simple way to share thoughts, ideas and opinions with other people. (Idea: Why not start your own forum, just for your friends or family?)

Web:
  http://communities.msn.com/
  http://messages.yahoo.com/
  http://www.ezboard.com/
  http://www.msnbc.com/bbs/

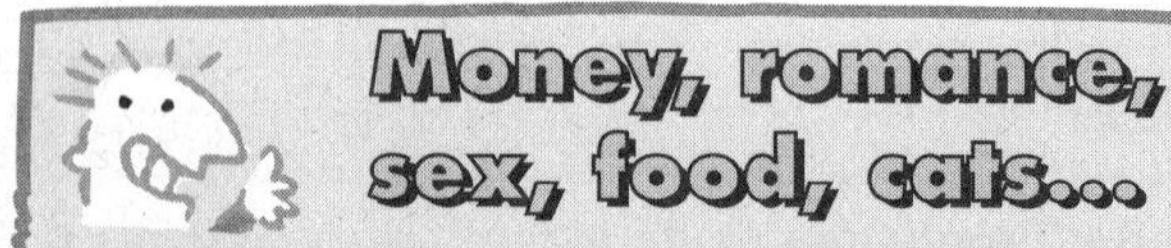

Want to join the discussion? Let me help you find the right Usenet groups.

Harley Hahn's Master List of Usenet Newsgroups:
"All the newsgroups fit to print."

Flames

Within Usenet, a flame is a message that contains an angry or abusive response to a previous message. A flame might be a complaint, a criticism of someone's ideas, or a good old-fashioned, mean-spirited tongue-lashing. The next time you feel like a good argument, join one of these groups and see what it is like to play with the people who live to complain.

Usenet:
alt.flame
alt.flame.abortion
alt.flame.airlines
alt.flame.rush-limbaugh

Harley Hahn's Master List of Usenet Newsgroups

Usenet is a worldwide system of discussion groups. To access Usenet, you use a program called a newsreader. (Usenet was originally designed to carry local news between two universities in North Carolina. Thus, for historical reasons, Usenet groups are often referred to as newsgroups, even though they don't carry news.) Both Internet Explorer and Netscape come with a newsreader program. With Internet Explorer, the program is Outlook Express. With Netscape, the program is built into the browser. There are between 20,000 and 60,000 different newsgroups (depending on whose numbers you believe). However, most of these groups are not of general interest and do not have worldwide distribution. Moreover, many newsgroups are "bogus", that is, non-existent or filled with spam (unsolicited advertising). To help you find the groups you want, I have created Harley Hahn's Master List of Usenet Newsgroups. Go to my Web site and you can search for newsgroups by topic, by name, or by looking for a particular keyword. I have taken a great deal of time and checked all the groups, keeping only those in the thirteen major hierarchies as well as throwing out all the bogus groups. I then wrote a short, accurate description for each group and placed it in a category, and organized the whole list to be easy to search. Enjoy.

Web:
http://www.harley.com/usenet/

Moderated Newsgroups

With most Usenet groups, anyone can post (send) any message he wants whenever he wants. This freedom is what makes Usenet so powerful. However, for some groups, such freedom doesn't work well: there are too many off-topic postings and too much spam (unsolicited advertising). One solution is to create a moderated group. One person, called a moderator, receives all the postings, and he or she decides which ones are actually sent to the group. Many Usenet groups are moderated, which cuts down on the spam and increases the usefulness of the newsgroup. This FAQ (frequently asked question list) explains moderated newsgroups, including the difference between moderation and censorship, what it takes to become a moderator and where to find resources for moderators.

Web:
http://www.faqs.org/faqs/usenet/moderated-ng-faq/

Net Abuse

Heavy cross-posting, spamming, and annoying commercial advertising are at the top of the list of Ways to Abuse Your Net Privileges. Read about the latest sins against the laws of Net etiquette, thoughts and ideas on the concept of minding our manners, and general ranting and raving about people who rant and rave.

Web:
http://www.cybernothing.org/faqs/
   net-abuse-faq.html
http://www.faqs.org/faqs/net-abuse-faq/

Usenet:
alt.current-events.net-abuse
alt.current-events.net-abuse.spam
news.admin.net-abuse.bulletins
news.admin.net-abuse.email
news.admin.net-abuse.misc
news.admin.net-abuse.policy
news.admin.net-abuse.sightings
news.admin.net-abuse.usenet

Check out page 706.

Newsgroup Catalogs

There are thousands of Usenet discussion groups (newsgroups) and it's not always easy to find the ones you want. These resources can help. You can search for the groups you want by name, by keyword, or by looking through a particular hierarchy.

Web:
    http://www.cyberfiber.com/
    http://www.tile.net/news/

Picture Grabbing Software

There are lots of pictures posted to Usenet (and some of them are even non-pornographic). If you like looking, you'll love these programs. They will visit your favorite groups, snarf out all the pictures automatically, and save them on your hard disk, where you can peruse them at your leisure. I like these programs, and they sure save me a lot of time. (My research requires me to look at lots of pictures...)

Web:
    http://www.allpicturez.com/
    http://www.binaryboy.com/
    http://www.binnetwork.net/~bnr/bnr.html
    http://www.kbrowning.com/
    http://www.newsbin.com/
    http://www.newsrobot.com/sbnews/frsbnews.html
    http://www.nijico.com/
    http://www.techsono.com/pixnewslite/
    http://www.tifny.com/
    http://www.zeonews.com/

Usenet Announcements

Stay informed on the latest new discussion groups that are cropping up in Usenet. The **.newgroups** group is where people post when they want to propose a new group. The **.newusers** group is a place where periodic explanations about Usenet are posted for the benefit of new users.

Usenet:
    news.announce.conferences
    news.announce.important
    news.announce.newgroups
    news.announce.newusers

Picture Grabbing Software

Do you like to watch? Well, there are oodles of free pictures just waiting for you on Usenet.

Grab yourself some picture grabbing software and soon you'll have more pictures than you know what to do with (but I bet you'll figure it out).

Usenet Culture Talk and General Discussion

Usenet has a culture all its own. Once you spend a lot of time on Usenet, you will get a feeling for its energy, its customs, its vocabulary and its importance: in other words, its culture. This is the group where you can discuss all these subjects.

Usenet:
    alt.culture.usenet

Usenet Discussion Group Administration

It's bound to happen. When you get thousands of people posting to Usenet, someone is going to decide that things need to get more organized. The **news.admin** groups are a central point for administrative topics relating to Usenet, such as the dissemination of information, statement of policies, and the relating of technical details about forming and moderating Usenet groups.

Usenet:
    news.admin
    news.admin.censorship
    news.admin.hierarchies
    news.admin.misc
    news.admin.policy
    news.admin.technical

Usenet for New Users

Usenet consists of many different discussion groups. Through the years, millions of people have participated in Usenet and, in that time, a good many conventions have been established. If you are a newcomer, there is a lot to learn. One way to start is to read the articles in **news.newusers.questions**, a group for new users. If you have any questions, this is a good place to post them, as there are experienced people who read this group and answer questions. In addition, I have some extra material that can help you. First, on my Web site, I have a short article will orient you to Usenet. (The article is also printed in the front part of this book.) Second, in my book *Harley Hahn's Internet Advisor,* you will find a more comprehensive discussion of Usenet, in which I explain everything you need to understand to get started and to use Usenet well.

Web:
　http://www.harley.com/usenet/whatis-usenet.html

Usenet:
　news.groups.questions
　news.newusers.questions

Usenet Hierarchies

Within the name of a Usenet group, the first part of the name indicates the hierarchy (major category) to which the group belongs. For example, when you see the names **alt.politics.usa** and **alt.sex.stories**, you can tell they are part of the **alt** (alternative) hierarchy. When you see the name **comp.infosystems.www**, you know the group is part of the **comp** (computer) hierarchy. Here are the most important hierarchies (the ones I want you to remember): **alt** (alternative), **bionet** (biology), **biz** (business), **comp** (computers), **humanities** (arts and humanities), **k12** (K-12 education), **misc** (miscellaneous), **news** (Usenet itself), **rec** (recreation), **sci** (science), **soc** (society) and **talk** (debate). However, there are literally hundreds of different hierarchies, most of them devoted to a particular geographical area, language or organization. This Web site has a large list of Usenet hierarchies along with a brief description. If you encounter a strange name that you don't understand, look here for help.

Web:
　http://www.faqs.org/faqs/usenet/hierarchy-list/

Usenet News Servers (Commercial)

I go to a lot of trouble to make sure that all the resources I choose for this book are free. So why am I giving you information about services that cost money? There are free news servers on the Net, in fact lots of them. However, if you really like Usenet, it may be worth a few bucks for you to use a reliable, well-maintained news server that you can count on.

Web:
　http://www.airnews.net/
　http://www.altopia.com/
　http://www.mammothnews.net/
　http://www.news-service.com/
　http://www.newscene.com/
　http://www.newsfeeds.com/
　http://www.supernews.com/
　http://www.triton.net/tritonnews/
　http://www.usenetserver.com/

Usenet News Servers (Free)

To access Usenet discussion groups (usually called "newsgroups"), you need access to a Usenet news server. Normally, your ISP would provide such access. If it doesn't, or if you don't like the service, there are many news servers around the Net you can use for free.

Web:
　http://freenews.maxbaud.net/
　http://newssearch.pilum.net/
　http://www.arcwebserv.com/jumpsite/usenet.html
　http://www.findolin.de/
　http://www.netwu.com/newswolf/
　http://www.wnabb.freeserve.co.uk/list.htm

> **Hint: You can skip directly to step #4 (unless today is Friday and there is a cat in the room).**

Usenet Newsreaders

To read and send articles to Usenet discussion groups, you use a program called a newsreader. Your browser can act as a newsreader, but if you use Usenet a lot, you may want to use a program that works better than a browser. Here are places where you can find newsreaders for different systems. If you take the time to try the various programs and choose the one you like best, you will greatly enhance your Usenet experience. However, if you are a beginner, many of the newsreader features won't make sense to you, so you should reevaluate once you have gained some experience.

Web:

http://cws.internet.com/news.html
http://www.forteinc.com/agent/
http://www.microplanet.com/gravity/
http://www.pure-mac.com/usenet.html
http://www.tin.org/
http://www.usenetopia.com/
http://xnews.newsguy.com/

Usenet:

alt.sys.amiga.thor
alt.usenet.offline-reader.forte-agent
alt.usenet.offline-reader.forte-agent.modified
alt.usenet.pirated.agent
news.software.nn
news.software.readers

Usenet Search Engines

Usenet is a vast system of thousands of discussion groups. (For historical reasons, the discussion groups are called "newsgroups".) A Usenet search engine allows you to specify keywords, and then search a large archive, looking for all the newsgroup articles that contain those keywords. Millions of people around the world participate in Usenet every day, so being able to find what you need is a tremendous resource.

Web:

http://groups.google.com/

Do, do, do. (Now.)

Web-Based Usenet Access

The basic way to read and post Usenet articles is by using a program called a newsreader. Your newsreader acts as a news client and contacts a news server on your behalf. However, there is another way you can access Usenet: you can use one of these these Web sites. They will display Usenet articles for you on Web pages, and allow you to post articles of your own. This means you can read Usenet articles as if they were regular Web pages, so you don't have to learn how to use a newsreader program. If you are a casual Usenet user, this may be all you need. However, if you want to use Usenet a lot, you are better off with a real newsreader.

Web:

http://groups.google.com/
http://www.mailgate.org/
http://www.newsone.net/
http://www.usenet-replayer.com/

VICES

Bingo

Feel the rhythm. It builds slowly as the caller announces the numbers and letters: B15, G59, O65... Slowly your card begins to fill in. One square, then another, then another. I21, N32, B13... Will you win this time? You start to sweat. You can feel your blood pressure rising and your heart pounding. I17, O65, G47... You only have two more squares to fill. Now one more square. I30, O64, B2... and somebody else wins. Never mind. The next game is about to start.

Web:

http://www.bingoace.com/
http://www.bingobugle.com/reviews.html
http://www.bingoseek.com/
http://www.club-king.com/

Caffeine

I can't stand still. All this great information about caffeine, and I have to read, read, read. Right away. Now. Lotsa links and I have to look at them all. Click, click, click. Go faster. I'll go get another Jolt while I'm waiting.... Okay, I'm back. Click on another one. Right away. Cool. All this caffeine stuff. I can't stand still.

Web:

http://faculty.washington.edu/chudler/caff.html
http://www.coffeefaq.com/
http://www.faqs.org/faqs/caffeine-faq/

Usenet:

alt.drugs.caffeine

Be careful, or bingo will control you. Here is an example from real life.

When I was working on this ad, I called a friend of mine (who loves bingo) to talk to her about it. But I couldn't reach her, and do you know why? Because she was playing bingo!

In other words, she passed up the chance to talk to a charming, sensitive, sophisticated man in order to slavishly follow her desires.

Bingo. Can *you* handle it?

Casino Gambling

The gambling (sorry, "gaming") industry spends a lot of effort to make sure your casino experience is as pleasant as possible, considering the fact that you are going to give them a significant amount of money and receive nothing in return. To help in this effort, they provide well-maintained gambling (sorry, "gaming") rooms, an attentive staff, a variety of games, economical hotel accommodations, and special rewards for big spenders. The gambling (sorry, "gaming") industry has a carefully maintained image, but behind the scenes there is a lot more going on than you realize. If you are new to casinos, start by using the Net to learn the basic rules of the games and get some experience. Then check up on what the serious recreational gamblers are discussing and see what comps the various casinos are offering. (A comp is something free given to gamblers, such as a free room or a free meal). I read a message from someone who said, "$2,800 play got me $17 cash back, a $20 comp to their deli, and a free baseball cap." Wow! Who knows? Maybe you'll do even better.

Web:

http://www.americancasinoguide.com/Promotions/
    promotions_main.shtml
http://www.casinocenter.com/
http://www.casinoworldnews.com/
http://www.onlinecasinonews.com/

A
B
C
D
E
F
G
H
I
J
K
L
M
N
O
P
Q
R
S
T
U
V
W
X
Y
Z

Chocolate

While chocolate is not one of the Seven Deadly Sins, it tastes good enough to be. If you are hooked on chocolate, check out these Web sites, if for no other reason than to enjoy the recipes for chocolate desserts. The Usenet discussion groups will give you access to chocolate chat even after all the supermarkets are closed.

Web:
  http://www.exploratorium.edu/chocolate/
  http://www.faqs.org/faqs/food/chocolate/faq/
  http://www.hhhh.org/cloister/chocolate/
  http://www.virtualchocolate.com/

Usenet:
  alt.food.chocolate
  rec.food.chocolate

Cigar Smoking

Cigar smoking really doesn't have a lot to do with smoking. Cigar smoking is all about image, social bonding and oral gratification. With that in mind, let me help you find what you need on the Net. These Web sites contain information about choosing and smoking cigars, along with explanations of the appropriate cultural accoutrements—in other words, everything you need to ensure that, as a cigar smoker, you are projecting the proper image and enjoying the right amount of social bonding. For oral gratification, you're on your own.

Web:
  http://www.cigaraficionado.com/
  http://www.cigarfriendly.com/
  http://www.cigargroup.com/
  http://www.cigarweekly.com/
  http://www.fujipub.com/cigar/
  http://www.top25cigar.com/

Usenet:
  alt.smokers.cigars

Listserv Mailing List:
  List Name: cigar-l
  Subscribe to: listserv@listserv.american.edu

Majordomo Mailing List:
  List Name: cigars
  Subscribe to: majordomo@listserv.prodigy.com

Cigarette Smoking

The idea behind these Web sites is that, if you are going to smoke, you should do it well. Smokers as a whole have need of certain resources that these sites provide: information about particular political issues, places to buy tobacco products, comparisons of various brands of cigarettes, and so on. (Personal note. Having gone to medical school and worked in hospitals, I can tell you categorically—anyone who could see what the end-stage of cigarette smoking looks like would never smoke, even moderately. If you like to smoke, imagine yourself in a hospital room, with a body ravaged by years of tobacco. Just trying to sustain enough breath to walk to the bathroom is a major achievement. Think about what it looks like when a surgeon cuts into your lower jaw and pulls it open in a vain effort to remove the cancer at the back of your throat. I have seen all of this and a lot more. Take my word for it, there are a great many adjectives you can use to describe what happens to a person who smokes for years, but "cool" is not one of them.)

Web:
  http://www.forces.org/
  http://www.smokersclub.com/
  http://www.tobaccolovers.com/

Usenet:
  alt.smokers

Drinking

Drinking alcohol is the most popular of all the acceptable vices, and the best part is that people have developed so many customs and so much mythology that a person who drinks can say to himself, "I'm doing much more than simply ingesting a drug that will have a particular biochemical effect on my brain cells; I am actually partaking in a highly developed social and gustatory ritual." So let me enhance the experience by showing you where to find information about alcoholic drinks. You'll find more recipes than you can shake several swizzle sticks at in a month of Saturday nights.

Web:
  http://www.drinkboy.com/
  http://www.mathu.com/cc-irc.htm
  http://www.webtender.com/
  http://www2.potsdam.edu/soc/hansondj/funfacts/
    funfacts.html

Usenet:
  alt.alcohol

Flirting

Flirting is the activity of making playful advances to another person, usually for romance, sex, or both. If you want to be a successful flirt, focus on making the other person feel good. Use eye contact, listen, be self-confident, be respectful and show a sense of humor. As with many other activities in life, successful flirting is not so much what you do, but how you do it. Hint for Men: The next time you see a beautiful woman, go up to her and say, "Hi, my name's Harley. Didn't I write about you in one of my books?" (Well, it always worked for me...)

Web:
  http://www.flirt.com/advice/susan/
  http://www.flirtzone.com/keys.htm
  http://www.flirtzone.com/tips.htm
  http://www.sexuality.org/flirtadv.html

Gambling and Oddsmaking

When you are not sitting in a smoke-filled room taking chances with your money, fill your urges with some great gambling and oddsmaking resources on the Net. The Web sites will show you hints and tips about gambling, and in the Usenet groups you can talk about various gambling games.

Web:
  http://www.acesguidetogambling.com/
  http://www.gambling-newsletter.com/
  http://www.gamblingwiz.com/
  http://www.learnhowtoplay.com/

Usenet:
  alt.gambling
  rec.gambling
  rec.gambling.blackjack
  rec.gambling.blackjack.moderated
  rec.gambling.craps
  rec.gambling.misc
  rec.gambling.other-games
  rec.gambling.poker
  rec.gambling.sports

> ## Television is bad for you.

Hangovers

It's a shame when something that can be fun causes so much misery later. But it's the same with any fun thing—sex, alcohol, excess food or roller coasters. There is always a risk of ensuing nausea or headache afterward. Don't be alone in your misery. Share stories and sure cures for hangovers. Learn from the people who never let the prospect of pain slow them down.

Web:
  http://www.hairytongue.com/
  http://www.hungover.net/
  http://www.soyouwanna.com/site/syws/hangover/
    hangover.html
  http://www.webtender.com/handbook/
    antihangover.html

Usenet:
  alt.hangover

Horse Racing

And they're off! You feel the adrenaline rush through your veins and into your fast-beating heart. Your pulse quickens and you break out in little beads of perspiration. You clutch the ticket in your fist and hope like heck that your horse comes in first, since you just bet your lunch money. In the whole history of horse racing, there probably was someone, somewhere, who went to the races just to watch the animals run around the track, but for everyone else there is only one important reason to follow this sport: gambling. If you are a horse-racing fan, you can meet up with other fans and discuss strategies and handicapping. When you need hard data, the Web sites contain enough information to choke a horse (not that you ever would, of course).

Web:
  http://www.bloodhorse.com/racing/
  http://www.espn.go.com/horse/
  http://www.racetracks.com/
  http://www.thoroughbredtimes.com/

Usenet:
  alt.sport.horse-racing
  rec.gambling.racing

Listserv Mailing List:
  List Name: hracing
  Subscribe to: listserv@listserv.louisville.edu

Lotteries

Why work all your life and feel the satisfaction of successfully making your way in the world when you can buy a lottery ticket and have the chance to win your fortune all at once? Lottery fans, get together and discuss the lotteries on Usenet, or see all the lottery resources that are on the Web, such as number generators, lottery news and helpful software.

Web:
  http://www.aboutlotto.com/
  http://www.interlotto.com/
  http://www.lottoshop.com/

Usenet:
  rec.gambling.lottery

Lying

We all know we shouldn't lie, but are white lies okay? What about lying when the cause is a good one? Is lying *ever* okay? As a general rule, no. Life can be hard enough at times just dealing with reality. When someone misleads you, even if they mean well, your vision of that part of the world will be wrong, and your actions and judgments will be skewed. And if you are the person who lied, you will find that, over time, you will have to exert more and more ingenuity explaining away your previous lies in a consistent manner. You should recognize that lying covers more than intentionally telling a falsehood. There are also lies of omission, where you create or perpetuate a lie by *not* saying something. Don't fool yourself, these are still lies. In general, lying is a highly destructive habit that always ends up causing more trouble than the lie was supposed to avoid in the first place. On the other hand, cultivating the habit of telling the truth has a wonderful side effect: you will become a better person, naturally, because you know you will never be able to lie about your actions.

Web:
  http://webhome.idirect.com/~readon/lies.html
  http://www.connectingwithkids.com/archives/
    goodlie.html
  http://www.liespeopletell.com/
  http://www.open2.net/trust/downloads/docs/
    kantiantrust.pdf
  http://www.parenthoodweb.com/articles/
    phw102.htm
  http://www.scu.edu/ethics/publications/iie/v6n1/
    lying.html
  http://www.straightdope.com/classics/a4_094b.html

Pipe Smoking

You know you are addicted when the sweet, rich scent of pipe tobacco makes you all goose-pimply and gives you urges to dress in velvet smoking jackets. Even if you don't like to smoke a pipe, it's fun to go in those tobacco shops with the rich wood paneling and case after case of sweet-smelling leaves.

Web:
  http://www.pipe-smokers.co.uk/pipes.htm
  http://www.pipes.org/asp_FAQ.html
  http://www.pipesandtobaccos.com/
    pipesandtobaccos/info/faq.htm
  http://www.pipesmokerscouncil.org/beginners.htm

Usenet:
  alt.smokers.pipes

Poker

Tom, Dick and Harry sat down to an all-night poker game.

Tom and Dick were completely self-taught and had no particular strategy. Harry had just spent several days learning about poker techniques on the Internet.

Who do you think won all the money?

(Actually, it was Tom, but Harry had the most fun.)

Poker

Poker is the most popular card game for gambling in a social setting. Poker is also one of the three most important pastimes that define the essence of masculinity (the other two being watching the Three Stooges and killing spiders). Poker is based on the idea that various combinations of cards are ranked from low to high. At the start of the game, each player is dealt a number of cards. Based on the value of their cards, the players make bets that are put together to form a pot. At the end of the game, the player with the highest hand wins the pot. Although poker has a number of variations, there are two basic forms: draw poker, in which your cards are seen only by you and are hidden from your opponents, and stud poker, in which some of the cards are dealt face up and, hence, are visible to everyone. In the long run, success in poker depends greatly on the odds of getting particular combinations and your ability to understand the related statistics. However, psychology is also significant, as bluffing (betting when you know you have a low hand) and outguessing your opponents are important parts of the game.

Web:
> http://www.conjelco.com/pokglossary.html
> http://www.faqs.org/faqs/gambling-faq/poker/
> http://www.playwinningpoker.com/articles/mz/
>   howto1.html
> http://www.pokermike.com/poker/
> http://www.pokerpages.com/
> http://www.seriouspoker.com/dictionary.html

Usenet:
> rec.gambling.poker

Stealing

In 1971, Abbie Hoffman published a book that jumped to the best-seller lists and, in less than a year, sold more than a quarter of a million copies. This book was refused by tens of publishers. Stores refused to carry it and the media refused to accept advertisements for it. The name of the book? "Steal This Book". When he wrote the book, Hoffman (1936-1989) was a well-known Yippie radical and member of the Chicago Seven. (If you are not sure what this is, ask an old person.) Steal This Book was a compendium of rip-off tricks and survival techniques. Today, in the ultimate irony, Hoffman's book is available for free on the Net. To complement it, I have included some sites with information about stealing. (The fine print: Stealing is wrong, so don't do it. This is only for fun.)

Web:
> http://www.shine.net.au/shinemag/bguide/
>   shoplifting.htm
> http://www.tenant.net/Community/steal/steal.html
> http://www.thespoon.com/stories/shoplifting.html
> http://www.thingy.apana.org.au/~fun/rabelais/
>   shoplift.html

Strip Clubs

It's nice when you go to a bar or club and you get the opportunity to see some nice scenery. And it doesn't really have to be anything special like glorious vistas that make you believe there is a God. Just something interesting will do, like a man or woman wearing nothing but strategically placed tassels as they gyrate in the vicinity of your seating area.

Web:
> http://www.sexwork.com/dancers/stripclubs.html
> http://www.sexykitten.com/
> http://www.tuscl.com/

Virtual Slot Machine

When you can't take the time to hit the slots in Vegas, at least stop on the Web to see if you can hit the jackpot. Start off with a few coins, pull the handle and see if you can win more coins.

Web:
> http://www.onlineslotplayer.com/free_slots.html
> http://www.state.mlive.com/slots/
> http://www.ulster.net/~jamihall/java/Slot/Slot.html

VIDEO AND MULTIMEDIA

Animation Showcases

There are a lot of people creating collections of cool, creative animations that they want to share on the Net. Here are some showcases where you can browse through a large number of homemade animations and marvel at the work of all the talented, witty people who have so much time on their hands.

Web:
  http://www.mondominishows.com/
  http://www.urbanentertainment.com/0/
  http://www.wildbrain.com/
  http://www.wired.com/animation/

CD-RW Drives

A CD-RW (CD-rewritable) drive is a wonderful addition to your PC. I have one and I love it. A CD-RW drive can not only read CDs, it can write to them in two different ways. First, it can make exact copies of music CDs and CD-ROMs, and it can make custom music CDs (using the songs you want). Second, CD-RW drives can use special blank CDs (CD-RWs) as rewritable storage devices. Once you format a CD-RW, you can access it like a regular disk. CD-RW discs are inexpensive and can hold up to 530 MB of data (after formatting). Thus, once you have a CD-RW drive, you can have as much extra storage as you want, which makes it great for backups. Hints: (1) When it comes to buying a CD-RW drive, faster is better. (2) If the drive is not built into your computer, have someone else install it for you.

Web:
  http://www.cdrfaq.org/
  http://www.cdrwcentral.com/
  http://www.osta.org/technology/cdqa.htm
  http://www.pcguide.com/ref/cd/cdrw.htm

Usenet:
  comp.publish.cdrom.hardware
  comp.publish.cdrom.multimedia
  comp.publish.cdrom.software

DVD

DVD (Digital Versatile Disc or Digital Video Disc) is an optical disc storage system that is faster and more powerful than regular CD technology. A DVD disc holds a lot more data than a CD, and a single disc can store both video and audio, as well as computer data. DVDs are widely used to distribute movies and, as such, will soon replace videotapes and laserdiscs. One day, DVDs may also replace audio CDs, CD-ROM discs and video game cartridges.

Web:
  http://www.dvddemystified.com/dvdfaq.html
  http://www.dvdfile.com/
  http://www.dvdlink.co.uk/
  http://www.dvdreview.com/
  http://www.dvdtalk.com/
  http://www.dvdtown.com/

Usenet:
  alt.video.dvd
  rec.video.dvd.advocacy
  rec.video.dvd.marketplace
  rec.video.dvd.misc
  rec.video.dvd.players
  rec.video.dvd.tech
  rec.video.dvd.titles

IRC:
  #dvdforum (EFnet)
  #dvdr (EFnet)

Watch as the future approaches—in high-resolution full-color interactive video with digital sound.

Flash

Flash is a product from Macromedia that allows you to create Web presentations using video, audio, animation and graphics. If you know what you are doing, you can do some awesome things. These resources can help you learn what you need to know to be the flashiest person on your virtual block. (The **macromedia.com** page is the home of the official Macromedia Web site.)

Web:
  http://www.flashfruit.com/
  http://www.flashkit.com/
  http://www.flashmagazine.com/flash4.htm
  http://www.kirupa.com/developer/
  http://www.macromedia.com/software/flash/
  http://www.visualintensity.com/flash.php

Usenet:
  alt.macromedia.flash

IRC:
  #flash (DALnet, EFnet, Undernet)

Someone has given you a file that contains a movie with irrefutable proof that the Pope is one of the aliens who masterminded the JFK conspiracy cover-up. However, your software cannot handle that type of file!

The Net can help. Go to the *Multimedia File Formats* Web resources and find the program you need to convert or view the file.

Once again (thanks to the Net), the truth will be revealed.

MIME Format

MIME (Multi-purpose Internet Mail Extensions) is the system used to attach various types of files to email messages. It is MIME that allows you to send and receive pictures, video, documents, and so on. For the most part, MIME works behind the scenes. To send a file, you tell your mail program to "attach" the file to an outgoing message. When you receive such a file, your mail program should "detach" it automatically (if not, you can tell the program to do so explicitly.) If you would like to find out more about how MIME works, here is the information.

Web:
  http://www.faqs.org/faqs/mail/mime-faq/
  http://www.hunnysoft.com/mime/

Usenet:
  comp.mail.mime

MPEG Video Resources and Software

The name "mpeg" (named after the Moving Picture Experts Group) refers to a family of standards used for encoding audio-visual information in a digital compressed format. At these Web sites you can find an overview of mpeg, as well as news, software, a FAQ, installation guides, and much more.

Web:

http://mpeg.telecomitalialab.com/
  http://www.bmrc.berkeley.edu/frame/research/ mpeg/
  http://www.dasound.com/programs/mpeg/
  http://www.datacompression.info/MPEG.shtml
  http://www.mpeg.org/

Multimedia File Formats

As an Internet user, you are going to encounter all different kinds of files. So what do you do when you find something your browser doesn't understand? Suppose you download a file named **harley.au** from the Web, but you are not sure whether you should look at it, listen to it or eat it. All the answers and more are in this wonderful, comprehensive guide to strange but true file formats.

Web:
  http://www.lib.rochester.edu/multimed/contents.htm

Multimedia Resources

No doubt about it. Multimedia is a frontier, and a lot is happening all at once. In order to stay where you are, you need to read as fast as you can. In order to keep up, you need to read twice as fast as that. So start here, with news, features, reviews and tech talk—enough info to keep you in the multimedia groove indefinitely.

Web:

http://www.newmedia.com/
http://www.smh.com.au/multimedia/

Usenet:

comp.multimedia

PC Video Hardware

When it comes to using a PC, what you get is what you see. The video hardware you use has a lot to do with how much you enjoy using your computer and the Internet. This Usenet group is where people discuss any topic related to PC video hardware: monitors, computers, video cards, flat-panel displays, video accelerators, video capture cards, and more. The Web site contains the FAQ (frequently asked question list) for the group.

Web:

http://www.faqs.org/faqs/pc-hardware-faq/video/

Usenet:

comp.sys.ibm.pc.hardware.video

Streaming Audio and Video

Streaming is a system in which audio or video data is sent to your computer as a continuous stream. The data is played as it arrives, making for an uninterrupted presentation. These resources provide sources for streaming audio and video broadcasting, as well as information about the tools you need to listen and watch.

Web:

http://www.icecast.org/
http://www.shoutcast.com/
http://www.shoutclub.com/
http://www.streamalot.com/
http://www.streamingmediaworld.com/

Video Creation

The difference between an entertaining video and one that no one wants to see is usually in the care and skill that went into the creation of the video. If you have mounds of videos collecting neglect, take a few moments to read this information and see if the idea of planning and editing your videos to create something real special appeals to you. If so, it won't be long before you are the envy of your family and friends, enjoying the respect that, as one of my readers, you firmly deserve. The only bad part is you will have to put up with Steven Spielberg and George Lucas dropping by all the time to beg you for ideas. (If this happens, do what I do, and tell them you don't see anyone without an appointment.)

Web:

http://www.datavideo-tek.com/datavideo2/
    nav&bkg_elements/resources/resources.htm
http://www.digitalvideosolutions.com/
    Guide0001.htm
http://www.focusinfo.com/articles/
http://www.hardwarecentral.com/hardwarecentral/
    tutorials/923/1/
http://www.uemedia.com/CPC/editorsnet/
http://www.videoguys.com/edit.htm

Video Glossary

The world of video, especially computer video, has a lot of specialized terminology. However, you need never feel lost. If you read or hear a word you don't understand, check the glossaries at these Web sites. Before you know it, you will be talking like a pro. ("What do you mean the machine doesn't have a flying erase head? I need to make a telecine transfer.")

Web:

http://www.bavc.org/glossary.htm
http://www.videonics.com/video-glossary.html

> There's no such thing as too much bandwidth.

WEATHER

Climate Data Catalog

This is no farmer's almanac. Don't count on the ache in your knees or the singing of crickets to tell you what the weather is going to be like. Get access to oceanic datasets, surface climatologies, air-sea data, sea surface temperatures, and Navy bathymetry.

Web:

http://ingrid.ldgo.columbia.edu/

Climate Diagnostics Center

You're leaning on the fence talking to the neighbor about life and the weather when he says, "In all my born days, I reckon this is the hottest summer I can ever remember." And when you think about it, you suspect he might have a point. Don't let the mystery of his remark keep you up at night. Utilize the Climate Diagnostics Center to see exactly how the weather has been not only for your lifetime, but for the last few centuries. Interesting climatological data is used to track persistent anomalies and to see how this affects short-term weather.

Web:

http://www.cdc.noaa.gov/

Climate Monitoring

The Climate Monitoring and Diagnostics Laboratory (CMDL) is part of the National Oceanic and Atmospheric Administration in Boulder, Colorado. The CMDL studies the atmosphere, looking at specific components that can change the Earth's climate. At its Web site, you will find research information in such areas as aerosol gases and the greenhouse effect, and depletion of the global ozone layer.

Web:

http://www.cmdl.noaa.gov/

Yes, you and I are right.

Hurricane Hunters

You may find it hard to believe, but there are people who actually fly right into hurricanes. They call themselves Hurricane Hunters, and they belong to the 53rd Weather Reconnaissance Squadron, part of the U.S. Air Force reserve. The Hurricane Hunters fly in and out of the eye of a hurricane in order to take accurate measurements of the internal pressure, the wind speed and the location of the center. These measurements allow the forecasters to make much more accurate predictions as to the characteristics and path of the storm. I bet you'll really enjoy visiting the Hurricane Hunters' Web site. The pictures and information are fascinating, and you can take a "cyberflight" into the eye of a hurricane. Usually these kinds of things are lame, but not here. Nothing is lame for the hurricane hunters.

Web:

http://www.hurricanehunters.com/

Hurricanes and Typhoons

Hurricanes and typhoons are powerful tropical storms that originate in the equatorial regions. They bring large amounts of rain and fierce winds and are capable of causing severe damage if they travel inland. When such a storm originates in the Atlantic Ocean or Caribbean Sea, the storm is called a hurricane. If it originates in the Pacific or Indian Ocean, it is called a typhoon. These sites provide information about upcoming tropical storms, as well as technical data about the storms themselves.

Web:

http://typhoon.atmos.colostate.edu/forecasts/
http://www.nhc.noaa.gov/

Marine Weather Observations

When you have been working hard all day and you want to go down to the beach to snorkel, it would be a handy thing to know in advance what the water temperature is like. That way, you will know whether or not to wear your wetsuit. You can find out this information and more from this site. Just click on a coastal region to get information on water temperature, wave height and frequency, and wind conditions.

Web:

http://www.oceanweather.com/data/

Meteorology Resources

Meteorology is the study of the atmosphere. Broadly speaking, there are two branches of meteorology: atmospheric dynamics and atmospheric physics. Atmospheric dynamics, part of fluid dynamics, deals with macroscopic phenomena on the scale of clouds to the entire planet. For example, this branch of meteorology would deal with thunderstorm complexes. Atmospheric physics studies processes that affect air parcels as they move through the atmosphere, for instance, the characteristics of the ozone layer or the physics of water vapor within clouds. Within these two branches, there are many specialties and sub-specialties such as atmospheric chemistry, cloud physics, meteorological optics, synoptic meteorology (day-to-day weather forecasting) and mesameteorology (short-term weather forecasting).

Web:
  http://www.datasync.com/~farrar/met.html
  http://www.faqs.org/faqs/meteorology/
    net-resources/
  http://www.usatoday.com/weather/askjack/
    wfaq0.htm

Meteorology Talk and General Discussion

It may be that no one does anything about the weather, but that doesn't stop us from talking about it. Join the discussion on Usenet and talk about the weather and all facets of meteorology.

Usenet:
  sci.geo.meteorology

Space Weather

It's a total drag when you are leaving Earth's gravitational influence, and you find out the weather in space is really not suitable. Next time, plan ahead. First, learn a bit about conditions in space, especially solar flares. Then check out today's space weather. You can see a current image of the sun, X-ray flux data, and get detailed information on solar flaring and the geomagnetic field.

Web:
  http://www.sec.noaa.gov/SWN/

Storm Chasing

The diameter of a tornado can vary from a few feet to as wide as a mile. Rotating winds within a funnel can reach a velocity of up to 300 mph (480 km/hour). However, the enormous risk posed by these storms is not enough to scare off certain types of people, called "storm chasers". Storm chasers will travel hundreds of miles, hot on the trail of storm activity. Their goals are to learn more about the storm and experience certain types of storms firsthand. Some storm chasers just want to have something exciting to do in their spare time. These sites offer lots of information about storm chasing, including pictures, anecdotes and late-breaking storm news.

Web:
  http://www.srh.noaa.gov/oun/skywarn/
    spotterguide.html
  http://www.stormpages.com/alarry8/
  http://www.stormtrack.org/
  http://www.wildweather.com/

Usenet:
  bit.listserv.skywarn

Chase a tornado.

Weather Images

When the weather is so cold that only an inebriated polar bear would go outside, don't even think of leaving the house before checking the latest pictures on the Net. There are a variety of different satellite images and maps to keep you apprised of what is happening on the surface of our planet. If you are a meteorologist, you will also be interested in some of the weather visualization tools.

Web:
  http://weather.unisys.com/
  http://www.weatherimages.org/

Weather Radar

There is a lot more to the weather than licking your finger to see which way the wind is blowing. Nobody knows this better than professional meteorologists, who use radar maps to study patterns and changes in the Earth's weather systems. If you would like to see what it is like being a professional meteorologist, visit one of these sites and choose a weather map that looks good. Then, making sure your friends are watching, stroke your chin and make some thoughtful remarks. (If you're not sure what to say, I suggest, "I don't like the looks of that low pressure area over the Ozarks.")

Web:
  http://vortex.plymouth.edu/
  http://www.earthwatch.com/SKYWATCH/
    RDUS2D.html
  http://www.rap.ucar.edu/weather/radar.html

Weather Reports: Canada

I grew up in Canada and you can believe me when I tell you they have a lot of weather up there. In fact, they have so much, they sometimes send their extra weather down to the United States. (And some people say Free Trade is bad.) If you want the official information about Canadian weather, connect to these Web sites, where you will find the latest weather forecasts, maps, satellite images, surfing forecasts, and so on.

Web:
  http://weatheroffice.ec.gc.ca
  http://www.canadianweather.com/
  http://www.msc-smc.ec.gc.ca/cmc/
  http://www.theweathernetwork.com/

Weather Reports: Europe

Once you are on the Net, timely weather reports for Europe are only a few mouse clicks away. If you live in Europe, you'll find all the information you need for your local area. If you are planning a trip, you can check the forecasts. Personally, I like to check the European weather in the winter, when it is warm in California (where I live) and cold and miserable everywhere else. But then, we all have our hobbies.

Web:
  http://www.eurometeo.com/english/
  http://www.europe.cnn.com/weather/
  http://www.flightline.co.uk/weather/weather.htm
  http://www.weather.net/fn/nexor.europe.html

Weather Reports: International

Here are weather reports for just about everywhere in the world. Once you have Net access, no matter where you are or what you are planning, there is no excuse for letting the environment rain on your parade.

Web:
  http://weather.noaa.gov/weather/ccworld.html
  http://www.cnn.com/weather/
  http://www.usatoday.com/weather/forecast/
    wglobe.htm

Weather Reports: United States

The next time you attend a costume party, go as a weather forecaster. Dress up in clothing suitable for a television broadcast, set up your computer and point to one of these Web sites. You'll find weather images and information just like they use on television. Stand in front of the computer and smile and point a lot. Your costume will be so convincing probably nobody will recognize you. (If they do, smile authoritatively and ask if they want your autograph.)

Web:
  http://www.absoluteweather.com/
  http://www.nws.noaa.gov/
  http://www.rainorshine.com/
  http://www.usatoday.com/weather/wfront.htm
  http://www.uswx.com/us/wx/

Weather Warnings

Many of the most severe weather events are predictable, and these predictions are available on the Net. If you live in an area that is susceptible to hurricanes, floods, tornadoes, thunderstorms or winter storms, it is easy to be forewarned. Even when the weather is fine, I find it interesting to check these sites, because something is always happening somewhere.

Web:
http://iwin.nws.noaa.gov/iwin/nationalwarnings.html
http://kamala.cod.edu/svr/

The Outside World

Living on the Internet is fine, but the outside world has two important advantages: (1) there is pizza, and (2) there is a lot of empty space where you can do stuff.

However, the outside world has some significant disadvantages. High up on the list is that there is just altogether too much weather.

So before you actually commit yourself to going outside, use the Internet to check the weather report for your area. Why take a chance when the information is only a few keystrokes away?

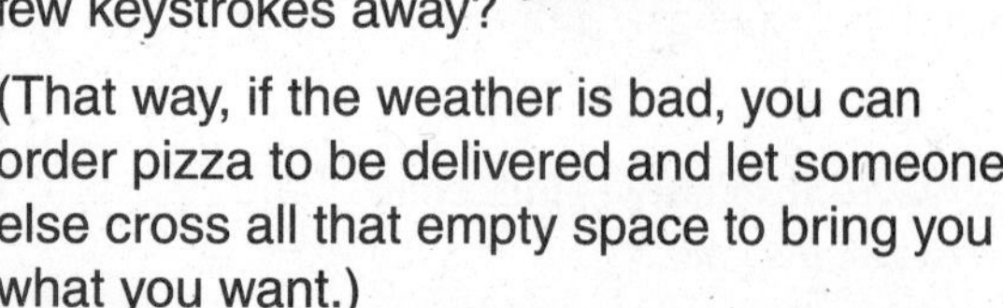

(That way, if the weather is bad, you can order pizza to be delivered and let someone else cross all that empty space to bring you what you want.)

Animated Gifs

A gif is an image that is stored using the gif format. (The name means "graphics interchange format".) An animated gif contains more than one image in the file. When your browser displays an animated gif, the series of images is displayed sequentially, providing for a primitive type of animation. These Web sites contain information that explains all about animated gifs: what they are, how to make them and how to use them effectively.

Web:
http://members.aol.com/royalef/gifmake.htm
http://www.3d-animated.com/
http://www.animationfactory.com/
http://www.webreference.com/dev/gifanim/

ASP Pages

ASP (Active Server Pages) is a system that allows you to use programming to control the content of a Web page. To use ASP, you insert lines of a program, written in a scripting language, right into the HTML that creates a page. Or, for more power, you can use ActiveX controls within a development environment such as Visual Basic or Visual C++. ASP allows you to perform tasks such as creating Web pages dynamically, using cookies, manipulating text files, retrieving information from a database, and using session variables (a type of global variable) to pass values from one Web page to another.

Web:
http://www.4guysfromrolla.com/
http://www.asp-help.com/
http://www.asp101.com/
http://www.aspalliance.com/
http://www.aspin.com/
http://www.aspwire.com/
http://www.programmersresource.com/

Listserv Mailing List:
List Name: asp-l
Subscribe to: listserv@list.emwac.cz

Bad Web Site Design

One of the best ways to learn how to do something well is to study what happens when people do it poorly. Here's a collection of links to Web pages that just do not cut the HTML mustard. Study them carefully, along with the commentary, and it won't be long before you are a better, finer Web page designer.

Web:
> http://www.users.nac.net/falken/annoying/main.html
> http://www.webpagesthatsuck.com/

Bandwidth Bandits

The term "bandwidth" is used to describe the amount of information being copied from one place to another. For example, if many people visit your Web site, you might say that it is a high bandwidth site. If a particular site is rarely visited, you could call it a low bandwidth site. So what is a bandwidth bandit? When you design a Web page that has pictures and graphics, you normally keep the images on your Web server. When someone visits your Web page, his browser gets the images from your server. From time to time, you may see a picture or graphic on someone else's page that you would like to use on your own page. The proper thing to do is to download copies of the images to your own server (and, if you are dealing with original art, to ask permission). Some people—the so-called bandwidth bandits—do not copy images to their own server. Instead, they just point to the original pages within their HTML. This means that each time somebody visits one of the bandit's pages, the browser must impose on other Web sites to get the images. In other words, when a person points to other people's images, he artificially increases the demands on those sites and becomes a bandwidth bandit. Don't do this.

Web:
> http://www.absolutecross.com/bandit.htm
> http://www.thesitewizard.com/archive/
>   protectimages.shtml
> http://www.wanderers.com/wanderer/direct/

> ### Change is up to you.

Cascading Style Sheets

HTML was designed to define the content of Web pages. In the original version of HTML, there were few ways to specify how that content should be displayed. Naturally, Web page designers want as much control as they can get over the exact layout of the page. Cascading style sheets (CSS) are an enhancement to basic HTML that allows you to have all the control you need. You can specify margins, colors, fonts, backgrounds, white space, and much more. You use CSS by attaching one or more style sheets to your HTML document. In order to create the final image, the browser applies each style sheet to the document. (The application of multiple style sheets to a single HTML page is called "cascading".) Here is a simple example of how CSS might be used. Say that a large company has several Web servers with many Web pages. There can be a general style sheet that is used for all the Web pages produced by the company. This will give all the Web pages a common appearance. A particular department might have a style sheet for all the Web pages they produce. Within that department, a Web designer could have his own style sheet. Thus, when you look at a Web page from this company, your browser might apply three different style sheets to render the final appearance of the page.

Web:
> http://www.blooberry.com/indexdot/css/
> http://www.htmlhelp.com/reference/css/
> http://www.pageresource.com/dhtml/indexcss.htm
> http://www.w3schools.com/css/

CGI Scripts

CGI stands for "Common Gateway Interface", a mechanism by which a Web server can process data that you enter into a form. The program that runs when you enter data is called a CGI script. These Web sites explain what CGI is and how it works. You will also find a collection of CGI scripts that you can use or modify. Note: Creating CGI scripts requires programming skills.

Web:
> http://www.1001tutorials.com/cgitut/
> http://www.cgidir.com/Tutorials/
> http://www.faqs.org/faqs/www/cgi-faq/
> http://www.scriptarchive.com/

Usenet:
> comp.infosystems.www.authoring.cgi

IRC:
> #cgi (Undernet)

Chat Facilities for Your Web Site

What could be better than people all over the world visiting your Web site? People all over the world chatting on your Web site. Start your very own chat room today and see what your fans have to say for themselves.

Web:

    http://www.infinitechat.com/addchat.htm
    http://www.javazoom.net/jzservlets/jzchat10/
       jzchat.html
    http://www.okchat.com/
    http://www.webchatting.com/addchat.htm
    http://www.weirdoz.org/visualchat/

Color Charts

There will be times when you want to control the colors on your Web pages as closely as you can. The best way to do so is to specify the colors numerically. Each specific color corresponds to a six-digit hexadecimal—base 16—number. (In decimal—base 10—our regular system, we use the digits 0 through 9. In hexadecimal, we use 16 digits: 0, 1, 2, 3, 4, 5, 6, 7, 8, 9, A, B, C, D, E and F.) For example, when you create a Web page, if you specify the color "00CC99" you get a greenish-blue. These Web sites have tools to make it easy to find the color you want and its numeric code.

Web:

    http://www.gotomy.com/color.html
    http://www.hypersolutions.org/rgb.html
    http://www.paletteman.com/
    http://www.zspc.com/color/index-e.html

Decorating Web Pages for Holidays

It's a holiday, but are you ready? Sure you are, because you prepared ahead of time, using all this free holiday clip art, graphics and designs. Happy Web-day.

Web:

    http://members.cyberz.net/jkeepes/holiday.htm
    http://www.fantasyrealm.com/Holiday/
    http://www.graphics-by-celeste.com/
       holiday_graphics/index.shtml
    http://www.graphicsring.com/holidays/
    http://www.patswebgraphics.com/holiday.html
    http://www.web-holidays.com/clipart/

Color Chart

My advice is to take control of the colors on your Web page by finding the ones you want and specifying them exactly.

I know someone who didn't. He designed an entire Web site, trusting his Web editing program to use the right colors. Without thinking, he finished all the pages and unloaded them to the Web server.

Within minutes, his life was exposed as being a total sham.

Discussion Groups for Your Web Site

Why not offer your visitors a chance to discuss ideas with one another? These resources make it easy for you to add discussion groups (also called forums or message boards) to your Web site. Aside from offering such services to the general public, you can also set up a private discussion group for your family or friends. The best part? Because it's on your Web site, *you* will be in control. Note: These resources are free, but your visitors will have to look at ads.

Web:

    http://www.amazingforums.com/
    http://www.beseen.com/board/
    http://www.boardhost.com/
    http://www.ezboard.com/
    http://www.voy.com/

Dynamic HTML

Dynamic HTML (DHTML), an extension of regular HTML, can enhance the functionality of your Web pages. For example, you can layer multiple images on top of one another, make elements on the page interactive, and, using cascading style sheets, control the exact placement of all text and images. DHTML also makes it easier to write scripts and to manipulate objects.

Web:

> http://msdn.microsoft.com/workshop/author/dhtml/
>   dhtml.asp
> http://www.dhtmlcentral.com/
> http://www.dynamicdrive.com/
> http://www.htmlguru.com/
> http://www.thelinkzone.com/webmaster/html/
>   dhtml.html
> http://www.tips-tricks.com/dy.html
> http://www.w3schools.com/dhtml/

Frames

Frames are Web page building blocks that allow you to divide a page into independent sections. Within each frame, you can control how data is to be displayed. These Web sites offer tutorials that will help you learn about frames and how to use them. Special request: Not everybody likes to use frames. Unless the nature of your data is such that it demands frames, please take the time to ensure that your Web pages work properly for people who choose to view them without frames.

Web:

> http://www.manda.com/frames/
> http://www.sharkysoft.com/tutorials/frames/
> http://www.weballey.net/frames/

> **The best business letters always include a free sample. Send one to your boss today.**

Free Web Site Hosting

Would you like to have your own Web site? Of course you would. So where are you going to put it? Some Internet service providers will give you free space for your Web site. But if this isn't the case for you, here are some places that will host your Web space for no charge. Is there a catch, you ask? Well, of course. First of all, you will be limited in how much space you are allowed. Second, you and your visitors may have to look at a lot of advertising. Third, if you try to present objectionable material (such as X-rated pictures), you may be censored. Finally, your name, email address and any other information you volunteer might be used for mailing lists and telemarketing. Still, free is free.

Web:

> http://angelfire.lycos.com/
> http://geocities.yahoo.com
> http://www.1accesshost.com/
> http://www.freeservers.com/
> http://www.freewebspace.net/
> http://www.freeyellow.com/
> http://www.tripod.lycos.com/

Guestbooks

When someone visits you at your home, you know they were there. But when somebody looks at your Web site, you have no way of knowing that you had a visitor. Of course, one of the nice things about the Net is that it is anonymous, and you don't want to force everyone who goes to your Web page to tell you who they are. But it is nice if you have a way for people to leave you a message and for other people who visit to read the messages. To do this, you use what's called a guestbook. If you are a programmer, you can create your own guestbook facility. But it's much easier to let someone else do the work. Here are some resources that make it easy for you to put your own personal guestbook at your own personal Web site.

Web:

> http://guestbooks.pathfinder.gr/
> http://www.dreambook.com/
> http://www.guestbook.de/
> http://www.guestpage.com/
> http://www.theguestbook.com/

HTML Editors

The content and design of Web pages is described by a system called HTML (Hypertext Markup Language). Broadly speaking, there are two ways to create Web pages. You can use a WYSIWYG (what you see is what you get) editor or an HTML editor. With a WYSIWYG editor, you manipulate the various elements of the page and make them just the way you want. Behind the scenes, the editor creates the appropriate HTML for you automatically. Both Microsoft and Netscape give away free WYSIWYG editors with their suites of Internet software: Frontpage Express (Microsoft) and Composer (Netscape). If you want more control over the Web page creation process, you can use an HTML editor. Such editors have sophisticated features to help you create and maintain HTML just the way you want it.

Web:

> http://cws.internet.com/32advhtml.html
> http://tucows.tierranet.com/htmlbeginner95.html
> http://tucows.wau.nl/htmledit95.html
> http://wp.netscape.com/download/
> http://www.microsoft.com/windows/ie/downloads/

It's not generally well known, but God used an HTML editor to design the universe.

(Why do you think everything lines up so well?)

> **Angular momentum makes the world go round.**

HTML for Advanced Users

You're at a party and you have your eye on a hot prospect you've been dying to talk to. You stake your claim at the onion dip, knowing at any minute she will come over, because who can resist onion dip? Finally she does and you strike up a conversation, ready to talk about something meaningful. Then she asks, "Don't you find it terribly inconvenient that, when you get the **rel** and **rev** attributes mixed up within a **<link>** tag, the relationships get all mixed up?" So what are you going to do—tell her that women have trouble understanding relationships? Be prepared for situations like this by reading up on all aspects of HTML (Hypertext Markup Language) *before* you go to a party.

Web:

> http://www.blooberry.com/indexdot/html/
> http://www.htmlgoodies.com/tutors/master.html
> http://www.htmlhelp.org/reference/html40/
> http://www.w3.org/markup/

Usenet:

> comp.infosystems.www.authoring.html

Listserv Mailing List:

> List Name: **adv-html**
> Subscribe to: **listserv@bama.ua.edu**

Majordomo Mailing List:

> List Name: **html**
> Subscribe to: **majordomo@mail.serve.com**

Majordomo Mailing List:

> List Name: **htmlhelp**
> Subscribe to: **majordomo@listserv.prodigy.com**

IRC:

> #html (DALnet, EFnet, Undernet)

HTML for Beginners

HTML (Hypertext Markup Language) is a system that describes the various elements used to create a Web page. To make a Web page, you create an HTML file that contains data along with special instructions (called "tags") that tell a browser how the data should be displayed and processed. You then put the HTML file where it can be accessed by a Web server. When someone gives the address of that file to their browser, the browser will contact your Web server and request a copy of the file. When the file arrives, the browser will read the HTML and display the data appropriately. If the HTML tells the browser that your Web page needs extra files (such as images or photos), the browser will request those as well and display them on the page. (This is why you often see your browser make more than one connection to a Web server even though you are only looking at a single page. Each image must be retrieved separately.) HTML is complex and, to create really good Web pages, you need to spend some time learning the details and experimenting. Here are some Web sites to help you get started. How do you know which HTML beginner's guide to read? Look at a few and pick the one that makes the most sense to you.

Web:
  http://builder.cnet.com/webbuilding/pages/
    Authoring/Basics/
  http://wdvl.internet.com/Authoring/HTML/
  http://www.december.com/html/
  http://www.htmlgoodies.com/primers/basics.html
  http://www.webdeveloper.com/html/
    beginners_html.html

Five Reasons Why You Should Learn HTML

(1) It's fun, it's legal, and the high lasts for weeks.

(2) Making your own Web site will give you a sense of freedom, independence and confidence that will mark you as a giant among men (or women).

(3) Your mother would be so proud of you.

(4) One person I know didn't learn HTML, and within a few years, his life degenerated so much that all he could do was watch TV and read USA Today.

(5) If all the people who know HTML were laid end to end, they would be very surprised.

Icons for Fake Awards

In the beginning, the idea sort of made sense: someone would look at a lot of Web pages and judge which ones were the very best. Those very best Web sites could display a special icon showing that they had achieved recognition, like a four-star restaurant mentioned in a guide book. What happened next should have been predictable, because it's a lot easier to give awards to other people than it is to actually do something creative on your own. The number of people willing to judge other people's work proliferated and, today, there are literally hundreds of awards on the Net. The whole thing has become rather silly. To help make it even more silly, here is a Web site that contains a whole bunch of icons for fake awards. Put one of these icons on your site, and you can thumb your nose at the entire award culture. Now, *that's* an idea that deserves an award.

Web:
  http://www.jwp.bc.ca/saulm/html/award/award.htm

Image Maps

An image map is a picture in which the various points correspond to URLs (Web addresses). When the image map is displayed on a Web page, the user can jump to the different URLs by clicking on different parts of the picture. For example, say you are designing a Web site to show specific information about each of the states in the U.S. You could use an image of the country that shows all the states, and then define an image map so that a person could jump to information about a particular state simply by clicking on it. The information in these resources will help you understand image maps, and show you how to create them for your own Web pages.

Web:
  http://www.coffeecup.com/mapper/
  http://www.cris.com/~automata/tutorial.shtml
  http://www.ihip.com/

Usenet:
  comp.infosystems.www.authoring.images

Meta Tags

A meta tag is an HTML statement that you place on your page for one of three reasons. First, a meta tag can be used to store information about the document, such as the name of the author or an expiration date. Second, you can use a meta tag to make something happen to the page automatically, such as playing a sound or jumping to another page. Finally, you can use a meta tag to hold keywords that will be noticed and indexed by various search engines. If you would like to attract a lot of the "right" people to your Web site, learning how to use meta tags to catch the eye of the search engines can help a lot. Is it fun to use these tags? Well, as Will Rogers once said, "I never meta tag I didn't like."

Web:

http://www.addme.com/meta.htm
http://www.metatagbuilder.com/
http://www.northernwebs.com/set/
    design_notes_0.html
http://www.philb.com/metatag.htm
http://www.searchenginewatch.com/webmasters/
    meta.html
http://www.webdeveloper.com/html/
    html_metatags.html

Promoting Your Web Site

There are millions of Web pages on the Net, so how do you get noticed? These resources will help you get the recognition you deserve. Before long, visitors from all over the Net will be beating an electronic path to your virtual door.

Web:

http://websiteawards.xe.net/dvworksheet.htm
http://www.accusubmit.com/promote.html
http://www.addme.com/
http://www.jimworld.com/
http://www.promotionworld.com/
http://www.the-vault.com/easy-submit/
http://www.uswebsites.com/submit/

The biggest cause of fatigue is boredom.

Tables

Within HTML, you use tables to display information in rows and columns. Aside from using them to present data in a tabular format, you can also employ tables to create margins and to control spacing. These Web sites will teach you about tables, what they can do, and how to use them well.

Web:

http://htmlgoodies.earthweb.com/tutors/tbl.html
http://www.bagism.com/tablemaker/
http://www.lib.berkeley.edu/TeachingLib/HTML/
    tables.html
http://www.netscape.com/assist/net_sites/
    tables.html
http://www.pageresource.com/html/table1.htm
http://www.webmist.com/webtutor/tables/

Transparent Gifs

A transparent gif is an image, in gif format, in which one color is designated as being "transparent". When the image is displayed on a Web page, the browser will change the places where the transparent color is used to be the same as the background color. The effect is to create an image that fits nicely into the background. Making transparent gifs is easy—if you have the right tools.

Web:

http://www.gifart.com/tip15.shtml
http://www.goddess.hispeed.com/goodies/misc/
    tutorials/tgifs.htm
http://www.grafx-design.com/08photo.html
http://www.mindworkshop.com/alchemy/
    gifcon.html
http://www.mit.edu:8001/tweb/map.html
http://www.webdevelopersjournal.com/software/
    transgif.html
http://www.wise-women.org/tutorials/ps1/

Using HTML Well

When you use HTML well, your pages look good and are easy to read. These Web sites will help you teach yourself how to use HTML well. There are lots of tips, explanations and links to tools. Most important, you will find examples you can use for your own Web pages.

Web:

http://wdvl.internet.com/Quadzilla/
http://www.ology.org/tilt/cgh/

Web Authoring FAQ

Before you create your next Web page, take a few minutes to read this FAQ. It contains practical answers to common HTML questions. I guarantee that when you read the FAQ, you'll find at least a few places where you will say to yourself, "So, that's how it works."

Web:

http://www.htmlhelp.com/faq/wdgfaq.htm

Web Authoring FAQ

There are two important reasons why you should read the Web Authoring FAQ (frequently asked question list).

First, if you design your own Web pages, the questions and answers in this FAQ will save you a lot of time.

Second, if you get invited to the White House to visit the President and he takes you to a formal reception where you are introduced to the Romanian ambassador, you will have something to talk about.

Web Development Resources

If you are a Web site developer, you have the difficult task of knowing everything and keeping up on all the changes. These Web sites will help you stay in tune with your colleagues and find the resources you need to do your job. Read about usability and design principles, compatibility, quality assurance, optimization, news and conferences. Find out about XML, VRML, Java, CSS, CGI, graphics, servers, and more.

Web:

http://www.ahref.com/
http://www.articlecentral.com/default.asp
http://www.builder.com.com/
http://www.useit.com/alertbox/
http://www.wdvl.com/
http://www.webdeveloper.com/
http://www.webdevelopersjournal.com/
http://www.webreference.com/
http://www.webreview.com/

Web Page Backgrounds

One way to spice up your Web page is to use a background. These Web sites provide lots of different textures and images you can use. Be careful, however, to exercise restraint. In most cases, anything unusual will look bad and be hard to read. Remember, even if a Web page looks good on your monitor, other people may not see it the same way you do, so be conservative.

Web:

http://www.artistic-designers.com/bkgds/
http://www.cgs-designs.com/backgroundsonly/
http://www.free-backgrounds.com/
http://www.the.enchantress.net/loe2.html
http://www.windyweb.com/design/gallery/
    backgrounds.htm

Web Page Counters

Why be different when you, too, can have a counter on your Web page? (There are even cats on the Net who have access counters on their Web pages.) Here are some resources that tell you how to put a counter on your page and offer some great samples of counter digits.

Web:

http://sm6.sitemeter.com/
http://www.counterart.com/
http://www.ipstat.com/
http://www.merlet.com/counterlinks.htm
http://www.sparklit.com/counter/

Web Page Creation Talk and General Discussion

Once you start to create your own Web pages, you will realize how helpful it can be to talk to other people. This Usenet group is for discussion of topics related to creating Web pages. You can discuss HTML, design style, techniques, tips, and so on.

Usenet:

comp.infosystems.www.authoring.misc

Web Page Images: Graphics, Backgrounds and Clip Art

If you want to dress up your Web pages, there are a great many graphics, icons, pictures and backgrounds available for free. However, please do not go overboard. I look at a lot of Web pages, and I can tell you that far too many of them are overloaded with superfluous graphics. Think twice before you put lots of images on your pages, and think three times before you use any background that is more than a simple color. As you use the Web, make a note of the pages you like the best, and use them to give you ideas for your own site. After all, why shouldn't your Web site be as cool as you are?

Web:
http://www.animfactory.com/
http://www.backgroundcity.com/
http://www.barrysclipart.com/
http://www.graphicsfreebies.com/
http://www.graphxkingdom.com/
http://www.thefreesite.com/freegraphics.htm
http://www.webplaces.com/html/clipart.htm

Web Page Images: Photographs

If you are going to say something, say it with pizazz—and that's exactly what these resources will help you do. Here are photographs that you can use to create imaginative and attractive visual highlights for your Web site.

Web:
http://gallery.yahoo.com/
http://www.freefoto.com/
http://www.freeimages.co.uk/
http://www.yahooligans.com/downloader/pictures/

Have you ever taken
a sheepdog to a
classical music performance
in Cleveland, Ohio?
If not, you haven't lived.

Web Page Validation

There are a variety of browsers used on the Net and they don't all work exactly the same. When you create a Web page, it's nice to check that your HTML will work well with various browsers. These sites contain Web page validation tools that can help you ensure that the HTML you write is as portable as possible. These tools are sophisticated and provide an in-depth analysis that would be impossible to do by hand.

Web:
http://validator.w3.org/
http://watson.addy.com/
http://www.alertra.com/
http://www.netmechanic.com/
http://www.resourcehelp.com/html_validate.htm

You can validate
a parking receipt.

You can validate a legal
document.

You can even validate your
best friend's feelings.

But when you put your own
Web site on the Net, the only
thing anyone will care about
is whether or not you have
validated the HTML.

> **Sorry I can't stay and talk. I promised my mother I would take her donkey bowling.**

Web Publishing Resources

With a good Web page editor, you don't have to be technical to create a Web page. All you need to do is type the text, insert some pictures, and keep moving stuff around until you think it looks good. However, if you would like to make your pages look even better, these resources will help you take your Web skills to the next level. You'll find HTML tutorials, a glossary, information about meta tags, color charts, forms, graphics, templates, style sheets, and more.

Web:
   http://hotwired.lycos.com/webmonkey/
   http://htmlgoodies.earthweb.com/
   http://www.accessplace.com/publish.htm
   http://www.cnctek.com/wpublnks.html
   http://www.howtoweb.com/corner/resource.htm
   http://www.sitepoint.com/

Web Site Marketing

Would you like to sell ad banners and generate revenue from your Web site? These Web sites contain serious information for serious marketers, but there are tips and resources for everyone. Actually, I think these resources should be entitled, "How to Make Your Web Site as Annoying as Possible". Please, please, promise me you won't use blinking banners, popup ads and frames with ads that automatically refresh themselves every thirty seconds.

Web:
   http://www.clickz.com/
   http://www.cyber-robotics.com/
   http://www.netb2b.com/

Web Site Polls

Find out what your visitors think by putting a poll on your Web site. Polls are a great way to invite people to come back again and again. You can ask people what they think of an issue that relates to the topics covered by your Web site; or you could ask more general questions, such as what people think about the latest movies, sports teams or political happenings. One more idea: When you implement a new feature on your site, ask your visitors what they think of it.

Web:
   http://webpoll.sparklit.com/
   http://www.freepolls.com/
   http://www.globalguestpoll.com/
   http://www.go2poll.com/
   http://www.mypoll.net/

Web Site Postcards

Snazz up your Web site by letting your visitors send custom electronic postcards. It won't be long before electronic postcards from your site will be electronic collectors' items, and people from all over the electronic world will be beating an electronic path to your electronic door.

Web:
   http://www.dropcard.com/
   http://www.mypostcards.com/bas/

Web Site Programs

Much of the tricky stuff you see on Web pages requires some programming. So why not get someone else to do the work? There are lots of pre-written Web page programs available for free on the Net. You may have to learn a bit of technical stuff, but once you do, you'll be in Web page heaven with tons of wonderful doodads that allow you to customize your Web site up the wazoo: access counters, password access controls, Web site search engines, email forms, calendars, calculators, tools for buttons, fonts, menus, tickers, and much, much more.

Web:
   http://javascript.internet.com/
   http://www.freecode.com/
   http://www.javapowered.com/werks.html
   http://www.scriptsearch.com/

Web Site Search Engines

Once your Web site starts to get a lot of content, it's helpful to give your visitors a way to search for what they want. All they have to do is type in a word or two and, within seconds, they'll see links to the pages they want. Once you have a local search engine, you can integrate it into your overall design, and make your navigation aids simpler. These resources provide free Web site search engine services. Try them all and see which one you like best.

Web:

http://intra.whatuseek.com/
http://www.atomz.com/
http://www.freefind.com/
http://www.picosearch.com/
http://www.searchenginewatch.com/resources/
  software.html

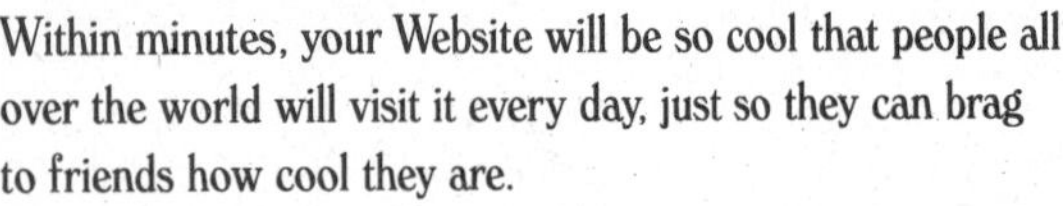

Web Site Search Engines

Connect your site to a Web site search engine facility, and – faster than you can say "epistemological empiricism" – anyone on the Net will be able to search through all the information on your site looking for anything they want.

Within minutes, your Website will be so cool that people all over the world will visit it every day, just so they can brag to friends how cool they are.

Web Style Manual

It is a good idea to learn something about design before you create your own Web page. Try reading this style manual, loaded with information on document design, navigation, site structure, Web page design, efficient use of the Web, design integrity, and much more. There is plenty of information for both beginning and advanced users.

Web:

http://www.info.med.yale.edu/caim/manual/
  contents.html

Webmasters

Running a Web site requires you to be knowledgeable about a part of the world that never stops changing. Moreover, Web site management has a way of using all your time. Still, you do need to keep up. These webmaster resources will help you stay ahead of the newest trends. They also provide the type of resources you need, especially if you are a professional webmaster. In case you are the type of person who likes to join organizations, I have also included the Web site for the International Webmasters Association.

Web:

http://www.freefever.com/
http://www.iwanet.org/
http://www.kresch.com/resources/
http://www.webmasterstation.com/

Usenet:

alt.www.webmaster

XML

XML (Extensible Markup Language) is a meta-language that allows you to define your own markup languages. (HTML, for example, is a markup language.) In general, XML has the potential to provide wonderful improvements in the way we create Web pages. However, XML is complex and not yet supported in all its rich fullness by the popular browsers. If you like to live on the leading edge of Web page design, you'll enjoy learning about XML.

Web:

http://www-106.ibm.com/developerworks/xml/
http://www.devx.com/xml/
http://www.ibiblio.org/xml/
http://www.skew.org/xml/tutorial/
http://www.ucc.ie/xml/
http://www.w3.org/XML/
http://www.xml.com/
http://www.xml.org/
http://www.xmldir.com/
http://www.xmlfiles.com/

Usenet:

comp.text.sgml
comp.text.xml

Majordomo Mailing List:

List Name: xml-dev
Subscribe to: majordomo@ic.ac.uk

WEB: SOFTWARE

ActiveX

ActiveX, designed by Microsoft, is a complex system designed to integrate programs with interactive Internet content. In particular, Web sites can use ActiveX tools to create multimedia effects, interactive objects and complex programs. With ActiveX, your browser can download programs from Web sites and then execute those programs on your computer. The programs can even interact with your own software (such as your word processor, database, spreadsheet, and so on). ActiveX's main competitor is Java, developed by Sun Microsystems.

Web:
  http://download.cnet.com/downloads/0-10081.html
  http://www.microsoft.com/com/tech/activex.asp

Ad Blocking Software

I hate commercials. I hate junk mail. I hate spam. I hate telemarketing. And I particularly hate advertisements, especially on the Web. But I'm not the only one. There are many smart people on the Net who also dislike ads, and out of antipathy comes invention. Here is software that will block ads for you as you look at Web pages. Now, throughout this book, I only put in resources that are free. However, in this case, I am making an exception, because I feel the service of blocking ads is so valuable. Some of these programs cost money (although you can try them for free, and they don't cost much anyway). Using an ad blocking program will make your Internet experience more enjoyable in two ways. First, you won't have to look at ads. Second, Web pages will load faster because you won't have to wait for ads to download (be transferred) to your computer.

Web:
  http://www.adsubtract.com/
  http://www.adwiper.com/
  http://www.guidescope.com/products/
  http://www.junkbusters.com/ht/en/ijb.html
  http://www.webwasher.com/

Browsers

A browser is an Internet client program you use to access the Web. Modern browsers can also read Usenet discussion groups, and send and receive mail. To extend the capabilities of a browser, you can use programs called "plug-ins". These Web sites have news about the browser industry, including a feast of rumors, news and tips. There are also lists of available browsers, in case you want to try a new one. (There are a lot more than you might think.)

Web:
  http://browsers.evolt.org/
  http://webtips.dan.info/brand-x/
  http://www.freewarehome.com/Internet/
    Web_Browsers_t.html
  http://www.sofotex.com/download/Browsers/
  http://www.upsdell.com/browsernews/
  http://www.w3schools.com/browsers/

Internet Explorer Browser

Microsoft's Internet Explorer (IE) is one of the two most popular browsers on the Web (the other one being AOL's Netscape). IE is more than a standalone browser. It is a complex program that is designed to be part of Windows. IE is also designed to work in an integrated manner with many other Microsoft programs, including Outlook Express (an email program and Usenet newsreader), FrontPage Express (a Web page editor), and Windows Media Player (a multimedia player). Here is what I think you should do. First, use this Web site to get the latest version of Internet Explorer (it's free), if you don't already have it. Then, from within IE, pull down the Tools menu and select "Windows Update". This will connect you to a Web site where you can see all the available programs (also free) and choose the ones you want. At the very least, get the Windows Media Player and the Web Accessories.

Web:
  http://www.microsoft.com/windows/ie/

Holy cow. Look what's in "Religion".

Java

Java is a complex system designed to support programs that can be downloaded from the Web and run automatically. For example, when you are visiting a Web site, selecting a particular link might send a program to your computer, where it will be run by your browser (which knows how to run Java programs). Why is Java important? On its own, a browser can only do so much. It can download and display data. It can also play sounds, show you pictures and images, and so on. But the capabilities of a browser are limited to what is built-in, or what is added by using plug-in or helper programs. With Java, it is possible to write a program to do just about anything, and then put that program on a Web site. When someone visits the site, the program is sent to his or her computer, where it is executed. Java is also important because it is the focus of a huge effort to build an Internet environment that can be run on various types of computers and other devices. Although Java was originally developed by Sun Microsystems, many other companies are riding along. Java's main competitor is ActiveX, developed by Microsoft.

Web:

http://www.ibiblio.org/javafaq/
http://www.java.sun.com/
http://www.javaboutique.internet.com/
http://www.javacoffeebreak.com/
http://www.javashareware.com/
http://www.lundin.info/

Usenet:

alt.www.hotjava
comp.lang.java
comp.lang.java.advocacy
comp.lang.java.announce
comp.lang.java.api
comp.lang.java.beans
comp.lang.java.corba
comp.lang.java.databases
comp.lang.java.gui
comp.lang.java.help
comp.lang.java.machine
comp.lang.java.misc
comp.lang.java.programmer
comp.lang.java.security
comp.lang.java.softwaretools
comp.lang.java.tech
comp.lang.javascript

Listserv Mailing List:

List Name: **advanced-java**
Subscribe to: **listserv@discuss.develop.com**

Listserv Mailing List:

List Name: **java**
Subscribe to: **listserv@discuss.develop.com**

Listserv Mailing List:

List Name: **java**
Subscribe to: **listserv@yorku.ca**

IRC:

#openjava (EFnet)

Javascript

Javascript is a language that allows programmers to write small programs (scripts) that can be imbedded in the HTML for a Web page. When your browser reads the HTML, it interprets the Javascript and performs whatever function the program tells it to do. Javascript can be used for all kinds of interesting and useful effects on a Web page. And you can use it even if you aren't a programmer: if you find a script you like—on somebody else's page or on an archive—you can copy it to your page. (Of course, if the script is original work, you should ask for permission.)

Web:

http://www.faqs.org/faqs/computer-lang/java/
  javascript/
http://www.javascript.com/
http://www.jfind.com/
http://www.wsabstract.com/javaindex.shtml

Usenet:

comp.lang.javascript

Majordomo Mailing List:

List Name: **javascript-developer-talk-list**
Subscribe to: **majordomo@maillist.peak.org**

IRC:

#javascript (Undernet)

"Look," said Java, "there's an apple tree. I sure could use an apple."

"Why don't you climb up and get one?" suggested ActiveX.

"Okay," said Java, "but could you please hold my wallet for me?" "No problem," said ActiveX.

So Java climbed the tree and picked an apple. After Java came back down, ActiveX returned the wallet.

"Wait a minute," said Java. "All the money is gone."

"Oh, that's a service charge," said ActiveX.

"A service charge?" said Java. "What for?"

"For making sure your wallet was safe while you were climbing the tree."

Javascript Archives

You don't have to be a programmer to use Javascript on your Web pages. Here are some Web pages with lots and lots of free scripts, yours to snarf at will.

Web:
   http://jakarta.apache.org/builds/scripts/projects/
   http://javascript.internet.com/
   http://www.javafile.com/
   http://www.javashareware.com/cfscripts/jscripts.cfm
   http://www.wsabstract.com/cutpastejava.shtml

Link Checkers

If your Web site contains a lot of links to other sites, you have a problem. How do you keep the information up to date? A link checker is a program that automates the process of testing links to see if they still work. As someone who spends a lot of time checking Web sites, I can tell you that link checkers have their place, but they are far from perfect, and they don't take the place of a smart person checking lists of links by hand.

Web:
   http://home.snafu.de/tilman/xenulink.html
   http://lithops.mastak.com/hlv/
   http://www.cyberspyder.com/cslnkts1a.html
   http://www.davecentral.com/urlcheck.html
   http://www.linkchecker.kyosoft.com/features.htm
   http://www.linklint.org/

Lynx

Lynx is a text-based Web browser that runs under a variety of operating systems including Unix, VMS, DOS, Windows and OS/2. I like Lynx because it is fast (no graphics) and easy to use. Even if you have the most powerful graphical computer around, give Lynx a try. When you are after pure information, no browser is faster.

Web:
   http://www.lynx.browser.org/

Mozilla Browser

Within the world of Unix and the Internet, there has been a long tradition of free, open software. Today, many people depend on such open products: Linux and FreeBSD (types of Unix), Perl (a scripting language), Apache (a Web server), and many more, including all the programs associated with the Free Software Foundation. On January 23, 1998, the Netscape company announced that they would become part of this tradition by distributing their browser for free and by making the source code readily available. (This was before AOL bought Netscape.) The new, open-source browser, was renamed Mozilla. Mozilla is now maintained by an international community of programmers.

Web:
   http://www.mozilla.org/

Netscape Browser

Netscape is one of the two most popular browsers on the Web (the other one being Microsoft's Internet Explorer). What we refer to as "Netscape" is actually a collection of programs called Netscape Communicator. This collection includes a browser (named Navigator), an email program (Messenger), a Web page editor (Composer), an instant messenger program (AOL Instant Messenger), and a scheduling program (Calendar). The browser can also act as a Usenet newsreader. All of these programs are available for free. Netscape, by the way, is owned by AOL.

Web:
   http://browsers.netscape.com/browsers/

Plug-Ins

A plug-in is a program designed to enhance the capabilities of a browser by processing a particular type of data that the browser cannot handle on its own. For example, if you visit a Web site that has music videos, you cannot look at the videos unless you have a plug-in that can process that type of video data. Your browser comes with various plug-ins, but there will be times when you need others. These Web sites provide information about plug-ins and how to get them. (Note: Within Internet Explorer, many of the jobs carried out by Netscape plug-ins are done by ActiveX controls. However, Internet Explorer is designed to use Netscape plug-ins.)

Web:

http://cws.internet.com/32plugins.html
http://wp.netscape.com/plugins/
http://www.plugins.com/
http://www.wdvl.com/Software/Plugins/
http://www.web3d.org/vrml/browpi.htm

Pop-up Blocking Software

Of all the Web-based ads, the most annoying are the pop-up ads. Because pop-up ads are displayed in separate windows, you have to manually close each one. Moreover, some ads are programmed so that when you close them, they spawn even more windows. The solution is to use pop-up blocking software. (I do, and I think it's great.) Note: If you already use an ad-blocking program, you may find that it blocks pop-up ads. However, if it isn't doing a good enough job, you will have to use a separate pop-up blocker.

Web:

http://www.anarelion.com/aalku/WebWindowKiller/
http://www.emsproject.com/FS
http://www.panicware.com/product_dpps.html
http://www.searchsleuth.com/
http://www.southbaypc.com/noads/

Need to get the word out?
Use the Net.

RealPlayer

RealPlayer is an audio/video program from RealNetworks that allows you to use streaming technology to listen to audio and watch video over the Net. RealPlayer also makes it possible to listen to live broadcasts, such as radio stations or special events. Your browser may already come with RealPlayer. If not, you can find the software you need here. You can also start here to look for some of the many places around the Net that use RealPlayer to broadcast.

Web:

http://www.real.com/

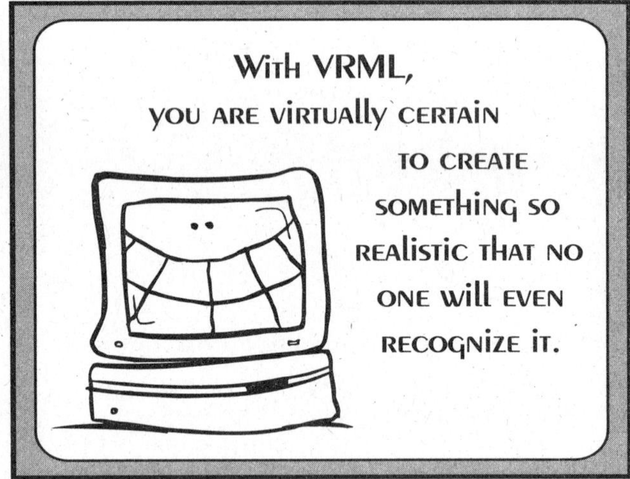

VRML

VRML (Virtual Reality Markup Language) is a system used to create three-dimensional objects. Using VRML, designers can create imaginary 3-D worlds that you can visit and explore. To do so, you need either a browser that handles VRML or a VRML plug-in for a regular browser. These resources will help you learn how to use VRML, as well as find any tools you may need.

Web:

http://www.refraction.com/vrml/
http://www.sics.se/dce/dive/
http://www.web3d.org/vrml/vrml.htm

Usenet:

comp.lang.vrml

Web Browser Talk and General Discussion

When you use the Web, your experience starts and ends with a browser. The browser you use very much colors your experience, so it is no surprise that people have strong opinions about what they like and what they dislike. In addition, the Web browser industry is fast-moving and highly competitive, with new browsers, plug-ins and related technology appearing all the time. All of this makes for a lot to talk about when it comes to browsers, and these Usenet groups are the places to be. (Take my browser, please.)

Usenet:

comp.infosystems.www.browsers.mac
comp.infosystems.www.browsers.misc
comp.infosystems.www.browsers.ms-windows
comp.infosystems.www.browsers.x

Web Log Analysis

A Web log is a file, kept on a Web server, in which information is stored about how the Web pages on that server are being accessed. To make sense of this information, you must use a Web log analysis program. You can use such a program to tell you how many people have been to your site, what pages are the most popular, what pages or images might be missing, which browsers people are using, and more.

Web:

http://www.davecentral.com/webstat.html
http://www.kresch.com/resources/Log_Analyzer/
http://www.programfiles.com/xq/asp/catid.475/qx/

Web Server Talk and General Discussion

When you connect to a Web site, your browser requests data from a program called a Web server. Web servers are complex software systems that require a fair amount of care and feeding. These are the Usenet groups in which you can discuss Web servers: what is available, how they work, tips, questions, answers, and lots and lots of opinions.

Usenet:

comp.infosystems.www.servers.mac
comp.infosystems.www.servers.misc
comp.infosystems.www.servers.ms-windows
comp.infosystems.www.servers.unix

98Lite

98Lite is a utility that will make your Windows 98 system smaller, faster and more stable. To do so, 98Lite removes most of Internet Explorer, as well as a lot of superfluous files and program. Using 98Lite can be beneficial if you have an older computer you want to speed up, or if you are a software minimalist who hates the junk that Microsoft stuffs down your computer's throat. However, 98Lite is only for people who know what they are doing (you know who you are), so be careful.

Web:

http://www.litepc.com/

Desktop Themes

A desktop theme defines the look of your Windows environment: the background you see on the desktop, the colors, the mouse pointer, and so on. Using these free resources, you can jazz up your desktop with fun, colorful themes, many of which also come with screensavers. Windows itself comes with a few extra themes, but there are a *lot* more available on the Net.

Web:

http://themes.tucows.com/
http://www.desktopdecor.net/#themes
http://www.freedesktopthemez.com/
http://www.galttech.com/desktop.shtml
http://www.passtheshareware.com/themes.htm

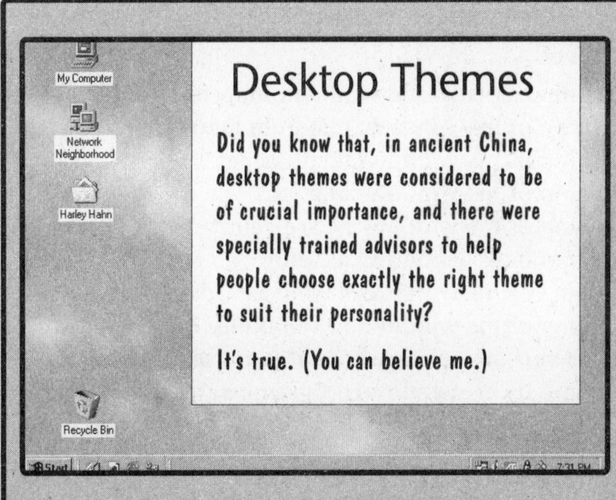

Desktop Themes

Did you know that, in ancient China, desktop themes were considered to be of crucial importance, and there were specially trained advisors to help people choose exactly the right theme to suit their personality?

It's true. (You can believe me.)

Windows 2000/NT

Windows 2000 is a family of operating systems used to run commercial computers. There are actually two main branches of the family: Windows 2000 Professional, the single-user system, and Windows 2000 Server, used to run servers. The first Windows NT systems were released in July 1993. In October 1998, Microsoft announced that all new versions of Windows NT would be named Windows 2000. Thus, Windows 2000 is the replacement for Windows NT. Windows 2000 has many of the features of NT and Windows 98. In particular, it can run the same 32-bit applications. One important advantage of Windows 2000 is it is more stable, requiring, in Microsoft's words, "fewer planned and unplanned system restarts". As we segue into the new century, and memories of NT fade like a politician's promises after the election, here are some resources to help you understand the vagaries of Windows 2000/NT and to communicate with the people who tend to the care and feeding of these systems. (And may all your restarts be happy ones.)

Web:

  http://www.bhs.com/
  http://www.entmag.com/
  http://www.jsifaq.com/
  http://www.microsoft.com/ntserver/
  http://www.microsoft.com/ntworkstation/
  http://www.microsoft.com/windows2000/
    professional/
  http://www.microsoft.com/windows2000/server/
  http://www.ntfaq.com/
  http://www.ntsecurity.net/
  http://www.ntware.com/
  http://www.win2000mag.net/

Usenet:

  comp.os.ms-windows.nt.admin.misc
  comp.os.ms-windows.nt.admin.networking
  comp.os.ms-windows.nt.advocacy
  comp.os.ms-windows.nt.misc
  comp.os.ms-windows.nt.pre-release
  comp.os.ms-windows.nt.setup
  comp.os.ms-windows.nt.setup.hardware
  comp.os.ms-windows.nt.setup.misc
  comp.os.ms-windows.nt.software.services
  comp.os.ms-windows.programmer.nt.kernel-mode

IRC:

  #win2000 (EFnet)
  #windows2000 (EFnet)

Windows Applications Talk and General Discussion

There is a lot of discussion about the various types of applications that run under the various types of Windows. You will find these groups to be invaluable when you encounter one of those mysterious Microsoft-based problems that make you wonder if Man is really Nature's last word. Look for the Usenet group that is closest to what you need to talk about. These groups are good places to send a question.

Usenet:

  comp.os.ms-windows.apps
  comp.os.ms-windows.apps.comm
  comp.os.ms-windows.apps.compatibility.win95
  comp.os.ms-windows.apps.financial
  comp.os.ms-windows.apps.misc
  comp.os.ms-windows.apps.utilities
  comp.os.ms-windows.apps.utilities.win3x
  comp.os.ms-windows.apps.utilities.win95
  comp.os.ms-windows.apps.word-proc

Windows CE

Windows CE is a Microsoft operating system used with small portable computers, such as PDAs and palmtops, as well as some video game systems. Windows CE can also be used with small specialized computers called embedded systems, which are used within larger machines, such as cars, microwave ovens and VCRs. In general, Windows CE is Microsoft's entry in the we-want-to-control-the-world sweepstakes and, as such, deserves your every attention. (By the way, the name "CE" used to stand for consumer electronics, although no one will admit it now.)

Web:

  http://windowsce.kensai.com/faq/
  http://www.cearchives.com/
  http://www.ceglobe.com/
  http://www.cewindows.net/
  http://www.hpc.net/
  http://www.pocketpcwire.com/
  http://www.windowscewebring.com/

Usenet:

  comp.os.ms-windows.ce

Windows Drivers

A driver is a complicated program that acts as an interface between an operating system (such as Windows) and a hardware device. Windows comes with many built-in drivers, but when you start adding your own hardware to the computer, you may have to start searching to find the driver you need. Even if you do have all the drivers required by your system, there will be times when you may want to update to a newer version. Sometimes, updating to newer drivers can eliminate mysterious problems.

Web:
http://www.drivershq.com/main.asp
http://www.helpdrivers.com/
http://www.winguides.com/drivers/

Windows Fine-Tuning

Once you get used to Windows, you will find that there are a number of small idiosyncrasies that annoy you. Well, they annoy everyone else, too. This site has advice and procedures you can use to make Windows do what you want (some of the time anyway). I have found lots of great hints here. Hint: Don't visit thise site unless you have a lot of time. I guarantee you will get distracted and spend half the night trying things.

Web:
http://www.annoyances.org/

Would you like to learn how to smooth out some of the rough spots in Windows? Check out the **Windows Annoyances** Web site for tips and secrets. Remember, Microsoft may deal the cards, but how you play them is up to you.

Windows Glossary

In the beginning, there was a word. And then, another word, and yet another word, and on and on. And finally, we found ourselves with a huge amount of technical terminology that only a nerd could understand. The next time you are reading about Windows and you encounter a word you don't understand, check with the Windows glossary: your permanent online nerd replacement.

Web:
http://www.intelinfo.com/
    microsoft_windows_glossary.html
http://www.jegsworks.com/lessons/win/glossary.htm
http://www.orlando.co.uk/glossary.htm

Windows Magazines

Here are some Web sites maintained by various Windows magazines. If you want to keep up on Windows news—especially developer issues—these are good places to spend some time. Personally, I find skimming through the Web sites a lot more fun than reading the print versions of the magazines.

Web:
http://www.winntmag.com/
http://www.zdnet.com/windows/

Windows Networking Talk and General Discussion

There are a variety of places to discuss Windows networking. First, there are a number of Usenet groups. It is a good idea to use the one that is most appropriate to your interests, although there is considerable overlap and cross-posting. Second, you can join the IRC channels for real-time networking talk.

Usenet:
comp.os.ms-windows.networking.misc
comp.os.ms-windows.networking.ras
comp.os.ms-windows.networking.tcp-ip
comp.os.ms-windows.networking.win95
comp.os.ms-windows.networking.windows

IRC:
#windows2000 (EFnet)
#windows98 (Undernet)
#windowsnt (DALnet, EFnet, Undernet)

Windows News

Behind the scenes, the world of Windows never stops. Microsoft is always making changes, creating new products and announcing new plans. Actually, it's all a plot. They want to lull you into a false sense of complacency, then—BLAM!—hit you with brand new "must have" software. Don't let anybody pull the operating system wool over your eyes. Keep up on the news, and people will invite you to parties just to hear you talk about the new version of Windows.

Web:
   http://www.labmice.net/w2karticles.htm
   http://www.swaine.com/windows.html
   http://www.wininformant.com/
   http://www.winplanet.com/
   http://www.winsupersite.com/

Usenet:
   comp.os.ms-windows.announce
   comp.windows.news

Windows Official Web Sites

Microsoft's official Web site offers access to official resources for Windows Me, 98, 95, NT, 2000 and XP. These are good places to look for the latest official free programs and utilities, official announcements, offical marketing info, and all the propaganda you need to throw your own Bill Gates' birthday party.

Web:
   http://www.microsoft.com/ntserver/
   http://www.microsoft.com/ntworkstation/
   http://www.microsoft.com/windows2000/
   http://www.microsoft.com/windows95/
   http://www.microsoft.com/windows98/
   http://www.microsoft.com/windowsme/
   http://www.microsoft.com/windowsxp/

Windows Pre-releases

The life cycle of a Windows operating system goes like this: (1) Wait and wait a long time for a new version. (2) Beta release: use a beta version of the new operating system for a long time. (3) Go to 1. When we are in the throes of a beta, you can participate in this Usenet discussion group to find out what everyone else is doing. This is also a good place to send questions when something strange happens and you need some help.

Usenet:
   comp.os.ms-windows.pre-release

Windows Programming

Here is a large selection of resources devoted to the topic of programming in the Windows environment. Topics cover general programming as well as more specific subjects like controls, graphics, memory management, multimedia, networking and tools.

Web:
   http://www.msdn.microsoft.com/
   http://www.windx.com/

Usenet:
   comp.os.ms-windows.programmer.controls
   comp.os.ms-windows.programmer.graphics
   comp.os.ms-windows.programmer.memory
   comp.os.ms-windows.programmer.misc
   comp.os.ms-windows.programmer.multimedia
   comp.os.ms-windows.programmer.networks
   comp.os.ms-windows.programmer.ole
   comp.os.ms-windows.programmer.tools.mfc
   comp.os.ms-windows.programmer.tools.misc
   comp.os.ms-windows.programmer.tools.owl
   comp.os.ms-windows.programmer.tools.winsock
   comp.os.ms-windows.programmer.vxd
   comp.os.ms-windows.programmer.win32
   comp.os.ms-windows.programmer.winhelp
   comp.windows.ms.programmer

Windows Pre-releases

Windows is so much fun that most people can hardly stand it. And the best part is that, each time Microsoft releases a new version, the world becomes a better place to live.

The new version of Windows is definitely worth waiting for, but if the wait is too much for you, relax. There is a Usenet discussion group where you can talk about pre-release versions of Windows right now.

Windows Questions and Answers

These mailing lists are dedicated to Window's 95/98 questions and answers. When you are completely stuck, and the possibility of useful tech support seems like a figment of Mr. Bill's overactive imagination, this mailing list is a godsend. Send in your question and you may get an answer from some kind soul somewhere on the Net. Of course, you have a responsibility, too. If you see a question you can answer, please do so and help someone else.

Listserv Mailing List:
List Name: **win95-l**
Subscribe to: **listserv@peach.ease.lsoft.com**

Listserv Mailing List:
List Name: **win98-l**
Subscribe to: **listserv@peach.ease.lsoft.com**

Windows Registry

The registry is the central location that stores all of Windows' configuration data, including data related to the Windows system, the hardware, applications and user preferences. You can do a lot of cool things, and solve some problems, if you know how to manipulate the registry. Windows 95 and 98 come with a registry editor program (**regedit.exe**). Windows 98 also has a program called Registry Checker that finds and fixes registry problems automatically (it runs each time you start Windows). However, it is crucial that you learn what you are doing before you make any changes, because it is possible to harm your system irrevocably. An easy way to manipulate the registry safely is to use the Microsoft program TweakUI, which is one of the Microsoft PowerToys. Here are some resources to help you understand the registry. In particular, you can read about TweakUI and the PowerToys. I have also included two relatively benign but useful registry tools: Regclean (from Microsoft) and EasyCleaner.

Web:
http://fileforum.betanews.com/
 detail.php3?fid=963771680
http://www.activewin.com/tips/reg/
http://www.eons.com/registry.htm
http://www.microsoft.com/technet/win98/reg.asp
http://www.winguides.com/registry/
http://www.woram.com/

Windows Resources

If you use Windows, I promise you—you will eventually need technical information. When that happens, try looking on the Net. I have chosen these Web sites as good, all-around places to help you find what you need. Aside from technical information, there are also other types of resources: discussion forums, software archives, event info, online magazines, and links to other Windows-related sites.

Web:
http://www.activewin.com/
http://www.anotherwin95.com/
http://www.labmice.net/
http://www.refdesk.com/win95.html
http://www.winpicks.com/

Windows Setup

The installation and configuration of Windows is supposed to be automatic and is supposed to work perfectly. However, once in awhile, perhaps even too seldom to mention—I don't want you to think I am a complainer—something goes wrong. Thus, we have Usenet groups just for discussion of Windows installations and other related miracles of modern life.

Usenet:
comp.os.ms-windows.setup
comp.os.ms-windows.setup.win3x
comp.os.ms-windows.setup.win95
comp.os.ms-windows.win95.setup

Windows Startup

When Windows starts, a lot of stuff happens, but figuring it out is not always straightforward. Startup instructions are contained in a number of places: (1) the config.sys, autoexec.bat, system.ini and win.ini files, (2) the Startup folder, and (3) the registry. When you have a mysterious Windows problem, or if want to tune your system, it can really help to know what is happening where. This information will help.

Web:
http://support.microsoft.com/support/kb/articles/
 q188/8/67.asp
http://support.microsoft.com/support/kb/articles/
 q273/7/38.asp
http://www2.whidbey.com/djdenham/

Windows XP

Windows XP is a member of the Windows family of operating systems. (According to Microsoft, XP stands for "experience".) With Win XP, Microsoft has merged the most important features of their consumer operating systems, Win 95/98/Me, with the security and reliability of their business operating systems, Win NT/2000. In the process, Microsoft has finally weaned their consumer operating system from the old DOS architecture. How good is Win XP? Well, in the words of Bill Gates, "Windows XP is the best operating system Microsoft has ever built." (And if you can't trust Bill Gates, who *can* you trust?)

Web:
> http://thor.prohosting.com/~1cls/windows_xp.htm
> http://windowsxp.devx.com/
> http://www.microsoft.com/windowsxp/
> http://www.windowsxpuser.com/
> http://www.zdnet.com/products/stories/reviews/
>   0,4161,2809517,00.html

WOMEN

Abortion

About 14 days after conception, a fertilized egg (zygote) attaches itself to the wall of the uterus. At this point, the developing baby is called an embryo. After 8 weeks, it is called a fetus. Somewhere between 20 to 28 weeks, the fetus becomes viable— that is, mature enough that it might survive on its own outside the uterus. An abortion occurs when a pregnancy is terminated after the zygote attaches to the uterus, but before the fetus is viable. If an abortion occurs naturally, it is called a miscarriage. If an abortion is induced for a good reason, it is called a therapeutic abortion. One of the volatile questions of our age is when, if ever, should it be allowable to induce an abortion? The arguments are important because they go to the heart of what it means to be human and to be alive. In many countries, therapeutic abortion is a significant political and religious issue. Clearly, this is a problem that the human race is going to have to sort out over a period of years.

Web:
> http://www.religioustolerance.org/abortion.htm

Usenet:
> alt.abortion
> alt.abortion.inequity
> talk.abortion

Disgruntled Housewife

It's easy to understand why a full-time housewife might feel less than fulfilled (unless she is married to a writer, in which case "disgruntled housewife" is an oxymoron). I love this site and you will too. The writing is excellent, the content is fascinating, and the wit is sharp. Disgruntled Housewife is one woman's "guide to modern living and intersex relationships". But to say Disgruntled Housewife is merely a guide is like saying Martha Stewart is merely a housewife. The talent, the effort and the hubris are both inspiring and engaging. Martha may embrace the art and science of homemaking, but only Disgruntled Housewife is courageous enough to take on the rest of the world.

Web:
> http://www.disgruntledhousewife.com/

Feminism

Modern feminism as a social movement began to grow from the civil rights and peace movements in 1967-1968. The basic idea is that men and women should be treated as economic, social and political equals. Today, radical feminists still support the movement with awe and pride, while other, more fashionably conservative women talk about feminism between clenched teeth and tight lips. In the middle is the large group of women and men who contemplate feminism and gender from a thoughtful, neutral point of view. Whatever your personal beliefs, you are welcome to join the mailing list. Remember, though, it is not a battleground to prove whether feminism is inherently good or evil. It is a place for thoughtful folks to share information on women, politics and economics.

Web:
> http://www.faqs.org/faqs/feminism/
> http://www.feminist.com/
> http://www.feminist.org/
> http://www.ifeminists.com/
> http://www.io.com/~wwwave/

Listserv Mailing List:
> List Name: femisa
> Subscribe to: listserv@csf.colorado.edu

Feminism Talk and General Discussion

If it weren't for feminists, men wouldn't have anything to grumble about except the President's Address to the Nation interrupting the football game. It's been proven through history that women are good at organizing themselves and getting things done, and they've shown it once again in Usenet. Join one or all of these groups and discuss feminism in all its forms.

Usenet:
  alt.feminism
  alt.feminism.individualism
  soc.feminism

Gender and Computing

For the longest time, computers have been "a guy thing". Why is that? Read articles put up by Computer Professionals for Social Responsibility that cover topics such as women in computer science, feminism, and cross-gender communication.

Web:
  http://www.cpsr.org/program/gender/

Gender and Sexuality

There's no escaping it. Gender and sexuality issues run rampant among the population, spurring arguments, thought-provoking discussion and philosophical meanderings. Read articles and papers about gender and sexuality, and explore other feminist resources available at this site.

Web:
  http://www.eserver.org/gender/

Gynecological Exams

Gynecology is the branch of medicine that deals with the female reproductive system and its interaction with the rest of the body. Having a regular gynecological examination is important for your long-term health. Moreover, you should have a gynecologist who knows you, so if a problem arises, you will have someone to see. However, if you've never been to a gynecologist before, you may be anxious. These Web sites contain information to help you. Read an overview of an exam, so you will know what to expect and how to prepare. There are also hints on how to find a doctor, as well as a glossary and a reading list.

Web:
  http://www.mckinley.uiuc.edu/health-info/
    womenhlt/gyneexam.html
  http://www.obgyn.net/women/women.asp
  http://www.shs.unc.edu/library/articles/gynexam.html

History of Women's Suffrage

Looking back at history, it is obvious that the more women are involved in government, the better everything works. But it took the world a long time to figure that out. In 1848, a group of American women adopted a resolution, referred to today as the Seneca Falls Declaration, in which they declared their support for political equality and called for universal suffrage (the right for both men and women to vote). But it was not until 1920 that the United States passed into law the 19th Amendment to the constitution: "The right of citizens of the United States to vote shall not be denied or abridged by the United States or by any State on account of sex." The history of the suffrage movement is characterized by bravery, persistence and foresight. It is important for all of us to learn about the suffragettes and their accomplishments. When we reflect that, today, there are still many countries where women are denied basic political rights, it is clear that the work of the original suffragettes is still unfinished.

Web:
  http://lcweb2.loc.gov/ammem/naw/nawstime.html
  http://www.dpsinfo.com/women/history/
    timeline.html
  http://www.pbs.org/onewoman/suffrage.html
  http://www.rochester.edu/sba/history.html
  http://www.spartacus.schoolnet.co.uk/resource.htm

Midwifery

You just never know when it's going to happen. You'll be stuck in an elevator or on the subway with a pregnant woman in labor. What will you do then? Plan ahead and get some information on midwifery so you will always be prepared. Articles, information on organizations, and links to other resources are a few of the things that are available.

Web:
   http://www.gentlebirth.org/archives/
   http://www.midwifeinfo.com/
   http://www.motherstuff.com/html/2midwifery.html

Usenet:
   sci.med.midwifery

Majordomo Mailing List:
   List Name: midwife
   Subscribe to: majordomo@fensende.com

National Organization for Women

The National Organization for Women (NOW) is a U.S. political organization dedicated to women's rights and feminist philosophy. NOW was established on June 30, 1966, and since that time has evolved and reinvented itself more than once. The NOW Web site has information regarding violence against women, lesbian rights, women-friendly workplaces, affirmative action, abortion, global feminism, economic equality, and so on.

Web:
   http://www.now.org/

Notable Women

History tends to be written by the people in charge, and for most of history, the people in charge have been men. There have been a great many important and accomplished women, but it can often be difficult to track down information about them. These resources will help you learn about many of the most notable women who ever lived.

Web:
   http://www.distinguishedwomen.com/
   http://www.greatwomen.org/

Rape and Sexual Assault

Rape refers to having sexual intercourse by force, intimidation, or without legal consent. The term "sexual assault" encompasses rape as well as other sexual crimes, including abuse. Rape and sexual assault have been a major problem in every society in history. If you have been raped, or you want to learn how to prevent such assaults, you will find resources here to help you. In particular, you can find a place to call if you need immediate help. If you like to argue politics, please remember that rape is a volatile subject, and you are going to encounter a lot of exaggerated and inaccurate information of all types.

Web:
   http://mova.missouri.org/sapg.htm
   http://www.amie.org/abuse/
   http://www.escapinghades.com/
   http://www.feminist.org/911/resources.html
   http://www.rainn.org/
   http://www.rapevictimadvocates.org/

Usenet:
   talk.rape

Listserv Mailing List:
   List Name: stoprape
   Subscribe to: listserv@listserv.brown.edu

Notable Women

Look at this list:

Susan B. Anthony
Colette
Marie Curie
Amelia Earhart
Emma Goldman
Georgia O'Keeffe
Madonna
Eleanor Roosevelt
Margaret Thatcher

Who's missing?

Why, you, of course. Better check with the
Notable Women
Web sites to see if they've got your name yet.

Your mantra is "vegetable fried rice". Say it over and over, and you will become enlightened.

Voices of Women

This is a marvelous archive of stories and articles by women. There are many different topics, so no matter what you feel like at the moment, I bet you'll find something you want to read.

Web:
  http://www.voiceofwomen.com/

Women in Congress

Women have been running homes for years, so they might as well run the House, too. Learn about the women in Congress by reading their online biographies.

Web:
  http://www.mith2.umd.edu/WomensStudies/
  GovernmentPolitics/WomeninCongress/

Women's Online Communities

Here are hip, comfortable places for you to hang out on the Net. You can chat with other people or read—and there is a lot to read. There are articles about many different topics, all of interest to the inquiring female mind. Once you get started at these sites, you might have trouble getting your work done. There are too many informative, fun, bite-sized things to enjoy.

Web:
  http://www.herplanet.com/
  http://www.neosoft.com/~acoustic/www.html
  http://www.thenetworkforwomen.com/
  http://www.totalwoman.com/
  http://www.womenfolk.com/
  http://www.wowwomen.com/

Women's Resources

There are an enormous number of resources on the Net related to women and women's issues: discussion forums, women's organizations, health, family, poetry and writing, feminism, spirituality and education.

Web:
  http://www.cyberwomanspace.com/
  http://www.feminist.com/resources/links/
  http://www.library.wisc.edu/libraries/
  WomensStudies/others.htm
  http://www.mrssurvival.com/
  http://www.sheknows.com/
  http://www.siliconsalley.com/
  http://www.women.com/
  http://www.wwwomen.com/

Women's Studies

Women's Studies is a general term, referring to the organized study of culture and history from a woman's perspective. There are a great many academic Women's Studies programs, and they vary enormously. If you are interested in this area for research or study, you'll find a large variety of resources on the Net.

Web:
  http://libraries.mit.edu/humanities/WomensStudies/
  wscd.html
  http://umbc7.umbc.edu/~korenman/wmst/links.html
  http://www.mith2.umd.edu/WomensStudies/
  http://www2.h-net.msu.edu/~women/

Women's Talk and General Discussion

Women: there is a place for you to go to talk with other women about anything you want. The mailing list offers a nice women's space to discuss your personal observations, interests, news, upcoming events and anything else that is relevant to your daily life. If you don't mind anyone jumping into the conversation, try the Usenet group.

Web:
  http://www-unix.umbc.edu/~korenman/wmst/
  forums.html

Usenet:
  soc.women

Listserv Mailing List:
  List Name: women-l
  Subscribe to: listserv@listserv.aol.com

WORLD CULTURES: CITIES

Amsterdam

Amsterdam (area population 2,100,000) is the capital of the Netherlands as well as its largest city. It is situated on the Ij and Amstel rivers and is an important port, connected by canals to both the North Sea and the Rhine River. Amsterdam is one of the great cities of Europe, dating from the 14th century, with a long history of culture and commerce. It is the location of one of the most important stock exchanges in the world, and for many years has been a center of the diamond-cutting industry. The architecture of the city is striking. Because of the soft ground, the city is built on wooden piles, and there is an extensive canal system with many old beautiful buildings along the waterways and numerous bridges. When I was in Amsterdam, I found great pleasure in just walking around. (Of course, I am a simple fellow.) Amsterdam is a popular tourist destination with many attractions, including the Rijks Museum (where you can see Rembrandts), the municipal museum (where you can see Van Goghs), legalized prostitution and soft drugs.

Web:
  http://www.amsterdam.nl/e_index.html
  http://www.amsterdamhotspots.nl/
  http://www.channels.nl/
  http://www2.holland.com/amsterdam/gb/

Usenet:
  alt.cities.amsterdam

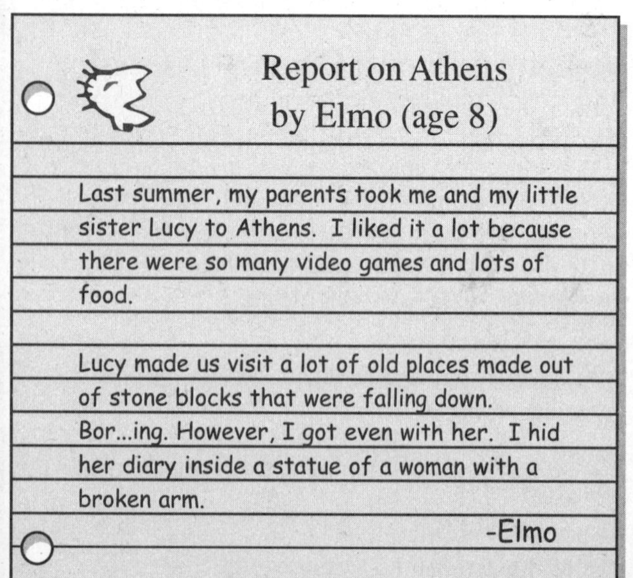

Athens

Athens (area population 3,500,000) is the capital of Greece. The name of the city comes from Athena, the ancient Greek goddess of wisdom and knowledge. Athens is more than the largest, busiest, most important city in modern Greece. It is also the cultural center of the ancient Greek world, the home of Plato and Socrates. Be sure to visit the Acropolis (where you'll find the Parthenon). It is on a hilltop that affords a spectacular view of much of the city. 1n 1896, Athens was the site of the first modern Olympic Games, and in 2004, the city will once again be host to the Summer Games. Athens has a lot to see and a lot to do, but I have to admit, my favorite memories are related to the food. Greek food smells and looks extremely inviting, and has the interesting quality that, no matter how much they put on your plate, you'll think you want more.

Web:
  http://www.athens-culture.ids.gr/english/
  http://www.athens-today.gr/
  http://www.athensguide.com/
  http://www.culture.gr/maps/sterea/attiki/
    athens.html

IRC:
  #athens (Undernet)

Beijing

Beijing (area population 9,200,000) is the capital of the People's Republic of China. Its history is a long one: in 1057 B.C., the city was made the capital of the region by King Wu. (The name "Beijing" dates from 1421 A.D.) Beijing is located in the northeastern part of China, and contains some of the most famous places in the country: the Forbidden City (the old Imperial city), Tiananmen Square, the Temple of Heaven, and the Summer Palace. Beijing is also close to the Great Wall. The city is very large, about 10,400 square miles (16,800 sq km), and consists of 18 districts and counties. (The only larger Chinese city is Shanghai.) Beijing is more than the seat of the federal government. The city is a major industrial area, as well as the financial, educational, and transportation center of the country.

Web:
  http://www.chinavista.com/travel/virtualtours.html
  http://www.travelchinaguide.com/cityguides/
    beijing.htm
  http://www.worldexecutive.com/cityguides/beijing/

Cairo

Cairo (area population 15,100,000) is the largest city in Egypt, as well as its capital. Cairo is located in the northeastern part of Egypt, near the head of the Nile River delta, close to many of the pyramids and to the Sphinx. Cairo was first settled as a military camp about 642 A.D., and as a city in 968. Cairo was conquered in 1517 by the Ottoman Empire, in 1798 by Napoleon, and in 1801 by Great Britain. In 1922, the British declared Egypt to be independent, while retaining control of much of the government as well as the Suez Canal. At about the same time, a king was appointed to rule the country. It was not until the Revolution of 1952, that the British and the king were overthrown, making Cairo an independent Egyptian city. Modern Cairo is one of the most important financial and commercial centers in the Middle East. As a city, Cairo is a *very* intense place: it is noisy, polluted, chaotic and teeming with people. This may or may not appeal to you.

Web:

  http://www.cairotourist.com/
  http://www.lonelyplanet.com/destinations/africa/
    cairo/
  http://www.worldexecutive.com/cityguides/cairo/

Jerusalem

"Ten measures of beauty were bestowed upon the world; nine were taken by Jerusalem, and one by the rest of the world." Jerusalem (area population 658,000), the most well-known city in Israel, is truly a world city. A spiritual center for Judaism, Christianity and Islam, Jerusalem is a city with connections to people all over the world.

Web:

  http://www.jerusalem.muni.il/jer_main/
    f1_main.asp?lng=2
  http://www.md.huji.ac.il/vjt/
  http://www.virtualjerusalem.com/

Las Vegas

Las Vegas (area population 1,750,000) is a city that shouldn't really be there. The city is in the Nevada desert, more or less in the middle of nowhere. However, Las Vegas is the mecca of the gambling world and, as such, has, over the years, developed a very sophisticated tourist industry based on gambling, entertainment, gambling, shopping, gambling, family activities, gambling, glamor and gambling.

Web:

  http://www.goingtovegas.com/
  http://www.lasvegas.com/
  http://www.lasvegastourism.com/
  http://www.vegas.com/

Usenet:

  alt.vacation.las-vegas

London

London (area population 11,850,000), the capital of Great Britain, is located on both sides of the Thames River in southeastern England. It is one of the world's greatest ports, and is also a world center for finance, industry and culture. London is the home of some of the most famous landmarks in the world, including Westminster Abbey, Hyde Park, Buckingham Palace, Big Ben, the Tower of London, and the University of London. London is also the home of one of my favorite foods, mushy peas. When I visited the city, I had a good time walking around, going to the theater, and riding on the Tube (subway). I especially appreciated that all the people took the trouble to learn how to speak English, although, as you may notice, they do have a strange accent.

Web:

  http://www.a-london-guide.co.uk/
  http://www.explore-london.co.uk/
  http://www.londonnet.co.uk/

Usenet:

  alt.cities.london

New York

New York (area population 21,400,000) is the largest city in the United States. It is located at the mouth of the Hudson River on the Atlantic coast of southern New York state. New York was founded by the Dutch in 1624, who named it New Amsterdam. During the Second Dutch War (1664-67), the British took the city from the Dutch and renamed it in honor of the Duke of York. New York consists of five well-known boroughs: Manhattan (an island, known as "the City"), the Bronx, Brooklyn, Queens, and Staten Island (Richmond). New York is the financial and cultural center of the U.S., the home of Wall Street, the Statue of Liberty, the Empire State Building, as well as many museums, galleries, stores, restaurants, theaters and ethnic neighborhoods. When I am in New York, I like to ride the subway, eat pizza and visit Central Park. All I can say is, I love New York in June, how about you?

Web:
  http://home.nyc.gov/
  http://www.newyork.com/
  http://www.ny.com/

Usenet:
  alt.cities.new-york

Paris

Ah, romance. There is nothing more romantic than being with your very special person, relaxing after a romantic candlelight dinner in front of a warm fireplace, snuggled quietly together taking a multimedia tour of Paris on your computer. If you get a chance, you may even enjoy visiting the city in person. Paris (area population 9,800,000) is the capital and largest city in France. The city is located on the Seine River in north-central France. While you are there, you can visit the Louvre (a wonderful museum), the Eiffel Tower, the Latin Quarter, the Sorbonne (a university) and Notre Dame Cathedral. When I visited Paris, my favorite things were the garden at the Palace of Versailles, a tour of the Paris sewer system, and lots of wonderful French food.

Web:
  http://www.paris.org/
  http://www.parisfranceguide.com/
  http://www.smartweb.fr/

Usenet:
  alt.cities.paris

IRC:
  #paris (DALnet, EFnet, Undernet)

Rio de Janeiro

Rio de Janeiro (area population 12,250,000) is the second largest city in Brazil. (The largest is São Paulo.) Rio, as it is commonly called, is in the southeast of the country, on Guanabara Bay. The city is the principal port of Brazil, the home to one of the world's most famous beaches, the Copacabana. Rio was founded in 1555, by the French Huguenots (Protestants who fled the oppression of Louis XIV). In the 1560s, the city was captured by Portugal. In 1763, it became the capital of Brazil, but it was replaced in 1960 by the newly created city of Brasilia. Rio is also the cultural center of the country, home of the famous pre-Lent Carnival. People who live in Rio are called Carioca.

Web:
  http://www.certameguide.com/rjing/aboutrj/
    index.html
  http://www.destinationrio.com/
  http://www.ipanema.com/
  http://www.worldexecutive.com/cityguides/
    rio_de_janeiro/

Rome

Rome (area population 3,300,000) is located on the Tiber River in west-central Italy, and was founded about 700 B.C. By the 2nd century B.C., Rome controlled most of central and southern Italy. Over the years, its influence expanded until it became the headquarters of a large empire encompassing most of the Western world. By the end of the 5th century A.D., the Roman Empire had collapsed. In 800 A.D., Rome became the center of the long-lasting Holy Roman Empire. Modern Rome is the capital of Italy and the largest city in the country. The Vatican City, an independent state serving as the world center of Roman Catholicism and the home of the Pope, is contained within the boundaries of Rome. It must be a nice place. Every time I talk to the Pope, he asks me when I am coming to visit.

Web:
  http://www.gotoroma.com/
  http://www.loc.gov/exhibits/vatican/toc.html
  http://www.lonelyplanet.com/destinations/europe/
    rome/
  http://www.members.aol.com/donnclass/
    Romelife.html
  http://www.stuardtclarkesrome.com/

Usenet:
  alt.cities.rome

San Francisco

San Francisco (area population 7,250,000) is one of the cultural centers of the United States. The city is located on the west coast of California, where the Pacific Ocean meets the mouth of San Francisco Bay (a strait called the Golden Gate). San Francisco was first settled in the 18th century, but its growth dates from 1848, when California joined the United States, gold was discovered, and San Francisco received a large influx of prospectors and adventurers. In 1906, the city was devastated by a severe earthquake followed by a large fire. San Francisco is one of the most popular tourist centers in the U.S., offering a wide variety of attractions and cultural diversity. I love visiting San Francisco, and here are some of my favorite things to do: (1) Take the streetcar all the way to the ocean, walk on the beach, and then visit the zoo. (2) Take the BART (subway) to Berkeley (where I used to live), and walk around the university, browse the used books stores on Telegraph Avenue, then enjoy dinner at Fondue Fred's. (3) Visit the Exploratorium, an enormous hands-on science museum. (4) Go roller skating in Golden Gate Park. (5) Have dinner at the Stinking Rose (a garlic restaurant) in North Beach, and then visit the City Lights bookstore.

Web:
  http://www.ci.sf.ca.us/
  http://www.metroactive.com/
  http://www.sanfrancisco.com/
  http://www.sfchamber.com/

IRC:
  #sanfrancisco (EFnet)

Tokyo

Tokyo (area population 34,900,000) is situated on the island of Honshu at the head of Tokyo Bay, an inlet of the Pacific Ocean. Tokyo was founded in the 12th century, at which time it had the name Edo. In 1868, Tokyo became the capital of the Japanese Empire. Modern Tokyo is the capital and cultural center of Japan. The city is relatively new, having been almost completely destroyed by a combination of a large 1923 earthquake and fire, and World War II bombing raids. Tokyo is a major manufacturing and transportation center, has more than 100 colleges and universities, and is one of the economic centers of the world. The city has many well-known landmarks including the Meiji and Hie shrines, ancient temples, the Korakuen landscape garden, and the large Ginza shopping and entertainment area. If you look carefully, you will also find some of my books translated into Japanese.

Web:
  http://www.boulevards.com/tokyo/
  http://www.ima-chan.co.jp/guide/
  http://www.metropolis.co.jp/
  http://www.pandemic.com/tokyo/

Vienna

Vienna (area population 1,875,000), the capital of Austria, is located on the south bank of the Danube River in northeastern Austria. Vienna was originally a Celtic settlement. From 1278 to 1918, the city served as the center of the Austrian Empire under the Hapsburgs. In the 18th century, Vienna was an important cultural center under the reign of Maria Theresa, being the home of Haydn, Mozart, Beethoven and Schubert. In later years, Vienna was also the home of Freud, Brahms and Mahler. When I was in Vienna, I had a wonderful time. Although German is the native language, English is understood widely. Vienna is the best place in the world to (1) spend time in a coffeehouse, (2) go to the opera, and (3) wait in line. One of the things I liked best was that, when I looked in the phone book, I saw a large number of Hahns. This may or may not be important to you.

Web:
  http://www.lonelyplanet.com/destinations/europe/
    vienna/
  http://www.vienna.at/pubs/redaktion/new-english/
  http://www.virtualvienna.net/

Washington, D.C.

Washington, D.C. is the capital of the United States. The actual city itself lies within a special area called the District of Columbia. The metropolitan Washington area (population 7,850,000) also encompasses parts of northeast Virginia and southwest Maryland. In many ways, Washington is a city of superlatives. It contains more political power than any city in the world, it has the world's largest library (the Library of Congress), the largest museum complex in the world (the Smithsonian Institutions: 16 museums and galleries, and the National Zoo), the world's largest concentration of think tanks, and on and on. For a tourist, Washington is a never-ending buffet of things to do, monuments to see, and places to walk. I once had the experience of visiting the city in the middle of winter during one of the most extreme snowstorms in its history. Because of the weather, the official city was shut down, and I had a wonderful time wandering the cold, snowy streets.

Web:
  http://www.dcchamber.org/ ·
  http://www.dcpages.com/
  http://www.washington.org/
  http://www.washingtondc.worldweb.com/

Usenet:
  alt.cities.washington

WORLD CULTURES: COUNTRIES AND REGIONS

Africa

Africa is a large continent with many different cultures. Here are some resources to help you explore the art, societies, languages, literature, music and customs of Africa. To start, here is a proverb from Nigeria: "Until lions have their own historians, tales of the hunt shall always glorify the hunter."

Web:
  http://www.africaguide.com/
  http://www.africaonline.com/
  http://www.afrika.no/
  http://www.geographia.com/indx06.htm
  http://www.newafrica.com/culture/

Usenet:
  soc.culture.african

Listserv Mailing List:
  List Name: **h-afrlitcine**
  Subscribe to: **listserv@h-net.msu.edu**

Antarctica and the Arctic

The Arctic is the northernmost part of the Earth, centered around the North Pole. The Antarctic is the southernmost part of the Earth, centered around the South Pole. What these two regions have in common are their extreme, very cold, virtually uninhabitable climates. The Arctic, however, is one large, frozen sea (the Arctic Ocean), while the Antarctic contains a large continent, Antarctica. In 1959, 12 countries signed the Antarctic Treaty, stating that Antarctica would not be controlled by any one country, and the continent would only be used for science and exploration, not for military activities. In 1985, 35 countries signed another treaty, agreeing that there would be no human access to the land outside of designated research zones. In 1991, exploration for oil or minerals was banned for 50 years.

Web:
  http://arcticcircle.uconn.edu/
  http://www.70south.com/home
  http://www.arctic.at/
  http://www.arcticwebsite.com/
  http://www.cmdl.noaa.gov/obop/spo/
  http://www.theice.org/

Asia

Asia has many cultures and peoples, each with its own history, traditions and customs. There are 240 different languages that are spoken by at least one million people each. Perhaps even more incredible, there are 12 languages that are spoken by more than 100 million people. (Here is the list, in order, starting from the top: Mandarin, Hindi, Spanish, English, Bengali, Arabic, Russian, Portuguese, Japanese, German, French, Malay-Indonesian.) Clearly, Asia is one of the best continents in the entire world.

Web:
  http://newton.uor.edu/departments&programs/
    asianstudiesdept/
  http://www.asiaondemand.com/
  http://www.interknowledge.com/indx04.htm
  http://www.southasia.net/

Usenet:
  soc.culture.asian

IRC:
  #asian (DALnet, EFnet, Undernet)
  #asianchat (DALNet)
  #asianpop (EFnet)

Australia

Australia is the smallest continent on Planet Earth, conveniently located southeast of Asia, between the Pacific and Indian Oceans. The Commonwealth of Australia includes a few external territories: the island of Tasmania, Christmas Island (the location of Santa's summer cottage), the Cocos Islands, the Coral Sea Islands, Norfolk Island, Heard and McDonald Islands, and a portion of the Antarctic Territory. The original inhabitants are thought to be Southeast Asian seafaring colonists. In 1770, the English Captain James Cook sailed into Botany Bay and claimed the eastern coast of Australia for Great Britain. The first British settlement was a penal colony. Australian geography is generally flat and arid and is the exclusive home of the platypus, koala, kangaroo, and wine of questionable parentage.

Web:
  http://www.api-network.com/vl/
  http://www.australianaustralia.com/
  http://www.bubl.ac.uk/link/a/australianculture.htm
  http://www.csu.edu.au/australia/culture.html

Usenet:
  alt.fan.countries.australia
  soc.culture.australia
  soc.culture.australian

IRC:
  #australia (Undernet)

Brazil

In the year 1500, the Brazilian territory was claimed for Portugal by Pedro Alvares Cabral and was officially part of Portugal until 1822, when the Brazilians declared their independence. The Federative Republic of Brazil is the largest country in South America, occupying half the continent and having the fifth highest population in the world. Brazil has abundant natural resources: fertile land (on which is grown coffee, cocoa, bananas, corn, citrus, sugar cane, soybeans, cotton and tobacco), and vast deposits of metals, minerals and gems (iron, manganese, chromium, uranium, platinum, quartz, coal and industrial diamonds). Brazil contains the Amazon basin, which is the home of the world's largest rainforests.

Web:
  http://www.maria-brazil.org/
  http://www.vivabrazil.com/

Usenet:
  soc.culture.brazil

IRC:
  #brasil (Undernet)

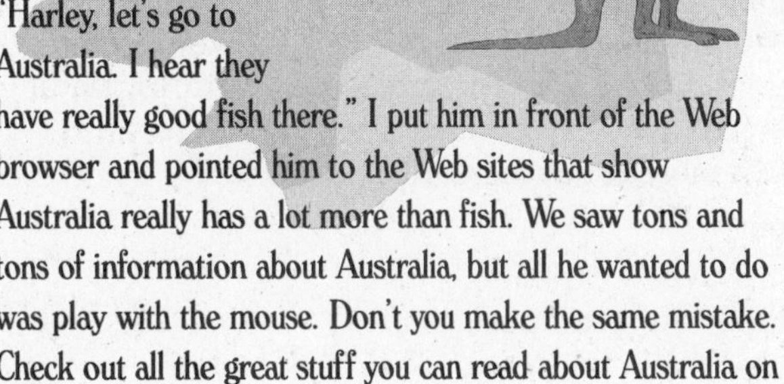

Cajun Culture

In 1755, the British and the French were gearing up for a war in the New World and, as a preliminary courtesy, the British authorities in Acadia (at the far east of Canada) kindly asked the French colonists to either renounce their religion (Catholicism) and swear allegiance to England, or could they please remove themselves to another part of the planet. What followed was a massive, haphazard migration that ended with a large number of French Acadians settling in the southern part of Louisiana, where they established small farms. (The word "Cajun" comes from the original French pronunciation of "Acadia".) Today, there is still a well-established Cajun culture—spreading through 22 of Louisiana's 64 parishes (counties)—and centered around the city of Lafayette. Cajun food has a large variety of specialties such as jambalaya, gumbo, turtle sauce piquante and crawfish bisque. What I like best is that Cajun is the only culture in which one of the traditional musical instruments is the triangle (the other instruments being the fiddle and the accordion). As you can see, when it comes to food or music, Cajun culture has something for everyone.

Web:
  http://www.cajunculture.com/
  http://www.suite101.com/welcome.cfm/
    cajun_culture

Usenet:
  alt.culture.cajun

Caribbean

After many months of working on a book, there's nothing like going to the Caribbean with a beautiful woman and spending your days snorkeling or lying around on the beach. If that's what you like to do on your vacation, check out some of the Caribbean resources on the Net. You will find travel and tourist guides, links to other Internet sites, pictures, reading material, news, current weather conditions, and much more about the Caribbean.

Web:
http://www.caribinfo.com/
http://www.caribseek.com/
http://www.hwcn.org/~aa462/carib.html

Central America

Central America is the part of North America that separates the Pacific Ocean from the Caribbean Sea and stretches from Mexico to Colombia. The countries of Central America are Belize, Guatemala, Honduras, El Salvador, Nicaragua, Costa Rica and Panama. The area is culturally rich, and parts of it are exquisitely beautiful. Central American climate varies from tropical to cool. Its chief exports are bananas, coffee, and T-shirts that say, "My parents went to Central America and all I got was a lousy banana and a package of coffee."

Web:
http://www.centramerica.com/
http://www.travel-guide.com/navigate/region/
    cam.asp

Usenet:
soc.culture.el-salvador

Listserv Mailing List:
List Name: centam-l
Subscribe to: listserv@listserv.acsu.buffalo.edu

CIA INFO FOR YOU

The American Central Intelligence Agency is so secret that its budget is not even made public. (I don't even know if they have enough money to buy copies of my Internet books.) What I do know is that the CIA spends a lot of time and effort keeping track of all the countries of the world. And you can get it all (the non-secret stuff anyway) for free. This resource is invaluable for anyone who is planning to create his own military alliance.

Chile

When you look at a map of the west coast of South America, the most striking thing you see is the shape of the country of Chile. Although Chile is about 2,600 miles (4,180 km) long, it has an average width of only 110 miles (177 km), making it the narrowest large country in the world. (In fact, the coastline is longer than the width of the United States.) Because it is surrounded by virtually impassable barriers, Chile was unknown to the outside world until the middle of the 15th century, when it was occupied by the Incas. In 1541, Chile was colonized by Spain, from which it declared its independence in 1818. The country of Chile includes Easter Island, the island with the large statues, even though it is 2,300 miles (3,700 km) from the mainland.

Web:
http://www.interknowledge.com/chile/
http://www.lonelyplanet.com/destinations/
    south_america/chile_and_easter_island/
http://www.thebestintheworld.com/chile.asp

Usenet:
soc.culture.chile

Listserv Mailing List:
List Name: chile
Subscribe to: listserv@listserv.uh.edu

Majordomo Mailing List:
List Name: chile-l
Subscribe to: majordomo@freeteam.xs4all.nl

IRC:
#chilevirtual (Undernet)

> You are right. (If anyone doesn't believe you, show them this page.)

China

The People's Republic of China, located in central and eastern Asia, is the most highly populated country in the world. Geographically, China is the third-largest country (after Russia and Canada) and is one of the world's leading producers of minerals, as well as having huge reserves of coal and oil. China is the home of very old civilizations. The first documented Chinese civilization was the Shang dynasty, which lasted from 1523 B.C. to 1027 B.C. Outside of China, people know the country as being famous for its philosophers (such as Confucius and Lao-Tze), the Great Wall (a 25-foot high, 1,500-mile long barrier, completed in the 3rd century B.C. in an attempt to keep out invaders), and its culinary contributions to American cuisine.

Web:
  http://sun.sino.uni-heidelberg.de/igcs/
  http://www.chinapage.org/
  http://www.chinatoday.com/
  http://www.chinavista.com/travel/virtualtours.html

Usenet:
  alt.culture.china
  soc.culture.china

IRC:
  #china (DALnet, Undernet)

CIA World Factbook

The CIA World Factbook makes for wonderful reading: it contains detailed information about every country and territory in the world.For each country you will find data about geography, people, government, the economy, transportation, communication and defense. This is a fantastic resource with which you should become familiar; you never know what you will find. For example, I found out that 97 percent of Canadians over 15 years old can read and write. (The others, presumably, depend on a graphical user interface.)

Web:
  http://www.odci.gov/cia/publications/factbook/

Country Studies Area Handbooks

This resource consists of a series of books prepared by a division of the U.S. Library of Congress and sponsored by the Department of the Army. These books are fabulous resources, each one describing a separate country. You will find information about the people of that country, its government, social institutions and history. Whenever I want to learn about a particular country, this is where I go first.

Web:
  http://lcweb2.loc.gov/frd/cs/cshome.html

Czech Republic

The Czech Republic has some of the most beautiful scenery and interesting culture in Eastern Europe. Take some time to browse this Internet site, and you will find a great many resources to guide you through the Czech Republic. Here is my hint for staying out of trouble: just memorize this phrase— *To je moc drah*—and use it as much as possible.

Web:
  http://www.cia.gov/cia/publications/factbook/geos/
    ez.html
  http://www.czech.cz/
  http://www.locallingo.com/

Usenet:
  soc.culture.czecho-slovak

Egypt

Take a guided tour of Egypt without ever having to leave your seat. See pictures and learn a little of the history and culture of the land of the great pyramids. You can even download pictures of some of those great pyramids, the Temple of Osiris and the Nile, and then send them to your friends on the Net, saying, "Having a great time. Wish you were here."

Web:

http://www.egyptsearch.com/
http://www.sis.gov.eg/
http://www.touregypt.net/
http://www.wildegypt.com/

Usenet:

alt.culture.egyptian
soc.culture.egyptian

IRC:

#egypte (Undernet)

France

France is a country in Western Europe and is more agricultural than most people realize. Roughly 30 percent of the land is used for livestock, while another 30 percent is used for crops such as wheat, corn, barley, sugar beets and potatoes. France is also a well-known producer of wine, second only to Italy. Throughout its history, France has been embroiled in many wars and conflicts. Between 58-51 B.C., the area—which was known as Gaul—was conquered by Romans under Julius Caesar. In more modern times, France has been involved in the Crusades, the Hundred Years War, the Seven Years War, the American Revolution, the French Revolution, the July Revolution, the February Revolution, the Franco-Prussian War, and the two World Wars. All this and they make great cheese, too.

Web:

http://fr.yahoo.com/
http://www.france.com/francescape/regions/
    discover.html
http://www.franceway.com/

Usenet:

alt.france
soc.culture.french

IRC:

#france (Undernet)

Germany

The Federal Republic of Germany is located in north-central Europe. Germany is a mountainous country with the Black Forest (famous for its cuckoo clocks and toys) to the west and the Bavarian Alps (famous for its cream pies) to the south. Like its neighbor to the west (France), Germany has been involved in many wars and conflicts through the years, and was the base for two of the world's most powerful and ambitious military leaders: Napoleon and Hitler. As a result, Germany has faced a huge amount of political and social upheaval in its history. After World War II, the country was divided into parts that were occupied by various Allied forces. The country was not completely reunified until October 3, 1990.

Web:

http://de.yahoo.com/
http://www.goethe.de/uk/saf/enindex.htm
http://www.insidegermany.com/

Usenet:

soc.culture.german

IRC:

#germany (DALnet, Undernet)

Hungary

Hungary is located in central Europe on the Danube River and is the home of Lake Balaton, the largest lake in Europe. Being located centrally, Hungary suffered by being overrun by various groups of invaders, in particular the Magyars, Turks, Austrians and Soviets. Hungary is a beautiful country with more than 1,000 lakes and many parks and protected areas. One of the most famous Hungarians of all time is Franz Liszt (1811-1886), the piano virtuoso and composer.

Web:

http://www.go2hungary.com/
http://www.hungary.org/
http://www.insidehungary.com/
http://www.lonelyplanet.com/destinations/europe/
    hungary/

Usenet:

bit.listserv.hungary
soc.culture.magyar

Listserv Mailing List:

List Name: hungary
Subscribe to: listserv@hermes.gwu.edu

Immigration

If your goal is to move to the United States, you'll want to know all about green cards, temporary visas, citizenship, the visa lottery and various types of asylum. In the Usenet groups, you'll find discussions about immigrating to other countries, as well as specific groups for Canada, Australia, New Zealand and the U.S.

Web:
  http://www.cs.uu.nl/wais/html/na-dir/us-visa-faq/
    .html
  http://www.immigration.com/
  http://www.ins.usdoj.gov/

Usenet:
  misc.immigration.australia+nz
  misc.immigration.canada
  misc.immigration.misc
  misc.immigration.usa
  soc.subculture.expatriate

India

With more than 900 million people, India is the second-most populous country in the world (after China). India's people represent many cultures and traditions, and speak many different languages, with Hindi and English predominating. To a foreigner, India is a mysterious place: a country divided by caste, ethnicity and custom. However, it is also the largest democracy in the world.

Web:
  http://www.anything-indian.com/
  http://www.india-today.com/
  http://www.indianholiday.com/india/
  http://www.lonelyplanet.com/destinations/
    indian_subcontinent/india/

Usenet:
  soc.culture.india
  soc.culture.indian
  soc.culture.indian.bihar
  soc.culture.indian.delhi
  soc.culture.indian.gujarati
  soc.culture.indian.info
  soc.culture.indian.jammu-kashmir
  soc.culture.indian.karnataka
  soc.culture.indian.kerala
  soc.culture.indian.marathi
  soc.culture.indian.telugu

Indigenous Cultures and Peoples

From the 15th to the 20th century, Europeans explored much of Africa, the Americas and Asia. During this time, the Spanish, Portuguese, English, French and Dutch established many colonies around the world, mostly in areas that were already occupied by indigenous peoples. By the mid-20th century, virtually all of these colonies became independent, some of them having evolved into great countries, such as the United States, Canada and Australia. However, for several centuries, the indigenous peoples and their cultures had been suppressed, resulting in the creation of an underclass. Although these people are diverse, they do have much in common, including spiritual practices, a close association with nature, and a history of being repressed.

Web:
  http://www.bloorstreet.com/300block/aborl.htm
  http://www.cwis.org/wwwvl/indig-vl.html
  http://www.nativeweb.org/

Usenet:
  soc.culture.native

Indonesia

Indonesia is in southeast Asia and is made up of more than 3,000 islands, from the Malaysian mainland to New Guinea. The main islands of Indonesia are Java, Kalimantan (Borneo), Celebes (Sulawesi), Bali, Timor, the Moluccas (Maluku), Irian Jaya (West New Guinea) and Sumatra (home of Sherlock Holmes's infamous giant rat). Indonesia, which used to be known as the Dutch East Indies, gained its independence from the Netherlands in 1949. Ranked by population, Indonesia is the fourth largest country in the world, and is home to more than 250 different languages and dialects. Indonesia produces a variety of exports, including petroleum, natural gas, exotic rainforest hardwoods, rubber, palm oil and cinchona (an evergreen tree that is a source of quinine).

Web:
  http://indonesia.elga.net.id/
  http://www.lonelyplanet.com/destinations/
    south_east_asia/indonesia/

Usenet:
  alt.culture.indonesia
  soc.culture.indonesia
  soc.culture.indonesian

Ireland

Ireland has more than three and a half million people in an area about the size of West Virginia. The Irish people have a well-known culture—literature, music, dance, folklore—as well as highly developed social customs. They also have a political history that certainly qualifies as "interesting". Meet, chat and drink with Irish people on the Net, and use the Web to explore the leprechaun-loving Emerald Isle.

Web:
   http://www.goireland.com/
   http://www.insideeire.com/
   http://www.ireland.com/
   http://www.islandireland.com/

IRC:
   #ireland (DALnet, EFnet, Undernet)

Israel

The State of Israel is located on the eastern Mediterranean sea and was formed in 1948, after the United Nations divided Palestine into Jewish and Arab territories. About 85 percent of the population of Israel is Jewish, and the official languages are Hebrew and Arabic. For decades, the Jews and Palestinians have been fighting over the land, both groups having strong feelings of ownership. Despite a great deal of political tension, Israel has a large tourist industry. About 7 percent of the population of Israel lives on either a collective farm (kibbutz) or an agricultural co-op (moshav).

Web:
   http://www.goisrael.com/discoverisrael/
   http://www.mfa.gov.il/mfa/home.asp
   http://www.sabranet.com/
   http://www.shamash.org/

Usenet:
   soc.culture.israel

On the Net, everybody knows you're cool.

Italy

In ancient times, Rome, the capital of modern-day Italy, established an empire that lasted 500 years and contributed mightily to world culture. Today, Italian food, fashion, language and art are all influential outside of their native home. To find out about Italy, there are many resources on the Net you can use, as well as Usenet and IRC for discussion. (All this talk about Italy is making me hungry. I wish I had some spaghetti right now.)

Web:
   http://it.yahoo.com/
   http://www.initaly.com/
   http://www.lonelyplanet.com/destinations/europe/
      italy/

Usenet:
   alt.italia
   soc.culture.italian

IRC:
   #italy (Undernet)

Japan

Japan (Nippon) is an archipelago off the northeast coast of Asia. The country has four main islands—Hokkaido, Honshu, Shikoku and Kyushu—as well as other smaller ones. Japan is an old country, first settled in 660 B.C. Two thirds of the land consists of mountains, the most famous being Mount Fuji. Japan has a democratic form of government with a prime minister as chief executive, and an emperor as symbolic head of state. Legislative power resides with the national legislature (called the Diet), consisting of a House of Representatives and a House of Councillors.

Web:
   http://www.japan-guide.com/
   http://www.jinjapan.org/
   http://www.nihongo.org/english/
   http://www.yahoo.co.jp/

Usenet:
   soc.culture.japan
   soc.culture.japan.moderated

IRC:
   #japan (Undernet)

Korea

The Korean Peninsula was first unified into a single political entity in 668 A.D. During the 19th and 20th centuries, Korea was much affected by the political and military machinations of other countries. During World War II, it was agreed by the major powers that, after Japan (which had invaded Korea) was defeated, the country would become an independent state. Unfortunately, at the Yalta Conference in 1945, the leaders of the United States, England and the Soviet Union agreed in secret to divide the Korean Peninsula in order to make it easier to disarm the Japanese: the U.S. would occupy the south, the Soviets would occupy the north. Well, you can guess what happened. As with other famous divisions in history—such as East and West Germany, North and South Vietnam, and North and South Dakota—one part became communist while the other developed into a Western-style something or other. Today, Koreans are a people divided: North and South Korea share the Korean Peninsula, but that is about all they share.

Web:
  http://welcome.korea.com/
  http://www.korea.net/
  http://www.lonelyplanet.com/destinations/
    north_east_asia/south_korea/
  http://www.suite101.com/welcome.cfm/korean_culture

Usenet:
  alt.talk.korean
  soc.culture.korean

IRC:
  #korea (Undernet)

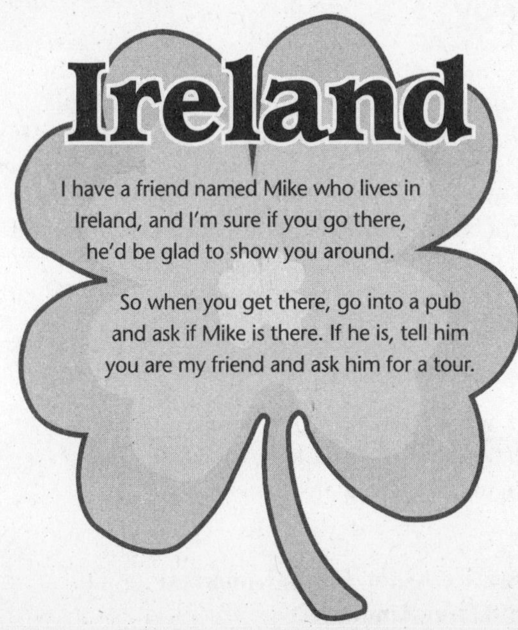

Latin America

Latin America is a descriptive term referring to the countries of Central and South America. These countries include Argentina, Belize, Bolivia, Brazil, Chile, Colombia, Costa Rica, Cuba, the Dominican Republic, Ecuador, El Salvador, Guatemala, Haiti, Honduras, Mexico, Nicaragua, Panama, Paraguay, Peru, Uruguay and Venezuela. In all of these countries the official language is Spanish, with the exception of Brazil (Portuguese), Haiti (French) and Belize (English).

Web:
  http://lanic.utexas.edu/
  http://www.americanetworld.com/
  http://www.latinamericalinks.com/
  http://www.latinworld.com/

Usenet:
  soc.culture.latin-america

IRC:
  #latino (Undernet)

Malaysia

Malaysia is an independent federation in southeast Asia, consisting of the southern Malay Peninsula and the northern portion of the island of Borneo. In its early history, Malaysia was part of the British protectorates, but achieved its independence in 1963. Malaysia has 4,800 km of coastline and more than 200 islands. Culturally, Malaysia consists of a number of diverse ethnic groups, the main ones being Malays (58%), Chinese (26%) and Indians (7%). There are also indigenous peoples, the Sabah and the Sarawak. The Malaysian constitution recognizes Islam as the official religion. In principle, every citizen has the right to practice his or her own religion, although, in practice, Islam predominates over Buddhism (Chinese) and Hinduism (Indians). The official language is Malay, although other languages are commonly spoken, including English, Chinese, and numerous tribal languages. The capital city of Malaysia is Kuala Lumpur.

Web:
  http://www.asinah.net/malaysia.html
  http://www.cia.gov/cia/publications/factbook/geos/
    my.html
  http://www.lonelyplanet.com/destinations/
    south_east_asia/malaysia/

Usenet:
  bit.listserv.berita
  soc.culture.malaysia

A B C D E F G H I J K L M N O P Q R S T U V W X Y Z

Mexico

Mexico is a large country bordered to the north by the United States and to the south by Belize and Guatemala. Mexico's indigenous population was conquered by Spain in the early 16th century and regained its independence in 1822. You can read more about Mexico and its people and culture by checking out the Web sites.

Web:
> http://www.lonelyplanet.com/destinations/
>   north_america/mexico/
> http://www.mexconnect.com/
> http://www.mexonline.com/

Usenet:
> alt.mexico
> soc.culture.mexican

Middle Europe

The first question one must ask when contemplating whether to join a discussion group relating to Middle Europe is: What *is* Middle Europe? It's defined as the countries lying between the Mediterranean/Adriatic and Baltic Seas and between the German/Austrian borders and the former Soviet Union. That settled, the second question would be: What is the list about? Just about everything. The list is unmoderated, and topics cover history, culture, politics, economics and current events.

Listserv Mailing List:
> List Name: mideur-l
> Subscribe to: listserv@listserv.acsu.buffalo.edu

Morocco

Moonlight in Morocco. It sounds so exotic. What a great movie that would make. The first scene shows a man sitting in front of the computer looking at a Web page about Morocco. He reads all about the culture, cooking and history of this country. He decides to go, and while he's there he has a daring adventure, finds love, and the final scene shows him with a beautiful woman, riding a camel into the sunset. This could be you. Go read about Morocco.

Web:
> http://www.lexicorient.com/morocco/
> http://www.marweb.net/morocco/
> http://www.morocco.com/

New Zealand

New Zealand consists of two main islands about 1,500 miles east of Australia and 8,200 miles southwest of Fargo, North Dakota. The two islands are called North Island and South Island, although the origin of these names is lost to antiquity. The New Zealand Web sites have a wonderful collection of information. You can learn about famous people from New Zealand such as Edmund Hillary (the first man to climb Mount Everest), Ernest Rutherford (who pioneered our understanding of atomic structure), and Kate Shepphard (notable women's suffragist). You can also find information about the Maori (aboriginal people), New Zealand English, read a translation of Jules Verne's encounter with rampaging kiwis (large New Zealand birds), and much, much more. If you are planning a trip to New Zealand, check the Net for travel information before you leave. After all, you don't want to make a wrong turn and end up in Fargo, North Dakota.

Web:
> http://www.newzealand.com/
> http://www.nz.com/guide/
> http://www.nz.com/mainpage.html

Usenet:
> soc.culture.new-zealand

Norway

Norway is a country in northern Europe, in the western portion of the Scandinavian peninsula. Norway is rugged and mountainous, and is the home of the largest glacier field in Europe, Jostedalsbreen. The country is a constitutional monarchy, and has two official languages, both of which are forms of Norwegian: Bokmål and Nynorsk. Famous Norwegians include Henrik Ibsen (author), Edvard Grieg (composer), and Edvard Munch (painter).

Web:
> http://www.norway.org/
> http://www.norwaypost.no/
> http://www.norwegian-scenery.com/

IRC:
> #norway (DALnet, EFnet, Undernet)
> #oslo (EFNet, Undernet)

Peru

The Republic of Peru is a Spanish-speaking country on the west coast of South America. The capital of Peru, Lima, includes the port of Callao. Much of Peru lies within the Andes mountains, and the country is particularly susceptible to earthquakes. (In 1970, 50,000 people were killed by a big quake.) Peru produces copper, silver, petroleum, sugarcane, fish, cotton and coca (from which cocaine is made). Peru has been inhabited for well over 10,000 years and was home to the Incas who, before the Spanish Conquest, established an empire that stretched from northern Ecuador to central Chile.

Web:

http://www.interknowledge.com/peru/
http://www.peru-explorer.com/
http://www.peru.com/peruinfo/ingles/index.html

Usenet:

soc.culture.peru

IRC:

#peruanos (Undernet)

Poland

The Republic of Poland is a country in central Europe, bordered on the north by the Baltic Sea. Between the 14th and 16th centuries, Poland enjoyed prosperity and a flourishing culture. In the 16th and 17th centuries, Poland lost much of its territory to Sweden and Russia. In the late 18th century, the remaining portion of Poland was partitioned into three sections by Prussia, Austria and Russia. As a result, Poland, as a country, vanished from the map of the world. However, Poland had strong nationalistic traditions and came back into existence after World War I, its borders being fixed by the Treaty of Versailles in 1919.

Web:

http://www.gopoland.com/
http://www.insidepoland.com/
http://www.polandonline.com/

Usenet:

soc.culture.polish

Listserv Mailing List:

List Name: poland-l
Subscribe to: listserv@listserv.acsu.buffalo.edu

IRC:

#polska (Undernet)

Portugal

The Portuguese Republic is located in southwest Europe on the western Iberian Peninsula (which it shares with Spain), and includes the Madeira Islands and the Azores in the Atlantic Ocean. Most people don't know that Portugal is a major supplier of the world's cork. (If it wasn't for Portugal, most of the champagne in the world would be flat.) Portugal is also known for its vineyards, olive groves and almond trees, but, due to antiquated farming techniques, the Portuguese are unable to produce enough food for their own country. (However, they do have lots of cork.) In the 15th century, Portugal was at a peak, with territories extending into Asia, Africa and America. Portugal's decline began in the 16th century when Spain began to take over various Portuguese territories, and, through the years, many of the remaining territories have declared their independence. Today, Portugal is a relatively small but stable country.

Web:

http://home.online.no/~nancys/portugal/index2.html
http://www.portugal.org/indexhtml/index2.html
http://www.portugalvirtual.pt/

Usenet:

soc.culture.portuguese

IRC:

#portugal (DALnet, EFnet, Undernet)

The last time I went to Mexico, I spent the whole time looking for jumping beans. I looked all over. I found friendly people, beautiful weather, interesting places to visit, and wonderful beaches and mountains, but no jumping beans.

The funny thing was, when I got back, I found a can of lima beans lying on the floor of my kitchen, where they had fallen from the cupboard.

Isn't it funny how life works? You can travel all around the world, only to find that what you really wanted was in your very own home the whole time.

Russia

The Russian Federation occupies most of eastern Europe and northern Asia. It extends 5,000 miles (8,000 km) from the Baltic Sea to the Pacific Ocean, crossing eleven time zones and covering more than a tenth of the Earth's land area. Geographically, it is the world's largest country and ranks sixth in population. The Russian climate varies from extreme cold in northern Russia and Siberia (Verkhoyansk, Siberia, is the world's coldest settled place) to subtropical along the Black Sea. Generally speaking, we can think of Russia as being divided into European Russia and Asiatic Russia. Most of the population lives in European Russia, making Russia an important European power.

Web:

http://www.city.ru/
http://www.insiderussia.com/
http://www.lonelyplanet.com/destinations/europe/
    russia/

Usenet:

soc.culture.russia
soc.culture.russian
soc.culture.russian.moderated
soc.culture.soviet

IRC:

#russia (EFnet, Undernet)
#russian (DALnet, EFnet, Undernet)

Saudi Arabia

The Kingdom of Saudi Arabia occupies most of the Arabian Peninsula in the Middle East. Saudi Arabia is an arid desert country that controls 25 percent of the world's oil reserves. The holy cities of Mecca and Medina are both located in Saudi Arabia. The majority of Arabs adhere to the Wahhabi sect of Islam. There are also some Muslim Arabs, called Bedouin, who rove in tribal groups, headed by a sheikh. Their main livelihood is breeding camels and sheep.

Web:

http://www.lonelyplanet.com/destinations/
    middle_east/saudi_arabia/
http://www.saudi-pages.com/

Usenet:

alt.culture.saudi

Slovakia

Slovakia, a country in central Europe, was more or less under Hungarian rule until 1918, at which time it became part of Czechoslovakia. On January 1, 1993, Czechoslovakia split into Slovakia and the Czech Republic. On the Net, you can find maps, statistics, pictures, accommodation and transportation guides, and political, historical and tourist information.

Web:

http://www.heartofeurope.co.uk/
http://www.insideslovakia.com/
http://www.slovakia.org/

Spain

Spain lies in southwestern Europe, on the north shore of the Mediterranean Sea. In the 16th and 17th centuries, Spain had a powerful navy, which enabled the country to assemble a large empire and colonize much of the New World. The 18th and 19th centuries, however, saw Spain lose most of its empire, due to economic and political instability. In the 20th century, Spain remained neutral through two world wars, although it did suffer from a devastating civil war (1936-1939). Modern day Spain is one of the cultural centers of Europe, as it has been for centuries and, outside the major cities, is still very much an agricultural country.

Web:

http://es.yahoo.com/
http://www.cia.gov/cia/publications/factbook/geos/
    sp.html
http://www.red2000.com/spain/index-eng.html
http://www.travelinginspain.com/

Usenet:

soc.culture.spain

Sweden

Sweden has a population of 8.8 million people, 85 percent of whom live in the southern half of the country. Sweden is one of the oldest continuously existing countries on the entire planet, being over a thousand years old. In that thousand years, Sweden has given the world much to be thankful for: food and drink (especially vodka), automobiles, furniture, as well as a model for highly socialized democracy.

Web:

http://www.insidesweden.com/
http://www.royalcourt.se/net/royal+court
http://www.swedeninfo.com/

IRC:

#sweden (DALnet, EFnet, Undernet)

Taiwan

Taiwan (which used to be called Formosa) is an island nation off the southeast coast of China. Taiwan was first settled by the Chinese in the 7th century. It was later held by Holland, then China again and then Japan. In 1945, after World War II, control of Taiwan passed back to China. However, in 1949, the Nationalists (led by Chiang Kai-shek) were expelled from mainland China by the Communists and settled in Taiwan where they set up a government in exile. Today, Taiwan is still completely separate from China, although the two countries have significant cultural and economic ties.

Web:
http://taiwan.asiadragons.com/
http://www.lonelyplanet.com/destinations/
    north_east_asia/taiwan/
http://www.taiwandc.org/

Usenet:
alt.taiwan.republic
soc.culture.taiwan

IRC:
#taiwan (DALnet)

Thailand

Thailand (once called Siam) occupies a central position in southeast Asia, both geographically and politically. The country was first established in the mid-14th century, but spent much of its history being dominated by other countries. In 1932, Thailand became a constitutional monarchy. Today, the Thai people are united in three ways: via the Buddhist religion, through their love for freedom, and by their support of the monarchy.

Web:
http://www.mahidol.ac.th/thailand/
http://www.siamweb.org/thailand/
http://www.tat.or.th/index2.html

Usenet:
soc.culture.thai

IRC:
#thailand (Undernet)
#tnet (EFnet)

United Kingdom

The United Kingdom, or U.K., is in western Europe and consists of Great Britain (England, Scotland and Wales) and Northern Ireland. The U.K. is governed by a constitutional monarchy and is one of the world's leading industrial nations. The U.K.'s contributions to world culture are legion: the Royal Family, well-mannered soccer fans, afternoon tea, and Monty Python, not to mention a longstanding contribution to the world of food and haute cuisine.

Web:
http://uk.yahoo.com/
http://www.insideuk.com/
http://www.ukindex.co.uk/

Usenet:
soc.culture.british

IRC:
#england (DALnet, EFnet, Undernet)
#uk (EFnet, Undernet)

United States

American culture, inventiveness and business influence all have an enormous effect on the world at large. Here are the places to discuss what America is and how it fits into the global community. Talk, argue and meet new friends, all at the same time. For information about the United States, these Web sites will help you explore the land of the free and home of the brave from your living room. (You do need to supply your own hot dog and apple pie.)

Web:
http://www.50states.com/city/regions.htm
http://www.odci.gov/cia/publications/factbook/
    geos/us.html
http://www.usacitylink.com/

Usenet:
soc.culture.african-american
soc.culture.african.american.moderated
soc.culture.usa

IRC:
#usa (DALnet, EFnet)

> # The body is the
> # servant of the mind.

Venezuela

Venezuela is located on the northern coast of South America on the Caribbean Sea. In 1499, a Spanish explorer named an offshore island Venezuela, meaning "little Venice". The explorer called the island "little Venice" because the inhabitants of the island built their huts above the water on stilts. The name was eventually used for the mainland area.

Web:

http://www.odci.gov/cia/publications/factbook/
geos/ve.html
http://www.think-venezuela.net/
http://www.venezuelatuya.com/eng.htm

Usenet:

soc.culture.venezuela

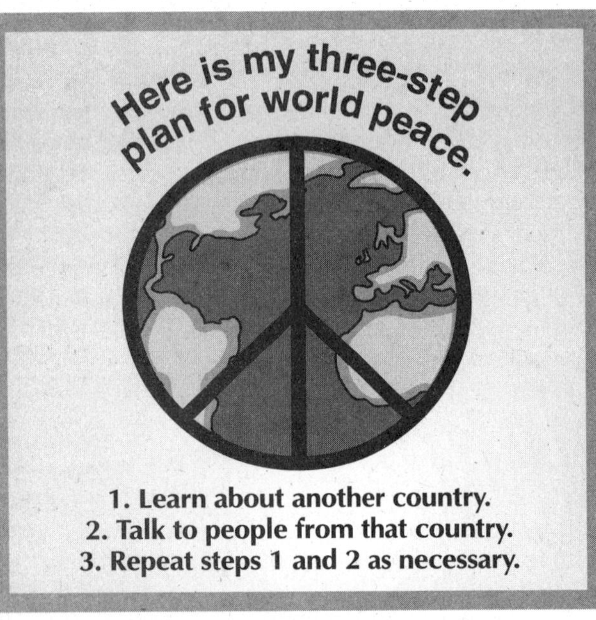

World Culture Talk and General Discussion

As more and more of the world connects to the Net, we become closer to one another and more and more like a global village. Today, problems and conflicts anywhere in the world are of concern to everyone. These discussion groups are for talking about general world and cultural issues.

Usenet:

soc.culture
soc.culture.intercultural
soc.culture.misc
soc.culture.multicultural

World Heritage List

Around the world, there are many cultural and natural sites that are part of the common heritage of people everywhere. In order to help preserve these sites, the World Heritage Committee, working under the auspices of UNESCO, identifies such places and publishes information about them in the World Heritage list.

Web:

http://fp.thesalmons.org/lynn/world.heritage.html
http://www.unesco.org/whc/nwhc/pages/sites/
main.htm

WRITING

Bad Writing Contest

Anyone can write poorly, but can you write worse than thousands of other people? If so, you may want to enter the annual Bulwer-Lytton Fiction Contest. All you have to do is write one sentence—a sentence that pretends to be the opening of a bad novel. This contest has been run since 1982, and, if your stomach for atrocious writing is strong, you can peruse the winners by visiting this Web site. The contest is named for a Victorian historical novelist, Edward George Bulwer-Lytton (1803-1873), who wrote a story that begins: "It was a dark and stormy night; the rain fell in torrents—except at occasional intervals, when it was checked by a violent gust of wind which swept up the streets (for it is in London that our scene lies), rattling along the house-tops, and fiercely agitating the scanty flame of the lamps that struggled against the darkness..."

Web:

http://www.bulwer-lytton.com/

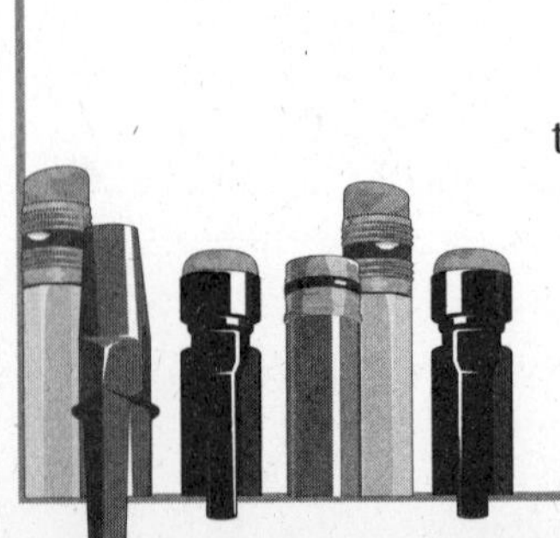

Copy Editing

Copy editing is a process in which text is checked for mistakes. Every writer, no matter how good, needs a copy editor for two reasons: first, copy editors are specialists, trained to recognize and correct written mistakes, and second, it is difficult for a writer to notice his or her own mistakes. Having a second person read the text makes a big difference. In general, copy editors are overworked, underpaid and under-appreciated. This is a shame, because copy editing is a necessary part of the writing process and some copy editors demonstrate a dedication to their craft and a degree of professionalism that would be difficult to overpraise.

Web:

    http://www.copydesk.org/
    http://www.theprices.com/4artTW1.htm
    http://www.theslot.com/sharp.html

Listserv Mailing List:

    List Name: copyediting-l
    Subscribe to: listserv@indiana.edu

Freelance Writing

Does the romance of uncertain work, low remuneration, no benefits and a complete lack of guarantees sound appealing to you? Good. You're ready to be a freelance writer. As a freelancer, you will have to find your own work and negotiate your fees and conditions, so here's some information to get you going. Once you do, you'll be able to set your own hours, work at home, live without a boss hanging over your head, and generally be the captain of your own ship. Now, doesn't that sound better?

Web:

    http://www.freelanceonline.com/
    http://www.freelancewriting.com/
    http://www.poewar.com/articles/beginner.htm
    http://www.worldwidefreelance.com/
    http://www.writershome.com/
    http://www.yudkin.com/flfaq.htm

> **Here is the latest news: There is no important news. You can now return to enjoying your life.**

Literary Agents

A literary agent is a person who represents you and your work. The main job of an agent is to sell what you create, along with subsidiary rights. You pay an agent commission on the money you receive for the work he or she sells—most agents charge 15 percent. All money is sent to the agent, who deducts the commission and then sends the remainder to you. (Agents are not fools.) Do you need an agent? There is no easy answer. Within some genres, such as computer book publishing, using an agent is optional. In other areas, such as screenwriting, it is difficult to get a movie studio to even look at you if you are not represented professionally. Remember, though, agents are not managers; all they do is sell. It is up to *you* to build your career. If you need an agent, these resources will help you find one. To get you started, I have some tips. One, when you sign a publishing agreement, everything is negotiable, even— as Isaac Asimov once pointed out—your name and the date. Two, and this is very important, pay a lawyer who is familiar with the publishing industry to read every contract *before* you sign it. Does this apply to the contract a literary agency wants you to sign when you hire them? Yes, yes and yes. Three, everything is negotiable. Four, do not ever pay anyone to "read" your work. Five, everything is negotiable. Six, avoid agents who try to steer you toward a particular commercial editing service. Seven everything is negotiable. Eight, beware of agents who collect a 15 percent commission and then try to charge you for extras, such as phone calls, faxes and photocopying. Nine, everything is negotiable.

Web:

    http://www.authorlink.com/agents.html
    http://www.jkelman.com/agents/
    http://www.talewins.com/Role.htm
    http://www.wga.org/agency.html

A B C D E F G H I J K L M N O P Q R S T U V W X Y Z

Mystery and Crime Writing

Are you a mystery writer? Would you like to be one? These Web sites have lots of useful information for mystery and crime writers. On Usenet, the **rec.arts.mystery** group is the place to discuss mystery plays, books and films. The other groups are where people talk about actual and imaginary crimes. These are good places to visit when you need inspiration or information.

Web:
> http://www.acwl.org/
> http://www.johnmorganwilson.com/writingcraft.htm
> http://www.redinkworks.com/mystery_writers.htm
> http://www.writing-world.com/links/mystery.html

Usenet:
> **alt.crime**
> **alt.true-crime**
> **rec.arts.mystery**

Mystery and Crime Writing

Here is the world's shortest mystery story that involves all of the following ideas:

- murder
- romance
- royalty
- a great detective
- the Internet
- Microsoft Windows
- a small blue sock

"Darling, I told you not to look in my small blue sock," she said, as she lovingly shot him through the heart.

The Great Detective leaped up from behind the couch. "After spending two years chasing you through fifteen countries, Contessa, I was finally able to track you down by analyzing the information on your Web page."

"I'll come quietly," she said, "but please tell me one thing."

"Yes?" said the Great Detective.

The mysterious, red-haired woman looked into his eyes and breathed a deep sigh of despair. "Do you have any idea how to get rid of that Network Neighborhood icon?"

(to be continued...)

Prose

These bite-sized morsels of prose make the perfect afternoon brain snack. No matter what tickles your fancy, the variety of stories will have something for you. Read or share, it's up to you: just remember, if you don't use it, you'll lose it.

Usenet:
> **alt.prose**
> **rec.arts.prose**

Publishers

Looking for a publisher or for information about a specific publisher? Here's the information you need to find the company that is good enough to publish *your* work. You'll also find information about online publishers who can sell your books electronically over the Net. Hint: Once your book comes out, check your publisher's Web site to make sure your work is given the prominence it deserves.

Web:
> http://archive.museophile.sbu.ac.uk/publishers/
> http://www.coredcs.com/%7emermaid/epub.html
> http://www.lights.com/publisher/
> http://www.literarymarketplace.com/lmp/

Query Letters

You write a query letter to an editor when you have an idea you are trying to sell. Sometimes you will already have a completed manuscript, and you will want to send part of it (say, the first chapter) along with your query. In this case, the query letter is also a cover letter. It is important that you learn how to write such letters well: after all, you are a professional writer, and you will be judged on all your writing, letters included. My advice is to put the editorial process in perspective. What are editors? They are just poor saps whose job it is to find writers. Without you and me, they have no reason to exist. So the better you write your letter, the easier it is for them to pay you money, and the faster we can all get back to work.

Web:
> http://www.eclectics.com/articles/query2.html
> http://www.poewar.com/articles/query_letter.htm
> http://www.underdown.org/covlettr.htm

Romance Writing

Do you want to be a romance writer? Good, because a lot of people need you. Romance novels are popular for a variety of reasons, the most important of which is that men simply do not pay enough attention to women. If you happen to have a husband or boyfriend who reads Harley Hahn books, you know that your man is intelligent, sensitive, emotional (in a good way) and altogether desirable. However, many women find that their mates do not quite measure up, and an escape into romantic fantasy is a welcome relief. Thus, if you are a romance writer or aspiring romance writer, you are fulfilling an important function in our society and your responsibilities are great. Remember, the Net is always there to help you stay in touch with your colleagues and do your research.

Web:
   http://www.likesbooks.com/write.html
   http://www.nettrends.com/romanceauthors/
   http://www.romance-central.com/
   http://www.rwanational.com/
   http://www.writerswrite.com/messages/
      romance.html

Listserv Mailing List:
   List Name: rw-l
   Subscribe to: listserv@maelstrom.stjohns.edu

Science Fiction Writing

Allow yourself to linger on the words, your eyes playing gently back and forth across the pages of your latest sci-fi, fantasy or horror novel. That's right: *your* novel (or *your* story or screenplay). Would you like to be a writer in one of these genres? Here are some resources to help. (And here's the secret of being a writer. If you want to be a writer, you have to write every day, and you will probably have to write for at least several years just to learn your trade. So start now. Right now. Today. No excuses.)

Web:
   http://www.marketlist.com/
   http://www.sff.net/
   http://www.sfwa.org/

Usenet:
   rec.arts.sf.written

Screenplay Archives

If you are working on a screenplay, you definitely need something to do when you are not writing. The Net is always available with plenty of relevant distractions, and the best possible distraction is to read someone else's screenplay. There are lots of great screenplays available online. Even if they don't help you pay the bills, at least you will have something to read between now and the time your electricity is shut off.

Web:
   http://sfy.iv.ru/
   http://www.screentalk.org/gallery.htm
   http://www.script-o-rama.com/snazzy/dircut.html
   http://www.scriptdude.com/frames/scriptindex.html

Screenwriters and Playwrights

Do you have dreams of becoming a successful screenwriter or playwright? Here are some resources that will help: information for screenwriters and playwrights as well as some general writing resources. The Usenet group is for the discussion of writing screenplays and other related topics. The mailing list is for writers, agents, producers and other people who are interested in screenwriting.

Web:
   http://www.screenwritersforum.com/
   http://www.visualwriter.com/
   http://www.wga.org/
   http://www.wordplayer.com/

Usenet:
   misc.writing.screenplays

Listserv Mailing List:
   List Name: collab-l
   Subscribe to: listserv@lists.psu.edu

Screenplays

I have a friend who is a screenwriter, and she won't let me look at her current screenplay until it is finished. But do I care? No, because I can go to the Net and look at as many screenplays as I want.

Speechwriting

You know, of course, that when you listen to an Important Person make a speech, he or she did not write the words. Important People have speechwriters: skilled and imaginative writers who make a living telling other, less skilled and imaginative people what to say. If writing speeches appeals to you, visit these Web sites for a lot of useful information. One of the sites also has a great collection of speeches in history.

Web:
http://www.davegustafson.com/speech/
http://www.executive-speaker.com/res_m.html
http://www.nvo.com/speechwriters/
   tipswritingperformingspeeches/
http://www.saxton.com.au/greatspeeches.html

Technical Writing

Technical writers create exposition, words that explain. A technical writer must be able to master a complex subject, and then describe it for a casual reader who needs to understand the relevant facts and ideas. This mailing list is for discussion of all aspects of technical writing. The Usenet group is the same as the list, so you only need to read one of them.

Web:
http://www.poewar.com/articles/twfaq.htm
http://www.raycomm.com/techwhirl/
http://www.writerswrite.com/technical/

Usenet:
bit.listserv.techwr-l

Listserv Mailing List:
List Name: techwr-l
Subscribe to: listserv@listserv.okstate.edu

Writer's Block Magazine

When you need a break from typing, spend some time browsing through the latest copy of this online writers' magazine. The articles are for professional writers and editors. You will find essays, reports on technology, book reviews, interviews, and more.

Web:
http://www.writersblock.ca/

Writers' Resources

When you're not writing, you might as well be cruising the Net looking at writers' resources. These Web sites will help you find a huge variety of writing information. So much that you will be exploring for hours and hours, and the best part is it all counts as work.

Web:
http://www.absolutewrite.com/
http://www.authorlink.com/
http://www.jkelman.com/
http://www.pw.org/
http://www.sharpwriter.com/
http://www.writerswrite.com/

Writers Talk and General Discussion

Being a writer is great way to live, because you get to sleep in and work in your pajamas all day. Writers tend to be solitary people, either from personal inclination or circumstance. Spending a large number of hours slaving over a hot computer makes it difficult for people like us to find time to go outside and meet people. That's why these discussion forums are so wonderful. You can check in, read the new messages and post some of your own, all without leaving the house. This means that, as writers, we can fulfill our social needs without having to actually meet anyone in person. Wow. Now, if I could only figure out how to download some cold spaghetti for breakfast.

Web:
http://www.ability.org.uk/writers_chat.html
http://www.freelancewriting.com/yabbprivate/yabb/
   YaBB.cgi
http://www.missouri.edu/~writery/index2.html
http://www.scalar.com/mw/
http://www.writersbbs.com/

Usenet:
misc.writing

Listserv Mailing List:
List Name: writers
Subscribe to: listserv@mitvma.mit.edu

IRC:
#writers (EFnet)

Writing for Children

A *lot* of people want to write for children. If you are going to be successful, you must be persistent, skillful, knowledgeable, experienced, talented and lucky. When it comes to information, the Net can help. These Web sites have lots of resources including answers to FAQs, a glossary of common terms, and information about agents and submissions. The Usenet group is a place where real writers hang out, and if you spend some time there, you will definitely learn something.

Web:
  http://www.cynthialeitichsmith.com/
    writingforkids.htm
  http://www.scbwi.org/
  http://www.signaleader.com/childrens-writers/
  http://www.underdown.org/magazines.htm
  http://www.write4kids.com/

Usenet:
  rec.arts.books.childrens

Writing Jobs

A lot of companies and organizations need writers. And why not? Writers are among the most useful, talented, valuable people in the world. If you are one of these lucky people, check and see what's available. Remember, if they could write, they wouldn't need *you*.

Web:
  http://www.sunoasis.com/
  http://www.writerswrite.com/jobs/
  http://www.writetools.com/jobs.html

Writing Markets

There are a lot of magazines and newspapers that buy articles from freelancers, as you will see when you take a look at these resources. I bet you'll be surprised how big the market really is. Here is a hint if you are not yet an experienced professional. It can be hard to sell your writing when you don't have a track record. However, some of the publications in the writing market lists are looking for free articles. To help you get started, why not spend some time writing for such publications? You'll not only have fun and develop your skills, you'll learn how to deal with magazines and editors.

Web:
  http://www.worldwidefreelance.com/markets.htm
  http://www.writerswrite.com/paying/
  http://www.writetools.com/jobs.html#market

TIDBITS

What should homeowners know about THROWING STUFF AWAY?

When a storage area is full, you have no room to move stuff around, and it is difficult to get at the things you want. Thus, your overall goal is to discard enough of your possessions so that all your closets, drawers, cupboards and storage areas are at *least* 1/3 empty.

I realize that you will have to be ruthless, so here is how to make it easy.

Let us pretend that, exactly one year ago, you put an imaginary red tag on every item that you own. Over the last year, whenever you used an item for the first time, you removed the tag. Now, as you go through a storage area, look at each item in turn and ask yourself, "Does this still have the red tag on it?" If so, throw it out.

See how easy it is?

There is, of course, one exception. It is okay to keep anything of sentimental value indefinitely, as long as the item is not too large. For example, you would never throw away family photos or Baby Lydia's first shoes. However, it is okay to get rid of the car that Junior rebuilt when he was a teenager.

Once you have your home organized, how do you keep everything under control? Just follow this one simple rule:

Whenever you bring anything into the house that has to be stored, you must throw away something else that is at least the same size.

For example, if you have a lot of shirts in your closet, you can bring in a new shirt whenever you want, as long as you throw away an old shirt at the same time.

(Note: This system is not applicable to pets and relatives.)

ZINES

American Folk

American Folk is where I found out about egg-in-a-frame: a breakfast treat in which an egg is cooked within a frame made by cutting a hole in a piece of toast. Celebrate contemporary American culture—families, traditions, kitsch—by reading this down-home zine, guaranteed to give you a warm feeling inside. (And if that doesn't work, make yourself an egg-in-a-frame.)

Web:

http://www.americanfolk.com/

Bad Girl Zines

Zines by girls with attitude. Bad girls with attitude. Bad grrls with attitude. Grrls with bad attitude. Thoughtful. Brazenly pithy. Girls. Grrls. Bad. Attitude. Yep. Zines by girls with attitude.

Web:

http://www.bitchmagazine.com/
http://www.geekgirl.com.au/
http://www.nofuncharlie.com/whirlingcervix/
  intro.html
http://www.purpletights.com/

Bad Subjects

Thinking for yourself is Bad. Thinking in ways that are not mainstream or that are radical is Bad. That's why Bad Subjects is so good. Check out the zine that promotes the questioning of old ways and tries to show how politics applies to everyday life.

Web:

http://www.eserver.org/bs/

Fray

Fray uses cool HTML and a so-hip design to showcase rants, articles and stories. When I visited, I saw stuff—and that is exactly the *mot juste*—related to work, hope and vices. Weep it and read.

Web:

http://www.fray.com/

Glassdog

Glassdog is a thought-provoking, well-designed literary zine with thought-provoking, well-written things to read. You'll enjoy the essays, as well as the section called Overheard: random snippets of conversation and opinions that were not meant to be public knowledge.

Web:

http://www.glassdog.com/

Mad Dog Weekly

Have you ever wanted to write your own screenplay? I live in California where everyone is a screenwriter (or has an option on a TV series), so I can tell you, before you can write a screenplay you need to pitch (sell) the concept. But where do you get the concept? Just sashay over to Mad Dog and use the Plot-o-Matic. Just type a few words, make some selections, and click on the button. Before you can say, "Get Tom Cruise on the horn!" you'll have a brand new film concept, suitable for pitching. (And while you are there, read some of the articles. After all, this is a humor zine.)

Web:

http://www.maddogproductions.com/

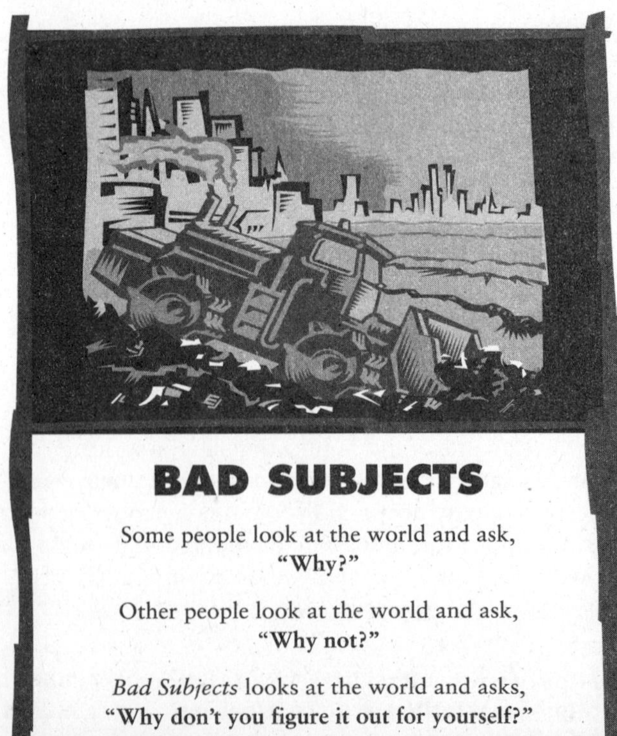

Pigdog Journal

Let's put it this way. If you are tired of the ordinary, and you want to look at the world turned upside down through the transparent cup of literary what-have-you, you need to read the Pigdog Journal. It may not lull you to sleep after a restless day of fighting the world, but it sure as heck will make you feel better to get your brain running on all six cylinders. Pigdog: it takes the "biz" out of bizarre, and shovels it straight to you.

Web:
   http://www.pigdog.org/

Majordomo Mailing List:
   List Name: pigdog-l
   Subscribe to: majordomo@bearfountain.com

Popular Culture Zines

The best thing about popular culture is that it is so *accessible*. Just turn on your TV, pick up a newspaper, or listen to the radio, and there it is: popular culture. So if you can't get away from it, you might as well understand it. These popular culture zines are filled with commentary, reviews, rants and articles. Read about television, art, politics, technology, movies, books, fashion, music and celebrities. Boy—talk about culture.

Web:
   http://www.hissyfit.com/
   http://www.onthewallnow.com/
   http://www.spankmag.com/
   http://www.zinebook.com/

Salon

There was a time, before television and radio, when cultured and intelligent people would gather at someone's house in order to talk. This was known as a "salon". At a salon, people would think for themselves (instead of repeating what they heard on the news and talk shows), and elegant and stimulating conversation was considered valuable. This Web site seeks to capture the spirit and philosophy of the salon days, when thinkers, writers and scholars would sit in comfortable chairs and discuss ideas. You are invited to visit.

Web:
   http://www.salon.com/

Zine Lists

Making your own zine is the rage. In zine-land, nothing is sacred. Zines cover topics as mainstream as education, politics and philosophy, and as bizarre as hyperactive armadillos and free verse about plastic lawn ornaments.

Web:
   http://www.ezine-dir.com/
   http://www.ezine-universe.com/
   http://www.ezinehub.com/
   http://www.pilot-search.com/links/Zines/

Zine Talk and General Discussion

I read a lot of different zines, and one thing I can tell you: people who make zines like to talk to other people who make zines. So, if you are the zine-type, there are plenty of people waiting to talk to you on Usenet. Find out what's good, what's bad, and what's cooking in the zine community.

Usenet:
   alt.binaries.zines
   alt.ezines
   alt.zines
   rec.mag.fsfnet

ZOOLOGY

Arachnology

Arachnology is the study of arthropods belonging to the class Arachnida. Arachnids include spiders, scorpions, mites and ticks. Most arachnids are carnivorous. All arachnids have a body divided into two parts, a cephalothorax and an abdomen. Arachnids have four pairs of segmented legs (compared to insects that have a separate head, thorax and body, and three pairs of legs). My cat, The Little Nipper, is an amateur arachnologist, although he has a more utilitarian attitude toward spiders and other arachnids: he plays with them, and then he eats them.

Web:

  http://www.americanarachnology.org/
  http://www.qmuseum.qld.gov.au/features/spiders/
  http://www.ufsia.ac.be/Arachnology/
    Arachnology.html

Intrigue, Privacy, Secret Stuff...

Entomology

Entomology is the study of insects, the largest class of the phylum Arthropoda (invertebrates). Entomologists recognize more than 750,000 described species of insects, although it is thought that there may be as many as 5,000,000 different species in the world. As a general rule, insects are long, narrow, and bilaterally symmetrical (sort of like Calista Flockhart). Their bodies are composed of ringlike segments, grouped into the head (eyes, antennae and mouthparts), thorax (legs and wings), and abdomen. The surface of the body consists of hardened plates, called sclerites, separated by membranous areas called sutures. Here is an easy way to make money. Go into a bar where entomologists hang out. Find a group that has been drinking a lot, and bet them that insects have more than 10 abdominal segments. When they scoff at you and take the bet, whip out a magnifying glass and a couple of bugs. "Look here," you can tell them, "these appendages at the end of the abdomen are really a greatly reduced segment. So, even though it doesn't look like it, there are actually 11 segments in the abdomen." (Hint for guys: This is a great way to meet girls.)

Web:

  http://folk.uio.no/mostarke/forens_ent/
    forensic_entomology.html
  http://www.ent.iastate.edu/list/
  http://www.insects.org/
  http://www.msstate.edu/entomology/ENTPLP.html

Usenet:

  sci.bio.entomology.homoptera
  sci.bio.entomology.lepidoptera
  sci.bio.entomology.misc

Listproc Mailing List:

  List Name: bugnet
  Subscribe to: listproc@listproc.wsu.edu

Listserv Mailing List:

  List Name: entomo-l
  Subscribe to: listserv@listserv.uoguelph.ca

Ethology Talk and General Discussion

Ethology is the study of animal behavior. A simplistic view of animals would say that a particular type of behavior is either instinctual or learned. However, modern thought holds that much of what we observe cannot be explained so simply. We have come to realize that much depends on an interaction between an animal's genetic inheritance and its environment when it is young. I find the ethology discussions on the Net fascinating, and even if you are not a biologist, you may enjoy reading what people have to say.

Web:
   http://www.biosis.org.uk/zrdocs/zoolinfo/behav.htm
   http://www.usask.ca/wcvm/herdmed/
      applied-ethology/

Usenet:
   sci.bio.ethology

Listserv Mailing List:
   List Name: ethology
   Subscribe to: listserv@segate.sunet.se

Herpetology

Herpetology is the branch of zoology that studies reptiles and amphibians. Reptiles are dry-skinned vertebrates, usually scaly and cold-blooded. They have low-hanging bodies with four short legs (except snakes) and long tails. They breathe air, live on land (mostly) and have thick, waterproof skins. The most well-known reptiles are snakes, turtles and crocodiles. Amphibians have moist skins, without scales or with tiny scales. They deposit their eggs in or near water. Young amphibians start life as water-breathing tadpoles, and grow into air-breathing adults. The most well-known amphibians are frogs, toads, salamanders and newts.

Web:
   http://elib.cs.berkeley.edu/aw/
   http://gto.ncsa.uiuc.edu/pingleto/herp.html
   http://research.amnh.org/herpetology/
   http://www.embl-heidelberg.de/~uetz/
      livingreptiles.html
   http://www.herpetology.com/
   http://www.open.ac.uk/daptf/

Usenet:
   sci.bio.herp

Ichthyology

There are close to 21,000 different species of fish in the world. Fish have adapted to an underwater environment. They breathe oxygen dissolved in water with the use of gills, and have maintained the same general physical characteristics throughout their history. Biologists divide fish into three classes: the most primitive jawless fish are called Agnatha; fish with cartilage and no true bones, such as sharks and rays, are called Chondrichthyes; bony fish, the ones with which most people are familiar, are called Osteichthyes. Generally speaking, the study of fish can be divided into two basic disciplines. Ichthyology is the scientific study of fish: their physiology, habitat, history and characteristics. The second basic discipline is social ichthyology, the study of people with fish-like faces. If you are a social ichthyologist, you are more or less on your own, but I can send you a picture of my old high school chemistry teacher.

Web:
   http://www.fishbase.org/search.cfm
   http://www.flmnh.ufl.edu/fish/
   http://www.nefsc.nmfs.gov/faq/

Malacology

Malacology is the study of mollusks: the second largest invertebrate phylum, which includes clams, oysters, scallops, bivalves, gastropods (such as snails), squid and octopus. Some mollusks are so small as to be almost invisible to the human eye. Other mollusks are large. A giant squid has been found that measured 70 feet (21.3 meters) long. Most mollusks live in water or at shoreline in the tidal zone. They live inside shells and have soft bodies, as well as a "foot" that allows them to move around. (Some mollusks, such as the octopus, have a shell that is enclosed by their body.)

Web:

http://home.wxs.nl/~spirula/crossref.htm
http://www.biosis.org.uk/zrdocs/zoolinfo/
   grp_moll.htm
http://www.conchology.uunethost.be/
http://www.il-st-acad-sci.org/malacol.html
http://www.si.edu/resource/faq/nmnh/mollusk1.htm

Listserv Mailing List:

List Name: conch-l
Subscribe to: listserv@listserv.uga.edu

Mammals

What makes a mammal a mammal? Well, let's say you're in a bowling alley, standing at the snack bar waiting for a hot dog. You look up and see a warm-blooded vertebrate with hair or fur, a four-chambered heart, a relatively large brain, and mammary glands (don't stare). Chances are, you are looking at a mammal. The first mammals developed from reptiles about 200 million years ago. Today, there are more than 4,000 recognized species. My favorites are the Felis catus (domestic cats), Mesocricetus auratus (hamsters), Equus caballus (horses), and Homo sapiens (people).

Web:

http://nmnhwww.si.edu/msw/
http://www.abdn.ac.uk/mammal/
http://www.mammalsociety.org/

Listserv Mailing List:

List Name: mammal-l
Subscribe to: listserv@sivm.si.edu

Marine Life

When you need to find out how Ctenophora differ from Platyhelminthes, it's comforting to know that the Net will not let you down. If you have a question about a marine animal, there is a good chance that the answer is at one of these Web sites. The Usenet groups are for discussing dolphins, whales and deep-sea biology.

Web:

http://ourworld.compuserve.com/homepages/jaap/
http://www.mbl.edu/
http://www.whaletimes.org/

Usenet:

alt.animals.dolphins
alt.animals.whales
bionet.biology.deepsea

Nematology

The phylum Nematoda comprises the roundworms, small organisms that live in water or soil. Some of the nematodes, such as pinworms or hookworms, can cause illness in people, although most nematodes feed on bacteria, fungi and other organisms found in the soil. There are nearly 20,000 known species of nematodes, and they are among the most numerous multi-cellular animals in the world. If you were to look at a nematode under a microscope, you would see an outer body wall, an inner digestive tube and a fluid-filled cavity between the two. Thus, some people describe a nematode as being a tube within a tube. Think about this: the next time you pick up a handful of soil, you are probably holding more nematodes in your hand than the total number of people you have met in your whole life. Now throw away all the soil except a gram or so. Put it in your palm and look at it. That gram of soil contains more organisms, of one type or another, than the number of human beings on Earth.

Web:

http://kbn.ifas.ufl.edu/kbnstein.htm
http://nematode.unl.edu/
http://www.barc.usda.gov/psi/nem/what-nem.htm

Listserv Mailing List:

List Name: nema-l
Subscribe to: listserv@crcvms.unl.edu

Ornithology

Birds belong to the class Aves and are characterized by having wings, a streamlined body covered with feathers, light bones, a four-chambered heart (like mammals), a fast metabolism, a relatively large brain, acute hearing, little sense of smell and no external ears. Ornithology, the study of birds, is one of the few sciences where amateurs often make important contributions, usually in the area of bird populations, by making notes about where various types of birds have been sighted.

Web:
  http://www.aves.net/the-owl/
  http://www.nmnh.si.edu/birdnet/
  http://www.ornith.cornell.edu/
  http://www.ornithology.com/

Primates

Primates are the biological order to which human beings belong. Broadly speaking, there are two basic types of primates, grouped according to physical traits: the sub-order Prosimii (the lower primates), and the sub-order Anthropoidea (higher primates). Prosimii, which have longer snouts, include shrews, lemurs, lories and bushbabies. Anthropoidea, which have shorter snouts, include marmosets, monkeys, gibbons, gorillas, chimpanzees, orangutans and human beings. Primatology, a subfield of anthropology, is the the study of nonhuman primates.

Web:
  http://www-ls.lanl.gov/wjt/
  http://www.asp.org/
  http://www.indiana.edu/~primate/primates.html
  http://www.primate.wisc.edu/pin/

Strange Animals

This Web site discusses the mistakes scientists have made in relation to animal life. Read about sea monsters, dragons and dinosaurs, as well as forgeries and frauds perpetrated by scientists. There are also some fascinating drawings, made by scientists, that show various types of monsters.

Web:
  http://www.strangescience.net/

Zoological Resources

Slippery, slimy, creepy, crawly, furry or scaly, these sites probably have it covered. Here are some nice collections of resources such as Web sites, databases, museums, Web servers and image galleries related to zoology.

Web:
  http://www.biolinks.org/Biology/Zoology/
  http://www.biosis.org/free_resources/
    resource_guide.html
  http://www.madsci.org/libs/areas/zoology.html

Index

Main subject headings are shown in **bold**

*Main subject headings are shown in **bold***

*Main subject headings are shown in **bold***

*Main subject headings are shown in **bold***

*Main subject headings are shown in **bold***

*Main subject headings are shown in **bold***

*Main subject headings are shown in **bold***

*Main subject headings are shown in **bold***

*Main subject headings are shown in **bold***

*Main subject headings are shown in **bold***

A Personal Invitation
from Harley

*Harley Hahn, best-selling
Internet author of all time,
and The Little Nipper.*

Would you like an easy way to use the resources in this book, without having to type in long Web addresses?

Visit my Web site at **www.harley.com,** and sign up to access an online version of this book.

And, if you have kids, find out how they can access an online version of The Little Nipper's Internet Clubhouse, the special kids' section in the center of this book.

While you are at my Web site, you'll also be able to:

Have fun with Harley Hahn's List of 25 Things To Do When You Should Be Working.

Read stories, essays, and other writing, only available online.

Sign up for my free newsletter.

Send me a personal message. . . and much, much more.

So, take a moment right now and come visit me, on the Net, at: **www.harley.com.**